multinational
management

A Strategic Approach 4e

John B. **Cullen**
Washington State University

K. Praveen **Parboteeah**
University of Wisconsin, Whitewater

THOMSON
＊
SOUTH-WESTERN

Australia · Brazil · Canada · Mexico · Singapore · Spain · United Kingdom · United States

THOMSON

SOUTH-WESTERN

Multinational Management: A Strategic Approach, 4th Edition
John B. Cullen and K. Praveen Parboteeah

VP/Editorial Director:
Jack W. Calhoun

VP/Editor-in-Chief:
Melissa Acuna

Senior Acquisitions Editor:
Michele Rhoades

Assoc. Developmental Editor:
John Abner

Marketing Manager:
Kimberly Kanakes

Assoc. Content Project Manager:
D. Jean Buttrom

Manager of Technology, Editorial:
John Barans

Technology Project Editor:
Kristen Meere

Manufacturing Coordinator:
Doug Wilke

Compositor:
International Typesetting and
Composition

Art Director:
Tippy McIntosh

Internal and Cover Designer:
c miller design

Cover Images:
©Getty Images

Production House:
LEAP Publishing Services, Inc.

Printer:
Quebecor World
Dubuque, IA

Library of Congress Control Number:
2006939530

For more information about our
products, contact us at:

Thomson Learning Academic
Resource Center

1-800-423-0563

Thomson Higher Education
5191 Natorp Boulevard
Mason, OH 45040
USA

To les deux

J & J

and

To Kyong, Alisha and Davin and to my parents Balmik and Sita

BRIEF CONTENTS

CONTENTS

part two   ## Strategy Content and Formulation for Multinational Companies   217

part four   Strategy Implementation for Multinational Companies: Human Resource Management   511

part five   **Strategy Implementation for Multinational Companies: Interaction Processes   637**

T he globalization of markets and companies; the growing importance of the emerging markets of India and China; and the global impact of wars, terrorism, and even disease define the nature of today's business. Developing and making strategic choices are the mainstays of successful decision making in this increasingly complex global environment. To help students develop the essential skills needed to formulate and implement successful strategic moves in the competitive global environment, *Multinational Management: A Strategic Approach, 4e,* continues the strong tradition of providing a thorough review and analysis of the latest research on international management. In addition, we bring a distinctive method to the teaching and learning of international management by using a strategic perspective as a unifying theme to explore the global economy and the impact of managerial decisions. This text remains the first international management text that uses this critical emphasis on strategic decision making as the cornerstone of its approach.

Successful multinational managers view the world as an integrated market where competition and collaboration evolve from almost anywhere and anyone. At the same time, these managers must appreciate the wide array of differences that exist in cultures and social institutions. This text considers how cultural differences affect strategies and operations and gives the student an appreciation of how social institutions such as the economic system, the polity, the educational system, and religion play an important role in any multinational operation. As such, the reader is not limited to understanding multinational management from the perspective of any one nation or group.

New to This Edition

The entire text has been updated to reflect current research and examples from the field of international management. Specific revisions to the text material include the following:

New Topical Areas: All chapters include the latest developments in the field.

➤ **Chapter 3 The Institutional Context of Multinational Management** has been updated and now contains important information on social inequality and its impact for multinational management.

part two

➤ **Chapter 5 Strategic Management in the Multinational Company: Content and Formulation** now includes a section on outsourcing within the context of the value chain.

➤ **Chapter 6 Multinational and Participation Strategies: Content and Formulation** now includes a section on political risk and what companies can do to mitigate political risk.

➤ **Chapter 7 Small Businesses and International Entrepreneurship: Overcoming Barriers and Finding Opportunities** provides greater emphasis on the importance of international entrepreneurship to both countries and multinational companies and also discusses some of the cross-cultural factors determining the growth of international entrepreneurship.

➤ **Chapter 8 Organizational Designs for Multinational Comanies** now includes an extensive discussion of knowledge management, adding a timely and interesting topic to the traditional discussion of multinational organizational structures. This reflects the growing importance of knowledge management systems to multinationals.

Focus on Emerging Markets Feature: This edition includes a new feature focusing on the growing importance of emerging markets in Asia, Latin America and Europe. Each chapter includes a discussion of the many opportunities and threats presented by emerging markets in the context of the chapter. Many of these examples emphasize the two dominant emerging markets, namely India and China.

Multinational Management Skill Builders: In this fourth edition, we update the skill-building activities at the end of every chapter to give learners an opportunity to apply the chapter material to solve practical multinational management problems.

Chapter Cases: All chapters now have their own cases with specific case-based discussion questions. Case topics reflect the current global environment and cover most of the world's continents. For instance, some cases pertain to companies operating in the world's biggest markets such as India and China. As an example, a new case on McDonald's in India provides valuable insights into the Indian markets and the approaches used by McDonald's to succeed in this market. Cases also include companies in the Czech Republic and Poland to reflect the challenges faced as these countries transition to more market-based economies. Cases on Asian economies, such as South Korea and Japan, illustrate some of the difficulties these countries are facing as they try to deal with an environment that is counter to collectivist values. For instance, a new case on Nissan and Carlos Ghosn provides important information on Japan and Goshn's approach to dealing with cultural differences to his own advantage. Cases on companies in Latin American countries such as Argentina and El Salvador illustrate some of the unique challenges multinationals located in these countries are facing. Finally, some cases from Europe and Canada show that these places also represent particular difficulties for multinationals.

Current Data: All chapters have been updated to include the latest research, examples, and statistics in multinational management, creating the most accurate and current presentation possible. Highlights include the following:

➤ Current multinational management examples can be found in the Case in Point and other chapter features, including Multinational Management Briefs, Multinational Management Challenges, and Multinational Management Skill Builders

➤ Updated tables and figures using recent findings on multinational leadership from *GLOBE: The Global Leadership and Organizational Behavior Effectiveness Research Program*

➤ Updated tables and figures using recent findings on organizational behavior issues from the *World Values Survey* and the *International Social Survey Program*

➤ Updated tables and figures using recent publications from the latest World Bank's *World Trade Report*, other critical information from the United Nations Conference on Trade and Development (UNCTAD) and the United Nation's *World Investment Report*.

➤ Prepublication information from the authors' own research on the effects of social institutions of work values and international recruiting

➤ A large selection of new cases

Pedagogical Approach

Multinational Management: A Strategic Approach, 4e, provides a thorough review and analysis of multinational management. In addition, this text includes several unique pedagogical learning tools:

Strategic Viewpoint: The strategic viewpoint found in the text provides a unifying theme that guides the reader through the material. This theme highlights for students the process multinational companies engage in when deciding to compete in the global economy and the management consequences of these strategic choices.

Comparative Management Issues: Multinational managers must learn to understand the strengths, weaknesses, and strategies of competitors from anywhere in the world. In addition, they must know when and how to adapt their organizational practices to accommodate local situations. Where applicable, the comparative sections of the text assist students in understanding the complexities of the cultures and business practices of other nations.

Review of Management Principles: The text contains several chapters that assume limited background knowledge in management. These topics include strategic management, organizational design, human resource management, and organizational behavior. For students with limited previous coursework in management, or who need a review, each chapter provides background primers with a brief explanation of key concepts and ideas.

Small Business and Entrpreneurship Applications: Unlike most international management texts, this book offers the multinational activities of small businesses a prominent position. An entire chapter focuses specifically on the problems and prospects for entrepreneurs and small businesses looking to become multinational competitors.

Application Based: Each chapter gives the learner three different opportunities to apply the knowledge gained from reading the chapter: Multinational Management Skill Builders, chapter Internet Activities (located on the book Web site www.thomsonedu.com/management/cullen), and end-of-chapter cases. These exercises simulate the challenges that practicing multinational managers encounter on the job.

Key Features

Chapter Cases and Multinational Management Skill Builders: End-of-chapter projects include cases and activities, which give the learner the opportunity to apply text material to real-life managerial problems.

Integrating Cases: Each major section offers at least one full-length case that requires the integration of material from all preceding chapters. These cases were chosen to challenge the reader with the complexities of the global environment.

Extensive Examples: Throughout the text, many examples enhance the text material by showing actual multinational management situations. These examples are illustrated in six different formats:

➤ *Preview Case in Point:* These brief cases open each chapter and focus the reader's interest on the chapter content.

➤ *Focus on Emerging Markets:* New to the 4th edition, these brief cases discuss relevant chapter issues and how they apply to emerging markets.

➤ *Case in Point:* Real-life examples of multinational companies that discuss relevant topics in each chapter.

➤ *Multinational Management Challenge:* Cases that explore challenging situations faced by multinational managers using actual companies and situations.

➤ *Multinational Management Brief:* Brief examples that further explain an issue discussed in the text.

➤ *Comparative Management Brief:* Examples of management issues that are influenced by a unique cultural or social institutional setting.

Models as Examples: To further explain key principles, extensive sets of models created by the authors offer visual aids for students to draw upon as they study the material.

Learning Aids: The Multinational Management Electronic Study Tools for students, product support Web site, and supporting video make learning easy and fun while exposing the learner to the complex issues of multinational management. In addition, included on the product support Web site are Internet Activities that challenge students to use Internet resources in locating international business information. The Web site also contains an extensive selection of Internet links to resources and information that are updated regularly.

Contents

The text is structured into five major parts. Part 1 is divided into four chapters, namely three introductory chapters that provide essential background on the nature of multinational management and a fourth chapter on international ethics. These chapters address the challenges facing managers in the new global economy, how national cultures affect management, the institutional context of multinational companies, and the ethical challenges facing multinationals.

Part 2 includes three chapters that review how multinational companies formulate successful strategies to compete internationally. Chapter 5 provides a broad overview of strategic management with multinational implications. Chapter 6 focuses on the strategies required to "go international." Chapter 7 applies the concepts from the previous two chapters to the unique problems faced by smaller, entrepreneurial organizations.

Part 3 addresses the management systems used to implement multinational strategies. Specifically, Chapter 8 considers how multinational companies design and structure their organizations to implement these strategies. Chapter 9 examines the management and design issues involved in building international strategic alliances. Chapter 10 considers how companies can use e-commerce in multinational operations.

Part 4 contains two chapters dealing with the human resource management issues related to strategy implementation. Topics considered include international human resource practices and the adaptation of these practices across cultures.

Finally, Part 5 continues to examine strategy implementation at the level of the individual in the organization. Chapters consider international negotiation and cross-cultural communication, motivating people for different nations, and leadership challenges in multinational companies.

Ancillary Materials

Multinational Management: A Strategic Approach, 4e offers a highly intensive learning and teaching package of ancillary tools for both students and instructors. These supplements to the text give students and instructors many options for learning and teaching the text content.

For Instructors

Instructor's Manual with Test Bank (ISBN# 0-324-36137-8): This book offers instructional materials, case solutions and questions, a full test bank, and a full set of transparency masters. For this fourth edition, we continue to provide case solutions for each chapter in a consistent format. Instructors are provided with a list of suggested questions and solutions. Furthermore, instructors are provided with a synopsis and case objectives that show the academic value of each case. Another important addition to this edition is that the authors have provided clear lessons that can be learned from the assigned cases. These lessons are stated with direct reference to the chapter content and provide an added avenue to demonstrate the relevance of the concepts discussed in the applicable chapters as they apply to real companies.

PowerPoint® Slide Presentations (ISBN# 0-324-36132-7): The authors have created more than 450 slides illustrating the concepts of each chapter. These are located on the Instructor's Resource CD-ROM or can be found on the Web site at www.thomsonedu.com/management/cullen.

ExamView (ISBN 0-324-36132-7): ExamView Computerized Testing Software, located on the Instructor's Resource CD-ROM, contains all of the questions in the printed test bank. This program is an easy-to-use test creation software compatible with Microsoft Windows. Instructors can add or edit questions, instructions, and answers, and select questions by previewing them on the screen, selecting them randomly, or selecting them by number. Instructors can also create and administer quizzes online, whether over the Internet, a local area network (LAN), or a wide area network (WAN). Contact your South-Western/Thomson sales representative for ordering information.

Instructor's Resource CD-ROM (ISBN# 0-324-36132-7): This CD-ROM includes the key instructor support materials—Instructor's Manual, Test Bank, ExamView and PowerPoint Slides—and provides instructors with a comprehensive capability for customizing lectures and presentations.

Web Site: Visitors to the Web site (www.thomsonedu.com/management/cullen) will find the above teaching ancillaries available for download in the password-protected Instructor Resources section. For students, Internet Activities and key Web site references related to international business for each chapter. are provided

Video (ISBN# 0-324-20354-3): The video to accompany *Multinational Management: A Strategic Approach, 4e,* uses real-world companies to illustrate international business concepts as outlined in the text. Focusing on both small and large businesses, the video gives students an inside perspective on the situations and issues that global corporations face.

Multimedia Cases from Harvard Business School Publishing: Thomson Higher Education is the exclusive higher education distributor of select interactive e-learning materials from Harvard Business School Publishing (HBSP). Thomson combines its leading business and economics textbooks with Harvard Business School Publishing's robust interactive media assets to help professors enhance student productivity and learning in the classroom. *Multimedia Cases* from Harvard Business School bring text material to life with animated charts, audio, and video segments to highlight a case's business dilemmas. Available on CD, HBSP Multimedia Cases are inexpensive and easy to use. They can take students to places that are difficult to reach with conventional paper cases. Most of these cases are extensions of the print cases from Harvard Business School Cases and offer another layer by extending the experience in an interactive form. These cases will typically take 1–3 class periods to complete. The **Zara Fast Fashion Multimedia Case** is recommended for International Management courses. For more information, contact your Thomson representative or visit http://www.thomsonedu.com/hbsp.

For Students

Web Site: The web site offers for students Internet Activities and key Web site references related to international business for each chapter.

Multinational Management Electronic Study Tools (ISBN# 0-324-36133-5): Available to be packaged at no charge with the textbook, access to this resource-rich Web site provides students with supporting material such as dynamic quiz questions, electronic flash cards, a PowerPoint presentation in note-taking form, "Hot Links" to Web sites that contain information about companies and concepts covered in the text, key terms and concepts, maps, and a copy of the *2006 CIA World Factbook.*

World Map: Included with new copies of the text is a full-color Rand McNally World Map.

Acknowledgments

Numerous individuals helped make this book possible. Most of all, we must thank our families for giving us the time and quiet to accomplish this task:

➤ Jean Johnson, Professor of Marketing at Washington State University, an experienced internationalist—and John's wife—read and commented on all chapters. Her insights were invaluable, as was her suggestion to organize the book around the strategic management perspective.

➤ Kyong Pyun, Praveen's wife, was very patient during the revision process. She stayed calm and collected, although Praveen did not help much with Davin, the 6-month-old! However, she was able to get a break as she prepared the chapter PowerPoint presentations for the text. Praveen's 5-year-old daughter, Alisha, made sure Praveen got regular breaks, stopping by regularly for conversations.

This text would not be possible without the support of a team of professionals. Our initial thanks go to John Szilagyi, former Executive Editor of South-Western's management list, who encouraged us to write the fourth edition. The commitment of Sr. Marketing Manager Rob Bloom to the first edition helped make possible the continued success of this book. Developmental Editor John Abner worked diligently and with patient tact to keep us on track. Our thanks also go to the numerous other professionals who made this text possible including: Kimberly Kanakes, Marketing Manager; Vicky True, Manager of Technology, Editorial; Kristen Meere, Technology Project Editor; and Tippy McIntosh, Art Director. We also appreciate the hard work of individuals involved on the production side, particularly Content Project Manager, Jean Buttrom.

Several colleagues who read and offered insightful comments on this and previous editions include the following:

Carol Sánchez, *Grand Valley State University*

Raffaele DeVito *Emporia State University*

David F. Martin *Murray State University*

Anthony J. Avallone, Jr. *Point Loma Nazarene University*

Gerry N. Muuka *Murray State University*

Maru Etta-Nkwelle *Howard University*

Gary Baker *Buena Vista University*

Douglas M. Kline *Sam Houston State University*

Michael J. Pisani *Texas A&M International University*

Tracy A. Thompson *University of Washington, Tacoma*

Bonita Barger *Tennessee Technological University*

Dave Flynn *Hofstra University*

Mike Giambattista *University of Washington*

Kamala Gollakota *University of South Dakota*

Stephen Jenner *California State University, Dominguez Hills*

John A. Kilpatrick *Idaho State University*

Richard Lovacek *North Central College*

Scott L. Boyar *University of South Alabama*

Carl R. Broadhurst *Campbell University*

Linda L. Blodgett *Indiana University South Bend*

Joseph Peyrefitte *University of Southern Mississippi*

Lawrence A. Beer *Arizona State University*

Janet S. Adams *Kennesaw State University*

Manisha Singal *Virginia Tech*

The following case authors also deserve a special recognition for contributing their cases to this book: Suzanne Uhlen and Michael Lubatkin, "ABB in China: 1998"; Asianweek.com & Sang-Hun Choe, "Old corporate ways fade as new Korean generation asserts itself"; Mark Andersen and Joan Winn, "Anglo-American College in Prague (AAC): The Challenge to Lead in Post-Communist Czech Republic"; Krystyna Joanna Zaleska, "Organizational and National Cultures in a Polish/U.S. Joint Venture"; Sonia Ferencikova, "Transition at Whirlpool-Tatramat: From Joint Venture to Acquisition"; Marlene Reed and Rochelle R. Brunson, "The Fleet Sheet" and "Skoda Auto 'The Czech Carmaker'"; Kris Opalinski and Walter Good, "Airview Mapping, Inc."; Southwest Case Research & Nan Muir Bodensteiner, "Haute Innovations- International Virtual Teams Case Scenario"; Stanley D. Nollen, Karen L. Newman, and Jacqueline M. Abbey, "PBS (B): The ABB PBS Joint Venture in Operation"; Sandeep Krisnamurthy, "The Failure of Boo.com"; Thunderbird, The American Graduate School of International Management & Robert Grosse and Carlos Fuentes, "STS Manufacturing in China: Mark Hanson Returns from Vacation" and "Enersis: Global Strategy in the Electric Power Sector"; Gareth Evans, "The Road to Hell"; Asia Case Research Journal & Syed Aqeel Tirmizi and Faiza, "Management Appraisal at Attock Refinery Limited"; Thunderbird, The American Graduate School of International Management & Caren Siehl and Scott Hessell, "Cadet Uniform Services: Cleaning Up in the Cleaning Business"; Thunderbird, The American Graduate School of International Management & Karen Walch with research assistance from Arturo Callau, Thomas Cornell, Paolo Crozzoli, Nina Erichsen, Ana Maslesa, Guenadi Milanov, Markus Nelson, Vijay Parmar, Eduardo Saldana, and Olaf Svanks, "The AT&T/BT Joint Venture Negotiations"; Nina Hatvany and Vladimir Pucik, "Chiba International, Inc."; Stephen M. Hills, G. Keong Leong, and P. Roberto Garcia, "Grupo UNIKO"; North American Case Research Association, "Argentina Suites: A Case Study"; Laura Pinkus Hartman, "Tee-Shirts and Tears: Third World Suppliers to First World Markets;" James W. Bronson and Graham Beaver, "Harley-Davidson and the International Market for Luxury Goods;" Thunderbird, The American Graduate School of International Management & Roy Nelson, "Dell's Dilemma in Brazil: Negotiating at the State Level;" Thunderbird, The American Graduate School of International Management & John Millikin, Dean Fu, and Koichi Tamura, "The Global Leadership of Carlos Ghosn at Nissan;" and Thunderbird, The American Graduate School of International Management & Kishore Dash, "McDonald's in India."

John B. Cullen
K. Praveen Parboteeah

John B. Cullen

John Cullen is Professor of Management at Washington State University where he teaches courses on international management, organizational theory, strategic management, and business ethics. He has also taught on the faculties of the University of Nebraska, the University of Rhode Island, Waseda and Keio Universities in Japan (as a Fulbright lecturer), and the Catholic University of Lille in France. He received his Ph.D. from Columbia University. He consults regularly with U.S. and Japanese organizations regarding international strategic alliances and the management of ethical behavior.

Professor Cullen is the author or co-author of four books and over 60 journal articles, which have appeared in journals such as *Administrative Science Quarterly, Journal of International Business Studies, Academy of Management Journal, Organization Science, Journal of Management, Organizational Studies, Management International Review, Journal of Vocational Behavior, American Journal of Sociology, Organizational Dynamics,* and the *Journal of World Business.* He also has given over 100 presentations at national and regional meetings. His major research interests include the effects of national culture and social institutions on managers and workers, the management of trust and commitment in international strategic alliances, ethical climates in multinational organizations, and the dynamics of organizational structure. Professor Cullen serves or has served on various editorial boards including the *Academy of Management Journal* and *Advances in International Management* and reviews for major journals in management and international business.

K. Praveen Parboteeah

K. Praveen Parboteeah is an Associate Professor of International Management in the Department of Management, University of Wisconsin–Whitewater. He received his Ph.D. from Washington State University, holds an MBA from California State University–Chico and a BSc (Honors) in Management Studies from the University of Mauritius.

Parboteeah's research interests include international management, ethics, and technology and innovation management. He has been actively involved in developing alternative models to national culture to explain cross-national differences in individual behaviors. He has published over 20 articles in journals such as the *Academy of Management Journal, Organization Science, Decision Sciences, Small Group Research, Journal of Business Ethics, Management International Review, Journal of World Business,* and *Journal of Engineering and Technology Management.*

Parboteeah has received numerous awards for his research. He was the 2005 Western Academy of Management Ascendant Scholar. He has also received Best Paper Awards from the Academy of Management and Global Information and Technology Management Association. Most recently, he was awarded a Certificate of Excellence for Outstanding Research by the University of Wisconsin–Whitewater and the Research Award by the College of Business.

Parboteeah has been involved in many aspects of international education at the University of Wisconsin–Whitewater. He chairs the International Business Committee and is currently developing a strategic plan for the college. He is also the coordinator for exchanges with two French universities, namely ESC Rouen and the Burgundy School of Business in Dijon. He has also lectured in many countries including Mexico, South Korea, Germany, and the U.K.

Of Indian ancestry, Parboteeah grew up on the African island of Mauritius and speaks English, French, and Creole. He currently lives in Whitewater, Wisconsin, with his South Korean wife Kyong, daughter Alisha, and new son Davin. He has traveled extensively around the world.

Foundations of Multinational Management

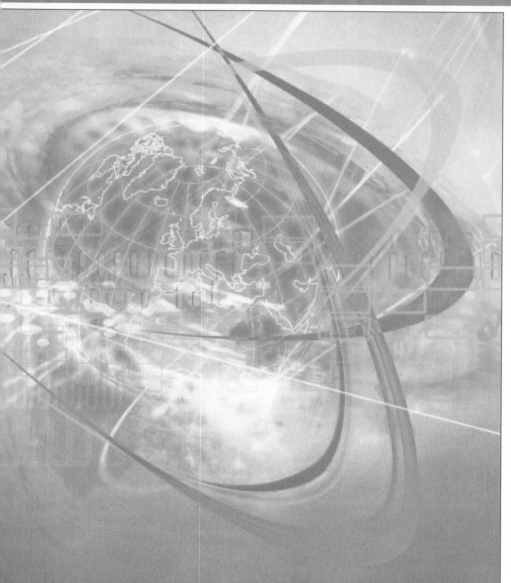

Multinational Management in a Changing World

Learning Objectives

After reading this chapter you should be able to:

- Define multinational management.
- Understand the characteristics of a multinational company.
- Understand the nature of the global economy and the key forces that drive globalization.
- Know the basic classification of the world's economies.
- Identify the characteristics of the next generation of multinational managers.

Preview CASE IN POINT

Global Opportunities

Cyworld is South Korea's major Internet-based social network. It was created in 1999 by four graduates of the Korea Advanced Institute of Management and Technology, Korea's equivalent of MIT. Today, close to one-third of the South Korean population uses Cyworld for a variety of activities including checking messages and uploading pictures for viewing by others. Nearly 90 percent of South Koreans in their 20s are registered with Cyworld, making their penetration much more successful than MySpace in the United States. Cyworld is planning a U.S. release soon to compete with the widely successful MySpace.

Not too many people have heard of Laksmi Mittal, an Indian-born entrepreneur who now owns the biggest steelmaker in the world. He represents the global dealmaker of today's world with operations in numerous locations from Eastern and Central Europe to America and Asia. His most recent acquisition is Arcelor, one of Europe's prized and profitable steelmakers. Mittal had to fight a strong insider European culture to make the merger happen.

Josh Pollock is a 31-year-old who recently opened a restaurant in Shanghai, China. While living in China, Pollock was frustrated with the poor quality of Western food and saw an opportunity for such a restaurant. He picked Kunming, a growing city with a significant university population. His restaurant, Salvador Coffee House, offers hard-to-find items such as fresh coffee, bagels, and home-made ice cream. The restaurant venture has been very successful, and Pollock is planning to open restaurants in other cities.

Sources: Schonfeld, Erick. 2006. "Cyworld attacks." Business 2.0, August, pp. 84–89; Shwartz, Nelson D. 2006. "Emperor of steel." Fortune, Huly 24, pp. 100–108; Sloan, Paul. 2006. "East meets—and eats—West." Business 2.0, August 2006, p. 76.

As the three examples in the Preview Case in Point show, businesses and individuals, whether from the old or new economy, increasingly see the entire world as a source of business opportunities. The world is becoming one connected economy in which companies conduct business and compete anywhere and with anyone, regardless of national boundaries. In a global economy, any company or individual from any country can become a competitor. The Internet crosses national boundaries with the click of a mouse, allowing even the smallest businesses to go global immediately. Consequently, companies can no longer afford the luxury of assuming that success in their home market equates to long-term profitability—or even survival. Furthermore, although the integrated global economy presents challenges and threats such as terrorism, war, and recession, there are significant opportunities for most companies. Consider the following Focus on Emerging Markets.

What does this mean to the student of international business? With companies increasingly looking at global rather than domestic markets, managers of the next century will have little choice but to be multinational in outlook and strategies. Consequently, all students of business should have at least a basic background in multinational management. Simply put, **multinational management** is the formulation of strategies and the design of management systems that successfully take advantage of international opportunities and respond to international threats. Successful multinational managers are executives with the ability and motivation to meet and beat the challenges of multinational management.

To provide you with basic background in multinational management, this book introduces you to the latest information on how managers throughout the

Multinational management

The formulation of strategies and the design of management systems that successfully take advantage of international opportunities and respond to international threats.

Focus on Emerging Markets

Growing Opportunities

According to experts, the middle class in emerging markets will grow to 800 million people with more than $1 trillion to spend annually. This large middle class in countries such as China, India, Russia, and Brazil will largely exceed the combined population of the United States, Western Europe, and Japan. Furthermore, this middle class aspires to live a more comfortable life by owning U.S. and Western branded products. This suggests tremendous opportunities for multinationals.

Of the many emerging markets, China clearly presents significant potential. China has enjoyed sustained growth over the past three years and is now the largest importer of many commodities. It is also the largest supplier of a number of manufactured goods. In fact, for many countries such as South Korea, Japan, Chile, Cambodia, and Thailand, both China's imports and exports have doubled over the period from 2000 to 2004.

India is also poised to become a dominant trade player in the next decade. Similar to China, India's economy has grown tremendously with real growth of gross domestic product of more than 6 percent over the past decade. Experts see important developments in trade, labor, and capital that will provide important opportunities to multinationals.

Sources: Based on Business 2.0. 2006. "The emerging global middle class." July, 96; Wilson, Beth Anne, and Geoffrey N. Keim. 2006. "India and the global economy." Business Economics, 41(1), pp. 28–36; World Trade Organization. 2006. World Trade Report 2006. Geneva: World Trade Organization.

world respond to the challenges of globalization. You will see how businesses, both large and small, deal with the complexities of national differences in cultures, economies, and political systems. You will learn how multinational managers use their understanding of these national differences to formulate strategies that maximize their companies' success in globalizing industries. Because having good strategies is not enough to succeed in today's economy, you will learn how multinational managers carry out their multinational strategies. First, the book explains how managers design organizational and human resource systems for multinational companies. Second, it shows how multinational managers develop motivational and leadership strategies that work in any national setting. In addition to these issues, you will see some of the challenges that multinational managers face in dealing with ethics and social responsibility in different national cultures. To give you insights into the real world of multinational management, you will find several types of examples in this and the following chapters. Preview Cases in Point show you examples of how multinational companies are dealing with a key issue that is discussed in the chapter. Cases in Point give information on how actual multinational companies deal with the issues currently under review in the text. Multinational Management Briefs give you further details and examples that extend the discussions in the chapters. Multinational Management Challenges describe problems and dilemmas faced by real multinational managers for which there is no easy answer. Comparative management briefs provide some examples of management issues that are influenced by a unique cultural or social institutional setting. Finally, the Focus on Emerging Markets feature reflects the growing importance of emerging markets in world trade. Each chapter discusses examples of the many opportunities and threats presented by selected emerging markets.

Multinational management takes place within the multinational company. What is a multinational company? The next section gives a definition and brief introduction to the major players in multinational competition.

The Nature Of The Multinational Company

The **multinational company** is broadly defined as any company that engages in business functions beyond its domestic borders. This definition includes all types of companies, large and small, that engage in international business. Most multinational companies, however, are also multinational corporations—the companies are publicly owned through stocks. Most often, when you see references to MNCs in the popular business press, the reference is to multinational corporations. The largest multinationals are all public corporations. (Exhibit 1.1 lists the top twenty multinational corporations ranked by sales revenue.)

As the list shows, the largest corporations are in the petroleum industry.[1] The latter is not surprising given the recent increase in oil prices. However, out of the top ten companies, four are automotive companies and big consumers of the oil industry. Wal-Mart is the only retailer among the top ten companies.

Where are most of the global multinationals located? Exhibit 1.2 lists the 15 cities with the most Fortune Global 500 companies. As you can see, global multinationals are not concentrated only in major Western cities. Prominent new competitors can be found in cities such as Seoul, South Korea and Beijing, China. Furthermore, Tokyo, Japan currently has the most Fortune Global 500 companies among the major cities around the world. This exhibit also shows

Multinational company

Any company that engages in business functions beyond its domestic borders.

EXHIBIT 1.1   The Largest Companies in the World

Rank (2005)	Rank (2004)	Company Name	Main Industry	Headquarters Country	Revenues (million US$)
1	3	Exxon Mobil	Petroleum	USA	339,938
2	1	Wal-Mart stores	Retail	USA	315,654
3	4	Royal Dutch Shell	Petroleum	Netherlands	306,731
4	2	BP	Petroleum	Britain	267,600
5	5	General Motors	Automobile	USA	192,604
6	11	Chevron	Petroleum	USA	189,481
7	6	DaimlerChrysler	Automobile	Germany	186,106
8	7	Toyota Motor	Automobile	Japan	185,805
9	8	Ford Motor	Automobile	USA	177,210
10	12	ConocoPhillips	Petroleum	USA	166,683
11	9	General Electric	Electronics	USA	157,153
12	10	Total	Petroleum	France	152,360
13	17	ING Group	Insurance	Netherlands	138,253
14	16	Citigroup	Finance	USA	131,045
15	13	Axa	Insurance	France	129,839
16	14	Alianz	Insurance	Germany	121,406
17	15	Volkswagen	Automobile	Germany	118,376
18	30	Fortis	Insurance	Belgium/ Netherlands	112,351
19	60	Credit Agricole	Banking	France	110,764
20	19	American International Group	Insurance	USA	108,905

Sources: Adapted from Fortune 2006. "Fortune Global 500." http://www.fortune.com/fortune/global500

that global companies are located anywhere in the world and are not confined to European or U.S. cities. Furthermore, the recent entry of both Beijing and Seoul in the list also provides some evidence of the increased importance of Asia in global trade.

What kinds of business activities might make a company multinational? The most apparent activity, of course, is international sales. When a company produces in its own country and sells in another country, it engages in the simplest level of multinational activity. However, as you will see in much more detail later in the text, crossing national borders opens up more multinational options than simply selling internationally.

To introduce some of the multinational options, consider the following hypothetical U.S. company that produces and sells men's shirts. As a domestic-only company, it can buy the dye, make the fabric, cut and sew the garment, and sell the shirt, all in the United States. However, the firm might not be able to compete successfully using this approach. The U.S. market may be stagnant, with competitive pricing and lower profit margins. Competitors might find higher-quality fabric or dye from overseas suppliers. Competitors might find lower production costs in low-wage countries, allowing them to offer lower prices. What can this company do?

EXHIBIT 1.2   **Location of Global Companies**

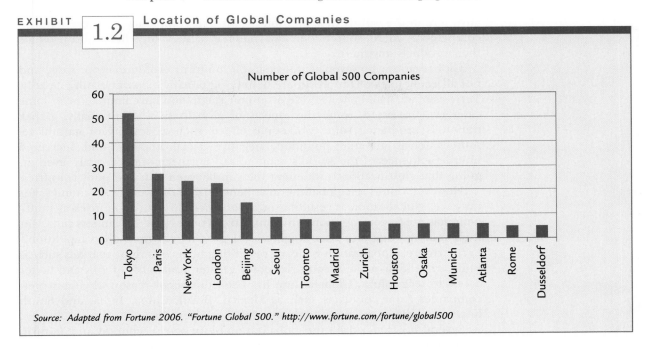

Source: Adapted from Fortune 2006. "Fortune Global 500." http://www.fortune.com/fortune/global500

As a multinational company, the firm might sell the shirt to overseas buyers in countries with less competition and higher prices. Several other multinational activities also might increase its competitive strength. For example, this company might locate any of the steps in obtaining raw materials or completing production in another country. It might buy the highest-quality dye from Italy, use the lowest-cost, high-quality fabric producers in Hong Kong, and have the cutting and sewing done in Vietnam with very low labor costs. For any of these steps, the company might contract with local companies in another country, or it may own its own factories within another country. As you will see in later chapters, multinational companies must develop strategies and systems to accomplish all or some of the multinational business tasks of this hypothetical U.S. company.

Next, we will consider the forces that drive the new economic reality that faces the next generation of multinational managers and multinational companies.

The Globalizing Economy: A Changing (But Not Always Stable) Environment For Business

Trade barriers are falling, and world trade among countries in goods and services has grown faster than domestic production over the last decade. Money is flowing more freely across national borders. allowing companies to seek the best rates for financing anywhere in the world and allowing investors to look for the best returns anywhere in the world. All these processes represent a trend known as **globalization.** Globalization is the worldwide trend of the economies of the world becoming borderless and interlinked—companies are no longer limited by their domestic boundaries and may conduct any business activity

Globalization

The worldwide trend of economic integration across borders that allows businesses to expand beyond their domestic boundaries.

anywhere in the world. Globalization means that companies are more likely to compete anywhere, source their raw material or R&D anywhere, and produce their products anywhere.

Globalization, however, is not a simple uniform evolutionary process, and not all economies of the world are benefiting equally or participating equally. Terrorism, wars, and a worldwide economic stagnation have limited, or in some cases even reversed, some the aspects of globalization. Additionally, globalization is producing some worrisome effects such as scarcity of natural resources, environmental pollution, negative social impacts, and increased interdependence of the world's economies.[2] Furthermore, some are even arguing that globalization is widening the gap between rich and poor countries.

However, others see globalization as beneficial to the world's economies. For instance, globalization is resulting in lower prices in many countries as multinationals are becoming more efficient. Lower prices give consumers more for their money while also encouraging local productivity through competition.[3] Furthermore, globalization is clearly benefiting many emerging markets such as India and China as these countries enjoy greater availability of jobs and better access to technology. Globalization has been the major reason why many new companies from countries such as Mexico, Brazil, China, India, and South Korea are among the new dominant global competitors.

Several key trends drive the globalization of the world economy and, in turn, even with shakeups to the world economy, force businesses to become more multinational to survive and prosper. Some of the most important trends include falling borders, growing cross-border trade and investment, the rise of global products and global customers, the growing use of the Internet and sophisticated information technology, privatizations of companies formerly owned by governments, the emergence of new competitors in the world market, and the rise of global standards of quality and production.

Before discussing the key globalization trends that affect multinational managers and their companies, it is useful to look at some commonly used classifications of the world's countries. The classifications roughly indicate a country's gross domestic product (GDP) and the growth in GDP. The classifications are not exact, but they simplify discussions of world trade and investments.

Countries of the World: The Arrived, the Coming, and the Struggling

Exhibit 1.3 shows some divisions of the world's economies based roughly on classifications used by the United Nations and *The Economist*. Developed countries have mature economies with substantial per capita GDPs and international trade and investments. The developing countries, such as Hong Kong, Singapore, South Korea, and Taiwan, have economies that have grown extensively over the past two decades yet have sometimes struggled recently, especially during the setbacks of the Asian crisis in the late 1990s. Other developing economies to watch are what the UN calls the transition economies of Central and Eastern Europe, such as the Czech Republic, Hungary, Poland, and Russia. Transition economies are countries that have changed from government-controlled, mostly Communist economic systems to market or capitalistic systems. The former systems relied on state-controlled organizations and centralized government control to run the economy. In the transition to free market and capitalistic systems, many government-owned companies were converted to private ownership. The market, not the government, then

Developed countries

Countries with mature economies, high GDPs, and high levels of trade and investment.

Developing countries

Countries with economies that have grown extensively in the past two decades.

Transition economies

Countries in the process of changing from government-controlled economic systems to capitalistic systems.

EXHIBIT 1.3   **Selected Economies of the World**

Developed Economies	Developing Economies	Transition Economies	Emerging Markets
Australia	Hong Kong	Czech Republic	Argentina
Austria	Singapore	Hungary	Brazil
Belgium	South Korea	Poland	China
Britain	Taiwan	Russia	Chile
Canada	Malaysia		Colombia
Denmark	Indonesia		India
France	Thailand		Mexico
Germany			Philippines
Italy			South Africa
Ireland			Turkey
Japan			Venezuela
Netherlands			
Spain			
Sweden			
Switzerland			
United States			

Sources: Adapted from Economist. 2003 "Markets and data, weekly indicators." http://www.economist.com, June 7; Economist. 2006. "Emerging markets and interest rates." August 5, p. 65.

determines the success of companies. Several of these transition economies, such as Hungary, Poland, Slovakia, and the Czech Republic, have developed market economies and are now members of the European Union.

Finally, **emerging markets** are those countries that are currently between developed and developing countries and are rapidly growing. Although it is difficult to determine the exact list of emerging markets, prominent countries such as India, China, Brazil, and Russia are considered emerging markets. Furthermore, some of the emerging markets also show up on the transition economies list.

The term *emerging markets,* coined by the World Bank around 25 years ago, represents those markets that present tremendous opportunities for all multinationals.[4] In fact, emerging markets have around five-sixths of the world's population with only half of the output. Furthermore, the purchasing power in many emerging markets has been increasing steadily. It is therefore not surprising to see that emerging markets now account for 40 percent of exports compared to only 20 percent in 1970. Recent trends also show that developed countries' trade with emerging markets has been growing twice as much compared to trade with each other.[5]

Less developed countries (LDCs) have yet to show much progress in the evolving global economy. They are the poorest nations and are often plagued with unstable political regimes, high unemployment, and unskilled workers. Most of these countries are located in Central and South America, Africa, and the Middle East. However, recent trends suggest that the LCDs are experiencing significant growth in their share of world trade with sharp increases in the past

Emerging markets
Countries that are currently between developed and developing countries and are rapidly growing.

Less developed countries (LDCs)
The poorest nations, often plagued with unstable political regimes, high unemployment, and low worker skills.

three years.[6] Furthermore, it is important to note that developed country markets are becoming less important to LCDs for exports. China has been very aggressive in promoting trade with LCDs and now account for one-third of all exports from LCDs.

With this overview of the major economies of the world, we can now look more closely at the driving forces of the new world economy. Exhibit 1.4 illustrates these important forces. Each of these driving forces is discussed below.

Borders Are Disintegrating: The World Trade Organization and Free Trade Areas

General Agreement on Tariffs and Trade (GATT)

Tariff negotiations between several nations that reduced the average worldwide tariff on manufactured goods.

In 1947, several nations began negotiating to limit worldwide tariffs and encourage free trade. At that time, worldwide tariffs averaged 45 percent. Seven rounds of tariff negotiations reduced the average worldwide tariffs on manufactured goods from 45 percent to less than 7 percent. These negotiations were known as **GATT, the General Agreement on Tariffs and Trade.**

Negotiations in Uruguay began in 1986 and ended in 1993 with agreements to reduce tariffs even further, liberalize trade in agriculture and services, and eliminate some non-tariff barriers to international trade, such as excessive use of health regulations to keep out imports.[7] The Uruguay talks also established the

EXHIBIT 1.4   The Globalizing Economy

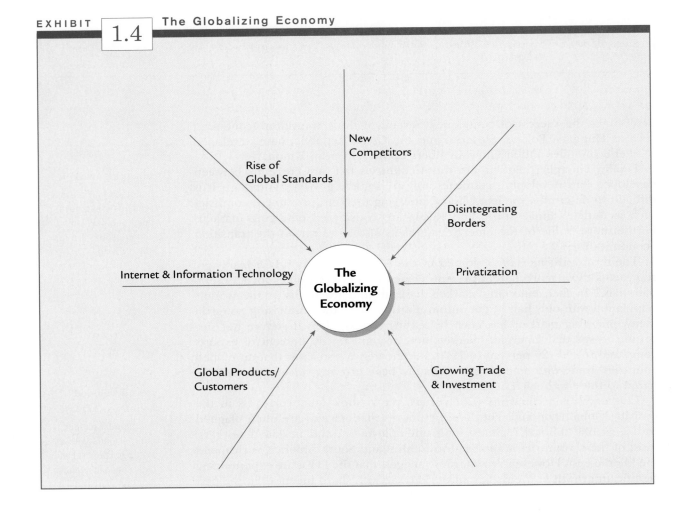

World Trade Organization (WTO) to succeed GATT. The WTO provides a formal structure for continued negotiations and for settling trade disputes among nations. There are now 144 nations in the WTO, up from 92 when the 1986 GATT talks began, including 29 of the UN-classified least-developed countries. Thirty more countries, including Russia, seek WTO membership. Since 1995, tariffs on industrial products have fallen from an average of 6.3 percent to 3.8 percent.[8]

In March 1997, trade ministers from countries representing 92 percent of world trade in information technology products agreed to end tariffs on trade in software, computer chips, telecommunications equipment, and computers. By the year 2005, this $500 billion a year trade should be mostly tariff free. The immediate expected result is that, with tariffs eliminated, high-tech exports to Europe from Asia and the United States should double. Developing countries, even those not party to the agreement, will likely also benefit. Prices should go down on products such as phones, faxes, and computers that are produced in tariff-free locations.[9]

Is free trade working? The WTO thinks so, and the data seems to support its conclusion. Since the early GATT agreements, world trade has grown at more than four times the output of the world's gross domestic product. This suggests that the world's economies are increasingly more intertwined and mutually stimulated.

There are, however, critics. Some argue that the WTO favors the developed nations because it is more difficult for poorer nations to compete in a non-regulated world. Environmentalists note that free trade encourages large multinational companies to move environmentally damaging production to poorer and often environmentally sensitive countries. That is, commercial interests have priority over the environment, health, and safety. Labor unions see free trade leading to the migration of jobs from higher wage countries to lower wage countries. You can see the WTO's counter arguments on its web site at http://www.wto.org/.

The WTO is an evolving organization, and its goal of free trade for all is still not achieved. Not all major world players are WTO members, and trade discussions continue over specific products. The next Multinational Management Brief describes some of the more major challenges the WTO is facing.

The WTO is not the only group encouraging the elimination of trade barriers. Regional trade agreements or free trade areas are agreements among groups of nations to reduce tariffs and develop similar technical and economic standards. With the breakdown of the Doha talks, regional trade agreements are very likely to continue growing in importance.[10] Such agreements have usually led to more trade among the member nations. Some argue that these agreements are the first step toward complete globalization. Others criticize the agreements as benefiting only trade-group members and being harmful for the poorer nations left out of the agreements, such as the Caribbean countries that are not members of NAFTA.[11] From a practical point of view, regional agreements benefit world trade more than they hurt it. Although they do benefit member countries the most, such agreements are more politically manageable than worldwide trade agreements.[12]

Within the last few years, the number of regional trade agreements reached 170, more than double the number that existed in 1992 (WTO Secretariat 2005). In addition, between January 2004 and February 2005 alone, the WTO was notified of 43 regional trade agreements. This is the most agreements any period has seen and provides evidence of the popularity of regional trade

World Trade Organization (WTO)

A formal structure for continued negotiations to reduce trade barriers and a mechanism for settling trade disputes.

Regional trade agreements

Agreements among nations in a particular region to reduce tariffs and develop similar technical and economic standards.

Multinational Management **Brief**

World Trade Organization Meltdown

The most recent WTO meeting provides evidence of the major challenges facing the WTO as it strives for trade liberalization. The meeting in Geneva was meant to continue intensive negotiation started in the capital of Qatar, Doha. The Doha talks were initiated after the September 11 attacks in 2001 and placed special focus on helping poorer nations develop their economies through exports through the elimination of trade barriers in richer countries.

The recent meeting, however, ended in suspended talks with the WTO Director-General Lamy recommending a "time-out" for all negotiating parties. This collapse in negotiations is seen as the result of many of WTO's members' unwillingness to stray from their entrenched positions. For instance, the European Union (EU) blamed the United States for its unwillingness to reduce agricultural subsidies. However, the United States also blamed the EU for its refusal to reduce its farm import tariffs. Furthermore, both the EU and the United States also blamed many of the developing countries, such as India and Brazil, for their inflexibility in cutting barriers to provide market access for their industrial and service products.

What is the future of the Doha talks? Many are uncertain about the next phase. All talks and deadlines have been currently suspended, and there is no new timetable to complete the rounds. Lamy, the Director-General, has no intention yet to propose a date to continue the meeting.

Sources: Based on Economist. 2006. "The future of globalization," July 29, p. 11; Klapper,, Bradley S. 2006. "5 years of WTO crash amid bickering." Seattle Times, July 25, p. C1.

agreements. As another example, it is estimated that just East Asia will have around 70 trade deals by the end of 2006.

The three largest groups account for nearly half of the world's trade. These groups are the EU, NAFTA, and APEC.

The **EU**, or **European Union**, includes 25, members, namely Austria, Belgium, Britain, Cyprus, Czech Republic, Denmark, Estonia, Finland, France, Germany, Greece, Hungary, Ireland, Italy, Latvia, Lithuania, Luxembourg, Malta, the Netherlands, Poland, Portugal, Slovakia, Slovenia, Spain, and Sweden. Although the idea of the European Union originated during World War II, the EU took off in 1992 since countries have allowed goods and services to move across borders without customs duties and quotas. More recently, they adopted a unified currency called the European Economic and Monetary Union, or EMU. EU member countries currently represent 450 million individuals and are an area of significant economic importance. The EU is also currently considering applications for membership from countries such as Bulgaria, Croatia, Macedonia, Romania, and Turkey. You can check the current status of the EU at http://europa.eu.int.

The **North American Free Trade Agreement (NAFTA)** links the United States, Canada, and Mexico in an economic bloc that allows freer exchange of goods and services. After the agreement went into effect in the early 1990s, all three countries saw immediate increases in trade. However, the Mexican economy soon went into a tailspin, with inflation running as high as 45 percent.[13] Emergency loans from the United States helped stabilize the situation, and by 1996, Mexico had paid back the loans—before the due date. The next step for NAFTA may be FTAA or the Free Trade Area of Americas. This group

European Union (EU)

Austria, Belgium, Britain, Denmark, Finland, France, Germany, Greece, Ireland, Italy, Luxembourg, the Netherlands, Portugal, Spain, and Sweden, plus Norway and Switzerland in the related European Free Trade Area.

North American Free Trade Agreement (NAFTA)

A multilateral treaty that links the United States, Canada, and Mexico in an economic bloc that allows freer exchange of goods and services.

will include not only the United States, Canada, and Mexico but also most other Caribbean, Central American, and South American nations.

When compared with the EU or NAFTA, the **Asia-Pacific-Economic Cooperation (APEC)** is a looser confederation of nineteen nations with less-specific agreements on trade facilitation. However, ultimate goals call for total free trade in the Pacific region by 2020.[14] Some of the major players in APEC include China, the United States, Japan, Taiwan, South Korea, Hong Kong, Australia, Singapore, Thailand, and Malaysia. Exhibit 1.5 shows all the major regional trade agreements and their member countries.

Sell Anywhere, Locate Anywhere: Trade and Foreign Investment Are Growing But Setbacks are Part of the Challenge

World trade among countries (imports and exports) grew at an average rate of 6.5 percent per year between 1990 and 2000,[15] slowed to 4 percent by 2004, and grew again to 6 percent in 2005[16] Exhibit 1.6 shows the leading exporting and importing countries based on data published by the WTO. Note that the combined countries of the EU now lead the United States in exporting. Exhibit 1.6 also shows that nearly half of the more than $5 trillion in world trade is among the European Union, the United States, and Japan. This trading group is sometimes called the **TRIAD**. However, China is now in third place in imports and exports and is rapidly gaining on the TRIAD countries.

Multinational companies not only trade across borders with exports and imports but also build global networks that link R&D, supply, production, and sales units across the globe. The result is that cross-border ownership, called foreign direct investment, is on the rise, more than doubling between 1998 and 2001.[17] **Foreign direct investment (FDI)** occurs when a multinational company from one country has an ownership position in an organizational unit located in another country. Fueled by cross-border mergers and acquisitions, such as the merger of Chrysler and Daimler-Benz, cross-border ownership was especially high in the late 1990s and up to 2000.

Foreign direct investment soared by more than 36 percent between 1996 and 2000 and reached a record of more than $1.5 trillion in 2000.[18] Following a pattern similar to international trade, FDI declined to $735 billion in 2001, less than half of the previous year, and declined another 25 percent in 2002. However, the most recent figures show that the global environment for FDI is improving significantly.

The importance of emerging markets is also reflected in the growth of FDI in these economies. Exhibit 1.7 shows the growth of FDI in a few emerging markets and selected developed countries. Most of the emerging markets such as Romania, India, South Africa, and Russia saw significant and steady increases in foreign direct investment. Furthermore, these countries show positive inflows of investment when outward FDI is deducted from the inward FDI. It also should be noted that China saw strong increases of FDI from $52.7 billion in 2002 to $72.4 billion in 2005.[19]

Who gives and who gets these investments in the global economy? With inflows of $165 billion, the UK passed the United States as the world's largest recipient of FDI. However, this large figure reflects the fact that many UK-based companies were targets of cross-border takeovers.[20] Furthermore,

Asia-Pacific-Economic Cooperation (APEC)

A confederation of 19 nations with less specific agreements on trade facilitation in the Pacific region.

TRIAD

The world's dominant trading partners: European Union, United States, and Japan.

Foreign direct investment (FDI)

Multinational firm's ownership, in part or in whole, of an operation in another country.

EXHIBIT 1.5   Regional Trade Agreements around the World

Andean Common Market
- Bolivia
- Colombia
- Ecuador
- Peru
- Venezuela

ASEAN (Association of Southeast Asian Nations)
- Brunei Darussalam
- Cambodia
- Indonesia
- Lao People's Democratic Republic
- Malaysia
- Myanmar
- Philippines
- Singapore
- Thailand
- Vietnam

Baltic countries
- Estonia
- Latvia
- Lithuania

CEPGL (Economic Community of the Great Lakes Countries)
- Burundi
- Democratic Republic of the Congo
- Rwanda

APEC (Asia-Pacific Economic Cooperation)
- Australia
- Brunei Darussalam
- Canada
- Chile
- China
- Hong Kong, China
- Indonesia
- Japan
- Malaysia
- Mexico
- New Zealand
- Papua New Guinea
- Peru
- Philippines
- Republic of Korea
- Russian Federation
- Singapore
- Taiwan
- Thailand
- United States of America
- Vietnam

UEMOA (West African Economic and Monetary Union)
- Benin
- Burkina Faso
- Côte d'Ivoire
- Guinea-Bissau
- Mali
- Niger
- Senegal
- Togo

CACM (Central American Common Market)
- Costa Rica
- El Salvador
- Guatemala
- Honduras
- Nicaragua

Bangkok Agreement
- Bangladesh
- China
- India
- Lao People's Democratic Republic of Korea
- Sri Lanka

EFTA (European Free Trade Association)
- Iceland
- Liechtenstein
- Norway
- Switzerland

EU (European Union)
- Austria
- Belgium
- Denmark
- Finland
- France
- Germany
- Greece
- Ireland
- Italy
- Luxembourg
- Netherlands
- Portugal
- Spain
- Sweden
- United Kingdom

COMESA (Common Market for Eastern and Southern Africa)
- Angola
- Burundi
- Comoros
- Democratic Republic of the Congo
- Djibouti
- Egypt
- Eritrea
- Ethiopia
- Kenya
- Madagascar
- Malawi
- Mauritius
- Namibia
- Rwanda
- Seychelles
- Sudan
- Swaziland
- Uganda
- Zambia
- Zimbabwe

BSEC (Black Sea Economic Cooperation)
- Albania
- Armenia
- Azerbaijan
- Bulgaria
- Georgia
- Greece
- Moldova
- Romania
- Russian Federation
- Turkey
- Ukraine

CARICOM (Caribbean Community)
- Antigua and Barbuda
- Bahamas
- Barbados
- Belize
- Dominica
- Grenada
- Guyana
- Jamaica
- Montserrat
- Saint Kitts and Nevis
- Saint Lucia
- Saint Vincent and the Grenadines
- Suriname
- Trinidad and Tobago

ECO (Economic Cooperation Organization)
- Afghanistan
- Azerbaijan
- Islamic Republic of Iran
- Kazakhstan
- Kyrgyzstan
- Pakistan
- Tajikistan
- Turkey
- Turkmenistan
- Uzbekistan

UMA (Arab Maghreb Union)
- Algeria
- Libya
- Mauritania
- Morocco
- Tunisia

CIS (Commonwealth of Independent States)
- Armenia
- Azerbaijan
- Belarus
- Georgia
- Kazakhstan
- Kyrgyzstan
- Moldova
- Russian Federation
- Tajikistan
- Turkmenistan
- Ukraine
- Uzbekistan

OECS (Organization of Eastern Caribbean States)
- Anguilla
- Antigua and Barbuda
- British Virgin Islands
- Dominica
- Grenada
- Montserrat
- Saint Kitts and Nevis
- Saint Lucia
- Saint Vincent and the Grenadines

continued

EXHIBIT 1.5   Regional Trade Agreements around the World (continued)

FTAA (Free Trade Area of the Americas)

Antigua and Barbuda
Argentina
Bahamas
Barbados
Belize
Bolivia
Brazil
Canada
Chile
Colombia
Costa Rica
Dominica
Dominican Republic
Ecuador
El Salvador
Grenada
Guatemala
Guyana
Haiti
Honduras
Jamaica
Mexico
Nicaragua
Panama
Paraguay
Peru
Saint Kitts and Nevis
Saint Lucia
Saint Vincent and the Grenadines
Suriname
Trinidad and Tobago
United States of America
Uruguay
Venezuela

GCC (Gulf Cooperation Council)

Bahrain
Kuwait
Oman
Qatar
Saudi Arabia
United Arab Emirates

EU (European Union and Accession countries)

Member states:
Austria
Belgium
Denmark
Finland
France
Germany
Greece
Ireland
Italy
Luxembourg
Netherlands
Portugal
Spain
Sweden
UK

New member states:
Cyprus
Czech Republic
Estonia
Hungary
Latvia
Lithuania
Malta
Poland
Slovakia
Slovenia

Ascension States:
Romania
Slovakia
Turkey

ECOWAS (Economic Community of West African States)

Benin
Burkina Faso
Cape Verde
Côte d'Ivoire
Gambia
Ghana
Guinea
Guinea-Bissau
Liberia
Mali
Niger
Nigeria
Senegal
Sierra Leone
Togo

LAIA (Latin American Integration Association)

Argentina
Bolivia
Brazil
Chile
Colombia
Cuba
Ecuador
Mexico
Paraguay
Peru
Uruguay
Venezuela

MSG (Melanesia Spearhead Group)

Fiji
New Caledonia
Papua New Guinea
Solomon Islands
Vanuatu

SADC (Southern African Development Community)

Angola
Botswana
Democratic Republic of the Congo
Lesotho
Zambia
Zimbabwe
Malawi
Mauritius
Mozambique
Namibia
Seychelles
South Africa
Swaziland
United Republic of Tanzania

ECCAS (Economic Community of Central African States)

Angola
Burundi
Cameroon
Central African Republic
Chad
Congo
Democratic Republic of the Congo
Equatorial Guinea
Gabon
Rwanda
Sao Tome and Principe

MERCOSUR (Southern Cone Common Market)

Argentina
Brazil
Paraguay
Uruguay

SAARC (South Asian Association for Regional Cooperation)

Bangladesh
Bhutan
India
Maldives
Nepal
Pakistan
Sri Lanka

MRU (Mano River Union)

Guinea
Liberia
Sierra Leone

CEMAC, former UDEAC (Central African Customs and Economic Union)

Cameroon
Central African Republic
Chad
Congo
Equatorial Guinea
Gabon

NAFTA (North American Free Trade Agreement)

Canada
Mexico
United States of America

Source: Adapted from UNCTAD (UN Conference on Trade and Development). 2003. "Prospects for global and regional FDI ows, UNCTAD's worldwide survey of investment promotion agencies." Research Note. May 14.

EXHIBIT **1.6**   **Who's Selling, Who's Buying: The World's Leading Exporters and Importers**

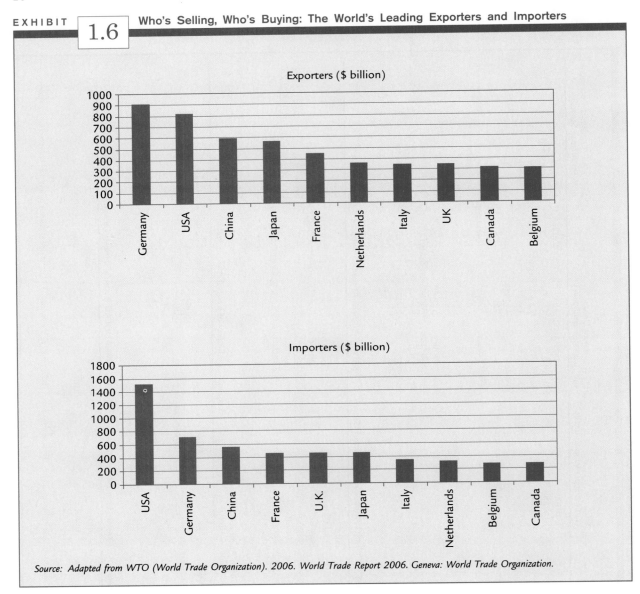

Source: Adapted from WTO (World Trade Organization). 2006. World Trade Report 2006. Geneva: World Trade Organization.

although developed countries still lead the world in terms of inward investments, the share of FDI for developing and emerging nations is growing steadily.[21] For instance, Brazil received inflows of $15 billion in 2005, confirming its position as the top emerging market FDI recipient outside Asia. Furthermore, some African countries also have seen significant investment with overall growth in Africa exceeding 4.5 percent in 2004.[22] Despite these changes, smaller countries still lag behind and will see less than significant inflows of FDI.

What does this mean for individual companies? Trends suggest that FDI will stay steady, with mergers and acquisitions playing an important role in these markets. Perhaps the most important implication is that multinational companies now manufacture and sell anywhere. The Case in Point on page 18 shows

EXHIBIT **1.7**   **Foreign Direct Investment Trends in Selected Markets**

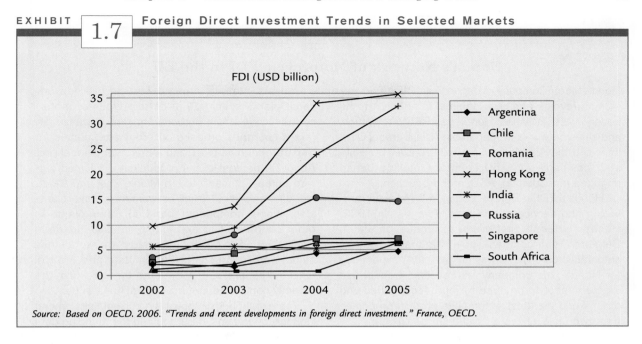

Source: Based on OECD. 2006. "Trends and recent developments in foreign direct investment." France, OECD.

how Honda Motor Company of Japan used FDI to create a European network of interrelated operations.

Although the TRIAD countries dominate the bulk of world FDI and will continue to do so in the immediate future, astute multinational managers also are looking to other areas of the world for future investments. Specifically, emerging markets will continue to attract significant inflows of FDI. As we will see throughout the text, many countries such as India, China, Brazil, Russia, and others will continue to present tremendous opportunities. Multinationals will likely continue the investment flows to play a role in these markets. Furthermore, although the developing countries may provide the great opportunities for multinational companies, they also are among the most risky locations in the world. We usually think of two types of risks in multinational business: economic and political. As you will see in more detail in Chapter 5, political risk is anything a government might do (or not do) that might adversely affect a company. In extreme circumstances—and now very rarely—governments have expropriated or taken over foreign firms with little or no compensation. More often, though, a government's instability and the uncertainty of its reactions to foreign investment are most important. Economic risk considers all factors of a nation's economic climate that may affect a foreign investor. Government policies affect some of these factors such as mandating artificially high or low interest rates. Other factors, such as a volatile exchange rate, may respond to economic forces from outside the country.

Despite the promise of international trade, three factors outside of the control of multinationals have the potential to slow global trade down. First, the recent increases in oil prices have the potential to slow down global trade because many countries are heavily dependent on oil imports.[23] Fortunately, this surge in prices has not yet produced damaging effects similar to the 1970s oil crisis as many developed countries have become more efficient in their oil use. Furthermore, the gradual price change has been due mostly to demand

CASE IN POINT

Honda's Network of Motorcycle FDI in the EU

Honda Motor Company of Japan is a global producer of motorcycles and automobiles. In addition to its headquarters in Japan, Honda has R&D, production, and sales networks in four areas: Asia, Europe, Oceania, and the Americas. In total, there are 100 affiliated companies in 150 countries outside Japan engaged in marketing, R&D, and production.

Honda's FDI in Europe began in 1961 with marketing and service activities in Germany. In 1963, Honda started its first overseas production unit in Belgium. That company now manufactures only automobile parts, but it was an invaluable experience for Honda. The company learned that it could use Western labor to produce for both local tastes and other world markets. Automobile production comes from two state-of-the-art plants in the UK.

Honda has taken advantage of the ease of trade among EU nations to integrate its European operations into one large network. In this network, some plants specialize in certain types of motorcycles for the whole European market. Plants in different countries produce different size models for the European market and other world locations. About 60 percent of the production is shipped outside Europe, primarily to the Middle East and Africa. Not all plants produce all components. Some plants also supply component parts to other plants in other countries. For example, Montessa Honda in Spain produces no engines. Most of its engines come from production sites in Italy and France. R&D takes place in Germany, the UK, and the recently completed motorcycle R&D unit in Italy.

The exhibit below shows the current links among Honda's operations in Europe and the founding date of each operation. There are also supply links to North and South America and Japan.

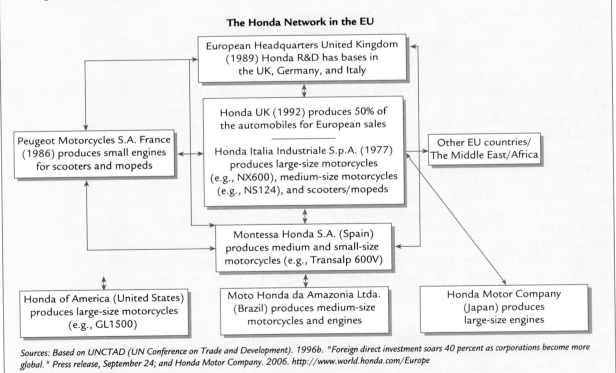

The Honda Network in the EU

European Headquarters United Kingdom (1989) Honda R&D has bases in the UK, Germany, and Italy

Honda UK (1992) produces 50% of the automobiles for European sales

Honda Italia Industriale S.p.A. (1977) produces large-size motorcycles (e.g., NX600), medium-size motorcycles (e.g., NS124), and scooters/mopeds

Peugeot Motorcycles S.A. France (1986) produces small engines for scooters and mopeds

Other EU countries/ The Middle East/Africa

Montessa Honda S.A. (Spain) produces medium and small-size motorcycles (e.g., Transalp 600V)

Honda of America (United States) produces large-size motorcycles (e.g., GL1500)

Moto Honda da Amazonia Ltda. (Brazil) produces medium-size motorcycles and engines

Honda Motor Company (Japan) produces large-size engines

Sources: Based on UNCTAD (UN Conference on Trade and Development). 1996b. "Foreign direct investment soars 40 percent as corporations become more global." Press release, September 24; and Honda Motor Company. 2006. http://www.world.honda.com/Europe

issues (as opposed to supply shock), giving countries time to adjust their policies. However, future trade growth will likely hinge on changes in oil prices.

Natural disasters also have become more prevalent and have the potential to disrupt international trade. For instance, the Indian tsunami severely affected five countries, namely India, Indonesia, Maldives, Sri Lanka, and Thailand. Furthermore, hurricanes Katrina and Rita have resulted in losses valued between $70 billion and $130 billion. Fortunately, these natural disasters have not had severe impact on trade so far. Except for Maldives, all of the other countries affected by the tsunami have seen continued growth. As such, the impact of future disasters will depend on how connected the size of affected areas and the degree of connected with global trade.[24]

Finally, international terrorism is seen as one of the most important threats to international trade. The September 11 attacks resulted in a slowdown in trade, and the recent bombings in London and Madrid have also had significant impact. Furthermore, the recent bombings in Bali have had a negative effect on the tourism industry.[25] However, these terrorists' acts seem to have had more short-term and localized effects so far. Nevertheless, if future terrorist acts occur, more companies will see increases in their insurance premiums affecting the transaction costs of their operations. As more insurance companies become reluctant to provide such insurance, costs of doing business internationally may increase significantly and may slow global trade.

The Internet and Information Technology Are Making It All Easier

The explosive growth in the Internet as well as in the capabilities of information technology increases the multinational company's ability to deal with a global economy. The Internet makes it easy for companies to go global since any web site can be accessed by anyone in the world. Thus, companies and individuals can shop anywhere and sell anywhere. Consider some of these data. The global online population numbers more than 600 million. The United States has 29 percent of global Internet access, followed by Europe with 23 percent and the Asia-Pacific region with 13 percent. Latin America has two percent. However, Europe has passed the United States' lead in Internet use, and e-commerce will end early in this decade.[26]

Because of the importance of this growing trend, Chapter 9 in this text discusses the impact of the Internet on multinational management in detail.

Electronic communication such as e-mail and the World Wide Web allows multinational companies to communicate with company locations throughout the world. Information technology expands the global reach of an organization. Multinational companies can now monitor worldwide operations to an extent never before possible. Text and graphic information can flow to any part of the world nearly instantaneously. Headquarters, research and development, manufacturing, or sales can be located anywhere there is a computer. Because employees, suppliers, and customers are geographically dispersed, organizations are becoming virtual—linked by networks of computers. Information technology makes it all happen.

Information technology is also spurring a borderless financial market. Investors are going global, and companies of the future will get their financing not in local stock or bond markets but in global markets that seek the best companies worldwide. Consider this *BusinessWeek* comment, which captures the feel of financial markets of the next century:

It's January 20, 2015, a fine summer day in Sydney. You stroll up to a Citibank automated-teller machine and, after the eye retina scan log on, a computer in Bombay greets you, and you get down to business. First, you shift

10,000 Euros into today's special—a NAFTA-dollar certificate of deposit issued by GEC Capital in Rome. Equities are looking good, so you punch in an order for 500 shares of Teléfonos de México on the New York Stock Exchange. Then, at the press of a button, an account officer in Singapore comes onto the screen to answer your questions about a loan for your factory in Argentina.[27]

However, as we will see in Chapter 7 on small businesses, information technologies are allowing small companies to get access to resources worldwide (capital, human resources, and machinery) very easily. Consider the following Case in Point.

Information technologies make available many new tools that facilitate business operations. For instance, Voice-Over-Internet Protocol (VOIP) companies such as Skype now allow employees to communicate worldwide at very low costs. WIKI companies allow companies to set up collaborative networks at very low cost. Instant messaging through MSN Messenger and AOL also allow employees to stay in constant communication. Finally, increasingly sophisticated search engines such as Google also allow anyone to find crucial information. Many smaller companies typically use such searches to find suppliers or manufacturers in emerging markets such as India or China.

The use of information technology and the Internet also are speeding up another globalization driver. Since many companies now use the Web to search for suppliers, it is easier to be a global customer.

The Rise of Global Products and Global Customers

Although large differences still exist among countries in terms of national cultures and political and economic systems, the needs of customers for many products and services are growing more similar. For example, fast-food chains such as McDonald's, aircraft manufacturers such as Boeing, and automobile makers such as Toyota each have individual products that are quite similar and successful throughout the world. In industries where customers'

C A S E   I N   P O I N T

Kidrobot

Kidrobot produces action figurines and other collectible dolls. In just over three years, Kidrobot founder Paul Budnitz grew the company from literally no sales to $5.5 million in sales. How did Budnitz achieve such success? He relies heavily on the many opportunities brought along by development in information technologies. The company uses Basecamp, a web-based collaboration tool, to integrate design teams in New York and manufacturers in China. Instead of spending thousands of dollars flying designers around the world similar to larger companies, Budnitz can instantly access design changes through a monitor and make such designs accessible to others in the company. If the company is not satisfied, it can e-mail the manufacturers and changes are made rapidly. Once Kidrobot is satisfied with the design, it can have the Chinese office produce and send a prototype within days. The simplicity afforded by intense use of cheap information technologies allows Kidrobot to juggle 40 toys at various stages of production and to bring toys from design to production within a month. In contrast, well-established companies such as Mattel are hampered by bloated design and production staffs and can take more than a year to bring toys to market.

Source: Based on Copeland, Michael V., and Andrew Tilin. 2005. "The new instant companies." Business 2.0, June, pp. 83–94.

needs are similar across national boundaries, global competition is more likely.[28]

Along with the rise of worldwide customer needs, a new type of customer is more common—the global customer. Global customers search the world for their supplies without regard for national boundaries. Price and quality affect the purchase decision more than nationality. At present, most global customers are companies making industrial purchases. This explains why 70 percent of the global e-commerce comes from business-to-business transactions. However, with the globalization of mail-order businesses and the increased use of web stores for purchasing consumer goods, including everything from athletic equipment to PCs, soon anyone can be a global customer. The Case in Point below may indicate the types of individual global purchasing that the future holds.

Similar customer needs and globally minded customers link economies because companies can produce one product for everybody, and anyone can buy anything from anywhere. These trends will continue as developing nations become more than sources of cheap production and become the sources of the greatest consumer growth.

The State Is Getting Out of Business

Privatization is the sale of government-owned businesses to private investors usually through stock or direct sale to other companies. The total value of government sell-offs rose sharply in the 1990s, peaking at $160 billion in 1998.[29] From 1988 to 1998, Western Europe had 52 percent of the privatizations; Asia and the Pacific region had 23 percent; and Latin America had 15 percent. Currently, state-owned enterprises (SOEs) are largely obsolete in Spain, Portugal, and the United Kingdom.[30] By 2002, European privatizations slowed to less than $20 billion. Low stock prices and previous sales accounted for much of the drop.[31]

Privatization

The sale of government-owned businesses to private investors.

CASE IN POINT

The Global Tennis Racquet

In spite of the recent strength of the dollar, the author considered $270 for the Prince tennis racquet too steep in the Lille, France sporting goods store. A quick check on the World Wide Web, however, showed me that the same racquet cost only $149 (plus $15 next-day air shipping) in the United States. It was also nice to see pictures of the racquet and read the evaluations.

Being a global shopper, I ordered the racquet by e-mail delivered to my U.S. address by next-day air. The racquet was then shipped by two-day air from Pullman, Washington to Lille, France for about $45 in U.S. currency. Import duty drove the total cost up to around $220, but I had my new racquet and saved around $50. Someday my electronic order will go directly to the Prince manufacturing plant in China. They will then ship it directly to me anywhere I happen to be in the world, avoiding the transportation costs from China to the Prince distribution center, from the distribution center to the mail-order house, from the mail-order company to my U.S. address, and then to France—maybe without any tariffs at all.

The hope for these countries is that privatization will not only make their companies more globally competitive but also will attract foreign investors who can bring up-to-date technology and management practices. For multinational companies from other nations, the privatization in the developing world offers opportunities for bargain-basement investments. Buying formerly government-owned companies can be an easy way to gain access to new production facilities, often with local-government incentives such as several years of tax-free operations.

Two types of privatization contribute to the global economy—one in the developed world and another in the developing world. The developed countries use privatization to make formerly government-controlled enterprises more competitive in the global economy. They represent the bulk of the dollar value of privatizations. These privatizations are driven by reductions in government trade protection, which often led government-owned organizations into complacency. Without protection from global competitors, newly privatized companies are forced to meet worldwide standards of quality and efficiency or face bankruptcy. When old government monopolies go public, foreign firms are often first in line to acquire the new organizations. For example, Ameritech Corp, one of the U.S. Baby Bells, was part of a consortium that purchased 49.9 percent of Belgacom, the privatized Belgian phone company.[32]

The developing nations use privatizations to jump-start their economies or to speed the transition from a communist system to a capitalist system. For example, the break from socialism was apparent when the former Soviet Union privatized the enormous SOEs: Lukoil (petroleum), Gazprom (natural gas), and Syzainvest (telecommunications). Foreign investment in Latin America hit record levels in 1999 and 2000[33] due to opportunities for multinational firms to invest in local companies. Latin America had 70 percent of the privatizations of the developing nations in the late 1990s.[34]

Multinational firms often acquire the best companies in the developing world. For example, when Bosnia's privatization program came online with 80 companies for sale in late 2000, Germany's Heidelberger Zement bought 51 percent of Cement Plant Kakanj, the country's biggest cement maker. This was the first company sold. It has a modern plant and a high demand for its high-quality cement. Experts agree, however, that it may be difficult to privatize the other companies. Like many operations from the transition economies in Russia and Eastern Europe, these old state companies are incapable of competing in the world economy. They have outdated equipment, poor management, and a bloated workforce, all vestiges of a time when they did not have to compete.[35] However, privatizations that originate with stock offerings also have proven successful.

However, recent trends suggest that privatization opportunities are starting to dry up in many of the established European emerging markets such as Poland, the Czech Republic, and Hungary. While 2003 saw 80 percent of EU foreign investment go to these three countries, investors are now turning their attention to South Eastern European countries, Russia, and the Commonwealth of Independent State countries. Privatization opportunities are numerous in South Eastern European countries such as Slovakia (airports and utilities), Romania (telecommunications and oil companies), and Bulgaria (banking sector).[36] The Case in Point on page 23 discusses the example of Turkey and privatization opportunities in its banking industry.

New Competitors Are Emerging

The free-market reforms in emerging countries are creating a potential group of new competitors in the world market. Who are some of these companies to watch? Exhibit 1.8 shows selected top 25 companies from the *Business Week* annual scoreboard of the top 100 emerging-market companies. Of these 100 emerging-market companies, 44 are from China, 21 are from India, and 12 are from Brazil, with other countries represented including Egypt, Russia, Turkey, Thailand, and Indonesia.[37]

C A S E   I N   P O I N T

Privatization in Turkey

As Turkey continues talks to gain membership in the European Union, more investors are becoming interested in Turkish privatization opportunities. In 2004 alone, Turkey raised around $2.1 billion through privatization projects. There are future plans to privatize companies involved in oil refineries, steel and iron industry, telecommunications industry, and the Turkish airline.

The rush to invest in Turkey can be explained by the significant potential presented by Turkey. Turkey has had a strong and stable economic environment over the past four to five years. Furthermore, Turkey has a predominantly young population, with a median age of 33 in 2005, and it is experiencing rapid growth. Additionally, recent increases in payment cards, such as credit and debit cards, have been among the highest in Europe, suggesting that people are willing to spend.

The banking industry in Turkey presents the most opportunities. Many of the first-tier banks have seen significant investment from companies such as Hong Kong Shanghai Bank, General Electric, and BNP Paribas. Many investors are keeping an eye on the second-tier banks to get access to the Turkish market.

Source: Based Bedell, Denise. 2005. "The investment magnet." Global Finance, 19, 9, pp. 91–94; Krebsbach, Karen. 2006. "Turkey's strong growth beckons Western banks." USBanker, 116, 1, p. 16.

In many cases, these new competitors had to survive brutal competition in their domestic markets to become successful. By competing every day with both domestic rivals and Western multinationals, they were able to develop strategies to generate profits at very low prices. However, operating in emerging markets gives companies significant cost advantages. Consider the Case in Point on page 25.

Global trade has two important effects in developing new competitors. First, when the large multinationals use developing countries as low-wage platforms for high-tech assembly, they facilitate the transfer of technology. Workers and companies in developing countries often learn new skills when the large multinationals use them for low-cost production and assembly. In countries where the workers are well educated and motivated, the former assemblers often become the creators rather than the builders of advanced technologies. Second, aggressive multinational companies from emerging-market countries are also expanding beyond their own borders. Consider the Case in Point on page 25 for Cemex S.A. from Mexico. It shows not only how smaller competitors can grow to challenge any company but also how information and web technology can be used successfully.

The Rise of Global Standards

Increasingly, especially in technical industries, global product standards are common. For example, you can buy an AA battery anywhere in the world, and it will fit in your flashlight. One driving factor is that, when a product standard is accepted globally or regionally, companies can make one or only a few versions of a product for the world market. This is much cheaper than making 100 different versions for 100 different countries. Component makers also benefit since they can take advantage of the same efficiencies with fewer product designs.

Certainly there are still many diverse technical standards throughout the world. For example, Europe and North America have different formats for TVs and VCRs. Differences in electrical currents and plugs are common examples

EXHIBIT 1.8   The Top Emerging Market Companies

Company	Revenues (USDb)	Country	Industry
Petrobras	56.3	Brazil	Petroleum
Gazprom	48.9	Russia	Petroleum
China Mobile	30.1	China	Telecommunication
Koc Holding	18	Turkey	Diversified Industries
America Movil	17	Mexico	Telecommunication
Shanghai Baosteel	15.8	China	Steel
Cemex	15.3	Mexico	Building materials
CVRD	15.1	Brazil	Mining
Lenovo Group	13.4	China	Computers
Haier	12.8	China	Home appliances
CNOOC	8.7	China	Petroleum
MNC Norilsk Nickel	7.2	Russia	Mining
Huawei Technologies	5.9	China	Telecommunication
Tata Motors	5.8	India	Automotive
Severstal	4.9	Russia	Steel
Hisense	4.2	China	Electronics and appliances
Embraer	3.8	Brazil	Aerospace
Sadia	3.6	Brazil	Food and beverage
Orascom	3.3	Egypt	Telecommunication
Techtronic Industries	3	Hong Kong	Power tools
Mahindra	2.9	India	Auto and tractors
Tata Consultancy	2.8	India	IT
Wipro	2.3	India	IT
Infosys	2	India	IT
Ranxaby Labs	1.2	India	Pharmaceuticals

Sources: Adapted from BusinessWeek. 2006. "The top 25 emerging markets." July 31, p. 43.

ISO 9001:2000

The current name for the technical and quality standards of the International Organization for Standardization.

ISO 14000

The current name for the environmental protection standards of the International Organization for Standardization.

faced daily by international travelers. However, many electronic devices are now smart enough to overcome these differences. Power sources for computers, for example, often can adjust automatically for differences in voltage.

As new products are introduced into the world market, there is increasing competitive pressure to save money by developing one product for everyone. Thus, the company that can establish its standard as dominant either regionally or worldwide has a tremendous strategic advantage. For example, Motorola of the United States is locked in a fierce competitive battle with Finland's Nokia and Sweden's Ericsson over setting the standard for the next generation of digital cell-phone technology.

Consistency in quality also has become a requirement for doing business in many countries. The International Organization for Standardization (ISO) in Geneva, Switzerland has developed a set of technical standards known originally as ISO 9000, now called the **ISO 9001:2000** series (International Standards Organization 2006). There also are environmental protection standards known as **ISO 14000**.

CASE IN POINT

Orascom Telecom, Egypt

Orascom Telecom, based in Cairo, Egypt, is a fast-growing telecommunications company with operations in many of the world's top emerging markets. Naguib Sawiris, Orascom's chairman, saw potential in emerging markets from the day he founded the company. As of the first quarter of 2006, Orascom had 35 million subscribers, representing a 101 percent increase in subscribers from the previous year. The company also recently added Italy's Wind Telcommunicazioni to its growing empire.

How has Orascom been so successful while established European rivals have had difficulty breaking into emerging markets? Sawiris believes

that the low costs of operations in emerging markets give Orascom a significant advantage over European rivals. Orascom can operate at a tenth of expenses relative to European rivals as engineers and salespeople tend to be much less expensive in emerging markets. The sustained level of growth in these markets also has enabled Orascom to keep spreading fixed costs over a larger base of subscribers. It also helps that the company is headquartered in Egypt as this gives the company an edge over European rivals in understanding emerging markets.

Source: Reed, Stanley. 2006. "This mobile upstart really gets around." BusinessWeek, July 31, p. 49.

In 1992, ISO compliance became part of product-safety laws in many European countries. Many large European multinationals such as Germany's Siemens now require suppliers to be ISO-certified. As a result, in order to do business in the EU, the pressure is increasing for the United States and other countries to adopt ISO quality requirements and standardization.[38]

Complying with global standards has been beneficial to companies. Consider the Multinational Management Brief on page 26.

CASE IN POINT

No Longer Local

Cemex S.A. de C.V. is the world's third largest cement company. This Mexican company has 56 plants in 30 countries. Based on size of foreign assets, Cemex ranks second on the World Investment Report's list of top 50 transnational corporations from developing nations. According to *BusinessWeek,* it also is in the top 25 emerging market companies in market value. It has the highest profit margins of any cement company in the world.

Founded in the early 1900s, Cemex reached the number one rank in Mexico in the late 1980s. In the 1990s, the company went multinational. During the last decade, Cemex doubled its production capacity and tripled its revenues largely by acquiring companies outside of Mexico. It now owns, either completely or in part, ten companies from other developing countries and three from developed countries.

Cemex CEO Lorenzo Zambrano is a technology enthusiast. Cemex has invested more than $200 million in a state-of-the-art computerized information

system. This system gives managers real-time information on inventory, delivery schedules, quality records, and even oven temperatures at Cemex's operations in Spain, Venezuela, Colombia, Panama, the Philippines, Indonesia, and the United States. Most recently, Cemex tied its information system into global positioning satellites that allow managers to find the shortest route to customers. Delivery time dropped from an average of three hours to 20 minutes. Cemex uses web technology to let customers place and track orders, called e-selling. It uses an extensive intranet to encourage organizational learning by sharing information across national boundaries.

Source: Based on BusinessWeek Online. 2002. "Scoreboard: The top 200 emerging markets companies." July 15th; BusinessWeek. 2006. "The top 25 emerging markets." July 31, p. 43; Economist. 2001. "The Cemex way." http://www.economist.com. January 14; Smith, Geri. 1999. "Concrete benefits from a plunge into cyberspace." http://businessweekonline.com, April 29; UNCTAD. 2002. World Investment Report. New York and Geneva: United Nations; Cemex. 2006. http//: www.cemex.com.

Multinational Management **Brief**

Metro Cash and Carry and Process Standardization

Metro Cash and Carry is part of the Metro Group, a German retailer that ranks among the top three in the world. It has operations around the world and is the global market leader in wholesale cash and carry. The retailer is reputed for its ability to deliver fresh meat, fruits and vegetables around the world. How did it achieve such competence in delivering freshness? An important factor is that the company has strictly standardized procedures with respect to how it deals with its supply chain around the world. At a minimum, Metro's 90,000 employees are required to satisfy strict international professional standards in whatever they are doing. This standardized process has allowed the company to have all employees, departments, and subsidiaries around the world on the same page.

Sources: Dziobaka-Spitzhorn, 2006. "From West to East." Performance Improvement, 45, 6, pp. 41–47.

The next section discusses the type of managers that will succeed in the global economy of the future by describing some of the characteristics of the next generation of multinational managers.

The Next Generation Of Multinational Managers

Consider what the experts say about the need for multinational managers and leaders:

> *It takes more than a lot of frequent flyer miles to become a global leader. Today's cosmopolitan executive must know what to do when competitive advantage is fleeting, when change becomes chaos, and when home base is the globe.*[39]
>
> *We need global leaders at a time when markets and companies are changing faster than the ability of leaders to reinvent themselves. We have a shortage of global leaders at a time when international exposure and experience are vital to business success. And we need internationally minded, globally literate leaders at a time when leadership styles are in transition around the world.*[40]

To become global leaders and keep pace with the dizzying rate of globalization, most managers will need additional strengths to meet its challenges. According to some experts, the next generation of successful multinational managers must have the following characteristics:[41]

Global mindset

One that requires managers to think globally, but act locally."

- *A global mindset:* A person with a **global mindset** understands that the world of business is changing rapidly and that the world is more interdependent in business transactions. A global mindset requires managers to think globally, but act locally." Managers must see similarities in the global market while still being able to adapt to local conditions in any country. A global mindset is necessary for all employees, from the CEO to the rank and file, if a company is to support and implement a global strategic vision.
- *The ability to work with people from diverse backgrounds:* In the global economy, customers, partners, suppliers, and workers often will come from

locations other than the company's home country. The next generation of multinational managers will build on their awareness of cultural differences to succeed in these cross-cultural relationships. Successful organizations will require all employees to work well with diverse groups of people.

- *Emotionally intelligent:* There is growing evidence that being able to manage one's emotions, or emotional intelligence, is a crucial requirement for the multinational manager. Previous research has shown that emotional intelligence prepares the manager to better adjust to and deal with new cultures and people.
- *A long-range perspective:* A short-term view seldom succeeds in the new global economy. Credited with responsibility for turning Motorola into a global player, former CEO Robert W. Galvin put a representative in Beijing more than ten years ago. Now Motorola is the largest U.S. investor in China. Successful companies must be persistent to overcome the complexities of dealing with the international environment.
- *The ability to manage change and transition:* Although a long-term view favors survival in the global environment, the global economy is volatile and unpredictable. This will require leaders with the skills to effectively implement many organizational changes.
- *The ability to create systems for learning and changing organizations:* Organizations competing in the global economy will face rapidly changing and complex environments. These organizations will need to tap the talents of all employees concerning what is going on in the world and in the organization. They will need to coordinate complex interdependencies among business functions (e.g., marketing and manufacturing) across national boundaries. The next generation of multinational leaders will be responsible for building the organizations that can meet the needs of evolving strategies for global competition.
- *The talent to motivate all employees to achieve excellence:* The ability to motivate has always been a hallmark of leadership. In the next generation of organization, the leader will face additional challenges of motivation. Employees may come from any country and may live in any country. Leaders will face the motivational challenge of having employees identify with the organization rather than with their country. Leaders also will need to develop motivational strategies that transcend cultures.
- *Accomplished negotiating skills:* All business transactions require negotiation. However, leaders in the global economy will spend considerably more time negotiating cross-culturally. This will be more challenging as well as more necessary.
- *The willingness to seek overseas assignments:* The next generation of leaders will have significant international experiences. They will demonstrate management skills and success in more than one cultural environment.
- *An understanding of national cultures:* In spite of the pressures of globalization to treat the world as one market, large differences still exist among national cultures. No multinational leader or business can succeed without a deep understanding of the national cultures in which they do business. Multinational managers often will be required to learn two or more additional languages as well as the nuances of local cultural differences.

Can you develop the skills necessary to be a successful multinational manager? One of the first tasks is to learn all you can about multinational management and international business. In the next section, we will discuss how this text can contribute to this goal.

Multinational Management: A Strategic Approach

Why should you study multinational management? In today's Internet-connected world, you may have little choice but to be a multinational manager. Foreign competition and doing business in foreign markets are daily facts of life for today's managers. The study of multinational management helps prepare you to deal with this evolving global economy and to develop the skills necessary to succeed as a multinational manager. This text will introduce some of the basic skills of multinational management.

It takes a strategic approach to multinational management, focusing on how multinational managers formulate and implement strategies to compete successfully in the global economy. **Strategy** is defined here as the maneuvers or activities that managers use to sustain and increase organizational performance. **Strategy formulation** is the process of choosing or crafting a strategy. **Strategy implementation** includes all the activities that managers and an organization must perform to achieve strategic objectives.

From the perspective of the multinational company and managers, strategies must include maneuvers that deal with operating in more than one country and culture. Thus, multinational strategy formulation takes on the added challenges of dealing with opportunities and competition located anywhere in the world. Similarly, multinational strategy implementation carries added challenges, including the need to develop complex management systems to carry out strategies that reach beyond domestic boundaries.

The rules of competition are constantly evolving. Today's multinationals face an environment that is drastically different from the environment that multinationals faced in the past. A company can be a dominant player but can lose its competitive edge rapidly. As we examine international management from a strategic perspective, it is important to understand the trends that will shape the future business environment. These include:[42]

- *Blurring of industry boundaries:* Information and other communication technologies have made industry boundaries less clear. For instance, the South Korean company Samsung now produces products ranging from televisions to cell phones to microprocessors. This blurring of boundaries make it much harder to identify and understand competitors.
- *Flexibility matters more than size:* Recent events suggest that being big may no longer be useful. Consider that many giants such as GM, Microsoft, Dell, and IBM have all hit market caps. As outsourcing, alliances, and partnering gather steam, companies are finding that they can convert many fixed costs into variable costs. Such changes make scale less useful.
- *Find your niche:* Multinationals have traditionally strived to be the leader in their respective industries. However, such thinking is now changing. Kim and Mauborgne's[43] Blue Ocean Strategy suggest that finding those uncontested niches also leads to success. In fact, many companies are finding that they can do well by finding niches and satisfying the needs in that niche. Consider the Multinational Management Brief on page 29.
- *Hypercompetition:* The new environment is characterized by intense competition coming from companies located in all parts of the world. Businesses

Strategy

The maneuvers or activities that managers use to sustain and increase organizational performance.

Strategy formulation

Process by which managers select the strategies to be used by their company.

Strategy implementation

All the activities that managers and an organization must perform to achieve strategic objectives.

Multinational Management **Brief**

Chaliyuan and the Chinese Cell Phone Industry

Shouji jiayouzhan or "cell-phone" gas stations can now be found almost everywhere in cities and towns in China. With approximately 340 million cell phone users, there is tremendous demand for power sources to recharge these cell phones. While other companies have considered cell phone recharging as an unimportant side business, Chaliyuan has gone aggressively after the market. It produces as many as 75 percent of cell-phone-charging machines currently found in China. The phone kiosk is equipped with as many as 24 cords to accommodate a variety of phones and other digital devices such as digital cameras and laptops. The company charges the equivalent of 12 cents for a 10-minute recharging time. As cell phone use grows steadily in China, the company has tremendous growth potential. Additionally, the company also is considering other uses such as advertising for their kiosks.

Sources: Shi, Ting. 2005. "A gas pump for 300 million phones." Business 2.0, June, p. 78.

cannot expect to be stable and be around for a long time. For instance, consider that Haier, a Chinese company that entered the U.S. market in 1999, is now the top-selling brand of dorm fridges. It also is the market leader in home wine coolers and ranks third in freezers.

- *Emphasis on innovation and the learning organization:* Successful companies are going to those that can draw on local knowledge to innovate and compete globally. For instance, many of the successful South Korea and Japanese companies were able to use their domestic markets as tests to improve and launch their products globally. To achieve such success, any multinational will need to develop the appropriate mechanisms and systems to integrate the local knowledge to produce value for the company.

Given the above, a fundamental assumption of this book is that successful multinational management requires managers to understand their potential competitors and collaborators.[44] Consider:

When you understand your competitors and yourself, you will always win. (Sun Tzu, The Art of War.)

Multinational companies and managers must be prepared to compete with other firms from any country. In addition, they must be prepared to collaborate with companies and people from any country as suppliers, alliance partners, and customers. To accomplish these tasks means that multinational managers must understand more than the basics of national culture. They must understand how people from different nations view organizational strategies and organizations. To provide such a background, this text devotes several chapters to comparative management—the comparison of management practices used by people from different nations.

Summary and Conclusions

This chapter provided you with key background information that supports the study of multinational management. The chapter defined multinational management and the multinational company. You saw examples of the world's largest multinationals. However, as the Preview Case in Point showed, companies of all sizes can be multinational.

Because we exist in a globalizing world, considerable attention has been devoted to the forces that drive globalization. These are key environmental issues that affect every multinational company and its managers. World trade and investments are growing rapidly, but not always consistently, making all economies more linked and creating both opportunities and threats for both domestic and multinational companies. New competitors, strong and motivated, are coming from developing nations in Asia, the Americas, and the transitioning economies of Eastern Europe. Customers, products, and standards are becoming more global. The increasing sophistication and lower cost of information technology fuel the development of global companies that can more easily manage worldwide operation.

Multinational managers of the next generation will need skills not always considered necessary for domestic-only managers. This chapter described key characteristics of successful multinational managers as identified by several experts. Perhaps the most encompassing characteristic is the global mindset. Managers with a global mindset understand the rapidly changing business and economic environment. They can see the world as an integrated market, yet appreciate and understand the wide array of differences in the world cultures and social institutions.

The next two chapters in this section will begin building the foundation of your global mindset. You will see how cultural differences affect business practices. You will see not only how understanding national culture is crucial to your success as a multinational manager but also how social institutions such as religion and law influence multinational management. This combination of national culture and social institutions is called the national context.

After reading this text, you should have the foundation for understanding the latest challenges and practices of multinational management. However, the field is dynamic, and your learning will never be complete. Successful multinational managers will view the understanding of their field as a lifelong endeavor.

Discussion Questions

1. Discuss how any company can become a multinational company. What are some of the options available to companies that allow them to use international markets and locations competitively?

2. Discuss some reasons why reductions in world trade barriers are driving the world toward a global economy.

3. Consider how things such as wars, terrorist act, and bird flu might alter the progression of globalization. What should a multinational manager do to deal with these situations?

4. Discuss the differences between foreign trade and foreign direct investment.

5. Discuss some of the advantages and disadvantages of setting up production in developing nations. Consider the benefits of market growth and the risk of the venture. Consider the position of Motorola discussed in the text. If you were the CEO, would you think that Motorola made the right move?

6. Look at the information on developing economies and hot competitors discussed in the text. Where do you think the next generation of world-class competitors will come from? Why?

7. Discuss the characteristics of a next generation multinational manager. How can you develop those characteristics through education and experience?

8. What are some of the new rules of competition today? How are these new rules going to affect global trade?

Multinational Management **Skill Builder**

Interview a Multinational Manager

Step 1. In teams or as an individual, contact a current or former multinational manager. Where can you find a multinational manager? Perhaps some are close by. In a business college, many graduate students and professors have had work experience as a multinational manager. Also, the parents of many students are similarly experienced. Most likely, however, you will need to contact a company and ask to speak with the individual in charge of international operations. Don't overlook small companies. Although it may not be a full-time responsibility, many companies still have someone responsible for international sales.

Step 2. Set up an appointment for an interview.

Step 3. Arrive on time, professionally dressed with a list of prepared questions. Some possible questions include:

What circumstances led you to assume a position with international responsibilities?

What are the major challenges in the international part of your job?

How would you describe the international strategy of your company?

How important is international work to advance in your company?

How do you deal with and prepare for cultural differences?

Do you ever have to manage directly employees from other countries? If so, what are the challenges in doing that?

How are people selected for international assignments?

Do you face any unique ethical situations in your job?

Endnotes

[1] Lustgarden, Abrahm. 2006. "Fortune Global 500." Fortune, July 24, pp. 95–98.

[2] Lamy, Pascale. 2006. "Humanizing globalization." *International Trade Forum*, 1, pp. 5–6.

[3] *Economist*. 2006. "The future of globalization," July 29, p. 11.

[4] *Economist*. 2006. "Climbing back," January 21, p. 69.

[5] Ibid.

[6] WTO (World Trade Organization). 2006. *World Trade Report 2006*. Geneva: World Trade Organization.

[7] *Economist*. 1996a. "All free traders now?" December 7, pp. 23–25.

[8] *Economist*. 2003. "Heading east." http://www.economist.com, March 27.

[9] WTO (World Trade Organization). 2000. *Annual Report* (2000). Geneva: World Trade Organization.

[10] *Economist*. 2006. "In the twilight of Doha," July 29, pp. 69–70.

[11] *Economist*. 1996a. "Spoiling world trade." December 7, pp. 15–16.

[12] Lubbers, R. F. M. 1996. "Globalization: An exploration." *Nijenrode Management Review*, p. 1.

[13] Boscheck, Ralph. 1996. "Managed trade and regional preference." In IMD, *World Competitiveness Yearbook 1996*, pp. 333–44. Lausanne, Switzerland: Institute for Management Development.

[14] *Economist*. "Spoiling world trade."

[15] WTO (World Trade Organization). *World Trade Organization: Trading into the Future* (2002) Geneva: World Trade Organization.

[16] WTO (World Trade Organization), *World Trade Report 2006*.

[17] UNCTAD (UN Conference on Trade and Development). 2002. *World Investment Report*. New York and Geneva: United Nations.

[18] UNCTAD (UN Conference on Trade and Development). 2000. *World Investment Report*. New York and Geneva: United Nations;

UNCTAD (UN Conference on Trade and Development). 2000. "World FDI flows exceed US$ 1.1 trillion in 2000." UNCTAD Press Release, December 7.

[19] *OECD*. 2006. *"Trends and recent developments in foreign direct investment."* France, OECD.

[20] Ibid.

[21] Ibid.

[22] UNCTAD (UN Conference on Trade and Development). 2005. *Trade and development report, 2005*. New York and Geneva: United Nations.

[23] Ibid.

[24] WTO (World Trade Organization), *World Trade Report 2006*.

[25] Ibid.

[26] NUA Internet Surveys. 2003. http://www.nua.ie/surveys.

[27] Javetski, Bill, and William Glasgall. 1994. "Borderless finance: Fuel for growth." *BusinessWeek*, November 18, pp. 40–50.

[28] Yip, George S. 2002. *Total Global Strategy II*, Englewood Cliffs: Prentice Hall.

[29] Megginson, William. 2000. "Privatization." *Foreign Policy*, http://www.findarticles.com, Spring.

[30] Ibid.

[31] *Economist*. 2002. "Coming home to roost." http://www.economist.com, June 27.

[32] Javetski, Bill, Gail Edmondson, and William Echikson. 1996. "Believing in Europe: U.S. companies are plowing billions into the Old World—and shaking up its business practices in the process." *BusinessWeek*, International Edition—Europe, cover story, October 7.

[33] UNCTAD (UN Conference on Trade and Development). 2000. "World FDI flows exceed US$ 1.1 trillion in 2000." UNCTAD Press Release, December 7.

[34] World Bank. 2000. *Global Development Finance*. Washington, DC: World Bank.

[35] Dizarevic, Eldar. 2000. "Hot cakes." *Business Central Europe*, http://www.bcemag.com, December.

[36] Hawser, Anita. 2006. "Attention turns to the new wave." *Global Finance*, 20, 1, pp. 30–31.

[37] Marsh, Peter. 2006. "Companies from emerging markets setting the pace." http://www.ft.com.

[38] Levine, Jonathan B. 1992. "Want EC business? You have two choices." *BusinessWeek*, October 19, pp. 58–59.

[39] Rhinesmith, Steven H., John N. Williamson, David M. Ehlen, and Denise S. Maxwell. 1989. "Developing leaders for the global enterprise." *Training and Development Journal*, April, pp. 25–34.

[40] Rosen,, Robert H., Patricia Digh, Mashall, Singer, and Carl, Phillips. 1999. *Global Literacies: Lessons on Business Leaders and National Cultures*. Riverside, NJ: Simon & Schuster.

[41] Beamish, Paul J., Peter Killing, Donald J. Lecraw, and Allen J. Morrison. 1994. *International Management*; Gabel, Racheli

Shmueli, Shimon L. Dolan, and Jean Luc Cerdin. 2005. "Emotional intelligence as predictor of cultural adjustment for success in global assignments." *Career Development International*, 10, 5, pp. 375–95; Moran, Robert T., and John R. Riesenberger. 1994. *The Global Challenge*. London: McGraw-Hill.

[42] Hitt, Michael A., Barbara W. Keats, and Samuel M. DeMarie. 1998. "Navigating in the new competitive landscape: Building strategic flexibility and competitive advantage in the 21st century." *Academy of Management Executive*, 12, 4, pp. 22–42; Kim, Chan W., and Renee Mauborgne. 2005. "Value innovation: A leap into the blue ocean." *The Journal of Business Strategy*, 26, 4, pp. 22–28; Morris, Betsy. "The new rules." *Fortune*, July 24, pp. 70–87.

[43] Kim and Mauborgne, "Value innovation: A leap into the blue ocean."

[44] Hamel, Cary, and C. K. Prahalad. 1989. "Strategic intent." *Harvard Business Review*, May–June, pp. 63–76.

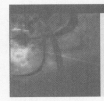

CHAPTER CASE
ABB in China: 1998

"I want to make ABB a company that encourages and demands innovation from all of its employees, and a company that creates the environment in which teamwork and innovation flourish," declares ABB's CEO Göran Lindahl. In seeking new growth, CEO Göran Lindahl is escaping the long shadow of his predecessor Percy Barnevik. The former CEO of ABB, Percy Barnevik, was argued to be one of the most successful international managers in Europe.

ABB, the world leader in electrical engineering, is a US$35 billion electrical engineering group, with companies all over the globe. It operates primarily in the fields of reliable and economical generation, transmission and distribution of electrical energy.[1] Much has been written about the worldwide company. In 1996 ABB was ranked in the top 40 listed by Fortune 500. Recently, the company announced its newest reorganization making it more up-to-date with the global world, as the current CEO, Göran Lindahl, expressed.[2] In 1997, Göran Lindahl took over from Percy Barnevik as CEO of the technology giant ABB, and is feeling the demanding market and shareholder pressures.

ABB has different priorities in different markets. Western Europe and North America are the company's biggest markets. However, the high-potential markets are the Middle East, Africa, Latin America and Asia. These markets are growing fast and ABB expects to have half of its customers in these regions not long into the next century. The priority is on building local manufacturing, engineering and other forms of added value. ABB wants to integrate these operations into the global networks to obtain full synergy effects and economies of scale.

During 1998 it was shown that the industrial production in OECD countries, in which ABB performs about 75 percent of its total business, continues to grow, although at a slower pace than the strong growth rates a year ago. Overall, industrial production in Europe is lower than a year ago, but still high compared with historical levels. Current economic activity in North America is slowing compared with the strong economy of recent years. In Latin America, high interest rates are delaying the financial closing of projects in an environment of reduced economic activity. The Indian economy is slowing due to reduced exports as a result of its strong currency compared with others in the region. Southeast Asia is gradually stabilizing at a low level, with reduced consumption and investments.

As a result of the ongoing economic uncertainty, overall global demand is forecast to remain soft in the near future. ABB expects to benefit with its well-established local presence around the world from higher demand in various industries and world markets. Appropriate cost cutting, continued selective tendering and successful working capital reduction programs are expected to continue contributing positively to the ABB Group results. The company recognizes the world to be rapidly changing and increasingly unpredictable. Efforts have paid off and the Group has taken its opportunities in Asia and positioned itself for future growth in what is seen to be "the world's most dynamic market—China."[3]

The interest in China is growing steadily and companies in Japan, the western European countries, the United States and elsewhere today view the Chinese market as having enormous potential. With a population of a billion and a growing economy, it seems to be worthwhile to gain a foothold in the market.[4] On the one hand, China represents a huge and largely untapped market. The Chinese market alone is potentially bigger than that of the United States, the European Community, and Japan combined! On the other hand, China's new firms are proving to be very competitive, and China's culture is quite different from that of the West. However, the Chinese market growth remains relatively good for enterprises such as Procter & Gamble, Motorola, Nestlé and ABB. This market acts as a lifeboat to many of the worldwide companies suffering from the financial crisis in the rest of South East Asia.

Nevertheless, discussions exist about China devaluating its currency, which might also drag China down into the crisis. Yet the country has not shown any visible scratches from the surrounding crisis. China seems to be unshakable and analysts are still valuing China as the country of the future.[5] Thus, the changes in China are creating both opportunities and threats for established worldwide companies. This is a country that, according to Management Today, will be one of the top 10 economies in the world by the year 2010.[6]

Chinese Influence

China will enter the next century as the rising power in Asia after two decades of astonishing economic growth that has transformed the country and that has given rise to new challenges.[7]

Many cities in China have more than five million inhabitants. It is a country that has had a growing economy, which cannot be compared to that of any other country during almost three decades.[8] It is argued that China is not like any other developing country, due to the rapid changes that are taking place in certain areas. In some areas, such as with home electronics,[9] the development has surpassed the development in Western countries, while in other areas, China lags far behind.

The Chinese culture and society is more than five thousand years old with a unique cultural heritage of philosophy, science and technology, societal structures and traditional administrative bureaucracy.[10] With this in mind it is no wonder, according to researchers, that conflicts often occur between Chinese and foreign cultures. This is caused by foreign managers being accustomed to other values and norms, some of which are not acceptable in China.[11]

In the current half-year reports from worldwide companies, a distinct trend is noticed, according to Dagens Industri.[12] The more focus that the companies have put on basic industry, the more the Asian crisis tends to affect these companies. However, China can save these companies and others, especially those companies operating in the business of infrastructure.[13] Now that the Cold War with China has ended, economic growth is stabilizing and the country is demanding a speedy reconstruction. The country has begun to enjoy unprecedented strategic latitude for the first time in 200 years, and it no longer faces the threat of aggression from superior powers. Ahlquist, Magnus as editor,[14] This has enabled the country to focus on economic developments as the driving force of both its domestic and foreign policies. According to Professor Yahuda, China's leaders are basing their legitimacy on providing stability and continued high levels of prosperity. The need for economic development is fueled by many other factors, such as providing employment for a vast population that increases by some 15 million people a year. In addition, there are significant regional inequalities that can be addressed only by further economic development.[15]

China is expected to evolve into a hybrid system of authoritarianism, democracy, socialism, and capitalism. Also recognized are the internal problems the country faces, such as environmental disasters, political struggles, and tensions between the emerging entrepreneurial economy and the vast parts of China still under state control.[16] Today China receives the most direct investment and foreign aid of any developing country. Many companies are eager to establish their presence in China, which, it is argued, attracts more than its proportionate share of investments.[17] However, "westerners cannot expect to know how China will develop and need to expect that the Chinese will always be different from them. Instead of trying to change China, they should look for positive steps that take their differences into account."[18]

According to China's Premier, Zhu Rongji, China is indeed the largest market in the world. However, due to the problem of duplicate construction, there is a problem of oversupply in some areas. Nevertheless, the Premier states that the market is far from being saturated.[19] Since China opened up its doors to the outside world in the late 1970s, a large number of foreign investors have gained rich returns from their investments, yet some have ended in failure. Some guiding keys to ensuring successful business in China, according to China Daily, include:[20]

- Making long-term strategies for the Chinese market. Competition is intensifying and market exploitation needs time and patience. Foreign companies eager to get a quick return are usually disappointed at the results.
- Localizing staff. They are familiar with the local business environment.

- Being aware of changes in policies and regulation. China is in a process of transforming from a planned economy to a market economy. Various policies and regulations are being revised and replaced, while new ones are being issued. Foreign investors must keep informed of the ongoing changes.
- Undertake practical market research. Due to social, economic, and cultural differences, practical and down-to-earth market research is a must before and during investment in China.

Chinese Cultural Influence

There is a consensus among several authors that China has a traditional respect for age, hierarchy and authority.[21] This originates from the Confucian concept of li (rite, proprietary), which plays an important role in maintaining a person's social position. Li can be seen today in the existing traditional bureaucracy and in vertical relationships concerning centralization of decision-making, and in corruption to some extent, which is acceptable in such a cultural context.[22]

Second, the family is viewed as an essential social unit and there is a strong tendency to promote the collective or the group. Members within the family or group must maintain harmonious relationships and these social relations are seen as more important than the individual.[23] Thus, the family or clan norms are adopted as the formal code of conduct, and members are bound to these standards. Other research found that in modern China, business and industrial enterprises were perceived as an extension of the family system.[24]

Third, the concept of "face" (mianzi) is seen as an important characteristic. As Ju noted, the general idea of mianzi is related to "a reputation achieved through getting on in life through success and ostentation."[25] Mianzi also serves to enhance harmony within the family or group, so that the positive is expressed publicly and any conflicts remain private.[26] Hong has found that the concept of mianzi still plays an important role in social relationships and organizational behavior.[27] However, Yuan points out that there are two sides to this concept.[28] The first includes the individual's moral character, and the strong fear of losing this limits the person's behavior. The second aspect of mianzi involves assertions about a person, which is not seen quite as seriously as the former type of loss of face.[29]

The importance of personal relations (guanxi) is the fourth characteristic. According to Hong, persons with guanxi usually share a common birthplace, lineage, surname or experience, such as attending the same school, working together or belonging to the same organization.[30] A comparative study of decision-making in China and Britain has revealed that Chinese managers use their personal guanxi more widely to exchange information, negotiate with planning authorities and accelerate decision-making processes than do managers from British firms.[31] As it is, the network transmits information, and because contacts and cooperation are built on trust, it is seen as very serious if that trust is broken. If a trust is broken, the whole network will soon know about the incident and it is maintained that the person involved will have a hard time doing business again.[32]

A company that has been doing business on the Chinese market since 1919 is ABB. At that time this was the first product delivery to China, and it was not until 1979 that ABB established its first permanent office. Almost 11 years later, the heart of almost every chairman of an energy company started to pound with excitement if it heard the words "Asia" and "electricity." There were billions to be had from the booming demand for electricity in Asia.[33] But in recent years, the emerging Asian market has slowed down due to the financial crisis in the area. At the moment it seems as if China is the only country not affected by this financial crisis, and consequently, there are many companies that are now trying to be successful in China.

ABB is argued to be a company with a good position on the Chinese market, due to good performance, delivery, autonomy and its good name. Today the company has 9 representative offices and 15 joint ventures, and the number of employees has grown in four years from approximately 1,000 to 6,000 employees in China.

Local Roots

The strategy of ABB is to use its global strength to support the needs of its local customers around the world. However, in China, ABB has a fairly high import duty on its products, which limits how much the company can sell. The idea of setting up local production in China was to increase the market share, as most Chinese customers do not have foreign currency[34] and are consequently forced to buy locally produced goods with the local currency. Furthermore, the reason for ABB to localize in China was not to achieve lower production costs, as some locally supplied components are actually more expensive in China than elsewhere. It was rather to be closer to the local market, and therefore facilitate a few local modifications to the products and provide shorter delivery times to the customer.

The phrase "think global, act local" is said to reflect ABB's fundamental idea of strong local companies working together across borders to gain economies of scale in many areas.[35] In spite of ABB's claims to respond swiftly and surely to market conditions,[36] some of the products in China are not truly adapted to the local market. Most of the products are designed for the IEC-international standard association based in Europe. The company manufactures products that have to be tested according to different norms and standards. For example, North America ABB follows the ANSI-standard, and Canada ABB follows the CSA-standard.

However, some of ABB's products would not pass a type test based on the Chinese standards. That is not because the quality is too low; on the contrary, the quality of ABB products is sometimes too high. The quality of some of the products has evolved far beyond the requirements of Chinese standards; therefore these ABB products cannot meet local Chinese standards. The Chinese standards are based on what the local manufacturer can produce, because the country does not have much other information. As one manager at ABB in China stated,

We are not going to redesign our products in order to meet the standards, for the obvious reasons: Why should we take our quality out? Why shall we take the advances out? It does become an issue from time to time. Chinese are very risk averse, if we have not done the type test in China. It is more to cover themselves in case something goes wrong.

Some managers feel that when ABB tries to adapt the products to the Chinese local standard, there is a negative response. The customer regards Western standards as superior and is actually asking for the superior product. The Chinese customers are seen as tough and sometimes demand more tests than ABB's products have gone through. Another reason put forward is insufficient feasibility studies when setting up new joint ventures in China. This delays the work when new information has to be collected about the market conditions. This aspect originates from the speed of changes in China and the difficulty for the company to catch up with what is going on.

However, when the so-called "type tests" of the product have been done, the company cannot change the design, due to the high costs involved in this test. Some criticism has been heard that ABB should adapt more to the Chinese situation, which the company cannot respond to concerning the technical design, because then the tests have to be done all over again. Of course, it is different from product to product; for some of the products, as one manager said,

We have to adapt to the configurations the customers have a demand for, because they have an option—go to the competitor.

Still in most cases, the local ABB companies in China are not allowed to change the products other than according to agreements with the licensee. The reason for that is that the technology partners[37] have the overall view of the quality and performance. The ABB corporation definitely does not want to have different product performance from different countries. The products must have the same descriptions, so that they are seen as the same product all over the world. Consequently the local ABB company can only do a few modifications to the standard product for the specific customer and cannot change the technology involved. The technology partners have a few alternatives that meet the demands of the Chinese customers, and these products are also tested, but do not necessarily meet the Chinese standards.

The local ABB company tries to follow the ABB Group's policy, to be close to the customer and responsive to his or her needs.[38] In China, however, contracts are not commonly used, and this frequently obstructs satisfying many customer demands.

They keep on saying this is China and you should adapt to the Chinese way: Ok, if you want to buy a Chinese product that's fine, but this is our product—here are the terms and conditions. You can't just give in to that; otherwise you will kill your company, because they expect you to

accept unlimited liability and lifetime warranty, and the risks to which you would expose your company would eventually lead to its shutting down, so you just cannot do that.

ABB feels that to be close to the customer is the best guarantee that local requirements are met.[39] However, the headquarters in Zurich has also set up some rules about the kind of contracts that the local subsidiaries shall sign worldwide. In China contracts are something rather new, and many Chinese customers do not want it that way. The consequence is that some ABB companies in China do not use the standard ABB contract and are actually responsive to the customers' needs. When another ABB company comes to the same customer to set up a standard contract, the customer will refer them to the previous ABB company who did not seem to find the contract necessary. The question asked by the confused customer is said to be,

Why do you then have to use a standard contract when the other ABB didn't?

Profit Centers

ABB's strategy is to take full advantage of its economies of scale and at the same time be represented by national companies in many home markets where some 5,000 entrepreneurial profit centers are attentive to every local customer. These companies are independent and have to stand on their own economically. The individual company's profit can easily be compared to revenue. The individual ABB company is measured on its own performance and needs. It is recognized that the profit centers are efficient for decentralization and that the organization can act relatively fast. This enables the company to be sensitive and responsive to potential problems. Each company has a fair amount of autonomy, making the individual company flexible. Even though ABB brochures state that the strategy of having profit centers enables the easy transfer of know-how across borders,[40] the direction is pretty much one way—from the technology partners, Business Areas and Country level to the subsidiary—rather than a two-way exchange.

Nevertheless, some conflicts of interest have occurred because the local ABB company and all other licensees are more or less dependent on their licensors in Europe.[41] In the local ABB company's

case, one of their technology partners is measured like the others, on performance and profit. If it gives the local ABB company support, it will cost the former money, and likewise, if it sells the local ABB company components, it wants to make a profit. The consequence is that it is charging the local ABB company 25-100 percent over and above the cost of its parts.

So in the end you end up calling them as little as possible and we end up buying parts from local suppliers that probably we should not buy from local suppliers. And we reduce our quality. They have great profit figures, we have some profit figures but there are some real serious problems along the way.

The technology partner argues that the prices are high because first it has to buy from its supplier and then sell to the local ABB company. This makes the products more expensive. The technology partners also pay for the "type tests" and all the product development.[42]

Conflicts of this sort have been occurring for a long time within ABB, but nobody has yet found a solution. It is difficult for a company like ABB, which is working with so many different products, markets, and in different cultures, to have anything other than sole profit centers. If the profit centers did not aim for a profit when selling within the ABB Group, then the companies would no longer be independent companies. Being independent is seen as a strength, and therefore it would be against the laws of nature if the companies were not always aiming for a profit. Nonetheless, between these independent companies with profit centers there are some extreme examples:

Our partner in Y-country was selling the finished product in China before. Now he sells the parts to the joint venture in China and wants to charge more for the parts than he did for the finished product, and that is because it is in his interest and he will be evaluated on his performance. If he does not do that, his profits will be too low and he will be blamed for it. So he has got to do what he has got to do. That is what he is motivated to do and that is what he is going to do.

To some extent the technology partners are selling indirectly to the Chinese market using non-official agents to avoid a high import tax and the high market price that exists on the Chinese market. ABB China is trying to force ABB companies to use only two official channels for ABB goods into the Chinese market-the locally produced by the local ABB company and the directly imported from a technology partner.

Structure

ABB is a huge enterprise with dispersed business areas, which encompass the three segments: Power Generation, Transmission & Distribution and Industrial Building systems. However, this recently has been changed and divided into six segments. Before the reorganization, every country had its national ABB head office, dealing with all the company business in that particular country. The other dimension of the matrix structure reflects the clustering of the activities of the enterprise into 36 Business Areas (or BAs). Each Business Area represents a distinct worldwide product market. Simplified, each BA is responsible for worldwide market allocation and the development of a worldwide technical strategy for that specific product line. Additional responsibilities for the BA are to coordinate who shall supply or deliver where, and also to work as a referee in potential disagreements between companies within the ABB Group.

However, in China, as in most developing countries, there is no BA in place and the decision-power of the country management is consequently closer at hand. The power of the decision-making tends to rest more heavily on the country level than on the BA level. Disagreements between licensees in Western countries and subsidiaries in China have been, and are occurring, due to different business orientations. The local subsidiary in China has two or more licensors in western countries, from which they buy components. Some of the licensees sold these components themselves before the local subsidiary was set up in China. In some cases the licensee feels that the market in China was taken from them and that they therefore can compensate for potentially lost sales only by charging the Chinese subsidiary a higher cost. Consequently, if the disagreeing partner seeks the BA as a referee in this kind of case, the following happens and is explained by one manager:

The BA are looking at the global business—we can increase our global business if we set up a joint venture in China. But the technology partner can't increase their business if we set up a joint venture in China . If we set up a joint venture in China the technology partner wants to increase its business also, they are going to do some work, and of course want something for it. The BA is really powerless to push those along.

To date, the licensors have been paying for all the technology development, which is the reason for charging a higher price for the components they are selling. Since the enterprise is divided into 5,000 profit centers and because each of these profit centers wants a profit when selling a component or product, there have been some shortcomings in the coordination and cooperation between the licensors and the local Chinese subsidiary.

The licensor in X-country makes the same breakers that the local ABB company does and faces the same problems with quality. For example, in Germany, they do not inform their licensee in China, who will also run into the same problem with quality in the near future. The problem is also discussed at the local ABB company, but if it suggests changes to the licensor, the licensor will evaluate on the basis of benefits to itself. Since they are going to invest their own resources, they are, of course, going to invest in areas beneficial to themselves first, or else charge the local ABB company extra. The consequences are thus summarized as follows:

We have had some things that would really help us here in China . But I don't even bother, because I know the reaction.

Over 80 percent of what the Centers of Excellence produce is going to be exported,[43] making it important that the partners of the licensor manage the contemporary challenges and opportunities that can emerge. However, the BA divides the world markets into different areas in which the specific ABB companies are to be a first source.[44] Between some of the licensors and the local ABB company, this has resulted in certain disputes. For example,

We are responsible for the Peoples Republic of China's market and are supposed to be the sole source (or rather first source) because we have the expertise for this market. Our technology partner in X-country quotes into this market on a regular basis, does not inform us, and competes against us, and takes orders at a lower price. This can destroy our position in the marketplace.

According to the licensor, it does not quote in the local ABB company's market because a customer with foreign currency will prefer imported products. The licensor argues that it does not go into the Chinese market and offer its products, but does get inquiries from ABB in Hong Kong and deliver to it. Hong Kong sells the products directly to the Chinese customer after having increased the original price several times higher in China than in Europe. It is a decision of the ABB China management that the Hong Kong coordinated sales force shall sell the local ABB company's products on the Chinese market among imported products and locally joint venture produced products. It helps to have sales coordination when deciding whether the products should be imported or not.

The technology is owned today by the Centers of Excellence in Europe or so-called licensors who pay for all the product development. ABB has chosen these licensees to be responsible for the company's world source of this specific technology. These units are responsible for developing new products and look after the quality. They arrange technical seminars about the technology, and by keeping special technology parts at only their factory. The strategic decision to keep special parts and the drawings of these parts at only one chosen factory enables the company to secure itself against competitors copying its products. Consequently, these parts will not be localized or purchased in China. However, for one products group (THS) there has been an organizational change, including the establishment of a unit called CHTET, which shall now own all new technology that is developed and also pay for the product development. This change now involves all product groups.

Multicultural

The current fashion, exemplified by ABB, is for the firms to be "multicultural multinationals" and be very sensitive to national differences.[45] Barnevik did debate that a culturally diverse set of managers can be a source of strength. According to Barnevik, managers should not try to eradicate these differences and establish a uniform managerial culture. Rather, they should seek to understand these cultural differences, to empathize with the views of people from different cultures, and to make compromises for such differences. Barnevik believes

that the advantage of building a culturally diverse cadre of global managers is to improve the quality of managerial decision making.[46]

ABB in China is typified by a culturally diverse set of managers with a mixture of managerial ideas, derived from the different managers' national backgrounds, different values, and different methods of working. It then depends on which stage in personal development the manager has reached if he or she is going to be influenced and absorb the new climate. Or as one manager said,

If you are close to being retired you might not change so much, there isn't much point. But you can't work in the same way as you do at home-it just wouldn't work.

According to another manager, ABB is a very international company with a great deal of influence from Scandinavian culture. However, it is a mixture of many cultures and it really depends on where the ABB company is located. In China the ABB culture is influenced by Chinese culture, by the environmental circumstances and by the laws. It is stricter in China than it is, for example, in Europe, because there are more rules. In spite of that, the managers do not feel that the result is a subculture of the ABB culture, rather a mixture of managers from different cultures- "we are a multidomestic company."

However, the top level of the ABB management is seen to be far away from the daily life at the subsidiary level in China, such as at the Local ABB company. Or as one manager expressed, "between that level and here, it's like the Pacific Ocean." All the managers agree that what the top level, including Barnevik and Lindahl,[47] says sounds very good and that is how it should be. Some managers continued the discussion and expressed this difference:

Sounds like I'm working for a different ABB than these guys are. What they talk about is really good and that is how it should be. But then when I sit back and go into the daily work and say that's not at all how it is. Somewhere along the line something gets lost between the theory and ideas at that level which is quite good. But when you get down to the working level and have to make it work something really gets lost along the way.

Expatriates

It is the BA with its worldwide networks that recommends, after suggestions from local offices, who is going to be sent as an expatriate to China or any other country. Thereafter, it is a cooperation between the BA and the country level, but it is the latter that finally decides which potential foreign expatriate is appropriate. However, it is important that an expatriate be able to fit into the system when coming to China with the high costs involved in being there. It is estimated that an expatriate costs the company about $0.25 million a year, due to the high taxes the company is paying to have a foreign employee.

ABB's identity is supported by a coordinating executive committee and an elite cadre of 500 global managers, which the top management shifts through a series of foreign assignments. Their job is intended to knit the organization together, to transfer expertise around the world, and to expose the company's leadership to differing perspectives.[48]

However, ABB in China is not yet a closely tied country unit for several reasons. First, the expatriates come from the outside and most of their contacts are back in the home country. Most expatriates feel that the home office does not understand how difficult it can be to work abroad and that they need support. "Sometimes it just feels like I'm standing in the desert screaming," one expatriate expressed. The home office feels that the expatriates can be a burden because they need so much support. It is the home office, along with the BA, that selects candidates for foreign placement, even though it has brief or no knowledge, of how it is to work in that country. However, it would be impossible to have insights into how the working conditions are in the other operating countries.

Concerning growing a strong country unit, the expatriates are stationed in China on assignments for a relatively short time period, and are thus less able to build up informal networks. Few efforts are put into establishing an informal network, because the few contact persons the managers have today will eventually return home after a while and there is no formal way of contacting the replacing person. Of course, there is the formal LOTUS Notes,® which is a computer-based network with all managers worldwide included, but it is said to be deficient in building the preferred strong country unit within China. Finally, the managers do not feel they can offer the time to establish informal networks to be rebuilt due to the replacement of expatriates every two to three years. A worldwide policy within the company limits the expatriates to operating as such for not more than five years at a time. Executives have questioned this policy, saying that

It is during the first year you learn what is going on and get into your new clothes. During the second year you get to know the people and the system, the third year you apply what you learned and the fourth year you start to make some changes and this is very specific for developing countries.

Three years ago the expatriates did not get any information or education about the country-specific situation before being sent out to ABB's subsidiaries in China. Today, when there are about 100 expatriates with 25 different nationalities in China, it has changed, but it is mostly up to the individual to collect material and prepare for the acclimatization. Within the worldwide corporation there is no policy of formal training before one is sent out as an expatriate; rather, it is up to the home office of the expatriates to prepare the managers for the foreign assignments. Some argue that "you could never prepare for the situation in China anyway, so any education wouldn't help." Others say that this has resulted in a lot of problems with the expatriates, which results in even higher costs for the company if the expatriate fails.

When the contract time as an expatriate is finished, he or she may feel unsure about placement for him or herself back home. Thus, it is important for the expatriate to have close contact with the home office and make use of the free trips home. In most cases the expatriates do not know what will happen when the contract expires and they are to return back home.

The Chinese Challenge

According to ABB they prefer to send out managers with 10–15 years of experience. However, the task is difficult when the location may be in a rural area overseas and most managers with 10–15 years experience have families who are less likely to want to move to these areas. Sometimes a manager gets sent to China when the company does not want to fire him.

So instead they send the manager to where the pitfalls are greater and challenges bigger and potential risks are greater.

It is found throughout the research that most expatriates have strong feelings about living in and adapting to the new environment in China. Newly arrived expatriates seem to enjoy the respect they get from the Chinese, and several managers delightedly expressed,

> I love it here, and how could you not, you get a lot of respect just because you're a foreigner and life is just pleasant.

Other expatriates that have stayed a bit longer disliked the situation to a great extent and a number of expatriates have asked to leave because their expectations about the situation in China have not been fulfilled.[49]

One country-specific situation is how to teach the Chinese employees to work in teams. The worldwide company ABB is especially focusing on creating an environment that fosters teamwork and promotes active participation among its employees.[50] This is a big challenge for Western managers (the expatriates) because the Chinese employees have a hard time working in a group, due to cultural and historical reasons. Some of the local ABB companies have failed in their attempt with team working, ad hoc groups and the like, because they have been in too much of a hurry. Or, as one manager said,

> Here in China the management needs to encourage the teamwork a little bit, because it is a little against the culture and the nature of the people. This is not a question of lack of time for the managers, but I do not think we have the overall commitment to do it. Some of us feel strongly that we should, others that we can't.

Another consequence is expatriate management does not have the understanding or the commitment to teach local employees the company values, a situation that has resulted in unacceptable quality at some companies.

ABB has a great advantage in comparison to other worldwide companies due to its top priority of building deep local roots by hiring and training local managers who know their local markets.[51] Replacing expatriates with local Chinese employees, where the local employees are set to be successors to the expatriates after a certain number of years, shows the commitment to the philosophy of having a local profile. However, as the Chinese employees are coming from an extremely different system from the western expatriates, it takes quite a long time for the former to get exposed to western management practices. To ease this problem and to teach western management style, ABB China, among other companies, has recently set up an agreement with a business school in Beijing to arrange training for Chinese employees with good management potential. This is specific for ABB China because in developed countries the employees are responsible for their own development.[52] Recently ABB had its own school in Beijing for Chinese employees to learn ABB culture and management. Unfortunately, this school had to close due to the profit-center philosophy, where even the school had to charge the individual ABB companies for teaching their employees.

ABB is sending about 100 local Chinese employees to an ABB company in a Western country every year. After problems with several employees quitting after training, ABB has set up precautions with a service commitment. The employee (or new employer) has to pay back the training investment if he or she quits or that the employee signs an agreement that he or she will continue working for ABB for a certain number of years. The problem with local employees quitting after ABB's investment in training also has been experienced in India and Thailand. It is shown in the personnel turnover rate, approximately 22 percent within ABB China, that many local employees are aiming for the experience of working for an international company such as ABB and then move on to a better-paying job.

However, by having local employees, the local ABB company is responsive to local conditions and sensitive to important cultural objectives such as the Chinese "guanxi."[53] It has been decided that the local employees should take care of the customer contact, since the expatriates are usually stationed for only a few years at one location and are consequently not able to build up strong connections with customers.

Reorganization

The organization is decentralized based on delegated responsibility and the right to make decisions in order to respond quickly to customers' requirements. In the core of this complex organization are two principles: decentralization of responsibility and individual accountability. These principles have been very relevant in China, which is a relatively young country for ABB to be operating in.[54] Decentralization is highly developed and the expatriate[55] managers have a wide responsibility that would normally demand more than one specialist in a western company. However, in some instances the organization is criticized for being too centralized.

The changes in China happen very fast, and according to ABB brochures, the greatest efficiency gains lie in improving the way people work together.[56] Within the ABB China region, communication has its shortcomings. Companies with overlapping products or similar products do not exchange information to any large degree or coordinate their marketing strategies. On the technical side, communication is used frequently, which can be seen when a manager usually receives up to 100 e-mails per day from other ABB employees. However, tactics for building up effective informal communication are lacking between most ABB companies operating in China. The distances are large, and accordingly, a meeting demands greater efforts than in almost any other country in the world.

According to the former CEO, Percy Barnevik, the purpose with the matrix organization is to make the company more bottom heavy than top heavy—"clean out the headquarters in Zurich and send everybody out, have independent companies operating in an entrepreneurial manner," as one respondent mentioned. It is further maintained in the company brochures that these entrepreneurial business units have the freedom and motivation to run their own business with a sense of personal responsibility.[57]

However, the result from the matrix organization in China is ABB subsidiaries have ABB China's objectives (the country level) and the Business Areas' (BA) objectives to follow. ABB China is measuring how the different companies are performing within China. The BA, on the contrary, is measuring how the specific products are performing on a worldwide basis and what the profitability is for the products. Each BA has a financial controller, and each country level has one also.

Rarely are the two coordinated, or do they meet. So you end up with one set of objectives from each . . . Duplication! Which one shall you follow?

According to the ABB Mission Book, the roles in the two dimensions of the ABB matrix must be complementary.[58] It demands that both the individual company and the headquarter level are flexible and strive for extensive communication. This is the way to avoid the matrix interchange becoming cumbersome and slow. It is seen to be the only way to "reap the benefits of being global (economies of scale, technological strength, etc.) and of being multidomestic (a high degree of decentralization and local roots in the countries in which we operate)."

For many years ABB was widely regarded as an exemplary European company, yet it is undergoing a second major restructuring within four years. CEO Göran Lindahl says that restructuring is aimed at making the organization faster and more cost efficient.[59] Due to the demands of a more global market, there are reasons for getting rid of the regional structure and to concentrate more on the specific countries. The reorganization has basically dismantled one half of the matrix: the country management. Henceforth, the BAs will manage their businesses on a worldwide basis and there will no longer be the confusion caused by BA and country management setting different objectives. At the same time, segments are split up (many BAs form a segment) to make them more manageable (e.g., the Transmission and Distribution segment has been split into two segments: Transmission and Distribution). To conclude, the general managers of the individual joint ventures and other units will have only one manager above them in the organization that has a global view of the business. In China, it also means the dismantling of the Hong Kong organization as well as the Asia Pacific organization.

According to Göran Lindahl, the reorganization is preparation for a much faster rate of change on the markets and for the company to be able to respond more effectively to the demands of globalization. It is seen as an aggressive strategy to create a platform for future growth.

Future Vision

CEO Göran Lindahl was appointed in 1997 to be the new president and chief executive of ABB. His view of the future is that it can no longer be extrapolated, but can be forecast by creativity, imagination, ingenuity, innovation-action based not on what was, but on what could be. The corporate culture needs to be replaced by globalizing leadership and corporate values. ABB is focusing on this by creating a unified organization across national, cultural, and business borders.

On the path towards the next century, ABB is going to focus on several essential elements: a strong local presence; a fast and flexible organization; the best technology and products available; and excellent local managers who know the business culture, are able to cross national and business borders easily, and who can execute your strategy faster than the competition.[60]

We are living in a rapidly changing environment, and our competitors will not stand still. In the face of this great challenge and opportunity, enterprises that adapt quickly and meet customer needs will be the winner, and this is the ultimate goal of ABB.[61]

CASE DISCUSSION QUESTIONS

1. Why is ABB restructuring again, so soon after its last restructuring?
2. How well is ABB doing in China? What effect does the Chinese culture have on the manner that companies conduct their business?
3. Will ABB's restructuring efforts resolve some of the problems it is experiencing in China?
4. Should ABB even be in China? Does their presence in China enhance their worldwide advantages?
5. What challenges does China present to ABB's current expatriate policies?

CASE CREDIT

Suzanne Uhlen, Lund University, and Michael Lubatkin, University of Connecticut. Reprinted with permission. This case is to serve as a basis for classroom discussion rather than to illustrate either effective or ineffective handling of an administrative situation.

CASE NOTES

[1] 100 years of experience ensures peak technology today, ABB STAL AB, Finspong.

[2] Dagens Industri, August 13, 1998, p. 25.

[3] Ibid.

[4] Usunier, Jean-Claude, Marketing across Cultures.

[5] Dagens Industri, July 2, 1998.

[6] Management Today, April 1996, by David Smith, p. 49.

[7] Ahlquist, Magnus as editor, The recruiter's guide to China, by preface of Professor Michael Yahuda.

[8] Bizniz, Sept. 30, 1997.

[9] Examples include VCD-player, CD-ROM player, mobile telephones, beepers, and video cameras.

[10] Garten, Jeffrey E., "Opening the Doors for Business in China," Harvard Business Review, May-June, 1998, pp. 160–172.

[11] Månadens Affärer, Nov. 11, 1996, searched through AFFÄRSDATA via http://www.ad.se/.

[12] Dagens Industri, August 19, 1998, searched through AFFÄRSDATA via http://www.ad.se/.

[13] Ibid.

[14] The recruiter's guide to China, by preface of Professor Michael Yahuda.

[15] Ibid.

[16] Garten, Jeffrey E., "Opening the Doors for Business in China," Harvard Business Review, May-June, 1998, pp. 167–171.

[17] See a recent report from The Economist, www.economist.com, in October 1998.

[18] Hong Yung Lee, "The implications of reform for ideology, state and society in China," Journal of International Affairs, vol. 39, no. 2, pp. 77–90.

[19] An interview with Premier Zhu Rongji in china Daily, March 20, 1998, p. 2.

[20] China Daily, Business Weekly, Vol. 18, No. 5479, March 29-April 4, 1998, p. 2.

[21] Hoon-Halbauer, Sing Keow, Management of Sino-Foreign Joint Ventures; Yuan Lu, Management Decision-Making in Chinese Enterprises.

[22] Ibid.

[23] Ma, Jun, Intergovernal relations and economic management in China.

[24] Laaksonen, Oiva, Management in China during and after Mao in enterprises, government, and party.

[25] Ju, Yanan, Understanding China, p. 45.

[26] Hwang, Quanyu, Business decision making in China.

[27] Hong Yung Lee, "The implications of reform for ideology, state and society in China," Journal of International Affairs, Vol. 39, No. 2, pp. 77–90.

[28] Yuan Lu, Management decision-making in Chinese enterprises.

[29] Yuan Lu, Management decision-making in Chinese enterprises.

[30] Hong Yung Lee, "The implications of reform for ideology, state and society in China," Journal of International Affairs, Vol. 39, No. 2, pp. 77–90.

[31] Yuan Lu, Management decision-making in Chinese enterprises.

[32] Månadens Affärer, Nov. 11, 1996.

[33] The Economist, Oct. 28, 1995, searched from http://www.economist.com.

[34] Due to China still being a quite closed country, Chinese people are not able to obtain foreign currency, other than in very limited amounts.

[35] ABB, "The art of being Local," ABB Corporate Communications, Ltd., printed in Switzerland.

[36] ABB Brochure, "You can rely on the power of ABB." ABB Asea Brown Boveri, Ltd., Department CC-C, Zurich.

[37] Technology partner (in this case) = Center of Excellence (CE), = Licensors.

[38] ABB's Mission, Values, and Policies.

[39] HV Switchgear, ABB, ABB Business Area H. V. Switchgear, Printed in Switzerland.

[40] ABB Asea Brown Boveri, Ltd., You can rely on the power of ABB, Department CC-C, Zurich.

[41] Licensing is defined here as a form of external production where the owner of technology or proprietary right (licensor) agrees to transfer this to a joint venture in China which is responsible for local production (licensee).

[42] During the study this has changed to some degree, due to a unit called CHTET being introduced.

[43] http://www.abb.se/ in November 1997.

[44] First source = you are the first source, but if you cannot meet the customers' requirements, the second source steps in.

[45] The Economist, Jan. 6, 1996, searched from http://www.economist.com.

[46] Ibid.

[47] Göran Lindahl is the present CEO, Chairman of the Board.

[48] The Economist, Jan. 6, 1996, searched from http://www.economist.com.

[49] There are two types of common, but false, expectations expatriates have when coming to China. Either they believe they are going to make a lot of money or they are going to experience the old Chinese culture—a culture that, most of the time, does not correspond to the culture of today in China.

[50] ABB's Mission, Values, and Policies, Zurich, 1991.

[51] ABB, "The art of being Local," ABB Corporate Communications, Ltd., printed in Switzerland.

[52] ABB's Mission, Values, and Policies, Zurich, 1991.

[53] Guanxi = connections, relations.

[54] ABB set up its first office, a representative office, in 1979.

[55] An expatriate is a person who has a working placement outside the home country.

[56] ABB Asea Brown Boveri, Ltd., You can rely on the power of ABB, Department CC-C, Zurich.

[57] ABB Asea Brown Boveri, Ltd., You can rely on the power of ABB, Department CC-C, Zurich.

[58] ABB's Mission, Values, and Policies.

[59] Dagens Industri, August 13, 1998, p. 25.

[60] "Meeting the Challenges of the Future," Presentation given to the Executives Club of Chicago, October 16, 1997.

[61] ABB, "Leading the way in efficient and reliable supply of electric power," ABB Transmission and Distribution, Ltd., Hong Kong.

Culture and Multinational Management

Learning Objectives

After reading this chapter you should be able to:

- Define culture and understand the basic components of culture.

- Identify instances of cultural stereotyping and ethnocentrism.

- Understand how various levels of culture influence multinational operations.

- Apply the Hofstede, GLOBE, and 7d models to diagnose and understand the impact of cultural differences on management processes.

- Appreciate the complex differences among cultures and use these differences for building better organizations.

- Recognize the complexity of understanding new cultures and the dangers of stereotyping and cultural paradoxes.

Preview CASE IN POINT

Different and the Same—Explorations in Culture

The poem "We and They" by Rudyard Kipling captures some of the feelings associated with intercultural experiences.

Father, Mother, and Me
Sister and Auntie say
All the people like us are We,
And everyone else is They.
And They live over the sea
While we live over the way,
But—would you believe it?—They look upon We
As only a sort of They!

We eat pork and beef
With cow-horn-handled knives.
They who gobble Their rice off a leaf
Are horrified out of Their lives;
While They who live up a tree,
Feast on grubs and clay,
(Isn't it scandalous?) look upon We
As a simply disgusting They!

We eat kitcheny food.
We have doors that latch.
They drink milk and blood
Under an open thatch. We have doctors to fee.
They have wizards to pay.
And (impudent heathen!) They look upon We
As a quite impossible They!

All good people agree,
And all good people say,

All nice people, like us, are We
And everyone else is They:
But if you cross over the sea,
Instead of over the way,
You may end by (think of it!) looking on We
As only a sort of They!

Source: Rudyard Kipling, "We and They." 1923. In Craig Storti, 1990. The Art of Crossing Cultures. Yarmouth, Maine: Intercultural Press, pp. 91–92.

The Preview Case in Point shows the feelings that many people have when they meet people from other cultures. They see behavior that they have trouble understanding. They see, hear, smell, and taste things that are strange and unpredictable. However, in today's business world, these seemingly strange people are often your customers, employees, suppliers, and business partners.

To remain competitive and to flourish in the complex and fast-changing world of multinational business, multinational managers look worldwide not only for potential markets but also for sources of high-quality and less expensive raw materials and labor. Even managers who never leave their home country must deal with markets and a workforce whose cultural background is increasingly diverse. Those managers with the skills to understand and adapt to different cultures are better positioned to succeed in these endeavors and to compete successfully in the world market.

Conducting business with people from other cultures will never be as easy as doing business at home. However, you can improve the chances of success at cross-cultural business interactions by learning more about the nature of culture and its effects on business practices.

Throughout this text you will be exposed to numerous cultural differences in management practices from countries around the world. To help you better understand these cultural underpinnings of management, this chapter considers two basic questions: (1) What is culture? and (2) How does culture affect management and organizations? Chapter 13 also considers the impact of cultural differences on business, but from the perspective of culture's effects on negotiation and communication. Other chapters show how an understanding of cultural differences in management practices can contribute to the more effective management of multinational organizations.

What is Culture?

Culture

The pervasive and shared beliefs, norms, and values that guide the everyday life of a group.

Culture is a concept borrowed from cultural anthropology. Anthropologists believe that cultures provide solutions to problems of adaptation to the environment. Eskimos, for example, have by necessity a large number of words to deal with the nature of snow. Culture helps people become attached to their society. It tells us who we are and to what groups we belong. Culture provides mechanisms for continuation of the group. For example, culture determines how children are educated and tells us when and whom to marry. Culture pervades most areas of our life, determining, for example, how we should dress and what we should eat.

Anthropologists have numerous and subtle different definitions of culture.[1] However, for the purposes of this book, with its focus on multinational management, culture is defined as the pervasive and shared beliefs, norms, and values that guide the everyday life of a group. These beliefs, norms, and values are expressed to current group members and passed on to future group members through cultural rituals, stories, and symbols.

Cultural norms both prescribe and proscribe behaviors. That is, they tell us what we can and cannot do. For example, norms prescribe when and whom we can marry and what clothes we can or cannot wear to a funeral or to the office. Cultural values tell us such things as what is good, what is beautiful, what is holy, and what are legitimate goals for life. Cultural beliefs represent our understandings about what is true. For example, most people in the United States accept the scientific method as a valid way of discovering facts. In contrast, other cultures may have the belief that facts can only be revealed by God.

Cultural symbols, stories, and rituals communicate the norms, values, and beliefs of a society or a group to its members. Each generation passes its culture to the next generation by symbols, stories, and rituals. A particular culture is continuously reinforced when people see symbols, hear stories, and engage in rituals.

Rituals include ceremonies such as baptism and graduation as well as the tricks played on a new worker or the pledge to a sorority or fraternity. Stories include such things as nursery rhymes, proverbs, and traditional legends (such as the U.S. legend that George Washington could not tell a lie). Symbols may be physical, such as national flags or holy artifacts. In the workplace, office size and location can serve as a cultural symbol. North American managers, for example, use large offices with physical barriers such as outer offices as symbols to communicate their power. In contrast, Japanese managers avoid physical barriers. They prefer instead to locate their desks at the center of communication networks where their desks are surrounded by coworkers.

Culture is pervasive in societies. It affects almost everything we do, see, feel, and believe. Pick any aspect of your life, and it is likely affected by your culture. What you sleep on, what you eat, what clothes you wear, how you address your family members and boss, whether you believe that old age is good or bad, what your toilet looks like, all respond to cultural differences. In each of these areas, societies develop pervasive cultural norms, values, and beliefs to assist their members in adapting to their environments.

Although culture is pervasive, not all aspects of culture are directly observable, especially to the outsider. We can see overt behaviors such as the Japanese executive's bow or the robust handshake of the North American. This easily observable aspect of culture is called the front stage of culture.[2] As in a stage play, it is what we see on stage, but it does not necessarily reflect people's thoughts and emotions.

Only insiders or members of the culture understand other aspects of culture. These aspects are called the back stage of culture. For example, when the Japanese businessman tells his U.S. colleague that something "is difficult" and twists his head a little to one side, he is really saying something else: "It is impossible, but I don't want to say 'no' directly." To understand this deeper meaning of culture, you must go beyond simple observation and view the world through the eyes of the members of a particular culture. This usually happens only when you live in a culture for some time and learn to speak the language of that culture.

Because culture affects so many aspects of our lives, many of the core values, norms, and beliefs about what should happen in everyday life are taken for granted. People do not consciously think about how culture affects their behaviors and attitudes. They just do what they believe is "right and natural" (see the Preview Case in Point). Even the members of a specific society may not fully understand why they behave in a particular manner in their culture.

Cultural norms

Prescribed and proscribed behaviors, telling us what we can do and what we cannot do.

Cultural values

Values that tell us such things as what is good, what is beautiful, what is holy, and what are legitimate goals for life.

Cultural beliefs

Our understandings about what is true.

Cultural symbols

These may be physical, such as national flags or holy artifacts. In the workplace, office size and location can serve as cultural symbols.

Cultural stories

These include such things as nursery rhymes and traditional legends.

Cultural rituals

Ceremonies such as baptism, graduation, or the tricks played on a new worker, or the pledge to a sorority or fraternity.

Pervasive

The idea that culture affects almost everything we do, everything we see, and everything we feel and believe.

Front stage of culture

The easily observable aspect of culture.

Back stage of culture

Aspects of culture that are understood only by insiders or members of the culture.

Cultural values

Values that tell us such things as what is good, what is beautiful, what is holy, and what are legitimate goals for life.

Cultural norms

Prescribed and pro-scribed behaviors, telling us what we can do and what we cannot do.

Cultural beliefs

Our understandings about what is true.

Shared cultural values, norms, and beliefs

The idea that people in different cultural groups have similar views of the world.

Levels of culture

These include national, business, and occupa-tional and organiza-tional culture.

Another key component of the definition of culture is that **cultural values, norms,** and **beliefs** must be **shared** by a group of people: The group must accept that, for the most part, the norms, values, and beliefs of their group are correct and compelling.[3] "Correct and compelling" means that, although people in any culture do not all behave the same way all the time, behaviors are pre-dictable most of the time. Imagine, for example, the chaos that would exist if we did not have norms to guide our driving. For example, when driving on two-lane roads in Ireland, drivers routinely pass slower vehicles even when faced with oncoming traffic. Unlike in the United States, oncoming drivers expect this tactic and routinely move to the breakdown lane. Although this norm is dif-ferent from that in the United States, the majority of people in Ireland manage to drive without running into each other.

For the multinational manager, the importance of understanding and dealing with cultural differences is unavoidable. To succeed cross-culturally, multinational managers must learn as much as they can about the important cultural norms, values, and beliefs of the societies in which they work. They also must learn to recognize the important symbols, values, and rituals of a culture. Such knowledge helps the multinational manager understand the "why" be-hind the behavior of their customers, workers, and colleagues. The following Case in Point shows how one U.S. company faced a challenge caused by a lack of cultural sensitivity to local religious beliefs and rituals.

The next section expands our discussion of culture by looking at how the various levels of culture affect the multinational manager in the business world.

Levels of Culture

The international businessperson needs to be aware of three **levels of culture** that may influence multinational operations. These levels include national

CASE IN POINT

Cultural Misunderstandings

Thom McAn is a shoe company that recently began operations in Bangladesh. When the firm's shoes first went on sale, a riotous protest occurred, result-ing in injury to more than 50 people. Why? The Thom McAn signature, which appears in a nearly illegible imprint on the sole of each shoe, looked similar to the Arabic script for "Allah" (God). In the Muslim world, the foot, especially the sole of the foot, is con-sidered unclean. For example, you should not show the sole of your shoes to guests. In this case, it looked as if Thom McAn was desecrating the name of God by asking the Bangladeshis to walk on it.

Consider some other possible cultural misunder-standing below:

- You spend considerable time preparing for your meeting in Tokyo. Your meeting goes well, and you are able to answer all questions about the

proposed joint venture without hesitation. How-ever, you do not hear from your contacts when you get back to the United States. Why? During your proposal, you crossed your ankle over your knee, something considered rude in Japan.
- Your meeting with your Chinese counterparts goes very well. After the negotiations end, you exchange gifts with your Chinese hosts. However, your gift is met with looks of disapproval. Why? Your gift was an expensive clock with the corporate logo. Unfortunately, clocks tend to be reminders of funerals in China.

Source: Based on Llorente, Elizabeth. 2006. "A little cultural savvy can go a long way toward sealing a deal: Avoid faux pas that can cost business." The Record, February 7: p. X28; Morrison, Terri, Wayne A. Conaway, and George A. Borden. 1996. "Kiss, bow or shake hands?" http://www.biztravel.com; Penzner, Betty. 2006. "The art of Chinese business etiquette: Ancient traditions form the basis of strategy." AFP Exchange, May, 26, 4: pp. 61–63.

EXHIBIT 2.1   **Levels of Culture in Multinational Management**

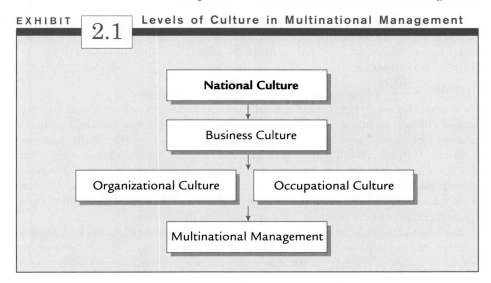

culture, business culture, and the occupational and organizational cultures. Exhibit 2.1 shows the levels of culture that affect multinational management.

National Culture

National culture is the dominant culture within the political boundaries of the nation-state. The dominant national culture usually represents the culture of the people with the greatest population or the greatest political or economic power. Formal education is generally taught and business is usually conducted in the language of the dominant culture.

Political boundaries, however, do not necessarily reflect cultural boundaries. Many countries, such as Canada and Singapore, have more than one major cultural group within their political boundaries. Even states with relatively homogeneous cultures have various subcultures, representing regional and rural/urban cultural differences that affect business transactions.

Most business takes place within the political boundaries of the nation-state. As such, the dominant culture of the nation-state has the greatest effect on international business. In particular, the dominant national culture usually influences not only the language of business transactions but also the nature and types of laws that govern businesses.

As we will see in Chapter 3, all major social institutions—religious beliefs, education, the family, politics, law, and economics—are closely intertwined with national culture. The family and educational system serve as the major transmitters of cultural heritage. Cultural norms, values, and beliefs are passed on through what individuals learn at home and in school. Political and economic systems evolve within the constraints of national culture. For example, cultures with strong beliefs regarding the differences among the social classes may evolve into a centralized, paternalistic political system. The laws and legal system of a country reflect in a formal way the cultural norms that guide behavior. Religion is closely intertwined with culture in the sense that it prescribes and proscribes beliefs, values, and norms for everyday actions. Each religion has its own principles that guide behavior. Buddhists, for example, must abstain from lying, killing, stealing, and sexual wrongdoing. Christians are guided by principles in the Bible that prohibit similar behavior, and Muslims follow the Koran and its guidelines for living.

National culture
The dominant culture within the political boundaries of the nation-state.

A detailed description of how each social institution relates to national culture is beyond the scope of this chapter. However, Chapter 3 shows how various social institutions combine with culture to affect local business practices and multinational operations.

Business Culture

Business culture

Norms, values, and beliefs that pertain to all aspects of doing business in a culture.

To a large degree, when multinational managers express concern with the impact of culture on international operations, they focus on how national cultures influence business operations. They ask, "How do the _____ (Germans, Indians, Japanese, Koreans, South Americans, Africans, Israelis, etc.) do business?" What concerns these managers is the **business culture.** More than cultural differences in business etiquette, business culture represents norms, values, and beliefs that pertain to all aspects of doing business in a culture.[4] Business cultures tell people the correct, acceptable ways to conduct business in a society.

Each national culture produces its own business culture. As such, business cultures are not separate from the broader national culture. Rather, the more pervasive national culture constrains and guides the development of business culture in a society. In any society, business closely interweaves with the broader culture's values, norms, and beliefs. Examples include the priorities given to age and seniority, the role expectations for women with their families, and expectations concerning how superiors should behave toward subordinates.

At a very broad level, business culture, as a reflection of national culture, influences all aspects of work and organizational life. This includes how managers select and promote employees, lead and motivate their subordinates, structure their organizations, select and formulate their strategies, and negotiate with other businesspeople. Much of what you read in this text will help you understand how national and business cultures affect organizations and management. The

---

C A S E   I N   P O I N T

Mexican Business Culture

The majority of Mexican businesses are small and are run by families. Even the larger businesses often have strong family ties. Because of the traditionally paternalistic nature of these organizations, jobs often go to family members and trusted friends of family members. Although education and training do count, management positions often are assigned based on relationships with the corporate family. Loyalty to one's superior is a major factor in obtaining promotions.

Mexican organizations are hierarchical, with power used and expected to be used by top management. This organizational structure results in many layers of management and slow decision making. Building trust is a key component of Mexican business culture and can speed up decision making for foreign firms. However, impatience is perceived as a weakness in Mexican culture, so foreign multinational managers should avoid moving too quickly.

The technical requirements of producing a product (e.g., production efficiency) do not dominate the administration and structure of the organization. Being sensitive to the needs of one's colleagues and subordinates and maintaining relationships often are higher priorities. Managers often base their decisions on custom and intuition rather than on formal analyses. An ideal workplace is free of excessive stress resulting from competition or conflict.

In Mexican business culture, work is considered a necessary evil, not the focus of life. Work provides support for life, family, and leisure. Unlike the Americans to the north, the "normal" person balances the demands of work and leisure.

Source: Based on Executive Planet. 2006. http://www.executiveplanet. com; World Trade Press. 2003. "Global Road Warrior." http:// www.worldcel.com/; Gomes, J. Eduardo Aguilar. 1993. "Mexican corporate culture." Business Mexico. August: pp. 8, 9, 38; and Kras, Eva S. 1995. Management in Two Cultures. Maine: Intercultural Press.

preceding Case in Point on Mexican business culture describes some of the practices considered typical in that culture. Consider the following Focus on Emerging Markets discussing the evolving business culture in China.

Business culture also guides everyday business interactions, and the business cultures of different nations vary widely in the codes of conduct that represent proper business etiquette. As we see in the Focus on Emerging Markets, what to wear to a meeting, when and how to use business cards, and whether to shake hands or embrace are examples of business etiquette that vary according to national cultures.

Understanding the basic business etiquette of a business culture is a minimal requirement for the multinational manager. In Germany, "Show up half an hour late [for a business meeting] and it makes no matter how bad the traffic and how tight your schedule. You've likely lost the appointment and may have a tough time getting another."[5] The following Comparative Management Brief,

---

Focus on Emerging Markets

Business Culture in China

China's business culture is undergoing dramatic and constant change. China's Cultural Revolution actually sent many young professionals to work in rural areas while also denying education to others. As such, because most Chinese enterprises were state-owned, most Chinese did not have the opportunity to study business-related areas to help craft the Chinese business culture. However, over the past two decades, more Chinese have had the chance to pursue business education and careers and are helping define the Chinese business culture.

Although Chinese business culture is rapidly evolving, there are a number of key issues that need to be addressed when doing business in China. These issues include:

- *Understand that business moves slowly:* Business happens at a much slower pace in China than in the United States. Companies wanting to do business may need to visit China numerous times before purchasing or negotiation anything.
- *Know the organizational hierarchy:* Chinese companies remain very hierarchical, and it helps to know the highest individuals at the negotiating table as they most likely are the decision makers.
- *Get it in writing:* Chinese companies are reluctant to say no, and what may seem to have been agreed upon may become a major barrier in the long term. It is important to get as much of the agreements in writing as possible for future consideration.
- *Respect Chinese business etiquette:* Individuals hoping to do business with Chinese companies should respect many aspects of Chinese business etiquette. For instance, it is strongly advisable to dress conservatively and to arrive promptly for appointments. The negotiator also is expected to present business cards with both hands. It is advantageous to carry business cards with English on one side and Chinese on the other. Chinese companies also treat their visitors with lavish banquets, and negotiators should expect to participate in some form of drinking.

Source: Based on Hannon, David. 2006. "Dos and DON'Ts of doing business in China." Purchasing, May 18, 135, 8: pp. 52–54; Penzner, Betty. 2006. "The art of Chinese business etiquette: Ancient traditions form the basis of strategy." AFP Exchange, May, 26, 4: pp. 61–63.

Comparative Management **Brief**

Knowing Your Business Etiquette in Egypt, Germany, and Japan

Business etiquette in Egypt, Germany, and Japan is more formal than in the United States. Conservative dress in dark business suits and formal polite interactions are the norm. People seldom use first names. The Germans prefer honorific titles (e.g., "Herr [Mister] Doctor"). The Japanese prefer the suffix *san*, as in *Tanaka-san*, as a polite form of address. In deference to Muslim culture, women multinational managers in Egypt should not expose arms or have low-cut tops in front or back. Skirts should be below the knees.

Business cards are expected in Germany, but they are essential in Japan. The Japanese use business cards (*meishi*) as a form of introduction. Business cards help the Japanese place an individual in the appropriate context, in terms of both the prestige of one's company and one's position in the company. The Japanese may study you and your *meishi* for several minutes without any other interaction. Many Westerners may find this use of time disconcerting and wonder what is happening. Egyptians also exchange business card during introductions. However, unlike the Japanese who exchange cards among all present, top Egyptian managers may only exchange cards with those of similar rank. Like the Japanese, Egyptian seating arrangements are based on rank, so it is important for foreigners to clearly define their hierarchy.

The Germans keep separate business and family lives. They seldom conduct business after 5 p.m. In contrast, the Japanese workday will run to sundown, and after that, eating and drinking with colleagues and business partners will continue to 10 or 11 p.m. Because of this cultural expectation, a Japanese wife might be embarrassed if her husband, the manager, routinely came home at 6 p.m. This would suggest that he was rejected by his colleagues. In Japan, multinational managers should expect to be entertained after business hours. The formality of the office often breaks down in ritualized drinking, as the Japanese view this as a way to really understand you in a relaxed situation. At 9 a.m. the next morning, however, all the formality of the previous day will return.

The interaction between business and socializing is more complex for the Egyptian. Egyptians socialize before, during, and after business transactions. Interruptions are common in meetings as managers respond to telephone calls and visits from family and friends. Several meetings may go on at the same time. Constant hospitality offerings in the form of light refreshments are also common.

Source: Based on Craighead's International Business, Travel, and Relocation Guide 2000. Detroit: Gale Research; Executive Planet. 2006. http://www.executiveplanet.com; World Trade Press. 2003. "Global Road Warrior." http:// www.worldcell.com/

dealing with Egypt, Germany, and Japan, describes essential elements of business etiquette for doing business in these countries.

Occupational Culture and Organizational Culture

Although differences in national and business cultures usually present challenges to the multinational manager, distinct cultures also develop around work roles and organizations. These cultures are called the occupational and organizational cultures.

Different occupational groups, such as physicians, lawyers, accountants, and craftspeople, have distinct cultures called **occupational cultures.** Occupational cultures are the norms, values, beliefs, and expected ways of behaving for people in the same occupational group, regardless of their organizational employer.

Occupational cultures

Distinct cultures of occupational groups such as physicians, lawyers, accountants, and craftspeople.

In spite of the importance of national and business cultures, the multinational manager cannot ignore differences in occupational cultures. To demonstrate this point, a study by Hofstede,[6] which included more than 40 different national cultures, found that people with similar jobs often had very similar cultural values. Moreover, the people from the different occupational groups were often more similar to one another than to people from their own national cultures.

The existence of an occupational culture is more prevalent for professional and technical occupations, such as physicians. This distinction occurs because professionals have similar educational backgrounds and have access to the free flow of technical information across national boundaries.

During the last decade, managers and academics realized that the concept of culture also applied to individual organizations. Differences in organizational cultures seemed to answer questions such as why two organizations with similar structures and strategies have different performance levels and why the merger of two otherwise successful companies failed. In particular, the idea of an organizational culture helps us understand how organizations are affected by more than their formally designed systems, such as the organizational structure.

Vijay Sathe defined **organizational culture** as "the set of important understandings (often unstated) that members of a community share in common."[7] Edgar Schein of MIT added that these assumptions, values, and beliefs concerning the organization are discovered and created when members learn to cope with external and internal problems, such as developing a strategy or the criteria for allocating organizational rewards. When coping strategies—such as Hewlett-Packard's "management by wandering around"—work successfully, they are taught to new members as "the correct way to perceive, think, and feel in relation to those problems."[8]

Seldom do organizations have only one organizational culture, nor perhaps should they. Because organizational subunits (i.e., divisions, departments) all face different situations, most subunits develop distinct subcultures. Subunits may retain many of the overall characteristics of the parent company, but, for example, few would expect an R&D department to have the same culture as a manufacturing plant.

Although various parts of the organization may have different organizational cultures, it is important to note that organizational cultures also may have as important an influence on employees as the national culture does. For instance, consider that many U.S. companies promote the use of first names as a way to encourage employees to bond and feel comfortable with each other. Such practices may not work well in more hierarchical societies such as Germany and France where is important to respect titles and hierarchy. However, organizational cultures in smaller firms may actually make the use of first names more acceptable since smallness encourages employees to be more familiar with each other. As such, it is critical for the multinational manager to understand the influences of the various levels of culture on employees. In the next section, we discuss some of the more popular national culture frameworks.

Organizational culture

The norms, values, and beliefs concerning the organization shared by members of the organization.

Cultural Differences and Basic Values: Three Diagnostic Models to Aid The Multinational Manager

Multinational managers face a complex array of cultures that challenge their ability to manage. To help you understand the important ways in which national and business cultures differ so that you can manage successfully in the various cultures in which you do business, the following sections describe three popular cultural models. The models can help you understand ways in which national and business cultures differ and thereby help you manage successfully in the various cultures in which you do business.

The Dutch scientist Geert Hofstede introduced the first model in the early 1980s and continued his research on national culture for over two decades.[9] Management scholars now use Hofstede's work extensively as a way of understanding cultural differences. We call his model the **Hofstede model of national culture**. Hofstede developed his cultural model primarily based on differences in values and beliefs regarding work goals. It has easily identifiable implications for business by providing a clear link between national and business cultures. It also serves an important role as a basis for extensive research on cross-cultural management.[10] You will see later in the text numerous examples of Hofstede's ideas providing the background for understanding differences in management practices.

The second model is the most recent development of a national culture framework as represented by the **Global Leadership and Organizational Behavior Effectiveness (GLOBE) project**.[11] This model, based heavily on Hofstede's national culture model, includes nine cultural dimensions. However, only two of those nine dimensions are developed independently of the Hofstede model. We will, therefore, focus our discussion of the GLOBE national culture model on these two dimensions.

Finally, the third model created by Fons Trompenaars is called the **7d culture model** since it represents seven dimensions of culture. This model comes from extensive and continuing cross-national research by Fons Trompenaars and his colleagues.[12]

All three models equip managers with the basic tools necessary to analyze the cultures in which they do business. Furthermore, these approaches also provide useful terms to help you understand the complexities of different cultural values. By using these models, you will develop an initial understanding of important cultural differences and key cultural traits.

The next section provides more detail on the Hofstede model, followed by a briefer section describing the GLOBE model. The section concludes with Trompenaars' 7d model.

Hofstede's Model of National Culture

To describe national cultures, Hofstede[13] uses five dimensions of basic cultural values. These values address issues of:

1. Power distance: expectations regarding equality among people.
2. Uncertainty avoidance: typical reactions to situations considered different and dangerous.
3. Individualism: the relationship between the individual and the group in society.
4. Masculinity: expectations regarding gender roles.
5. Long-term orientation: a basic orientation toward time.

Hofstede's framework was based on 116,000 surveys from 88,000 employees of IBM subsidiaries around the world. Although the original sample included 72 countries, Hofstede used only those countries that had more than 50 responses.[14] Hofstede thus identified four of these cultural value dimensions in the reduced sample of 40 countries.[15] However, the database was later

Hofstede model of national culture
A cultural model mainly based on differences in values and beliefs regarding work goals.

Global Leadership and Organizational Behavior Effectiveness (GLOBE) project
Recent large scale project based on Hofstedes model to determine nine cultural dimensions of 62 countries.

7d culture model
A seven-dimension cultural model based on beliefs regarding how people relate to each other, how people manage time, and how people deal with nature.

expanded to include 10 additional countries from three regions: Arab countries and East and West Africa. Later research by Hofstede and others added to the number of countries studied and introduced the fifth dimension, long-term orientation.[16]

Research on the long-term orientation dimension was unique. Rather than using survey questions developed by Western researchers, Michael Bond and several Chinese colleagues designed a new survey based on questions developed by Asian researchers reflecting Confucian values. Hofstede and Bond have related the long-term orientation to the recent economic growth in the minidragons of the rising Asian economies.[17]

Hofstede's Cultural Model Applied to Organizations and Management

The following section defines Hofstede's dimensions of national culture. It also adapts and extends this work[18] to show how cultural values affect numerous management practices in different cultures. The management practices considered in the discussion of Hofstede's model include:

1. Human resources management

   a. Management selection (how people are chosen for jobs)
   b. Training (what the focus of job training is)
   c. Evaluation and promotion (what counts to get ahead)
   d. Remuneration (what accounts for differences in pay)

2. Leadership styles (how leaders behave)
3. Motivational assumptions (beliefs regarding how people respond to work)
4. Decision making and organizational design (how managers structure their organizations and make decisions)
5. Strategy (effects of culture on selecting and implementing strategies)

First, we consider power distance followed by discussions of the other dimensions noted previously.

Power Distance

Power distance concerns how cultures deal with inequality. It focuses on (1) the norms that tell superiors (bosses, leaders) how much they can determine the behavior of their subordinates and (2) the values and beliefs that superiors and subordinates are fundamentally different kinds of people.

High power distance countries have norms, values, and beliefs such as:[19]

Power distance
Expectations regarding equality among people.

- Inequality is fundamentally good.
- Everyone has a place; some are high, some are low.
- Most people should be dependent on a leader.
- The powerful are entitled to privileges.
- The powerful should not hide their power.

Organizations in countries high on power distance use management systems and processes that reflect a strong concern with hierarchy. As shown later in the chapter with Exhibit 2.7, Latin American, Latin European, and Far Eastern countries demonstrate the highest levels of power distance.

The concern for hierarchy and inequality in organizations is rooted in early socialization in the family and school. In high power distance cultures, children are expected to be obedient to parents and elders. This deference continues as long as parents are alive. When children enter school, teachers assume the role of dominance. Children must show extreme respect and seldom challenge a teacher's authority. Later in life, organizations assume many of the roles of parents and teachers.

In high power distance countries, the ideal people for a managerial job come from a high social class or have graduated from an elite university. These characteristics define the person as having the intrinsic or built-in qualities of a leader. Who you are in terms of elite associations is more important than past performance. Leaders and subordinates expect large wage differences between management and workers.

The basic motivational assumption in high power distance countries is that people dislike work and try to avoid it. Consequently, managers believe that they must adopt a Theory X leadership style; that is, they must be authoritarian, must force workers to perform, and must closely supervise their subordinates. Similarly, employee training emphasizes compliance (following orders) and trustworthiness.

Organizational structures and systems match the assumptions regarding leadership and motivation. Decision making is centralized. Those at the top make most of the decisions. The close supervision of workers requires many supervisors and a tall organizational pyramid (an organization with many levels). Strategic decisions in high power distance countries are influenced by the need to maintain and support those in power.

The following Comparative Management Brief describes how differences in power distance affect specific U.S. and Mexican business practices.

Exhibit 2.2 gives a summary of these managerial implications for power distance. The next section considers uncertainty avoidance.

Uncertainty Avoidance

Uncertainty avoidance

How people react to what is different and dangerous.

Uncertainty avoidance relates to norms, values, and beliefs regarding a tolerance for ambiguity. A higher uncertainty avoidance culture seeks to structure social systems (politics, education, and business) where order and predictability are paramount, and rules and regulations dominate. In such a culture, risky

---

Comparative Management **Brief**

Respect and Power in Mexico vs. Respect and Fair Play in the United States

In describing Mexican business culture, a high power distance culture, Marc J. Erlich, a psychologist who works with U.S. businesses in Mexico, noted:

> Within Mexican society, there is a tendency to respect those in power. The boss's respectability is manifested by maintaining a definite social distance, through an unwillingness to delegate.
>
> Fair play, shared responsibility, and playing by the rules are characteristics of respect for the [North] American. Respect is earned, not given. North of the border, the ability to be one of the team reflects responsibility.
>
> The U.S. executive frequently perceives Mexican submission to authority as a lack of resolve and an unfortunate passivity. The Mexican will typically view the U.S. executive's insistence on fair play and desire to delegate as an inability to accept the power associated with position.

Source: Based on Erlich, Mark J. 1993. "Making sense of the bicultural workplace." Business Mexico. August: p. 18.

EXHIBIT
2.2
Management Implications of Power Distance

Management Processes	Low Power Distance	High Power Distance
Human Resources Management		
Management Selection	Educational achievement	Social class; elite education
Training	For autonomy	For conformity/obedience
Evaluations/Promotion	Performance	Compliance; trustworthiness
Remuneration	Small wage difference between management and worker	Large wage difference between management and worker
Leadership Styles	Participative; less direct supervision	Theory X; authoritarian, with close supervision
Motivational Assumptions	People like work; extrinsic and intrinsic rewards	Assume people dislike work; coercion
Decision making/Organizational Design	Decentralized; flat pyramids; small proportion of supervisors	Tall pyramids; large proportion of supervisors
Strategy Issues	Varied	Crafted to support the power elite or government

Sources: Adapted from Hofstede, Geert. 1980. Culture's Consequences: International Differences in Work-Related Values. London: Sage; Hofstede, Geert. 1991. Cultures and Organizations: Software of the Mind. London: McGraw-Hill; and Hofstede, Geert. 1993b. "Cultural dimensions in people management." In Vladimir Pucik, Noel M. Tichy, and Carole K. Barnette, Globalizing Management. New York: Wiley, pp. 139–158.

situations create stress and upset people. Consequently, people avoid behaviors such as changing jobs.

High uncertainty avoidance countries have norms, values, and beliefs such as:[20]

- Conflict should be avoided.
- Deviant people and ideas should not be tolerated.
- Laws are very important and should be followed.
- Experts and authorities are usually correct.
- Consensus is important.

The business cultures in countries high on uncertainty avoidance have management systems and processes that make organizations and employees dependable and predictable. People in such cultures react with stress and anxiety when the rules of behavior are not clear in organizational settings. Generally, Nordic and Anglo countries are low on uncertainty avoidance while Latin European and Latin American countries are high. As the Case in Point on page 58 shows, Belgian students have little uncertainty when deciding whether to enter their professors' offices.

In high uncertainty avoidance cultures, entry-level people are chosen for their potential fit with and loyalty to the organization. Managers follow the logic, "If people are like me, come from my town or my family, then I understand them and trust them more." This minimizes interpersonal conflict, reduces potential employee turnover, and makes people more predictable.

In some cultures, uncertainty regarding employees is further reduced by selecting and promoting people with specialized expertise. Employers seek out people who will be loyal and committed to them and to the organization. Later, seniority, long-term commitment to the organization, and expertise in the area of management become the prime basis for promotion and payment. Both managers and employees believe that loyalty to the organization is a virtue and that conflict and competition should be avoided.

Uncertainty Avoidance in a Belgian University and In Negotiations

Belgium ranks in the top 10 percent (91st percentile) on Hofstede's uncertainty avoidance dimension. As a result, one expects Belgian organizations to have many of the characteristics for high uncertainty avoidance, as shown in Exhibit 2.3. This seems true even for Belgium's universities.

At the University of Leuven, an old Belgian university, three lights stand over a professor's door: green, yellow, and red. Students wishing to see their professor must ring a bell and wait for an appropriate response. Green means come in; yellow means wait a few minutes; and red means go away. There is no ambiguity in these situations. Students do not have to interpret the situation to see if the professor is busy. In contrast, most students from the United

States, a low uncertainty avoidance country (21st percentile), would probably find this degree of formality impersonal at best and perhaps even insulting.

Negotiations also are impacted by the level of uncertainty avoidance. For instance, negotiators from high uncertainty avoidance countries such as Greece are more likely to ask for specific commitments when negotiating for product volumes, delivery schedules, and standards. In such cases, discussion of delays may be of great concern to negotiators from high uncertainty avoidance countries.

Source: Based on Gannon, Martin J., and Associates. 1994. Understanding Global Cultures. Thousand Oaks, CA: Sage; McGinnis, Michael A. 2005. "Lessons in cross-cultural negotiations." Supply Chain Management Review, April, 9, 3: pp. 9–10.

Task-directed leaders give clear and explicit directions to subordinates. This reduces ambiguity regarding job expectations. The boss tells workers exactly what to do. Task-directed leaders are the preferred leaders in high uncertainty avoidance cultures. Such leaders make subordinates less anxious, since subordinates know exactly what is expected of them. Similarly, organizations in these cultures have many written rules and procedures. Like the situation produced by the task-directed leader, extensive rules and procedures tell employees exactly what the organization expects of them. Consequently, employees believe that these rules should not be broken.

In contrast, leaders in low uncertainty avoidance cultures favor more flexibility and allow subordinates more choices on the job. The design of their organizations also builds in more freedom. There are fewer rules and regulations. There are also more subordinates per manager, which results in less supervision and greater autonomy for workers.

People in high uncertainty avoidance cultures do not like risk, and they often fear failure. As decision makers, they are conservative. Thus, it is unlikely that individual managers choose risky strategies for their organizations. Hofstede[21] notes, however, that low or high uncertainty avoidance does not necessarily relate to success. Innovations may be more likely in low uncertainty avoidance countries like the United States, but implementation of innovations may be more likely in high uncertainty avoidance countries such as Japan.

Exhibit 2.3 summarizes the managerial implications of uncertainty avoidance.

Individualism/Collectivism

Individualism
The relationship between the individual and the group in society.

The values, norms, and beliefs associated with **individualism** focus on the relationship between the individual and the group. Individualistic cultures view people as unique. People are valued in terms of their own achievements, status, and other unique characteristics.

Collectivism
A set of cultural values that views people largely through the groups to which they belong.

The cultural values associated with individualism are often discussed with the opposing set of values, called **collectivism.** Collectivist cultures view people

EXHIBIT
2.3
Management Implications of Uncertainty Avoidance

Management Processes	High Uncertainty Avoidance	Low Uncertainty Avoidance
Human Resources Management		
Management Selection	Seniority; expected loyalty	Past job performance; education
Training	Specialized	Training to adapt
Evaluation/Promotion	Seniority; expertise; loyalty	Objective individual performance data; job switching for promotions
Remuneration	Based on seniority or expertise	Based on performance
Leadership Styles	Task-oriented	Nondirective; person-oriented; flexible
Motivational Assumptions	People seek security, avoid competition	People are self-motivated, competitive
Decision Making/Organizational Design	Larger organization; tall hierarchy; formalized; many standardized procedures	Smaller organizations; flat hierarchy, less formalized, with fewer written rules and standardized procedures
Strategy Issues	Averse to risk	Risk Taking

Sources: Adapted from Hofstede, Geert. 1980. Culture's Consequences: International Differences in Work-Related Values. London: Sage; Hofstede, Geert. 1991. Cultures and Organizations: Software of the Mind. London: McGraw-Hill; and Hofstede, Geert. 1993b. "Cultural dimensions in people management." In Vladimir Pucik, Noel M. Tichy, and Carole K. Barnette, Globalizing Management. New York: Wiley, pp. 139–158.

largely in terms of the groups to which they belong. Social groups such as family, social class, organization, and team all take precedence over the individual.

Countries high on individualism have norms, values, and beliefs such as:[22]

- People are responsible for themselves.
- Individual achievement is ideal.
- People need not be emotionally dependent on organizations or groups.

In contrast, collectivist countries have norms, values, and beliefs such as:[23]

- One's identity is based on group membership.
- Group decision making is best.
- Groups protect individuals in exchange for their loyalty to the group.

Countries with low individualism have collectivist norms, values, and beliefs that influence a variety of managerial practices. Organizations in collectivist cultures tend to select managers who belong to favored groups. Most often, the favored group is the extended family and friends of the extended family. Being a relative or someone known by the family becomes more important than an individual's personal qualifications. In contrast, people in highly individualistic societies, such as the United States (the most individualistic society by Hofstede's measurement), often view favoritism toward family and friends as unfair and perhaps illegal. In such societies, most people believe that job selection should be based on universalistic qualification. Universalistic qualification means that the same qualifications apply universally to all candidates. The cultural belief is that open competition allows the most qualified individual to get the job.

Organizations in collectivist cultures base promotions mostly on seniority and age. People tend to move up the organizational hierarchy by being promoted with their age cohort (people of the same age). People feel that a major reward for working is being taken care of by their organizations, a type of organizational paternalism. The senior managers in the organization act as father figures. Unlike individualistic societies, where people expect extrinsic rewards such as money and promotions, managers in collectivist societies use "a call to duty" as an emotional appeal to work for the good of the group.

In some collectivist cultures, older senior managers ultimately make important decisions. Such collectivist cultures also tend to rank high on power distance. However, other collectivist cultures prefer group decision making. Two factors favor greater participation and influence on decision making by people throughout the organization. First, because people in the organization are family members or trusted friends, privileged information flows up and down the organizational hierarchy. Second, as an extended family or at least a close-knit group, there is pressure to account for the feelings and desires of all members. However, because of the need to take into account the input or feelings of group members, strategic decision making in collectivist cultures can be slow.

The effects of collectivism on aspects of various Asian countries are described in the following Multinational Management Brief.

Exhibit 2.4 summarizes the managerial implications of high individualism versus collectivist (low individualism) norms, values, and beliefs.

Masculinity

Different cultural expectations for men and women occur in all societies. In all cultures, men and women receive different socialization and usually

---

Multinational Management **Brief**

Asian Countries and Collectivism

Chinese businesspeople outside the People's Republic of China, whom Hofstede calls "the overseas Chinese," have developed highly performing businesses in Taiwan, Hong Kong, and Singapore, as well as throughout the world. Many of their organizations, however, lack all the trappings of modern management. They tend to be feudal (i.e., dominated by the entrepreneur father), family owned, and small, and have few if any professional managers. Most focus on only one product, and cooperation with networks of other small organizations is based on personal family friendships.

There are seldom any formal systems within or between organizations—only networks of people guided roughly by Confucian ethics. For example, in the father-dominated family firm, Confucian ethics dictate that the son must show respect and obedience to the father and the father must protect and show consideration for the son. In a practical sense, this means that the father will dominate organizational decision making. As the son gets older, he may be given considerations such as managing a new firm venture. However, on inheriting the family firm, brothers may engage in more horizontal decision making because their family obligations are less vertical.

This family aspect to business is not unique to China. Japan and South Korea are also collectivistic societies, and how businesses operate is also determined by collectivism. For instance, many Western-based companies are readily willing to sever relationships with suppliers in an effort to cut cost. However, this practice is not acceptable in Japan where collectivism encourages Japanese companies to hold long-term and often personal relationships with suppliers.

Source: Based on Dvorak, Phred. 2006. "Managing: Making U.S. ideas work elsewhere: Firms work to adapt management theory to local practices." Wall Street Journal, May 22: p. 31; Hofstede, Geert. 1993a. "Cultural constraints in management theories." Academy of Management Executive 7: p. 1; and Syu, Agnes. 1994. "A linkage between Confucianism and the Chinese family firm in the Republic of China." In Dorothy Marcic and Sheila M. Puffer (editors). Management International. Minneapolis: West.

EXHIBIT 2.4   **Management Implications of Individualism**

Management Processes	Low Individualism	High Individualism
Human Resources Management		
Management Selection	Group membership; school or university	Universalistic based on individual traits
Training	Focus on company-based skills	General skills for individual achievement
Evaluation/Promotion	Slow, with group; seniority	Based on individual performance
Remuneration	Based on group membership/ organizational paternalism	Extrinsic rewards (money, promotion) based on market value
Leadership Styles	Appeals to duty and commitment	Individual rewards and punishments based on performance
Motivational Assumptions	Moral involvement	Calculative; individual cost/benefit
Decision Making/Organizational Design	Group; slow; preference for larger organization	Individual responsibility; preference for smaller organizations
Strategy Issues	Incremental changes with periodic revolutions	Aggressive

Sources: Adapted from Hofstede, Geert. 1980. Culture's Consequences: International Differences in Work-Related Values. London: Sage; Hofstede, Geert. 1991. Cultures and Organizations: Software of the Mind. London: McGraw-Hill; and Hofstede, Geert. 1993b. "Cultural dimensions in people management." In Vladimir Pucik, Noel M. Tichy, and Carole K. Barnette, Globalizing Management. New York: Wiley, pp. 139–158.

perform different roles. A variety of studies shows that, in most—but certainly not all—cultures, male socialization has a greater emphasis on achievement, motivation, and self-reliance. In contrast, the socialization of women emphasizes nurturance and responsibility.[24]

As a cultural dimension, **masculinity** represents the overall tendency of a culture to support the traditional masculine orientation. That is, higher masculinity means that the business culture of a society takes on traditional masculine values, such as emphases on advancement and earnings. However, within each culture, there remain gender differences in values and attitudes.

High masculinity countries have norms, values, and beliefs such as:[25]

Masculinity
Tendency of a society to emphasize traditional gender roles.

- Gender roles should be clearly distinguished.
- Men are assertive and dominant.
- Machismo or exaggerated maleness in men is good.
- People—especially men—should be decisive.
- Work takes priority over other duties, such as family.
- Advancement, success, and money are important.

In highly masculine societies, jobs are clearly defined by gender. There are men's jobs and women's jobs. Men usually choose jobs that are associated with long-term careers. Women usually choose jobs that are associated with short-term employment, before marriage and children. However, smaller families, delayed childbirth, pressure for dual-career earnings, and changing national cultural values may be eroding traditional views of masculinity. Consider the cases for working women in Japan and Sweden as described in the Comparative Management Brief on page 62.

In addition to clear work-related roles based on gender, work in masculine cultures tends to be very central and important to people, especially men. In cultures like Japan, men often take assignments for over a year in other cities or other countries while other family members remain at home.

Comparative Management **Brief**

Working Women in Japan and Sweden: Contrasts in Cultural Masculinity

Japan, the highest-ranking masculine culture, now faces a challenge to its traditional cultural values regarding masculinity and the role of women. Japanese companies expect that most women, even college graduates, will quit their jobs by the age of twenty-five. Women occupy most of the part-time jobs and have less access to the fabled lifetime employment than do men. However, with the slowdown in the Japanese economy, many women are not leaving as expected. The popular Japanese press now has many stories about companies that "have problems with their women." Such phraseology reflects the conflict of changing values regarding masculinity in Japan. Although there are traditional cultural expectations about what women "should" do regarding work and family, there is no legal or accepted way to force Japanese women to leave their jobs when they choose to remain employed.

Perhaps because of strong norms of equality, the Nordic countries rank lowest in masculinity. In contrast to masculine Japan, where support for working women, such as day care, is rare, the Swedish government provides day care to all who need it. Since more than 85 percent of Swedish women work outside the home, day care is essential. In addition, with the birth of a child, one year of parental leave is available for both parents. Approximately 20 percent of the men take this option.

Source: Based in part on Gannon, Martin J., and Associates. 1994. Understanding Global Cultures. Thousand Oaks, C: Sage.

In the high masculinity culture, recognition on the job is considered a prime motivator. People work long hours, often work more than five days a week, and take short vacations. In most low masculinity countries, work typically has less centrality. People take more time off, take longer vacations, and emphasize the quality of life. There are, however, some exceptions. In the highly masculine Mexican culture, for example, gender differences are strong but work is less central. The cultural value is that people "work to live."

In masculine cultures, managers act decisively. They avoid the appearance of intuitive decision making, which is often regarded as feminine. They prefer to work in large organizations, and they emphasize performance and growth in strategic decision making.

Exhibit 2.5 shows the major effects of high masculinity on work and organizations. The next section deals with the impact of long-term orientation on work and organizations.

Long-Term Orientation

Long-term orientation

A basic orientation toward time that values patience.

Because we only have data on the **long-term (Confucian) orientation** for a few countries, Hofstede and others have produced less research on how this orientation relates to work and organizations. Consequently, the discussion on this issue is more speculative than some of the observations discussed previously.

Because of the need to be sensitive to social relationships, managers in cultures high on long-term orientation are selected based on the fit of their personal and educational characteristics to the company. A prospective employee's particular skills have less importance in the hiring decision than they do in cultures with short-term orientation. Training and socialization for a long-term commitment to the organization compensate for any initial weaknesses in work-related skills. Organizations in cultures with short-term orientation, in

EXHIBIT **2.5**   **Management Implications of Masculinity**

Management Processes	Low Masculinity	High Masculinity
Human Resources Management		
Management Selection	Independent of gender, school ties less important; androgyny	Jobs gender identified; school performance and ties important
Training	Job-oriented	Career oriented
Evaluation/Promotion	Job performance, with less gender-based assignments	Continues gender-tracking
Remuneration	Less salary difference between levels; more time off	More salary preferred to fewer hours
Leadership Styles	More participative	More Theory X; authoritarian
Motivational Assumptions	Emphasis on quality of life, time off, vacations; work not central	Emphasis on performance and growth; excelling to be best; work central to life; job recognition important
Decision Making/Organizational Design	Intuitive/group; smaller organizations	Decisive/individual; larger organization preferred
Strategy Issues	Preference for consistent growth	Aggressive

Sources: Adapted from Hofstede, Geert. 1980. Culture's Consequences: International Differences in Work-Related Values. London: Sage; Hofstede, Geert. 1991. Cultures and Organizations: Software of the Mind. London: McGraw-Hill; and Hofstede, Geert. 1993b. "Cultural dimensions in people management." In Vladimir Pucik, Noel M. Tichy, and Carole K. Barnette, Globalizing Management. New York: Wiley, pp. 139–158.

contrast, must focus immediately on usable skills. Managers do not assume that employees will remain with the company for an extended time. They cannot be assured of a return on any investment in employee training and socialization.

In short-term oriented cultures, leaders use short-term rewards that focus on pay and rapid promotion. Employees in long-term cultures value security, and leaders work on developing social obligations.

Hofstede[26] notes that Western cultures, which tend to have short-term orientations, value logical analysis in their approach to organizational decisions. Managers believe in logically analyzing the situation for their company and following up with a solid game plan. In contrast, Eastern cultures, which rank highest on long-term orientation, value synthesis in organizational decisions. Synthesis does not search for the correct answer or strategy. Rather, synthesis takes apparently conflicting points of view and logic and seeks practical solutions. Not surprisingly, organizations in short-term oriented cultures are designed and managed purposefully to respond to immediate pressures from the environment. Managers often use quick layoffs of "excess" employees to adjust to shrinking demand for products. Organizations in long-term oriented cultures are designed first to manage internal social relationships. The assumption is that good social relationships eventually lead to successful organizations. The difference between long- and short-term cultures is apparent in the goals companies set in strategic decision making. Managers in countries such as the United States want immediate financial returns. They are most comfortable with fast, measurable success. Countries with more long-term orientations do not ignore financial objectives, but they prioritize growth and long-term paybacks. The long time horizons allow managers to experiment and seek success by developing their "game plans" as they go along. In the following Multinational Management Brief you can see how goals differ between U.S. and Japanese firms.

Multinational Management **Brief**

U.S. and Japanese Strategic Goals

One study of the top firms in Japan and the United States showed distinct differences between the companies in terms of goals. Although firms from both countries considered financial performance important, the Japanese firms emphasized additional goals that would affect long-term financial performance. In addition, because Japanese stockholders also emphasize long-term investments, the Japanese companies face little pressure to respond to immediate stockholder gains. Consider these rankings with regard to strategic goals for U.S. Fortune 500 firms and their Japanese equivalents:

Goals	U.S.	Japan
Return on Investment	1	2
Stockholder Gain	2	9
Increase Market Share	3	1
Introduction of New Products	7	3

Source: Based on Kagono, T., I. Nonaka, K. Sakakibara, and A. Okumura. 1985. Strategic vs. Evolutionary Management: A U.S. Japan Comparison of Strategy and Organization. Amsterdam: North-Holland.

Exhibit 2.6 summarizes the managerial implications of long-term (Confucian) orientation.

EXHIBIT 2.6   Management Implications of Long-Term Orientation

Management Processes	Short-Term Orientation	Long-Term Orientation
Human Resources Management		
Management Selection	Objective skill assessment for immediate use to company	Fit of personal and background characteristics
Training	Limited to immediate company needs	Investment in long-term employment skills
Evaluation/Promotion	Fast; based on skill contributions	Slow; develop skills and loyalty
Remuneration	Pay, promotions	Security
Leadership Styles	Use incentives for economic advancement	Build social obligations
Motivational Assumptions	Immediate rewards necessary	Subordinate immediate gratification for long-term individual and company goals
Decision Making/Organizational Design	Logical analyses of problems; design for logic of company situation	Synthesis to reach consensus; design for social relationships
Strategy Issues	Fast; measurable payback	Long-term profits and growth; incrementalism

Sources: Adapted from Hofstede, Geert. 1980. Culture's Consequences: International Differences in Work-Related Values. London: Sage; Hofstede, Geert. 1991. Cultures and Organizations: Software of the Mind. London: McGraw-Hill; and Hofstede, Geert. 1993b. "Cultural dimensions in people management." In Vladimir Pucik, Noel M. Tichy, and Carole K. Barnette, Globalizing Management. New York: Wiley, pp. 139–158.

To apply Hofstede's model to specific countries, look at Exhibit 2.7. It displays the percentile ranks of selected countries on five of Hofstede's dimensions of national culture.

EXHIBIT 2.7

Percentile Ranks for Hofstede's Cultural Dimensions for Selected Countries by Cultural Cluster (100 = highest; 50 = middle)

Cultural Group/ Country	Power Distance	Uncertainty Avoidance	Individualism	Masculinity	Long-Term Orientation
Anglo:					
Australia	25	32	98	72	48
Canada	28	24	93	57	19
Great Britain	21	12	96	84	27
United States	30	21	100	74	35
Arab:					
Arab countries	89	51	52	58	n/a
Far Eastern:					
China	89	44	39	54	100
Hong Kong	73	8	32	67	96
Singapore	77	2	26	49	69
Taiwan	46	53	19	41	92
Germanic:					
Austria	2	56	68	98	n/a
Germany	21	47	74	84	48
Netherlands	26	36	93	6	65
Switzerland	17	40	75	93	n/a
Latin America:					
Argentina	35	78	59	63	n/a
Colombia	70	64	9	80	n/a
Mexico	92	68	42	91	n/a
Venezuela	92	61	8	96	n/a
Latin European:					
Belgium	64	92	87	60	n/a
France	73	78	82	35	n/a
Italy	38	58	89	93	n/a
Spain	43	78	64	31	n/a
Near Eastern:					
Greece	50	100	45	67	n/a
Iran	46	42	57	35	n/a
Turkey	67	71	49	41	n/a
Nordic:					
Denmark	6	6	85	8	n/a
Finland	15	42	70	13	n/a
Norway	12	30	77	4	n/a
Sweden	12	8	82	2	58
Independent:					
Brazil	75	61	52	51	81
India	82	17	62	63	71
Israel	4	66	66	47	n/a
Japan	32	89	55	100	n/a

Sources: Adapted from Hofstede, Geert. 1980. Culture's Consequences: International Differences in Work-Related Values. London: Sage; Hofstede, Geert. 1991. Cultures and Organizations: Software of the Mind. London: McGraw-Hill; and Hofstede, Geert. 1993b. "Cultural dimensions in people management." In Vladimir Pucik, Noel M. Tichy, and Carole K. Barnette, Globalizing Management. New York: Wiley, pp. 139–158; Ronen, S., and O. Shenkar. 1985. "Clustering countries on attitudinal dimensions: A review and synthesis." Academy of Management Review, September.

To interpret this exhibit you need to understand percentiles. The percentiles shown in the exhibit tell you the percentage of countries that rank below each country. For example, the United States has the highest scores on individualism, so its percentile rank tells you that 100 percent of the countries are equal to or below the United States on individualism. A percentile rank of 75 percent tells you that 75 percent of the other countries have equal or lower ranks on a cultural dimension.

To simplify generalizations from Hofstede's data, the table groups countries by country clusters.[27] **Country clusters** are groups of countries, such as Anglo, Latin American, and Latin European, with roughly similar cultural patterns. Although cultures differ within these broad classifications, such summaries are useful for condensing cultural information. They are also useful to predict likely cultural traits when specific information is not available on a national culture.

Next, we consider the GLOBE model of culture.[28] This model is heavily based on Hofstede's dimensions, and we focus mainly on the two dimensions unique to the model.

Country clusters

Groups of countries with similar cultural patterns.

GLOBE National Culture Framework

The GLOBE project involves 170 researchers who collected data on 17,000 managers from 62 countries around the world.[29] Using the Hofstede model as the base, the GLOBE researchers conceptualized and developed nine cultural dimensions. Of these nine dimensions, only two are independent of the Hofstede model. The seven GLOBE dimensions similar to Hofstede's model include assertiveness orientation and gender egalitarianism (similar to masculinity-femininity), institutional and family collectivism (similar to individualism-collectivism), future orientation (similar to long-term orientation), power distance, and uncertainty avoidance.[30] Given the similarity with Hofstede's dimensions, many of the implications discussed earlier for Hofstede's cultural dimensions would also apply for the similar GLOBE dimensions. However, we focus on the two dimensions unique to the GLOBE project.

The cultural dimensions unique to the GLOBE project include performance orientation and humane orientation. **Performance orientation** refers to the degree to which the society encourages societal members to innovate, to improve their performance, and to strive for excellence. This dimension is similar to Weber's Protestant work ethic and reflects the desire for achievement in society.[31] Countries such as the United States and Singapore have high scores on performance orientation while countries such as Russia and Greece have low scores on the dimension. Javidan, Dorfman, de Luque and House[32] argue that countries that have high performance orientation scores tend to favor training and development while in countries low on performance orientation, family and background are more important. In societies with high performance orientation, people are rewarded for taking initiative and for performing with the belief that one can succeed by trying hard. In contrast, low performance orientation societies reward harmony with the environment, emphasizing loyalty and integrity while regarding assertiveness as unacceptable. Exhibit 2.8 summarizes some of the management implications of performance orientation.

Humane orientation is an indication of the extent to which individuals are expected to be fair, altruistic, caring, and generous. In high humane orientation societies, need for belongingness and affiliation is emphasized more than needs such as material possessions, self-fulfillment, and pleasure. Less humane oriented societies are more likely to value self-interest and self-gratification.[33]

Performance orientation

The degree to which the society encourages societal members to innovate, to improve their performance, and to strive for excellence.

Humane orientation

An indication of the extent to which individuals are expected to be fair, altruistic, caring, and generous.

EXHIBIT **2.8**   **Management Implications of Performance Orientation**

Management Processes	High Performance Orientation	Low Performance Orientation
Human Resources Management		
Management Selection	Based on individual achievement and merit	Emphasize seniority and experience
Training	Value training and development	Value societal and family relationships
Evaluation/Promotion	Based on merit and achievement	Based on age
Remuneration	Pay, promotions	Tradition
Performance Appraisal	Systems emphasize results	Systems emphasize integrity and loyalty
Leadership Styles	Have "can do" attitude	Emphasize loyalty and belongingness
Motivational Assumptions	Value bonuses and rewards	Value harmony with environment and quality of life
Communication	Value direct and to-the-point communication	Value subtlety and ambiguity in communication

Sources: Adapted from House, R., P. Hanges, M. Javidan, P. Dorfman, and V. Gupta. 2004. Culture, Leadership and Organizations: The GLOBE Study of 62 Societies. Thousand Oaks, CA: Sage Publications.

Countries such as Malaysia and Egypt score highly on humane orientation while France and Germany have low scores. As such, companies in high humane orientation countries such as Egypt are generally expected to be caring and offer benefits that seem unusual for U.S. companies. For instance, companies may offer tuition assistance to employees' children, paid family vacations, or even home appliances.[34] Exhibit 2.9 discusses some of the management implications of humane orientation.

The GLOBE data shows that countries can be categorized by 10 clusters and that these clusters differ with respect to the nine cultural dimensions. Clusters

EXHIBIT **2.9**   **Management Implications of Humane Orientation**

Management Processes	High Humane Orientation	Low Humane Orientation
Relationships	Others are important (i.e., family, friends, and community	Self-interest is emphasized
Leadership Styles		
Style	More consideration-oriented leadership	Less consideration-oriented leadership
Concern for Subordinates	Individualized/holistic consideration	Standardized/limited consideration
Approach	More benevolent	Less benevolent
Relationship with Subordinates	More personal and less informal	More informal and less personal
Motivational Assumptions	Need for belongingness	Power and material possessions motivate people
Company Role	Provide support to employees	People expected to solve problems on their own

Sources: Adapted from House, R., P. Hanges, M. Javidan, P. Dorfman, and V. Gupta. 2004. Culture, Leadership and Organizations: The GLOBE Study of 62 Societies. Thousand Oaks, CA: Sage Publications.

in the GLOBE project include the Anglo cluster, the Confucian Asia cluster, the Eastern Europe cluster, the Germanic Europe cluster, the Latin America and Latin Europe cluster, the Middle East cluster, the Nordic Europe cluster, the Southern Asia cluster and the Sub-Saharan cluster. Exhibit 2.10 shows the various clusters and the corresponding cultural scores. You can refer to Exhibit 15.8 in Chapter 15 to see which countries are included in each cluster.

To use the seven GLOBE dimensions similar to Hofstede's dimensions, you can readily apply many of the management implications discussed earlier for Hofstede's cultural dimensions. Next we consider the model developed by Trompenaars and his colleagues. You will see that this model is also similar in some respects to Hofstede's, but it contains more dimensions and deals with a broader array of countries.

7d Cultural Dimensions Model

The 7d cultural model builds on traditional anthropological approaches to understanding culture. Anthropologists argue that culture comes into existence because all humans must solve basic problems of survival.[35] These challenges include how people relate to others such as family members, supervisors, friends, and fellow workers; how people deal with the passage of time; and how people relate to their environment. All cultures develop ways to confront these basic problems. However, the solutions are not the same, which is why cultures differ significantly.

Five of the seven dimensions of the 7d cultural model deal with the challenges of how people relate to each other. Each dimension is a continuum or range of cultural differences. The five dimensions that deal with relationships among people include:

1. Universalism versus particularism: the choice of dealing with other people based on rules or based on personal relationships.
2. Collectivism versus individualism: the focus on group membership versus individual characteristics.
3. Neutral versus affective: the range of feelings outwardly expressed in the society.
4. Diffuse versus specific: the types of involvement people have with each other ranging from all aspects of life to specific components.
5. Achievement versus ascription: the assignment of status in the society based on performance (e.g., college graduation) versus assignment based on heritage.

The two final dimensions deal with how a culture manages time and how it deals with nature. They include:

6. Past, present, future, or a mixture: the orientation of the society to the past, present, or future or some combination of the three.
7. "Control of" versus "accommodation with" nature: nature viewed as something to be controlled versus something to be accepted.

Exhibit 2.11 gives a summary of the 7d model and the issues addressed by each dimension. The following sections define the dimensions and show their managerial applications.

Universalism versus Particularism

Universalism and **particularism** pertain to how people from a culture treat each other based on equally applied rules versus personal relationships. In a

Universalism

Dealing with other people based on rules.

Particularism

Dealing with other people based on personal relationships.

EXHIBIT 2.10 The GLOBE Model of Culture

Cluster	Performance Orientation	Assertiveness	Future Orientation	Humane Orientation	Institutional Collectivism	In-group Collectivism	Gender Egalitarianism	Power Distance	Uncertainty Avoidance
Anglo	High	Medium	Medium	Medium	Medium	Low	Medium	Medium	Medium
Confucian Asia	High	Medium	Medium	Medium	High	High	Medium	Medium	Medium
Eastern Europe	Low	High	Low	Medium	Medium	High	High	Medium	Low
Germanic Europe	High	High	High	Low	Low	Low	Medium	Medium	High
Latin America	Low	Medium	Low	Medium	Low	High	Medium	Medium	Low
Latin Europe	Medium	Medium	Medium	Low	Low	Medium	Medium	Medium	Medium
Middle East	Medium	Medium	Low	Medium	Medium	High	Low	Medium	Low
Nordic Europe	Medium	Low	High	Medium	High	Low	High	Low	High
Southern Asia	Medium	Medium	Medium	High	Medium	High	Medium	Medium	Medium
Sub-Saharan Africa	Medium	Medium	Medium	High	Medium	Medium	Medium	Medium	Medium

Sources: Based on Javidan, Mansour, Peter W. Dorfman, Mary Sully de Luque, and Robert J. House. 2006. "In the eye of the beholder: Cross cultural lessons in leadership for project GLOBE." The Academy of Management Perspectives, February, 20, 1: pp. 67–90.

EXHIBIT **2.11**   **The 7d Model of Culture**

Cultural Dimension	Critical Question
Relationships with People:	
Universalism vs. Particularism	Do we consider rules or relationships more important?
Individualism vs. Collectivism	Do we act mostly as individuals or as groups?
Specific vs. Diffuse	How extensively are we involved with the lives of other people?
Neutral vs. Affective	Are we free to express our emotions or are we restrained?
Achievement vs. Ascription	Do we achieve status through accomplishment or is it part of our situation in life (e.g., gender, age, social class)?
Perspective on Time:	
Sequential vs. Synchronic	Do we do tasks in sequence or several tasks at once?
Relationship with the Environment:	
Internal vs. External Control	Do we control the environment or does it control us?

Sources: Adapted from Trompenaars, Fons, and Charles Hampden-Turner. 1998. Riding the Waves of Culture: Understanding Cultural Diversity in Global Business. New York: McGraw-Hill.

universalistic culture, the "right" way to treat people is based on abstract principles such as the rules of law, religion, or cultural principles such as "Do unto others as you would have them do unto you." Thus, universalism suggests that there are rules or appropriate and acceptable ways of doing things and we look to those precise guides in all situations.

In contrast, in particularistic cultures, rules represent only a rough guide to life. Each judgment represents a unique situation and the "right" way of behaving must take into account who the person is and his or her relationship to the one doing the judgment. In particularistic cultures, rules may be in place and fully recognized, but people expect exceptions to be made for friends, family relations, and others. The focus is on situation-to-situation judgments and the exceptional nature of circumstances as they change.[36]

In developing his 7d model, Trompenaars uses dilemmas that show the contrasts in cultural values. Consider the following dilemma and the different cultural assumptions that people use to make the "right" choice.

One of the dilemmas used to show differences between universalistic and particularistic cultures concerns the story of a motorist hitting a pedestrian while going 35 miles per hour in a 20-mile-per-hour zone. The driver's lawyer notes that if a witness says the driver was only going 20 miles per hour, the judge will be lenient. The question is this: Should a friend who is a witness be expected to or feel obligated to testify to the lower speed? In universalistic cultures such as the United States and Switzerland, more than 93 percent say no—the principle of telling the truth supercedes friendship. In particularistic cultures such as South Korea, Nepal, and Venezuela, close to 40 percent say yes— friendship supercedes the law.[37]

No culture is purely universalistic or particularistic. However, the tendency to lean in one direction or the other influences business practices and relationships between business partners from different cultures. In particular, more universalistic cultures tend to use contracts and law as a basis for business. Managers from such cultures often have difficulty when written documents are ignored and the personal relationships between partners become paramount. Consequently, managers from universalistic cultures doing business in particularistic cultures must be sensitive to building relationships. However, managers from particularistic cultures must make efforts to realize that the emphasis on law and contract does not mean a distrust of the business partner in a universalistic culture.

Exhibit 2.12 gives a brief description of universalism and particularism as cultural dimensions and shows the managerial implications for doing business in each cultural context.

Individualism versus Collectivism

In the preceding sections, we examined Hofstede's view of individualism and collectivism. The 7d model considers the same distinctions. That is, in collectivist societies people are defined by their group memberships including family, organization, and community. Responsibility, achievement, and rewards are often group-based. In individualistic societies, people are trained from childhood to be independent, and each person assumes individual responsibility for success or failure.

Although the 7d view of individualism is similar to Hofstede's in its concept, the rankings of countries do not match exactly. One explanation for this difference may be that Trompenaars' ranking comes from more recent data. Another reason is that the 7d model uses a different methodology from Hofstede's model and captures more subtle aspects of the individualism–collectivism continuum.

EXHIBIT 2.12   **Universalism versus Particularism: Differences and Managerial Implications**

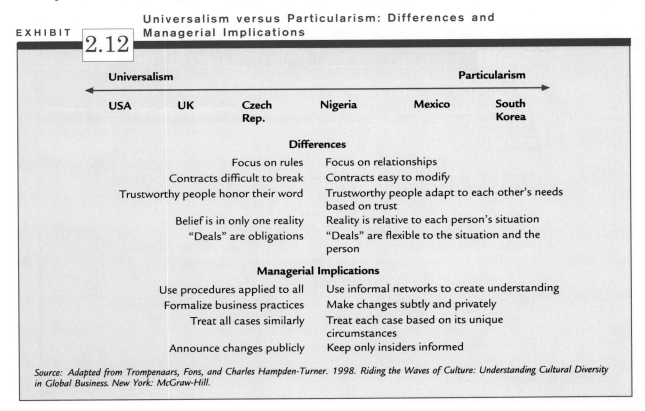

Universalism					Particularism
USA	UK	Czech Rep.	Nigeria	Mexico	South Korea

Differences

Focus on rules	Focus on relationships
Contracts difficult to break	Contracts easy to modify
Trustworthy people honor their word	Trustworthy people adapt to each other's needs based on trust
Belief is in only one reality	Reality is relative to each person's situation
"Deals" are obligations	"Deals" are flexible to the situation and the person

Managerial Implications

Use procedures applied to all	Use informal networks to create understanding
Formalize business practices	Make changes subtly and privately
Treat all cases similarly	Treat each case based on its unique circumstances
Announce changes publicly	Keep only insiders informed

Source: Adapted from Trompenaars, Fons, and Charles Hampden-Turner. 1998. Riding the Waves of Culture: Understanding Cultural Diversity in Global Business. New York: McGraw-Hill.

One of the questions that Trompenaars used to look at cultural differences in individualism asked about typical organizations in each country. One choice represented organizations where individual work and individual credit were common. The other choice represented group work and group credit. In the more collectivist societies such as India and Mexico, fewer than 45 percent of the workers said that their jobs involved individual work with individual credit. Somewhat surprising was the finding that the former Eastern Bloc countries of the Czech Republic, Russia, Hungary, and Bulgaria were the most individualistic in their organizations, ranking ahead of the United States.

Exhibit 2.13 gives a brief description of the individualism and collectivism cultural dimensions and the managerial implications of doing business in each cultural context.

Neutral versus Affective

Neutral versus affective
The acceptability of expressing emotions.

The **neutral versus affective** dimension of the 7d model concerns the acceptability of expressing emotions. In cultures with a more neutral orientation, people expect that interactions are objective and detached. The focus is more on the task and less on the emotional nature of the interaction. People emphasize achieving objectives without the messy interference of emotions. In contrast, in cultures with a more affective orientation, all forms of emotion are appropriate in almost every situation. Expressions of anger, laughter, gesturing, and a range of emotional outbursts are considered normal and acceptable. The natural and preferred way is to find an immediate outlet for emotions.[38]

You can test yourself on this dimension by responding to one of Trompenaars' dilemmas. How would you respond in a negotiation if your partner called your proposal insane? People from neutral cultures will attempt to hide their emotional reactions to this insult. Revelation of the hurt would show weakness and vulnerability. People from affective cultures would react immediately. They realize that such a reaction shows that they are insulted, but they believe that their partner should know this. This is expected behavior and is not viewed negatively by people in an affective culture.[39]

EXHIBIT 2.13

Individualism versus Collectivism: Differences and Managerial Implications

Individualism				Collectivism
Czech Rep.	UK	Nigeria	Egypt	Japan

Differences

Focus on "me" or "I"	Focus on "we"
Individual achievement and responsibility	Group achievement and responsibility
Individual decision making	Decision making by groups

Managerial Implications

Use individual incentives such as pay for performance	Focus on group morale and cohesiveness
Plan for turnover	Expect low turnover
Provide for individual initiative	Set group goals

Source: Adapted from Trompenaars, Fons, and Charles Hampden-Turner. 1998. Riding the Waves of Culture: Understanding Cultural Diversity in Global Business. New York: McGraw-Hill.

Exhibit 2.14 gives a brief description of the neutral versus affective cultural dimension and the managerial implications of doing business within each cultural context.

Specific versus Diffuse

The cultural dimension, **specific versus diffuse**, addresses the extent to which an individual's life is involved in his or her work relationships. In a specific-oriented culture, business is segregated from other parts of life. People in business-exchange relationships and work relationships know each other, but the knowledge is very limited and for very specific purposes. In such societies, written contracts frequently prescribe and delineate such relationships. Conversely, in diffuse-oriented cultures, business relationships are more encompassing and involving. In diffuse-oriented cultures, the preference is for an involvement of multiple areas and levels of life simultaneously; truly private and segregated spaces in life are quite small. In doing business, the parties come to know each other personally and more thoroughly and become acquainted with each other across a variety of life's dimensions and levels.[40]

The example Trompenaars uses to test the differences between specific and diffuse cultures concerns a boss who asks a subordinate to help him paint his house. In specific cultures, most people believe that the worker has no obligation to help his boss because the boss has no authority over him outside of work. In diffuse cultures, people feel an obligation to help the boss in any way possible although it is beyond the requirements of the job.[41]

Exhibit 2.15 gives a brief description of the specific versus diffuse cultural dimension and the managerial implications of doing business in each cultural context.

Specific versus diffuse

The extent to which all aspects of an individual's life are involved in the individual's work relationships.

EXHIBIT 2.14   Neutral versus Affective: Differences and Managerial Implications

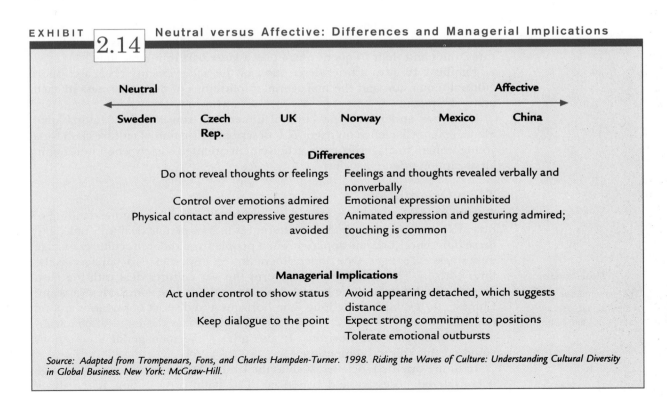

Neutral					Affective
Sweden	Czech Rep.	UK	Norway	Mexico	China

Differences

Do not reveal thoughts or feelings	Feelings and thoughts revealed verbally and nonverbally
Control over emotions admired	Emotional expression uninhibited
Physical contact and expressive gestures avoided	Animated expression and gesturing admired; touching is common

Managerial Implications

Act under control to show status	Avoid appearing detached, which suggests distance
Keep dialogue to the point	Expect strong commitment to positions
	Tolerate emotional outbursts

Source: Adapted from Trompenaars, Fons, and Charles Hampden-Turner. 1998. Riding the Waves of Culture: Understanding Cultural Diversity in Global Business. New York: McGraw-Hill.

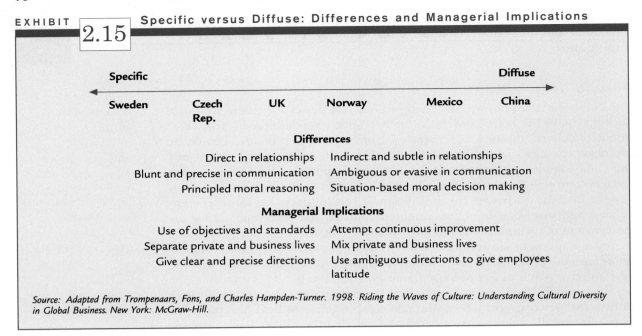

EXHIBIT 2.15   **Specific versus Diffuse: Differences and Managerial Implications**

Specific ← → Diffuse

Sweden   Czech Rep.   UK   Norway   Mexico   China

Differences

Direct in relationships	Indirect and subtle in relationships
Blunt and precise in communication	Ambiguous or evasive in communication
Principled moral reasoning	Situation-based moral decision making

Managerial Implications

Use of objectives and standards	Attempt continuous improvement
Separate private and business lives	Mix private and business lives
Give clear and precise directions	Use ambiguous directions to give employees latitude

Source: Adapted from Trompenaars, Fons, and Charles Hampden-Turner. 1998. Riding the Waves of Culture: Understanding Cultural Diversity in Global Business. New York: McGraw-Hill.

Achievement versus Ascription

Achievement versus ascription

How a society grants or gives status.

The dimension identified as **achievement versus ascription** addresses the manner by which a particular society accords or gives status. In achievement-oriented cultures, people earn status by their performance and accomplishments. In contrast, when a culture bases status on ascription, one's inherent characteristics or associations define status. For example, ascription-oriented societies often assign people status based on schools or universities attended or a person's age. Ascribed status does not require any justification. It simply exists. In such cultures, titles and their frequent usage play a large part in interactions.[42]

Exhibit 2.16 gives a brief description of the achievement versus ascription cultural dimension and the managerial implications of doing business in each cultural context.

To better understand this cultural dimension, consider the Multinational Management Challenge on page 75. It describes a situation of culture clash for a young woman manager from an achievement-oriented society when working in an ascription-oriented society.

Time Orientation

Time horizon

The way cultures deal with the past, present, and future.

To coordinate any business, managers must have some shared understanding of time. Experts on culture find vast differences in how people deal with time, and these differences become apparent when people from different cultures engage in business exchanges. One dimension of time of importance to managers is the time horizon. The **time horizon** concerns the way cultures deal with the past, present, and future and the boundaries among these time zones. Mexicans and Chinese, for example, have long time horizons and distinct boundaries among the time zones.[43] Exhibit 2.17 on page 76 summarizes the cultural characteristics of different time horizons. It also gives some managerial implications based on this cultural dimension.

In future-oriented societies, such as the United States, organizational change is considered necessary and beneficial. The static organization is the dying

EXHIBIT **2.16**   **Achievement versus Ascription: Differences and Managerial Implications**

Achievement					Ascription
Norway	Ireland	Austria	Japan	Hong Kong	Argentina

Differences

Use title only when relevant	Use of titles common and expected
Superiors earn respect through job performance	Respect for superior shows commitment to organization
Mixture of age and gender in management	Background and age main qualification for management

Managerial Implications

Emphasize rewards and respect based on skills and accomplishments	Emphasize seniority
Senior-level managers defer to technical and functional specialists	Use personal power of superior for rewards
	Emphasize the chain of command

Source: Adapted from Trompenaars, Fons, and Charles Hampden-Turner. 1998. Riding the Waves of Culture: Understanding Cultural Diversity in Global Business. New York: McGraw-Hill.

organization. For both people and organizations, one assumes that competition stimulates higher performance. It is assumed that individuals can influence the future. Both managers and workers assume that hard work now can lead to future success.

Multinational Management **Challenge**

Achievement-Based Management in an Ascription-Based Culture

What happens when young and previously successful managers from achievement-oriented Western societies find themselves in an ascription-based culture? Ms. Moore, a successful 34-year-old female manager from a U.S. company, takes a promotion as director of marketing in Ankara, Turkey. She has international experience in Britain and is confident that she can replicate her success at winning the support and trust of her subordinates and colleagues.

Within a few months, Ms. Moore finds her authority eroding. Hasan, a 63-year-old Turk, gradually and consciously takes over her authority as the boss and becomes the driving force behind marketing projects. Although everyone recognizes that Ms. Moore's marketing knowledge is much greater than Hasan's, her attempts to manage her function meets with increased resistance. The company follows Hasan's direction although results are not satisfactory. Later, Ms. Moore learns that her predecessor, a U.S. man her age, was fired for "failure to command local managers."

If you were sending a young, female manager to this assignment, what strategies would you recommend?

Source: Based on Trompenaars, Fons, and Charles Hampden-Turner. 1998. Riding the Waves of Culture: Understanding Cultural Diversity in Global Business. New York: McGraw-Hill.

EXHIBIT **2.17** **Time Horizon: Differences and Managerial Implications**

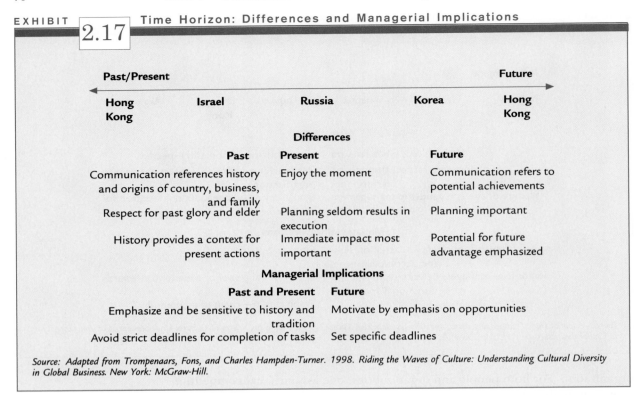

Past/Present ← ... → Future

| Hong Kong | Israel | Russia | Korea | Hong Kong |

Differences

Past	Present	Future
Communication references history and origins of country, business, and family	Enjoy the moment	Communication refers to potential achievements
Respect for past glory and elder	Planning seldom results in execution	Planning important
History provides a context for present actions	Immediate impact most important	Potential for future advantage emphasized

Managerial Implications

Past and Present	Future
Emphasize and be sensitive to history and tradition	Motivate by emphasis on opportunities
Avoid strict deadlines for completion of tasks	Set specific deadlines

Source: Adapted from Trompenaars, Fons, and Charles Hampden-Turner. 1998. Riding the Waves of Culture: Understanding Cultural Diversity in Global Business. New York: McGraw-Hill.

In past-oriented societies, people often assume that life follows a pre-ordained course based on traditions or the will of God. As such, strategic planning for the organization has little importance. A changing organization is suspicious to both employees and society. Stability is revered. Within these organizations, it is thought that senior people make the best decisions because they have the authority and wisdom to know the right way. Symbols and rituals dominate the organizational culture.

To consider your own time horizon, ask yourself how long ago your past started and ended, how long ago your present started and ended, and when your future will start and end. Trompenaars uses similar questions to measure the time horizons of different cultural groups.[44]

Internal versus External Control

Internal versus external control

Beliefs regarding whether one controls one's own fate.

The cultural dimension of **internal versus external control** concerns beliefs regarding control over one's fate. This cultural dimension is perhaps best reflected in how people interact with their natural environment. Does nature dominate us, or do we dominate nature?

To measure this dimension, Trompenaars and his colleagues present managers with the following options: "It is worthwhile trying to control important natural forces like the weather" and "Nature should take its course, and we just have to accept it the way it comes and do the best we can."[45] Arabic countries such as Bahrain, Egypt, and Kuwait are the most fatalistic with fewer than 20 percent of managers choosing the option of control over nature. This contrasts with more than 50 percent of the managers from Spain and Cuba who choose the option of control over nature.

Exhibit 2.18 summarizes the internal versus external cultural dimension and its managerial implications.

EXHIBIT **2.18**

Internal versus External Control: Differences and Managerial Implications

Internal Control ←——————————————————————→ External Control

| Poland | Brazil | Greece | Ethiopia | China |

Differences

Dominate the environment	Emphasis on compromise
Show convictions	Harmony and adjustment is good
Focus on self or own group	Adaptation to cycles

Managerial Implications

Emphasize authority	Emphasize patience
Dominate subordinates	Build and maintain relationships with subordinates, equals, and superiors
	Emphasize win-win relationships

Source: Adapted from Trompenaars, Fons, and Charles Hampden-Turner. 1998. Riding the Waves of Culture: Understanding Cultural Diversity in Global Business. New York: McGraw-Hill.

Differences in the cultural values regarding relationships with nature can affect how organizations and managers approach strategic and operational problems. In cultures where it is believed that nature dominates people, managers are likely to be fatalistic. They believe that situations must be accepted and reacted to rather than changed. In such cultures, people do not emphasize planning and scheduling. Work schedules must adjust to other priorities, such as family.

In contrast, where cultural values support the notion that people dominate nature, managers tend to be proactive. They believe that situations can be changed. Strategic plans and operations reflect the belief that obstacles can be conquered. What works is what is important. Organizations focus on using concrete data that suggest the best way to solve problems.

This section concludes our examination of the 7d view of culture. Similar to Exhibit 2.7 for the Hofstede model, Exhibit 2.19 gives percentile rankings for these dimensions for selected countries.

In the next section we discuss new information on a dimension of culture not considered by the major models, but generally recognized as key for conducting multinational business transactions.

Propensity to Trust: A Cultural Dimension of Increasing Importance

A growing concern of multinational businesspeople is the development of trusting relationships with business partners including strategic alliance partners, suppliers, distributors, and customers. Consequently, managers and academic researchers have begun to investigate differences among cultures in terms of how and when people trust each other.[46]

The common hypothesis is that individualistic societies, with their focus on self-interested behavior rather than what benefits the group,[47] have values that

EXHIBIT 2.19 — Percentile Ranks for The 7d Model Cultural Dimensions for Selected Countries

	Universalism	Individualism	Neutral	Specific	Achievement	Past Orientation	Future Orientation	Internal Control
Argentina	n/a	n/a	21	n/a	8	n/a	n/a	59
Australia	n/a	71	69	73	84	32	n/a	78
Austria	n/a	n/a	90	60	3	n/a	n/a	63
Belgium	n/a	52	46	n/a	n/a	n/a	n/a	43
Brazil	n/a	19	46	n/a	34	18	n/a	73
Bulgaria	n/a	84	81	n/a	29	n/a	n/a	20
Canada	95	74	77	80	92	n/a	47	88
China	26	26	85	3	58	82	89	2
Cuba	n/a	n/a	4	n/a	11	n/a	n/a	98
Czech Rep.	16	100	56	37	45	n/a	84	n/a
Denmark	n/a	61	33	70	82	n/a	n/a	80
Egypt	n/a	10	2	n/a	n/a	n/a	n/a	n/a
Ethiopia	n/a	n/a	100	97	37	n/a	n/a	24
Finland	n/a	58	50	63	76	n/a	n/a	39
France	63	n/a	25	53	71	77	74	90
Germany	n/a	35	35	40	61	64	53	34
Greece	42	32	38	40	55	n/a	n/a	51
Hong Kong	n/a	n/a	92	87	13	100	100	29
Hungary	79	94	58	23	47	n/a	n/a	n/a
India	21	16	83	27	18	9	39	27
Indonesia	47	n/a	85	17	n/a	36	39	32
Ireland	84	48	23	n/a	95	n/a	n/a	71
Italy	n/a	n/a	31	n/a	66	n/a	16	43
Japan	58	6	98	57	53	59	63	n/a
Kenya	n/a	n/a	n/a	n/a	26	n/a	n/a	17
Malaysia	n/a	29	25	43	n/a	n/a	n/a	n/a

(continued)

EXHIBIT 2.19   Percentile Ranks for The 7d Model Cultural Dimensions for Selected Countries (Continued)

Country								
Mexico	n/a	13	50	n/a	63	n/a	n/a	n/a
Netherlands	n/a	55	63	93	n/a	41	32	54
Nigeria	53	81	69	13	n/a	n/a	n/a	76
Norway	n/a	n/a	44	50	100	23	n/a	95
Pakistan	n/a	42	n/a	n/a	n/a	n/a	n/a	n/a
Philippines	n/a	n/a	15	33	21	n/a	n/a	n/a
Poland	37	87	96	90	39	27	n/a	100
Portugal	n/a	39	67	n/a	74	n/a	n/a	46
Romania	68	90	n/a	n/a	n/a	n/a	n/a	n/a
Russia	5	97	17	10	42	50	11	12
Korea	11	n/a	n/a	n/a	24	91	79	61
Singapore	32	23	69	47	68	73	5	10
Spain	n/a	68	4	n/a	32	55	n/a	93
Sweden	89	45	63	100	79	86	68	22
Switzerland	100	n/a	29	67	50	68	58	49
Thailand	n/a	n/a	58	n/a	16	n/a	n/a	56
UK	74	65	n/a	83	87	45	26	68
USA	n/a	77	54	77	97	14	21	66
Russia	5	97	17	10	42	50	11	12

Sources: Computed from data reported in Trompenaars, Fons, and Charles Hampden-Turner. 1998. *Riding the Waves of Culture: Understanding Cultural Diversity in Global Business.* New York: McGraw-Hill.

allow one person to take advantage of another person.[48] Symbolic statements such as "let the buyer beware" seem to support this cultural value in societies such as the United States. Alternatively, people often presume that collectivist cultures with their strong in-group ties and long-term relationships have a stronger predisposition for trusting each other, especially toward in-group members. Such logic leads some trust theorists to hypothesize that people from individualistic cultures enter relationships expecting opportunism and thus have low trust expectations.[49]

However, the evidence from research[50] suggests the opposite. It seems that people from individualistic cultures are more predisposed to trust others than people from collectivist cultures. For example, Americans, representing a highly individualistic culture, tend to have significantly higher levels for trust of other people than do the Japanese, representing a highly collectivist culture.[51]

Recent research by the World Values Study Group[52] provides perhaps the most comprehensive information, in terms of number of countries considered, on cultural values regarding trust. The World Values Survey (WVS) contains interview data on 45 societies (not all of which are nation-states) and is based on national sampling of adults 18 and over with a total sample of nearly 90,000 individuals.

To provide additional information of cross-cultural differences in trust, the author reanalyzed the original WVS data focusing on questions related to trust. As an indicator of general predisposition to trust, the WVS asked respondents whether they agreed with the statement: "Generally speaking, would you say that most people can be trusted or that you can't be too careful in dealing with people?" The dichotomous response categories were: "Most people can be trusted" and "Can't be too careful." Exhibit 2.20 shows the percentage of respondents in each society responding, "Most people can be trusted."

Nordic countries had the highest levels of trust. The United States ranked ahead of the more collectivist countries of Japan and South Korea. This was surprising because the business practices of these two countries are often characterized as based on trust more than legal contracts. However, China, another collectivist society, had levels of general trust similar to the Nordic countries.

This somewhat surprising summary of cultural differences in people's propensity to trust reveals that some common stereotypes regarding cultures may be false. It also shows that cross-cultural business interactions often begin with invalid assumptions regarding the nature of people.

After reading the forgoing sections on cultural models and cultural differences in trust, you should have acquired two skills. First, you can apply the models and your knowledge of trust to diagnose and understand the basic cultural values of a society. Second, you can apply this information to assess how the characteristics of a particular culture affect business operations. Later chapters will build on your knowledge of culture and the concepts introduced here. However, developing an in-depth understanding of any culture goes beyond the simply application of cultural models. The successful multinational manager will seek information continually from all sources. Consider, for example, how Exhibit 2.21 shows that proverbs provide less formal insights into national cultures.

Lastly, the chapter concludes with some cautions for all who venture into international operations.

EXHIBIT **2.20**   **Levels of General Trust in People**

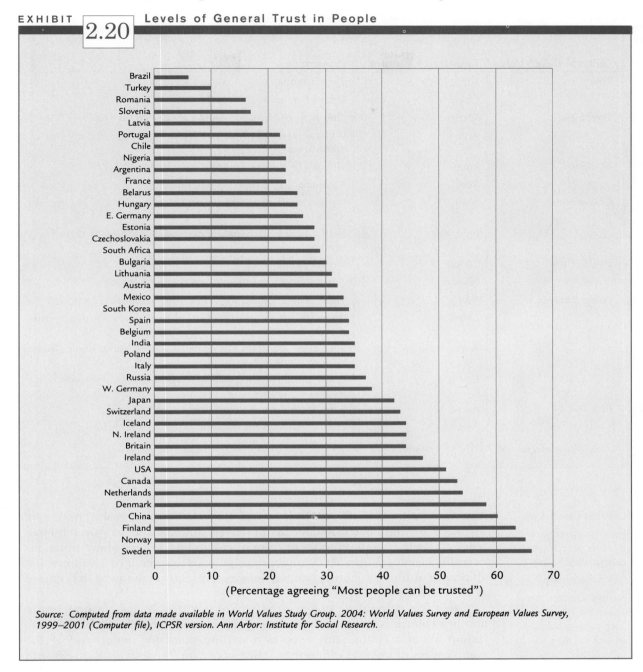

(Percentage agreeing "Most people can be trusted")

Source: Computed from data made available in World Values Study Group. 2004: World Values Survey and European Values Survey, 1999–2001 (Computer file), ICPSR version. Ann Arbor: Institute for Social Research.

Caveats and Cautions

Although understanding the cultures of the people and organizations with which you work is crucial for international business success, multinational managers in particular must realize that cultures provide only broad guidelines for behavior. Consider that, for instance, while the United States scores very highly on individualism, it has the highest percentage of charity giving in the world (clearly a collectivistic behavior). Similarly, while many of the Latin

EXHIBIT | 2.21 | Proverbs: Windows into National Cultures

Cultural Belief/Value	Country or Culture	Proverb
Time	U.S.	Time is money.
	China	Drips of water wear through stone.
Directness	Mexico	Only little children and drunks always tell the truth.
	Arab	If I have regretted my silence once, I have regretted my chatter many times.
Modesty	Japan	The nail that sticks up gets pounded down.
	Korea	A barking dog is never a good hunter.
Collectivism	Arab	My brother and I against my cousin. My cousin and I against the stranger.
	Indonesia	Both a light burden and a heavy burden should be carried together.
Value of age	Turkey	Beauty passes, wisdom remains.
	Nigeria	The elders of a community are the voice of God.
Power distance	Romania	There is no good accord where every man would be a lord.
	China	When you are an anvil, hold still. When you are a hammer, strike at will.
Fate	Arab	Man does not attain everything he desires; winds don't always blow as the vessels wish.
	China	A wise person adapts to circumstances as water conforms to the jar that contains it.
Risk	Korea	Even if it is a stone bridge, make sure it is safe.
	Arab	Only a fool tests the depth of water with both feet.

Sources: Wederspahn, Gary M. 2003. "Proverbs: windows into other cultures," http://www.executiveplanet.com/business-culture

Cultural paradoxes

Where situations in reality seem to contradict cultural prescriptions.

Stereotyping

When one assumes that all people within a culture behave, believe, feel, and act the same.

American cultures prefer warm interpersonal relationships, researchers were surprised to find that Costa Ricans preferred automatic tellers over human tellers.[53] Such examples represent cases of **cultural paradoxes** where situations in reality seem to contradict cultural prescriptions. However, if one assumes that all people within one culture behave, believe, feel, and act the same, it is known as **stereotyping.**

Using the cultural stereotype—the typical way people act—to understand another culture is not necessarily wrong if it is used carefully. Broad generalization about a culture can serve as a starting point for understanding the complexities of cultural differences. Most books on "how to do business with the _____" (name a culture) use stereotypical cultural generalizations. Such books can be used to understand comparisons between cultures rather than understand the variations within a single culture. After considering such information, however, the multinational manager must realize that organizational and occupational cultures differ within any national context and that individuals vary widely within each level of culture.

Consequently, management functions such as planning, organizational design, and personnel management must account for differences in occupational and organizational cultures as well as in national culture. Similarly, successful leadership, motivation, and development of individual employees must adjust for expectations based not only on all levels of culture but also on the unique characteristics of each employee.

Perhaps the greatest danger facing the multinational manager regarding culture is **ethnocentrism.** Ethnocentrism occurs when people from one culture believe that theirs are the only correct norms, values, and beliefs. The ethnocentric person may look down on people from other cultures and may consider people from other cultural groups backward, dirty, weird, or stupid. To offset the tendency of ethnocentrism, many anthropologists believe that one can understand another culture only if one adopts the position of **cultural relativism.** This is the philosophical stance that all cultures, no matter how different, are correct and moral for the people of those cultures.

Few multinational managers, however, are so ethnocentric that they fail to realize that people from other cultures just do things differently. Rather, the danger is a subtle ethnocentrism. Managers may find it difficult to remain entirely neutral in response to other cultures. For example, things such as the variations in pace of work in other countries, the unwillingness of subordinates to take responsibility, and practices such as bribery often frustrate North American managers. Early in an overseas assignment especially, managers must be wary of judging subordinates in terms of the manager's own cultural values. "Why don't they do it right, as we do?" is a common ethnocentric reaction.

The following Multinational Management Challenge shows that it is not always easy for the multinational manager to determine how sensitive to be to other

Ethnocentrism

When people from one culture believe that theirs are the only correct norms, values, and beliefs.

Cultural relativism

A philosophical position arguing that all cultures, no matter how different, are correct and moral for the people of those cultures.

Multinational Management **Challenge**

Can Cultural Adaptation Go Too Far?

Eric Bouvier was executive assistant to the managing director of a joint venture between a major European pharmaceutical company and a small but growing Korean pharmaceutical company. Bouvier spoke fluent Korean and served the company well as a cultural bridge between director Pascale Comont and Young Lim, his Korean counterpart.

After two years on the job, Comont became concerned about changes in Bouvier's behavior. Bouvier was no longer acting French. After his marriage to a Korean woman, he no longer socialized with his French expatriate colleagues, preferring instead to go to local bars with the Korean managers after work. In addition, whenever a disagreement arose between Comont and the Korean management team, Bouvier would side with the Koreans. He would simply tell Comont, "It's just the Korean way."

Although Comont initially found this behavior only mildly irritating, the issue came to a head over a personnel decision. When Comont fired a Korean manager for incompetence, Bouvier and Lim secretly had the man transferred to another division of the Korean parent company. When confronted with this situation, Bouvier simply explained it was his "moral duty to take care of subordinates—to protect their family and their reputation." As Comont pondered what to do, he wondered whether the issue of cultural sensitivity had gone too far.

Source: Based on Yoshino, Michael. 1989. "John Higgins: An American goes native in Japan." In Tom L. Beauchamp, Case Studies in Business, Society, and Ethics. Englewood Cliffs, NJ: Prentice-Hall, pp. 234–39.

cultures. The U.S. manager in this case is seen by his boss as over-identifying with Korean culture and not identifying enough with the culture of the parent organization.

Given the complexities and subtleties associated with national cultures, multinational managers have to work diligently to adequately understand the culture in any society. Often this process can take years of living and working in the new country. Chapter 11 discusses some of the ways multinationals can provide some cultural training to their managers to take foreign assignments in a new culture. Multinationals may use low-rigor teaching methods (e.g., classroom training through case studies, films, books, and lectures) whereby participants are involved in passive learning. However, multinationals also use high-rigor methods lasting longer than low-rigor approaches and relying on experiential learning, language training, and interactions with locals. Some universities are going as far as using cross-cultural simulations and drama to teach understanding of new cultures.[54]

Regardless of the training method, Osland and Bird[55] suggest that culture students should keep a few things in mind when learning about a new culture. These points include:

- *Question and analyze situations disconfirming stereotypes:* Stereotypes are useful to simplify a new culture. However, effective expatriates are the ones who can question and adapt their stereotypes as they interact with locals.
- *Seek cultural mentors:* Understanding a new culture is much easier with the help of local managers who are willing to help. Cultures are often too complex and subtle, and decoding such nuances is only possible with the help of an insider.
- *Get in-country training beyond factual or conceptual knowledge:* Serious scholars of cultures need to go beyond passive culture courses. It is important to get on-site training where they can learn real solutions to cross-cultural dilemmas.
- *Learn situation-specific cultural schemas:* Different situations may require different forms of responses. Successful culture students are the ones who can learn what rules and norms apply in what situation.

Summary and Conclusions

After completing this chapter you should know that culture has a variety of levels that affect multinational managers and organizations. However, the descriptions and examples of cultural effects on management are broad illustrations. No one book or chapter could do justice to the immense variety of cultures that exist in the world. This chapter hopes only to sensitize readers to the extremely complex and subtle influences that culture has on management and organizations.

The models of cultural values proposed by the GLOBE researchers, Trompenaars and his colleagues, and Hofstede provide basic concepts for analyzing cultural differences. They are tools to help you understand

a culture and to help you adjust business practices to various cultural environments.

The most successful multinational managers will realize that understanding a different culture is a never-ending learning process. They will prepare for their international assignments by studying all that they can about the country in which they will work. This includes the study of more than business etiquette. Understanding the national culture as well as important historical, social, esthetic, political, and economic trends builds a foundation. They will study the language. Few can really get behind the front stage of culture without speaking the local language. Finally, they will be sensitive and observant, continually adjusting their behavior to what works locally.

In this chapter, you received only a brief introduction. As you read later chapters, especially those with a comparative focus, you will broaden your understanding of cultural differences. You also will learn to seek advantage in differences and to avoid looking at culture as a potential obstacle to successful multinational operations.

Discussion Questions

1. Identify five cultural rituals, stories, or symbols from your native culture. Examples might include national holidays, the country's flag, nursery rhymes, childhood traditional stories, and sayings, such as "A stitch in time saves nine." Discuss how each of these communicates cultural values, norms, and beliefs.

2. Define and contrast back-stage and front-stage culture. Discuss how someone not familiar with your culture could misunderstand a front-stage behavior.

3. Discuss several ways that stereotyping and ethnocentrism limit successful multinational management.

4. Define levels of culture, and discuss the interrelationships among the levels.

5. Compare and contrast Hofstede's model of culture with the 7d model. Which model do you think is more valuable for managers? Why?

6. Compare and contrast the GLOBE model with the 7d model.

7. Pick three countries from Exhibits 2.7 and 2.19. Summarize and discuss the managerial implications of cultural differences by applying the Hofstede and 7d models.

8. What are cultural paradoxes? How can a manager prepare for such paradoxes?

Multinational Management **Skill Builder**

A Briefing Paper

Step 1. Read the following scenario.

You are a recent college graduate and a junior-levelexecutive in a midsize multinational firm. Your CEO will depart next week on a one-month business trip to meet potential joint-venture partners in Saudi Arabia, Poland, Hong Kong, Germany, Greece, and Brazil. Because of your expertise in international business, the CEO has asked you to prepare a cultural brief dealing with the national and business cultures where she will be visiting. She does not want to make any cultural faux pas. She expects a high-quality oral and written presentation. Since this is your first major assignment, it is important that you perform well. First impressions are lasting, and your job may depend on it.

Step 2. Your instructor will divide the class into six groups and assign each group at least one country.

Step 3. Using sources on the World Wide Web and in the library, research general cultural issues such as (but not limited to) basic cultural norms, values, and beliefs that may affect work (e. g., attitudes toward work in general, the role of the family in work, food and diet, the role of religion, language). Research specific business cultural issues such as expectations regarding dress, appointments, business entertaining, business cards, titles and forms of address, greetings, gestures, gift giving, language of business, interaction styles, time for deals to close, and the potential reactions to a woman executive.

Step 4. Present your findings to the class.

Endnotes

1 Kroeber, A. L., and C. Kluckhohn. 1952. "Culture: A critical review of concepts and definitions." *Papers of the Peabody Museum of American Archaeology and Ethnology*, 47: p. 1.

2 Goffman, Erving. 1959. *The Presentation of Self in Everyday Life.* Englewood Cliffs, N.J.: Prentice-Hall.

3 Terpstra, Vern, and Kenneth David. 1991. *The Cultural Environment of International Business.* Cincinnati, Ohio: South-Western.

4 Ibid.

5 *Craighead's International Business, Travel, and Relocation Guide 2000.* Detroit: Gale Research.

6 Hofstede, Geert. 1980. *Culture's Consequences: International Differences in Work-Related Values.* London: Sage.

7 Sathe, Vijay. 1985. *Culture and Related Corporate Realities.* Homewood, IL: Irwin.

8 Schein, Edgar H. 1985. *Organizational Culture and Leadership.* San Francisco: Jossey-Bass.

9 Hofstede, Geert. 2001. *Culture's Consequences: International Differences in Work-Related Values* (2d ed.) Beverly Hills, CA: Sage.

10 Ibid.

11 House, R., P. Hanges, M. Javidan, P. Dorfman, and V. Gupta. 2004. *Culture, Leadership and Organizations: The GLOBE Study of 62 Societies.* Thousand Okas, CA: Sage Publications.

12 Trompenaars, Fons, and Charles Hampden-Turner. 1998. *Riding the Waves of Culture: Understanding Cultural Diversity in Global Business.* New York: McGraw-Hill. 2000. http://www.7d-culture.nl/.

13 Hofstede, *Culture's Consequences: International Differences in Work-Related Values* (2d ed.).

14 Kirkman, Bradley L., Kevin B. Lowe, and Cristina B. Gibson. 2006. "A quarter century of Culture's Consequences: A review of empirical research incorporating Hofstede's cultural values framework." *Journal of International Business Studies*, 10, 4: pp. 1–36.

15 Hofstede, *Culture's Consequences: International Differences in Work-Related Values.*

16 Hofstede, Geert. 1991. *Cultures and Organizations: Software of the Mind.* London: McGraw-Hill; Hofstede, Geert and Michael Harris Bond. 1988. "The Confucian connection: From cultural roots to economic growth." Organizational Dynamics 16: pp. 4, 4–21.

17 Hofstede and Bond, "The Confucian connection: From cultural roots to economic growth."

18 Hofstede, *Culture's Consequences: International Differences in Work-Related Values*; Hofstede, *Cultures and Organizations: Software of the Mind*; Hofstede, *Culture's Consequences: International Differences in Work-Related Values* (2d ed.).

19 Hofstede, *Culture's Consequences: International Differences in Work-Related Values* (2d ed.).

20 Hofstede, *Culture's Consequences: International Differences in Work-Related Values.*

21 Hofstede, *Culture's Consequences: International Differences in Work-Related Values* (2d ed).

22 Hofstede, *Culture's Consequences: International Differences in Work-Related Values.*

23 Ibid.

24 Ibid.

25 Ibid.

26 Hofstede, *Cultures and Organizations: Software of the Mind.*

27 Ronen, S., and O. Shenkar. 1985. "Clustering countries on attitudinal dimensions: A review and synthesis." *Academy of Management Review*, September.

28 House, Hanges, Javidan, Dorfman, and Gupta. *Culture, Leadership and Organizations: The GLOBE Study of 62 Societies.*

29 Ibid.

30 Leung, Kwok, Rabi S. Bhagat, Nancy R. Buchan, and Cristina B. Gibson. 2005. "Culture and international business: recent advances and their implications for future research." *Journal of International Business Studies*, 36: pp. 357-78.

31 House, Hanges, Javidan, Dorfman, and Gupta. *Culture, Leadership and Organizations: The GLOBE Study of 62 Societies.*

32 Javidan, Mansour, Peter W. Dorfman, Mary Sully de Luque, and Robert J. House. 2006. "In the eye of the beholder: Cross cultural lessons in leadership for project GLOBE." *The Academy of management Perspectives*, February, 20, 1: pp. 67-90.

33 House, Hanges, Javidan, Dorfman, and Gupta. *Culture, Leadership and Organizations: The GLOBE Study of 62 Societies.*

34 Javidan, Dorfman, de Luque, and House, "In the eye of the beholder. Cross-cultural lessons in leadership for project GLOBE."

35 Kluckhohn, Florence, and F. L. Strodtbeck. 1961. *Variations in Value Orientations.* New York: Harper and Row.

36 Trompenaars, Fons. 1994. *Riding the Waves of Culture: Understanding Diversity in Global Business.* Chicago: Irwin; Trompenaars and Hampden-Turner. *Riding the Waves of Culture: Understanding Cultural Diversity in Global Business.*

37 Trompenaars and Hampden-Turner. *Riding the Waves of Culture: Understanding Cultural Diversity in Global Business.*

38 Trompenaars, *Riding the Waves of Culture: Understanding Diversity in Global Business*; Trompenaars and Hampden-Turner. *Riding the Waves of Culture: Understanding Cultural Diversity in Global Business.*

39 Trompenaars and Hampden-Turner. *Riding the Waves of Culture: Understanding Cultural Diversity in Global Business*, p. 79.

40 Trompenaars, *Riding the Waves of Culture: Understanding Diversity in Global Business*; Trompenaars and Hampden-Turner. *Riding the Waves of Culture: Understanding Cultural Diversity in Global Business.*

41 Trompenaars and Hampden-Turner. *Riding the Waves of Culture: Understanding Cultural Diversity in Global Business.*

42 Trompenaars, *Riding the Waves of Culture: Understanding Diversity in Global Business*; Trompenaars and Hampden-Turner. *Riding the Waves of Culture: Understanding Cultural Diversity in Global Business.*

43 Trompenaars and Hampden-Turner. *Riding the Waves of Culture: Understanding Cultural Diversity in Global Business.*

44 Ibid.

45 Ibid.

46 Johnson Jean L., and John B. Cullen. 2000. "The bases and dynamics of trust in cross-culture exchange relationships." In M. J. Gannon and K. L. Newman, (editors), Handbook of Cross-Cultural Management. London: Blackwell. Chapter 18.

47 Triandis, H. C. 1995. *Individualism and Collectivism.* Boulder, CO: Westview.

48 Williamson, O. E. 1996. *The Mechanisms of Governance.* New York: The Free Press.

49 Downey, P. M., J. P. Cannon, and M. R. Mullen. 1998. "Understanding the influence of national culture on the development of trust." Academy of Management Journal, 23 (3), pp. 601–20.

50 Yamagishi T., K. S. Cook, and M. Watabe. 1998. "Uncertainty, trust, and commitment formation in the United States and Japan." *American Journal of Sociology*, 104 (July), pp. 195–94.

51 Ibid.

[52] World Values Study Group. 2004. *World Values Survey and European Values Survey*, 1999-2001, (Computer file) ICPSR version. Ann Arbor: Institute for Social Research; Inglehart R., M. Basañez, and A. Moreno. 1998. *Human Values and Beliefs: A Cross-Cultural Sourcebook*. Ann Arbor: University of Michigan Press.

[53] Osland, Joyce S., Allan Bird, June Delano, and Mathew Jacob. 2000. "Beyond sophisticated stereotyping: Cultural sensemaking in context." The Academy of Management Executive, February, 14, 1: pp. 65–79.

[54] Lewis, Maureen Maguire. 2005. "The drama of international business: Why cross-cultural training simulations work." Journal of European Industrial Training, 29, 7: pp. 593–98.

[55] Osland, Bird, Delano, and Jacob, "Beyond sophisticated stereotyping: Cultural sensemaking in context."

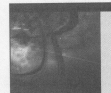

CHAPTER CASE

Organizational and National Cultures in a Polish/U.S. Joint Venture

This case looks at differences in cultural values and beliefs of Polish and U.S. managers employed in a joint venture in Poland. The case comes from data collected from interviews with Polish and expatriate U.S. managers.

Background

The U.S./Polish Company The company was a joint venture with a Polish partner and a wholly owned subsidiary of a U.S. multinational corporation located in Poland. The U.S. company started operations in Poland in 1990. The joint venture started two years later.

The joint venture was a small, nonbureaucratic organization with 140 employees. Everybody knew each other and a family type of relationship existed among the managers. Both local Polish managers and U.S. expatriates reported a friendly work climate even though all top managerial positions were held by the U.S. expatriates.

Polish Attitudes Regarding U.S. Management When asked why they chose to work for this company, Polish managers often described U.S. business as "real," "healthy," "tough," "honest," and "fair," although they had never had the opportunity to work with U.S. Americans before. In addition, they felt that features of Polish national culture such as "ability to work in difficult situations" and "experience of struggle with hardship of communism" combined well with American management expertise. In addition, Polish managers reported that working for a U.S. company was a major bonus for their future success and careers. Multinational corporations give employment security because they have a low risk of bankruptcy. In comparison with state companies, the organization was perceived as having a very efficient

organizational design dedicated to efficiency and profit making. Reflecting on his experience in state-owned operations, a Polish manager from the Customer Service Operation unit noted:

The basic difference between state companies and this company is that the organization of U.S. firms contains many necessary and indispensable elements. Whereas, in Polish companies, many elements were not needed and, even in some cases, disturbed the effective functioning of the company as a whole. Profit was not a major goal, only apparent activities. Many jobs and even whole companies were created when they were not needed. They were unproductive. Here we have only jobs and departments which help the company to function effectively.

The Polish managers expressed a great deal of enthusiasm and excitement for learning U.S. business know-how. Polish managers felt that they learned something new each day, not only from formal training but also from on-the-job training. Often Polish managers compared the company to a university. For the first time since entering a market economy, they felt they had the opportunity to learn business functions such as marketing, distribution, and logistics. These pro-American attitudes created an eagerness among the Polish managers to accept expatriate ideas concerning new work priorities. The attitudes also worked to legitimate the power and leadership of the U.S. Americans in the company.

The Polish managers believed that, unlike under the previous communist system, the new organization encouraged the development of the individual. They believed that the U.S. system of management inspired self-expression and achievement. It respected individuals and their unique personalities. There was a strong belief that hard work would bring success. Talented people who were willing to work could advance and succeed.

These organizational values were quite new for the Polish managers. In their previously state-controlled organizations, competence and good performance were not the main bases for a promotion and compensation. Party membership was the key to a successful managerial career. Rewards and promotions depended on fulfilling a political role rather than on achieving economic goals.

The Cultural Conflicts

In spite of the very positive attitudes of the Polish managers toward a U.S. management style, there were still many conflicts between expectations based on Polish cultural traditions and an organizational culture based on the national culture of the United States.

Managerial Selection Many Polish employees wanted to be hired immediately as managers, without any experience in basic business functions. The magic word "manager" was associated by them with a higher status and success. U.S. managers, however, felt that "you had to earn your spurs first." The U.S. expatriate District Manager recalled:

> *People applying for positions in the sales department do not want to do basic business first, to be a sales representative, they want to be immediately managers. People that I interview want to be only managers. How you can manage sales representatives if you don't know what they do? They lack a concrete answer for my question.*

Merit, Age and Seniority The corporate culture encouraged rewards primarily based on competence in key skills and performance against objective criteria. Both local and expatriate managers believed that individuals were appointed and promoted based on their knowledge and professional expertise. This situation often resulted in much younger managers having older subordinates. As one U.S. manager from the Finance Department stated:

> *The company gives a lot of authority to young people very quickly. You never know, the guy who is looking younger than you could be a vice president already.*

Although Polish managers appreciated promotions based on competence, the issue of age

presented some problems of adjustment. Traditional expectations hold that, when one is young, it is impossible to be knowledgeable and have the necessary experience and competence to manage successfully. As a Polish assistant manager from the Marketing Department admitted:

> *I prefer to have an older boss because it would be very stupid if I have a boss younger than me. He has less life experience and a shorter marriage. He is younger and he is not authority to me. I would prefer someone who has more life experience. I realize that it is a very Polish thing that I find this to be a problem.*

The Salary System Polish managers expressed difficulty in adjusting to the confidentiality of the new salary system. The Polish and U.S. managers differed in the beliefs regarding what information was personal and what information should be public. Polish managers wanted to know as much about each other's salaries as possible. They had no problems asking another employee about exactly how much they were paid. To the Polish managers, this served as a means of establishing their relative status. As a Polish assistant Brand Manager indicated:

> *I like this system but I would like to know how I am in comparison with the others. If I knew that the person who works together with me had a higher salary than me, I would be very unhappy.*

For the expatriate U.S. Americans, however, it was not part of the company culture to reveal explicit salary information. Salary information was considered personal and confidential. Most felt that revealing salary information disrupted the family climate of the organization. Instead, the Americans expressed faith in the system of assessment and reward allocation. As the expatriate head of the Finance Department noted:

> *Poles make mistakes when they say: "Americans don't share salaries in this system." I would say it is not that straightforward at all. In the American system, in our company's system, we don't share specifics on what any one person makes. We try very hard to share the system by which you make more salary. We make it very clear that your salary is based on your performance. If you perform well you will make a lot of money.*

Team Goals Working not only for your own interests but also for the success of the team or the whole company was a challenge for many Polish managers. This was especially true for those who had their initial managerial experiences in a state-controlled economy. One Polish manager noted:

> Americans want to hire the best, because the organization will gain from them and you as a boss should be not afraid if you hire a person who is more clever than you. You will benefit from it because the company will benefit. In state companies you had to protect yourself by not cooperating—a new, better employee was your potential enemy.

Another Polish assistant Marketing Manager mentioned:

> In a state company, if somebody has a problem, he or she solves it with their own interests in mind. Here we are thinking in terms of the benefit of the whole company. I made a mistake and I regarded it as my mistake because I was responsible for it. But the problem was judged [by the Americans] as a problem and loss for all of us. This is a different way of thinking, and this is the attitude of this company. Success belongs to everybody and so does failure. This is better than making one person responsible for it.

The Psychological Contract From the perception of the Polish managers, the organization required them to accept a new psychological contract between organization and the individual. On the one hand, they felt positive about the degree of personal involvement and responsibility in the daily activities of company affairs. On the other hand, they were confused where to draw the line between professional and private lives. Many of the Polish managers felt that, for them to succeed as employees, the organization demanded too much of their private lives. As the Polish Marketing Manager said:

> Americans look differently at the firm. They associate themselves very closely with it. They are part of the firm. In the past I never felt such a relationship with the firm.

Another Polish District Manager mentioned:

> This new way of thinking, that you have to have a strong psychological connection with the firm, surprised me. You have to show you are interested. In the past you escaped from your job as quickly as possible.

Trust A U.S. cultural trait found surprising by Polish employees was the perception of an underlying good faith in people. Both the company culture and the expatriate managers had positive valuations regarding the intentions of people within the organization. As a Polish accountant stated:

> What was new for me was that Americans have the assumption that you are acting for the good of the firm and that you are honest and that people are good. If you go to a restaurant for a business meal, nobody will tell you that you are nasty and that you used the company money and did it for a bad purpose.

A Polish assistant Brand Manager added:

> A positive attitude toward people, trust in people—this is a basis for everything. Americans don't wait to catch you in a mistake. We are more suspicious of people. Our immediate assumption is that a person wants to do something bad.

The Polish managers expressed much more negative attitudes regarding the nature of people. These were evidenced in many aspects of the daily business life of the organization: subordinate–superiors ("My boss wants to harm me"), employee–peers ("My colleagues would only criticize me"), customer–product ("Americans are trying to sell us bad products"), employee–product ("I don't believe in the value of this product"). A U.S. expatriate Brand Manager describing the Polish managers indicated:

> I have never met a group of people that was more skeptical of the future and more distrusting. Everyone we do business with is convinced that we are dumping a less quality product on the market. The Polish customer is very skeptical. They don't believe that they can get products as good as anybody else in the world.

Distrust, fear, and a disbelief that the boss wishes well for the employees were common attitudes observed by the U.S. expatriates. One U.S. expatriate from Customer Service Operations remarked:

> Sometimes they [the Polish managers] don't understand that the company is trying to do the right things for individuals. Sometimes there will be questions which assume that the employer is going to take advantage of them and is going to treat locals badly. It is not a good assumption that the company and manager are not trying to help them if they have a problem.

Informality U.S. managers valued blunt and direct speaking. Saying exactly what you mean was considered a virtue, and the U.S. managers had a low tolerance for ambiguity. Therefore, expatriate managers took most explanations at face value. Reacting to this, Polish managers often described Americans as very "open," "direct," "spontaneous," and "natural" during communication. However, this style of communication clashed with the indirect communication habits of Polish employees. As the American head of the Marketing Department stated:

> Communication with Polish employees is difficult, especially when an employee has a problem. There is a general unwillingness to talk directly about oneself and one's problems. Poles will gladly talk about somebody else. They will not talk about their own needs. They don't like direct questions about things which are important to them. Perhaps it is considered impolite, too bold, or inappropriate for them.

Polish managers adapted to the U.S. directness by developing an informal network of communication among themselves. This informal network served as a buffer between the U.S. and Polish managers. To deal with their U.S. superiors, Polish managers first talked among themselves. Then one person would become responsible for going to a U.S. manager and telling him or her about someone else's problems. Expatriate managers found it unusual when subordinates who needed to communicate problems resorted to this informal channel. However, this buffer in communication provided a comfort zone for the Polish managers. As the Polish assistant Marketing Manager noted:

> Poles more easily criticize things among themselves, but it is difficult for them to criticize things in the presence of Americans. It is as if they don't believe in their strengths, and are afraid that their opinions are either untrue or irrational. They are afraid of being funny.

Americans also introduced an informal style of communication by addressing everyone in the office on a first-name basis. Expatriates expressed the belief that their organizational culture provides an opportunity to "lead by competence, not by formality in relationships between superiors and subordinates." They were proud of their openness and equality in forming business relations. To the expatriates, those Polish managers who resisted the informality appeared to be cold and distrusting. Expatriates interpreted it as the "director syndrome," or an example of an attitude from the communist-controlled past. The expatriate head of the Sales Department described it as follows:

> I respect their history. I respect the cultural aspects. Every time they call me "Mister Director" I remind them to call me by my first name. I am constantly telling them that I have a culture, too. This company has a culture, one that I want to build here. I don't like the environment that formality fosters and the environment that it creates. It is a barrier for effective communication. You almost have too much respect, and then you stop talking to me, soon you stop coming and saying, "I have a problem."

The majority of Polish managers adjusted to the norm of a first-name basis very quickly in dealing with the Americans. However, this did not mean that they wished to be on a first-name basis when speaking among Polish managers, especially with their Polish subordinates. Using first names for older people or for superiors is not a Polish norm. Some Polish managers were afraid that they would lose the ability to lead by being so informal. They believed that distance between superiors and subordinates helped them in direct management of lower staff. The Polish head of the Human Resource Department said:

> There are some people in the firm with whom I will never be on a first-name basis. I am on a first-name basis with some people and on a Ms./Mr. basis with others. I don't know why, but I will not change that.

Informality also contrasted with Polish views that managers should symbolically show their status and success. Polish managers gave much value to formality, titles, and signs of status, such as having a good make of car. Superiors were expected to have these trappings as a demonstration of their authority over subordinates. In contrast, the U.S. expatriates regarded many of these status symbols as counterproductive and meaningless. A U.S. Brand Manager mentioned:

> Poles are passionate about getting ahead in status. People are looking for examples of badges to wear for the rest of the populace to

know that you have made it. My boss must be in a big car. "What car are you going to drive?" I was asked by a Pole in the first meeting in Poland.

Positive Feedback on the Job There were significant differences between Polish managers and expatriate Americans in the type of feedback given on the job. Consistent with U.S. views of management practices, the U.S. managers were quick to recognize achievements publicly and privately. Polish managers were generally positive about this approach and perceived it as motivating. However, in spite of this reaction, positive feedback was not a popular management technique among the Polish managers. They preferred to give criticism and generally negative feedback in front of subordinates and peers. Reacting to the U.S. approach, a Polish District Manager described the situation as follows:

If you are good, Americans can send you a congratulatory letter. Once I had got such a letter from an American colleague of mine even though he had no particular responsibility for my job. He was not my boss. I would never think of doing so. It was so spontaneous.

Conclusions

Coming from a culture that lacked experience and contact with U.S. businesses before 1989, Polish managers generally had positive but stereotypical views of U.S. business practices. In the short term, such attitudes played a highly motivating role in attracting managers to the joint venture. In the long term, however, despite the initial enthusiasm, basic cultural differences may lead to disillusionment among Polish managers.

CASE DISCUSSION QUESTIONS

1. What are some important cultural differences between the Poles and the U.S.?
2. Using the Hofstede's and 7d cultural dimension model, explain some of the cultural differences noted in the case.
3. What are some institutional explanations for how the Pole workers are reacting to US management style?
4. How can the joint venture take advantage of the initial enthusiasm of the Polish managers to build a stronger organization?
5. What cultural adaptations would you suggest to the US expatriates managers regarding their management styles?

CASE CREDIT

This case was prepared in 1992 by Krystyna Joanna Zaleska of the Canterbury Business School, University of Kent, Canterbury, England, while a postgraduate student at the Central European University, Prague. Reprinted with permission of the author.

The Institutional Context of Multinational Management

Learning Objectives

After reading this chapter you should be able to:

- Understand the national context and how it affects the business environment.
- Understand the influence of the institutional context of countries on individuals and organizations.
- Define social institutions and understand the basic forms of social institutions.
- Understand how social institutions influence both people and organizations.
- Understand the basic economic systems and their influence on multinational operations.
- Understand the basic stages of industrialization and their implications for multinationals.
- Understand the world's basic religions and how they shape the local business environment.
- Develop an understanding of education and its effects on multinational operations.
- Understand social inequality and its implications for multinationals.
- Understand the importance of the national context and its connection with other international management areas.

Preview CASE IN POINT

Search for Global Talent

According to McKinsey & Co., close to 33 million young professionals live in low-wage countries. The number of graduates from universities in low-wage countries is growing at an annual rate of 5.5 percent compared to only 1 percent for high-wage countries. In contrast, there are only 15 million such professionals with university degrees and experience living in eight of the high-wage nations. Such changes and an increased pressure on multinationals to lower costs will mean that more multinationals from developed nations will shift their critical workforce to labor markets in developing countries. Furthermore, although wages are increasing in high-profile locations such as Bangalore, Shanghai, and Prague, multinationals are now moving to other places such as Jaipur, India and Chengdu, China. Such trends suggest that many of the emerging markets will remain very attractive locations for professional talent.

Why are these countries producing such high-quality talent? Consider, for instance, the case of India. India has one of the most competitive educational systems in the world. India has produced some of the best talent in the fields of science, information technology, medicine, and engineering. Such an impressive workforce has been possible in large part due to a high-quality and highly competitive educational system provided by both private and public institutions. In fact, some even argue that India's business schools (Institutes of Management) most likely have some of the hardest entrance test of any program around the world.

China is also presenting multinationals with a huge and relatively inexpensive pool of talent. Many multinationals are now investing heavily in research and development in China, as evidenced by the growth of foreign-invested centers from 200 in 2002 to about 750 in 2006. This increased attraction of China as an innovation center is due largely to its supply of educated individuals. China currently graduates about five million individuals annually, of which one-fifth major in science or engineering. Furthermore, multinationals incur lower costs hiring both engineers and researchers in China.

Sources: Based on Chen, Kathy, and Jason Dean. 2006. "Low costs, plentiful talent make China a global magnet for R&D." Wall Street Journal, March 13, p. A1; Hansen, Fay. 2006. "The great global talent race." Workforce Management 85, 7, 1, pp. 20–23; Mazumdar, Sudip. 2006. "Grades and politics." Newsweek International Web Version http://www.msnbc.com; Punoose, Rukhmini. 2006. "India's edge." Newsweek Web Version http://www.msnbc.com

I n Chapter 2, we discussed some of the ways societies can be compared on the basis of national cultures. However, as the Preview Case in Point shows, there are other elements of a society besides national culture, such as education, that can produce important business-related differences among societies. These elements may sometimes even encourage individuals to adopt values that may not be consistent with their national cultures. It is important to understand these key elements, namely the dominant institutional context of any society, to appreciate the influence they have on both individuals and organizations.

Understanding the institutional context of countries is extremely critical to better multinational management. At a basic level, a complete understanding of any society cannot be fully achieved unless both the national culture and the institutional context are examined.[1] Both are key elements of societies, and both have important influences on issues that are related to strategic multinational management. Exhibit 3.1 shows a model of how the national context (i.e., institutional context, national culture, and business culture) leads to national differences that have implications for the business environment of any country.

The **national context** is made up of the respective national cultures and social institutions of any society. As we saw in Chapter 2, the national cultures of any society shape the important norms, values, and beliefs in any society. These cultural components provide important sources of influence on the business culture and what are acceptable and correct ways of doing business. However, closely intertwined with national cultural forces are social institutions such as the economic system, religion, and education. As we will see later in this chapter and in other chapters, they also represent significant influence on norms, values, and beliefs of people and have implications for the business culture. Social institutions evolve within the constraints of national culture not only to shape the values and beliefs of individuals but also to provide the business context within which some organizational forms can exist and some industries can flourish.

As the Preview Case in Point shows, social institutions have important influences on individuals and the business environment in any society. In concert with national culture, social institutions help shape the business culture. Furthermore, the social institutions also create induced-factor conditions (i.e., the science-oriented educational system in Eastern Europe has produced a supply of skilled engineers in these countries) that add to the resources of any society. In turn, this national context provides the environment that influences how firms are formed and how they approach multinational strategic management.

This chapter will provide a basic understanding of the institutional context of societies. In the next section, we discuss briefly the main elements of the

National context

National culture and social institutions that influence how managers make decisions regarding the strategies of their organizations.

EXHIBIT   3.1   The National Context and Multinational Companies

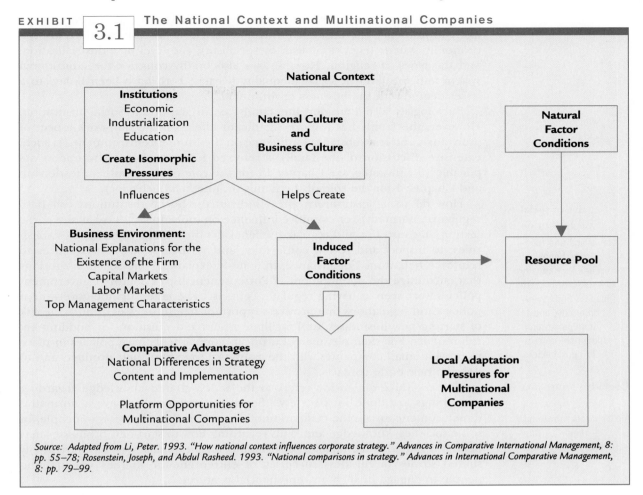

Source: Adapted from Li, Peter. 1993. "How national context influences corporate strategy." Advances in Comparative International Management, 8: pp. 55–78; Rosenstein, Joseph, and Abdul Rasheed. 1993. "National comparisons in strategy." Advances in International Comparative Management, 8: pp. 79–99.

institutional environments of countries, namely social institutions and how they influence society. In subsequent sections, we discuss each of these social institutions in depth and their implications for multinational strategic management. We conclude this chapter by looking at some of the ways social institutions are connected to later chapters in the text.

Social Institutions and Influence on Society

A **social institution** can be defined as "a complex of positions, roles, norms, and values lodged in particular types of social structures and organizing relatively stable patterns of human resources with respect to fundamental problems in . . . sustaining viable societal structures within a given environment."[2] In addition to national culture, social institutions have profound effects on people's immediate conditions of life and provide the context that affects psychological differences among people. Similar to national culture, social institutions provide boundaries and norms that prescribe how people will behave. In other words, social institutions provide people with behavioral guides when facing different social situations.

Social institution

A complex of positions, roles, norms, and values organizing relatively stable patterns of human resources with respect to sustaining viable societal structures within a given environment.

We consider three key social institutions that have been shown to be most likely to influence the business environment. These social institutions are the economic system (e.g., capitalism or socialism), the level of industrialization, and the types of religion. However, we also briefly consider the educational system and the level of social inequality because both have been linked to a lesser degree with the business environment.

Sociologists also consider the family as an important social institution. However, the family has a more significant effect on the non-work aspect of individuals and less substantial influence on the business environment. As such, extensive discussion of the family is reserved for later chapters whenever applicable (for instance, see Chapter 15 for the role of the family on leadership and Chapter 4 for the role of the family on unethical behavior).

How do social institutions affect individuals? Social institutions can have regulative, normative, or cognitive influence on individuals.[3] A **regulative social institution** constrains and regularizes behaviors through its capacity to establish rules, to inspect and review conformity, and to manipulate consequences to reinforce behaviors. For instance, in a study explaining the social institutions that encourage the development of entrepreneurship, a country's government policies were seen as having regulatory effects.[4] The latter include government policies and regulations that provide support for new businesses, reduce the risk of starting new businesses, and facilitate resource acquisition for budding entrepreneurs. For example, many European governments have policies in place to provide small companies with the assistance to export their products and to develop new trade contacts.[5]

The **cognitive dimension** refers to the widely shared knowledge regarding how things are done in a society.[6] Social institutions that have a normative dimension encourage the dissipation of some shared information to people. In some societies, knowledge and skills regarding how to start new businesses may be widely shared and available. For example, most capitalist societies have widely shared stories of business successes of entrepreneurs, thereby encouraging people to engage in such entrepreneurial ventures.

Finally, the **normative dimension** refers to the values and norms promulgated by the social institutions. With regards to our example of social institutions encouraging the development of entrepreneurial ventures, the normative dimension is an assessment of the degree to which people admire entrepreneurial activities and new product innovation.[7]

Social institutions have effects on individuals as well as organizations. However, in the case of organizations, social institutions, especially the legal and political systems, help define what are legitimate and correct management practices in a particular society. Organizations in that society tend to adopt similar management practices. This pressure from social institutions to follow similar paths in management practices is called **organizational isomorphism**.[8] Within a nation, isomorphism leads organizations to become similar to each other but different from organizations located in other nations.

Experts identify three types of isomorphism (or pressures for similarity) that are important for organizations: coercive isomorphism, mimetic isomorphism, and normative isomorphism. **Coercive isomorphism** means that social institutions coerce or force organizations to adopt certain practices. For example, in both Taiwan and Italy, extended family expectations of living and working together combine with national economic and legal policies to encourage the existence of small firms and discourage the development of large firms.[9]

Regulative social institution
Constrains and regularizes behaviors through its capacity to establish rules, to inspect and review conformity, and to manipulate consequences to reinforce behaviors.

Cognitive dimension
Refers to the widely shared knowledge regarding how things are done in a society.

Normative dimension
Refers to the values and norms promulgated by the social institutions.

Organizational isomorphism
Pressure from social institutions to follow similar paths in management practices.

Coercive isomorphism
Social institutions coerce or force organizations to adopt certain practices.

Consider the example of the coercive effects of governmental regulations on Asian value chains described in the Case in Point.

Mimetic isomorphism means that organizations purposefully copy the strategies of the most successful organizations. When people start new organizations or change ongoing organizations, they often imitate what seems to work most successfully. This imitation leads to organizations becoming similar to one another within a particular nation.

Normative isomorphism means that organizations indirectly copy the designs, cultures, and strategies of other organizations by conforming to professional and technical norms. Normative isomorphism differs from mimetic isomorphism because copying occurs largely without conscious effort. For instance, movements of employees among companies, availability of the same trade publications, and informal discussions among managers from different organizations can gradually introduce similarity among a group of organizations.

The preceding paragraphs show that social institutions have significant influences on both individuals and organizations within countries. In the next few sections, we look at a number of the most important social institutions that impact the business environment of most societies.

Economic Systems

The **economic system** is the "interrelated network or system of beliefs (concerning work, property, constructs, and wealth), activities (extraction, production, and distribution), organizations (business firms, labor unions, consumer associations, regulatory agencies) and relationships (ownership, management, employment, sales) that provide the goods and services consumed by the members of a society."[10] Economic systems are usually reflected in their governments' influence, specifically in terms of whether productive activities are state owned or privately owned.

Economic systems can be typified by the extremes of capitalism and socialism with mixtures of elements of both in the mixed economy. The **capitalist or market economy** refers to an economic system where production activities are "decentralized to private-property-rights holders (or their agents) who carry out these activities for the purpose of making profits in a competitive market."[11] In

Mimetic isomorphism

Organizations purposefully copy the strategies of the most successful organizations.

Normative isomorphism

Organizations indirectly copy the designs, cultures, and strategies of other organizations by conforming to professional and technical norms.

Economic system

System of beliefs (concerning work, property, and wealth), activities (extraction, production, and distribution), organizations (business firms, labor unions), and relationships (ownership, management) that provide the goods and services consumed by the members of a society.

Capitalist or market economy

System where production is decentralized to private owners who carry out these activities to make profits.

C A S E   I N   P O I N T

Regulations and the Asian Supply Chains

As multinationals keep the sustained pace of growth in many Asian markets, they are facing increased challenges due to the regulatory environment. Governments in many Asian countries have many rules, regulations, and policies in place that add substantial cost to the value chain resulting in very inefficient logistics. For instance, 100 percent of imports entering Sri Lanka are inspected while only 2 percent of German imports have to be inspected. Similarly, countries such as Thailand and Vietnam require numerous approval signatures for most exports while only two

are need in other places such as Australia and Canada. In addition to such red tape and other challenges in handling customs and port handling, multinationals have to contend with facilitation fees, which are effectively bribes to speed up customs clearance. Such regulatory environments in these countries add almost 5 to 15 percent to any company's supply chain. Reforms in these countries would likely make for much more competitive supply chains.

Source: Based on Bangkok Post. 2006. "Regulatory impacts on Asian supply chains." April 26, p. 1.

Socialist or com-
mand economy

Production resources
are owned by the
state and production
decisions are cen-
trally coordinated.

Mixed economy

Combines aspects of
capitalist and social-
ist economies.

contrast, the **socialist or command economy** is one where production resources are owned by the state and production decisions are centrally coordinated.[12] The ideal socialist economies pursue collective goals such as social equality and solidarity. Finally, the **mixed economy** combines aspects of the capitalist and socialist economic systems. In such economies, certain sectors of the economy are left to private ownership while other sectors such as health care and education are run by the state. The state determines that some sectors of the economy cannot be run by private interests and thus intervenes and takes control of such sectors. The state makes resource allocation and production decisions. Countries such as Sweden, France, Denmark, Italy, and India are examples of mixed economies.

Although it is impossible to cover all possible business implications, economic systems have three major implications for strategic multinational management. At a basic level, decisions to operate in a country can be made based on the dominant economic type. For instance, if a multinational expects to operate relatively free from governmental interference, it may want to set up operations in more capitalist societies such as the United States and Britain. However, if multinationals expect to do business in mixed economies like France and Italy, they should expect to subordinate their economic goals and respect social objectives. Emerging markets also present peculiar challenges for investors. Consider the following Focus on Emerging Markets.

Focus on Emerging Markets

Joint Ventures and Governmental Interference in China

Among emerging markets, China has presented investors with especially significant challenges related to government interference. Such governmental interference has been abrupt, complex, and ambiguous. Foreign investors often find it very difficult to predict, verify, and even control such interference. To further compound the problem, greater decentralization and deregulation has meant that investors also have to deal with local governmental interference as well as the central government agencies.

Research by Luo shows how companies deal with these difficulties when forming joint ventures in China. A critical aspect of most joint ventures is the international joint venture contracts governing how the joint ventures are operated. These contracts necessarily incorporate three important components, namely term specificity (the degree to which contractual terms are clearly specified), contingency adaptability (the degree to which companies can adapt to changing situations), and contractual 'obligatoriness' (the degree to which companies are bound by the contract). Using surveys from 110 executives involved in international joint ventures, Luo showed that the more the respondents experienced governmental interference, the more they rated the joint venture contract as containing contingency adaptability. In other words, the more there is governmental interference, the more the contract needs to leave room for adaptation to new situations. Luo also found that governmental interference had a negative impact on contract specificity because the more the government intervened the less possible it was to specify the contract clearly. Such research provides some important guidelines regarding how companies need to structure their contract to counteract Chinese local and central governmental interventions.

Source: Based on Luo, Yadong. 2005. "Transactional characteristics, institutional environment and joint venture contracts." Journal of International Business Studies, 36, pp. 209–30.

The Focus on Emerging Markets clearly shows the impact of governmental interference on a multinational's operations. As a rough guide, multinational managers may want to consider the **index of economic freedom** to determine the extent of governmental intervention in different countries. Since 1995, the Heritage Foundation, a U.S.-based research foundation, has been constructing the index. It defines the index as "the absence of government coercion or constraint on the production, distribution, or consumption of goods and services beyond the extent necessary for citizens to protect and maintain liberty itself." The index includes 10 indicators ranging from trade policy (i.e., the degree to which the government hinders free trade through tariffs), taxation policies, and the level of governmental intervention in the economy to property rights (freedom to accumulate private property) and regulation (i.e., ease of obtaining a business license). The foundation assigns scores of 1 through 5, with 1 being the highest degree of economic freedom. Exhibit 3.2 shows selected top and bottom 10 countries on the 2003 score.

The indices shown in Exhibit 3.2 are not surprising. Capitalist societies such as the United States, Australia, the United Kingdom, Singapore, and Hong Kong figure prominently in the list of top 10 countries. Communist societies such as Cuba and North Korea are in the bottom 10. Additionally, countries with repressive governments such as Zimbabwe and Libya are also in the bottom 10. The more mixed economies such as Italy, Portugal, France, and Spain also

Index of economic freedom

Determines the extent of governmental intervention in a country.

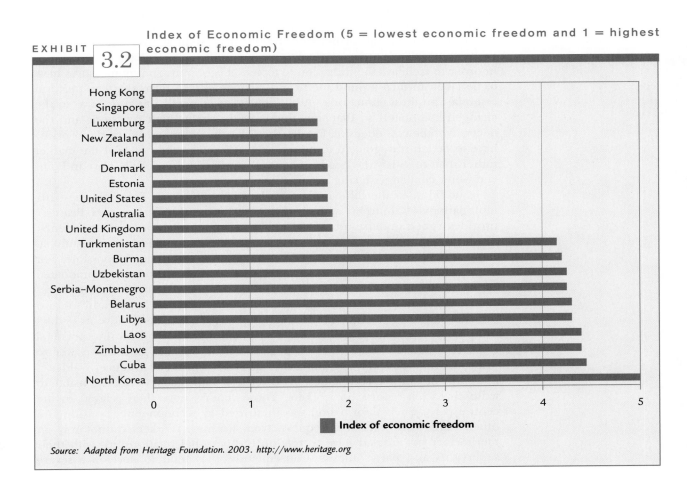

EXHIBIT 3.2   Index of Economic Freedom (5 = lowest economic freedom and 1 = highest economic freedom)

Source: Adapted from Heritage Foundation. 2003. http://www.heritage.org

have higher scores that reflect the high degree of governmental intervention. Similarly, both Japan and Korea have higher indices since both countries have very involved governments in the business sphere.

A second important implication for multinational strategic management related to economic systems are the **market transitions** that many societies are going through as they move from socialism to a more market-based system. The post 1980s saw a large number of countries in Russia, Eastern Europe, and Asia (i.e., China and Vietnam) undergo marked attempts by the governments to infuse heavy doses of capitalism. For most multinationals, such open market policies have presented incredible opportunities as they provide these companies with new markets and access to skilled but relatively cheaper labor. An important aspect of this transition for many multinationals has been an increase in international strategic alliances with local companies, as described in more detail in Chapter 9.

An important component of this market transition for most multinationals has been to understand socialism and its effects on both people and organizations in order to better understand the workers' reactions to market mechanisms. Under socialism, most enterprises were mere factories with no need for cost control.[13] Often these enterprises did not have any strategic planning, accounting, or marketing departments. Furthermore, central planners guaranteed survival and inefficiencies of these firms by setting up prices that were not accurate reflection of costs. Instead, prices were kept low to sometimes encourage heavy consumption of goods that were manufactured according to the central planners. Banks also were managed according to the needs of central planners. Loans were often made to enterprises on the basis of connections and personal relationships rather than credit worthiness.

It is not difficult to understand then what multinationals have to experience in order to facilitate the transition to a market economy. Drastic measures have to be taken to turn around inefficient companies into firms that can perform essential business functions. Additionally, managers' thinking has to be changed completely so that they understand management functions and the necessity to be cost effective. Finally, the financial system and firms (and price) have to be left unregulated to more accurately reflect the needs of the market rather than to satisfy the needs of central planners. Consider the Case in Point and other challenges facing multinationals.

In addition to the difficulties described in the Case in Point on page 101 multinationals have to be aware of the effects of socialism on workers. Pearce[14] provides a good understanding of what workers go through in socialist societies. She argues that a basic function of governments is to provide the institutional framework that makes impersonal exchanges among strangers possible. For instance, if the scope of businesses expands beyond what can be accommodated by friendship or family arrangements, individuals need institutional structures so that they can trust strangers to complete their end of the bargain. In socialist societies, however, the government is considered as non-facilitative as it does not provide the structure to ensure that people can depend on interpersonal trust. It is actually more likely that government officials have the power to distribute rewards and make important salary decisions. For instance, Walder,[15] in a study of Chinese companies, discusses how supervisors were responsible to write character reports on workers. Those reports were then relayed to the central party. Such information was then used to accommodate housing and other scarce consumer-item requests from workers. Workers cannot rely on meritocracy but instead have to rely on the personal relationships with their supervisors and party officials. Consequently, they tend to develop a severe

Market transitions

Changes societies go through as they move from socialism to a market-based economy.

C A S E   I N   P O I N T

Laying Off Workers in Lithuania and Other Challenges

Most firms transitioning to a market-based system find that they are seriously overstaffed and thus have a need to fire a significant portion of their workforce. However, firing workers may not always be easy. Often when countries are transitioning to a market-based economy, they enact laws to protect workers. These laws allow workers to unionize and bargain collectively. Additionally, the law requires that workers can be fired only with the approval of the unions.

In a study in Lithuania, a company tried to layoff 30 engineers. The company finally was able to secure union approval to lay off the engineers. However, when the engineers were informed of their dismissal, they immediately formed a new union and refused permission to lay off their members!

In Hungary, a new law that was passed as a result of the transition to the market economy allows companies to pay their suppliers only when the products are delivered. However, there regularly are delivery delays. For instance, if a company is scheduled to deliver a product in November but is able to deliver only in March of the following year, the company cannot pay the supplier. The company, however, must pay up front if it wants to keep access to reliable suppliers. Otherwise, when the supplier receives the order, it places the order at the bottom of its priorities, and both supplier and firm spend the rest of the time negotiating delivery of the product.

Source: Based on Pearce, Jone L. 2001. Organization and Management in the Embrace of Government. Mahwah, NJ: Lawrence Erlbaum Associates.

distrust of each other as they are all competing for the same limited rewards. Additionally, they tend to focus their energies on refining their personal networks rather than performance as the former is more likely to help with success.

Multinationals have incredible challenges as they hire employees in former socialist societies. At a basic level, they need to train these workers to trust each other. As multinationals use team-based approaches to designing work, they are finding that workers are reluctant to cooperate and work with each other. Furthermore, multinationals also need to change the mentality that personal relationships are key components of success. As they introduce more open systems based on meritocracy, they are sometimes facing significant opposition from these employees. Consider the Comparative Management Brief on page 102 showing the various challenges private firms have faced with regards to human resource policies in China and the response to these challenges.

A closely related third and final implication is privatization efforts in many countries including Russia, China, and some African countries. **Privatization** refers to the transfer of state ownership to private individuals.[16] The latter is also a critical part of understanding economic systems as they represent important efforts of formerly socialist societies to embrace a more market-based economy. Such efforts represent significant opportunities for U.S businesses. For instance, there are more than 400 public joint stock companies on the privatization list of Russia currently, and it is predicted that the list will grow bigger.[17] Furthermore, in 2002, it was predicted that state property valued at 35 billion rubles (around $1.19 billion) was privatized[18] in Russia. Similarly, there are now discussions of a second wave of privatizations in China although much of that privatization may be available only to locals.[19] Exhibit 3.3 on page 103 shows selected countries and the amount of money raised by privatization efforts in 2000.

Privatization of state businesses is seen as an effective way to encourage companies to become more efficient. Private owners are given a new powerful

Privatization

Transfer of state ownership to private individuals.

Comparative Management Brief

Human Resource Management Challenges in China

The 1950s Iron Rice Bowl policy was based on the notion that workers had the right to lifetime employment and a wide range of social programs such as housing, schools, and medical care. Additionally, the long isolation emphasized by communism resulted in a complete elimination of the human resource management function. China now is transitioning to a market economy, and companies are finding that they are facing major challenges as they try to adapt market-based approaches to the human resource management function.

In face-to-face interview with 10 individuals closely linked to private firms in China, a number of significant challenges were described. For instance, because the old system emphasized personal networks and ties, private firms find that Chinese managers tend to hire relatives and friends and to overstaff. Additionally, Chinese workers in these firms were not accustomed to do more than what was specified in their job description. They were often risk-averse. Finally, job appraisals and rewards were very difficult to do, especially when good relations with workers and government officials had to be maintained.

In addition to these challenges, other research suggests that the Chinese contextual environment has resulted in other problems. For instance, the planned economy and the "cultural revolution" have emphasized loyalty at the expense of initiative among workers. Furthermore, the lack of business education in the past means that China is currently suffering from a severe shortage of qualified professionals. This situation has resulted in a very mobile workforce where employees do not hesitate to change jobs frequently to take advantage of high demand for qualified individuals. Multinationals also find it risky to bring Chinese employees to train in Europe because such training makes the employee more attractive to other firms when he or she returns to China.

Source: Based on Bruton, Garry D., David A. Ahlstrom, and Eunice S. Chan. 2000. "Foreign firms in China: Facing human resources challenges in a transitional economy." SAM Advanced Management Journal, Autumn, pp. 4–36; Jaussaud, Jacques, and Xueming Liu. 2006. "La GRH des personnels locaux dans les enterprises etrangeres en Chine: Une approche exploratoire." Revue de Gestion des Ressources Humaines, 59, pp. 60–71.

incentive to turn around formerly state-run businesses, namely profits. Multinational companies have the prospect of investing in companies that present significant opportunities in terms of access to local markets and to relatively cheaper local labor. Consider the Focus on Emerging Markets regarding privatization in emerging markets.

Most proponents of privatization argue that privatization leads to better standard of living for workers as the pursuit of profit leads to better performance and, therefore, better pay. Do employees share this view? In a study of a Turkish cement company purchased by a French conglomerate, 150 employees were surveyed on their attitudes regarding privatization efforts.[20] The workers were asked a variety of questions related to job security. For instance, they were asked if they preferred higher income rather than job security. Not surprisingly, employees indicated that job security was more important for them. They also were asked about the effects of privatization on job security in their firms and in general. Most of the workers felt that privatization was detrimental to job security. In contrast, the managerial group was less pessimistic about the effects of privatization on job security. Managers believed that job security was not necessarily lower under the privatization reforms.

EXHIBIT **3.3**   Global Amounts Raised from Privatization (in U.S. dollars million)

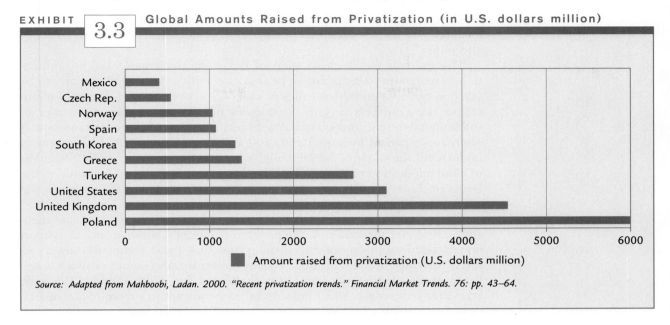

Source: Adapted from Mahboobi, Ladan. 2000. "Recent privatization trends." Financial Market Trends. 76: pp. 43–64.

Workers were also interviewed regarding their feelings on the effects of privatization on wages. They generally felt that privatization did not necessarily result in better wages for them. In fact, many of them preferred the previous state's minimum wage policies. They also did not feel that under privatization wages were more closely linked to how hard they were working. They argued that if privatization was truly meant to reflect a closer link between effort and hard work, then firms should rather be sold to employees.

Focus on Emerging Markets

Privatization in Emerging Markets

Emerging markets present tremendous potential as the massive privatization wave continues. Even as the pace of privatization slows in stable countries such as Poland, the Czech Republic, and Hungary, other countries such as Slovakia, Romania, Bulgaria, Serbia, and Croatia all present tremendous opportunities. For instance, foreign investors can currently participate in privatization efforts of the Bratislava and Kosice airports and the local electricity provider in Slovakia. The banking sector in Romania also represents tremendous opportunities for foreign investors. Serbia is currently exploring offers from 10 international companies to buy the majority state-owned Mobi 63, a mobile phone operator.

Major emerging markets such as India and China also present tremendous opportunities. Both countries have experienced tremendous growth and have significant market power through their rising middle class. For instance, both China and India have some of the fastest growing telecommunication markets due to the privatization of important industries.

Source: Based on BBC Monitoring European. 2006. "Privatization of Serbia's only private mobile operator begins." May 16, p. 1; Business Wire. 2005. "India has one of the fastest growing telecommunication markets due to the expanding middle class and the privatization of key industries." December 22, p. 1; Hawser, Anita. 2006. "Attention turns to the new wave." Global Finance, 20, 1, pp. 30–31.

Similar to their responses for job security, managers' views were different from employees. They felt that privatization made a closer link between effort and wages.

This example clearly shows some of the major challenges faced by multinational companies participating in privatization efforts. Special efforts have to be taken in order to understand what workers are experiencing. It is unrealistic to expect these workers to give up decades of economic expectations and to suddenly adopt the market-based approach. In fact, because privatization is often accompanied by large layoffs and significant changes, it is important to understand the workers. Additionally, it is critical to examine the effectiveness of blind application of Western-based management techniques. However, as the Focus on Emerging Markets shows, privatization will continue to present significant investment potential for foreign investors.

Clearly, economic systems have important implications for strategic management of multinationals. As the previous paragraphs show, economic systems impact relationships among companies and how these companies are structured. Specifically, the transition of many former socialist countries to a market-based approach presents significant challenges for multinationals. However, economic systems also affect individuals. As we will see in subsequent chapters, economic systems affect how workers view work and even how they justify ethical behaviors.

In the next section, we consider another critical social institution, namely the levels of economic development through different degrees of industrialization.

Industrialization

Industrialization

Cultural and economic changes that occur because of how production is organized and distributed in society.

The application of the steam engine to the gathering and production processes is largely used to explain the Industrial Revolution in Europe.[21] The latter eliminated excessive reliance on the use of animal power and allowed the building of and use of new machines and equipment that were very effective in resource use. This new ability to gather and transform resources allowed rapid development in many of the Western societies through large factories with large number of workers assembled around networks of machines. Such changes dramatically influenced all aspects of society.

Pre-industrial society

Characterized by agricultural dominance and shaping of the economic environment.

Industrialization refers to the cultural and economic changes that are brought about by fundamental changes in how production is organized and distributed in society. Industrialization can be categorized in several ways. In **pre-industrial society,** agriculture dominates and shapes the economic environment. In pre-industrial societies, religious norms and tradition are emphasized while social mobility is discouraged.[22] Occupational placement tends to be based on ascription (family background), and social status is largely determined through inheritance. An **industrial society** tends to be characterized by the dominance of the manufacturing or secondary sectors. Such societies reflect the prevalence of technological development that makes rapid economic growth possible. Industrial societies tend to require wider ranges of skills in their workforce relative to pre-industrial societies. Occupational placement is based on universalistic criteria such as achievement. Finally, the **postindustrial society** emphasizes the service sector. The dominance of employment by the service sector leads to a drastic expansion of the role of formal education as there is a need for highly skilled workers with specialized skills. Exhibit 3.4 shows selected countries and the distribution of employment by primary, secondary, and tertiary sectors.

Industrial society

Characterized by the dominance of the secondary or manufacturing sectors.

Postindustrial society

Characterized by emphasis on the service sectors.

EXHIBIT **3.4**   **Distribution of Production Activities by Sector**

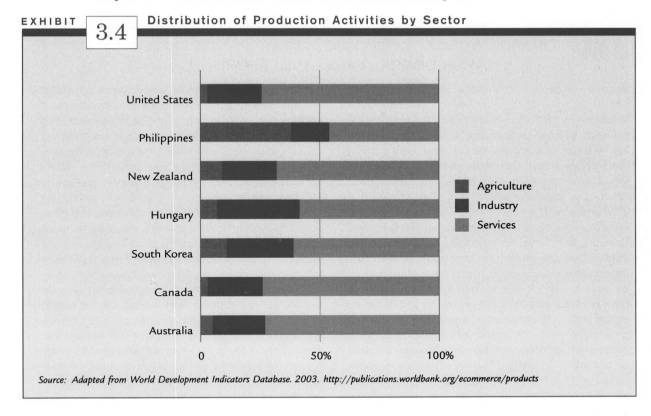

Source: Adapted from World Development Indicators Database. 2003. http://publications.worldbank.org/ecommerce/products

The level of industrialization has important implications for strategic multinational management. First, there is a direct correspondence between the level of economic development and industrialization. As such, pre-industrial societies tend to be the least economically developed. Multinational companies can use such indicators to determine the feasibility of doing business in pre-industrial societies. Given that the long-term prospect of a business in any country is dependent on the market size and income, pre-industrial societies tend to provide fewer opportunities. However, it is also important to note that pre-industrial societies also provide relatively cheap labor compared to more industrialized societies. It is therefore not surprising to see that many companies tend to locate their plants in pre-industrial countries. Yet another important issue to consider is that pre-industrial societies tend to have poorer infrastructure and business support. It may be more costly to operate in such societies because the multinational company may have to provide its own infrastructure and support services. Many African countries are unfortunately found in the pre-industrial category and multinationals have generally shunned most of them because of political instability. However, as the Case in Point on page 106 shows, the future for some African countries is bright, and multinationals have to be aware of the role they can play in such developments.

Industrial societies tend to be more economically developed than pre-industrial societies. As technological development makes it possible to shift production to the manufacturing sector, there are important changes in the economic environment of the society that impact strategic management. Instead of emphasizing tradition and communal obligations heavily influenced by religious norms typical of pre-industrial societies, industrial societies tend to

C A S E   I N   P O I N T

What Does the Future Hold for Africa?

With the exception of nations like Botswana and Mauritius, few African economies have been able to sustain growth in real per capita gross domestic product, another indicator of industrialization. The reality shows that African nations have been growing much more slowly than other developing nations. Why have most African countries been left behind in terms of industrialization? It is often argued that after many African nations experienced independence from the three major colonizers, namely France, Belgium, and Great Britain, their respective elites established one-party rule "promising stability and economic development in return for a monopoly on political power." However, these countries did not have previous experience in governing and in capital accumulation. Furthermore, any outward-oriented growth potential was viewed with suspicion because it was seen as foreign interference from the previous colonizers. Consequently, most governments, because of internal pressures, engaged in more state-led and inward-looking industrialization efforts. Coupled with internal strife and governments' response to interest groups, African nations did not achieve much economic progress.

Multinational companies nevertheless have significant roles to play in Africa's future development and growth. Africa has significant physical and human resources and represents significant market opportunities. As the continent wrestles with the failings of most autocratic regimes, many African countries are gradually moving towards multiparty regimes with an emphasis on political stability. As more and more African countries gain political freedom, the economic environment will become more conducive to capital accumulation and growth. As such, multinational companies will have a significant role to play as investors. As a rough guide for investment decisions, multinational companies may want to consider liberal democracy indices, i.e., the extent to which a political system enables political liberties and democratic rule. The exhibit shows the political democracy indices for selected African countries. A score of 100 indicates an absolute liberal democracy, and a score of 0 indicates an absolute dictatorship.

Source: Based on Ndulu, Benno J., and Stephen A. O'Connell. 1999. "Governance and growth in SubSaharan Africa." Journal of Economic Perspectives 13, pp. 41–66.

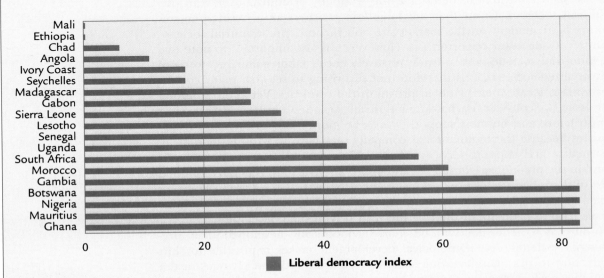

Source: Adapted from Bollen, Kenneth. 1993. "Liberal democracy: Validity and method factors in cross-national measures." American Journal of Political Science. 37: 1207–1230.

favor innovation and individualism. Economic achievement becomes the top priorities for industrial societies, and discipline and achievement-oriented norms predominate.[23] Industrial societies tend to present significant opportunities for multinational companies. Multinational companies have access to an environment that is very favorable to businesses and a labor force that is often educated and motivated. Additionally, industrialized societies tend to have governments that are usually favorable to businesses. Multinational companies can generally expect that their business endeavors will be facilitated. Furthermore, industrial nations tend to present less non-market risks, such as government appropriation, to businesses. Exhibit 3.5 shows materialist scores of selected countries. These scores provide indications of the degree to which societies value such goals as economic growth and maintaining discipline, both indicators of the degree of industrialization.

As Exhibit 3.5 shows, many countries that are currently undergoing industrialization processes (e.g., China, Hungary, India, and Brazil) have high rankings on the materialist index. This suggests that individuals in such societies are achievement oriented and favor material gains. The emphasis on economic achievement suggests that multinational companies are well advised to motivate employees with monetary rewards.

In addition to shaping norms for individuals, industrialization also has implications for how industries are shaped. In that respect, it is important to note that industrialization can take many forms and have different effects based on other conditions reflected in the society. In some cases, industrialization efforts can be inward-oriented where local industries are promoted in order to satisfy the domestic market and preserve foreign exchange.[24] In contrast, some countries also have more outward-oriented industrialization strategies where foreign investment is encouraged and exporting is heavily promoted.

EXHIBIT 3.5   Materialist Values for Selected Countries

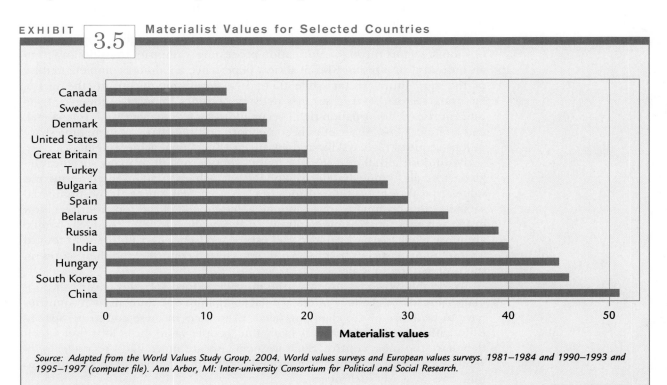

Source: Adapted from the World Values Study Group. 2004. World values surveys and European values surveys. 1981–1984 and 1990–1993 and 1995–1997 (computer file). Ann Arbor, MI: Inter-university Consortium for Political and Social Research.

Kuruvilla's[25] study of industrial relations/human resource policies in India, Malaysia, the Philippines, and Singapore shows that industrialization strategies had drastic effects on human resource policies in the country. For instance, the low-cost export-oriented industrialization strategy of the Philippines has encouraged industrial relations/human resources policies that emphasize cost containment and efforts to limit unionism. In order to be competitive as a low-cost producer, Philippines manufacturers have to be offered low cost labor with minimal union interference. In contrast, both Malaysia and Singapore have shifted from a low-cost-oriented export strategy to a higher-value-added export strategy. As a consequence, both countries found that they also had to change their cost containment industrial relations/human resources policies to favor workplace flexibility and skills development. This change was necessary to have access to a skilled workforce necessary for the new demands of the industrialization strategy. Finally, India, in an effort to become self-sufficient, adopted an import-substitution-oriented industrialization strategy. Because the state and unions had strong ties and because the focus of inward-oriented industrialization is to satisfy local demands, there was never an urgent need to adopt collaborative and flexible industrial relations policies. The result was that the "choice of institutional industrial relations governing industrial relations was geared toward the protection of labor rights and labor power."[26] Recent economic liberalization efforts in India are now encouraging changes toward more flexibility in industrial relations.

This discussion shows that degrees of industrialization have drastic impact on how the business environment of any society is shaped. It is therefore imperative for multinational companies to clearly understand the stage of industrialization and other types of industrialization to determine which areas of their businesses are affected.

A postindustrial society is characterized by the domination of the service sectors in production activities.[27] In such a society, the source of productivity and growth tend to come from the generation of knowledge as applied to all economic sectors through information processing. Countries transitioning from an industrial to a postindustrial society experience an almost complete demise of the agricultural sector while there is a significant decline in the manufacturing sector. Because services delivery becomes important, there is a significant rise of "information-rich" occupations such as managerial, professional, and technical jobs. As societies become more postindustrial, an increasing share of jobs requires higher skills and advanced educational achievements.

Postindustrialization is leading to a postmodern shift in many societies. Inglehart, et. al.[28] argue that the disciplined and achievement-oriented norms and values typical of industrialized societies have reached a peak. In postindustrial societies, the "emphasis on economic achievement as the top priority is now giving way to an increasing emphasis on the quality of life."[29] As such, people are more likely to espouse individual expression values and a movement toward a more humane society. Exhibit 3.6 shows selected countries and their scores on the post-materialist scale.

As Exhibit 3.6 shows, many of the most developed societies have high post-materialist scores. As such, multinational companies operating in such countries have to be aware of the changing needs of workers in these countries. Specifically, with regards to work, it is likely that people value those jobs over which they have the most control. Such workers also are more likely to prefer non-economic incentives rather than monetary rewards. Companies should strive to find ways to satisfy such needs.

EXHIBIT **3.6**   **Postmaterialist Values for Selected Countries**

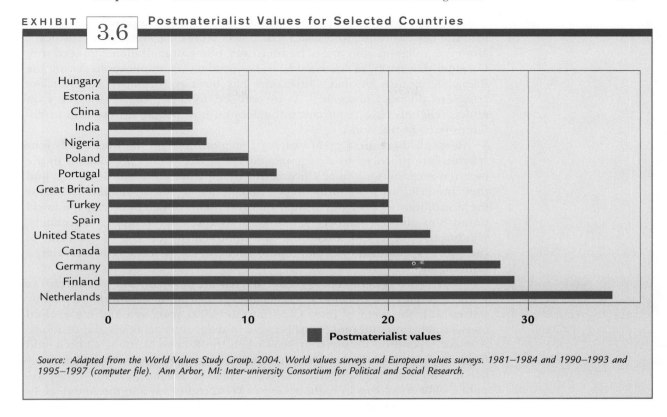

Source: Adapted from the World Values Study Group. 2004. World values surveys and European values surveys. 1981–1984 and 1990–1993 and 1995–1997 (computer file). Ann Arbor, MI: Inter-university Consortium for Political and Social Research.

In this section, we described some of the possible effects of industrialization on societies. Specifically, we looked at industrialization levels and how they affect individuals as well as organizations. In the next section, we consider another critical social institution, namely religion.

Religion

A **religion** can be defined as a shared set of beliefs, activities, and institutions based upon faith in supernatural forces.[30] Religions continue to be an important aspect of most societies. The reemergence of Christianity in the United States, the rise of Islamic fundamentalism in the Middle East, the rapid growth of Protestantism in Latin America, and the religious devotion in the former Soviet Union and Eastern Europe all signal that religions continue to be pervasive and important.[31]

Religions and work and their interrelationships form the very foundations of human society.[32] In fact, the link between religion and how societal systems are structured for economic purposes form the basis of Weber's[33] famous formulation of the Protestant work ethic. Weber, a famous German sociologist, proposed that the domination of Protestant religions led to the emergence of modern capitalism in Western Europe. He argued that Protestant beliefs emphasize hard work, creation of wealth, and frugality. This combination of values allowed individuals to work hard to accumulate wealth. However, because their beliefs encouraged them to reinvest the wealth rather than to spend it, they formed the basis of the Western European capitalist expansion.

Religion

Shared set of beliefs, activities, and institutions based on faith in supernatural forces.

Religions have important influences on society. Religions provide individuals with the way of dealing with issues that reflect individual wishes and activities.[34] However, religions also affect business and other organizational procedures. Consider that Islam, as discussed later, has productivity implications during the Ramadan months or that Christianity has obvious consumer behavior implications during Christmas.[35] As we will see, for instance, in Chapter 4 on ethics, religions have important influences on how people do business in different parts of the world.

Although there are a great variety of religions around the world, only four religions are practiced by a large percentage of the world's population. In the next few sections, we look at Christianity, Islam, Hinduism, and Buddhism and their implications for multinational strategic management. Exhibit 3.7 shows the distribution of religions around the world both in percentage of the world population and in number of followers. As the exhibit shows, Christianity, Hinduism, Islam, and Buddhism are followed by almost 71 percent of the world's population while approximately 20 percent are considered nonreligious.

Christianity
Religion based on the life and teachings of Jesus.

"**Christianity** is a faith based on the life, teachings, death, and resurrection of Jesus"[36] and is clearly the most practiced religion around the world. Christianity started with the birth of Jesus Christ around 2006 years ago and has evolved considerably into different forms because of many internal feuds and divisions. A major separation occurred in 1054 when the Roman Catholic Church split from the Eastern Orthodox Church. The majority of Orthodox Christians today live in Russia, Serbia, Bulgaria, Romania, Albania, Poland, and the Czech Republic while most Roman Catholics live in Western Europe and the Americas. In 1517, yet another major division occurred in Christian history. Disillusioned with the Roman Catholic Church's authority and practices, Martin Luther, a German monk and priest, initiated different interpretations of the Bible that led to the Protestant branch of Christianity.

Despite the many divisions among Christianity, Christians all share the same belief that Jesus is the incarnation of God who was sent to clean the sinfulness

EXHIBIT 3.7 Religion by Percentage of World Population and Approximate Number of Followers

Religion	Percentage of world population following religion	Number of followers
Christians	33.60%	1,900,174,000
Nonreligious	20.50%	1,163,189,000
Muslims	18.25%	1,033,453,000
Hindus	13.50%	764,000,000
Others	7.33%	414,725,000
Buddhists	5.99%	338,621,000
Sikhs	0.36%	20,204,000
Jews	0.24%	13,451,000
Confucians	0.10%	6,334,000
Jains	0.07%	3.951,000
Shintoists	0.06%	3,387,000

Sources: Adapted from Fisher, Mary P. 1999. Living Religions, 4th ed., Upper Saddle River, N.J.: Prentice-Hall.

of humanity. Jesus is often associated with love and allows humans to connect with God through penance, confessions of their sins, self-discipline, and purification.

The impact of Protestantism on the development of capitalism is seen as major evidence of the link between religion and economic structuring of societies. Because Protestantism emphasized wealth and hard work for the glory of God, it allowed the focus on goals attached to economic development and wealth accumulation. In contrast, Catholics were more likely to question the pursuit and accumulation of wealth. This difference explained the sustained development of capitalism in the Western Protestant societies.

In general, Christians agree "on the value and dignity of human life, labor, and happiness."[37] There is a general support for the freedom to accumulate wealth and possessions. However, human greed and selfishness is nevertheless viewed with contempt, and attempts are made to ensure that there is equality of opportunity and fairness for the less fortunate. Additionally, Christianity, through the Ten Commandments, provides the basis for what are considered ethical behaviors. Although not all individuals follow these commandments, they are nevertheless seen as norms guiding behaviors with respect to such things as theft (You shall not steal), murder (You shall not kill), and protection of private property (You shall not covet your neighbor's house...or anything that is his). As such, multinational companies have access to environments that are conducive to conducting business.

The essence of **Islam** as described in the *Qur'an* is the submission to the will of *Allah* (God). Islam can be traced back to Muhammad, a prophet born in 570 AD. However, unlike Christians' view of the divinity of Christianity's founder Jesus, Muslims do not ascribe divinity to Muhammad. Rather, he is seen as the messenger of *Allah's* (God) revelations and the last in a line of prophets starting with Adam, through Moses, Jesus, and Abraham.[38] Islam is currently the second largest of the world's religion and has adherents in countries in Africa, the Middle East, China, Malaysia, and the Far East. It continues to grow rapidly in many countries, especially in Europe.

Islam

Religion based on the submission of the will to Allah (God).

Muslims live in a society that is heavily influenced by Islamic standards and norms. Islam provides encompassing guidance in all spheres of life, both social and economic. Those who serve *Allah* and accept the reality and oneness of *Allah* go to paradise in the afterlife.[39] Muslims also believe that *Allah* wants them to live according to the *Shari'ah* (Law). The *Shari'ah* requires Muslims to follow five pillars, namely Confession, Prayer, Alms-giving, Fasting, and Pilgrimage to Mecca.[40]

These pillars have important implications to multinational strategic management. First, if a multinational company is operating in a Muslim country, it has to accommodate the Muslim's need to pray five times a day. Muslims need to pray in the early morning, noon, mid-afternoon, sunset, and evening.[41] Furthermore, during the Ramadan, a month of fasting, multinational companies will face some decline in productivity. During that month, Muslims are not allowed to eat, drink, smoke, and even take medicines from dawn till dusk. As such, multinational managers are advised to take the necessary steps to ensure that business activities are not disrupted. The month is also considered very spiritual, and multinational companies should expect their workers to be more concerned with sacred matters and a heightened spiritual atmosphere.

The alms-giving pillar also has critical implications for multinational strategic management and how Islam views business. In general, the *Qur'an* is supportive of entrepreneurship and earning of profits through legitimate business activities. The *Qur'an* also allows accumulation and protection of private property. However, Muslims are naturally concerned with issues of social justice and fairness. As such, Muslims are likely to condemn the pursuit of profits through exploitation of others. Multinational companies thus have to ensure that their business activities are conducted in a socially just manner. They also have to ensure that some form of alms giving is practiced. Muslims (and organizations) are required to share the accumulated wealth by charitable giving to the poor. This practice is seen as necessary to decrease social inequalities and personal greed. Multinational companies may be well served by participating in such donations.

An important consequence of Islam's condemnation of exploitation of other's is that Islam prohibits the payment or receipt of interest. Islam regards payment or acceptance of interest a serious sin. Such practices are not just ideals but are actually respected in many countries, including Pakistan. In such countries, governments have instituted financial laws declaring interest as illegal. For a multinational company operating in a Muslim country, the prohibition of interest presents a serious challenge. However, many Muslim societies have been working in profit-sharing plans to avoid the payment or receipt of interest. For instance, if a multinational company borrows money from a bank in a Muslim country, it should expect to be asked to share the profits from the investment as an alternative to interest payment. Multinational companies should thus be prepared to formulate creative but acceptable ways to manage their finances.

Multinational firms are likely to be presented with significant opportunities in the Muslim countries over the next few years. For instance, it has been estimated that the Middle East alone has approximately 300 infrastructure projects representing $45–$60 billion of possible private investment over the next decade.[42] It is also likely that multinational companies will have to provide significant financing for the projects. The challenges of financial exchanges will become more salient and will have to be dealt with. Consider the Comparative Management Brief on page 113 and the challenges of Islamic laws.

A final multinational strategic management implication of Islam pertains to the role of women in Muslim countries. Although the *Qur'an* puts men and women on equal footing as individuals, there are different guidelines regarding the roles of men and women.[43] While the man's role is to work and support the family, the woman's role is to provide care and stability to the family in the home. It is therefore not surprising to see that many Muslim societies are strictly separated by gender. Multinational companies have to be aware of implications of their business actions based on gender roles. For instance, it is not advisable for multinational companies to post women in Muslim countries in executive positions given the largely male-dominated sector. Additionally, human resource management practices need to take into consideration the limited role of women in such societies. There has been much progress in many Muslim societies regarding gender roles. However, respecting such traditional gender roles is clearly an important factor for any multinational firm operating in a Muslim country.

Hinduism

Acceptance of the ancient traditions of India that are based on the Vedic scriptures.

Hinduism is a broad and inclusive term referring to those individuals who respect and accept the ancient traditions of India, "especially the Vedic scriptures and the social class structure with its special respect for *Brahmans* (the priestly class)."[44] Unlike Christianity and Islam, Hinduism has no specific founder, and Hindus place no special significance on historical events or

Comparative Management **Brief**

Islamic and Financial Operations

In an effort to revitalize its economy after the Gulf War, the Kuwaiti government embarked on a strategy of attracting foreign investment to make up for the deficits incurred through reconstruction. However, Kuwait is an Islamic society and has to respect the *Shari'ah*, or religious laws, which has prohibitions against receiving or paying interest. In addition to the only well-known financial aspect of Islam, the *Shari'ah* also prohibits uncertainty and gambling. As a consequence, it is important for all contracts to be specified in great detail. Additionally, because futures and options have speculative natures, they are considered as gambling and are illegal. Such prohibitions represent significant challenges for international capital providers.

The EQUATE (Ethylene Products from Kuwait) project was a joint venture between Petrochemical Industries Company, a subsidiary of the Kuwaiti national oil company, and Union Carbide Corporation. The joint venture was formed to finance the construction and operation of a $2 billion petrochemical plant. It faced a number of significant challenges as the financing details were being dealt with. For instance, the venture wanted part of the financing for the project to come from Islamic banks in an effort to involve Kuwaiti citizens and investors in the project. However, the Islamic banks could not loan the money directly—the banks had to be involved directly in the venture so they could share in the profits instead of earning interest. Eventually, the Islamic banks purchased assets and leased the assets to the joint venture. As such, compared to a regular loan, such financial arrangements present significant challenges. With ownership of assets in a company comes ownership risk. For instance, how much should these Islamic banks be liable for if the plant causes serious environmental damage? One way that this problem was addressed was to place these assets in a special purpose vehicle with limited liability. Yet another challenge pertained to the leasing aspect of the financial arrangement whereby the Islamic banks owned the assets while the venture was the actual user of the assets. As with any lease agreement, the Islamic banks are responsible for maintaining the assets of the plant and for insuring against losses that may occur should the assets break down. A major challenge for the venture was to ensure that the Islamic banks took such insurance and maintenance precautions. Another challenge dealt with the application of the law in the event of default. For instance, should Islamic or other law apply to the contract? Additionally, the Islamic investors were at great disadvantage if payments were late because of their inability to collect penalty interest. Such interest would have to be donated to charities. Finally, in the event of a bankruptcy, the Islamic bank still owned the assets and would be able to claim them from the venture. However, such actions would destroy the ongoing value of the project and reduce any chance of recovery.

Recent interviews with top executives of Islamic banks in the United Kingdom also reveal some of the challenges facing Islamic financial institutions. For instance, each bank tends to appoint its own Islamic Shariah committee, resulting in widely different standards from one bank to another. Such practices make it harder for these Islamic banks to gain acceptance. Furthermore, there are significant tensions between British banking regulatory bodies and Islamic banks. For instance, many Islamic banks' unwillingness to guarantee their customers' deposits makes it less likely for the relevant British regulating bodies to grant them banking licenses. Islamic banks also face significant burdens because of taxation issues. British taxation laws allow interest to be tax-deductible. However, Islamic laws allow profits to be represented as an alternative to interest. Such profits, however, are not tax-deductible.

Source: Based on Esty, Benjamin C. 2000. "The EQUATE project: An introduction to Islamic project finance." Journal of Project Finance 5, pp. 7–20; Karbhari, Yusuf, Kamal Naser, and Zerrin Shahin. 2004. "Problems and challenges facing the Islamic banking system in the West: The case of the U.K." Thunderbird International Business Review, 46, 5, pp. 521–543.

sequences of events. Rather, Hinduism, through the Vedic scriptures, is seen as timeless and eternal. There are currently about 760 million Hindus residing in India, Malaysia, Nepal, Suriname, and Sri Lanka. Many of the Hindus outside of India typically share ancestors from India.

The quest for *Brahman* is the ultimate goal for most Hindus. *Brahman* refers to the ultimate reality and truth and to the "sacred power that pervades and maintains all things."[45] However, to discover the *Brahman*, one needs to look into one's *atma* or soul. Hinduism generally believes in the reincarnation of the *atma* based on one's *karma*, or the effects of one's past actions. As such, if one tries hard to live life according to the principles of *dharma* or principles of righteousness and moral order, one will be reincarnated in successively favorable *atmas* until one reaches *Brahman*.

The importance of spiritual achievement is an important value for most Hindus. Weber, in a comparison with Protestant values, argued that this emphasis on spiritual achievement conflicts with entrepreneurial desires. He argued that compared to devout Protestants, devout Hindus are less likely to engage in entrepreneurial pursuits. In fact, Hindus believe that the sole pursuit of wealth accumulation makes the search for *Brahman* difficult. The reality for multinational companies has nevertheless been contrary to Weber's predictions. India has seen a growth spurt in new business creations, and multinational managers find that workers are motivated and creative.

One aspect of Hinduism that is most likely to have implications for multinational companies in India is the caste system. The caste system refers to ordering of Indian society based on four occupational groups. The highest caste includes the priests, followed by the kings and warriors, and then merchants and farmers. The fourth caste includes the manual laborers and artisans. Although the caste system seems unfair and is illegal in India, its main purpose was to create a higher law that would subordinate individual interests for the collective good. It remains a dominant feature of life in India today. As such, multinational companies operating in India have to be aware of the caste system. For instance, having a lower caste member supervise higher caste individuals can be problematic. Additionally, members of lower castes may have promotion ceilings in organizations because of their caste membership. Finally, when meetings are held, it is important to consider how the various castes interact.

Consider the experience of FoodWorld supermarket chains in India.[46] When they were opening new retail supermarkets in India, they had to hire and train managers. However, a retail manager is not seen as having a high social status in India, and only members of the lower caste were willing to take such jobs. Given the pervasiveness of the caste system in India, these workers as well as customers felt that they had significantly lower status. As such, training programs had to be designed to emphasize confidence in the workers in order to get them to perform their duties adequately. Furthermore, a major challenge was to find ways to alleviate the concerns of the more traditional Indian customers who may not want to make contact with someone from a lower caste.

Some, however, argue that the caste system is slowly dying. The Case in Point on page 115 provides evidence of some fundamental changes in Indian society and how it views the caste system.

Hinduism's teachings and philosophies have other implications for multinational strategic management. Hinduism provides clear guidelines regarding ethical behaviors, among which respect for one's parents and performing one's duty are prominent. Coupled with the caste system, most people have clearly

C A S E   I N   P O I N T

Is the Caste System Dying?

The villagers of Seetanagaram were tired of their water pumps breaking down frequently. Despite their complaints to local officials, these pumps would seldom be repaired. The women would then have to walk two hours to get water from the Sarada River, and the water would often make them sick. Things changed when Mr. Rao, a 23-year-old resident, was sent to attend the pump repair training program offered by a British Charity, Water Aid. After he attended the training, his services were much in demand. However, Mr. Rao is a member of the *Dalit* caste, or untouchable, a fifth class below the four castes described earlier. Furthermore, Seetanagaram is a very segregated village where the upper castes live in a separate colony and even exclude the *Dalits* from participation in marriages and festivals. At the beginning, the upper-caste members were reluctant to interact with the *Dalits*. However, faced with the possibility of nonfunctioning pumps, the upper castes gradually accepted the idea of a *Dalit* helping them fix the pumps. Programs by Water Aid to help train 490 lower-caste villagers

and other similar programs are slowly eroding the caste-based prejudice systems.

The political environment also shows some evidence that the caste system is slowly eroding. India currently is considering extending quotas in various occupations to ensure that the lower castes get a fair representation. Furthermore, Indian companies also are implementing voluntary plans to accommodate a larger proportion of lower castes in the workforce. Some companies are considering offering better educational and training opportunities while other companies are investigating coaching classes to encourage lower castes to achieve higher education. The Indian government also is considering offering tax breaks to those companies offering employment to lower-caste people in poorer areas.

Source: Based on Economist. 2006. "Asia: Caste and cash; India." April 29, p. 67; Harding, Luke. 2002. "Indian villagers given a taste of equality: Lower-caste Dalis trained to fix pumps gain clean water and modicum of respect." The Guardian, December 7, p. 20; and Waldman, Amy. 2003. "Mayawati embodies outcasts' political rise; She is India's first Dalit chief minister." Seattle Times, May 4, p. A26.

defined paths that they should be engaged in. Multinational companies would be well-advised to take such guidelines into consideration. The Hindu's respect for parents also has business implications. Multinationals will often find that families run Indian businesses and that the elder males in the business typically make major decisions. As such, multinational companies should be ready to accept such influence even though they may be dealing with younger family members. Finally, Hindus also believe that they should aim for four goals in life, namely spiritual achievement, material prosperity, pleasure, and liberation, although the aims vary depending on the stage of life.[47] Nevertheless, multinational firms should be aware that Hinduism does not condemn the pursuit of material possessions and that they can generally expect an environment that is conducive to business and wealth accumulation.

Buddhism refers to the broad and multifaceted religious tradition that focuses primarily on the reality of worldly suffering and on the ways one can be freed from such suffering. Gautama Buddha, born as a prince around the six century BC in India, founded Buddhism. Buddhist accounts of the life of Buddha suggest that his father tried to protect him from seeing suffering to prepare him as a king. Buddha was, however, dissatisfied with the impermanence of life, and when he turned 29, he abandoned all riches to become "a wandering ascetic, searching for truth."[48] Today, Buddhism is very popular in Europe and the United States although most of its followers are found in countries such as Cambodia, China, Japan, Korea, Laos, Sri Lanka, and Thailand.

The essence of Buddhism is based on the idea that craving and desires inevitably produce suffering. It is, however, possible to reach a state where there

Buddhism

Religious tradition that docuses primarily on the reality of world suffering and the ways one can be freed from suffering.

is no longer any suffering. Buddha proposed that to remove the suffering, one had to follow the Eightfold Path of Right understanding, Right intention, Right speech, Right action, Right livelihood, Right effort, Right mindfulness, and Right concentration. Buddhism also believes that the way to end suffering is to meditate to train and soothe the mind to ultimately reach enlightenment or *Nirvana.*

Nanayakkara's[49] interpretations of Buddha's teachings suggest that Buddha saw poverty as the major reason for the decline of ethical behavior in society. Buddhism therefore prescribed a work ethic that encouraged workers to engage in their best efforts and promoted qualities such as taking initiative, persistence, and hard work. Laziness is seen as a very negative quality and is heavily discouraged. As such, multinational companies should expect workers who have a generally positive view of work. However, it is important for multinational managers to be aware that Buddhism proposes a work ethic that emphasizes teamwork and ethical means to achieve success at work. Multinational companies would be well advised to provide environments that take advantage of such values.

Buddhism is also based on the notion that there is no separate self and that all beings are interconnected and interdependent. Such beliefs affect how people treat each other. Buddhists see boundless compassion and love as "sublime states," and Buddhism provides actual practical guidance to live according to such high ethical standards and selflessness. Multinational managers should thus be aware of their actions and ensure that decisions are made within such ethical boundaries. Although Buddhism does not necessarily condemn wealth creation and profit, multinational companies nevertheless need to understand that a company exists for the betterment of society and other beings.

Given that Buddhism has a stronger emphasis on compassion and love, it has even been suggested that Western profit-oriented companies should adopt Buddhist principles. In that context, Gould[50] proposes that employees (and multinational managers) engage in a number of exercises that can enhance an ethical orientation to business. For instance, it is advised that everyone should be considered as a mother, father, brother, or sister. By doing so, one is more careful about the consequences of one's actions on others. Furthermore, the compassion and love inherent in considering others as close relatives may be helpful to deal with the employee diversity of multinational companies. A second Buddhist principle is the acknowledgement that the positive action of others makes life possible. Hence, multinational managers should recognize the efforts of their workers through ethical treatment. Such actions are likely to result in long-term gains. Finally, it is important to understand that although work is a key component of life, there are other areas that need to be balanced. Multinational companies can respect a balanced work design for their workers.

These descriptions of the four major world religions show that they all have implications for how the economic environment is shaped. A final issue that multinational companies should be aware of is religiosity. **Religiosity** is an indication of the importance of acceptance of the core philosophies of religion in one's life. A usual indication of religiosity is the level of church (or other relevant religious meeting place) attendance. There are wide variations in religiosity across countries, and multinational companies have to be aware of these differences. Understanding country-level religiosity is useful because it gives multinational companies a general indication of how responsive they need

Religiosity

Indication of the importance of acceptance of the core philosophies of religion in one's life.

to be to such religious needs. However, the economic effects of religiosity are undeniable.[51] Religiosity has been shown to be positively linked to favorable attitudes toward work and also to be linked to how people allocate their time. It is also possible that individuals in those countries that have higher religiosity have less stressful lives because of the social support provided by church attendance. Multinational managers should be aware of such effects of religiosity. Exhibit 3.8 shows the religiosity of selected countries from the World Values Survey.

In this section, we looked at four of the world's main religion and some implications for multinational strategic management. In the next section, we look at two final social institutions, namely education and social inequality. Both represent key aspects of most societies although their effects on multinational strategic management may not be as substantial as the other three social institutions.

Education

Education refers to the "organized networks of socializing experiences which prepare individuals to act in society" and "is also a central element in the table of organization of society, constructing competencies and helping create professions and professionals."[52] Education is seen as a critical path to economic development and progress. Most countries want to achieve universal educational enrollment[53] as education enables society to instill the skills, attitudes, behaviors, and knowledge that allow people to demand more and give

Education

Organized networks of socialization experiences that prepare individuals to act in society.

EXHIBIT 3.8   Religiosity for Selected Countries

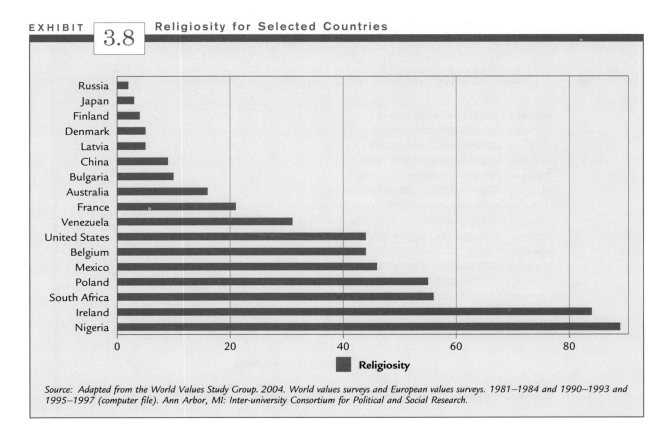

Source: Adapted from the World Values Study Group. 2004. World values surveys and European values surveys. 1981–1984 and 1990–1993 and 1995–1997 (computer file). Ann Arbor, MI: Inter-university Consortium for Political and Social Research.

more to society. Such exchanges enhance the expansion and modernization of society.

Education has obvious implications for multinational strategic management. At a basic level, educational levels give an indication of the skill and productivity of workers in any society.[54] The more educated workers are, the more skills they possess, and the more likely they are to contribute to a country's production, both in products and services. As you will see in Chapter 11 and 12 on human resource management issues in the international context, educational systems have implications for how labor force issues are approached and how policies are implemented. For instance, the educational systems determine the nature of the workforce. Additionally, having an abundant supply of well-educated individuals allows countries to facilitate the absorption of technology from developed countries. Multinational companies can thus gauge the educational levels of various countries they are involved in to determine what to expect from their workers. In that respect, multinational companies can look at the mean years of education or educational attainment scores to get an idea of human capital potential in a society. Exhibit 3.9 shows the educational attainment scores for a selected number of countries.

The educational attainment score reported in Exhibit 3.9 gives a very rough estimate of the educational potential of any society. However, education also varies widely in terms of its focus. As you will see in Chapter 11 on international human resource management, some societies have educational systems that value only academic education while others like Germany have a balance between the academic and vocational aspects of the workforce. Multinational companies also may be interested in the skills and experience that can be potentially gained from the educational system of the country. They should also consider the test scores of students on internationally comparable tests. For

EXHIBIT 3.9   Educational Attainment for Selected Countries (in Average Years of School)

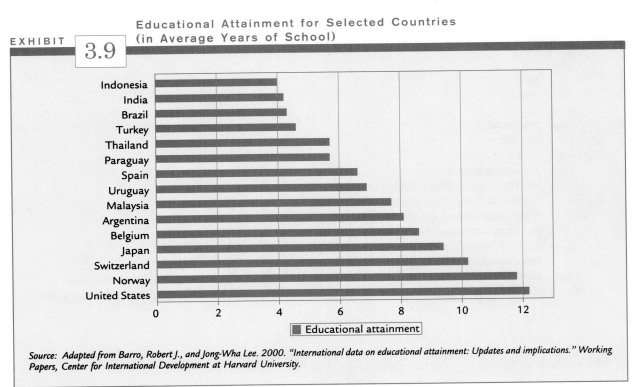

Source: Adapted from Barro, Robert J., and Jong-Wha Lee. 2000. "International data on educational attainment: Updates and implications." Working Papers, Center for International Development at Harvard University.

instance, the test scores on mathematics and science as conducted by the International Evaluation of Educational Achievement and International Assessment of Educational Progress provides a good idea of the quality of the future workforce and its preference for specific areas. If a multinational company is engaged in high-level research and development, it may find that location in countries with high mathematics and science scores provides access to an abundance of skilled workforce that is naturally inclined toward scientific projects. Exhibits 3.10 and 3.11 show the mathematics and science scores for the top 10 countries respectively.

As the exhibits show, many of the East Asian nations such as Japan, South Korea, Singapore, and Hong Kong figure prominently on the list. It is therefore not surprising to see that these countries have very active and innovative economic sectors that rely heavily on scientific progress. However, it also is important for multinational companies to note the relatively high scores of

EXHIBIT **3.10**   **Mathematics Scores for the Top 10 Countries**

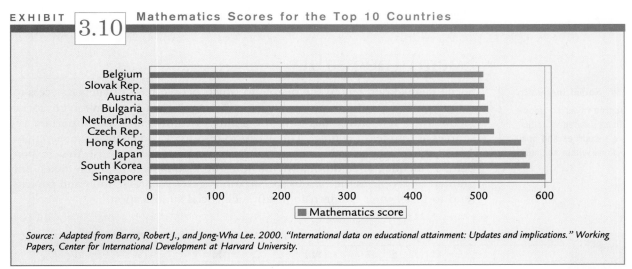

Source: Adapted from Barro, Robert J., and Jong-Wha Lee. 2000. "International data on educational attainment: Updates and implications." Working Papers, Center for International Development at Harvard University.

EXHIBIT **3.11**   **Science Scores for the Top 10 Countries**

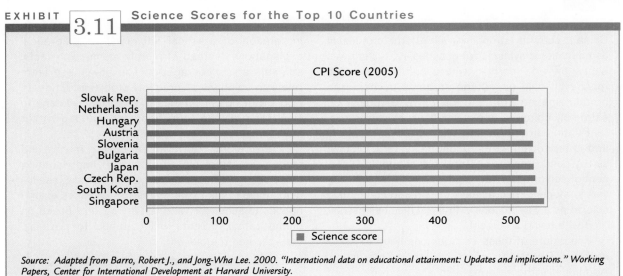

Source: Adapted from Barro, Robert J., and Jong-Wha Lee. 2000. "International data on educational attainment: Updates and implications." Working Papers, Center for International Development at Harvard University.

some Eastern European countries such as the Czech Republic, Bulgaria, and Hungary. These countries have very strong educational programs that emphasize science curricula. As such, multinational firms have access to a very skilled and inexpensive workforce in these societies.

A final issue is the extent to which educational systems actually encourage students to be innovative and creative. In that context, many Asian societies have been grappling with the redesign of educational systems that are extremely competitive at the secondary level but that rely heavily on rote learning. Consider the Case in Point below and the challenges facing China.

The Case in Point shows that many Asian societies tend to have students who go through extreme hardship to succeed. Multinational companies have to be aware that their workforce in such societies has gone through schooling experiences based on rote memorization. This is not to suggest that Asian countries are not creative. However, different training methods may be necessary to encourage the workforce to be creative.

This section shows that education has important effects on how societies are structured economically. In the next and final section, we look at social inequality.

Social Inequality

Social inequality

Degree to which people have privileged access to resources and positions within societies.

Social inequality refers to the degree to which people have privileged access to resources and positions within societies.[55] In societies that have high social inequality, a few individuals have the ability to control and use important resources as sources of control. This access to resources also enables the select few to use this power to gain access to even more power and to use that to perpetuate inequality. Additionally, the level of inequality is typically taken for granted by people as the various socialization agents such as schools and parents tend to teach their children to justify such social stratification.

C A S E   I N   P O I N T

Educational Redesign in China

China is currently struggling with efforts to redesign its educational system. For decades, its system was based on rote learning where both parents and teachers would encourage students to memorize brutal amounts of information and cram for extremely competitive examinations. However, current critics argue that the system stifles creativity and is producing a very unhappy student force. A survey conducted in 2002 found that about 50 percent of senior secondary students and first year university students had actually considered committing suicide as a way to cope with the difficulties associated with being a student.

The nature of these changes has been to reformulate textbooks to make them more interesting. Additionally, the reforms also are geared toward

integration of practical situations to theoretical explanations. Instead of merely memorizing facts, students are encouraged to see how these facts relate to solutions to practical problems. Students also are being encouraged to be imaginative and to view texts as the foundation for learning rather than as sacred books.

These reforms, however, are costing money, and many schools are having difficulties implementing these changes. Some also argue that as long as students have to take near impossible entrance examinations to secondary and tertiary schools based on memorization, parents will continue to pressure their children the old way.

Source: Based on Economist. 2003. "Roll over, Confucius." January 25, pp. 40–41.

Social inequality has important implications for multinational management. As you will see in the next chapter on international ethics, multinational companies are facing significant criticisms for their operations in countries with high social inequalities. Many multinational firms often face negative publicity for low wages or child labor, and the high levels of social inequality further magnify such publicity. As such, many multinational companies are realizing that it is sometimes in their interest to be more socially responsible to mitigate social inequalities. Consider the Case in Point , which considers social inequality from a gender perspective.

As the Case in Point shows, social inequality can have important implications for location decisions. Many multinational companies now actively avoid countries with high inequalities to prevent potential negative publicity. As we will see in the next chapter on ethics and social responsibility, many key ethical issues arise in countries with high forms of social inequalities. In that context, multinational companies can consider the GINI index as an indicator of the degree of social inequality. The GINI index measures the degree to which people's income deviates from a perfectly equal income distribution. Exhibit 3.12 shows the GINI index for selected countries where a 0 indicates perfect equality while 100 indicates perfect inequality.

Few cross-cultural studies have examined the role of social inequality on work-related variables. However, in an innovative study of 30,270 individuals from 26 nations, Parboteeah and Cullen[56] showed that social inequality negatively impacts the degree to which people are attached to work. Social

CASE IN POINT

Gender Inequality and Chiquita Bananas

Multinational companies involved in trading bananas have been under intense pressure to improve the labor conditions of both their workers and the workers of their suppliers. In that context, Chiquita has developed a comprehensive corporate social responsibility policy. A major component of this policy is a voluntary code of conduct, which both Chiquita and its independent producers must implement. However, a survey of Nicaraguan women banana workers revealed that the code of conduct has not made much difference in the lives of these workers. Why has the code been less effective for Nicaraguan women and women in other countries? Prieto-Carron argues that, among other factors, structural gender inequalities have mitigated the effectiveness of such codes. The banana industry employs approximately 482,000 women in countries such as Guatemala, Honduras, Nicaragua, Colombia, and Ecuador. However, most of these women are involved in very low-paying, high-hour packing jobs. They face significant inequalities compared to their male counterparts. Additionally, they also are employed in a very seasonal industry, and many more women workers are usually available to perform these jobs. Coupled with a social context where domestic violence and negative perception of women are common, women workers have faced much harder working conditions because of such inequalities.

What can Chiquita do to reduce such gender inequalities? Most experts agree that improving the conditions of women is a challenging task. However, local governments and companies can work to provide equal pay for equal work. Furthermore, gender awareness training may be useful to encourage male workers to change their perception of their female counterparts. Additionally, more female supervisors can be hired to reduce cases of sexual harassment and systems can be implemented so that women can safely report incidents and violators can be sanctioned. Finally, companies also can be proactive and work to provide a better environment for maternity rights.

Source: Based on Prieto-Carron, Marina. 2006. "Corporate social responsibility in Latin America." Journal of Corporate Citizenship, 21, pp. 85–94.

EXHIBIT 3.12   GINI Index for Selected Countries

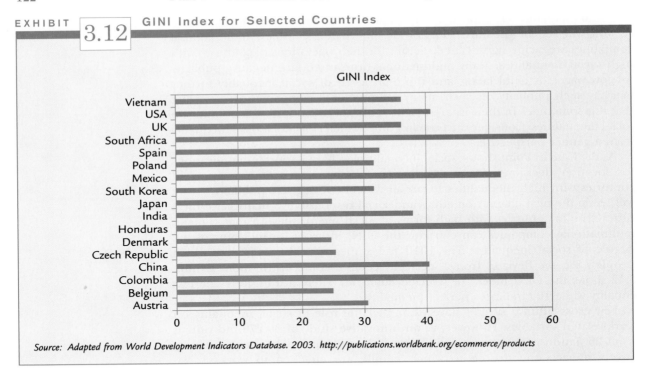

Source: Adapted from World Development Indicators Database. 2003. http://publications.worldbank.org/ecommerce/products

inequality provides job opportunities only to some highly placed individuals. Furthermore, high levels of social inequality also may result in more demoralized workers suspicious of their "exploiters." It is therefore less likely that people in high-social-inequality societies see work as more important in their lives. In fact, high levels of social inequality likely result in a less favorable work environment.

This study clearly shows the importance of social inequality and potential impact on multinational companies.

The National Context and International Management

Social institutions are key aspects of understanding the business environment in any country. In conjunction with national cultures as described in Chapter 2, social institutions shape norms, values, and beliefs that determine acceptable and unacceptable business practices. However, the national context's role is not only limited to shaping of business practices. The national context has significant influence on a company's strategy. For instance, you will see in Chapter 6 on multinational strategies that the national context determines the comparative advantage of nations, which ultimately determines which strategies multinational companies choose. The concept of comparative advantage refers to the idea that countries prosper when they can produce goods with the lowest relative cost of production. Thus, countries that have educational systems that emphasize sciences have a comparative advantage through the supply of skilled but cheaper workforce. For instance, India is gradually becoming the center for software development because of a ready access of software engineers. The national context also determines the global platform, namely the areas of business that can be performed the best in a country. For instance, most pharmaceutical companies tend to be located around universities and other research and development laboratories in more industrialized nations because of the crucial dependence of that sector on research.

The national context also plays an important role in the human aspect of international management. For instance, as you will see in Chapter 15 on leadership, the educational and family system has important implications as to who is seen as an effective leader. The national context is also seen as a determinant of the nature of the relationship between workers and their superiors. Furthermore, the national context also determines how people view work and sets the stage for motivation in an international context, as discussed in Chapter 14. As you will see, the transition from socialist systems to more market-oriented systems means that people now place even more value on monetary rewards, again showing the importance of the national context on individuals. Finally, the national context also influences how multinational companies approach human resource management policies. As you will see in Chapter 11 and 12 on human resource management issues in an international context, the national context determines how multinational companies should design human resource management policies in various countries and also what to expect from the labor force.

Additionally, although the national context may be causing some convergence, there will still be differences in terms of which designs work best for multinational companies. As we will see in Chapter 8 on organization design, the national context has an important influence on how organizations are designed. For instance, the heavy state involvement in emphasizing large family companies in South Korea has resulted in large conglomerates known as *chaebols*. In contrast, the influence of the Chinese family traditions whereby inheritance has to be divided equally among the sons has resulted in networks of smaller firms in Taiwan.

These examples clearly show the impact of the national context on international management. As we get into more substantive areas in the next few chapters, we will get a chance to examine the national context in more depth.

Summary and Conclusions

To get a full understanding of any society, it is essential to understand both national culture and the institutional context. Toward this goal, we first look at a model to examine how both national culture and social institution combine to form the national context that influences the business culture of any society. This chapter then complements Chapter 2 by providing more specific background information on four important social institutions and their implications both for companies and for the people they employ.

First, the chapter defined social institutions and provided an explanation of how social institutions affect individuals and organizations. Social institutions have regulative, normative, and cognitive influence on individuals. We also describe how social institutions encourage organizations to become similar through isomorphic forces. These include mimetic, normative, and coercive isomorphism.

The chapter described the economic systems, especially with reference to the extreme types of economic systems. It was shown that in societies arranged along socialist systems, the government owns the systems of production while in capitalist systems private, individuals make production decisions. Lodged between these two extremes is the mixed economy. Three major implications of economic systems for multinational strategic management were then discussed. These implications included the extent of governmental intervention in the business arena, the transition from a socialist economy to a market economy, and the privatization efforts in many countries.

The institutional context also includes industrialization. In that context, the chapter discussed pre-industrial, industrial, and postindustrial societies and their implications for multinational strategic management. Pre-industrial societies are typically less developed and thus present significant challenges for multinational companies. In contrast, industrial societies tend to be more economically advanced with the manufacturing sector dominating the economic environment. Finally, in the postindustrial society, services become the dominant sector, and people start shifting from achievement values to more quality-of-life values.

Religion is also an important social institution in most societies. We discussed four of the major religions around the world, namely Christianity, Islam,

Hinduism, and Buddhism. The chapter also outlined the important business implication for each of these religions.

Another social institution discussed was education. Educational systems have important implications regarding the available skills and experiences of the workforce in any society. However, other aspects of educational systems such as the emphasis on sciences and mathematics were also discussed.

Finally, we saw that social inequality can also have important implications for multinational companies. The chapter concludes with the theme that social institutional differences are going to be important now and in the future. We looked at the importance of these social institutions (and the national context) by showing how they are linked to most of the upcoming chapters. We concluded by arguing that successful multinational managers are the ones who can properly assess the institutional context of the society in which they operate and who can design work environments that fit the institutional context.

Discussion Questions

1. Define social institutions. How do social institutions affect individuals? Illustrate your answer with examples for each of the regulative, normative, and cognitive influences.

2. What is organizational isomorphism? Describe the three types of organizational isomorphism. Discuss examples of each isomorphic pressure.

3. What are the three major types of economic systems? What are the effects of economic systems on how organizations are structured in societies?

4. What are some implications of the market transition that many formerly communist societies are experiencing? What are some major challenges companies are facing in such societies as they try to motivate workers?

5. Why has Africa lagged behind other countries in economic development? What can multinational companies do to encourage economic progress in Africa?

6. What are the major philosophies of each of the world's four major religions? Pick two religions and discuss how they affect the business environment.

7. Discuss specific Buddhist principles and how they can be applied to help multinational managers become more ethical.

8. How does the educational system influence the business environment in a country?

9. What is social inequality? What important areas of business can social inequality impact?

Multinational Management **Skill Builder**

A Briefing Paper

You have just been informed that your company has agreed to a joint venture in a company in the Czech Republic. You not only will provide new technology to manufacture light bulbs but also will have to provide your managerial expertise to manage and motivate workers. Your understanding is that you will take over the managerial aspects of the joint venture at the

beginning and gradually will train Czechs in management positions.

Using the World Wide Web and the library, research general issues such as Czech culture, Czech workers' attitudes toward work, the appropriateness of Western-based motivational practices typically used in your company in the Czech Republic, and the managerial potential of Czech workers. Identify key challenges you will face as you make the merger work. Discuss some potential solutions to these challenges. Discuss some of the training methods you may want to use as you train Czechs to become managers. What are some challenges you may face when you try to train Czechs to become managers?

Present your findings to the class.

Endnotes

[1] Schooler, C. 1996. "Cultural and socio-cultural explanations of cross-national psychological differences." Annual Review of Sociology 22, pp. 323–49.

[2] Turner, J. H. 1997. The Institutional Order. New York: Addison-Wesley Educational Publishers, p. 6.

[3] Scott, Richard. 1995. Institutions and Organizations. London: Sage.

[4] Busenitz, Lowell W., Carolina Gomez, and Jennifer W. Spencer. 2000. "Country institutional profiles: Unlocking entrepreneurial phenomena." Academy of Management Journal 43, pp. 994–1003.

[5] Reynolds, P. D. 1997. "New and small firms in expanding markets." Small Business Economics 9, pp. 79–84.

[6] Kostova, Tatiana. 1997. Country institutional profiles: Concept and measurement. Academy of Management Best Paper Proceedings, pp. 180–89.

[7] Busenitz, Gomez, and Spencer, "Country institutional profiles: Unlocking entrepreneurial phenomena."

[8] Zucker, L. G. 1987. "Institutional theories of organization." Annual Review of Sociology 13, pp. 443–64.

[9] Orru, Marco. 1991. "The institutional logic of small-firm economics in Italy and Taiwan." Studies in Comparative International Development 26, pp. 3–28.

[10] Olsen, M. E. 1991. Societal Dynamics: Exploring Macrosociology Englewood Cliffs, NJ: Prentice-Hall, p. 35.

[11] Tsoukas, Haradimos. 1994. "Socio-economic systems and organizational management: An institutional perspective on the socialist firm." Organization Studies 15, pp. 21–45.

[12] Ibid.

[13] Healey, Nigel M. 1996. "Economic transformation in Central and Eastern Europe and the commonwealth of independent states: An interim report." Contemporary Review 268, pp. 229–36.

[14] Pearce, Jone L. 2001. Organization and Management in the Embrace of Government. Mahwah, NJ: Lawrence Erlbaum Associates.

[15] Walder, A. G. 1986. Communist Neo-Traditionalism. Berkeley: University of California Press.

[16] Brada, J. C. 1996. "Privatization is transition—Is it?" Journal of Economic Perspectives, pp. 67–86.

[17] BBC Monitoring Former Soviet Union. 2003. "Russian government lines up more companies for privatization in 2003." April 21.

[18] Kim, Ken I., and Anna Yelkina. 2003. "Privatization in Russia: Its past, present, and future." SAM Advanced Management Journal Winter, pp. 14–21.

[19] Batson, Andrew. 2003. "China's new privatization may elude foreigners." Wall Street Journal, May 14, p. A12.

[20] Cam, Surham. 1999. "Job security, unionization, wages and privatization: A case study in the Turkish cement industry." Sociological Review 47, pp. 695–714.

[21] Turner, The Institutional Order.

[22] Blau, Peter and Otis Duncan. 1967. The American Occupational Structure. New York: Wiley.

[23] Inglehart, Ronald, Miguel Basanez, and Alejandro Moreno. 1998. Human Values and Beliefs: A Cross-Cultural Sourcebook. Ann Arbor, MI: University of Michigan Press.

[24] Gereffi, Garry, and Donald L. Wyman. 1990. Manufacturing Miracles: Paths of Industrialization in Latin America and East Asia. Princeton, NJ: Princeton University Press.

[25] Kuruvilla, Sarosh. 1996. "Linkages between industrialization strategies and industrial relations/human resource policies: Singapore, Malaysia, the Philippines, and India." Industrial and Labor Relations Review 49, pp. 635–57.

[26] Ibid, 652.

[27] Bell, Daniel. 1973. The Coming of Postindustrial Society. New York: Basic Books.

[28] Inglehart, Basanez, and Moreno, Human Values and Beliefs: A Cross-Cultural Sourcebook.

[29] Ibid, 10.

[30] Stark, Rodney, and William S. Bainbridge. 1985. The Future of Religion. Berkeley, CA: University of California Press.

[31] Iannaconne, Laurence R. 1998. "Introduction to the economics of religion." Journal of Economic Literature 36, pp. 1465–96.

[32] Harpaz, Itzhak. 1998. "Cross-national comparison of religious conviction and the meaning of work." Cross-Cultural Research 32, pp. 143–70.

[33] Weber, Max. 1958. The Protestant Ethic and the Spirit of Capitalism. (Translated by T. Parsons). New York: Scribner's.

[34] Terpstra, V., and K. David. 1991. The Cultural Environment of International Business. Cincinnati, OH: South-Western.

[35] Harpaz, "Cross-national comparison of religious conviction and the meaning of work."

[36] Fisher, Mary P. 1999. Living Religions (4th ed.). Upper Saddle River, NJ: Prentice Hall, p. 273.

[37] Ludwig, Theodore M. 2001. The Sacred Paths (3rd ed.). Upper Saddle River, NJ: Prentice Hall, p. 425.

[38] Fisher, Living Religions.

[39] Ibid.

[40] Ludwig, The Sacred Paths.

[41] Ibid.

[42] Esty, Benjamin C. 2000. "The EQUATE project: An introduction to Islamic project finance." Journal of Project Finance 5, pp. 7–20.

[43] Ludwig, The Sacred Paths.

[44] Ibid, 64.

[45] Ibid, 84.

[46] Wylie, David. 1996. "Foodworld supermarkets in India." In Thompson A. A. & A. J. Strickland. Strategic Management. Eleventh Edition, Boston, MA: Irwin/McGraw-Hill.

[47] Ludwig, The Sacred Paths.

[48] Ibid, 117.

[49] Nanayakkara, S. 1992. Ethics of Material Progress: The Buddhist Attitude. Colombo: The World Fellowship of Buddhist Activities committee.

[50] Gould, Stephen J. 1995. "The Buddhist perspective on business ethics: Experiential exercises for exploration and practice." Journal of Business Ethics 14, pp. 63–70.

[51] Iannaconne, "Introduction to the economics of religion."

[52] Meyer, John W. 1977. "The effects of education as an institution." American Journal of Sociology 83, pp. 55–77.

53 Meyer, John W., Francisco O. Ramirez, and Yasemin N. Soysal. 1992. "World expansion of mass education, 1870–1980." *Sociology of Education* 65, pp. 128–49.

54 Barro, Robert J., and Jong-Wha Lee. 2000. "International data on educational attainment: Updates and implications." Working Papers, Center for International Development at Harvard University.

55 Olsen, *Societal Dynamics: Exploring Macrosociology.*

56 Parboteeah, K. Praveen, and John B. Cullen. 2003. "Social institutions and work centrality: Explorations beyond national culture." *Organization Science*, 14, 2, pp. 137–48.

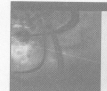

Anglo-American College in Prague (AAC): The Challenge to Lead in Post-Communist Czech Republic

As Jansen Raichl sat alone preparing for a special meeting at Anglo-American College in Prague (AAC) where he would face frustrated teachers and students, he reflected on the institution that he had so painstakingly built and tended over the last 3 years. He feared that, despite the personal and financial sacrifices he had made, his dream of pioneering an alternative higher educational institution in Central Europe was crumbling before his eyes. Enrollment had dropped from 120 to 60 students. According to his best estimates, AAC would finish the 1993–1994 academic year with a deficit of 76,000Kc (about $2,500USD) on an estimated income from tuition of 4,500,000Kc for the year. The institution was on the verge of bankruptcy, barely able to pay faculty salaries let alone purchase much-needed equipment. He feared virtual mutiny among the staff, most of whom he had carefully selected and had relied on to support him and promote the college to the outside world.

Raichl had carefully kept operating costs low, because he knew that this was the key to AAC's survival. "I don't think of it as a business. For me and most of the volunteers it was an academic/educational project first. There's nothing specifically Czech about it. What was unique was the postrevolutionary atmosphere which was very favorable but has since evaporated. [Westerners] don't realize the sacrifices students make to come here."

Its education program, although not a luxury product, was perceived as expensive for Czechs used to tuition-free state universities. But compared to a foreign university education, it was a price-competitive alternative. Raichl believed that he had laid the foundation for a high-quality institution, despite the lack of acceptance and prestige among the established university community. The existing Czech government's reluctance to provide any avenues for state accreditation of the colleges programs only made it harder to get local recognition for the educational work that the college was doing.

The college's first semester in 1991 had ended with a deficit. Theoretically, AAC's original 51 students should have generated a budget surplus. Unfortunately, most of the students had not paid the full announced tuition fees, and expenses exceeded income twofold. Despite a few small donations, corporate support for the college had remained low, and its financial base had always been too small to support its ambitions. Its facilities were well below the level of that expected in American or Western European countries; its student services were virtually nonexistent.

Low wages had contributed to the continuous turnover of lecturing staff, few of whom had academic credentials beyond a master's degree. Many viewed their association with AAC as a philanthropic endeavor or an interesting entry on their resumes. Despite Raichl's best efforts, frequent staff changes, lack of financial resources, and personal differences contributed to internal tensions. Two of Raichl's original founding partners had left AAC before the fall of 1993, certain AAC was on its deathbed. Several others had left to set up a competing American International University in Prague. If this new college succeeded, AAC had no hope of surviving.

Even with these very real problems, AAC had survived 3 years despite student frustration over a lack of administrative support, too few classes, and an absence of traditional student services such as a library or computer lab. Raichl believed that AAC's strength lay in the dedication of its ever-changing, but young, energetic and inspiring staff of lecturers and administrators. The low professor/student ratio and the informal and friendly relationships between students and lecturers did much to make up for some of the shortcomings in other areas.

By 1994, the Anglo-American College had been formally registered as a nonprofit foundation. In keeping with statutory requirements for foundation status, AAC formalized its management and board of directors. Raichl assumed the title of chancellor; Pavel Mach and Petr Suk had taken the positions of AAC treasurer and property manager, respectively. Dr Ladislav Venys, from the Center for Freedom and Democracy, had recently agreed to join the nascent AAC board. However, in May 1994, as the spring term was coming to an end, student and faculty discontent was at its highest point, and Raichl was at a loss as to what to do. He was not yet ready to give up, but he knew he needed help managing the day-to-day affairs of AAC. As he stared out the window, he sighed, "This time the problems are too big for me to fix by myself."

1989: The Velvet Invasion

In *The Rough Guide,* Rob Humphreys describes the November 1989 Czechoslovak break from Soviet communism "the most unequivocally positive of all the anti-Communist upheavals in Eastern Europe. True to their pacifist past, the Czechs and Slovaks shrugged off forty-one years of Communist rule without so much as a shot being fired. In the parliamentary elections the following summer, the Communists were roundly defeated and Vaclav Havel, a playwright of international renown with an impeccable record of resistance against the previous regime, was chosen as president. The euphoria and unity of those first few months evaporated more quickly than anyone could have imagined, and just three years after the revolution, against most people's predictions, the country split into two separate republics."[1]

Soon after the 1989 revolution, thousands of foreigners looking for adventure started streaming into Prague, and they found it. There was a wide variety among those who came: students, would-be writers, would-be artists, would-be entrepreneurs, and a few professionals working for multinationals.

Some just came to hang out. They left their home countries to step back in time into "The Golden City," capital of Bohemia. The Czechs were being invaded by foreigners again, but this time it was peaceful.

There were a lot of nationalities that moved to Prague in the early 1990s, but the Americans came in the greatest numbers. Most estimates said at the peak there were at least 20,000; some said there were as many as 40,000. This was the Velvet Invasion.

Why were so many drawn to the "City of 100 Spires"? First of all, it was new and exciting. This magical city had been barred from most foreigners until the revolution, because it was on the unfortunate side of the Iron Curtain. Now it was open for all, sitting at the crossroads of Europe. The architectural brilliance of this city cannot be adequately described—one must simply see it to believe it. Fortunately, Prague was never destroyed by bombs like so many other cities during the world wars. Few cities have splendors that compare with the Prague Castle, the Charles Bridge, Old Town Square, the countless inspiring churches, the old world cobblestone streets, and the Vltava river separating the still-distinct districts of the city. Europe's oldest active synagogue is in Prague. Music and theater, public means of expression even under communism, flourished. The great composers Dvorak or Smetana could be enjoyed in the National Theater or the Baroque State Opera; and as the Czechs are proud to remind, this is the city in which Mozart chose to premier his "Don Giovanni."

The opening of the doors of central Europe brought new market opportunities. International companies moved in quickly, bringing their own management teams and marketing professionals. Few native Czechs understood the fast and varied pace of Western-style commerce. The established university programs offered little free-market knowledge or understanding, so people with degrees from foreign universities were in high demand. Employers paid a premium for people with MBA training and actively sought people with good English skills, since English was quickly becoming the common language of business.

The Czech University System After the 1989 Revolution

The university system in the Czech Republic predates the first republic. Charles University, founded in 1348, established four faculties of law, medicine, philosophy, and theology that exist to this day. By 1913, the Czech lands were among the most industrially developed part of Europe. The alliance of the Czech and Slovak Republics in 1918 was a "visionary achievement of liberal nationalists,"[2] a strategic move designed to preserve political autonomy, religious freedom, and economic independence after the fall of the Hapsburg empire. Despite limited resources, the Czechoslovak Republic maintained a successful economy through market competition with foreign-trade controls, recognition and enforcement of private property rights, and a heavy reliance on democracy. Taking advantage of the Republics geographical location, the Prague College of Commerce was founded in 1919 as the center for education in trade and economics. Czechoslovakia grew in national sovereignty and independence until the Munich conference in 1938, when Nazi Germany took control.

During World War II, all Czech universities were closed, but they were reopened under the support and control of the Communist Party in 1953. Over the next four decades, the state universities were, in general, teaching rather than research institutions, with research being the domain of a few state-run institutes. Because of the weight of Soviet dogma, modern approaches to such social science subjects as politics and sociology were limited to the dissident intellectual community. Although theories of "capitalist" economics were relatively freely discussed in some of the country's research institutes, the study of capitalist business methodologies was by definition excluded from university curricula.

After the Velvet Revolution, the new government moved quickly to develop a macroeconomic strategy for the transition to a market economy and put in place a new legal structure to support private enterprise. On the microeconomic level, government policy was concentrated on massive privatization schemes and eliminated state-dictated pricing policies. At the end of 1992, the Czech and Slovak Republics divided along ethnic borders, but the principles of democracy and capitalism had remained as a strong foundation for the constitutions and legal systems of both countries.

In May 1990, the Czechoslovak Federal Parliament passed a Law on Higher Educational Institutions, which was expected to be the first step of a larger program of educational reform. The law guaranteed academic freedom and made universities self-governing. It initiated a period of rapid change, which led to the establishment of new links among higher education institutions both domestically and abroad. Required courses in soviet economy and Russian language were dropped. [Russian was still offered but increasingly students were choosing English or German as their second-language emphasis. Language instruction began at the basic (elementary) school level, and all Czech students were required to study two foreign languages.] Several groups of teachers were sent to Germany and England for programs in free-market economics and Western business practices. The University of Economics began a period of curriculum reform to include business degrees in finance and accounting, international relations, business administration and management, and public administration. Although much was achieved, there were neither the resources nor the professors to do much more than point the way toward university renewal.

Despite the slow pace of curriculum reform, interest in higher education in the Czech Republic was increasing. The increase in applicants for matriculation to university programs reflected increases in globalization, increases in disposable income, the rising social prestige of education in society, the temporary boom in students resulting from the country's highest birth rate in 1977–1978, and the growing financial rewards of higher education in the labor market. A survey of salary differentiation conducted in 1993 showed that in the state sector, those with higher education earned 45.5 percent more than those with only basic (elementary) school. In the now privatized sector, the respective percentage difference was 51 percent for the university educated; 32 percent for those who completed secondary school (gymnasium); and 13.1 percent for those with vocational training.

Although the content in business-related courses had started to change markedly in 1990, the structure of university education had not. Most disciplines were technical in nature, and the majority of college degrees were in engineering or economics. Curricula were fairly standardized, and classes were typically in large-lecture formats with optional small-group tutorials ("seminars"). Most evaluation was done during an examination period that lasted up to two weeks at the end of each semester. The exams were usually administered and graded by teams of teachers and standardized for each course. The structure of university studies was a variation of the German model, with three levels. The first period of study, lasting for 3 years, leading to degree of bachelor [Bakalar], was not considered a valid qualification on its own. It was rather a staging post on the way to the magister [Mgr] or engineer [Ing.] title, which was usually awarded after an additional 2 to 3 years of study.

As the demand for competent Western-educated managers increased, so did the number of new providers of management education. The Czech Republic's first English-language MBA program was a joint venture established in 1990 between the University of Economics, Prague, and the Rochester Institute of Technology in New York. The Czech Management Center, under sponsorship from the University of Pittsburgh, began English-language MBA education in 1991 in a refurbished 150-room hotel and training facility that used to host Communist Party dignitaries, about 25 miles east of Prague. These graduate-level programs were viewed as elite institutions, taking on as students those graduates from the traditional university programs who had high-level technical and language skills. The early success of these institutions paved the way for other entrants from England, France, and Germany over the next few years.

At the same time, undergraduate program offerings within the state university system remained largely unchanged. While state accreditation mandated strict standards that hindered curriculum and pedagogical reform, these programs were well established, highly regarded, and virtually free. (Most universities in Europe had no tuition fees for citizens; however, books and housing were not provided by the state. In the Czech Republic, most students lived with their parents and commuted to school. Students from small towns were given dormitory housing at modest rates.) However, funding and space constraints dictated enrollment standards, which resulted in fewer than 50 percent of qualified high school graduates gaining university admission. Most Western European countries guaranteed admission for any student meeting the entrance requirements.

The Czech Ministry of Education projected a 25–30 percent increase in the 18-year-old enrollment by the year 2000, at which point 40,000+ new students were expected to be accepted into the state university system annually. The Ministry estimates assumed that the number of students eligible for higher education would decrease by 10 percent, while the number of children entering secondary education would decrease by 20 percent during the same period, making this target easier to reach. The Ministry also estimated a decrease of approximately 12 percent in the size of the working population between 1989 and 1993, largely a result of population demographics.

Seizing an Opportunity

In 1989, 26-year-old Jansen Raichl was living in London, watching the revolutionary events speed by in his home country, Czechoslovakia. Raichl, who had studied mathematics and English at Charles University in Prague, had left Prague in 1987 and was completing coursework for a BA degree in sociology at the University of London. Excited to finally see the end of communism, Mr. Raichl started thinking of the opportunities that might open up back home now that the playwright cum activist, Vaclav Havel, had been elected president of the first Czechoslovak democracy since the dissolution of the First Republic in 1938. Raichl's courses at London University became the catalyst for an idea to build a college "that would help my country westernize and prove that the Czechs were able to do sophisticated things, in contrast to what the British media propaganda claimed."

In 1989, there were a total of 36 universities in Czechoslovakia, all of which offered English-language instruction, but none of which offered undergraduate degree programs conducted in English. The changing focus of the Czech economy and the restructuring process that began in 1989 created a demand for degree programs in business and the humanities and competence in English, which was rapidly becoming the language of international business in Central Europe. Enrollment caps in the state universities limited by government funding exacerbated this situation, and many young Czechs began to seek university degrees in nearby countries, despite the high tuition charges imposed on noncitizens of those countries. It became clear that there was a reservoir of young, English-speaking Central Europeans who wanted to study in Great

Britain or the United States but who could not afford the living expenses and fees that such study would require. This would be the niche Raichl wanted to target.

Raichl distributed leaflets around the campus of London University and put advertisements in a London newspaper soliciting volunteers to help him start a Western-style college in Prague. Jansen Raichl's mother, Dr. Vlasta Raichlová, had remained in Prague and was able to lay the groundwork and gather support from friends and colleagues. In 1991, with about $3,000 start-up capital, most of which he had saved on his own, Jansen Raichl returned to Prague to found the nonstate, nonprofit educational foundation for the Anglo-American College (AAC). Dr. Raichlová, a lawyer, nominally served as AAC's first president, and helped recruit and register students, and secure classroom space.

AAC began as a loose association of friends and colleagues. Dr. Raichlová's colleague Ing. Z. Leypold-Iglová was AAC's first director. Jansen Raichl acted as secretary. Raichl's London recruiting efforts yielded AAC's first teachers. Pavel Mach and Petr Suk, both Czechs, joined Raichl in 1993 and proved invaluable in understanding the Czech bureaucracy and working with the Czech authorities. Pavel Mach became Raichl's trusted and loyal administrator, Petr Suk, who spoke no English, had helped find premises when AAC was evicted from its original location.

AAC Starts its First Semesters

During the summer of 1991, AAC began recruiting both full-time and part-time students to study politics and history; business management and accountancy; and law. All programs would follow the European university 3-year model. (Throughout Europe, graduation from "high school" or "gymnasium" included completion of the equivalent of 1 year of college at an American university.) The Anglo-American College opened in September 1991 on a shoestring budget. The college had no permanent premises, no library, and no computer laboratory. Classes that year were held during the evening in retired high school classrooms.

AAC's first class was comprised of 51 students. In addition to native Czechs, the student body included four Nigerians, two Ethiopians, one student from the U.A.E., and one from Lithuania. Raichl understood that, until AAC could build its reputation, the college would

be viewed as a "college of last resort" for those gymnasium graduates who either did not want to leave Prague or who had failed to get into any Czech university. However, Raichl also knew that there were many able students who would view AAC as a better alternative to the rigid Czech university system and who would welcome an opportunity to improve their English-language competence.

Although its first emphasis was upon recruiting Central Europeans, Raichl and his AAC colleagues believed that its stress on global perspectives, international staffing, and modern teaching methods would eventually attract foreign students to AAC and thus create a truly multicultural college community. A student profile showed that, of the 78 students who were enrolled at the start of the 1992–1993 academic year, 28.3 percent of AAC's foreign students came from Africa; 21.7 percent came from Serbia-Montenegro; 21.7 percent came from Bosnia and Croatia; 6.4 percent came from the United States and Canada; and 2.6 percent came from other countries. The acceleration of the civil war in former Yugoslavia and the collapse of the educational system there did much to maintain a high rate of foreign enrollment at AAC.

From the beginning, recruiting qualified teaching staff with modern ideas was a challenge. In the newly emerging post-1989 private sector, such talented and educated people were at a premium, and the rewards in the university sector were pitifully small. The ex-dissidents who did take up university teaching were a small and disparate group who were not always up to date in their teaching methods or efficient as academic managers. Fortunately, AAC attracted a surprisingly high number of teachers willing to teach at least one class a semester, despite the paltry salary of $175 per month per class. This was because of the high number of expatriates who had moved to Prague in the early 1990s seeking adventure and opportunities. Though lacking in experience, most of these teachers were highly motivated and wanted to give something back to the local community while they were guests in Prague, the magical "City of 100 Spires."

There was little control over syllabi, course requirements, and information covered in classes. Most instructors used whatever format they had gone through in their home university. Classes run by American and British teachers were typically very interactive, a distinct departure from traditional Czech classrooms, with most instructors requiring student presentations as a significant evaluation component. These factors contributed to AAC's becoming a favorite recruiting source for multinational companies.

Each year, AAC attracted more students, almost in spite of itself. It was clear that the best things about AAC in the early 1990s were the students and the sincere altruism that motivated the founders, teachers, and administrators. However, the college was poorly organized and managed; it was always walking the razor's edge financially and, except for the law school, which had a separate administration and a coherent curriculum, academic standards were generally low.

Signs of Trouble

Despite the vision, hard work, and enthusiasm of its founders, AAC facilities did not convey an image of professionalism or permanence. In 1993, AAC facilities were three classrooms and a small office for Raichl and the copy machine in a run-down apartment building. In March of that year, the U.S.-based Printed Heritage Preservation Society had sent several shipments of books to the AAC. These were mainly pre-1980s discards from American university libraries, mixed with more recent publishers remainders. Although many of the books, and especially the good reference works included, were a good basis for setting up a college library, many more were on subjects that were not of primary interest to the college. The lack of a proper library and up-to-date textbooks added to the difficulties in providing students with the instructional materials they needed. AAC instructors were continually scrounging for teaching materials and begging copy services to provide text material for their students. There were no computers for students and, although thousands of books had been donated to AAC, the books were in storage and not available to the students.

Raichl had found teachers through any means possible, but there was virtually no screening process. Mark Andersen recalls, "I heard about AAC from a friend who had taught a law class for one semester and asked me to meet with Jansen Raichl about teaching a business class. I met with Jansen and all he needed to hear was that I had my MBA,

and then he said I could teach whatever I wanted to. I chose marketing but requested that there not be more than 25 students in my class, so that there could be adequate class participation. Jansen assured me I would not have more than that number. On the first day of class, I had 62 students show up. Students were sitting on the floor and many were very upset, understandably."

Despite the enthusiasm and self-motivation of many staff and students, there were too few administrators to attend to the organizational and outreach needs of the college. Jansen Raichl, as AAC's leader, was being pulled in all directions because he managed external relationships with other universities, accreditation efforts, fund-raising, recruitment of students, registration, scheduling of classes, recruitment of teachers, payroll, renting and maintenance of classroom space, student records, and relationships with corporations that were interested in hiring AAC students. By 1994, most of Raichl's original partners had either moved on to other jobs or had left out of frustration with Raichl's leadership, leaving him with only one full-time assistant, Pavel Mach, a loyal but inconsistent sidekick in the mode of a Sancho Panza to Raichl's Quixote.

Raichl did not delegate. Largely due to the lack of finances, which precluded hiring more staff, Raichl attempted to handle everything himself. "Pavel Mach was a loyal administrator in whom I had full confidence," explained Raichl. "There were many other competent people around, but often their visions differed from mine so I could not rely on them. I know I lack the skills needed to motivate others. Lately, the permanent crises are exhausting me."

When complaints were voiced to Raichl, he often became angry and confrontational. Raichl was obviously intelligent and had a strong, sarcastic sense of humor, but he was not considered by many students as sympathetic to their concerns. At the same time, many students had a soft spot for Raichl because they knew he struggled to keep AAC alive when nearly all of his other cofounders had left. However, this soft spot was shrinking as student frustration grew. Raichl cared deeply about AAC's success, and he was afraid that without his control of the day-to-day operations and finances, the institution would fail. Increasingly, he frustrated students and teachers with his unpredictable outbursts and quirky personality. His management style rarely intimidated anyone; most seemed to feel "Well, there goes Jansen" or "That's just Jansen's style."

AAC's constant financial problems and personal frictions began to fray Raichl's nerves. He had put much of his own money into this project and took only a minimal salary in return. In its second and third year of operation, some of the lecturers salaries for the final semesters were not paid until the beginning of the following semester, when new tuition fees made this possible. Keeping the college going became a balancing act in which current income always had to be used to settle outstanding debts.

Meanwhile, it was becoming more obvious that Pavel Mach was having some difficulties handling his job; missed deadlines and late payroll (which was done in cash payments, much like most companies in the country at that time) increased in frequency. Beneath the surface, Mach, like Raichl, cared deeply about AAC's success, but did not know how to achieve that success.

Preparing for a Civil War

In September 1993, with 120 students enrolled, it looked as if the AAC would at last reach a break-even point. However, during that fall, tempers of AAC faculty and staff reached a boiling point. The students also showed signs of discontent. At the beginning of the semester, students held a meeting to discuss if or how they would protest against AAC's administration to express their concern over the lack of services, lack of class offerings, and uneven teaching quality. Internal dissension was building between the faculty and administration because the faculty felt they were not receiving support from the administration.

Although the departure of some of the original founders lessened some of the internal tension, their threat of starting a competing American International University in Prague (AIUP) finally came to fruition, further endangering AAC's tenuous situation. AIUP started its first semester in February 1994, and as a result AAC's enrollment dropped to 60 students. Raichl realized that he needed help. He agreed to hire someone to help him with the day-to-day management of college affairs, but AAC was unable to find somebody he trusted to take the job. Several people were approached and a Czech

woman was offered the job but she turned it down. Negative attitudes among students and teachers had strained relationships and threatened to further tarnish AAC's public image.

As he prepared for his meeting with the teachers and students, Raichl feared that they would ask him to relinquish his control. Most of the instructors were young Americans, idealistic and enthusiastic, but not used to taking orders or living frugally. They did not understand that the college was in danger of bankruptcy without his diligence and philanthropy. Did any of these foreigners understand the importance of AAC's mission? Could a new management team run AAC any better than he had? Should he step down entirely and let the college flounder? What would it take to resolve the conflicts and make AAC the institution he knew it could be? As he mulled over the possibilities, he was convinced that a turnaround was possible, but he was unsure of the role he should—or could—take.

CASE DISCUSSION QUESTIONS

1. What are some of the major problems currently facing Anglo-American College?
2. Which aspects of the Czech Republic's communist past have contributed to Anglo-American College's problems? Could most of these problems have been predicted?
3. If you were Raichl, how would you approach the meeting with discontent instructors and students? What would you tell them?
4. Finally, what would you do next to save the college? Would you relinquish control to a new management team?

CASE CREDIT

The authors wish to thank AAC faculty and students for their cooperation in the preparation of this case. We are especially indebted to Jansen Raichl and Richard Jones for providing information about AAC's early years. This case was written solely for the purpose of stimulating student discussion and learning. All events and individuals in this case are real, but some names have been disguised.

CASE NOTES

[1] Humphreys, R., *Czech & Slovak Republics*, 4th Edition (London: Rough Guides, Ltd., 1998).

[2] Krauthamer, K., "Where Is My Home?" *The Prague Post*, October 27, 1998, p. 2B.

4

Managing Ethical and Social Responsibility Challenges in Multinational Companies

Preview CASE IN POINT

The Growing Responsibility of Multinationals

How responsible are multinational managers for working conditions and the use of child labor in overseas production facilities? For example, should the U.S. shoe or garment manufacturer be concerned if its goods are produced by subcontractors (at the lowest competitive cost) using child-labor sweatshops in Asia? Is it the duty of retailers to worry about where and how the goods they sell were produced? Increasingly, such issues are becoming important to multinational companies that source their production in the lowest-cost areas of the world. Such issues also attract public and governmental attention.

In response to these issues, a growing number of U.S. multinational companies—Levi Strauss, Nordstrom, Wal-Mart Stores, and Reebok International—actively monitor wages, working conditions, workers' rights, and safety in their production facilities. Levi is among the most active. It routinely sends inspectors to Southeast Asia to inspect working conditions in factories from Indonesia to Bangladesh. Even over the objections of some senior managers and board members, Levi CEO Robert D. Haas took action. He dropped two of the cheapest labor sites, China and Burma, from its manufacturing locations because of unsatisfactory working conditions.

Levi Strauss even went further with its plants in Bangladesh. When the company discovered that two sewing subcontractors employed young children, it was faced with a dilemma. Children without jobs frequently beg or prostitute themselves for money. Levi, however, did not want to have these children fired. The solution that won the company great praise was to ask the subcontractors to remove these children from the factory, and Levi would continue to pay their wages while they attend school full time. These children were then guaranteed their jobs back when they reached maturity at age 14.

Many companies are also taking active steps to implement global ethics program to ensure that their employees around the world adhere to their ethics standards. For instance, Deloitte Touche

Tohmatsu has appointed a chief ethics partner in most of its member firms and an ethics officer in each country in which it operates. Even Wal-Mart is putting more emphasis on its global ethics program by hiring someone to run its global ethics office.

Sources: Based on Davids, Meryl. 1999. "Global standards, local problems." Journal of Business Strategy. January/February: pp. 38–43; Marion, Vivian. 1996. "What's fit to buy?" Lewiston Morning Tribune, June 30, pp. 1e, 5e; Maher, Kris. 2004. "Global companies face reality of instituting ethics program." Wall Street Journal, Nov. 9, p. b8; Mesure, Susie. 2006. "World's most reviled retailer seeks ethics guru." The Independent, Mar 4, p. 45; and Zachary, G. Pascal. 1994. "Levi tries to make sure contract plants in Asia treat workers well." Wall Street Journal, July 28, pp. A1, A5.

The Preview Case in Point shows how multinational firms are facing growing ethical issues. This chapter will review basic knowledge of business ethics and will build on this knowledge to discuss ethical and social responsibilities unique to multinational management.

Managers at all levels face ethical issues every day. "If I fire a poorly performing employee, what will happen to his children?" "If we can get cheap child labor overseas, and it is legal there, should we use it because our competitors do?" "Should we refuse to give a bribe to an underpaid government official and lose the contract to our competitor's weaker product?" "Should we dump our waste in the river knowing well that it would pose pollution risks although it is acceptable in the country?"

Why is so much attention being paid to ethical issues in multinational companies? Graham and Woods[1] argue that there are approximately 60,000 multinationals operating across country borders today. However, an overwhelming majority of these multinational companies and their 500,000 subsidiaries are based in developing countries. Multinational firms have access to vast financial, capital, and human resources, and such access provides power that limits the ability of the developing countries' governments to regulate these multinational companies. In some cases, the governments of developing countries are not willing to regulate as they compete for foreign investment.

The next Case in Point discusses many of the perceived negatives associated with globalization and multinational companies.

Despite the negatives, some have argued that multinational companies bring benefits such as the creation of jobs and wealth and technology transfer to developing nations. Whether these negative perceptions are real or not, multinational firms will have to deal with these problems. Dealing with such issues is not easy. However, with a better understanding of key ethical problems in multinational management, you can make more informed ethical judgments. This chapter will provide some of the background and skills required to deal with the ethical situations faced by multinational managers.

What are International Business Ethics and Social Responsibility?

Before you can understand the ethical dilemmas faced by multinational managers, you need a working definition of business ethics. Most experts consider

CASE IN POINT

Negatives Associated with Multinational Companies

Globalization has made it possible for thousands of multinational companies to operate in places that would not have been possible before. For instance, multinationals often conduct oil exploration in African nations while other multinationals outsource footwear and clothing to Asian countries. This expanded activity has brought increased attention to the many negatives associated with these large companies. These negatives include:

- *Destruction of local sector/companies:* Multinational companies, by virtue of their size, can instantly strip the ability of local firms to meet their credit obligations and can force them into bankruptcy. They also can borrow money at much better rates and leave little for local firms.
- *Environmental and other pollution:* Multinational firms are often seen as major environmental polluters because they often take advantage of weak or absent local environmental regulations.

- *Undermining of local governments and social programs:* Multinationals, because of their power, can often pressure local governments to give tax breaks or other benefits for locating in that country. Such tax breaks may mean that important social programs cannot be supported.
- *Creation of inequalities:* Multinational companies are often perceived to create various forms of inequalities. Income inequalities occur because multinationals tend to pay higher wages than local firms. Multinationals also create economic inequalities by emphasizing global trade and investment in some areas at the expense of other areas.
- *Labor market exploitation:* Multinational companies are also accused of exploiting local labor markets and paying low and inadequate wages.

Source: Based on Goulet, Denis. 2004. "Is sustainable development possible in a globalized world?" Humanomics, 21, 1/2, pp. 3–16; Graham, David, and Ngaire Woods. 2006. "Making corporate self-regulation effective in developing countries." World Development, 34, 5, pp. 868–883.

business ethics as one application of the broader concern for all ethical behavior and reasoning. In this broad sense, ethics pertain to behaviors or actions that affect people and their welfare. A decision by managers to knowingly sell a useful but dangerous product is an ethical decision. Ethics deal with the "oughts" of life—that is, the rules and values that determine what goals and actions people "ought" to follow when dealing with other human beings.[2]

Although economic logic (i.e., making money) dominates business decision making, most business decisions also have consequences for people (workers, suppliers, customers, society). Thus, ethical decision making permeates organizational life. For example, decisions such as those regarding product safety, layoffs, closing or relocating a plant, or the truthfulness of an advertisement have consequences for people. When managers make such decisions, they make decisions with ethical consequences—whether consciously or not.

However, it is important to remember that ethical questions seldom have clear or unambiguous answers that are accepted by all people. For example, it is possible to produce automobiles safer than those currently on the market. However, if such vehicles were required by law, they would be extremely expensive (meaning only the rich could drive); would probably result in smaller automobile-production plants (putting people out of work); would likely require larger engines (increasing oil consumption and pollution); and would likely reduce profits (violating the ethical responsibilities of the managers to stockholders). Thus, for the automobile manufacturers, there is always an ethical dilemma of whether a vehicle is sufficiently safe versus sufficiently affordable.

International business ethics pertain to those unique ethical problems faced by managers conducting business operations across national boundaries.

International business ethics

Those unique ethical problems faced by managers conducting business operations across national boundaries.

International business ethics differ from domestic business ethics on two accounts. First, and perhaps most important, international business is more complex because business is conducted cross-nationally. Different cultural values and institutional systems necessarily mean that people may not always agree on what one "ought" to do. Expatriate managers may face situations where local business practices violate their own culturally based sensibilities or their home-country laws. Second, the very large multinational companies often have powers and assets that equal those of some of the nations with which they deal. Managers in these large and powerful multinationals face challenging ethical dilemmas regarding how to use this power. The example of Levi Strauss in this chapter's Preview Case in Point illustrates how one CEO uses his company's assets in ways that benefit several stakeholders, including the company and the people in the developing nations that produce Levi's products.

The concept of **corporate social responsibility** is closely related to business ethics. Corporate social responsibility refers to the idea that businesses have a responsibility to society beyond making profits. That is, corporate social responsibility means that a company must take into account the welfare of other constituents (e.g., customers, suppliers) in addition to stockholders. While business ethics usually concern the ethical dilemmas faced by managers as individuals, corporate social responsibility is usually concerned with the ethical consequences of policies and procedures of the company as an organization. Monitoring the working conditions of your suppliers, paying for the education of the children of workers, and donating money to the local community are examples of corporate social responsibility in action. Consider the following Case in Point.

In practice, ethics and social responsibility are not easily distinguished. Usually, procedures and policies in a company regarding social responsibility reflect the ethical values and decisions of the top management team.[3] For example, as shown in the Preview Case in Point, Levi's decision to engage in the socially responsible action of monitoring the working conditions of its suppliers reflects the ethical beliefs of Levi CEO Robert D. Haas regarding these issues.

> **Corporate social responsibility**
>
> Idea that businesses have a responsibility to society beyond making profits.

C A S E   I N   P O I N T

Social Responsibility in Various Global Companies

Social responsibility usually means going beyond complying with ethical standards. For instance, while it is ethical not to hire children, social responsibility involves paying for the education of the children of workers. The Zero Hunger program in Brazil is a good example of social responsibility. Multinational companies such as IBM, Ford, Bayer A.G., and Unilever are all working with the Zero Hunger program to eradicate poverty in Brazil. Ford recently became the first automaker in Brazil to set up a social responsibility department. It is donating 440 pounds of food for every truck sold and is now working with unions on adult literacy programs. Ford has also donated spare cars and spare parts to a mechanics school for underprivileged adolescents. Similarly, Asea Brown Boveri (ABB) has partnered with the World Wide Fund for Nature to direct some of its donations to rural electrification in Africa. The partnership chose the remote village of Ngrambe in Tanzania to install a diesel-based generator to supply electricity. ABB also has trained numerous technicians in the village hoping that they will be able to develop a business model so that the villagers can financially support the project.

Source: Based on Egels, Niklas. 2005. "CSR in electrification of rural Africa." The Journal of Corporate Citizenship, 18, pp. 75–85; Smith, Tony. 2003. "In Brazil, companies help poor: Da Silva makes battle on poverty popular." International Herald Tribune, April 1, p. 11.

The ethical and social-responsibility issues faced by multinational companies are complex and varied. Exhibit 4.1 identifies some of the stakeholders in the multinational company and shows typical problems faced by the multinational company that affect these stakeholders.

EXHIBIT 4.1

Areas of Ethical and Social Responsibility Concerns for the Multinational Company

Stakeholder Affected	Ethical/Social Responsibility Issue	Example problems for the MNC
Customers	Product safety	Should an MNC delete safety features to make a product more affordable for people in a poorer nation?
	Fair price	Should a sole supplier in a country take advantage of its monopoly?
	Proper disclosures and information	Should an MNC assume the cost of translating all its product information into other languages?
Stockholders	Fair return on investment	If a product is banned because it is unsafe in one country, should it be sold in countries where it is not banned to maintain profit margins?
		What should a company do if it is found that the corporate executives have been involved in accounting scandals? What protection measures should be taken to protect shareholders' interests?
		How much should CEOs be paid? Should shareholders ignore extremely generous severance packages?
	Fair wages	Should a company pay more than market wages when such wages result in people living in poverty?
	Safety of working conditions	Should a company be responsible for the working conditions of its suppliers?
Employees	Child labor	Should an MNC use child labor if it is legal in the host country?
	Discrimination by sex, race, color, or creed	Should a company assign a woman to a country where women are expected to remain separate from men in public?
	Impact on local economies	Should an MNC use transfer pricing and other internal accounting measures to reduce its actual tax base in a foreign country?
Host Country	Following local laws	Should an MNC follow local laws that violate home-country laws against discrimination?
	Impact on local social institutions	Should an MNC require its workers to work on religious holidays?
	Environmental protection	Is an MNC obligated to control its hazardous waste to a degree higher than local laws require?
Society in General	Raw-material depletion	Should MNCs deplete natural resources in countries that are willing to let them do so?

As Exhibit 4.1 shows, multinational companies are faced both with primary and secondary stakeholders. **Primary stakeholders** are directly linked to a company's survival and include customers, suppliers, employees, and shareholders. In contrast, secondary stakeholders tend to be less directly linked to the company's survival and include the media, trade associations, and special-interest groups.[4] However, although it may seem that secondary stakeholders have less impact for multinational companies, recent examples show that secondary shareholders are as important as primary shareholders in terms of impact. Consider, for example, that Shell Oil has been forced to acknowledge its relationship with a corrupt government in Nigeria. Similarly, the agricultural giant Monsato has been forced to deal with secondary stakeholders such as Greenpeace and Friends of the Earth as it tries to develop agricultural biotechnology products.[5] Such examples show that addressing the needs of both types of shareholders is critical.

How can international managers deal with the constant ethical challenges such as those in Exhibit 4.1? To succeed and be profitable in a socially responsible fashion, multinational company managers must weigh and balance the economic, legal, and ethical consequences of their decisions. The next sections discuss how managers must analyze situations with ethical consequences. The first section presents an overview of basic ethical philosophies used by managers as guides for ethical decision making. The second section deals with national differences in business ethics and social responsibility. The third section considers the development of transnational business ethics—an ethical system for the multinational company that does not rely on the ethical principles and philosophies of any one country. In the final section, we consider the practical considerations of balancing the needs of the company and managerial actions with ethical consequences.

Ethical Philosophy

In this section, we examine two ways to consider ethical decision making. The first comes from traditional ethical philosophy. The second is a contemporary philosophical view of how we can think about ethics.

Traditional Views

Two basic systems of ethical reasoning dominate ethical philosophy. These are the teleological and the deontological.

In **teleological ethical theories,** the morality of an act or practice comes from its consequences. The most popular teleological theory is **utilitarianism.** Utilitarianism argues that what is good and moral comes from acts that produce the greatest good for the greatest number of people. For example, from a utilitarian perspective, one might argue that stealing a loaf of bread to feed a hungry family is moral because eating the bread is crucial for the family's survival. Many multinational economic decisions are made using utilitarianism. For instance, a multinational company can choose a plant location among countries by doing a cost-and-benefit analysis, which represents one of the most popular applications of utilitarianism.

In contrast to teleological ethical theories, **deontological ethical theories** do not focus on consequences. Rather, *actions by themselves have a good or bad morality regardless of the outcomes they produce.* For example, a person who chooses not to steal a loaf of bread because it is immoral to steal, even if people starve because of this action, behaves ethically according to some deontological arguments. In this

---

Primary stakeholders

People directly linked to a company's survival, including customers, suppliers, employees, and shareholders.

Secondary stakeholders

People less directly linked to a company's survival, including the media, trade associations, and special-interest groups.

Teleological ethical theory

One that suggests that the morality of an act or practice comes from its consequences.

Utilitarianism

Argument that what is good and moral comes from acts that produce the greatest good for the greatest number of people.

Deontological ethical theory

Focus on actions that, by themselves, have a good or bad morality regardless of the outcomes they produce.

case, the moral principle forbidding stealing, common in many religious doctrines, takes precedence over a bad outcome. Similarly, deontology would argue that closing a plant is unethical as workers are not being treated with dignity.

Some ethical philosophers who believe in deontological ethical theories argue that morality is intuitive and self-evident—that is, moral people just know what is right because it is obvious how an ethical person should behave. Other ethical philosophers argue that we cannot rely on intuition. Instead, we should follow an essential moral principle or value such as the Golden Rule or a concern for justice. Still other deontologists argue for a more comprehensive set of moral principles or rules that can guide our behavior, such as the Ten Commandments, the Koran, or the Bible.[6]

Moral Languages

Another more contemporary way of looking at ethics, favored by Thomas Donaldson, an expert on international business ethics, broadens the rough distinction between teleological and deontological ethical theories. Donaldson argues that international business ethics is best understood by focusing on the "language of international corporate ethics."[7] According to Donaldson, **moral languages** describe the basic ways that people use to think about ethical decisions and to explain their ethical choices. The six basic ethical languages identified by Donaldson include:[8]

Moral languages

Description of the basic ways that people use to think about ethical decisions and to explain their ethical choices.

- *Virtue and vice:* This language identifies a person's good or virtuous properties and contrasts them with vices. For example, temperance might be contrasted with lust. People or groups who exhibit or who have virtuous characteristics are seen as ethical. It is not so important what results from an action, but rather the virtuous intent of the action.
- *Self-control:* This language emphasizes achieving perfection at controlling thoughts and actions, such as passion. It is apparent in Buddhist and Hindu views of the world but also appears in many Western traditions, such as in the philosophy of Plato and the control of "appetites."
- *Maximizing human welfare:* This is the basic language of the utilitarian view of ethics, emphasizing the greatest good for the greatest number of people. For example, using this language of ethical thought, one might argue that exposing a few people to dangerous chemicals is okay if most people in the society benefit.
- *Avoiding harm:* Like the emphasis on the greatest good for the greatest number, this language of ethics also sees good or bad in the consequences of behavior or action. However, rather than maximizing benefits, it focuses on avoiding unpleasant outcomes or consequences. For example, one might argue: "If it doesn't hurt anyone, it's okay."
- *Rights/duties:* This language focuses on principles that guide ethical behaviors. The principles specify duties that are required, such as the duties of a parent to care for a child. The principles also specify the rights that people have, such as the right to free speech. According to Donaldson, the language of rights and duties fits well in a legal context.
- *Social contract:* The social-contract language structures ethics as a form of agreements among people. These agreements need not be written but may be taken for granted by those concerned. In this sense, what is ethical is what the people in our culture or in our organization have come to agree is ethical.

The moral philosophies provide a language or structure for thinking about ethical decisions and dilemmas. They help the manager understand the philosophical bases for his or her decision making and the ethical or social-responsibility policies of a company. International managers face the additional challenge of understanding the cultural and institutional contexts surrounding their ethical decision making. The next section shows how culture and social institutions come into play in the complexities of ethical decision making.

National Differences in Business Ethics and Social Responsibility

As with most multinational business practices, national culture and social institutions also affect how businesses manage ethical behavior and social responsibility. Exhibit 4.2 gives a simple model of the relationships among national culture, social institutions, and business ethics.

As discussed in Chapter 2, national culture through the cultural norms and values influence important business practices—such as how women and minorities are treated on the job, attitudes toward gift giving and bribery, and expectations regarding conformity to written laws. Similarly, social institutions

EXHIBIT 4.2   A Model of Institutional and Cultural Effects on Business Ethics Issues and Management

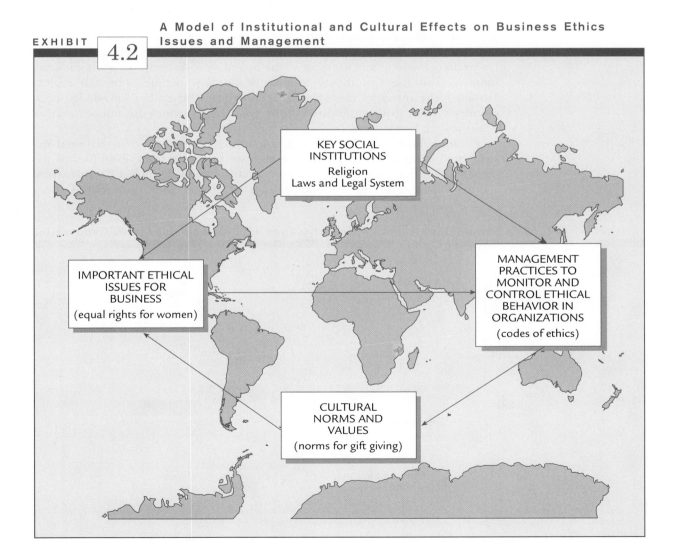

described in Chapter 3, such as religion and the legal system, are probably the key institutions that affect what ethical issues are important in a society and how they are typically managed.

Although there is no comprehensive body of knowledge identifying exactly how national culture and social institutions affect business ethics and under what conditions, recent work by Cullen, Parboteeah, and Hoegl[9] suggests that there are possible applications to multinational ethics. Basing their study on Messner and Rosenfeld[10] institutional anomie theory, they argue that specific national culture and social institutions are likely to encourage people to break norms and thereby justify ethically suspect behaviors. They argue that societies with national cultural values of high achievement (i.e., people value achievement), high individualism (i.e., people value their own personal freedom), high universalism (i.e., people are more ambitious because they expect to be treated fairly), and high pecuniary materialism (i.e., people have higher materialist tendencies) are likely to have a higher degree of people engaging in deviant acts such as crime. In addition to these national culture values, they also specify that social institutions such as industrialization, economic system, family, and education should be related to the breaking of norms. They suggest that societies with higher levels of industrialization, more capitalist systems, lower degrees of family breakdown, and more accessible education should encourage more deviance. Testing their theory on 3,450 managers from 28 countries, the researchers find support for most of the hypotheses. As such, the multinational manager can use this theory to understand how people approach ethics. However, the manager can often only infer from his or her knowledge of a country's social institutions and culture what ethical issues are important and how they are best managed.

To show other examples and anecdotal evidence of how the national institutional context affects business ethics, we now give some examples of international differences in business-ethics management. Exhibit 4.3 summarizes the results of one study on the ratings of ethical issues considered most

EXHIBIT 4.3   The Management of Key Ethical Issues in U.S. and European Companies

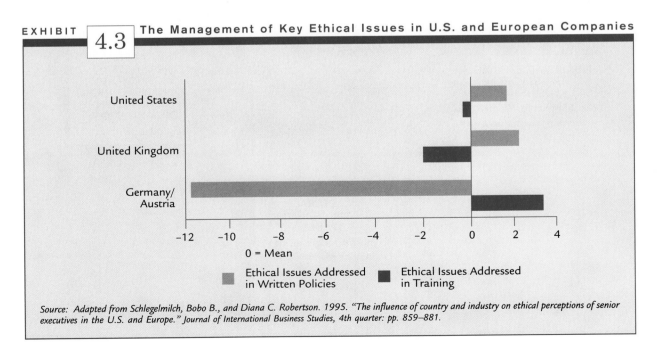

Ethical Issues Addressed in Written Policies
Ethical Issues Addressed in Training

0 = Mean

Source: Adapted from Schlegelmilch, Bobo B., and Diana C. Robertson. 1995. "The influence of country and industry on ethical perceptions of senior executives in the U.S. and Europe." Journal of International Business Studies, 4th quarter: pp. 859–881.

important by senior U.S. and European executives.[11] Of course, a broader range of ethical issues or a larger sample of countries would produce more differences than those in the example here. However, although these managers all come from Western democracies, cultural differences and historical, legal, and political traditions influence which ethical issues managers deem important.

Why is the United States so different from the other countries on the ethics of HRM issues? U.S. cultural norms emphasize the value of individual freedom. Compatible with these norms, the U.S. legal system has developed extensive prohibitions against discrimination and extensive laws regulating HRM issues. Consequently, U.S. managers ranked personnel issues as requiring the greatest concern for their ethics management.

Why are the German and Austrian managers more concerned with political issues? Perhaps because of recent legal and popular challenges to the historically close (and mutually self-serving) interactions between industry and political leaders, the German and Austrian managers have above-average concerns for ethical issues related to politics.

Although limited in national coverage, these examples show that to identify key ethical issues in a society, multinational managers must be attuned to cultural, legal, and political traditions. These traditions affect people's beliefs concerning what ethical issues are important and, as you will see next, how they should be managed.

The techniques of managing ethical behavior in organizations also reflect cultural and institutional differences. Exhibit 4.4 shows the management techniques preferred by the same group of managers reported on in Exhibit 4.3. Consistent with their practice of a heavy emphasis on training, and in comparison to managers from other countries, Germans used training for ethical control

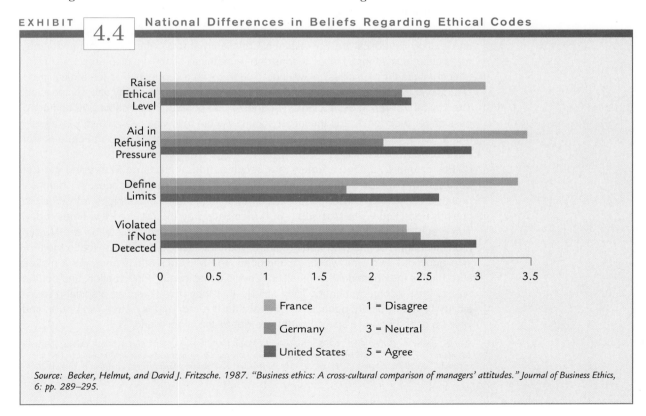

EXHIBIT 4.4   **National Differences in Beliefs Regarding Ethical Codes**

France   1 = Disagree
Germany   3 = Neutral
United States   5 = Agree

Source: Becker, Helmut, and David J. Fritzsche. 1987. "Business ethics: A cross-cultural comparison of managers' attitudes." Journal of Business Ethics, 6: pp. 289–295.

most often and relied little on written policies. U.S. and British managers seemed to think that having the written policies was sufficient for ethics management.

Aside from the effect of other social institutions on defining important ethical issues, as we saw in Chapter 3, religions are important aspects of societies and can have a powerful impact on the nature of business ethics. Although this is most apparent in states where there is a close relationship between a particular religious hierarchy and the government, religious values impact business ethics even in more secular states. For example, the Judeo-Christian traditions of values and beliefs regarding ethical behavior dominate the ethical philosophies of most Western countries. Similarly, as shown in the Comparative Management Brief on religion and business ethics, other religious traditions can influence what people believe is good and correct actions at work.

Because of its extensive legal control over the management of ethical behaviors, the United States is unique in the world. The next section discusses a major law governing ethical behavior in international business that has possibly the greatest impact on U.S. multinational companies.

Questionable Payments and the U.S. Foreign Corrupt Practices Act

In addition to the many possible ethical issues discussed in Exhibit 4.1, a particular ethical difficulty for many U.S. multinational companies revolves around

Comparative Management **Brief**

Religion and Business Ethics

It is typically claimed that all religions tend to provide some guidelines regarding ethics and leading the ethical life. For instance, Christianity, through the Ten Commandments, gives clear indications of what is considered unethical. Hinduism also prescribes clear ethical values through classical writings. Buddhism also suggests that the ethical life is clearly one lived where humans and nature coexist through harmony and compassion. The concept of *ren* in Confucianism suggests that people should show love and compassion for their family and the larger society. As the following example shows, all religions tend to provide some ethical prescriptions that have implications for multinational companies.

For example, although Turkey is a secular state, there is an increasing merger between the values espoused in the Koran and business practices. A voluntary group of executives, called the Musiad, try to combine Islamic teachings with Western business practices. The Musiad's 1,800 members pray the required five times a day. The group is male-dominated, with only two female members. They follow the Muslim prohibition against charging *riba* (interest), and they feel it is a moral obligation to provide good pay and safe working conditions. The Musiad's ethics committee makes sure that its members don't drink alcohol, avoid conspicuous consumption, and donate part of their income to charity. They believe that they must exercise a social responsibility to their society because they feel that the money they earn "isn't ours, and we'll be asked how we spent it when we get to the other world."

Sources: Based on Doxey, John. 1995. "Bringing the Koran to the corner office." BusinessWeek Online, February 13; Huang, Y. 2005. "Confucian love and global ethics: How the Cheng brothers would help respond to Christian criticisms." Asian Philosophy, 15, 1, pp. 35–60; Parboteeah, K. Praveen, Martin Hoegl, and John B. Cullen. 2006. "Religion and ethically suspect behaviors: A multidimensional approach." Western Academy of Management Meeting Proceedings.

the issue of bribery, or what some call questionable payments. In many societies, people routinely offer bribes or gifts to expedite government actions or to gain advantage in business deals. "Grease money" can speed importing or exporting of goods or cause customs agents to look the other way. A gift or a kickback may be expected for a purchasing agent to select your company's product over another. Words for these types of actions exist in all countries. For example, in Mexico the bribe is known as *mordida,* the bite; in France the *pot-de-vin,* jug of wine; in Germany, the "N.A.," an abbreviation of *nutzliche Abagabe,* the useful contribution; and in Japan, the *jeitinho,* the fix.[12]

Corruption and bribery can have devastating effects on societies. Compte, Lambert-Mogiliansky and Verdier[13] argue that companies typically make up for bribery by increasing the contract price by the amount of the bribe. As such, many developing countries suffer because they are charged higher prices. However, companies also routinely use poorer-quality products or materials to cover for the bribe, thus resulting in inferior products. Furthermore, corruption can also result in collusion among firms, resulting in even higher prices. As such, corruption and bribery usually result in higher public spending, lower quality projects, under-mined competition, and inefficient allocation of resources. Additionally, some also argue that corruption discourages entrepreneurship as bribery becomes a form of taxation.[14] Such impediments to entrepreneurship affect investment growth and development, leading to lower economic performance.[15]

To understand the level of corruption in countries, multinational companies can rely on the corruption perception index (CPI). The CPI, developed by Transparency International, gives an idea of the levels of perception of corruption within countries. Exhibit 4.5 shows the CPI for selected countries where higher CPIs indicate the least corruption.

Another important bribe index in Exhibit 4.6 shows estimates of the extent of bribery of public officials accepted from companies within leading exporting countries when doing business in emerging market economies. Emerging market economies included countries such as Indonesia, Poland, Nigeria, Colombia,

EXHIBIT 4.5   Corruption Perception Index for Selected Countries

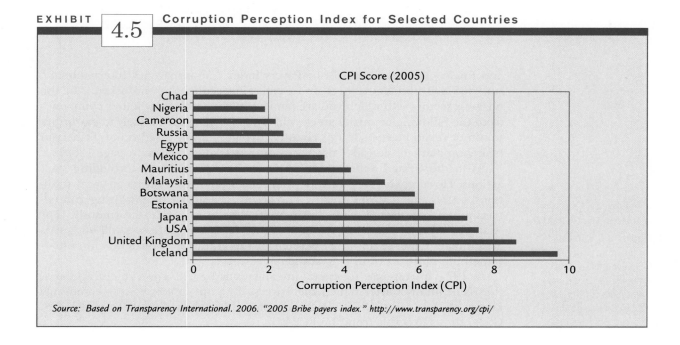

Source: Based on Transparency International. 2006. "2005 Bribe payers index." http://www.transparency.org/cpi/

EXHIBIT **4.6**

Levels of Bribery Paid by Leading Exporting Countries in Emerging Market Countries

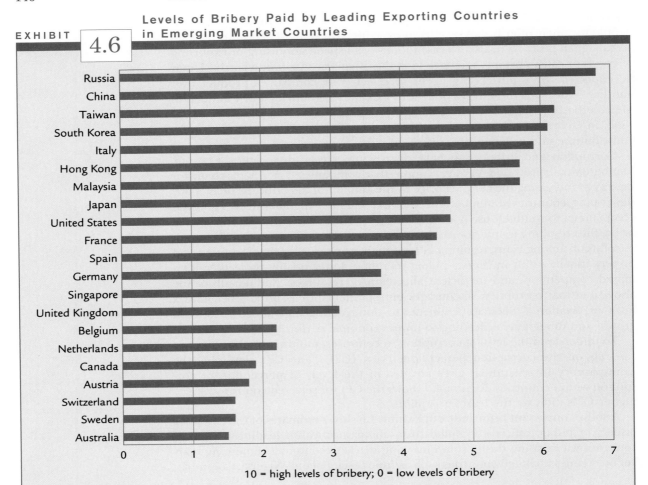

10 = high levels of bribery; 0 = low levels of bribery

Source: Adapted from Transparency International. 2006. "2005 Bribe payers index." http://www.transparency.org/cpi/

and Russia. To create this "Bribe Payers Index," Transparency International[16] surveyed 835 business leaders in 15 emerging economies and asked: "In the business sectors with which you are familiar, please indicate whether companies from the following countries are very likely, quite likely, or unlikely to pay bribes to win or retain business in this country." To get further insights into bribery in emerging markets, consider the Focus on Emerging Markets on page 183.

As in the United States, most countries have formal laws forbidding such actions. However, because of wide differences among countries in legal traditions, enforcement varies greatly. The accepted amount of gift giving and entertainment associated with business transactions varies enormously. For example, even for academic-research grants, Japanese professors will budget as a legitimate expense about 20 percent of the grant for entertainment costs—something unheard of in U.S. academic research.

In 1977, in response to several investigations by U.S. government agencies, President Jimmy Carter signed the **Foreign Corrupt Practices Act**—commonly known as the **FCPA**.[17] Exhibit 4.7, on page 184, taken directly from the U.S. Code, shows excerpts from the FCPA.

Foreign Corrupt Practices Act (FCPA)

Forbids U.S. companies to make or offer illegal payments or gifts to officials of foreign governments for the sake of getting or retaining business.

Focus on Emerging Markets

Corruption and Corruptibility in Post-Communist Europe

Post-communist European countries suffer from the perception that bribes are always necessary to get things done. Research has shown that the frequent bureaucratic encounters between citizens and officials do actually reveal that individuals make extensive use of contacts, presents, and bribes to navigate such bureaucracies. But does the presence of high levels of corruption reflect the values of individuals? In a study of 6,000 members of the public and 1,300 officials, Miller provides some insights on corruption in the Czech Republic, Slovakia, Bulgaria, and the Ukraine. Findings suggest that a majority of the public and officials in these countries abhor the use of presents and bribes to influence officials. However, more that half of these officials were willing to accept some small gift or were willing to justify others accepting small payments. The exhibit below illustrates some of these findings.

As the exhibit above shows, most individuals in these societies condemn bribes, suggesting that bribes are inconsistent with their values. However, they are also willing to give or accept bribes, suggesting that they are corruptible. Such findings suggest that external pressures play a big role in encouraging people to accept or give bribes. These findings are also noteworthy in that hopefully bribery can be reduced in the long run through the reduction of such external pressures.

Sources: Based on Miller, William L. 2006. "Corruption and corruptibility." World Development, 34, 2, pp. 371–380.

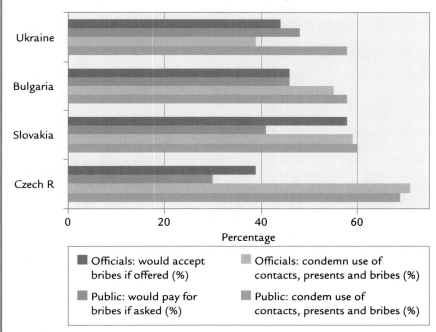

Corruption in Emerging Markets

Legend:
- Officials: would accept bribes if offered (%)
- Public: would pay for bribes if asked (%)
- Officials: condemn use of contacts, presents and bribes (%)
- Public: condem use of contacts, presents and bribes (%)

Source: Adapted from Miller, William L. 2006. "Corruption and corruptibility." World Development, 34, 2, 371–80.

EXHIBIT 4.7   Excerpts from the Foreign Corrupt Practices Act

Prohibited Foreign Trade Practices

It shall be unlawful for *any domestic concern* or for any officer, director, employee, or agent of such domestic concern or any stockholder thereof acting on behalf of such domestic concern, to make use of the mails or any means or instrumentality of interstate commerce corruptly in furtherance of an offer, payment, promise to pay, or authorization of the payment of any money, or offer, gift, promise to give, or authorization of the giving of anything of value to any foreign official for purposes of—

A. influencing any act or decision of such foreign official, political party, party official, or candidate in his or its official capacity, or

B. inducing such foreign official, political party, party official, or candidate to do or omit to do any act in violation of the lawful duty of such foreign official, political party, party official, or candidate, or

C. inducing such foreign official, political party, party official, or candidate to use his or its influence with a foreign government or instrumentality thereof to affect or influence any act or decision of such government or instrumentality, in order to assist such issuer in obtaining or retaining business for or with, or directing business to, any person.

Also prohibited is any offer, payment, promise to pay, or authorization of the payment of any money, or offer, gift, promise to give, or authorization of the giving of anything of value *when given to any person, while knowing* that all or a portion of such money or thing of value will be offered, given, or promised, directly or indirectly, to any foreign official, to any foreign political party or official thereof, or to any candidate for foreign political office, for purposes of A through C above.

Definitions

(1) The term *"domestic concern"* means any individual who is a citizen, national, or resident of the United States; and any corporation, partnership, association, joint-stock company, business trust, unincorporated organization, or sole proprietorship which has its principal place of business in the United States, or which is organized under the laws of a State of the United States or a territory, possession, or commonwealth of the United States.

(2) The term *"foreign official"* means any officer or employee of a foreign government or any department, agency, or instrumentality thereof, or any person acting in an official capacity for or on behalf of any such government or department, agency, or instrumentality.

(3) A person's state of mind is *"knowing"* with respect to conduct, a circumstance, or a result if—

   (i) such person is aware that such person is engaging in such conduct, that such circumstance exists, or that such result is substantially certain to occur; or

   (ii) such person has a firm belief that such circumstance exists or that such result is substantially certain to occur.

Knowledge is established if a person is aware of a high probability of the existence of such circumstance, unless the person actually believes that such circumstance does not exist.

(4) The term *"routine government action"* means only an action which is ordinarily and commonly performed by a foreign official in such cases as obtaining permits, licenses, or other official documents to qualify a person to do business in a foreign country. The term "routine governmental action" does not include any decision by a foreign official whether, or on what terms, to award new business to or to continue business with a particular party, or any action taken by a foreign official involved in the decision-making process to encourage a decision to award new business to or continue business with a particular party.

(5) The term *"interstate commerce"* means trade, commerce, transportation, or communication among the several States, or between any foreign country and any State or between any State and any place or ship outside thereof.

Exceptions

A. Facilitating or expediting payment to a foreign official, political party, or party official the purpose of which is to expedite or *to secure the performance of a routine governmental action* by a foreign official, political party, or party official.

B. The payment, gift, offer, or promise of anything of value that was made, *was lawful under the written laws and regulations of the foreign official's, political party's, party official's, or candidate's country;* or

(continued)

EXHIBIT 4.7   Excerpts from the Foreign Corrupt Practices Act (Continued)

C. The payment, gift, offer, or promise of anything of value that was made, was a *reasonable and bona fide expenditure,* such as travel and lodging expenses, incurred by or on behalf of a foreign official, party, party official, or candidate and was directly related to the promotion, demonstration, or explanation of products or services; or the execution or performance of a contract with a foreign government or agency thereof.

Penalties

1. Any domestic concern that violates this section shall be fined not more than $2,000,000 and shall be subject to a civil penalty of not more than $10,000 imposed in an action brought by the Attorney General.

2. Any officer or director of a domestic concern, or stockholder acting on behalf of such domestic concern, who willfully violates this section shall be fined not more than $100,000, or imprisoned not more than 5 years, or both.

3. Any employee or agent of a domestic concern who is a United States citizen, national, or resident or is otherwise subject to the jurisdiction of the United States (other than an officer, director, or stockholder acting on behalf of such domestic concern), and who willfully violates this section, shall be fined not more than $100,000, or imprisoned not more than 5 years, or both.

4. Any officer, director, employee, or agent of a domestic concern, or stockholder acting on behalf of such domestic concern, who violates this section shall be subject to a civil penalty of not more than $10,000 imposed in an action brought by the Attorney General.

5. *Whenever a fine is imposed upon any officer, director, employee, agent, or stockholder of a domestic concern, such fine may not be paid, directly or indirectly, by such domestic concern.*

Sources: U.S. Code, Title 15—Commerce and Trade, Chapter 2B—Securities Exchanges, Section 78dd–1.

The FCPA forbids U.S. companies to make or offer payments or gifts to foreign government officials for the sake of gaining or retaining business. However, the FCPA does not prohibit some forms of payments that may occur in international business. Payments made under duress to avoid injury or violence are acceptable. For example, in an unstable political environment, a company may pay local officials "bribes" to avoid harassment of its employees. Small payments that just encourage officials to do their legitimate and routine jobs are okay. Payments made that are lawful in a country are also acceptable. These "grease" payments must not seek illegal ends but just speed up or make possible normal business functions, such as necessary paperwork.

A tricky component of the FCPA for U.S. companies is the law's reason-to-know provision. The reason-to-know provision means that a firm is liable for bribes or questionable payments made by agents hired by the firm—even if members of the firm did not actually make the payments or see the payments being made. To take advantage of a local person's knowledge of "how to get things done" in a country, U.S. multinational managers often use local people as agents to conduct business. If it is common knowledge that these agents use part of their fees to bribe local officials to commit illegal acts, then the U.S. firm is breaking U.S. law. If, however, the U.S. firm has no knowledge of the behavior of the agent and no reason to expect illegal behavior from the agent, then the U.S. firm has no liability under the FCPA. A person is considered "knowing" if the person actually knows an illegal bribe will be given, knows that the circumstances surrounding the situation make it likely that an illegal bribe will be given, or is aware of the high probability that an illegal act will occur.

Exhibit 4.7 also shows the types of penalties included in the FCPA. Note that penalties can be given to individuals as well as to companies and that individual fines cannot be paid by the company. In a recent case, a former executive from

Lockheed Martin Corp. was convicted of bribing an Egyptian parliamentarian to facilitate the sale of three C-130 cargo planes. This individual now faces a sentence of 18 months in prison and a $125,000 fine.[18]

Effects of the Ethics Gap

Ethics gap

Idea that U.S. political and legal social institutions create greater coercive and normative pressures for U.S. businesses to follow ethical standards.

Legislation like the FCPA and the proliferation of ethical codes in U.S. corporations has caused some experts to argue that there is an **ethics gap** between the United States and the rest of the world. The ethics gap does not mean that the United States has a more ethical culture than other countries. Rather, it means that U.S. political and legal social institutions create greater coercive and normative pressure for U.S. businesses to follow ethical standards.

Does the FCPA hurt business? Soon after the passage of the FCPA, many business leaders felt that U.S. corporations would be at a competitive disadvantage when conducting business in countries prone to bribery. One early survey found that 78 percent of 1,200 U.S. senior executives felt that the law put U.S. companies at a disadvantage.[19] To address this question, several years after the law went into effect, John Graham[20] looked at changes in the U.S. share of the import markets for the 51 countries that account for the majority of U.S. exports. Dividing the countries into two groups, one in which business practices traditionally allow bribery and the other in which bribery is frowned upon, Graham found no effect on U.S. overseas sales for either group.

However, more recent evidence suggests that, although the FCPA may not have caused U.S. businesses to fall behind, it has blocked some gains in export market share and extent of U.S. ownership in foreign countries. Harvard University economist James R. Hines, Jr. estimates that U.S. direct investment in and exports to "corrupt" countries declined substantially when compared with competitors' investments in the same countries. U.S. Trade Representative Mickey Kantor estimates that successful use of bribery by companies from other countries costs the United States $45 billion a year. One study by the U.S. Commerce Department tracked 100 business deals worth an estimated $45 billion in which U.S. competitors used bribes. Eighty percent of the business went to the foreign competition.[21] Such findings have encouraged some U.S. politicians and managers to pressure other nations to follow U.S. rules. But should they?

Growing international trade relationships also have resulted in calls for universal codes of ethics for the control of the ethical behavior of multinational companies and their employees. The following section discusses some of the current trends and proposals.

Toward Transnational Ethics

Globalization dramatically increases contact among people from different ethical and cultural systems. This contact is creating pressure for ethical convergence and the development of transnational agreements among nations to govern business practices. For example, the Case in Point on page 187 shows that the battle against corrupt relationships between business and government is growing.

Next, we review some of the trends toward ethical convergence and transnational ethical agreements.

Pressures for Ethical Convergence

In spite of the wide differences in cultures and in social institutions, there are growing pressures for multinational companies to follow the same rules in

C A S E   I N   P O I N T

Corruption Attacked Around the World

No nation is free from ethical violations in business practices. However, there are wide differences in how national legal systems prosecute violations and the degree to which the public tolerates ethical violations. For instance, a common joke in Asia is that it is futile to pursue contracts without a sizable checkbook since bribery is a normal part of doing business. However, some evidence now suggests that there is a worldwide trend to clean up business practices, especially unethical business relationships with government. The growing power of shareholders challenges the once cozy relationship between business and government, from Paris to Seoul to Mexico City. Ordinary citizens, prosecutors, and the press are challenging the corporate elite and clamoring for more ethical corporate governance. Consider the following examples.

Investigators in Korea found that 35 Korean *chaebols* (conglomerates) gave approximately $369 million in bribes to former President Roh Tae Woo. Leading the bribery list were the chairmen of giant *chaebols* Samsung (with $32 million) and Daewoo (with $31 million in bribes). However, the Chairman of Hyundai is also facing prosecutors for another bribery scandal. Both the chairman and his son are accused of creating slush funds to bribe South Korean public officials. These exposures and the resultant severe sentences are expected to reduce illegal payoffs in Korea. Additionally, they may make Korean businesses more competitive because companies will now compete based on merit and will avoid the excess costs of bribery.

Instead of waiting to be prosecuted, some companies are starting to be more proactive about bribes and corruption. For instance, DaimlerChrysler recently admitted to making improper payments to officials in several countries in Africa, Asia, and Eastern Europe. Furthermore, DaimlerChrysler has also fired the executives involved in these bribery allegations. The company wants to take the necessary steps to ensure that the multinational company operates ethically.

At the international level, the World Bank and the IMF have stopped lending or have threatened to stop lending to countries such as Kenya, Nigeria, and Indonesia where corruption and bribery has stifled economic growth. Twenty-nine members of the OECD and five nonmembers signed a "bribery convention," which, like the U.S. Foreign Corrupt Practices Act, requires each country to make it a crime to bribe a foreign office to win or retain business.

Source: Based on Brull, Steven, and Margaret Dawson. 1995. "Why Korea's cleanup won't catch on." BusinessWeek Online, International Edition, December 18; Economist. 1999. "A global war against bribery." Economist.com, January 16:Story_1D=182081; Nag, Arindam. 2006. "Carmaker comes clean over bribery." DowJones Newswire, March 12, p. 1; Rossant, John. 1995. "Dirty money." BusinessWeek Online, International Edition, December 18; Woods, Walter. 2006. "Hyundai scandal delays 2nd plant." The Atlanta Journal-Constitution, April 25, p. C4.

managing ethical behavior and social responsibility. This is called **ethical convergence.** There are four basic reasons for ethical convergence.

1. The growth of international trade and trading blocs, such as NAFTA (North American Free Trade Agreement) and the EU, creates pressures to have common ethical practices that transcend national cultures and institutional differences. Predictable interactions and behaviors among trading partners from different countries make trade more efficient. Furthermore, many of these trade organizations and other international associations are developing measures to reduce corruption. Consider the following Case in Point on page 188 reducing global corruption.

2. Interaction between trading partners creates pressure for imitating the business practices of other countries. As the people from different cultural backgrounds increase their interactions, exposure to varying ethical traditions encourages people to adjust to, imitate, and adopt new behaviors and attitudes.

3. Companies that do business throughout the world have employees from varied cultural backgrounds who need common standards and rules regarding how to behave. As such, multinational companies, especially

Ethical convergence

Refers to the growing pressures for multinational companies to follow the same rules in managing ethical behavior and social responsibility.

CASE IN POINT

Reducing Global Corruption

With globalization, the potential for corruption is enhanced. Consequently, there has been stronger interest and efforts among various trade organizations to implement measures to combat corruption. Consider the following examples:

- *OECD Anti-bribery:* The convention, similar to the FCPA, requires that participants make bribery of officials a crime. Participants are also required to demonstrate that adequate measures are taken to sanction those involved in bribery. This convention, which went into effect in February 1999, has been ratified by all OECD members except Slovenia.
- *United Nations Convention Against Corruption:* This convention, adopted in 2003, includes legislation similar to the OECD convention. It requires members to criminalize bribery of government officials.
- *Inter-American Convention Against Corruption:* This convention went into effect to handle cross-

country bribery in the Western hemisphere. It has been ratified by 23 of the 35 members of the Organization of American States.
- *European Union on the Fight Against Corruption:* This convention applies to members of the European Union and prohibits bribery of public officials within countries.
- *Other Conventions:* The following regional associations are either implementing or have implemented measures to curb bribery. These include the African Union and the Convention on Preventing and Combating Corruption (July 2003) and the Pacific Basin Economic Council and its Statement on Standards of Transactions Between Business and Governments (November 1997).

Source: Based on Gleich, Oren, and Ryan Woodward. 2005. "Foreign corrupt practices act." The American Criminal Law Review, 42, 2, pp. 545–71; Organization for Economic Cooperation and Development. 2005. "Bribery: Does the OECD convention work." The OECD Observer, 246/247, pp. 20–21.

the transnationals, often rely on their corporate culture to provide consistent norms and values that govern ethical issues.

4. An increasing number of business watchdogs, such as ethical investment company and nongovernmental organizations, also are encouraging multinational companies to become more ethical.

Not only is there a moral pressure to eliminate corrupt activity, but there is increasingly a financial pressure. Extensive corruption costs money, makes businesses less competitive internationally, and risks embarrassing scandals.

Prescriptive Ethics for the Multinational

Prescriptive ethics for multinationals

Suggested guidelines for the ethical behavior of multinational companies.

Donaldson, an expert in international business ethics, argues that the three moral languages of avoiding harm, rights/duties, and the social contract should guide multinational companies. He advocates **prescriptive ethics for multinationals;** that is, multinational companies should engage in business practices that avoid negative consequences to their stakeholders (e.g., employees, the local environment). While multinationals retain basic rights, such as seeking a fair profit, these rights also imply duties, such as providing a fair wage to local employees. The multinational company also has a social contract between itself and its stakeholders. This contract, even if taken for granted, defines the nature of the relationships. For example, when a multinational company enters a country, it accepts the social contract to follow local laws.

These three moral languages are the easiest to specify in written codes such as contracts and international laws. Donaldson believes that these moral languages are most appropriate for managing ethical behaviors among culturally heterogeneous multinationals—that is, regardless of their national-culture background, companies can agree with their stakeholders on the basic rules of moral behavior.[22]

For Donaldson's ideas to work, there must be a code of conduct to guide multinational companies that is independent of national boundaries. These codes must include prescriptive and proscriptive rules to guide multinational behavior. Prescriptive rules tell multinational managers and companies what they should do while proscriptive rules tell them what they cannot do.

Some scholars argue that such ethical guides currently exist based on various international agreements and on the codes of international governing bodies, such as the United Nations and the International Labor Office.[23]

Exhibit 4.8 summarizes ethical stipulations for the multinational company derived from the following international sources:

- The United Nations Universal Declaration of Human Rights
- The United Nations Code of Conduct on Transnational Corporations
- The European Convention on Human Rights
- The International Chamber of Commerce Guidelines for International Investment
- The Organization for Economic Cooperation and Development Guidelines for Multinational Enterprises
- The Helsinki Final Act
- The International Labor Office Tripartite Declarations of Principles Concerning Multinational Enterprises and Social Policy

The principles in the code of conduct for the multinational company shown in Exhibit 4.8 have two basic supporting rationales. The first rationale comes from the basic deontological principles dealing with human rights, such as the right to work and the right to be safe. To a large degree, the international agreements specify the rights and duties of multinational companies that are presumed to be transcultural—that is, the basic ethical principles apply for all, regardless of a company's country of origin or its current business location. The second rationale for the types of issues addressed in the code comes from the history of experiences in international business interactions.[24] For example, because multinational companies often ignore the environmental impact of their operations in other countries, several international agreements specify the duties of the multinational company regarding the environment.

In spite of the existence of extensive agreements and organizations governing multinational ethical behavior, there are several reasons why multinational companies may not follow the ethical principles summarized in Exhibit 4.8:[25]

- *Governments make agreements:* Most international agreements are between governments, not the multinational companies themselves. However, multinational companies do fall under the jurisdiction of the governments involved in the pacts.
- *The agreements have only voluntary compliance:* Without an international enforcement agency, some argue that it is impossible to expect multinational firms to follow any code of ethical behavior.[26]
- *Not all governments subscribe to the agreements:* Governments often reflect their own geopolitical interests and cultural and religious biases. Even if they are a party to the agreements governing multinational-company behaviors, governments may choose to ignore them.
- *Each of the agreements is an incomplete moral guide to the company:* It is probably impossible to arrive at an agreement that can cover all the ethical consequences of a firm's operations.

EXHIBIT   4.8   **A Code of Conduct for the Multinational Company**

Respect Basic Human Rights and Freedoms

- Respect fundamental human rights of life, liberty, security, and privacy
- Do not discriminate on the basis of race, color, gender, religion, language, ethnic origin, or political affiliation
- Respect personal freedoms (e.g., religion, opinion)

Maintain High Standards of Local Political Involvement

- Avoid illegal involvement in local politics
- Don't pay bribes or other improper payments
- Do not interfere in local government internal relations

Transfer Technology

- Enhance the transfer of technology to developing nations
- Adapt technologies to local needs
- Conduct local R&D when possible
- Grant fair licenses to use technology

Protect the Environment

- Follow local environmental-protection laws
- Actively protect the environment
- Repair damage to the environment done by company operations

- Help develop local standards
- Provide accurate assessments of environmental impact of the company
- Provide complete disclosure of the environmental effects of operations
- Develop standards to monitor environmental effects

Consumer Protection

- Follow local consumer-protection laws
- Ensure accurate and proper safety disclosures

Employment Practices

- Follow relevant policies and employment laws of host nation
- Help create jobs in needed areas
- Increase local employment opportunities and standards
- Provide local workers stable employment and job security
- Promote equal employment opportunities
- Give priority to local national residents when possible
- Provide training opportunities at all levels for local employees
- Promote local nationals to management positions
- Respect local collective-bargaining rights
- Cooperate with local collective-bargaining units
- Give notice of plant closings
- Do not use threat of leaving country in collective-bargaining dealings
- Provide income protection to terminated workers
- Match or improve local standards of employment
- Protect employees with adequate health and safety standards
- Provide employees information on job-related health hazards

Sources: Adapted from Getz, Kathleen A. 1990. "International codes of conduct: An analysis of ethical reasoning." Journal of Business Ethics 9: pp. 567–78; and Frederick, William C. 1991. "The moral authority of transnational corporate codes." Journal of Business Ethics 10: pp. 165–177.

Although the sources of agreements that govern the ethical behavior of multinational companies are diverse and are not always enforceable, the agreements are useful. They provide a safe guide to ethical management for multinational managers. It is likely that, if one follows the code of conduct shown in Exhibit 4.8, both in individual behavior and in guiding a company, one will generally be on safe ethical and legal ground in nearly all situations. However, to ensure that the code of ethics is effective in preventing unethical behaviors, practitioners[27] suggest a number of "best practices" steps:

- *Leading by example:* International executives and other managers need to adhere to the code of ethics since employees often base their behaviors on their superiors.
- *Making ethics part of the corporate culture:* Multinational managers need to make sure that employees are fully aware of ethical guidelines and codes and "live" them through training programs, handbooks, and clear communication channels. Similarly, when new employees are hired, they need to be carefully screened for consistency with the code of ethics and also to be trained.
- *Involving employees at all levels:* Codes of ethics are clearly more effective when affected parties are involved in making the rules. As such, not only are more people going to be aware of these guidelines, but they also are more likely to know how they apply to practical situations.
- *Setting and monitoring goals:* Codes of ethics need to be embodied in performance indicators (e.g., code of conduct awareness and signatures, training records, help-line trends) that are monitored to determine the effectiveness of the program.
- *Effective integration in business processes:* A code of ethics is only effective if employees clearly know how it affects them. Multinational companies should develop policies and procedures regarding how to implement the code of ethics.
- *Open discussion of ethics and other ethical issues:* Managers need to regularly address ethical issues of great importance. Employees also need to feel free to voice their ethics-related concerns when necessary.

This list is not necessarily comprehensive, but it provides some basic steps to ensure that the code of ethics works. The following Multinational Management Brief on page 192 discusses Citigroup's efforts to change the corporate culture to become more ethical.

The next section concludes this chapter with a focus on ethical decision making for the individual multinational manager.

The Ethical Dilemma in Multinational Management: How Will you Decide?

The potentially wide differences in ethical systems and in how ethics are managed create dilemmas for multinational managers. This section looks first at the issue of what ethical system one should use—your own country's or that of the host country. It concludes with a description of an ethical decision model for the multinational manager.

Ethical Relativism versus Ethical Universalism

Throughout our study of multinational management, this text shows the extensive effects of differences in cultural values on all areas of management. However, this is nowhere more apparent than in the difficulties multinational

Multinational Management **Brief**

Building an Ethical Culture at Citigroup

Most financial institutions have received their share of attention for ethical lapses in the 1980s and 1990s. Citigroup, a leading global financial services company operating in more than 100 countries with more than 200 million customers, has not escaped such negative attention. Furthermore, Citigroup was forced to close its private bank in Japan because of the unethical behaviors of a few employees. Additionally, it was also being questioned for potentially damaging activities in Europe.

When Charles Prince took over as CEO in 2003, he set the goal of making Citigroup the most respected financial services company in the world. To understand why there were so many ethical lapses, Prince traveled around the world and spoke to 30,000 employees, representing 10 percent of Citigroup's workforce. Not surprisingly, one major culprit was the intense focus on short-term financial results or "making the numbers." This focus on short-term results combined with drastic cost-cutting measures led to a company focusing exclusively on results at the expense of employees.

To change the culture and integrate more ethics, Prince launched the Five Point Plan in March 2005. The Plan is centered around three major themes: (1) responsibility to customers by always putting customers first and providing products/advice with the highest level of integrity, (2) responsibility to employees by providing the environment where employees can realize their potential and where diversity is championed, and (3) responsibility to the company by putting the company's long-term interest ahead of short-term results through respect of local cultures and involvement in local communities.

To implement this ambitious plan, Citigroup embarked on a number of major initiatives including extensive ethics training for all employees on an annual basis and expanded management training. The human resource department is also playing an important role by developing plans to better appraise employees. Initiatives to promote diversity are also being implemented. The HR department has also revamped performance appraisals to balance profits and ethics. Finally, Citigroup is also encouraging two-way communication between employees and managers. Even Prince is involved in bimonthly conversations with senior managers.

Source: Based Harker, John. 2005. "Ethics and strategy innovation at Citigroup." Strategic HR Review, 4, 6, pp. 16–19.

---

companies face in determining how to deal with ethical differences among the countries in which they do business. Do you impose your own country's ethical system everywhere you do business or do you follow the maxim, "When in Rome, do as the Romans do"?

In Chapter 2, the text introduced the concept of cultural relativism. As you remember, cultural relativism represents the philosophical position of the science of anthropology: All cultures are legitimate and viable as a means for people to guide their lives—that is, what people consider right or wrong, pretty or ugly, good or bad, depends on their cultural norms and values.

Ethical relativism

Theory that each society's view of ethics must be considered legitimate and ethical.

There is a similar concept in business ethics, called **ethical relativism**. Ethical relativism means that a multinational manager considers each society's view of ethics as legitimate and ethical. For example, if the people in one country believe something like assisted suicide to be morally wrong, then for them it is morally wrong. If, on the other hand, people from another country believe that assisted suicide is morally correct, then for them it is not immoral. For multinational companies, ethical relativism means that when doing business in a country managers need only follow local ethical conventions. Thus, for example, if bribery is an accepted way of doing business in a country, then it is okay for a multinational manager to follow local examples, even if it would be illegal at home. Consider the following Comparative Management Brief.

The opposite of ethical relativism is **ethical universalism.** Ethical universalism holds that there are basic moral principles that transcend cultural and national boundaries. All cultures, for example, have rules that prohibit murder, at least of their own people.

The difficulty in using ethical universalism as a guide for multinational business practices is that there is little agreement on which moral principles exist in all cultures. Moreover, even when the same principles are used, there is no guarantee that all societies use the principles in the same way. For example, two societies may prohibit murder. However, so that the group has a better chance of surviving, a society with food resources marginal for survival may force the aged to commit suicide or may kill newborn girls to keep the population

Ethical universalism

Theory that there are basic moral principles that transcend cultural and national boundaries.

Comparative Management **Brief**

Chinese Guanxis: Are They Ethical?

Most experts agree that the Chinese economy will continue experiencing tremendous growth. The opportunities for business in China will likely stay strong. However, doing business will also become more complex and challenging. Consider the case of guanxis, which are special relationships among Chinese companies that rely on trust, favor, and interdependence. Companies that are within the same network or guanxi are bound by expectations of reciprocal obligations and are expected to give preferential treatments to other members within the same network. As such, Western companies have often argued that such arrangements lead to unethical behaviors, bribery, and corruption. In the absence of a good legal infrastructure, guanxis lead to unethical behaviors as members within the same network engage in under-the-table dealings and give preferential treatment to each other.

However, for the Chinese, a guanxi network is indispensable for efficiently doing business and is therefore ethical. Guanxis substitute for the poorly developed legal and distribution systems in China. For instance, instead of dealing with complicated administrative procedures regarding distribution whereby export companies may be faced with complex customs clearance rules and difficulties with securing raw materials and finished goods, these companies are more likely to develop special relationships with local customs officials and other trading firms in order to ensure smooth and speedy delivery. Similarly, the Chinese are more likely to engage in conflict resolution based on trust within their network rather than rely on the open but poorly developed commercial laws.

As such, for the ethical relativist, guanxis are acceptable as they represent legitimate views of Chinese business society. Furthermore, most foreign companies find that they need to rely on these personal connections to do business. However, ethical universalists most likely view guanxis as unethical as they violate transparency norms.

Sources: Based on Chan, Ricky Y.K., Louis T.W. Cheng, and Ricky W.F. Szeto. 2002. "The dynamics of guanxi and ethics for Chinese executives." Journal of Business Ethics 41: pp. 327–36; Graham, John L. and N. Mark Lam. 2003. "The Chinese negotiator." Harvard Business Review, October, pp. 29–39; Lieberthal, Kenneth, and Geoffrey Lieberthal. 2003. "The great transition." Harvard Business Review, October, pp. 13–27; Su, Chenting, M. Joseph Sirgy, and James E. Littlefield, 2003. "Is guanxi orientation bad, ethically speaking? A study of Chinese enterprises." Journal of Business Ethics 44: pp. 303–12.

down. They certainly do not consider this "murder," but rather an ethical way to ensure the survival of the group. Most societies tolerate some form of killing, such as in executions of criminals or in wars. Even though people die by human action, these acts are not defined as murder but as legitimate acts of society.

For the multinational company, however, there are practical problems for following either ethical relativism or ethical universalism. Some ethicists argue that cultural relativism, while a necessary condition for conducting unbiased anthropological research, cannot be applied to ethics. Thomas Donaldson, for example, argues that multinational companies have a higher moral responsibility than ethical relativism.[28] He notes that, at the extreme, ethical relativism can become convenient relativism. Convenient relativism occurs when companies use the logic of ethical relativism to behave any way that they please, using the excuse of differences in cultures. Donaldson gives the example of child labor in developing countries. In some cases, children as young as seven years of age work for a pittance wage producing products that eventually are used by large multinational companies.

Extreme moral universalism also has its pitfalls. The assumption that one can identify universal ethics that all people should follow can lead to a type of ethnocentrism that Donaldson calls cultural imperialism. That is, managers who assume that they know the correct and ethical ways of behaving can easily view the moral systems of foreign cultures as inferior or immoral. This is particularly dangerous when the multinational is a big and financially powerful company with subsidiaries located in the developing world.

Individual Ethical Decision Making for the Multinational Manager

Although companies develop policies, procedures, organizational cultures, and business practices that have ethical consequences, individual managers ultimately must make decisions.

The first duty for a manager is to consider whether a decision makes business sense. This is called the economic analysis. In the economic analysis, the prime interest focuses on making the best decision for a company's profits. However, if profits alone guided ethical decision making, managers could worry little about how their decisions affected anyone except the owners of the company. Some argue that this is not ethics at all since businesses could engage in deceptive and dangerous practices with only the marketplace to control their actions.

After considering the business impact of a decision, multinational managers must consider the legal and ethical consequences of their actions.[29] Exhibit 4.9 shows a decision flowchart that illustrates the issues multinational managers must consider beyond profits when confronted with ethical decisions.

In the legal analysis of an ethical problem, the manager focuses first on meeting the laws of the country in which his or her company is operating, or, if required, the laws of the home country as well. Should the law not forbid something, it is ethical. In a combination of pure economic and legal analyses, managers should seek to maximize profits within the confines of the letter of the law. The law in this sense provides the "rules of the game" under which companies and people compete. Since different countries have different legal systems, a multinational manager using only a legal analysis of an ethical problem is free to behave within the law in each country, provided that his or her own country does not require following its own laws. Some scholars, such as the Nobel Laureate Milton Friedman, believe that profit maximization—within the rules of the game of open and free competition—is the main ethical

Convenient relativism
What occurs when companies use the logic of ethical relativism to behave any way they please, using the excuse of differences in cultures.

Economic analysis
Of an ethical problem, focuses on what is the best decision for a company's profits.

Legal analysis
Of an ethical problem, focuses on only meeting legal requirements of host and parent countries.

EXHIBIT   4.9   **Decision Points for Ethical Decision Making in Multinational Management**

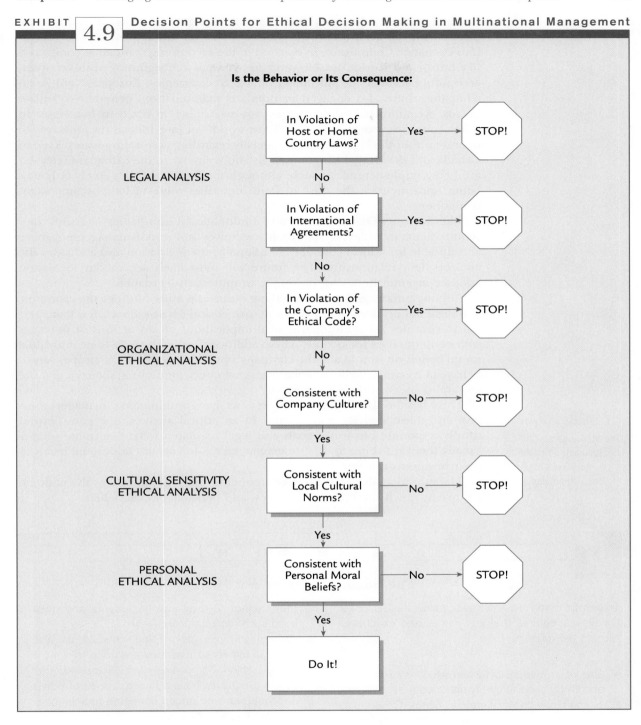

responsibility of business.[30] Many multinational managers also believe that the legal analysis includes not only a test of whether a behavior or its consequences meet legal standards in the home and host countries, but also a comparison against international standards. These standards come from the international agreements among nations, identified earlier, and the resulting code, summarized in Exhibit 4.9.

An important legislation that pertains to legal behavior with ethical implications is the 2002 Sarbanes-Oxley Act. This act was approved by the Securities Exchange Commission in reaction to the accounting scandals at companies like Enron and WorldCom. However, as we saw at the beginning of this chapter, accounting scandals do not affect only U.S. companies. European and Asian companies have also engaged in numbers manipulation, generally to inflate profits. As multinational companies get even more involved in businesses in other countries, executives around the world will face increasing pressures to operate within the legal bounds, especially regarding accounting issues. Even in Canada and the United Kingdom, legislations similar to the Sarbanes-Oxley Act are being implemented. As such, although the Sarbanes-Oxley Act is only now being implemented, the Case in Point describes some of its most important components.

The Sarbanes-Oxley Act requires multinational companies to satisfy new requirements in order to hold their executives and senior management more accountable for ethical conduct. Additionally, the legislation also addresses the auditor-client relationship. The future will most likely see similar legislation adopted around the world, making it an important legislation.

Although managers in profit-making businesses must consider the economic and legal implications of any decision with ethical consequences, few managers fail to consider the additional ethical implications of any actions or practices with consequences for people. These additional issues include their individual moral beliefs on how to act, the company's policies regarding the proper way to behave in treating all constituents (e.g., customers, employees, society), and the cultural context of the ethical issue.[31]

Ethical analysis
One that goes beyond focusing on profit goals and legal regulations.

Thus, besides the economic and legal analysis, multinational managers must give an **ethical analysis** to problems. In an ethical analysis, one goes beyond simply responding to profit goals and legal regulations. To determine what is "really the right thing to do," managers take into account additional issues in their business decisions.

The ethical analysis has three components: one's organization, the national culture in which the business operates, and personal ethical beliefs.

CASE IN POINT

The Sarbanes-Oxley Act

To prevent Enron-like financial scandals, the Sarbanes-Oxley Act requires that companies and executives respect the following rules:

- *Executive responsibility and accountability:* CEOs and CFOs need to certify under oath the accuracy of their company's financial filings. Other rules include requiring executives to promptly disclose sales of shares in the company. Executives cannot sell shares if other employees cannot.
- *Auditor responsibility:* Auditors are also prohibited from doing certain non-audit work. They are also required to change clients after five years. Finally,

they cannot destroy any documents and must keep such records for five years.

- *Company responsibility:* Filing schedules are also being modified so that they are done in a more timely fashion. Companies must disclose whether senior executives have adopted a code of ethics and whether their audit committee has an independent financial expert.

Source: Based on Bednarz, Ann. 2003. "Legislation refocuses corp. reporting systems." Network World, http://www.nwfusion.com; Economist. 2003c. "Wishy-washy." February 1, p. 60; Hall, Linda A., and Chris Gaetanos. 2006. "Treatment of Section 404 compliance costs." The CPA Journal, 76, 3: pp. 58–62; and Messmer, Max. 2003. "Does your company have a code of ethics?" Strategic Finance, April, pp. 13–14.

In the organizational ethical analysis, managers must look to their written codes of ethics and the unwritten norms of the company culture. Many organizations have ethical codes that specify the principles by which managers must guide their decision making and behaviors. When referring to the ethical code as a guide, managers use deontological ethical reasoning—they know and follow the written rules. In addition, all organizations have company cultures that have unwritten rules that prescribe or proscribe behaviors. In some companies, for example, all managers would know informal rules, such as, "Profit is more important than the environment as long as you follow the letter of the law" or "Give the bribe if it gets the job done and no one gets hurt or caught." A manager might better understand the ethical bases of the company's culture by understanding the moral language used. For example, is it maximizing the greatest welfare or is it avoiding harm?

Multinational managers are guests in other nations. As such, their ethical decision making must go beyond legal constraints and following company rules and cultural norms. The managers must ask themselves whether what they are doing is consistent with and respectful of local cultural norms. For example, should they have employees work on a religious holiday in one country because other units throughout the world are having regular business days?

A manager may begin these analyses at different points. For some issues, one may consider personal moral beliefs first. For other issues, it may make more sense to consider the law. At some point, however, after considering all components in managerial decision making, the manager must make a personal moral judgment. Is it right for you? You are ultimately responsible. Most courts of law throughout the world will not accept the defense "The organization made me do it."

Thus, for the multinational manager, the purely ethical issues in a decision must be weighed against the economic and legal analyses that also influence the decision. A business must make a profit to survive; people don't want to go to jail or be fined; and most people want to behave ethically as they understand it. Often there will be no easy answer. For example, should a manager move a factory to a country with a cheaper labor force—even if it hurts the people who will lose their jobs? Should a multinational company sell potentially dangerous but useful products to a Third World country because the people in that country can only afford the cheaper but less safe products? Should a multinational company ignore the use of child labor by some of its suppliers if the company realizes the children's families desperately need the money and their competitors will use these suppliers if they don't?

When faced with such complex conflicts among economics, law, and ethics, how do managers know if they are behaving ethically? Although there is no resolution to every ethical dilemma faced by every individual and in every culture, one aid to ethical decision making is to analyze one's decisions using philosophical ethical theories.

Unfortunately, there is no single accepted ethical theory or system that managers can use for a guide when they face difficult ethical problems. Philosophers have debated for millennia the merits of various systems. However, there are generally accepted ethical theories that managers can use to help understand ethical problems and the nature of their ethical decisions.

Although an ethical analysis such as that suggested in Exhibit 4.9 does not provide the "right" answer to an ethical problem, it does offer an understanding of the reasons behind ethical choices. It also raises the businessperson's awareness regarding the ethical nature of business decisions.

Summary and Conclusions

The multinational manager faces ethical challenges similar to the domestic manager, but the challenges are magnified by the complexity of working in different countries and cultures. Part of this chapter provided essential background information on business ethics useful for ethics management in all settings. Understanding the relationship between ethics and social responsibility; how ethical philosophies underlay much of our ethical reasoning; and the differences among financial, legal, and ethical analyses provide a starting point for understanding international business ethics.

Unlike the domestic-only manager, the multinational manager must be able to assess how a country's social institutions and culture will affect his or her ability to manage ethical behavior. The examples showed that differences in legal and religious institutions and basic cultural values often lead to different perceptions of what is ethical in business. Although there is some evidence of a convergence in business ethics due to the increase in international trade and investment, a multinational manager can never be too sensitive to issues as important as moral behavior in another culture.

Besides understanding the cultural setting in which they operate, multinational managers can never ignore their home country laws. In this regard, the U.S. manager probably faces the strictest constraints. The FCPA represents an important law that constrains U.S. managers from behaving in ways that, while accepted in other societies, are off limits to U.S. managers. All multinational managers, regardless of national origin, should be aware of the international agreements to which their country is party. Following the summary of these agreements, as shown in Exhibit 4.8, will likely help managers avoid legal and ethical difficulties in their international operations.

The chapter concluded with a decision model for making ethical decisions in a multinational setting. Although the model does not tell you what to do, it does provide a variety of issues that a manager should consider. Managing ethically in the international environment is not always easy, but certainly it is a challenge that will continue to grow with increasing interactions among nations.

Discussion Questions

1. Discuss some of the issues that make international business ethics more complex than domestic business ethics.

2. What is ethical relativism? What are some of the dangers of using ethical relativism to justify all ethical decisions?

3. How do legal and ethical analyses differ? Give some examples. Can a manager behave ethically just by following the host country's laws? Explain.

4. Discuss the difference between teleological and deontological theories of ethics. Give examples of how an international manager might appeal to either type of theory when faced with the opportunity to offer a bribe.

5. How do social institutions and culture affect the practice of business ethics in different countries? How do these differences affect managers who take the moral positions of ethical relativism and ethical universalism?

6. Discuss the arguments regarding whether businesses from other nations should follow the U.S. FCPA.

7. Discuss reasons why there is a trend toward a universal code of business ethics.

Multinational Management **Skill Builder**

Rex Lewis's Ethical Dilemma

Step 1. Reread the section on Thomas Donaldson's views on moral languages.

Step 2. Read the following scenario.

Rex Lewis is a 25-year-old manager for ICS Corp., a small U.S. manufacturer of dietary supplements. After graduation, Mr. Lewis worked at company headquarters in Lexington, Nebraska in a variety of positions. As a former international business major, Mr. Lewis jumped at the chance to take a position as country manager in Matinea. Mr. Lewis studied the Matinean language for four years and visited the country for a summer while an undergraduate. He feels confident that he can handle this position since he has both the managerial and cultural experience.

ICS's major product is supall, a dietary supplement that is inexpensive to produce and can provide children with all of their basic nutritional needs. This product is very attractive to poor countries such as Matinea, where agricultural production is not sufficient to feed the population and recent droughts have made the situation even worse. Although cheaper than a well-rounded basic diet, one child's monthly supply of supall costs about one-quarter of an average worker's salary at current prices, and most families are quite large.

In his first week in Matinea, Mr. Lewis makes a variety of startling discoveries. In spite of the relatively high price of SUPALL, demand in the Matinean market is quite strong. Moreover, ICS is making a 50 percent return on SUPALL! Now Mr. Lewis realizes why the revenues from SUPALL have been able to support his company's crucial R&D research on other products. When he worked back in the United States, the CEO told him personally that if ICS doesn't come up with new products soon, the big companies will soon have a SUPALL-type product, and the price will fall drastically.

Mr. Lewis, who considers himself a good Christian, begins to wonder whether the price is fair for the Matineans. The price of SUPALL is cheaper than food, but it takes virtually all of a family's income to buy it. Yet, ICS needs the profits to survive. Mr. Lewis has the authority to set prices in the country, but he must justify his decision to headquarters back in the United States.

Step 3. Divide the class into six teams, one for each moral language. Each team represents a version of the ICS Corp. but with a corporate culture dominated by one of the moral languages.

Step 4. As a team, review Exhibit 4.9 and conduct the relevant analyses. Come to a consensus and give a recommendation to Rex Lewis.

Step 5. Present and discuss your findings with the entire class.

Endnotes

[1] Woods, Walter. 2006. "Hyundai scandal delays 2nd plant." *The Atlanta Journal-Constitution,* April 25, p. C4.

[2] Buchholz, Rogene A. 1989. *Fundamental Concepts and Problems in Business Ethics.* Englewood Cliffs, N.J.: Prentice Hall.

[3] Cullen, John B., Bart Victor, and Carroll Stephens. 1989. "An ethical weather report: Assessing the organization's ethical climate." *Organizational Dynamics,* 18: p. 50–62.

[4] Ferrell, O.C., John Fraedrich, and Linda Ferrell. 2005. *Business Ethics.* New York: Houghton Mifflin Company.

[5] Hall, Jeremy, and Harrie Vredenburg. 2005. "Managing stakeholder ambiguity." *MIT Sloan Management Review,* 47, 1, p. 11–13.

[6] Buchholz, *Fundamental Concepts and Problems in Business Ethics.*

[7] Donaldson, Thomas. 1992. "The language of international corporate ethics." *Business Ethics Quarterly 2: p. 271–281.*

[8] Ibid.

[9] Cullen, J.B., K. Praveen Parboteeah, and Martin Hoegl. 2004. "Cross-national differences in managers' willingness to justify ethically suspect behaviors: A test of institutional anomie theory." *Academy of Management Journal* 47, 3: pp. 410–421.

[10] Messner, S.F., and R. Rosenfeld. 2001. *Crime and the American Dream.* Belmont, CA: Wadsworth.

[11] Schlegelmilch, Bobo B., and Diana C. Robertson. 1995. "The influence of country and industry on ethical perceptions of senior executives in the U.S. and Europe." *Journal of International Business Studies,* 4th quarter: pp. 859–881.

[12] Mendenhall, Mark E., Betty Jane Punnet, and David Ricks. 1994. *Global Management*. Cambridge, Mass.: Blackwell.

[13] Comte, O., A. Lambert-Mogiliansky, and T. Verdier. 2005. "Corruption and competition in procurement actions." *The Rand Journal of Economics, 36, 1: pp. 1–15.*

[14] Bayar, Guzin. 2005. "The role of intermediaries in corruption." *Public Choice, 122: pp. 277–298.*

[15] Soon, Lim Ghee. 2006. "Macro-economic outcomes of corruption: A longitudinal empirical study." *Singapore Management Review, 28, 1, pp. 63–72.*

[16] Transparency International. 2006. "2005 Bribe payers index." http://www.transparency.org/cpi/

[17] Gleich, Oren, and Ryan Woodward. 2005. "Foreign corrupt practices act." *The American Criminal Law Review, 42, 2: pp. 545–571.*

[18] Borrus, Amy, Stewart Toy, and Peggy Salz-Trautman. 1995. "Investigations: A world of greased palms." *BusinessWeek Online,* November 6.

[19] *BusinessWeek.* 1983. "The arbitrary act splits executives," September 19, p. 16.

[20] Graham, John. 1983. "Foreign Corrupt Practices Act: A manager's guide." *Columbia Journal of World Business,* 18: pp. 89–94.

[21] Borrus, Toy, and Salz-Trautman, "Investigations: A world of greased palms"; Koretz, Gene. 1996. "Bribes can cost the U.S. an edge: In some spots, honesty doesn't pay." *BusinessWeek Online,* April 15.

[22] Donaldson, Thomas. 1989. *The Ethics of International Business.* New York: Oxford University Press; Donaldson, "The language of

international corporate ethics."; Donaldson, 1992, "The language of international corporate ethics."

[23] Frederick, William C. 1991. "The moral authority of transnational corporate codes." *Journal of Business Ethics* 10: pp. 165–177; Getz, Kathleen A. 1990. "International codes of conduct: An analysis of ethical reasoning." *Journal of Business Ethics, 9: pp. 567–578.*

[24] Frederick, "The moral authority of transnational corporate codes."

[25] Ibid.

[26] Velasquez, Manuel. 1992. "International business, morality, and the common good." *Business Ethics Quarterly,* 2: pp. 27–40.

[27] Coughlan, Richard. 2003. "Demystifying business ethics." *Successful Meetings,* May: pp. 33–34; Everson, Miles, Charles Ilako, and Carlo di Florio. 2003. "Corporate governance, business ethics, and global compliance management." *ABA Bank Compliance,* March/April: pp. 22–32; Messmer, Max. 2003. "Does your company have a code of ethics?" *Strategic Finance,* April, pp. 13–14.

[28] Donaldson, Thomas. 1992. "Can multinationals stage a universal morality play?" *Business and Society Review,* pp. 51–55.

[29] Hosmer, Larue Tone. 1987. *The Ethics of Management.* Homewood, IL: Irwin.

[30] Friedman, Milton. 1970. "The social responsibility of business is to increase its profits." *New York Times Magazine,* September 13, pp. 122–126.

[31] Victor, Bart, and John B. Cullen. 1988. "The organizational bases of ethical work climates." *Administrative Science Quarterly* 33: pp. 101–125.

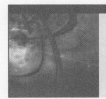

Tee-Shirts and Tears: Third World Suppliers to First World Markets

"The hottest places in hell are reserved for those who, in a period of moral crisis, maintain their neutrality."

— *Dante*

Recent media attention has heightened our awareness of labor conditions in third world countries. While Americans otherwise may have been able to write off substandard labor conditions as another case of cultural variations, these recent cases garnered domestic interest as a result of the parties involved. Their names are about as American as apple pie: The Gap, Kathie Lee Gifford, even Michael Jordan. These are the contractors, the investors, the spokespeople who represent "sweatshops" where, allegedly, young girls are allowed only two restroom visits per day and, allegedly, the days sometimes consist of twenty-one straight hours of work.

Labor Conditions in the United States

America's garment industry today grosses $45 billion per year and employs more than one million workers.[1] Uproar began in the Fall of 1995 when Secretary of Labor Robert Reich announced the names of several large retailers who may have been involved in an El Monte, California, sweatshop operation. Notwithstanding the fact that the retailers are not liable for the conditions if they have no knowledge of them, the companies involved in this situation agreed to adopt a statement of principles which would require their suppliers to adhere to U.S. federal labor laws.[2] Reich followed this announcement with an appearance on the *Phil Donahue Show* where he discussed a situation at another

plant that employed Thai workers at less than $1.00 per hour and kept its workers behind a barbed-wire fence. Retailers respond that it is difficult, if not impossible to police their suppliers and subcontractors, who may total more than 20,000 in some cases. And the pressures of the situation are only becoming worse. The apparel industry, which has borne the brunt of Reich's focus, is highly competitive, and extremely labor-intensive. Competition from companies in other countries that do not impose similar labor condition requirements is fierce. Consequently, one is not surprised to learn that a 1994 Labor Department spot check of garment operations in California found that 93% had health and safety violations.[3]

Manufacturers may have a bit more to be concerned about than retailers. Reich has recently invoked a little-used provision in the Fair Labor Standards Act that holds manufacturers liable for the wrongful acts of their suppliers and that allows for the confiscation of goods produced by sweatshop operations.

Reich has now appealed to the retailers and manufacturers alike to conduct their own random spot checks. "We need to enlist retailers as adjunct policemen. At a time when business says to government, 'Get off our back. We can do it ourselves,' we're giving them the opportunity," Reich notes.[4] In June, 1995, Reich established a consortium to police working conditions made up of manufacturers. The group, called "Compliance Alliance," will police contractors conducting regular audits and will identify firms that pay less than minimum wage or otherwise violate the provisions of the Fair Labor Standards Act.[5]

The Clinton Administration's voluntary Model Business Principles, published in May, 1995, are relevant to this discussion. The principles encourage all businesses to adopt and implement voluntary codes of conduct for doing business around the world and suggest appropriate code coverage. In addition, under former secretary Robert Reich's direction, the Department of Labor has established a "No Sweat" campaign to encourage American apparel manufacturers to end sweatshop labor throughout the world.[6] The campaign is based on the belief that consumers will be willing to pay more for garments under a manufacturer guarantee on the label that the product was made without sweatshop labor. On the other hand, critics of the campaign claim that the proposed label is like "the Good Housekeeping seal of approval to a kinder, gentler sweatshop,"[7] and that the agreement to monitor conditions and to use these labels does not go far enough, basically calling for practices already adopted by firms.

American Attention Drifts Toward Other Countries

Neil Kearney, general secretary of the International Textile, Garment and Leather Workers' Federation, describes the garment workplace as follows:

> The reality today is that most of the 30 million jobs in the fashion industry around the world are low paid, often based in export processing zones where worker rights are usually suppressed. Wages are frequently below the subsistence level and falling in real terms. . . . Management by terror is the norm in many countries. Workers are routinely shoved, beaten, and kicked, even when pregnant. Attempts to unionize are met with the utmost brutality, sometimes with murder.[8]

Once the American public considered its own conditions, it looked to other countries to see how labor was treated there. Following Reich's slap on the hand to American manufacturers, media attention turned toward the conditions in third world countries and toward American responsibility for or involvement in those conditions. In 1970, there were 7,000 multinational companies in the world. Today, there are more than 35,000.[9] The topic of conditions in those multinationals was destined for afternoon talk shows once it was announced that television personality Kathie Lee Gifford endorsed a line of clothing that had been made for Wal-Mart in

Honduran sweatshops. These operations employed underage and pregnant women for more than 20-hour days at $0.31 per hour. The conditions were extremely hot and no worker was allowed to speak during the entire day.

The situation was brought to the attention of the press by Charles Kernaghan, director of the National Labor Committee based in New York City. Kernaghan informed Gifford, and the press, of the conditions in the plant and asked her to respond. Gifford's immediate response was to immediately break off her relationship with the company.[10] Unfortunately, this is not what is always best for the exploited workers. Instead, Kernaghan impressed upon her the need to remain involved and to use her position and reputation to encourage a change in the conditions at the plants.

These arguments may remind the reader of those waged several years ago regarding divestment from South Africa. Proponents of investment argued that the only way to effect change would be to remain actively involved in the operations of the South African business community. Others argued that no ethical company should pour money into a country where apartheid conditions were allowed to exist. The same arguments can and have been made about conducting business in third world countries, and Gifford found herself right in the middle of them.

The El Salvadoran Labor Environment

El Salvador is a country that has been ravaged by internal conflicts culminating in a civil war that lasted for many years. In 1992, with the advent of peace, the country sought to rebuild what it had lost during wartime and is now considered one of the fastest growing economies in Latin America.[11] The objective of the El Salvadorans involved in the rebuilding process was to help the poor to overcome the conditions of poverty, dependence and oppression that they had experienced during the conflict. While the objectives of private investors may be different, all seem to share a common interest in social stability and development. Economist Louis Emmerij notes that the leading cause of social unrest is "the lack of sufficient and renumerative employment opportunities, bad living conditions, and the lack of perspective and hope."[12]

In developing countries like El Salvador, long-term strategies for improving a poor household's ability to generate disposable income on a sustained basis must consider if households have the skills, education, and know-how to allow them to operate in the market. These strategies include support for training and education, access to markets and access to technology and credit. A large part of the labor problem in the *maquiladores* is the lack of agreement between the workers and management as to the minimum level of productivity expected per day, the level of compensation for a worker who achieves that level, and who should assume the burden of training in order to increase productivity.

Yet, low wages are the prime magnet for multinational firms coming to El Salvador. In 1990, a glossy full-color advertisement appeared in a major American apparel trade magazine showing a woman at a sewing machine and proclaiming, "Rosa Martinez produces apparel for U.S. markets on her sewing machine in El Salvador. *You* can hire her for 57 cents an hour." One year later, the same ad announced that Rosa's salary had gone down—*"You* can hire her for 33 cents an hour."[13] It appears that the publicists felt that Rosa's salary originally looked too high, in the eyes of the market players.

Critical to understanding these conflicts is an understanding of the Salvadoran culture itself. Salvadoran workers are not exempt from the consequences of their history. When they enter the work place, they expect to be exploited and do not trust management. In addition, as a result of the repressive conditions in El Salvador during the war, the society suffers from a general lack of candor and a tendency on the part of individuals to protect themselves by not telling the truth.[14] But this quality is different from the deception that occurs in American business dealings. In this situation, it serves as a means of self-protection in a culture that offers little else. Moreover, the government does not protect individual and business interests, thereby allowing cartels to develop, flourish, and continue.

The author of this case had the opportunity to travel to El Salvador in 1996 in order to observe a class in financial administration at an El Salvadoran university. During the course of a quiz in the class, the professor had reason to leave the classroom for a moment. Upon his return, he found that the students were now collaborating on the answers to the quiz. During the discussion that later ensued regarding the students' actions, the students articulated a need to help each other to succeed. They felt that they should bind together in order to help them all to move forward. If this meant helping a colleague who did not have time to study because he had to work to support his family, in addition to attending school, that seemed acceptable, if not necessary and ethical.[15]

During that same course, the graduate students (most, if not all, of whom worked full time in professional positions) were asked to identify the principal barriers to trust in Salvadoran business relationships, and the means by which those barriers could be broken down. Students responded as follows (translated from Spanish):

> One barrier is that the big businesses are formed at the level of families and friends that form a close nucleus, prohibiting others from entering. The government does not enact laws to guarantee business interests and growth without the intervention of stronger, "bully" businesses.
>
> There is a failure of information—only certain people have access to the most important, business-related information. There is no requirement that business share information, even at a level that would mimic the American SEC requirements.
>
> Create legal mechanisms that sanction companies violating the rules. These sanctions do not exist. Companies use illicit means to take advantage of their competitors and employing the same means is the only way to compete.
>
> The period since the war has seen an increase in vandalism at an individual and corporate level, making it difficult to carry on a business.[16]

Consider the expectation of conflict in this scenario recounted by Fr. David Blanchard, Pastor of the Our Lady of Lourdes Church in Calle Real Epiphany Cooperative Association:

> In February of 1994, the cooperative had a serious labor conflict. The women became quite adept at sewing lab coats. But in February, 1994, when the only contract available was for sewing hospital bathrobes, a serious labor conflict arose. Unfortunately, the women who were elected by their peers to negotiate with the contractor made some serious errors in judgment when they calculated the time required to sew this item.

At the time, some women were earning 80 colones daily (twice the minimum wage). Most were making 50 colones. Only a few apprentices were making less than the minimum wage.

With the transition to sewing bathrobes, production and therefore income, was cut in half. Six of the highest wage earners subsequently staged a sit-down strike at their machines, claiming that they were being oppressed. Father Blanchard asked, "Who negotiated your contract?"

"Our representatives," they said.

"Who elected your representatives?"

"We did."

"Who will suffer if this work is not completed?"

"We will."

These women had entered this project with no prior skills. They had received high-quality and expensive technical, legal and social training. They were all self-employed, but when their wages plunged, they felt oppressed, frustrated and angry, and ended up leaving the cooperative. . . . Some of these women will continue to suffer in poverty. It is certain that they are victims. But they are the victims of hundreds of years of oppression and not of the immediate circumstances sewing hospital bathrobes. They responded to the problems created by the lack of education and their lack of abilities by generating conflict.[17]

Blanchard remarks that Salvadoran industrialists and managers are even more strident in generating conflict in the work place. For instance, consider the case of the Mandarin factory and many other similar plants throughout El Salvador.

The Mandarin Plant and its Labor Conditions

The San Salvador Mandarin International plant was established in order to assemble goods to be shipped to the U.S. under contract with major U.S. retailers such as The Gap and Eddie Bauer. The plant was built in the San Marcos Free Trade Zone, a zone owned by the former Salvadoran Army Colonel Mario Guerrero and created with money from the Bush Administration's U.S. Agency for International Development (USAID). David Wang, the Taiwanese owner of the plant, subsequently hired Guerrero as its personnel manager. In addition, the company also hired ex-military, plain-clothed armed guards as

security for the plant.[18] Factories in El Salvador, as in the U.S., need protection for workers, personal property and for real property.

While personnel managers are not security guards, such appointments have become commonplace with Salvadoran industrialists precisely because they expect conflict in the workplace. However, in many situations, their personnel managers generate the conditions of conflict and attempt to control the conflict through the same methods employed during wartime.[19] For example, Colonel Guerrero himself told the workers at one point, "I have no problem, but perhaps you do; either the union will behave, leave, or people will die."[20]

While The Gap was one of the first companies to have a code of conduct for overseas suppliers (along with Reebok) this strategy might not be effective in the El Salvadoran business environment. Charles Kernaghan, Director of the National Labor Committee in Support of Democracy and Human Rights in El Salvador (NLC), believed that a preexisting code of conduct was practically useless and stated the following in an interview with *Business Ethics Magazine* in June, 1996:

Consider the history of El Salvador's military, which specialized in the killing of nuns and priests and trade unionists. It is laughable to think that these same people will carry out a company's code of conduct. And there were no legal avenues to challenge any violation because the ministry of labor there is so ill-funded and ill-trained. So you can't depend on the laws. And the women were afraid to speak out.[21]

The following is a summary of events leading to the current situation between the Gap and the Mandarin plant, written by Charles Kernaghan, the Director of the National Labor Committee in Support of Democracy and Human Rights in El Salvador (NLC), a coalition of groups with shared interests in workers' rights.

Women maquiladora workers under attack in El Salvador at a plant producing for J.C. Penney, The Gap, Eddie Bauer, and Dayton-Hudson.

In late January, 1995, the women at Mandarin organized a union—the first union ever established in a free trade zone in El Salvador. At the time, the Salvadoran government and the Maquiladora Association pointed to Mandarin as living proof that workers' rights and unions are respected in El Salvador. Reality proved otherwise.

Mandarin International immediately lashed out at the new union, at first locking out the workers and then illegally firing over 150 union members. The company hired two dozen ex-military plain-clothed, armed "security guards." The women workers were told their union will have to disappear one way or another or "blood will flow."

Groups of five workers at a time are now being brought before their supervisors and told to renounce the union or be fired. Union leaders are followed around the plant by company security guards. At work, the women are forbidden to speak to one another. Colonel Guerrero himself has told workers at the San Marcos zone, "I have no problem, but perhaps you do . . . either the union will behave, leave, or people may die."

These women want their union and they are struggling to keep it alive, but they are afraid. Along with the threats, the company is now systematically firing—a few each week—every union member and sympathizer. They cannot hold out much longer. They are appealing for solidarity.

The Salvadoran Ministry of Labor, which could be fining Mandarin $5,700 a day for violating the Labor Code, has done nothing to reinstate the fired workers or demilitarize the plant.

Mandarin produces clothing for J.C. Penney, The Gap, Eddie Bauer, and Dayton-Hudson (now Target Corporation). These companies have codes of conduct, which are supposed to govern their offshore operations, but the workers at Mandarin had never heard of or seen any of these codes. No codes of conduct are posted in the San Marcos free trade zone.[22]

Conditions at Mandarin/Why the Workers are Struggling For a Union

For eight hours of work at Mandarin, an employee earns $4.51 for the day or 56 cents an hour. This comes to $24.79 for the regular 44-hour work week. However, overtime at Mandarin is obligatory, and if you do not stay for extra shifts whenever they demand it, even if it is at the last minute, you are fired the next day. A typical week includes at least eight hours of obligatory overtime.

Conveniently for itself, Mandarin pays the workers in cash in envelopes which do not list regular hours worked or overtime hours, or at what premium it was paid. This makes it almost impossible for the young workers to keep track of whether they are receiving proper pay.

The Mandarin plant is hot and the workers complain of constant respiratory problems caused by dust and lint. There is no purified drinking water, and what comes out of the tap is contaminated and has caused illnesses. The bathrooms are locked and you have to ask permission to use them—limited to twice a day—or you are "written up" and fired after three such sanctions.

Talking is prohibited during working hours. The women say the piece-rate quota for the day is very high, making the work pace relentless. The supervisors scream at the workers to go faster. The women told us of being hit, pushed, shoved, or having had the garment they were working on thrown in their face by angry supervisors.

The workers say that if you are sick, the company still refuses to grant permission for you to visit the Social Security health clinic during working hours. Nor does Mandarin pay sick days. There is no child care center, which is a critical issue for the women, most of whom are mothers.

Working under these conditions, you earn $107.45 a month, $1,397 for the entire year, if you are paid your Christmas bonus. These wages provide only 18.1% of the cost of living for the average family of four.

The women say that even by scrimping and eating very cheaply just to stay alive, meaning going without meat, fish and often milk, food for a small family of two or three people still costs over 1,000 colones a month, or $114.29, which is more than they earn. Rent for three small basic rooms costs around $57 a month, which they cannot afford. There are other basic expenses as well. Round-trip bus transportation to and from work can cost over $6.00 a week. Tuition for primary school costs $8.00 a month. For a maquiladora worker to eat a simple breakfast and lunch at work costs approximately $2.50 a day. The wages of the maquila workers cannot possibly meet their expenses. Many of the Mandarin workers are forced to live in tin shacks, without water and often lacking electricity in marginal communities on vacant land, along roadsides or polluted river banks. Asked if they had a T.V., a radio, or a refrigerator, the workers laughed. They could not afford those things, we were told. All the

Mandarin workers can afford to purchase is used clothes shipped in from the U.S.

It is a myth on the part of the multinationals and their maquiladora contractors that the cost of living in El Salvador is so much less than in the United States, that 56 cents an hour is really not a bad wage. In El Salvador, a "Whirlpool" washer costs $422.26, which is equal to 17 weeks' worth of wages for a maquiladora worker. A refrigerator costs $467.35, or 19 weeks' worth of wages. A queen-sized bed costs $177.85 on sale, or more than seven weeks of wages. A maquiladora worker would have to work three and a quarter hours to afford a quarter-pound cheeseburger, which costs $1.82. A two-pound box of Pillsbury pancake mix costs $2.67, or nearly five hours of wages.

We asked mothers, now that they are working in the maquiladoras, if their children were better off. They told us no, that with their wages they simply could not afford the right food for their children. In Honduras and the Dominican Republic, there is growing evidence that malnutrition is rising among the children of maquiladora workers.

How the Maquiladora System Works

Mandarin sews women's 3/4 sleeve T-shirts for The Gap, which had $3.6 billion in sales last year and made over $300 million in profits. The Gap T-shirts made at Mandarin sell for $20 each in the U.S.

A production line of 40 workers at Mandarin produces 1,500 The Gap T-shirts a day. These T-shirts sell for $30,000 in the U.S. ($20 × 1,500). The 40 Mandarin workers who make these 1,500 T-shirts earn, collectively, $180.23 for the day (40 × $4.50/day wages). This means that the Mandarin workers earn .6%, or just a little more than one-half of one percent of the sales price of the Gap shirt they make. What happens to the other 99.4%?

Under the U.S. government's Caribbean Basin Initiative trade and aid benefits, maquiladora exports from El Salvador to the U.S. grew by an amazing 3,800% between 1985 and 1994, increasing from $10.2 million to $398 million. The number of maquiladora workers producing for the U.S. market increased 14-fold, from 3,500 to 50,000. At the same time, the real wages of the maquiladora workers were slashed 53%—to the current 56 cents an hour or $4.50 a day, which provides only 18% of a family's basic needs.

This is what trade benefits look like from the perspective of the maquiladora worker on the ground. This is what happens when worker rights are divorced from trade and denied in reality. From the perspective of The Gap, however, it means the system is working fine.

Mandarin and its Young Workers

What kind of a company is Mandarin? Child labor came into focus as an issue toward the end of 1994, following the release of a U.S. Labor Department study and a Senate Hearing, where the National Labor Committee showed a short film documenting child labor in Honduran maquiladoras producing for the U.S. In February, 1995, afraid it might get caught, Mandarin summarily fired at least 100 minors between 14 and 17 years old who had been illegally hired. In El Salvador, minors can work only with special authorization from the Labor Ministry, and even then they cannot work more than seven hours a day. Mandarin, of course, worked the minors like everyone else, including forcing them to work overtime. Given that the average work week was 52 hours at Mandarin, this means that the minors were illegally forced to work 17 hours a week more than they should have by law (7 hours × 5 days = 35; 52 − 35 = 17).

Mandarin, J.C. Penney, The Gap, Eddie Bauer, and Dayton-Hudson (now Target Corporation) have the responsibility to pay these fired minors back wages in the form of overtime payments to compensate them for the 17 hours a week they were forced to work illegally.

It is also interesting to note the absence of the Salvadoran Labor Ministry here as well. Even when it comes to monitoring and protecting child labor, the Ministry is nowhere to be found. It would be worthwhile to ask to see the Ministry's records on Mandarin.

There are No Labor Rights in El Salvador

Any attempt to organize in the booming maquiladora sector in El Salvador must be clandestine. The mere mention of a union, even the suspicion of interest, will get you fired.

Between 1992 and 1994, maquiladora exports from El Salvador to the U.S. leapt nearly 2.5-fold, growing from $166 million to $398 million. The number of maquiladora plants soared 73% from 120 in April 1992, employing 30,000, to 208 assembly companies by December 1994, employing 50,000. The most recent figures show that the surge is continuing. A comparison of January and February, 1994, with the same two months of this year shows maquiladora exports from El Salvador to the U.S. increasing 60%—a growth rate faster than any other country in the region.

During this same boom period over the last three years, the International Labor Organization (ILO) estimates that at least 1,000 workers have been illegally fired in El Salvador for trying to organize in the maquilas. In a devastating report on El Salvador released at the end of April, 1995, the ILO concludes: "...to speak of union freedoms and the right of unionization in the maquiladora enterprises is impossible, quite simply because such rights do not exist...." This comes on top of an April 6 ILO condemnation of El Salvador for permitting systematic and grave abuses of worker rights, including assassinations, beatings, arrests, and illegal firings for union activity.

The history of worker rights violations at Mandarin fits the above to a "t."

A History of Repression at Mandarin

In November, 1993, the maquiladora workers at Mandarin formed a local union. The minute the company was notified that the Ministry of Labor had granted legal status to a union at its plant, management illegally fired 100 workers, including the entire leadership of the new union. When the workers fought this, the Ministry of Labor said it could not help and that they would have to turn to the courts (where such a case would drag out for at least two years). Mandarin then told the fired workers point blank to accept the firings, take your severance pay and clear out, or else you will be blacklisted and never again work in the maquila.

This fits in with what we were told in August, 1992, during a National Labor Committee/*60 Minutes* investigation in El Salvador. Posing as potential investors, we met with John Sullivan, who directed USAID's private sector program in El Salvador during the Bush Administration. Sullivan told us we would not have to worry about unions in the free trade zones, since zone management used a computerized blacklist to prevent the unions from penetrating the zones.

Sullivan also told us that we could make a lot of money in El Salvador, where there were world class wages, about 40 cents an hour. If we put our workers on piece-rate and raised the production quota, we could make even more money. Further, Sullivan encouraged us to fire our workers every year—keeping them on a year-to-year contract—rather than allow severance benefits to build up. Lastly, the USAID official suggested we form a Solidarista Association—a phony company union—which would help increase our security from disturbances. As we shall see, Mandarin did all these things.

Repression at Mandarin Worsens

Facing such repression, it was not until January, 1995, that the workers at Mandarin were able to reorganize their union—the Union of Workers of the Mandarin International Company (SETMI). The union was organized by the Democratic Workers Central (CTD), which maintains fraternal relations with the AFL-CIO. When the Ministry of Labor granted SETMI legal status, it became the first union ever recognized in a free trade zone in El Salvador.

The Minister of Labor told union leaders that he would see to it that the union was accepted without delay by the Mandarin company. This was a time of considerable pressure on labor ministries across Central America and the Caribbean to demonstrate concrete advances in the respect for worker rights. In October, 1994, the National Labor Committee was able to delay U.S. Congressional approval of $160 million a year in increased tariff benefits to maquila companies across the region until worker rights conditions improved.

However, despite promises from the Labor Minister, when the company was notified on February 7 that a legal union had been established at Mandarin, it responded by locking out all 850 workers the next day.

Mandarin representatives said that they would rather fire all of the workers than accept a union. The workers refused to leave the industrial park and spent that day and night camped out in front of the factory. On the following morning, February 9, one of the San Marcos Free Trade Zone administrators, Ernesto

Aguilar, and several security guards attacked and beat a number of the women. Aguilar punched one woman in the face several times until she was bleeding badly.

An emergency commission was formed to mediate a resolution to the crisis, made up of National Assembly deputies, United Nations delegates, representatives of the Human Rights Ombudsman's Office, several Labor Ministry officials—including Inspector General Doctor Guillermo Palma Duran—as well as union officials and Mandarin management. At 6:00 P.M., February 9, an agreement was reached and signed by all of the participants.

Mandarin committed itself in writing to end the lock-out, to strictly comply with the Salvadoran Labor Code from this point forward, to recognize the union, and to continue negotiations to reach a collective contract. The company also stated that there would be no reprisals against union members.

Between the day Mandarin signed the agreement, along with officials from the Labor Ministry, and today, Mandarin has illegally fired over 150 union members, in a systematic campaign to destroy the union and spread fear among the workers. The agreement Mandarin signed was not worth the paper it was written on.

The Ministry of Labor could be fining Mandarin $5,700 a day for violating the country's labor code but, for lack of power or will, nothing has been done.

Colonel Guerrero has responded to the workers' attempt to organize to defend their basic rights by "militarizing" his San Marcos Free Trade Zone. Colonel Guerrero hired ex-military people both as zone administrators and armed security guards. One of his administrators, Colonel Amaya, told the women at Mandarin that every single union affiliate at the plant will be fired until the union disappears, which is exactly what is happening. As has already been pointed out, over 150 union members have already been illegally fired, including the entire union leadership—something which is clearly prohibited by the Salvadoran Labor Code.

Five at a time, workers are being brought into management's offices and told to renounce the union or be fired.

Mandarin has brought in nearly two dozen ex-military to act either as plain-clothed, armed security guards or to pose as mechanics so that they can spy on the workers. Armed guards are posted at all four Mandarin entrances. Whenever union leaders must move about the plant, armed company security guards follow them. If workers are seen speaking to a union leader, the guards immediately intervene. During working hours, the workers are not allowed to speak to each other.

Colonel Amaya, along with the security guards, has told the women workers that "blood will run" if the union does not leave Mandarin and the San Marcos Zone.

The union leaders fear that even their homes are at times under surveillance. On April 25, Mandarin's Chief of Production, Liou Shean Jyh, along with his bodyguard and two other company staff, went to the home of union leader Alonso Gil Moreno. When he refused to let them enter his home, they pushed the door open. Their message was simple: renounce the union. They also offered him a bribe.

Mandarin was worried that despite the systematic repression and threats, the union continued to grow. Even under these conditions, 300 workers had signed up to affiliate to the union. It was clear, that if it were not for the fear of losing one's job, the overwhelming majority of the 850 workers would side with the union. The union was asking for a secret ballot to determine support for their union.

Mandarin's response has been to step up the pace of the firings and to demand that workers join Mandarin's Solidarista Association or lose their job.

The union was about to be destroyed.

The Workers Fight Back

The U.S. State Department's latest "Country Reports on Human Rights Practices for 1994" (released in February, 1995) observes that in El Salvador's maquiladora sector, there are both documented cases of the illegal firing of union organizers and of physical abuse being used in the maquiladoras. In the face of these abuses, the State Department concludes: "[Salvadoran] Government actions against violations have been ineffective, in part because of an inefficient legal system and in part because of fear of losing the factories to other countries." Nor can the workers turn to the Ministry of Labor for protection. According to the State Department report, "The Ministry [of Labor] has very limited powers to enforce compliance, and has suffered cutbacks in resources to carry out certification and inspection duties, which curb its effectiveness."

The ILO report, mentioned earlier, found the Labor Ministry to be so underfunded and its staff so poorly paid that "this precarious situation in terms of human and financial resources is the best guarantee that not even legally recognized labor rights in the area of union freedom are applied in the companies."

As of Monday, May 15, Mandarin had fired around 100 union members. Every day more unionists were being systematically dismissed. Mandarin was picking up the pace in its campaign to wipe out the shrinking union.

On Monday, May 15, at 9:30 A.M., the union called a work stoppage to protest the mass of illegal firings. As the union leaders stood up to announce the work stoppage, company goons moved in and attacked the union leaders. At one point seven company guards were punching and kicking Dolores Ochoa. They broke her leg. Marta Rivas and Esmeralda Hernandez were also beaten. Elisio Castro Perez, General Secretary of the SETMI union, was beaten and detained for several hours by company security guards.

Once again, Mandarin responded by locking out all 850 employees and firing 50 more union members, including the union's entire leadership. Another commission was formed and another agreement was reached with the company. At 8:00 P.M. Monday evening, Mandarin committed itself to reopen the plant the next morning and to reinstate all of the fired workers.

As in the past, this agreement turned out to be worthless. When the fired workers showed up on Tuesday morning, May 16, the armed guards refused to let them enter the plant. When the union protested, the guards again roughed up the women.

At this moment, the union workers and their supporters—a majority of workers—have stopped working and left the plant to stand in solidarity with their fired sisters and brothers.

The workers are desperate and they are asking for our solidarity.

The Workers' Demands

The fired workers want their jobs back and they want their union and they want their security guaranteed. They specifically seek:

1. The immediate reinstatement, with back pay, of all fired workers;

2. The demilitarization of the Mandarin plant and the San Marcos Free Trade Zone, which means removing the armed security guards;

3. To end completely the firings, the repression, the threats being directed against union affiliates and their supporters;

4. Mandarin's strict compliance with the Labor Code, including the union's right to organize free of company reprisals;

5. That Mandarin negotiate in good faith a collective contract with the SETMI union.

As North Americans became more and more aware of the working conditions in El Salvador, they began to take action against the retailers. On August 16, 1995, more than one hundred workers from UNITE (Union of Needles Trades and Industrial & Textile Employees) demonstrated in front of a Gap outlet store in downtown Toronto in protest of the working conditions at Gap suppliers. At the same time, thousands of miles south of Toronto, Guerrero claimed that "the working conditions here are good for us and good for the Salvadoran workers, but bad for those seeking to keep jobs in the United States . . . [Without the jobs in the maquilas,] young women would have few other work options apart from prostitution or crime."[23] The story becomes further blurred, however, when Guerrero's comments are compared with an earlier statement by Mandarin owner David Wang in connection with the wages paid to Mandarin workers: "If you really ask me, this is not fair."[24]

Workers' wages make up less than 1% of the retail cost of The Gap shirts. Is it any wonder that the company made $310 million in 1994 and paid its CEO Donald Fisher $2 million plus stock options?" [25]

From The Gap Sourcing Principles & Guidelines: "Workers are free to join associations of their own choosing. Factories must not interfere with workers who wish to lawfully and peacefully associate, organize, or bargain collectively. The decision whether or not to do so should be made solely by the workers." [26]

Based on claims of a violation of its sourcing principles and in an effort to ameliorate the situation, The Gap decided to discontinue its relationship with the Mandarin (following in the footsteps of other previous Mandarin contractors such as Eddie Bauer, Liz Claiborne, J. Crew and Casual Corner); however, this action prompted strong cries of concern from labor activists. Contrary to the intentions of The Gap, this resolution was viewed as irresponsible and lacking in accountability.[27] Those concerned with the rights of workers in El Salvador contested The Gap's decision, claiming that this would be the worst possible solution to the problems in a country where 60% of the labor force is unemployed.[28] As a result of other pullouts, the Mandarin has had to cut its work force from 1,300 to 300, and 32 other maquilas have already shut down.[29] "Instead of acting responsibly and seeing that conditions are improved at Mandarin, The Gap is trying to wash its hands and to shift production to other maquilas in other countries with equally bad conditions."[30]

The Gap's original perspective is not without its supporters. Joan Spero, business executive and Secretary of State for Economic Affairs, explains, "A world community that respects democracy and human rights will provide a more hospitable climate for American trade and commerce.... Repression fosters instability in the long run and puts investment at greater risk of expropriation and loss."[31] Consider as well the following comments of John Duerden, former President of Reebok:

> As a public company, we have an ethical responsibility to build value for Reebok's shareholders—but not at all possible costs. What we seek is harmony between the profit-maximizing demands of our free-market system and the legitimate needs of our shareholders, and the needs and aspirations of the larger world community in which we are all citizens.[32]

"A Victory for All of Us Who are Determined to Eliminate Sweatshops at Home and Abroad"[33]

The situation took a drastic turn in December, 1995, when Reverend Paul Smith called a meeting between The Gap Senior Vice President for Sourcing, Stan Raggio, The Gap sourcing guidelines director, Dottie Hatcher, The Gap consultant James Lukaszewski, Reverend David Dyson of the Interfaith Center for Social Responsibility and Charles Kernaghan (NLC). The Gap was feeling pressure from all sides. On the one hand, labor, religious, consumer, solidarity, children's and women's groups were arguing for dramatic changes in working conditions.

On the other hand, the National Retailers' Federation contested the complaints and encouraged The Gap to ignore the demonstrations.

The Gap responded to the consumers, issuing a letter stating that it is "committed to ensuring fair and honest treatment of the people who make [its] garments in over 40 countries worldwide,"[34] and, in the words of the NLC, "took a major step forward in accepting direct responsibility for how and under what conditions the products it sells are made."[35] As a result of the meeting, The Gap agreed to implement an independent monitoring system in El Salvador, using the Human Rights Ombudsperson in El Salvador to monitor factories' compliance with its labor guidelines, as long as the Mandarin agreed to rehire the fired union activists.

The NLC and others saw this decision by The Gap as a benchmark against which all other multinational retailers will be measured. Says Kernaghan, "The message is clear: If you make it, you are responsible."[36] Not everyone agrees with Kernaghan's assessment. Larry Martin of the American Apparel Manufacturer's Association believes otherwise: "They've [labor] given us a black eye that most of us don't deserve. Most of us monitor contractors we use here and offshore."[37] One might understand Martin's concerns for the rest of American retailers when one considers the comments of U.S. Labor Secretary Robert Reich, "This raises the question for other big retailers who haven't moved in this direction—why not?" United Auto Workers, "The Gap Agrees to Improve Conditions in Overseas Plants," *Frontlines,* http://www.uaw.org/solidarity/9601/frontlinesjan96.html (January 1996) p. 1.

The Monitoring Process Begins

The Gap's reputation and image since the December 15, 1995, meeting has been rehabilitated in connection with workers' rights.[38] In fact, the response was almost instantaneous. On December 22, 1995, the Department of Labor added The Gap to its list of "good guy" businesses (the "Fair Labor Fashion Trendsetter List") that have pledged an attempt to avoid selling products manufactured in sweatshops.[39] The Gap consulted with Aaron Cramer, Director of the Business and Human Rights Program at California's Business for Social Responsibility (an association of over 800 firms for clearinghouse and consulting purposes). Cramer contacted several individuals in El

Salvador to discuss the most effective means by which to establish the independent monitoring system at the Mandarin. One of these individuals was Father David Blanchard, Pastor of Our Lady of Lourdes in the Calle Real Epiphany Cooperative Association, and Father Esteban Alliete, Pastor of Santiago in Ciudad Delgado Vicariate for Human Development. Their evaluation of human rights monitoring in El Salvador follows:

The Monitoring of Human Rights in the Marketplace: The Case of El Salvador

Your letter of February 5, 1996 asks to define independent monitoring.

First, the monitoring of human rights must be assumed by Salvadoran organizations. This is important because of the characteristics of organized labor, traditions of work, and work codes that are unique to El Salvador. For example, in the United States, unions choose to support one or another (and sometimes both) political parties in an election. They do this to maximize their interests. In El Salvador, the relationship of political parties to unions is often the reverse. Political parties establish and control unions as a means to expand their power base.

Understanding the union's role in a labor dispute thus demands understanding the political culture that surrounds the conflict. Therefore, those who monitor the labor conflict in El Salvador must be independent of both the union, the political allies of that union and management. But they must be close enough to this situation to interpret accurately the possible sources and manifestations of the conflict.

The best agency to do this in El Salvador is the government Procurator for Human Rights. The Procurator for Human Rights guarantees that government offices function in ways that respect human rights. The Procurator is responsible for the supervision of the ministry of labor, which must assure compliance with work codes. It provides vigilance over the ministry of justice which must prosecute violations. It monitors the role of the security forces.

Should additional verification be required, the Vicariate for Human Development of the Archdiocese of San Salvador and the Human Rights Office of the University of Central America (IDUCA) both enjoy an international reputation for fairness and objectivity. The Vicariate for Human Development of the Archdiocese includes the social secretariat and CARITAS, both of which have promoted productive enterprises,

and of course, Tutela Legal. In addition to its legal staff, IDUCA also has access to economists, academics in the faculty of management and business administration and other important intellectual resources.

Not to focus the monitoring process in local agencies such as these seriously undermines reconstruction efforts in El Salvador. These agencies have earned their right to speak out for justice. The vicariate for Human Development and IDUCA have paid for this right with the blood of faithful colleagues. The Procurator's Office for Human Rights was created as a result of the 1992 peace accords. Its integrity is unblemished and it deserves a chance to take its place in the forum for human rights.

You ask how the effectiveness of the monitoring process should be measured. There are two measurable criteria.

First, as Lic. Maria Julia Hernandez has pointed out, each factory should minimally be made to follow the law. This includes the right to organize. Cases of violations should be prosecuted. The number of cases prosecuted and the results of these cases should be published.

Secondly, over the long term, the work force will become more qualified and more productive. When the minimal legal requirements are respected, a stronger work force has greater possibility to negotiate the value of its labor collectively and individually. The result will be seen in greater productivity, profits and an increased standard of living for the work force.

How can an independent monitoring process be established in a cost-effective manner? It would certainly reduce costs greatly if monitoring is concentrated in Salvadoran institutions. Perhaps the interfaith Center on Corporate Responsibility and the National Labor Committee can collaborate asking the private foundations and donors who support your efforts to contribute to the Procurator for Human Rights, Tutela Legal and the IDUCA. Eventually, such monitoring will have to receive its support from local sources— workers, unions and corporations.

You ask how independent monitors should present their findings. Honestly. Individual cases should not be presented as representing a pattern. When patterns exist, they should be clearly presented. Also, all parties should attempt to depersonalize the way cases are presented and strive for objectivity. Where real cases of suffering and abuse exist, these should be treated immediately. Suffering should not be exploited to achieve a public relations victory.

Your question, "how should we gain input from concerned organizations in Central America?," suggests that the independent monitoring is something that should be done from outside, with data obtained from local organizations. Our response is that local organizations should gather the data; they should analyze this data and present their findings to organizations such as yours for dissemination.

Monitoring began and problems ensued. An impasse was reached in March, 1996, followed by a Resolution Declaration regarding the rehiring of union activists at the plant. The Resolution also included a commitment of the signatories to:

1. peace and harmony among workers;
2. the maintenance of the existent peace between workers and management;
3. insofar as possible, a promise to aggressively contact and encourage clothing retailers and manufacturers to direct orders to Mandarin International to help demonstrate that agreement and independent monitoring can and will work.[40]

By April, 1996, the Mandarin plant was in serious trouble. David Wang, owner of the plant, informed the monitoring team at an April 18 meeting that there was an 80% chance that the plant would have to be closed by May, 1996. Wang claimed that only a miracle would keep the plant from closing. Fr. Blanchard responded, "I personally believe in miracles, but they are nothing to base a business on."[41] The problem at the Mandarin plant was not much different that at any other manufacturing plant: contracts. The Mandarin was not going to be able to stay afloat without additional contracts. Its renewed contract with The Gap was simply insufficient alone to satisfy the financial needs of the plant. Because Wang believed the closing was imminent, he refused to provide the monitoring team with the information it required to conduct its responsibilities.

At the same time, The Gap hired two Central American Sourcing Compliance Officers "whose sole responsibility [was] to ensure that Gap contractors operated in full compliance with local laws and [its] Code of Vendor Conduct."

Moreover, the Salvadoran Minister of Labor established a government commission to review conditions in the free trade zone and indicated that foreigners would no longer be permitted to monitor the implementation of work codes in El Salvador. Ibid. This begs the question of why The Gap doesn't simply allow the El Salvadoran government to monitor the work conditions of the plant? Father Blanchard offers the following response:

We must consider what are the global consequences for disbanding this effort after less than one month in existence.

For example, recently we have learned that the Commerce Department of the United States has informed the international fishing industry that it will not allow the importation of shrimp that are caught with nets that also snare turtles. All fisherman who use nets and who wish to sell their produce in the United States must use turtle-free nets. What is more, the industry must allow independent monitoring by outside agencies.

Salvadoran law permits the use of turtle-snaring nets. The United States has no authority to control the Salvadoran shrimp industry (one of the largest sources of external revenue for the Government of El Salvador). It has complete authority to determine the conditions under which shrimp may be imported into the United States.

The question remains: why not simply rely on the government of El Salvador to supervise compliance, especially given the importance of the shrimping industry in this country.

The answer lies in norms for the modernization of government and general guidelines for development being promulgated by the World Bank, the InterAmerican Development Bank and other loaning agencies. Governments that contribute to international loaning agencies insist on downscaling government and allowing compliance to be monitored by the private sector in alliance with independent monitoring groups. In this scheme, Congress passes the law defining the kinds of nets that are required in the shrimp industry; people concerned about the welfare of turtles contribute to organizations like the International Wildlife Fund to guarantee that these laws are enforced; organizations like the International Wildlife Fund in turn collaborate with the fishing industry to guarantee that the norms are followed. When all is said and done, if nobody cares about the welfare of turtles, the laws are not passed and compliance never takes place. What is good for turtles is also good for human beings.[42]

The Story Continues

Not only do these events continue to occur in El Salvador in connection with the Mandarin plant and others in the Free Trade Zone, but these same issues are also prevalent elsewhere throughout the world. A recent study by the Committee for the Defense of Human Rights in Honduras found that 90% of the women who work in assembly plants there are forbidden to join a union.[43] The same study also found that women between ages 15 and 30 were required to submit to pregnancy tests and to pledge to use contraceptive pills in order to ensure attendance on the job, rather than pregnancy leave.[44] Ralph Lauren's Chaps brand shirts are made under martial law in Myanmar where workers are paid only $.06 per hour for their assembly.[45] Notwithstanding these conditions, the United States apparel industry has increased its imports from Myanmar 330% since 1992.[46]

Further atrocities are evidenced by these comments made by Douglass Cassel, Director of the International Human Rights Law Institute, before the Chicago Council of Foreign Relations.

Shell in Nigeria

A hands-off stance was adopted by Shell Oil last year when Nigeria executed author and environmental activist Ken Saro-Wiwa. For years Saro-Wiwa had led an activist group of the Ogoni ethnic minority in the Niger River Delta. The Ogoni claimed that Shell drilling and pipelines had polluted their waters and poisoned their lands, ruining not only their environment but their livelihoods, which depended on fishing and farming.

And, they claimed, they did not benefit from this exploitation of their land. Although Shell says it has supported dozens of community projects and recently boosted its budget for environmental improvements to over $100 million, the Ogoni say that most of the oil money that stayed in Nigeria went into the pockets of corrupt military officers.

In the early 1990s, members of Saro-Wiwa's group allegedly sabotaged Shell's equipment, to the point where Shell ceased operations in Ogoniland in 1993. Still, to preserve its investment, Shell called upon—who else?—the local authorities.

Now in normal circumstances, summoning the gendarmes to protect one's property would seem to be the proper thing to do. In Nigeria, however, it is akin to calling in the Mafia. Nigeria is ruled by a corrupt, repressive, military regime, currently headed by General Sani Abacha. Its most recent election resulted in the imprisonment of the civilian winner.

When Shell called, the colonels responded predictably: by allegedly razing thirty Ogoni villages, killing more than 2,000 Ogoni, and displacing some 80,000.

But even this did not suffice to quell the unrest. So the regime had Mr. Saro-Wiwa and several other activists arrested, jailed, and prosecuted on trumped-up murder charges. British Prime Minister John Major later called the trial "fraudulent." At its conclusion last October, Saro-Wiwa and his co-accused were sentenced to death.

As the trial unfolded and its unfairness became apparent, international protests mounted. Yet Shell kept mum. When the death sentence was announced, protests poured in from the United Nations Human Rights Commission, the United States and British governments, South African Nelson Mandela, Amnesty International, and countless others.

But not from Shell, whose joint venture with Nigeria's state oil company supplies more than half the revenue for General Abacha's regime. "It is not for a commercial organization," the company explained, "to interfere with the legal processes of a sovereign state such as Nigeria."

Only after the General's Military Council confirmed the death sentences did Shell's Chairman send a last-minute letter "requesting clemency on humanitarian grounds." But this gesture was too little, too late; a few days later, Ken Saro-Wiwa and his colleagues were hanged.

Before the dirt on Saro-Wiwa's grave could settle, Shell announced that it would go ahead with a $4 billion joint venture natural gas plant in Nigeria. Its partner: General Abacha's state oil company.[47]

The Sullivan Principles

Still, during the 1970s and 80s, there was one striking experiment in corporate codes of conduct for human rights: The Sullivan Principles for South Africa. Developed by Reverend Leon Sullivan, a General Motors Board member, these principles were initially adopted in 1977 by twelve U.S. firms including GM. By 1986, some 200 of the 260 U.S. corporations doing business in South Africa had adopted the Sullivan Principles.

By adopting the Sullivan Principles, these firms adopted unprecedented, far-reaching commitments to corporate social responsibility toward human rights violations—albeit limited to a single country, and spurred by a desire to deflect a growing call for divestment from that country.

Sullivan firms committed themselves not only to racially nondiscriminatory employment, but also to pay fair wages well above the minimum cost of living; to provide managerial training programs for Blacks and other non-whites; to provide them supportive services for housing, health care, transportation and recreation; and to use their corporate influence to help end apartheid in South Africa. And each firm's performance was subject to outside audit and public reports by A.D. Little.

Might events in Nigeria have turned out differently, had Shell undertaken similar commitments for the Ogoni?

Far-reaching as they were, however, the Sullivan Principles failed both in their ostensible goal—to bring down apartheid—and in their tactical goal—to offer a publicly palatable alternative to divestment from South Africa. By 1977, even Reverend Sullivan pronounced his principles a failure and disassociated himself from their further use. When apartheid ultimately did fall in South Africa, it was not because of the Sullivan Principles.

Northern Ireland: The MacBride Principles In the mid-1980s, a similar experiment called the MacBride Principles was initiated for Northern Ireland. Their purpose differs from the Sullivan Principles: they aim not to deflect divestment (for which there has been no serious support) but instead to secure equal treatment for Catholic workers in Protestant-majority Northern Ireland. Their content is more limited, focusing on non-discrimination, without mandating higher wages and social services.

MacBride firms do, however, make one unusual commitment with potential applications elsewhere: to make reasonable, good faith efforts to protect the personal safety of their Catholic workers not only at the work place but while traveling to and from work.

As of February, 1995, 32 of the 80 publicly traded U.S. firms operating in Northern Ireland had signed on to the MacBride Principles. Sixteen states, including Illinois, and more than 40 cities, including Chicago, have passed MacBride Principles laws.

Another highly publicized case of substandard working conditions involves the Nikomas Gemilang factory in Serang, Indonesia (where 1.2 million pairs of Nike shoes—more than a third of its products—are constructed each month), where the resolution has not come so quickly as with The Gap. In Serang, workers faint from exhaustion, humiliation of the workers is commonplace and, in contrast to Nike spokesperson Michael Jordan's multi-multimillion dollar salary, the workers earn $2.23 per day. One labor activist comments, "From the outside it looks like heaven, but for workers on the inside, it's hell."[48] In fact, only one worker interviewed at the Nikomas factory had even heard of Nike's Code of Conduct.[49]

New York Times columnist Bob Herbert claims that the problem is that Nike overlooks atrocities such as the government-sponsored murder of thousands of innocent civilians "if there is a large enough labor force willing to work for next to nothing."[50]

In response to questions concerning his role as Nike spokesperson, Michael Jordan said, "It is up to Nike to do what they can to make sure that everything is correctly done. I don't know the complete situation. Why should I? I'm trying to do my job. Hopefully, Nike will do the right thing."[51] On the other hand, consumers are concerned. Herbert reported in another *New York Times* article that a woman from New York wrote the paper to state that she "simply cannot sit back and watch my two children frolic in their vacation surf knowing that other children suffer to enable my kids to have cute bathing suits."[52]

Other companies are well known for their intolerance of inhumane conditions. Levi Strauss and Timberland received accolades for their 1993 decision to discontinue operations in China as a result of that country's stance on human rights. Reebok, as well, refused to operate in China under its martial law conditions following the Tian An Men Square massacre in 1990. In 1992, Sears, Roebuck and Co. refused to import products produced by prison or other involuntary labor in China.[53] Recently, Talbots, K-Mart, and J.C. Penney have introduced compliance programs specifically implementing monitoring procedures for suppliers.[54] Talbots' policy requires that a supplier must *actively* work to prevent sweatshop abuses if that supplier wants to do business with Talbots.[55]

Multimillion dollar globalized firms have the opportunity to make a difference in the countries in which they conduct business. That difference may be for the worse if they are seen to condone the poor labor conditions and treatment of workers in those countries or may be for the better if they use their financial leverage to force a change in the conditions. But what is the responsibility of a foreign firm? If The Gap's costs increase as a result of its activities in El Salvador, are its customers willing to pay the price? If Nike's shoes cost more at the store, will its sales go down? The ultimate question of responsibility appears to be on the shoulders of every person with a dollar to spend.

CASE DISCUSSION QUESTIONS

1. The Gap has demanded certain quality working conditions of the Mandarin for the Mandarin workers? Since the Mandarin's cost will increase due to this change in working conditions, who should shoulder the burden? The GAP?

2. Assume that the Gap is now required to pay higher prices for the merchandise. What is their ethical responsibility to remain a Mandarin customer when other firms might now be more competitive?

3. The Gap was persuaded to resort to an independent monitoring system in order to ensure compliance with its Code of Vendor Conduct. What alternatives exist for a firm that does not have the resources to install independent monitors in each of the countries it conducts business?

4. How would you go about establishing an independent monitoring team? Who should be on the team and how would you ensure accurate reporting?

CASE CREDIT

This case was prepared by Laura Pincus Hartman, Kellstadt Graduate School of Business, DePaul University, as a basis for classroom discussion rather than to illustrate either effective or ineffective handling of an administrative situation. Copyright © 1997 by Laura Pincus Hartman.

Copyright South-Western and Thomson Learning Custom Publishing (ISBN 0-324-00303-X). For information regarding this and other CaseNet® cases, please visit CaseNet® on the World Wide Web at http://casenet.thomson.com.

CASE NOTES

[1] Dept. of Labor, "No Sweat Initiative: Fact Sheet." http//www.dol.gov/dol/esa/public/forum/fact.htm

[2] Susan Chandler, "Look Who's Sweating Now," *BusinessWeek* (Oct. 16, 1995): pp. 96, 98. [In March, 1996, 72 Thai workers at the El Monte sweatshop were awarded more than $1 million in backwages in connection with the scandal. George White, "Sweatshop Workers to Receive $1 Million," *L.A. Times* (Mar. 8, 1996): p. B1.]

[3] Ibid. p. 98. The study also found that 73% of the garment makers had improper payroll records, 68% did not pay appropriate overtime wages, and 51% paid less than the minimum wage.

[4] Ibid., p. 96. Self-inspection may also be necessitated by the drop in the number of inspectors assigned by the Labor Department to investigate wage and hour law violations. Since 1989, that number has fallen from almost 1000 to less than 800. Ibid., p. 98; Andrea Adelson, "Look Who's Minding the Shop," *New York Times* (May 4, 1996): p. 17.

[5] Stuart Silverstein, "Self-Regulatory Group to Police Clothes Makers' Work Conditions," *L.A. Times* (June 20, 1995): p. D1.

[6] Pat Widder, "'No Sweat' Proposal Aims to Prevent Abuses of Labor," *Chicago Tribune*, April 15, 1997, electronic version; Barbara Sullivan, "Label Plan Gets Mixed Reaction," *Chicago Tribune*, April 15, 1997, electronic version.

[7] Sullivan, op. cit, p. 2.

[8] http://www.dol/gov/dol/opa/public.forum/kearney.txt.

[9] Douglass Cassel, "Human Rights Violations: What's a Poor Multinational To Do?" remarks before the Chicago Council on Foreign Relations, Feb. 7, 1996, p. 10.

[10] "Gifford Counters Sweatshop Charges," May 2, 1996, p. 40 (Reuters).

[11] Michael McGuire, "Lost in the Junkyard of Abandoned U.S. Policy," *Chicago Tribune*, Sec. 2 (April 7, 1996): p. 1, 4.

[12] Louis Emmerij, *Social Tensions and Social Reform: Toward Balanced Economic, Financial and Social Policies in Latin America* (Washington, DC: Social Agenda Policy Group, Inter-American Development Bank, 1995) p. 7, cited in letter from Fr. David Blanchard, Pastor, O.L. Lourdes in Calle Real Epiphany Cooperative Assn. to Aaron Cramer, Director, Business and Human Rights Program, Business for Social Responsibility, February 6, 1996, p. 2.

[13] Bob Herbert , "Sweatshop Beneficiaries," *New York Times* (July 24, 1995): p. A13.

[14] Letter from Fr. David Blanchard, Pastor, O.L. Lourdes in Calle Real Epiphany Cooperative Assn. to Aaron Cramer, Director, Business and Human Rights Program, Business for Social Responsibility, February 6, 1996, p. 8, citing research by Fr. Ignacio Martin-Baro, a social psychologist and one of the six Jesuit priests slain in November 1989 at the University of Central America in El Salvador. The war has additional effects on the people of El Salvador, even if they were not alive at the time of the recent conflicts. For example, one American student recorded in his journal, "9/3/95: One of the little children handed me an old bullet that he must have found. I imagine there must be many bullets out there in the field. I just wanted the day to be over, for me and for this little boy." (Student manuscripts, in possession of the author.)

[15] First-hand experience of the author, February, 1996.

[16] Student Manuscripts, in possession of the author (June, 1996).

[17] Letter from Fr. David Blanchard, Pastor O.L. Lourdes, in Calle Real Epiphany Cooperative Assn. to Aaron Cramer, Director, Business and Human Rights Program, Business for Social Responsibility, February 6, 1996, p. 5.

[18] Terry Kelly, "The GAP: Brutality Behind the Facade," part of *World History Archives* located at http://neal.ctstateu.edu/history/world.history/archives/canada/canada002.html, p. 1 (1995).

[19] Letter from Fr. David Blanchard, Pastor, O.L. Lourdes in Calle Real Epiphany Cooperative Assn. to Aaron Cramer, Director, Business and

Human Rights Program, Business for Social Responsibility, February 6, 1996, p. 6.

[20] Terry Kelly, "The GAP: Brutality Behind the Facade," part of World History Archives located at http://neal.ctstateu.edu/history/world.history/archives/canada/canada002.html, p. 2 (1995).

[21] Mary Scott, "Going After The Gap," *Business Ethics Magazine* (May/June, 1996): p. 20.

[22] Charles Kernaghan, *Urgent Action Alert* (June 3, 1995), http://www.miyazaki-mic.ac.jp/classes/compoliss/ElSalvadorlabor.html.

[23] Letta Taylor, "Salvadoran Clothing Factory Accused of Worker Abuse," *Roanoke Times and World News* (Dec. 31, 1995): p. D4.

[24] Bob Herbert, "Not A Living Wage," *New York Times* (Oct. 9, 1995): p. A17.

[25] Terry Kelly, "The GAP: Brutality Behind the Facade," part of *World History Archives* located at http://neal.ctstateu.edu/history/world.history/archives/canada/canada002.html, p. 2 (1995).

[26] Gap, Inc., *Code of Vendor Conduct*, Section VIII, 1996. See also Christian Task Force on Central America, "Urgent Action El Salvador," http://www.grannyg.bc.ca/CTFCA/ act1295a.html (Nov. 29, 1995) p. 1.

[27] Letta Taylor, "Salvadoran Clothing Factory Accused of Worker Abuse," *Roanoke Times and World News* (Dec. 31, 1995): p. D4; Joanna Ramey, "Worker Rights Groups Slam Gap for Ending El Salvador Contract," *Women's Wear Daily*, Nov. 30, 1995.

[28] Letta Taylor, "Salvadoran Clothing Factory Accused of Worker Abuse," *Roanoke Times and World News* (Dec. 31, 1995): p. D4.

[29] Ibid.

[30] Christian Task Force on Central America, "Urgent Action El Salvador," http://www.grannyg.bc.ca/CTFCA/act1295a.html (Nov. 29, 1995) p. 2.

[31] Douglass Cassel, "Human Rights Violations: What's a Poor Multinational To Do?" remarks before the Chicago Council on Foreign Relations, Feb. 7, 1996, p. 9.

[32] Ibid.

[33] Words of Jay Mazur, UNITE President, in National Labor Committee, *"Gap Victory,"* http://www.alfea.it/coordns/work/industria/gap-victory.html (Feb. 1996).

[34] Christian Task Force on Central America, "Urgent Action El Salvador," http://www.grannyg.bc.ca/CTFCA/act1295a.html (Nov. 29, 1995).

[35] National Labor Committee, "Gap Agrees to Independent Monitoring Setting New Standard for the Entire Industry," http://www.alfea.it/coordns/work/industria/gap.agrees.html.

[36] Industrial Workers of the World, "Unions Win Victory in Gap Battle," *The Industrial Worker*, http://fletcher.iww.org/~iw/feb/stories/gap.html (February, 1995). See also Mary Scott, "Going After The Gap," *Business Ethics Magazine* (May/June 1996): p. 18–20

["What the Gap has done is historic. It will be a good pilot project to see if third party monitoring works," said Conrad McKerron, social research director of Progressive Asset Management.]

[37] Paula Green, "The Gap Signs Accord on Conduct Code with U.S. Labor Group," *The News-Times*, http://www.newstimes.com/archives/dec2295/bzf.htm (12/22/95), p. 2.

[38] See, e.g., Paula Green, "The Gap Signs Accord on Conduct Code with U.S. Labor Group," *The News-Times*, http://www.newstimes. com/archives/dec2295/bzf.htm (12/22/95); Mary Scott, "Going After The Gap," *Business Ethics Magazine* (May/June, 1996): pp. 18–20.

[39] Stuart Silverstein, "Labor Department Adds Gap Inc. to 'Good Guy' Retailer List," *L.A. Times*, Dec. 22, 1995, p. D2.

[40] Resolution Declaration, March 22, 1996, signed by: David Wang (Mandarin International), Hector Bernabe Recinos (Centra), David Blanchard (Archdiocese of San Salvador), Maria Julia Hernandez (Tutela Legal del Archdiocese), Benjamin Cuellar (Univ. of Central America), Lucia Alvarado Portan (Mandarin International Workers Assn.), and Eliseo Castro Perez (for former SETMI union leaders).

[41] Memo from Fr. David Blanchard to Mark Annerm, Coordinator, Independent Monitoring Team, April 19, 1996, p. 1.

[42] Memo from Fr. David Blanchard to Mark Annerm, Coordinator, Independent Monitoring Team, April 19, 1996, pp. 5–6.

[43] Thelma Mejia, "Slaves for Hire," *Chicago Tribune*, 45., sec. 13 (June 22, 1997): p. 10.

[44] Ibid.

[45] National Labor Committee, "Ralph Lauren and Warnaco Working Hand in Hand with Brutal Dictators in Burma," *Urgent Action Alert (June 13, 1997): p. 1.*

[46] Ibid.

[47] Douglass Cassel, "Human Rights Violations: What's a Poor Multinational To Do?" remarks before the Chicago Council on Foreign Relations, Feb. 7, 1996.

[48] Mark L. Clifford, "Pangs of Conscience: Sweatshops Haunt U.S. Consumers," *BusinessWeek* (July 29, 1996): p. 46.

[49] Ibid., p. 47.

[50] Bob Herbert, "Nike's Bad Neighborhood," *New York Times* (June 14, 1996): p. A15.

[51] Bob Herbert, "Nike's Pyramid Scheme," *New York Times* (June 10, 1996): p. A19.

[52] Bob Herbert, "Buying Clothes without Exploiting Children," *New York Times* (August 4, 1995): p. A27.

[53] Douglass Cassel, "The Gap: Getting Serious about Sweatshops," broadcast on *World View*, WBEZ, 91.5FM (Jan. 3, 1996), p. 3.

[54] Office of Public Affairs, U.S. Dept. of Labor, "Reich Applauds Significant Steps Taken by Retailers to Combat Worker Abuses in the U.S. Garment Industry," press release, June 17, 1996.

[55] Ibid.

STS Manufacturing in China: Mark Hanson Returns from Vacation

I t was late February 1998 and a bitterly cold day in Shenyang as Mark Hanson made his way to his office at STS Manufacturing (STS), a joint venture between Shanrong Manufacturing of China (Shanrong) and Tellsan Products of the United States (Tellsan). STS manufactured components for automotive steering assemblies and was a supplier to Volkswagen's joint ventures with Shanghai Automotive Industry Corp. and First Auto Works. Hanson, the young general manager of the joint venture, had just returned from a long overdue week's vacation in Thailand. As he began going through the stack of paperwork and messages on his desk, Hanson realized that just because he had been away for a week, the issues and problems in the joint venture had not disappeared. Moreover, after working at Tellsan for 18 months, he was seriously questioning whether or not Tellsan had made the right decision about even being in China.

China's Foreign Investment Climate

Understanding the challenging business environment that China poses for foreign investors requires some knowledge of China's history and relations with the outside world. One of the oldest civilizations on earth, stretching back some five thousand years, China's history was both impressive and tragic. It was impressive in the tremendous technological innovations that have come from China, including paper money, gunpowder, printing press, and fertilizer. It was tragic in that famine, poverty, warlordism, civil war, and encroachment and conquest by outside forces have characterized much of China's recent history. In the last two hundred years of China's history, foreign powers have carved up China into spheres of influence, imposed their own legal systems within Chinese territory, imported opium on a massive scale to settle imbalances in trade accounts, and brutally massacred hundreds of thousands of Chinese citizens. This history shaped China's often suspicious and volatile relationship with the outside world and partially accounted for China's leeriness toward foreign investors. Despite all of this, China has at times admired and welcomed foreigners and their technologies. However, at other times China rejected foreigners and everything they had to offer. As early as 1792 the Chinese emperor dismissed Western attempts to engage in trade, stating, "We possess all things and have no need for the strange or ingenious manufactures of foreign barbarians."

From 1948 to 1978, China was in the midst of an inward-looking phase and had limited contact with the outside world. The door was closed to outside investors and capitalism. With Mao Tse Tung's death in 1976 and the realization that China's economic progression required new technologies and skills from the West, China's new leader, Deng Xiao Ping, opened the door to outside investors and began loosening the government's iron grip over economic activity. Gradually, market forces were allowed to play a more significant role in the economy. Referring to the cautious and gradual manner in which China would make this transformation to a more market-based economy, Deng said, "You cross the river by stepping on the stones." This statement captured the incremental and cautious manner by which China was attempting to introduce market forces and, once again, allow foreigners a foothold in the Chinese economy.

Beginning in the countryside under the Household Responsibility System, family and collective farms were allowed to sell some of their produce in an open market, and government quotas for production were gradually reduced. Similar to the farm sector, manufacturing enterprises were encouraged to locate buyers and sell products at market-determined prices once quotas were satisfied. Over time, as quotas were diminished and more products flowed to the expanding market segment of the economy, the percentage of total goods sold at market prices in China far exceeded goods produced for quota. As this occurred, China began to resemble a market economy, although not a privatized one. By 1997, privatization had not occurred in China on a significant scale. Despite the lack of privatization, China was able to develop an incentive-based system harnessing the motivations of individuals and firms. Incentives to produce arose from the government allowing an increasing percentage of household or firm earnings to remain in the hands of the workers and managers. Under Mao, all income was repatriated to the central government ministries in Beijing and then distributed as the leadership saw fit. There was no linkage between firm or farm performance and the welfare of its employees.

This changed under Deng Xiao Ping. Although this system of complete and arbitrary control over the economy changed as market forces were introduced, some decisions remained in the hands of the government planning authorities. Decisions of a more strategic nature such as the decision to expand into new markets or the building of factories remained under the control of often multiple supervisory ministries at the local, provincial, and central government levels.

Another significant milestone in China's effort to interject market forces into their economy involved relaxation of restrictions on products produced. Prior to the policy change, firms were limited to producing products that were clearly associated with the ministry of which they were a part. For example, Shanghai Pharmaceutical Factory No. 1 was restricted to producing pharmaceuticals because of its ownership by the Shanghai Municipality's Ministry of Pharmaceuticals, which was in turn controlled by the central government's Ministry of Pharmaceuticals located in Beijing. Similarly, a firm associated with the Ministry of Posts and Telecommunications could not venture beyond producing telecommunications-related products. Policy reform relaxed these restrictions and allowed firms to invest wherever they discovered a market opportunity, regardless of the industrial sector/ministry to which they belonged. This change undermined the silo nature of the Chinese economy and complicated the task of foreign investors in understanding the Chinese market. Whereas prior to the reform it was relatively simple to identify potential joint venture partners and competitors, the removal of restrictions on investment and the breakdown of the silos meant that both potential partners and/or competitors could come from any sector.

All the reforms, while providing annual double-digit growth rates in the economy and raising the living standards of the Chinese people, had the additional effect of decentralizing decision-making and undermining the control of the central government. By introducing a myriad of policy changes and decentralizing decision-making, foreign investors were constantly confronted with contradictory regulations coming from central, provincial, and local government authorities. While China deserved considerable credit in creating a legal framework of rules and regulations governing foreign investment where none existed prior to 1978, the lack of consistency in enforcement continued to confound investors. Furthermore, limited private ownership of property and the socialization of ownership meant that managers in state-owned enterprises did not necessarily view rate of return as a primary objective. Instead, multiple government agencies, each with their own agenda, competed to influence decision-making in a bureaucratic free-for-all. Managers were often evaluated and promoted to positions not on the basis of merit or rate of return, but on the basis of how politically astute they were in catering to the interests of other higher-level government officials in other ministries.

In 1998, although the door for foreign investors was open and market forces were becoming prominent in China's economy, the Peoples' Republic of China (PRC) government tightly controlled and regulated all the activities of foreign firms operating in China. Issues for foreign investors such as plant location, market access, technology transfer, and foreign exchange management were just a few of the areas exposed to government regulation and constant meddling.

The Chinese Automobile Industry

The Chinese automobile industry in early 1997 was suffering from serious overcapacity. Although 1996 sales increased by 19% to 382,000 units, capacity reached more than 700,000 units and was growing quickly with new investments under way by General Motors, Daimler-Benz, Citroën, Honda, and other firms. The Chinese government announced that it would not license any more automobile manufacturing joint ventures and revised its projections for future car demand from 1.2 million units in 2000 to 850,000. Adding to the competition was rampant smuggling of vehicles from Japan and South Korea, which was estimated to have reached 100,000 units.

Most of the foreign automobile firms in China were struggling. For example, in 1993 Peugeot began investing in its joint venture plant in Guangzhou to increase production to 150,000 units. In 1996 the Peugeot plant produced less than 3,000 units, down from 6,600 in 1995. Citroën produced only 13,000 vehicles in 1996, even though its joint venture agreement permitted production of up to 300,000 units. Nevertheless, Citroën was expanding steadily. With the possible exception of Peugeot, none of the automakers appeared willing to withdraw from China, and Japanese firms, latecomers to China, were scrambling to gain a foothold.

Shanghai VW, the joint venture between Volkswagen and Shanghai Automotive Industry Corp., was unique in two respects: it was the only foreign joint venture to be profitable, and the only one to have achieved commercially viable levels of production. Shanghai VW was formed in 1984 as the first foreign automotive venture in China. By 1996, Shanghai VW was producing more than

200,000 vehicles and had built strong supply and distribution channels. Nevertheless, until recently, Shanghai VW had minimal serious competition and, consequently, invested little in product development. The Santana model produced by Shanghai VW was more than a decade old. In addition, Volkswagen's second joint venture with First Auto Works in Changchun, formed in 1988 to produce the Jetta model, was in serious difficulty. Sales in 1996 were 25,000 units, half the target output and far less than the plant's 150,000-unit capacity. The joint venture lost just over $100 million in 1996.

STS Manufacturing (STS)

STS was formed in 1994 as an equity joint venture between Shanrong Manufacturing of China and Tellsan Products of the United States. Tellsan had a 60% equity share in the venture and Shanrong had 40%. Tellsan's relationship with Volkswagen in China was linked to the firm's experience as a Volkswagen supplier in Germany through a majority-owned German-based joint venture. Tellsan had been encouraged by Volkswagen to invest in China to support its increased investment and, in particular, the joint venture with First Auto Works. Because the First Auto Works–Volkswagen business was doing poorly, STS had not achieved its performance objectives. In 1997 the venture lost close to $1.5 million, and 1998 did not look like it would be much better.

The joint venture with Shanrong epitomized the problems foreign companies often experienced when venturing with a local Chinese partner. While Tellsan had highly motivated shareholders in the United States with the clear objective of maximizing profits, it was often difficult for the Tellsan team to comprehend what was motivating Shanrong. Part of this was due to the multiple lines of authority that criss-crossed the Shanrong organization. While the Chinese National Automotive Industrial Corporation (CNAIC) assumed lead responsibility for all automobile assembly operations in China, including the First Auto Works, as a parts supplier, Shanrong was under the direction and influence of multiple bureaucracies including, but not limited to, the Liaoning provincial government and the provincial level authorities of the Ministry of Machinery Industry (MMI). The Liaoning provincial government's interest was in maximizing the contribution of the joint venture to the development of Liaoning province as a whole. In turn, MMI's provincial arm, the Chinese Heavy Machinery Bureau had responsibility for maximizing the growth and profitability of a broad range of machinery industries, of which steering assemblies was only one.

Wu Fan was the joint venture's Deputy General Manager. He was appointed at about the same time as Mark Hanson. Mr. Wu's hometown was Fushun, a sizeable town 60 kilometers east of Shenyang. Shenyang is Liaoning's largest city and the location of the provincial government. Mr. Wu was considered to be a promising manager with a strong future within the MMI. At 42, he was one of the oldest Chinese employees at the joint venture. As was typical of individuals his age in China, Wu was a victim of the Cultural Revolution. Because of his education and visibility, he had been forcibly sent to the countryside to be reeducated and work as a peasant for four years in the early 1970s. Trained as an engineer at China's prestigious Qinghua University, his work experience included serving as the Chief Engineer and Party Secretary at other MMI plants. Wu also held advisory positions within the planning department of the CNAIC and the State Science and Technology Commission. The latter organization was responsible for China's acquisition of foreign technologies.

Career paths for Shanrong executives involved advancing up the organizational ladder within MMI, often moving to larger manufacturing facilities within the same industrial sector or moving into management positions within the provincial level of the MMI or another bureaucracy. The factors that determined career advancement for Shanrong executives went well beyond the narrowly focused, merit-based criteria that Tellsan executives operated under. Guanxi, or connections, was an important factor affecting promotions in China's highly relationship-oriented society. Mr. Wu was known for having a particularly broad range of connections.

Mark Hanson was 34 years old and the second general manager in the joint venture. The first general manager was Steve Johnson, an American from Tellsan. Johnson had been quite effective in getting the plant built and production started. However, his relationship with Wu had been strained by various issues. In August, 1996 Johnson returned to Tellsan in the United States and was replaced by Hanson. Hanson had a master's degree from a well-known Southwestern business school and had studied Chinese. Although not fluent, he understood enough to hold a basic conversation. After graduation in 1993, Hanson worked with a large automotive supplier before joining Tellsan in 1995.

Quality Issues at STS

STS produced a steering wheel assembly for the new VW 2000 sedan widely sold in China. Quality standards had to be high for this precision part but, unfortunately, problems with quality control had plagued the joint venture from the very beginning. Production was falling further and further behind schedule, largely because of the high failure rate in the final inspection. The joint venture was not even close to achieving the same level of productivity as comparable plants in Toledo and Germany. Prior to July 1996, the Shenyang plant had been limited to assembling kits and had not attempted to manufacture component parts from raw materials. Now, STS was struggling to manufacture several precision components for the steering wheel assembly. For each component, the failure rate remained too high.

At a meeting in December 1997, Wu Fan made three recommendations to address the problem: 1) the quality standards could be lowered slightly; 2) additional line workers could be hired; and 3) the highest precision products could be manufactured during overtime work where management could be more discriminating in selecting the workers.

Hanson and Dietrich Werner, Tellsan's Director of Operations and Chief Engineer, did not believe any of the three options were viable long-term solutions because each failed to identify and address the fundamental problem. First, the quality standards at STS were no higher than those achieved at Tellsan's two other plants in Toledo and Germany. Moreover, to ensure quality components in China, VW had recently acquired suppliers of other precision components similar to the steering wheel assembly. If the quality at STS could not be improved, there was a real risk that VW would shift sourcing to one of STS's highly competent competitors, or begin producing the assembly itself.

Second, the ratio of line workers in Shenyang to the number of line workers in Germany and Toledo was 5:1 and 6:1, respectively. All three plants used comparable manufacturing equipment and processes. When forming the joint venture in 1995, Tellsan had agreed to keep on the payroll a much larger number of workers from Shanrong's existing plant than they needed. As far as

Hanson and Werner were concerned, many, if not most, of STS's workers were already redundant.

Third, while using select high-quality workers on an overtime basis to produce critical components had been a strategy successfully employed by many Sino foreign joint ventures operating in China, STS management wanted to avoid what would be at best a temporary solution. Instead, Hanson and Werner decided to probe deeper to uncover the fundamental problem and find a solution. Upon close investigation, they found that the causes of the quality problem at STS were multiple and complex and were more deeply entrenched than STS executives had anticipated.

Despite all the work that Hanson, Weinrich, and Hanson's predecessor had done over the past three years, the sobering reality was that below the management level STS had a total absence of a quality control system, no notion of continuous improvement, and no comprehension of quality being more broad-based than testing end products and throwing the defective ones away. In one instance, Werner found that instead of regularly replacing contaminated chemical solutions with clean solution, the workers were simply reusing solution in order to conserve. In other instances, workers could be observed filing precision components manually to meet specifications. Particularly alarming was that there seemed to be no focus on prevention of problems. Quality control involves process control, statistical control, efforts to narrow deviations, and corrective action, all of which seemed to be missing. When a problem appeared, it was perceived to be a random idiosyncratic event and no effort was expended to determine the root cause.

Werner did not believe that technical and engineering skills were the problem: China has the best reverse engineers in the world. Give them the plans, specifications, tool designs and a step-by-step process sheet and they can manufacture virtually anything without the assistance of foreign engineers.

Werner described the cultural problems surrounding quality and lean production efforts: Our partner has a core group of managers assigned to work in the joint venture and these people make all the decisions. Lean manufacturing is an easy subject to discuss but it takes years of experience to implement. There is a physical side that is relatively easy to understand. There is a psychological side that is based on leadership and a willingness to empower teams to manage their own destiny. Lean manufacturing is based on assigning responsibility to lower levels of the organization. To the Chinese, this shatters their view of the world and the Confucian notion of hierarchy and orderliness. Decision-making in China happens at the top of the organization, not the bottom. Below the senior management level hardly anybody makes decisions. The Chinese view of hourly workers is that they make parts. They don't need to be thinking about safety and continuous improvement and quality; somebody else in the organization is responsible for that.

Supplier Selection

Local content was a key element of China's automotive policy. Nevertheless, Hanson realized that the Chinese operating environment offered several challenges; and from the perspective of one of his colleagues, "the deck is stacked against us." First, the partner said that Tellsan could not use suppliers based in the United States. Then, Shanrong began exerting pressure on Tellsan to select suppliers from firms in Shanrong's network. The longer Hanson spent in China, the more he realized how important networks were to Chinese organizations and how impenetrable they could appear to non-Chinese. Shanrong was involved in several other joint ventures and made it clear that it expected these joint ventures would become STS suppliers. In one case, Shanrong wanted Shen-Tech, a joint venture between Shanrong and a German firm, to be a key supplier for STS. After six weeks of extensive reviewing, Tellsan concluded that Shen-Tech was not qualified to get the business. Another firm was selected as the supplier. However, Shanrong was determined that Shen-Tech would get the business. Land for Shen-Tech's expansion had been acquired across from the STS plant site. In September 1997, a review was held with the government so that Tellsan could try to disqualify Shen-Tech as a supplier. Tellsan offered Shen-Tech part of the business but the offer was refused. The issue remained undecided.

In another case, Shanrong's choice of a supplier for a critical rotary part did not pass the quality review. The supplier's management then suggested that the specifications could be changed. Not surprisingly, Hanson said no. Next, the firm called a meeting and announced a recovery plan that would allow them to meet the quality standards. To the two Tellsan managers at the meeting, it was clear that the supplier was hoping for a miracle. Hanson said no again. Other Shanrong suppliers were expanding with the hope of getting STS business, even though these firms had not gone through the quality assurance process. Shanrong had analyzed its strategic objectives for STS and came up with a list of components that it funneled to its supplier base, without any input from Tellsan.

Hanson explained some further concerns: We have had, and continue to have, a whole lot of detailed questions from the Liaoning government and the other people reviewing this. The problem is that they don't understand the scope or the business challenges. They have been soured by other joint venture experiences and want this joint venture to be a showcase. They were more interested in the facade on the STS administration building—they had artist renderings that look like Las Vegas hotels. They knew they would be parading politicians through and making this a technology showcase.

Our partner agrees that we have to have quality components. But, if it comes down to the wire and there are two suppliers with equal quality and Shanrong's supplier is 5% higher, we know who will get the business. We have agreed that we will help improve China's supplier base, so we know that we will have to balance what we said we would do with our financing plan.

We have some leverage because we are sticking to the objectives of the deal. We are not going to budge off that. We are trying to make it clear to our partner that you guys need to realize that you are not an export player. You have a huge stigma regarding quality. You can make almost anything but it is going to fall apart in two days. Moreover, now that we have been designated a "trusted company" with the Customs Administration, we can expedite the processing of component parts through Customs and save some inventory costs and shipping time there. Although we have noticed that the duties on a select range of our imported components have been gradually inching upward.

We are also in the middle of what has been a lengthy negotiation with the Ministry of Foreign Trade and Economic Cooperation (MOFTEC) to establish our own import-export corporation. Once in-house, this could save us the 11/2% commission that we currently pay the Chinese Heavy Machinery Bureau's foreign trade corporation every time we import or export a part. It's hard to tell the politicians from the people who run the plants. I took a team of six Tellsan executives on some supplier visits. On one of the plane trips we had a representative from China's Heavy Machinery Bureau with us. We had a reception and sitting at the table, each with their own interpreter, was the Heavy Machinery representative and a project manager from the MMI. Also present were representatives from the provincial divisions of the State Science and Technology Commission, State Planning Commission, and the Liaoning Customs Administration. They talked candidly about the planned economy and how they were trying to change.

Training

The joint venture agreement specified that joint venture employees would receive various types of training and that Tellsan would participate in the process, both in China and in the United States. But the training efforts were getting bogged down in numerous delays involving arguments over the selection of candidates for the training, costs, problems with travel documents, etc.

We are trying to use the best systems Tellsan has and shoot for very high standards. We do not want to compromise just because this is China. But we are having lots of problems with our partner. The joint venture agreement says that Tellsan will assist in training STS employees and the joint venture will be required to pay its fair share of the costs. Recently, we had two engineers scheduled to go to Toledo. Three days before they were supposed to leave, we found out they had no visas. Shanrong was supposed to have applied for visas weeks ago. We had to shorten the training period and the only reason we got the visas was because the embassy did us a favor. So far, the three trips we have planned for STS Chinese employees have run into travel problems with travel documents that we have had to fix. Each time we are assured by Shanrong that it won't happen again and each time it does. We have one guy who has told us he does not to expect to work since he is in the Communist Party.

Also, if STS suppliers have to be trained by Tellsan, Tellsan's view is that STS should pay for the training, not Tellsan. Because of the disagreements about the responsibility for startup costs for the previous two months, we, meaning Tellsan, have instituted a policy of getting a written agreement from our partner before spending any training money. Unfortunately, the policy is solving few disagreements, and only slowing things down because Shanrong managers are reluctant to sign any agreements.

STS and Tellsan Headquarters

Just before he went on vacation, Hanson had a long conversation with Jack Pitfield, his boss in Toledo, Ohio. They discussed a variety of different issues and as the conversation went on, Pitfield expressed frustration with the pace of change in the joint venture.

Pitfield: Mark, you have been telling me about these problems for a year-and-a-half but nothing seems to get resolved. What is the problem?

Hanson: Well, Jack, this is China and things move a bit more slowly than in the States.

Pitfield: I have been hearing that "this is China" ever since we first decided to get involved in the joint venture. Now that the business is up and running, and we have a 60% share in the business, I expect you to make some decisions to get things under control. Maybe our partner will not be too crazy about some of these decisions, but you need to empahsize that we are the majority owner and for some things, we are going to do it the Tellsan way.

Hanson: It is not that easy. My predecessor did that once and it took us over a year to get the relationship back to what it was.

Pitfield: If we can't use our majority ownership position, why do we have it? I just came back from our German joint venture and I can assure you that we certainly take advantage of our majority position. Why, just last week our partner wanted to . . .

With that, the line went dead, "Perhaps fortunately," thought Hanson. "All I need is another lecture about how our German joint venture works like clockwork and STS is a disaster. Pitfield just does not understand what we are up against here. If we use our majority position and outvote our partner, we will kill this relationship."

What Next?

Hanson explained some of the issues surrounding the partner relationship:

Every single issue with our partners involves a protracted negotiation. If we say ten, they will say five. It doesn't matter whether the issue is significant or not. If we say let's do "Y" because "Y" makes sense, they will challenge us. It is as if they must leave a meeting with a lower number than we proposed, even if our first number was the right one. When we go to meetings we talk for two hours to see who will turn the lights on. Often we will agree on something on Monday, and then on Tuesday they will deny that we had an agreement. They will even sign off on an issue and then want to renegotiate. Or, they will keep delaying until it is too late to do what we want to do and we have to do it their way. Even minor decisions require senior management approval. There is a tremendous unwillingness for anybody in our partnership to accept risk. When I try to explain to Pitfield and other people in the United States why things are moving slowly, they just say, "What is the problem—make a decision!"

We are not doing business just with Shanrong. Nobody there has the power to make decisions. We get frustrated and then we realize that we are really doing business with China, Inc.

I am used to following a system and being evaluated on performance. Our partner gets assessed on relationship-building. There are certain objective steps that must be followed to achieve an outcome. Our partner finds the objective steps very difficult to understand.

We are dealing with talented people in Shanrong. The top people assigned to the STS project are the best they have. Unfortunately, when you get below these people the talent leaves a lot to be desired. The depth of management is a function of relationships. And the senior people don't know how to delegate. As a result, lots of things fall through the cracks. When things go wrong, we are not sure whether our partner is deliberately trying to mess things up, or they genuinely don't know how to get things done but won't tell us because they would lose face.

Hanson's Dilemma

Hanson glanced across the bare concrete floor of the spartan room and saw Dietrich Werner busy at his desk. Despite outside temperatures in the upper 20s, without any prior notice, the heat in the plant and administrative offices had been turned off by the Ministry of Energy in order to conserve electricity. Since typing on the computer was almost impossible wearing gloves, all the managers and staff had cut off the fingertips of their gloves so that they could type and still keep the remainder of their hands warm. Conditions were even colder at the other end of the factory where the Shanrong managers' offices were located, because that part of the factory had virtually no insulation.

As Hanson sorted through the mass of paper that had accumulated in his absence, he decided that the first thing to do was to establish some priorities. The problem was where to start. What were the most critical problems? Pitfield expected action, quickly, but Hanson knew that as far as Shanrong was concerned, the most pressing problem was that workers were beginning to grumble about rumors of layoffs. Without reducing headcount and solving the quality problem and getting quality suppliers, the joint venture had a grim future. To make matters worse, Mr. Wu had just told Hanson that the municipal government was planning a new highway that might require STS to give up some land or even move the factory. In contrast to Hanson's uncertainty and concerns, Mr. Wu not only did not share his opinion, he was proposing a very expensive banquet to celebrate four years of the special relationship between Shanrong and Tellsan. "How," Hanson wondered, "can I convince my partner that the problems at STS are serious and the future of the joint venture is far from certain?"

CASE DISCUSSION QUESTIONS

1. Is China a market economy? What role have foreign companies played in China's fast-paced growth since the reform began? How does the Chinese government perceive foreign enterprises operating in China? What has been the history of China's relations with the outside world and how does this history influence its behavior toward foreign firms on Chinese soil?
2. What is happening to the Chinese automobile industry?
3. Why was STS Manufacturing formed?
4. Describe Mark Hanson's job. How is he evaluated? What skills should a JV general manager have in order to do his or her job properly?
5. Describe Mr. Wu's job. Who does he report to? What are his likely motivations?
6. What are the issues that Mark Hanson must deal with and why have they arisen?
7. What are the most important issues? Where should Mark Hanson devote most of his energy? How should he deal with the issues? What is an appropriate action plan?

McDonald's in India

I do not see anything wrong with McDonald's doing business in India. After all, it is not McDonaldization that we know of; it is a Big MaCcommodation.

A Senior Bureaucrat in New Delhi

In October 1996, McDonald's opened its first Indian outlet in Vasant Vihar, an affluent residential colony in India's capital, New Delhi. As of November 2004, McDonald's has opened a total of 58 restaurants, mostly in the northern and western part of India (Exhibit 1).[1]

While McDonald's opened 34 restaurants in five years (by 2001), 58 restaurants in eight years (by 2004), it is now planning to add more than 90 new restaurants in the next three years.[2] Although the initial scenes of crowds lining up for days outside the McDonald's restaurants in Delhi and Mumbai are no longer seen, Indian consumer response to McDonald's products still remains very strong.

The ten McDonald's I visited in Mumbai and Delhi were packed with young people, children, and young parents enjoying ice creams, spicy potato wedges (instead of the usual french fries), and Happy Meals. The growth of McDonald's in India is not as rapid as in China (Exhibit 4). But its growth is nevertheless impressive. How did McDonald's do it? How did a hamburger chain become so prominent in a cultural zone dominated by non-beef, non-pork, vegetarian, and regional foods such as *chola bhatura, kababs, bhaji, samosa, dosa, vada, sambar, bhelpuri,* and rice? The answer to this question lies in McDonald's carefully planned entry and expansion strategy in accordance with India's changing political, economic, and cultural landscape in the 1990s.

The Indian Food Service Industry

With more than five thousand ethnic communities represented, India has a very diverse population. Each region and subregion in India has distinct food traditions and preferences. Indian consumers typically maintain their distinct food habits even after migrating to different parts of the country. In large cities and metropolitan areas, some restaurants serve only specialty regional foods. Some regional fast foods such as *samosa, kababs, chola bhatura, pakoda, aloo-paratha, poori-bhaji, dosa,* and *sambarvada* are popular among Indian consumers and are available in both specialty and multi-cuisine restaurants throughout India.

EXHIBIT **1**   **Map of India**

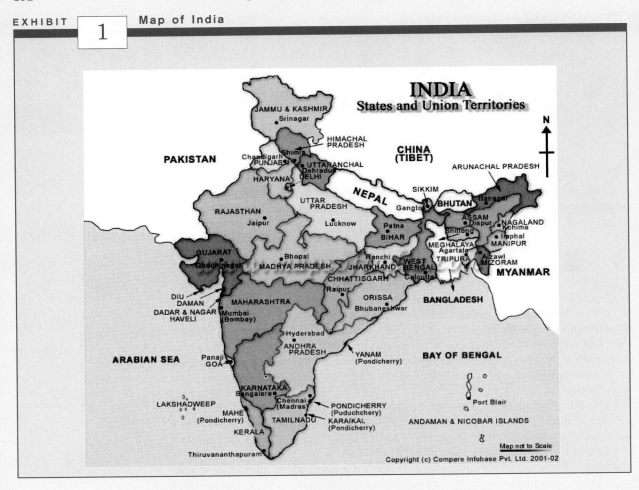

Most Indians prefer to eat home-cooked foods and take immense pride in the varieties of food cooked at home. For most Indians, home-cooked foods are considered fresh, healthy, and inexpensive. Given the distinct dietary habits and food preference of Indian consumers, it is not surprising that until the early 1990s Western fast food chains had largely ignored Indian markets. As a result, Nirulas, the only notable Indian fast food chain, has been able to dominate the Indian market in fast food service sales.

There are approximately 22,000 registered restaurants in India. In addition, there are more than 100,000 *dhabas* (small roadside food stalls) that sell a variety of foods in cities and on highways. By 1998, there were approximately 1,568 registered hotels in India, half of which have their own restaurants.[3] In addition, large to medium-range canteens serve the food needs of various institutions such as hospitals, prisons, defense establishments, schools, colleges and universities, railways, airlines, government establishments, and private companies.

Since 1994, India's food imports have been growing more than 37% per year. Half of India's food imports are agricultural items such as cereals, vegetables, fruits, wheat, and nuts. One of the significant problems of the Indian food industry is an inefficient food chain between farmers and consumers. About 20% of India's food production is wasted because of too many intermediaries, poor infrastructure, and poor transportation facilities. Considerable inefficiency in the food distribution system cuts farmers' income while raising consumer food prices. Although India is the world's third largest food producer, its processing industry is very small compared to other countries in Asia, Europe, and the United States. Despite the lack of a well-developed food processing industry, India's imports of processed consumer foods have traditionally remained low.

Since the early 1990s, India's food service sales have significantly increased. India's processed and fast food markets have shown considerable potential for growth. A number of factors have driven increased processed and fast food sales:

- Growing Income

   The long-term growth trend in India is improving. The past three decades have seen a steady acceleration. Average annual growth in GDP per head climbed from 1.2% in the 1970s to 3% in the 1980s and 4% in the 1990s. From 1972 to 1982, GDP growth averaged 3.5% a year—the so-called "Hindu rate of growth." As a result of India's decade-long liberalization of economic policies, the growth rate climbed to 6% from 1992–2002 and is likely to reach 7% by 2010.[4] If this rate is maintained, GDP per person will double in only 18 years. However, high GDP growth is confined to only the few states with coastal access and high levels of urbanization. The fastest-growing Indian states in 1991–2001 were Delhi, Maharashtra, Karnataka, West Bengal, and Gujrat. These states enjoyed annual average economic growth of 6–8%, which is comparable to East Asian economies during the same period. But the economies of poor states like Bihar, Uttar Pradesh, Madhya Pradesh, Orissa, and Assam grew by a dismal annual average of 2% over the same period.[5]

   Not surprisingly, income distribution is highly skewed in India. Just 20% of the richest Indians share more than 40% of the national income (Exhibit 2).

   Exhibit 3A gives a profile of average annual household income distribution in India. According to a study by National Applied Economic Research (2004), the number of households with an annual income over Indian Rupees (Rs.) 1 crore (US $228,351) has grown by 26% since 1995–96 to

EXHIBIT   2   India's Socio-Economic Profile

GDP (US$ billions, 2003)	658.2
GDP (PPP US$ billions, 2003)	3,033.0
GDP per capita (PPP US$, 2004)	3,100.0
GDP per capita annual growth rate % (1999–2004)	6.8
Total Population 2005 (millions)	1,080.0
Annual Population growth rate (%) 1999–2015	1.3
Urban Population (as % of total, 1975)	21.3
Urban Population (as % of total, 2004)	28.1
Population under age of 15 (as % of total, 2004)	31.7
Life expectancy at birth (2003)	63.0
Adult literacy rate (% age 15 and above, 2003)	59.5
Population below national poverty line % (1999–2000)	29.0
Share of Income or Consumption % (richest 20%) 2000	43.3
Share of Income or Consumption % (poorest 20%) 1999	8.9

Source: World Development Report 2003, The World Bank (New York: Oxford University Press, 2003); Human Development Report 2003, UNDP (New York: Oxford University Press, 2003); Economist Intelligence Unit, 2005.

EXHIBIT   **3A**   Income Distribution and Market Size in India (2004)

Average Annual Income in US $	% of Households	Number of Households (millions)
0–1,000	32	64.4
1,001–2,000	40	78.4
2001–3,000	13	26.3
3,001–5,500	8	15.2
> 5,500	7	13.4
Total	100	197.7

Source: India Economics, Merrill Lynch, Lafferty estimates, Lafferty Ltd., Cards International, February 24, 2005; India: The Structure of Poverty, World Resource Institute, Washington, D.C., May 19, 2004.

20,000 in 2001–02. By 2009–10, it will increase more than seven times to 1,40,000 households. In the Rs. 50 lakh (US $114,180) to Rs. 1 crore (US $228, 351) bracket, the number of households is expected to increase from 40,000 in 2001–02 to over 250,000 in 2009–10.

Exhibit 3B describes the change in average annual household income distribution of low, lower, and high middle class in India's urban and rural areas from 1989–90 to 2001–02. It also provides a projection in income distribution of low, lower, and high middle class for the year 2009–10. In the 11 years following 1989–90, the total number of households increased by 32%, although the average size of Indian households has declined from 5.9 people per household in 1990 to 5.2 in 2001. What is important is that the number of low-income urban households has been approximately halved, from 14.9 million households in 1989–90 to 7.6 million in 2001–02. The number of low-income rural households has also declined from 69 million in 1989–90 to 58 million in 2001–02. The growth in incomes in the top band has been experienced by both urban and rural households, both of which have roughly doubled as a share of the total population over the 1990s.[6] The members of these households have higher disposable income and have shown greater propensity to spend on fast foods.

- Population Growth and Urbanization
  According to the 2001 census, India's population grew at a rate of around 2% a year during the previous decade. This was a marked decline from earlier decades of population growth of around 3% annually. Nevertheless, India added 181 million people between 1990-2001, more than the total population of Brazil.[7] According to the forecast of Goldman Sachs (an American investment bank), the reason why India is expected to outperform Brazil, Russia, and China, as well as the "rich world" (i.e., United States, Canada, France, Germany, United Kingdom), is that it is the only country where the population will continue to grow for the next 50 years and where the proportion of working-age people will increase well into the 2020s.[8]

  The percentage of urban population in India has increased from 21% in 1975 to more than 28% in 2004 (Exhibit 2). It is likely to increase to 36% in 2025.[9] Most high-income Indians prefer to live in urban areas. Over 70% of affluent urban Indian consumers live in the ten most populated and cosmopolitan cities in India: Mumbai, Delhi, Kolkata, Pune, Chennai, Hyderabad, Bangalore, Ahmedabad, Ludhiana, and Nagpur. The number of dual income

EXHIBIT   **3B**   **Middle-Class Income Distribution in India (Rs, 2001–2002 prices)**

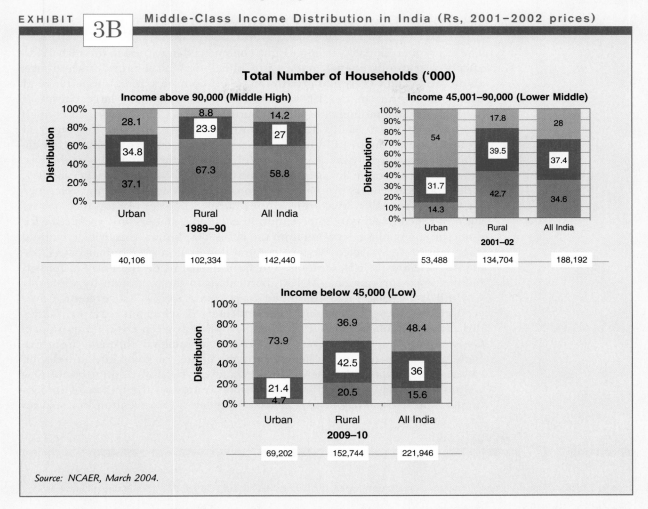

Total Number of Households ('000)

Income above 90,000 (Middle High) — Urban / Rural / All India, 1989–90
(Urban: 37.1 / 34.8 / 28.1; Rural: 67.3 / 23.9 / 8.8; All India: 58.8 / 27 / 14.2)
40,106 — 102,334 — 142,440

Income 45,001–90,000 (Lower Middle) — Urban / Rural / All India, 2001–02
(Urban: 14.3 / 31.7 / 54; Rural: 42.7 / 39.5 / 17.8; All India: 34.6 / 37.4 / 28)
53,488 — 134,704 — 188,192

Income below 45,000 (Low) — Urban / Rural / All India, 2009–10
(Urban: 4.7 / 21.4 / 73.9; Rural: 20.5 / 42.5 / 36.9; All India: 15.6 / 36 / 48.4)
69,202 — 152,744 — 221,946

Source: NCAER, March 2004.

households, where both husband and wife work, is slowly increasing in urban areas. Like their husbands, full-time working women spend most of their time away from home. As a result, there has been a dramatic change in the way Indian working wives shop and organize family meals. Packaged rice, prepared yoghurt, packets of flour, frozen chickens, and marinated mutton (goat or lamb meat) are fast replacing curdling, grinding, and handling of market-bought fowls and haunches of mutton. Not surprisingly, even some Indian consumers have started opting for meals away from home on working days. The growing popularity of Delhi's Waiters on Wheels (WOW), a supply agency delivering meals to people's doorsteps from 30 different restaurants at the same price as one would pay in the restaurants, is an example of India's changing food service landscape.[10] High income and growing urbanization have also contributed to a shift in the traditional Indian food habits.

High-income urban dwellers are seeking variety in their choice of foods and are willing to spend more on international cuisine, including fast foods. Consequently, a growing number of domestic fast food outlets, home delivery, take-away restaurants, and American restaurant chains, such as Kentucky Fried Chicken (KFC), TGI Friday's, Domino's Pizza, Pizza Hut, McDonald's, and Baskin Robbins, have opened in the last few years.

India's Economic Liberalization

The effort of McDonald's to enter India commenced in earnest in the early 1990s after it successfully opened outlets in China.[11] Exhibit 4 provides some facts about McDonald's entry and growth into select countries. India's wide range of economic reforms in the 1990s, coupled with a potentially large consumer market (with 300 million consumers, almost as big as China), provided enough incentives for McDonald's to enter into the Indian market. Executives at McDonald's were aware of India's deep suspicion of foreign companies. After all, India's colonization by the British for over three centuries started with the East India Company's trade linkages. Not surprisingly, after its independence in 1947, Indian political leaders propounded vigorously the *swadeshi mantra* (preference for national products). Accordingly, they pursued policies of economic nationalism in which heavy state intervention in economic matters and preference for domestic companies continued until the late 1980s. India's sensitivity to cultural imperialism, the so-called Western cultural domination over Indian values, traditions, religious beliefs, customs, and food habits, made the entry of foreign multinational corporations (MNCs), particularly in the food industry, difficult.

Until late 1980s, India continued to pursue a *dirigiste* (state control over economic matters) and *autarkic* (self-sufficient) development strategy. Under this strategy, public sector-led economic growth was given critical importance. Government control over the economy was maintained through protective trade policies; price control; licensing requirements for companies to relocate existing facilities, establish new plants, expand production, and introduce new technology or new product lines; severe constraints on the in-flow of foreign capital and technology; and extensive regulatory intervention on market

---

EXHIBIT   **4**   **McFactoids**

- Ray Kroc, founder of McDonald's Corporation, opened his first McDonald's in 1955 in Des Plaines, Illinois.

- McDonald's is the largest global fast food-service retailer, with more than 30,000 restaurants in 120 countries serving 47 million customers daily, and more than 1.5 million employees worldwide.

- The first McDonald's restaurant outside of North America opened in Costa Rica on December 28, 1970.

- In Russia, McDonald's opened its first restaurant on January 31, 1990. As of June 2001, it has opened 60 restaurants in that country.

- McDonald's opened its first restaurant in the People's Republic of China (Shenzhen Special Economic Zone) on October 8, 1990. It opened its outlet in Beijing in 1992. As of June 1999, it has opened 235 outlets in that country.

- There are 164 McDonald's in three countries in Africa: South Africa, Egypt, and Morocco.

- McDonald's opened its first restaurant in Japan in 1971. As of September 30, 2001, Japan has 3,717 McDonald's restaurants.

- McDonald's opened its first restaurant in Singapore in 1979. As of September 30, 2001, Singapore has 124 McDonald's restaurants.

- McDonald's opened its first restaurant in India in 1996. As of November 2004, India has 58 McDonald's restaurants.

- McDonald's opened its first restaurant in Pakistan in 1998. As of September 30, 2001, Pakistan has 18 McDonald's restaurants.

Source: "McAtlas Shrugged," Foreign Policy, May/June 2001, p. 30; Seema Shukla, "McIndia," Business Today, November 25, 2001, p. 61; James L. Watson, "China's Big Mac Attack," Foreign Affairs, May/June 200, p. 120.

activities. Companies were forced to import at the government-fixed exchange rate. The inefficiency of the public sector and the government's policy to support loss-making public firms by budget outlays and loans from nationalized banks led to a considerable slowing down of the Indian economy. Such strategies produced a low economic growth rate (the so-called Hindu rate of growth) of 3.5% between 1965 and 1980.

By the late 1980s, India began to borrow heavily from both commercial sources and the World Bank and Asian Development Bank to finance its growing budget deficits. The major portion of the government's fiscal deficit was incurred by its inability to control the expansion of public sector employment, subsidies, military expenditure, and interest payments. By 1990, India's economic situation was in a critical stage. In June 1991, India faced a severe balance of payment crisis as its foreign exchange reserve plummeted to an all-time low of $1.2 billion, barely sufficient to pay for two weeks of vital imports. Besides, by 1991 the central government's budget deficits reached a record high of 8.4% of GDP. The inflation rate, which for most of the 1970s and 1980s remained at a single digit, went up to 17%; external debt increased from $21 billion in 1980 to over $ 71 billion; and the debt-to-service ratio increased to an unmanageable 32% of GDP.[12]

In response to this severe macroeconomic crisis, India's newly formed government, under the leadership of Prime Minister Narasimha Rao of the Congress (I) party, introduced a series of economic reforms designed to decrease government control in the economy and move toward an increasingly market-based economy. Exhibit 5 outlines some of the major policy reforms of 1991. India's economic liberalization policies were designed to create a market-friendly environment to attract MNCs and foreign direct investment. While a number of U.S.-based fast food chains like KFC and Pizza Hut rushed to the Indian market in the early 1990s as result of the Indian government's liberalization policies, McDonald's did not enter the Indian market until 1996. Instead, it spent about six years in planning, extensively researching Indian consumer tastes, product development, and supply chain arrangement before opening its first outlet in 1996.

McDonald's Road Map for India

Emphasis on Local Management

McDonald's has given the adage of "think global, act local" a concrete shape in India. The company's localization strategy is clearly manifest in the critical area of management. McDonald's decided to set up two joint ventures on a 50:50 basis with two local entrepreneurs in Mumbai and Delhi. In Mumbai, Amit Jatia's company, Hardcastle Restaurants Private Limited, was selected to own and manage McDonald's restaurants in the western region. In Delhi, Vikram Bakshi's Connaught Plaza Restaurants Private Limited was chosen to own and manage McDonald's restaurants in the northern region. Both Vikram Bakshi and Amit Jatia are responsible for running McDonald's in India. Vikram Bakshi has extensive background in real estate development in Delhi, while Amit Jatia, a vegetarian, has a chemicals and textile business background in Mumbai. It was not their backgrounds, however, that won the confidence of the Big Mac's management. Rather, it was their business plan emphasizing India-centric management strategies and their easy access to bureaucracy so critical to effective government relations building.

EXHIBIT   5

Summary of Economic Reforms and Changes in the Indian Economy (1991–93)

Industrial Reform

Abolition of industrial licensing	Industrial licensing abolished for all but 18 strategic industries. Earlier, licenses were required not only for new industries, but also to make any change in the existing ones.
Removal of control over capacity expansion	Under Monopoly and Restrictive Trade Practices (MRTP) Act, large firms were prevented from expanding their existing industrial capacity. This was removed.
Participation of foreign firms in new projects	Automatic approval granted for projects involving foreign equity investment up to 51% in high priority industries such as transportation, power, infrastructure-related, etc.
Privatization	List of industries reserved for public sector reduced from 17 to 6. Private sector participation is allowed in industries on the reserved list.
Price liberalization	Prices of most controlled items such as steel, petroleum, and coal liberalized.

Capital Market Reform

Liberalization of foreign investment	Foreign Exchange Regulation Act (FERA) was amended to make it easier for foreign firms to take more than 40% stake in Indian firms.
	Foreign institutional investors such as pension funds and mutual funds were allowed to invest in Indian capital market after registering with the independent authority called Security and Exchange Board of India (SEBI).
Access to global capital markets	Indian firms were allowed to raise debt and equity in global capital markets. Rupee convertibility on current account No longer necessary to purchase raw materials and capital goods at government-fixed exchange rates.

Tax Reform

Reduction of income tax rate	Corporate taxes lowered from 65% to 45%. Personal income tax rate reduced to 40% and exemption limit raised.
Abolition of wealth tax	Wealth tax on all financial assets, including shares, securities, bonds, and bank deposits abolished.

Labor Market Reform

Exit policy	No real progress. Companies with a workforce of over 300 cannot retrench workers without authorization from the government.

EXIM Policy Reform

Reduction of tariff structure	Customs duties on raw materials and finished goods lowered from 110% to 65% and on capital goods from 110% to 25%. Requirement on import licenses removed.
	Import duties on machinery for agriculture, horticulture, forestry, poultry, etc., reduced from 100% to 25%.
	Importation of consumer goods remains restricted.

"Politically Correct" Strategy

In the beginning, McDonald's was faced with two challenges of the Indian market: (1) how to avoid hurting religious sensibilities of Indian consumers; and (2) how to avoid political confrontation with Indian government and political activists. McDonald's managers were well aware of the fact that political activists can create trouble for foreign-based fast food chains, as demonstrated in the case of politically organized agitation against KFC in Bangalore in January 1996. With two local managing directors (Bakshi and Jatia) playing critical roles, McDonald's took a series of politically correct strategies to deal with the initial challenges of the Indian market. Since India's majority Hindus (80% of India's population) revere cows as sacred and 150 million of Indian Muslims do not eat pork, beef and pork have been a "complete no-no" from the start. Instead, McDonald's introduced a mutton-based "Maharaja Mac" in India, as opposed to its flagship beef-based Big Mac elsewhere.[13] Other items—such as the tantalizing McAloo Tikki Burger (breaded potato and pea pattie)—were added to the menu to lure India's middle class. Approximately 75% of the menu available in McDonald's in India is Indianized and specifically designed to woo Indian customers (Exhibit 6).

Employment Opportunity

India has come a long way from opposing the entry of MNCs to encouraging them to expand their business operations in India. Today, every expansion move McDonald's makes is received well by government officials. An important reason for this shift in attitude is the ability of the company to generate quality and long-term employment opportunities for Indians. McDonald's typically employs local people, and the average McDonald's restaurant in India employs more than 100 people in all kinds of positions—cashiers, cooks, managers, etc. Besides, every expansion also brings additional income and employment opportunities to India's agricultural work force, which is very pleasing to government officials. As Devinder Singh, a post-graduate economics student of Delhi School of Economics in Delhi University, put it: "McDonald's is now seen as a small- or medium-scale industry and is thus considered as useful for generating additional employment opportunities. As long as McDonald's serves this purpose, government support will follow."[14]

Green Sensitivity

In India, there is a vocal group of environmental and animal activists who oppose the entry of fast-food chains like KFC and McDonald's. Maneka Gandhi, former environment minister in the central government, and Dr. Vandana Shiva, director of the Research Foundation for Science, Technology and Ecology, are the prominent leaders of this group. According to this group's campaign, junk food chains like McDonald's and KFC destroy ecological balance and cause severe behavioral disorders because of their fatty and unhealthy foods, which have excessive levels of monosodium glutamate (MSG). Besides, they also campaign that these food chains are anti-poor and cater only to the rich segment of the Indian society.

To counter such negative campaigns, McDonald's has instituted a special fund to support green movements in Delhi. In Mumbai, in addition to financial contributions, it sponsors various community-related activities—such as "keep your city clean"—to promote environmental consciousness. In some of its restaurants in Delhi's residential areas like Vasant Vihar and Noida, McDonald's has put up pro-environment advertisements like "We Love Green." As a part of its attempt to increase awareness for an active and healthy lifestyle, McDonald's has sponsored and promoted several highly visible sports-related activities, including the recently concluded and very well attended "Olympic Day Run" in June 2005 in Vadodara in the state of Gujrat. Besides, McDonald's is currently focusing on fine tuning its fast food image by

EXHIBIT   6   McDonald's Menu in India (May 2001)

ITEM	ITEM
A LA CARTE	**FRIES**
Maharaja Mac	Regular
McChicken Burger	Medium
McChicken Burger with Cheese	Large
Filet-o-Fish	Wedges
McBurger	**BEVERAGES**
McBurger with Cheese	Regular Coke
McVeggie Burger	Medium Coke
McVeggie Burger with Cheese	Large Coke
McAloo Tikki Burger	Regular Fanta
McAloo Tikki Burger with Cheese	Medium Fanta
Salad Sandwich	Large Fanta
Pizza McPuff	Regular Sprite
Chicken McGrill	Medium Sprite
Chicken McGrill with Cheese	Large Sprite
Extra Cheese	**McSHAKES**
Extra Condiments	Chocolate
HAPPY MEALS (with regular drink and toy)	Strawberry
McBurger	Vanilla
Pizza Puff	Mineral Water 500 ml
Salad Sandwich	Coffee
McAloo Tikki	Tea
Chicken McGrill	Toned Milk
VALUE MEALS (with wedges and regular drink)	**DESSERTS**
McAloo Tikki	Soft Serve
Chicken McGrill	Vanilla
Salad Sandwich	Pineapple
Pizza Puff	Hot Fudge
MEAL COMBOS (with medium fries and medium drink)	Soft Serve Cone
McVeggie	Apple Pies
McVeggie with Cheese	
Maharaja Mac	
McChicken	
McChicken with Cheese	
Filet-o-Fish	
Upsize	

adding health food options to its product lists in terms of offering more baked or toasted options as opposed to fried patties. McCurry Pan, introduced in 2003, was the first baked dish option, and many more are being developed.

Corporate Citizenship: Giving Back Is Good Business

The executives of McDonald's understand it well that giving back to society is not just a one-way street (benefiting the recipients of corporate volunteerism). It is also a critical element of a company's brand and reputation. Giving back to the community brings benefits that far exceed any costs—whether it's in terms of strengthening the brand name or generating positive political capital that translates into more official support for company's expansion strategy. Thus, as a part of its corporate citizenship strategy, McDonald's has been involved in many community-related projects in India. Most of its projects are, however, directed toward children. One of its most popular community programs in Mumbai is called McDonald's Spotlight, which is an annual interschool performing arts competition. This competition is open to all secondary schools (standards 5th to 10th). The popularity of McDonald's Spotlight is evident from the number of schools participating in it. From 28 schools in 1998, the figures have increased to 120 schools in 2003.

Since 2002, McDonald's has been participating in World Children's Day on November 20 that coincides with United Nations' Universal Children's Day. On this day, McDonald's restaurants all over the world come together to raise funds for a charity of their choice. Since India has already been celebrating Children's Day on November 14 (that coincides with the birthday of India's first Prime Minister, Jawaharlal Nehru), McDonald's thought it appropriate to link these two days in India to create what is known as World Children's Week. Thus, instead of World Children's Day, McDonald's celebrates World Children's Week from November 14–20 in all its restaurants in India, during which funds are raised to finance various educational programs for children. One such popular initiative by McDonald's in Mumbai is known as the *Blue Dot* initiative that supports educational programs for the girl-child. In the Indian society, where the girl-child is always less favored than a boy, such an initiative by McDonald's has generated a lot of goodwill among Mumbai's politicians and community organizations that are working toward improving the status of the girl-child.

Another successful program sponsored by McDonald's is the Pulse Polio program that aims to make India polio-free by the year 2005. Partnering with the Rotary Club and local health organizations in Mumbai, McDonald's has been setting up inoculation booths outside its restaurants in Mumbai since 2001 to provide free polio vaccine to the children up to the age of five years during the polio eradication drive week once a year. McDonald's has also sponsored such popular children programs as the Millennium Pune Festival, Millennium Dreamers Global Recognition program (a talent search program for children between 8 to 15 years) in collaboration with UNESCO and Disney World Resort in Florida, and Interschool Science Quiz contest (where more than 180 schools from Mumbai participate every year) in collaboration with the Nehru Science Center, Mumbai. Needless to say, such community-related programs have earned official support for McDonald's and have helped its brand and reputation.

Pricing

Much of the McDonald's growth in India can be attributed to its pricing strategy. Since, on an average, each household spends about 50% of income on food and beverages in India, food prices are always a sensitive issue (Exhibit 7).

Even the Indian middle class, despite their much improved income level, remains very price sensitive. Accordingly, McDonald's has pursued what Amit

EXHIBIT **7**   Household Expenditures (% of total), 1998–99

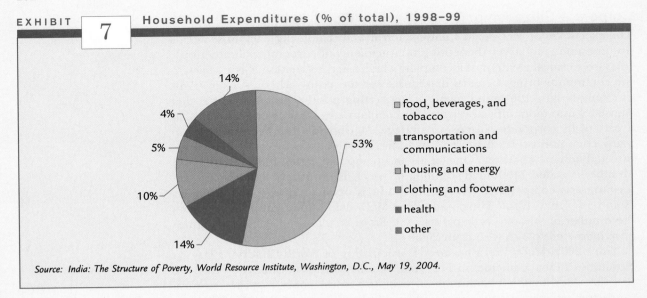

- food, beverages, and tobacco
- transportation and communications
- housing and energy
- clothing and footwear
- health
- other

53%
14%
14%
10%
5%
4%

Source: India: The Structure of Poverty, World Resource Institute, Washington, D.C., May 19, 2004.

Jatia, the company's managing director in the Western region, calls "purchasing power pricing" or the customer's ability to pay. The adoption of such a pricing strategy in India offers a useful country-specific insight on possible price differences of the company's products on the basis of purchasing power parity (PPP) calculations across countries as provided by the so-called Big Mac Index (Exhibits 8 and 9).

Worldwide, McDonald's has achieved success by tapping middle-class households. But in India, while McDonald's has been able to get a larger share of rich and upper-middleclass population, it has not been as successful at

EXHIBIT **8**   The Big Mac Index Concept

The Economist, a weekly news magazine published in the United Kingdom, introduced its Big Mac Index in 1986 to explain the concept of purchasing power parity (PPP). Given the consistency of McDonald's Big Mac product across countries, its price is used by *The Economist* to calculate exchange rates adjusted for purchasing power for a sample of countries. The idea of the Big Mac as a measure of purchasing power parity is based on the Law of One Price, according to which the exchange rate should adjust to equate prices of the same products between countries. By comparing the price of a Big Mac in any two cities in different countries, the exchange rate can be readily calculated that would make the prices equal (Exhibit 9). For example (as shown below), if a Big Mac costs US$2.90 in the United States and 10.41 yuan in China, then the exchange rate should be 3.59 yuan per U.S. dollar, so that the same Big Mac costs the same in New York and Shanghai.

Calculating the Big Mac PPP rate

PPP Yuan/US$ = Chinese price of a Big Mac in yuan divided by U.S. price of a Big Mac in US$
= Yuan 10.40 / US$2.90
= 3.59 Yuan/US$, which is the exchange rate that will exist if the Law of One Price holds exactly

The above example makes it clear that the calculation of purchasing power parity is based on equal prices in both countries, rather than necessarily equal purchasing power for consumers. Given that the average per capita income in China in 2004 was US$5,225, while in the U.S. the average was US$34,770, it is clear that Chinese would not have the same purchasing power as the average American in that year. It would cost a Chinese consumer about 6.5 times as much as a percentage of his/her income to buy a Big Mac, even if the price were the same in both countries. Not surprisingly, a Big Mac costing 10.40 yuan in China may very well be a luxury good. In fact, in many countries, this is exactly the case.

Source: Adapted from Robert Grosse and Adrian E. Tschoegl, "The Manager's Guide to Big Macs," unpublished paper, July 2004.

EXHIBIT 9   Big Mac Index

	Big Mac prices in local currency	Big Mac prices in dollars	Implied PPP of the dollar	Actual dollar exchange rate May 2004	Under (−)/over (+) valuation against the dollar (%)
United States	$ 2.90	2.90	—	—	—
Argentina	Peso 4.35	1.48	1.50	2.94	− 49
Australia	A$ 3.25	2.27	1.12	1.43	− 22
Brazil	*Real* 5.39	1.70	1.86	3.17	− 41
Britain	£1.88	3.37	1.54	1.79	+ 16
Canada	C$ 3.19	2.33	1.10	1.37	− 20
Chile	Peso 1,401	2.18	483	643	− 25
China	Yuan 10.41	1.26	3.59	8.26	− 57
Czech Rep	Koruna 56.55	2.13	19.5	26.6	− 27
Denmark	DKr 27.75	4.46	9.57	6.22	+ 54
Egypt	Pound 10.00	1.62	3.45	6.17	− 44
Euro area	2.74	3.28	1.06	1.20	+ 13
Hong Kong	HK$ 12.01	1.54	4.14	7.80	− 47
Hungary	Forint 531	2.52	183	211	− 13
Indonesia	Rupiah 16,101	1.77	5,552	9,097	− 39
Japan	¥ 262	2.33	90.3	112	− 20
Malaysia	M$ 5.05	1.33	1.74	3.80	− 54
Mexico	Peso 24.01	2.08	8.28	11.54	− 28
New Zealand	NZ$ 4.35	2.65	1.50	1.64	− 8
Peru	New Sol 8.99	2.57	3.10	3.50	− 11
Philippines	Peso 69.02	1.23	23.8	56.1	− 57
Poland	Zloty 6.29	1.63	2.17	3.86	− 44
Russia	Rouble 42.05	1.45	14.5	29.0	− 50
Singapore	S$ 3.31	1.92	1.14	1.72	− 34
South Africa	Rand 12.41	1.86	4.28	6.67	− 36
South Korea	Won 3,199	2.72	1,103	1,176	− 6
Sweden	SKr 29.87	3.94	10.3	7.58	+ 36
Switzerland	SFr 6.29	4.90	2.17	1.28	+ 69
Taiwan	NT$75.11	2.24	25.9	33.5	− 23
Thailand	Baht 58.87	1.45	20.3	40.6	− 50
Turkey	Lira 3,950,000	2.58	1,362,069	1,531,008	− 11
Venezuela	Bolivar 4,399	1.48	1,517	2,972	− 49
India*	**Rs 34.00**	**0.75**	**11.7**	**45.3**	**− 74**

Calculating over (under) valuation: PPP Yen/US$ = Tokyo price of a Big Mac in Yen divided by U.S. price in US$ = (Yen 262)/(US$2.90) = 90.3

Over (under) valuation = The PPP exchange rate minus the actual exchange rate, divided by the actual exchange rate = (90.3 − 112)/112 = −20% (that is, US$ has to fall by 20% against the Yen—Yen has to appreciate from 112/US$ to 90 yen/US$—for the rate to reach Big Mac PPP).

*Big Mac is not sold in India. In its place, Big Mac's substitute Majaraja Mac's price is given here.

Source: Adapted from The Economist, May 29, 2004, pp. 71–72; and Robert Grosse and Adrian E. Tschoegl, "The Manager's Guide to Big Macs," unpublished paper, July 2004. Data for India is author's calculation.

effectively tapping the middle-class and lower middle-class segments. Capturing the latter segment is critical as McDonald's starts entering into smaller cities. But this section has mainly stayed away because of a widely prevailed perception that McDonald's is expensive. This is the reason why the company cut prices on its vegetable nuggets from Rs 29 to Rs 19, and the soft service ice cream cone from Rs 15 to Rs 7 in 1997.[15] In September 2001, McDonald's offered its enormously popular *shudh shakahari* (pure vegetarian) Veg Surprise (a veggie burger) for Rs 17. With this price, McDonald's was able to sell the veggie burger 40% more than what it expected within a month between September and October of 2001.[16] In March 2004, McDonald's launched a Happy Price menu under which it sells four of its burger products at Rs20 each. This has led to a 25% increase in customers.[17] Clearly, the McDonald's strategy has been to increase sales volume of its products by making its products available at an affordable price.

McDonald's has been offering value meals in a range of prices—Rs 29, Rs 39, Rs 49, Rs 59, Rs 79, and Rs 89. McDonald's has employed this value-ladder strategy to ensure affordability and thus attract the widest section of customers. As Vikram Bakshi, McDonald's managing director of the Northern region in India, explains, "Our clear strategy is to bring the customers in initially and provide a range of entry-level products so that they can try new items and graduate to the higher rungs. Thus, if a customer starts with a McAloo Tikki Burger (breaded potato and pea pattie), what he graduates to finally is a vegetarian burger. Or, if a customer starts with a Chicken Kabab burger, what he graduates finally to is the McChicken." Such strategy has helped its volume business.

Another strategy that seems to have gone well with Indian customers is what the company calls the 80-20 menu board—80% visual and 20% descriptive. The main objective of the company is to make it easier for customers to understand what the 29, 39, 49, 59, 79, and 89 rupee options are. Coupled with the pricing range, McDonald's quick service, convenience, and no-tips environment have attracted many school- and college-going customers, as well as young middle-class families.

The most important reason for McDonald's pricing flexibility is its well-established supply chain arrangement, which ensures efficiency and speed in distribution. Besides, huge increases in volume sales and food processing technology have been helping the company to offset its cost.

Supply Chain Management

Another critical strategy was to set up a well-established supply chain in India in order to achieve three objectives: (1) to operationalize its globally practiced QSCV (quality, service, cleanliness, and value) principle; (2) to enjoy flexibility in pricing; and (3) to launch a new product when necessary. To achieve these three objectives, McDonald's often uses an outsourcing model in all its markets. In some cases, it also actively imports. But given India's relatively higher import duties and foreign exchange fluctuations, McDonald's decided early on to source its raw materials from the local suppliers to the maximum extent possible. Currently, McDonald's only imports the process control equipment that allows it to dish out burgers and other orders within its super-fast time frames. The company, however, sources 95% of its raw materials from 38 local suppliers.[18] Fresh lettuce comes from Delhi, Pune (Maharashtra), Nainital, and Ooty (Uttar Pradesh); cheese comes from Dynamix Dairies located in Baramati (Maharashtra); buns come from Cremica Industries in Phillur (Punjab) and Shah Bector and Sons in Khopoli (Maharashtra); pickles come from Global Green Company in Hyderabad (Andhra Pradesh); sauce comes from Bector

Foods in Phillur (Punjab); and chicken patties, vegetable patties, pies, and pizza puffs come from Vista Processed Foods in Taloja (Maharashtra) (Exhibit 10). The entire supply distribution is the responsibility of AFL Logistics Ltd., a joint venture between Airfreight and Coughlin in the U.S., and Radhakrishna Foodland (P) Ltd. in Thane, Maharashtra.

Setting up a well-coordinated supply chain was not easy, given India's poor transportation and storage infrastructure, as well as its lower-quality agricultural products. Thus, six years prior to the opening of its first restaurant in India, McDonald's and its international suppliers worked together with local Indian companies to develop products that meet the rigorous quality standards McDonald's demands. An underlying principle in product development was to strictly adhere to the Indian government's regulation on food, health, and hygiene and to exceed the government's standards. To do so, McDonald's transferred its state-of-the-art food processing technology to India, enabling Indian businesses to grow by improving their ability to compete in today's international markets.

McDonald's has worked with local Indian suppliers to consistently improve the quality and increase greater yields of agricultural products. For instance, it helped farmers of Trikaya Agriculture Company to grow high-quality lettuce year round in Ooty, Pune, Delhi, and other regions. McDonald's shared with Trikaya advanced agricultural technology and expertise like utilization of drip irrigation systems that reduce overall water consumption and agricultural

EXHIBIT 10   Suppliers for McDonald's in India

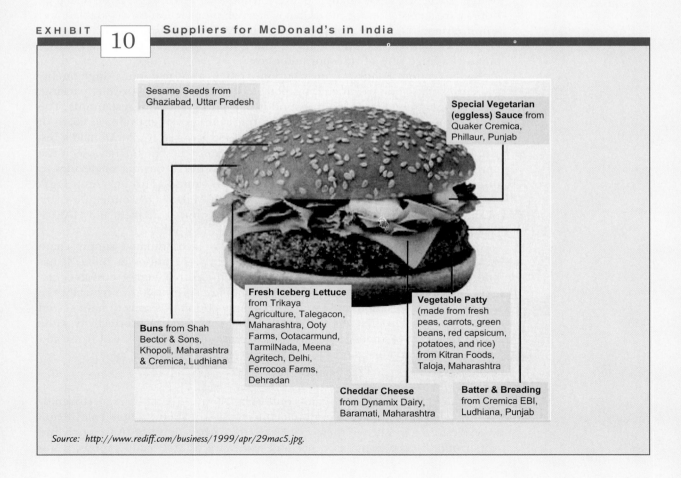

Sesame Seeds from Ghaziabad, Uttar Pradesh

Special Vegetarian (eggless) Sauce from Quaker Cremica, Phillaur, Punjab

Fresh Iceberg Lettuce from Trikaya Agriculture, Talegacon, Maharashtra, Ooty Farms, Ootacarmund, TarmilNada, Meena Agritech, Delhi, Ferrocoa Farms, Dehradan

Vegetable Patty (made from fresh peas, carrots, green beans, red capsicum, potatoes, and rice) from Kitran Foods, Taloja, Maharashtra

Buns from Shah Bector & Sons, Khopoli, Maharashtra & Cremica, Ludhiana

Cheddar Cheese from Dynamix Dairy, Baramati, Maharashtra

Batter & Breading from Cremica EBI, Ludhiana, Punjab

Source: http://www.rediff.com/business/1999/apr/29mac5.jpg.

management practices. For quality control, Trikaya's post-harvest facilities now include a large cold storage facility, a cold chain consisting of a pre-cooling room to remove field heat and large refrigerated vans with humidity controls. To ensure standardization and higher quality, Vista International, which supplies the pies, nuggets, and vegetable and chicken patties, built a new facility in 1996 with help from McDonald's. This new facility has insulated panels, temperature control, and chill rooms. Vista International has obtained American Institute of Bakers and Hazard Analysis Critical Control Points (HACCP) certification for quality standards.[19]

In some cases, Indian companies like Dynamix Dairies had the technology but no market for their milk derivative products. By associating with McDonald's, Dynamix Dairies has seen a regularly growing expansion of its market. Now, it not only supplies products to McDonald's restaurants in India, but also has an export order of approximately US$12 million per year.

Radhakrishna Foodland (P) Ltd., which is responsible for getting products from various suppliers and delivering products to various McDonald's outlets, has earned an excellent reputation in maintaining a tight "delivery-on-time" schedule. This is possible because of the company's installation of enterprise resource planning (ERP) software, which provides data of what is selling where. This way, the company is able to anticipate demand in each retail outlet and place orders with producers accordingly. With the help of McDonald's, the company has set up a trucking fleet to move supplies to restaurants at short notice. Each of the company's delivery trucks has three degrees of refrigeration—a freezer section for meats, a cold refrigerator section for vegetables, and a nonrefrigerated section for paper cups, napkins, and plastic cutlery. This way, each truck delivers multiple items at one go and saves the company and restaurants a huge sum of transportation cost.

Radhakrishna Foodland distribution center also maintains high-quality standards in cleanliness, including personal hygiene for the drivers, packing, and checking temperatures of the food it transports to various restaurants. The company maintains detailed data logs to track the movement of each batch of food items. In case of a complaint about a food item at any McDonald's restaurants, the data logs help the company to identify the batch from which the particular food item came. Then the company issues a warning or decides to discontinue the batch from which the food item came.[20] This ensures a high-quality standard of food items delivered to each McDonald's outlet. Not surprisingly, the company has obtained American Institute of Bakers and HACCP certification for quality standards.

Such meticulous planning in setting up a well-coordinated supply chain system has paid rich dividends to the McDonald's operations in India. It has minimized costs, optimized quality control, and ensured higher customer satisfaction, which is so very essential for the company's growth. More critically, the improved transportation and food processing technology seems to have served as an important catalyst for increasing India's agricultural productivity while raising farmers' incomes. This has scored very well on the political front and won the government's goodwill.

Location

The initial openings of McDonald's outlets in Delhi and Mumbai were driven by affordability and brand recognition factors. Given the metropolitan culture and wide Western exposure of these two large cities, where most of India's rich and upper middle-class population live and are aware of McDonald's foods, it was logical for the company to open its initial outlets in these two cities. Besides, the inhabitants of both Mumbai and Delhi love to experiment with a wide variety of foods. This obviously suited McDonald's brand of foods. In addition, McDonald's has two large distribution centers in these two metros. Needless to say, opening up restaurants in these two cities would drive down the opportunity and transaction costs.

Logistics play a critical role in McDonald's location strategy. As a part of its Quick Service Restaurant (QSR) business, McDonald's has initially decided to open its outlets only within a 500-km radius of its main distribution centers in Delhi and Mumbai. This is the reason why McDonald's has not opened a single outlet in metropolitan cities like Kolkata in the eastern part of India, despite the city's huge urban and cosmopolitan character.

Besides Delhi and Mumbai, other places where McDonald's has opened up restaurants are satellite cities located near Delhi (such as Noida, Gurgaon, and Faridabad), or Mumbai (such as Pune); places with tourist appeal (such as Jaipur, Mathura, and Shimla); and cities with an eating-out culture (such as Ahmedabad, Chandigarh, and Bangalore). The McDonald's outlet in Ahmedabad in the state of Gujrat is an interesting case. Ahmedabad is largely a vegetarian city. But, like other metropolitan Indian cities, Ahmedabad has a significant number of eating-out customers. Given long lines of people at the counter, it seems that McDonald's well-balanced menus of vegetarian and nonvegetarian items has provided enough choice and space for customers of this city.[21]

McDonald's has partnered with the state-owned oil company, Bharat Petroleum Corporation Ltd. (BPCL), to set up restaurants at the latter's petrol stations in and around Delhi to make it more convenient for automobile-driving consumers. BPCL is the leading petroleum retailer in India and has the largest number of petroleum stations in and around Delhi. It is important to note the shift in government attitude toward MNCs that led to a successful partnership between McDonald's and the largest state-owned company.

Keeping an eye on the huge potential for eating out venues for lower middle-class Indians, McDonald's has partnered with a railway station and bus station in Delhi to open its outlets: Delhi Metro Rail Corporation, and the overcrowded Delhi's Inter-State Bus Terminus, where thousands of people pass through daily on their way to different destinations. More importantly, to tap the automobile-driving consumers, business travelers, and tourists, McDonald's has set up drive-through outlets in Delhi and along national highways. Two drive-through outlets on the Delhi-Agra and Mumbai-Pune highways have proven to be successful. The company has plans to open more drive-through outlets in Delhi and Mumbai and along national highways—such as the Delhi-Jaipur highway, Delhi-Ambala highway, and Delhi-Ludhiana highway. Again, as with all of its restaurants, the move to set up these new restaurants has been driven by business prospects, logistics, and supply chain.

In order to tap into the business of shopping mall and film-going customers, McDonald's has set up outlets at shopping malls and new multiplexes in metros like Delhi and Mumbai. The success of its outlet at the Crossroads in Mumbai is evidence that a strategic location outside a mall can bring in customers in hordes. Given the premium pricing in the shopping mall, it is not surprising to see that many people are content with window-shopping at the Crossroads. But they do not mind spending a few rupees at McDonald's for a burger or spicy fries. More important, families with children are happy to spend at least 7 rupees to buy an ice cream for their children. Thus, while most shopowners at the mall are hard-pressed to break even, the lines at the McDonald's counters seem unending. A similar trend is seen at the newly opened multiplex in Delhi's Vikaspuri.

Cultural Sensitivity

Since the mid-1980s, Indian society has undergone a dramatic shift in social values. The traditional caste-defined view of Indian life, which undervalues social and economic mobility, and the dominance of the Brahmanical culture's disdain toward commerce have been challenged by the middle class in contemporary Indian society. Getting rich and enjoying a good life has become the new mantra of social existence for the Indian middle class. With more income and more purchasing power, the status-conscious Indian middle class now seek to buy good quality consumer products and spend more money on food and entertainment. In metropolitan cities, extensive foreign media exposure and the Internet revolution have contributed to the emergence of a new social attitude which accepts Western values and culture. The contemporary Indian society can be understood on the basis of a 70/30 dynamic. While 70% of Indians are still traditional, poor, and live in rural areas, 30% of Indians (more than 300 million people) have emerged as rich, modern, Western-exposed, English-speaking, urban dwellers.

In India's metropolitan cities, the young and rich have embraced the spirit of American culture.[22] America has come to be associated with success, productivity, and a good life. This growing acceptance corresponds to the big impact of the American influence on Indian business, education, and entertainment. The U.S. is India's largest trading partner, investor, and business collaborator. Top U.S. corporations like General Electric, General Motors, Ford, Citibank, Coca Cola, Pepsi, Microsoft, IBM, and Intel are entrenched in India. American universities in general, and a few in particular like Harvard, Wharton, Columbia, Princeton, and Massachusetts Institute of Technology (MIT), are instantly recognized in India and have become the most preferred destinations for today's generation. The growing popularity of Western pop culture, MTV, Hollywood movies, and American-type fast food are all a part of this new social acceptance of the urban-based Indian rich and middle class.

The image of McDonald's as a premier American fast food chain fits well with this changing Indian socio-cultural landscape. For many, McDonald's has become an important stop on the way to Harvard or MIT, a place that provides an opportunity to "connect" with the world outside India. For its part, McDonald's has also introduced several new products specifically for Indian consumers in order to get accepted and successfully blend into local Indian culture. Of course, introducing local products for the local palate is not a new concept at McDonald's. The Teriyaki Burger in Japan, Croque McDo in France, the Maharani Burger in Malaysia, a green pepper burger in Singapore, a Thai burger with a Thai curry paste, spaghetti in the Philippines, spicy chicken with rice in Indonesia, and spicy seafood noodle in China are some of the examples of its localization strategy. But what is unique in the context of India is the company's willingness to replace its core product, beef-based Big Mac.

Given the fact that an overwhelming majority of Indians (about 83%) do not eat beef or pork, the introduction of the Maharaja Mac (a mutton-based burger) by McDonald's seems to be an appropriate cultural fit. Contrary to popular belief, however, India is not a predominantly vegetarian country. About 20% of India's population is completely vegetarian (Exhibit 11). A closer look at state-level food habits in India reveals that food preferences vary widely among the

EXHIBIT   11   Indian Food Preferences—Vegetarian vs. Nonvegetarian

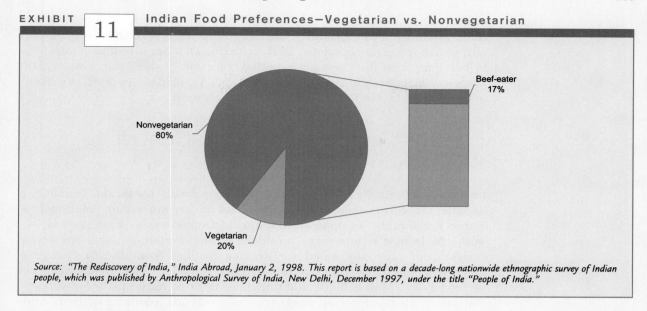

Source: "The Rediscovery of India," India Abroad, January 2, 1998. This report is based on a decade-long nationwide ethnographic survey of Indian people, which was published by Anthropological Survey of India, New Delhi, December 1997, under the title "People of India."

country's 30 states and six union territories. About 69% of Gujrat is vegetarian; 60% of Rajasthan; 54% of Punjab and Haryana; 50% of Uttar Pradesh; 45% of Madhya Pradesh; 34% of Karnataka; 30% of Maharashtra; 21% of Tamil Nadu; 16% Andhra Pradesh and Delhi; 15% of Assam; 6% of Kerala, Orissa, Bihar, and West Bengal; and less than 5% in northeastern states/union territories (Manipur, Mizoran, Nagaland, and Arunachal Pradesh). While part of this vegetarianism is economic, a more compelling force is ethical and even religious. Jains avoid meat totally, while many Buddhists in India are vegetarian. Brahmins, Saivite non-Brahmins of South India and several Vaishnavite sects across the country avoid meat. Interestingly, though, Brahmins of East India, Kashmir, and the Saraswats of the southwest eat fish and mutton. But even among meat-eaters, beef is taboo.[23]

For vegetarian consumers, McDonald's offers veggie burgers, which are very popular among the vegetarians in India. Like the Maharaja Mac, the veggie burger has gone through a rigorous testing procedure and detailed planning. Sanjiv Mediratta, McDonald's quality assurance and product development manager for India, had test-marketed this veggie burger in 1994 in McDonald's outlets located in three Asian population-dominated towns of London—Southhall, Ilford, and Hounslow—before launching the product in India in 1996.[24] Further, McDonald's has sought to enforce strict standards in product development and cooking so as not to ruffle cultural sensitivities of the vegetarian consumers of the Indian society. All foods are strictly segregated into vegetarian and nonvegetarian lines and separate utensils are used for cooking vegetarian and nonvegetarian foods. French fries in India are not flavored with beef tallow, as is the case in the United States and elsewhere. Even the mayonnaise and ice cream contain no eggs.[25]

Indians typically spend more money on eating out and purchasing new products during festival seasons. To capitalize on the spending habits of Indian consumers, McDonald's has often sought to launch new products, the so-called "fourth flavor,"[26] during India's festival season, which falls between September and November. Some of the major and popular religious festivals in India during September and November are *Navratras, Dussehra,* and *Diwali,* when even nonvegetarian Hindus turn vegetarian. Given this dynamic, McDonald's decided to launch a new product called Veg Surprise, a vegetable burger laced with Indian spices, in September 2001, achieving an impressive sales figure 40% higher than what the company expected. Likewise, *Paneer Salsa*, a vegetarian wrap, was introduced in 2003. Given its growing popularity, this product is likely to be adopted by McDonald's in global markets soon.

Family-Centric and Child-Centric Strategy

In India, McDonald's has positioned itself as a family restaurant. Family has become the cornerstone of its strategy. Its outlets are called "McDonald's Family Restaurants," as opposed to simply McDonald's as in other parts of the world. McDonald's restaurants provide a clean, comfortable, and stress-free environment especially suited for working families. With India's changing family system in metropolitan cities, where the extended family is no longer the preferred way of living, McDonald's has become an attractive place for working and busy young parents on weekdays. On weekends, residents of Delhi and Mumbai bring their children to McDonald's so that they can relax, while their children play in McDonald's hugely popular play places.

Like its other worldwide locations, McDonald's targets children as their main clientele in India. Children in India may not have the purchasing power comparable to their Western counterparts, but they are still the center of the universe in the Indian family system, and they can actually pull the parents to visit a place time and again. Children are an enormously powerful medium for relationship building in India. They not only influence markets in terms of the parental decision-making to buy certain kinds of products, they are also future consumers. After all, brand impressions, once formed, can stay for a lifetime.

Thus, McDonald's has done everything possible to attract children. When one of its outlets was opened in South Mumbai, a children's parade was organized all along the popular Marine Drive, led by McDonald's mascot, Ronald, who was accompanied by a 40-feet long float depicting the various tourist destinations in Mumbai. Its "Happy Meals" and the accompanying Lego toys are a great attraction for children. McDonald's play places—appropriately called Fun Zones—appeal to children and their parents, because they are considered safe, reliable, hygienic, and kid-friendly. Kids like McDonald's outlets because they are brightly lit and full of young people. During their visits, kids are showered with knickknacks. The Noida outlet near Delhi even has a low-height order counter for children. McDonald's outlets provide the kids with a hassle-free experience where no one tells them "sit down," "don't move," or "keep out of my way."

McDonald's also promotes birthday parties complete with cake, candles, and toys in television advertising aimed directly at kids. In some Indian cities like Mumbai, Delhi, and Bangalore, birthday parties are all the rage for upwardly mobile youngsters. Given that most young people in these cities live in small, overcrowded flats, McDonald's has become a convenient and welcoming place for birthday celebrations.

McDonald's has become a popular place for many jean-clad teenagers, who use the outlet as a venue to meet their boyfriends/girlfriends, still a tricky issue among Indian middle-class families. McDonald's appeals to India's new Westernized elites because its food is clean, safe, and reliable. India's upwardly mobile middle-class families show considerable interest in enjoying what is often described as the "McDonald's experience"—i.e., eating McDonald's food in a clean, friendly, and fun-filled environment with quick and accurate services.

McDonald's offers attractive new promotions from time to time to attract more young adults to its outlets. One such promotion—"Music Meal," launched in April 2005 in association with Coca-Cola India and Universal Music India—became extremely popular with young men and women. Through this promotional campaign, young people were offered free tickets to an exclusive hugely popular Bombay Vikings show upon collection of four McDonald's mini-CDs, which come with a large meal combo order. By engaging young customers with fun and new promotions that are in tune with their changing desires, McDonald's has been able to increase its business volume considerably over the past years.

McDonald's has introduced other innovations that appeal to customers of all ages in India. In some of its newly opened restaurants, McDonald's has provided lounges for senior citizens to relax and taste its food. For people used to a traditional restaurant environment, in which waiters lead patrons to sitting places, McDonald's in Delhi's residential areas has made special arrangements, where several crewmembers are present to direct families to available sitting places. Most Indians love to have sweet desserts after a meal. Keeping this in mind, McDonald's has opened several very popular Cold Kiosks in Mumbai and Delhi. These Cold Kiosks, which are located either inside the main outlet or adjacent to the McDonald's outlet, offer customers an innovative range of cold desserts such as ice creams with unusual flavors like bubble gum, green apple, and peach.

Most Indians believe in fate, and fate-driven success or failure is a way of life. There may not be frequent discussion in public discourse, but the powerful concept of *Karma* in Hinduism and reward for good *Karma* still continues to be a critical and almost subconscious determinant of Indian social existence. Not surprisingly, one of McDonald's most popular attractions has been the instant scratch-and-win prizes on a daily and weekly basis (Exhibit 12). The daily drawn prizes include color televisions, cell phones, Panasonic camcorders, VCRs, music systems, microwave ovens, and even scooters. The weekly prizes promise a family vacation to various places outside India. There is also a monthly jackpot prize of a Mahindra Bolero jeep and other high-ticketed items available. Aptly named the "Lucky Itch," these prizes have become enormously popular for the fate-driven Indian psyche, i.e., "if you are lucky, you are successful and win big."

For people who still want to eat at home or are unable to visit restaurants because of lack of transportation, traffic jams, and overcrowded eating places, McDonald's has introduced its popular home-delivery (McDelivery) services. For another section of rich middle-class families in Delhi and Mumbai who prefer to enjoy watching movies, cricket matches at home, or just for plain relaxation away from cooking, McDonald's home-delivery services (where food is delivered usually hot) have become popular and convenient. McDonald's has achieved about a 15% increase in sales as a result of starting home deliveries from some of its stores.

Challenges Ahead

It is too early to say that McDonald's has succeeded in India. Nine years after McDonald's first set up in India, the burger giant has yet to make any net profit. According to McDonald's management, each McDonald's store in India takes

EXHIBIT   12   McDonald's Enticement (itch karo, rich bano)

Source: McDonald's in Mumbai, India (May 21, 2001).

about five to seven years to break even. Part of the reason for this long break-even period has to do with the investments required per store in terms of expensive process control equipment (that the company imports from abroad) and acquiring prime location real estate properties. However, compared to 12–13 years that McDonald's takes to break even in any new country the company enters, India's break-even time is actually more favorable. One reason for the quicker breakeven in India is the reduction in the per-store investment that McDonald's has managed to achieve with indigenization. McDonald's per-store investment in 2003-2004 was 33% less than its per-store investment in 1996 in India.

Going by McDonald's expansion, an impressive 50% annual revenue growth since 1997, and growing popularity, it is reasonable to argue that McDonald's operations in India have achieved decent success.[27] McDonald's couldn't have achieved the success without appealing to new generations of consumers—children 3 to 14 and their busy parents' nurturing needs. In a recent survey by Synovate, a global market research agency, 20% of young Indians between the ages of 8 and 24 reported their preference for McDonald's products, followed by Pizza Hut (11%) and then KFC (2%).[28] No amount of advertising and brilliant promotions could have done the trick alone. In India, McDonald's did not create a market where none existed. It merely responded to an opportunity presented by the changing Indian socio-cultural values and sustained economic liberalization.

McDonald's strategy of positioning itself as a family restaurant with an emphasis on local menus and local values seems to be working well in India. But to what extent McDonald's can continue its growth in India remains uncertain. McDonald's is more than just another American fast food chain. It carries a symbolic load of Americanness—American variant of capitalism and its overwhelming domination over the global economy. It is also a symbol of American cultural imperialism.[29] For this reason, McDonald's operations in India, like other parts of the world, will continue to face opposition from religious fundamentalists, environmentalists, protectionists, animal rights activists, and antiglobalization protestors.[30] Already, McDonald's outlets in Delhi and Thane (on the outskirts of Mumbai) have been the targets of violent protests from the Hindu militant groups led by the Shiv Sena (the right-wing Hindu nationalist group) after the company was sued in the United States over the use of beef extract on its French fries.[31] McDonald's public assurance that it does not use any animal extract in vegetarian foods in India and the clearance certificate the company got from the government agency Brihanmumbai Municipal Corporation (BMC) took the steam out of this kind of politically motivated violent protests for the time being.[32]

In March 2005, McDonald's outlet in Ahmedabad in the western state of Gujrat became a target of protest from the ruling BJP (Bharatiya Janata Party) party workers, following the U.S. decision to deny the BJP party's leader and the Chief Minister of Gujrat Narendra Modi a diplomatic visa on the ground of his alleged involvement in the Godhra train carnage, where hundreds of people were killed as a result of Hindu-Muslim communal riots. Denouncing the U.S. decision as an insult to India's sovereignty, the BJP party workers organized protest rallies in Ahmedabad with placards like, "Throw out all American goods and Americans from Gujrat."[33] With increased deployment of police force and the central BJP leaders' advice not to attack the American companies, the protest fizzled out. But it may erupt again.

In India, McDonald's is likely to face constant pressure to increase its product range. Until now, the company has responded well to varying customers' tastes and preferences by introducing new products. But given India's fragmented regional cultures, where no single food preference predominates, McDonald's needs to develop new products on a regular basis. Developing new products adds complexity and cost and raises the risk of error. It also runs counter to McDonald's culture and history. Yet, if McDonald's does not do it on a regular basis, the company's popularity will be short-lived. It will be difficult for the company to meet the range of different competitors, most notably the homegrown Nirula's, which offers a variety of products at reasonable prices.

In order to grow, McDonald's needs to expand to other cities and towns in India rather than concentrating in Delhi, Mumbai, and a few other metropolitan cities. For expansion to succeed, McDonald's can no longer depend on its processing and distribution centers in and around Delhi and Mumbai. Given India's poor transportation and road facilities, the logistical bottleneck of transporting food items from one place to another will add to the cost of its products. It needs to build new processing and distribution centers in other cities for In India, McDonald's is likely to face constant pressure to increase its product range. Until now, the company has responded well to varying customers' tastes and preferences by introducing new products. But given India's fragmented regional cultures, where no single food preference predominates, McDonald's needs to develop new products on a regular basis. Developing new products adds complexity and cost and raises the risk of error. It also runs counter to McDonald's culture and history. Yet, if McDonald's does not do it on a regular basis, the company's popularity will be short-lived. It will be difficult for the company to meet the range of different competitors, most notably the homegrown Nirula's, which offers a variety of products at reasonable prices. In order to grow, McDonald's needs to expand to other cities and towns in India rather than concentrating in Delhi, Mumbai, and a few other metropolitan cities. For expansion to succeed, McDonald's can no longer depend on its processing and distribution centers in and around Delhi and Mumbai. Given India's poor transportation and road facilities, the logistical bottleneck of transporting food items from one place to another will add to the cost of its products. It needs to build new processing and distribution centers in other cities for operational efficiency. This requires additional investment, and the cost cannot be easily passed on to the consumers. Price increase is the last thing that McDonald's can afford if it wants to succeed in its expansion strategy in India. Already, for most people, McDonald's is associated with high prices. Many critics therefore argue that McDonald's will never become part of mass culture in India because most people can't afford a Maharaja Mac.

Despite these challenges, the outlook is positive for McDonald's in India. It may remain as a restaurant for rich and middle-class people in the near future. But these are the classes that have extra money to spend on food and entertainment. The growing popularity of McDonald's-type fast food is only one dimension of a much larger Indian trend toward culinary adventurism associated with rising affluence of 30% of Indians. Rajesh Chauhan, the marketing manager of the newly opened superplex in Delhi's Vikas Puri, where the newly opened McDonald's is attracting streams of well-dressed and well-mannered people, states with a calm smile, "Personally, I like Maharaja Macs."[34] This view was echoed by Pramod Chatterji, an Indian Airlines Pilot, who said, "McDonald's offers just another option for eating out, and their products really taste good."[35] While eating a Maharaja Mac in a McDonald's located in Delhi's crowded Connaught Place shopping area, Sandeep Kohli, a tourist taxi driver in Delhi, said, "I do not mind eating at McDonald's once a while if I can afford it."

More critically, support for McDonald's operations in India comes from an unexpected quarter. A senior high-ranking bureaucrat in his mid-40s, who occasionally visits McDonald's outlets in Delhi with his two children, observed, "I do not see anything wrong with McDonald's doing business in India. After all, it is not McDonaldization (cultural imperialism) that we know of, it is a Big MacCommodation (cultural accommodation)," referring to the Indianization of McDonald's products.[36]

Local adaptation, no doubt, has contributed to McDonald's business growth in India. As Vikram Bakshi, Managing Director of McDonald's India, sums up, "Good Planning is absolutely necessary when you go into any country. Very clearly, you have to understand the culture; you have to understand how you intend to be relevant to the consumer in that country. I don't think any brand, no matter how big it is, can take the market lightly. And I think the biggest mistake is when you think you have a big brand and that everyone is overwhelmed by it. Because whatever the brand, it has to be relevant to the consumer of that country."

By providing country-specific relevant products—Maharaja Mac and about 70% Indianization of its products—McDonald's has been able to triumph over its last great frontier. Or has it, really?

CASE DISCUSSION QUESTIONS

1. What are some of the contextual issues for McDonald's in India? What are some of the more prominent social institutions at work?
2. Given the challenging country context of India, why has McDonald's done well in India?
3. What are some of the future challenges that McDonald's has to deal with in India? How would you resolve these challenges?
4. What are some of the important lessons of McDonald's operation in India?

Endnotes

[1] In November 2004, McDonald's entered the southern part of India with its first restaurant in Bangalore, the so-called Silicon Valley of India.

[2] "McDonald's to Open 90 Outlets in Three Years," *Business Standard,* June 24, 2005.

[3] *USDA Foreign Agricultural Service GAIN Report #IN9082,* U.S. Embassy,New Delhi, November 14, 1999, pp. 2–3.

[4] Dani Rodrik and Arvind Subramanian, "Why India Can Grow at 7 Percent a Year or More: Projections and Reflections," IMF Working Paper, July 2004.

[5] EIU, Business India Intelligence, January 26, 2005, Vol. 12, No. 2, pp. p. 5.

[6] NCAER (National Council of Applied Economic Research) survey report, March 9, 2004.

[7] "Looking on the Bright Side: India's Economy Is Revving Up," *The Economist,* February 21, 2004, p. 13.

[8] In a widely circulated report on the growth prospects of BRIC (Brazil, Russia, India, China), Goldman Sachs predicted that over the next half century growth will slow sharply in the world's six big rich countries and in Brazil, Russia, and China. But India will continue to experience an annual average growth of more than 5%, and by 2032 its GDP will be bigger than Japan's. By 2050, India's national income per head in dollar terms will have multiplied 35-fold. Goldman Sachs, *Global Economic Paper No 99: Dreaming with BRICs: The Path to 2050,* October 2003, http://www.gs.com/insight/research/reports/report6.html. Also see the follow-up report by Goldman Sachs, *Global Economic Paper No 112: The G8: Time for a Change,* June 2004, http://www.gs.com/insight/research/reports/report15.html.

[9] Tim Dyson, Robert Cassen, and Leela Visaria, *Twenty-First Century India: Population, Economy, Human Development and the Environment,* Oxford University Press, 2004.

[10] See Adirupa Sengupta, "Living Up to the Choices Offered by the Free Market," *India Abroad,* August 29.

[11] For background information about McDonald's and its history, see *McDonald's: Behind the Arches* by John F. Love (New York: Bantam Books, 1995); *Grinding it Out: The Making of McDonald's* (Chicago: H. Regnery, 1977) written by McDonald's Corporation founder Ray Kroc with Robert Anderson; *Big Mac: The Unauthorized Story of McDonald's* (New York: Dutton, 1976) by Max Boas and Steve Chain; and the McDonald's Web site.

[12] See Montek Singh Ahluwalia's commentary on India's Reform, *Columbia Journal of Business,* 29: p. 1 (Spring 1994), p. 7.

[13] Maharaja Mac is made of two all-lamb patties, special sauce, lettuce, cheese, pickles, onions on a sesame seed bun.

[14] See Interview, New Delhi, May 17, 2004.

[15] Bhanu Pande and Aarti Dua, "Big Mac's Appetite for Growth," *Business Standard,* August 29, 2000, p. 4.

[16] Seema Shukla, "McIndia," *Business Today,* November 25, 2001, p. 58.

[17] Pooja Kothari, "Brand-Equity—Shaking It Up at McDonald's," *The Economic Times,* October 13, 2004.

[18] Seema Shukla, "McIndia," *Business Today,* November 25, 2001, p. 62.

[19] Hazard Analysis Critical Control Point (HACCP) is a systematic approach to food safety that emphasizes prevention of illness or presence of microbiological data within suppliers' facilities and restaurants rather than its detection through inspection. Based on HACCP guidelines, control points and critical control points for all McDonald's major food processing plants and restaurants in India have been identified. The HACCP verification is done at least twice a year and is certified.

[20] Neera Bhardwaj, "The Making of McQuality," *Business India,* August 24, 1998, p. 19.

[21] Vinod Mathew, "McDonald's Set to Enter Veg Territory," *Business Line,* February 18, 2002.

[22] For growing acceptance of American culture, see Sudeep Chakravarti, Nandita Chowdhury, and Stephen David, "Americana: Like, This is it!" *India Today,* February 9, 1998, pp. 17–19.

[23] See D. Balasubramanian, "Changes in the Indian Menu over the Ages," *The Hindu,* October 21, 2004; for details about India's demography and food preference. Also see "The Rediscovery of India," *India Abroad,* January 2, 1998. This report is based on a decade-long nationwide ethnographic survey of Indian people, which was published by Anthropological Survey of India, New Delhi, December 1997, under the title of "People of India."

[24] Interview, New Delhi, May 17, 2003.

[25] This information is prominently displayed in all McDonald's outlets in India. On June 1, 2002, McDonald's Corporation said it would pay $10 million to Hindu, vegetarian, and other groups more than a year after a Seattle lawyer, Harish Bharti, sued the fast food chain, alleging it failed to disclose the use of beef flavoring in its french fries. In the same press release, McDonald's clearly stated that it does not use the beef flavoring for fries sold at its restaurants in India.

[26] McDonald's terminology for products that are temporarily added to the menu.

[27] For this assessment, see "McDonald's Plans to Explore South Indian Market," *The Economic Times,* April 30, 2002.

[28] Chandrima S. Bhattacharya, "Rich Kids Eat, Drink and Wear Videshi," *The TeleGraph,* July 10, 2005.

[29] Several books and articles have explored the cultural impact of McDonald's expansion around the globe, including *To Russia with Fries* (Toronto: M&S, 1997) by George Cohon with David Macfarlane, which tells the story of how McDonald's opened its first restaurant in Russia; *Golden Arches East: McDonald's in East Asia* (Stanford: Stanford University Press, 1997) edited by James L. Watson, which looks in particular at China; and Maoz Azaryahu's "McIsrael? On the 'Americanization' of Israel" (*Israel Studies,* March 31, 2000). Thomas L. Friedman offers his "Golden Arches Theory of Conflict Prevention" in *The Lexus and the Olive Tree: Understanding Globalization* (New York: Farrar, Straus & Giroux, 1999). Theodore C. Bestor provides an example of how the spread of other cuisines has affected local tastes and cultures in "How Sushi Went Global" (*Foreign Policy,* November/December 2000).

[30] For opposition to McDonald's operations in various countries, see Francis Rocca, "America's Multicultural Imperialism," *American Spectator*, Vol. 33, No. 7, September 2000, pp. 34–38. McInformation Network, an independent group of McDonald's critics, has created its own Web site where readers can learn about protests against McDonald's worldwide, including the much publicized McLibel Trial in Britain. For more information about that trial, also see John Vidal's *McLibel: Burger Culture on Trial* (New York: New Press, 1998). For a survey of European reaction to McDonald's, see Carla Power's "McParadox" (*Newsweek*, July 10, 2000). John Stopford's "Think Again: Multinational Corporations" (*Foreign Policy*, Winter 1998–99) gives a good overview of how today's multinational companies operate. For outlooks on McDonald's future, read Ken Kurson's "Surprise Dread: McDonald's Future Is Smelling Worse than Its Restaurants" (*Esquire*, April 2001); and financial press releases on McDonald's Web site. See how mad cow disease is affecting McDonald's in Andrew Edgecliffe-Johnson's "Beef Concerns Hit McDonald's" (*Financial Times*, March 15, 2001).

[31] "Quit India, Shiv Sena Tells McDonald's," http://www.businessworldindia.com/archive/990621/strategy1.htm.

[32] "Animal Flavouring—McDonald's Indian Arm Says It's Clear," *Business Line*, March 9, 2002, http://www.blonnet.com/2002/03/09/stories/2002030901530600.htm.

[33] "Security Beefed Up for U.S. Companies in Gujrat," *The Economic Times*, March 19, 2005.

[34] Interview, New Delhi, December 28, 2003.

[35] Interview, New Delhi, December 28, 2003.

[36] Interview, New Delhi, December 28, 2003.

Strategy Content and Formulation for Multinational Companies

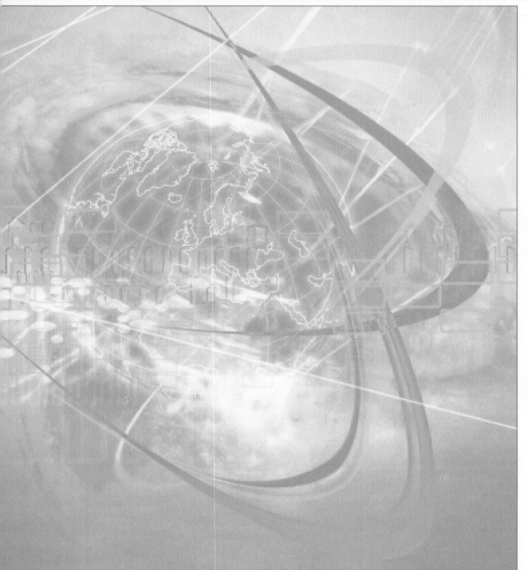

Strategic Management in the Multinational Company: Content and Formulation

5

Learning Objectives

After reading this chapter you should be able to:

- Define the generic strategies of differentiation and low cost.
- Understand how low-cost and differentiation strategists make money.
- Recall multinational examples of the use of the generic strategies.
- Understand competitive advantage and the value chain and how it applies to multinational operations.
- Understand how offensive and defensive strategies are used by multinational firms.
- Understand the basics of multinational diversification.
- Understand how the traditional strategy formulation techniques, industry and competitive analysis, and company situation analysis are applied to the multinational company.
- Realize that the national context affects both the convergence and divergence in strategies used by multinational companies.

Preview CASE IN POINT

Airbus and Boeing: The Continuous Battle

Only three years ago, Airbus had surpassed Boeing in sales volume of commercial planes. Airbus, designed by European governments through mergers of European manufacturers, was touted as the model of collaboration. Airbus developed the A380, believing that airline companies would want an airplane that could carry 550 or more passengers between hubs from which travelers would then transfer to their destination. The A380 would outdo Boeing's 747 as the world's largest commercial jet. In contrast, Boeing assumed that there is a market for passengers willing to pay a premium for long distances (8,000 miles, which is 2,000 miles more that any plane can currently fly nonstop). It is currently developing the Dreamliner, the company's first new plane in 10 years. The Dreamliner has a lightweight structure and new engines, making it 20 percent more efficient than other similar planes carrying more than 200 passengers.

In the space of three years, Airbus's fortunes have dramatically changed. It now faces severe delays with delivery of its A380s to customers. Although none of the 16 airlines with orders of 159 A380s are backing out of their orders, many are considering seeking extensive compensation for these delays. Airbus dramatically underestimated production times and is now facing its worst manufacturing crisis as workers scramble to finish 500 kilometers of electrical wiring for each plane. Furthermore, Airbus executives are also under investigation for selling their shares shortly before the delays in production were announced. To compound problems, the A350, which is Airbus's answer to Boeing's Dreamliner, has been viewed as inadequate by the industry.

Boeing, in contrast, seems to be enjoying better times. As the price of gas continues to soar, more airlines are paying attention to fuel efficiency. As such, Boeing has been booking hundreds of orders for the 787 Dreamliner. So far, 36 different customers have placed orders for 383 planes, suggesting that Boeing may break even sooner on the

Dreamliner than Airbus does on the A380. However, given the complexities of developing new planes, it is possible that Boeing also may face delays as it attempts to deliver the first Dreamliner in 2008.

Sources: Based on Daily Mail. 2006. "Setback for Boeing's Dreamliner." June 20: p. 68; Michaels, Daniel. 2006. "Leading the news: Airbus scrambles to fix wiring problems; Effort aims to put production, delivery of 380 back on track." The Wall Street Journal Asia, June 26: p. 3; Phillips, Don. 2006. "A380 trips but has fans free flow." International Herald Tribune, June 29: p. 15; Sachdev, Ameet. 2006. "Success not going to the head of Boeing boss." Knight Ridder Tribune News Service, June 23: p. 1; The Times. 2006. "Fasten your seatbelts: As Airbus loses altitude, Boeing looks on anxiously." June 20: p. 19.

The Preview Case in Point indicates how rapidly firms must adjust their strategies in the new competitive landscape. Although Airbus had been seemingly enjoying a good market position, its fortunes changed quickly because of major changes in its environment, both internally (e.g., delays in delivering the A380) and externally (e.g., sustained increases in the price of fuel). Successful companies are going to be the ones that will be able to accurately predict and be prepared for such changes. Furthermore, the environment facing companies has never been more complex than now. Companies now face global competition, extreme difficulty to predict environments, rapid technological change, hypercompetitive markets, and an increasing emphasis on price and quality for more demanding customers.[1] As an example, consider how new technologies are forcing television, telecommunications, and utilities companies to compete with each other in what were previously distinct industries. In this highly competitive environment, the multinational managers in these organizations craft the basic competitive strategies that they hope will guide their companies to profitability and long-term success. This chapter introduces the basic strategies that all multinational managers must be prepared to face and to master.

To develop an understanding of these strategies, this chapter presents the major components of the strategic management process. The chapter has three main sections. The first section provides background on basic strategic content applied to the multinational firm, including the strategic options available to companies. The second main section reviews the basic principles of strategic formulation with applications for the multinational company, including the processes by which managers analyze their industries and companies to select a strategy for their company. The third and final section shows how institutional forces lead to both national differences and similarities in the choices of strategies for multinational firms.

After reading this chapter, you should understand how the basic elements of the strategic management process apply to multinational operations. You also should understand how the multinational manager is faced with more complex challenges than those faced by a domestic-only manager.

Basic Strategic Content Applied to the Multinational Company

What is a strategy? Hambrick and Fredrickson[2] argue that statements such as "Our strategy is to be the low-cost provider" or "Our strategy is to provide excellent customer service" are not really strategies. These statements only represent elements of strategies. Rather, a **strategy** is the central, comprehensive, integrated and externally oriented set of choices of how a company will achieve its objectives. Ideally, a strategy needs to address important areas:[3]

- *Arenas:* A company needs to be able to decide which businesses it wants to be in. To be meaningful, the stated arena has to be as specific as possible.
- *Vehicles:* A properly stated strategy also needs to include the vehicles a company will use to create a presence in specific markets or products. For a multinational company considering entry into new foreign markets, the strategy needs to include the ways by which such international expansion will occur. Consider the Multinational Management Brief.
- *Differentiators/Economic Logic:* A company also needs to decide what ways it will use to win over customers. As you will see later, companies have various generic approaches they can use to compete in their markets.
- *Sequencing:* A company also needs to decide in what sequence and at what pace major decisions will be made. For instance, for a multinational company, a major question is to decide which country to enter at what time.

Multinational companies use many of the same strategies practiced by domestic companies. An overview of common organizational strategies to address these components is provided next. For students with coursework in strategic management, this will serve as a partial review. However, the discussion illustrates specifically how multinational companies use basic strategies. In particular, the Cases in Point and Multinational Management Briefs show how real multinational firms use basic strategic options in international business. After this introductory chapter, the text focuses on the strategic options that are unique to the multinational company.

Competitive Advantage and Multinational Applications of Generic Strategies

Generic strategies represent very basic ways that both domestic and multinational companies achieve and sustain competitive advantage. **Competitive advantage** occurs when a company can outmatch its rivals in attracting and maintaining its targeted customers. Porter[4] identifies the two primary generic

Multinational Management **Brief**

Liberty Global and the Global Cable Industry

Liberty Global, based in Douglas County, Colorado, calls itself the largest cable company outside of the United States. More than 15.2 million customers use its video, phone, and Internet services. For instance, if a person signs up for high-speed Internet in Tokyo, it is likely coming from Liberty Global. Similarly, if a teenager watches MTV in Budapest, it is likely coming from Liberty Global's cable operations in Eastern Europe. If someone wants to watch a soccer game in Santiago, it is probably from VTR, another Liberty Global cable subsidiary. How did Liberty Global achieve such international presence? Its vehicle for international entry into these various markets was simply to acquire 12 cable companies around the world. Liberty Global spent more than $4 billion to buy cable companies in countries as far away as Switzerland and Australia.

Source: Based on Potter, Beth. 2006. "Branching out globally after acquiring 12 cable companies worldwide, newly formed Liberty Global faces big challenges." Denver Post, March 14: p. C01.

Strategy
The central, comprehensive, integrated and externally oriented set of choices of how a company will achieve its objectives.

Generic strategies
Basic ways that both domestic and multinational companies keep and achieve competitive advantage.

Competitive advantage
When a company can outmatch its rivals in attracting and maintaining its targeted customers.

strategies that companies use to gain competitive advantage as differentiation and low cost.

Companies that adopt a **differentiation strategy** find ways to provide superior value to customers. Superior value comes from sources such as exceptional product quality, unique product features, rapid innovation, or high-quality service. For example, BMW competes in the world market by providing customers with very high-quality and high-performance sport touring cars. Caterpillar competes worldwide in its heavy construction equipment business by offering not only high-quality machinery but also, more important, after-sales service committed to delivering spare parts anywhere in the world.

Companies that adopt a **low-cost strategy** produce or deliver products or services equal to those of their competitors. However, low-cost companies find the means to produce their products or to deliver their services more efficiently than the competition. That is, they lower the costs of their products without sacrificing a quality acceptable to customers. The cost savings that improve efficiency may occur anywhere from the creation of the product to its final sale. Examples include finding sources of cheaper raw materials, employing cheaper labor, using more efficient production methods, and using more efficient delivery methods. Porter[5] notes, for example, that Korean steel and semiconductor firms often perform well against U.S. and Japanese firms, using low-cost strategies. These Korean firms save money with low-cost and productive labor combined with advanced and efficient production methods.

How Do Low-Cost and Differentiation Firms Make Money?

Differentiation leads to higher profits because people will often pay a higher price for the extra value provided by the superior product or service. Levi's jeans have higher prices in the world market because of the special appeal of the Levi's brand. The Swiss firm Tobler/Jacobs can charge more for its specially produced chocolate than Hershey can for its mass-produced product. Tobler/Jacobs uses higher-quality ingredients, a longer processing time, and specialized distribution channels. These factors produce a higher-quality product that commands a higher price.[6]

High quality, service, or other unique characteristics of a differentiated product usually increase costs; that is, it takes more expensive labor or higher-quality materials to make a differentiated product or to provide a differentiated service. In addition, to make customers aware of the special value of their products or services, firms must spend more on marketing. Consequently, to provide a good profit margin, the differentiating company must charge higher prices to offset its additional costs.

Low-cost firms produce products or services similar to their competitors in price and value. Their competitive advantage and their additional profits come from cost savings. Every dollar, mark, or yen they save contributes to the bottom line by increasing their profit margins. Exhibit 5.1 shows how the relationships among costs, prices, and profits work for the differentiator and the low-cost strategist compared to the average competitor. As Exhibit 5.1 shows, both the differentiator and the low-cost strategist have higher profits than the average competitor. The Multinational Management Brief on Ryanair (page 224) shows how a low-cost competitor is gaining market share over other competitors.

EXHIBIT **5.1**   Costs, Prices, and Profits for Differentiation and Low-Cost Strategies

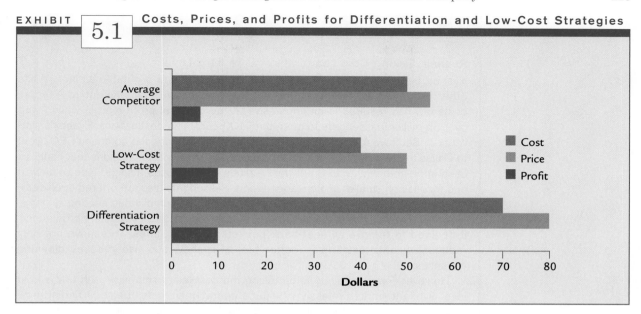

Porter[7] identifies another competitive issue regarding the two basic generic strategies, called the **focus strategy,** which is based on competitive scope. **Competitive scope** represents how broadly a firm targets its products or services. For example, companies with a narrow competitive scope may focus only on limited products, certain types of buyers, or specific geographical areas. Companies with a broad competitive scope may have many products targeted at a large range of buyers. Auto manufacturers such as BMW target a high-income market with a few models while most U.S. and Japanese auto manufacturers target a broad-income market with many models. Exhibit 5.2 shows the four subdivisions of Porter's generic strategies. These include the basic differentiation and cost-leadership strategies with their broad-market or narrow-market options.

Focus strategy

Applying a differentiation or low-cost strategy to a narrow market.

Competitive scope

How broadly a firm targets its products or services.

Competitive Advantage and the Value Chain

A firm can gain a competitive advantage over other firms by finding sources of lower cost or differentiation in any of its activities. These range from getting necessary raw materials, through production, to sales, and to eventual follow-up with after-sales service. For example, a company may find cost savings with cheaper raw materials or cheaper labor in other countries. A

EXHIBIT **5.2**   Porter's Generic Strategies

| | Source of Competitive Advantage | |
Scope of Competitive Target	**Lower Cost**	**Differentiation**
Broad Market	General cost leader	General differentiator
Niche Market	Focused cost leader	Focused differentiator

Source: Adapted from Porter, Michael E. 1990. Competitive Advantage of Nations. New York: Free Press.

Multinational Management **Brief**

Ryanair: Taking Cost Leadership to the Next Level

Ryanair has become one of Europe's most popular and profitable airlines. While other European airlines struggle, Ryanair's obsessive commitment to keeping costs low has resulted in an impressive 22 percent net profit margin while flying over 35 million passengers to more than 100 European destinations. Ryanair's similarity to Southwest Airlines is not coincidental as O'Leary, the company CEO, went to Dallas to meet Southwest Airlines executives to learn some lessons that could be used in Ireland. Similar to Southwest Airlines, Ryanair uses a single type of aircraft and focuses on smaller and cheaper airport. Passengers also are offered open seating, meaning that Ryanair does not need to maintain complicated seating systems. However, Ryanair has also found other innovative ways to cut costs. For instance, it decided to remove all seat-back pockets in its airplanes. This move not only reduces weight, resulting in better fuel efficiency, but also reduces cleaning expenses.

However, Ryanair seems to be taking the cost-leadership approach to the next level. While it works tirelessly to reduce operational costs, it also is finding new ways to get more revenue from each traveler. For instance, Ryanair charges passengers for all amenities on the plane, and last year, in-flight beverages generated $61 million in revenues. Similarly, Ryanair started charging $3.50 per bag for checked-in luggage and expects to save $36 million in fuel and handling costs. Ninety-eight percent of Ryanair's customers buy their tickets online, making its web site the largest travel site in Europe. This has enabled Ryanair to use its web site for marketing purposes while also getting commission on other items such as car rentals or hotel rooms. Ryanair is also selling advertising opportunities through repainting of the exterior of the planes. Finally, Ryanair will likely offer in-flight online gambling in 2007 and expects to generate significant revenues from these activities.

Ryanair's goal is to offer the ultimate in cost leadership: free air travel. Will it be successful? Some think that the company can achieve that goal. Consider that it already offers free travel for more than a quarter of its passengers.

Source: Adapted from Maier, Matthew. 2006. "A radical fix for airlines: Make flying free." Business 2.0, April, pp. 32–34.

---

multinational company may base its differentiation on the excellent R&D produced by its subsidiary located in a country where high-quality engineering talent is cheap. Many multinational software-design companies, for example, take advantage of the very high number of quality engineers in India and Singapore.

Value chain

All the activities that a firm uses to design, produce, market, deliver, and support its product.

One convenient way of thinking about a firm's activities is called the **value chain.** Michael Porter uses the term "value chain" to represent all the activities that a firm uses "to design, produce, market, deliver, and support its product."[8] The value chain identifies areas where a firm can create value for customers. Better designs, more efficient production, and better service all represent value added in the value chain. Ultimately, the value a company produces represents what customers will pay for a product or service. Exhibit 5.3 shows a picture of the value chain. Later, you will see that the value chain provides a useful way of thinking about how multinational companies operate.

Porter divides the value chain into primary and support activities. These activities represent (1) the processes of creating goods or services and (2) the

EXHIBIT   **5.3**   The Value Chain

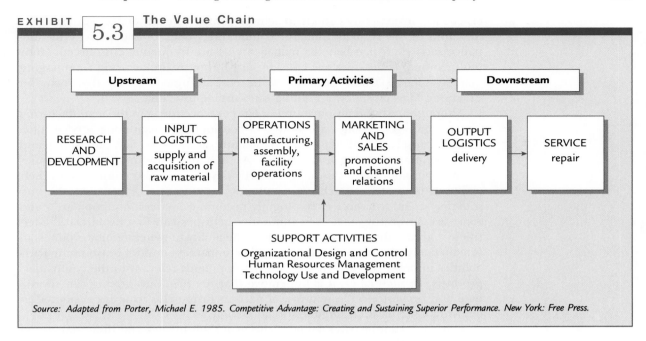

Source: Adapted from Porter, Michael E. 1985. Competitive Advantage: Creating and Sustaining Superior Performance. New York: Free Press.

organizational mechanisms necessary to support the creative activities. *Primary activities* involve the physical actions of creating (or serving), selling, and providing after-sale service of products. Early activities in the value chain, such as R&D and dealing with suppliers, are called *upstream*. Later value-chain activities, such as sales and dealing with distribution channels, represent *downstream* activities. *Support activities* include systems for human resources management (e.g., recruitment and selection procedures), organizational design and control (e.g., structural form and accounting procedures), and a firm's basic technology.

The utility of the value chain is that it allows companies to assess the cost levels associated with the different activities to determine its internal cost structure.[9] Comparing internal cost structure against the industry or other competitors provides the multinational company with information about the efficiency of its various internal activities relative to competitors. However, this benchmarking exercise also provides important guidance regarding which internal activities are sources of internal cost advantage or cost disadvantage. To become more competitive, most multinational firms need to find ways to correct cost disadvantages.

Although there are other ways to correct internal cost disadvantages, one of the most popular and controversial ways is outsourcing. **Outsourcing** represents a deliberate decision to have outsiders or strategic allies perform certain activities in the value chain.[10] Merrifield[11] argues that if current trends continue, about half of U.S. manufacturing jobs will be outsourced to more than 28 emerging countries over the next 10 years. However, outsourcing is not solely limited to manufacturing. Consider that 28 developing, low-wage countries currently offer about 4.3 million engineers who have the skills to work for U.S. multinational companies and that soon about 10 percent of U.S. service jobs may be outsourced.[12]

When should a multinational company outsource? In general, outsourcing makes sense if an outsider can perform a value-chain task better or more cheaply.[13] However, tasks that are outsourced should the ones that are not

Outsourcing

A deliberate decision to have outsiders or strategic allies perform certain activities in the value chain.

crucial to the company's ability to achieve competitive advantage. For example, functions of low strategic value or commodities (e.g., billing services, maintenance services, fringe benefits management) are frequently outsourced. Many multinational companies are considering shifting manufacturing to emerging markets such as China because of the cost savings. Consider the Focus on Emerging Markets below regarding outsourcing to China.

Although traditionally outsourcing has been occurring in the manufacturing section, more companies are now also considering outsourcing service functions. For instance, skilled jobs in architecture, accounting, law, publishing, and insurance are now being sent abroad.[14] As such, more multinational companies are now considering outsourcing key activities that can also contribute to their ability to innovate and achieve competitive advantage. For instance, the outsourcing of information technology is becoming increasingly popular,[15] and some are advocating that even innovative activities can be outsourced.[16] Merrifield[17] argues that few companies have the ability to generate new products to remain competitive. He also suggests that companies consider outsourcing R&D abilities in order to look for the best developments relevant to the companies' products. In such cases, it is imperative that the firm outsourcing can coordinate and orchestrate the network of partner firms. This issue is considered in depth in Chapter 8 on Organizational Design.

Exhibit 5.4 summarizes some of the major advantages and disadvantages of outsourcing. Multinational companies need to balance such costs and benefits to determine whether they want to outsource and then which activities to outsource.

Focus on Emerging Markets

Outsourcing Manufacturing to China

China's recent economic growth and its easing of rules and regulations mean that more companies are considering outsourcing manufacturing to China. However, before any outsourcing commitment is made, it is essential to understand some of the following key issues:

- *The local business environment:* Multinational companies considering outsourcing manufacturing to China need to carefully consider the local business environment. China is a big country that has large variations in business conditions and customs, and it is important to understand and adapt to such differences.
- *Availability and cost of resources:* Multinational firms cannot assume that labor is inexpensive everywhere in China. Interior provinces such as Sichuan and Anhui do provide cheaper labor while the coastal areas such as Shanghai and Guandong are experiencing skilled labor shortages. Energy supply also varies greatly from location to location.
- *Local contacts:* Multinational companies need to respect local officials if they want to be successful. It is therefore imperative to have face-to-face meetings to build such respect and relationships.
- *Local laws:* Multinational companies find it challenging to navigate the legal environment in China. The levels of government and inconsistencies in application of laws and regulations can frustrate outsourcing plans.

Source: Adapted from Pan, Alexander. 2006. "Manufacturing in China? Key facts for getting started." Financial Executive, April, 22, 3: p. 19.

EXHIBIT 5.4   Advantages and Disadvantages of Outsourcing

Benefits	Risks
Allows company to reduce costs on peripheral activities and labor and focus resources on core business	Danger of outsourcing too many activities thereby diluting core capabilities
Improves ability to innovate when company partners with suppliers who have cutting-edge technology	Security risks as companies can better control data and information if they are stored on in-house equipment
Reduces risk exposure to changing technology or buyer needs as partners shoulder such burdens	Theft of critical intellectual capital as legal environment in other countries may not adequately deal with such infractions
Flexibility to respond to changing demands because company is not tied to in-house capabilities	Language and cultural barriers also cause frictions and inefficiencies
Allows company to access new and useful expertise through suppliers	Costs to negotiate, manage, and maintain outsourcing contracts can be high

Source: Based on Dhar, Subhankar, and Bindu Balakrishnan. 2006. "Risks, benefits, and challenges in global IT outsourcing: Perspectives and practices." Journal of Global Information Management, July–September, 14, 3: pp. 39–69; Kakumanu, Prasad, and Anthony Portanova, 2006. "Outsourcing: Its benefits, drawbacks and other related issues." Journal of American Academy of Business, September, 9, 2: pp. 1–7; Merrifield, Bruce. 2006. "Make outsourcing a core competency." Research Technology Management, May/June, 49, 3: pp. 10–13; Thompson, Arthur A. Jr., A.J. Strickland III, and John E. Gamble. 2007. Crafting and Executing Strategy. McGraw-Hill. Homewood, IL: Irwin.

The value chain thus identifies the areas in the input, throughput, and output processes where multinational companies can find sources of differentiation or lower costs. To achieve higher value or lower costs for its products or services than its rivals do, the company must take advantage of the distinctive competencies in its value chain. What distinctive competencies are and where they come from is the topic of the next section.

Distinctive Competencies

Distinctive competencies are the strengths anywhere in the value chain that allow a company to outperform rivals in areas such as efficiency, quality, innovation, or customer service.[18] Distinctive competencies come from two related sources: resources and capabilities. **Resources** are the inputs into a company's production or services processes. Resources can be tangible assets such as borrowing capacity, buildings, land, equipment, and highly trained employees. Resources can be intangible assets such as reputation with customers, patents, trademarks, organizational knowledge, and innovative research abilities. **Capabilities** represent the ability of companies to assemble and coordinate their available resources in ways that lead to lower costs or differentiated output.

Thus, resources provide a company with potential capabilities. They are the raw materials—much like a person's athletic or intellectual potential—that become capabilities only when used effectively. In turn, capabilities are the building blocks of a distinctive competence. However, although capabilities are the prerequisite of building distinctive competencies, this is not enough. To result in long-term profitability and success, capabilities must lead to a sustainable competitive advantage. Next, we consider how companies achieve this state.

Sustaining Competitive Advantage

For a company to have long-term profitability, a successful low-cost or differentiation strategy must be sustainable. **Sustainable** means that strategies are not easily neutralized or attacked by competitors.[19] Sustainability is traced to the

Distinctive competencies
Strengths that allow companies to outperform rivals.

Resources
Inputs into the production or service processes.

Capabilities
The ability to assemble and coordinate resources effectively.

Sustainable
Strategies not easily defeated by competitors.

nature of a company's capabilities. Capabilities that lead to competitive advantage must have four characteristics.[20] They must be valuable, rare, difficult to imitate, and nonsubstitutable.

Valuable capabilities create demand for a company's services or products or give companies cost advantages. Rare capabilities are those that a company possesses but that no competitor or only a few competitors also possess. For example, Boeing and Airbus are two companies with the rare technological capability to design and manufacture large commercial aircraft.

As shown in the preceding discussion of the generic strategies, providing customers superior value or finding a way to deliver products or services at lower cost results in increased profit margins. Competitors seek high profits by imitating or substituting for these capabilities. Thus, sustainable or long-term competitive advantage comes from having capabilities that not only meet the requirements of valuable and rare but also are difficult to imitate or are nonsubstitutable.

Difficult-to-imitate capabilities are not easily copied by competitors. One of the most imitated sources of lower costs in the international marketplace is cheap labor. Competitors with access to the same international labor pools quickly duplicate any cost advantage of locating manufacturing facilities in countries with cheap labor. In addition, wage rates in countries with cheap labor often rise faster than productivity, gradually undermining cost advantages based on cheap labor.

Nonsubstitutable capabilities leave no strategic equivalent available to competitors. For example, many early e-commerce companies such as Amazon.com developed capabilities to conduct business over the Internet. Not only have these models been easy to copy, but competitors have also substituted for these capabilities by outsourcing such procedures as web site building and translation. In contrast, consider the example of Toyota in the Case in Point on page 229. It shows how Toyota uses strategic capabilities that competitors have found difficult to copy or for which they have been unable to create substitutes.

Exhibit 5.5 summarizes the relationships among resources, capabilities, distinctive competencies, and eventual profitability.

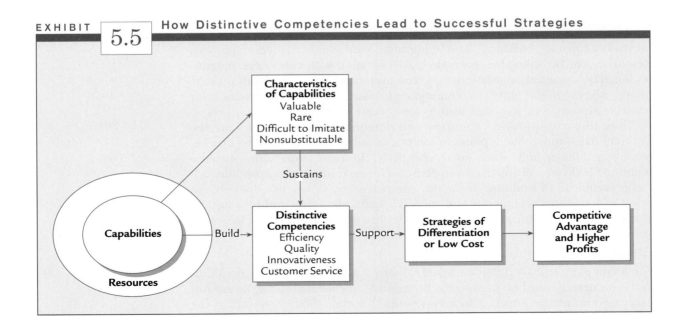

EXHIBIT 5.5   How Distinctive Competencies Lead to Successful Strategies

C A S E   I N   P O I N T

Toyota's Distinctive Competencies Along the Value Chain: Strategic Capabilities in Cost Reductions, Quality, and Service

Toyota is Japan's No. 1 automaker. Its competitive advantages over other automakers from Japan, Europe, and the United States are the firm's distinctive competencies in cost reduction and high-quality materials and service. Upstream in the value chain, to bring new models to market more quickly and cheaply, Toyota combines manufacturing and production engineering. This eliminates mistakes in production design and reduces cost. Designing a new model takes only 18 months while many competitors take up to 30 months. Toyota designs cars with an objective of fewer parts, fewer production machines, and faster production times. For example, Toyota's redesigned Corolla model had 25 percent fewer parts, was 10 percent lighter, and was more fuel efficient. Of the one billion dollars necessary to design a new model and build the plants to produce it, tools and machinery can account for three-quarters of the cost.

The mastery of *kanban,* the just-in-time production system, provides a basis of cost reduction and customer service. Not only do suppliers deliver materials just-in-time, as now happens for many U.S. manufacturers, but the whole value chain also works just-in-time.

Downstream, in the marketing and sales component of the value chain, Toyota dealers use online computers to order models directly from the factory.

A built-to-order car can be built in as little as five days using its virtual production system. The system precisely calculates the types and timing of parts to arrive on the assembly line exactly when needed for a particular mix of production. Even with this design flexibility, Toyota uses only 14 person-hours to assemble a car, compared with 22 for Honda and Ford. However, Toyota also has distinctive competencies in developing engines that are more fuel efficient than the American Big Three automakers. Given the current fuel prices, it is not surprising to see Toyota gaining further market share as evidenced by a 14.4 percent increase in sales while GM sales fell by 26 percent from a year earlier. Furthermore, the manufacturing efficiency also translates into bigger profits, with Toyota's average profit margin per vehicle at 9.4 percent compared to GM's 3-percent margin. Thus Toyota has the advantage not only of being the cost leader but also of being perceived by consumers as being among the highest-quality manufacturers.

Sources: Based on Bunkley, Nick. 2006. "Gas prices stall U.S. sales of big vehicles: Detroit's Asian rivals benefit, helped by fuel-efficiency reputation." International Herald Tribune, June 5: p. 11; Jiji Press English News Service. 1999. "Toyota shrinks car production time to 5 days." August 6; Peterson, Thane. 2000. "Toyota's Fujio Cho: Price competition will be brutal." http://www.businessweek.com. April; and Williams, Chambers G. III. 2003. "Toyota strategy includes San Antonio expansion." Knight Ridder Tribune Business News. February 7.

Besides these very basic strategies, companies also develop strategies that directly target rival firms. The following section reviews some of these strategies from the vantage point of the multinational company.

Offensive and Defensive Competitive Strategies in International Markets

Besides using the basic generic strategies in their operations, multinational companies use several strategic moves called **competitive strategies.** Competitive strategies can be offensive or defensive. In offensive strategies, companies directly target rivals from whom they wish to capture market share. For example, an attacking company may suddenly drop its prices or add new features to its products that compete with its rival's products. In defensive strategies, companies seek to beat back or discourage the offensive strategies of rivals. For example, a firm might match a rival's lower prices or give distributors volume discounts to discourage customers from shifting to a rival's products.

Competitive strategies

Moves multinational firms use to defeat competitors.

Examples of **offensive competitive strategies** include direct attacks, end-run offensives, preemptive strategies, and acquisitions.[21] Descriptions of each strategy follow.

- *Direct attacks:* Direct attacks include price cutting, adding new features, comparison advertisements that show lesser quality in a competitor's products, or going after neglected or poorly served market segments.
- *End-run offensives:* With these strategies, companies try to avoid direct competition and seek unoccupied markets. Usually, in international competition, unoccupied markets are countries ignored or underserved by competitors.
- *Preemptive competitive strategies*: These strategies involve being the first to gain a particular advantageous position. Advantages might include getting the best suppliers of raw material, buying the best locations, or getting the best customers. In international markets, being the first company with a global strategy can bring great advantages. For example, a multinational company can seek the best raw material in any country. It also can work to become the first company to have its brand recognized worldwide.
- *Acquisitions:* This can be the most effective competitive strategy against rivals since the acquired competitor no longer exists. An acquisition occurs when one firm buys its competitor. However, if the purchased company does not contribute to the overall company performance, the strategy may not contribute to bottom-line effectiveness. For the multinational firm, acquiring a firm from another country might include other strategic benefits besides profit, such as improving geographical coverage or strengthening the firm's position in important countries.

Usually, multinational managers analyze the strengths and weaknesses of their competitors separately in each country. Different countries represent different markets and often require different attack strategies. Consequently, managers develop country-specific plans for dealing with their competitors and deciding whether to attack, take an end-run approach (avoid direct competition), or, possibly, acquire the rivals.

In a competitive industry, all managers should expect attacks from rival firms. To counteract these attacks, companies use **defensive competitive strategies**. Defensive strategies attempt to reduce the risks of being attacked, convince attacking firms to seek other targets, or blunt the impact of any attack. Companies may defend at several points on the value chain. For example, a firm may sign exclusive contracts with the best suppliers, thus blocking competitors' access to raw materials. A company can introduce new models that match competitors' lower prices. A firm may get exclusive contracts with distributors or provide better warranties or after-sales service. To scare off potential challengers, firms also make public announcements of their willingness to fight. Rivals then realize that an attack will be costly, and they often decide it is not worth the risk. Attacked firms can also **counter-parry,** a popular strategy for multinationals. In international markets, the counter-parry fends off a competitor's attack in one country by attacking it in another country, usually the competitor's home country. This strategy draws resources from the competitor and weakens its attack. It is most successful when the rival firm is forced to protect its established home markets. Kodak used this strategy to defend against Fuji. When Fuji attacked Kodak in the U.S. market, Kodak countered by attacking Fuji in Japan. Goodyear used the same strategy against Michelin. When Michelin attacked Goodyear with low prices in the United States, Goodyear countered by attacking Michelin in Europe.

Next, we discuss how multinational companies use diversification in the international marketplace.

Multinational Diversification Strategy

Most of the strategic options discussed to this point pertain to the operation of a single business. Consequently, these strategies are called **business-level strategies.** However, many corporations have more than one type of business. Strategies for multi-business companies are called corporate level strategies. **Corporate-level strategies** concern how companies choose their mixture of different businesses. When a company moves from a single type of business into two or more businesses, this is called diversification. There are two basic types of diversification: related and unrelated.

In **related diversification,** companies start or acquire businesses that are similar in some way to their original or core business. These similarities can exist all along the value chain. Firms choose related diversification for three basic reasons: sharing activities, transferring core competencies, and developing market power.[22] Following the value chain, sharing activities can include common purchasing of similar raw material; common production of similar components; and shared sales forces, advertising, and distribution activities. Companies such as Honda transfer core competencies across units by using similar technologies in their internal combustion engines for motorcycles and lawn mowers. Nike transferred its core competency in brand recognition when it added a clothing line to its athletic-shoe operations. Firms use related diversification to build market power by attacking rivals with multipoint competition or competition in more than one area and by vertical integration. Vertical integration allows firms to internalize supply (e.g., coffee growing for a company like Starbucks) or downstream (e.g., direct sales) components of their value chain. This results in greater profits if the integration leads to lower costs or improved bases of diversification.

In unrelated diversification, firms acquire businesses in any industry. Their main concern is whether a business represents a good financial investment.[23] Businesses can be acquired as long-term investments. Usually, in this case, the acquired firm has potential for growth, but it does not have the financial or other resources necessary to grow without help. To reach its potential, the acquired company needs the parent company's financial or managerial resources. Businesses can also be acquired as short-term investments. In this case, the parent company hopes to sell off the acquired firm's assets for more than the cost of acquisition. In addition, some firms look for businesses in industries with different economic cycles. In this way, the parent firm can remain profitable even if one industry is in an unprofitable economic cycle.

Like domestic companies, multinational firms also pursue diversification strategies. Acquiring a business in another country is a quick way to gain a presence and often a recognized brand name. The multinational company with related diversification can also coordinate and use resources such as R&D from different businesses located anywhere in the world to gain competitive advantages. It also can more easily establish global brand names for different but related products. Diversified multinational companies can cross-subsidize, both across countries and across companies, to attack rivals in different countries. Cross-subsidization means that money generated in one country or from one company of a corporation provides resources to sister organizations in other countries or companies to undercut their local competition.

Business-level strategies
Those for a single business operation.

Corporate-level strategies
How companies choose their mixture of different businesses.

Related diversification
A mixture of businesses with similar products and markets.

Exhibit 5.6 shows a selection of Global Fortune 500 diversified multinational companies with their major lines of businesses.

Experts do not agree on which form of diversification is best for multinationals. However, recent research by Li and Wong[24] provides some understanding of the forms of diversification and consequent success in emerging markets. They argue that most research on diversification has been done in developed economies where the institutional environment is well developed. The adequately developed institutional environment enables multinational firms in such countries to find ways to compete effectively without worrying about institutional gaps. However,

EXHIBIT 5.6   **Examples of Diversified Multinationals**

Company (Headquarters Location)	Major Lines of Business	Countries	Revenues ($ million)	Profits ($ million)
GE (U.S.A.)	Aircraft engines, aerospace, appliances, communications and services, electrical distribution and control, financial services, industrial and power systems, lighting, medical systems, motors, NBC, plastics, transportation	100+	152,866.00	16,819.00
Siemens (Germany)	Automation and drives, automotive systems, computers, industrial projects and technical services, mobile information and communication, information and communication networks, medical engineering, power distribution and transmission, power generation, production and logistics system, building technologies, business services, design and exhibition, financial services, real estate management, transportation systems	190	91,493.20	4,144.60
Nestlé (Switzerland)	Drinks, dairy products, chocolate and confectionery, culinary products, frozen food and ice cream, food service products, hotels and restaurants, instant food and dietetic products, pet foods, pharmaceutical products and cosmetics, refrigerated products	113	69,825.70	5,405.40
Procter & Gamble (U.S.A)	Health, beauty care, industrial chemicals, beverages and food, laundry and cleaning detergents, food services and lodging, paper	140	51,407.00	6,481.00
Mitsui (Japan)	Iron and steel, non-ferrous metals, property, service, construction, machinery chemicals, energy, foods, textiles, general merchandise	88	32805.90	1127.10
Samsung (South Korea)	Mobile phones, television sets, camcorders, MP3 players, computers and related products, semiconductors, business telephone systems, networking, home appliances, fiber optics	50+	71,555.90	9419.50

Source: Based on Fortune. 2005. Global 500. http://money.cnn.com; Siemens. 2006. http://www.siemens; Mitsui. 2006. http://www.mitsui.co.jp; Procter & Gamble. 2006. http://www.pg.com; Samsung. 2006. http://ww.samsung.com/Products/index.htm; and General Electric. 2006. http://www.ge.com

most emerging markets suffer from key institutional voids in five important areas: poorly developed product, poor capital markets, poor labor markets, lack of laws and regulations, and improper enforcement of such contracts.[25] As such, to compete effectively, multinational firms in emerging countries can use diversification strategies to work around such institutional voids. For instance, consider the distribution challenges facing a multinational company as it attempts to achieve synergies across multiple businesses in India or China.

To be better able to face the gaps in the institutional environment, Li and Wong[26] argue that unrelated diversification is very useful. Unrelated diversification allows a multinational company to have better control over various institutional elements by internalizing such functions. For instance, a multinational company may have better control over the poor labor market by providing in-house training for its employees across its many businesses. Similarly, an unrelated diversification approach gives a multinational company better control over the financial market because the multinational firm can use its aggregate clout to secure funding.

Using data on 106 publicly traded Chinese firms, the authors find that unrelated diversification gives a company a better ability to manage its external institutional environment. However, Li and Wong[27] also find that related diversification is also useful as it allows firms to build a concentrated resource base. The authors recommend that managers assess the degree to which they will need to manage the institutional environment and the degree to which they will need to build and leverage resources and choose the appropriate forms of diversification. The related diversifier is better positioned to take advantage of economies of scale and business similarities (resource building), and the unrelated diversifier provides multinational companies the ability to internalize various markets (to manage institutions).

Strategy Content: Brief Conclusions

The first section of this chapter provided an overview of the content or makeup of basic strategies: generic, competitive, and diversification. Like solely domestic firms, multinational companies use these strategies to achieve and maintain competitive advantage over rivals. The next section reviews traditional strategy-formulation techniques applied to the multinational company.

Strategy Formulation: Traditional Approaches

There are several common techniques used by managers as aids in formulating their strategies. In general, strategy formulation represents the process by which managers select the strategy to be used by their company.

In this section, we review some of the popular types of analyses that provide managers with the information to formulate successful strategies. These analyses help managers understand: (1) the competitive dynamics of the industry in which they operate; (2) their company's competitive position in the industry, (3) the opportunities and threats faced by their company, and (4) their company's strengths and weaknesses. This information allows managers to choose strategies that best fit the unique situations of their companies.

Industry and Competitive Analyses

Industries identify the main competitive arenas of a company's businesses. To formulate good strategies, managers must understand their industries well. This

Strategy formulation

Process by which managers select the strategies to be used by their company.

involves understanding the forces affecting the industry, the economic characteristics of the industry, and knowing the driving forces of change and competition in the industry. Below we provide a review of these various techniques.

Porter's five forces model is a popular technique that can help a multinational firm understand the major forces at work in the industry and the degree of attractiveness of the industry.[28] The first important force facing any multinational company is the degree of competition among existing competitors in the industry. For instance, there is a high degree of competition among auto manufacturers globally, and such competition has significant influence on the profitability of the industry and what strategic moves the players make. The second force is the threat of new entrants. Companies need to consider the degree to which they may face new competitors in their industry. The threat of new entrants is generally dependent on barriers to entry as shown in the following Case in Point.

The next force in Porter's five forces model is the bargaining power of buyers. Bargaining power of buyers refers to the degree to which buyers of the industry's products can influence the competitors within that industry. Most experts argue that buyers are becoming increasingly sophisticated globally and will have an ever-growing influence on most industries. To remain competitive, most companies will have to create innovative products and services at low prices.[29] To understand any industry, multinational companies must also look at the bargaining power of suppliers. Suppliers tend to have high power if they can

Porter's five forces model

A popular technique that can help a multination firm understand the major forces at work in the industry and the degree of attractiveness of the industry.

CASE IN POINT

Barriers to Entry

Today's Internet revolution and cheap technology have made it easier to start a company. Traditional barriers to entry in many industries are slowly eroding, making any industry more accessible to start-ups. Cheap open-source programs allow anyone to launch new software easily. Any start-up can also get access to offshore manufacturers that can quickly produce prototypes from any design. The Web also provides any company with easy access to both consumers and beta testers.

Consider the case of Metrokane and its popular "Rabbit" corkscrew. For years, quality corkscrews were available only through specialty stores at high prices. For instance, Le Creuset's Lever Model, the first corkscrew that could uncork a wine bottle in less than two seconds, retailed for over $175. However, Riki Lane, the founder of Metrokane, hired a designer who made a corkscrew based heavily on Le Creuset's model. Metrokane's corkscrew, the Rabbit, quickly became a favorite, unsettling the venerable French company Le Creuset.

The experiences of Joe Kraus, Excite's founder, in starting new companies also provides evidence of falling barriers to entry. Kraus recently created a new start-up, Jot Spot, a server software that allows users to post and edit web pages as a collaboration tool in companies. Jot Spot currently has more than 20,000 corporate customers and is quickly becoming popular as a collaboration tool. Kraus suggests that there are a number of important barriers to entry that are falling, making it easier to start a company. For instance, he discusses how computer hardware is now much cheaper. While it cost him more than $60,000 to buy servers when he founded Excite, servers are now commodities and can be bought for less than $1,000. Similarly, both software and software engineers are now much cheaper. Open source programs have greatly reduced software costs while any company can easily hire programmers from locations such as India, Romania, and Russia for a fraction of the cost in the United States. Finally, search engines such as Google and pay-per-click advertising enable companies to advertise and reach their target much more effectively.

Sources: Based on Copeland, Michael. 2006. "Start last, finish first." Business 2.0, January/February, pp. 41–43; Heilemann, John. 2005a. "Retooling the entrepreneur." Business 2.0, November, pp. 42–45; Khemsurov, Monica. 2006. "Rabbit on a run." Business 2.0, January/February, p. 69.

exert significant influence on competitors within the industry. Consider that DeBeers controls a significant proportion of the supply of diamonds and has significant influence on the global diamond market.

The final force is the threat of substitutes. This force looks at the extent to which competitors are confronted with alternatives for their products. For instance, Netflix, the company that pioneered web-based DVD rental, and other competitors such as Blockbuster and Amazon.com are facing substitutes in the form of web-based movies-on-demand services.[30] In such cases, the threat of substitutes is high.

Although Porter's five forces is a powerful technique to understand the competition at the domestic level, it can also be very useful to multinational firms as they examine their industries in the various countries in which they are involved. It allows multinational firms to determine the attractiveness of the various industries in which they are involved and also to ascertain which forces require attention. Such analyses can be very helpful as strategies are crafted.

The next important step in understanding industries is to assess the dominant economic traits. The dominant economic characteristics of an industry affect how strategies work. Issues that influence strategy selection include market size, ease of entry and exit, and whether there are economies of scale in production.[31] For example, markets with high growth rates often attract new competitors. Companies in these industries must be prepared to evoke defensive strategies against the new rivals. Michael Porter argues that strategists must also monitor several driving forces of change in an industry.[32] These forces include the speed of new-product innovations, technological changes, and changing societal attitudes and lifestyles. For example, rapidly changing technology creates the risk of being quickly overtaken by competitors; firms must respond by emphasizing innovation. Industries are also affected by the extent of their competition. Increased competition comes from such forces as the power of key suppliers and buyers or the threat of potential new entries into the industry.[33] Knowing your industry can be the key to strategic survival.

An analysis of an industry helps the manager identify the important characteristics of companies and their products or services that lead to competitive success. For example, in some industries, speed to market with a new product might be the key. Intel maintains dominance in the microprocessor industry by continually beating its rivals to the market with the next generation of computer chips. In other industries, high-quality designs may be most important for competitive success.

The factors that lead to success in an industry are called **key success factors (KSFs)**. Each one of these factors can have different degrees of importance in different industries or within the same industry at different points in time. Possible KSFs include:[34]

Key success factors (KSFs)

Important characteristics of a company or its product that lead to success in an industry.

- Innovative technology or products
- Broad product line
- Effective distribution channels
- Price advantages
- Effective promotion
- Superior physical facilities or skilled labor
- Experience of firm in business
- Cost position for raw materials
- Cost position for production
- R&D quality
- Financial assets
- Product quality
- Quality of human resources

A knowledge of industry dynamics and KSFs helps both multinational and domestic managers formulate strategies that best achieve these key goals. With an understanding of what drives competition in the industry and what the successful firms do to achieve and maintain their profitability, managers can formulate strategies that have the best chance of success for their firms. The Case in Point shows how South African Breweries uses a knowledge of KSFs to defend its monopoly in the South African beer market.

Understanding an industry and identifying KSFs represent only some of the knowledge necessary to formulate successful strategies. Formulating the best strategies also demands that you understand and anticipate your competitors' strategies. One technique used to assess rivals is a competitor analysis. A **competitor analysis** profiles your competitors' strategies and objectives. It can help you select an offensive or defensive competitive strategy based on the current or anticipated actions of your rivals.

The competitor analysis has four steps. These include:

Competitor analysis

Profiles of your competitor's strategies and objectives.

1. Identifying the basic strategic intent of competitors. Strategic intent represents the broad strategic objectives of the firm, such as to be the market share leader or to be a company known for its technological innovation.

C A S E   I N   P O I N T

Mastery of Local KSFs: SAB Miller (South African Breweries Miller) Defends Its Local Markets

SAB Miller is one of the dominant players in the South African alcoholic beverages market with a 97 percent market share in beer and more than 60 percent of the liquor market. However, SAB Miller dominates the South African market not because its beers have a unique taste or quality but, rather, because the company has the distinctive competency to meet the complex demands of the local market.

The key success factor for selling beer in South Africa is mastery of the distribution channel. In South Africa, most beer is sold through *shebeens,* unlicensed pubs left over from apartheid when the sale of alcohol to blacks was illegal. Most *shebeens* are in poor and rural areas with bad roads and unstable supply of electricity. The government allows these pubs to exist to discourage the use of potentially lethal home brews.

SAB Miller does not sell directly to the illegal pubs but works through local distributors and independent truck drivers. Loyal to SAB, many of the truck drivers are former employees who started their delivery businesses with help from SAB. In remote towns and villages, SAB provides refrigerators and generators to make sure their beer is cold.

Foreign brewers often consider trying to break SAB's monopoly in South Africa. Consider, for instance, when Diageo launched Smirnoff Ice in 1999, SAB countered with a similar product named Brutal Fruit, which is now one of the best-selling flavored alcoholic drinks. Like Diageo, foreign companies would have to develop the competency to build a competitive channel in this unique region. SAB is also a cost leader with very efficient production allowing it to reduce prices by more than 50 percent during the last decade and to serve poor, price-sensitive customers.

Despite its merger with U.S.-based Miller, SAB Miller is also trying to stay close to its roots. SAB Miller is heavily involved in affirmative action and other socially responsible programs in South Africa. Furthermore, although the company's headquarters moved to London, six of the eight members of the executive committee and the chief executive are all South African nationals.

Sources: Based on Economist 2000. "South African Beer: Big lion, small cage." http:www.economist.com August 12; Reed, John. 2005. "How SAB Miller stayed dominant at home while aiming to go global." Financial Times, October 21: p. 12.

2. Identifying the generic strategies used and anticipated to be used by competitors (e.g., producing at the lowest cost). This helps managers determine which KSFs are currently most important to competitors and are most likely to be important in the future. For example, cheap labor cost might be an important KSF for a competitor's low-cost strategy.
3. Identifying the offensive and defensive competitive strategies currently used or anticipated to be used by rivals.
4. Assessing the current positions of competitors, such as identifying the market leader or companies losing market share.

Understanding current and anticipated competitive moves by rival firms allows managers to plan offensive or defensive strategies for their own firms. For example, if a competitor uses a differentiation strategy based on high-quality products, a company may attack by matching or exceeding that quality at a lower price.

To formulate their competitive strategies, multinational companies use a country-by-country competitive analysis. In this way, a company can plan competitive moves, using distinct competitive strategies against different competitors in different countries. Exhibit 5.7 shows hypothetical competitive profiles of four companies in different countries. Using this hypothetical illustration, a multinational manager might decide to avoid attacking Bronson, Inc. in its home market. Bronson is the dominant leader and has threatened retaliation.

Company-Situation Analysis

Each company faces its own unique situation in the competitive business world. Managers must understand what *their* particular company can and cannot do best, realistically assessing their company's resources and strategic capabilities. In addition, they must identify any opportunities for or threats to their company's unique position in the industry.

The most common tool for a company-situation analysis is called the **SWOT**. SWOT is an acronym for Strengths, Weaknesses, Opportunities, and Threats. The SWOT has an internal component, which focuses on an organization's *strengths* and *weaknesses,* and an external component, which focuses on *opportunities* or *threats* from the environment.

A strength is a distinctive capability, resource, skill, or other advantage that an organization has relative to its competitors. Strengths may come from technological superiority, innovative products, greater efficiencies and lower costs, human-resource capabilities, marketing and promotional strengths, or other factors. A weakness is any competitive disadvantage of a company relative to its competitors. To identify relevant strengths or weakness, managers must assess their distinctive competencies that can lead to sustainable competitive advantage when matched with an appropriate strategy. Relevant strengths and weaknesses are often industry-specific and depend on the KSFs in a company's industry. Companies attempt to build their strategies around their strengths. For example, if you can produce at lower costs, you can underprice your rivals. If you can innovate more quickly, you can be first to market with a new product.

Opportunities represent favorable conditions in a firm's environment. Threats are unfavorable conditions in the environment. Threats come from any changes that challenge a company's position in its industry: new competitors, such as Korean electronics makers in the United States, technological change,

SWOT

The analysis of an organization's internal strengths and weaknesses and the opportunities or threats from the environment.

EXHIBIT 5.7   A Hypothetical Country-by-Country Competitive Analysis of Rivals

Rivals	Strategic Issues	Countries			
		Canada	Mexico	France	Taiwan
Bronson, Inc. (United States)	➤Strategic Intent	Dominant leader	Maintain position	Dominant leader	Move into the top five
	➤Generic Strategies	Low cost	Low cost	Low cost	Differentiation based on foreign image
	➤Competitive Strategies	Defensive based on threat of retaliation	None	Offensive price cutting	Offensive price cutting
	➤Current Position	Market leader	Middle of the pack	Increasing share: No. 2	New entry
Leroux (Belgium)	➤Strategic Intent	Overtake the leader	Move up a notch	Dominant leader	Survive
	➤Generic Strategies	Differentiation based on brand name	Differentiation based on brand name	Differentiation based on brand name	Differentiation based on brand name
	➤Competitive Strategies	Price cutting based on counter-parry	Price cutting based on counter-parry	Provide resources for counter-parries	Price cutting based on counter-parry
	➤Current Position	Holding at No. 3	Market leader	New entry; too early to tell	Holding at No. 2
Shin, Ltd. (Singapore)	➤Strategic Intent	Gain and hold market share	Gain and hold market share	Gain and hold market share	Gain and hold market share
	➤Generic Strategies	Differentiation based on high quality	Differentiation based on high quality	Differentiation based on high quality	Differentiation based on high quality
	➤Competitive Strategies	Offensive by comparative advertisements	Offensive by comparative advertisements	Defensive, lock in long-term contracts	Defensive, lock in long-term contracts
	➤Current Position	Middle of the pack	Middle of the pack, but rising	Market leader	Market leader
Keio, Ltd. (Japan)	➤Strategic Intent	To catch and pass the leaders	To catch and pass the leaders	To catch and pass the leaders	To catch and pass the leaders
	➤Generic Strategies	Low cost based on cheap labor	Low cost based on cheap labor	Low cost based on cheap labor	Low cost based on cheap labor
	➤Competitive Strategies	Heavy discounts based on volume purchases	Heavy discounts based on volume purchases	Heavy discounts based on volume purchases	Heavy discounts based on volume purchases
	➤Current Position	New entry, rising fast	New entry, rising fast	Expected to enter this year	New entry, rising fast

political change, and changes in import regulations, for example. Opportunities often come from the same sources, although new markets may also constitute important opportunities. Consider the Multinational Management Brief on page 239 emerging markets and opportunities for insurance markets.

A threat for one company may represent an opportunity for another company. For example, Honda, Toyota, and Nissan view Europe as the next

---

Multinational Management **Brief**

Emerging Markets and Opportunities for Insurance Markets

Faced with a very saturated domestic market in the United States, multinational insurers have always had a tough time finding new markets. However, things have improved dramatically in the past decade, and many insurers are now faced with the challenge of choosing from a number of promising opportunities in emerging markets. For example, China remains very promising for multinational insurers with a potential market of 1 billion customers. The American Insurance Group's (AIG) success in China shows the potential of such emerging opportunities to a multinational firm's success. AIG started small, but it has enjoyed impressive compounded growth to become a dominant player in the market. However, other emerging markets in Eastern Europe (Poland, Slovakia, Czech Republic, Hungary, and Slovenia), Vietnam, Russia, and Turkey also present tremendous opportunities. For example, Turkey has a population of more than 70 million young people and also presents tremendous potential for growth. Recent surveys suggest that the insurance premium in Turkey rose by 40 percent in 2004 over the previous year. Furthermore, while analysts predict that both life and non-life insurance growth in industrialized countries will likely hover around 1.7 percent, they predict that such insurance growth in emerging markets will be greater than 7.4 percent.

Source: Based on Pilla, David. 2005. "Emerging opportunities." Best's Review, September 106, 5: pp. 56–58.

---

opportunity after the United States for their luxury models Acura, Lexus, and Infinity. BMW and Mercedes, however, view their Japanese rivals' moves into the upscale European car market as a major threat.

Successful firms monitor not only their industry, which is usually called the operating environment, but also the broader environment, which is usually called the general environment. The general environment includes all the social institutions (e.g., economy, politics) and cultural context discussed earlier as the national context. It also includes broad issues of technological change such as the evolution of the Internet that has provided opportunities for many new business forms as well as threats to established organizations.

The SWOT analysis for the multinational company is more complex than for the domestic company. This is especially true for assessing opportunities and threats. Multinational companies face more complex general and operating environments because they compete in two or more countries. Each country provides its own national context, which may present opportunities or threats different from those in another country.

Import or export barriers may also make exporting products or importing supplies prohibitively expensive. Volatile exchange rates may make an otherwise attractive business environment threatening. Local inflation may play havoc with prices for the international market. Changes in government policies may affect the ability to repatriate earnings (get the company's money out).

In conducting a SWOT, multinational managers must conduct extremely thorough analyses of the business environment in each country. A country-by-country SWOT is probably most prudent.

Corporate Strategy Selection

A diversified corporation has a portfolio (a selection) of businesses, with the primary goal of investing in profitable businesses. The major strategic question is deciding which businesses in the portfolio are targets for growth and investment and which businesses are targets for divestment or harvesting. Targets for growth and investment receive additional corporate resources because managers anticipate high returns. Targets for divestment are businesses that managers decide to sell or liquidate. Targets for harvesting are usually mature and profitable businesses that managers see as sources of cash for other investments.

One way of assessing a corporate business portfolio is through a matrix analysis. Several consultants and companies have developed their own business matrix systems to assess business portfolios. One popular method is the growth-share matrix of the Boston Consulting Group (BCG). It is used to decide how much of its resources a corporation should devote to any unit. The BCG growth-share matrix divides businesses into four categories based on the industry growth rate and the relative market share of the business in question. The most attractive businesses are those in fast-growing industries in which the business has a relatively large market share compared to the most successful firm in the industry. Businesses in this category are called "stars." In contrast, "dogs" are businesses with relatively low market shares in low-growth industries. "Cash cows" are businesses in slow-growth industries where the company has a strong market-share position. "Problem children" are businesses in high-growth industries where the company has a poor market share. For each type of business, the growth-share matrix has a suggested strategy. These strategies are shown in Exhibit 5.8.

EXHIBIT 5.8   The BCG Growth-Share Matrix for a Diversified Multinational Company

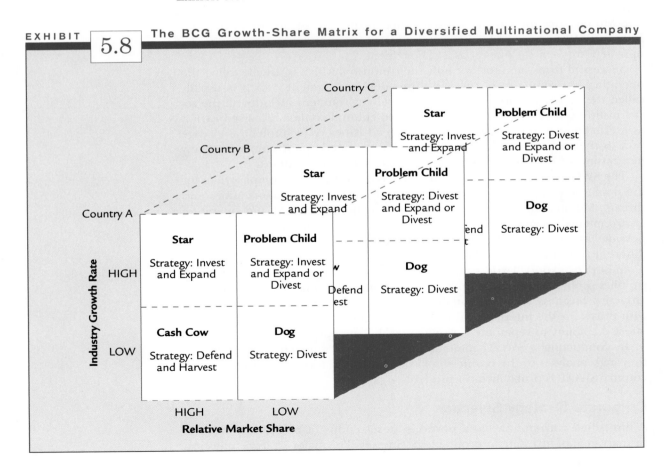

Another popular portfolio matrix is the GE Portfolio Matrix. This matrix contains nine cells based on high, medium, and low levels of industry attractiveness and strong, average, and weak levels of a business's competitive position in the industry. Some indicators of industry strength are market size and growth rate. Competitive position is based on the strategic capabilities of a business such as lower costs for production. This matrix is used to determine the competitive position of a business in its industry.

All matrices are used to help answer some basic strategy formulation questions:[35]

- Are businesses in attractive industries?
- Are most businesses growing?
- Are there sufficient cash cows to finance other potential growth businesses?
- Is the business portfolio well positioned for the future?
- Do the businesses have some strategic synergies?

For the diversified multinational company, the portfolio assessment becomes more complex. The added complexity occurs because market share and industry growth are seldom the same in all the countries in which a multinational competes. Thus, as illustrated in Exhibit 5.8 showing a cross-country BCG analysis, portfolio analyses must be conducted for each business in each country or region of operation.

The previous discussion provided a brief review of some analytical techniques used to formulate strategy for the multinational company. The challenge for the multinational manager is to use these and other techniques in the highly complex and evolving world of international competition. The next section shows how broader institutional forces can affect the choice of strategies for the multinational company and its competitors.

Organizations Alike: Globalization and Convergence

Some experts believe that many management practices, especially those related to strategy, are becoming more similar. This increasing similarity of management practices is called **convergence.** In fact, many of the multinational management examples given in this book show the effects of convergence. The examples come from organizations throughout the world and illustrate management practices readily copied and used by managers of all nationalities.

Convergence is most apparent with transnational firms. Multinational firms competing in the same industry tend to have similar structures and strategies regardless of the location of the company's headquarters. They use what they see as most effective. In addition, because they compete in worldwide markets, multinational companies seek not only uniform products and strategies but also strategies and ways of organizing that need not differ by national boundaries. Multinational managers also often lack deep-seated national cultural or societal identification. Their companies, not their nations, are more important to them.

The forces that lead companies to become transnational in strategy include coercive, mimic, and normative isomorphic pressures for similarity (see Chapter 3 for definitions). For example, agreements among countries, such as regional trade agreements and membership in the WTO, provide supranational regulatory environments that affect management practices. Cross-border competition,

Convergence

Increased similarity of management practices.

trade, mergers, and acquisitions provide more opportunities to learn about and copy successful managerial practices from anywhere in the world. Normative pressures for similarity come from the internationalization of business education and the movement of managers across borders. Exhibit 5.9 shows visually how these processes work.

The following points show in more detail how globalization pushes organizations to be more similar.

- *Global customers and products:* The similarity of customer demands and the increased likelihood that companies and people shop worldwide limits the options managers have in strategy and structure. This results in managers creating similar organizations with similar capabilities to serve similar customers.
- *Growing levels of industrialization and economic development:* This results in convergence because more organizations have the technical and financial capability to use similar technologies. In turn, the technologies used by organizations limit the strategy and design options available to managers.
- *Global competition and global trade:* International competition raises managerial awareness of what people in other countries are doing. The growth of U.S. managers' interest in Japanese management, for example, occurred because of increasing Japanese competition with U.S. companies. Increased trade means that managers interact more with each other and learn more about the strategies and structures of organizations from different societies. Both competition and trade encourage managers to mimic or copy what works in other nations.
- *Cross-border mergers, acquisitions, and alliances:* As with cross-border trade, when companies from different nations combine, such as the merger of Chrysler and Daimler Benz, managers combine the strategies and organizational designs from both nationalities. These combined organizations provide a wealth of information on the organizational practices of other societies. Later, parent organizations use this knowledge to change and improve their own organizations. They must find strategies and structures that work for all of the participating companies regardless of nationality.

EXHIBIT 5.9   The Effects of Globalization on the Convergence of Strategies for Multinational Companies

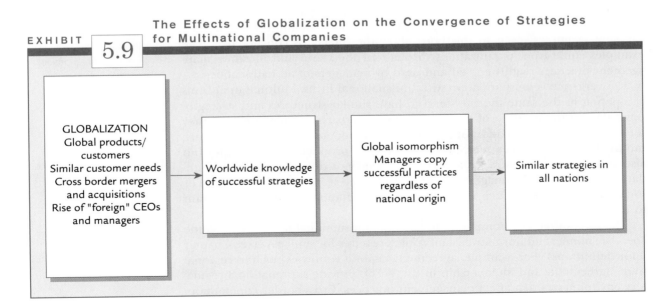

- *Cross-national mobility of managers:* Increasingly, organizations are looking for CEOs, managers, and technical experts from any country that can provide the highest level of talent. When managers cross borders, they bring with them the technical and managerial knowledge from their country of origin. This migratory knowledge increases mimic isomorphism or the ability of managers to copy strategies and designs from other countries.

- *Internationalization of business education:* Business education also serves to homogenize organizational practices. In particular, the large number of international students in U.S. and European MBA programs helps spread common business techniques. Many students return to their home countries with the intent of adopting management practices that best fit their national cultures. Cooperative MBA programs between universities in developing nations and partner universities in the United States and Europe also transfer management practices. Consider the Multinational Management Brief, which shows examples of the transfer of management knowledge through managers and education.

In spite of the trend toward convergence, national differences still affect the way many firms compete via their choices of strategies. Savvy multinational

Multinational Management **Brief**

Management Transfer

Many of the high-tech firms in Korea, India, and Taiwan are staffed with top executives who were educated in the United States and stayed on to work for a decade or more. Now they are returning to their homelands armed with technical and managerial expertise. John Gage, an executive at Sun Microsystems, estimates that half of the vice presidents of engineering in Taiwanese electronics companies originally worked for U.S. companies such as Hewlett-Packard or Sun. Former expatriates such as Hong Kong's Allan Wong are borrowing management systems learned from their former U.S. companies and adapting them to local needs. Wong, for example, is following his former company's (NCR) example by investing in continuing education for his managers as a technique for sustaining long-term growth. Chris Chang, a Texas Instruments veteran, advises a new chip manufacturing company in Shanghai. Right now he says of the $1.5 billion chip-making complex owned by Semiconductor Manufacturing International Corp., "It's a baby. But it's a baby elephant."

In China, approximately 25 universities have joint MBA programs with foreign universities and more than 40 run alone by Chinese universities. The Shanghai Municipal Government and the EU jointly finance the China Europe International Business School. Typical examples for U.S. universities include a program between Beijing's Qinghua University and MIT's Sloan School of Management and Washington University and the prestigious Fudan University in Shanghai. Additionally, some universities such as Beijing University's Guangha School of Management are also offering MBAs partnering with universities in Singapore and the U.K. Expectation is that the demand for MBAs in China will soar as local companies go international and more multinational firms enter China. Furthermore, increasingly, China's top universities are also requiring PhDs from foreign schools

Source: Based on Aiyar, Pallavi. 2006. "Excellence in education: The Chinese way." The Hindu, Feb. 17, p. 1; Engardia, Pete, Jonathan Moore, and Christine Hill. 1996. "As the miracle economies slow down, their hidden problems start to appear." BusinessWeek, December 2; Knight Ridder Tribune Business News. 2002. "Kimberly-Clark Corp. fires back in the diaper wars." December 12; Roberts, Dexter, Li Yan, and Sheridan Prasso. 2002. "To get an MBA is glorious." BusinessWeek. April 22, p. 14.

managers must understand these differences for three important reasons. First, managers in successful multinational firms must understand and anticipate the strategies of rivals from other countries. Second, managers in successful multinational firms must understand the strategies of potential business partners since cross-national partnerships often exist for any value-chain activity, from raw-material suppliers to downstream distribution. Third, strategies developed in one national context might be copied and modified to fit another national context.

To provide a better understanding of international rivals and collaborators, the chapter now presents an overview of how the national context leads to national differences in strategic management practices.

The National Context and Organizational Strategy: Overview and Observations

The national context has been discussed at length throughout this text. Following is a brief summary of the effect of the national context on organizational strategy and design. The national context represents the immediate environment where firms compete. These environments provide firms with nation-specific opportunities and threats. That is, there are specific combinations of opportunities and threats in a nation that are different from those in other nations. As a result, the varieties of national contexts lead to the flourishing of different industries and the prospering of different strategies.

More specifically, the national context affects organizational design and strategy formulation and content through the following processes:

- The social institutions and national and business cultures encourage or discourage certain forms of businesses and strategies in each nation. There are generally acceptable and unacceptable ways of conducting business. For example, isomorphic forces that encourage copying successful firms and responding to government policies create national similarities in strategy.
- Social institutions and national culture serve as barriers to the easy transfer of competitive advantages among countries. The culture and social institutions prevent or inhibit the easy copying of management practices from other countries.
- Each nation must rely on its available factor conditions for developing industries and the firms within industries. Factor conditions lead to the existence of each country's unique resource base. Local firms have the easiest access to local resources. Consequently, firms in a nation are most likely to favor similar strategies that take advantage of their unique bundle of local resources.
- Social institutions and culture determine which resources are used, how they are used, and which resources are developed. The resource base limits the strategic options available to firms in any nation.

The points just discussed provide a general picture of the processes by which national context affects strategic management. Multinational managers can generalize and apply these ideas to understand the actions of rivals or alliance partners in any country where their firm does business.

Summary and Conclusions

Few students who read this book will work in industries untouched by global competition. Many will work for multinational companies or their subsidiaries. Others will work for companies that may source their raw materials from international suppliers, sell to international customers, or compete with multinational companies (or all three). The business environment becomes increasingly global each day. Consequently, even the managers of domestic firms need to have a good understanding of multinational business strategy. This chapter provided a foundation and the basic terminology to understand the strategic issues facing the multinational manager.

The primary ingredients of multinational strategic management are based on general strategic management processes. Like domestic firms, multinational companies employ the generic strategies of low cost and differentiation. To compete with rival firms, multinational firms also use offensive and defensive competitive strategies. Diversified multinational firms can have both unrelated and related business portfolios. To formulate strategies, multinational managers use many of the same tools available to domestic managers.

Differing from the solely domestic firm, however, the multinational company always faces more complex situations. Basic strategies that work in one country may not work in another. Competitive strategies also must be considered on a country-by-country basis. The multinational company and its rivals are seldom in the same competitive positions in all the countries in which they compete. Although there are global trends of convergence in strategies, the institutional and cultural conditions favor different strategies by competitors from different nations. Multinational managers must be aware of these differences as they affect both collaborators and competitors. Because of these complexities, and the additional complexities of a multi-country economic and political environment, the multinational manager faces continuous challenges in strategy formulation.

The multinational manager also must realize that strategy is a combination of planned intent and adaptive reactions to changing circumstances. The techniques discussed in this chapter and in the following chapter refer to the planned aspects of strategy—what the manager determines is the best game plan given the nature of his or her company and the competitive and general environment in which the company must survive. Modifying or changing strategies in responses to new opportunities and new threats is a necessity in today's world of rapid cross-border competition.

Beyond the traditional strategic questions facing all managers, the multinational manager must confront other issues related to strategy. The next chapter deals directly with these issues. Chapter 6 introduces the "global vs. local" dilemma faced by multinational companies. For example, multinational companies must decide whether to sell one product worldwide or to make unique products for each country. Chapter 6 also introduces an array of strategies that multinational companies use to participate in different markets. For example, multinational companies must decide whether to export their products or to manufacture their products in other countries.

Discussion Questions

1. Discuss how a multinational firm might use a low-cost strategy in one country while using a differentiation strategy in another country.

2. Identify examples of how multinational companies have used the offensive competitive strategies discussed in the chapter.

3. How can a multinational competitor such as Wal-Mart attack multinational rivals using the counter-parry?

4. Discuss the advantages that multinational companies might have over domestic rivals in sustaining competitive advantage.

5. Identify and discuss the KSFs that are most likely to vary by national context. Explain your answer.

Multinational Management **Skill Builder**

Identifying Distinctive Competencies and Generic Strategies

Step 1. Choose a global industry, such as the automobile industry or the cell phone industry, and identify two to four major competitors in the industry.

Step 2. Research the selected companies in the popular business press and make a list of the unique capabilities of each company. Identify the location on the value chain where these capabilities exist.

Step 3. For each company, write a one-page analysis showing how these capabilities lead to distinctive competencies.

Step 4. For each company, write a one-page analysis showing how the company attempts to use its distinctive competencies to successfully implement a generic strategy. Note whether companies have different generic strategies for different products or for different market segments.

Endnotes

[1] Hitt, Michael A., B. W. Keats, and S. M. DeMarie. 1998. "Navigating in the new competitive landscape: Building competitive advantage and strategic flexibility in the 21st century." *Academy of Management Executive*, 12: pp. 22–42.

[2] Hambrick, Donald C., and James W. Fredrickson. 2005. "Are you sure you have a strategy?" *Academy of Management Executive*, 19, 4: pp. 51–62.

[3] Ibid.

[4] Porter, Michael E. 1990. *Competitive Advantage of Nations*. New York: Free Press.

[5] Ibid.

[6] Ibid.

[7] Ibid.

[8] Porter, Michael E. 1985. *Competitive Advantage: Creating and Sustaining Superior Performance*. New York: Free Press.

[9] Thompson, Arthur A. Jr., A. J. Strickland III, and John E. Gamble. 2007. *Crafting and Executing Strategy*. McGraw–Hill. Homewood, IL: Irwin .

[10] Ibid.

[11] Merrifield, Bruce. 2006. "Make outsourcing a core competency." *Research Technology Management*, May/June, 49, 3: pp. 10–13.

[12] Ibid.

[13] Kakumanu, Prasad, and Anthony Portanova. 2006. "Outsourcing: Its benefits, drawbacks and other related issues." *Journal of American Academy of Business*, September, 9, 2: pp. 1–7.

[14] Hall, Kevin G. 2006. "Moving up the chain: More complex jobs are moving offshore." *Little India*, January: p. 54.

[15] Dhar, Subhankar, and Bindu Balakrishnan. 2006. "Risks, benefits, and challenges in global IT outsourcing: Perspectives and practices." *Journal of Global Information Management*, July–September, 14, 3: pp. 39–69.

[16] Mahnke, Volker and Serden Ozcan. 2006. "Outsourcing innovation and relational governance." *Industry and Innovation*, June, 13, 2: pp. 121–125.

[17] Merrifield, "Make outsourcing a core competency."

[18] Hill, Charles, W. L. Jones, and Gareth R. Jones. 2001. *Strategic Management Theory*. Boston: Houghton Mifflin, p. 137.

[19] Aaker, David A. 1989. "Managing assets and skills: The key to sustainable competitive advantage." *California Management Review* 31: pp. 91–106.

[20] Barney, J.B. 1991. "Firm resources and sustained competitive advantage." *Journal of Management*, 17: pp. 99–120.

[21] Thompson, Strickland III, and Gamble, *Crafting and Executing Strategy*; Yip, George S. 2002. *Total Global Strategy II*. Englewood Cliffs, N.J.: Prentice Hall.

[22] Ibid.

[23] Thompson, Strickland III, and Gamble, *Crafting and Executing Strategy*.

[24] Li, Mingfang, and Yim-Yu Wong. 2003. "Diversification and economic performance: An empirical assessment of Chinese firms." *Asia Pacific Journal of Management*, June, 20, 2: pp. 243–265.

[25] Ibid.

[26] Ibid.

[27] Ibid.

[28] Thompson, Strickland III, and Gamble, *Crafting and Executing Strategy*.

[29] Hitt, Keats, and DeMarie, "Navigating in the new competitive landscape: Building competitive advantage and strategic flexibility in the 21st century."

[30] Heilemann, John. 2005. "Showtime for Netflix." *Business 2.0*, March, pp. 36–38.

[31] Thompson, Strickland III, and Gamble, *Crafting and Executing Strategy*.

[32] Porter, Michael E. 1980. *Competitive Strategy: Techniques for Analyzing Industries and Competitors*. New York: Free Press.

[33] Porter, Michael E. 1979. "How competitive forces shape strategy." *Harvard Business Review* 57, March–April, pp. 137–145.

[34] Pearce, John A. II, and Richard B. Robinson, Jr. 1994. *Strategic Management: Formulation, Implementation, and Control*. Burr Ridge, Ill.: Irwin; Thompson, Strickland III, and Gamble, *Crafting and Executing Strategy*.

[35] Thompson, Strickland III, and Gamble, *Crafting and Executing Strategy*.

Harley-Davidson and the International Market for Luxury Goods

Mission Statement:
"We fulfill dreams through the experience of motorcycling, by providing to motorcyclists, and to the general public, an expanding line of motorcycles, branded products, and services in selected market segments."

http://www.harley-davidson.com

In fiscal year 2005 Harley-Davidson produced 329,017 motorcycles. 62,510, or 19%, of these motorcycles were delivered to offshore markets and contributed $1.04 billion to the company's sales. These motorcycles, showcasing chrome and flawless paint, are intended to make a statement for their owners. It can be an expensive statement; 2007 base prices, f.o.b. factory, ranged from $6,595 for the smallest model, the venerable Sportster, to over $20,000 for the massive Electra Glide. Accessories, shipping, import tariffs, and other duties and licenses can more than double the factory price in offshore markets.

Harley-Davidson (H-D) produces and sells only heavyweight motorcycles under the H-D brand; the company also manufactures motorcycles under the Buell brand. The company has defined the heavyweight segment as motorcycles with engines displacing a minimum of 651cc. Following a decade of

short supply, the production of Harley-Davidson motorcycles rose markedly in the first five years of the 21st century. A portion of the rise in production was attributable to a radically new model, the V-Rod or VRSC. Introduced for the 2002 model year, Harley-Davidson's VRSC model, merged engineering from German auto manufacturer Porsche with H-D's classic design. The availability of motorcycles, along with the new VRSC model, has allowed, some might say forced, H-D to increase its focus on international markets. Whether domestic or international, Harley-Davidson motorcycles fall into the highest end of the market in terms of price, quality, and finish—the luxury segment of the motorcycle market.

International Market for Luxury Goods

Economists define luxury goods and services, as goods for which the demand increases at a proportionally faster rate than income. From a socio-cultural perspective, a luxury good is seen as a product at the highest end of the market in terms of design, quality, durability, performance, and price. The definition of luxury is not solely objective, it is also subjective as a function of the buyers' personal circumstances and the status the good conveys. The concept of luxury evolves constantly with the ever-shifting economic, demographic, socio-cultural,

Harley-Davidson Units Produced and Sold: 2001–2005									
H-D Units Sold	**2005**	**Change**	**2004**	**Change**	**2003**	**Change**	**2002**	**Change**	**2001**
Domestic	266,507	2%	260,607	10%	237,656	12%	212,833	14%	186,915
International	62,510	10%	56,682	6%	53,491	5%	50,820	7%	47,546
Total	329,017	4%	317,289	9%	291,147	10%	263,653	12%	234,461

and geopolitical climate. Classic luxury goods include haute couture items such as clothing, perfume, and luggage. Many product and service markets have a luxury segment, for example, cars, hotels, and even chocolate. Estimates of the 2005 global market for luxury goods vary, but range up to the $1 trillion estimate of the Boston Consulting Group.

- *United States* The United States (U.S.) consumes roughly 25% of the world's luxury goods. In 2005 the U.S. consumption of luxury goods grew by 11.6% over 2004. In the U.S. there are four million households that have an income of more than $1 million. It is this population that defines the luxury sector through its patronage. There are also 48 million households in the U.S. earning between $50,000 and $150,000. Although the purchase of luxury goods is relatively infrequent in these 48 million households, their collective purchase of luxury goods is a significant share of the market. The purchasers of luxury goods are not price-resistant, but they do wants to know what they get for the price. Thus, companies must demonstrate that not only are their products luxurious, but that they will also add value to the consumer's lifestyle.

- *Europe* Estimates for the size of the European luxury good market range from 25–40% of the global market. Europe is the spiritual home of luxury goods and the originator of many traditional brands, e.g., Louis Vuitton, Ferrari, and Chanel. European demographics bear many similarities to those in the U.S. However, in Europe income growth has been more evenly distributed across the population. Europe also has double the population of seniors. Those seniors control more wealth and are more likely to spend that wealth on luxury goods.

- *Japan* Japan is the home of the largest Louis Vuitton store; a fact that only seems appropriate given that 94% of Tokyo women in their 20s own something from Louis Vuitton. Japanese luxury goods retailers are seeing annual sales growth of 10–15% and they often charge 40% more than in the European market. Prestige is valued in Japanese culture and external signs of status are evident.

- *China* China, together with India and Russia, is part of what is seen as a "golden triangle" of the newly wealthy who are 'thirsty' for luxury goods. These growth markets are attractive to Western luxury-good

businesses whose sales have traditionally been concentrated on the U.S., Europe, and Japan. China is expected to pass Japan to become the world's second-largest purchasers of luxury goods by 2015, and to account for 29 percent of the world's luxury sales. Consumers are status-conscious, increasingly wealthy, hungry for brand image, and fanatical about shopping. A recent survey of young urbanites on the Chinese mainland found over 60% of them prone to buy high-end consumer goods. On the average, luxury goods consumption accounts for 4 percent of consumer spending, but in China, the proportion is estimated to be as much as 40 percent.

- *India* 1.6 million Indian households spend an average of $9000 a year on luxury items. India is the highest wage growth country in Asia. Multi-income families and increasing international exposure is driving a socio-cultural transition from saving to a spending. Sales of luxury products have risen by 20% per year and consumers want the latest models and exclusive editions. India's luxury-car market has tripled in the past five years despite import duties of about 100 percent.

- *Russia* Russia accounts for five percent of the global luxury goods market. Russia is producing today's most determinedly conspicuous consumers and may be the single fastest growing market for luxury goods. A lot of this spending is abroad as more than 23 million Russians travel outside the country each year. While the luxury market continues to develop in Russia, it is not yet saturated and the demand for exclusive and prestigious brands continues.

Consumption of luxury goods reflects a movement to a single luxury esthetic that incorporates influences from every corner of the globe. This means that a brand's ethnicity is no longer an indicator of where its owners are from, where the goods are produced, or who buys them, but rather is a matter of buyer preference—for anyone who can pay the price.

The International Heavyweight Motorcycle Market

In the U.S., H-D clearly trades on its image and the nostalgia to sell its traditional bikes. While Harley's quality and engineering is excellent, the technology of the company's traditional bikes lags behind that of competitors. The technology gap is largely intentional; customers are paying for an American icon. Harley-Davidson relies on something

Harley-Davidson Motorcycle Retail Sales by International Market					
	2005	**Change**	**2004**	**Change**	**2003**
U.S.	253.4	4.2%	243.2	7.1%	227.1
Canada	11.7	4.1%	11.2	14.6%	9.8
Europe	29.5	19.9%	24.6	–5.3%	26.0
Japan	11.4	11.1%	10.3	–0.9%	10.4
Other Mkt.	11.2	19.4%	9.3	11.0%	8.3
Total	317.2	6.2%	298.6	6.0%	281.6

other than nostalgia for an American icon to sell motorcycles in the international market. That something is the image and status that is conveyed by a luxury good. Like the traditional styling and dated mechanical movement of a Rolex watch, the value of a H-D motorcycle is in its status and image and not its technology.

Harley-Davidson has led the motorcycle industry in domestic unit sales of heavyweight bikes for 17 straight years. The company's domestic market share increased 9% from 2001 to 2005. The company faces a challenge in limiting availability to ensure high-markups for itself and its dealers, while maintaining market share in the face of stiff competition. Through an understanding with its dealers, a maximum of 20% of the production of H-D's traditional motorcycles is shipped offshore, while 33% of VRSC production is exported. Consequently, international sales as a percentage of H-D's total sales remain flat even as the number of motorcycles shipped offshore increases.

The European market is a particularly difficult one for Harley-Davidson and the company's market share is 10%. The market is an attractive one and heavyweight motorcycle sales are 64% of those in the U.S. market. Unlike the U.S. market, the H-D image and nostalgia doesn't sell many bikes in Europe. 70% of the European market is comprised of performance bikes, a market segment in which the traditional H-D offerings are not competitive. Harley-Davison's newest design, the V-Rod or VRSC, with its Porsche designed engine, competes in this market segment. Europeans differ in their tastes on a regional and national basis. Those that favor Italian flair have the option of the racy Ducati and similar bikes, while those that like Teutonic thoroughness

can opt for the highly refined BMW. Harley-Davidson would like to double its European market share over the next few years.

In 2005 Harley-Davidson sold over 11,400 motorcycles in Japan through a network of 81 dealers. The VRSC model is popular with Japan's twenty-something thrill junkies. Overall motorcycle ownership in Japan peaked in the mid-1980s and has been in a slow decline since that time. However, the decline in ownership has been largely limited to motorcycles less that 250cc. Japanese law currently does not allow a motorcycle driver to carry a passenger.

China and India offer large and fast growing motorcycles markets. In both countries motorcycles meet the basic transportation needs of millions of families and businesses. Each country currently consumes around six million new motorcycles each year with almost all bikes displacing 250cc or less. Price is the competitive issue and joint ventures between domestic companies and international motorcycle manufacturers like Honda and Kawasaki produce affordable motorcycles of good quality. One source estimates there are 300 Harley-Davidson motorcycles in Beijing and perhaps 2,000 in all of China. H-D has an agreement with China's Zonshen Motorcycle Group to develop the Chinese market and a Harley-Davidson dealership was opened on the outskirts of Beijing in 2006. Trade barriers at all levels remain a problem in the Chinese market. Import tariffs are also onerous in India, running over 90% for a heavyweight motorcycle. India's emission standards for bikes over 500cc are rigorous and exclude H-D's current products. Harley-Davison has engaged in talks with the government of India, but there is little reason to think India will change its regulations to permit the import of H-D motorcycles. Despite the vagaries of Indian regulations, Suzuki and Kawasaki have enjoyed modest success selling performance motorcycles in India.

Australia and New Zealand continue to be strong markets for H-D motorcycles. Australia in particular has roads and landscapes similar to those found in U.S. Harley-Davidson is seen as a symbol of the freedom of the open road and has a loyal and passionate following. The growth segment in the Australian motorcycle market is off-the-road or dirt bikes with 40% of the market. In 2004 H-D was the 6th largest selling motorcycle brand in Australia with only 2% of the motorcycle market.

New Heavyweight (651+ cc) Motorcycle Registrations by Market	2005	2004	2003	2002	2001
North America					
H-D & Buell	253.4	259.6	242.0	223.1	188.3
Other Manufacturers	264.2	271.2	253.5	251.9	234.5
Europe					
H-D & Buell	34.3	30.4	29.4	21.9	21.8
Other Manufacturers	298.5	305.8	293.7	281.6	271.8
Japan/Australia	N/A				
H-D & Buell		16.6	16.2	14.3	13.4
Other Manufacturers		45.3	42.7	49.6	48.7
Total	N/A				
H-D & Buell		306.6	287.5	259.3	223.5
Other Manufacturers		622.3	590.0	583.1	555.0

Other significant markets for H-D include Canada, Brazil, and Mexico. Harley-Davidson opened its first dealership in Moscow, Russia in 2005.

Competitors

According to Harley-Davidson:

> *"Competition in the heavyweight motorcycle market is based upon a number of factors, including price, quality, reliability, styling, product features, customer preference, and warranties. The Company emphasizes quality, reliability and styling in its products and offers a warranty . . ."*
> *(2005 Annual Report)*

All of Harley-Davidson's major competitors have their headquarters outside the U.S. Most of the major competitors are operating units of larger diversified companies, e.g., Honda, Yamaha, Kawasaki, Suzuki, and BMW. At least one of H-D's major competitors, Honda, manufactures its largest motorcycles in the U.S. A major exception to the larger diversified company rule is Ducati, an Italian company that is a leader in the European performance market. In addition to offshore competition, H-D faces domestic competitors. These companies include newer brands like Big Dog and Polaris, and a number of small custom shops that cater to the ultra-high end motorcycle market.

- **Ducati** Ducati is representative of Harley-Davidson's European competition. Ducati Motor Holdings is listed on both the Milan and New York stock exchanges. Ducati has adopted a cyberspace model selling motorcycles, accessories and clothing online, http://www.ducati.com. The company promotes its cyberspace model through participation in motorcycle racing where Ducati has dominated the world Superbike Championships for over ten years. Unlike Harley-Davidson, Ducati does not build bikes on the basis on nostalgia and comfort, rather Ducati sells style and performance based on technologically advanced designs. Ducatis are race proven bikes, sold for use on the street - the ultimate café racer. Like Harley-Davidson, Ducati employs a premium pricing strategy. Ducati customers tend to be younger and somewhat less affluent, consequently

Market Share as a Function of U.S. Heavyweight Motorcycle Registrations	2005	2004	2003	2002	2001	2000
Harley-Davidson	48.9%	49.5%	49.5%	47.5%	45.0%	45.6%
Buell	00.7%	00.7%	00.8%	00.7%	00.7%	01.2%
Honda	16.6%	18.7%	18.4%	19.8%	20.5%	18.5%
Suzuki	12.4%	10.2%	09.8%	09.6%	10.8%	09.3%
Kawasaki	8.9%	06.4%	06.7%	06.9%	08.0%	09.0%
Yamaha	6.5%	08.7%	08.5%	08.9%	07.9%	08.4%
Other	6.0%	05.8%	06.3%	06.6%	07.1%	08.0%

sales vary more with the economic cycle. Harley-Davidson's new V-Rod appears to be aimed squarely at the high-end of Ducati's customer base.

- **BMW** BMW's focus is on putting their best efforts into a small range of products, which makes their products unique in quality, style and performance. Their motorcycle production concentrates on three different series stressing superior quality. BMW's strategy is based on premium pricing and building the best motorcycle that money can buy by setting the standard in technology, environment, and safety in all of their product offerings. Each of their motorcycles portrays the traditional motorcycle image; however, the BMW brand also includes elements of sophistication and class in their products. All of BMW's motorcycles have high resale values; however, their high cost limits their market share.

  BMW is the only manufacturer of cars and motorcycles worldwide that concentrates on premium standards and outstanding quality for all of its product lines. Once a goal is attained, that goal becomes the starting block for a new challenge in their quest for creating the untouchable and unmatchable product. Throughout their quest and their commitment to enhancing their international presence, BMW has expanded with 23 production and assembly plants located in seven countries and BMW has marketing subsidiaries in 33 countries. BMW is synonymous with high quality and performance, which is reinforced by strong brand recognition and customer loyalty . . . for those who can afford it.

- **Honda** Honda is the leader in motorcycle manufacturing with 17% of the North American market, 22% of the European market, and 23% of the Asian-Pacific market. Honda combines excellent engineering and quality with highly automated manufacturing to achieve significant economies of scale. Honda has been able to leverage its low-cost advantage into global leadership.

  Honda is a diversified company that at one time surpassed Chrysler and Toyota in sales to become the third largest automobile company in the U.S. In addition to motorcycles and automobiles Honda manufactures ATVs, outboard motors, generators, lawn care equipment and other power products. Honda has a presence in the financial services industry providing financing options for motorcycle and automobile dealers and consumers. Honda's niche in the U.S.

motorcycle market is touring bikes. With up to 1500 cc water-cooled engines, Honda's touring bikes are high quality, refined, comfortable, and fuel-efficient.Honda's corporate culture is egalitarian with all employees, including the president, wearing the same uniform and sharing the same facilities. Input is sought from all levels of the company. Honda encourages creativity and is widely regarded as being the leader in 4-cycle gasoline engine technology. The company goes to considerable lengths to structure its operations around the needs of local markets. Honda is committed to continuing its leadership position through attention to markets, continual improvement and the introduction of new models and technologies.

- **Kawasaki** Kawasaki is a world leader in the transportation equipment and industrial goods industries with diverse product lines in each category. Kawasaki motors is focused on motorcycles, all-terrain vehicles, Jet Ski watercraft, utility vehicles, rail cars, wheels, robots, and engines for consumer products such as lawnmowers. Kawasaki is well known for providing a wide-range of products that offer high performance and low maintenance attributes. Kawasaki offers multiple models of motorcycles, which makes them competitive in many different facets of the industry including touring bikes, sport bikes, off-road bikes, dual-purpose bikes, street bikes, and police bikes.

  Kawasaki has a large international presence with production facilities in Southeast Asia, China, Europe, and the United States. They hold the third largest motorcycle market share in North America at 10%, the fourth largest market share in Asia/Pacific at 19%, and the fifth largest market share in European markets at 12%. One of Kawasaki's strategic initiatives is striving for continual improvement in operational efficiencies. This has led many U.S. companies to study Kawasaki and their methods/techniques, which are called KPS – The Kawasaki Production System. One of the key techniques used is high employee empowerment and involvement, which allows for a more efficient workflow in producing high-quality products. KPS assists Kawasaki in meeting the fluctuating needs of its customers because it allows them to produce units through just-in-time production, one-piece production, and mixed model production. KPS is vital in supporting their position of offering a wide variety of products throughout the motorcycle industry that services a diversified customer base and multiple target markets.

- **Suzuki** Suzuki manufactures automobiles, commercial vehicles, outboard motors, and ATV's. Suzuki is the third largest manufacturer of motorcycles lagging only Honda and Yamaha. Motorcycles comprise 19% of the company's total sales. Suzuki motorcycles have a significant international presence with sales in over 190 countries. 80% of Suzuki's total motorcycle sales are in offshore markets. Suzuki began using joint manufacturing efforts in foreign countries in 1993 and uses direct sales subsidiaries to reach customers. The joint manufacturing efforts require constant and dynamic technical cooperation between groups using cost reduction activities to achieve their on-going goal of providing a low-cost product. Efficiency is the backbone of Suzuki's low-cost position in the industry.

- **Yamaha** Yamaha has manufacturing facilities, distribution, and R&D operations in many international markets. Yamaha's focuses on tailoring its products to local market conditions. Yamaha Motor Company has a diverse product line including outboard motors, boats, personal watercraft, generators, golf cars, ATV's, snowmobiles, outdoor power equipment, race kart engines, accessories, apparel, and motorcycles. Yamaha produces a full-line of motorcycles ranging from scooters to heavyweights; however, their competitive advantage focuses on speed and high-performance racing bikes. Yamaha's motorcycle sales are strong globally as they currently hold the fifth largest market share in North America, the third largest market share in Asia/Pacific, and the second largest market share in Europe. Their target market throughout the world is the young and thrill-seeking consumer who sees riding as a sport.

The Harley-Davidson Company in 2006

Harley-Davidson is an American icon and has a loyal customer following that has been described as cult-like. The company has to be careful to not offend its traditional customers by going too far, too fast. With one notable exception, H-D's line of motorcycles are engineered and designed to evoke an earlier age. While the company has continuously been in business since 1903, today's company is the result of a leveraged buyout in 1981. The 1980s proved to be a difficult time and the company was often on the brink of

failure. The 1990s brought a complete reversal in H-D's fortunes with the demand for the company's motorcycles far outstripping supply. During this period it was not unusual for a buyer to have to wait as long as two years to take delivery on the company's most popular models. Profits soared and H-D became the darling of Wall Street. By 2005 management had narrowed the gap between demand and supply, but carefully manages growth to ensure its bikes are not too easy to come by. Managing the supply of Harley-Davidson motorcycles maintains high prices and permits H-D to avoid having to offer promotions and discounts to sell its product.

Harley-Davidson's premium pricing limits the number of younger buyers. Two-thirds of its customers are between ages of 35 and 54 of age. Recently H-D has redesigned some of its bikes to better accommodate female riders. The percentage of female buyers has reached 11% and continues to move slowly upward. H-D also offer motorcycle driver education courses, where 40% of the participants are women.

For the most part, the company has failed in its attempts to diversify into related industries. Its only real success has been Harley-Davidson Financial Services. Financial Services primary business is to provide financing and insurance to H-D dealers and buyers. In 1998 H-D moved to expand its presence within the motorcycle industry when it acquired the outstanding shares of the Buell Motorcycle Company. While sharing components and technology with H-D, the performance oriented Buell is intended to attract younger and non-traditional riders to the H-D family.

H-D Strategy In 2006 Harley-Davidson's strategy incorporates five related objectives: 1) increase sales, 2) achieve a stronger international presence, 3) attract more female buyers, 4) continuous operations improvement, and 5) launch new model variations. The company is increasing sales by decreasing the waiting time for most H-D models. In 2006 many customers could buy bikes off the show room floors and the waiting time for all but highly customized orders was down to two months. Supply is an area in which H-D must move cautiously. H-D management was forced to act on its limited production policy in early 2005. As the stock of production bikes in dealer showrooms built-up for the first time since the 1980s, Harley-Davidson instituted a 3% cut in motorcycle production. H-D maintained the cut was intended only to reduce the number of 2005 model-year bikes in dealers' showrooms in anticipation of the 2006 model-year release. H-D worked closely with union leaders and employees in making, what turned out to be a brief, production cutback.

Harley-Davidson needs to strengthen its international presence. Sales growth in the domestic market has slowed, while sales growth in the international market has increased. Timing for entry into some emerging international markets for luxury goods, e.g., China and Russia, appears to be optimal; while more established markets, e.g., Europe and Japan, are currently more receptive of H-D products. H-D is also seeing the need for contra-seasonal and contra-cyclical markets. Seasonality was not an issue for H-D when customers were waiting a year, or more, to take delivery on a motorcycle. Today, with supply approaching the domestic demand, the ability to move product into contra-seasonal or non-seasonal markets like the southern hemisphere, or much of Asia, is an attractive option. Access to the international market also offers H-D an outlet for product when economic downturns in the U.S. temporarily reduce demand. As a producer of luxury goods, H-D needs international market exposure; status and image are difficult to convey if the general public lacks knowledge of the good.

Since the start of the 21st century Harley-Davidson has demonstrated modest success in attracting female buyers. H-D interest in women buyers is one outcome of the company's inability to attract a significant number of young buyers. H-D found that taking women off the back of motorcycles was easier than attracting young buyers. Placing women in the driver's seat has required a mix of education, redesign, and promotion. Women buy bikes for many of the same reasons as men, but they want a bike that fits their physical needs. H-D accomplished this by offering model variants with seat positions that are lower to the ground, among other changes.

H-D Human Resources Management Harley-Davidson prides itself on open communication with its union and non-union employees and a team-based culture. Employees are involved in goal setting and this practice facilitates a shared vision of the company's direction. Self-directed work groups

are the norm. Departmental differences are minimized through a focus on cross-functional communications. These types of personnel practices are known as "partnering" at H-D; partnering results include increased employee motivation and a reduced need for supervision.

In 2005 the company employed approximately 9,000 employees in the manufacture of motorcycles. As a function of their geographical location, unionized employees are represented by one of two unions. Harley-Davidson has only incurred one strike since its AMF days and generally evokes a deep commitment from employees. Building consensus with union employees is H-D's standard practice. Resolving the occasional union grievance is left to the employee filing the grievance, the union-steward, the work group, and the work group's advisor (manager). The grievance resolution is considered binding by the union and the company.

Harley has a time-tested device for keeping up with customer demands and ensuring product quality. Half of the company's 9,000 employees ride a Harley-Davidson. Every employee, including the CEO, must go through a dealer to get a bike. This is just a testament to Harley-Davidson being a company driven by the Human Resources function. Fairness and equality are driving this company into the future with a workforce that believes that they are a part of something special.

H-D Operations Harley-Davidson has an ongoing production strategy of increasing the supply of its motorcycles, but at a rate less than that demanded by the market. To this end, the company continues to expand its manufacturing capacity. The company tries to position its product development staff in proximity to its manufacturing operations in order to ensure new product and model changes are coordinated prior to, and during, ramp-up.

A company operation in South America imports parts and sub-assemblies from the U.S. for final assembly in Brazil. Assembling the bikes in Brazil reduces duties and taxes, thus reducing the selling price and increasing the company's market. However, the volume of this facility remains under 1,000 units per year. Bikes for all other international markets are exported from the U.S.

Harley-Davidson actively practices quality management. The company continuously strives to improve

Harley-Davidson Manufacturing Facilities		
Wauwatosa, WI	422,000 sq. ft.	Powertrain
Menomonee Falls, WI	479,000 sq. ft.	Powertrain
Tomahawk, WI	189,000 sq. ft.	fiberglass parts & painting
York, PA	1,331,000 sq. ft.	parts fabrication, painting, & assembly
Kansas City, MO	330,000 sq. ft.	Sportster assembly, V-Rod powertrain
East Troy, WI (Buell)	40,000 sq. ft.	Buell assembly
Manaus, Brazil	30,000 sq. ft.	office & subassembly for local markets

the quality of its operations while controlling costs. Quality management related practices include statistical process control, employee involvement in operations related decisions, supplier participation, just-in-time inventory control, and partnerships with the company's unions. H-D trains its employees in the use of statistical methods and problem solving through its Leadership Institute courses. The company is proud of its relationship with employees and encourages employee involvement, emphasizing a highly flexible and participative workforce. The company employs this flexibility in cross-functional teams that review every aspect of the production process.

Harley-Davison strives to establish long-term mutually beneficial relationships with its suppliers. H-D involves suppliers in the design and manufacturing of its products and quality improvement programs. Harley requires that its suppliers be committed to annual cost reductions even when labor and material costs are rising. The company believes that vendor involvement results in improved products, the adoption of new technologies, and the smoother introduction of new products and product changes. Supplier involvement is not without its costs and led to an increase in the number of purchasing engineers from 4 to 30 in the 1990s. The involvement of suppliers has resulted in improvements in productivity and product quality, and a 4–5 day component inventory; all of which translates into an estimated savings of over $10,000,000 per year.

H-D Marketing August 2003 saw the culmination of Harley-Davidson's 100th anniversary celebration when an estimated 200,000 people participated in events in, and around, Harley's hometown of Milwaukee, Wisconsin. Riders came from every state and from every inhabited continent. H-D's anniversary was one of the biggest; some said the biggest, events in Milwaukee's history. Harley-Davidson's public exposure from the carefully orchestrated event was beyond price, but events and promotions are the norm for H-D. Countless features in the media focus on the company, its bikes, and the image of Harley riders. The company has a long history of successful promotion, and its bikes have "costarred" in numerous of major film productions.

The company's traditional advertising and promotional venues include dealer promotions and cooperative programs, magazine and direct mail advertising, and its famous H.O.G. customer events. The annual gathering in Sturgis, South Dakota has been the subject of public television documentaries. Harley-Davison's website, http://www.harley-davison.com, offers an interactive and exhaustive on-line catalog. Customers can order accessories and customize bikes with hundreds of options. It wasn't until 2002 that Harley-Davidson felt the need to advertise its products on television. The result of the company's marketing actions is that Harley-Davidson ranks near the top among iconic brands – ranking with Disney and Apple Computer.

Formed in 1983, the company sponsored Harley's Owner Group or H.O.G. has over one million members worldwide as of 2005. The Buell Riders Adventure Group, or BRAG is a 11,000 member strong counterpart to H.O.G. Both groups sponsor events, including national rides and rallies. The company also sponsors racing activities. Harley's buyers aren't locked into any social class. You are just as likely to find a CEO on a Harley as a worker off the assembly line. Harley owners are loyal with 90% of buyers reporting the intention of purchasing another Harley bike. Clearly image sells to this demographic, Harley ranks near the 100th percentile on the Brand Asset Valuator scale for such qualities as authentic, rugged, daring, dynamic, distinctive and high performance. As one Harley owner put it:

"What Harley-Davidson appeals to me is that we all think we're cooler than we really are."
(Milwaukee Journal Sentinel, August 24, 2003)

A creative tool in H-D's marketing program is its Authorized Rental and Tour program. Operated in the U.S. and overseas this program puts riders on "factory maintained" Harleys for guided tours. Included in the tour are some meals, lodging and a support vehicle to carry the heavy luggage and take care of any mechanical malfunctions. A lot of development ideas come from bike-riding employees and from employee attendance at Harley rallies held around the country. The company's marketing efforts were recognized when Harley-Davidson was inducted into the 2001 Marketing Hall of Fame. Their selection was based on "an outstanding job of building and sustaining their brand through smart marketing." The honor recognized what Harley followers have known for years: brand equity plus superior manufacturing has positioned Harley-Davidson as the elite manufacturer in the North American motorcycle market.

H-D Distribution Harley-Davidson products are sold through a network of 667 independently owned full-service dealerships in the U.S. The company maintains a European headquarters in England. Dealerships can be found in 36 European/Middle Eastern/African countries, 8 Asian countries and 15 Latin America countries. Most dealerships sell only Harley-Davidson and Buell products.

Uke's Harley-Davidson/Buell dealership in Kenosha, Wisconsin is fairly typical of Harley dealers. Uke's recently completed a new 54,000-square-foot facility alongside I-94. What may be unique to Uke's is a six-story glass tower that displays custom bikes like jewels in a showcase. The new building features a 15,000-square-foot showroom and a 10,000-square-foot service area. The basement is given over to the winter storage of customer's bikes, while the second-floor mezzanine houses a museum and art gallery. The architectural firm of Kubala Washatko of Cedarburg, Wisconsin, designed the new facility. Kubala Washatko has designed dozens of Harley dealerships around the U.S.

H-D Research and Development Harley-Davidson believes research and development is a key component of its ability to lead the touring bike market. The company maintains a 383,000 square foot product development center and a separate 43,000 square foot development center for the Buell product line. The product development centers are staffed with employees from styling, purchasing and

Harley-Davidson Dealership Locations

Country/Region	H-D/Buell Dealerships	H-D only Dealerships	Total Dealerships
U.S.A.	318	349	667
European	292	67	359
Asia/Pacific	77	102	179
Latin America	0	31	31
Canada	43	32	75

manufacturing, as well as supplier representatives. The practice is consistent with Harley-Davidson's commitment to quality management and results in seamless product development. Due to the increasing prevalence of environmental and safety regulations, the product development centers are staffed with professionals specializing in the regulatory process. The company has sought to be proactive in meeting environmental and safety regulations in both its products and facilities. The company spent $178.5 million in 2005, $170.7 million in 2004 and $150.3 million in 2003 on product development.

The company's products are in compliance with all current Federal and State emission and noise standards. The California Air Resources Board standards become increasingly stringent in model year 2008 and H-D will incur costs in complying with the new standards. A more pressing problem for H-D may come from more stringent noise standards in the European Union and Japan. Such standards may interfere with one of Harley's most sacred traditions, the bike's distinctive, and loud, exhaust.

H-D Motorcycle Unit According to Harley-Davidson:

"The motorcycle market is comprised of four segments: standard, which emphasizes simplicity and cost; performance, which emphasizes handling and acceleration; touring, which emphasizes comfort and amenities for long-distance travel; and custom, which emphasizes styling and individual owner customization."

(2005 Annual Report)

The company currently addresses all categories with its offerings from the Buell lineup in the standard and performance segments and with the H-D offerings in the performance, touring, and custom segments.

The company's motorcycle unit consists of Harley-Davidson Motor Company and the Buell Motorcycle Company. The motorcycle unit designs, manufacturers and markets primarily heavyweight bikes as well as motorcycle parts, accessories and merchandise. The company is the only major U.S. manufacturer of motorcycles and has led the heavyweight market since going public in 1986. The Motorcycle Industry Council figures give H-D a 48.9% share of the domestic heavyweight market for 2005. During 2004 the motorcycle unit generated 80.0% of the total net sales of Harley-Davidson, Inc.

Harley's heavyweight bikes are, by the company's own definition, more than 650cc of engine displacement. The company currently markets 33 models of performance, touring, and custom bikes with suggested retail prices up to $32,000 for a limited-edition factory customized model. These bikes are built on five basic chassis designs (Softail, Sportster, Dyna Glide, Touring, and the new VRSC, or V-Rod) and are powered by one of four 45-degree V-twin air-cooled engines ranging from 883cc to a huge 1690cc brute (the V-Rod utilizes a liquid-cooled engine). The company pioneered the touring heavyweight motorcycle and this segment includes well-equipped bikes with fairings, windshields, and luggage carriers. The custom segment includes the retro-look bikes that are typically highly customized through the use of chrome, paint, and accessories. These bikes sell for prices that are about 50% higher than competitor's comparable models.

The V-Rod or VRSC model is the first in a new series of bikes aimed at the "performance café-racer" market. The VRSC shares nothing with existing bikes and is equipped with the Porsche designed liquid-cooled, 60-degree V-twin, 1130cc, 110+hp, Revolution engine. It is the most expensive development project in the company's history, but Harley-Davidson has not revealed the numbers. The VRSC model has met grudging acceptance at best with H-D's traditional buyers, but has done well with non-traditional buyers and the international market. Harley's previous foray into the performance segment with its Buell line of motorcycles has met with only limited success.

Harley-Davidson manufactured and shipped 329,000 motorcycles in 2005 and expects to sell 350,000 in 2006. About half of all bikes are Harley's big street cruisers, like the Softail, that sell for around $17,000. Around 30% are the true heavyweight touring machines; equipped with fiberglass saddlebags, CD players, radios and cruise control, these bikes sell for $20,000+. The remaining bikes are mostly the $6,500+ Sportsters; with a cosmetic redesign for 2005–2006 the Sportster remains Harley's oldest, and most affordable, model.

CASE DISCUSSION QUESTIONS

1. Which of Porter's generic strategy is Harley Davidson using? Will this strategy work for all of the countries described in the case? Why or why not?
2. What does a Porter's five forces reveal for Harley Davidson? Is Harley Davidson operating in an attractive industry? Are there significant differences among the industries in the various regions?
3. What are some of the key success factors for companies involved in the industry? How does Harley Davidson compare to the other competitors?
4. Should Harley Davidson expand more aggressive internationally? Why or why not? Which countries are the most attractive candidates for expansion?

CASE CREDIT

Harley-Davidson, Inc. 3700 West Juneau Avenue Milwaukee, Wisconsin 53208 http://www.harley-davidson.com SIC: 3751-Motorcycles, bicycles & parts by James W. Bronson, University of Wisconsin-Whitewater and Graham Beaver, University of Brighton

CASE NOTES

1. Barret, R. (2005) "Harley-Davidson Stock Takes a Beating." *Milwaukee Journal Sentinel*, April 13.
2. "Company Profile: Harley-Davidson Motor Company-Product Development Center, Milwaukee." November 13, 2003. www.careerbuilder.com
3. Content, T. (2003) "Harley Looks To A New Breed Of Bike For Growth." *Milwaukee Journal Sentinel*, August 24.
4. Ducati., Annual Report, December 31, 2004.
5. "European Luxury Brands Chase China's Rising Wealth". *Taipei Times*. December 10, 2004. http://www.taipeitimes.com/News/worldbiz/archives/2004/12/10/2003214537
6. Fahey, J. (2002). "Love Into Money." *Forbes*, January 07: pp. 60–56.
7. Fitzgerald, Nora. (2006) "Dressing Russian Children to the Nines." *International Herald Tribune* , May 31. http://iht.com/articles/2006/03/06/opinion/rkid.php

8. Harley Davidson, Inc., Form 10-K, December 31, 2001.

9. Harley Davidson, Inc., Form 10-K, December 31, 2002.

10. Harley Davidson, Inc., Form 10-K, December 31, 2003.

11. Harley Davidson, Inc., Form 10-K, December 31, 2004.

12. Harley Davidson, Inc., Form 10-K, December 31,2005

13. "Harley-Davidson and Staples Elected to the 2001 Marketing Hall of Fame." *PR Newswire,* April, 27 2001: p. 1.

14. "Harley-Davidson: Marketing an American Icon." *Journal of Business and Design.* January 05, 2002. http://www.cdf.org/cdf/atissue/vol2_1/harley/harley.html

15. Johnson, M. (2003) "Thundering Across All Demographics." *Milwaukee Journal Sentinel,* August 24.

16. Klayman, B. (2005) "Harley-Davidson CEO Sees Strong Growth."

17. http://go.Reuters.co.uk/newsArticle.jhtml

18. "Luxury's new empire." *The Economist.* June 17, 2004.

19. http://www.economist.com/business/displaystory.cfm?story_id=2771531

20. Narayan, Shoba. "India's Lust for Luxe." *Time: Asia.* April 2006. http://www.time.com/time/asia/magazine/printout/0,13675,501060410-1179415,00.html.

21. Nauen, E. (2003) "Ride & Seek." *AARP The Magazine,* July/August: pp. 59–62.

22. Teerlink, R. & Ozley, L. (2000) *More Than a Motorcycle: The Leadership Journey at Harley-Davidson.* Boston, MA: Harvard Business School Press.

23. Teerlink, R. (2000) "Harley's Leadership U-Turn." *Harvard Business Review.* Jul/Aug 2000: pp. 43–48.

24. Weisman, Katie (2005) "America's take on New Luxury." *International Herald Tribune,* December 05.

25. Windle, Charlotte. "China luxury industry prepares for boom." BBC News. Sept. 27, 2005. http://news.bbc.co.uk/2/hi/business/4271970.stm

26. http://www.harley-davidson.com

27. http://www.hoovers.com

28. Zielinski, G. (2003) "Milwaukee Gears Up For Motorcycle Mania." *Milwaukee Journal Sentinel,* August 24.

Multinational and Participation Strategies: Content and Formulation

Learning Objectives

After reading this chapter you should be able to:

- Appreciate the complexities of the global–local dilemma faced by the multinational company.

- Understand the content of the multinational strategies: transnational, international, multidomestic, and regional.

- Formulate a multinational strategy by applying the diagnostic questions that aid multinational companies in solving the global–local dilemma.

- Understand the content of the participation strategies: exporting, alliances/IJVs, licensing, and foreign direct investment.

- Formulate a participation strategy based on the strengths and weaknesses of each approach and the needs of the multinational company.

- Understand political risk and ways a multinational can manage such risks.

Preview CASE IN POINT

Global Markets: The Jewelry Industry and Luxury Goods

For centuries, merchants have scoured the globe in search of precious stones and metals to fabricate into ornamentation worn by people from their country. The modern European jewelry industry was globalized during the colonial error when Europeans returned from Africa, Asia, and the New World with the raw material to produce their wares for sale on the continent.

The global model still exists for the industry. However, the dropping of trade barriers and the availability of real-time communication now allows even the smallest players to seek low-cost sourcing or sales worldwide, often without any intermediaries in the distribution channel. Referring to China, Wayne Emery, a jewelry store owner in Tacoma, Washington, notes: "Send them a sketch or a CAD file, and you'll get a finished piece pronto—well-made, ready for your stones to be set, and it'll cost you way less than half of what any local ship (or you) can do."

Finished products for retailers are also available from emerging markets. Brazil, for example, is becoming a world source for gemstones. The Brazilian Institute of Gems and Precious Metals, the industry trade association, has worked hard in the past few years to ease trade restrictions into the U.S. market. Brazilian raw stones and finished products are now shown in trade shows from New York to the Hong Kong Jewelry and Watch Fair.

Big time players like Tiffany & Co. are also getting closer to international suppliers. Working with Aber Resources, a mining operation in the tundra town of Yellowknife, Canada, Tiffany is cutting diamonds directly at the mine site. This "mine-to-market" scenario is based on free trade and streamlined supplier relationships.

The luxury goods market is also a global industry that has seen tremendous success in the past few years. The booming Chinese and Indian markets have been the major reasons why these companies have been so successful. Companies such as LVMH (with brands such as Louis Vuitton, Tag Heur, and Dom Perignon), Cartier, Gucci, Mont Blanc, Coach, and Bulgari have all seen double-digit sales and profit growth.

Sources: Based on Gomelsky, Victoria. 2003. "Going global: Spotting opportunities in emerging markets." National Jeweler pp. 97, 27–28; Forbes 2000 "Jewelry." September 11: p. 203; and Jones, Adam. 2006. "Global glamour: A wealthier world has been kind to luxury goods makers." Financial Times, June 5, pp. 1–3.

The Preview Case in Point describes two industries where almost any company can be a multinational strategist. In the case of jewelry companies, they can seek lower cost expertise or source lower-cost or higher-quality raw materials from anywhere in the world to enhance their competitive positions. However, makers of luxury goods can use similar marketing strategies around the world to sell similar products to wealthy customers. In both cases, we see global strategies being used to approach the international market.

In this chapter you will find a review of the essential strategies that multinationals use to bring their companies to international markets and compete successfully. Unlike those in the previous chapter, the strategies discussed here pertain specifically to international operations. In addition to the basic issues regarding strategy content and formulation, there are additional strategic issues specific to the multinational company.

This chapter contains three major sections. The first section introduces general strategies regarding multinational operations. The second section introduces the specific techniques that multinationals use to enter markets. The final section provides an understanding of the political risk, an important risk that many multinational companies face.

After reading this chapter, you should understand how global markets, products, competition, and risk influence the choice of a multinational strategy and the choice of a market-entry strategy. You also should understand that multinational managers face different and more complex challenges than those faced by domestic-only managers.

Multinational Strategies: Dealing with the Global–local Dilemma

A fundamental strategic dilemma faced by all multinational companies is how to compete internationally. We call this problem the global–local dilemma. On one hand, there are pressures to respond to the unique needs of the markets in each country in which a company does business. When a company chooses this option it adopts the **local-responsiveness solution.** On the other hand, there are efficiency pressures that encourage companies to de-emphasize local differences and conduct business similarly throughout the world. Companies that lean in this direction choose the **global integration solution.**

The solution for the **global–local dilemma,** whether local responsiveness or global integration, forms the basic strategic orientation of a multinational company.[1] This strategic orientation affects the design of organization and management systems as well as supporting functional strategies in areas such as

Local-responsiveness solution
Responding to differences in the markets in all the countries in which a company operates.

Global integration solution
Conducting business similarly throughout the world and locating company units wherever there is high quality and low cost.

Global–local dilemma
Choice between a local-responsiveness or global approach to a multinational's strategies.

production, marketing, and finance. Here we consider only strategic implications of the multinational companies' global–local dilemma. In later chapters, you will see how this fundamental problem of the multinational firm influences other areas of management, such as human resources management and the choice of an organizational design.

Companies that lean toward the local-responsiveness solution stress customizing their organizations and products to accommodate country or regional differences. The focus is on satisfying local customer needs by tailoring products or services to meet those needs. Forces that favor a local-responsiveness solution come primarily from national or cultural differences in consumer tastes and variations in customer needs. In addition, national differences in how industries work and political pressures can lead companies to favor local responsiveness. For example, government regulations can require a company to share ownership with a local company. Some governments also require companies to produce their products in the countries in which they sell.[2]

To the largest degree possible, multinational companies that lean toward a global integration solution reduce costs by using standardized products, promotional strategies, and distribution channels in every country. In addition, such globally oriented multinational firms seek sources of lower costs or higher quality anywhere in their value chain and anywhere in the world. For example, in such companies, headquarters, R&D, production, or distribution centers may be located anywhere they can provide the best value added with quality or lower cost.[3]

Neither responding to local customer needs nor selling the same product worldwide is a guarantee of success. Multinational firms must choose carefully for each product or business how global or local they orient their strategies. Later in the chapter, you will see some of the questions that managers must answer before selecting an appropriate multinational strategy. Before that, however, we will review the broad strategic choices for the multinational manager dealing with the global–local dilemma.

There are four broad multinational strategies that offer solutions to the global–local responsiveness dilemma: multidomestic, transnational, international, and regional. The multidomestic and transnational strategies represent the bipolar reactions to one side of the global–local dilemma. The international and regional strategies represent compromise positions that attempt to balance these conflicting drives.

Multidomestic Strategy

Multidomestic strategy

Emphasizing local-responsiveness issues.

The **multidomestic strategy** gives top priority to local responsiveness. The multidomestic strategy is in many respects a form of differentiation strategy. The company attempts to offer products or services that attract customers by closely satisfying their cultural needs and expectations. For example, advertisements, packaging, sales outlets, and pricing are adapted to local standards.

As with most uses of differentiation, it usually costs more for multinational companies to produce and sell unique or special products for different countries throughout the world. There are extra costs to adapt each product to local requirements, such as different package sizes and colors. Thus, to succeed, a multidomestic strategy usually requires the company to charge higher prices to recoup the costs of tailoring a product for local needs. Customers will pay this higher price if they perceive an extra value in having a company's products adapted to their tastes, distribution systems, and industry structures.[4]

A multidomestic strategy is not limited to large multinational companies that can afford to set up overseas subsidiaries. Even a small firm that only exports its products may use a multidomestic strategy by extensively adapting its product line to different countries and cultures. However, for larger organizations, with production and sales units in many countries, using a multidomestic strategy often means treating foreign subsidiaries as independent businesses. Headquarters focuses on the bottom line, viewing each country as a profit center. Each country's subsidiary is free to manage its own operations as necessary, but it must generate a profit to get resources from headquarters. Besides having its own local production facilities, marketing strategy, sales staff, and distribution system, the subsidiary of the multidomestic company often uses local sources of raw materials and employs mostly local people.

Transnational Strategy

The **transnational strategy** gives two goals top priority: seeking location advantages and gaining economic efficiencies from operating worldwide.[5] Using **location advantages** means that the transnational company disperses or locates its value-chain activities (e. g., manufacturing, R&D, and sales) anywhere in the world where the company can "do it best or cheapest" as the situation requires. For example, many U.S. and Japanese multinational companies have production facilities in Southeast Asian countries where labor is currently cheap. Michael Porter[6] argues that, for global competition, firms must look at countries not only as potential markets but also as "global platforms." A **global platform** is a country location where a firm can best perform some, but not necessarily all, of its value-chain activities.

Historically, international firms took advantage of the comparative advantage of their nations to compete on the world market. For example, the United States has had abundant natural resources. However, comparative advantage of a nation no longer gives competitive advantages only to the domestic firms. That is, the induced or natural resources available in different nations provide the transnational firm with the global platforms to boost location-based competitive advantages in costs and quality. For the most part, these resources support upstream activities in the value chain such as R&D and production. With upstream location advantages, the transnational can:

- locate subunits near cheap sources of high-quality raw material.
- locate subunits near centers of research and innovation.
- locate subunits near sources of high-quality or low-cost labor.
- seek low-cost financing anywhere in the world.
- share discoveries and innovations made in one part of the world with operations in other parts of the world.

Thus, a company adopting a transnational strategy can locate the activities in its upstream value chain based not only on lower costs but also on the potential for creating additional value for its products or services.

Location advantages also can exist for other value-chain activities. These include having locations for cheaper manufacturing, being close to key customers, and locations that serve the most demanding customers. Location in the Japanese market, for example, usually requires that a firm produce products with a quality level acceptable to the whole world. The Case in Point entitled "Bangkok: Welcome to the Detroit of the East" shows how several multinational automobile manufacturers use Thailand as a global platform for production and sales.

Transnational strategy

Seeking location advantages and gaining economic efficiencies from operating worldwide.

Location advantages

Dispersing value-chain activities anywhere in the world where the company can do them best or cheapest.

Global platform

Country location where a firm can best perform some, but not necessarily all, of its value-chain activities.

C A S E   I N   P O I N T

Bangkok: "Welcome to the Detroit of the East"; Getting More Mileage from the Third World

Welcome to the Detroit of the East. So reads the sign at the gate of the Eastern Seaboard Industrial Estate in Bangkok, Thailand. Site of manufacturing units of Ford and General Motors, the "Detroit" name symbolizes that these two companies account for almost one-third of region-leading Thailand's vehicle exports. Thailand represents Ford's largest investment in Asia. Toyota, Honda, Mitsubishi, and Isuzu also manufacture in Thailand.

Manufacturing in Thailand is not just for the local market although the ASEAN total market size is expected to be more than 2.5 million by 2010. Rather, Thailand is a manufacturing platform for both global and regional distribution. Isuzu and Mitsubishi use Thailand as the global manufacturing platform for pickup trucks. Ford's production capacity in Thailand is 130,000 units per year, with approximately two-thirds being exported out of Thailand. GM uses its state-of-the-art $650-million factory for export production to serve Europe, Africa, South America, the Middle East, and other Asian countries. BMW sees three phases of development for its new plant. First, build cars only for Thailand. Second, start exporting to other countries in the ASEAN regional trade association. Third, go transnational and source from or export to anywhere in the world.

One attraction of Thailand and other third-world nations is low labor costs. Wages are often less than one-tenth of those in home countries. In Thailand, for example, wages for Ford employees are about $120 a month but are still above local averages. Manufacturers also have the pick of the labor pool. GM had 20,000 applicants for its initial 650 jobs.

In the 1990s, many automakers spent billions of dollars developing state-of-the-art manufacturing facilities in the developing nations with the hope of a growing local demand. For the most part, demand has not reached expectations, and the automakers are looking to use this excess capacity worldwide. Honda now uses its plant in Thailand to supply its home market in Japan, the first Japanese manufacturer to try that strategy on the fickle Japanese market. Ford's most efficient factory in the world is in Brazil, and the new plant is the planned manufacturing site of a mini-support utility for the U.S. market. BMW produces its 3-series car in South Africa for shipment to the United States and Japan. The plant matches German quality standards and gets an extra bonus due to import-duty exemptions to the United States based on a law intended to increase trade with African countries.

Source: Based on Economist. 2000. "The revolution at Ford." August 7. http://www.economist.com; Hoovers. 2006. "Tri Petch Isuzu Sales Co. Ltd. Hoover's Company Information;" Phoosuphanusorn, Srisamorn. 2002. "Ford aims to double turnover in Thailand." Knight Ridder Tribune Business News, October 16; Santivimolnat, Santan. 2002. "Thailand's August auto exports jump more than 75 percent from last year." Knight Ridder Tribune Business News, October 4; Tilley, Robert. 2000. "Detroit moves east." http://www.asia-inc.com. October; Shirouzu, Norihiko. 2003a. "Ford sees tough road for core unit: Projections are disclosed for North American business as 4th-period loss narrowed." Wall Street Journal, January 22, p. A3; Shirouzu, Norihiko. 2003b. "Ford aims to speed up process of new-vehicle development." Wall Street Journal, February 20, p. B8; Zaun, Todd, Gregory L. White, Norihiko Shirouzu, and Scott Miller. 2002. "A global report—two-way street: Automakers get even more mileage from third world—low-cost plants abroad start to supply home markets, as quality picks up steam—elephants white and rented." The Wall Street Journal, July 31, p. A1.

Comparative advantage

That arising from cost, quality, or resource advantages associated with a particular nation.

Often costs or quality advantages associated with a particular nation are called national **comparative advantage**. This is different from *competitive* advantage, which refers to the advantages of individual firms over other firms. *Comparative* advantage refers to advantages of *nations over other nations*. For example, a country with cheaper and better-educated labor has a comparative advantage over other nations. Comparative advantage is important to organizations because they can use their nation's comparative advantages to gain competitive advantages over rivals from other nations.

Traditionally, scholars viewed comparative advantage as something from which only the indigenous or local organizations could benefit in world competition. Many Japanese and Korean organizations, for example, built their early competitive advantages on the cheap, high-quality, and motivated labor available in their countries. However, the transnational strategy has made this view somewhat out-of-date. The transnational views *any country* as a global platform where it can perform *any value-chain activity.* Thus, the comparative advantage of a nation is no longer just for locals. With increasingly free and open borders, any firm, regardless of its nation of ownership, can turn any national advantage into a competitive advantage—if the firm has the flexibility and willingness to locate anywhere.

Location advantages provide the transnational company with cost or quality gains for different value-chain activities. To reduce costs even further, transnationalist firms strive for uniform marketing and promotional activities throughout the world; these companies use the same brand names, advertisements, and promotional brochures wherever they sell their products or services. The soft-drink companies, such as Coca-Cola, have been among the most successful in taking their brands worldwide. When a company can do things similarly throughout the world, it can take advantage of economies of scale. Thus, for example, it is most efficient to have one package of the same color and size produced worldwide in centralized production facilities.

International Strategy

Companies pursuing **international strategies,** such as Toys "R" Us, Boeing, and IBM, take a compromise approach to the global–local dilemma. Like the transnational strategists, firms pursuing international strategies attempt to sell global products and use similar marketing techniques worldwide. Adaptation to local customs and culture, if any, is limited to minor adjustments in product offerings and marketing strategies. However, international-strategist firms differ from transnational companies in that they choose not to locate their value-chain activities anywhere in the world. In particular, upstream and support activities remain concentrated at home-country headquarters. The international strategist hopes that the concentration of its R&D and manufacturing strengths at home brings greater economies of scale and quality than the dispersed activities of the transnational. For example, Boeing in the United States keeps most of its production and development at home while selling planes such as the 757 worldwide with the same sales force. Its marketing approach focuses on price and technology, and even the price and payments are quoted and made in U.S. currency.

When necessary for economic or political reasons, companies with international strategies frequently do set up sales and production units in major countries of operation. However, home-country headquarters retains control of local strategies, marketing, R&D, finances, and production. Local facilities become only "mini-replicas" of production and sales facilities at home.[7]

> **International strategies**
>
> Selling global products and using similar marketing techniques worldwide.

Regional Strategy

The **regional strategy** is another compromise strategy. It attempts to attain some of the economic efficiency and location advantages of the more global transnational and international strategies combined with some of the local-adaptation advantages of the multidomestic strategy. Rather than having worldwide products and a worldwide value chain, the regional strategist manages raw-material sourcing, production, marketing, and some support activities within a particular region. For example, a regional strategist might have one set of products for North America and another for Mexico and South America. This strategy not only allows some cost savings similar to those of the transnational and international strategists but also gives the firm flexibility for regional

> **Regional strategy**
>
> Managing raw-material sourcing, production, marketing, and support activities within a particular region.

responsiveness. Managers have the opportunity to deal regionally with regional problems, such as competitive position, product mix, promotional strategy, and sources of capital.[8]

Regional trading blocs such as the European Union (EU) and North American Free Trade Agreement (NAFTA) have led to more uniformity of customer needs and expectations within member nations. Trading blocs also reduce differences in government- and industry-required specifications for products. As a result, within the trading bloc, companies can use regional products and regional location advantages for all value-chain activities. The rise of trading blocs has forced some former multidomestic strategists, especially in Europe and the United States, to adopt regional strategies. For example, Proctor & Gamble and Dupont have combined their subunits in Mexico, the United States, and Canada into one regional organization. With this strategy, these companies gain some of the advantages of local adaptation and some of the advantages of transnationalization.

Ghemawat[9] argues that there are various degrees of regional strategies and that multinational companies also need to choose the most appropriate form. The first form is the "home base strategy" where international expansion takes place by using the home base as R&D location to serve all international markets. For instance, Samsung considers its concentration of most R&D and production in South Korea as a source of competitive advantage. Samsung's home strategy is appropriate because of the relatively low costs of transportation relative to the product's value. The second form of regional strategy is the "hub strategy." In such cases, a company decides to set up regional bases to serve countries within the region. For instance, Toyota adopted a hub strategy when it set up manufacturing plants in the United States to serve the U.S. market. The third form of the regional strategy is known as the "platform strategy." While the hub strategy attempts to spread fixed costs across countries within a region, the platform strategy spreads fixed costs across regions. For instance, while cheaper fuel costs in the United States may have encouraged a hub strategy in the past because of the regional preference for vehicle power and size, recent trends suggest that more automotive companies will adopt platform strategies. In fact, Asian companies such as Toyota and Honda already have significant experience with smaller and more fuel-efficient cars and may adopt more platform-oriented strategies (i.e., use of similar fuel-efficient engines) across regions. Finally, multinationals following the "mandate strategy" use specific regions to specialize in specific functions or roles. For example, Whirlpool is following a mandate strategy by producing most of its small appliances in India.[10]

A Brief Summary and Caveat

Students of multinational management should realize that these strategies are general descriptions of multinational strategic options. Seldom do companies adopt a pure form of a multinational strategy. Companies with more than one business may adopt different multinational strategies for each business. Even single-business companies may alter strategies to adjust for product differences. In addition, governmental regulations regarding trade, historical evolution of the company, and the cost of switching strategies may prevent a firm from fully implementing a particular strategy.

Exhibit 6.1 summarizes the content of the four basic multinational strategies. Which strategy works best? Different companies use different approaches suiting their realities. Consider LG Electronics' successful localized approach in its various markets in the Focus on Emerging Markets on page 266.

EXHIBIT   **6.1**   **Multination Strategy Content**

Strategy Content	Transnational Strategy	International Strategy	Multidomestic Strategy	Regional Strategy
Worldwide markets	Yes, as much as possible, with flexibility to adapt to local conditions.	Yes, with little flexibility for local adaptation.	No, each country treated as a separate market.	No, but major regions treated as similar market (e.g., Europe).
Worldwide location of separate value-chain activities	Yes, anywhere, based on best value to company—lowest cost for highest quality	No, or limited to sales or local production replicating headquarters.	No, all or most value-chain activities located in country of production and sales.	No, but region can provide some different country location of activities.
Global products	Yes, to the highest degree possible, with some local products if necessary; companies rely on worldwide brand recognition.	Yes, to the highest degree possible, with little local adaptation; companies rely on worldwide brand recognition.	No, products produced in and tailored to the country of location to best serve needs of local customers.	No, but similar products offered throughout a major economic region.
Global marketing	Yes, similar strategy to global product development.	Yes, to the highest degree possible.	No, marketing focuses on local-country customers.	No, but region is often treated similarly.
Global competitive moves	Resources from any country used to attack or defend.	Attacks and defenses in all countries, but resources must come from headquarters.	No, competitive moves planned and financed by country units.	No, but resources from region can be used to attack or defend.

As the above shows, the array of strategic options for the multinational company means that managers must carefully analyze the situation for their company when formulating or choosing a strategy. The following section presents diagnostic questions that multinational managers can use to select a strategy appropriate for their company. These diagnostic questions guide multinational companies in resolving the global–local dilemma.

Resolving the Global–local Dilemma: Formulating a Multinational Strategy

The selection of a transnational, multidomestic, international, or regional strategy depends to a large degree on the globalization of the industry in which a company competes. Multibusiness companies need to consider the degree of globalization within all industries in which they compete.

What makes an industry global? George Yip calls the trends that globalize an industry the globalization drivers. **Globalization drivers** are conditions in an industry that favor the more globally oriented transnational or international strategies over the more locally oriented multidomestic or regional strategies.[11]

The globalization drivers fall into four categories: markets, costs, governments, and competition. Each of these areas has key diagnostic questions that the strategist must answer in selecting the degree of globalization of multinational strategies. The more positive the answer to each of these questions, the more likely that company should select a global transnational or international strategy.

Globalization drivers

Conditions in an industry that favor transnational or international strategies over multi-local or regional strategies.

Focus on Emerging Markets

LG Electronics' Success in Emerging Markets

LG Electronics is currently the world's top producer of air conditioners and is among the top three producers in other appliances such as washing machines, microwave ovens, and refrigerators. It is the dominant player in emerging markets like India in nearly every appliance and electronics category. Furthermore, although it is a relative newcomer in the Chinese market, LG has been successful and has achieved sales of $8 billion in China.

LG uses an in-depth localized strategy where it tries to understand the realities and subtleties of the local market by establishing local research, manufacturing, and marketing facilities. Such efforts come easy to LG, which pioneered the kimchi refrigerator in South Korea. Kimchi, which is made from fermented cabbage seasoned with garlic and pepper, is used with most meals in South Korea. However, it has a strong smell that can overpower other items when placed in a regular refrigerator. About 20 years ago, LG introduced a special refrigerator that has a separate compartment for kimchi. This product has been very successful, encouraging other competitors such as Samsung to also introduce a similar product.

LG's localization strategy in India provides a good understanding of its approach. To meet local Indian needs, LG offers refrigerators that have larger compartments for vegetables and water storage and surge-resistant power supplies to deal with frequent power outages. LG goes as far as customizing to local customers' color preferences, selling red refrigerators in the south and green in Kashmir. Furthermore, it also offers microwave ovens with darker interiors to mask staining from curries. Additionally, to take advantage of the Indian passion for cricket, LG also offers televisions that come with cricket video games.

LG's localization approach in emerging markets has been successful because it realized that customers in emerging markets generally do not yet have strong brand loyalties. By offering products adapted to the local needs, LG can start to build its own brand. For example, LG's research in other markets has resulted in products such as microwaves with preset shish-kebab heat settings in Iran and refrigerators with special compartments to store dates in the Middle East. Research in Russia also revealed that people are more likely to entertain indoors during the harsh winters. LG then developed a karaoke phone that can hold more than 100 Russian songs for the market. The phone has been very popular, selling more than 220,000 handsets in 2004.

Source: Based on Esfahani, Elizabeth. 2005. "Thinking locally, succeeding globally." Business 2.0, December, pp. 96–98.

Global Markets

- *Are there common customer needs?* Increasingly, in many industries, customer needs are converging. These include industries such as automobiles, pharmaceuticals, and consumer electronics. However, in industries where cultural differences, income, and physical climate are important, common customer needs are less likely.
- *Are there global customers?* Global customers are usually organizations (not individual consumers). They search the world market for suppliers. PC manufacturers usually become global customers for PC components.
- *Can you transfer marketing?* If you can use the same brand name, advertising, and channels of distribution, the industry is more global.

Costs

- *Are there global economies of scale?* In some industries, such as the disposable-syringe industry, no one country's market is sufficiently large to buy all the products of efficient production runs. To be cost-competitive, firms in this industry must go global and sell worldwide.
- *Are there global sources of low-cost raw materials?* If so, it pays to source your raw materials in those countries with this advantage. If not, it is probably cheaper to produce the product at home and avoid the additional costs of shipping and administration.
- *Are there cheaper sources of highly skilled labor?* If so, as with the case for raw materials, the strategic push is for companies to manufacture in foreign locations. The move of many U.S. manufacturing operations to Mexico and the use of manufacturing plants in Eastern Europe by German companies represent examples of the many companies seeking global sources of lower costs.
- *Are product-development costs high?* When they are, it is often more efficient to produce a few products that a company sells worldwide. Sometimes a single market cannot absorb high development costs. Toyota attempts a global strategy for its higher-end sedan (called Camry in the United States). Keeping as many parts as possible for internal components (the exterior is different in different countries), the company spreads development costs over the world market.

Governments

- *Do the targeted countries have favorable trade policies?* Government trade policies differ by industry and product. Import tariffs, quotas, and subsidized local companies are examples of policies that restrict global strategies. In Japan, for example, import restrictions and heavy subsidies of rice farmers keep foreign competition out and maintain domestic prices that often approach four times the world market price. Trade agreements such as the WTO and trading blocs such as NAFTA and the EU encourage global strategies by lowering governmental trade restrictions, at least among member nations.
- *Do the target countries have regulations that restrict operations?* Restrictions on foreign ownership, on advertising and promotional content, and on the extent of expatriate management present barriers to full implementation of a transnational strategy or an international strategy.

The Competition

- *What strategies do your competitors use?* If transnational or international companies successfully attack the markets of multidomestic companies, then the multidomestics may have to become more global.
- *What is the volume of imports and exports in the industry?* A high volume of trade suggests that companies see advantages in strategies that are more global.

A Caution

The increasingly popular strategy of going global by making uniform products for the world market can sometimes backfire. Cultural and national differences still exist, and even the transnational and international strategist must adjust to key differences in national or regional needs. However, managing the degree of local adaptation can also be a challenge. The Multinational Management Challenge on page 268 shows how McDonald's is searching for the right mixture.

Multinational Management **Challenge**

Find the Right Level of Local

Until recently, McDonald's was the quintessential model of international growth and success. At the peak of its international expansion, McDonald's opened 2,000 stores in 1996. When it opened its first store in Kuwait City, the drive-through line stretched for seven miles. The number of new store openings is now falling.

The McDonald's business model is based on rigid standards for cleanliness, speed, and uniformity of the experience if not exactly all of the products. Consistency in serving cheap food in familiar settings, whether it is Moscow, Idaho or Moscow, Russia, was the recipe for expansion. Although the form of its restaurant is a global product, McDonald's has always shown a local adaptation. It has veggie burgers in India, beer in most European stores, and even a drive-through for snowmobiles in Sweden.

The debate is whether the global product setting with some local adaptation is still a viable model for international competition. Some analysts note that the more McDonald's becomes local, the less it can position its product as an American experience. Without that mystique, local competitors who can often provide fast food at lower prices, attack McDonald's quick-and-cheap strategy. For instance, in India, McDonald's had to be very local from the day the first store was opened. It had to develop recipes from scratch and had to get these new items approved by the appropriate authorities. Care had to be taken to avoid beef and pork altogether to be sensitive to India's Muslim and Hindu customers. Furthermore, McDonald's had to devise a system to completely separate vegetarian items from non-vegetarian items across all activities in the value chain.

Similarly, in France, McDonald's is also becoming even more local. In some markets, gone are the trademark golden arches from restaurants that don't resemble the classic cookie-cutter model. Facing increased competition from fast baguettes, McDonald's has remodeled nearly 1,000 French stores into a more upscale image that is not uniform. Early signs show the strategy is working, but whether McDonald's can use the same model worldwide remains a question.

Sources: Based on Dutta, Devangshu. 2005. "The perishable food chain in India: Opportunities and issues." Just-Food, September, pp. 22–28; Ghazvinian, John, and Karen Lowry Miller. 2002. "Hold the fried: Mighty McDonald's has long been the epitome of Pax Americana. Lately the multinational giant has stumbled. Here's why." Newsweek, December 30, pp. 16–20; Leung, Shirley. 2002. "McHaute cuisine: Armchairs, TVs and espresso–is it McDonald's—burger giant's makeover in France boosts sales; big changes for fast food—some franchisees have a beef." The Wall Street Journal, August 30, p. A1.

Competitive Advantage in the Value Chain

The diagnostic questions just listed help managers decide whether to compete globally or locally in their industry. The globalization drivers represent a balance sheet of forces that move a company either toward transnational or international strategies on the one side, or regional or multidomestic strategies on the other. In addition, the location in the value chain of primary sources of a firm's competitive advantage influences the choice of a generic multinational strategy.

If most of a company's competitive advantages come from upstream in the value chain—as for example, from low-cost or high-quality design, engineering, and manufacturing (as with the Toyota example)—a company can often generalize these advantages worldwide. A transnational strategy or an international strategy becomes the likely choice. Conversely, if a firm generates most of its value downstream—in marketing, sales, and service—then it is well positioned to engage in a multidomestic strategy, which serves each market individually. Next, we discuss how the globalization drivers push some firms toward the transnational strategy and others toward the international strategy.

Some firms may have competitive strengths in downstream activities, such as customer service, but may compete in industries with strong globalization drivers. Other companies may produce high-quality products efficiently but may compete in industries with strong pressures for local adaptation. In such circumstances, multinational companies often compromise and select a regional strategy. For the firm with upstream competitive strengths, such as high-quality R&D, the regional strategy allows some downstream adaptation of products to regional differences. For the firm with downstream competitive strengths, such as after-market service, the regional strategy allows some of the economies of scale produced by activities such as centralized purchasing and uniform products.

Exhibit 6.2 shows how these factors and the pressures for globalization and local responsiveness combine to suggest different multinational strategies.

Transnational or International: Which Way for the Global Company?

In globalized industries, companies with global strategies tend to perform better than multidomestic or regional strategists because they can usually offer cheaper or higher-quality products or services. How do companies choose between these two approaches to globalization—the transnational and the international?

To select a transnational over an international strategy, the multinational manager must believe that the benefits of dispersing activities worldwide offset the costs of coordinating a more complex organization. For example, a company may do R&D in one country, parts manufacturing in another, final assembly in another, and sales in a fourth. Coordination of these activities across national borders and in different parts of the world is costly and difficult. In a later chapter, you will see some of the complexities of organizing a transnational company to accomplish these tasks. The transnational strategist, however, anticipates that the benefits of these dispersed activities in low-cost or high-quality labor and raw materials will offset the difficulties of coordination to produce better or cheaper products.

In contrast to the transnational strategist, the international strategist believes that centralizing key activities such as R&D reduces coordination costs and gives economies of scale. The cost savings from these economies of scale then offset the lower costs or high-quality raw materials or labor that the transnationalist can find by locating worldwide.

EXHIBIT 6.2   Multinational Strategies, Value-Chain Locations of Competitive Advantages, and Pressures for Globalization or Local Responsiveness

Global/Local Responsiveness Pressures	Primary Source of Competitive Advantage in Value Chain	
	Upstream	Downstream
High Pressures for Globalization	Transnational strategy or international strategy	Regional strategy compromise
High Pressures for Local Responsiveness	Regional strategy compromise	Multilocal strategy

The world's largest multinationals seldom adopt a pure international or transnational strategy. Most major multinational corporations, such as IBM, GM, and Siemens, have some mixture of transnational and international strategies. Multibusiness companies may be more international or transnational in different business lines. However, as information systems and communications systems become more sophisticated, many of the traditional international firms are developing transnational characteristics. Boeing, for example, has components of its aircraft produced in Japan and China.

Once multinational managers choose their basic strategic approach to the internationalization of their business, that is, their multinational strategy, they must also select the operational strategies necessary to enter different countries. The remainder of the chapter discusses these strategic operations in detail.

Participation Strategies: The Content Options

Participation strategies

Options multinational companies have for entering foreign markets and countries.

Regardless of their choice of a general multinational strategy (e.g., multidomestic or transnational), companies must also choose exactly how they will enter each international market in which they wish to do business. For example, multinational managers must decide: Will we export only? Or will we build our own manufacturing plant in the country? The strategies that deal with the choices regarding how to enter foreign markets and countries are called **participation strategies.** This section reviews several popular participation strategies, including exporting, licensing, strategic alliances, and foreign direct investment.

Exporting

Passive exporting

Treating and filling overseas orders like domestic orders.

Exporting is the easiest way to sell a product in the international market. The effort can be as little as treating and filling overseas orders like domestic orders, often called **passive exporting.** Alternatively, at the other extreme, a multinational company can put extensive resources into exporting with a dedicated export department or division and an international sales force. The various export options beyond passive exporting are discussed next.

Although exporting is often the easiest participation strategy, it is an important one. In the United States, most export sales in dollars go to large companies. The aircraft manufacturer Boeing, for example, receives over half of its revenues from exports. However, it is important to note that most U.S. exporters are small companies. As you will see in the next chapter, exporting is often the only strategy available to small businesses.

The U.S. government understands the importance of the economy. There are several governmental agencies that work closely with various states to provide assistance to small companies interested in exporting. Consider the following Case in Point.

Export Strategies

Indirect exporting

Intermediary or go-between firms provide the knowledge and contacts necessary to sell overseas.

Once a company moves beyond passive exporting, there are two general export strategies that multinational companies can use: indirect and direct exporting.

Smaller firms and beginning exporters usually find indirect exporting to be the most viable option. In **indirect exporting,** intermediary or go-between firms provide the knowledge and contacts necessary to sell overseas. Indirect exporting provides a company with an export option without the risks and complexities of doing it alone.

C A S E   I N   P O I N T

Export Assistance for the Small Company

The Export-Import Bank of the United States (http://www.exim.gov) is an independent federal government agency that assists small companies in exporting to new markets. Ex-Im Bank provides the financial tools (access to working capital and export credit insurance) to help small companies export goods and services to the global market. It also accepts credit and country risks that smaller companies cannot afford. For instance, it recently approved $300 million to be allocated to Nigerian banks in order to help develop the export sector in Nigeria for U.S. companies.

States also understand the importance of exporting to the local economy. Many states have special agencies that provide assistance to companies interested in exporting. Consider Illinois Global Partnership Program (IGP) (http://www.illinoisglobal.org), which was established in 2005 to provide small and medium businesses with the tools to succeed at an international level. IGP offers regular one-day seminars on best practices on important financial topics such as funding export working capital, offering more competitive terms at an international level, and benefits of foreign-currency invoicing. However, IGP recently partnered with Ex-Im Bank to make Ex-Im Bank's services more visible and accessible to Illinois companies. Illinois is one of the leading exporting states in the United States, and such programs are seen as very crucial.

Source: Based on Business Wire. 2006. "Illinois Global Partnership and Export-Import Bank of the United States collaborate to introduce new city-state partnership in Illinois: Initiative to help Illinois companies succeed in international business." June 8, p. 1.

The most common intermediaries are the **Export Management Company (EMC)** and the **Export Trading Company (ETC).** EMCs usually specialize in particular types of products or particular countries or regions. They may have both product and country specializations. Usually for a commission, they provide a company with ready-made access to particular international markets. For example, an EMC might specialize in fruit products for the Asian market, and an apple producer who wished to export to Japan would seek an EMC with that specialization. Good EMCs have established networks of foreign distributors and know their products and countries very well. Export Trading Companies are similar to EMCs and provide many of the same services. The ETC, however, usually takes title to the product before exporting. That is, the ETC first buys the goods from the exporter, and then resells them overseas. The most important advantage of an EMC or an ETC is that a company can quickly get into a foreign market at a low cost in management and financial resources.

In contrast to indirect exporting, **direct exporting** is a more aggressive exporting strategy. Direct exporters take on the duties of the intermediaries. That is, the exporters make direct contact with companies located in the foreign market. Direct exporters often use foreign sales representatives, foreign distributors, or foreign retailers to get their products to end users in foreign markets. At the highest level of investment, direct exporters may set up their own branch offices in foreign countries.

Foreign sales representatives use the company's promotional literature and samples to sell the company's products to foreign buyers. Sales representatives do not take title to products, nor are they employed by the direct exporters. Rather, sales representatives have contracts with companies that define their commissions, assigned territories, length of agreements, and other details. Unlike foreign sales representatives, foreign distributors buy products from domestic sellers at a discount and resell the products in a foreign market at a

Export Management Company (EMC)

Intermediary specializing in particular types of products or particular countries or regions.

Export Trading Company (ETC)

Intermediary similar to EMC, but it usually takes title to the product before exporting.

Direct exporting

Exporters take on the duties of intermediaries and make direct contact with customers in the foreign market.

profit. Typically, the foreign distributor is an intermediary selling to foreign retailers rather than to end users.

Some exporters sell directly to foreign retailers. For example, some Korean and Japanese exporters sell electronics products directly to large retail chains in the United States, such as Sears. Usually, for consumer goods, direct exporting requires at least one intermediary before the end user.

However, direct exporters, depending on their resources and local laws, can sell directly to foreign end users. This strategy often works better for selling industrial products to other organizations than for consumer products, such as microwave ovens for consumers. Some firms reach foreign consumers through traditional catalog sales or web site catalogs. L. L. Bean (outdoor clothing), Austad (golfing equipment), and Dell Computer (PCs) successfully market through direct mail internationally. REI's e-commerce venture in Japan rivals its more traditional catalog sales.

Licensing

Licensing

Contractual agreement between a domestic licenser and a foreign licensee (licenser usually has a valuable patent, technological know-how, trademark, or company name that it provides to the foreign licensee).

International **licensing** is a contractual agreement between a domestic licenser and a foreign licensee. A licenser usually has a valuable patent, technological know-how, trademark, or company name that it provides to the foreign licensee. In return, the foreign licensee provides royalties to the domestic licenser. Licensing provides one of the easiest, lowest-cost, and least risky mechanisms for companies to go international. Licensing, however, is not just for small companies or for companies with limited capital. Even the giant multinationals use licensing when the conditions are right. The following Case in Point shows how Disney is licensing its characters for use in European supermarkets.

Exhibit 6.3 shows the contents of a typical licensing agreement. The licensing agreement or contract provides the legal specifications of the relationship between the licensee and the licensor. These contracts can be quite complex. They deal with everything from specific descriptions of the licensed product or technology to how the licensing agreement will end. Usually specialized attorneys from both countries work to prepare a document valid in both countries.

CASE IN POINT

Disney and Licensing

Disney has very ambitious plans for its licensing divisions over the next five years. It anticipates licensing its characters for products such as toys, clothing, food, and consumer electronics. It is working closely with many of the larger retailers, such as U.K.-based Tesco, French-based Carrefour, and U.S.-based Wal-Mart and Target, to increase its licensing arrangements with many of the retailers' own brand products.

Disney also plans to become more closely associated with healthier foods for children. For example, Disney did not renew its 10-year global promotional contract with McDonald's. Instead, it is working to

license its characters to encourage children to eat healthier food. For instance, British-based Tesco has started selling satsumas, a citrus fruit, with stickers of "collectible" Winnie the Pooh-based characters. Children are encouraged to transfer these stickers to a sticker book. Disney plans to extend these licensing agreements to other fruits such as bananas and apples. In fact, it launched more than 300 new products during 2005, and it continually is working to extend licenses to other products.

Source: Based on Wiggins, Jenny. 2006. "Disney banks on Winnie formula." Financial Times, June 8: p. 18.

EXHIBIT
6.3   Content of a Licensing Agreement

What is Licensed	Conditions of Use	Compensation	Other Provisions
Know-how; Special knowledge or technology	*Who:* Which companies can use the licensed property (and whether the use is exclusive)	*Currency:* In what currency	*Termination:* How to end the agreement
Patents: The right to use inventions	*Time:* How long the license lasts	*Schedule:* When payments must be made	*Disputes:* What type of dispute resolution mechanism will be used
Trademarks: Brand names, such as Levi's	*Where:* In what countries the license can or cannot be used	*Method:* Payments may be lump-sum, installments, royalties as a percentage of profits	*Language:* What the official language of the contract will be
Designs: The right to copy the design of production or final products	*Confidentiality:* Provisions to protect trade secrets or designs	*Minimum payments:* Agreements regarding minimum royalty	*Law:* What country's contract law will apply
Copyrights: the use of intellectual property, such as book material or CDs	*Performance:* What exactly the licensee has to do	*Other:* Fees for technical assistance, product improvements, training, etc.	*Penalties:* What penalties are in place for lack of performance by either party
	Improvements: Rights of the licensee and licenser regarding improvements in licensed property		*Reports:* What and when the licensee must report
			Inspections and audits: What the rights of the licenser are

Source: Adapted from Beamish, Paul J., Peter Killing, Donald J. Lecraw, and Allen J. Morrison. 1994. International Management. Burr Ridge, IL: Irwin; Root, Franklin R. 1994. Entry Strategies for International Markets. New York: Lexington Books.

Some Special Licensing Agreements

Many international firms enter foreign markets using agreements similar to the basic licensing agreement. Like the more general forms of licensing, these agreements allow firms to operate in foreign countries without extensive capital investments.

International franchising represents a form of comprehensive licensing agreement. The franchisor grants to the franchisee the use of a whole business operation, usually including trademark, business organization, technologies and know-how, and training. Some worldwide franchisors, such as McDonald's, even provide company-owned stores. To standardize operations, franchisees agree to follow strict rules and procedures. The franchisor, in turn, receives royalties and other compensation, usually based on sales revenue. U.S. companies, such as Holiday Inn, McDonald's, 7-Eleven, and Kentucky Fried Chicken, dominate the use of franchising as an international participation strategy.[12] The Case in Point on page 274 gives some background on McDonald's franchising strategy.

Some international companies contract with local foreign firms to produce the international company's products. Similar to the typical licensing agreement, the foreign company uses the international firm's technology and specifications. They then produce products for their local market or other markets.

International franchising

Comprehensive licensing agreement where the franchisor grants to the franchisee the use of a whole business operation.

C A S E I N P O I N T

McDonald's Franchising

McDonald's is clearly one of the pioneers of global brand expansion. It started pushing international expansion in 1967, and more than half of its 31,500 restaurants are now found outside of the United States. Such rapid expansion has largely been possible through the use of franchising approaches.

For U.S. franchises, McDonald's typically finds and purchases the sites and builds the restaurant. The franchisees are then responsible for all of the equipment, décor, and landscaping. Franchisees also pay percentage-of-sales royalty and advertising fees. However, McDonald's has a developmental license arrangement in over 32 countries. In such cases, the entrepreneurs are responsible for all risks and investments. They also pay McDonald's royalties.

Worldwide, about 70 percent of McDonald's company-owned stores are franchised. In Europe, getting a franchise is a two-year process of screening and selection. Franchisee candidates must work at a store for two years and undergo mandatory training. Those individuals selected pay $45,000 for a twenty-year contract. Typically, start-up costs range from $455,000 to $768,500. An individual is expected to contribute between $100,000 and $175,000 of his or her own money to start the restaurant.

In return, McDonald's gets a base royalty of 5 percent of sales, another approximately 8.5 percent of sales for rent of the company-owned store, and an additional 3.75 percent of sales for the franchisee's contribution to advertising. All of these percentages come from gross sales and not profit. However, in spite of McDonald's seemingly heavy take, the average European store has a profit of $200,000 per year. Large, high-volume stores in major cities can triple that sum.

The table shows the some of the fees associated with opening a McDonald's franchise in Ireland.

McDonald's Franchise Fees in Ireland	
Variable Fees	
Rent of company-owned store	From 5.65% to 18.40% of Sales
Service fee	5.00% of Sales
National marketing fee	3.75% of Sales
Start-up Costs	
Purchase Price	£400,000
Security deposit	£10,000
Franchise fee	£30,000
Maximum borrowings	£264,000 for new restaurant; £330,000 for existing
Unencumbered cash required	£176,000 for new restaurant; £90,000 for existing
Total cost	£440,000

Source: Adapted from http://www.mcdonalds.com/countries/ireland/franchise/require/index.html. 2006.

Source: Based on http://www.mcdonalds.com. 2006; Nation's Restaurant News. 2005. "Studying McDonald's abroad: Overseas branches merge regional preferences, corporate directives." pp. 52–59; Spielberg, Susan. 2006. "McD to spin off stores to franchisees amid investor pressure." Nation's Restaurant News, February 6, 40, 6: p. 1.

Contract manufacturing

Producing products for foreign companies following the foreign companies' specifications.

However, unlike the typical licensing agreement, the international firm still sells the products and controls marketing. This form of agreement is called **contract manufacturing**. It represents another quick, low-cost entry mode, usually used for small markets not warranting direct investment.[13]

In **turnkey operations**, the international company makes a project fully operational before turning it over to the foreign owner. It is called turnkey because the multinational firm builds the project and trains local workers and managers on how to operate it. After this, the multinational firm gives the owners an operational project, one which they must simply "turn the key" to start.

Turnkey operations occur most often in public construction projects done by multinational companies for host governments. For example, an international construction company, such as Bechtel, might build a hydroelectric power plant for a Middle Eastern government. Besides building the plant, the construction company would provide training for workers and management. This would make certain that the plant is fully operational in the hands of local people.

International Strategic Alliances

International strategic alliances are cooperative agreements between two or more firms from different countries to participate in business activities. These activities may include any value-chain activity, from R&D to sales and service. There are two basic types of international strategic alliances: the equity international joint venture, known popularly as the IJV, and non-equity-based alliances, usually known as international cooperative alliances.

Equity international joint ventures (IJVs) exist when two or more firms from different countries have an equity (or ownership) position in a separate company. A multinational company may have a majority, minority, or equal ownership in the new company. A non-equity-based **international cooperative alliance (ICA)** exists when two or more firms from different countries agree to cooperate in any value-chain activity. This is a contractual agreement for cooperation and does not require setting up a separate company. For example, Ford and Renault have agreed to cooperate in the design, production, and sales of utility vans for the commercial market in Europe. The market for commercial vans is quite profitable, but not big enough for one company to invest in design and production.

Gaining increasing popularity during the last decade, international strategic alliances have become one of the dominant participation strategies for multinational firms. Even firms such as IBM and General Motors, which have resources for and traditions of operating independently, have turned increasingly to international strategic alliances as basic participation strategies.[14]

Foreign Direct Investment

Foreign direct investment (FDI) symbolizes the highest stage of internationalization. Although IJVs are a special form of direct investment (i.e., ownership is involved), usually FDI means that a multinational company owns, in part or in whole, an operation in another country. Unlike the IJV, a new firm is not created by parent companies.

Multinational companies can use FDI to set up any kind of subsidiary (R&D, sales, manufacturing, etc.) in another country from scratch. They can use FDI to acquire existing companies in another country.

According to the *World Investment Report*,[15] cross-border mergers and acquisitions (M&As) are a major driving force affecting FDI. From 1996 to 2000, cross-border M&As increased by an average of 49.8 percent. In spite of the post-9/11 recession, which hit the developed nations hard, resulting in a 47.5 percent decline in M&As, the total value of mergers and acquisitions was still greater in 2001 than in 1998. Unlike **greenfield investments**, which involve starting your own foreign company from scratch, M&As provide speed and access to propriety assets. According to the World Investment Report,[16] the rapid pace of technological change and the liberalization of foreign investment policies by numerous countries are the major driving factors leading to more M&As as a form of FDI. Exhibit 6.4 illustrates the driving forces behind cross-border M&A activity based on a United Nations report of worldwide levels of FDI.

Perhaps the most famous and largest of single mergers is that of U.S. Chrysler and German Daimler-Benz to create the company DaimlerChrysler—although

Turnkey operations

Multinational company makes a project fully operational and trains local managers and workers before the foreign owner takes control.

International strategic alliances

Agreement between two or more firms from different countries to cooperate in any value-chain activity from R&D to sales.

International cooperative alliance (ICA)

An agreement for cooperation between two or more companies from different nations that does not set up a legally separate company.

Foreign direct investment (FDI)

Multinational firm's ownership, in part or in whole, of an operation in another country.

Greenfield investments

Starting foreign operations from scratch.

EXHIBIT 6.4   The Driving Forces of Cross-Border M&As

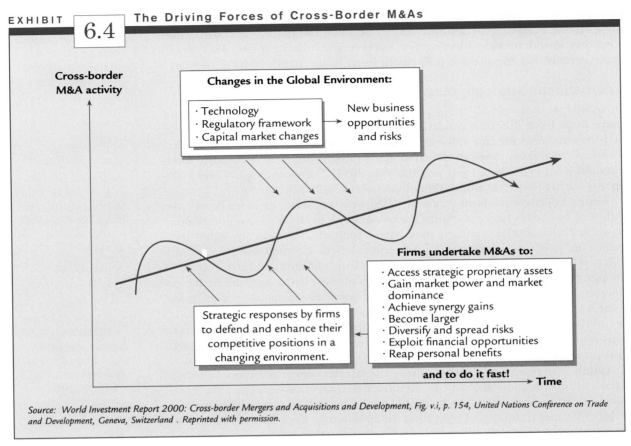

Source: *World Investment Report 2000: Cross-border Mergers and Acquisitions and Development, Fig. v.i, p. 154, United Nations Conference on Trade and Development, Geneva, Switzerland . Reprinted with permission.*

some would say that it is a merger of unequals with Daimler truly in charge. However, the biggest dealmaker is Vodafone with a value of $297.5 billion for 28 deals (DaimlerChrysler is a distant third at $54.6 billion). GE, the U.S. multinational firm, has made the most deals (228) but ranks only 11th in total value in a recent United Nations report.[17] Many other multinational firms are using privatizations in former Eastern bloc countries, Europe, and South America to acquire formerly state-owned firms. The decline of the Asian economies has also resulted in acquisition opportunities in Korea and Japan. Part ownership of a foreign company is also common in this area. For example, Ford has a controlling ownership of Mazda (33.4 percent), and Renault owns 36.8 percent of Nissan.

Reports by the Organization for Economic Cooperation and Development[18] also suggests that foreign direct investment stayed strong in 2005. Direct investment in OECD countries actually increased to $622 billion in 2005, representing an increase of 27 percent over 2004. However, foreign direct investment outflows actually fell by 8 percent to around $716 billion. The United Kingdom was the world's largest recipient of FDI in 2005 with inflows of $165 billion. However, the United States lost its role as the leading foreign investor to France, which led FDI with outflows of $116 billion in 2005. This large French outward investment can largely be explained by four very large acquisitions by French companies.

Some multinational companies set up foreign operations only to extract raw materials to support their production at home. This type of backward vertical integration is common in the steel, aluminum, and petroleum industries. Other companies set up foreign operations primarily to find low-cost labor, components, parts, or finished goods. Finished products or components are then shipped home or to other markets. Ford, for example, assembles some automobiles in Mexico and Thailand primarily for export. Market penetration, however, is the major motivation to invest abroad. Companies invest in foreign subsidiaries to have a base for production or sales in their target countries.[19]

The scale of FDI often changes as firms gain greater returns from their investments or perceive less risk in running their foreign operations. For example, a multinational manufacturing firm may begin with only a sales office, later add a warehouse, and still later add a plant or acquire a local company with the capacity only to assemble or package its product. Ultimately, at the highest scale of investment, the firm can build or acquire its own full-scale production facility.[20]

Exhibit 6.5 shows the leading FDI companies in the world from the developed and developing countries.

Although multinational companies have many options regarding how to participate internationally, the difficult questions focus on choosing the right participation strategy for a particular company and its products. The next section addresses these questions in detail.

Formulating a Participation Strategy

As in formulating any strategy, formulating a participation strategy must take into account several issues, including the basic functions of each participation strategy; general strategic considerations regarding the company and its strategic intent, products, and markets; and how best to support the company's multinational strategy. We will next deal with each of these issues in turn.

Basic Functions of Participation Strategies

Deciding on an Export Strategy

Exporting is the easiest and cheapest participation strategy, although it may not always be the most profitable. However, it is a way to begin to internationalize or to test new markets. Most companies will continue to export even as they adopt more sophisticated participation strategies. However, a company must answer the question: Which form of exporting should it choose?

Each export strategy has some advantages and some drawbacks. As with most business decisions, the greater potential profits of direct exporting are offset by considerations of greater financial risk and commitment of resources.[21] In addition, there are considerations regarding the needs and capabilities of the company. The following diagnostic questions can help multinational managers select the best export strategy for their company:[22]

- *Does management believe it must control foreign sales, customer credit, and the eventual sale of the product to the customer?* If yes, choose a form of direct exporting.
- *Does the company have the financial and human resources for creating an organizational position or department to manage export operations?* If not, choose a form of indirect exporting.
- *Does the company have the financial and human resources to design and execute international promotional activities (for example, international trade shows and*

EXHIBIT 6.5   World's Top Companies Ranked by Foreign Assets

All Companies (Assets in Billions of U. S. Dollars)

Assets		Company	Country	Industry
Foreign	Total			
221.2	222.3	Vodafone	United States	Telecommunications
159.2	437.0	General Electric	United States	Electronics
101.7	149.0	ExxonMobil	United States	Petroleum
93.3	141.9	Vivendi Universal	France	Diversified
75.2	303.1	General Motors	United States	Motor vehicles
74.8	122.5	Royal Dutch/Shell	Netherlands/United Kingdom	Petroleum
57.5	75.2	BP	United Kingdom	Petroleum
		Toyota	Japan	Motor vehicles
55.9	87.1	Telefónica	Spain	Telecommunications
44.9	131.5	Fiat	Italy	Motor Vehicles

Companies from Developing Economies (Assets in Millions of U.S. Dollars)

Foreign	Total	Company	Country	Industry
41.96	56.8	Hutchinson Whampoa, Ltd.	Hong Kong	Diversified
10.8	15.8	Cemex, S.A.	Mexico	Construction
8.7	17.7	LG Electronics	Korea	Electronic equipment
8.0	57.1	Petróleos de Venezuela S.A.	Venezuela	Petroleum exp.
7.7	36.6	Petronas	Malaysia	Petroleum
4.6	16.4	New World Development	Hong Kong	Diversified
3.9	10.4	Samsung Corporation	Korea	Diversified/trade
3.9	25.1	Samsung Electronics	Korea	Electronic equipment
3.8	4.4	Neptune Orient Lines	Singapore	Transport and storage
3.7	10.3	Companhia Vale Do Rio Doce	Brazil	Mining & quarrying

Source: Adapted from UNCTAD. 2002. World Investment Report 2002. New York: United Nations Conference on Trade and Development. Tables IV.1 and Table IV.10.

foreign-language advertisements)? If not, rely on the expertise of intermediaries; choose a form of indirect exporting.

- *Does the company have the financial and human resources to support extensive international travel or possibly an expatriate sales force?* If yes, choose a form of direct exporting.
- *Does the company have the time and expertise to develop its own overseas contacts and networks?* If not, rely on the expertise of intermediaries; choose a form of indirect exporting.
- *Will the time and resources required for the export business affect domestic operations?* If not, favor direct exporting.

When Should a Company License?

The decision to license is based on three factors: the characteristics of the product selected for licensing, the characteristics of the target country in which the product will be licensed, and the nature of the licensing company.

The Product   The best products to license use a company's older, or a soon-to-be-replaced, technology. Companies that license older technologies avoid giving potential competitors their newest innovations while using the license to profit from earlier investments.

Often, licensed products no longer have domestic sales potential. The domestic market may be saturated, or domestic buyers may anticipate new technologies. However, older technologies may remain attractive to the international market for several reasons. First, in countries where there are no competitors with recent technology, strong demand may still exist for the licensed product, even if it is based on older technology. Second, the foreign licensees may not have production facilities capable of producing the latest technology. Third, from the licensee firm's point of view, it may still have an opportunity to learn production methods or other information from a licensor's older technology.[23]

The Target Country   The situation in the target country may make licensing the only viable participation strategy. Factors that add costs to a product often make licensing more attractive than exporting. Trade barriers such as tariffs or quotas add costs to finished goods that can make exporting them unprofitable. In this situation, rather than transferring a physical product, a company can transfer the intangible know-how through a license. For example, a brewing company that exports kegs of beer may face stiff import tariffs. However, by licensing the brewing process to a local brewer, know-how is transferred, and tariffs or import quotas are avoided.

Similarly, transportation distance between two countries can add significant costs. To continue with the brewing-company example, beers are about 90 percent water—making them quite heavy to transport—and have a limited shelf life. Consequently, overseas shipping is bulky, heavy, and expensive. In such cases, when transportation costs can make a product prohibitively expensive in a target country market, it often makes more sense to license the technology to local producers.

Other issues associated with the target country affect the licensing decision. Sometimes it is the only option. For some military and high-technology products, local governments require that the production be done locally. In other situations, licensing is the low-risk option. Political instability or the threat of a government takeover of companies in the industry can make the lower risks of licensing more attractive. Since a firm neither contributes equity nor transfers products to the host country, it only risks losing the licensing income in an unstable environment. Finally, the market may simply be too small to support any investment larger than licensing.[24]

The Company   Some companies lack adequate financial, technical, or managerial resources to export or to invest directly in foreign operations. With licensing, however, the company does not have to manage international operations. There is no need for an export department, a foreign sales force, or an overseas manufacturing site. The company's managers need not know much about operations in the foreign country or how to adapt their product to local needs. The licensee assumes these chores and responsibilities. Thus, licensing is a low-cost option. It does not demand much from the licensing company, and it often is the most attractive option for small companies.[25]

Having more than one product makes it more advantageous for a company to license. Multi-product companies can license their more peripheral or sideline products but not their key or most important products. This protects their core technologies from potential competitors but still allows additional profits from licensing.[26]

Some Disadvantages of Licensing   Although a low-cost and low-risk strategy, there are four major drawbacks of licensing as a participation strategy:[27]

First and most important, licensing *gives up control*. Once an agreement is signed and the trademark, technology, or know-how is transferred, there is little the licensor can do to control the behavior of the licensee, short of revoking the licensing agreement. For example, a licensee may not market the product adequately or correctly.

Second, a company may create a *new competitor*. The licensee may use the licensor's technology to compete against it not only in the licensee's country but elsewhere in the world market. Even though a contract may prohibit future use of the technology or its use in other countries, local laws may not support this type of clause in the licensing agreement. In addition, even with the protection of local laws, the cost of foreign litigation may make enforcement too costly.

Third, *low income* generally results. Royalty rates seldom exceed five percent. Often licensees are less motivated to sell a licensed product with its shared profits than to sell its own, homegrown products.

Fourth, there are *opportunity costs* to licensing. That is, the licensee removes the opportunity to enter the country through other means, such as exporting or direct investment. Usually the licensing contract grants licensees the exclusive right to use trademarks or technologies in their countries, excluding even the licensor.

Why do Companies Seek Strategic Alliances?

Given the importance of strategic alliances to multinational companies, we consider strategic alliances separately in Chapter 9. Next, we consider a few issues briefly:

Why do companies seek strategic alliances? Several motivations lead multinational companies to use strategic alliances. Most of these reasons are based on the logic that two or more companies have different capabilities that, when combined, can lead to competitive advantages. Some of the reasons for forming alliances follow.

- *The Local Partner's Knowledge of the Market:* A major motivation of many foreign companies, especially the smaller ones, is that alliances allow them to take advantage of the local partner's knowledge of the local market. Usually, foreign companies seek partners with similar products who have a good knowledge of local buyers and local channels of distribution.
- *Government Requirements:* Especially in developing countries, local governments often require joint ventures as a condition of entry into the country. Local governments want to ensure that local people have an ownership position. In countries such as China and in many of the former Eastern bloc countries, the government itself is often a joint-venture partner.
- *Sharing Risks:* When two or more companies agree to cooperate on a project, they agree to share not only the potential profits of the relationship but also

the risks, should the venture fail. This motivation for entering an alliance becomes particularly popular when either the project is very risky, as for example with an unknown technology, or the project requires a heavy investment.

- *Sharing Technology:* Many companies seek alliances to find partners with complementary technological strengths. In combination, two or more companies often can bring a sophisticated product to market more quickly and with higher quality. This is the strategy used by the Japanese firm Toshiba and the Korean firm Samsung to improve their technological competitive advantages. They seek alliances with companies throughout the world to gain technical knowledge.
- *Economies of Scale:* By bringing the resources of two or more companies together, strategic alliances often provide the most efficient size to conduct a particular business. Small businesses may team up to compete successfully with larger global firms.[28] Even the world's largest firms, such as GE, team up with other companies to make products more efficiently. For example, none of the several European companies that collaborated to form Airbus could have afforded the level of investment necessary to start an aircraft-manufacturing company to compete with Boeing.
- *Low-cost Materials or Labor:* Alliances between partners from developed and developing countries often have dual motivations. The partner from the lesser-developed country seeks the technology, know-how, or capital investment from the developed country. The partner from the developed country seeks an opportunity to benefit from comparative advantages of the lesser-developed country. These advantages often include cheaper labor and untapped reserves of raw material.

Key Considerations in the Strategic Alliance Decision   Companies must assess their needs for and abilities to succeed in strategic alliances. Questions to consider include the following:

- *Could other participation strategies better satisfy strategic objectives?*
- *Does the firm have the management and capital resources to contribute to the relationship?*
- *Can a partner really benefit the company's objectives?*
- *What is the expected payoff of the venture?*

In addition to addressing these questions, to maximize their chances of success, companies must plan for the design and management of the alliance. In Chapter 9, we will discuss the management and design of strategic alliances in more detail.

Some Advantages and Disadvantages of FDI

All but the most experienced international firms usually try other forms of participation strategies before they select direct investment. Exporting, licensing, or alliances can prepare a firm for FDI and can minimize the chances of failure. In any case, however, the advantages and disadvantages of FDI must be weighed. Exhibit 6.6 summarizes the advantages and disadvantages of FDI.

Choosing a Participation Strategy: General Strategic Considerations

Once a multinational manager considers the general merits of each possible participation strategy, there are several broader strategic issues to consider as

EXHIBIT 6.6   Advantages and Disadvantages of FDI

Advantages	Disadvantages
➤ Greater control of product marketing and strategy	➤ Increased capital investment
➤ Lower costs of supplying host country with the firm's products	➤ Drain on managerial talent to staff FDI or to train local management
➤ Avoiding import quotas on raw material supplies or finished products	➤ Increased costs of coordinating units dispersed worldwide over long distances
➤ Greater opportunity to adapt products to the local markets	➤ Greater exposure of the investment to local political risks as expropriation
➤ Better local image of the product	➤ Greater exposure to financial risks
➤ Better after-market service	
➤ Greater potential profits	

Source: Adapted from Root, Franklin R. 1994. Entry Strategies for International Markets. New York: Lexington Books.

part of formulating a participation strategy. In particular, multinational managers must consider: (1) their company's strategic intent regarding profits versus learning; (2) the capabilities of their company; (3) local government regulations; (4) the characteristics of the target product and market; (5) geographic and cultural distance between the home country and target country; and (6) the tradeoff between risk and control.[29]

Strategic Intent

Although ultimately profit is the major goal of all firms, many companies enter international markets with less emphasis on the goal of short-term profit. Other goals—such as being first in a market with potential or learning a new technology—motivate their internationalization efforts. For example, many firms have entered China and the former Eastern bloc countries with the knowledge that profits are possible only in the distant future. In the meantime, their companies are learning the market and making the business contacts necessary to take advantage of future market potential. Joint ventures often serve these purposes well.

If the strategic goal is immediate profit, then entry strategies can be compared using more traditional market-forecasting techniques. Such techniques use the predicted sales to project estimated revenues for each participation strategy (for example, licensing versus exporting). Comparing the forecasted revenues to the costs associated with the investment yields a forecasted profit for each participation strategy. All things being equal, a company will choose the most profitable entry strategy.

Company Capabilities

What can a company afford? This fundamental question governs entry choice. For many companies, exporting is the only viable internationalization option. Companies also should consider human resource issues. Do they have the necessary managers to run a wholly owned subsidiary, to transfer to a joint venture, or even to supervise an export department? Production capabilities may be important if the company needs to adapt its products to foreign markets. Finally, even if a firm has the necessary managerial and financial resources to implement a participation strategy, the managers must be committed to using these resources.

Local Government Regulations

Dealing with the complexities of the legal system and government regulations often challenges many firms in their own countries. A company that decides to go international confronts a whole new set of regulations in the target market countries. Many questions must be considered: What kinds of import or export tariffs, duties, or restrictions exist? Excessive import tariffs, for example, may inflate the price of a company's products to a noncompetitive level. What kinds of laws restrict foreign ownership or participation in local firms? In some countries, majority ownership by foreign companies is unlawful. Other legal and regulatory issues also demand careful consideration. Depending on the product, a multinational company might select a participation strategy based on local-content laws (how much of the product or raw material must be produced or supplied locally), patent laws, consumer-protection laws, labor laws, tax laws, and so on.

Characteristics of the Target Product and its Market

Factors related to the product targeted for the international market affect the participation decision in several ways. For example, products that spoil quickly or are difficult to transport might be poor candidates for exporting, whereas products that need little adaptation to local conditions might be good candidates for licensing, joint ventures, or direct investment. Another key issue relates to how and where the product is sold. This means that a company must address the question of how to get the product to market. Can it use local channels of distribution? If not, the firm might explore exporting or joint ventures. If it can develop its own channels of distribution, direct investment might provide the best strategy.

Geographic and Cultural Distance

A great distance between two countries, either in geography or culture, affects the participation decision. Physical distance raises several issues. When the producing country is a great distance from the consuming country, exporting may be limited by excessive transportation costs. Even with direct investment for production, it is sometimes necessary to ship components or raw material from another country to the producing country. Distance also makes it more difficult for managers to communicate face to face, and local managers may feel "out of the loop" in corporate decision making.

Cultural distance can often be as important as, if not more important than, physical distance. Cultural distance represents the extent that two national cultures differ on fundamental beliefs, attitudes, and values. Usually, when two countries have distinctly different cultures, the foreign company initially avoids direct investment. Joint ventures, for example, are attractive in these situations because they allow local partners to deal with many local cultural issues. Licensing and exporting further remove the foreign company from direct dealings with the local culture.

Financial Risk of the Investments

Multinationals face financial risks from their investments. Such financial risks can be manifested in the volatility of returns, cash flows, or other financial measures.[30] An important determinant of financial risk is the economic system, which can be unstable and risky for multinational companies. For instance, currencies that fluctuate widely in value make international trade difficult.

Economic systems that have excessive inflation or recession can affect the profitability of local investments. The sustained increase in oil prices can also have a substantial impact on a multinational company's operations. Unless a joint venture or direct investment has a potential for extremely high profits, most companies stick to licensing or exporting in risky economic environments.

Need for Control

A company going international must determine how important it is to monitor and control operations overseas. Key areas for concern over control include: product quality in the manufacturing process, product price, advertising and other promotional activities, where the product is sold, and after-market service. Companies such as McDonald's that use uniform product quality for competitive advantage often have high needs for control. FDI usually provides the most control.

The Control-Versus-Risk Tradeoff

Usually, participation choices that increase control also have more risks. For example, exporting and licensing are low-risk ventures. However, exporting and licensing also surrender control over the product or service to another party. The various forms of FDI allow firms to maximize control, but they also expose the firm to the greatest financial and political risks. Exhibit 6.7 shows the tradeoffs between risk and control for common international-participation strategies.

To conclude this section, Exhibit 6.8 summarizes the preferred participation strategies for companies facing different conditions for the issues just discussed. Ultimately, and perhaps most important, participation strategies must align with the multinational strategy. Next, the text addresses this final issue in the section on formulating a participation strategy.

Participation Strategies and the Multinational Strategies

Should a transnational strategist use mostly FDI? Should an international strategist use mostly exporting? There are no simple answers to these questions. Even companies with the same multinational strategies may use different participation strategies in the same country. Some of the issues that multinational managers must consider in matching their multinational and participation strategies are discussed next.

Most multinational companies prefer combinations of participation strategies, depending on their reasons for being in a country. Each product and each market may require a different choice. The multinational manager must ask: Why do we want to be in this country? Are we in this market to get raw materials, manufacture products, or sell products? For example, raw-material extraction and manufacturing may favor FDI as a participation choice. A focus on sales only may favor exporting or licensing, especially if the market is small.

The answer to the question why a company is in a specific country follows from the choice of a general multinational strategy. Transnationalists seek location advantages and may be in any country for any value-chain activity. Multidomestics seek local adaptation. They must address the issue of whether this is best done by modifying home-country exports or by locating the entire value chain from R&D to service in each country. Thus, the basic diagnostic question for the multinational manager is what participation strategy best serves the firm's

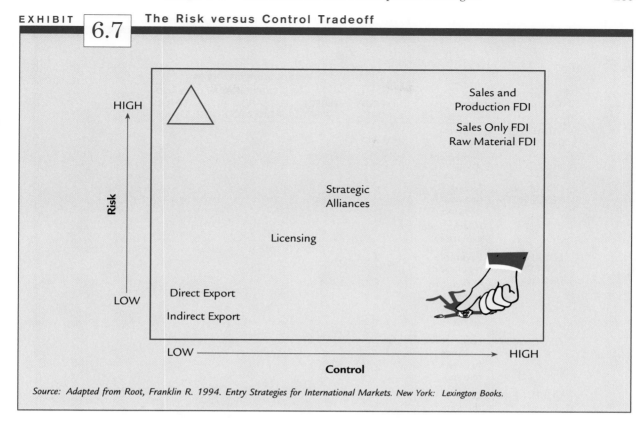

Source: Adapted from Root, Franklin R. 1994. Entry Strategies for International Markets. New York: Lexington Books.

objectives for being in a given country or region. In this sense, participation strategies represent the "nuts and bolts" regarding how a company is actually going to use international markets and country locations to carry out its more general multinational strategies. Exhibit 6.9 describes how companies with various multinational strategies might use the different participation options.

Participation Strategies: Synopsis

Companies of all sizes have the option to go international. With the growth of global competition, more and more companies will continue to seek international locations for R&D, raw materials, manufacturing, and sales. This section reviewed participation choices that companies can use to operate in the international marketplace. It also addressed the major issues a multinational manager must consider in formulating a participation strategy.

The selection of a participation strategy depends on a complex array of factors, including, but not limited to, the company's multinational strategy, its strategic intent, and its need for control of its products. Most multinational companies will choose a mixture of participation strategies to fit different products or different businesses.

Political Risk

In the previous section, we looked at some of the ways companies can participate in international markets. However, recent events at an international level suggest that more multinationals have to deal with political risk when making

EXHIBIT 6.8   Decision Matrix for Formulating Participation Strategies

Company Situation		INDIRECT EXPORT	DIRECT EXPORT	LICENSING AND CONTRACTS	IJVs AND OTHER ALLIANCES	FDI
					Participation Strategies	
STRATEGIC INTENT	Learn the market			👍	👍👍	👍👍👍
	Immediate profit	👍👍👍	👍👍👍	👍👍	👍	👍
COMPANY RESOURCES	Strong financial position				👍👍	👍👍
	International expertise				👍👍👍	👍👍👍
LOCAL GOVERNMENT PRODUCT	Favorable regulations		👍	👍	👍👍	👍👍
	Difficult to transport			👍👍	👍👍	👍👍👍
	Easy to adapt	👍👍	👍👍	👍👍	👍	👍👍
GEOGRAPHY	Long distance between markets			👍👍	👍👍	👍👍
CULTURE	Large differences between cultures	👍👍	👍	👍👍	👍👍👍	👍
NEED FOR CONTROL	High				👍	👍👍👍
RISK	Low	👍👍👍	👍👍👍	👍👍	👍	👍

👍 = Favorable conditions for participation strategy

👍👍 = More favorable conditions for participation strategy

👍👍👍 = Most favorable conditions for participation strategy

Source: Adapted in part from Root, Franklin R. 1994. Entry Strategies for International Markets. New York: Lexington Books.

entry decisions. Terrorist activities and wars are contributing to making political risk a more crucial factor in investment decisions today. Furthermore, while emerging markets present significant potential, many of these markets also suffer from higher degrees of political risk. As such, it is becoming more critical for multinational firms to be able to assess political risk before making investment decisions. In this final section, we look at political risk and what multinational companies can do to prepare for political risk.

Political risk refers to the impact of political decisions or events on the business climate in a country such that a multinational's profitability and feasibility of its global operations are negatively affected.[31] For example, consider Russia's politically motivated jailing of Mr. Khodorkovsky, the business tycoon;[32] the Ukraine's disputed recent elections resulting in presidential uncertainties;[33] the Brazilian government's insistence for both government agencies and private

Political risk

The impact of political decisions or events on the business climate in a country such that a multinational's profitability and feasibility of its global operations are negatively affected.

6.9   Participation Strategies and the Multinational Strategies

Participation Strategies	Multinational Strategies			
	Multidomestic	**Regional**	**International**	**FDI**
Exporting	Export uniquely tailored products to different countries	Export similar products to each region served	Export home-produced global products world-wide	Export global products produced in most-advantageous locations to any other country or region
Licensing	License local companies to produce products with flexibility to adapt to local conditions	License local companies to produce product with flexibility to adapt to regional conditions	License only when export barriers or other local requirements preclude imports from home country	License only when export barriers or other local requirements preclude imports from optimal production locations or when local risk factors or other barriers preclude FDI
Strategic cooperative alliances	Use when partner's knowledge is required for local adaptation of product or service	Use when partner's knowledge is required for regional adaptation of product or service	Use alliances for upstream value-chain activities when required by own resources (e.g., investment cost); use downstream alliance under same conditions as licensing	Use alliance for upstream value-chain activities when required by own resources (e.g., investment cost or knowledge); use downstream alliance under same conditions as licensing
FDI	Own full value-chain activities in each country—from raw materials to service	Own full value-chain activities in regions—distribute activities within regions for location advantages	Use for downstream sales and after-market services	Invest anywhere in the world for location advantages in sourcing, R&D, production, or sales

citizens to use only open-source software; and countries in turmoil such as Iran, Lebanon, and Sudan. In such cases, government actions or related incidences contribute to higher uncertainties in the business climate, and multinational firms have to carefully consider whether their investments can be potentially constrained by these government-related incidences.

Why should a multinational company be concerned about political risk? Many multinational companies understand that political risk can have a serious impact on their profitability. In fact, for some companies such as Royal Dutch/Shell and American International Group (AIG), political risk is so important that these companies have dedicated departments to assess political risk. However, recent changes accentuate the need for an increased understanding of political risk. For instance, while many multinational companies find that outsourcing production to locations such as India or Kenya can reduce costs, they also are discovering that workers in such locations work in very harsh conditions that can greatly accelerate the risk of social unrest.[34] Furthermore, the world is also becoming increasingly dependent on energy sources that come from locations with high political risk (Venezuela, Saudi Arabia, Nigeria). As we have already seen, political instability in these societies can have dramatic effects on multinational firms. Additionally, because the world is so connected today, political uncertainties in one country can have substantial effects on the world.

Given the importance of political risk, it is useful to understand some of the factors that influence political risk in any society. Bremmer[35] argues that all of the factors that can politically stabilize or destabilize a country play important roles in political risk assessments. Some of the most common factors are changes in the government, sudden shift in governmental policies or ideology, social unrest, passage of new laws, leadership changes and potential of unrest after such leadership changes, and level of corruption.[36] How can a multinational company assess these various factors? The Multinational Management Brief on Political Risk Assessment provides some important questions that a multinational company must ask before it decides to invest in a country.

Not all companies can be like Royal Dutch or AIG and afford their own department dedicated to understanding political risk. In these cases, there are various agencies that can provide services to multinational companies with regards to risk assessment. One of the most popular companies assessing country risk is the Economist Intelligence Unit (http://www.eiu.com), and multinational firms can consult its risk ratings to make investment decisions. The Economist Intelligence Unit assesses a number of country risks including:

- security risk (degree to which crime or other criminal activities such as kidnapping, burglary, and blackmail are likely to occur)
- political stability risk (the extent to which the government is stable)
- labor market risk (degree of harmony with employees and trade unions)
- legal and regulatory risk (effectiveness of judicial system to facilitate business operations)
- infrastructure risk (degree to which local infrastructure is well developed)
- tax policy risk (extent of tax burdens and risk on businesses)

Multinational Management **Brief**

Political Risk Assessment

Political risk assessment is a very subjective and difficult task. However, experts suggest that asking a number of key questions can provide some preliminary insights into the political risk of a market that a multinational firm is choosing to enter. These questions include:

- How durable and resilient is the political system?
- How peaceful have governmental transitions been in the past?
- What roles do other nongovernmental organizations, such as trade unions, churches, and the press, play in the country's political stability?
- Are there internal factors such as social, ethnic, or religious tensions that could result in social unrest or civil war?
- What is the level of corruption?
- How reliable is the rule of law?
- What is the likelihood that the country can be hit by natural disasters such as tsunamis or earthquakes?

Source: Based on Bremmer, Ian. 2005. "Managing risk in an unstable world." Harvard Business Review, June: pp. 51–60; Wade, Jared. 2005. "Political risk in Eastern Europe." Risk Management Magazine, March, 52, 3: pp. 24–29.

As such, multinational companies can consult such risk ratings to make decisions about the appropriateness of investment decisions. Exhibit 6.10 shows risk ratings for selected countries on selected risk criteria. It should be noted that the higher the scores, the higher the political risk in the country.

Given the impact of political risk on multinational companies, it is imperative that the appropriate steps are taken to assess and manage political risks. Several options are available for companies contemplating political risk management. Although there are private organizations offering political risk insurance, the governmental agency Overseas Private Investment Corporation (OPIC) (http://www.opic.gov) provides insurance against various risks such as political violence, foreign currency inconvertibility risks, expropriation risks, and other interference with business operations. However, such insurance can be expensive because it may not always be easy to quantify such risks. For some forms of insurance, insurers may simply not be able to offer protection. For example, many insurance underwriters are now hesitant to insure foreign-owned natural-resource-extraction companies operating in Latin American countries such as Bolivia, Ecuador, and Venezuela.[37] In such countries, recent government actions have greatly constrained the business operations of multinational firms.

However, if available, political risk insurance can be very beneficial. The Case in Point on page 290 shows how a U.S.-based company was able to continue operations in Rwanda largely because of OPIC insurance.

For regions with extremely high political risk, companies need to be aware of the added risks and budget accordingly. For instance, in locations such as Iraq and Afghanistan, a major component of the risk management is to work closely with agencies providing security. Security provision can be of the hard (high profile with large numbers of security staff or vehicles) or low (low-key detection

EXHIBIT 6.10   Risk Ratings for Selected Countries

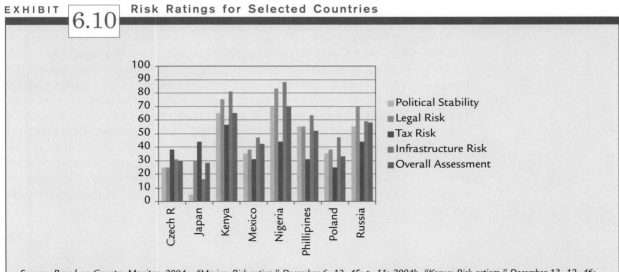

Source: Based on Country Monitor. 2004a. "Mexico: Risk rating." December 6, 12, 45: p. 11; 2004b. "Kenya: Risk ratings." December 13, 12, 46: p. 11; 2005a. "China: Risk ratings." January 17, 13, 2: p. 11; 2005b. "Uruguay: Risk ratings." January 24, 13, 3: p. 11; 2005c. "Russia: Risk ratings." January 31, 13, 4: p. 11; 2005d. "Japan: Risk ratings." February 21, 13, 6: p. 11; 2005e. "Nigeria: Risk ratings." February 28, 13, 7: p. 11; 2005f. "Philippines: Risk ratings." March 14, 13, 9: p. 11; 2005g. "Czech Republic: Risk ratings." April 4, 13, 12: p. 11; 2005h. "Poland: Risk ratings." April 18, 13, 14: p. 11.

C A S E   I N   P O I N T

Tea Importers Inc. in Rwanda

Tea Importers Inc. is a privately held company headquartered in Westport, Connecticut. It imports tea from around the world and is one of the few importers with investments in tea-producing countries. In 1978, the company obtained a loan from OPIC to start a 668-acres tea plantation and build a tea-processing facility in Rwanda. The company's investment was very successful, and Tea Importers Inc. was able to repay the loan in 1990.

During the 1990–1994 civil war in Rwanda, Tea Importers' tea factory was repeatedly shelled, and much of its equipment, such as cars and furniture,

was looted. However, Tea Importers Inc. had purchased OPIC insurance the day it began operations in Rwanda. Political-risk insurance from OPIC allowed the company to get four political-violence claims from losses it incurred during the civil war. Such insurance claims totaling $250,000 enabled Tea Importers Inc. to resume operation after the war. It has since expanded its processing facilities and remains a strong player in Rwanda's tea industry.

Source: Based on Overseas Private Investment Corporation. 2006. http://www.opic.gov.

systems) form.[38] As such, funds must be set aside to pay for these security measures. It is estimated that around 20 percent of the budget for projects needs to be set aside for security expenses in Afghanistan, and 30 percent needs to be set aside for security in Iraq.

Multinational companies can also rely on local partners to mitigate political risks. For instance, Japan's Sumito Chemical has agreed to a $4.3 billion joint venture with Saudi Arabia's Aramco to build a major petrochemical plant in Saudi Arabia.[39] Such ventures may help a company deal with local political risk. Furthermore, in a case study of various international firms, Lankova and Katz[40] showed that multinational companies often can take a high-involvement strategy where these companies develop a network of government, business, and public partners to help them face local political risks.

In sum, it is clear that multinational companies will continue to invest in countries with high levels of political risk. Many of the emerging markets that have the highest potential (e.g., Egypt, Colombia, Jordan) also have high levels of political risk.[41] However, such markets usually present tremendous potential. Furthermore, as Bremmer[42] argues, some of these markets may be so unstable that further instability does not have much influence. As such, it is imperative for multinational firms to adequately assess political risk and then devise the appropriate measures to manage such risks. Political risk assessment is a very subjective exercise and can vary greatly by region or industry. As a consequence, a multinational firm must be very diligent in assessing the correct degree of political risk and must adopt the appropriate measures.

Summary and Conclusions

The multinational manager faces an array of complex strategic issues. In the previous chapter, you saw how basic strategic-management issues apply to the situations faced by multinational firms. In this chapter, you built on that knowledge to see how multinational managers confront strategic issues unique to the multinational situation.

All multinational managers, in both large and small companies, must deal with the multinational dilemma of local responsiveness versus the global solution. The choice of a solution to this dilemma was called the multinational strategy—and each multinational strategy has its costs and benefits.

There are benefits to favoring local responsiveness, a form of differentiation. Either through the multidomestic or regional strategy, the multinational company can meet the needs of customers by country or region. Tailoring products or services for each country, the pure multidomestic strategy is the most costly, but it allows the company to deal specifically with differences in culture, language, and political and legal systems. The regional strategy, however, goes only part of the way toward local adaptation. Regional adaptation is balanced against the efficiencies of doing things similarly in a whole region.

International and transnational strategists see the world as one market. They try to have global products with global marketing. The goal is to produce high-quality products as efficiently as possible. The transnational strategist differs from the international strategist primarily by using worldwide locations or platforms to maximize efficiency and quality. The transnational will do anything anywhere.

For the multinational company, participation in the international market may occur anywhere in the value chain. At some point, all multinational firms must choose participation strategies that focus on the downstream activities of selling their products or services. All participation strategies, from exporting to FDI can be used for sales. Exporting focuses just on sales although there may be other strategic benefits, such as learning about the market. However, the other participation strategies, including licensing, strategic alliances, and FDI, serve other value-chain activities, including sales. For example, a multinational company might use a strategic alliance for R&D and sales in one country and use FDI for production and sales in another country.

In a globalizing world, the complexities of choosing multinational and participation strategies represent significant challenges to multinational managers. For example, the nature of the product, the government and political systems where the company locates, the risk of the investment, and the needs of the company to control operations (to name only a few issues) come into play in formulating strategic choices for the multinational company. The Cases in Point showed how practicing managers faced and responded to the challenge of formulating multinational and participation strategy.

Finally, political risk is becoming an increasingly important component of investment decisions. The final section discussed some of the components of political risk and the ways that multinational firms can manage such risks.

The next chapter will continue the discussion of strategic issues in multinational management. There you will see some of the problems unique to small entrepreneurial organizations. Many people mistakenly think of international business as the domain of the huge multinational corporations, such as Sony or GM. However, small- and medium-sized multinational companies are increasingly significant contributors to the growth of global trade.

Discussion Questions

1. Discuss the conditions when a transnational or international firm is likely to perform better than a multidomestic or regional strategist. Contrast this with the opposite situation, where the multidomestic firm is more likely to be successful.

2. Contrast the transnational and international strategies in their approach to location advantages.

3. Pick a product and analyze its globalization potential, using Yip's diagnostic questions.

4. How might a small manufacturing company become a global marketer?

5. You work for a small company that has an innovative, low-cost production method for laser disks. A Chinese firm approaches your CEO to license the technology. The CEO asks you to write a report detailing the potential risks and benefits of this deal.

6. You work for a small company that has an innovative low-cost production method for laser disks. A Belgian firm approaches your CEO to form a joint venture with your company. The CEO asks you to write a report detailing the risks and potential benefits of this deal.

7. Discuss some key issues to consider when choosing a participation strategy.

8. What is political risk? How can a multinational company manage political risk?

Multinational Management **Skill Builder**

Step 1. Read the case provided about Intel.
Step 2. In the table, describe the strategy content of Intel that matches the characteristics of the basic multinational strategies as described in the text.

Semiconductors were the most dynamic products in world trade during the period 1985–2000, when their exports grew from $26 billion to $235 billion. The demand for semiconductors comes mainly from the IT industries (computers, telecommunications and consumer electronics). By 2000, they represented 5 percent of world trade, up from 1.5 percent in 1985, and they accounted for 20 percent of the trade in high-technology non-resource-based manufactures, the most dynamic category of world trade.

In terms of ownership advantages, competition has been fierce in the semiconductor industry, and Intel, the market leader, has set the pace. It adapted better to the evolution of the industry in which there was a long period of fast growth (1982–1995), followed by consolidation (1995–1998), followed by a short boom and then a sharp fall.[1]

Intel jumped from seventh to first rank by sales in the semiconductor industry between 1983 and 2001, and is today by far the largest chipmaker in the world. Its sales increased 42 times between 1983 and 2000 before declining in 2001 as the IT market fell. It

Strategy Content	Transnational Strategy	International Strategy	Multidomestic Strategy	Regional Strategy
Worldwide markets				
Worldwide location of separate value chain activities				
Global products				
Global marketing				
Global competitive moves				

		The world's leading semiconductor manufacturers, 2001 (Billions of dollars)			
Rank 2001	**Rank 1983**	**Company (Home country/ region)**	**Sales 1983**	**Sales 2000**	**Sales 2001**
1	7	Intel (United States)	0.7	29.7	22.7
2	5	Toshiba (Japan)	0.9	11.0	7.2
3	3	NEC (Japan)	1.3	10.9	7.0
4	2	Texas Instruments (United States)	1.6	10.3	6.7
5	—	STMicroelectronics (EU)	—	7.8	6.3
6	—	Samsung Electronics (Republic of Korea)	—	10.6	5.1
7	1	Motorola (United States)	1.6	7.9	5.0
8	4	Hitachi (Japan)	1.0	7.4	4.7
9	—	Infineon (EU)	—	6.8	4.6
10	10	Philips (EU)	0.5	6.3	4.6
Total top 10			9.4	108.6	73.6
Semiconductor industry			17.4	204.4	139.0

Source: UNCTAD, based on IC Insights, cited by Semiconductor Electronics Resource Centre. http://www.dir-electronics.com and UNCTC. 1986.

accounts for about one-quarter of global sales in semi-conductors, mostly to the computer industry. It also accounts for one-quarter of the R&D undertaken by the industry, and has been the biggest investor during the past decade. Intel's capital expenses in 2001 were $7.3 billion. The company has developed significant technological and production advantages: it has been able to squeeze more transistors onto silicon wafers for computers than its competitors and it has developed larger silicon wafers, reducing fabrication costs, by about one third.[2]

Intel exploited its manufacturing prowess by integrating its production system and establishing identical plants in numerous locations to obtain the optimal global configuration of its production facilities. This system allowed the company to locate particular activities in the sites most suited for them. It kept the high-value elements of the semiconductor cost structure (wafer production and fabrication) predominantly in the United States and shifted the more labour-intensive assembly-and-testing activities to lower-cost sites. Thus, Intel has kept its production process internalized. More specifically, it has 13 fabrication plants and 11 assembly-and-testing sites in 7 countries. About half of its 86,200 employees work in its Technical Manufacturing Group. It has expanded internationally with fabrication facilities in Israel (1985 and 1999) and Ireland[3] (1993 and 1998) and concentrated its labour-intensive operations in Malaysia (1988, 1994, 1996 and 1997),[4] the Philippines (1979, 1995, 1997–1998),[5] Barbados (1977, later closed), China (1997, 2001) and Costa

Rica (1997 and 1999).[6] Today, about two-thirds of Intel's manufacturing workforce is in the United States, 11 percent in Malaysia, 8 percent in the Philippines, 4 percent in Ireland, 3 percent in Israel, 2 percent in Costa Rica and 1 percent in China. It is the leading national exporter from Ireland, the Philippines and Cost Rica, and ranks seventeenth among foreign exporters from China.

Many of Intel's competitors have reorganized their own international production systems, following Intel's lead and on the basis of the same overall intra-firm division of labour.[7] In the process, a number of firms have consolidated their activities. For example, Motorola has reduced the number of its plants from 29 to 14 since 1997, and Hitachi reduced its plants from 13 to 8, shifting production from Japan to China and Malaysia.

With regard to transnationalization, Intel's operations and its international production system are designed to distance itself from competitors by protecting its technological advantages inside subsidiaries strategically located in its home country, or in Ireland and Israel. In the case of assembly and testing facilities, it has expanded internationally to incorporate a few carefully selected sites in low-cost locations but always in fully-owned operations. It is an international production system that is hierarchical, integrated (with associated intra-firm trade) and based on tightly controlled subsidiaries. The semiconductor industry is thus a good example of a global value chain driven by carefully protected technological advantages.

Locational advantages also play a role. As technology-intensive stages in the semiconductor production

Intel's manufacturing sites, January, 2002

Country	City	Function	Year built	Current process technology	Employees
United States	Hillsboro, Oregon	Wafer fabrication	1978, 1992, 1996, 1999, 2003[a]	0.13-, 0.25-, 0.35-micron	16000
	Rio Rancho, New Mexico	Wafer fabrication	1980, 1993, 2002[a]	0.13-, 0.18-, 0.25-, 0.35-micron	5500
	Santa Clara, California	Wafer fabrication	1988	0.13-, 0.18-micron	8500
	Hudson, Massachusetts	Wafer fabrication	1994	0.28-, 0.35-, 0.50-micron	2700
	Chandler, Arizona	Wafer fabrication, assembly and testing	1996, 1999, 2001	0.13-, 0.18-micron	10000
	Dupont, Washington	Systems manufacturing	1996	—	1400
	Colorado Springs, Colorado	Wafer Fabrication	2001	0.18-micron	1845
Ireland	Leixlip	Wafer fabrication	1993, 1998, 2004[a]	0.18-, 0.25-micron	3400
Israel	Jerusalem	Wafer fabrication	1985	0.35-, 0.50-, 0.75-, 1.0-micron	800
	Qiryat Gat	Wafer fabrication	1999	0.18-micron	1500
Malaysia	Kulim	Board manufacturing, assembly and testing	1996, 1997	—	7790
	Penang	Assembly and testing	1988, 1994, 1997	—	
Philippines	Cavite	Assembly and testing	1997, 1998	—	5984
	Manila	Assembly and testing	1979, 1995	—	
China	Shanghai	Assembly and testing	1997, 2001	—	1227
Costa Rica	San José	Assembly and testing	1997, 1999	—	1845

Source: http://www.intel.com. January 2002.
[a] Estimated construction completion.

process can be separated from labour-intensive ones and the cost of transport is low relative to the value of the output, it is economical to pursue a global production strategy. In the case of Intel, the principal factors that the firm takes into account in establishing a new subsidiary for assembly and testing functions include the availability of a technical workforce, construction costs, the quality of infrastructure, logistics, business costs and supplier capabilities (http://www.intel.com/pressroom/). Host country incentives can be important as well. The

selection process for the plant that was located in Costa Rica exemplifies the interplay of these factors.[8] Intel's strategy of locating labour-intensive activities in low-wage areas, mainly in Asia, and then moving to yet lower-wage locations, has also been utilized by many of its competitors. They too have moved the more labour-intensive stages of their production to developing countries, often the same ones as Intel, thereby creating a clustering effect. As semiconductors enjoy unencumbered access to most

Winners and losers in semiconductor exports, 1985–2000 (Percent)[a]

Economy	1985	2000	Market share increase, 1985–2000[b]	Top 10 TNCs present[c] in winner economies
Principal winners				
China	0.14	8.82	8.7	Intel, Toshiba, NEC, Texas Instruments, ST, Motorola, Hitachi, Infineon, Philips, Samsung
Taiwan Province of China	2.72	10.64	7.9	Texas Instruments, Hitachi, Infineon, Philips
Malaysia	0.36	7.81	7.5	Intel, Toshiba, NEC, Texas Instruments, ST, Motorola, Hitachi, Infineon, Philips
Republic of Korea	0.76	4.01	3.2	Texas Instruments, Samsung
Philippines	0.23	3.07	2.8	Intel, Texas Instruments
Thailand	0.46	2.54	2.1	Toshiba, Philips
Costa Rica	—	1.41	1.4	Intel
Ireland	2.37	3.43	1.1	Intel, Motorola, NEC
Total	7.04	41.73	34.7	
Principal losers				
United States	29.97	15.40	–14.2	
Germany	8.76	3.39	–5.4	
France	6.52	1.71	–4.8	
Japan	13.83	10.27	–3.6	
Italy	3.28	1.14	–2.2	
United Kingdom	6.73	4.88	–1.8	
Hong Kong, China	3.92	2.11	–1.8	
Total	73.01	38.90	–33.7	

Source: UNCTAD, based on the United Nations' Comtrade database. 2002
[a] SITC 7599: parts and accessories of data-processing equipment.
[b] The concept of "market share increase" is based in the import market shares as calculated by the CAN computer programme on international competitiveness of UN-ECLAC, which is based on the United Nations' Comtrade database. The data are classified at 3 or 4 digits of the Standard International Trade Classification (Rev.2). The period of analysis is 1985–2000, in which the value of individual years represents 3-year rolling averages (two-year average of the year 2000) to emphasize the structural aspects of change.
[c] As of January 2002. Developing economies with semiconductor affiliates not mentioned here: Singapore (NEC, Texas instruments, ST, Hitachi, Infineon, Philips), Hong Kong, China (Motorola, Philips), Indonesia (NEC); Morocco and Malta (ST).

markets, market-access factors do not play a role in these locational decisions.

As a result, a handful of East and South-East Asian countries have registered high increases in their export-market shares in semiconductors, while some developed countries have experienced large declines. During the period 1985–2000, a total of eight winners (mainly from Asia) improved their shares by almost 35 percentage points, while seven, mainly developed, economies lost a similar percentage. In other words, a very high proportion of these trade gains and losses were accounted for by the relocation of the labour-intensive segments of semiconductor international production systems. Another factor was the arrival of newcomers in the industry from economies such as Taiwan Province of China and the Republic of Korea.

Source: UNCTAD. 2002. Used with permission.

NOTES

[1] During the first period, Japanese TNCs mounted a serious challenge to United States producers, winning significant market share (from 32.5 percent to 51.2 percent during 1982–1988), then falling back and reaching a low of 26.4 percent in 1998. The main United States transnational producers (Motorola, Texas Instruments, National Semiconductor, Intel and AMD) collectively reached bottom in 1989 (at 37.3 percent) before making a strong comeback (peaking with about 50 percent of the global semiconductor market share in the late 1990s). While United States and Japanese leaders were fighting for market shares, new producers were making inroads, more than doubling their market

shares, from 9 percent to about 20 percent over the period (based on data from the Semiconductor Industry Association)

[2] On Intel's lead in flash memory design technology, lithography, and capacity, see http://www.intel.com/intel/finance/presentations/pdf_files/nichols.pdf.

[3] By end 2000, Intel's investment in Ireland surpassed $3 billion. A new $2 billion wafer fabrication unit was under construction (http://www.intel.com/intel/community/ireland/index.htm).

[4] Intel's investment in Malaysia totalled $1.9 billion in 2000 (http://www.intel.com/intel/community/malaysia/index.htm).

[5] Intel's investment in the Philippines surpassed $1 billion by 2000 (http://www.intel.com/intel/community/philippines@index.htm).

[6] Intel's investment in Costa Rica was about $450 million (http://www.intel.com/costarica.index.htm).

[7] AMD is Intel's most direct competitor; however, it is not in the list of the top ten semiconductor makers.

[8] See Egloff, Enrique (2001). "CINDE: Costa Rican Investment and Development Board". Presentation at the UNCTAD Expert Meeting on the Impact of FDI policies on Industrialization, Local Entrepreneurship and the Development of Supply Capacity, 5–7 November (Geneva), mimeo. Rodríguez-Clare, Andrés (2001). "Costa Rica's development strategy based on human capital and technology: how it got there, the impact of Intel, and lessons for other countries." Draft prepared for UNDP, *Human Development Report,* February, mimeo. Shiels, Damien (2000). "Site selection for Intel's assembly and test plant #6." Presentation at the MIGA meeting on South America Investment Promotion Strategy Forum for Heads of Investment Promotion Agencies, 6–7 May (Rio de Janeiro), mimeo. Spar, Debora (1998). "Attracting high technology investment: Intel's Costa Rican plan," *FIAS Occasional Paper,* No. 11 (Washington D.C.: World Bank).

Endnotes

[1] Humes, Samuel. 1993. *Managing the Multinational: Confronting the Global–Local Dilemma.* New York: Prentice Hall.

[2] Ghoshal, Sumatra. 1987. "Global strategy: An organizing framework." *Strategic Management Journal* p. 8, 424–440.

[3] Doz, Yves L. 1980. "Strategic management in multinational companies." *Sloan Management Review* 21:p. 2, 27–46; Porter, Michael E. 1986. "Changing patterns of international competition." *California Management Review* 28:p. 2; Porter, Michael E. 1990. *Competitive Advantage of Nations.* New York: Free Press.

[4] Ghoshal, "Global strategy: An organizing framework."

[5] Bartlett, C. A., and S. Ghoshal. 1990. *Managing Across Borders: The Transnational Solution.* Boston: Harvard Business School Press.

[6] Porter, "Changing patterns of international competition."

[7] Hill, Charles W. L. 1994. *International Business: Competing in the Global Marketplace.* Burr Ridge, IL.: Irwin.

[8] Morrison, Allen J., David A. Ricks, and Kendall Roth. 1991. "Globalization versus regionalization: Which way for the multinational?" *Organizational Dynamics, Winter,* p. 17–29.

[9] Ghemawat, Pankaj. 2005. "Regional strategies for global leadership." *Harvard Business Review,* December: p. 98–108.

[10] Ibid.

[11] Yip, George S. 1995. *Total Global Strategy.* Englewood Cliffs, NJ.: Prentice Hall.

[12] Root, Franklin R. 1994. *Entry Strategies for International Markets.* New York: Lexington Books.

[13] Ibid.

[14] Beamish, Paul, J., Peter Killing, Donald J. Lecraw, and Allen J. Morrison. 1994. *International Management.* Burr Ridge, IL.: Irwin.

[15] UNCTAD. 2002. *World Investment Report: Transnational Corporations and Export Competitiveness.* New York: United Nations.

[16] UNCTAD. 2000. *World Investment Report: Cross-border Mergers and Acquisitions and Development.* New York: United Nations.

[17] UNCTAD, *World Investment Report: Transnational Corporations and Export Competitiveness.*

[18] Christiansen, Hans, and Ayse Bertrand. 2006. "Trends and recent developments in foreign direct investment." *Investment Division, OECD.* June: p. 1–26.

[19] Root, *Entry Strategies for International Markets.*

[20] Beamish, Killing, Lecraw, and Morrison, *International Management.*

[21] Wolf, Jack S. 1992. *Export Profits: A Guide for Small Business.* Dover, NH: Upstart Publishing Company.

[22] Ibid.

[23] Beamish, Killing, Lecraw, and Morrison, *International Management;* Root, *Entry Strategies for International Markets.*

[24] Beamish, Killing, Lecraw, and Morrison, *International Management.*

[25] Root, *Entry Strategies for International Markets.*

[26] Beamish, Killing, Lecraw, and Morrison, *International Management.*

[27] Root, *Entry Strategies for International Markets.*

[28] Beamish, Killing, Lecraw, and Morrison, *International Management.*

[29] Root, *Entry Strategies for International Markets.*

[30] Click, Reid W. 2005. "Financial and political risks in US direct foreign investment." *Journal of International Business Studies,* 36: p. 559–575.

[31] Click, "Financial and political risks in US direct foreign investment;" Wade, Jared. 2005. "Political Risk in Eastern Europe." *Risk Management Magazine,* March, 52, 3: p. 24–29.

[32] Bremmer, Ian. 2005. "Managing risk in an unstable world." *Harvard Business Review,* June: p. 51–60.

[33] Wade, "Political risk in Eastern Europe."

[34] Bremmer, "Managing risk in an unstable world."

[35] Ibid.

[36] Ibid; Wade, "Political risk in Eastern Europe."

[37] Ceniceros, Roberto. 2006. "Political risk insurers leery of Latin America." *Business Insurance,* May 29, 40, 22: p. 21–22.

[38] Baker, Greg. 2006. "Peace Dividends." *Financial Management,* March: p. 16–18.

[39] Bremmer, "Managing risk in an unstable world."

[40] Lankova, Elena, and Jan Katz. 2003. "Strategies for political risk mediation by international firms in transition economies: The case of Bulgaria." *Journal of World Business,* August 38, 3:p. 182.

[41] Davis, Chris. 2006. "Emerging markets still a good bet despite recent volatility: Long-term outlook remains strong but be careful, investors told." *South China Morning Post,* May 28: p. 15.

[42] Bremmer, "Managing risk in an unstable world."

Transition at Whirlpool-Tatramat: From Joint Venture to Acquisition

This case gives a description of the evolution of Whirlpool's participation strategy in Slovakia. Beginning first with a joint venture, Whirlpool eventually takes control of the whole operation.

The Joint Venture Partners

Whirlpool Corporation Whirlpool Corporation is one of the world's leading manufacturers and marketers of home appliances, such as washing machines, refrigerators and kitchen ranges. Its growth, from a domestic manufacturer in the United States to a firm with worldwide presence, is the result of a strategic decision taken in the mid-1980s.

Unable to find adequate growth potential in the United States appliance market, the company began its global expansion. By 1998, the company manufactured products in 13 countries and marketed them in approximately 170 countries. It employed over 59,000 people worldwide, and its net sales reached $10.5 billion (Whirlpool Corporation, 1999). Over ten years, the company had doubled the number of its brands, its employees and its revenues, and had tripled the number of countries in which it had manufacturing sites (Table 1).

Whirlpool's Western European operations started in 1989, when Whirlpool and N.V. Philips of the Netherlands formed a joint venture, Whirlpool Europe B.V. (WEBV). Its mission was to manufacture and market appliances in Europe. Originally, Whirlpool held a 53 percent stake in the joint venture; in 1991, it became the sole owner through the acquisition of the remaining shares.

Whirlpool Europe B.V. soon became the third largest household appliance producer in Europe, behind the Swedish company AB Electrolux and the German joint venture Bosch-Siemens Hausgeräte GmbH. After its acquisition of Philips' shares, Whirlpool began production in several European countries (France, Italy, Germany and Sweden). These sites achieved economies of scale by producing a minimum of 600,000 pieces per year per factory. However, the Western European market soon experienced a recession, which was reflected in disappointing sales and profits unlike at that time in the United States.

After the fall of the Berlin wall and the revolutionary wave in CEE, WEBV started looking for opportunities in the transition economies of Eastern Europe. Given the competitive pressure in Western Europe, as well as pressures on manufacturing

Item	1988	1998
Countries with manufacturing sites	4	13
Brands	14	25
Employees	29,100	59,000
Revenues (billions of dollars)	4.4	10.5

Table 1   A Decade of Whirlpool's Internationalization, 1988 and 1998

Source: Whirlpool Corporation, 1998b, and information provided by Whirlpool Slovakia.

costs, WEBV capitalized on the idea of opening new markets as well as using the low-cost competitive advantage of CEE by investing in Poprad, Slovakia.

Whirlpool Europe not only ranked as the third largest producer and marketer in Western Europe, but it also was the leader in CEE, where it had one manufacturing centre (in Poprad, Slovakia) and 10 sales offices. Whirlpool's strategy for Europe has evolved over time. During the 1990s, Whirlpool focused on closing the "value gap" between the costs of appliances relative to consumers' disposable income in Western Europe as compared to other major world markets, such as North America. That strategy was by and large successful, although at that time the whole industry was under cost pressures, as economic growth in Europe stagnated and consumers turned to lower-cost, less-featured products.

Through new products, the company undertook a dramatic restructuring of its entire line during the second half of the 1990s. Using extensive consumer and trade customer research, new products were introduced in every appliance category. In 1997, an estimated 60 percent of revenues came from these new products. In February 1998, Whirlpool CEO David Whitman commented on the situation in Europe: "Europe proved to be a bright spot for us in 1997, following two years of turbulent times. Our performance in Europe has consistently improved, quarter after quarter, following cost-reduction and productivity improvement efforts begun in 1996. Additionally, we continued to expand our business in Central Europe and other emerging markets by drawing from our expertise throughout our other European operations. As a result, Whirlpool remains the leading brand across the whole region" (Whirlpool Corporation, 1998a).

Tatramat Karol Scholz founded Tatramat in 1845 as a producer of nails and currycombs for grooming horses. After World War I, the company switched to producing domestic kitchen goods; after World War II, the company was nationalized. Under the 45 years of socialism, the company expanded to produce zinc-coated and painted barrels, water heaters, electric ovens and automatic washing machines. It began production of automatic top-loading washing machines (under license with VIVA of France) in 1969, and frontloading washing machines in cooperation with Elektronska Industrija of Yugoslavia in 1972. In Czechoslovakia, it was the number one manufacturer of automatic washing machines (202,500 units in 1990) and domestic water heaters (146,900 units). At the beginning of the 1990s, Tatramat employed approximately 2,300 people. It controlled 88 percent of the automatic washing machine market in Czechoslovakia, a near monopoly. The company derived about 12 percent of its revenues from exports. In 1990, its sales reached $48 million. The operating profit was about $3.2 million, resulting in an operating margin of 6.8 percent. Tatramat's washing machines were designed to meet the requirements of the Czechoslovak market.

In the late 1980s, Western brands were often too expensive, too complicated, or simply too large to appeal to the average Czechoslovak buyer. Tatramat also had an established distribution and servicing network in Czechoslovakia. This, along with a wide spread of the brand, meant cheaper distribution costs, cheaper servicing costs and lower advertising costs relative to imported brands. In addition, there was an untapped market for washing machines in Czechoslovakia. At the beginning of the 1990s, the penetration level for washing machines was only 58 percent. It was expected to rise to the levels of Western Europe (approximately 90 percent) within a decade. The demand for major consumer appliances was expected to increase gradually in Czechoslovakia and in neighboring countries as the region reoriented itself towards a market economy.

After the Velvet Revolution in 1989 in Czechoslovakia, Tatramat, as well as other Czech and Slovak companies, went through major changes. The communist government was overthrown and Czechoslovakia began to build a democratic society and a market economy. Although restructuring was difficult, and the year of 1990 was particularly hard, Czechoslovakia was considered to be among the leading and most successful countries in transition. Martin Ciran, the director of Tatramat and, subsequently, Whirlpool Slovakia, described the situation of Tatramat at that time as follows:

After 1988, State export subsidies that covered the difference between high domestic costs and low prices on foreign markets were gradually abolished in our country. It hit the sales of our main export article, frontloaded washing machines, very strongly. At that time we realized that our products were not competitive on the open

European market. We concentrated on top loaded washing machines because our main customers were all interested in top-loaders and we were able to increase the production of only one product at a time. Obviously, top-loaders and front-loaders were produced using different technology. In 1989–1990, we introduced abroad our new product, the MINI, fully designed by Tatramat. It was a failure because of its low quality and high price. It was simply an old concept; a new machine, but an old concept. Afterwards, we started to think about how to increase the competitiveness of our products. We considered the purchase of technology or licensed production. In 1989, prior to the revolution, I began looking for partners to supply technology for top-loading washing machines. We received bids from Philips, Thompson and Zanussi. We intended to improve the technical standards of our production as well as to increase production capacity. We realized that it was not enough to produce only 200,000 units per year, because studies showed us that we had to produce more than 300,000 per year to achieve scale economies.

Martin Ciran and other managers of the company visited the leading manufacturers of white goods in Western Europe and saw that even 300,000 washing machines per year were probably not enough. The best companies produced 600,000 to 1,000,000 units per year. They decided hence to change their products, to increase production, to share costs and to cut unit costs in order for the company to survive. Martin Ciran went on:

In the meantime, the COMECON market collapsed. We totally lost our foreign markets for washing machines and boilers; domestic demand also went down as a result of the difficulties of the first years of transition. There were fewer apartments built, fewer weddings. . . . People had other troubles and preferences than the purchase of a washing machine. We lost markets, we lost customers. In 1990, we fired about 100 people; in 1991, were fired 900, from an original of 2,300. We were lucky, because such a major lay-off did not lead to any special discontent. Employees got good compensation according to the law and some of them started to run their own small private businesses, which had not been allowed under socialism. It was also a time of so-called small privatization—the privatization of small shops, services etc. formerly owned by the State, which attracted some of our employees, too.

One of the primary challenges in the Czechoslovak transition and in the shift toward a market economy was privatization. On October 1, 1990, the Slovak Ministry of Economy transformed Tatramat from a State enterprise into a State joint stock company. At that time, ownership of assets, in the form of shares, was transferred to the National Assets Fund, under the administration of the Slovak Ministry of Privatization. As a joint stock company, the intention was to privatize Tatramat through vouchers. Companies owned by the National Assets Funds could establish joint ventures with foreign investors only after approval by the Slovak Ministry of Privatization.

Martin Ciran recalled:

We were transformed from a State-owned company into a State-owned joint stock company, one of the first companies in Czechoslovakia. In the meantime, the separate Czech and Slovak Governments became much stronger and federal Czechoslovak Government lost most of its power. It meant that our superior authorities were no longer the federal authorities in Prague but the Slovak authorities in Bratislava. The change of the form of the company also resulted in more power in the hands of management. We started to have a real feeling for new responsibilities, and we could do a lot of things without the approval from the State or State authorities. Although short of ownership, we had more competence and power. We could, for example, negotiate with foreign companies. After we recognized that the price for a license or a new technology was very high, we started thinking about capital investment or about a partner for a joint venture. It took us half to three-quarters of a year to understand that it would not be enough to produce new machines without access to markets. Under the new conditions brought by the revolution, it was possible to think about other forms of cooperation or alliance with foreign companies, not only about licensing. At that time, Volkswagen was preparing a deal with Skoda in the Czech Republic and with BAZ in the Slovak Republic, with the assistance of Credit Suisse First Boston. We also prepared a memorandum about us, followed by an offer for cooperation. This memorandum was sent in January 1991 to all prospective investors known worldwide, all leading companies in white goods. I cannot say that all the people in the company were eager for such cooperation with Western companies as I and my closest team were, but everybody felt it was necessary to do something.

Table 2 Tatramat Sales, 1988–1991 (Thousand units)				
Item	1988	1989	1990	1991
Washing machines	200.0	199.1	210.6	144.1
Water heaters	151.8	143.7	133.3	76.2

Source: Information provided by Tatramat.

After receiving the memorandum, Whirlpool, Electrolux, Bosch-Siemens and Thompson all declared their interest in possible cooperation. It is to be recalled that, at the end of the 1980s and at the beginning of the 1990s, Tatramat produced about 200,000 washing machines per year: 100,000 top-loading washing machines (the so-called MINI, 95 percent sold in the Czechoslovak market) and 100,000 front-loading machines (25 percent for the Czechoslovak market, 75 percent for exports, primarily to the socialist countries of Poland, Bulgaria, Yugoslavia and the German Democratic Republic—only 5,000 were sold on Western markets). At that time, various problems surfaced in the factory and its environment: high fixed costs, low productivity and quality, backward technology, products unsuitable for foreign markets, the abolition of State export subsidies, the collapse of the COMECON market, and a drop in demand on the domestic market. Tatramat sales dropped from around 350,000 units in 1988 to around 220,000 units in 1991 (Table 2). Finally, the devaluation of the Czechoslovak crown in 1990 tripled production costs.

At that time, Tatramat's management realized that a single purchase of technology would not solve all its problems. Market access was needed, and a partner who would be able to guarantee it. Tatramat's idea shifted from a purchase of technology or licensed production to capital investment or a joint venture. During the search for the right partner, it was realized that Whirlpool was the firm most interested in improving Tatramat's management and including Tatramat in its global network.

Motivations for an Alliance Between Whirlpool Europe B.V. and Tatramat

In 1990, the managers of WEBV realized that the changes in CEE brought about new opportunities and challenges for their company. They were attracted by the possibility of gaining new markets, as well as obtaining production facilities and a skilled labor force. Their facilities were not efficient, but they were low-cost in comparison to Western Europe. The privatization of State-owned factories opened the way for potential ownership and control. However, WEBV was not driven only by external reasons. It was also forced to look at new opportunities because of its internal problems: more limited success in Western Europe than expected, disappointing operating margins and the need to decrease costs.

Strategic Options for Whirlpool To solve some of the above-mentioned problems, WEBV could use various strategic options: exporting, joint venture, acquisition or greenfield investment in CEE. Every option had some advantages and disadvantages as listed below.

Exporting
➢ *Advantages:* Sales would increase, without assuming high risks.
➢ *Disadvantages:* Production costs would not be reduced, tariff barriers would remain.

Joint venture
➢ *Advantages:* Access to an existing facility, an existing brand, an existing labor force, an established market share, existing distribution facilities, an established local supplier base; low production costs; contact with authorities through the local partner; the potential to increase ownership control at a later stage.

➢ *Disadvantages:* Control would be shared, relationships and trust need to be built, labor force training would need to change local attitudes, need to overcome negative attitude towards the local brand name.

Acquisition
➢ *Advantages:* Full control plus all advantages of a joint venture mentioned above.

➤ *Disadvantages:* More resistance from the target firm and local government. In Czechoslovakia, takeovers had no precedence, resulting in more prejudice, resulting in less motivation or cooperation by the local partner; the facility and the labor force would be more difficult to change.

Greenfield

➤ *Advantages:* New facility, full control, own trained labor force, low costs.

➤ *Disadvantages:* No labor force at hand, more training needed, local competition, more obstacles from the Government and local authorities, more expatriates staff would be needed, no inherited market share, no previous brand-name recognition. A takeover would have been the best choice for Whirlpool. However, the legal system of Czechoslovakia and the resistance of the local managers as well as the Government did not allow going for this form immediately. Therefore, the most realistic choice for Whirlpool from a strategic point of view was a joint venture, with the possibility of a gradual increase in investment until a final takeover.

Strategic Options for Tatramat Tatramat's reasons for entering into the joint venture could be summarized as follows: drop in domestic demand, collapse of export markets in CEE, high and growing costs, obsolete technology, risk of massive lay-offs and a need to increase production to reach scale economies. To solve its problems, Tatramat had to choose between two strategic options: licensing or joint venture. Both options had some advantages and disadvantages as listed below.

Licensing

➤ *Advantages:* New technology, no partner to be accommodated, full control, access to training in technology, would keep producing both washing machines and water boilers under Tatramat's control.

➤ *Disadvantages:* No market access, technology and license fees may be high, no other know-how or skills inflow, no capital inflow.

Joint venture

➤ *Advantages:* Technology, capital, training capacity, know-how, and market access.

➤ *Disadvantages:* Profits and control to be shared, eventually leading to a loss of control over the enterprise. A joint venture seemed to be a better choice in comparison to a licensing agreement. Because the potential partners wanted only the washing machine unit, Tatramat's contribution could be only this part of production. The main question that remained was what to do with the water boiler segment. Other problems could be solved through gradually selling Tatramat's ownership to Whirlpool or by becoming a supplier to the joint venture.

Form of the Deal As seen from this analysis, the most suitable form for both partners was a joint venture. Tatramat was nevertheless concerned by the three conditions set by Whirlpool: the possibility of a gradual increase of Whirlpool's share in the joint venture, Whirlpool's unwillingness to include water boiler operations in the joint venture, and the call for an increase in the tariff protection of the local washing machine market. Tatramat was in a weak position vis-à-vis Whirlpool, and it decided to accept fully the first two conditions. It even managed to lobby for import tariffs.

Anatomy of the Deal: Main Problems and Outcomes

After complex negotiations, the contractual basis for the joint venture was created at the end of 1991, and it began operations in May 1992. Whirlpool contributed know-how in technology, production and marketing to the joint venture, and also bought 43.8 percent of the shares for $6 million (Figure 1). Tatramat's non-financial contribution consisted of intellectual property rights in the area of washing machine production, goodwill, buildings, machinery, land, and contracts. It kept 56.2 percent of the shares of the joint venture. The original agreement was signed for ten years.

With Whirlpool's investment, the original Tatramat company split into three separate entities: the joint venture Whirlpool-Tatramat became the number one washing machine producer in both the Slovak and Czech Republics; Tatramat itself continued to produce water heaters; and Tatramat-Quasar, a small joint venture with an Italian partner, continued to produce vending machines.

Whirlpool-Tatramat became a separate organization with its own sales staff, after-sales service and support, and local distribution facilities, located at the Poprad site.

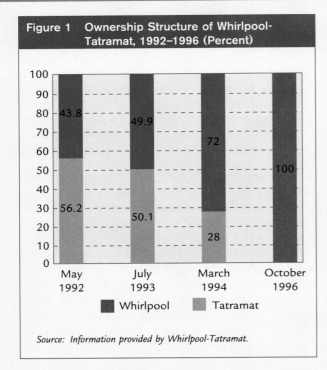

Figure 1   Ownership Structure of Whirlpool-Tatramat, 1992–1996 (Percent)

Source: Information provided by Whirlpool-Tatramat.

Whirlpool-Tatramat produced two types of top-loading washing machines: the old Tatramat MINI (under Tatramat's brand name), and the Whirlpool T-12 (under the Whirlpool-Philips brand name). The first T-12 rolled off the line in October of 1992. Even though results improved over time, the number of units produced in 1993 (59,000 MINIs and 39,000 T-12s) was below expectations.

Not only quantity but also quality became a critical problem in Poprad. As WEBV envisaged broadening Poprad's role to an international production platform for Western markets, the quality of Poprad's products had to meet the strict demands of Whirlpool and its customers. Quality had improved at Poprad during the years 1992 and 1993 but not enough forcing them to sell to mostly Czech and Slovak customers.

Employment levels significantly dropped after the establishment of the joint venture. Initially, 550 employees were transferred from Tatramat to the joint venture, and the remaining 750 employees stayed on the payroll of the Slovak parent company. In the case of management staff, Tatramat did not want to lose its best employees to Whirlpool-Tatramat, and therefore any transfer of white-collar workers was subject to its approval.

By 1993, employment at the joint venture was down to 219 (William Davidson Institute, 1994). However, productivity increased from 153 units per employee in 1992 to 199 units in 1993.

In July 1993 Whirlpool transferred $1.5 million to the joint venture, increasing its share in the joint venture to 49.9 percent (Figure 1). This amount was invested into a partial transfer of "hard" technology.

The external conditions of the joint venture also experienced a drastic change. In 1993, as a consequence of the division of Czechoslovakia, the local market for Whirlpool-Tatramat, with its location in Slovakia, diminished by two-thirds with the loss of the Czech Republic. However, Tatramat's brand name still enjoyed high name recognition in the Czech Republic, and the company maintained distribution facilities there. To catch up with the political changes, including new borders, and to avoid losses resulting from worsened operational conditions, Whirlpool-Tatramat established its own affiliate in the Czech Republic in May 1993.

Despite the loss of about $1.5 million in the first full year of operations, Whirlpool increased its share in the joint venture to 72 percent in February 1994 (Figure 1). Before Whirlpool's stake reached two-thirds of the joint venture, Tatramat had the right to nominate the chairperson of the board of directors and two other board members, compared to two seats for Whirlpool. After having obtained the two-thirds majority, Whirlpool got the Chairpersonship plus two additional seats. Moreover, as soon as Whirlpool reached two-thirds in the joint venture, the joint-venture agreement allowed it to decide, without the approval of Tatramat, on most important issues, such as plans, major contracts and financing. As Martin Ciran, Managing Director of Whirlpool-Tatramat since the beginning of its operations, recalled: "We were aware of the necessity of performance improvement, but we did not want to have our hands tied up by Tatramat, which faced big economic troubles at that time."

In 1994, production experienced moderate growth, with the production of T-12 more than doubling to 95,000 units (Table 3). The joint venture also produced the 11,000 MINIs that year, but it was the last year that the model was manufactured. The MINI was abandoned due to poor design, quality, declining sales and thin margins. Initially, in 1992 and 1993, the Whirlpool-Tatramat assembled

Table 3 Whirlpool-Tatramat's and Whirlpool Slovakia's Production, 1992–2000 (Thousand units)										
Type	Brand	1992	1993	1994	1995	1996	1997	1998	1999	2000
MINI	Tatramat	74	59	16	—	—	—	—	—	—
TL[a]	Whirlpool Ignis	5	39	95	219	267	349	381	495	585
FL	Whirlpool Ignis	—	—	—	—	—	1	140	275	360
Total		79	98	111	219	267	350	521	770	945

Note: TL: top-loaders, FL: front-loaders.
[a] The model T-12 has been produced since the beginning. In 1998, other top-loaders (Kireco and Alliance) were introduced.
Source: Information provided by Whirlpool Slovakia.

washing machines from kits imported from Amiens, France, where the T-12 was also made. The joint venture produced only the T-12 in 1995 and 1996.

In October 1996, Whirlpool bought out the remaining shares and became the sole owner of the company (Figure 1). The name was changed to Whirlpool Slovakia, and its headquarters and national sales office were moved from Poprad to the capital city, Bratislava. The following year the company exceeded, for the first time, the production targets outlined in the original joint venture agreement. A new front-loading model, the Tatry, was introduced in 1997 and production reached over half-a-million washing machines in 1998 and nearly one million by the year 2000. Although the capacity at Poprad made it the smallest of Whirlpool's European manufacturing centers, it remains the lowest-cost production facility.

Operational Issues

Since 1994, Poprad has begun to integrate vertically, producing more of its components in-house in an effort to reduce its reliance on the expensive Amiens components. Components account for 80 percent of a machine's costs. This, together with transport distance, customs regulations and problems with timely delivery from the Amiens site led to a decision to source as much as possible locally. While local content was only 3 percent in the first year, it reached 12 percent in 1994, 37 percent by the end of 1995, and 60 percent by the middle of 1997. This share has been maintained since then. In the mid 1990s, the plant had only 14 local suppliers; by 2000, it had 35.

With the creation of a local supplier network, the company succeeded in increasing production flexibility, reducing costs and avoiding import restrictions such as duty, import surcharges.

The total equity investment of Whirlpool, including the initial investment and the equity increases, reached about $11 million (including technology capitalized at $3 million) by 1996. The joint venture invested $14 million into production in 1992 to 1995. In the years 1996 through 1998, the company planned significant investments into new front-loading machines (the so-called Delta). This project was supposed to introduce a completely new front-loading machine for the European market. Later, Project Delta was changed to Project Tatry, with less investment and different technology, producing low-end frontloading washing machines. Investment into this model reached about $10 million by 1997. To prepare for the launching of this product, changes had to be made to production areas and technology, and a semi-robotic line for assembling was installed.

The total amount of Whirlpool investment into the Poprad plant reached $36 million by the year 2000. In comparison to "hard" technology, "soft" technology transfer has been more pronounced. Whirlpool introduced its management and incentive structures in Poprad. The company stressed the importance of communication with workers. Face-to-face meetings with management took place, explaining human resources practices previously unknown to the employees. After the first shock from Western management style in 1992 and 1993, employment gradually grew.

The human resources department adopted new policies, such as performance evaluation, pay for performance, a "recognition policy" to reward hard work and innovation, and "gainsharing" schemes in which additional wages were linked to company profits. It also emphasized the need for improving inter- and intradepartmental communication, and for training on specialized topics, such as teamwork, decision-making and individual thinking.

White-collar workers were trained in basic business skills, market economics, quality management, supplier quality, ISO 9000, English, computer skills, and Whirlpool philosophy and corporate culture. These training programmes were intended to increase managers' commitment to the firm and to spread the new corporate philosophy among workers. People were taught how to communicate, organize their workplace and how to increase productivity and the quality of work.

Additionally, the human resources department provided introductory courses on the Whirlpool Excellence System (WES). These courses were popular among Whirlpool Slovakia employees. According to the managers, it became a valuable tool for improving the work of the company. The region of Poprad had an unemployment rate of about 17 percent, and for Whirlpool this meant the possibility to ensure flexible work practices.

The human resources department received 400–500 job applications annually. Seventy percent of the candidates completed high-school education. Currently, workers' wages consist of a fixed part (73 percent on average) and a collective bonus (27 percent), depending on productivity, flexibility, quality and the level of absenteeism. A collective bonus was chosen as a way of encouraging cooperation among employees to work more efficiently at a lower level of absenteeism.

Since work there is considered to be intense, most employees at the Poprad plant are young with an average age of 28 years. The average manager is 38 years old, which is also considered to be young. This may reflect the fact that only young people were willing to join a *terra incognita*—a joint venture—when joint venture was established in 1992. They were trained by Whirlpool and were able to take their new positions quickly. In comparison to the Slovak average, they are well paid: during the first six years of Whirlpool's operations in Slovakia, only one employee had left the company. Currently, there is only one expatriate in Slovakia, an Italian national who serves as plant director in Poprad.

The joint venture was established with the aim to reach the productivity levels that was typical of other Whirlpool plants in Europe. The productivity in Poprad's plant increased significantly from 153 pieces

per employee in 1992 to 199 in 1993 and 323 in 1994. It reached 927 pieces per employee in 1997, which is far above the expectation and levels in similar plants (Table 3). Product quality has been a critical aspect of production at Poprad. As WEBV intended to expand Poprad's role as an international production centre to serve Western markets, Poprad's products had to meet Whirlpool's global quality requirements. Quality improvements in Poprad have been attributed to the training of employees in quality concepts, in-process checks and vertical integration, including greater internal control over the quality of components. During production, every machine is tested electronically, and 10 percent are taken off the assembly line and tested for 50 cycles. Additionally, 3 percent out of the 10 percent taken from the line are taken to the factory reliability lab where they are run through 250 cycles (corresponding to one year's usage) or 2,500 cycles (ten year's usage).

During the two first years (1992–1993), the company operated only in the Czech and Slovak markets because product quality at that time was too low to guarantee exports. In 1994, the company started to sell in Poland, Hungary and Argentina. In 1995, it entered into the Western European market. In 2000, about 90 percent of the output of Poprad was exported through the corporate distribution network. On balance, Whirlpool-Tatramat proved to be successful. Its performance has gradually improved. Its WES score rose from 238 in 1993 to 702 in 1997. Even the best Whirlpool plant in Europe managed to score only slightly better in 1997 (850). According to Whirlpool managers, the performance of Poprad has remained at the same high level since then.

Reasons for the Takeover of the Joint Venture by Whirlpool

The following reasons for the full takeover of the joint venture by Whirlpool could be identified:

➢ *The global strategy of Whirlpool.* Whirlpool and Tatramat were two unequal partners with two different goals: Since the beginning, the goal of Whirlpool was a gradual increase of its share in the joint venture with the aim of taking it over. It is consistent with its worldwide strategy of acquisitions and global control.

➢ *The economic problems of Tatramat.* Tatramat was not able to keep its share in the joint venture. In

1993, when it was time for the first significant investment to increase productivity, Tatramat was unable to contribute. This situation propelled a gradual increase in the share of Whirlpool in the joint venture. Under the worsened conditions, the goals of Tatramat to continue washing machine production and to survive the transition could be reached only at the expense of losing control over the joint venture. The hopes of Tatramat's management to obtain the dividends from a profitable joint venture and to improve its own difficult economic situation were not realized.

At the beginning of its operations, the joint venture was in the red, and the only way for Tatramat to get some cash was to sell its shares to the other partner. With this deal, each party nevertheless satisfied at least some of their needs: Whirlpool established production in a low-cost country, benefited from the local skilled labor force, reached a new market and created a new export base for other countries. Tatramat avoided going into bankruptcy, received cash and knowledge in various areas, including marketing, management and production.

Factors of Success at Whirlpool Slovakia

A Manager's Point of View According to Martin Ciran, "the very comprehensive and detailed joint venture agreement consisting of 30 pages and four appendices worked out by English lawyers from the Scadden Arps Company was one of the reasons for the success of the company. In each case of a misunderstanding, we referred to this agreement, and it really showed us the way out. On the other hand, you have several cases in Slovakia where a joint venture broke up because of a non-qualified agreement. After the collapse of the centrally run economy, the establishment of joint ventures was marked by a lack of hands-on experience on the Slovak side. Due to a shortage of reputable and experienced law firms, we chose a foreign company to draft the agreement and it was really worthwhile."

There is still more to that story. Martin Ciran described other success factors:

> Based on the joint venture agreement and the follow-up development of the ownership structure, the parent company Whirlpool practically had full managing and decision-making power in the company. Its approach has been very transparent and we got all the necessary knowledge and skills through training and technology transfer. On the other hand, Whirlpool's headquarters in Italy had agreed to the use and application of this knowledge. I would say mutual trust has been one of the basic points of our success. Furthermore, our people have been eager to learn and to apply new procedures. It was also essential that top management of the joint venture was young and not "afflicted by socialist working practices." It identified very quickly with the Whirlpool philosophy and corporate culture. The managers have transferred these values to other employees. We have implemented a new management system known as the Whirlpool Excellence System, quickly and successfully. In my opinion, the greatest change since the Tatramat days has not been in technological innovation or investment but in employee attitudes. The new thinking of our employees and their accomplishments in improving the working conditions at the facility and in making the production lines more flexible set the company apart from most of the other firms in Slovakia today. On top of that, the next very important success factor has been "not over investing." In other words, our company has a big cost advantage in comparison to Western European producers because of low debts. With high investment we would lose this advantage.

A Broader Approach to Success Factors Even though Martin Ciran mentioned many success factors, it is necessary to add that the story started with the investment of Whirlpool into a local monopoly producer. Hence, an immediate market share was guaranteed for the joint venture. This was important especially at the beginning of the operations when it was not possible to export products abroad due to their low quality. The monopoly position was also guaranteed in the joint venture agreement stipulating a non-competition clause. It did not allow the Slovak parent company to produce washing machines and excluded competition between affiliates and parent companies. Whirlpool could also realize classical first-mover advantages. The combination of a monopoly position, low-cost production and first-mover advantages has contributed to the success of Whirlpool Slovakia. It is interesting to note that Whirlpool insisted on market protection, but this was automatically abolished in the Czech

Republic after the split of Czechoslovakia and did not play any special role in Slovakia. The firm maintained its market share simply because imported goods were too expensive for the average Slovak costumer at the beginning of the 1990s. There were no other classical incentives (such as tax holidays) provided to Whirlpool.

The Performance of the Slovak Parent Company

The managers of Whirlpool were satisfied with the evolution of Whirlpool-Tatramat and later Whirlpool Slovakia. However, the situation in the Slovak parent company, Tatramat, has proved to be more complex. With the creation of the joint venture Whirlpool-Tatramat, and the splitting of the old Tatramat into washing machines and boilers production, the parent company Tatramat entered into a period of difficulties. The parent company Tatramat tried to adjust to its joint ventures with foreign partners. At the beginning of the 1990s, in addition to Whirlpool-Tatramat, it established Tatramat- Quasar, which produced vending machines with an Italian partner. At a later stage, it also established Scame-Tatramat with an Italian partner to produce plastic parts. As activities moved out from the parent firm into the joint ventures, Tatramat experienced a large decline in its labor force, especially in the first half of the 1990s, and at one point even faced bankruptcy. As initially expected, the sense of rivalry, jealousy and competition between Whirlpool-Tatramat and its Slovak parent company evolved during the first year of operations: Tatramat, located in the neighborhood of Whirlpool, has become its main local supplier. According to the Slovak managers of Whirlpool, Whirlpool's orders placed in Tatramat and its ventures created employment for about 200 persons there. Besides that, they argued that Whirlpool contributed to the creation of 400 more jobs in other Slovak companies. This means that one workplace established in Whirlpool created another job in supplier, service or distribution companies doing business with or for Whirlpool.

In the end, Tatramat survived its period of transition. In 2000, it reported a turnover of about $11 million, of which 75 percent came from export sales. It recorded a pre-tax profit of $ 0.15 million (compared with a loss of $0.6 million in 1997) with 520 employees.

Conclusions

The acquisition of Tatramat by Whirlpool is only one example out of many: since the middle of the 1990s, the strategy of investors in Slovakia has changed, especially among large multinational corporations (MNCs). The new trend is characterized by incremental takeovers. In several instances in the late 1990s, MNCs (including the biggest investor in manufacturing, Volkswagen) steadily increased their equity shares in joint ventures in Slovakia. There are a number of reasons for this new trend:

➤ The global strategies of MNCs;

➤ The weak, unequal position of the local partners in comparison to their foreign partners;

➤ The conflicts between the Slovak and foreign partners over the joint venture strategy;

➤ Conflicts over the control of key or common services such as energy, telecommunications and security (joint ventures are usually situated in the former plants of Slovak parent companies);

➤ Conflicts over pricing and transferring profits abroad;

➤ A lack of experience by local companies in how to deal with these issues (under socialism, cooperation with Western companies was not permitted);

➤ The inability or unwillingness of the Slovak partners to maintain their shares in the joint ventures;

➤ Financial difficulties of the Slovak partners forcing them to sell their shares in the joint ventures to their foreign partners;

➤ The success of MNCs in establishing their own communication channels with the authorities, in building positive public relations and in finding local managers for top positions, resulting in less reliance on local partners in these areas; and

➤ The recognition by MNCs that the transition process is irreversible and thus risk-sharing with local partners was no longer necessary.

Most MNCs that first established a joint venture with local partners in Slovakia have, in the meantime moved into the acquisition of shares (Whirlpool-Tatramat, Volkswagen-BAZ, Alcatel SELTesla, Henkel-Palma, Hoechst-Biotika, etc.). There are only a few exceptions—usually based on legal constraints, such as State participation in the telecommunication industry. Moreover, this situation is typical not only for Slovakia, but also for many other transition economies in CEE.

Like the best-known examples in Slovakia (Whirlpool and Volkswagen), similar developments occurred, for example, in Hungary with General Electric-Tungsram, in Poland with Gerber, and in the Czech Republic with Philip Morris. As soon as MNCs became sole owners, they tended to invest more into technology (however, they usually tried not to "over invest," i.e., not to lose the cost advantage and not to replace cheap labor by machinery). Most Governments seem to have no policy to prevent an "incremental takeover." Moreover, entry into the European Union—and the acceptance of its legal framework—may further limit the possibilities to block such acquisitions.

CASE DISCUSSION QUESTIONS

1. Would you have recommended a greenfield investment strategy for Whirlpool Slovakia rather than a joint venture? Explain your answer.
2. Would you have recommended a direct acquisition of Tatramat for Whirlpool rather than a joint venture? Explain your answer.
3. How would do you assess the control versus risk trade-off by Whirlpool?

CASE CREDIT

Sonia Ferencikova. 2002. "Transition at Whirlpool-Tatramat: From joint venture to acquisition." Transnational Corporations, 11, pp. 69–98. Used with permission of the author.

CASE NOTES

1. Fazio Maruca, Regina (1994). "The right way to go global: Interview with the Whirlpool CEO David Whitman," *Harvard Business Review*, 72, March–April, pp. 135–145.
2. Steinmetz, Greg and Carl Quintanilla (1998) "Tough target," *Wall Street Journal Europe*, 16, 50, p. 1.
3. William Davidson Institute (1994). "Whirlpool Tatramat, a.s." (Ann Arbor, MI: William Davidson Institute, University of Michigan School of Business Administration), mimeo.
4. Whirlpool Corporation (1996). *Annual Report 1996* (Benton Harbor, MI: Whirlpool Corporation).
5. —— (1998a). *Annual Report 1997* (Benton Harbor, MI: Whirlpool Corporation), p. 4.
6. —— (1998b). *Vision*, 1 (2) (March–April).
7. —— (1999). *Annual Report 1998* (Benton Harbor, MI: Whirlpool Corporation).

Small Businesses and International Entrepreneurship: Overcoming Barriers and Finding Opportunities

Learning Objectives

After reading this chapter you should be able to:

- Understand the basic definitions of small business and entrepreneurship.

- Explain how small businesses can begin as global start-ups or follow the stages of internationalization.

- Understand how small businesses can overcome barriers to internationalization.

- Identify when a small business or entrepreneur should consider going international.

- Understand how small businesses or entrepreneurs can find customers, partners, or distributors abroad.

- Understand how new venture wedge strategies can be used in foreign markets.

- Understand factors driving entrepreneurship at an international level.

Preview CASE IN POINT

A Boom in Small Businesses Going Global

Colite International Ltd. is a U.S. company that makes signs for businesses. In 1992, brothers Martin and Peter Brown bought a South Carolina local operation (they were the only employees) with little international experience. As one brother noted regarding going international: "No one else in our business was even thinking about it at the time." However, in 1996 when Lucent Technologies needed signs for its international operations, Colite got the contract and installed signs in 22 countries. "We had at least been to some of the countries and had enough contacts to get the signs installed," the brothers noted. By the early 2000s, they had more than $10 million a year in business with 55 employees in 80 countries. Nearly 30 percent of revenue comes from international sources.

How do they outcompete larger international rivals? The Brown brothers say they use speed, technology, and the Web to beat the competition. They take digital pictures of a customer's signs. They change the design and then post the design on their web site (http://www.colite.com) for the customer's approval. This process takes just 24 hours, and they deliver the signs within four weeks, beating the industry average of 10 weeks. They use a network of informal strategic alliances with foreign sign companies to do local installations following Colite's procedures and to provide local attention to customer needs.

Colite also launched an outdoor advertising company, Colite Outdoor, in 1999. Colite Outdoor provides billboard services primarily to the Latin American market. It has operations in Panama, Costa Rica, Guatemala, El Salvador, Nicaragua, and Honduras. Among its many clients, Colite has designed signs for companies such as Coca-Cola, Nestle, Exxon, FedEx, McDonald's, Shell, and 3M.

Colite is typical of the boom in exporting by small U.S. companies. One survey estimated that companies with fewer than 500 employees account for more than 30 percent of U.S. export dollars and represent 90 percent of the number of exporters.

Sources: Based on Barry, Doug. 2000. "From Appalachia to India: U.S. small businesses are going global." Business Credit 102, 6: pp. 49–50; Colite International. 2006. http://www. colite.com; Johnson, Derek. 2001. "Colite International's secrets." Signs of the Times, April; Lynch, Lorna. 2001. "The globalization model for 2001." Office.com; McClenahen, John S. 2000. "Global gold." Industry Week 249, 12: pp. 71–76.

Small businesses contribute significantly to most national economies. The Preview Case in Point shows the growing influence of smaller U.S. companies in the international market. Even in the developed nations of Europe, North America, and Japan, more than 98 percent of all businesses are small. In these countries, small businesses employ more than 50 percent of the workforce and produce nearly 50 percent of the countries' GNPs. During the recent periods of downsizing by large firms in the United States, small companies created more than two-thirds of the new jobs.[1] How important are small businesses to the U.S. economy? Consider the following facts regarding small businesses in the United States:[2]

- Small businesses represent 99.7 percent of all employing firms, employing about half of all private employees.
- Small businesses generate about 60 to 80 percent of all new jobs annually.
- Small businesses generate 13 to 14 times more patents per employee than larger firms.
- Small businesses employ almost 41 percent of all high-tech workers.
- Small businesses represent 97 percent of identified exporters, producing 28.6 percent of export value in 2004.

Given the importance of small businesses to the growth of national economies and to the increasing globalization of business, it is not surprising that small businesses seek opportunities outside their national boundaries—just as their larger brothers and sisters do. When going international, small businesses can use the same participation strategies and multinational strategies available to larger businesses. They can export, form a joint venture, license, and engage in FDI. Small businesses can also act like multidomestic strategists in product adaptation or develop transnational networks for supply, manufacturing, and distribution. In Korea, for example, small businesses account for approximately 40 percent of exports and 65 percent of Korean manufacturing FDI.[3]

Because they are small and often controlled by the entrepreneur or founder, small businesses face some circumstances different from those of larger multinational corporations. This chapter presents examples and reviews the barriers small businesses face and must overcome in internationalization. It also shows how some basic entrepreneurial strategies can serve small businesses in taking their products or services to the global marketplace. Topics covered in the chapter include defining the nature of a small business and an entrepreneur, identifying how small businesses go international—from global start-ups to the following stages of internationalization—identifying how small businesses break the barriers to internationalization, and the strategies companies can use to find international markets and to succeed in new international ventures.

What is a Small Business?

There are many definitions of what makes a "small" business. The United
Nations and Organization for Economic Cooperation and Development
(OECD) define small- and medium-sized businesses as those having fewer than
500 employees.[4] The popular press usually considers small businesses as those
with fewer than 100 employees. The U.S. Small Business Administration has a
more complex definition. The definition of small varies by industry and uses
both sales revenue and the number of people as indicators of size. For example,
to be classified as small by the U.S. Small Business Administration, annual receipts cannot exceed $17 million in the general construction industry but may
range up to $22 million in wholesale trade industries. In manufacturing in-
dustries, the maximum number of employees for small businesses ranges between 500 and 1,500, depending on specific industry.[5]

Internationalization
and the Small Business

How do small businesses go international? This section examines two ways by
which small businesses enter the international arena. First, some organizations
go international by following stages of international involvement. Each stage
leads to a greater involvement in international business. Second, organizations
can begin as global companies. They start international operations at the same
time they start domestic operations. The incremental view of internationalization for the small business is called the **small-business stage model**. Going global
from day one of the company's life is called a **global start-up** or **born-global firm**.
The next sections discuss these two processes of small-business internationalization in more detail.

The Small-Business Stage Model of Internationalization

The traditional view of small-business internationalization follows the stage model.
That is, small companies take an incremental approach to internationalization.
Such companies begin as passive exporters, filling international orders but not
actively seeking international sales. It is typically assumed that these companies
consider exporting only after they have a strong domestic base.[6] However, later,
the company may add an export department or an international division, with a
more proactive approach to international sales. Joint ventures and other forms of
direct investment follow. The stage model probably applies to the majority of
small-business efforts at internationalization. Most, but not all small businesses, do
not have the managerial and financial resources for immediate globalization.

The typical stages of internationalization for a small entrepreneurial business
include:[7]

- *Stage 1—Passive exporting:* The company fills international orders but does not
  seek export business. At this stage, many small-business owners do not realize
  that they have an international market.

- *Stage 2—Export management:* The CEO or a designated manager specifically
  seeks export sales. Because of resource limitations, most small businesses at
  this stage rely on the indirect channel of exporting (see Chapter 5). However,
  this stage is often a major change in orientation for the entrepreneur or small-
  business manager. Exporting is seen as an opportunity for new business.

- *Stage 3—Export department:* The company uses significant resources to seek increased sales from exporting. Managers no longer see exporting as a prohibitive risk. The key for most small businesses is finding a good local partner for distribution.

- *Stage 4—Sales branches:* When demand for the company's product is high in a country or region, it justifies setting up local sales offices. Small businesses must have the resources to transfer home managers to expatriate assignments or to hire and train local managers and workers to run these operations.

- *Stage 5—Production abroad:* Production moves a company beyond downstream value-chain activities. It allows companies to gain local advantages such as easy local product adaptation or production efficiencies. Companies may use licensing, joint ventures, or direct investment. This is often a very difficult stage for a small business because the cost of a failed direct investment can put the whole company at risk for survival.

- *Stage 6—The transnational:* Small size does not preclude a business from developing a globally integrated network that characterizes the transnational corporation. As we will see, some entrepreneurs begin their small businesses as transnationals.

Many small and some large companies find the deliberate process of internationalization by stages adequate for their strategic situation. Following the stage model allows companies to minimize their exposure to risk and develop their international expertise gradually. In contrast, other entrepreneurial companies have products that often require them to go international immediately or to move rapidly through the internationalization stages. In the next section, we discuss the growing phenomenon of global start-ups to show how rapidly some beginning businesses become global operations.

Small-Business Global Start-Up or Born-Global Firms

Global start-ups occur when companies begin as multinational companies. Impossible? Not in today's international marketplace. The Multinational Management Challenge on page 332 shows how one company was able to go global from its founding.

Global start-ups require unique conditions and organizations. One viewpoint argues that six key elements favor global start-ups.[8] Not surprisingly, these elements are similar to the globalization forces that favor transnational companies of all sizes. They include:

- *Dispersed human resources:* Conditions favor global start-ups when key skills exist in different locations throughout the world. To tap these human resources, companies must locate wherever the best and cheapest skills are found.

- *International sources of venture capital:* Conditions favor global start-ups when entrepreneurs have sources of capital from within their native country and from sources in other countries. When a company has a global presence, it can move quickly to the most available and cheapest sources of funds.

- *The existence of a global demand:* Conditions favor global start-ups when demand for the product or service exists in many countries. The existence of global demand was a key driving factor for Surftech, discussed in the foregoing Multinational Management Challenge, to go global immediately on founding.

- *The lack of a geographically protected market:* Conditions favor global start-ups if the flow of information and communication breaks down barriers of

Multinational Management **Challenge**

Can You Go Global from Day One? Surftech Did.

Surftech is a small manufacturer of molded surfboards. Fifty-year-old entrepreneur Larry French has turned his passion into a transnational business.

With boards that cost around $800, Surftech targets the high end of the surfing market. However, its boards are manufactured in molds unlike the typical high-end product, which is handcrafted and shaped by skilled artisans. After demonstrating that his boards could perform equally as well as the handmade versions, French convinced 25 of the top shapers in the world to make molds for his products. With an innovative manufacturing process and top designers in hand, he needed a production platform that could produce the boards in quantity. Like many transnational cousins, he found it—not in his native California, but in Thailand with a company skilled in producing sailboards.

Designers (shapers) from around the world produce a master. Then a mold is built, and four months later, boards ship from Thailand to warehouses in the United States (Florida, Hawaii, and California), Australia, Japan, New Zealand, and the United Kingdom.

Surftech sold only 75 boards during its first year of business. However, French consistently pursued the world's top surfers. The company now has the endorsement of most of these individuals and expects to sell between 18,000 and 20,000 boards in 2006.

"It's funny," French says. "We're running a sophisticated global business, but we're probably earning as much as the corner 7-Eleven. It's just not a business where you can have a machine churning out 200 parts an hour."

Sources: Based on Pitta, Julie. 2003. "Kowabunga! A surfin' safari supply chain." http://www.worldtrademag.com; Surftech. 2006. http://www.surftech.com

---

geography and allows competitors from other nations to imitate a new venture. Companies must go global immediately to gain a foothold in competitors' domestic markets.

- *The necessity of worldwide sales to support the venture:* Conditions favor global start-ups when no one market can produce sufficient sales to support the business. A company may capture near total market share in its domestic market but still not have sufficient sales revenue to survive. High-tech businesses with large R&D expenses often require the large sales of global markets to offset the cost of the R&D investment.

- *The potential to avoid later resistance to internationalization:* Conditions support global start-ups when it is easier to begin globally than to change to global later. All organizations develop a history and culture that, if initially successful, inhibit later change. Domestic success may squelch an entrepreneurial spirit and lead to missed international opportunities later in the organization's life.

How do companies following the traditional internationalization stages compare with born-global firms? Exhibit 7.1 shows some of the major differences on key aspects.

Although a global start-up is not always possible for a new venture, when the conditions are right, the global start-up represents an increasingly popular choice for many new companies. Although all entrepreneurial ventures are risky, global start-ups are more risky than domestic ventures. Nevertheless, even with the increased risk and complexity of immediately going international,

EXHIBIT **7.1** **Comparison of Traditional Internationalization Firms and Born-Global Firms**

Dimension/Attribute	Traditional Internationalization Stage Firm	Born-Global Firm
Managerial vision	Global from founding	International market developed after solid domestic market base
Previous global experience	Significant among founders	Low degree of previous global experience
Networking	Strong use of personal and business networks at both domestic and international level	Looser network with only foreign distributors playing a key role in internationalization efforts
International market knowledge	High from founding of firm	Low and slowly accumulating based on domestic market knowledge
Degree of innovation	High, though product differentiation based on leading-edge technology and technological innovativeness	Less innovative approach
Nature of international strategy	Niche-oriented and proactive international strategy to gain market share in key markets around the world	Broader market approach and more reactive strategic approach
Nature of relationship with foreign customers	Strong customer orientation and close or direct customer relationships	Indirect relationships through intermediaries at early stages of internationalization

Source: Based on Rialp, Alex, Josep Rialp, David Urbano, and Yancy Vaillant. 2005. "The born-global phenomenon: A comparative case study research." *Journal of International Entrepreneurship* 3: pp. 133–171.

global start-ups may offer the only avenue of success for new ventures in rapidly globalizing industries.[9]

Small-Business E-Commerce

To a large extent, technology has helped to level the playing field for small companies. Today, a small business in rural Maine can export machine parts to 38 countries, using the Internet. A woman in Mississippi can export food products to Canada. Handcrafted bowls from Colorado can be sold in Japan.[10]

Regardless of whether a small business uses a stage development model or a global start-up model of going international, a web site configured for e-commerce is a low cost and quick way to sell products across national borders. Chapter 10 provides a longer treatment of the challenges associated with cross-boarder e-commerce. However, some of the major benefits and challenges are listed below.[11] The Multinational Management Brief on page 335 regarding Internet Innovations for Small Businesses provides examples of strategic Internet use by small firms.

Advantages

- Ability of small firms to compete with other companies both locally, nationally, and internationally
- Possibility and opportunity for more diverse people to start a business
- Convenient and easy way of doing business transactions (not restricted to certain hours of operation; open 24 hours a day, seven days a week)

- An inexpensive way (compared to the cost of paper, printing, and postage prior to the Internet) for small business to compete with larger companies
- Makes domestic products available in other countries
- Small businesses, at least in the United States, that utilize the Internet have higher revenues, averaging $3.79 million compared to $2.72 million overall (IDC research).

Challenges

- Managing upgrades (anticipating business needs/application)
- Managing upgrades in several languages
- Managing shipping and returns
- Assuring security for a web site and the back-end integration with existing company system
- Avoiding being a victim of fraudulent activities online
- Receiving international payments
- Costs required to maintain the site
- Finding and retraining qualified employees

How important is e-commerce to small businesses? Consider the case of New Zealand and the organized efforts to improve electronic services to help small business. The government acknowledges the importance of small businesses to its economy, and it also realizes that having an e-commerce business strategy can go a long way helping small businesses. In 2001, the New Zealand government launched an e-government strategy to assist small businesses with respect to their information technology needs.[12] For instance, the government has created various web sites to provide core information, such as regulations and other information crucial to the development of small businesses. The web site can also serve as an online consultation tool where, for example, a small company can request guidance from a web site consultant regarding what policies or regulations should be considered when entering a new business area. The web site also allows local government or authorities to assist small businesses with respect to innovation. They can provide access to already developed intellectual property or other infrastructures at much lower costs.[13]

However, in spite of the expanding opportunities for small businesses to internationalize, there remain psychological and resource-related barriers. The next section reviews some of the obstacles that often prevent small businesses from going international, either by stages or by global start-ups.

Overcoming Small-Business Barriers to Internationalization

Conventional wisdom argues that small businesses face many barriers that retard their becoming multinational companies. Small size often means limited financial and personnel resources to dedicate to international activities. Small size can also mean a lack of sufficient scale to produce goods or services as efficiently as larger companies. Small companies often have top managers with limited international experience. These managers may have

Multinational Management **Brief**

Internet Innovations for Small Businesses

- ***Small business innovators use the Internet to leverage existing businesses and add value.***

  Owners use the Web to build an existing business. For example, by dramatizing the message, "We're not really selling boats—we're selling a lifestyle," a boat builder stimulates insurance sales and participation in regattas (*http://www.sumerset.com*).

- ***Small business innovators use the Internet and software to revamp the value chain.***

  Creative Woodworking, a high-tech woodworking operation based in Colorado, uses Internet technology to boost production capacity and efficiency. The company uses a variety of software to automate production while also using CAD/CAM models to help clients visualize products.

- ***Small business innovators use the power of the keyword search to reach distant markets with niche products.***

  Niche businesses like *http://www.dogbooties.com* gain visibility through the Internet that would be difficult to achieve any other way. The company *http://www.casketfurniture.com* offers "…entertainment centers that can be promptly converted into coffins, usually by just removing the shelves" (Business Week 2001). Taking a low-fat cookie onto a web site brought in $800,000 in combined retail and direct sales (*http://www.nopudge.com*) (U.S. Small Business Administration 2001). Dogbooties.com (*http://www.dogbooties.com*) reaches customers worldwide for the company's niche product, booties and other products for sled dogs or for any dogs that have tender paws that need protection from the cold or that simply have owners who want them to appear stylish. This may not seem to be a product that many people need, but actually the business has competitors such as REI, a major sporting-goods chain.

- ***Innovators make imaginative use of the Internet's visual capabilities.***

  Entrepreneurs market real estate, bed and breakfast rooms, and their designs for custom fireplaces using streaming video to give "you are there" virtual tours (*http://www.callelizabeth.com, http://www.innaccess.com/view, http://www.dukefire.com*). Or they post construction photos that allow customers to catch production errors before they become serious, which results in cost savings for the business.

Source: Sampson William. 2006. "Software gives small shop the edge." CabinetMaker. February 20, 2: pp. 30–35; Pratt Joanne H. 2002. E-Biz: Strategies for Small Business Success. Washington, DC: U.S. Small Business Administration Office of Advocacy, p. 22.

negative attitudes toward becoming multinational. Such managers view international ventures as too risky and not potentially profitable. Negative managerial attitudes and past success at home lead to organizational cultures with a strong domestic orientation.

Although many barriers to internationalization seem internal, small businesses also have to face contextual and other environmental issues that also magnify difficulties pertaining to international operations. These difficulties are even more salient in many of the emerging markets in Central and Eastern Europe. Consider the following Focus on Emerging Markets.

Focus on Emerging Markets

Small Business Barriers in the Transitional Economies In Central and Eastern Europe

Small businesses face significant barriers when going international. However, these barriers are even more challenging when they try to take advantage of emerging markets. In interviews with Australian small businesses involved in markets in Central and Eastern Europe, Freeman and Reid[14] identified the following major constraints, which are often outside of the control of these small businesses.

- *Geographic distance:* The strongest constraint facing small business owners in Australia was the geographic distance from their markets in Poland and the Czech Republic. Unlike larger firms that have more managers to send to negotiate or manage foreign operations, smaller businesses often rely on a few individuals who have to travel more often. Having to travel frequently to meet geographically dispersed partners can take a toll on the small business.

- *Lack of Central and Eastern European managers with decision-making authority:* Small businesses in Australia often had to deal with the existing Central and Eastern European staff's inability to make decisions. Such slow decisions can be very costly since time is critical for smaller businesses.

- *Psychic Distance:* Small businesses often have a hard time understanding local market conditions and the local culture and business etiquette. For example, they may not have access to training and other resources to gain such market and cultural knowledge. This is even more significant given that most of the interviewees in the study agreed that a small business will likely fail if no effort is made to understand and adapt to such differences.

- *Central and Eastern European middle managers' mindsets:* Although larger companies may be able to hire middle managers, train them, and wait until they acquire modern management techniques, many smaller businesses have to contend with middle managers who have worked under communism for many years. It is very challenging for small businesses to do well with such managers.

- *Finding reliable suppliers:* Small businesses often find it challenging to locate local suppliers. Decades of state-owned enterprises have not encouraged private enterprises to flourish. These small businesses face the challenge of having to find committed suppliers. Dealings with such suppliers and distributors can be difficult and sometimes unethical.

- *Bureaucracy and Regulations:* Small businesses also have to face the challenge of understanding and addressing governmental regulations and bureaucracy. While larger companies may have the resources to address such issues easily, smaller companies often have to contend with government regulations that have not changed much to address the needs of a market-based economy.

Source: Based Freeman, Susan, and Imogen Reid. 2006. "Constraints facing small Western firms in transitional markets." European Business Review 18, 3: pp. 187–213.

In spite of these difficulties with internationalization, many small businesses aggressively enter international markets and succeed. Next, we consider some of the barriers to internationalization and examples of how small businesses and entrepreneurs have overcome these barriers to achieve successful multinational operations.

Developing a Small-Business Global Culture

A **global culture** occurs when an organization has managerial and worker values that view strategic opportunities as global and not just domestic. At all levels of the organization, members share a common language to describe international operations. This common language gives organizational members a framework to interpret and understand their company's actions in the international arena.[15]

Generally, increased international competition and exposure to international markets have forced larger companies, such as those in the automobile industry, to develop more of a global culture. Survival made it necessary for top executives of all nationalities to respond to global competition.

Smaller businesses, however, often ignore international opportunities because key decision makers and the culture of their organizations view competition only as domestic. In a true global culture, entrepreneurial owners develop a global mindset for themselves and their companies. Thinking globally permeates everything that happens in the company. People believe that national boundaries are less relevant. They also believe that the company can do business and conduct value-chain operations (e.g., R&D, manufacturing, raising capital) anywhere in the world.

Several characteristics of the key decision makers in an organization affect the development of a global culture.[16] These include:

- *Perceived psychic distance to foreign markets:* This represents the extent to which managers believe that foreign markets are "just too different" for involvement. As the earlier Focus on Emerging Markets feature illustrated, Australian small businesses found the psychic distance from the Central and European markets to be a significant constraint.[17] However, when key managers overcome this belief, a global culture is more likely to develop.

- *International experience:* Managers with little training in foreign languages and little international travel often resist internationalization. However, managers with previous international experiences, even just personal travel and sightseeing, have a greater propensity to recognize global opportunities. Often even a chance meeting during a foreign vacation can trigger an international small-business venture.

- *Risk aversion:* Managers who are unwilling to take risks have difficulty supporting internationalization of the firm. Going international requires an entrepreneurial spirit and thus the willingness to face risks.

- *Overall attitudes toward international strategies:* Some managers just find the idea of international strategies too dangerous to the status quo. Others see international opportunities as beneficial to the company and to their careers. A global culture will develop when the owner/entrepreneur promotes company values that support and reward looking for international opportunities.

Furthermore, as Exhibit 7.1 showed, born-global firms likely have global cultures. In such companies, the founders or top managers already have very high levels of international experience.[18] They use that experience to influence all facets of operations. They are committed to internationalization and have a proactive international strategy where they readily apply learning across the various markets in which they are involved. Those companies with a global

Global culture

Managerial and worker values that view strategic opportunities as global and not just domestic.

culture and key decision makers that view the world as an opportunity will more likely become multinational companies. The Case in Point below shows how the international experience of the CEO helped one organization overcome the lack of a global culture.

Changing Attitudes of Key Decision Makers

Both the stage model and the global start-up model focus on the attitudes of the primary decision makers as key to the development of an international culture in small- or medium-sized businesses. For companies that internationalize their business through stages, each stage demonstrates the key executives' increasing commitment to internationalization.

Early in internationalization, managers perceive foreign markets as risky, with high costs to enter and low potential benefits. Because of these negative attitudes toward internationalization, most international sales for small- and medium-sized businesses come from countries that are close in culture and in geography. For example, most Canadian companies begin exporting first to their geographically and culturally similar neighbor to the south. These cautious moves to increase internationalization help top managers overcome initial skepticism regarding international markets. In later stages of internationalization, these attitudes change, with the international market often perceived as being more profitable than the domestic market.[19] Exhibit 7.2 shows that exporters and nonexporters in the U.S. industrial-equipment industry have quite different attitudes regarding internationalization.

Positive attitudes toward international markets are perhaps more necessary for global start-ups than for companies that move slowly into the global marketplace. Experts[20] argue that successful global start-ups require the founders to communicate a global vision to everyone in the organization. Managers use their global vision to help their companies become multinational from birth.

C A S E   I N   P O I N T

A Transnational Strategy Takes a Small Company to the *BusinessWeek* 1000

Dennis Gillings was chief executive of a four-year-old pharmaceutical research company with one U.S. location and only thirty-five employees. Gillings, however, had an international mindset. Raised in England but managing a U.S. business, he saw the unified EU market as a great opportunity for his company. Gillings reasoned that if he started European operations early in the unified EU, he would have a tremendous competitive advantage.

When Gillings proposed a European office for his four-year-old company, he now recalls, "Everyone within the company thought I was verging on crazy." He had an international mindset, but his company did not. To develop an international culture, he started cautiously. Gillings visited 30 prospective European customers before lining up sufficient work to open the London office. Within five years, Gillings' company, Quintiles Corp., had offices in five countries.

To develop a more international culture, Quintiles Corp. starts an operation with expatriate managers. However, the firm hires local managers as soon as possible to take advantage of local contacts. Quintiles uses a sophisticated electronic communication system to keep everyone in touch. Beginning as a small U.S. professional service business, Quintiles Corp. is the global leader of pharmaceutical services, a fast-growing *BusinessWeek* 1000 company with more than 16,000 employees in over 50 countries.

Source: Based on Quintiles Transnational Corp. 2006. http://www.quintiles.com; Mangelsdorf, Martha E. 1993. "Building a transnational company." Inc. Online. Archive/Doc. No. 03930921.

EXHIBIT **7.2**
Attitudinal Differences Concerning Internationalization for Small-Business Exporters and Nonexporters

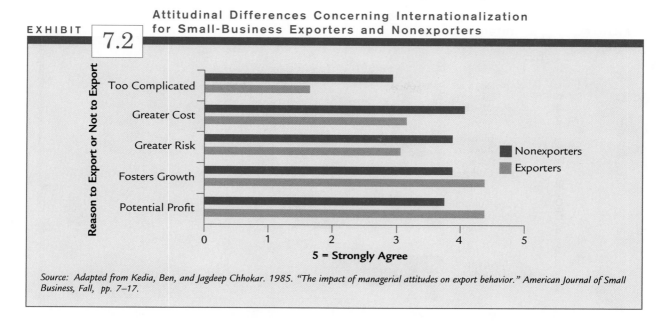

Source: Adapted from Kedia, Ben, and Jagdeep Chhokar. 1985. "The impact of managerial attitudes on export behavior." American Journal of Small Business, Fall, pp. 7–17.

Gaining Experience: Duties and the Personal Life of the Small-Business CEO

The effects of internationalization on the personal life and duties of the CEO may play a more important role in the international activities of small- and medium-sized companies than in larger firms. The owner of a small business is often the CEO and the driving entrepreneurial force in the business. Running a small business is already extremely time-consuming and challenging for small businesses involved only in the domestic market.[21] However, internationalization demands significantly more commitment, and when internationalization affects this individual, it threatens the whole underlying fabric of the organization.[22]

For a small firm, opening new markets is often the CEO's personal responsibility. Although small-company CEOs spend only 20 percent of their time managing export and other international functions, the CEO must be willing to incur more than economic costs for the venture.[23] There are social and business costs to the CEO who engages in internationalization. The CEO's responsibilities for the new international venture often result in increased travel and stress from undertaking a new venture. Many CEOs feel that these activities adversely affect family life. They also dislike being away from the daily management of their businesses.[24]

In addition, the job of the small-business CEO may change when the company becomes multinational. A study of Canadian manufacturers that had recently begun exporting found that more than 50 percent of the CEOs felt that their duties had changed since going international. The impact seemed to affect CEOs more than their workers. Only slightly more than 20 percent of the employees in the same companies had their jobs restructured and needed retraining due to the firms' international business.[25]

As new multinational managers, the Canadian CEOs also believed that they needed skill upgrading for international business. Exhibit 7.3 shows key skills that the CEOs felt they needed.

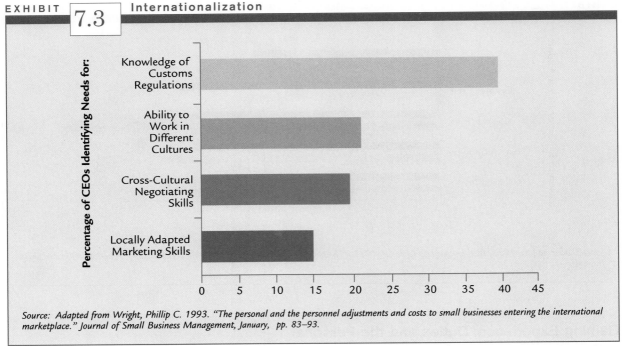

Source: Adapted from Wright, Phillip C. 1993. "The personal and the personnel adjustments and costs to small businesses entering the international marketplace." Journal of Small Business Management, January, pp. 83–93.

Is Size a Barrier for Small-Business Internationalization?

Larger firms have a greater tendency to enter export markets. They have more resources to absorb the risk of exporting and often have a greater incentive to export when domestic markets become saturated.[26] Furthermore, as we discussed earlier in the Emerging Markets Feature, larger firms have other advantages, such as having access to more qualified individuals who have the ability to negotiate with geographically dispersed partners.[27] In contrast, smaller businesses often have to rely on the same individuals involved in grueling travel. Larger firms also have more resources to invest in cross-cultural training to better understand the countries in which they operate and the local business and national culture. Such training tends to be less likely for smaller firms with limited resources.

Many academic researchers and small-business managers thus argue that only larger companies have the resources to become multinationals.[28] In fact, most studies find that the larger the business, the more likely the firm exports its products.[29] Even among those firms that do export, larger firms tend toward committed exporting while smaller firms tend toward passive exporting. Larger firms also serve more national markets. For example, one study of Canadian firms found that companies with total sales of more than $50 million exported on average to 27 while smaller firms averaged only slightly more than 12 countries.[30]

The above statistics show that small companies do suffer from the **liabilities of smallness.** Compared to larger firms, smaller firms find it more challenging to obtain and secure the necessary resources they need to internationalize. Furthermore, this liability of smallness also can inflate the **liabilities of foreignness** and **liabilities of newness.** [31] The liabilities of foreignness refer to the disadvantages associated with competing with local firms that are more familiar with the local context and have better local connections. The liabilities

Liabilities of smallness

The challenges facing small businesses in getting access to necessary resources to internationalize.

Liabilities of foreignness

Challenges facing small companies due to lack of knowledge of local market.

Liabilities of newness

A large percentage of new businesses fail within a year.

of newness refer to the operational challenges associated with starting a new business. These include issues such as financing, recruiting new employees, and marketing the product.

However, the liabilities of smallness may exist only in the initial internationalization decision. That is, larger size makes it easier for a company to begin exporting or direct investment. But once firms choose to take on an international venture, experts suggest that the international sales intensity of small firms equals or may even exceed that of larger firms.[32] **International sales intensity** represents the amount of international sales divided by the total sales of the company. Once involved in international ventures, small multinational companies often gain sales revenues proportionally equal to or greater than those of larger multinational companies.[33]

The study of Canadian firms discussed earlier[34] also shows how small multinational firms can outperform larger companies on international sales intensity. The researchers found that smaller companies using foreign direct investment produced more than 68 percent of their revenues from foreign sales compared to 48 percent for larger firms with similar investments. Similarly, smaller exporting firms were as likely as larger exporting firms to generate about one-third of their revenues from exporting.[35]

International sales intensity
Amount of international sales divided by total sales of the company.

Using the Small-Business Advantage

In spite of some barriers to internationalization, the small business has some advantages over larger and often more entrenched organizations. In fact, the trend-spotting author of *The Global Paradox,* John Naisbitt, predicts that small multinational businesses will have even greater advantages in the increasingly global economy. He argues that small companies can change products and internal operations faster to take advantage of evolving technologies. In contrast, larger organizations often must overcome extensive bureaucratic procedures when adopting new products or new management operations. The bureaucratic procedures of larger organizations slow down decision making, often leading to missed opportunities in the global marketplace.

For the small business, speed becomes the **small-business advantage.** When larger companies are slow to react to rapidly changing conditions, fast-moving entrepreneurs can use their competitive advantage of speed. Being first to market, they can capture significant sales before the larger competitors can react.[36] The small-business advantage is particularly important for the multinational company because, increasingly, the global economy requires fast change to take advantage of new markets.

Small-business advantage
Fast-moving entrepreneurs can use their competitive advantage of speed. Being first to market, they can capture significant sales before larger competitors react.

The Future: Falling Barriers to Multinational Small Businesses and More Global Start-Ups

Many of the barriers to small-business internationalization are becoming easier to overcome. Government programs that support small-business exporting and sales are expanding. High-impact trade agreements such as NAFTA and the WTO make trade less complex and reduce the resource requirements that previously held back many smaller firms. The rapid growth of international business information produced by governments and other sources such as the World Wide Web provide a wealth of readily available information to entrepreneurs regarding international opportunities. The Internet makes the world a click away. In turn, this knowledge of international business opportunities encourages more entrepreneurs to consider global start-ups and makes it easier for established small businesses to become multinationals.

The increase in the number of small businesses engaged in international activities also makes it easier for other businesses to develop a global culture. Now, potential international entrepreneurs not only have a better knowledge of business opportunities abroad but also can copy the cultures of other successful small multinational companies. In addition, as more managers gain experience in international business, negative attitudes among small-business owners and entrepreneurs toward international sales will decrease.

As shown, going international should become easier for the small firm. In fact, many experts suggest that the only way a small firm can survive and grow is by going international. Consider that exporting, the first phase in internationalization, can bring several important long-term advantages for the small business.[37] Exporting allows the small firm to increase sales volumes and income, thereby providing much needed cash flow to the firm. However, more important, exporting allows the small firm to better understand global markets through a better understanding of new cultures and the development of new contacts. Such activities can help the small firm's future foray into new markets and also can help the company become more competitive. Consider the Case in Point regarding SC Solar.

Although the barriers to small-business internationalization may be falling and there are significant benefits to going international, managers still need to assess whether their firm is ready to go international. The next section provides a series of diagnostic questions that can help small-business owners and managers make the internationalization decision. The following section describes how small businesses can make the contacts with customers and potential partners necessary to succeed in foreign sales.

When Should a Small Business Go International?

The small business must respond to many of the same questions as the larger business when considering multinational options. However, the limited number

---

C A S E   I N   P O I N T

SC Solar

From the day it was founded, SC Solar faced a very competitive market. The U.S. market has a glut of companies producing solar technology products, making it very difficult for companies to survive. Furthermore, a large percentage of demand for products using solar power comes from overseas markets, and the barriers to entry into these international markets are very high.

How did SC Solar deal with these challenges? The company realized that the only way to survive is to innovate and take advantage of international opportunities. The company started integrating solar technology into other products such as lighting systems, traffic management systems, and other related products. It also worked closely with U.S. Commercial Services and the South Carolina Export Consortium to identify and take advantage of international markets.

SC Solar's entry into the international market has been very successful. The company quadrupled its annual revenues with a very aggressive growth approach, most of which came from the international market. Furthermore, the company's long-term outlook seems very bright as the demand for solar-powered products continues to grow because of high energy costs due to high oil and gas prices.

Source: Based on Hilton, Gregory. 2005. "Knocking down export barriers to smaller firms." Business and Economic Review. July–September 51, 4: pp. 18–20.

of products or services—and the limited resources—of most small businesses make certain drivers of internationalization more important for them.

Affirmative answers to the following questions suggest that a small business is ready to become a multinational company.

- *Do we have a global product or service?* A global product or service can be sold worldwide with minimal changes for each country. Since small businesses seldom have the resources to adapt each product to local needs, producing a standard worldwide product makes globalization easier. As discussed in Chapter 6, if customers have similar needs, or customers seek a product or service from anywhere in the world, then there exists a greater opportunity for globalization.[38]

- *Do we have the managerial, organizational, and financial resources to internationalize?* Internationalization, even with the more simple participation strategies, requires significant availability of financial and personnel resources. Exhibit 7.4 gives some of the questions concerning resource requirements that a small business facing the prospect of going international needs to address.

- *Even if we do have the resources, are we willing to commit those resources and face the risks of internationalization?* Small-business managers must view internationalization as similar to other start-up ventures. For the right company, with the right products, the eventual returns from a new international venture may exceed the investment and make the exposure to risk worthwhile. To seek

EXHIBIT **7.4**

Questions to Consider in the Small-Business Decision to Go International

Management Objectives

- What is the reason for going international?
- How committed is top management to the internationalization decision?
- How quickly does management expect the internationalization effort to pay off?

Management Experience and Resources

- What in-house international expertise does the firm have (international sales experience, language capabilities, etc.)?
- Who will be responsible for the international organizational component of the company (e.g., export department)?
- How much senior management time should be allocated?
- What organizational structure is required?

Production Capacity

- How is the present capacity being used?
- Will international sales hurt domestic sales?
- What will be the cost of additional production at home or in a foreign location?
- What modifications of the product or service are required?

Financial Capacity

- What amount of capital can be committed to international production and marketing?
- What level of operating costs for international operations can be supported?
- What other financial requirements may compete with the internationalization efforts?
- By what date must the internationalization effort have positive returns?

Source: Adapted from U.S. Department of Commerce. 1998. Basic Guide to Exporting. Washington, D.C.: Government Printing Office.

these potential returns, managers must overcome the psychological and cultural boundaries already noted.

- *Is there a country in which we feel comfortable doing business?* Without the resources to understand the cultural and business practices in many countries, small-business managers often first seek international opportunities in national cultures similar to their own.

- *Is there a profitable market for our product or service?* Even with good products or services, a key question focuses on which countries to enter. For example, research by managers at Ekkwill Tropical Fish Farm indicated that collecting fish was a popular hobby in many countries. One-third of its production now goes to markets in Asia, Latin America, Canada, and the West Indies.[39]

- *Which country should we enter?* A thorough strategic analysis is required. Firms need to identify potential threats and opportunities by country. For example, current and future demand for a product may vary by country. Each country also has different competitors as well as different barriers to entry (e.g., tariffs, complex distribution systems). Exhibit 7.5 gives a summary of the steps that small businesses can follow to find customers abroad.

- *Do we have a unique product or service that is not easily copied by larger multinational companies or local entrepreneurs?* Although small firms may have the advantage of speed to market, large multinationals may use their advantage of economies of scale to imitate an innovation, using a lower-priced product. To maintain their competitive advantage over larger firms, small multinational companies must have rare resources (i.e., not easy to copy) and valuable

EXHIBIT **7.5**   **Steps in Picking a Foreign Market**

1. Screen Potential Markets

- Get statistics that show the extent of the relevant products exported to or produced in potential countries.
- Identify five to ten countries with large and fast-growing markets for the products. Examine the trends in the market in past years and different economic circumstances.
- Identify additional countries with smaller, newly emerging markets. These may provide first mover advantages.
- Target three to five of the most promising markets. Mix established markets with emerging markets, depending on management's tolerance for risk.

2. Assess Targeted Markets

- Examine market trends for company products or services and related products or services that could affect demand.
- Identify demographic trends (income, age, education, population, and so on) that identify the users of the company's products or services.
- Estimate the overall consumption of the product or service and the amounts provided by foreign and domestic producers.
- Identify sources of competition from domestic producers and other foreign competitors, including price, quality, features, and service.
- Identify local channels of distribution.
- Assess what modifications of the product or service are required.
- Identify cultural differences that may influence participation strategies available.
- Identify any foreign barriers to exporting or other participation options (tariffs, limitations on percentage of ownership, home-country export controls, etc.).
- Identify any foreign or home-country incentives to enter the market.

3. Draw Conclusions and Make the Choice

Source: Adapted from U.S. Department of Commerce. 1998. Basic Guide to Exporting. Washington, D.C.: Government Printing Office.

resources (factors that allow the company to produce a product or service valued by customers). These rare and valued resources may include technical superiority, innovation, or high quality. They give the company the muscle to produce continuously superior products or services.[40]

- *Do location advantages exist upstream in the value chain?* Internationalization of a small firm need not be just a downstream activity in the value chain, such as marketing. When there are advantages of lower cost or higher quality in supply or manufacturing, small multinational companies can seek the same location advantages available to larger companies by sourcing raw materials or manufacturing in other countries. For example, Northwest River Supply Corp., a small firm producing high-quality whitewater rafts in Moscow, Idaho, found significant cost advantages by manufacturing in Mexico. It could produce better-quality products with cheaper prices than its large-company competitors.

- *Can we afford not to be a multinational?* There are several factors, even for the small business, that may make becoming a multinational company necessary for survival. A shrinking home market may require a firm to internationalize to maintain sales revenue. Finding international sources of lower costs of raw material or production facilities may be necessary to match competitors' prices and maintain profit margins. Small multinational companies may find the positive image of being a multinational firm necessary for attracting new customers and attracting investors.

The next section reviews the use of different participation strategies for the small multinational company.

Getting Connected to the International Market

Participation Strategies

Small- and medium-sized multinational companies have the same participation options as do larger firms, including exporting, licensing, joint ventures, and foreign direct investment. Most often, however, the small business emphasizes exporting as its major international-participation strategy. For the small firm without knowledge of potential foreign customers or sufficient resources to set up an overseas sales office, indirect exporting makes the most sense. These firms use the services of ETCs or EMCs to get their products to the international market.

Among the various participation strategies, strategic alliances are also very popular. Consider the next Multinational Management Brief.

Finding Customers and Partners

To go international, small businesses must find ways to reach their foreign customers, either by direct contact or by teaming up with foreign partners (distributors, joint venture partners, or licensees) who deal with the ultimate customers. As with larger multinational companies, there is no set formula for finding partners or customers. Much depends on the nature of the product, the countries involved, and the nature and resources of the company involved. However, there are some standard techniques readily available to small multinational companies. In this section, we show some of these common **customer contact techniques**.

Customer contact techniques

Trade shows, catalog expositions, international advertising agencies and consulting firms, government-sponsored trade missions, and direct contact.

Multinational Management **Brief**

Small Businesses and International Joint Ventures

As discussed earlier in the chapter, small businesses face significant constraints in the form of the liabilities of smallness, liabilities of newness, and liabilities of foreignness. However, international joint ventures can help small companies overcomes these barriers when they enter international markets. In a study of 614 small Japanese businesses involved in 1,117 joint ventures in 43 countries, Lu and Beamish (2006) provide evidence of the benefits of international joint ventures to these small businesses. They find that having a local partner has a positive impact on the joint venture's profitability and also helps the Japanese businesses overcome some of the small-business constraints. Having a local partner provides the small Japanese firms with a primary source of local knowledge (overcoming liabilities of foreignness) and a partner that is already familiar with operations in that country (overcoming the liabilities of newness). The study also shows that the size of the partner had an impact on the longevity of the joint venture. Specifically, the findings show that the larger the size of the partner, the longer the joint venture lasts. This also points to the benefits of joint ventures in overcoming the liabilities of size by partnering with a much larger partner. However, larger partners also were more likely to exploit the smaller Japanese firms when the latter had low equity ownership in the joint venture.

Source: Based on Lu, Jane W., and Paul W. Beamish. 2006. "Partnering strategies and performance of SMEs' international joint ventures." Journal of Business Venturing 21: pp. 461–486.

- *Trade shows:* National and international trade shows give small businesses inexpensive mechanisms to contact potential customers or business partners. Trade shows give businesses the opportunity to set up displays of their products and to provide brochures and other documents that describe their product or service. Businesses may rent space at the shows individually or as part of a larger group. The U.S. Commerce Department now runs a virtual trade show and the web site offers constant access to U.S. suppliers and international buyers. The web site shows product descriptions, photos, and videos.[41]

- *Catalog expositions:* Catalog expositions are similar to trade shows except that a business does not have its product or people at the show. Rather, product catalogs, sales brochures, and other graphic presentations show a firm's goods or services at some site. Some U.S. embassies and consulates provide catalog expositions for U.S. goods. Because a company need only send printed matter, catalog expositions provide a low-cost way of testing international markets.

- *International advertising agencies and consulting firms:* International advertising agencies and consulting firms have offices throughout the world, often with specialists in different products or services. International advertising agencies can provide advertising and promotional services geared to a local national environment. Consulting firms often have a good knowledge of local regulations, local competitors, and local distribution channels. A business that uses these services can expect to pay significant compensation. However, local-market expertise and contacts may make the expenditure worthwhile.

- *Government-sponsored trade missions:* To foster growth in international trade, governments often sponsor trade missions. These missions represent companies or industries looking to open new markets in the countries visited. Host governments usually provide introductions to potential local sales representatives, distributors, and end users.

• *Direct contact:* Although it is often more difficult and costly, small-business entrepreneurs and managers can seek channel partners, joint-venture partners, and end users directly. If the managers/entrepreneurs can find key intermediaries—that is, potential alliance partners or distributors—or can get direct access to potential customers, then direct contact may work best.

Exhibit 7.6 shows some of the programs the U.S. government provides to businesses seeking international contacts or potential customers. Other countries provide similar services. Exhibit 7.7 shows some sources on the World Wide Web that any multinational company can access to find trade leads.

Ready to Go and Connected: A Synopsis

The forgoing sections provide the diagnostic questions a small-business person can use to decide when to take his or her business international. These questions focus first on whether a firm has the right products and adequate resources to go international. The questions then prompt the entrepreneur to consider the competition and the country environments where he or she hopes to do business.

EXHIBIT **7.6**   Selected U.S. Government Programs for Making International Contacts

Department of Commerce Contact Programs

➤ *Export contact list service:* provides mailing lists of foreign distributors, manufacturers, retailers, service firms, and government agencies.

➤ *Trade opportunities program (TOP):* provides sales leads from foreign firms that seek to buy or represent U.S. services or products.

➤ *Agent/distributor service (ADS):* a custom search service for U.S. exporters seeking foreign import agencies and distributors.

➤ *Commercial news USA (CNUSA):* provides an illustrated catalog and electronic bulletin boards available through U.S. embassies and consulates.

Department of Commerce Trade-Event Programs

➤ *Certified trade-fair program:* provides U.S. Department of Commerce assistance and support to trade-fair organizers who agree to give special assistance to small businesses and new-to-export businesses.

➤ *Foreign buyer program:* provides overseas promotional support for selected trade shows where U.S. businesses can meet potential foreign buyers, distributors, licensees, or joint-venture partners.

➤ *Matchmaker trade delegations:* organized and led by Department of Commerce personnel, these delegations introduce new-to-export and new-to-market firms to prescreened international prospects.

➤ *Trade missions:* similar to matchmaker delegations, these missions introduce U.S. makers and service providers to foreign contacts.

U.S. Department of Agriculture

➤ *Commodity and marketing programs:* provide businesses with data on consumption, trade, stocks, and marketing information on specific agricultural products.

➤ *High-value product services division:* provides trade shows, trade leads from overseas buyers with an interest in U.S. agricultural products, and free advertising of U.S. products overseas.

➤ *Trade assistance and planning (TAPO):* provides an information source for U.S. agricultural exporters.

Source: Adapted from U.S. Department of Commerce. 1998. Basic Guide to Exporting. Washington, D.C.: Government Printing Office.

EXHIBIT   7.7   International Trade Leads: A Web Sampler

International Import-Export Trade Leads

Tradeleadscenter.com is a brand new directory of import–export international trade leads. Directory helps you to find new partners worldwide. Trade Leads posting is free.

AfaceriOnline

AfaceriOnline is an international business-to-business marketplace that links buyers and sellers. Viewing of trade leads is by country and product.

AFRICA: MBendi - The African Trading Space

Hosted by the premier African business information site, trade inquiries posted can be searched by product and offer type. Companies wishing to buy or sell items can post and update trade inquiries. There is currently no charge to use this service but a fee-based subscription is required for e-mail notification.

B2BTradeholding

Trade leads from all over the world are posted on this web site. They are organized by category, but it is possible to search also by company names. Contact information as well as detailed products description is provided. A one-time fee of $24.95 (USD) is required to permanently list your company in the database.

Busytrade.com

Busytrade is a well-organized trade lead web site that offers a large amount of trade leads, products, company listings, and trade-show announcements. The site is easy to navigate through and offers both free and for-fee memberships.

EC21: Global B2B e-Marketplace

This global B2B portal brings together buyers, sellers, and trade organizations for international trade in the global marketplace by providing trade leads, company directories, and product catalogs. The site is also available in Chinese, Japanese, and Korean.

ecplaza.net

Ecplaza.net is a global B2B marketplace offering trade leads that include both offers to buy and sell. Product categories are diverse, and the site also publishes industry news and reports.

EUROPE: ECeurope.com

A business-to-business trading bulletin board that serves small- to medium-sized companies in accessing trade leads. Membership is required, but it is free.

FoodExnet

FoodExnet is a global B2B electronic marketplace offering trade leads in the food and beverages industry. This web site features an interactive platform where buyers and sellers can realize online trade activities.

fuzing.com

Fuzing.com is an international business trade web site that deals with trade leads for both finished goods and raw materials. Registration is required but is free to both buyers and suppliers.

Global Sources

Global Sources is a business-to-business media company that facilitates global trade, with a particular focus on the Chinese market, by providing information to international buyers and integrated marketing services to suppliers. Features search engine by product, supplier, or news. Free e-mail alerts are also available.

Global Trade Opportunities

From Global Trade Exchange, a site offering trade leads and a global trade directory. Offers to buy and sell are searchable by country and category using the Harmonized System (HS) Code categorization.

Go4WorldBusiness.com

The site connects businesses worldwide by providing information on buyers, suppliers, trade leads, and products.

NuDeal

NuDeal is a Canadian-based company that offers both local and international trade leads and company directory listings. Trade leads are sorted by category. Product catalogs and company listings are also available.

(continued)

EXHIBIT 7.7   International Trade Leads: A Web Sampler (continued)

International Buyer/Seller Connection
Publishes interests and needs from international buyers and sellers, including the company web site and contact details.

Trade Boss
Users can browse trade leads and company listings, but free registration is required to post information and to access trade lead and company details.

TradeGet.com
The site provides free information to international importers/buyers wanting to do business with pre-qualified exporters, manufacturers and suppliers. Product catalogs, exporters' directories, trade show listings, and market buy/sell services are offered. Free registration is required for some services.

Trade Opportunities Organisation
TradeOpportunities.com provides a database with information on buyers, suppliers, and trade opportunities worldwide.

TradeMatch
Through Tradematch, you can search for importers, exporters, or service providers doing business, or wanting to do business, in a specific region, on a specific product. Free registration is required.

TradeZone
TradeZone provides services for international trade, including trade leads and a trade bulletin board. The International Business Opportunities page provides access to a trade leads database for manufacturers, exporters, importers, trade services and opportunity seekers. Access to the database is free.

Wbiz.net
Wbiz.net is a trading place for exporters and importers. The site features business offers, product listings, and company directories. Product and company information is arranged by industry sector.

World Bank FundLine
FundLine is managed by the World Bank's Private Sector Development Department to facilitate communication between potential equity investors and enterprises. Its coverage includes countries in Central and Eastern Europe as well as the former Soviet Union. Last updated in 1999.

World Trade Link - International Trader's Board
This is a very active site that links buyers and sellers worldwide through the posting of trade leads.

WorldBid.com
WorldBid.com is an international network that brings together buyers and sellers from around the world for interactive trade. The site receives more than 1,000 new posts daily from over 70,000 companies worldwide. It also includes links to country-specific WorldBid web sites. Registration (for a fee) is required.

Source: Michigan State University. http://globaledge.msu.edu/ibrd/. 2006. Used with permission.

If the company is ready to go international and the foreign opportunities are attractive, then there exists a variety of mechanisms popular among small multinational businesses to make international contacts for customer and partners. The previous section reviewed many of the readily available sources. However, an enterprising small-business person will find that many more sources exist and that detailed research will increase the likelihood of the international venture's success. Finding the right overseas partner may be the most crucial decision of all.

Even with the right company, the right product, and a potential customer, a small business needs a good wedge to break into a new market. The next section shows how small businesses can use some traditional entrepreneurial wedge strategies in starting and building an international venture.

New-Venture Strategies for Small Multinational Companies

New ventures, whether initial start-up operations such as global start-ups or new international operations for an ongoing business, need some type of entry wedge to gain an initial position in a business opportunity. Karl Vesper, the renowned expert on new ventures, defines the **entry wedge** as "a strategic competitive advantage for breaking into the established pattern of commercial activity."[42] In this section, the chapter examines how some of the common entrepreneurship entry wedges work for the small multinational business. The section also includes numerous examples of small businesses using entry wedges for their multinational activities.

New Product or Service and First-Mover Advantage

One basic entrepreneurial wedge strategy focuses on being the first to introduce a new product or service.[43] This strategy tries to capture **first-mover advantage.** First-mover advantage occurs when the entrepreneur moves quickly into a new venture and establishes the business before other firms can react to the opportunity. To succeed, the new product or service must be not only innovative but also comprehensive. Comprehensive means that the product must meet customer expectations in areas such as warranty, customer service, and expected components. Without a comprehensive introduction, the new product or service is easy for competitors to imitate.

Technological leadership provides the most common source of first-mover advantage. The first company to use or introduce a new technology often has the best understanding of how to produce a product. It did the initial research and development and has the greatest familiarity with the product's characteristics. Such firms can build on this knowledge to keep ahead of competition by using their head start to introduce new product developments and innovations.

Several other situations give first movers an advantage. They may have first access to natural and social resources such as mining rights and close relationships with research universities. The first movers can choose the best locations not only for raw materials but also for proximity to customers. Finally, and perhaps more important in international business, first movers can have the best access to social relationships. Social relationships lead to the personal contacts necessary to build effective channels of distribution. They also lead to trust and commitment from business partners and customers.

The final advantage of being first comes from switching costs. **Switching costs** occur when customers face some loss in turning to a competitor's products. Customers become familiar with products, and they often invest time and effort learning to use the products. For example, many people do not switch between Apple- and Windows-based computers because they already know one operating system well. In addition, because of brand loyalty, many customers may not want to face the discomfort of switching to another brand of a product or service.

Copycat Businesses

Copycat businesses follow the "me too" strategy. A company adopts existing products or services. Competitive advantage comes from varying the nature of product or service characteristics or how the company provides the product or service.[44] Successful copycats do not copy existing businesses identically. They find a niche or slight innovation to attract customers away from existing businesses.

Entry wedge

Company's competitive advantage for breaking into the established pattern of commercial activity.

First-mover advantage

That of the entrepreneur who moves quickly into a new venture and establishes the business before other companies can react to the opportunity.

Technological leadership

Being first to use or introduce a new technology.

Switching costs

Expenses involved when a customer switches to a competitor's products.

Copycat businesses

Those following the "Me too" strategy, whereby they adopt existing strategies for providing products or services.

Sometimes the innovation can be as simple as a new location more convenient for customers. Consider the Case in Point about the Irish-based company, Intuition. How can companies find their niche and follow copycat strategy? Some suggestions for successful copycats include the following:[45]

- *Be the first to change to a new standard:* New standards of quality or internationally recognized specification standards offer powerful entry wedges for new competitors.

- *Go after the toughest customers:* Often established firms shy away from some customer groups. Highly price-sensitive or quality-sensitive customers may offer an opportunity for a niche market for the new competitor.

- *Play to minor differences in customer needs:* Established firms often ignore minor differences in customer needs and leave open an opportunity for doing new business with these customers.

- *Transfer the location:* A business that works in one part of the country may work equally well in another part of a country or in another country. The success of U.S. franchises like McDonald's throughout the world shows that this strategy is viable for creating a new business.

- *Become a dedicated supplier or distributor:* A dedicated supplier finds another firm that needs its goods or services and focuses all efforts on that major customer. For example, a small firm in the state of Washington provides cargo containers for Boeing airplanes. This small company serves Boeing directly and sells indirectly to users of Boeing jets throughout the world.

- *Seek abandoned or ignored markets:* The major players in any industry do not always serve every market fully and well.

- *Acquire existing business:* Acquiring an existing business is a common start-up strategy for small businesses in domestic markets. However, opportunities also exist in foreign countries to acquire businesses. In particular, formerly state-controlled businesses in Eastern Europe provide potentially good acquisition targets for entrepreneurs from around the world.

C A S E   I N   P O I N T

Intuition and Finding Your Niche

People seldom think of Ireland as a major resource for e-learning. However, Intuition, a company based in Dublin, Ireland, has carved an important niche providing computer-based training to the banking industry. It represents a textbook example of what small companies should do when they face the challenges of breaking into a large market: find what you do well and specialize in that in a niche. Intuition now boasts a very solid position in its niche as businesses call it for its services.

How did Intuition get to this point? It realized that to break into the large e-learning market, it needed to find a profitable niche. Intuition identified the financial sector as that profitable niche and now provides more than 250 hours of both introductory and advanced online training in various areas such as asset management, money markets, regulations, and corporate finance. However, the company also has been proactive in dealing with environmental conditions. As the market for online training has become more commoditized, Intuition has started offering classroom training to complement its online offerings. This allows Intuition to offer online training that is followed by classroom training. Additionally, Intuition is also developing customized software for specific banks since all banks don't deal with problems the same way.

Source: Based on Hosford, Christopher. 2006. "Selling strategies for small business." Sales and Marketing Management. April 158, 3: pp. 30–33.

As you may have realized, entrepreneurship plays a big role in small business creation. In the final section, we consider some key aspects of international entrepreneurship.

International Entrepreneurship

Entrepreneur

Person who creates new ventures that seek profit and growth.

New ventures

Entering a new market; offering a new product or service; or introducing a new method, technology, or innovative use of raw materials.

International entrepreneurship

The discovery, evaluation, and exploitation of market opportunities.

An **entrepreneur** creates new ventures that seek profit and growth. An entrepreneur deals with the risk and uncertainty of new and untested business. **New ventures** exist when a company enters a new market, offers a new product or service, or introduces a new method, technology, or innovative use of raw materials. Risk results from new ventures because their outcomes, such as survival and profitability, are variable. Some companies survive while others die. Some companies make a profit and grow while others remain small. Uncertainty results because the founder of a new venture can never fully predict which of the variable outcomes will befall his or her company.[46]

When applied to the international level, **international entrepreneurship** refers to the "discovery, evaluation and exploitation of market opportunities."[47] Why should an international management student be concerned about international entrepreneurship? Most experts consider entrepreneurship the driving force of all small businesses. Without an entrepreneurial spirit, few small businesses would exist. Thus, if we want to get a complete understanding of small businesses in any nation, we also need to examine the level of entrepreneurship in that country. At some point, it is necessary for the local entrepreneur to face the risk and uncertainty of starting the business.

However, entrepreneurship is also seen as the driver of innovation and economic development for any nation.[48] For instance, it is frequently posited that countries such as the United States and United Kingdom experienced rapid industrialization because the country context allowed entrepreneurial activities to flourish. As such, entrepreneurship not only creates new job but also generates new wealth and growth. Consider the Case in Point on entrepreneurship around the world.

C A S E   I N   P O I N T

Entrepreneurship Around the World

The role of entrepreneurship and small businesses in the economic development of Wales cannot be underestimated. Recent statistics show that about one-third of all Welsh small businesses are now exporting their products to other markets. Although a significant proportion of these exports are to the Euro-zone, Welsh companies also are actively exporting to North American markets. Such exports actively contribute to Wales' economy as these exports generate cash flow for local companies and create new jobs.

However, for a country like Peru, entrepreneurship is critical to combat poverty and underemployment. Because the country's formal sector cannot employ all of the available workers, Peru is very reliant on its micro-enterprises for survival and economic development. Such micro-enterprises, defined as companies with a maximum of 10 workers, constitute 96 percent of all entrepreneurial units and employ more than 45 percent of the economically active population.

Source: Jones, David. 2006. "Exporting Wales to the world: Small business make big impact in euro-zone." Daily Post, June 28:p. 22; Jackle, Annette E., and Carmen A. Li. 2006. "Firm dynamics and institutional participation: A case study on informality of micro enterprises in Peru." Economic Development and Cultural Change 54, 3: pp. 557–578.

Another important reason for an understanding of international entrepreneurship is that many multinational firms rely on entrepreneurs and small businesses to do business when entering a new country. Small businesses often can provide critical products or services that can facilitate a multinational firm's entry into a new country. Consider the challenges facing Handango when it entered the Japanese market.[49] Handango discovered that Japanese consumers do not use credit cards for purchases. Handango had to partner with a local small business to provide alternative payment options for its Japanese consumers. Furthermore, Low, Henderson, and Weiler[50] also argue that entrepreneurs play a very important role in bringing new ideas and innovations to the marketplace. As such, small businesses also can play an important role in assisting existing multinational companies in developing or offering new products that can improve productivity. For example, Pixalert, a small Dublin-based company, has developed innovative image-recognition software that can alert a company when employees are viewing inappropriate pictures online.[51] Viewing inappropriate images on the job results in a significant drop in productivity as well as potential corporate liability in sexual harassment issues. However, while traditional filters cannot detect images installed from flash drives or other means such as instant messaging, Pixalert's system can monitor image viewing through image analysis.[52]

Given the importance of entrepreneurship to economies and multinational companies, it is important to understand how entrepreneurial activities differ among nations. Busenitz, Gomez, and Spencer[53] provide some understanding of how the national context affects entrepreneurial rate. Similar to the discussion in Chapter 3, they argue that a country's national context can be categorized as having a regulatory dimension (laws and regulations that provide support for entrepreneurship), a cognitive dimension (knowledge and skills possessed by people to start new businesses), and a normative dimension (degree to which people value entrepreneurship). They tested their dimensions on individuals from six nations, and their findings provide support for their propositions. Such results are not surprising since some cultures encourage more risk taking. For instance, Hofstede's individualism measure has been linked with higher levels of entrepreneurial activity.

Similarly, institutional factors such as banking systems and the degree of capitalism of the nation can affect small businesses. For example, regulatory measures such as fiscal policies for entrepreneurs or other national policies toward innovation are likely to impact entrepreneurship.

Multinational companies may make location decisions based on the degree to which the country's inhabitants are entrepreneurial. In that context, Global Entrepreneurship Monitor (GEM) is an ongoing study of entrepreneurship activity around the world. The GEM research team has developed several measures of entrepreneurship and studies the cultural and institutional conditions that support the driving forces of contemporary economies. Exhibit 7.8 shows the total entrepreneurial activity (TEA) for selected countries.[54] The TEA represents the number of entrepreneurs (measured by starting new businesses) in a country per 100 of population.

EXHIBIT 7.8   Total Entrepreneurial Activity Ratings by Country

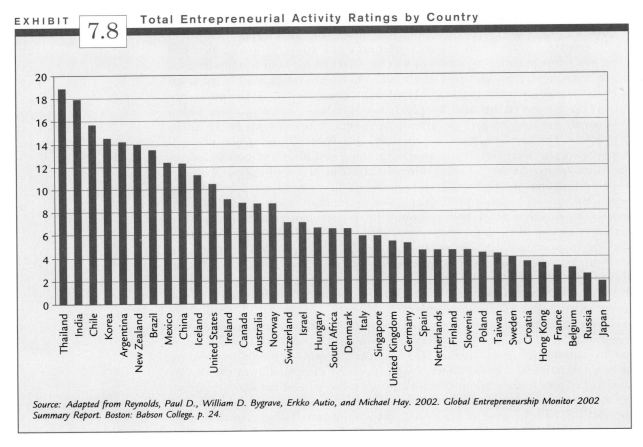

Source: Adapted from Reynolds, Paul D., William D. Bygrave, Erkko Autio, and Michael Hay. 2002. Global Entrepreneurship Monitor 2002 Summary Report. Boston: Babson College. p. 24.

Summary and Conclusions

Small businesses are important aspects of economies of all nations. Often they provide the most jobs, the most economic growth, and the most innovation. Increasingly, small businesses must face the challenges of becoming multinational companies and entering the international marketplace. Small businesses do, however, face some unique problems and prospects when entering global competition. In this chapter, therefore, we have extended the study of multinational and participation strategies to focus on situations with particular application to small multinational companies.

After defining the basic characteristics of a small business and entrepreneurship, we reviewed the processes by which small businesses go international— through stages or through global start-ups. Increasingly, global start-ups are replacing stages of internationalization, especially for high-tech entrepreneurial companies in fast-changing industries.

A small business must overcome certain traditional barriers that may inhibit its internationalization. The chapter discussed how small businesses develop a global culture, change the attitudes of key decision makers, gain crucial international experience, and overcome the size barrier of internationalization. The chapter also presented the diagnostic questions that a small-business person can ask in deciding when the company is ready to enter the international marketplace.

Crucial to a small business is finding ways to access foreign customers and business partners. Small businesses have the same participation-strategy options as larger firms. However, small businesses often do not have the in-house resources to identify or go directly to foreign customers. Fortunately, there are many public and private resources available to businesses wishing to become multinational. This chapter provided an overview of some resources pertinent to small businesses that are available from government and private sources. Increasingly, electronic media, such as the World Wide Web, provide easy and quick access to information on markets throughout the world. Exhibit 7.7 provided just a small sample of this growing source of multinational-business information.

For the small business, entering the international market is an entrepreneurial venture. Entrepreneurial ventures require successful entry-wedge strategies if the company hopes to have any chance of success. Traditionally, books on entrepreneurship consider entry-wedge strategies only in terms of the domestic market. This chapter, however, showed how entrepreneurial entry-wedge strategies could work in the global marketplace. Several Cases in Point showed how actual entrepreneurs used entry-wedge strategies to compete successfully with larger international rivals.

A full appreciation of small businesses is not possible without also understanding international entrepreneurship. Entrepreneurship is important to a country because it helps generate jobs and wealth. However, entrepreneurship is also critical to multinational companies as small businesses can provide larger companies with new ideas while also providing crucial products and services to these larger companies. The degree to which countries are entrepreneurial varies, and we looked at some of the reasons why such differences exist.

Small business will continue to be an important and growing component of international trade and investment. As a result, small-business managers will need many of the same multinational management skills used by managers from larger companies. This chapter provided you some background on key multinational strategy issues faced by the small-business person.

Discussion Questions

1. Why are small businesses important for most economies?

2. What are the advantages of a small business going international through incremental stages rather than as a global start-up?

3. The Multinational Management Challenge on Surftech showed a successful global start-up. Discuss the conditions that made this strategy the correct choice.

4. Identify two or three small-business barriers to internationalization. If you were a recently hired manager of a small business facing great opportunities in a foreign market, how would you go about overcoming these barriers?

5. As a recent business-college graduate, you have been asked by a small-business manager to help her decide whether she should enter the export market. What questions would you ask her and why?

6. Discuss ways that a small-business manager can make the contacts necessary to implement an exporting strategy.

7. Consider three of the suggested strategic moves for copycat businesses. What additional difficulties will a company face in using these strategies in the international market as opposed to the domestic market?

8. What is international entrepreneurship? What benefits do international entrepreneurs bring to multinational companies?

Multinational Management Skill Builder

Take a Product International

Step 1. Your instructor will divide the class into groups.

Step 2. Select an agricultural or industrial product produced in the region of the country where you are located. If possible, interview a small-business person concerning his or her perspectives on the international opportunities for the company's product. In the United States, one way of finding a potential business owner is through the small-business development centers attached to many U.S. universities. Your instructor may assign you a business or product.

Step 3. Using the steps shown in Exhibit 7.4 and information from World Wide Web sources (such as those in Exhibit 7.6) and your library, identify a foreign market or markets for the product or products.

Step 4. Using Web sources (such as those in Exhibit 7.6) identify potential trade shows, trading partners, or other intermediaries (e.g., ETCs) that would help you get the product to the international marketplace.

Step 5. Present your findings to your class, and to the small-business person, if possible.

Endnotes

[1] Organization for Economic Cooperation and Development [OECD]. 2002. *OECD Small and Medium Enterprise Outlook.* Paris: OECE Publication Services.

[2] U.S. Small Business Administration. 2006. "Advocacy: The voice of small business in government". June. http://www.sba.gov/advo

[3] Organization for Economic Cooperation and Development [OECD], Small and Medium Enterprise Outlook.

[4] Ibid.

[5] Scarborough, Norman M., and Thomas W. Zimmer. 1996. *Effective Small Business Management.* Upper Saddle River, N.J.: Prentice Hall.

[6] Rialp, Alex, Josep Rialp, David Urbano, and Yancy Vaillant. 2005. "The born-global phenomenon: A comparative case study research." *Journal of International Entrepreneurship* 3: p. 133–171.

[7] Dollinger, Marc J. 1995. *Entrepreneurship.* Burr Ridge, IL.: Irwin.

[8] Oviatt, Benjamin M., and Patricia Phillips McDougall. 1995. "Global start-ups: Entrepreneurs on a worldwide stage." *Academy of Management Executive* 9: p. 30–44.

[9] Ibid.

[10] U.S. Small Business Administration. 1999. *E-Commerce: Small Businesses Venture Online.* Washington, D.C.: Government Printing Office.

[11] Ibid.

[12] Locke, Stuart M. 2006. "E-local government strategies and small business." *Journal of American Academy of Business* 10, 1: p. 21–30.

[13] Ibid.

[14] Freeman, Susan, and Imogen Reid. 2006. "Constraints facing small western firms in transitional markets." *European Business Review* 18, 3: p. 187–213.

[15] Caprioni, Paula J., Stefanie Ann Lenway, and Thomas P. Murtha. 1994. "Understanding internationalization: Sense-making process in multinational corporations." In Tamir Agmon and Richard Drobnick (eds.), Small Firms in Global Competition, edited by Tamir Agmon and Richard Drobnick, New York: Oxford, p. 27–36.

[16] Dichtl, Drwin, Hans-Georg Koeglmayr, and Stefan Mueller. 1990. "International orientation as a precondition for export success." *Journal of International Business Studies*, 1st Quarter, p. 23–40.

[17] Freeman and Reid, "Constraints facing small western firms in transitional markets."

[18] Rialp, Rialp, Urbano, and Vaillant, "The born-global phenomenon: A comparative case study research."

[19] Calof, Jonathan L. and Wilma Viviers. 1995. "Internationalization behavior of small- and medium-sized South African enterprises." *Journal of Small Business Management*, October, p. 71–79; Miesenbock, Kurt J. 1988. "Small business and internationalization: a literature review." *International Small Business Journal* 6: p. 42–61.

[20] Oviatt and McDougall, "Global start-ups: Entrepreneurs on a worldwide stage."

[21] Dalin, Shera. 2005. "Owning a business isn't a 9-to-5 job." *St. Louis Post-Dispatch.* St. Louis. October 30: p. E6.

[22] Wright, Phillip C. 1993. "The personal and the personnel adjustments and costs to small businesses entering the international market place." *Journal of Small Business Management*, January, p. 83–93.

[23] Beamish P. W., and H. J. Munro. 1987. "Exporting for success as a small Canadian manufacturer." *Journal of Small Business and Entrepreneurship* 4: p. 38–43.

[24] Wright, "The personal and the personnel adjustments and costs to small businesses entering the international market place."

[25] Ibid.

[26] Bonacorsi, Andrea. 1992. "On the relationships between firm size and export intensity." *Journal of International Business Studies*, 4th Quarter, p. 605–633.

[27] Freeman and Reid, "Constraints facing small western firms in transitional markets."

[28] Bonacorsi, "On the relationships between firm size and export intensity."

[29] Christensen, C., Angela da Rocha, and Rosane Gertner. 1987. "An empirical investigation of the factors influencing export success of Brazilian firms." *Journal of International Business Studies*, Fall, p. 61–78.

[30] Calof, Jonathan L. 1993. "The impact of size on internationalization." *Journal of Small Business Management*, October, p. 60–69.

[31] Lu, Jane W., and Paul W. Beamish. 2006. "Partnering strategies and performance of SMEs' international joint ventures." *Journal of Business Venturing* 21: p. 461–486.

[32] Calof, "The impact of size on internationalization."

[33] Bonacorsi, "On the relationships between firm size and export intensity."

[34] Calof, "The impact of size on internationalization."

[35] Ibid.

[36] Scarborough and Zimmer, *Effective Small Business Management.*

[37] Hilton, Gregory. 2005. "Knocking down export barriers to smaller firms." *Business and Economic Review.* July–September 51, 4: p. 18–20.

[38] Yip, George S. 2001. *Total Global Strategy.* Englewood Cliffs, N.J.: Prentice Hall.

[39] Knowlton, Christopher. 1988. "The new export entrepreneurs." *Fortune,* June p. 6, 98.

[40] Barney, J. B. 1991. "Firm resources and sustained competitive advantage." *Journal of Management* 17: p. 99–120.

[41] Barry, Doug. 2000. "From Appalachia to India: U.S. small businesses are going global." *Business Credit* 102, 6: p. 49–50.

[42] Vesper. Karl M. 1980. *New Venture Strategies.* Englewood Cliffs, N.J.: Prentice Hall.

[43] Dollinger, *Entrepreneurship.*

[44] Vesper, New Venture Strategies.

[45] Dollinger, *Entrepreneurship.*

[46] Ibid.

[47] Baker, Ted, Eric Gedajlovic, and Michel Lubatkin. 2005. "A framework for comparing entrepreneurship processes across nations." *Journal of International Business Studies* 36: p. 492–504.

[48] Busenitz, Lowell W., Carolina Gomez, and Jennifer W. Spence. 2000. "Country institutional profiles: Unlocking entrepreneurial phenomena." *Academy of Management Journal.* October 43, 5: p. 994–1003.

[49] Bright, Beckey. 2005. How Do You Say "Web"? Planning to take your online business international? Beware; E-commerce can get lost in translation. Wall Street Journal, May 23, p. R11.

[50] Low, Sarah, Jason Henderson, and Stephan Weiler. 2005. "Gauging a region's entrepreneurial potential." *Economic Review-Federal Reserve Bank of Kansas City*, Third Quarter 90, 3: p. 61–89.

[51] Hosford, Christopher. 2006. "Selling Strategies for Small Business." *Sales and Marketing Management.* April 158, 3: p. 30–33.

[52] Ibid.

[53] Busenitz, Gomez, and Spence, "Country institutional profiles: Unlocking entrepreneurial phenomena."

[54] Minniti, Maria, William D. Bygrave, and Erkko Autio. 2005. "Global Entrepreneurship Monitor 2005 executive report." *GEM*, p. 1–67.

CHAPTER CASE
Airview Mapping, Inc.

I n early March 1994, Rick Tanner, the principal of Airview Mapping, Inc., started drafting plans for the upcoming summer season. For him, late winter typically involved making sales calls on the company's established and potential clients for the purpose of determining the expected demand for his services and then drafting his sales forecasts for the upcoming year.

Airview, which had traditionally dominated the aerial surveying markets of Central and Eastern Canada, had recently been faced with increasing competition from other air surveyors from across Canada in its traditional territories. The protracted recession of the early 1990s, combined with the anti-deficit measures introduced by all levels of government, had reduced the overall demand for geomatic services in Canada, producing significant overcapacity in the industry, including the particular markets in which Airview was involved.

This situation had already reduced the company's profits, but the real threat lay in the fact that the new competitors, once established in Airview's region, would stay there, permanently capturing a significant share of the Central Canadian market. These competitors, typically larger than Airview, could expand their market coverage, even if it meant creating a temporary operating base in a distant location. At the same time, their home markets were extremely difficult for small companies from other regions to penetrate due to their fierce price competition.

Rick realized that his company might face difficult times if he could not redirect his attention to some new areas of opportunity. His view was that these opportunities had to be found in international markets. He had already gathered some information on several foreign markets, which looked promising from the company's perspective. It was now time to review the overall situation and decide whether to attempt penetrating any of the identified foreign markets, and, if so, what entry strategy to choose.

The Company

Airview Mapping, Inc. was incorporated in November 1979 by a group of former employees of Aerosurvey Corporation Ltd., with Tom Denning and Rick Tanner as the principal shareholders of the new entity. For the first two years, the company operated without an aircraft, providing mapping services based on externally developed photogrammetric images to clients in Central Canada. Airview's early success provided sufficient capital to acquire an aircraft and a photographic processing laboratory, which, in 1981, was initially placed under the company's subsidiary, Airtech Services Ltd. The two operations were amalgamated in November 1983 under the parent company's name.

When Tom retired in 1990, Rick took over his duties as president and offered key employees 40% of the company's shares, retaining 60% himself.

Airview's sales grew steadily throughout the 1980s, from an annual level of $500,000 in 1981 to $1.2 million in 1989. Sales stabilized during the 1990s at a level of just over $1.1 million.

Airview had traditionally maintained an advanced level of technical capability, investing in the most up-to-date photographic, film processing, data analysis, and plotting equipment. This, combined with the technical expertise of the company's staff, had enabled them to build an excellent reputation for quality, reliability, and professionalism.

Product Line

With its extensive technological capabilities, Airview provided a range of services associated with the development of spatial images of terrain; referred to (in Canada) as *geomatics.* The company's primary specialization was related to its ability to acquire airborne images of objects, areas, or phenomena. Its image processing capabilities, however, provided an opportunity to complement its core offering by processing and analyzing externally acquired imagery. The range of services provided by Airview included:

Aerial Photography and Photogrammetry Aerial photography occupied a pivotal place in Airview's business. The majority of the complex services provided by Airview were initiated by taking photographs from the air. However, aerial photography was also a separate product, which, depending on the light spectrum applied during the picture taking, could provide information on forest growth and diseases, quality of water resources, wildlife migration, land erosion, and other physical features.

Photogrammetry involved a number of image-processing techniques using aerial photographs as a basis for the development of maps, composite views, or spatially referenced databases. Photogrammetry was distinguished from aerial photography by its capability to identify three-dimensional coordinates for each point on the captured image.

Aerial photography/photogrammetry was very capital intensive, requiring a specially prepared aircraft with specialized cameras and sophisticated photo-laboratory equipment. Airview was considered one of the best equipped aerial photography companies in Canada. Its survey aircraft, with a 25,000-foot photo ceiling was capable of producing photographs at scales of up to 1:10,000. A recently (1992) acquired Leica camera represented the latest in optical technology, meeting all calibration and accuracy requirements set by North American mapping agencies and accommodating a wide variety of specialized aerial film. Finally, Airview's photo laboratory, which was certified by the National Research Council, processed all types of aerial film used by the company.

Aerial Surveying Aerial surveying involved taking photographs with the purpose of defining and measuring boundaries and the configuration of particular areas on the earth's surface for a variety of uses, such as establishing ownership rights (cadastre); triangulation[1]; locating and appraising mineral resources, forests, and wild habitat; and detecting earth and water movements.

Mapping This area included the development of maps from either internally or externally acquired photographic images. Before the 1980s, map making had largely been a manual process of drawing the terrain's contours and elevations and then inserting the accompanying descriptive information. Since the early 1980s, however, the process had

been increasingly computer-driven. This resulted in a reduction in the manual labor required and in increased accuracy of the images produced. At the same time, the new technology permitted the storage of maps in a digital format, which created demand for converting maps from the traditional, analog format into a computer-based one.

CADD This area also dealt with map making, but based on computer-operated scanners supported by CADD/CAM (computer-aided design and drafting/computer-aided mapping) software. With this technology, the digitizing of analog images, such as existing maps or photographs, was fully automated. The scanners interpreted the subject image as a series of dots identified by their coordinates, colors, and illuminance and then produced their digital presentation. The computer-stored images could then be enhanced by adding descriptive information, using a process still performed manually by the CADD operators.

Consulting Over its 15-year history, Airview had developed a multidisciplinary team of specialists, whose expertise had also been employed in providing consulting services associated with the planning and execution of comprehensive mapping projects. This area involved advising clients on the optimal method of gathering spatial information, the interpretation of client-provided data, and supervising data-gathering projects conducted by the client or their subcontractors.

Data capture (aerial photography/photogrammetry) and data-processing (mapping and CADD) projects had traditionally generated (in equal proportions) around 90% of Airview's sales. The remainder had come from consulting projects (9%) and surveying (1%). By 1994, this sales distribution did not reflect the changing structure of the marketplace, where data capture had become a relatively small part of the overall scope of geomatic activities.

Customer Base

Airview Mapping, Inc. provided services to a variety of clients locally and nationally. The majority of the company's sales had traditionally come from the public sector. Over the period of 1991 to 1993, government agencies (both federal and provincial), local municipalities, and regional utilities in Ontario, Manitoba, and Saskatchewan had accounted for between 65% and 75% of the company's total dollar sales.

Agencies of the federal and provincial governments as well as provincial utilities were the company's most significant clients. Procurement by public tender, the significant size of individual contracts (from $50,000 to $100,000+), and clear specifications of requirements characterized these projects.

The private sector, accounting for the remaining 35% to 45% of Airview's sales, was represented predominantly by clients from the mining and resource sectors. These contracts were typically in the range of $20,000 to $40,000. Companies representing such diverse areas as construction, recreation, and environmental protection contracted for projects typically valued at up to $20,000 each. Companies from the private sector did not apply a rigorous procurement procedure and frequently needed guidance in defining (or redefining) the requirements of their projects.

Geographic Coverage

Airview concentrated its activities within a 1,200-mile radius of its headquarters in the provincial capital of one of the prairie provinces. In this local region, the company was able to deal directly with its clients and had a cost advantage over its competitors from other provinces. It included Northwestern Ontario, Manitoba, Saskatchewan, and Alberta, each contributing equally to the company's revenues.

The company had never attempted to expand beyond the Canadian market, even though the sizeable market south of the U.S.–Canada border was well within its 1,200-mile radius. In the past, this had been justified by the abundance of opportunities available in Canada and restrictions on foreign access to the U.S. market. However, this situation had recently changed on both counts, which caused Rick to consider changing his company's geographic orientation.

Organization And Staff

The production process associated with the services provided by Airview involved grouping activities into three functional areas; airplane operation and maintenance (two staff members), film development (two), and image processing/output (ten). Regular managerial, marketing, and administrative activities involved four additional staff.

Each production area (aircraft operations, photo lab, data capture, and data conversion) was assigned a coordinator responsible for quality assurance and overall coordination of the workload in the area. These coordinators also provided expert advice to their staff and were responsible for individual projects within their respective production areas.

Airview's production activities were characterized by the relatively small number of concurrent projects (4 to 6) and their modest size. This, combined with the well-trained staff (13 out of 18 had completed postsecondary education in geomatics-related fields), enabled the company to apply a skeleton project management structure.

Coordination of project work among different production areas was the responsibility of the production coordinator, Sean Coleman. Garry Howell was in charge of marketing. Tim Connors, who occupied the position of vice president, also acted as the general manager responsible for all projects. Rick, who was the company's president, oversaw general administration and communication with customers.

Pricing

Each price quotation was based on Garry Howell's assessment of the scope of work required to complete it. This was broken down by category of activity (aircraft operation, film processing, digitization of images, or image analysis). For each of these activity categories, a budget hourly rate was developed, based on historical cost figures (both direct and fixed), the budgeted number of hours for a given planning period, and the company's profit targets. Recently, rates had ranged from $25 for digitization of images to over $900 for aircraft flying time, with an overall average of some $70.

The initial price was determined by multiplying the estimated number of hours required in each category by its budgeted rate and then adding the figures for all activity categories involved in the project. This price was later adjusted by Rick's assessment of the competitive situation (in the case of a tendered bid) or his negotiations with the customer.

Generally, Airview's budgeted rates and—consequently—prices were within the average values prevailing in Canada. This situation reflected their general knowledge of the cost structure of the industry. Any undercutting of price tended to raise suspicions of lower standards. This being the case, the competition between bidders had severely squeezed profit margins, with many firms trying to survive by quoting their services on a break-even basis.

Financial Results

In the late 1980s and early 1990s, Airview had acquired advanced photographic and mapping equipment and computer hardware and software with a total value of close to $900,000. Financing for these acquisitions had been provided by bank loans and capital leases at interest rates ranging from 12.25% to 17.25%.

During the most recent two years, the cost of servicing this debt load had created a real strain on the company's cash flow, requiring an annual outlay of $200,000, split evenly between interest costs and repayment of the principal. This was extremely difficult for a company traditionally only generating a free annual cash flow in the range of $100,000 to $150,000.

Airview's operating cost structure was characterized by a high proportion of fixed costs. Currently, some 75% of direct costs and 83% of total costs did not vary with changes in their sales level. This cost structure might seem surprising for a business with some 60% of its direct expenses associated with wages and salaries. However, considering the unique nature of the professional qualifications of the company's staff, it was extremely difficult, if not impossible, to vary the number of staff in line with fluctuations in sales levels.

This situation reduced the company's profit at their current sales level, but, at the same time, created significant profit potential with a possible sales increase. It was estimated that the company, barely breaking even at its current sales of $1.1 million, could make over $200,000 in profits by increasing sales to $1.4 million.

Overall Strategic Profile

Viewed from a strategic perspective, Airview could be characterized as a locally based company with strong technical capabilities but limited expertise in marketing, particularly outside its traditional markets. Rick recognized the importance of having a clear understanding of his company's current position as well as its goals for the next few years. His analysis

of Airview's structure and performance led him to develop the company's corporate profile presented in Exhibit 1 (p. 362).

Industry Trends

The term *geomatics* was widely used in Canada to describe a variety of fields that acquired, managed, and distributed spatially referenced data. The term was generally applied to refer to several disciplines, including the following:

➤ Aerial photography

➤ Ground-based (geodetic) and aerial surveying—i.e., assessing and delimiting boundaries of land

➤ Mapping—i.e., cartography (map making based on ground measurements) and photogrammetry (converting photographic images and measurements into maps)

➤ Geographic Information Systems (GIS) —i.e., computer-based systems for the storage and processing of spatial information

➤ Remote sensing—i.e., satellite-borne images and measurements (quite often, airborne images were included in the remote sensing category)

The use of this general term, however, was limited to Canada. In other countries these disciplines were referred to by their individual names. On the other hand, the term *remote sensing* was frequently used to describe all satellite and airborne observations of the earth's surface, regardless of their purpose and the techniques applied. Although traditionally distinct, these disciplines were becoming increasingly integrated due to the commonality of the computer tools employed to acquire and process the spatial information and generate the final product.

The emergence of satellite-based remote sensing had also affected the geomatics industry worldwide. Its impact on air-based services had been largely positive, despite the fact that both technologies served the same user segments. Advances in satellite technology had received a lot of publicity, which sensitized users of geomatic services to the cost advantages of remote sensing in general and aerial photography/photogrammetry in particular. Consequently, those users who could not use satellite-based services turned to airborne imagery. In many cases, satellite trajectories limited the frequency with which information on a particular earth location could be gathered. This problem was further exacerbated by the prevalence of

EXHIBIT 1   Airview's Corporate Profile: Current versus Target (5-Year Perspective)

	Current	Target
Rank and Size	$1,100,000 sales	$2,000,000 + sales
	$0–$25,000 profits	$300,000 + profits
	18 employees	30 + employees
	Medium-sized aerial surveying company	Medium-sized GIS company
	No export sales	$700,000 + export sales
Product Line	Aerial photography—40%	Aerial photography—30%
	Mapping—30%	GIS—40%
	Surveying—1%	Mapping—20%
	CAD—20%	Commercial/consulting—10%
	Commercial—9%	3–5 concurrent projects
	5–10 concurrent projects	
Geographic Coverage	Canada—100%	Canada—60%
		International—40%
Performance Goals	Maintenance of cash flow	Sales/profit growth
	Profit margin	Market penetration
	Protecting market share	Technology adoption
		New product development
		Productivity
Strengths	Customer goodwill	Customer goodwill
	Technological expertise	Active marketing
	Aerial photography	Geographical diversification
	Digital imaging	Flexible offer
		Technological expertise
		Digital imaging
		Aerial photography
		System development
Weaknesses	Marketing	International exposure
	Narrow product line	
	Balance sheet	
Strategy	Passive	Active

cloud cover over certain territories. It was expected that, despite recent plans to increase the overall number of remote sensing satellites, aerial photography/photogrammetry would maintain its advantage in applications requiring high resolution capabilities (aerial images could produce resolutions in a 2 to 3 in. range versus a 10m range available from most satellites) and full-color capabilities.

Airview's Markets
In the first half of the 1990s, the Canadian geomatics industry was represented by over 1,300 firms from all geomatic disciplines, employing some 12,000 people. The largest number of firms were located in Quebec and Ontario, followed by British Columbia. The distribution of primary activities within the industry was as follows:

Major Line of Business	% of Total Establishments	% of Total Billings
Geodetic (ground) surveying	65%	53%
Mapping	9%	16%
Remote Sensing	5%	11%
Consulting	10%	4.5%
GIS	7%	12%
Other	4%	3.5%

The vast majority (86%) of geomatic firms were small establishments generating sales of less than $1 million. However, the remaining, small number of larger firms generated the majority (68%) of the industry's revenues. Airview belonged to the growing category of medium-sized businesses (10% of all establishments) with sales of between $1 million and $2 million.

The overall market size in Canada was estimated at $630 to $650 million and was dominated by local companies. The industry also generated some $120 million in foreign billings (mainly GIS hardware and software). Interestingly, the export of these services from Canada had traditionally been directed outside of North America and Europe and concentrated in Africa, Asia, and the Middle East.

Competition

Competition in the Canadian geomatics industry was on the increase. The current economic climate, characterized by fiscal restraint in both the private and government sectors, had reduced the growth rate of the demand for the services provided by the industry. As a result, geomatic companies, with their increased production capacities and reduced costs, had become more active in competing for the constant volume of business. This had resulted in a decrease in industry profitability. Overall industry profit levels were the same as in the early 1980s, despite a doubling of overall industry demand.

Global Opportunities Overview

By March 1994, Rick had spent considerable time reviewing global market opportunities for the company. He had taken a general look at several foreign markets, looking at such major factors as their overall size and growth prospects, political stability and entry barriers, competition, and the availability of funding for geomatic projects.

This step had resulted in rejecting the possibility of entering the markets of Western Europe, which—despite their size—were characterized by ferocious competition and limited growth prospects. Eastern Europe was felt to be too politically unstable (particularly the countries of the former USSR), lacked funding, and were fragmented along national borders.

Rick also felt that the distances associated with dealing with markets in Southeast Asia and Oceania would put a significant strain on the company's financial and human resources, particularly in view of increasing competition from locally based companies. On the other hand, other Asian markets lacked either the size or the financing required to support Airview's long-term involvement.

Finally, he decided that sub-Saharan Africa, although in dire need of the services offered by Airview, was either dominated by companies from their former colonial powers or could not afford any significant level of geomatics-related development, particularly in view of the declining level of support being received from international financial institutions like the World Bank.

On the other hand, Rick found the characteristics of some of the remaining regions quite interesting. Consequently, he decided to concentrate his deliberations on these markets, which included North America (the United States and Mexico), Latin America, and the Arab World (North Africa and the Middle East).

American Market

The U.S. market was somewhat different from its Canadian counterpart in that it had a larger proportion of geodetic and GIS firms among the 6,300 businesses in its geomatic industry. This larger proportional number of geodetic firms in the United States was due to its higher population density, which increased the need for cadastral surveying. At the same time, faster adoption of computers in a variety of industrial applications in the United States had stimulated demand for GIS applications and related services.

On the other hand, in comparison to the relative size of the U.S. and Canadian economies, the Canadian geomatic market was disproportionately large.

The American market was estimated at $3 billion in 1994; only five times the size of its Canadian counterpart or only half the relative difference in the size of the economies between the two countries. This disparity could be largely attributed to the structural differences between the economies of the two countries. Canada's economy was largely dependent on the mineral and forestry sectors; both industries that supported a relatively large geomatic industry.

The demand for geomatics services in the U.S. market was growing at a 15% annual rate and was particularly dynamic in the areas of airborne photography and (satellite) remote sensing, digital conversion of existing data, and consulting.

Access to U.S. Markets

In 1994, there were few tariff obstacles to entering the U.S. market. Previous barriers related to licensing and local presence requirements were being removed as a result of the passage of the North American Free Trade Agreement. In some cases, Canadian companies who had succeeded in penetrating the U.S. market indicated that it had been easier for them to cross the international border than to overcome provincial barriers within their home country.

Although there had been some opportunities in the U.S. geomatics market during the 1980s, Canadian firms had traditionally been reluctant to take advantage of them. For aerial surveying companies like Airview, one of the reasons was the fact that American aircraft maintenance and licensing requirements were much more lenient in the United States than in Canada. As a result, a company operating an aircraft out of Canada was not able to compete with American firms on price if there was any significant amount of flying time involved. Although these differences still remained, the recently falling value of the Canadian dollar had all but nullified the cost advantage previously enjoyed by U.S. companies.

In general, the level of competition in the United States was not much different from that in Canada except that the American firms, particularly the larger ones, marketed their services much more aggressively than did their Canadian counterparts.

User Segments

It was estimated that local and state governments accounted for some 25% of the total U.S. market for geomatic products and services and that close to half of all local/state budgets allocated to the acquisition of geomatic services was allocated for data capture purposes. The largest potential lay with the 39,000 municipal/county governments. A trend to modernize the land records and registration systems that document the 118 million land parcels in the United States was the most significant factor in stimulating the demand for data capture, their conversion into a digital format, their subsequent analysis, and graphical presentation.

The average contract performed for local/state governments ranged from $60,000 to $190,000 for aerial photography/photogrammetry services. Although the Northeast, Southeast, Southwest, and states bordering the Pacific Ocean accounted for the greatest demand, there was also an abundance of opportunities in the states closer to Airview's base, such as Minnesota (3,529 local government units), North Dakota (2,795), and South Dakota (1,767).

Federal government agencies represented the second largest user group, accounting for slightly less than 25% of the total U.S. geomatic market. Digital mapping was the major area of demand within this segment. This corresponded closely to Airview's principal area of expertise.

Contracts with the federal government ranged from $30,000 for surveying projects to $1.5 million for data-digitizing projects. On average, they tended to be larger in size than those with state and local governments and were typically awarded to larger firms. As a result of the U.S. federal government policy of decentralizing the contracting of services, the demand from this user sector was distributed across the country.

The third largest segment in the U.S. geomatic market was the demand from regulated industries, such as communication firms and gas and electric companies. They traditionally generated between 20% and 25% of the overall U.S. demand for geomatic services. Customers from this category were interested in more cost-efficient management of the large infrastructure under their administration. Consequently, they had been among the early adopters of GIS technology, and their major thrust was in implementing AM/FM (automated mapping and facilities management) systems that combined digital maps with information on the operation of their facilities.

The utilities market for geomatic services was spread across the United States, with the size closely related to the population density of individual regions. These regional markets were dominated by large companies, such as Baymont Engineering and AT&T, which—due to economies of scale—became very price competitive in catering to the utility sector.

Finally, the rest of the demand for geomatic services came from the private sector, with the most significant segments being the resource industries, viz. mining and forestry. The rate of adoption of GIS technology in this sector was rather slow, and remotely sensed data and basic mapping were the primary services contracted out by these firms.

The Mexican Geomatics Market

Overview By the early 1990s, Mexico had developed significant capabilities in geomatics. Between 40,000 and 50,000 people were employed in all surveying and mapping related disciplines. Yet, in view of the country's problems with rapid urbanization, deforestation, and land use change, local demand for geomatics products and services in the early 1990s exceeded the available supply in some product and service categories.

The primary demand for geomatics services in Mexico was created by cartographic agencies of the federal and state governments. The National Institute of Statistics, Geography, and Informatics (INEGI) had the primary responsibility for integrating the country's geographical data, carrying out the national mapping project and developing the national geographic information system.

Each state in Mexico was responsible for undertaking and maintaining a land survey of its territory and maintaining land cadastre. Therefore, state markets were the second largest in volume after the federal market.

Several large municipalities were also purchasers of geomatics products and services. In 1993–1994, they were in the process of establishing databases of property boundaries, partly in cooperation with SEDESOL (Directorate of Cartography and Photogrammetry) under the One Hundred Cities Program.

The private sector of the country was also a significant user of spatially referenced information. PEMEX, the state oil monopoly, was by far the largest of those users. It was also in the strongest position to acquire the most technologically advanced products and services in this area.

The total size of the Mexican market for geomatics services in 1993 was estimated at between $160 million and $200 million.

There were two cycles that affected the volume of geomatics work available in Mexico. First, there was the annual rainy season (June to September), which had a negative impact due to limitations on aerial surveying caused by inclement weather. Second, there was the change in Mexico's presidency every six years. As government agencies were the main purchasers of geomatic services, the political environment had a profound effect on business. In general, the first three years of any presidency resulted in minor projects, while the final three years were noted for major works.

The demand for geomatics services in Mexico was increasing. In addition, most Mexican companies competing for this business were interested in foreign participation, particularly if these relationships carried with them better technology and more modern equipment.

Mexico offered a significant operating benefit to Canadian aerial photography firms in that its weather patterns (the rainy season between May and September) counterbalanced those in Canada. This could enable Canadian exporters to utilize their aircraft and photographic equipment during the slow season in Canada (December through March).

Competition The Mexican geomatics industry was well developed in the traditional areas of ground surveying and cartography. However, its technological and human resource capabilities in the more technical areas, such as digital mapping and GIS were generally limited.

In the area of aerial mapping and surveying, there were about 20 companies, located mostly in Mexico City. Six of these companies, which owned their own aircraft, dominated the national market, whereas the remaining 14 were quite small, did not have their own aircraft, and were fairly new to the industry.

Market Access Public tender was the normal method for obtaining projects in Mexico. Most tenders were open to all companies, but some were by invitation only. The tendency was for contracts to go to those companies that had their own aircraft and the proper equipment. Subcontracting was a popular way for smaller companies to obtain a portion of larger projects.

If a foreign company was awarded a contract, it had to obtain permission from the state geography department and from the Mexican Defense Department. In addition, until 1996, foreign companies were not allowed to operate aircraft over Mexican territory without local participation.

The Latin American Geomatics Market

In the early 1990s, the geomatics market in Latin America was at an early stage of transition from traditional to digital technologies for data capture, analysis, and storage. Although general awareness of GIS and remote sensing was widespread, their adoption was largely limited to international resource exploration companies and some public institutions.

The market for geomatics products and services was dominated by the public sector on both the supply and demand sides. However, the private sector was becoming the primary growth area, particularly the resource sector (agriculture, forestry, mining, and energy), where significant investment programs created demand for cadastral surveying, mapping, and GIS. This demand potential, in turn, was providing a growth opportunity for local surveying and mapping companies. This industry had traditionally been dominated by government organizations (mostly military controlled), which, over the previous few years, had gained a significant degree of business autonomy and were actively competing in both local and international markets.

International financial institutions (IFIs), such as the World Bank and the Inter American Development Bank were very active in Latin America. As their major concern was economic development of the entire area, their activities were concentrated in the less developed nations of the region. The IFIs recognized the importance of infrastructure projects and their geomatics components and provided financial support for such basic services as topographic and property mapping and cadastral information systems. As a result of this fundamental focus, geomatics contract activity was not confined to the more economically advanced countries of the region. From the point of view of foreign-based geomatics companies attempting to enter the Latin American market, the IFI-sponsored contracts provided a very attractive opportunity since they were open for public tender.

It was anticipated that the Latin American market for geomatics products and services would grow significantly. It was estimated that from 1993 to 1998, the total demand for geomatics products and services in the region would increase from US $650 million to US $1,500 million.

The provision of spatial information and its conversion to a digital format, as well as the delivery of GIS applications and the provision of training to local staff, constituted the major demand area, expected to constitute three-quarters of the region's market.

Geographic Distribution Brazil was by far the largest market for geomatics products and services, with an estimated 50% of the total demand in the region.

Argentina, with the second largest territory and population in the region, was also the second largest market for geomatics products and services, accounting for 20% of Latin American demand.

Chile, with its significant resource sector, was the third significant geomatics market in the region with a 5% share of total demand.

Interestingly, Bolivia, with its relatively small population and economy, was a disproportionately large market for geomatics products and services (4% of the overall demand).

The other 13 countries of the region shared the remaining 21% of the Latin American market, with Venezuela and Colombia leading the group.

Competition By the 1990s, Latin American companies had developed substantial capabilities in the areas of surveying and mapping. The mapping sector in the region had originated from the military and, until recent years, had been protected from foreign competition by trade barriers. Consequently, the capabilities of local firms were significant, particularly in the larger countries such as Brazil and Argentina. More significantly, larger surveying and mapping companies had already invested in digital mapping technology and remote sensing. With their developed expertise and low labor and overhead costs, these firms had a significant advantage over their competitors from North America, Europe, and Australia. Their knowledge of the local market was an additional factor placing them ahead of competitors from other continents.

Larger Brazilian and Argentinean firms had used this advantage to penetrate the markets of the smaller countries of the region. Since each national market was characterized by wide fluctuations in the demand for geomatic services, the markets of other countries provided them with an opportunity to stabilize and, possibly, expand their sales. In view of this situation, service firms from outside the region had to compete on the basis of their technological and managerial advantage. Large scale projects, possibly involving digital imaging, provided the best opportunity to compete with local companies.

Despite all these impediments to foreign participation in the Latin American market, European companies had succeeded in capturing a significant share of the region's business. Their success was built on the strong business network established in the region by their home countries. Their penetration strategy was to establish their presence initially (through international assistance programs and the provision of training and education) and then to develop ties with local government agencies and companies from the private sector. European firms were also characterized by their ability to form consortia to pursue larger contracts. These consortia combined European technology and equipment with local labor and market experience.

American firms had achieved significant penetration of these markets for GIS hardware and software. However, their presence in the other sectors was less pronounced, probably due to their uncompetitive cost structure.

Australian geomatics firms involved in Latin America were typically affiliated with Australia's mining and forestry companies active in resource exploration activities in the region.

The Arab World (North Africa And The Middle East)

Countries of the Arab world were characterized by the dominance of their oil and gas industries in geomatics-related projects. Their economies and political systems were relatively stable and provided a good foundation for establishing long-term penetration plans by a foreign geomatics company. In addition, in their economic development, countries in this region were less dependent on international aid

than was the case of the countries of Latin America. Consequently, their approach to the development of topographic, cadastral, and administrative mapping was based more on long-term planning.

Countries in this region had developed their own companies, typically originating from the national cartographic agencies. In the early 1990s, these agencies still dominated the industry in the region, employing from 30% to 60% of the total number of personnel working in the geomatics field. However, their role had been steadily declining over the past few years.

At the same time, the level of development of locally based firms differed significantly among individual countries. Egypt, Iran, Jordan, Kuwait, Lebanon, Qatar, Syria, and Tunisia each had a substantial number of local specialists in the field (relative to their populations and territory), whereas Algeria, Libya, Iraq, Saudi Arabia, and Yemen had rather limited geomatics capability. Even more significantly, this latter group also had a relatively low proportion of geomatics specialists with university education.

The combined market size for geomatics services in the region was estimated at between $400 million and $600 million in the commercial sector. In view of the political situation in the region, some of the markets were characterized by restrictions on foreign access. Libya and Iraq, for example, were not open to Canadian companies. Also Syria, which had traditionally been very restrictive in granting foreign geomatics companies access to its market, was also of limited attractiveness to Canadian companies.

Iran was the country with the best opportunity for geomatics firms. The climate for Canadian firms in the country was favorable due to Canada's position as a noninvolved country and the technological advancement of the Canadian geomatics industry.

The major opportunities in Iran were associated with several national development programs in the areas of energy production (construction of hydroelectric and nuclear power stations and upgrading the country's power distribution system), expansion of the mining industry (production of iron ore, copper, aluminum, lead/zinc, and coal), the oil and gas sectors, and construction of the country's railway system.

Kuwait and Saudi Arabia had traditionally been the target markets for several Canadian geomatics firms. The expansion of the two countries' oil production and refining capacity had triggered major investment outlays in both countries (for a total of over $20 billion between 1992 and 1994) and would continue (albeit at a slower rate) for a number of years. These two national markets were dominated by American companies and any penetration effort there would require cooperation with Canadian firms from the construction, mining, or oil and gas sectors.

Tunisia represented an example of a country that had developed its own expertise in the area of cartography, which, in turn, had created demand for external assistance in the provision of more sophisticated products and services, such as digital mapping and GIS applications.

Egypt represented yet another type of geomatics market in the region. Its major thrust was now on environmental concerns. The country had developed an environmental action plan that addressed problems with water and land resources management, air pollution, marine and coastal resources, and global heritage preservation, all of which had a significant geomatic component. The cost of implementing Phase 1 of the plan was estimated at some $300 million over the period of 1993–1995.

Egypt also provided opportunities associated with a $3 billion power generation and distribution project and some $2 billion in construction projects associated with the expansion of the country's gas production and oil-processing capacity. Although the majority of work in the geomatics-related field was conducted by local companies, subcontracting opportunities were significant.

Egypt was also a significant market from another perspective. Historically, Egypt had exported its geomatics expertise to other Arab states. Consequently, penetration of this market could be used to leverage access to other markets of the region, particularly in conjunction with Egyptian partners.

Market Evaluation

In order to evaluate each of the four geographic regions from Airview's perspective, Rick developed a summary of the primary characteristics of each of the market areas under consideration. This summary is presented in Exhibit 2 on page 369.

He also reviewed several possible ways of establishing Airview's presence in any of the regional/national markets. He summarized his considerations as indicated in Exhibit 3 on page 370.

Discussion

In his considerations related to the choice of a potential, new, target market, Rick assumed that once he had arrived at a sensible, coherent marketing plan, Airview could apply for financial support from the government. In fact, he had already discussed this possibility with the Federal Business Development Bank. In addition, he could expect some assistance from the Program for Export Market Development if he chose to establish an office or participate in bidding for projects in a selected market. This assistance could cover 50% of their costs of travel and setting up a permanent foreign office.

His overall concerns included not only the immediate costs of implementing his marketing plan but also the process he should use to select the best market in view of its salient characteristics and the company's goals.

Rick's view of the American market was generally positive. His major concern was with price competition from local firms and possible fluctuations in the exchange rate, which over a short period of time might undermine their cost structure. At the same time, he felt that Airview's technological advantage in the United States was less significant than in other markets. Finally, he assumed that his best opportunity south of the border would be in GIS-related areas, which would require either a substantial investment in obtaining a greater degree of expertise in this area or a joint effort with a GIS company.

The Mexican market was also viewed positively, particularly after the anticipated lifting of flight restrictions in 1996. However, Rick felt that due to the high cost of their staff, Airview would probably be competitive only in complex projects involving both data capture and their conversion into a computer format. At the same time, he was attracted by the operating advantages of having the company's flying season extended beyond the current few summer months.

Latin America seemed to be too competitive to support Airview's solo entry. On the other hand, the region's fragmentation into many small national markets could prove challenging from an operating point of view. Rick felt that seeking an alliance with Canadian mining and resource companies, thereby successfully establishing their operations, might prove to be attractive, particularly if Airview's entry could be

EXHIBIT 2   Market Review

Market Characteristics	United States	Mexico	Latin America	North Africa and Middle East
Economic and Political Environment	Stable	Stabilizing	Stabilizing	Fluctuating
Access Restrictions	None	Local agent required No flying in Mexico	All mapping on-site in Brazil	Language Culture
Market Size	Large	Small	Medium	Medium-large
Entry and Operating Costs	Low	Medium	Medium	Medium-high
Growth	Slow, stable	High	High	High
Financing	Cash, immediate	Transfer, delays	Transfer problems IFIs	Ranging from cash to IFIs financing
Contract Procurement	Transparent, fair	Ambiguous, improving	Frequently ambiguous	Ambiguous
Major Products	Digital mapping, GIS	Cadastral mapping, GIS	Topographic and cadastral mapping	Topographic mapping, surveying
Long-Term Advantage (technology, expertise)	Limited advantage	Diminishing, but not disappearing	Slowly diminishing	Sustainable
Primary Customers	State and municipal governments	Federal and state governments	Federal governments Resource sector	Central cartographic agencies Resource sector
Pricing	Compeititve, but based on high local costs	Competitive, based on low local costs	Extremely competitive, based on low local costs	Relatively high costs
Competition	Local, very high	Local, U.S. high	Local, international, extremely high	Local, international, moderate
Entry Strategies	Direct bidding, local partner	Local partner or subsidiary	Network of agents or local partner IFIs projects	Local partner or agent IFIs projects
Strategic Advantages	Close, similar to the Canadian market	Entry to South America Technological advantage Active during Canadian slack	Technological fit Active during Canadian slack	Technological advantage Growing Less competition Long-term prospects
Expansion Opportunities	GIS consulting systems integration	Acquisition of local subsidiary	Training	CIDA project Libya after restrictions

supported by the provision of some elements of GIS. As in Mexico's case, the countries of Latin America provided the possibility of operating the company's aircraft during the Canadian off-season.

Finally, Rick regarded the markets of the Arab world with particular interest. Airview would definitely have a technical advantage over its local competitors in these markets. At the same time, pricing in this region seemed to be generally less competitive than in the other areas, whereas the similarity of the individual national markets, in most cases based on the demand created by the resource sector, would allow for gradual penetration of the region. At the same time, Rick realized that Airview's lack of experience in international markets in general and in the Arab world in particular would create a very challenging situation for the company's staff.

EXHIBIT 3   Airview Entry Strategies

Project-Oriented Penetration

This is a strategy suitable for small, niche-oriented firms. The company would have to target a specific area and seek a specific contract. Involvement would be limited to the scope of the specific contract. The main barrier to this approach could be associated with local presence requirements.

Establishing a network of local agents in the countries of interest in the region may provide access to information on upcoming tenders and allow for participation in the bidding process. Bidding for local contracts may serve as a foundation for establishing the company's presence in the region and could be treated as part of an entry strategy.

Subcontracting to Local Firms

This strategy offered the advantage of overcoming local presence restrictions.

Strategic Alliances

An alliance with a Canadian or foreign partner can work quite effectively, provided the firms complement one another in resources and business philosophies.

Establishment of Branch Office

This could be an effective way of overcoming local presence restrictions, provided the firm was sufficiently financed to undertake the costs of setting up such an operation. The choice of location would also be crucial in determining the success of such a venture.

A Corporate Buy-Out

This seemed a somewhat risky proposition, requiring both adequate financing, business acumen to succeed, and lack of restrictions on foreign ownership of local companies. If successful, however, the result would be an immediate presence in the selected market.

Establishment of Head Office Outside of Canada

Although this could enable a company to access the selected market, this possibility could only be considered for large and stable markets, such as the United States.

Foreign Ownership

Like the strategic alliance option, this can offer opportunities, particularly with U.S. firms, provided that this route is in keeping with the long-term goals of that firm and that the two firms are compatible.

Alliances with Local Geomatics Firms

An alliance with a local partner could be beneficial if based on the combination of local experience and inexpensive labor with Airview's equipment and data-processing and mapping capabilities.

Joint Ownership of a Local Company

Acquiring a local company in partnership with another Canadian company may provide some advantages if the partners' product lines complement each other. A provider of GIS software or system integrator may be a good candidate for joint ownership with Airview.

CASE DISCUSSION QUESTIONS

1. How would you characterize Airview's primary goals associated with its plans to expand internationally? How will these goals influence the company's evaluation of the various market opportunities?

2. How would you assess the export potential of Airview's services?

3. How would you evaluate each of the described markets from Airview's perspective? Which market(s) would you choose for Airview to enter?

4. Which of the indicated entry strategies would you suggest for your selected market(s)? Why?

5. What managerial issues would you consider in drafting an implementation plan for entering your chosen market?

CASE CREDIT

Prepared by Kris Opalinski and Walter S. Good of the University of Manitoba as a basis for classroom discussion rather than to illustrate either effective or ineffective handling of an administrative situation. The name of the company and its officers have been disguised. Support for the development of this case was provided by the Centre for International Business Studies, University of Manitoba. Used with permission of the authors.

CASE NOTES

[1] A specialized technique for defining an accurate three-dimensional coordinate system for determining the location and dimensions of objects on the earth's surface.

Škoda Auto (The Czech Carmaker)

I n the Fall of 2000, an interesting advertisement ran on British television concerning the Czech plant of Volkswagen. In the television spot, a very British executive in French cuffs, a chalk-striped suit, and with a posh accent is looking impressed as he is shown through an automotive assembly factory. Everything is state of the art, with robots working efficiently on the gleaming shop floor as a doughyfaced Czech explains the factor's rigorous quality control.

His Lordship comments, "Most impressive," and pantomimes a round of applause for some of the workers. "Well done," he tells them. Then he turns and says, confidentially, to his host, "And I understand you also make those funny little Škoda cars here."[1]

The advertisement indicated how far Škoda had come during its 100-year history. The company's Annual Report for 2000 had announced the production of 400,000 vehicles in that year—the most ever produced in a single year. This was in spite of negative tendencies in the global automobile industry. This was only one of many accolades the company had received, and one might wonder what the future held for a company that had lived the Cinderella story. However, any observer of the global automobile industry knew that the industry was becoming intensely competitive, and many firms that had once been profitable were suffering great losses and wondering if they could survive. In that type of environment, the company had to decide what should be their marketing strategy? Should they move beyond manufacturing and selling automobiles primarily in the Czech Republic and Germany to a global strategy that would include erecting plants and sending exports far beyond the present reach? Should the United States, one of the world's largest markets, be the destination of Škoda products? Indeed, the financial statements in the 2000 Annual Report, revealed several trends that might negatively impact the company.

Background on the Company

The company that would later become Škoda Automobile Company was first formed in 1895 when Vaclav Laurin, a mechanic, and Vaclav Klement, a bookseller, joined together to manufacture the Slavia bicycle in the town of Miladá Boleslav, Czechoslovakia about 40 miles to the northeast of Prague. Four years later, the company decided to begin the production of motorcycles. By this time, the company had a total workforce of 68 people.

Then in 1901, the company began using its motorcycle parts in the production of motor vehicles with four wheels and a 2-cylinder engine. The first automobile they produced was named the L & K Voiturette. A quarter of a century later in 1925, the company merged with Škoda Plzen (a producer of heavy equipment) and expanded its production of motor vehicles by producing trucks, buses, aircraft engines and agricultural machines. The company assumed the name Škoda and dropped the former brand name of Laurin & Klement. Škoda Plzen and Škoda Auto remained under the same roof until 1931 when they split and went their separate ways.

At this time, Škoda had a sleek and powerful model called the Superb that was even more desirable to own than a BMW—and more expensive. The time was when people bought a BMW if they did not have enough money to buy a Škoda Superb.

When the Nazis marched into Czechoslovakia in 1939, Hitler grabbed Škoda Auto and made it an armaments factory that was a part of the Hermann-Goering-Werke. He also ordered Škoda to move the steering wheel of its autos to the left side where it has remained ever since.

As soon as the war was over, the company was nationalized by the Soviets who had taken over the country and renamed it AZNP Škoda. Under the Soviets, the company gained a monopoly status as the only Czech passenger car manufacturer. With its glory days faded, the jokes began as the quality of the automobile began to slide. After 1960, Škoda began producing cars for the mass market that had little style and often looked like a metal box. As poor as their quality was, the Škoda was still ahead of its Eastern European counterparts such as Trabant, Wartburg and Lada.

After the Velvet Revolution in Czechoslovakia in 1989 when the Communist government resigned, a Republic was formed, and the writer Vaclav Havel was elected President. The government immediately began to seek a buyer for Škoda as a part of its privatization of national assets. That buyer was found, and on April 16, 1991, Škoda became the fourth brand of the Volkswagen Group after VW, Audi and Seat (the Spanish subsidiary). Volkswagen bought a 70 percent interest in the company, and the Czech government retained a 30 percent interest. In 1994, Volkswagen bought out the remaining 30 percent interest from the Czech government.

Interestingly, the name "Škoda" in the Czech language means "a shame," and the company in the 40 years of the Soviet regime certainly lived up to its name. It was unfortunate that the oldest car company in Eastern Europe fell greatly in both quality and prestige. Because of a lack of innovation, its models became outdated, its factories became inefficient and its workers were not well trained.[2] In fact, there were more than enough jokes about Škoda to go around. People would often ask, "Have you heard the one about—

"How do you double the value of a Škoda? Fill it with gasoline."

"What do you call a Škoda convertible? A dumpster."

"Why does the Škoda have a heated rear window? To keep your hands warm when you're pushing it."

These jokes grew out of the lack of emphasis on quality in nationalized companies. If consumers were forced to purchase automobiles from Soviet Union companies and were prevented from purchasing goods outside the region, there was no real incentive to produce a competitive automobile. Likewise, workers who were guaranteed by the government "lifetime employment" were not motivated to produce quality products in order to keep their jobs.

However, the new infusion of capital and emphasis on research and development from Volkswagen brought forth such popular models as the smaller Felicia and the larger middle-class model Octavia. These models began to steal market share from other car manufacturers in the highly competitive Western European small car market.

Škoda received such honors as the "F.I.A. World Cup for Manufacturers of 2-Litre-Cars 1994." In 2001, *Which? Magazine* of the United Kingdom rated

Škoda's new Fabia model (designed to replace the Felicia) as the safest car in the supermini class. Another magazine of the United Kingdom, *The Economist,* identified Škoda Auto as the most successful company in the post-Communist countries.

Economic Status of the Czech Republic in the Twenty-First Century

On November 17, 1989, a student rally for freedom began at Wenceslas Square in Prague, and within two weeks the Communist government had relinquished power to the government in what would later be referred to as a "Velvet Revolution." In 1993, Czechoslovakia split into two parts—the Czech Republic and Slovakia. The Czech Republic began to put into place laws to encourage privatization of national assets and the development of new entrepreneurial enterprises. The privatization of national companies took place by three means: A sale of the assets to outside owners (often companies from other countries); a management-employee buyout; and voucher privatization in which citizens were given vouchers for a minimal price that they could use to purchase the stock of national companies that were being privatized.

Dr. Jaroslav Halik, Professor at the Prague School of Economics, suggested the initial situation in the Czech Republic after the fall of Communism had the following characteristics: The country had many problems moving into a free market because of the heritage of the former Communist Society from 1948 until 1989. Some of these problems were low-quality products that could not compete in Western markets; the lack of incentives to produce high-quality products because employees had been assured of "lifetime employment" which restrained motivation; old and obsolete factory equipment; an economically and ecologically unsuitable structure of production; a monopolistic banking system that would take years to privatize; very little private money available in the Czech Republic to buy nationalized companies; an insufficient infrastructure; lack of development of managerial skills that would support the free market operation of businesses; a high degree of state ownership of businesses; a high concentration of production with very few SMEs (small and medium-sized enterprises); prices set by the government on the basis of cost; and a high degree of domestic products as opposed to imports from other parts of the world.

On the other hand, Dr. Havlik suggested there were some factors inherent in the Czech Republic that were not present in other Eastern European countries. (See Exhibit 1, "Comparison of Selected European Countries—2000.") These were as follows: A good financial position relative to other Eastern European countries; a stable market of consumer goods; a low rate of inflation; efficient agricultural market; a highly skilled labor force; close contacts with Western Europe; and a good standard of living.[3] In addition, wage rates in the Czech Republic were lower than other closely related Eastern European countries such as Poland and Hungary and certainly much lower than the wage rates of more developed economies. (See Table 1, "Comparison of Wage Rates in Czech Republic, Hungary, and Poland", p. 312.)

As compared to Hungary, Poland and Slovakia (the three other nations on track to be admitted to the European Union at the same time as the Czech Republic), the Czech Republic was doing quite well in 2000.

EXHIBIT 1   Škoda Auto: Comparison of Selected European Countries—2000

	Czech Republic	Hungary	Poland	Slovakia	Austria	France	Germany	United Kingdom	Japan	USA	Russia
Surface area (thous. km²)	79	93	323	49	84	551	357	244	378	9364	17075
Mid-year population (mil)	10,3	10,1	38,7	5,4	8,1	58,8	82,0	59,2	126,4	270,6	146,5
Live births per 1000 inhabitants	8,8	9,6	10,2	10,7	10,1	12,6	9,7	12,1	9,6	14,4	8,8
Deaths per 1000 inhabitants	10,6	13,9	9,7	9,9	9,7	9,2	10,4	10,6	7,5	8,8	13,6
Gross domestic product (USD bn, current prices, at exchange rate)	55,7	47,0	158,6	20,3	210,9	1451,8	2150,5	1403,4	3783,0	8699,2	276,7
Gross domestic product per capita (USD, current prices, at exchange rate)	5412	4649	4101	3766	26101	24669	26219	23928	29926	32153	1888
Consumer price index (1995 = 100)	130,6	166,7	153,7	116,3	103,8	104,0	104,3	109,3	102,5	107,0	216,7
Exports (USD mil)	26347	22955	27191	10720	62746	305492	543431	271849	388117	682497	74157
Exports per capita (USD)	2558	2271	703	1989	7766	5191	6626	4635	3070	2523	506
Imports (USD mil)	28783	25596	46494	13071	68187	286847	471447	314033	280618	944353	58935
Imports per capita (USD)	2794	2532	1202	2425	8439	4874	5748	5354	2220	3490	402
International reserves—minus gold (USD mil)	12542	9319	26432	2869	22432	44312	74024	32210	215471	70710	7801

Source: International yearbooks; data of national statistical offices; UN/ECE Geneva. 2000; Main Economic Indicators 3,4,7,8/00; International Financial Statistics. August, 2000.

TABLE 1   Comparison of Wage Rates in Czech Republic, Hungary, and Poland

Monthly Base Salaries in United States $	Czech Republic	Hungary	Poland
General Manager	$2,640	$3,220	$5,886
Chief Engineer	1,338	1,668	2,816
R&D Engineer	1,013	1,312	2,092
Skilled Machine Operator	377	371	607
Worker	227	237	443

Source: Hay International. October, 2000.

Status of the Company in the Twenty-First Century

The past several years have seen new records set in all areas of profitability by Škoda. In 1999, the company posted a net profit of Czech korunas 2.64 billion ($71 million) and increased its share of Czech exports to 10 percent. That year Škoda topped the Czech Top 100 Association's List as the most-admired domestic firms.

By the year 2000, Škoda produced a 3.34 billion koruna ($87 million) profit for parent company, Volkswagen. This amounted to a jump of 27 percent over the last year's profits of 2.63 billion koruna. (See Exhibit 2, "Profit and Loss Accounts for 1999–2000.") The balance sheets for 1999 and 2000 showed a significant increase in liabilities as well as equity for the year ending December 31, 2000. (See Exhibit 3, "Balance Sheets for 1999 and 2000.") The company had also enjoyed a healthy 62 percent increase in sales from 1996 to 2000 and a 17 percent increase from 1999 to 2000. (See Exhibit 4, "Key Performance Indicators.")

Škoda by the year 2001 had become the largest employer in the Czech Republic with 25,000 workers. It was now spending $750 million a year with Eastern European suppliers and purchasing parts and components from 260 Czech suppliers valued at $1.1 billion. During the first half of 2000, Volkswagen had purchased the remaining 30 percent of Škoda Auto shares following negotiations with the Czech government.

Two interesting figures for the company were the following:

1. Since the privatization of Škoda in 1991, production had risen from 170,000 cars per year to 451,000 cars in 2001; and
2. Although sales of new cars fell 2.5 percent in the Czech Republic in the first two months of 2001, car sales by Škoda increased 4.7 percent.

By 2001, Škoda automobiles were available in 64 countries, and the company was considering establishing a plant in India. Škoda also had established a plant in Poznan, Poland, where it assembled from kits about 93 units of the Felicia model a day and about 44 units of the Fabia model a day. The Felicia was also assembled in Sarajevo, Bosnia. Production of Octavia also began in 2001 in Russia. The vast U.S. market looked promising, and the company wondered if it was a market it should enter.

Although Škoda normally was privileged to receive excellent press coverage, with its new models, from time to time it found itself as the recipient of some

EXHIBIT   2   Škoda Auto: Profit and Loss Accounts for 1999–2000

(in CZK thousand)	2000	1999
Revenue from sales of merchandise	6,079,724	5,315,966
Costs of sales of merchandise	3,352,780	3,090,215
Sales margin	2,726,944	2,225,751
Revenue from sale of own products and services	130,203,513	105,092,907
Change in stocks of own production	102,666	304,289
Own work capitalized	13,782,839	1,120,344
Production	116,426,226	106,517,540
Material and energy consumption	102,643,387	77,335,789
Services	13,782,839	12,894,575
Consumption for Production	116,426,226	90,230,364
Value added	18,976,749	18,512,927
Personnel expenses	7,464,855	6,628,853
Taxes and charges	42,336	44,286
Depreciation and amortization of fixed assets	7,767,963	6,516,311
Revenue from sale of fixed assets and raw materials	1,862,988	1,102,763
Book value of fixed assets and raw materials sold	1,422,305	855,090
Other operating revenue	790,715	275,179
Other operating costs	717,015	653,741
Release of provisions and accruals	2,500,771	1,744,643
Creation of provisions and accruals	1,875,147	1,812,049
of which deferred costs	(290,743)	(207,842)
Release of provisions	488,690	426,994
Creation of provisions	108,000	301,011
Operating profit	5,222,292	5,251,165
Loss from financial operations	–1,028,957	–1,422,579
Profit from ordinary activities before tax	4,193,335	3,828,586
Extraordinary (loss)/profit	–17,946	–14,383
Profit before tax	4,175,389	3,814,203
Corporate taxes	839,076	1,176,929
Profit for the year after tax	3,336,313	2,637,274

unfortunate comments. In February 2001, Škoda unveiled a prototype of its new 4-door limousine at the Geneva Car Show. The prototype was called the "Octavia Long" and resembled the Volkswagen Pasat but was 10 centimeters longer. The automobile was intended for ministers, ambassadors and businesspeople. However, Czech Premier Milos Zeman complained about the price, delivery terms and size of the Octavia Long. He said that of all the Czech ministers, only Gregr Miroslav (who is short) would fit comfortably in the car.[4]

In February of 2001, Škoda Auto's management and labor unions agreed to a 10.1 percent pay raise for the year and the next year thus averting an announced strike. The unions had originally asked for a 12 percent hike, and Škoda management had originally offered 8 percent. To support the higher

EXHIBIT

3

Škoda Auto: Balance Sheets for 1999 and 2000

(in CZK thousand)	31.12.2000	31.12.1999
Assets		
Fixed assets	**39,174,741**	**33,687,219**
Intangible assets	223,302	309,402
Tangible assets	38,229,431	32,648,475
Financial Assets	722,008	729,342
Current Assets	**26,802,482**	**21,362,401**
Inventories	9,014,089	7,702,590
Receivables	16,945,579	11,998,388
Cash and cash equivalents	842,814	1,661,423
Other assets	683,754	560,704
Total Assets	**66,660,977**	**55,610,324**
Liabilities and shareholders' equity		
Equity	**26,032,625**	**22,700,302**
Share capital	16,708,850	16,708,850
Share premium and legal reserves	1,888,548	1,756,684
Profit/loss of the previous years	4,098,914	1,597,494
Profit/loss of the current year	3,336,313	2,637,274
Liabilities	**37,433,811**	**29,027,069**
Provisions for future liabilities and charges	4,284,200	4,948,709
Long-term liabilities	10,000,000	9,033,297
Short-term liabilities	18,299,611	12,045,063
Loans and overdrafts	4,850,000	3,000,000
Other liabilities	3,194,541	3,882,953
Total liabilities and shareholders' equity	**66,660,977**	**55,610,324**

pay, Škoda demanded greater productivity from its workers and announced that those who could not handle triple-shift production or computer-driven technology would have to leave. The company also announced an increase in the price of its automobiles in May of that year. The base price of the Fabia would rise by several hundred dollars and the cheapest Octavia would cost $10,335 instead of $9,585.

The plant at Miladá Boleslav was now an impressive structure of glass and steel which was designed by the famous architect Dr. Gunter Henn and based on the concept presented in Professor Hans-Joachim Warnecke's 1990 work, "The Fractal Factory."[5]

In May of 2001, the company also announced that it intended to build a testing facility for its cars on state-owned land. At that time, new car testing was often carried out in Germany. However, environmentalists were afraid that the facility would endanger plants and animals.[6]

The success of Škoda reverberated throughout Europe. The French automobile manufacturer Renault decided to invest in Automobile Dacia of Romania to produce a car that would sell for about $5,000 for the emerging

EXHIBIT | 4 | Škoda Auto: Key Performance Indicators

		1996	1997	1998	1999	2000
Vehicle production	cars	263,193	357,170	403,515	371,169	450,910
Vehicle sales	cars	279,363	373,451	400,269	376,329	448,394
of which imported	cars	16,907	16,096	2,957	0	0
Total revenue	CZK mill.	58,898	90,095	105,704	110,409	136,283
of which domestic	%	45	37	23	19	18
export	%	55	63	77	81	82
Profit after tax	CZK mill.	163	1,168	2,239	2,637	3,336
Fixed assets	CZK mill.	25,116	26,836	29,482	33,687	39,175
Current assets	CZK mill.	17,324	21,009	21,893	21,923	26,802
Equity	CZK mill.	26,469	17,997	20,236	22,700	26,032
Liabilities	CZK mill.	15,971	29,848	31,139	32,910	37,434
Cash flow	CZK mill.	5,179	7,710	8,795	9,780	10,756
Capital expenditure	CZK mill.	10,417	7,069	8,658	10,709	13,248
Employees	personnel	17,992	22,205	22,768	22,030	25,833
of which temporary	personnel	1,271	3,228	2,327	1,708	3,245
Equity as a percentage of equity and total liabilities	%	62.4	37.6	39.4	40.8	39.1
Fixed assets as a percentage of equity	%	105.4	67.1	68.6	67.4	66.5

markets of Eastern Europe. Likewise, General Motors invested $100 million in a partnership with Auto Vaz of Russia to produce an inexpensive mini-SUV for sale in that country and eventually be exported elsewhere.[7] Škoda itself had decided to produce 50 prototypes of the new mid-size Bentley in the Czech Republic in a move that shocked the United Kingdom automotive industry. Many people familiar with the global car industry wondered if one company could produce and sell an inexpensive car such as the Fabia and also the highly respected and expensive Bentley.

Trends in the World Automobile Industry

By 2001, the global automobile industry had become fiercely competitive. This industry which was so vulnerable to downturns in the business cycle, relied heavily upon a strong cash flow to weather such perils. Even the world's largest auto maker, General Motors, was suffering a bleak outlook as it struggled to survive the consumer malaise that set in after the events of September 11, 2001. Additionally, Toyota (the world's third largest automobile manufacturer) hit record highs with its sales. The company suggested the weaker yen and tough cost-cutting measures were responsible for their good fortune.

Another world automobile trend in 2001 was the growth in demand experienced in developing countries. Such substitute products as bicycles were being displaced by automobiles in these countries. Until shortly before 2001, cars were out of the reach of most Chinese—even the middle class. But as incomes increased and tariffs on imported cars began to fall after Beijing's accession to the World Trade Organization and imported models began to flood the market, domestic producers were forced to cut their prices.[8]

A price war was heating up in late 2001 with sticker prices on Chinese cars falling by as much as 15 percent. In the first years of the twenty-first century 100 state-owned car companies still existed in China, and most were losing money. The Government was encouraging the merger of many of these firms to achieve economies of scale. Industry projections suggested that the strongest potential growth in automobile sales would be in the developing countries of Asia, South America, Eastern Europe and Africa rather than the mature economies of Western Europe, North America and Japan.

In making plant location decisions, companies normally considered the following factors: labor costs, energy costs, access to a work force that had the right skills, access to the necessary infrastructure (roads, railroads, favorable political climate) and closeness to important global markets.[9] The Škoda plant in the Czech Republic had been a good selection for Volkswagen for those reasons. There was also a tendency to move to just-in-time inventory systems at automobile manufacturers around the world which caused suppliers to move their operations closer to auto plants. This movement was occurring around the Škoda plant at Miladá Boleslav as well.

Not only were mergers of automobile companies being considered in China, but there was a strong movement worldwide to an amalgamation of companies within the industry. Unfortunately, many of the cross-border mergers and joint ventures in the industry have had a difficult time surviving. For instance, the joint venture between General Motors and Saab cost General Motors $2 billion which would be difficult to recoup. In addition, Ford bought Jaguar in the early 1990s and invested approximately $5 billion in that model. However, observers suggested this purchase could actually end up being profitable for Ford. Other global ventures that did not have positive outcomes were Ford-ACE, Chrysler-Lamborghini, Chrysler-Rootes, Renault-Volvo, BMW-Rover, and Volkswagen-Rolls. For the high cost of acquisition, the automobile companies might have more easily created their own new models.[10]

Questions for the Future

As Škoda looked to the future, there were several important decisions that would have to be made to help the company stay competitive in the coming years. The global car manufacturing industry was becoming more highly competitive than ever before. The market structure was changing as the industry went from a primarily national to a regional and finally a global marketplace. One question Škoda had to deal with was whether to continue the movement of assembly plants abroad when the Czech Republic had such inexpensive labor. Also, the United States, the largest automobile market in the world, had not been targeted as a destination for the Škoda. Would the success of the past continue to fuel the company in the future? What were trends in the world automobile market that might impact the company in the coming years? Were there trends in the recently published 2000 Annual Report's Profit in the Loss Accounts and the Balance Sheets that might negatively impact the company in the future.

CASE DISCUSSION QUESTIONS

1. Identify challenges faced and opportunities available to companies in the Czech Republic as they have moved from nationalized to privatized entities.

2. Perform a SWOT analysis for Škoda.

3. Analyze how well Škoda fits within the Volkswagen group.

4. Identify appropriate strategies for a company operating in the global car manufacturing environment.

CASE CREDIT

This case was prepared by Marlene M. Reed, Samford University, and Rochelle R. Brunson, Alva Community College, and is intended to be used as a basis for classroom discussion. All rights are reserved to the authors. Copyright © 2002. Used with permission.

REFERENCES

1. *The Fleet Sheet,* April 25, 2001.

2. *The Fleet Sheet,* June 18, 2001.

3. Flint, Jerry (January 1999). Global math. *Ward's Auto World,* Volume 35, Issue 1, p. 15.

4. Halik, Jaroslav (June 5, 2001). Lecture at the Prague School of Economics.

5. Kimberley, William (June 2001). Škoda: An Eastern Europe success. *Automotive Manufacturing & Production,* Volume 13, Issue 6, pp. 26–28.

6. Kovarow, Steven (April 23, 2001). Czech carmaker Škoda moving up. *USA Today,* p. 3–B.

7. Mudd, Tom (September 18, 2000). The last laugh. *Industry Week,* Volume 249, Issue 15, pp. 38–44.

8. Roberts, Dexter, and Webb, Alysha (June 17, 2002). Motor nation. *Business Week,* Issue 3787, pp. 44–45.

9. *Škoda Auto Annual Report,* 2000.

10. Yip, George S. (Fall 1989). Global strategy in a world of nations? *Sloan Management Review,* pp. 29–41.

Endnotes

1. Mudd, Tom (September 18, 2000). The last laugh. *Industry Week,* Volume 249, Issue 15, pp. 38–44.

2. Kovarow, Steven (April 23, 2001). Czech carmaker Škoda moving up, *USA Today,* p. 3–B.

3. Halik, Jaroslav (June 5, 2001). Lecture at the Prague School of Economics.

4. *The Fleet Sheet,* June 18, 2001.

5. Kimberley, William (June 2001). Škoda: An Eastern Europe success. *Automotive Manufacturing & Production,* Volume 13, Issue 6, pp. 26–28.

6. *The Fleet Sheet,* April 25, 2001.

7. Kovarow, Steven (April 23, 2001). Czech carmaker Škoda moving up, *USA Today,* p. 3-B.

8. Roberts, Dexter, and Webb, Alysha (June 17, 2002). Motor nation. *Business Week,* Issue 3787, pp. 44–45.

9. Yip, George S. (Fall 1989). Global strategy in a world of nations? *Sloan Management Review,* pp. 29–41.

10. Flint, Jerry (January 1999). Global math. *Ward's Auto World,* Volume 35, Issue 1, p. 15.

The *Fleet Sheet*

Marlene M. Reed/Professor, School of Business,
Samford University, Birmingham, Alabama
Rochelle R. Brunson/Department Chair, Management Development
Alvin Community College, Alvin, Texas

At precisely 8:00 A.M. on Monday, April 3, 2000, faxes began printing out simultaneously in the offices of English-speaking companies all over the Czech Republic. Among the news of the Czech Republic translated into English that day was an interesting political insight gleaned from two newspapers:

> "The Washington Post *wrote that Madeleine Albright is the weakest U.S. Secretary of State since the early 1970s and is now only popular in Prague. Euro quips that that's not so bad: The only place Vaclav Havel* [1] *is now taken seriously is in Washington."*

It was this kind of honest, straightforward evaluation of the Czech economy and government that had made the *Fleet Sheet* so popular to foreign companies and their managers. For Erik Best, founder of the *Fleet Sheet*, there were many decisions to be made concerning the future of the company as well as his own future.

He had begun the business on February 22, 1992, because of a perceived short-term need by Western companies rushing into Czechoslovakia after the Velvet Revolution for economic and political information that they could understand. He had envisioned that in a few years these companies would train Czech nationals to take over their operations in the country, and the English-speaking Westerners would withdraw. That had not happened, and he now wondered if he had a "going concern" that lacked a sound organizational and legal structure to survive into the future. He also wondered how long an operation such as his would continue to be a viable venture because of rapidly-changing technology and greater access to news through the Internet. Erik was now 37 years old, and he knew he needed to make some decisions for the future.

Erik's Education and Early Work Experience

Erik was born in North Carolina; and when he was 11 years old, his family moved to Montana. He went to high school there and wrote for the high school newspaper. He also became a part-time staff sports writer for the *Missoulian*—the local newspaper. Near the end of his Senior year in high school, Erik was offered a journalism scholarship to Vanderbilt University; however, he turned it down because at that time he was not sure he wanted to be a journalist. In the back of his mind, he had thought for some time that he wanted to be involved in business or politics or perhaps both. He decided to attend Georgetown University, and he received a degree in Foreign Service from Georgetown in 1985.

In the summers while working on his undergraduate degree at Georgetown, he also studied the Russian language at Middlebury College in Vermont; a school well known for its concentration on international affairs. He subsequently received a Master's Degree in Russian from Middlebury in the Summer of 1985. Perhaps the educational experience that had the greatest impact upon Erik's life was a required four months' stint in Moscow. When he had completed his degree at Middlebury, he entered the M.B.A. program at the University of North Carolina at Chapel Hill and received his M.B.A. degree in 1987.

The Move to Prague

Erik Best, a fluent speaker of the Russian language and one conversant in other Slavic languages, became enamored with the historic changes taking place in Eastern Europe. Never in the 20th Century, had the opportunity existed to be a part of such a great transformation. Never before in history had countries formerly living under a Socialist government with centrally-planned economies tried to make the transition to a free market economy where Adam Smith's "Invisible Hand" would be responsible for moving resources into their most advantageous usage.

Therefore, when the offer was made to Erik by the M.B.A. Enterprise Corps to join them in their work in Czechoslovakia, he quickly accepted. In February of 1991, Erik packed his bags and moved to Prague. He immediately fell in love with the country and found the Czech language very similar to Russian. In explaining his love of Prague to others, Erik would state, "I have always loved music, and there is no city in the world so rich with music as Prague. There are classical concerts daily in concert halls, churches, town squares, on the breathtaking Charles Bridge, private chambers, large public halls and under street arches. There are violinists and accordianists playing on street corners and in Metro stations. I have heard that there are more musicians per capita in the Czech Republic than anywhere else in the world. After all, it was in Prague that Mozart wrote the opera *Don Giovanni* and found greater acclaim than in his own Austria. It was also the home of composers Dvorak and Smetana. This is one of the reasons I feel at home in this city."

The Situation in Eastern Europe

In the early 1990s, the breakup of centralized Socialist economies was occurring all over Eastern Europe. Simultaneously, there was a rapid growth of the private sector in Russia and the surrounding countries of Poland, Czechoslovakia, and Hungary. One of the challenges in the burgeoning market economies was creating small businesses out of large enterprises and also launching entirely new ventures where none had been before. In fact, the development of the small business sector had been the most successful manifestation of the movement to a market economy. Small businesses had also been the greatest success story in the privatization process. Auctions of small businesses and the restitution of property in these countries had led to the restoration of some family businesses.

However, numerous problems beset these newly-created companies. In some cases, the venture was merely additional work added to one or two other jobs to keep the entrepreneur afloat with increasingly higher inflation rates and increasingly stagnant wage rates. Many small businesses were forced into operating illegitimately to deal with unfair and cumbersome legal procedures in the regulatory environment, or to avoid the attention of the Mafia or corrupt officials. It became very difficult to work out a secure contract for lease of property, and the banking system was not equipped to deal with the needs of small business.[2]

Another serious problem was the lack of experience in running private businesses that existed in Eastern Europe. Most hopeful entrepreneurs had lived all of their lives in a Socialist economy and had no training or knowledge related to the way in which one becomes an entrepreneur. It was into this environment that many organizations from the West sent consultants to assist with the revitalization of the economy as a free market. The M.B.A. Enterprise Corps was one such operation.

Origination of Idea for the *Fleet Sheet*

After working in Prague for a year, it became clear to Erik that international companies that had established offices and operations in the Czech Republic had difficulty in obtaining accurate and timely information on political and economic trends in the country upon which to make business decisions. From his work as a management consultant, he knew that decision makers in companies are very busy, and those operating in the Czech Republic would need information that was very concise and written in English. At the time, no such product was available in the country. It occurred to him that a 1-page faxed bulletin would be the best format for such a paper. The fax was also an inexpensive medium to use. He knew that in the beginning there would not be much news to report, and a 1-page sheet of paper would probably hold all he needed to print.

By early 1992, he had worked out all of the details to begin the business; and on February 22nd he published the first issue. Erik believed that if he had 4 or 5 subscribers in the first month, the product would be successful. In fact, approximately 15 to 20 subscribers signed up in the first month of operations. By early Spring of 2000, there were somewhere in the neighborhood of 1,000 subscribers receiving the *Fleet Sheet* on a regular basis.

Believing that the life cycle of his product would be relatively short, Erik took little thought to establishing a permanent structure for his business. He set it up as a sole proprietorship, and did not bother with a business plan since the operations of the company were uncomplicated and easy to establish. By 2000, he had 8 staff members in the company. Some of the staff came in the very early morning to review newspapers and begin translating the news from Czech to English. Other members of the staff came in around 7:30 A.M. and were involved in distribution and client support. Erik assumed the major responsibility for picking out the most important news to be translated and distributed in the *Fleet Sheet*. He believed a key competitive advantage of the *Fleet Sheet* was its emphasis on a quality product that reported useful Czech economic and political news. Occasionally, the *Sheet* had made a person unhappy by interpreting something incorrectly. However, if Erik agreed with the person's argument, he would admit it and print a retraction. He had found it important to listen to customer complaints and recognize the needs of the customer. He attempted to treat his readers as equal partners. The name for his paper came from the fact that it was issued in a timely manner, and also in reference to Fleet Street in London where all of the major newspapers once resided before moving to the Docklands.

The Pricing Strategy

Erik realized immediately that the major publication constraint would be the number of people he could physically fax copies of the *Fleet Sheet* to in a short period of time. This was primarily due to the fact that he knew there would be a limitation on the number of telephone lines that he could get. He also knew that another constraint was the budget of the companies and when they needed to have the news. The larger multinational companies, he speculated, would be willing to pay a higher price to get the information very early in the morning. On the other hand, smaller companies beset with fewer complicated decisions would probably be willing to pay a lower price to have the information later in the day. Some businesses might need the information only once a week.

On the basis of this assessment, Erik constructed a pricing structure that averaged $3 to $4 per day for the customer who wanted the *Fleet Sheet* faxed to the him or her early in the morning, and for the smaller companies who needed the *Fleet Sheet* faxed to them only once a week, the price would drop to $.50 to $.75 an issue. There would be intermediate pricing between the two end points. Therefore, the large companies and lawyers for whom "time is money," could have access to all of the Czech political and economic news early in the morning so that they could make astute and timely decisions based upon realistic information. The companies that did not need information in a timely manner could enjoy the benefit of a discounted price for the information. The graduated pricing strategy would also make the distribution of the paper manageable. It seemed to be an effective pricing strategy: Pricing based upon when the subscriber receives the news. The attractiveness of the pricing strategy was that anyone could afford the *Fleet Sheet*.

In order to insure the timeliness of the paper, Erik initially guaranteed the larger companies that if they did not receive their fax of the *Fleet Sheet* before 9:00 A.M. each day, it would be free. However, the fax was never late, and Erik simply dropped this guarantee since no one worried about getting a fax late.

Marketing of the *Fleet Sheet*

The marketing of the *Fleet Sheet* was multi-pronged. The first thing that Erik did was to advertise in English-language publications such as the *Prague Post, Business Central Europe* (published by *The Economist*), *The American Chamber of Commerce Newsletter* and in the Czech press in very select publications read by the elite. He was surprised that his subscribers had been not only people from English-speaking countries, but also the Dutch, French, German and even some Czech companies that realized having the news abbreviated for them saved valuable time.

The company also engaged in direct marketing. They found out about new companies moving to town from the American Chamber of Commerce, people Erik met, personal contacts and by word of mouth. With all new contacts, the company immediately apprised them of the product they were offering. Erik found that his satisfied subscribers let other people know about the service, and many new customers came from referrals. One reason his subscribers had been well satisfied was because Erik made an effort to dig into the important issues facing businesses in the Czech Republic. He also attempted to give people analysis rather than a simple reporting of the news. He found that clients read the *Fleet Sheet* because of the selection of articles that were covered.

A more recent addition to his marketing activities had been using E-mail to whet the appetite of potential subscribers. (See Exhibit 1, "E-mail Synopsis of *Fleet Sheet*.") Whenever anyone E-mailed him, Erik immediately added their name to a list of people who receive a summary of the day's *Fleet Sheet* articles twice a week. The purpose of this was to acquaint them with the value of subscribing to the *Fleet Sheet* for daily faxes. Understanding the animosity some people have to receiving "junk Emails," Erik added a notice at the bottom of the E-mail that explained:

If you do not wish to receive such messages in the future, please simply let us know and we will remove your name from our list.

EXHIBIT 1   E-Mail Synopsis of *Fleet Sheet*

Subj: **In today's Fleet Sheet**
Date: 11/20/00 12:43:19 AM Central Standard Time
From: info@fleet.cz (Fleet Sheet/E.S. Best)
To: info@fleet.cz
From today's Fleet Sheet:

(MFD/1) The four-party coalition won a big victory in the Senate elections yesterday, gaining seats in 16 of the 19 races in which it had candidates. ODS and CSSD lost their Senate majority and will not be able to elect the chairman of the Senate or push through constitutional changes on their own. The top position in the Senate is now held by Libuse Benesova of ODS, but she lost to Helena Rognerova of the 4C. ODS won just eight of the 27 Senate seats at stake, and CSSD managed only one victory. An independent candidate won the final seat. The communists (KSCM) failed to win any seats. One seat had been decided in the first round in favor of the 4C. Of the 81 total Senate seats, the 4C now has 39, to 22 for ODS, 15 for CSSD, three for KSCM and two for independents. Voter turnout was less than 20%. Vaclav Klaus responded to this by saying the Senate should be reformed so that its elections become part of the regional elections. (MFD/8) Jiri Leschtina of MFD says it will be interesting to see whether the Senate results lead anyone from within ODS and CSSD to break the loyalty pact and take a firm stance against Klaus and Zeman.
*

(HN/2) The results of the Senate elections reduce the chance that Vaclav Klaus will succeed Vaclav Havel as President. The results suggest that a candidate close the 4C and Havel has a better chance. The results also make it unlikely that the constitutional amendment to reduce the powers of the President will win approval. If passed, the President's power to pick Bank Board members would be limited.
*

(HN/3) CEO Jaroslav Mil of CEZ said that if price were the top priority, the sale of the state's stakes in âEZ and the regional electricity distributors could bring Kc 200- 300bn in privatization. If synergies were sought with the natural-gas distributors, he said, the amount could be higher. However, if things such as maintaining employment and coal output play a role, this amount cannot be expected, he said. In this respect, he said he could imagine a requirement that a certain amount of output be guaranteed by the buyer. He also said he sees no reason why one Czech company should not be able to offer gas, water and electricity. He also indicated that he expects more use of nuclear power in the future. (HN/P9) CEZ's stock hit a low for the year of Kc 85 and might fall more.
*

(MFD/2) Klaus got a bit touchy at ODS campaign headquarters yesterday after the first results of the Senate elections were announced. When an MFD photographer made a call during Klaus' live interview on Czech TV, Klaus grabbed the man's cellphone out of his hand and tossed it into the corner. "How can he dare (talk on the phone) while I'm being interviewed?" Klaus asked. (MFD/3) Milos Zeman, for his part, refused to face defeat and didn't even show up at CSSD campaign headquarters.

Few people ever asked to have their names removed, and many signed up as regular subscribers. This was probably because the E-mail was only sent to individuals whom Erik believed would have an interest in Czech news.

In the late 1990s, Erik developed a web site for his company. The web address was http://www.fleet.cz. (See Exhibit 2, "Home Page of *Fleet Sheet*" Home page and Final Word) He believed that the web site had enormous market potential for his company. It would now be possible for the company to place a

EXHIBIT 2   *Fleet Sheet* Home Page and Final Word

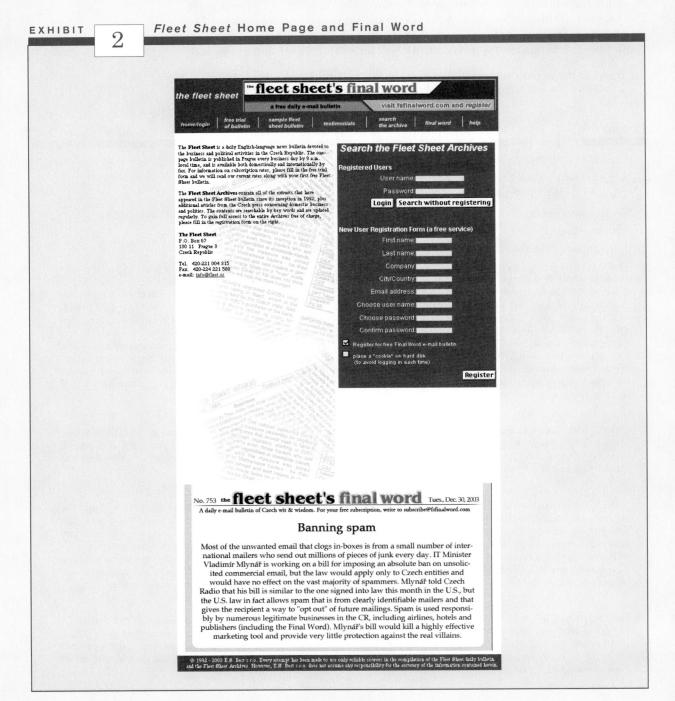

page on the web site that was a sampling of the *Fleet Sheet* for interested individuals and companies. Erik believed this had the potential to generate an even greater number of subscribers than did the E-mail synopses.

In the past, Erik had offered the entire archives on disk. A company would pay about $500 a year to subscribe to the service. However, he decided to put all of his archives from the past 8 years on the web site. The service was free, but one had to register to have access to it. This registry began to generate a good source of names for the E-mail synopses which were intended to develop enough interest from the reader to cause him or her to subscribe to the fax service.

Erik hoped that his web site would be of sufficiently high quality for people to continue to read it. He was gambling on the belief that a company could make more money in the long run by using its archives as a marketing tool to generate more subscriptions than by selling the archives as some companies such as the *Wall Street Journal* had done.

People occasionally asked Erik why he didn't go to E-mail entirely as the medium for publishing and distributing the *Fleet Sheet*. His response was, "There is the problem of protecting intellectual property. Unless you can encrypt it, you may have a copyright infringement of your material. In fact, Stephen King's most recent story which was published originally on the Internet was encrypted, but someone broke the code. Another problem with encryption is that the message can only be sent to a specific person—not a company. Therefore, there are some real problems with encrypting the information on the Internet."

Hurdles for the Business

Unlike most start-up businesses, the *Fleet Sheet* was profitable from the very beginning. Erik made an early decision to rent office space and computers initially. Whenever it became clear that the *Fleet Sheet* was a viable business, he did invest in some assets for the company such as necessary equipment.

Concerning the success of the company, Erik mused, "The revenues of the company have grown every year because the Czech Republic was seen early as the darling of the West, and they also received a great deal of media attention. Under more realistic conditions, many of the companies would not have come here." However, in the last couple of years of the 1990s, there had been a decline in subscribers. Erik often contemplated how recent world economic events might be affecting the circulation of the *Fleet Sheet*.

As to the last hurdle, Erik commented, "We have had to fend off 6 or 7 competitors who began to offer the same service that we were offering—a faxed bulletin with important political and economic news. It was a blatant rip-off of our product. The success of the *Fleet Sheet* drew other companies into the market."

Erik speculated:

> The drastic price reduction the competition offered in the beginning served to lower the overall revenue size of the market. I have often wondered if there is a big enough market to support ONE such publication over the long run, much less numerous competitors in a smaller revenue pool.

However, he also observed:

> The reason we survived was due to the overall quality of the paper. Business people know quality when they see it, and they immediately know that the Fleet Sheet *is professionally done.*

Government regulations which had been devastating to many businesses in the Czech Republic had been minimal for the *Fleet Sheet*. The company did not require a large number of licenses or drug approvals as did the large pharmaceutical companies operating in the country. However, they had been faced with government bureaucracy—especially in the distribution of their product. The Government informed them that they had to send the *Fleet Sheet* to hundreds of libraries at the company's own expense. This, of course, would have made the company non-profitable and no one would have read the paper anyway. They decided to take a risk and send the paper to only selected libraries where they believed there was a greater chance of someone actually reading the *Fleet Sheet*. Fortunately, the regulation was changed in the early part of 2000 so that the company would no longer be required to distribute the paper in this manner.

In the late 1990s, Erik decided to add an advertisement to the *Fleet Sheet*. The ad was priced at $400 a day and was rotated among 4 or 5 different companies' ads. (See Exhibit 3, "*Fleet Sheet* with Ad.") If he should decide to add another advertisement, Erik would probably have to add another page to the fax. Faxing charges are minimal, the primary cost would be additional staff to prepare another page. However, he wondered if the primary focus of the paper—relevant information in a concise format—would be maintained. People don't mind taking the time to read 1 page of the most concise political and economic news of the day, but would they read 2 pages?

In the Spring of 2000, there were around 800 subscribers to the *Fleet Sheet* paying an average of $2.50 each per day to receive the publication. In addition, each additional subscriber brought in 90% in profits and only 10% in variable costs. Erik speculated about whether a new format with two pages would actually reduce—rather than increase—subscribers.

Erik had always used Adobe Acrobat to format the paper, and the faxed paper was very easy to read. If he went to an E-mail publication of the paper altogether, there could be a text format that would not be limited to one or two pages. But he wondered if that would affect the integrity of the product. They had done so well in the past with the concise format of a 1-page fax. Would people actually sit at their computers and read through a lengthy E-mail the way they read through a newspaper or fax that they can hold in their hands? Erik speculated, "If you could produce the same experience of reading a newspaper on the Internet, it would be good. However, our present computer monitors prevent this from occurring." Erik also wondered how a company could build a brand name and attract a loyal readership over the Internet. On the Internet, one must click through so many pages to get to the desired material, that the opportunity cost of one's time becomes very expensive.

When Erik began his venture in 1992, he firmly believed it would be a short-term operation bridging the gap until a new economy was established and other sources of information became available. With that in mind, he had spent little time pondering an appropriate legal structure for the business. He had initially set the business up as a sole proprietorship, but now he wondered if he should have established it as an LLC. He would also have developed a long-term strategy for the company. He wondered if it was too late to develop a business plan for the *Fleet Sheet* and alter its legal structure. He knew he would have to fill out some forms and notify the United States Government of his actions, but perhaps he should do that. Erik wondered if a change in the legal structure of the organization would have capital gains tax implications if he decided to sell the business. He never assumed the business would last this long or he might have spent more time in planning rather than starting the business up in two weeks.

EXHIBIT **3**   *Fleet Sheet* with Ad

the fleet sheet

No. 2999	*Today's news, today* Prague, Tues., Dec. 30, 2003

Euro (fixing)	32.505	-0.015
Dollar	26.009	-0.235
Pound	46.168	-0.125
Slovak crown 100	79.011	-0.036
3-month Pribor	2.07	0.00
Dow Jones	10450.0	+1.2%
DAX	3952.7	+1.3%
Nikkei	10500.6	+0.8%
České Radiokom.	345.50	+0.6%
Český Telecom	287.50	-0.3%
ČEZ	145.25	+1.7%
Erste Bank	3210.0	+1.9%
Komerční banka	2414.00	+1.2%
Philip Morris ČR	15398.0	+1.6%
Unipetrol	66.39	+1.9%
PX 50	656.9	+1.15%

Business

(MFD/1) A poll by SC&C found that many Czechs associate EU accession next year with higher prices. Some price increases will take effect immediately in Jan., while others will be timed to coincide with EU accession on May 1. Consumers are stocking up on such things as gasoline, alcohol and prepaid phone cards at the old prices. The SC&C poll found that 26.8% of respondents fear price increases next year, compared to 16.7% who fear losing their job and 9.9% who fear accession. Most respondents consider 2003 to be an average year. Most young respondents thought it was a good year, while older respondents and low wage-earners tended to be more pessimistic. (MFD/B4) EU entry will mean higher prices for imports from some non-EU countries of such things as bananas, rice, tuna, bicycles and CDs. (MFD/6) MFD pictures Klaus in a cartoon working on his New Year's address. "Bad things come in threes," he says. "First the floods, then the drought, then EU entry."

(MFD/7) Oskar said it expects a single-digit decrease in calling levels during the first months of next year, due to the sharp VAT increase. T-Mobile said it expects calling traffic to return to its previous level after a few months. Český Telecom expects about 100,000 people to give up their fixed lines because of the higher tax.

(HN/1) Some building & loans have been unable to handle all the customers seeking to sign contracts by the end of the year, before the state subsidy declines next year. ČMSS said that it expects to serve as many as 10,000 customers a day this week. About 2m new contracts are expected this year. Next year, though, this should drop to just six figures, according to ČMSS. Building & loans will use the promise of loans to attract new customers next year. (LN/6) Some clients are using very high target savings levels - such as Kč 1m - as a way to guarantee the higher state subsidies for many years to come.

(HN/13) Pre-Christmas internet sales quadrupled this year. Czech shoppers bought more-expensive items on line, such as DVD players and digital cameras.

(HN/18) Landowners claim that a planned new law for specifying the price and length of their leases of land to farmers is unconstitutional. One version of the bill would allow farmers to continue to pay today's artificially low rates. Farmers welcome the law and favor long lease periods.

(MFD/9) Škoda Auto is offering bonuses of up to Kč 90,000 on Octavias. (EU/62) Škoda does not expect its planned new Octavia to cannibalize its sister brands.

(HN/1) The terms for reserving and paying for tickets to next year's hockey championships were so tight that many people risk losing their reservations. Tickets went on sale shortly before Christmas and had to be paid for within seven days. Due to the holidays, payment orders needed to be submitted many days in advance. Sazka said it will wait an extra day or two and will then put any tickets that have not been paid for on sale in early Jan. (MFD/D1) Some people are threatening to sue Sazka for not honoring ticket reservations that were made in the summer. Sazka blamed the situation on the Hockey Union.

(HN/13) The CR attracted 40 investments this year into IT and service centers, from companies such as Accenture, DHL, Honeywell and ExxonMobil. Investment into the 15 largest of them will exceed Kč 17bn. (DHL accounts for Kč 16bn of this, and HN gives no figure for Accenture, Honeywell and ExxonMobil.) These 15 investments are expected to lead to 4,386 new jobs. (EU/62) Separately, Škoda Auto Chairman Vratislav Kulhánek said the decade-long tax breaks given to foreign investors are "perverse." Many of the companies would come anyway, he said, and CzechInvest pays no attention to whether the new investments will threaten the existence of thriving businesses. CzechInvest's policies in general need to be examined, he said.

(HN/17) One of the pillars of Český Telecom's strategy is to remain in a business only if it is No. 1 or No. 2 on the market, according to HR Director Imrich Gombar. Layoffs will be closely linked to this. Job cuts are planned preliminarily for the end of each of the first three quarters of 2004. On average, employees will get about eight months' wages as severance pay.

(HN/2) Charges are expected to be filed early next year in what HN calls the biggest corruption affair since 1989. Karel Srba, Pavel Jaroš, Alex Šatánek and other former top-level employees of the foreign ministry are suspected of profiting from state contracts. [HN's article was written by Sabina Slonková. Srba has already been found guilty of conspiring to kill her.]

(HN/17) Czech Railways chose Kapsch again to supply a GSM-R network.... Due to changes in U.S. rules, large PR agencies active here will no longer disclose their annual results.... Ruhrgas will shift its 24% stake in Pražská plynárenská Holding to E.ON. (EU/8) The SEC launched a Kč 100m computer system for detecting trading fraud. (MFD/5) On Jan. 10, Mountfield will launch discounts of "up to 100%" on garden tools and swimming pools.

Politics

(P/1) Stanislav Gross said KDU-ČSL Chair Miroslav Kalousek should join the cabinet. Kalousek said he is willing to enter into talks with ČSSD and US-DEU about a fourth cabinet seat for KDU. He ruled out any reshuffling of KDU's three seats.

(MFD/2) Czech TV will air a taped three-minute toast by Václav Havel at midnight on New Year's Eve. Václav Klaus will give his live New Year's address 13 hours later. (MFD/4) Separately, architect Bořek Šípek said he will wait for Klaus' term to expire to carry through with his idea of erecting 25 small buildings in the Castle grounds for representing EU countries. The project is supported by Havel but has been rejected by the current Castle administration.

(HN/4) Jiří Svoboda, who led the Communist Party for three years in the early 1990s, said the shift of voters away from ČSSD to the Communists is due mainly to two things. First, ČSSD makes one decision as a party and another on the cabinet level (such as in the case of the Iraq war), and this confuses voters. Second, voters perceive that the use of "repressive elements," such as wiretaps, is on the rise, and this reminds them of pre-1989 days.

(HN/3) Interior Minister Stanislav Gross said he has the feeling that Viktor Kožený does not meet the conditions set forth in the election law for running for office. Kožený has said that he plans to run for the European Parliament next year.

Society

(MFD/4) Two youths shot by security guards while allegedly trying to force their way into a nightclub in Most have died, and a third was charged with disorderly conduct. The guards have so far not been charged. A police car was called to the scene, but the officers reportedly remained in the vehicle while the shots were fired.

(MFD/1) Another flu epidemic is expected after New Year's, and it could be worse than the pre-Christmas epidemic. MFD quotes an epidemiology official from Ústí nad Labem as saying that anyone with a fever should seek medical attention.

(HN/13) About 25,000 Czechs are spending the holidays at the beach, up 25% from last year. Accommodations are cheap, income is up, the weather at the beach is warm, and there isn't much snow in the mountains. Favored destinations include Egypt, the Canary Islands and Thailand.

Published by 9 a.m. Mon-Fri except holidays by E.S. Best s.r.o., P.O. Box 67, 130 11 Prague 3. Tel. 420 221 004 315 Fax 420 224 221 580 info@fleet.cz Unauthorized use or copy prohibited. © 2003
MK ČR E 6106 MIC 46593 ISSN 1210-5279 89Kč www.fleet.cz

Erik's Dilemma

Erik wondered if this business could survive indefinitely into the future. He also wondered what factors would have an impact on its remaining as a "going concern." Some foreign companies had already begun to close their offices in the Czech Republic because of the difficulties of doing business there, and the German banks were beginning to focus on Germany and not other countries. Even if the multinationals decided to stay in the country and there continued to be a market for the *Fleet Sheet*, he wondered what format it might take in the future. And then there was the question of the Internet. Would people have such quick access to data on the Internet that a service such as his would become obsolete?

Erik also thought about future competition. Would other companies try to offer the service he was offering at a lower price? Would subscribers be enticed by lower prices even though the quality of the product might be inferior?

When Erik had first begun his business, he was not making what he considered an adequate salary; and he often speculated that it would be very easy to close the business and go to work somewhere else. However, by the Spring of 2000, the business was doing so well that he was making a very good salary that might be difficult to duplicate somewhere else. Erik thought it humorous to contemplate all of the problems that one encounters when a business becomes successful.

CASE DISCUSSION QUESTIONS

1. What are the potential difficulties of starting a business in a transition economy?
2. Prepare a SWOT analysis for the *Fleet Sheet*.
3. What are the key success factors of *Fleet Sheet*?
4. What is the relationship between education, experience, personal skill and entrepreneurship for Erik Best?
5. What did you learn about entrepreneurship from this case?

6. Erik Best did not prepare a business plan for starting *Feet Sheet*. What type of operation would benefit most from a business plan?

CASE CREDIT

Used with permission of the authors, Professor Marlene M. Reed, Samford University and Rochelle R. Brunson, Alvin Community College. Exhbits used courtesy of Erik Best and *The Fleet Sheet*.

Endnotes

[1] Vaclav Havel was the gifted writer who was elected the first President of Czechoslovakia after the dissolution of Communism and was serving his last term in office.

[2] Lyapura, Stanislav, and Allan A. Gibb (1996). "Creating Small Businesses Out of Large Enterprises," *Small Business in Transition Economies*. Intermediate Technology Publications, Ltd., London: pp. 34–50.

Management Processes in Strategy Implementation: Design Choices for Multinational Companies

part three

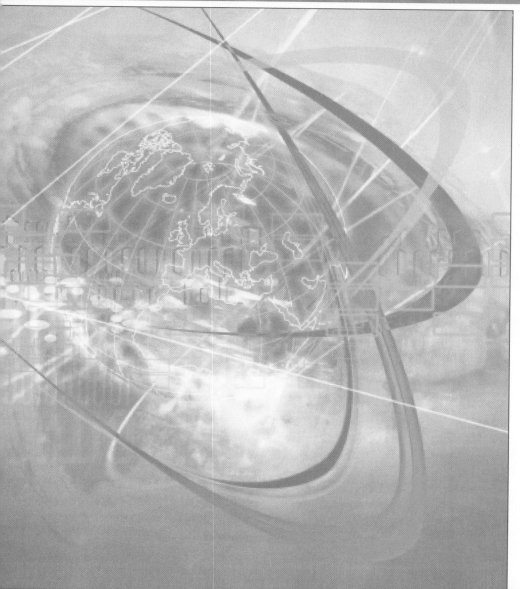

Organizational Designs for Multinational Companies

8

Preview CASE IN POINT

Intel's Organizational Design for Global Competition

Intel has 11 fabrication plants worldwide today. These plants produce the chip sets and microprocessors on silicon wafers. These products then are sent to assembly and test sites where they are cut into appropriate components and tested. The company has six assembly and test sites worldwide.

Worldwide, Intel plants are tightly controlled and fully owned. This protects proprietary technology. Intel keeps upstream value-chain activities in fabrication plants in the United States, Ireland, and Israel. Lower technology assembly and test sites are chosen for cost advantages in labor.

For all fabrication factories, Intel has a "copy exactly" organizational form that duplicates all processes including, for example, the flow of materials, equipment, and training, from a development plant to a high-volume production plant. Although at first glance this may seem a rigid organization, Intel claims that the "copy exactly" organizational form results in a flexible factory network. Technical resources are shared continuously via a virtual factory network that allows engineering improvements to be shared instantaneously and implemented simultaneously at all Intel factories throughout the world. Additional advantages are that this organization limits Intel's vulnerability from natural or man-made disasters. Should an event stop production in one factory, partially completed wafers can be finished in another factory with equal specifications and quality so that Intel's manufacturing need not stop.

Sources: Based on Intel. http://www.intel.com/. 2006; United Nations Conference on Trade and Development (UNCTAD). 2003. World Investment Report. United Nations: New York and Geneva.

The best multinational strategies do not ensure success. Implementation of a multinational business strategy requires that managers build the right type of organization—that is, managers try to design their organizations with what they believe are the best mechanisms to carry out domestic and multinational strategies. As shown in the Preview Case in Point, Intel hopes that its innovative network organizational design will provide the right support for their global strategies in the next decade. In this chapter, you will see other design choices and consider the complexities of organizing for international competition.

This chapter discusses the organizational-design options available to implement the various multinational strategies. What is organizational design? **Organizational design** represents how organizations structure subunits and coordination and control mechanisms to achieve their strategic goals. This chapter shows how having the right organizational design is crucial for multinational companies to achieve their multinational strategic goals.

The choices regarding how to set up an organization are complex and varied. Each organizational design has costs and benefits regarding the best way to deliver a product or service to the domestic or international customer. Some organizational designs for multinational companies favor flexibility. These designs provide managers with the organizational tools to deliver products adapted to different national or regional markets or to take advantage of resources located in different regions of the world. Other organizational designs favor efficiency. These designs provide managers with organizations best suited to deliver low-cost products worldwide.

Before considering specific designs for multinational organizations, the chapter presents a survey of organizational design and a summary of basic background knowledge on organizational structure. Building on this information, the chapter then discusses the organizational structures used by multinational companies. However, because organizational structure effectively breaks down the organization in terms of logical entities, it is also necessary to implement various mechanisms to help integrate these entities. The chapter then gives a summary of the basic coordination and control mechanisms available to multinational companies to integrate the various building blocks. Finally, most experts agree that knowledge is crucial in today's increasingly competitive and ambiguous environment. In the final section of this chapter, we look at knowledge management and related design issues.

Organizational design

How organizations structure subunits and use coordination and control mechanisms to achieve their strategic goals.

The Nature of Organizational Design

The two basic questions in designing an organization are: (1) How shall we divide the work among the organization's subunits? and, after that, (2) How shall we coordinate and control the efforts of the units we create?[1]

In very small organizations, everyone does the same thing and does everything. There is little reason to divide the work. However, as organizations grow, managers divide work first into specialized jobs. Different people perform different tasks. Later, when enough people are doing the same tasks and a supervisor is required, managers divide their organizations into specialized subunits. In smaller organizations, the subunits are usually called departments. In larger organizations, divisions or subsidiaries become the major subunits.

Once an organization has specialized subunits, managers must develop mechanisms that coordinate and control the efforts of each subunit. For example, a manufacturing company must make sure that the production department produces the goods to be available at the time when the marketing department promised the customers. Similarly, a multinational company must ensure that its foreign operations support the parent company's strategic goals. Some companies monitor their subunits very closely. They *centralize* decision making at company headquarters to make certain that the production and delivery of products or services conform to rigid standards. Other companies give subunits greater flexibility by *decentralizing* decision-making control. Later in the chapter, we will discuss why multinational companies might choose tight or loose control of their subunits.

There is no one best organizational design. The choice of an organizational design depends mostly on the choice of strategy. Some design options are more effective for implementing different strategies. In addition, the choice of design options depends on the firm's resources. To modify an organizational design successfully requires that companies have the necessary personnel to staff newly created organizational subunits and the financial resources to support the new organization. For companies operating internationally, the key issue is the degree to which a company has a local responsiveness or global strategic orientation.

Why should multinational companies be concerned about organizational design? In today's world characterized by hypercompetition and ambiguous industry boundaries, it has never been more crucial to pay attention to organizational design issues. Many companies such as GM, IBM, Sears, and Kodak suffered major setbacks and saw their profits fall dramatically in the last decade because of their poor organizational design. While the new global competition demanded flexibility and speed, these companies had very bloated bureaucratic structures that made it difficult to adapt rapidly to new environmental conditions.[2] A properly aligned organizational design allows a multinational company to respond quickly to its environmental demands. As such, it is not surprising that IBM has worked hard to eliminate management layers as it changed from a hardware producer to a service provider.[3]

A Primer on Organizational Structures

Before you can understand the organizational structures necessary for multinational strategy implementation, you need some basic knowledge of organizational structure. To provide this background, the next section gives a brief review of the basic structural options available to managers in designing their organizations. Students who have had course work on organizational design will find this a review.

Organizations usually divide work into departments or divisions based on functions, geography, products, or a combination of these choices. Each way of organizing has its advantages and disadvantages. Companies adopt one or a combination of these subunit forms based on management's beliefs concerning the best structure or structures to implement their chosen strategies. In this chapter, some of the advantages and disadvantages of each choice will be explained.

Functional structure

Has departments or subunits based on separate business functions, such as marketing or manufacturing.

The Basic Functional Structure

In the **functional structure**, departments perform separate business functions such as marketing or manufacturing. The functional structure is the simplest of organizations. As such, smaller organizations usually have functional structures. However, even larger organizations often have some functional subunits. Since most organizations use charts to display their organizational structure, the chapter shows each type of organization using exhibits of hypothetical or real organizational charts. Exhibit 8.1 shows an organizational chart for a generic functional structure.

Why do organizations choose a functional structure? The major reason to choose a functional structure for a subunit is efficiency. The functional structure gets its efficiency from economies of scale in each function. Economies of scale result because there are cost savings when a large number of people do the same job in the same place. For example, the organization can locate all marketing or manufacturing people in one subunit, with one staff support group, one telephone system, and one management system. However, because functional subunits are separated from each other and serve functional goals, coordination among the units can be difficult. Responses to changes in the environment can be slow. As such, the functional structure works best when organizations have few products, few locations, or few types of customers. It also works best when the organization faces a stable environment where the need for adaptation is minimal.[4]

Organizations face a variety of situations that can undermine the effectiveness of the functional structure. Functional structures can lose effectiveness and efficiency when organizations have many products, serve different customer groups, or locate in widely dispersed geographical areas. The most common reaction by managers to these situations is to organize departments or divisions by product or geography.

The Basic Product and Geographic Structures

Product structure

Has departments or subunits based on different product groups.

Geographic structure

Has departments or subunits based on geographical regions.

The structural arrangements for building a department or subunit around a product or a geographic area are called the **product structure** and the **geographic structure,** respectively. Exhibits 8.2 and 8.3 show simple product and geographic structures.

Product or geographic organizations must still perform the functional tasks of a business (e.g., marketing, accounting). In contrast to the functional structure, however, product or geographic organizations do not concentrate functions in separate subunits. Instead, functional tasks are duplicated for each product department or geographic-area department. The duplication of these functional tasks usually requires more managers and more people to run the organization.

EXHIBIT **8.1**   **A Basic Functional Structure**

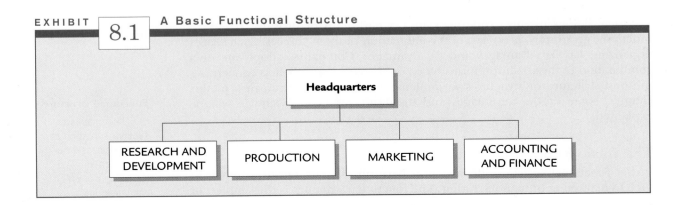

EXHIBIT 8.2   **A Basic Product Structure**

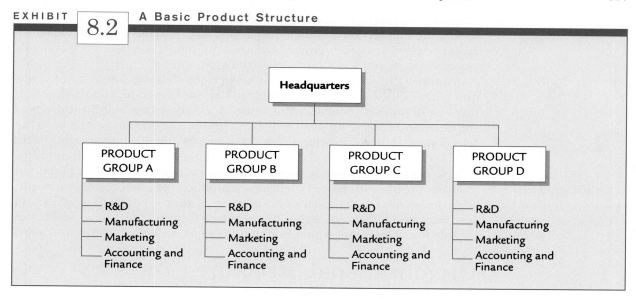

EXHIBIT 8.3   **A Basic Geographic Structure**

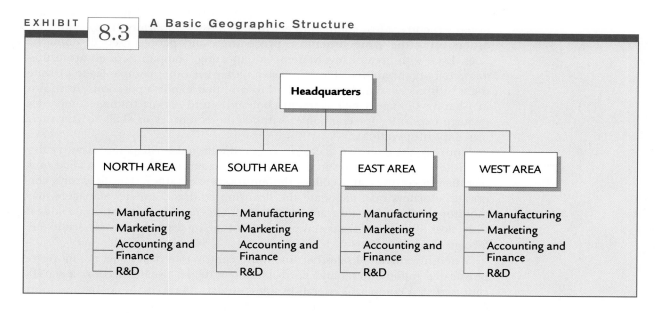

Duplication of functions also suggests the greatest weakness of the product or geographic structures—the loss of economies of scale in functions. These organizations are usually less efficient than the purely functional organization.

Managers accept the loss of functional efficiencies in product or geographic organizations for two reasons. First, as customer groups and products proliferate, the cost of coordination and control across functions also grows, offsetting basic functional efficiencies. Second, even for small organizations, product and geographic organizations can have competitive advantages over the more efficient functional structure.

The geographic structure allows a company to serve customer needs that vary by region. That is, the geographic structure sets up a mini-functional organization in each region. Rather than one large functional organization that serves all customers, the smaller, regional, organization focuses all functional activities on serving the unique needs of the regional customer. Because the organization focuses on specific customer groups, managers can more easily and quickly identify customer needs and adapt products accordingly.

Managers choose product structures when they believe that a product or a group of products is sufficiently unique to require focused functional efforts on one type of product or service. This structure creates strong coordination across the functional areas to support the product group. The pressures that lead to the selection of product structures are the products' unique or changing technologies or the association of different customer groups with different products.

Few organizations adopt purely organizational forms. Each organization faces unique tradeoffs based on efficiency, product types, and customers' needs. They design their organizations with mixtures of structures that they believe will best implement their strategies. These mixed-form organizations, which can include functional, geographic, and product units, are called **hybrid structures.**

Hybrid structures

Mixes functional, geographic, and product units.

Organizational Structures To Implement Multinational Strategies

When a company first goes international, it seldom changes its basic organizational structure. Most companies act first as passive exporters. They simply fill orders using the same structures, procedures, and people used in domestic sales. Even with greater involvement in exporting, companies often avoid fundamental organizational changes. Instead, they use other companies to provide them with international expertise and to run their export operations. As shown in Chapter 6, export management companies and export trading companies manage exporting for companies without the resources or skills to run their own export operations.

Similarly, the choice of licensing as a multinational participation strategy also has little impact on domestic organizational structures. The licensor need only negotiate a contract and collect the appropriate royalties. The licensor's corporate attorneys may negotiate the licensing contract, and its managers may monitor the licensing contract. However, the licensee's organization must deal with most of the organizational problems of taking a product or service to the foreign market.

When international sales become more central to a firm's success, more sophisticated multinational and participation strategies usually become a significant part of a company's overall business strategy. As a result, companies must then build appropriate organizational structures to manage their multinational operations and implement their multinational strategies. The following sections focus on the structural options for companies using the multinational and participation strategies discussed previously.

The Export Department

Export department

Coordinates and controls a company's export operations.

When exports become a significant percentage of company sales and a company wishes greater control over its export operations, managers often create a separate **export department.** A separate department shows that top management believes that the investment of human and financial resources in exporting is necessary to sustain and build international sales. The export department deals with all international customers for all products. Managers in the export department often control the pricing and promotion of products for the international market. People within the department may have particular country or product expertise. Export-department managers have the responsibility to deal with export management companies, with foreign distributors, and with foreign customers. When the company uses a direct exporting strategy, sales representatives located in other countries may also report to the export-department management. Exhibit 8.4 shows a hypothetical organization with a functional structure and an export department.

As companies evolve beyond initial participation strategies of exporting and licensing, they need more sophisticated organizational structures to implement more complex multinational strategies. These more complex structures include the international division, the worldwide geographic and products structures, the worldwide-matrix structure, and the transnational-network structure.

Before discussing the more complex multinational structures in detail, some background is necessary on the types of subunits multinational companies set up in foreign countries.

Foreign Subsidiaries

The more complex multinational organizational structures support participation strategies that include direct investments in a foreign country. This means setting up an overseas subunit of the parent firm. These subunits are called foreign subsidiaries. Foreign subsidiaries are subunits of the multinational company located in countries other than the country of the parent company's headquarters. Foreign subsidiaries are a growing component of international business. For example, the United Nations estimates worldwide that there are over 65,000 multinational corporations with more than 850,000 foreign subsidiaries employing nearly 25 million people.[5] Siemens, the German giant, reported 900 fully-owned and 400 majority-owned subsidiaries in its 2005 statements. Other multinational organizations such as Total, Asea Brown Boveri (ABB), and Daimler-Chrysler all report associations with more than 1,000 entities each while General Electric reports ownership in more than 8,000 subsidiaries.[6]

Foreign subsidiaries
Subunits of the multinational company that is located in another country.

EXHIBIT 8.4   A Functional Structure with an Export Department

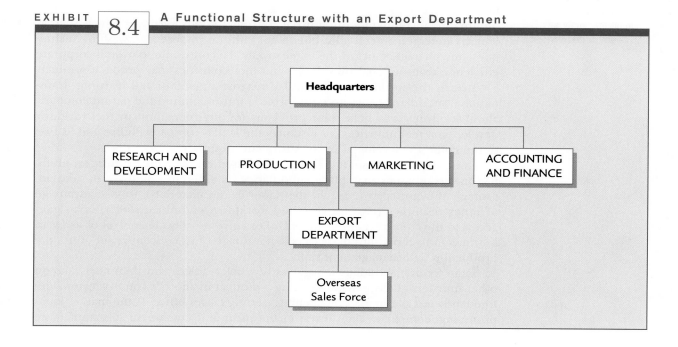

Multinational firms have varying control over their subsidiaries.[7] Some multinational companies retain active control by maintaining a board that is active in subsidiary management. Such forms of control tend to be more typical of joint ventures in emerging markets in India and China where the multinational firm wants to control the subsidiary's activities. The second form of control is the "rubber stamp" board, which tends to be required by law. Such boards are more likely to be formal, and they merely approve the subsidiary's activities. However, most multinational companies use the third form of control where the multinational firm avoids managing the local subsidiary and leaves management decisions up to the subsidiary. The latter arrangement is seen as necessary to ensure that local subsidiaries stay as lean and mean as possible.

In addition to the forms of control, multinational companies use several types of foreign subsidiaries. For companies pursuing a multidomestic strategy, the foreign subsidiary often becomes a smaller version of the parent company.[8] This type of subsidiary is called the **minireplica subsidiary.** It uses the same technology and produces the same products as the parent company. However, it runs on a smaller scale. By producing products or services strictly for the local market, the minireplica can adapt to local conditions and support the multidomestic strategy.

Minireplicas use few expatriate managers. Local managers run the organization, often with little influence from headquarters. Because of its autonomy from headquarters, the minireplica is usually a profit center. In a profit center, corporate headquarters evaluates local managers based on the unit's profitability, using financial-performance information such as return on investment. Seldom do minireplicas contribute to corporation-wide goals such as providing R&D or manufacturing for other locations around the world.

At the opposite end of the spectrum from the minireplica is the **transnational subsidiary.** This type of subsidiary supports a multinational-firm strategy based on location advantages. The transnational subsidiary has no companywide form or function. Each subsidiary contributes what it does best for corporate goals.

To respond to local conditions, a transnational subsidiary in one country may produce some products that it adapts to the local tastes. For example, multinational companies often make consumer goods locally. Products such as laundry detergents need adjustments for cultural preferences, washing techniques, and characteristics of the water supply. To contribute to overall corporate efficiency, transnational subsidiaries in other countries may produce products for sale in the worldwide market. To increase organizational learning, transnational subsidiaries anywhere can provide information to the parent company about local markets, help solve problems for any other unit in the world, or develop new technologies. For instance, the Dutch company Philips had its first stereo color TV developed by its Australian subsidiary.[9]

To implement transnational strategies based on location advantages, multinational companies may place subsidiaries in different countries to take advantage of factor costs (e.g., cheaper labor or raw materials), to take advantage of other resources (e.g., an educated workforce or unique skills), or to gain access to the country. For example, DuPont gives worldwide control of its Lycra business to its Swiss subsidiary to take advantage of its concentration of unique production and management skills.

Some foreign subsidiaries begin as only sales offices and then later take on other functions. Before manufacturing a product in another country, companies frequently test the market by opening a foreign sales office. If the market looks promising, companies then invest in the plant and equipment to manufacture

Minireplica subsidiary

Smaller version of the parent company, using the same technology and producing the same products as the parent company.

Transnational subsidiary

Has no companywide form or function—each subsidiary does what it does best or most efficiently anywhere in the world.

locally. In contrast, other subsidiaries begin and remain as suppliers of raw materials for the parent company or other subsidiaries. These units often have no manufacturing or sales capacities. For example, major oil companies such as British Petroleum use many of their subsidiaries only to supply raw material. Finally, some multinational companies use their subsidiaries as offshore production or assembly plants for export back to the headquarters' country.

Most subsidiaries are neither pure minireplicas nor pure transnationals. Rather, foreign subsidiaries take many different forms and have many different functions. Multinational companies choose the mix of functions for their foreign subsidiaries based on several issues, including (1) the firm's multinational strategy or strategies, (2) the subsidiaries' capabilities and resources, (3) the economic and political risk of building and managing a subunit in another country, and (4) how the subsidiaries fit into the overall multinational organizational structure.

Foreign subsidiaries provide the structural building blocks for running multinational operations; that is, once companies move beyond simple exporting, foreign subsidiaries become key parts of the organizational designs used by multinational companies to implement their multinational strategies. With the background knowledge of the nature of foreign subsidiaries, we will now consider how multinational companies use the various organizational structures to implement their multinational strategies.

International Division

As companies increase the size of their international sales force and set up manufacturing operations in other countries, the export department often grows into an international division. The **international division** differs from the export department in several ways; it is usually larger and has greater responsibilities. Besides managing exporting and an international sales force, the international division oversees foreign subsidiaries that perform a variety of functions. Most often, these are sales units. However, units that procure raw material and produce the company's products in other countries are common. The international division also has more extensive staff with international expertise. Top management expects these people to perform functions such as negotiating licensing and joint-venture agreements, translating promotional material, or providing expertise on different national cultures and social institutions.

Exhibit 8.5 gives an example of an international division in a domestic product structure. In this example, the international division handles all products and controls foreign subsidiaries in Europe and Japan and a general sales force in the rest of Asia.

The international-division structure has declined in popularity among the large multinational companies.[10] For multiproduct companies operating in many countries, it is not considered an effective multinational structure.[11] However, for companies of moderate size with a limited number of products or country locations, the international division remains a popular and potentially effective organization.

Why do companies often abandon their international divisions as they expand international operations in terms of products and country locations? There are several reasons. First, too many products often overwhelm the capacities of the international division. In sales, for example, it is difficult for people in the international division to know the whole product line and sell it worldwide. Second, when the number of locations in different countries grows,

International division

Responsible for managing exports, international sales, and foreign subsidiaries.

EXHIBIT **8.5**   **An International Division in a Domestic Product Structure**

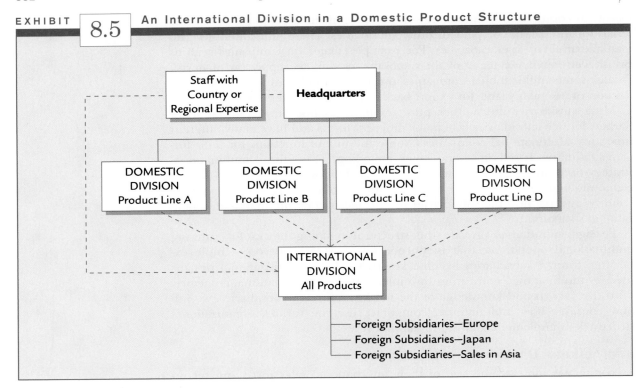

it is difficult for the international division to manage multidomestic or regional adaptations. How can a remote headquarters division know local needs and adapt products and strategies accordingly?

Third, the international division makes it more difficult to implement international strategies using worldwide products or location advantages. Because the international division separates international concerns from the headquarters-based product divisions, these divisions are less likely to look at the world as one market. Divisions have a product focus and not a market focus. Home-based product divisions are also less likely to view worldwide production or R&D locations as global platforms. Rather, for most companies with international divisions, the domestic market is king, and international issues are the international division's "problem."

To deal with the shortcomings of the international-division structure, multinational companies have several options. These include the worldwide product structure, the worldwide geographic structure, the matrix structure, and the transnational-network structure. The following section discusses the worldwide geographic and product structures.

Worldwide Geographic Structure and Worldwide Product Structure

Worldwide geographic structure

Has geographical units representing regions of the world.

In the worldwide geographic structure, regions or large-market countries become the geographic divisions of the multinational company. The prime reason to choose a worldwide geographic structure is to implement a multidomestic or regional strategy. Since a company with a multidomestic or regional strategy needs to differentiate its products or services by country or region, it needs an organizational design with maximum geographic flexibility. The semiautonomous regional or country-based subunits of the worldwide geographic structure provide that flexibility to tailor or develop products that meet the particular needs of local or regional markets. Often differences in an area's product or service needs or in channels of distribution enhance the need for a geographic structure. Exhibit 8.6 shows a geographic structure used by Royal Vopak, a Dutch multinational company that specializes in the distribution of chemicals.

For practical purposes, even for the multidomestic strategist, country-level divisions usually exist only when a country's market size is sufficiently large or important to support a separate organization. Separate divisions often make economic sense for large market countries such as the United States, France, Germany, or Japan. Regional divisions combine smaller similar countries such as, for example, a Southern European division for Italy, Spain, and Portugal.

EXHIBIT **8.6**   **Royal Vopak's Worldwide Geographic Structure**

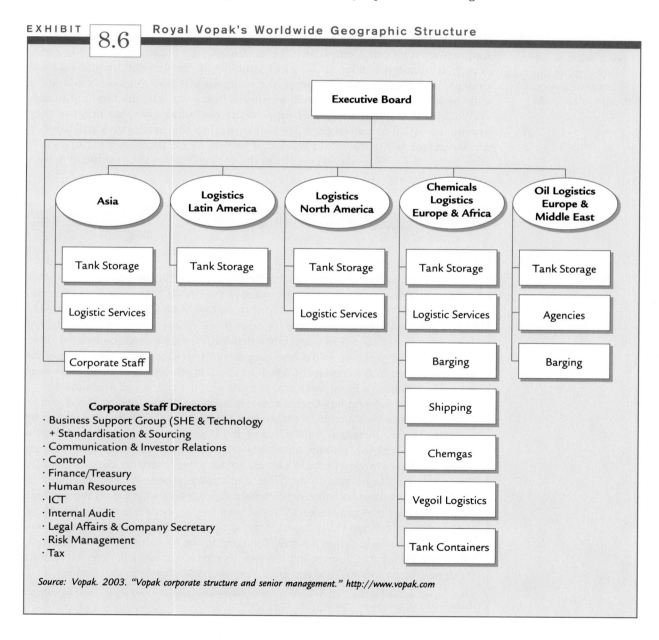

Source: Vopak. 2003. "Vopak corporate structure and senior management." http://www.vopak.com

For the regional strategist, combinations of countries are as large as possible, based on similarities in customer requirements balanced against the efficiencies of uniform products. However, it is interesting to note that Toyota made some important changes to its geographic structure. While both its sales operations and planning operations groups were previously organized by region (domestic and overseas), Toyota has decided to integrate both operations by combining the domestic and overseas divisions.[12] As a global company, Toyota wants more coordination among the various regions, including Japan, to implement the most appropriate growth strategy from a global perspective.

However, as the emerging markets gain importance, some companies are also shifting their attention to these markets. Consider the Focus on Emerging Markets below.

Worldwide product structure

Gives product divisions responsibility to produce and sell their products or services throughout the world.

Product divisions form the basic units of worldwide product structures, as shown in Exhibit 8.7. Each product division assumes responsibility for producing and selling its products or services throughout the world. The product structure supports strategies that emphasize the production and sales of worldwide products. It is usually considered the ideal structure to implement an international strategy. In the international strategy, the company attempts to gain economies of scale by selling worldwide products with most upstream activities based at home.

Worldwide product structures support international strategies because they provide an efficient way to organize and centralize the production and sales of similar products for the world market. The worldwide product structure sacrifices regional- or local-adaptation strengths derived from a geographic structure

Focus on Emerging Markets

Cisco and Emerging Markets

Cisco's organizational structure has traditionally been of the geographic type or what Cisco calls "theatres." These theaters included the United States, Americas International, Europe, the Middle East and African market, Asia Pacific, and Japan. This organization made sense for Cisco because these different regions had sufficient demand and need for product adaptation that they needed a separate theatre. However, the recent explosion in the emerging markets for Cisco and changes to other markets has led to the creation of a new geographic structure to include an emerging market theatre, a European markets theatre, and a U.S. and Canada theatre.

Cisco's restructuring has been necessary because of new geographic developments. For instance, Cisco has realized that the emerging markets represented by countries in Latin America, the Caribbean, the Middle East and Africa, and Russia and Eastern European markets have tremendous potential as these regions invest heavily in new networking capabilities. By creating the Emerging Markets Theatre, Cisco is hoping to be able to apply the appropriate processes and resources to meet the unique needs of these new markets. Cisco feels that the many regions represented in the Emerging Markets Theatre have similar needs and that by creating a special division devoted to the region, it can apply knowledge learned across the various markets to help deliver tailored solutions to the local markets. Furthermore, Cisco also hopes that, by creating the new division, it can show its commitment to these new emerging markets and create demand and growth for the future.

Source: Based on Business Wire. 2005. "Cisco System announces three new geographic theatres: New "emerging markets" theatre created to drive growth." June 6.

EXHIBIT **8.7**   **A Worldwide Product Structure**

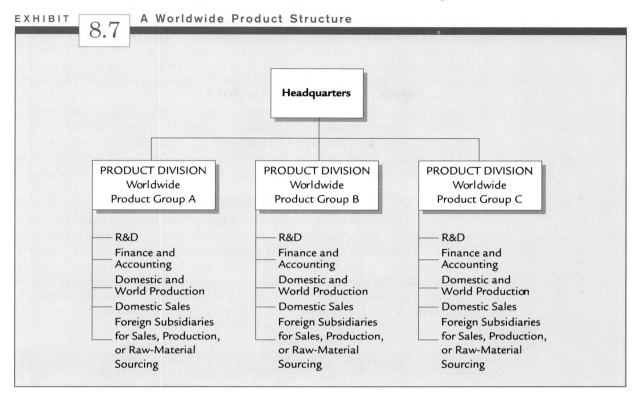

to gain product-development and manufacturing economies of scale. For example, Ford Motor Company implemented its Ford 2000 strategy by scrapping Ford of Europe and centralizing product engineering and design in Detroit. It created product groups called "Vehicle Centers" that had worldwide responsibility to develop new trucks and cars. This more product-oriented design has resulted in substantial cost savings from using fewer global suppliers and eliminating duplication in product development.[13] However, the current view is that Ford's worldwide product organization lost touch with local customers in Europe.[14] A danger for Ford—or any other company that emphasizes product over geography—is that the cost savings from more efficiently produced products may not offset revenue losses when products fail to please the local market.

In the ideal worldwide product structure, all the value-chain functions, with the exception of sales, would remain in the company's home country. However, this is seldom possible because strategic, logistical, or political considerations lead a worldwide product structure company to perform some functions (e.g., supply, manufacturing, or after-market service) in foreign locations. In these cases, product-division headquarters still centralizes control of R&D, manufacturing, and international marketing strategy. When they are used, foreign subsidiaries have little autonomy.

Foreign subsidiaries in the worldwide product structure may produce worldwide products/components, supply raw materials, or specialize only in local sales. However, they serve product goals directed from product-division headquarters. Production or supply subsidiaries often have little concern for their local markets. For the sales subsidiaries, there is minimal local adaptation of the headquarters-directed worldwide marketing strategy. Manufacturing subsidiaries in the product structure may produce component products for the global market and export these products back to the division's home country for final assembly. In this case, sister sales subsidiaries may then reimport the finished product for local sales.[15] For example, the U.S. aircraft manufacturer Boeing produces many of its aircraft components outside the United States. Its subsidiaries return these components to the United States for final assembly. Later, airlines in many of the producing countries buy the completed Boeing planes.

In the competitive world of consumer products, P&G is moving away from a multidomestic sales strategy to a product orientation, as described in the following Multinational Management Challenge. To accomplish this shift in strategic orientation, the firm must dismantle its geographic units and build a new product-based organization. What problems would you anticipate in this change?

Hybrids and Worldwide Matrix Structures

Both the worldwide product structure and the worldwide geographic structure have advantages and disadvantages for multinational strategy implementation. The product structure best supports strategies that emphasize global products and rationalization (worldwide products using worldwide, low-cost sources of raw materials and worldwide marketing strategies). The geographic structure best supports strategies that emphasize local adaptation (managers are often local nationals and are sensitive to local needs). Most multinational companies,

---

Multinational Management **Challenge**

Can P&G Change Its Structure?

Procter & Gamble is a $38 billion company with operations in 160 countries. Recently, however, P&G has been losing market share to multinational rivals such as Unilever and Colgate-Palmolive. The problem, according to Durk Jager, the Dutch CEO of this U.S. giant, is that the company is too slow to introduce new products and too inefficient in its organizational structure. The solution: Organization 2005.

In the old P&G model, country or region-level operations were separate fiefdoms, allowing country managers veto power over R&D and sales and marketing decisions. In contrast, the new structure abandoned the 100 geographic profit centers and replaced them with seven global business units (GBUs) representing product categories: fabric and homecare, food and beverages, feminine hygiene, beauty cream, tissues and towels, baby care, and healthcare. To support these global product divisions in their local marketing, P&G added eight market development organizations based on regions.

It remains to be seen how P&G will coordinate dominant product divisions with their less powerful geographic units. As P&G's CEO admits, "this is an area we've been struggles with" and "we've been flexing our models." Currently P&G gives more authority to country managers in newer markets where adaptation is important and, depending on the similarity of customer needs regarding the product, emphasizes either the global product division or the regional units for profit responsibility and resource allocation.

Sources: Based on Bell, Steve. 1999. "P&G forced by rivals to change old habits." Marketing, June 17, pp. 15–19; Economist. 1999a. "Procter's gamble." June 12; Economist. 2002. "Ford in Europe: In the slow lane." October 7; Lublin, Joann. 2001. "Division problem—place vs. product: It's tough to choose a management model—Exide tore up system based on countries for one on centered battery lines—rolling over European fiefs." Wall Street Journal. (Eastern edition). New York . June 27, p. A1; and Murphy, Brian P. 1999. "Bulky P&G looks for speed." Money, pp. 28, 11, November, pp. 50–3.

however, adopt strategies that include both concerns for local adaptation as well as for the economic and product-development benefits of globalization. Consequently, most large multinationals have structures that are hybrids, or mixtures of product and area units. The nature of the product determines the emphasis given to the product or geographic side of the company (How global are the products?) and the nature of the markets (How complex and different are the major markets?).

At Sony Corporation headquarters, for example, worldwide product group managers exercise broad oversight over their businesses. However, Sony also focuses on regional needs by dividing global operations into four zones: Japan, North America, Europe, and the rest of the world. The consumer products giant, Unilever PLC, has a regional structure with local managers in three areas: Africa/Middle East, Latin America, and East Asia/Pacific. However, managers in Europe and North America report to worldwide product coordinators.[16] Similarly, Unilever gives most power to the global product units when customers have similar needs worldwide. When customer needs vary by country or region, they emphasize geographic unit power with product groups under local management.[17]

One evolving form of hybrid structure that attempts to solve global product and local markets needs is called the **front–back hybrid structure**.[18] The front–back hybrid divides the organization into two line sub-organizations. The front side has units based on geography to provide a multidomestic or regional focus. The backside has units based on product groups to capture global economies of scale in R&D and production. Essentially, this organization divides the value chain where upstream activities are global and downstream activities are local.

Exhibit 8.8 shows a chart for a front–back hybrid structure for Tetra Pak. Tetra Pak produces paper and plastic packaging for liquid foods. It specializes in aseptic packages that allow products such as milk and juice to be kept without refrigeration. Citibank and Xerox are also examples of companies that use variants of the front–back hybrid. These structures are usually very complex since it is often not clear which side controls profit and loss and which side is a cost center. One possibility is that enough functions are moved to the geographic units that they become responsible for profit and loss while the back side is a cost center taking care of R&D, procurement, and manufacturing, the costs of which are transferred to the geographic units. With Tetra Pak, regional and country units receive material and manufacturing equipment from the global product units. Geographic units then manufacture the packages using sizes, colors, and labeling to match local needs.[19]

To balance the benefits produced by geographic and product structures and to coordinate a mixture of product and geographic subunits, some multinationals create a worldwide matrix structure. Unlike hybrid organizations, the **worldwid e matrix structure**, shown in Exhibit 8.9, is a symmetrical organization: it has equal lines of authority for product groups and for geographic divisions. Ideally, the matrix provides the structure for a firm to pursue both local and more global strategies at the same time. Geographic divisions focus on national responsiveness, and product divisions focus on finding global efficiencies. The matrix structure works well only when there are nearly equal demands from the environment for local adaptation and for product standardization with its associated economies of scale. Without these near-equal demands, the organization tends to evolve into a product or geographic structure, based on which side is more important for competitive advantage.

Front–back hybrid structure

Splits the value chain into worldwide product divisions for upstream activities and geographical units for downstream activities.

Worldwide matrix structure

Symmetrical organization, usually with equal emphasis on worldwide product groups and regional geographical divisions.

EXHIBIT **8.8**   **Tetra Pak's Front–Back Hybrid Structure**

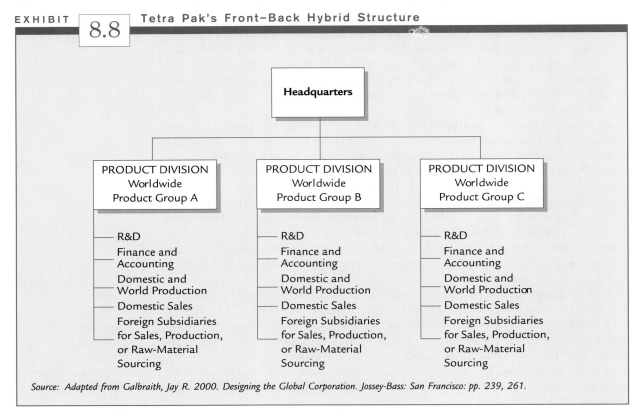

Source: Adapted from Galbraith, Jay R. 2000. Designing the Global Corporation. Jossey-Bass: San Francisco: pp. 239, 261.

In theory, the matrix produces quality decisions because two or more managers reach consensus on how to balance local and worldwide needs. Managers who hold positions at the intersection of product and geographic divisions are called "two-boss managers" because they have a boss from the product side of the organization and a boss from the geographic side of the organization. Product bosses tend to emphasize goals such as efficiency and using worldwide products while geographic bosses tend to emphasize local or regional adaptation. The conflict in these interests is intended to balance globalization and localization pressures. As such, for managers at all levels, the matrix requires continual compensation for product needs and geographic needs.

To succeed at balancing the inherent struggles between global and local concerns, the matrix requires extensive resources for communication among the managers. Middle- and upper-level managers must have good human-relations skills to deal with inevitable personal conflicts originating from the competing interests of product and geography. The middle-level managers must also learn to deal with two bosses, who often have competing interests. Upper-level managers, in turn, must be prepared to resolve conflicts between geographic and product managers.

Is the matrix worth the effort? During the 1980s, the matrix structure was a popular organizational solution to the global–local dilemma. More recently, however, the matrix has come under fire because consensus decision making between product and geographic managers has proved to be slow and cumbersome. In many organizations, the matrixes became too bureaucratic, with too many meetings and too much conflict. Some organizations, such as the Royal

EXHIBIT **8.9**   **A Worldwide Matrix Structure**

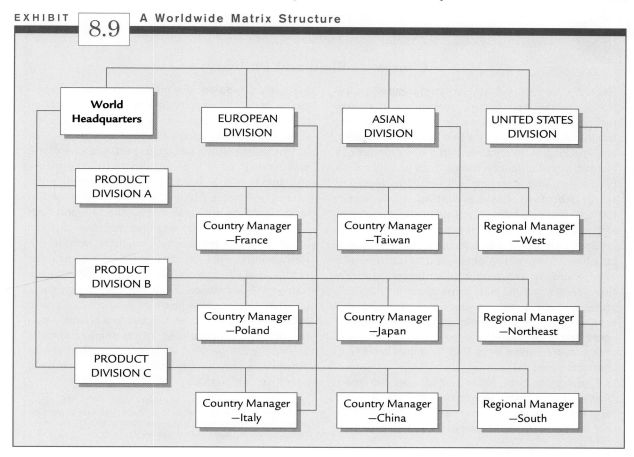

Dutch/Shell Group, discussed in the following Case in Point, abandoned their matrixes and returned to product structures. Other organizations have redesigned their matrix structures to be more flexible with speedier decision making. In the more flexible matrixes, management centralizes key decisions in the product side or geographic side of the matrix, depending on the need. For example, geographic areas with unique characteristics may require the freedom to have more unique strategies. Facing such a situation, AT&T and Owens-Corning Fiberglas Corp. created highly autonomous units in China. They believed that the local Chinese and Asian markets are so dynamic that local managers (both Chinese and expatriates) need a great deal of freedom to seek opportunities.[20]

The evolving intensity and complexity of competition in international business has created the evolution of strategies beyond geography and product foci. We saw earlier that this resulted in the transnational strategy. To carry out a transnational strategy effectively, a new organizational form has also arisen. This is the transnational-network structure.

The Transnational-Network Structure

The **transnational-network structure** represents the newest solution to the complex demands of being locally responsive while taking advantage of global economies of scale and seeking location advantages such as global sources of knowledge. Like the matrix, the transnational network tries to gain all the

Transnational-network structure

Network of functional, product, and geographic subsidiaries dispersed throughout the world, based on the subsidiaries' location advantages.

C A S E   I N   P O I N T

Change at Shell and Philips

Recently, Cornelius A. J. Herkstruter, chair of the Royal Dutch/Shell Group, announced a radical restructuring of his company. In a speech delivered simultaneously to corporate headquarters in London and The Hague, he declared that the matrix was out. Instead, global product divisions such as exploration, production, and chemical will report to teams of senior executives. These executives will have centralized decision-making power no longer shared with country or functional managers.

Shell's old matrix was quite complex. Most matrix structures combine two organizational designs, usually geography and product, for the multinational firm. Shell's matrix was three dimensional, with some managers having functional, product, and area bosses! For example, a finance executive could have a functional boss (e.g., chief financial officer), a country-level boss, and a product boss (e.g., chemical products).

The current chair believes that, over the years, Shell's complex matrix resulted in too much bureaucracy. The matrix required too many managers. In addition, the meetings and consensus decision making of the matrix slowed decision making. To remain competitive in the oil industry, industry analysts believe Shell must cut many management positions and be quicker to identify business opportunities.

Philips, the Dutch electrical giant, was one of the earliest multinational companies to use the matrix structure. It had a structure combining product and country divisions. For instance, the head of the washing-machine division in Italy had to report both to the head of the washing-machine division in Italy and the top washing-machine head in the Netherlands. This created major difficulties for Philips, and there were continuous accountability problems. For instance, it was not easy to determine whether the country head or product head was responsible for profits and losses in a country. As a result, Philips reorganized into a number of units around the company's main businesses. The national offices are now held accountable for these units based around products.

Source: Based on Dwyer, Paula, and Heidi Dawley. 1995. "The passing of 'the Shell man': An era ends as Royal Dutch/Shell vows to centralize power." BusinessWeek Online. International Edition, April 17; Economist. 2006. "Survey: The matrix master." January 21.

advantages of the various structural options. It combines functional, product, and geographic subunits. However, unlike the symmetrical matrix structure, the transnational network has no basic form. It has no symmetry or balance between the geographic and product sides of the organization. Instead, the transnational network links different types of transnational subsidiaries throughout the world. Nodes, the units at the center of the network, coordinate product, functional, and geographic information. Different product-group units and geographic-area units have different structures, and often no two subunits are alike. Rather, transnational units evolve to take advantage of resources, talent, and market opportunities wherever they exist in the world. Resources, people, and ideas flow in all directions.

As discussed earlier in the Case in Point, The Dutch multinational Philips Electronics N.V. is one example of a transnational network.[21] Working in sixty different countries, the company produces products as diverse as defense systems and light bulbs. There are eight product divisions with more than sixty subgroups based on product similarity. The product divisions have subsidiaries throughout the world. Subsidiaries may focus on only one product or on an array of products. Subsidiaries can specialize in R&D, manufacturing, or marketing for world or regional markets. Some subsidiaries focus only on sales. Some units are highly independent of headquarters while headquarters tightly controls other units.

In terms of geography, Philips divides the world into three groups. "Key countries" such as the Netherlands and the United States produce for local and world markets and control local sales. "Large countries" such as Mexico and Belgium have some local and worldwide production facilities and local sales. "Local business countries" are smaller countries that are primarily sales units and that import products from the product divisions' worldwide production centers in other countries. All these design choices by Philips attempt to optimize efficiency, organizational learning, and local responsiveness.[22]

Exhibits 8.10 and 8.11 show two different perspectives on how one can look at Philips' very complex transnational-network structure. One views geographic links among locations while the other looks at the functions of different locations. Another company often considered to have the prototypical transnational structure is ABB. The first Case in Point on page 394 discusses the transnational-network structure of ABB, termed a "loose matrix" by its former CEO.

The basic structural framework of the transnational network consists of three components: dispersed subunits, specialized operations, and interdependent relationships.[23] The transnational network structure uses the flexible transnational subsidiaries, discussed earlier, as the basic structural unit.

Dispersed subunits mean that management locates subsidiaries anywhere in the world where they can benefit the company. Some subsidiaries take advantage of lower factor costs (e.g., lower labor costs); other units provide information on new technologies, new strategies, and consumer trends. All subunits try to tap worldwide managerial and technical talent. Consider the second Case in Point on page 394, showing how two companies use engineers in different countries to produce key products.

Specialized operations mean that subunits can specialize in particular product lines, different research areas, and different marketing areas. Specialization builds on the diffusion of subunits by tapping specialized expertise or other resources anywhere and everywhere in the company's subsidiaries. Philips, for example, has eight research labs located in six countries. Some units have broad mandates, such as Philips' central laboratory in Eindhoven. Other units focus on specific areas, such as the laboratories for solid-state electronics work at Redhill in the United Kingdom.[24]

Interdependent relationships must exist to manage dispersed and specialized subunits. In interdependent relationships, units share information and resources continuously. To do this, transnationals usually build communication systems based on the latest technology. For example, GE Appliances' CEO J. Richard Stonesifer begins each Friday at 7:00 A.M. in a video conference with colleagues in Asia. For the next five hours, he follows the rising sun with more video conferences with managers from the Americas to Asia.[25] Ford creates "virtual teams" of design engineers from Europe, Japan, and the United States. These engineers communicate electronically, sharing both written material and design drawings.

The Multinational Management Brief on page 395 gives additional real-world examples of the various transnational activities just discussed.

Beyond The Transnational: Is there a New Structure For The Multinational?

Some evidence now suggests that the transnational network is not the end of the evolution of the structure of the multinational. Professor Yves Doz and his colleagues argue that a new structure is emerging called the **metanational**.[26] The metanational company is "a large, entrepreneurial multinational firm that

Dispersed subunits

Subsidiaries located anywhere in the world where they can most benefit the company.

Specialized operations

Subunits specializing in particular product lines, different research areas, or different marketing areas.

Interdependent relationships

Continuous sharing of information and resources by dispersed and specialized subunits.

Metanational structure

An evolution of the transnational network structure that develops extensive systems to encourage organizational learning and entrepreneurial activities.

EXHIBIT 8.10   Geographic Links in the Philips Transnational Structure

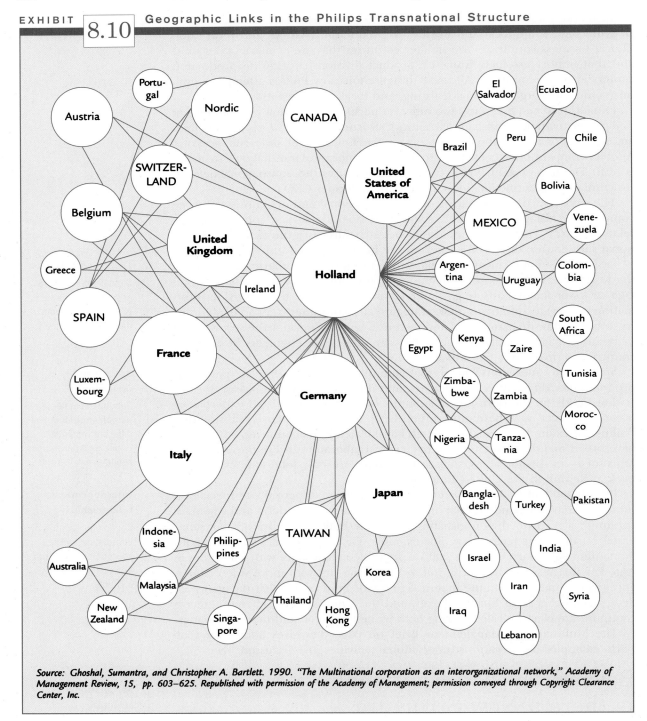

Source: Ghoshal, Sumantra, and Christopher A. Bartlett. 1990. "The Multinational corporation as an interorganizational network," Academy of Management Review, 15, pp. 603–625. Republished with permission of the Academy of Management; permission conveyed through Copyright Clearance Center, Inc.

is able to tap into hidden pockets of innovation, technology, and market now scattered around the world, especially in emerging markets."[27]

In many regards the metanational structure is like the transnational network. It is a networked organization with different types of platforms around the world. Also like the transnational, the metanational company is a centerless organization

EXHIBIT 8.11 Product Links in the Philips Transnational Structure

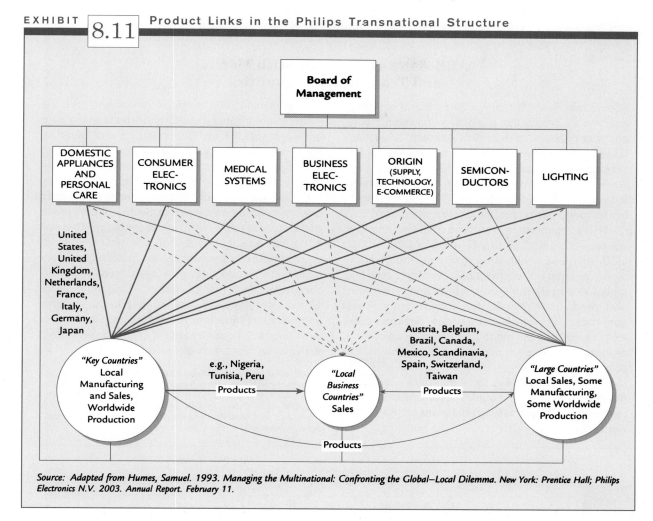

Source: Adapted from Humes, Samuel. 1993. Managing the Multinational: Confronting the Global–Local Dilemma. New York: Prentice Hall; Philips Electronics N.V. 2003. Annual Report. February 11.

that reduces hierarchy and places critical decision making in the peripheral units or nodes throughout the world. The characteristic that differentiates the meta-national from the transnational is the metanational's overriding objective to learn from anywhere in the world and to share this knowledge with the rest of the company. The metanational organization uses the latest in virtual connectivity to link team members anywhere in the world.

Characteristics of the metanational structure include:[28]

- Nonstandard business formulas for any local activity
- Looking to emerging markets as sources of knowledge and ideas, not just for local labor
- Creating a culture and advanced communication systems that support global learning
- Extensive use of strategic alliances to gain knowledge for varied sources
- High levels of trust between partners to encourage knowledge sharing
- A centerless organization that moves strategic functions away from headquarters and to major markets
- A decentralization of decision making away from headquarter and to managers who serve the key customers and strategic partners.

CASE   IN   POINT

ABB—An Organization with Matrix and Transnational Qualities

Asea Brown Boveri (ABB) is a Swiss-based electrical-equipment company that is bigger than Westinghouse and that hopes to take on GE. Although headquartered in Zurich, Switzerland, the company's 13 top managers speak only English at their meetings. English is the one common language, but it is a foreign language to all but one manager. The choice of meeting language personifies the global culture of ABB.

ABB's organization is a loose and decentralized matrix, according to Percy Barnevik, ABB's former CEO. ABB has about 100 country managers, most of whom come from the host country. Sixty-five global managers head product divisions from several product segments: transportation; process automation; environmental devices; financial services; electrical equipment; and electric-power generation, transmission, and distribution. The matrix produces two-boss managers at the level of 1,100 local companies. These local company managers must deal with their country-level boss on local responsiveness and their global manager on worldwide efficiency.

The organization is transnational because the matrix is not balanced and the functions of the subunits are not uniform. Depending on the situation, country or global-product bosses may have control. The organizational culture of ABB encourages sharing technology and products within product lines. For example, ABB's U.S. steam-turbine business uses techniques developed in Switzerland to repair the machines built with U.S. technology. There is not a bias against things "not invented here." Management expects even locally run factories to participate in global coordination. For example, 31 power-transformer factories located in 16 countries share all their performance data monthly through global segment headquarters in Mannheim, Germany. If even one factory has a problem, global headquarters expects solutions from all factories.

Source: Based on Taylor, William. 1991. "The logic of global business: An interview with ABB's Percy Barnevik." Harvard Business Review, March–April, pp. 91–105; Rapoport, Carla. 1992. "A tough Swede invades the U.S." Fortune, June 29, pp. 76–79; Ferner, Anthony. 2000. "Being local worldwide: ABB and the challenge of global management." Relations Industrielles, Summer, pp. 527–529.

CASE   IN   POINT

Talent is Everywhere—Finding Low-Cost Talent in a Borderless Company

Fueled by advances in telecommunications and the Information Superhighway, cities such as Taipei, Edinburgh, and Singapore are emerging as centers for technological breakthroughs and worldwide product developments. Multinational companies with subsidiaries in such locations can find talented workers in fields ranging from software development to architecture. For example, Motorola, Inc. used 75 local Singapore engineers to design its Scriptor pager. Northern Telecom Ltd. expects to employ 250 Chinese engineers in Beijing to develop and produce software, cellular phones, and multimedia devices.

One big attraction of the overseas intellectual workforce is price. For example, in Taiwan, qualified design engineers for circuit boards earn about $25,000 annually. In China or India, the same top-level talent costs less than $10,000. Equivalent talent in California or Boston costs from $60,000 to $100,000. Similarly, when ClariPhy, an Irvine, California-based semiconductor company was looking to hire engineers, it decided to look for engineers in Argentina. Although Argentina has a plentiful supply of top engineers, there is less competition for these engineers. ClariPhy was able to hire eight engineers for a third of the cost of engineers in the United States.

Source: Based on BusinessWeek Online. 1994c. "High-tech jobs all over the world," November 18; Copeland, Michael V. 2006. "The mighty micro-multinational." Business 2.0, July, pp. 107–114.

Multinational Management **Brief**

Transnational Activities

Since the transnational model has no fixed organizational components and activities, consider how the following companies include transnational activities in the organizational designs.

- *Flattened hierarchies for quick decision making:* Asea Brown Boveri (ABB) operates in more than 140 countries but still has only one layer of management between the top ranks and the business units.

- *Decentralized R&D for short product life cycles:* Nokia, the Finnish cellular phone maker, puts R&D at the plant level at five factories around the world. Concurrent engineering takes place, and the culture supports sharing any valuable engineering information with plants in all country locations.

- *Finding global products:* Texas Instruments created a team with the mandate to search the company worldwide for possible global products.

- *Tapping worldwide talent:* ABB designs locomotives in Switzerland and tilting trains in Sweden. Singapore engineers designed a new pager for Motorola.

- *Integrating the workforce:* To build a collaborative culture between workers in Singapore and workers in their sister plant in the United States, Motorola brought the workers to a Colorado resort for Outward Bound-style team-building games.

- *Using e-mail, information systems, voiceover Internet protocol and WIKIs(server software that allows users to create or change website content):* Unilever PLC has 31,000 employees worldwide communicating by e-mail or Lotus Notes. The Mexican company Cemento Mexicanos can tell with one keystroke the energy use in an oven from its Spanish subsidiary.

Source: Based on Beamish, Paul W., J. Peter Killing, Donald J. Lecraw, and Allen J. Morrison. 1994. International Management. Burr Ridge, IL: Irwin; BusinessWeek Online. 1994b. "Grabbing markets from the giants," November 18; BusinessWeek Online. 1994d. "Tearing up today's organization chart," November 18; Coepland, Michael V. 2006. "The mighty micro-multinational." Business 2.0, July, pp. 107–114; Forteza, Jorge H., and Gary L. Neilson. 1999. "Multinationals in the next decade." Strategy & Business, 16, Third Quarter, pp. 1–11.

The current Internet revolution and the Web also have led to the creation of another new form of multinational company, the **micro-multinational**.[29] Micro-multinational companies are smaller organizations that take advantage of the Web to operate globally from Day One. Consider the example of Sundia (http://www.watermelonworks.com), an international fruit and juice company created by Bradford Oberwager from his San Francisco home office. Today, Sundia still operates in Oberwager's home but employs workers in the United States, India, and the Philippines to sell its products in the United States or Europe. For instance, if a customer calls Sundia within the United States, the phone system forwards the call to a call center in the Philippines. At the call center, the order is taken and then relayed to the nearest warehouse to the customer. The nearest warehouse, which in this case is located in Wisconsin, sends the product to the customer. At the same time, the warehouse also informs the accounting office in India of the transaction, and the Indian accounting office processes the bill for the customer. The bill is then sent to the headquarters in San Francisco, and the customer is billed. As such, Sundia has taken full advantage of the Web to grow into an international juice company.

Micro-multinational

Company that uses web technology and the Internet to go global from the day it is founded.

Although the micro-multinational company is a relatively new form of organization, it will likely become more popular in the future with rapid developments in information technology. Although the micro-multinational structure shares some similarity with the transnational structure, it is important to note some of its unique characteristics:[30]

- Micro-multinational companies operate as born-global firms from the day they are founded, and they operate everywhere around the world.
- They are willing to start operations and hire workers from around the world and from where it makes the most sense to do so.
- They are more likely to use various state-of-the-art technology for communication purposes. Such technologies include voiceover Internet protocol (Skype), instant messaging (MSN Messenger), WIKIs (MediaWiki), and other online meeting services.

Multinational Strategy and Structure: An Overview

Exhibit 8.12 shows the relationship between the choice of multinational strategy and the choice of an organizational structure. The connections between the boxes for each strategy also show typical ways that multinational structures evolve.

EXHIBIT 8.12   Multinational Strategy, Structure, and Evolution

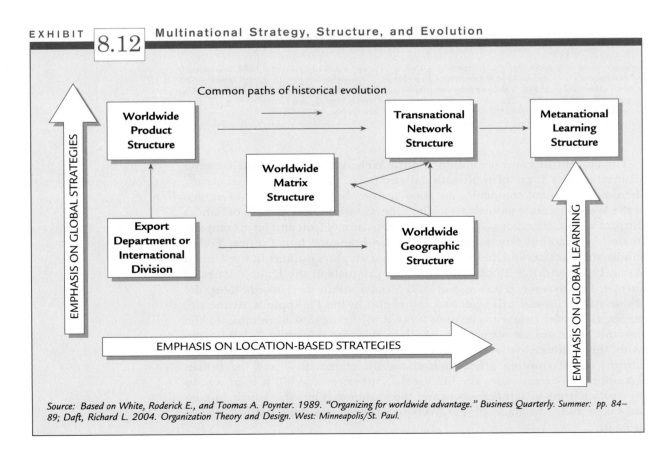

Source: Based on White, Roderick E., and Toomas A. Poynter. 1989. "Organizing for worldwide advantage." Business Quarterly. Summer: pp. 84–89; Daft, Richard L. 2004. Organization Theory and Design. West: Minneapolis/St. Paul.

Strategies of national or regional responsiveness (i.e., the multidomestic or regional strategies discussed in Chapter 6) suggest the use of geographic structures. An international strategy suggests that managers use a product organization and have worldwide products.

Most companies support their early internationalization with export departments or international divisions. Later, as Exhibit 8.12 suggests, and depending on the globalization of their strategy, companies evolve into worldwide product or geographic structures. After this, because of the dual demands of local-adaptation pressures and globalization, many companies move toward a matrix or transnational-network structure. Most companies, however, never quite reach the pure matrix, transnational, or metanational state. Instead, they most often adopt hybrid structures with some matrix and transnational qualities. Recently, because of the globalization of more products and the competitive efficiencies gained with global products, there is a growing tendency of large multinational companies to give product divisions increased power and to create more transnational subsidiaries.

Up to this point, we have discussed how to divide the organization into units that best support different strategies. Next, we will see how these units are brought together to accomplish organizational goals.

Control and Coordination Systems

Selecting different types of subunits to perform specialized tasks and responsibilities represents only one of the major decisions multinational companies make regarding organizational design. In addition, top managers must design organizational systems to control and coordinate the activities of their subunits. This is a difficult task. Foreign subsidiaries differ widely by geographic location, local markets, cultures, and legal systems, as well as by the talents and resources available to the subsidiary.[31] This section reviews systems used by multinational companies to control and coordinate their dispersed activities.

For multinational companies, organizational control represents the procedures used to focus the activities of subsidiaries in directions that support the company's strategies. **Control systems** help link the organization vertically, up and down the organizational hierarchy.

Two basic functions of control systems help focus the activities of the multinational company's subunits to support company-wide strategic goals and objectives. First, control systems measure or monitor the performances of subunits regarding their assigned roles in the firm's strategy. Second, control systems provide feedback to subunit managers regarding the effectiveness of their units. Measurement and feedback help top management communicate strategic goals to subordinates. In addition, measurement and feedback—combined with reward systems (e.g., promotion and pay)—help direct subordinates' behavior in appropriate directions.

Coordination systems help link the organization horizontally. They provide information flows among subsidiaries so that they can coordinate their respective activities. For example, in implementing its strategy, Ford plans to use advanced information systems so that designers in Europe, the United States, and Japan can coordinate their efforts in designing cars for the world market. Engineers will be able to communicate directly and share complex design

Control system
Vertical organizational links, up and down the organizational hierarchy.

Coordination system
Horizontal organizational links.

information instantaneously. More detail on control and coordination systems follows.

Design Options for Control Systems

There are four broad types of control systems: output control, bureaucratic control, decision-making control, and cultural control.

Output control systems assess the performance of a unit based on results, not on the processes used to achieve those results. When used in multinational companies, top management and local management usually negotiate output goals for foreign subsidiaries. These output goals must support the overall corporate strategy. Control occurs as headquarters evaluates subsidiaries and rewards local managers depending on how well the subsidiaries achieve the output goals.

Responsibility for profit is the most common output control. As noted before, **profit center** is the name given to a unit controlled by its profit or loss performances. Companies compare such units by looking at each profit center's profit or loss. The minireplica subsidiary, discussed earlier, often is a profit center. These profit-center subsidiaries usually set their own strategies, hire local workers, and act independently from the multinational company's headquarters. Top managers judge the success of the unit and the unit's managers based on the profits generated for the parent company.

Besides profit, other outcomes such as market share, developing new technologies, and supplying high-quality raw materials provide performance targets used to control multinational subsidiaries. For example, companies with transnational strategies and structures may evaluate each of their subsidiaries differently. One subsidiary may be evaluated based on its development of worldwide products, and another subsidiary may be evaluated on its market penetration by capturing market share.

Bureaucratic control systems focus on managing behaviors, not outcome, within the organization. Typical bureaucratic-control mechanisms include budgets, statistical reports, standard operating procedures, and centralization of decision making.[32] These systems work as follows:

- *Budgets set financial targets for expenditures during specific time periods.* **Budgets** control subsidiary behavior by providing rules that limit how much the subsidiary can spend on any activity. Budgets focus on controlling costs and usually emphasize efficiency goals. That is, efficient subunits produce more output (service or products) on a fixed budget.
- *Statistical reports provide information to top management on nonfinancial outcomes.* For example, a service organization might report on the number of customer complaints each week. A manufacturing organization might report on the number of units produced or the number of units rejected by quality control.
- *Standard operating procedures (SOPs) provide the rules and regulations that identify the approved ways of behaving.* For example, SOPs might prescribe that all subsidiaries should follow a standard practice for personnel evaluations.

Decision-making control represents the level in the organizational hierarchy where managers have the authority to make decisions. Upper management seldom makes all decisions in the organization. However, in decentralized organizations, lower-level managers make a larger number of more important decisions. In centralized organizations, higher-level managers make most of the important decisions. In most worldwide product structures, control over the

Output control system
Assesses the performance of a unit based on results, not on the processes used to achieve those results.

Profit center
Unit controlled by its profit or loss performance.

Bureaucratic control system
Focuses on managing organizational processes through budgets, statistical reports, standard operations procedures, and centralization of decision making.

Decision-making control
Level in the organizational hierarchy where managers have the authority to make decisions.

functional and strategic activities (i.e., production, finance, marketing, and product strategies) is centralized in the product division headquarters. Local country-level subsidiary managers deal only with local administrative, legal, and financial affairs.[33] In contrast, decentralized decision making is more common in worldwide area structures. Local country or regional subsidiaries have considerable autonomy from headquarters. Transnational network structures have no general tendency for decision-making control. The transnational company has several headquarters, each controlling different types of decisions depending on local expertise and the strategic situation. Depending on the strengths of a subsidiary, decision making may be centralized in the headquarters' nodes or passed down to lower levels.

Cultural control systems use the organizational culture (see Chapter 2 for a review) to control behaviors and attitudes of employees. Strong organizational cultures develop shared norms, values, beliefs, and traditions among workers. Such cultures encourage high levels of commitment and support for the organization. Workers and managers understand management goals and direct their efforts in support of these goals. Many experts now argue that a strong organizational culture may be the only way to link a dispersed multinational company with managers from many different national cultures.

Cultural control is the favored control mechanism for transnational-network structures. Although transnational organizations continue to use bureaucratic and output-control mechanisms, the uncertainties and complexities of the international environment make these more formal control mechanisms less effective than culture. For example, budgets or output goals set at Paris headquarters may not be timely for changing situations in Budapest or Singapore. Instead, headquarters relies on the commitment of local managers to corporate goals and trusts that they will adjust appropriately to local conditions.

The Royal Dutch/Shell group has a long tradition of using its strong global culture to bring cohesion to operating companies in more than a hundred countries. In spite of consistently being one of the most profitable companies in the world, Shell is changing its geographic structure to more of a product structure. The challenge for Shell will be to maintain its excellent system of cultural control while gaining the efficiencies of the new product organization. Consider the following Multinational Management Challenge. Do you think that Shell will succeed?

Multinational companies use all the control mechanisms to varying degrees, depending on their particular structure. Exhibit 8.13 shows the relationships between the control mechanisms and basic multinational organizational structures.

Design Options for Coordination Systems

There are six basic horizontal coordination systems: textual communication (memos or reports in electronic or paper form), direct contact, liaison roles, task forces, full-time integrators, and teams.[34] We discuss first the mechanisms that provide the least amount of coordination and then continue to the mechanisms that provide the greatest amount of coordination.

All organizations use textual communication, such as e-mail, memos, and reports, to coordinate the activities of subunits. Units report on their activities, keeping other units aware of problems, output levels, innovations, or any other important information. With the increased availability of low-cost computer equipment, most memos and reports no longer appear on paper. Companies use e-mail or postings to local web sites. Such electronic communication is particularly popular for multinational companies since they need rapid interaction over long distances and across many time zones.

Cultural control system

Uses organizational culture to control behaviors and attitudes of employees.

Multinational Management **Challenge**

Shell's Worldwide Family—How Must It Change?

Until the recent centralization of power in product-division heads, the Royal Dutch/ Shell group was a geographic organization with highly independent operating companies in more than 100 countries. To bring cohesion to these units with widely different national interests and conditions and to a headquarters with binational heritage (British and Dutch), Shell developed a strong corporate culture. This culture encourages people to identify with the parent company even while focusing on local interests. The building block of this cultural glue comes from the numerous international assignments of the typical Shell manager. Many managers serve in more than four different nations during their Shell careers.

The evolution of the Shell group into a product organization may result in a shift of control mechanisms. When profit and loss responsibilities are transferred to the product-division headquarters, output control will increase in importance. It remains to be seen if Shell can benefit from both its strong culture and output control at product-division level.

Sources: Based on Humes, Samuel. 1993. Managing the Multinational: Confronting the Global—Local Dilemma. New York: Prentice Hall; Dwyer, Paula, and Heidi Dawley. 1995. "The passing of 'the Shell man': An era ends as Royal Dutch/ Shell vows to centralize power." BusinessWeek Online, International Edition, April 17.

EXHIBIT 8.13   **Use of Control Mechanisms in Multinational Organizational Structures**

Multinational Structures	Control Systems			
	Output Control	**Bureaucratic Control**	**Decision-Making Control**	**Cultural Control**
International-Division Structure	Most likely profit control	Must follow company policies	Some centralization possible	Treated like other divisions
Worldwide Geographic Structure	Profit center most common	Some policies and procedures necessary	Local units have autonomy	Local subsidiary culture often more important
Worldwide Product Structure	Unit output for supply; sales volume for sales	Tight process controls for product quality and consistency	Centralized at product-division headquarters	Possible for some companies but not always necessary
Matrix Structure	Shared profit responsibility with product and geographic units	Less important	Balanced between geographic product units	Culture must support shared decision making
Transnational-Network Structure	Used for supplier units and some independent profit centers	Less important	Few decisions centralized at headquarters; more decisions centralized in key network nodes	Organizational culture transcends national cultures; supports sharing and learning; the most important control mechanism

Direct contact

Face-to-face interaction of employees.

Direct contact means that managers or workers interact face to face. For multinational companies, direct contact often requires sophisticated video conferencing and knowledge of a common language. For example, GE Medical Systems uses nearly 1,000 hours of teleconferencing in a year. Ford has computer-aided design and manufacturing links between two continents to allow its engineers in Europe and the United States to communicate design and engineering ideas.[35]

Liaison roles are specific job responsibilities of a person in one department to communicate with people in another department. A liaison role is only part of a manager's job responsibilities. For example, in a multinational company, one manager in each country subsidiary might be given the responsibility of coordinating marketing efforts within a region of the world. **Full-time integrators** are similar to liaison roles, but they have coordination as their sole job responsibility. Often product managers are full-time integrators. Product managers coordinate the development of their product with design teams, the production of their product with the manufacturing departments, and the sales and promotion of their product with marketing. In the multinational company, they often serve as a link between the production units and local-country operations.

Task forces are temporary teams created to solve a particular organizational problem such as entering a new market. They usually link more than one department. For example, to take advantage of new market opportunities in China, Unilever assembled a group of Chinese-speaking troubleshooters selected from its 100 country operations and sent them to China. The troubleshooters built plants, planned strategy and organization, and returned to their home countries when they had completed their task.[36]

Teams are the strongest coordination mechanisms. Unlike task forces, which have a short-term life span, teams are permanent units of the organization. Teams come from several organizational subunits to specialize in particular problems. For example, a team doing new-product development might include a scientist from R&D and managers from production and marketing. In a multinational example, Texas Instruments uses permanent special-project teams, called Nomads, to set up chip-fabrication plants anywhere in the world—from Italy to Singapore.[37]

As with the various control options, most multinational companies use several if not all of the coordination mechanisms. However, matrix and transnational-network structures have very high needs for coordination. In these types of organizations, one sees a greater use of the more elaborate control mechanisms of task forces, full-time integrators, and teams. For transnational networks, with their extensive geographic dispersion of subunits, teams are increasingly virtual units with members seldom meeting face-to-face. As such, given the importance of teams as a coordination mechanism, we consider this issue in more depth.

Teams

As more multinational companies are facing the pressures to meet both local and global customer needs through the integration of design and development expertise spread around the world, they are making increased use of teams.[38] Teams give global companies the ability to better coordinate the work and expertise of individuals located around the world, to develop and launch new products, and to become more flexible. Consider the example of International Truck and Engine Corporation that created cross-functional project teams of employees located in Canada, the United States, and Mexico to help create its new products.[39] By combining the top individuals in the various areas of engineering, manufacturing, finance, and project management in these cross-functional teams, International Truck and Engine Corporation hopes to find

---

Liaison roles

Part of a person's job in one department to communicate with people in another department.

Full-time integrator

Cross-unit coordination is the main job responsibility.

Task force

Temporary team created to solve a particular organizational problem.

Team

Permanent unit of the organization designed to focus the efforts of different subunits on particular problems.

Global virtual team

Groups of people from
different parts of the
world who work to-
gether by using infor-
mation and
communication tech-
nologies such as in-
tranets, web meetings,
WIKI's, e-mails, and
instant messaging.

ways to bring products to market more rapidly while also becoming more productive. Furthermore, the new global workplace is also seeing an increased use of **global virtual teams** Global virtual teams are groups of people from different parts of the world who work together by using information and communication technologies such as intranets, web meetings, WIKI's, e-mails, and instant messaging.[40]

Although global teams are popular, they face significant hurdles. Many of these challenges are associated with the difficulties with having team members with diverse cultural backgrounds located in different parts of the world. Previous surveys and empirical research identify the following as the most significant problems:[41]

- *Team members' native languages are different:* Although English may be widely becoming the shared language for teams, research suggests that team members around the world may not always have the same level of familiarity with the shared language. Such differences in understanding of the shared language can lead to significant problems and sometimes to mistakes and confusion.

- *Differences in cultural background:* Differences in cultural backgrounds can also be a significant challenge for team members working from different parts of the world. As an example, team members may have different perceptions of time and may not respond similarly to deadlines. (See Chapter 2 for other potential differences.)

- *Global teams dominated by headquarters' perspectives and experiences:* Although teams can be formed to tackle global projects, often the headquarters can have significant influence on the objectives, agendas, and initiatives of such teams. Such biases may occasionally lead to missed opportunities and misuse of the diversity of knowledge and perspectives on issues.

- *Major challenges in building team collaboration:* While it is difficult to build team collaboration in domestic teams, the lack of regular face-to-face meetings makes it especially challenging to build trust and collaboration. Sometimes, global team members may not have met each other, making it challenging to build trust, cohesion, and collaboration.

- *Challenges in meeting programmatic objectives:* The peculiar situations facing global teams also make it harder for multinational companies to keep such projects on track and within budget. Keeping a project on schedule and budget requires discipline and focus. However, it is usually difficult to get people focused and disciplined when they are located in different areas and may already have significant tasks to do.

However, despite these challenges, multinational companies can take steps to ensure that their global teams collaborate to function effectively. These steps include:[42]

- *Build relationships and trust:* Important steps have to be taken to encourage global team members to get to know each other to build trust. For instance, initial face-to-face meetings should be organized not only to let team members learn about each other but also to set project goals and roles. Some even suggest that the first meeting should last a minimum of three days. However, if traveling is too expensive, conference calls or other means can be used regularly to build relationships. It is advisable to use the time at the start of such meetings to encourage global team members to get to know each other on a personal level. This can be done by assigning a full-time communication specialist who can plan and manage both information flows and communication across teams. For instance, a communication specialist may request team members to provide more extensive feedback when necessary. Or the specialist can educate the team members about the pros and cons of the various forms of communication such as e-mail and videoconferencing.

- *Devote significant attention to project planning and hold project progress meetings regularly:* Ensuring that projects are completed on schedule and on budget is already difficult with domestic teams. However, the added complexity of team members located around the world suggests that multinational companies need to devote significant resources to planning the project. All team members should be made aware of the goals and time line of the project. The project leader should send clear messages about the key issues and how they relate to the strategic objective of the team. Furthermore, regular team meetings should be held to inform team members of progress. Corrective actions can also be implemented as necessary.

- *Cultural, language, and active-listening training:* Global teams can only function if team members are all on the same wavelength. Multinational companies need to devote resources to train global team members appropriately and to assess their level of cultural competency. Language training may also be appropriate to bring some level of language commonality to all team members. For instance, many of the prescriptions discussed in Chapter 13 on International Negotiation regarding communication with non-native speakers should be followed. Furthermore, global teams may fail because they consider lengthy discussions a waste of time. Group members must be trained to be sensitive to different communication styles and to practice active listening to avoid overlooking important issues.

- *Be aware of team-development stage:* Team research suggests that teams usually go through various stages as they progress to higher productivity. However, these stages are especially critical for global teams. As such, global team leaders should be aware of the team stage and provide adequate support. For instance, at the forming stage, the team leader should provide ample opportunity for the team members to get to know each other. At the storming stage, there's a higher likelihood of conflict, and the global team leader should find ways to address such conflict, which can be magnified because of the use of impersonal technologies to communicate. Care should be take to defuse conflict stemming from such issues.

This section completes our consideration of organizational design by showing how managers can control and coordinate the various types of subunits that multinational organizations employ. In the final section, we look at knowledge management, a design issue that is becoming increasingly crucial for most multinational companies.

Knowledge Management

In Chapter 7 on participation strategies, we saw that most multinational companies now face a very chaotic and "blurry" environment. Industry boundaries are now very ambiguous, and companies are facing intense competition. Product life cycles also are being increasingly compressed, and most multinational companies are facing severe information overload.[43] To face such challenges, most experts agree that it is becoming increasingly critical for companies to make optimal use of the knowledge available to them to build an innovative culture. Knowledge is the filtered information that has value to any company. As such, most experts agree that knowledge is the most important source of sustainable competitive advantage as multinational companies face shifting markets, rapid product cycles, and hyper-competition.[44] Companies must implement systems to manage knowledge. In this final section, we examine some of the critical design issues related to knowledge management.

Knowledge management

Systems and mechanisms to ensure that the right form of knowledge is available to the right individual at the right time.

Knowledge management refers to the systems, mechanisms, and other design elements of any organization to ensure that the right form of knowledge is available to the right individual at the right time.[45] Why is it so critical for companies to better manage their knowledge? For domestic companies, adequately managing knowledge can be very instrumental in generating new knowledge, which can then lead to innovation and value creation.[46] However, for multinational companies, knowledge management is even more critical as they face some unique challenges. Many multinationals now have to face forces for both global integration and local differentiation while achieving global innovation. As such, multinational companies need to be able to implement systems that are capable of combining worldwide knowledge from local sources to create and transfer innovation to new products for international markets. Appropriately managing knowledge can give multinational companies the means to create the global flexibility they will need to survive.[47]

Explicit form knowledge

Knowledge that can be found in records or databases and that can be easily transferred.

Tacit knowledge

Knowledge that resides within employees and is dependent on the organization's context.

To understand how to develop a knowledge-management system in a multinational organization, it is first necessary to distinguish between the various types of knowledge. Knowledge can be of the **explicit form**,[48] found in records or other repositories of information.[49] For example, DuPont has a number of knowledge repositories or databases at different levels that are accessible to employees globally through various intranet systems.[50] Because explicit knowledge is typically stored in some form, it can usually be codified and can be transferred easily to other employees. In contrast, **tacit knowledge,** represents the knowledge that usually resides within employees and is dependent on the organization's culture and context. Tacit knowledge is usually seen as the most important form of knowledge because it is more critical to innovation and competitive advantage. For example, tacit knowledge is reflected at DuPont through the social network of people (e.g., vendors, customers, contractors, universities) that R&D employees have access to for guidance and consultation when they are facing problems.

How can a multinational company develop an effective knowledge-management system? The first step is to identify potential barriers to knowledge sharing within the organization. Barriers can exist at various levels, including the individual and organizational levels.[51] Sharing knowledge across companies located in different parts of the world also introduces a number of cross-cultural and geographic distance-related challenges. Exhibit 8.14 summarizes some of the most important individual, organizational, and cross-cultural problems.

To build a knowledge-management system, multinational companies must assess the degree to which these barriers exist and implement appropriate actions to reduce the influence of such barriers. For instance, the multinational firm can take the appropriate steps to communicate to employees about the necessity to share knowledge. Individual employees should be motivated,

EXHIBIT **8.14**   Knowledge Management Barriers

Individual Barriers

- Lack of time or interest to share knowledge
- Lack of understanding of importance of sharing knowledge
- Lack of trust of others impedes knowledge sharing
- Use of hierarchical position or power to encourage sharing of explicit rather than tacit knowledge
- Poor communication skills

Organizational Barriers

- Lack of communication of importance of knowledge management
- No strategic alignment between organization's mission and objectives and knowledge-sharing strategy and initiatives
- Lack of sufficient mechanisms (both online and face-to-face) to share knowledge
- Lack of reward systems to foster and encourage knowledge sharing
- Communication flows restricted to one direction as reflected in the organizational hierarchy
- Internal strife and conflict among business units

Cross-cultural Barriers

- Language barriers
- Cultural differences
- Time-zone and other geographic distance-related challenges

Source: Based on Riege, Andreas. 2005. "Three-dozen knowledge-sharing barriers managers must consider." Journal of Knowledge Management 9, 3: pp. 18–35; Voelpel, Sven C., and Zheng Han. 2005. "Managing knowledge sharing in China: The case of Siemens ShareNet." Journal of Knowledge Management, 9, 3: pp. 51–63.

encouraged, and rewarded to capture and disseminate the appropriate knowledge to others in the organization as needed.[52] Furthermore, the organizational structure should be aligned with the need for knowledge management. Taller hierarchical structures are obvious barriers to information flow, and important steps need to be taken toward a flatter and more fluid structure. Finally, it should be noted that an important aspect of knowledge management is the use of computer-based technology.[53] Computer and web-based technologies allow multinational companies to create simple data repositories to store explicit knowledge. However, use of computer-based technologies also enables multinational companies to make use of tacit knowledge through various tools such as networking, collaborative commerce, and other decision-support systems. DuPont uses Lotus Notes to allow its R&D personnel to collaborate and consult with other in-house and outside experts on various matters.[54] As such, it is important for multinational companies to invest in the necessary technology to provide the necessary integrative platform for individuals located around the world.

In addition, best practices show that multinational companies need to address the following if they want to develop a successful knowledge-management system:[55]

- *Identify/support knowledge activists:* Multinational companies need to identify and support those individuals who are willing to make the network function successfully. Network activists have a good understanding of the importance of such networks and will coordinate the work of other members to make the network a reality.

- *Make knowledge management part of the general strategy:* **Multinational companies need to frame knowledge-management systems as an integral part of the general corporate strategy. For instance, it is important for the multinational organization to communicate the importance of knowledge-management systems to the organization's innovation processes. By communicating the importance of knowledge management, the multinational company can get more individuals to support the knowledge networks within the organization. Such support is critical if the system is to be implemented successfully.**

- *Provide financial and human resources support:* **Knowledge-management systems require both time and money commitments. For example, the knowledge network may need the creation of mailing lists, web sites, employee meetings. The multinational company must understand that the necessary resources need to be provided to support such important activities.**

- *Emphasize importance of communication:* **As mentioned earlier, tacit knowledge is often most valuable to innovation. However, tacit knowledge is usually the result of years of experience and learning. As such, intense communication is necessary to give members of the network time to be able to decode and appreciate the complexity of such tacit knowledge.**

- *Celebrate success:* **By collecting and communicating success stories, multinational companies can show the value of knowledge-management systems and can reduce resistance to such systems. Furthermore, the multinational company also can show appreciation for individuals who promote sharing within the organization. Such celebration of success not only shows the commitment of the organization to its knowledge-management systems but also may encourage others to explore new ways to collaborate.**

Summary and Conclusions

Good strategies by themselves will never guarantee successful multinational operations. Good implementation is equally important. Perhaps the most important part of strategy implementation is having the right organizational design to carry out strategic intents, goals, and objectives. This chapter provided a review of how multinational companies use organizational designs to implement multinational strategies. Organizational design concerns the choice of subunits (how to divide work) and the choice of coordination and control mechanisms (how to focus the efforts of the subunits).

As supporting background, the chapter reviewed the basics of organizational structure. Functional, product and geographic structures were described and pictured. They also were compared and contrasted for their strengths and weaknesses. A knowledge of

these basic structures is necessary because functional, product, and area structures are the building blocks for the organizational structures used by multinational companies.

As companies internationalize their strategies, they usually progress from using an export department or international division to more complex organizational structures. To use more complex structures, multinational companies need foreign subsidiaries to conduct value-chain activities (e.g., manufacturing) in other countries. Some of these subsidiaries are minireplicas—small reproductions of the home-country organization. Other subsidiaries are transnational—they can do anything or be anywhere depending on the local strengths and the parent company's needs. Companies use different types of subsidiaries depending on the structures that they choose.

If companies adopt a multidomestic or regional multinational strategy, then they usually favor a worldwide geographic structure. This structure emphasizes responding to local markets. In contrast, the worldwide product structure supports the more global international strategy. It is an organizational form that facilitates building and selling global products. Hybrid and matrix structures support companies with mixtures of strategies for different products and businesses. These structures try to combine some of the benefits of both the geographic and product structures. The transnational-network structure goes beyond the matrix and hybrid. It has no set form, and its subsidiaries respond uniquely to global efficiency pressures, company-learning needs, or local needs, as the strategic situation dictates. The step beyond the transnational-network structure is the metanational structure where organizational learning and virtual sharing of information become the drivers of the organization.

Organizational designs are not complete without integration mechanisms. These mechanisms link subunits and coordinate their activities. Control systems such as bureaucratic and cultural control link the organization vertically. Coordination mechanisms such as task forces and teams link the organization horizontally. Multinational organizations use all these integration mechanisms. However, for the multinational company, cultural control is often considered most important. A strong organizational culture helps the multinational company bridge the national cultures of its employees.

Finally, an important component of today's multinational companies is knowledge-management systems. Knowledge-management systems allow the multinational company to encourage sharing of valuable expertise of individuals often located around the world. To implement such systems successfully, the multinational organization must assess barriers to knowledge sharing and implement knowledge networks through the consideration of various factors discussed earlier.

Discussion Questions

1. You work for a company with three major products. Your CEO has decided to sell these products in the international marketplace. She asks your advice in setting up an organizational structure. What issues would you discuss with her regarding the company's international strategy before making any recommendations?

2. What are the advantages of a worldwide product structure over a worldwide area structure? What type of company would most likely choose each type?

3. What are the costs and benefits of having a matrix structure?

4. What transnational activities might be possible for a small company with only an export department or an international division?

5. Identify some areas in multinational companies where cultural control might work better than bureaucratic control.

6. What cultural values must a metanational company encourage so that alliance partners and dispersed subsidiaries share knowledge?

7. What are virtual teams? What benefits can virtual teams bring to multinational companies?

8. What are some of the typical problems multinationals face when using teams as integration mechanisms? What can multinational companies do to address these problems?

9. What are knowledge-management systems? How can knowledge-management systems be appropriately designed?

Multinational Management **Skill Builder**

Build an Organization Structure for P&G

Step 1. Procter & Gamble is a major multinational corporation headquartered in the United States. Review the popular business press (e.g., *Wall Street Journal, Fortune, Economist, BusinessWeek*, etc.) over the last year for articles on P&G's operations around the globe.

Step 2. Given this background information, design a multinational structure that you think can best implement P&G's strategies for different products. An overview of P&G's geographic locations and major global products is presented here.

Step 3. Prepare a written or oral report showing your design and providing a rationale for the structural choices.

P&G's Worldwide Locations and Starting Dates of Operations

Algeria, 2001	Denmark, 1992	Indonesia, 1970	Panama, 2000	Tanzania, 1997
Argentina, 1991	Egypt, 1986	Ireland, 1980	Peru, 1956	Thailand, 1985
Australia, 1985	El Salvador, 1988	Israel, 2001	Philippines, 1935	Turkey, 1987
Austria, 1966	Estonia, 1995	Italy, 1956	Poland, 1991	Uganda, 1995
Azerbaijan, 1998	Federal Republic of	Japan, 1973	Portugal, 1989	Ukraine, 1993
Bangladesh, 1995	Yugoslavia, 1996	Kazakhstan, 1996	Puerto Rico, 1947	United Arab
Belarus, 1995	Federation of Bosnia-	Kenya, 1985	Romania, 1994	Emirates, 2001
Belgium, 1955	Herzegovina, 1998	Korea, 1988	Russia, 1991	United Kingdom,
Brazil, 1988	Finland, 1971	Latvia, 19995	Saudi Arabia, 1957	1930
Bulgaria, 1994	Former Yugoslav	Lebanon, 1959	Singapore, 1969	United States,
Canada, 1915	Republic of Mace-	Lithuania, 1997	Slovak Republic,	1837
Caribbean Islands,	donia, 1998	Malaysia, 1969	1993	Uzbekistan, 1996
1986	France, 1954	Mexico, 1948	Slovenia, 1996	Venezuela, 1950
Chile, 1983	Germany, 1960	Morocco, 1958	South Africa, 1994	Vietnam, 1994
China, 1988	Ghana, 1998	Netherlands, 1964	Spain, 1968	Yemen, 1995
Colombia, 1982	Greece, 1960	New Zealand, 1985	Sri Lanka, 1996	
Costa Rica, 1995	Guatemala, 1985	Nicaragua, 1985	Sweden, 1969	
Croatia, 1991	Honduras, 1985	Nigeria, 1992	Switzerland, 1953	
Czech Republic,	Hong Kong, 1969	Norway, 1993	Syria, 1998	
1991	Hungary, 1991	Pakistan, 1989	Taiwan, 1984	

Source: Adapted from Procter & Gamble. 2003. Facts about P&G 2002–2003 Worldwide. Cincinnati: Procter & Gamble.

P&G Global Product Groups and Product Types		
Product Groups	**Product Types**	**Net Sales (millions)**
Baby, Feminine and Family Care	Baby Diapers, Baby Wipes, Baby Bibs, Baby Change and Bed Mats	$11.9
	Toilet Tissue, Paper Towels And Facial Tissue	
	Feminine Protection Pads, Pantiliners & Tampons	
Beauty Care	Cosmetics	11.6
	Deodorants	
	Fragrances	
	Hair Coloring	
	Skin Care	
Fabric & Home Care	Bleach	8.1
	Care for Special Fabrics	
	Dish Care	
	Fabric Conditioners	
	Household Cleaners	
	Laundry Detergent	
	P&G Chemicals	
	Cosmetics	
Food & Beverage	Beverages	3.8
	Snacks	
Health Care	Oral And Personal Care	5.0
	Pet Health And Nutrition	
	Prescription Drugs	
	Water Filtration	

Source: Adapted from Procter & Gamble. 2003. Facts about P&G 2002–2003 Worldwide. Cincinnati: Procter & Gamble.

Endnotes

[1] Jones, Gareth R. 2007. *Organizational Theory, Design and Change.* Upper Saddle River, NJ: Pearson-Prentice Hall.

[2] Ibid.

[3] Glader, Paul. 2006. "It's not easy being lean; How many managers make for an efficient company? Layers 'slow decisions down'." *Wall Street Journal, June 19:* p. B1.

[4] Duncan, Robert. 1979. "What is the right organization structure? Decision tree analysis provides the answer." *Organizational Dynamics,* Winter.

[5] United Nations Conference on Trade and Development (UNCTAD). 2003. *World Investment Report.* New York and Geneva: United Nations.

[6] Brellochs, Jochen, and Ulrich Steger. 2006. "Most multinationals now derive most of their value from subsidiaries. So, why do so few have robust systems in place to ensure that principles of governance are applied consistently across their organizational networks?" *Financial Times,* June, 2: p. 4.

[7] Ibid.

[8] Beamish, Paul W., J. Peter Killing, Donald J. Lecraw, and Allen J. Morrison. 1994. *International Management.* Burr Ridge, IL: Irwin.

[9] Bartlett, Christopher A., and Sumantra Ghoshal. 1989. *Managing across Borders: The Transnational Solution.* Boston: Harvard University Press.

[10] Humes, Samuel. 1993. *Managing the Multinational: Confronting the Global–Local Dilemma.* New York: Prentice Hall.

[11] Stopford, J. M., and L. T. Wells, Jr. 1972. *Managing the Multinational Enterprise.* New York: Basic Books.

[12] Toyota. 2006. "Toyota Announces Board of Directors and Organizational Changes." June 23. http://www.toyota.co.jp

[13] *BusinessWeek Online. 1994.* "Borderless management: Companies strive to become truly stateless." May 23; Treece, James B., Kathleen Kerwin, and Heidi Dawley. 1995. "Ford: Alex Trotman's daring global strategy." *BusinessWeek Online,* April 3.

[14] *Economist. 2000.* "Ford in Europe: in the slow lane." October 7; *Economist.* 2002. "From baron to hotelier." May 9; Lublin, Joann. 2001. "Division problem—place vs. product: It's tough to choose a management model—Exide tore up system based on countries for one on centered battery lines—rolling over European fiefs." *Wall Street Journal.* (Eastern edition). New York . June 27, p. A1.

[15] Beamish, Killing, Lecraw, and Morrison, *International Management.*

[16] *BusinessWeek Online,* "Borderless management: Companies strive to become truly stateless."

[17] *Economist,* "From baron to hotelier."

[18] Galbraith, Jay R. 2000. *Designing the Global Corporation.* San Francisco: Jossey-Bass.

[19] Ibid.

[20] *BusinessWeek Online.* 1994. "High-tech jobs all over the world." November 18.

[21] *Economist.* 2006. "Survey: The matrix master." January 21.

[22] Ghoshal, Sumantra, and Christopher A. Bartlett. 1990. "The multi-national corporation as an interorganizational network." *Academy of Management Review,* pp. 15, 603–625; Humes, *Managing the Multinational: Confronting the Global–Local Dilemma;* Philips Electronics N.V. *2003. Annual Report.* February 11.

[23] Bartlett and Ghoshal, *Managing across Borders: The Transnational Solution.*

[24] Ibid.

[25] *BusinessWeek Online,* "High-tech jobs all over the world."

[26] Doz, Yves, J., José Santos, and Peter Williamson. 2001. *From global to metanational: How companies win in the knowledge economy.* Boston: Harvard Business School Press.

[27] Fisher, Lawrence M. 2002. "STMicroelectronics: The metaphysics of a metanational pioneer." *Strategy & Business,* 19, Third Quarter pp. 2–10.

[28] Ibid.

[29] Copeland, Michael V. 2006. "The mighty micro-multinational." *Business 2.0, July,* pp. 107–114.

[30] Ibid.

[31] Cray, David. 1984. "Control and coordination in multinational corporations." *Journal of International Business Studies,* Fall, pp. 85–98.

[32] Daft, Richard L. 2004. *Organization Theory and Design.* Minneapolis/St. Paul: West; Jones, *Organizational Theory, Design and Change.*

[33] Beamish, Killing, Lecraw, and Morrison, *International Management.*

[34] Daft, *Organization Theory and Design.*

[35] *BusinessWeek Online,* "Borderless management: Companies strive to become truly stateless."

[36] *BusinessWeek Online.* 1994. "Tearing up today's organization chart." November 18.

[37] *BusinessWeek Online,* "High-tech jobs all over the world."

[38] Barczak, Gloria, Edward F. McDonough III, and Nicholas Athanassiou. 2006. "So you want to be a global project leader?" *Research Technology Management,* May/June, 49, 3: pp. 28–35.

[39] Rosswurm, Gretchen, and Patricia Bayerlein. 2004/2005. "Overcoming barriers to global success at International." *Strategic Communication Management,* December/January, 9, 1: pp. 14–17.

[40] Brake, Terence. 2006. "Leading global virtual teams." *Industrial and Commercial Training,* 38, 3: pp. 116–121.

[41] Barczak, Gloria, and Edward F. McDonough III. 2003. "Leading global product development teams." *Research Technology Management,* November/December, 46, 6: pp. 14–18; Barczak, McDonough III, and Athanassiou, "So you want to be a global project leader?"; Rosswurm and Bayerlein, "Overcoming barriers to global success at International."

[42] Barczak, McDonough III, and Athanassiou, "So you want to be a global project leader?"; Kumar, Janaki Mythily. 2006. "Working as a designer in a global team." *Interactions,* March/April: pp. 25–27; Rosswurm and Bayerlein, "Overcoming barriers to global success at International."

[43] Davis, Joseph G., Eswaran Subrahmanian, and Arthur W. Westerberg. 2005. "The 'global' and the 'local' in knowledge management." *Journal of Knowledge Management,* 9, 1: pp. 101–112.

[44] Ibid.

[45] Wang, Junxia, Hans Peter Peters, and Jiancheng Guan. 2006. "Factors influencing knowledge productivity in German research groups: Lessons for developing countries." *Journal of Knowledge Management* 10, 4: pp. 113–126.

[46] Voelpel, Sven C., and Zheng Han. 2005. "Managing knowledge sharing in China: The case of Siemens ShareNet." *Journal of Knowledge Management,* 9, 3: pp. 51–63.

[47] Davis, Subrahmanian, and Westerberg, "The 'global' and the 'local' in knowledge management."

[48] Schönström, Mikael. 2005. "Creating knowledge networks: Lessons from practice." *Journal of Knowledge Management,* 9, 6: pp. 17–29.

[49] Riege, Andreas. 2005. "Three-dozen knowledge-sharing barriers managers must consider." *Journal of Knowledge Management* 9, 3: pp. 18–35.

[50] Davis, Subrahmanian, and Westerberg, "The 'global' and the 'local' in knowledge management."

[51] Riege, "Three-dozen knowledge-sharing barriers managers must consider."

[52] Ibid.

[53] Holsapple, Clyde W. 2005. "The inseparability of modern knowledge management and computer-based technology." *Journal of Knowledge Management,* 9, 1: pp. 42–52.

[54] Davis, Subrahmanian, and Westerberg, "The 'global' and the 'local' in knowledge management."

[55] McKenzie, Jane. 2005. "How to share knowledge between companies." *Knowledge Management Review,* November/December 8, 5: pp. 16–19; Schönström, "Creating knowledge networks: Lessons from practice;" Wang, Peters, and Guan, "Factors influencing knowledge productivity in German research groups: Lessons for developing countries."

CHAPTER CASE

Haute Innovations— International Virtual Teams Case Scenario

Synopsis

As technology communication tools become more advanced and markets more global, cross-border virtual teams are becoming more prevalent. This fictional case study uncovers some of the trials and tribulations of an international virtual team working toward the development and production of an innovative video game product. The manager of the team has to make crucial decisions to keep her team on track and up to speed as they race to the finish line of a successful prototype.

Company Background

Haute Innovations was started by Robert "Bob" Grady on December 3, 1984 to produce video gaming software to compete with such early video game development companies as Atari. With little start-up funding, Bob decided to rent a house in Houston, Texas where he set up his offices on the bottom floor and lived upstairs. He hired two of his close college buddies to design and develop video games. They met with immediate success when they sold conceptual gaming software designs to an arcade manufacturer.

Bob developed his initial business attitudes around experimentation, being on the cutting edge of gaming programming and having fun. He hired young, promising programmers who were not "business types" but who had the wild imaginations that were needed to create visually intensive graphics and stimulating

---

Company Profile

Name: Haute Innovations

Company inception date: December 3, 1984

Company size: approximately 1000 employees worldwide

1998 Net income: $1.6 billion, $500 million dedicated to Research and Development

Main product: handheld video games and video game programming

Headquarters: Houston, Texas

Site locations:

   Houston, Texas—Main headquarters

   Montgomery, Alabama—United States manufacturing plant

   Oslo, Norway—European headquarters

   Copenhagen, Denmark—Research & Development

   Stockholm, Sweden—European manufacturing plant

Team: Bob Grady, Nan King, Georg Lonson, Carl Jensen, Ingrid Hans

Goal: Create a prototype of a voice interactive video game.

Budget: Generous. President's pet project

Deadline for prototype: July 1, 1999

Team Profile

Robert "Bob" Grady   Title: President

Role on this project: Moneybags, Idea approver Location: Houston, Texas

Profile: Robert is a 38-year-old entrepreneur that started this company after he graduated from the University of Alabama with an undergraduate degree in Finance. He is very creative and described as "full of energy." Known for his pet projects and lack of hands-on involvement over these projects—advantages of owning your own company. As long as he is in the black, his company is doing well enough to satisfy him. Even though he does not care to manage, he wants to be kept well informed. Owns a ranch in Palestine, Texas where he holds his annual company meetings.

Nan King, MBA   Title: Research and Development Director

Role on this project: Team Lead, R & D Specialist, Benchmark analyst

Location: Houston, Texas

Profile: Nan is a 35-year-old "go-getter" that joined Haute Innovations after receiving her MBA from Southern Methodist University in Dallas, Texas in 1995. Her background includes working as an R&D consultant with such companies as Texas Instruments and Sega. She is accustomed to being the leader and keeping employees on task.

Georg Lonson   Title: Creativity Director

Role on this project: Idea GeneratorLocation: Oslo, Norway

Profile: Georg is a 29-year-old programmer with a background in comic book design. Known for his humor and ability to come up with the wild ideas. Bob met Georg at a local Norwegian bar, SMUGET, where their personalities clicked. Georg showed Bob his comic book designs and Bob knew that he had to have him on the team.

Carl Jensen   Title: Design Consultant

Role on this project: Design, Quality Assurance Location: Copenhagen, Denmark

Profile: Carl is a 35-year-old design engineer. He is quiet and shy—especially when it comes to making decisions about important issues but solves every design problem with exceptional creativity. He works very well with CAD to get his ideas on paper and prefers to meet his teams face to face. He's not very comfortable with advanced software—prefers to have everything in design blueprints as opposed to just looking at a computer screen.

Ingrid Hans   Title: Prototype Specialist

Role on this project: Overseer of prototype development Location: Stockholm, Sweden

Profile: Ingrid is a 42-year-old prototype specialist for small/handheld video products. She is the local contact in Stockholm for Bob—he places a tremendous amount of faith and expectation in her to control the European production. Her English communication skills tend to waiver on occasion—especially when there are problems with the team. Bob hopes this won't be a problem . . .

---

games. They set up their computers and design boards in his house and programmed typically until all hours of the night. They considered it challenging fun rather than a "real job." From watching the gaming market, Bob had bigger plans for his business and started to consider his options.

Initially, the company only developed the programming behind the video games and subcontracted to a computer manufacturer to actually produce and package the games for sale. After three years of operation, Bob decided that it would

be to his company's advantage to incorporate manufacturing for expansion, quality control, and efficiency purposes. From his profits, he reinvested capital to purchase a small plant in Montgomery, Alabama from Wang Computers with an existing but primitive clean room for technology hardware development. They shifted into manufacturing without many problems and soon needed further expansion to meet their demand.

After a much needed vacation to Scandinavia in 1989, Bob decided that a prime opportunity to stay ahead of the "game" would be to open a European headquarters in Oslo, Norway. This predominately English-speaking country had two big advantages: they liked working with Americans and the companies thrived on the cutting edge technology. Bob purchased a small business office, set up his European headquarters, and hired programmers and support staff to begin his operation.

In 1994, he decided to open a European plant to accelerate his production and lower his costs for the European market. Building a new manufacturing plant in Norway was basically out of the question because of the cost of land and building. He considered many places in Europe but decided that with Stockholm's advances in technology and forward thinking environment purchasing an existing manufacturing plant there would be his best bet. He could retool the plant and then custom train Swedish employees to manufacture the product to his quality specifications. He hired Ingrid Hans, a developer and manager, to oversee quality assurance and proper development of Haute Innovations' products. An R&D site in Copenhagen was added via acquisition just this year.

Haute Innovations experienced much success from the beginning due to Bob's ability to understand both technology and the financial aspect of running a business. He took many risks (that luckily paid off) and considered continued expansion essential. He also placed a tremendous amount of faith in the employees and programmers that he hired—he did not want to "manage" them but rather let them mutually adjust and self-monitor their performance. Often, his programmers set more challenging goals than Bob would have imagined. Setbacks occurred, but Bob didn't mind taking risks as long as everyone learned from them. Bob was so laid back that as long as his programmers produced a quality end product near deadline and near budget, he was happy. He relied on teams to work together and troubleshoot issues that were out of his specialty. For the most part, these business practices worked well.

Project Formation

On October 1, 1998, Bob called for inner-company résumés to form a development team that would create a prototype for a voice interactive video game. The technology had been developed to participate interactively with toys that were due to be released for Christmas sales. Sensing the products would be tremendously popular, he came up with the idea that he could go beyond virtual reality and actually have voice activated instruction applied to handheld video games. This initial product would be very expensive, but it would be Haute Innovations' chance to really make its cutting edge mark. Bob decided this would be his pet project and he developed what he felt was a liberal budget to get the project to a prototype state.

The deadline for résumé submission was November 15, 1998 and he received a total of 15 résumés from which to select. He had never designed a team exactly this way before but was hoping to gain an advantage by picking eager participants who were also the best and brightest. He was very pleased because all of his international divisions submitted a few résumés from which he could select quality individuals. He contemplated the fact that the experts he wanted all resided in different countries, but decided that he had quality professional people working for him and they would overcome any problems this might present. He assumed their years of experience would mitigate the need for team training. A product such as this would be ideal for global markets and he wanted to be sure the design team understood this and designed it accordingly. This would be his first international virtual team to work on a project of this scale.

The team was announced on December 1, 1998 with their initial phone conference meeting on December 2, 1998. During the initial phone conference, Bob laid out his expectation that the team was to stay in constant open communication and arrive at effective decisions to produce the prototype. Since this product would be on the cutting edge of technology, it was Bob's decision to manufacture the prototype in Sweden—to remove it from the American element. The designs were to be created and tested in the United States, but the actual prototype markup would be completed at the Stockholm plant, by the European developers. The team exchanged e-mail addresses, day and night phone numbers, bio information, and quickly determined their job roles.

Nan, who is located at the main headquarters in Houston, Texas, assumed the role of team leader of the prototype team. With a watchful eye always on the calendar, she is very mindful of ensuring that any of her teams stay on task. Her main role on this team is to make sure the group receives what they need, when they need it, to get the prototype to her on time and reasonably on budget. She often fights the tendency to micromanage, yet insists on regular updates and frequent, often perceived as excessive, communication. She is a stickler for paperwork and integrated design documents.

Georg Lonson, who is located at the European headquarters in Oslo, Norway, is the creativity director over a small group that designs the casings for the toys. It is his responsibility to ensure that his group builds the casing model to Carl Jensen's specifications and then makes it attractive so that consumers will buy it. This is especially important in gaming toys because children and young adults will buy bright eye-catching toys. He must also deal with outside plastics and metal brokers.

Carl Jensen, the design consultant in Copenhagen, Denmark, is the head of a five-person team of design engineers that plans, designs, and builds the inner workings of the video games. He is a highly trained engineer who is more focused on his successes, rather than those of his design team. He is kept on as the head of the team because of his ability to spur everyone to truly innovative designs. His previous successes are the company's most popular products.

Ingrid Hans, the prototype specialist at the European manufacturing plant in Stockholm, Sweden, has the job of bringing it all together and developing it for mass production. She has somewhat limited experience in working with vendors and suppliers but has tremendous knowledge of her manufacturing line and its capabilities. She claims she would much rather work with the automated lines than have to talk with others. Ingrid works very well in a one-on-one situation but not under extreme stress. Nan is well aware of her situation, but agreed with Bob that she would be able to handle the manufacturing inputs into the development of this prototype. Nan raised the issue of an initial team face-to-face meeting and some team training to help them go "virtual" but everyone agreed they were eager to get to work

designing their own working groups. Meetings would come later.

Work on the initial designs began. Each member of the virtual team assembled their working groups and solicited confidential input from outside vendors and prior alpha and beta testers as appropriate. Everyone on the team embraced concurrent design principles and acted accordingly. Detailed work schedules were compiled at each site and Nan facilitated the development of an integrated design-to-prototype document that noted all critical interfaces, hand-offs, and milestones for the virtual team. Upstream and downstream concerns at each interface were captured in checklists. Nan discussed the critical interfaces and scheduled handoff dates with each member of the team and made sure everyone agreed to them. Little did she know that while everyone verbally agreed with her, doubts ran rampant. When the team shared the document with their working groups at home, deadlines were considered challenging bordering on impossible. A teleconference was scheduled for the last week of January to discuss initial design issues.

The teleconference made them painfully aware of the fact that everyone had their favorite features and difficult trade-off decisions were inevitable. Thanks to the variety of computer aided design tools on the company intranet, all aspects of the design project were captured and documented. Some decisions were easy once everyone had accessed the full information. Other decisions seemed impossible—everyone stuck with their favorite solution and conflict ruled the day. Some conflicts once resolved improved the design. Other conflicts were starting to get personal . . . They realized it was time to meet face-to-face.

The team had their first and it turned out their only face-to-face meeting at the annual company meeting in the first weekend of March. Bob's ranch provided the means for privacy and relaxation for the team to get to know more about each other. They engaged in the team-building activities that had been scheduled and joked about how late in the life of their team they were finally getting to know one another. They talked about their families, and just had fun together. Between fishing on the lake and picnics, the whole team reviewed the first designs, made some difficult decisions (ones that seemed impossible only a week earlier) and met with Bob. Bob gave his suggestions for modification and then his mark of approval. In the fast and furious three months that the team had been working together, no serious problems had surfaced. However, they knew the most difficult times were at hand. Moving from design to prototype would be the true test. At the annual meeting, questions were raised about their changing roles, how they were going to meet such a demanding schedule, and who was going to take the managerial lead now that Bob had given his approvals. Some on the team expressed their desire for more of Bob's leadership. They felt he could really give their project the push it needed to stay on track. They asked him to visit their respective working groups. Unfortunately Bob's laid back attitude and lack of hands-on style didn't fit. Bob reassured them that Nan would be there for them for project direction and to provide needed resources and coordination. Nan was pleased that he recognized her and started thinking of ways to keep the lines of communication open, the creative juices flowing and conflicts to a minimum. She knew these would be critical to the project's success and she fretted about them for the rest of the weekend. She came up with a list of common pitfalls of virtual teaming and felt her team was vulnerable on all counts. Everyone else enjoyed the rest of the weekend and then returned to their respective locations. The pace intensified.

The work started off at a good pace but then the schedule began to be overbearing. The "I told you we couldn't possibly do this in this time frame" comments surfaced in every working group. The virtual team (v-team) members started to not respond to e-mail, phone calls, and even ignored faxes labeled urgent. They were not very forthcoming with information during conference calls. Nan became more demanding and intensified her forthcoming communication requirements and the team members became defensive and even more closemouthed. They were overwrought with their individual problems and scrambled to find solutions within their groups without keeping other virtual team members informed.

Major conflicts arose when minor changes in one area created big problems for others. Add to that the ill will that developed when it took days and days for the change specifications to be communicated. For

example, the materials supplier had excuses as to why motherboards were failing tests when a design flaw was discovered. The redesign changed the specs on the casing materials which then arrived cracked and the vendor was refusing to replace the items. Some of the newest equipment delivered to the Sweden plant to be used in the development of the prototype and manufacturing of the new product was not functioning correctly and the vendor was on holiday. Finally, out of extreme frustration, v-team members began to call Nan at all hours to complain about each other. They all had the perception that their internal problems were minimal—everything was someone else's fault.

Nan, usually calm and collected, began to have sleepless nights and health problems. When she really thought about the problems everyone was calling her about, she realized that she was only hearing the tip of the iceberg. She knew of the schedule and integration problems but knew little of the internal problems in each working group. When she questioned Ingrid about concerns at her site, she responded that she did not want to bother others with her issues and that she thought she had proper control over it. Nan wondered if the other team members were hiding similar issues. Nan decided that she was going to need to be a more involved manager of this virtual team. She wondered what other issues were out there festering. She was in for more problems.

To Complicate Matters. . . .

As Nan started to dig deeper into the health of her team, she found many situations that she was unaware of within her group. She had never dealt with a completely international virtual team, especially when developing a cutting edge prototype. Some of the problems were not too much of a surprise because they are typical of virtual teams but the international distance only accentuated the negative effects of the problems. Some of the problems compounded by the international dimension follow.

Ingrid complained that she was always having difficulty speaking to the manufacturing plant in Alabama because of the time differences. The United States–based plant only worked in two shifts for a total of a 16-hour day. Ingrid would call at 4:00 P.M. her time and could never get in touch with the plant manager. She would leave messages and they would not respond until late in the afternoon. Since Haute Innovations is an open information sharing environment, the American-based plant had her home phone number and would just call her at home in the middle of the night. At first, she was so happy to receive a returned call that she did not complain, but the phone calls became more frequent and for less important reasons.

Not only are Haute Innovations' employees dealing with time zones, they are affected directly by different working schedules and quality of life standards. The Scandinavian standard is to work from 9:00 A.M. to 4:00 P.M. and then to spend the remaining time with their families and friends. They take their holidays and personal time very seriously because of their high standard of quality living and family values. In the United States, the standard working time is 8:00 A.M. to 5:00 P.M., although that is rarely ever followed. The American professionals work much longer hours and drive themselves to achieve a higher quality bank account. They work through their holidays and family time so that they may move up the proverbial promotional ladder. This caused resentment from the American side of the company because they felt that the Europeans were really slacking and not working hard. The Scandinavians perceived they were working smarter and more efficiently to achieve their daily goals, where the Americans were more apt to waste time and company resources.

Carl complained that the American standard operating procedures were too strict and that he felt confined when Nan started inflicting them on his European team. Part of their culture is to have a long working lunch over a few beers while sitting outside a café. This just seemed inappropriate to Nan, so she suggested that the European side cut out the alcohol and socializing in the middle of the working day and often scheduled conferences at the lunch hour. This bothered the whole European group but they did not express it directly to her. They instead built a complaint alliance where they sneered about the "American" rules to make each other feel better. This drove a large wedge between the European and American team, without the Americans even knowing about it.

For the whole virtual development team, there were serious concerns about the stress factor to get the prototype to production level readiness by July 1. As the deadline approached, they felt a general lack of social support. Nan justified this to herself because it happens in all "virtual teams" but she did not quite know how to help. She thought that Bob had built a solid group of very talented people that would work well together. But they were lacking crucial team elements that help defray stress, namely humor and social activities. Because they are all in different countries, it is difficult for them to just "get together" to blow off steam. They sent a few humorous e-mails back and forth, but because of language barriers and wording differences, the interpretations were just not the same. Georg complained that Ingrid would be blunt and less than helpful over the phone and her e-mails were interpreted as being curt. This just added to his stress.

As the stress increased at the Swedish manufacturing plant, Ingrid cut off others by not e-mailing and returning phone calls only when she knew that her other team members would not be in the office. She was so bogged down in her own problems with external issues and plant difficulties that she began to ignore everyone else. Nan knew that this behavior is very typical of stressed team members but Ingrid ignoring everything that was not in her direct line of sight was unacceptable. The final straw was when Ingrid refused to speak English. She claimed she needed to think and it was just too difficult to have to explain her thinking in English. She brought in an interpreter, but Carl was having difficulty being understanding of the communication filter. Carl's native tongue is Danish but he communicates in perfect business English, French, and German. Ingrid was not so lucky—she natively communicated in Swedish only. Her English was not a high priority in her own family, and even though the Swedish schools made her take five years of it, she still struggled. Ingrid was the key team member to pull the whole project together for the deadline and the whole team was growing more concerned that the prototype would not be ready. Despite Nan's anticipation of some of the above issues they seemed to blindside her. She was always a hands-on manager and meant to travel more for the critical face-to-face interaction she knew was important but the timing never seemed right.

Table 1   Team Issues

	Differences between Domestic and International Teams	Combined Needs for Successful Multinational Teams
Managerial Attributes		
Managerial Style		
Communications		
Tools—Technology		
Cross Cultural Issues		
Team Composition and Establishment		
Budget		
Managing Conflict		

The final crises was that what appeared at first to be a minor flaw in the design threatened to necessitate major changes unless the flaw could be worked out in the prototyping phase. Everyone had his or her own idea of how to fix it. Everyone wanted a quick and simple solution that would avoid major changes in the design. Everyone knew the costs of a major change this far into the life of a development effort would be substantial. Yet, they also know that the cost of design changes grows exponentially over the life of the project, fix it now or risk even more later.

Current Situation

With three weeks until the prototype is due in Nan's office, the team is still having difficulties. Nan is now faced with trying to get the group to solidify again and push toward the finish line. She walked into Bob's office, plopped down into his leather chair, and exhaled.

Nan: "Bob, I need your help."

Bob: "What do you think went wrong?"

Nan: "I don't know, I thought I had control over the situation but so much happened that they did not tell me about. Could we consider pushing the prototype date back two weeks?"

Bob: "Definitely not! With the Christmas season sales to start in October, we must have the prototype in full production by the end of August. We just do not have the time to delay! They are just going to have to work together to reach their goal."

Nan: "Bob, you do realize that you may be acting a little unreasonable? The team has worked hard but they just need a little help to get back on the right path. Some input from you, some recognition of their hard work could go a long way."

Bob: "Nan, I really want you to handle this. . . ."

Nan walked back to her office and sat down to contemplate her next move. She grabbed a legal pad and quickly sketched out a team issues table (see Table 1) to help her make some sense of the situation. What should she do? Nan thought that with their sound beginning, the face-to-face team bonding, and the lines of communication she tried to maintain, that these issues would not come up. What should she do now?

CASE DISCUSSION QUESTIONS

1. What is your perception of a virtual team? List some key characteristics. Now, give a general description of Haute Innovations' team. How does the Haute Innovations' team fit into your description of a v-team in general?

2. What do v-teams have going for them? What are the strengths of the international virtual team in this scenario and in general?

3. What problems are they having? (Stick to those you recognize in the case scenario.) Suggest solutions.

4. Complete Table 1: Team Issues to assist Nan. How should team members use their time together and time apart to maximize their chances for success?

5. What types of communications tools would a v-team utilize? Which of these tools facilitate the product design task of the team? Revisit the communications issues that this team is experiencing as identified in Table 1. How does the team/task benefit from communicating and working as an international v-team? What could the team manager do to help with the communication problems and facilitate the task?

6. List some barriers to successful virtual teaming. What barriers do you see with this team? How could the team overcome these barriers?

CASE CREDIT

Nan Muir Bodensteiner, University of Houston-Clear Lake. Reprinted with permission from the author and the Southwest Case Research Association.

International Strategic Alliances: Design and Management

9

Learning Objectives

After reading this chapter you should be able to:

- Know the steps for implementation of successful international strategic alliances.

- Understand how multinational companies link value chains in international strategic alliances.

- Understand the importance of choosing the right partners for alliances.

- Know the important characteristics to look for in potential alliance partners.

- Know the differences between equity-based international joint ventures and other types of international cooperative alliances.

- Know the basic components of an international strategic alliance contract.

- Understand the control systems and management structures used in alliance organizations.

- Appreciate the unique problems in human resource management faced by managers in alliance organizations.

- Realize the importance of interfirm commitment and trust for building successful international strategic alliances.

- Understand how multinational companies assess the performance of their international strategic alliances.

- Know when companies should continue or dissolve their international strategic alliances.

Preview CASE IN POINT

Strategic Alliances in Emerging Markets

Emerging markets such as India, China, Russia, Brazil, and South Africa continue to enjoy good health largely due to maturing economic policies. Many of the emerging markets have taken steps to control potentially damaging economic factors such as inflation while maintaining strict monetary and fiscal policies. These emerging markets present tremendous potential for multinational companies as they consider taking advantage of significant cost benefits and the rising middle class in these countries. Consider that, in the next decade, more than 800 million people in China, India, Russia, and Brazil will qualify as middle class with more than $1 trillion to spend on products.

Many multinational companies also find that if they want to take advantage of such markets, they need to form strategic alliances with local companies. For example, McDonald's recently signed a significant deal with the Chinese company Sinopec. Sinopec currently runs almost 30,000 gas stations and is growing by about 500 stations annually. McDonald's is hoping to create thousands of drive-through restaurants at many of Sinopec's locations. It anticipates that the alliance will give it a powerful means to attract younger and more affluent Chinese who are more likely to drive. Another company, Saks Fifth Avenue, is also considering entering Shanghai as a means to test the Chinese markets.

India also presents significant strategic alliance opportunities. For instance, many Indian manufacturers are becoming a significant force in the global pharmaceutical supply chain. The future will likely see growing alliances in that industry.

Sources: Based on Business Wire. 2006. "Saks Incorporated Announces Saks Fifth Avenue's Planned Expansion into China; Saks Fifth Avenue to Open on the Historic Bund in Shanghai in Venture with Roosevelt China Investments." April 18. pp. 1–4; Litterick, David. 2006. "Fast food McDonald's takes meals on wheels to China." The Daily Telegraph, June 21, p. 1; Van Arnum, Patricia. 2006. "Asian producers raise their profiles in the global pharmaceutical value chain." Pharmaceutical Technology, May, 30, 5: pp. 70–76.

As the Preview Case in Point shows, emerging markets will likely continue to enjoy good economic health and provide tremendous potential for multinational companies. As such, because strategic alliances are fast and flexible ways to gain complementary resources, they are increasingly among the most popular strategies that companies use to develop new products and to expand into these new geographic areas or markets. In fact, a recent worldwide study by Accenture (formerly Anderson Consulting) found that major multinational companies expect alliances to account for up to 40 percent of company value in the next five years.[1] However, the same study found that only 30 percent of the alliances were considered outright successes by top management.

Why do alliances fail to meet expectations? The most common reason is a poorly designed or managed alliance organization—not a poor strategic choice of entering the alliance. Increasingly, strategic alliances involve companies from two or more nations. Foreign partners often have the most attractive resources or skills that make them the strategic alliance partners of choice. However, partnering with a company from a different nation further compounds the management difficulties. As such, the student of multinational management needs an understanding of international strategic-alliance operations and management.

In Chapter 6, you saw the importance of the strategic alliance as an international participation strategy. This chapter shows how international strategic alliances can succeed and reviews the latest in alliance-management techniques. Issues discussed include: where to link in the partnering companies' value chain, selecting a partner for a strategic alliance, the options available for designing alliances, HRM issues in managing successful strategic alliances, the importance of building trust and commitment, and how to assess the performance of strategic alliances.

Although strategic alliances are attractive for a variety of reasons (see Chapter 6), they are inherently unstable and provide significant management challenges. Estimates of failure rates range from 30 to 60 percent. Partners may fail to deliver, partners may disagree on how to run the business, and even profitable alliances can be torn by conflict. Successful alliances must make strategic sense, but they also require good implementation. In this chapter, you will see the steps necessary to implement a successful strategic alliance. A model of these steps is presented in Exhibit 9.1. We will follow the model in our discussion.

Where to Link in The Value Chain

Chapter 6 showed you the many benefits of strategic alliances. These benefits include gaining access to a local partner's knowledge of the market, meeting government requirements, sharing risks, sharing technology, gaining economies of scale, and accessing lower-cost raw materials or labor. The objectives a firm hopes to achieve determine where multinational companies link in the value chain.

Consider Exhibit 9.2. It shows two value chains and the common areas that companies link to gain strategic benefits from an alliance.

Alliances that combine the same value-chain activities often do so to gain efficient scales of operations, to merge compatible talents, or to share risks. These alliances are attractive when no one company is big enough, has the necessary talent, or is willing to take on an enormously risky venture. In R&D

EXHIBIT 9.1   **Implementing A Strategic-Alliance Strategy**

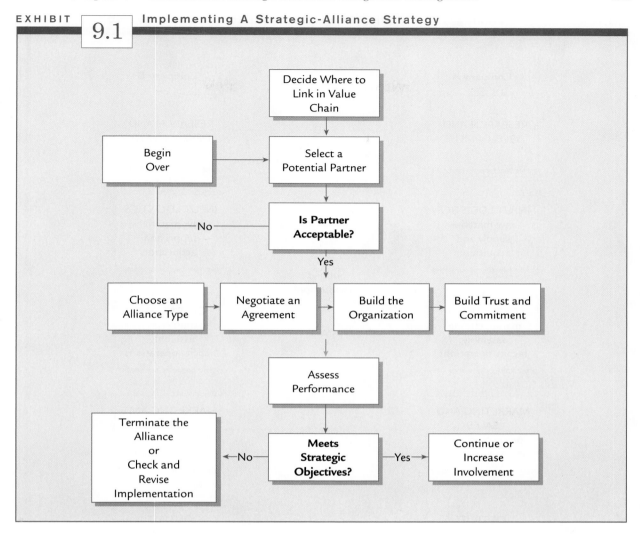

alliances, for example, high-tech multinational companies often use joint research and development to merge different technical skills or to share the risks of developing new or costly technologies. The alliance of IBM, Toshiba, and Siemens illustrates these points. These companies bring together engineering talent from three nations with the hope of discovering the next generation of computer chips. Why not do it alone? R&D in computer chips is a highly risky and expensive venture, which no one company wants to attempt by itself. Just the design of the chip and the fabrication processes costs in the billions. The Case in Point on page 423 describes how the British defense industry used strategic alliances to face new market realities by combining the R&D aspect of the value chain.

In operations alliances, multinational companies often combine manufacturing or assembly activities to reach a profitable volume of activity. For example, General Motors Corp. and Renault SA of France have an alliance to develop and market pickup trucks and vans targeted at the light commercial truck market.[2] These companies intend to work together to produce light commercial trucks for the European market. Leadership skills and a focus on results and values have made this alliance between GM and Renault a success.[3]

EXHIBIT   9.2   Linking Value Chains in Strategic Alliances: Some Examples

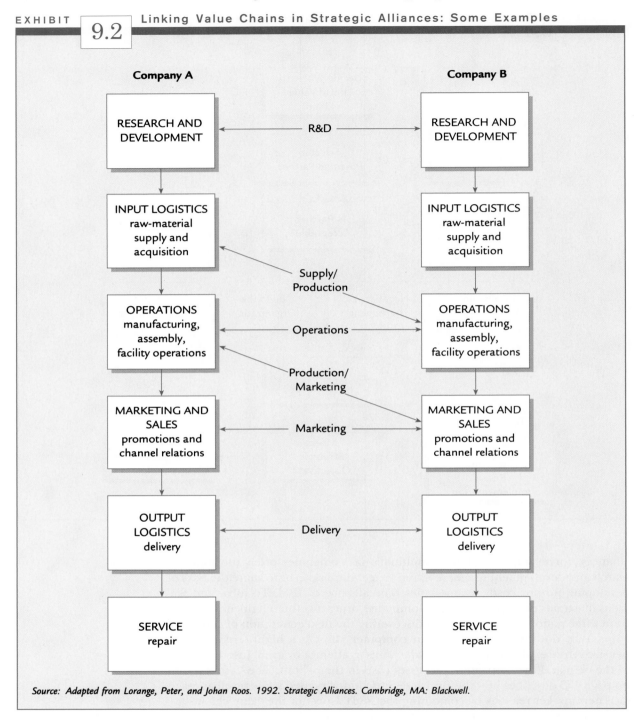

Company A   **Company B**

RESEARCH AND DEVELOPMENT ← R&D → RESEARCH AND DEVELOPMENT

INPUT LOGISTICS raw-material supply and acquisition

Supply/ Production

INPUT LOGISTICS raw-material supply and acquisition

OPERATIONS manufacturing, assembly, facility operations ← Operations → OPERATIONS manufacturing, assembly, facility operations

Production/ Marketing

MARKETING AND SALES promotions and channel relations ← Marketing → MARKETING AND SALES promotions and channel relations

OUTPUT LOGISTICS delivery ← Delivery → OUTPUT LOGISTICS delivery

SERVICE repair   SERVICE repair

Source: Adapted from Lorange, Peter, and Johan Roos. 1992. Strategic Alliances. Cambridge, MA: Blackwell.

Marketing and sales alliances allow multinational companies to increase the scope and number of products sold. They also allow partners to share distribution systems. Sometimes partners even share logos. In the KLM/Northwest Airlines alliance, the companies share advertising that notes their joint

C A S E   I N   P O I N T

British Defense Industry and Strategic Alliances

For most of its existence up to the early 1990s, the British defense industry was a protected industry. While other industries had to deal with the challenges of the common European market, the arms manufacturing sector was excluded from any treaties because of its strategic importance to most countries. As a result, the British defense industry evolved into a culture emphasizing research and development with more scientific or engineering-based personnel at the expense of finance or marketing. The British government was willing to support the best weapons technology regardless of the costs.

Recent changes, however, are placing increased pressure on the industry to become more cost effective. For instance, factors such as reduction of the defense budget, massive increases in costs because of increased use of technology, and liberalization of previously protected domestic markets are forcing British defense firms to find ways to adapt to these new conditions. British defense companies can no longer rely on the existence of guaranteed and lucrative deals.

Recent surveys of a representative sample of British defense executives show that British defense firms have reacted to the new circumstances by engaging in more cross-border alliances, primarily with U.S. firms. U.S. firms tend to invest the most in R&D and, thus, produce the leading-edge defense technology. As such, U.S. defense companies tend to be seen as more attractive because British firms can have access to much needed technology while also working with U.S. firms to develop new technology at lower costs. However, executives also maintain that the United States represents significant market potential.

Source: Based on Butler, Colin J. 2005. "Changes in industry structure and competition: The use of strategic alliances by UK defence manufacturing firms." Strategic Change. January/February, 14, 1, pp. 15–24.

reservation-and-route systems. In the automobile industry, alliance partners often share each other's dealer systems.

Output alliances to deliver a service are perhaps most popular in the airline industry. International alliances such as those between KLM and Northwest, Swissair and Delta Airlines, and British Airways and USAir deliver their services jointly through a process called code sharing (the sharing of reservation codes). In this way, passengers can buy an international ticket in one airline's country, fly to the partner's country, and get continuing flights with the same ticket on the partner's airline.

Alliances linking upstream and downstream components of the value chain can serve the objectives of low-cost supply or manufacturing. Some supply/operations alliances attempt to find partners where one partner provides low-cost sources of supply or components and the other partner does the manufacturing. Operations/marketing links can work similarly. One company provides a source of low-cost manufacturing for another company's eventual sales. For example, because of increasing wages in their own countries, many Japanese and Korean companies formed production/marketing alliances with low-wage Southeast Asian companies. Production and assembly occur at the low-cost site, and the Japanese and Korean companies do the downstream marketing and sales.

Operations/marketing alliances can also provide access to markets. This use of the operations/marketing alliance tends to occur when the producing firm needs a local partner with knowledge of local sales and distribution systems. This type of alliance can be necessary when local governments require local participation in foreign businesses. It is often an initial participation strategy for a company with limited knowledge of a foreign market.

For U.S. companies, the majority of international strategic alliances occur in operations. Exhibit 9.3 shows the mixture of value-chain links for the nearly 800 publicly announced international strategic alliances created by U.S. multinational companies during a four-year period.[4]

The links discussed so far and illustrated in Exhibits 9.2 and 9.3 are only some of those possible for international strategic alliances. In building alliances, each company must determine which of its value-chain activities can be enhanced by the relationships. After deciding which value-chain link or links are necessary to achieve its strategic objectives, management faces what is generally considered the most important step in implementing a strategic alliance—selecting the right partner.

Choosing a Partner: The Most Important Choice?

Most experts attribute success or failure of strategic alliances to how well the partners get along. Especially early in the relationship, the parties must believe

EXHIBIT **9.3**   Value-Chain Links in U.S. International Strategic Alliances

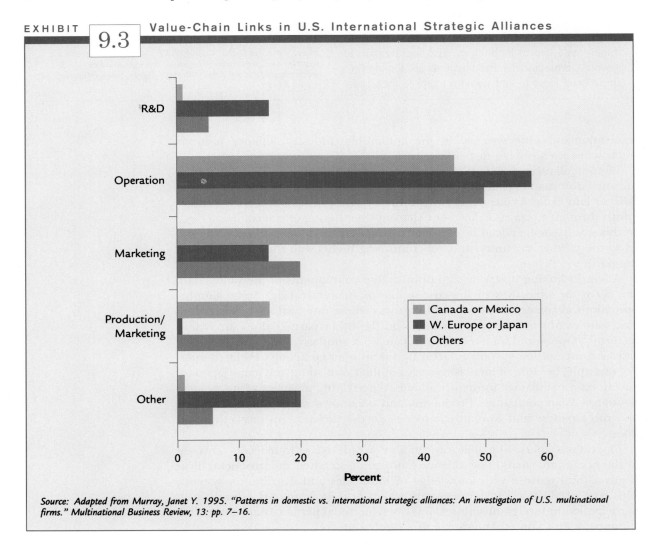

Legend:
- Canada or Mexico
- W. Europe or Japan
- Others

Source: Adapted from Murray, Janet Y. 1995. "Patterns in domestic vs. international strategic alliances: An investigation of U.S. multinational firms." Multinational Business Review, 13: pp. 7–16.

that they have a good partner who can deliver promised contributions and whom they can trust. The following Case in Point shows some of the difficulties that can occur when a company makes mistakes in partner selection.

Experts identify several key criteria for picking an appropriate alliance partner:[5]

* *Seek strategic complementarity.* Before forming the strategic alliance, potential partners must have a good understanding of each other's strategic objectives for the venture. Each should know what the other hopes to achieve from the venture, both in the short term and in the long term. It is not necessary, however, that partners have the same objectives. While similar strategic objectives, such as rapid growth, are beneficial, objectives can be complementary. For example, a U.S. or Japanese firm may have an advanced computer component-manufacturing technology attractive to a Chinese firm. The Chinese firm may dominate the Chinese market and could provide a potential powerful sales and distribution outlet for the alliance partner. These companies have complementary strategic objectives. The U.S. or the Japanese company desires growth in its Chinese market share, and the Chinese company desires access to the other side's advanced manufacturing technology.

* *Pick a partner with* **complementary skills.** Partners must contribute more than money to the venture. Each partner must contribute some skills or resources that complement those of the other partner. J. Michael Geringer asserts that technical complementarity is most important.[6] A typical complementary alliance, for example, occurs when one company (usually the foreign country) contributes technical skills and another company (usually a local company from the host country) contributes marketing skills. Another recommendation is to find partners with similar but not identical products or markets. This avoids the increased difficulties of working with direct competitors.[7]

Strategic complementarity
The alliance partners' strategies are complementary.

Complementary skills
One that enhances but does not necessarily duplicate an alliance partner's skills.

CASE IN POINT

Picking the Wrong Partner

When the U.S. steelmaker, Carpenter Technology from Reading, Pennsylvania, invested $45 million for a 19 percent stake in a joint venture with Walsin Lihwa Corp. of Taipei, Taiwan, it hoped for a profitable venture. Unfortunately, the local partner could not deliver. Plans to build a high-tech stainless steel and carbon bar plant met resistance from the Taiwanese government. Local farmers protested the location, delayed the installation of electric power, and the plant opened two years late. In the meantime, a competitor added similar products, so Carpenter's profits didn't materialize. In three years, Carpenter dropped its interest to 5 percent. Two years later, the company abandoned the venture. Robert Cardy, chairman and CEO of CarTech, noted. "That one didn't work out the way it had been planned...there was more of a speculative interest by the Taiwanese than we found comfortable sometimes."

The alliance between Telia and Telenor, Sweden's and Norway's largest telecom companies, also made sense on paper. In 1999, the companies merged, creating one of the largest mergers in Nordic history. However, the alliance soon started going wrong as allegations of cheating and other issues emerged. An analysis of the breakdown revealed that, although the alliance looked perfect in theory, both companies may not have spent enough time picking a partner. Issues such as lack of trust and cultural differences (although these national cultures are supposed to be similar) showed that not enough time was devoted to analyze the subtleties of the partners.

Source: Based on Bagsarian, Tom. 2000. "The lessons learned from overseas partnerships." Iron Age New Steel 16, pp. 34–37; Strategic Direction. 2006. "Create successful international mergers and alliances." 22, 1: pp. 25–28.

- *Seek out companies with compatible management styles.* Lord Weinstock, the managing director for 27 years of Britain's General Electric Company (not related to the U.S. company GE), is a strategic alliance expert. He has seen many alliances succeed and fail. One recent failure, an alliance of GEC with Germany's Siemens, flopped. Consultants noted that Siemens is an engineers' company, consistent with many values in German business culture, and GEC is a financiers' company. The managers simply didn't get along. Weinstock noted that for alliances to succeed, "You have to suppress the ego—it's absolute poison in a joint venture."[8]

- *Seek a partner that will provide the "right" level of mutual dependency.* As in any marriage, mutual dependency means that companies must rely on each partner to contribute to the relationship. With a good match, partners feel a mutual need to supply their unique resources or capabilities to the strategic alliance. Both partners see their contribution as critical to the success of the relationship and, ultimately, to the success of the strategic alliance. The best level of mutual dependency is balanced. With balanced dependency, both companies feel equally dependent on the outcome of the venture. Geringer[9] suggests maintaining this mutual dependency by building safeguards into the strategic-alliance agreement. These might include types of "alimony" payments and restrictions on entering the same business over a specified period. The "alimony" payments would require payments to the partner if the relationship should break up before a specified period.

Anchor partners

A partner that holds back the development of a successful strategic alliance because it cannot or will not provide its share of the funding.

- *Avoid the "anchor" partner.* **Anchor partners** hold back the development of a successful strategic alliance because they cannot or will not provide their share of the funding. Potential partners should study carefully each other's financial position and investment plans. A potential partner with a weak division or expansion in other areas may drain financial support from the alliance. If a potential partner is financially weak but still attractive for other reasons, precautions are advised. For example, a contract might specify that the division of the alliance's profits (or other alliance outputs) among the partners will vary in proportion to each partner's financial contribution to the venture.

Elephant-and-ant complex

Occurs in strategic alliances when two companies are greatly unequal in size.

- *Be cautious of the "elephant-and-ant" complex.* The **elephant-and-ant complex** occurs when two companies are greatly unequal in size. For an international strategic alliance between companies of unequal size, managers must consider serious potential problems. First, the larger firm may dominate the smaller firm, controlling the strategies and management of the alliance. Second, the corporate cultures probably differ to a significant extent. For example, bureaucracy and slower decision making usually characterize larger and older companies. Smaller companies are often more entrepreneurial and informal. Thus, because of cultural differences, a small firm's executives may see the larger firm's managers as ignoring the immediate problems of the venture. The larger partner's executives may see the smaller partner's managers as less professional. In spite of these potential problems, however, elephant-and-ant alliances do succeed. When other factors, such as complementary skills, exist, managers find ways to overcome size differences. Analysis of the strategic alliance between Telia and Telenor, discussed earlier in the Case in Point also shows that the "elephant-and-ant" complex may have played a role in the alliance's failure.[10] A close look at the alliance shows that Norwegian nationalistic feelings emerged when the country's largest telecom company, Telenor, was being treated poorly by Sweden's Telia. In such cases, the "elephant-and-ant" complex was reflected in the perception that a big-country company (Sweden, the elephant) was bullying a small-country company (Norway, the ant). Exhibit 9.4 contrasts in more detail some of the incentives and concerns for small businesses in "elephant-and-ant" international strategic alliances.

- *Assess operating-policy differences with potential partners.* Marriage partners need to work out how to squeeze the toothpaste, when to have dinner, who makes the beds, who cleans the house, and all the other operational details of running a household. Similarly, potential partners in a strategic alliance most likely have operational differences in how their companies are run on a day-to-day basis. Accounting policies, human resource management policies, financial policies, reporting policies, and so on, may all differ because of organizational or cultural differences. For example, potential European partners may want to close operations during certain holiday periods. Potential Japanese partners may want the strategic alliance to respect the age hierarchy of management. For the strategic alliance to function smoothly, and before the strategic alliance comes into operation, partners should agree on mutually satisfactory operational policies.

- *Assess the difficulty of cross-cultural communication with a likely partner.* Even if partners speak each other's languages, cross-cultural communication is never as easy as within one's own culture or organization. Managers must expect slower communication and more errors of understanding. For example, in a joint venture between a Japanese company and the U.S. aircraft manufacturer Boeing, the agreement required that fuselage panels be produced with a "mirror finish." The Japanese workers interpreted this literally. They polished the metal to a mirror finish. The result was excessively high labor costs and the need for further discussion to resolve the meaning of "mirror finish."[11]

The following Multinational Management Brief discusses some of the key questions to ask when picking a partner.

After finding potentially satisfactory partners, multinational mangers from all companies involved in the alliance must decide on the form of the alliance that they wish to build. Next, we consider the popular choices in types of international strategic alliances.

EXHIBIT 9.4

International Strategic Alliances for Small Multinational Companies: Incentives and Concerns

Incentives	Concerns
➤ Gain Legitimacy Act as a seal of approval	➤ Relative level of contribution Must commit relatively more assets than larger firm
➤ Develop Links in Distribution Channel Use large firm's existing channels	➤ Entering a large scale of operations Lack of experience with large-scale operations
➤ Access to Resources Help speed access to market	➤ Risk of unequal proprietary information disclosure Access to smaller firm's information easier
➤ Diversify Risk Share risk with richer partner	➤ Mismatch of interacting managers Small firm entrepreneur with large firm functional or product specialists
	➤ Loss of control Concerns of large firm dominate relationship

Source: Adapted from Peridis, Theodoros. 1992. "Strategic alliances for smaller firms." Research in global Strategic Management. 3: pp. 129–142.

Multinational Management **Brief**

Picking an Alliance Partner

Picking an alliance partner can be a very difficult task. However, Jagersma, in extensive interviews with 106 chief executives and top managers from 89 global companies, suggests that multinational companies need to ask a number of questions about the potential partner. These questions are seen as "make-or-break questions." The interview participants advised companies to avoid the cross-border alliance if the potential partner answers "no" to any of the questions:

- *Can the partner deliver as required to make the alliance successful?*
- *Can both partners agree on clear goals and objectives for the strategic alliance?*
- *Have there been attempts to minimize potential for competition and friction with the partner? Does the potential partner have any alliances with your competitors?*
- *Does the potential partner share with you a vision about how the cross-border strategic alliance might evolve?*
- *Is the partner willing and able to contribute the necessary skills and resources to ensure that the alliance is successful?*
- *Does the partner have a history of success with previous strategic alliances?*
- *Have you compared the potential partner with other partners in terms of value creation?*
- *Does the cross-border alliance fit with your vision of your alliance network in the future?*

Source: Based on Jagersma, Peter Klaas. 2005. "Cross-border alliances: Advice from the executive suite." The Journal of Business Strategy, 26, 1: pp. 41–50.

Informal international cooperative alliances

A non-legally binding agreement between companies to cooperate on any value-chain activity.

Formal international cooperative alliances

A nonequity alliance with formal contracts specifying what each company must contribute to the relationship.

International joint ventures

A separate legal entity in which two or more companies from different nations have ownership positions.

IJV

International joint venture.

ICA

International cooperative alliance.

Choosing An Alliance Type

There are three main types of strategic alliances:[12] **informal international cooperative alliances, formal international cooperative alliances, and international joint ventures.** International joint ventures are usually called **IJVs** and international cooperative alliances are usually called **ICAs.** Exhibit 9.5 outlines the major differences among the types. We consider each of these next.

Informal and Formal International Cooperative Alliances

Informal ICAs are agreements between companies from two or more countries that are not legally binding. They can be agreements of any kind and can provide links between companies anywhere on their value chains. For example, a local company might agree informally to market and sell a foreign firm's products in exchange for exclusive distribution rights. Although neither firm would be legally bound to continue this relationship, the companies might use this informal agreement as a test of their ability to work together in agreements that are more formal. If it does not work, the alliance can end at any time.

Since there is no legal protection from a contract, managers usually limit the scope of their involvement with the other company. This means that there is usually a reluctance to dedicate sizable resources to the relationship, such as product changes for the partner's benefit. In addition, multinational companies in informal alliances resist revealing a company's proprietary information to the partner. Proprietary information refers to information that a company considers its own and wants to keep secret from competitors. An example might be special manufacturing processes.

EXHIBIT **9.5**   **Types and Characteristics of International Strategic Alliances**

Alliance Type	Degree of Involvement	Ease of Dissolution	Visibility to Competitors	Contract Required	Legal Entity
Informal International Cooperative Alliance	Usually limited in scope and time; a marriage of convenience	Easy, at the convenience of either side	Often unknown to competitors	No	None
Formal International Cooperative Alliance	Deeper involvement requiring exchange of proprietary company knowledge and resources	More difficult to dissolve before end of contract because of legal obligations and commitment of resources by companies	Often visible to competitors through announcements in business press but details can be secure	Yes	None
International Joint Venture	Deep involvement requiring exchange of financial, proprietary company knowledge, and managerial resources	Most difficult to dissolve because companies invest significant resources and have ownership in a separate legal entity	High visibility because joint venture company is a separate legal entity	Yes	Yes, separate company

A higher degree of involvement between or among companies occurs with the formal ICA. This type of alliance usually requires a formal contract specifying exactly what each company must contribute to the relationship. Contributions to the relationship could be managers, technical specialists, factories, information or knowledge, or money. To make some strategic gain that a single company cannot do by itself, companies must usually share some knowledge, skill, or specialized resources through a formalized ICA. This sharing of proprietary information or knowledge raises the level of involvement between the companies. It means that both companies must give away something valuable to the partner to get something in return. In addition, in combination with the obligations specified in a contract, this sharing of proprietary knowledge makes backing out of a formal alliance more difficult than for alliances with informal agreements.

Formal ICAs are very popular in some high-tech industries because of the high costs and risks of R&D. This is particularly true in the semiconductor industry. The following Multinational Management Brief shows some of the reasons why.

The next level of alliance involvement is the international joint venture.

International Joint Ventures

An international joint venture (IJV) is a separate legal entity owned by parent companies from different countries—companies have an equity or ownership position in an independent company. The simplest IJV occurs when two parent companies have 50/50 ownership of the venture. International joint ventures are becoming increasingly popular as a means for global companies to join forces by sharing resources.[13]

Not all joint ventures have only two partners although two-partner joint ventures are probably the most common. When a large number of companies form a joint venture, the resulting IJV is often called a consortium. Airbus Industries, for example, is a consortium that includes Aérospatiale from France, Messerschmitt Böklow Blöhm from Germany, British Aerospace, and Construcciones Aeronáuticas from Spain.

Multinational Management **Brief**

Semiconductor Alliances

The semiconductor industry produces the "chips" that drive computers and provide memory for storage. It is a fast-moving industry in which companies must innovate continuously. Strategic alliances are very popular because companies can share talent and risk and move products faster from research to the market. Consider these snapshots of some of the international strategic alliances planned or in place:

- *Samsung Electronics Co.:* Looking for partners for $1 billion chip-manufacturing plants in Europe, Asia, and the United States. Signed a chip-purchasing agreement with NEC Corp. of Japan.
- *IBM, Toshiba, and Siemens:* Signed an eight-year, $1 billion agreement to produce the next generation of chips for the 21st century. Two hundred engineers from the three countries report to a Toshiba manager located at IBM's Advanced Semiconductor Technology Center located in New York. An informal side of the agreement allows Toshiba to share with another company (Motorola) technology developed with its IBM and Siemens partners.
- *Texas Instruments:* Teamed with Hitachi, Sharp, Canon, and Motorola to develop memory-chip technology.
- *Fujitsu:* Allied with Advanced Micro Devices Inc. for research and production of EPROMs (electronically programmable read-only memories) and flash chips. They split the cost of a $700 million plant and bought 5 percent of each other's stock as insurance for the deal. AMD also has a relationship with Sony for microprocessors.
- *Beijing Stone Group Company:* Created the company Mitsubishi-Stone Semiconductor Co with Mitsubishi Electric Corp. This $2 billion investment will produce state-of-the-art SRAM chips in two new fabs in the special economic development zone of Shezhen.
- *STMicroelectronics:* Swiss-based STMicroelectronics formed an R&D alliance with two of its competitors, Freescale and Philips, to produce semiconductors. By combining revenues, the alliance has one of the highest R&D spending powers in the industry.

Source: Based on Glain, Steve. 1995. "Samsung mounts big push to diversify." Wall Street Journal, February 10, p. A6; Katz, Jonathan. 2006. "Friendly competition." Industry Week, January, 255, 1:p. 15; Lei, David. 1993. "Offensive and defensive uses of alliances." Long Range Planning, 26: pp. 32–34; Port, Otis, Richard Brandt, Neil Gross, and Jonathan B. Levine. 1992. "Talk about your dream team." BusinessWeek Online, June p. 27; Pecht, Michael, Weifeng Liu, and David Hodges. 2000. "Newer fabs in Chin." Semiconductor International 23, pp. 156–160; Singer, Peter. 2005. "Wafer processing." Semiconductor International, December, 28, 13:p. 24.

Companies need not have equal ownership to form a joint venture. Often one partner will have a majority ownership. In some countries, the local law requires that the local partner has the dominant ownership position. In such cases, for example, the foreign company could not own more than 49 percent of the IJV's stock in a two-company venture. Companies may also increase or decrease their ownership share. Prior agreements may require a foreign company to surrender its ownership after a limited time. The first McDonald's in Russia, for example, was a joint venture designed to revert eventually to sole Russian ownership. Some parent companies also increase or decrease ownership depending on the IJV's performance or the parent company's strategic goals. One company may buy out its partner and take over the joint venture as a wholly owned subsidiary.

One difficulty in determining the initial ownership of a joint venture arises from equity contributions other than cash. It is not necessary for companies to contribute equal monetary shares to a venture to have equal equity positions. Partners may bring resources to the venture other than financial resources. If the partners accept that the resources contributed have an economic value, then these resources become part of a firm's equity contribution to the venture. For example, one parent company in a 50/50 joint venture may contribute only its advanced technology, whereas the other partner may provide all of the financial contribution.

The choice of an international alliance type is similar to the choice of a participation strategy discussed in Chapter 6. The alliance types range from those that are flexible and informal and require minimal investment to those that are legally binding, require heavy investment, and are difficult to dissolve. The choice of form depends on the strategic intent of the firm, the nature of the firm's products and industry, the resources of the firm, and the requirements of the country of location.

Formal ICAs and IJVs require formal agreements. Next you will see some of the issues considered by multinational managers in negotiating alliance agreements.

Negotiating The Agreement

After picking a partner or partners for an IJV or a formal ICA, it is necessary to negotiate and sign contractual agreements. Similar to licensing agreements, alliance contracts are the legal documents that bind partners together. The formal agreements, however, are never as important as the ability of managers to get along. Exhibit 9.6 shows some of the questions that must be addressed as IJV negotiation issues.

Negotiations for alliance agreements have no consistent timetable or form. Some companies sign agreements almost immediately after they receive a proposal. Other agreements can take years for companies to complete. For example, the joint venture partnerships that eventually resulted in the first McDonald's in Russia took nearly ten years of negotiations. In some situations, even when both parents sign a partnership agreement, the alliance venture never gets off the ground. One or both parents fail to deliver, and the venture dissolves.

In general, experts recommend that negotiation teams with technical and negotiation experience negotiate any alliance agreement. The types of preparation for this cross-cultural negotiation would follow the steps discussed later in Chapter 13 on international negotiations.

Once a firm has a partner and an agreement, it is necessary to build the organization to run the alliance. This includes organizational design and human resource management issues. First, we consider structure and design.

> **IJV negotiation issues**
>
> Include points such as equity contributions, management structure, and "Prenuptial" agreements regarding dissolution of the relationship.

Building The Organization: Organizational Design In Strategic Alliances

The design of strategic alliances depends on the type of alliance chosen. Informal ICAs often have no formal design issues. Managers from different companies cooperate without any formal control. Formal ICAs may require a separate organization unit housed in one of the companies, with employees

EXHIBIT 9.6   **Selected Questions for a Strategic-Alliance Agreement**

For Both ICAs and IJVs

- What products or services does the alliance produce?
- Where is the new alliance located?
- Under which country's law does the agreement operate?
- What are the basic responsibilities of each partner? These might include issues such as which company provides the production technology, the plant location, the training of the workforce, the marketing expertise.
- What are the partners' contributions of senior managers?
- What are the partners' contributions of other employees?
- How will royalties or profits be divided?
- How should the company be controlled?
- How is the company organized?
- Who owns new products or technology developed by the new company?
- To whom and where will the strategic alliance sell its products?
- Is a prenuptial agreement needed?
- How can the alliance be dissolved?

Primarily for IJVs

- What is the name of the new IJV company?
- What are the equity contributions of each partner?
- What is the makeup of the IJV's board of directors?

from all the parents. The IBM/Toshiba/Siemens alliance located in New York is an example of an organizational unit setup for an ICA. However, some formal ICAs may share information or products with minimal organizational requirements. For example, two airlines may book each other's routes but need no common organization. IJVs, however, are separate legal entities. This requires that parent companies set up a separate organization for the IJV to carry out the objectives of the alliance.

In this section, we consider two key issues in managing an alliance organization: decision-making control and the management structure. These design issues are applicable mostly to IJVs but also to formal ICAs that require organizational settings. For example, the IBM/Toshiba/Siemens alliance created an organization headquartered at an IBM location but managed by a Toshiba engineer.

Decision-Making Control

Parent companies must consider two major areas of decision making when designing their alliance organizations: operational decision making and strategic decision making. Operational decisions include management decisions associated with the day-to-day running of the organizations. For example, the size of production runs and the hiring of assembly line workers represent operational decisions. Strategic decisions focus on issues that are important to the long-term survival of the alliance organization. For example, opening a new plant and introducing a new product are strategic decisions.

Majority ownership of an IJV does not necessarily mean that the parent company controls operational and strategic decision making for the IJV. Similarly, providing the location for a formal ICA does not mean that the parent controls operational and strategic decision making for the alliance. Depending on each partner's skills, parent companies may agree to assign different managerial decision-making duties to different partners.

In the IJV, strategic decision making usually takes place at the level of the IJV's board of directors or the top management team. To gain more control over strategic decision making, some IJV parent companies place more of their managers on the IJV company's board of directors or on the IJV's top management team. IJV parent companies that wish to control the operational decision making of the IJV usually have most of their people serving as mid- to lower-level managers.

In nonequity ICAs, strategic decision making usually remains with the parent companies. Alliance managers focus on operational decision making related to delivering the product or knowledge to the parent companies.

Management Structures

The mix of strategic and operational decision-making control among alliance partners is often complex and unique to each relationship. However, to formalize the nature of decision-making control in a strategic alliance, partners must choose a management structure. Management structures specify formally the division of control responsibilities among partners. There are five typical management control structures used by multinational companies for their ICAs or IJVs. These include:[14]

- *Dominant parent:* The **dominant parent** is usually the majority owner of an IJV or, in some cases (especially where majority ownership is not possible), the major contributor of critical resources to an ICA. In this structure, one parent controls or dominates strategic and operational decision making. Its managers hold most of the important positions in any IJV or ICA organization. For IJVs, the dominant parent treats the IJV as if it were just another one of its subsidiaries.

- *Shared management:* In the **shared management structure**, both parents contribute approximately the same number of managers to positions such as the board of directors, the top management team, and the functional areas of management (e.g., production or marketing).

- *Split control:* The **split-control management structure** is similar to the shared management structure in that partners usually share strategic decision making. However, at the functional level (e.g., marketing, production, and research and development), partners make decisions independently. Often one partner has a unique skill or technology that it does not want to share completely. This partner insists on independent decision making in these protected areas.

- *Independent management:* In the **independent management structure**, the alliance managers act more like managers from a separate company. This structure is more characteristic of mature IJVs—IJVs must be legally separate organizations—and seldom occurs in ICAs. Especially for operational decisions, IJV managers have nearly complete decision making autonomy. Because of their independence, IJVs with this structure often recruit managers and other employees from outside the parent companies' organizations.

- *Rotating management:* Key positions in the management hierarchy rotate between or among partners in the rotating management structure. For

Dominant parent

The majority owner or contributor who controls or dominates strategic and operational decision making of the alliance.

Shared management structure

Occurs when both parent companies contribute approximately the same number of managers to the alliance organization.

Split-control management structure

Partners usually share strategic decision making but split functional-level decision making.

Independent management structure

Alliance managers act more like managers from a separate company.

example, the alliance's top manager or management team may change each year. Each partner then appoints its own managers on a rotating basis. The rotating management structure is popular with alliance partners from developing countries. It serves to train local management and technical talent and transfer this expertise to the developing country.[15]

Choosing a Strategic Alliance Management Structure

Many characteristics of the alliance relationship influence the choice of a management structure. Usually, if one parent has a dominant equity position or contributes the most important resources to the alliance, this dominant parent will favor a dominant management structure, at least for strategic decision making. Alliance partners with equal ownership shares (for IJVs) or equal resource contributions (for ICAs) tend to avoid the dominant management structure. Instead, they adopt one of the more balanced managerial control systems, such as the shared, split, or rotating structures.

Management structures can change as companies' needs change or their contributions to the alliance change. When an Italian motorcycle helmet manufacturer found that inexperienced Belarussian managers had difficulty running the operation, it faced a serious challenge to the viability of the IJV. The Multinational Management Challenge on page 435 shows how the company solved the problems. How would you react?

Additional considerations in the choice of a management structure relate to the strategic and organizational characteristics of the parent companies and the nature of their industry. That is, parent company and industry characteristics make different management structures more effective or more attractive to the companies involved.[16] A recent summary of alliance research summarized several of the factors that multinational managers take into account when designing a management structure for their international strategic alliances. These include:[17]

- If partners have *similar* technologies or know-how and they contribute this knowledge *equally* to the alliance, partners prefer a shared management structure.
- If partners have *different* technologies or know-how and they contribute this knowledge *equally* to the alliance, partners prefer split management structures.
- If the alliance has more strategic importance to one partner, a dominant management structure is more likely.

For joint ventures in particular:

- Mature joint ventures move to independent structures as the joint venture's management team gains more expertise.
- Joint ventures in countries with a high degree of government intervention produce IJVs with local partner dominance.
- Independent management structures are more likely when the market is expanding, the venture does not require much capital, or the venture does not require much R&D input from its parents.

All organizations need more than the formal control and coordination systems set up by management. An equally important key for building successful alliances is finding the right people to staff the alliance organization. As such, we now consider the human resource management (HRM) issues in alliance management.

Multinational Management **Challenge**

Finding the Right Management Structure

AGV is a small but highly successful Italian manufacturer of motorcycle helmets. Although AGV has only 190 employees, it is the second leading producer of helmets in the world. AGV exports to more than 30 countries and has nearly 2,000 sales outlets in different countries.

Seeking a presence in the former Soviet republics and a cheaper source of raw materials, AGV formed a joint venture with Steklovolokno, a fiberglass producer located in Belarus. AGV took a 40 percent ownership share in the joint venture company called Agv Polspo.

Management control problems surfaced quickly. As the minority owner, AGV was forced to use local managers from the Belarus partner. The Italian side discovered that these managers, trained and developed in a formerly state-run organization, had no concept of marketing and no concept of meeting time goals in production. To solve the problem, AGV first attempted retraining. It brought 30 managers to Italy for training in the AGV management methods. However, the Belarussian managers proved reluctant to change their old practices, and this program was eventually abandoned.

To gain dominant management control of the venture, AGV bought an additional 20 percent of Agv Polspo. It then installed an Italian CEO and Italian managers in sales and production. Because of the cost and difficulty of hiring and maintaining expatriate managers in Belarus, AGV saw this as only an intermediate step. It recruited and trained mostly younger Belarussian managers who eventually filled the positions held by Italian expatriate managers. Agv Polspo is now a successful company exporting its helmets to 17 countries.

Sources: Based on United Nations Economic Commission for Europe & ILO. 1993. "The management challenge in Belarus: The case of AGV-Polotsk." In Management Development in East-West Joint Ventures, pp. 33–36, New York: United Nations; Agv Polspo. 2003. http://www.agvpolspo.narod.ru/

Building the Organization: Human Resource Management In Strategic Alliances

The HRM functions of international strategic alliances include recruiting and staffing for all alliance positions and evaluating alliance personnel. These issues are made more complex because managers and other employees come from two or more companies and from two or more national cultures.

Experts identify several critical HRM problems and issues that multinational managers must address in the implementation of international strategic alliances:[18]

- *HRM planning:* Many companies spend considerable time and effort planning the strategic use of strategic alliances. Perhaps just as important to the eventual success of the alliance is the communication of that strategic intent to the employees who will staff the alliance organization; that is, employees at all levels need to understand why the alliance exists and need to be aware of the parent companies' goals for the alliance.

- *Parent involvement:* The degree of parent-company involvement in the alliance's human resource functions depends largely on the age, size, and intended life span of the alliance organization. Newer organizations, especially those with dominant parent or revolving management structures, tend to maintain HRM practices inherited from parent companies. However, for IJVs in particular, due to the need to mesh two or more organizational and national cultures into a legally separate organization, HRM practices soon become different from either parent. In addition, as all alliance organizations get older and larger, they tend to develop their own organizational cultures. This often leads to a need for their own HRM practices.

- *Staffing the alliance management and technical personnel:* Selecting managers or a technical specialist for an assignment in an international strategic alliance is a crucial but risky decision. On one hand, these individuals must have the necessary abilities to contribute the skills required to ensure the success of the alliance. Companies must resist the temptation to unload unwanted personnel on the alliance. On the other hand, parent companies must realize that an IJV or ICA assignment may last a long time. Managers, engineers, or other employees may never return to the parent company. Both of these immediate and long-term staffing needs of the alliance require that parent companies ensure that they have enough management and technical talent to give the alliance the necessary people.

- *Staffing the alliance workforce:* Most ICAs involve the exchange of primarily technical and managerial personnel. However, independent IJV organizations often hire lower-level workers who are not employees of the parent-company owners. In these situations, partners must determine if local workers with the required skills are available at the IJV location. Local labor supply, labor laws, and local cultural values regarding work also determine HRM planning for an IJV. For example, an IJV may require skilled workers that are scarce at the IJV location. In such a case, HRM planning must include the necessary training of the local workforce.

- *Assigning managers strategic or operations tasks:* Depending on the form of managerial control structure and the type of international strategic alliance, parent companies must assign the proper number and types of managers. Crucial to this decision is whether the managers will take primarily strategic or operational roles in the alliance. Managers with strategic-level decision-making responsibility usually have more experience and come from higher levels of management in the parent companies. Operations-level managers, such as a production manager, usually come from lower levels of the parent company's management.

- *Performance assessment:* People who work in alliances need performance assessment for retention, promotion, and salary decisions. However, whenever two or more companies cooperate, it is unlikely that their performance-assessment techniques match exactly. As such, it is usually best to avoid adopting the system of one partner. This may lead to unavoidable cultural biases against employees from partner companies. In the early life of an alliance, performance judgments of employees may follow their parent-company guidelines. Managers or other employees from each parent are evaluated on the bases of their parent companies' performance-evaluation systems. Later, it is common for joint performance review committees to take over performance evaluation from the parent companies as the alliance venture matures.

- *Loyalty:* Managers and other employees in ICAs or IJVs may feel a dual loyalty—to their parent organization and to the alliance organization. The intensity of loyalty tends to vary with the term of the alliance assignment. If employees perceive that they are "on loan" from their home organization, as is more often true with ICAs than with IJVs, they will usually remain loyal to the parent company. If employees believe that their assignments to the alliance organization are long term, they will usually develop a stronger loyalty to the alliance. Multinational managers must realize that loyalty to the alliance organization and the parent company can and should vary depending on the nature of an individual's assignment. Dealing with this fact must be a part of a strategy for human resource management for all alliance organizations.

- *Career development:* To motivate managers or other employees to perform successfully in international strategic alliances, the IJV or ICA assignment must be relevant to a future career and must provide some job security. As with many international assignments, there is often a fear that one will be forgotten while away from the home organization. Companies actively pursuing multinational strategies based on international strategic alliances must provide clear information on how alliance assignments fit into an employee's career path and planning. For assignment to long-term joint ventures or cooperative alliances, the career ladder may exist entirely within the alliance.

- *Cultural differences:* The cultural differences inherent in all forms of international strategic alliances operate at all levels of culture, especially the national, business, and organizational levels. Different culturally based HRM practices can result in conflict over HRM practices. For example, the Japanese concern for age seniority or the U.S. concern for promotions based on individual achievement regardless of age affect many U.S./Japanese alliances because parent companies cannot resolve differences in HRM policies.

- *Training:* Managers, engineers, and other employees who work together in international strategic alliances perform better if they have prior training to develop cross-cultural interaction skills. The amount of required investment in training depends on the degree of cultural differences between national cultures, the length of the assignment, and the international experience of the employees of the alliance. Larger cultural differences, long-term assignments, and employees with limited international experience require more training.

The following Case in Point discusses recent research and the critical role of appropriate HR policies in a strategic alliance.

Exhibit 9.7 summarizes many of the key issues for successful HRM practices in strategic alliances. A strategic alliance is like a marriage. Without mutual trust and commitment, the relationship will fail. We now examine how these issues are handled in strategic alliances.

Commitment and Trust: The Soft Side of Alliance Management

A common theme among managers from both failed and successful strategic alliances is the importance of building mutual trust and commitment among

CASE IN POINT

Role of HR in Strategic Alliance Success

Strategic alliance experts suggest that a number of key factors, such as readiness to learn, willingness to adapt and be open, and strategic congruence, play important roles in the success of a strategic alliance. However, a recent empirical study based on interviews from 30 key informants and a survey of 143 alliance managers in the United Kingdom show that HR was the second most important factor in ensuring strategic alliance success. Why is HR so critical to alliance success? Having the right people in place is critical, and the HR department often determines who will staff the alliance. For instance, one interviewee noted that personnel from both partners often do not want to accept that they can learn from the alliance. However, if the HR department selects those individuals who are open to new ideas and are willing to learn, there is more

likelihood that the alliance can progress and that learning can occur. Allocation of key individuals to an alliance also demonstrates the commitment of the partner to the alliance. In fact, another interviewee in the study observed that while some alliance partners discussed the strategic importance of the alliance on numerous occasions, they would only staff the alliance with "dead wood." By sending the appropriate individuals, partners can signal their commitment to making the alliance work. Appropriate involvement of the alliance's HR function makes certain that the best individuals are assigned to the alliance, thus ensuring success.

Source: Based on Taylor, Andrew. 2005. "An operations perspective on strategic alliance success factors: An exploratory study of alliance managers in the software industry." International Journal of Operations & Production Management, 25, 5/6: pp. 469–490.

partners. No matter how mutually beneficial and logical the venture may seem at its start, without trust and commitment, the alliance will either fail entirely, or it will fail to reach its strategic potential.[19]

The Importance of Commitment and Trust

Commitment

In a strategic alliance, occurs when partners take care of each other and put forth extra effort to make the venture work.

Attitudinal commitment

The willingness to dedicate resources and efforts and face risks to make the alliance work.

Fair exchange

In a strategic alliance, occurs when partners believe that they receive benefits from the relationship equal to their contributions.

Commitment in a strategic alliance means taking care of each other and putting forth extra effort to make the venture work. Committed partners are willing to dedicate resources and effort and face risks to make the venture work. This is called **attitudinal commitment.** Formally, attitudinal commitment is the psychological identification with the relationship and a pride of association with the partner and with the alliance.

Aspects of attitudinal commitment in international strategic alliances are expressed in many ways, including the following: a fair financial commitment; a commitment to support the partner's strategic goals; a commitment to the partner's employees; and a commitment to understand the culture, politics, and economics of the partner's country.

If all partners involved in the alliance demonstrate these aspects of commitment, the venture will develop based on the principle of **fair exchange.**[20] Fair exchange means that all partners believe that they receive benefits from the relationship that equal their contributions.

Why is commitment important? The marriage of two or more distinct companies from different cultures creates a strong potential for conflict and mistrust. Without a sense of mutual obligation to each other and to the alliance, partners often fail to work out problems. Instead, they retreat to their own companies or cultures leaving issues unresolved and often feeling that the venture is not worth the effort. As Henry Lane and Paul Beamish[21] point out, "A successful relationship requires constant attention and nurturing. As one executive explained, 'Good local partners have to be cherished and taken care of.'"

EXHIBIT **9.7**   **HRM Issues in Strategic Alliances**

HRM Planning	Training and Development
➤ Communicate strategic intent ➤ Take a long-term dynamic approach	➤ Train for cross-cultural competence ➤ Make sure training includes all partners ➤ Build a career structure of IJV participation

Staffing	Appraisals and Rewards
➤ Give time for staffing decisions ➤ Provide high quality people to the alliance ➤ Don't depend on the partner for staffing	➤ Appraise based on long-term goals ➤ Build incentives for strategic goals—learning or profits ➤ Tie rewards to global strategy

Source: Adapted from Pucik, Vladimir. 1988. "Strategic alliances, organizational learning, and competitive advantage: The HRM agenda." Human Resource Management 27, pp. 77–93.

Commitment also has a practical side, **calculative commitment.** Calculative commitment comes from the evaluations, expectations, and concerns about the future potential for gaining rewards in a relationship. Businesses require tangible outcomes for a relationship to continue. A recent study of commitment in IJVs suggests that commitment increases when both partners achieve their strategic goals. These goals may be financial or other strategic goals such as market entry or learning a new technology. However, it is not necessary that partners have the same strategic goals for the relationship to endure or grow in commitment.[22] Perhaps, like any marriage, if partners select each other carefully, it is easier to develop complementary strategic goals and eventual commitment to the relationship.

Trust and commitment usually go hand in hand. As with commitment, there are two forms of trust. **Credibility trust** is the confidence that the partner has the intent and ability to meet its obligations and make its promised contributions to the alliance. Trust is also the confidence that the partner will behave with goodwill and with fair exchange, called **benevolent trust.**[23]

The development of trust between partners in an alliance may take time. Alliance partners often begin a relationship suspicious of each other's motives. Typical fears and questions include the following: Do they want to steal my technology? Are they trying to take me over? Am I building a new competitor? Am I giving away too much? Will they or can they provide what we agreed on? Such initial suspicions make trust difficult.

Most experts on trust believe that trust builds in what are called "trust cycles." Just like people in relationships, partners in IJVs and ICAs often feel vulnerable. This early vulnerability makes partners tentative in their involvement in the relationship and reluctant to reveal true motives, business "know-how," or technology. Gradually, as each side deals repeatedly with its partner, suspicion declines and reciprocal trust grows.[24] Exhibit 9.8 shows an example of the trust and commitment cycle in strategic alliances.

Why is trust important? Successful cooperation requires alliance participants to contribute quality inputs into the alliance organization. When partners do not trust each other, they hold back information or take unfair advantage of each other if given the opportunity. When this happens, the alliance seldom produces all the mutual benefits possible from cooperation. As discussed earlier

Calculative commitment

Alliance partner evaluations, expectations, and concerns regarding potential rewards from the relationship.

Credibility trust

The confidence that the partner has the intent and ability to meet promised obligations and commitments.

Benevolent trust

The confidence that the partner will behave with good will and with fair exchange.

EXHIBIT
9.8
The Trust/Commitment Cycle

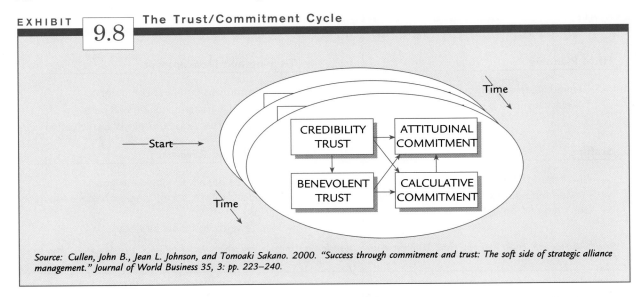

Source: Cullen, John B., Jean L. Johnson, and Tomoaki Sakano. 2000. "Success through commitment and trust: The soft side of strategic alliance management." Journal of World Business 35, 3: pp. 223–240.

in the case of the alliance between Telia and Telenor, Norway's and Sweden's largest telecom companies respectively, trust was a critical issue that led to the breakdown of the alliance. Although the CEOs trusted each other during the pre-alliance phase, the individuals involved during the implementation did not carry over the trust.[25]

Trust is also necessary because formal contracts can never identify all the issues that arise in strategic alliances. It is impossible to write a contract with sufficient detail to cover every foreseeable situation. Much of what happens between partners in alliances develops informally as the alliance matures. In addition, the technology and know-how of organizations contain "tacit knowledge." Tacit knowledge includes rules, procedures, and ways of doing things that are parts of the organization's culture. They are not written down, and often people are not aware that they exist. As a result, for two organizations to share sensitive knowledge and go beyond the details of a formal contract, trust must exist. What happens if trust is lost and evolves into a distrust cycle? Consider the following Multinational Management Challenge, which shows some of the difficulties faced by Pepsi with its joint-venture partner in China.

Building and Sustaining Trust and Commitment

Multinational managers need to consider several key factors to build and sustain commitment and trust in international strategic alliances, including the following:[26]

- *Pick your partner carefully:* As a major step in alliance implementation, picking a partner must include consideration of more than potential strategic complementarity and resource contributions. Alliance partners must believe that they can trust each other, and they must believe that mutual commitment is possible.

- *Know your strategic goals and those of your partner:* Mutual revelations of strategic goals build a crucial step in the trust cycle. It also allows partners to realize early in the relationship whether they can commit to each other's strategic goals. However, alliance partners must realize that strategic goals for the ICA or IJV may change.

Multinational Management **Challenge**

Pepsi seeks a divorce

"Divorce is not a pleasant thing; you only go through it where there is no alternative. We have found them impossible to work with. They have totally destroyed any basis for cooperation."

—Wah-Hui Chu, president of Pepsi's China regarding a local IJV partner

The attraction of gaining access to a city of 10 million led Pepsi to create a joint venture with Sichuan Radio and Television Industrial Development Co., a subsidiary of the province's Bureau of Radio, Film, and Television. Although the Chinese company had no knowledge of the beverage industry, most foreign investments in China require local partners—so Pepsi saw this as a way to gain local government favor. Pepsi's Chu noted, "They came to us and said they could secure government approval to set up the business, and off we went. It wasn't a pure commercial decision. You could call it an arranged marriage." Pepsi invested $20 million into the factory, which resulted in only 27 percent ownership. However, it retained the right to 50 percent of the board.

Although the assembly line is still pumping out bottles of cola, the international joint venture between Pepsi and the Sichuan provincial government in China, Sichuan Pepsi-Cola Beverages Co., has deteriorated. Once a symbol of China's economic reforms, the IJV is now an embarrassment for both partners. How could such a promising venture go into the distrust cycle?

Pepsi's side:

- The partner looted the company, using funds for fancy vacations and cars. Managers submitted multiple copies of receipts to pad reimbursements.
- The general manager of the IJV, appointed by the local partner, did not follow company policies regarding sales areas.
- The partner changed the ownership structure.
- The partner blocked Pepsi's auditors from looking at factory books.

The local side:

- Managers dismissed talks of improper use of company monies.
- We must sell outside the markets assigned by Pepsi to make a profit—managers' bonuses depend on it.
- Pepsi's accusations are exaggerations of long-unresolved conflicts designed to lead to the replacement of the factory's management.
- Pepsi is practicing "commercial hegemonism."

In what amounts to a public admission of failure, Pepsi filed papers to dissolve the partnership. An international arbitrator in Stockholm will consider the case. However, with a market of 70 million people in Sichuan province, Pepsi intends to stay and will seek other partners or will go it alone without a partner.

Sources: Based on Goodman, Peter S. 2002. "Pepsi seeks 'divorce' in China: Subsidiary seeks to dissolve partnership that runs bottling plant in Sichuan Province." The Washington Post, September 28, p. E01.

- *Seek win–win situations:* To achieve and maintain mutual commitment in an alliance, there must be a balance in which each side gains something of importance from the relationship. Although the outcomes from the alliance need not be the same, both sides must perceive them as a fair exchange if commitment and trust are to evolve.

- *Go slowly:* Participants in international strategic alliances must realize that problems arise and take time to work out. Trust and commitment develop in cycles and not necessarily all at once.
- *Invest in cross-cultural training:* As in all international ventures, managers with cross-cultural sensitivity and language competence will likely have more success in understanding partner needs and interests. Quality cross-cultural interactions between partners' employees will avoid conflict and misunderstandings and lead to greater trust and commitment between partner companies.
- *Invest in direct communication:* To overcome national, business, and organizational cultural differences, alliance partners are more successful at building trust and commitment when they deal with issues face-to-face.
- *Find the right level of trust and commitment:* Exhibit 9.9 shows the trade-off between the vulnerability that comes with trust and commitment and their benefits.

In addition to efforts to build trust and commitment, another key issue that needs to be addressed in a strategic alliance is learning. Multinationals involved in alliances need to make efforts to ensure that they are learning appropriately from the partnership. Learning and knowledge-management issues are discussed in depth in Chapter 8 on Organizational Designs for Multinational Companies.

Companies form IJVs or ICAs to benefit their companies either in the short or long term or both. As with all strategic decisions, companies must assess the

EXHIBIT 9.9   The Right Level of Trust and Commitment

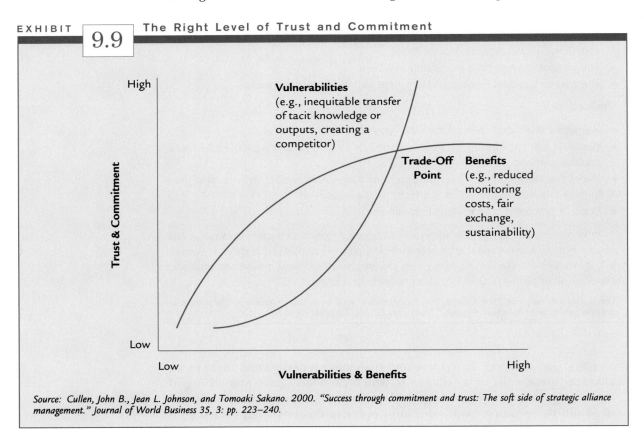

Source: Cullen, John B., Jean L. Johnson, and Tomoaki Sakano. 2000. "Success through commitment and trust: The soft side of strategic alliance management." Journal of World Business 35, 3: pp. 223–240.

performance of their strategies. In the next section, we consider the complex problems of assessing the performance of international strategic alliances.

Assessing the Performance of an International Strategic Alliance

Like all business ventures, strategic alliances should contribute eventually to their parents' profitability. When the strategic intent of the alliance is to produce immediate results, assessment of the alliance's performance is not difficult. Standard financial and efficiency measures of performance, such as profit, sales revenue, or number of units produced, are common. Often such alliances, particularly IJVs, become stand-alone profit centers that provide direct financial benefits to the parents. Profit-center alliances produce and sell their own products on the open market. Parents evaluate profit-center strategic alliances similarly to their other corporate divisions, based on traditional financial profitability ratios, such as return on investment.

Other types of strategic alliances provide mostly indirect strategic contributions to parents. Such alliances may never generate profits from the alliance organization. Rather, these strategic alliances produce other valued outputs such as new technologies with potential benefits for their parents. Indirect benefits from strategic alliances may come from penetrating risky markets, learning new markets or technologies, developing new technologies, overcoming local political barriers, developing a presence in a market, or supporting other competitive tactics.[27]

Boeing's ventures with Japanese companies provide one example of indirect benefits from alliances. Boeing uses alliances with Japanese aircraft-component makers as a defensive strategy. These alliances prevent its competitor, Airbus, from working with the Japanese. Another example is McDonald's joint-venture operations in Russia. McDonald's wanted to be the first fast-food chain in this emerging market—even though managers realized that profits would be hard to repatriate and that the venture would eventually convert to complete Russian ownership.

Eventually, all companies hope to make money from their ICA or IJV investments. The alliance itself may not produce the profit, but the knowledge gained may allow the parents to succeed in the future. In the meantime, however, how can upper management assess the performance of a strategic alliance and the performances of the managers responsible for the ICA or IJV? What is distinctive about IJV and ICA performance criteria?

Financial performance measures alone are seldom good indicators of performance for strategic alliances created for indirect strategic benefits. Depending on the unique objectives of the alliances, parent companies must develop more subjective performance criteria. These criteria include factors such as creating harmony among the partners, identifying product adaptations for a new market, or capturing market share to gain first-mover advantages over their competitors.[28]

The recent research emphasis on relational aspects of alliances has also spurred interest in other forms of alliance performance measures.[29] For instance, some have proposed "alliance satisfaction" as a measure of alliance performance while others emphasize other measures such as goal accomplishment. Additionally, some also have argued for alternatives to more direct measures of performance such as duration of the alliance whereby early

IJV and ICA performance criteria

Often must include criteria other than financial, such as organizational learning.

termination suggests failure.[30] However, most measures have problems, and the best measure depends on the nature of the alliance. For instance, duration may not be an appropriate measure since most alliances are formed with the explicit notion that the alliance will be dissolved once its goals have been achieved. Early termination of an alliance may sometimes imply that the goals of the alliance have been achieved faster than expected.

Assessing the performance of all types of alliances demands that parents match the strategic objectives of their alliances with the measures used for assessment. If immediate profit is the strategic goal, then profit must be in the assessment. If long-term goals, such as learning a new market or technology, are the main goals of the alliance, then immediate profit must be de-emphasized in favor of other performance measures.

Exhibit 9.10 shows a list of potential performance measures that parent companies use to evaluate their strategic alliances.

Not all alliances achieve their strategic intent; therefore, managers must plan for how to handle a nonperforming alliance. The next section addresses this issue.

If The Alliance Does Not Work

If the alliance fails to meet strategic goals, managers have two basic choices (see Exhibit 9.1). Providing that they keep their same strategic intent, they can negotiate an end to the agreement or improve their implementation.

EXHIBIT 9.10   Selected Performance Criteria for Strategic Alliances

Management Processes	Competitive
➤ Good partner relationships—no conflict or handled well ➤ High worker morale ➤ Meeting goals of social responsibility ➤ Development of human resources ➤ Dealing with the local government	➤ Gaining market share ➤ Minimizing knowledge leakage to partners (knowledge not intended for partners) ➤ Affecting competitors (e.g., preventing them from gaining a foothold in the country)
Organizational Learning	**Marketing**
➤ Understanding a new market ➤ Learning a new technology ➤ Improving R&D cycle times ➤ Developing new management techniques ➤ Developing innovative technologies ➤ Generating other potential opportunities	➤ Total sales ➤ Customer satisfaction ➤ Insights into customer needs ➤ Facilitating the sale of other products
	Financial
	➤ Return on investment ➤ Return on assets

Source: Adapted from Anderson, Erin. 1990. "Two firms, one frontier: On assessing joint venture performance." Sloan Management Review. Winter, pp. 19–30; Gomes-Casseres, Ben. 1998. "Strategy before structure." The Alliance Analyst, August.

The art of managing strategic alliances is in knowing when to quit and when to invest more time and resources in building the relationship. There are really no hard-and-fast rules, and each case is unique. Often, the personal relationships among alliance managers become the key for turning around a nonperforming alliance.

A particular danger in all questionable alliance relationships is escalation of commitment.[31] **Escalation of commitment** means that managers continue in relationships longer than necessary because of past financial and emotional investments. Consider the case of Global One, the three-way alliance between Deutsche Telekom, France Telecom, and Sprint, created in 1994.[32] Despite higher-than-expected losses and significant turmoil, the alliance existed for six years. This was even more surprising because many outside analysts consistently voiced their views that the alliance was a mistake. In such cases of escalation of commitment, alliance partners believe that "just one more day" or "just a little more money" will make the relationship work and make their past investments worthwhile. The truly difficult choice is in knowing when to take the loss and dissolve the alliance.

Improving the implementation means going over each step in the implementation process to determine what, if any, changes can be made. Perhaps, for example, partners failed to develop an appropriate design for the alliance organization or chose a weak alliance manager. Of course, if one side decides that it just has the wrong partner, it must dissolve the relationship and, if necessary, seek another alliance partner.

A recommended strategy of alliance formation is to plan for the end of the alliance from its beginning. Alliance contracts can contain "prenuptial" agreements, which specify how the alliance can be dissolved. These agreements note the procedures to end the alliance and review periods when both sides must agree to keep the alliance alive. They may also specify penalties for early termination of the contract by either side. The advantage of including such agreements up front, before the alliance begins, is that negotiations occur in a positive and friendly stage of the relationship. They do not occur later when there is often conflict between the partners and a high level of distrust.

The death of a strategic alliance should not be confused with a failed relationship. Many alliances are intended to be short term. Once partners achieve their strategic goals, they both go their own ways. For example, an alliance may end after a new technology is developed, a new market is penetrated, or a temporary product gap is remedied. In addition, IJVs are often acquired by one of the partners and move to the next level of direct investment.

Next we consider the role of the parent company in managing a portfolio of international joint ventures.

> **Escalation of commitment**
> Companies continue in an alliance relationship longer than necessary because of past financial and emotional investments.

Learning to Partner: Building A Dedicated Strategic Alliance Unit and Key Lessons from Cross-Border Alliances

Alliances are so common in today's global business environment—the Global 500 average 60 each—that companies are developing specialized units to manage the design of strategic alliances. These specialized units provide processes and procedures that, for example, help managers identify the need for an alliance, evaluate partners, negotiate agreements, structure the alliance organizations, and develop specific performance indicators.

Experienced multinational companies that have had many alliances are taking the experience of what has worked and what has failed and are developing templates of successful practices. A recent study shows that multinational companies such as HP and Lucent Technologies with alliance-management units outperform companies without such a function.[33] However, alliance-management units do not work for all companies. Typically, only the very large multinational companies have enough alliances to dedicate the resources necessary to create a specialized unit for alliance management.

As we saw in this chapter, strategic alliances are likely to become more crucial in the future as multinational companies take advantage of emerging markets as well as try to lower costs. To conclude this chapter, we look at some of the some key lessons learned from successful cross-border alliances based on Peter Jagersma's[34] interview and survey of key individuals involved in successful cross-border alliances. These include:

- *Understand and appreciate business and cultural differences:* Successful cross-border alliances can only be possible if the partners recognize cultural and business differences and adapt to such differences.
- *Keep strong executive support:* Successful cross-border alliances are the ones that consistently retain strong executive support. Involvement of the executive shows commitment and support of the alliance.
- *Communicate:* Communication is crucial to the cross-border alliance's success. Nothing is worse than two partners having different visions for the alliance.
- *Negotiate logic before control:* It is imperative for partners to identify potential areas of opportunities and synergies (the pie) before negotiating on how to allocate the profit and ownership issues (the slices).
- *Commitment, trust and dedication:* Successful cross-border alliances are those where partners are committed to the alliance and are willing to commit the resources and personnel (including senior management time) to make the alliance work.
- *Have "checkpoint" as the alliance is being implemented:* It is important to build in "go/no go" checkpoints to ensure that the partners are informed and satisfied with progress and development.
- *Review alliance's viability:* Multinational companies need to review any alliance frequently to determine if the alliance is viable and beneficial.

Summary and Conclusions

The use of international strategic alliances as a major participation strategy continues to grow in international business. Implementing this strategy demands a good knowledge of the problems and prospects associated with alliance management. This chapter provided a basic understating of issues in alliance management, including where to link in the value chain, how to select a partner, how to design an alliance organization, HRM practices in an alliance, how to build trust and commitment in an alliance, how to assess performance, and what to do if the alliance fails.

Perhaps the most important decision in managing successful strategic alliances is picking the right partner. Picking a compatible partner with the appropriate skills determines the eventual fate of most strategic alliances.

Strategic alliances have no set structure for ownership, decision-making control, or management control. Partners must negotiate structures that support their mutual strategic goals. The ICA or IJV manager faces HRM problems similar to those in all international operations. However, there is added complexity because parent companies must come to some agreement regarding the HRM practices used in alliance organizations.

Most experts consider trust and commitment as basic foundations for IJV or ICA success, second only to picking the right partner. Commitment and trust take on such importance because not everything can be stated in a contract. For long-term success, partner companies must trust each other to deliver agreed-upon outputs and to not take advantage of partners in the relationship.

Because strategic goals for strategic alliances are varied and subtle, the performance of an IJV or ICA is often difficult to determine. Usually, companies expect a strategic alliance to generate more than short-term financial returns. Objectives such as organizational learning and market penetration often represent major goals of alliances and must figure strongly in their performance assessment.

Strategic alliances are inherently unstable and many will fail. Consequently, when an international strategic alliance fails to meet strategic goals, multinational managers must be prepared to improve their implementation efforts or to abandon the alliance. However, many strategic alliances will die natural deaths when they meet their strategic objectives or are bought out by one of the parent companies.

International strategic alliances are now so common among the major multinational companies that many have formalized the process of implementing alliance processes and organizations. Eli Lilly calls its unit the Office of Alliance Management.[35]

Discussion Questions

1. What are the characteristics of a good partner in a strategic alliance? How do these partner traits help make a strategic alliance successful?
2. Which of the alliance contract issues shown in the text do you think are most important? Why?
3. Discuss some costs and benefits of the different management structures available for a strategic alliance. Under what conditions should a firm choose any particular structure?
4. What types of personnel are usually assigned to strategic alliances? For each type of personnel, what kind of impact does the IJV assignment have on future careers?
5. What are some of the difficulties of assessing IJV or ICA performance? How do these differ for companies with different strategic goals?
6. Why is trust and commitment so important to strategic alliances? How can a partner demonstrate trust and commitment to a joint venture?

Multinational Management **Skill Builder**

Compare and Contrast International Joint Venture Contracts

Most multinational companies have many joint ventures or strategic alliances. Your task is to identify the alliances of a company you select.

Step 1.   Go to http://contracts.corporate.findlaw.com/ and search for joint venture or alliance contracts. There are many available that include well-known companies.

Step 2.   Select two contracts for alliances in the same industry and make a summary list of the major points covered.

Step 3.   Compare and contrast these contracts regarding inclusiveness and detail of points covered versus the flexibility of the relationship.

Step 4.   Search the Web and see if the venture still exists.

Endnotes

[1] Accenture. 2006. http://www.accenture.com

[2] Kimberley, William. 2001. "Renault and GM target the light truck market." http://www.autofieldguide.com. December.

[3] *Strategic Direction.* 2006. "Create successful international mergers and alliances." 22, 1: pp. 25–28.

[4] Murray, Janet Y. 1995. "Patterns in domestic vs. international strategic alliances: An investigation of U.S. multinational firms." *Multinational Business Review* 13: pp. 7–16.

[5] Geringer, J. Michael. 1988. *Joint Venture Partner Selection.* Westport, Conn.: Quorum Books.

[6] Ibid.

[7] Main, Jeremy. 1990. "Making global alliances work." *Fortune,* December 17, *pp.* 121–126.

[8] Ibid.

[9] Geringer, *Joint Venture Partner Selection.*

[10] *Strategic Direction,* "Create successful international mergers and alliances."

[11] Geringer, *Joint Venture Partner Selection.*

[12] Lorange, Peter, and Johan Roos. 1992. *Strategic Alliances.* Cambridge, Mass.: Blackwell.

[13] Kealey, Daniel L, David R. Protheroe, Doug MacDonald, and Thomas Vulpe. 2006. "International projects: Some lessons on avoiding failure and maximizing success." *Performance Improvement,* March, 45, 3:p. 38.

[14] Gray, Barbara, and Aimin Yan. 1992. "A negotiations model of joint venture formation, structure, and performance: Implications for global management." *Advances in International Comparative Management* 7: pp. 41–75; Killing, J. P. 1988. "Understanding alliances: The role of task and organizational complexity." In *Cooperative Strategies in International Business,* edited by F.J. Contractor and P. Lorange, pp. 241–245. Lexington, Mass.: Lexington Books.

[15] Vernon, R. 1977. *Storm over Multinationals.* Cambridge, Mass.: Harvard University Press.

[16] Vernon, R. 1977. *Storm over Multinationals.* Cambridge, Mass.: Harvard University Press.

[17] Ibid.

[18] Datta, Deepak K., and Abdual M. A. Rasheed. 1993. "Planning international joint ventures: The role of human resource management." In *Multinational Strategic Alliances,* edited by Refik Culpan, pp. 251–271. New York: International Business Press; Lorange, Peter. 1986. "Human resource management in multinational cooperative ventures." *Human Resource Management* 25, 1:pp. 133–148;

Pucik, Vladimir. 1988. "Strategic alliances, organizational learning, and competitive advantage: The HRM agenda." *Human Resource Management* 27, pp. 77–93.

[19] Taylor, Andrew. 2005. "An operations perspective on strategic alliance success factors: An exploratory study of alliance managers in the software industry." *International Journal of Operations & Production Management,* 25, 5/6:pp. 469–490.

[20] Lane, Henry W., and Paul W. Beamish. 1990. "Cross-cultural cooperative behavior in joint ventures in IDCs." *Management International Review* 30, Special Issue, pp. 87–102.

[21] Ibid.

[22] Cullen, John B., Jean L. Johnson, and Tomoaki Sakano. 2000. "Success through commitment and trust: The soft side of strategic alliance management." *Journal of World Business* 35, 3: p. 223–240; Cullen, John B., Jean L. Johnson, and Tomoaki Sakano. 1995. "Japanese and local partner commitment to IJVs: Psychological consequences of outcomes and investments in the IJV relationship." *Journal of International Business Studies* 26, 1: pp. 91–116.

[23] Johnson, Jean L., John B. Cullen, Tomoaki Sakano, and Hideyuki Takenouchi. 1996. "Setting the stage for trust and strategic integration in Japanese–U.S. cooperative alliances." *Journal of International Business Studies* 27: pp. 981–1004.

[24] Johnson, Cullen, Sakano, and Takenouchi, "Setting the stage for trust and strategic integration in Japanese–U.S. cooperative alliances;" Ring, Peter Smith, and Andrew H. Van De Ven. 1992. "Structuring cooperative relationships between organizations." *Strategic Management Journal* 13, pp. 483–498.

[25] *Strategic Direction,* "Create successful international mergers and alliances."

[26] Cullen, Johnson, and Sakano, "Success through commitment and trust: The soft side of strategic alliance management."

[27] Lei, David. 1993. "Offensive and defensive uses of alliances." *Long Range Planning* 26: pp. 32–44.

[28] Anderson, Erin. 1990. "Two firms, one frontier: On assessing joint venture performance." *Sloan Management Review,* Winter, p. 19–30.

[29] Rahman, Noushi. 2006. "Duality of alliance performance." *Journal of American Academy of Business,* September, 10, 1: pp. 305–311.

[30] Ibid.

[31] Cullen, Johnson, and Sakano, "Japanese and local partner commitment to IJVs: Psychological consequences of outcomes and investments in the IJV relationship."

[32] Delios, Andrew, Andrew C. Inkpen, and Jerry Ross. 2004. "Escalation in international strategic alliances." *Management International Review,* 44, 4:pp. 457–479.

[33] Dyer, Jeffrey H., Prashant Kale and Harbir Singh. 2001. "How to make strategic alliances work." Sloan Management Review, 42: pp. 37–44.

[34] Jagersma, "Cross-border alliances: Advice from the executive suite."

[35] IBM Institute for Business Values. 2002. "Leveraging knowledge management across strategic alliances." http://www.ibm.com

PBS (B): The ABB PBS Joint Venture in Operation

The PBS board meeting to make the decision whether or not to accept the ABB proposal for a joint venture lasted 18 hours. In the end, the PBS board voted in favor and the joint venture was agreed upon. Several legal and contractual issues were quickly resolved, and the deal was signed in late December 1992.

Structure and Organization

ABB První Brnénská Strojírna Brno, Ltd. (ABB PBS) was a joint venture in which ABB has a 67 percent stake and PBS a.s. has a 33 percent stake. The PBS share was determined nominally by the value of the land, plant and equipment, employees, and goodwill. ABB contributed cash and specified technologies, and assumed some of the debt of PBS. The new company started operations on April 15, 1993.

The ABB PBS Company was a joint venture in its formal structure and governance. PBS a.s. had seats on the board, had part ownership, and was a supplier to the joint venture. The core operations of PBS a.s. were its Brno-based power generation business, its experience with turnkey operations, and its engineering and manufacturing capabilities with its customer base of installed equipment. The joint venture included the turnkey power plant business, boilers, and turbines (but not turbochargers). All of the PBS facilities in Brno and the outlying plant in Mikulov that made turbine blades went into the joint venture. In sum, about 4,000 employees from PBS a.s. went to the joint venture; about 3,400 remained in PBS a.s. About 80 percent of the revenue of PBS a.s. became part of the joint venture.

Profit was to be divided in 2/3–1/3 shares according to ownership when it was earned and distributed; initial plans called for reinvestment of all profits and no dividends paid out to corporate parents.

ABB PBS was organized by product lines: power plants, turbines, boilers, and external services (the latter was added in 1995). Centralized functions such as marketing, finance, human resources, quality control, and information systems reported vertically to the general director and are matrixed horizontally with the business units or product divisions. The internal service division (maintenance) served the four product divisions. Each product division also had some of the same functions (Exhibit 1).

ABB PBS was assigned geographic regions as its market territories by the ABB power generation segment and used the ABB selling network in these territories. Other ABB companies in the same lines of business had other territories, so head-to-head competition among ABB sister companies for the same customers was minimized.

The ABB regional selling network assisted ABB PBS to identify business opportunities. ABB PBS was the prime contractor for projects that are obtained. For turbines and boilers that were not part of a turnkey project, or in cases in which another ABB company was the primary contractor, ABB PBS participated as a subcontractor. ABB PBS had its own vice-president for export sales and an export sales force for direct selling as well as selling in cooperation with the ABB regional network.

In the domestic market, ABB PBS continued to use its own sales force and customer contacts. There were two domestic competitors, Škoda Turbiny (a company in the Škoda Koncern) and Vitkovice, whose principal business was steel.

Business Goals and Objectives

Financial Performance Business for the joint venture in its first two full years was good in most aspects. The 1995 results showed substantial progress toward meeting the joint venture's strategic goals adopted in 1994 as part of a five-year plan. One of the goals was that exports should account for half of total orders by 1999. (Exports had

EXHIBIT **1**   ABB PBS Organizational Chart in 1995

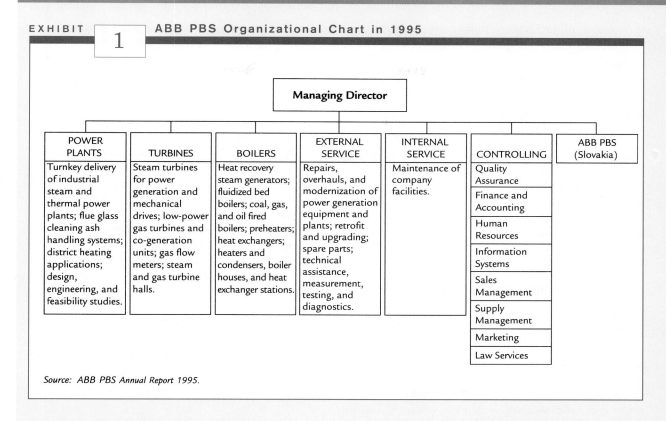

Source: ABB PBS Annual Report 1995.

accounted for more than a quarter of the PBS business before 1989, but most of this business disappeared when the Soviet Union collapsed.) In 1995 exports increased as a share of total orders to 28 percent, up from 16 percent the year before.

The external service business, organized and functioning as a separate business for the first time in 1995, did not meet expectations. It accounted for five percent of all orders and revenues in 1995, below the 10 percent goal set for it. The retrofitting business, which was expected to be a major part of the service business, was disappointing for ABB PBS, partly because many other small companies began to provide this service in 1994, including some started by former PBS employees who took their knowledge of PBS-built power plants with them. However, ABB PBS managers hoped that as the company introduced new technologies, these former employees would gradually lose their ability to perform these services, and the retrofit and repair service business would return to ABB PBS.

ABB PBS dominated the Czech boiler business with 70 percent of the Czech market in 1995, but managers expected this share to go down in the future as new domestic and foreign competitors appeared. Furthermore, the west European boiler market was actually declining because environmental laws caused a surge of retrofitting to occur in the mid-1980s, leaving less business in the 1990s. Accordingly, ABB PBS boiler orders were flat in 1995.

Top managers at ABB PBS regarded business results to date as respectable, but they were not satisfied with the company's performance. Cash flow was not as good as expected. Cost reduction had to go further. "The more we succeed, the more we see our shortcomings," said one official.

Restructuring The first round of restructuring was largely completed in 1995, the last year of the three-year restructuring plan. Plant logistics, information systems, and other physical capital improvements were in place. The restructuring included:

➤ Renovating and reconstructing workshops and engineering facilities

➤ Achieving ISO 9001 for all four ABB PBS divisions (awarded in 1995)

➤ Transfer of technology from ABB (this was an ongoing project)
➤ Installation of an information system
➤ Management training, especially in total quality assurance and English language
➤ Implementing a project management approach

A notable achievement of importance to top management in 1995 was a 50 percent increase in labor productivity, measured as value added per payroll crown. However, in the future ABB PBS expected its wage rates to go up faster than west European wage rates (Czech wages were increasing about 15 percent per year), so it would be difficult to maintain the ABB PBS unit cost advantage over west European unit cost.

The Technology Role for ABB PBS The joint venture was expected from the beginning to play an important role in technology development for part of ABB's power generation business worldwide. PBS a.s. had engineering capability in coal-fired steam boilers, and that capability was expected to be especially useful to ABB as more countries became concerned about air quality. (When asked if PBS really did have leading technology here, a boiler engineering manager remarked, "Of course we do. We burn so much dirty coal in this country, we have to have better technology.")

However, the envisioned technology leadership role for ABB PBS had not been realized by mid-1996. Richard Kuba, the ABB PBS managing director, realized the slowness with which the technology role was being fulfilled, and he offered his interpretation of events:

ABB did not promise to make the joint venture its steam boiler technology leader. The main point we wanted to achieve in the joint venture agreement was for ABB PBS to be recognized as a full-fledged company, not just a factory. We were slowed down on our technology plans because we had a problem keeping our good, young engineers. The annual employee turnover rate for companies in the Czech Republic is 15 or 20 percent, and the unemployment rate is zero. Our engineers have many other good entrepreneurial opportunities. Now we've begun to stabilize our engineering workforce. The restructuring helped. We have better equipment and a cleaner and safer work environment. We also had

another problem, which is a good problem to have. The domestic power plant business turned out to be better than we expected, so just meeting the needs of our regular customers forced some postponement of new technology initiatives.

ABB PBS had benefited technologically from its relationship with ABB. One example was the development of a new steam turbine line. This project was a cooperative effort among ABB PBS and two other ABB companies, one in Sweden and one in Germany. Nevertheless, technology transfer was not the most important early benefit of the ABB relationship. Rather, one of the most important gains was the opportunity to benchmark the joint venture's performance against other established western ABB companies on variables such as productivity, inventory, and receivables.

Management Issues

The toughest problems that ABB PBS faced in the early years of the joint venture were management issues. There were two: How to relate to ABB sister companies in other countries, and how to transform the human capital of the company.

Relationships with Other ABB Companies Managing a joint venture company was always difficult, and joining a global corporation compounded the start-up challenges. The Czech managers at ABB PBS had to learn fast. One set of problems arose from the relationship of ABB PBS to its ABB sister companies. Richard Kuba and his colleagues were accustomed to working together with other companies on big projects; before the Velvet Revolution, PBS worked with other companies in the Škoda group. But ABB was different. Cooperation coexisted with competition, and that was outside Kuba's experience. Sibling rivalry among companies was very much a fact of business life, he discovered. Kuba related an unhappy episode about his company's unfamiliarity with these business relationships. He said:

We underestimated the cultural differences between Czechs and other west European people. We have to learn how to say "no." We have to be better in claim management. We have to fight more in order to succeed in this environment.

This fact of corporate life was confirmed by Erik Fougner, the ABB country manager in the Czech Republic, who also noted that excess capacity in Europe caused the older ABB companies to be particularly anxious about the arrival of the Czech newcomer. Some were concerned that there would not be room for three ABB power generation industry companies in Europe in the future.

Human Capital Transformation The physical and organizational restructuring of ABB PBS was nearly completed by 1996. The transformation of the thinking and behavior of employees had just begun. The ways that were adaptive, or at least tolerated, under central planning would not succeed in a competitive market economy. Changing employees' "mentality"—the term used by Czech managers—was human capital restructuring. It was proving very difficult to do, and it was going very slowly.

In several respects, ABB PBS was nicely positioned to accomplish human capital restructuring. The top management of the joint venture was stable, it was thoroughly Czech but with a keen awareness of the mentality issues, and the ABB parent company tried to offer assistance in a variety of ways. Czech management was supported by two or three expatriates taking non-executive positions in project management, supply management, and workshop planning.

The ABB PBS managers believed a background of knowledge of local history, culture, and business practices was essential. These Czech managers, as in most Czech companies, knew they had to change the attitudes and behaviors of their employees. Richard Kuba said,

> It is easy to change the structure of the company, and it is easy to change the facilities, but it is not easy to change people's minds. Employees don't yet understand the consequences of their actions. They don't take responsibility. There is low unemployment so they can leave and get a less stressful job instead of taking responsibility here.

ABB PBS had never laid off any employees for lack of work. Managers appreciated the good reputation this brought the company, but they also wondered if it dampened employees' motivation to work hard. Without the threat of layoff, would managers' human resource initiatives be listened to?

Fougner, a Norwegian located in Prague since 1992, saw the same "mentality" problem:

> This is a bigger challenge than I thought it would be. The first level of change in Czech companies comes easily. To make nice new offices and new factory layouts is quite simple. But the transfer of real human resource learning is slow. Responsibility and initiative are poor because it was not rewarded for two generations in these formerly centrally planned economies. Under central planning, you were given a task, you did it, and nothing bad would happen to you. The tasks themselves were compartmentalized—I did mine and you did yours. I did my duty so I'm okay. Even managers did not see the whole picture and could not take responsibility for it. The functional organization of companies [with the archetypal "functional chimneys"] made it worse.

What could be done? The company took three approaches. At the corporate level, ABB PBS tried to instill a sense of mission. The annual report for 1995 noted the efforts of top management to find agreement on corporate goals and values in order to strengthen employee identification with the company.

ABB, the parent company, tried to assist, but did not want to send too many expatriates to ABB PBS. Rather, local managers had to bring about the mentality changes themselves. ABB loaned some of the people from its internal consulting unit to the joint venture on a part-time basis. Their job was to train the (local) trainers, and to sit beside the production and engineering managers and supervisors and work through attitude change material with them. Line managers were the ones who would implement the human capital restructuring, not personnel managers.

The compensation system was the third line of attack. Before the Velvet Revolution, factory worker pay at PBS was based on a piece rate system that was surprisingly common in the Czech Republic. However, it was badly manipulated so that it did not motivate workers to raise output. Real or imagined equipment problems or shortages of parts—both of which occurred frequently—would excuse workers from meeting desired rates of output, or workers would stockpile output and then slack off. The system fostered the attitude among some workers that "you get a wage to show up, and anything extra you do gets you extra pay." This attitude reflected working conditions under communism where wages were an entitlement rather than a payment for labor services rendered.

ABB PBS introduced a new incentive pay scheme that was not without its problems. Employees were accustomed to stability and predictability in earnings. Another problem was that the time horizon for the incentive pay was too long—year-long profit sharing schemes were too distant for production workers because they could not see the link between their performance and their reward that far ahead. The scheme was modified in 1996 to reintroduce some smaller discretionary bonuses that were granted when the bonus-worthy work took place.

The Future

The ABB PBS joint venture was only three years old in the spring of 1996. By that time, the legal privatization of industry in the Czech Republic was essentially completed. The first five years of the transition from central planning to market economy for Czech companies was over. This meant that some of the most extreme external stresses on companies, such as loss of markets and lack of finance, were behind them. The Czech economy appeared to be strong and growing.

By 1996, most of the major restructuring of ABB PBS was completed. Most of the easier internal changes had been made. Plant and equipment had been improved, and product quality was in good shape. Richard Kuba and his colleagues had accomplished a lot, but they were not satisfied. Some

of the hard changes were yet to be made, and the outlook for the company was mixed.

Doing business in competitive western markets was much more rugged than Kuba expected. Financial results were sufficient given the difficult business conditions the company faced, but they were not good enough for a mature market economy. Kuba knew there was overcapacity in the industry worldwide. There were tens of relatively small companies like his, and some of them would not survive. Belonging to the ABB network had advantages of course, but it also brought problems. Cooperation with ABB sister companies in marketing and technology was mirrored by competition and sibling rivalry with companies from cultures with which Kuba and his colleagues were unfamiliar. Internally, the transformation of ABB PBS's considerable human capital required renewed focus. Kuba could not rest easily yet.

CASE DISCUSSION QUESTIONS

1. How does the joint venture meet the needs of both companies? Where does it fall short?
2. What are likely to be the greatest challenges for the joint venture? What role might cultural differences between ABB and PBS play?
3. What actions are necessary for ABB PBS top management to undertake to secure the long-term success of the company?

CASE CREDIT

By Stanley D. Nollen, Karen L. Newman, and Jacqueline M. Abbey, of the School of Business, Georgetown University, Washington, D.C. 20057. Copyright © by the Case Research Journal and Stanley D. Nollen, Karen L. Newman, and Jacqueline M. Abbey.

Multinational E-Commerce: Strategies and Structures

10

Learning Objectives

After reading this chapter you should be able to:

- Define the forms of e-commerce.
- Appreciate the growing presence of e-commerce in the global economy.
- Understand the structure of the Internet economy.
- Identify the basic component of a successful e-commerce strategy.
- Know the basic multinational e-commerce business models.
- Identify the practicalities of running a multinational e-commerce business.
- Understand the function of enablers in multinational e-commerce operations.

Preview CASE IN POINT

The Global Internet Economy

The Internet and electronic commerce (e-commerce) is seen as drastically changing how international business is done. The Internet allows any company to create a virtual and global presence to conduct operations around the world. The Internet also allows a multinational company to dramatically alter the way it presents and communicates with global customers. Web presence can give any company the ability to advertise and present useful information that is seen as critical in influencing purchasing decisions. In fact, product-based web sites are becoming increasingly important as an advertising medium. Furthermore, the Internet enables companies to analyze their value chain to become more efficient and competitive by implementing e-commerce initiatives across their value chains.

It is predicted that this trend will accelerate in the future. Consider the following facts supporting the Internet economy and e-commerce:

- The latest figures (March 2006) suggest that approximately 16 percent of the world or 1.02 billion consumers now has access to the Internet. As countries like China and India continue to develop their Internet infrastructure, this access will accelerate.
- In countries such as South Korea, Iceland, Denmark, Germany, Norway, and the United Kingdom, more than 55 percent of households have access to the Internet. As an example, online sales in the United Kingdom are expected to increase to nearly $55 billion in 2007, an increase of 51 percent over 2006.
- Broadband, which is considered one of the fastest modes of Internet connection, continues to grow at a rapid pace.
- By 2006, close to 27 percent of Internet users in Central and Eastern Europe will go online at least once a month. E-commerce spending in Central and Eastern Europe is expected to reach

$17.6 billion by 2006, with 90 percent of spending in business-to-business transactions.

- According to Forrester Research, online retail sales in the United States are expected to increase from $172 billion in 2005 to more than $329 billion in 2010, representing a 14 percent compound growth over the five-year period.
- The United Nations predicts that 18 percent of purchases made by firms and individuals will be conducted online.
- Only 36.5 percent of the global online population are native English speakers, followed by Chinese (12.2 percent), Japanese (9.5 percent), Spanish (8 percent) and German (7 percent).
- Business Web users are three times more likely to make a purchase when using an e-commerce site in their own language.

Sources: Adapted from; Cyr, Dianne, Carole Bonanni, John Bowes, and Joe Ilsever. 2005. "Beyond trust: Web site design preferences across cultures." Journal of Global Information Management. 13, 4, October–December, pp. 25–54; Interactive Media in Retail Group 2006; Internet Economy Indicators 2001, http://www.Internetindicators.com; Slyke, Craig Van, France Belanger, and Varadharajan Sridhar. 2005. "A comparison of American and Indian consumers' perceptions of electronic commerce." Information Resources Management Journal. 18, 2, April–June, pp. 24–40.

Although still small by comparison to the traditional economy, the Internet economy is booming and growing faster than any other business trend in history. As shown in the Preview Case in Point, the Internet economy is not only growing exponentially but it is also a worldwide phenomenon. Consequently, multinational managers must be knowledgeable in all aspects of e-commerce and must be prepared to use the Internet as a new global platform for multinational business transactions.

Earlier chapters discussed many of the intricacies involved in developing multinational strategies and building the organizations to implement these strategies effectively. This chapter will show that new opportunities exist for companies to expand their multinational operations via the Web and the Internet.

Many of the issues involved in doing multinational business over the Web are similar to those faced by traditional multinational companies. However, the next generation of multinational managers must address many unique issues in formulating and implementing multinational strategies for the Internet economy.

This chapter will provide essential background on the nature of e-commerce and the Internet economy. First, the chapter considers basic e-commerce strategies, structures, and operations. Second, the chapter considers issues unique to the multinational company including the costs and benefits of globalizing via the Internet, basic multinational e-commerce models, and practical issues associated with multinational e-commerce such as web-site design. After reading this chapter and considering the array of multinational management issues considered earlier, you should gain a good understanding of and appreciation for the e-commerce challenges multinational companies must face now and in the immediate future.

The Internet Economy

What Is E-Commerce?

E-commerce refers to the selling of goods or services over the Internet. These goods or services include those delivered offline, such as UPS shipping a book purchased through Amazon.com to a customer anywhere in the world. They also include goods and services delivered online, such as downloaded computer software. When most people talk about e-commerce, they focus on two types of transactions. The first type is business-to-consumer transactions such as buying toys from eToys. The acronym **B2C** is commonly used to refer to these transactions. The second type represents selling among businesses, or business-to-business transactions. This is the **B2B** component of e-commerce. B2B transactions make up 70 to 85 percent of current e-commerce business. This high proportion of B2B relative to B2C is expected to continue in the future.[1]

One of the most important reasons for the significance of B2B e-commerce comes from the revolution in supply chain management made possible by electronic links between businesses and suppliers. Information sharing between business customers and suppliers allows suppliers to know what their customers want and allows businesses to know price, availability, and product characteristics immediately.

For example, Ericsson, the Swedish mobile phone giant, has gone to paperless procurement. It uses the company's local network or intranet to find approved suppliers. The intranet provides links to the supplier's web sites, and a purchase is made within predefined levels. Prior to this system, Ericsson spent an average of $100 on every order processed. The reduction in paperwork has reduced the average transaction cost to $15.[2] Similarly, Microsoft uses an intranet procurement process called Microsoft Market that reduced its business purchase transaction costs from $60 to $5.[3] Exhibit 10.1 shows how e-commerce activities work along the value chain.

E-commerce
The selling of goods or services over the Internet.

B2C
Business-to-consumer transactions.

B2B
Business-to-business transactions.

EXHIBIT 10.1   E-Commerce Value Chain

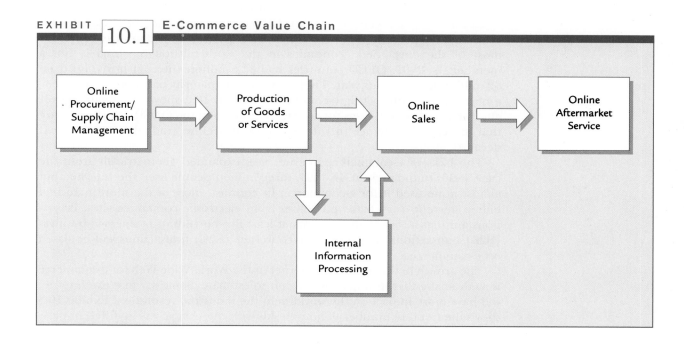

Recent longitudinal research in the United States confirms the pervasiveness of Internet usage across the value chain. A large number of firms were studied in 1998 and 2000. Researchers found that the top ten uses of the Internet for the companies had shifted from information posting in 1998 to more strategic operations in 2000. For instance, in 1998, the top ten Internet uses in these companies included activities such as product information, advertising, customer suggestions, newsletters, and job information. However, in 2000, the top Internet uses included new categories such as selling products, recruiting operations, and project coordination. The most interesting finding showed that all companies experienced increased Internet use across the value chain. The companies surveyed were making increased use of the Internet to facilitate value-chain activities such as human resources, sales, advertising and other operations.[4] This study shows that the future will likely see more e-commerce at all levels of the value chain.

In addition to these e-commerce models, the Internet has spawned other forms of business transactions. eBay is a global player in the **C2C** (consumer-to-consumer) business of auctions. Anyone can sell something online and place bids for items. Other forms of business transactions to consider might be **C2B** (consumer-to-business). Examples of these firms include price comparison web sites such as http://www.addall.com, which searches online bookstores throughout the world to provide price comparisons and shipping and delivery information.

What is the current global presence of e-commerce? Recent reports from OECD (Organization for Economic Cooperation and Development) use two indicators.[5] One is the number of secure servers. A **secure server** is an Internet host that allows users to send encrypted data so that those outside the connection cannot see the information. Such servers are necessary for e-commerce to thrive because they encourage users to send credit card information over the Internet. A second indicator of the presence of e-commerce is the number of **Internet hosts**. Any computer connected to the Internet with its own Internet Protocol address is considered a server in OECD statistics. An Internet Protocol address is a unique address that a computer has on the Web so that other Internet users can access the public information on the computer.

According to a recent report,[6] OECD countries dominate the Internet with more than 90 percent of the world's Internet hosts. OECD countries represent most of the developed economies in the world although China is not a member. By 2002, OECD countries had 112 million Internet hosts, up from 82 million the previous year. They also had the majority of secure web servers, a necessity for conducting e-commerce. Exhibit 10.2 shows the secure server and Internet host rankings for selected countries in the OECD. Projections are that the U.S. dominance in Internet use will decline gradually over the next decade.

The basis of e-commerce, Internet use, expanded geometrically from the early 1990s to the present. In 1991, three million people used the Internet, but almost none used it for e-commerce. In contrast, most of the more than half billion current users make purchases from electronic commerce sites. Projections are that in less than five years at least five percent of business-to-business (B2B) transactions and business-to-consumer (B2C) transactions will be based on e-commerce.

The growth in the use of the Internet or the World Wide Web for e-commerce is so dramatic that its impact is difficult to estimate. Some say that the Internet will have more impact on the world than the industrial revolution. Exhibit 10.3 shows the trend in number of households with Internet access in different parts

C2C

Consumer-to-consumer transactions.

C2B

Consumer-to-business transactions.

Secure server

An Internet host that allows users to send and receive encrypted data.

Internet hosts

Computers connected to the Internet with its own IP address.

EXHIBIT
10.2

Internet Hosts (per thousand inhabitants) and Secure Servers (per million inhabitants) in OECD Countries

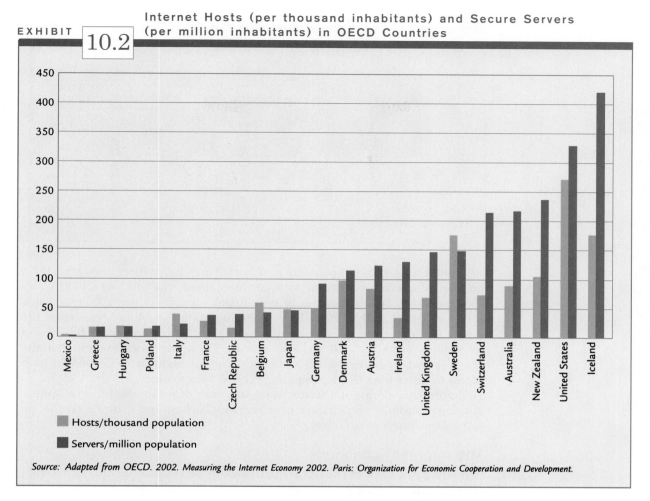

Hosts/thousand population

Servers/million population

Source: Adapted from OECD. 2002. Measuring the Internet Economy 2002. Paris: Organization for Economic Cooperation and Development.

of the world according to recent estimates.[7] Such consistent growth suggests tremendous opportunities for multinational companies to use the Internet as a tool for conducting business worldwide at any point in the value chain from procurement of raw materials to eventual sales. China also presents companies with significant opportunities. Consider the following Focus on Emerging Markets.

The OECD[8] sees broadband development as a critical aspect of the Internet and e-commerce. Broadband is a combination of digital technologies that allows rapid transmission of data and other digital services, often simultaneously. It is seen as a major reason why people adopt information and technology products and services. In turn, the OECD believes that such adoption can result in economic growth, facilitating social and cultural development and even innovation. Broadband also allows small and medium firms to benefit from higher efficiency through faster information exchanges. The OECD[9] also argues that broadband adoption can benefit governments through the efficient and increased availability of high interest services such as health, education, and other social services.

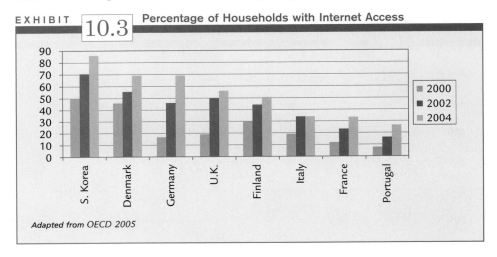

EXHIBIT 10.3   Percentage of Households with Internet Access

Adapted from OECD 2005

Exhibit 10.4 shows the number of broadband subscribers over time for a number of selected countries. As the exhibit shows, the selected OECD countries have seen steady increase of broadband subscribers per 100 inhabitants over the period 2001 to 2005. Even emerging markets such as Mexico and the Czech Republic have seen dramatic increases in the number of broadband subscribers over the 2001 to 2005 period. These increases suggest that the Internet and e-commerce will continue its progression as more people have access to faster ways to transmit and received information.

Before considering the strategy and structure of using e-commerce in multinational business, the chapter next provides background material on the nature of the Internet economy.

The Internet Economy

According to a team of experts at the University of Texas at Austin, the Internet economy has four layers.[10] These layers are (1) the Internet infrastructure, (2) the applications infrastructure, (3) the Internet intermediaries, and (4) the Internet commerce layer.

Focus on Emerging Markets

The Internet in China

China has seen tremendous growth in Internet use over the past few years. It is estimated that in 2006, China had approximately 110 million web surfers, second only to the United States. The Chinese government estimates that the 2006 online revenues were valued at nearly $69 billion, representing a growth of 58 percent over 2005. Analysts predict that China will have the world's leading online commerce by 2010. But although China presents tremendous opportunities, multinationals also have to contend with some challenges. China's Web is constantly being monitored by more than 30,000 people to filter and delete prohibited phrases. The Chinese Web also is being targeted by scam artists and criminals ready to take advantage of naïve customers through phishing and spamming.

Source: Adapted from Barboza, David. 2006. "110 million surfers can buy sex and drugs, but Regorm is still illicit." New York Times. March 8, C1.

EXHIBIT 10.4 **Broadband Penetration**

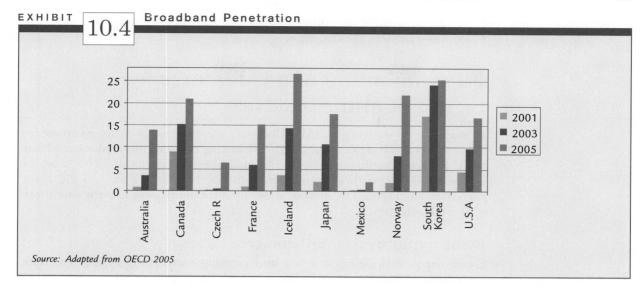

Source: Adapted from OECD 2005

Layer 1 is the backbone of the Internet including Internet service providers (ISPs), telecommunication companies, and the manufacturers of networking systems. Companies on this level include:

- Communications (Qwest, MCI, WorldCom)
- Internet Service Providers (Mindspring, AOL, Earthlink)
- Networking (Cisco, Lucent, 3Com)
- Hardware (Dell, Compaq, HP)

Layer 2 includes the companies and consultants that build web systems and supporting software. Companies on this level include:

- Consultants (Scient)
- Commerce applications (Netscape, Sun, IBM)
- Web development software (Adobe, Netobjects)
- Search engine software (Verity)
- Web-enabled databases (Oracle)

Layer 3 includes a new type of company that provides linking services on the Internet and derives its revenues from commissions, advertising, and membership fees. Examples of these companies include:

- Online travel agencies (TravelWeb, Travelocity.com)
- Online brokerages (Etrade)
- Content aggregators (Cnet, Zdnet)
- Online advertising (Yahoo!)

Level 4 includes companies that conduct commercial transactions over the Web. Amazon.com and drugstore.com provide examples of companies from this layer. Other examples include:

- E-retailers (wine.com, diamond.com)
- Manufacturers selling directly (hpshopping.com, Dell)
- Subscription-based companies (vrbo.com)

- Transportation services (most airlines)
- Shipping services (FedEx, UPS)

Fundamentals of e-commerce Strategy and Structure

E-commerce is evolving quickly. However, the failures of many e-commerce start-ups demonstrate that the Internet economy is not without risks. Each layer of the Internet economy has its threats and opportunities. Exhibit 10.5 provides a summary of these threats and opportunities. In this section, you will learn current strategies used by successful e-commerce companies to overcome some of these challenges.

Steps for Successful E-Commerce Strategy

E-commerce strategizing is a new and evolving management challenge. The multinational manager must build on sound, basic strategizing as a prelude to

EXHIBIT 10.5   E-Commerce Business Models: Openings and Barriers for Going Global

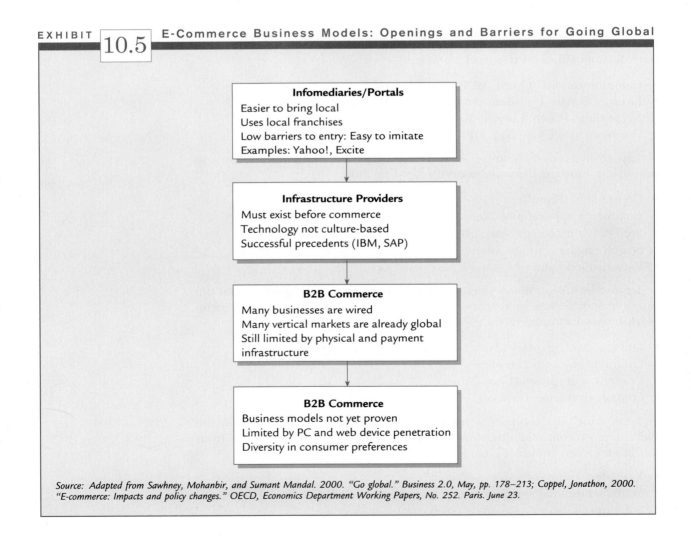

Infomediaries/Portals
Easier to bring local
Uses local franchises
Low barriers to entry: Easy to imitate
Examples: Yahoo!, Excite

Infrastructure Providers
Must exist before commerce
Technology not culture-based
Successful precedents (IBM, SAP)

B2B Commerce
Many businesses are wired
Many vertical markets are already global
Still limited by physical and payment infrastructure

B2B Commerce
Business models not yet proven
Limited by PC and web device penetration
Diversity in consumer preferences

Source: Adapted from Sawhney, Mohanbir, and Sumant Mandal. 2000. "Go global." Business 2.0, May, pp. 178–213; Coppel, Jonathon, 2000. "E-commerce: Impacts and policy changes." OECD, Economics Department Working Papers, No. 252. Paris. June 23.

multinational operations. Experts[11] suggest key basic steps for building a successful e-commerce strategy. These include:

- *Leadership.* Successful e-commerce is only possible through dynamic and strong leadership. At a minimum, CEO and senior executives should strongly believe in the benefits of an e-commerce approach. They also should have expertise in order to objectively assess the company's position on e-commerce in order to craft the most appropriate e-commerce strategy.

- *Build on current business models and experiment with new e-commerce models.* Search for ways to use the e-commerce business to reduce costs or enhance services offered by the traditional business. E-commerce transactions can be cheap, yet they can add value to customers. Customers can get timely updates such as American Airlines Alert, an e-mail service to notify customers of changes in schedules.

- *Meet the challenge of developing an e-commerce organization.* The basic choice involves the distinction between a separate autonomous entity for e-commerce business and a seamless integration into the current model. The integrated model works best when it is difficult to separate e-commerce from the existing organization without confusing the customer. This also requires senior management commitment to using the Internet aggressively as part of the company's strategy. Not only senior management but also the entire firm must be prepared to embrace the e-commerce model as did Egghead Software when it moved entirely to a Web-based business.

- *Allocate resources to the e-commerce business.* A successful e-commerce strategy must commit financial, human, and technological resources to developing e-commerce capabilities. If these capabilities do not exist within the organization, then selected e-commerce operations are outsourced to third parties or to strategic alliance partners. Many companies such as Wal-Mart, Kmart and Target have made supply-chain arrangements with their suppliers for their online customers.

- *Build a superior e-commerce infrastructure as a basis of a differentiation strategy.* Possible sources of differentiation include the following. Build web sites with superior online experiences. Gulfstream, for example, sells multimillion-dollar jets on its interactive site (http://www.gulfstreampreowned.com).[12] Personalize the interaction to each customer. Streamline and simplify transactions. Some companies even use web sites to offer product information to guide customers to their stores. For instance, both Office Depot and Best Buy provide their customers the ability to buy products in their store. Even Amazon.com can direct its customers to Borders if the customers don't want to wait for their books to be shipped.

- *Have an e-commerce strategy.* Companies should ensure that e-commerce is not implemented haphazardly. The company can use some of the techniques discussed in Chapter 5 on strategic management to implement a strong and adequate strategic e-commerce plan. Some of the most recent experiences suggest that a well-positioned brand name is very critical for repeat purchases. However, companies need to ensure that they offer reliable customer service as customer service often is seen as being more critical than a strong brand. It also is not always necessary to offer the same products as in physical locations. Companies such as Office Depot typically offer more products online while companies such as Costco have smaller and more specialized product offerings.

- *Develop appropriate e-commerce systems.* **Appropriate systems need to be implemented to fully benefit from e-commerce.** There has to be a cultural transformation in the way information flows through the organization. The company has to work hard to remove traditional barriers to ensure that there are increased coordination and information flows among the various functional areas such as manufacturing, sales, service, and shipping. Any company serious about e-commerce must also align human resource policies and compensation with desired e-commerce goals.
- *Measure success.* Companies need to have metrics in place to measure e-commerce success. Obvious output success measures include web site hits, number of new e-commerce customers, e-commerce revenue, and number of customers learning about new products to purchase through other channels. Companies also can assess other process success measures such as degree of top management commitment to e-commerce and assessment of e-commerce integration across internal and external operations.

There are a number of other things that multinationals should avoid if they want to be successful at e-commerce. Exhibit 10.6 provides a summary of e-commerce "don'ts" based on best practices.

The Internet economy has spawned numerous new companies. At the same time, it has provided opportunities for traditional companies to use this evolving business tool. Next, you will see one of the major issues faced by traditional companies when they add e-commerce to their current businesses.

E-Commerce Structure: Integrated or Autonomous

Each company needs to decide how e-commerce fits into its existing organizational design and management systems. Writing in the *Harvard Business Review*, Ranjay Gulati of Northwestern University and Jason Garino of the Boston Consulting Group[13] call this the "right mixture of bricks and clicks." They mean that companies must decide how much to integrate their evolving Internet operations into their traditional business operations. In the evolving e-commerce jargon, traditional business operations are often called the **brick-and-mortar** part of the company.

Brick-and-mortar

Traditional or nonvirtual business operation.

The degree of integration between brick-and-mortar operations and the Internet business can occur anywhere in the value chain from procurement of raw material to after-sales service. Additionally, the degree of integration can

EXHIBIT 10.6   Don'ts of E-commerce

> Don't treat online customers as secondary or inferior customers. Treat them like regular customers and give them the needed attention.
> Don't rely on technology as a solution for all of your problems. Technology can be useful only if wisely used.
> Don't compete solely on price. Online customers also appreciate value-added services such as convenience and selection.
> Don't rely solely on self-service and automated systems. Similar to traditional customers, online customers also like to talk with people when they have
> Market appropriately. You don't want to wait for customers to find you.

Source: Based on Lager, Marshall. 2006. "E-commerce best practices." Customer Relationship Management, 10, 6, pp. 22–25, 27.

range from the near-seamless operation of an Office Depot to the mostly independent operations of Barnes & Noble and Barnesandnoble.com.

Each choice has benefits. The independent operation can move faster and be more entrepreneurial when freed from corporate bureaucracy. It can seek funding from the deep pockets of venture capitalists willing to invest in e-commerce companies. The integrated operation, on the other hand, can benefit from cross-promotion of shared products, shared customer information, increased large-quantity purchasing leverage, and economies of scale by using the same distribution channels.[14]

The choice between seamless integration and a fully autonomous unit is not simple and seldom is clear cut. The best option for most companies is something in between. As with most strategy implementation issues, managers must evaluate their company's particular situation to make an informed decision. Exhibit 10.7 shows a decision model with the questions that managers must consider when choosing the best level of integration for the e-commerce unit.

Although Exhibit 10.7 provides useful guidance regarding the appropriate level of integration, recent experiences suggest that more companies in the U.S. are taking steps to integrate their online and offline channels.[15] Customers are getting more sophisticated about their purchases and often use channels that

EXHIBIT 10.7   Key Decisions in the Web Business Integration Versus Separation Decision

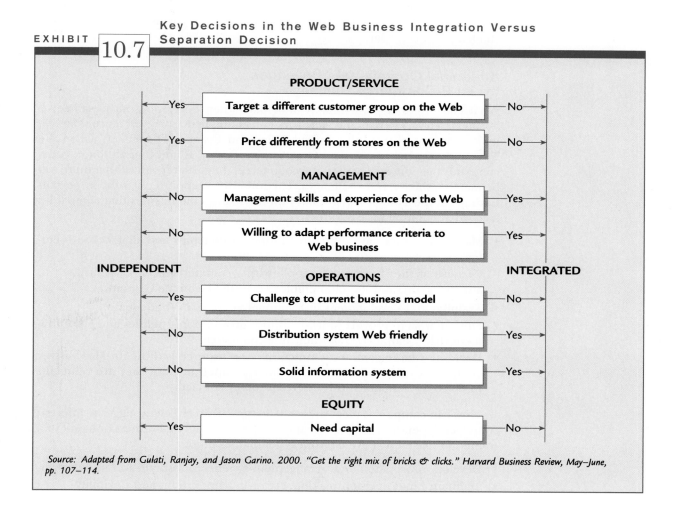

Source: Adapted from Gulati, Ranjay, and Jason Garino. 2000. "Get the right mix of bricks & clicks." Harvard Business Review, May–June, pp. 107–114.

offer the best prices. These customers get frustrated if they are not informed of appropriate pricing or inventory differences between a retailer's online and offline offerings. The following discusses some of the ways companies can integrate their online and offline operations:[16]

- *Keep customers informed.* Most retailers find it impossible to maintain the same pricing and inventories on their web sites and in their stores. However, this discrepancy does not have to be a source of frustration for consumers. Companies often find that their customers appreciate being informed of such differences.
- *Integrate business operations.* Retailers can add value for their customers by integrating their business operations. For instance, some retailers such as Costco allow consumers to return products purchased online in stores while others like Best Buy allow consumers to pick up products in a store that were purchased online.
- *Share customer data across channels.* More companies are realizing the benefits of sharing customer data across channels. For instance, retailers can send tailored product emails based on store purchases. Segmentation campaigns cross channels (online vs. in-store) can be compared to get better insights on customer purchasing behaviors.

Although the level of e-commerce integration is a crucial decision in implementing an e-commerce strategy, there are numerous other operational challenges to consider.

Additional Operational Challenges for an E-Commerce Business

What challenges can a company anticipate when developing an e-commerce business? Towers Perrin, the New York consulting firm, surveyed more than 300 major companies from the United States and Europe. The survey, called the Towers Perrin Internetworked Organization Survey, found that although many companies see the advantages of e-commerce, they also recognize that there will be many problems and challenges. The following section reports the important findings of the Towers Perrin survey on the management issues that companies face when running an e-business.

- Many companies have difficulty finding partnerships and alliances with customers or third parties.
- Because of the shortage of people with e-commerce skills, it is difficult to attract, retain, and, develop employees in the e-commerce unit.
- Training and development in e-commerce are not yet adequate.
- Finding ways to provide individuals with growth opportunities and job fulfillment drives employee retention in e-commerce.
- Deciding what e-commerce functions to outsource is difficult. Most survey companies outsource many e-commerce functions, but they are reluctant to do so for functions with direct customer contact.

How can companies meet these challenges? Towers Perrin suggests different strategies depending on whether the company is a pure e-business or a unit of a traditional business. Pure e-business companies must:

- Develop information and management systems to respond to rapid growth.
- Maintain rapid decision making, creativity, innovation, and flexibility.

- Build external relationships with e-commerce support companies and customers.
- Attract and retain e-commerce-capable talent.
- Develop an effective management team.

Traditional companies with e-commerce units must:

- Build a common vision and commitment to the e-commerce operation throughout the organization.
- Change the organizational structure to emphasize quick reconfiguration of assets and capabilities.
- Change the organizational culture to create a supporting environment for e-commerce.
- Attract and retain e-commerce-skilled employees.
- Alter HR programs to suit the different skill requirements of e-commerce employees.

Exhibits 10.8 shows the organizational changes multinational companies are making to implement their e-commerce strategies.

However, as more companies and institutions take advantage of e-commerce and its applications, companies are facing a new and important challenge: e-commerce security[17] E-commerce security refers to the degree to which customers feel that their private, personal information can be safeguarded in the hands of online companies collecting such information. Hundreds of millions of people around the world provide personal information on the Internet as they browse or purchase products and services online.[18] How such information is collected and stored and what is done with it is a source of obvious concern for most Internet users. Furthermore, attacks on popular web sites are increasing rapidly. Such attacks have resulted in theft of credit card numbers of thousands of customers. Specific industries such as online banking are suffering significant Internet attacks through phishing and Trojan horses.[19] Banking regulators suggest that online bank frauds may drain from two to five percent of a bank's overall revenue. Furthermore, recent observations suggest that cyber-criminals are becoming increasingly sophisticated.[20] Instead of attacking operating systems and Internet services on the Web, cyber-criminals now are focusing on applications and other network devices operating systems. Cyber-criminals are also emphasizing specific vulnerabilities within certain companies.

As the Internet becomes a crucial medium of international trade and commerce, countries are also being urged to improve Internet security. Both European Union and ASEAN (Association of South East Asian Countries including Singapore, Thailand, Malaysian, and Indonesia) are being encouraged to improve Internet security and also minimize abuse as many online scams and phishing tend to originate in some of these member countries.

Multinationals also are being encouraged to take appropriate measures to beef up their Internet security. Specifically, most companies need to be concerned about a number of information security issues.[21] These include 1) confidentiality (making sure that private information is protected), 2) availability (ensuring that information is accessible to authorized users), 3) integrity (ensuring that the information collected is accurate and reliable), and 4) authentication (having systems in place to ensure that persons using the systems are legitimate). Companies are also under increased pressure to protect the privacy of individuals as more and more personal information is being

E-commerce security
Degree to which customers feel that their private and personal information is safeguarded by companies collecting such information.

Recent and Expected Organizational Changes in Major Multinational Companies Building E-Commerce Businesses

10.8

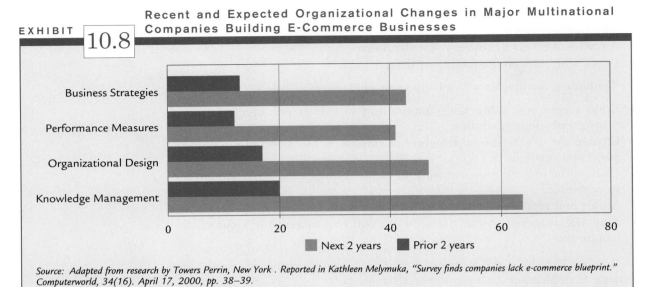

Source: Adapted from research by Towers Perrin, New York . Reported in Kathleen Melymuka, "Survey finds companies lack e-commerce blueprint." Computerworld, 34(16). April 17, 2000, pp. 38–39.

collected, stored, and shared by companies involved in industries such as health care, banking and finance, travel, and the government.[22]

To ensure that these Internet security issues are addressed, experts[23] suggest the following:

- *Use firewalls, intrusion detection software, and antivirus shields.* Multinational companies need to have systems in place to keep outsiders from entering private networks. Various companies specialize in providing technologies to protect a company's network.

- *Encrypt data.* Most companies and multinationals are transmitting and transporting huge amounts of data over fiber optics communication lines and servers or hard drives. As more instances of data theft emerge, it is critical for companies to adequately encrypt data so that they are meaningless if they fall into the hands of criminals.

- *Require two-phased authentication.* To prevent unauthorized access to information, more multinationals are now requiring two-phased authentication. Such systems require two forms of identity, namely a password and some identity token such as a key fob or other device. There also is an increased use of biometrics (the measurement of physiological or behavioral characteristics of individuals such as fingerprints or retina) as a source of identity.[24] Although biometrics technology is relatively new, more companies are going that way as it provides an unambiguous means to identify people.[25]

- *Use web site monitoring tools.* Multinationals are well advised to use technology to monitor web sites to detect any unusual page requests or other suspicious activity. Monitoring will provide some warning if a web site is being attacked or is about to be attacked.

- *Abide by privacy rules.* Most multinationals are required to disclose data collection practices before personal or other private information is collected.[26] Consumers and web users must have the choice to decide whether to allow collected information to be used for other purposes. Consumers also must have the ability to review and correct collected data.

The preceding sections reviewed the basic strategies, structures, and challenges managers face when developing an e-commerce business. The following sections will discuss some of the additional challenges faced when companies choose to move their e-commerce operations into the multinational domain.

Globalizing through the Internet

The increase in information exchanges and efficiency due to the Internet and e-commerce has made it possible for companies to reach customers worldwide to become global companies. However, the Internet also is enabling the emergence of a new form of multinational, the **born-global firms**.[27] As we saw in Chapter 7 on Small Businesses as Multinational Companies, from the day they are created, born-global firms are able to obtain a significant portion of their revenues from sales in international markets. Unlike other companies that tend to operate in the domestic market and then gradually expand to foreign markets, born-global firms tend to adopt a global view of markets and develop competitive advantages to succeed in the various markets.[28] Recent research suggests that born-global firms increasingly are appearing in large numbers in industrialized countries with more than 1,000 born-global firms estimated in the United States[29] and others in countries such as Denmark and Australia.[30]

Although the above shows that a web site immediately gives the entire world access to a company's products or services, many of the challenges of globalization faced by traditional brick-and-mortar companies remain. A company still must solve the global–local dilemma discussed in detail in Chapter 6. Managers must decide whether the company's products or services are global in content and delivery or whether they require localization to national or regional levels. E-commerce companies also must address the traditional multinational business problems relating to national and business cultures and national institutional contexts (e.g., currencies/payments, local laws, and infrastructure for delivery or procurement). Other chapters consider these issues in more detail. This section adds to the understanding of multinational strategy formulation and implementation by considering some issues unique to the e-commerce operation.

Born-global firms

Firms that generate a significant portion of their revenues from international sales the day they are founded.

Multinational E-Commerce Strategy Formulation

The Nature of the Business

What kind of e-business is easiest to take global? To a large degree, it depends on the types of products or services offered through e-commerce. The next section reviews these differences.

According to e-commerce experts, Mohanbir Sawhney and Sumant Mandal,[31] e-commerce companies work in three areas. Some move bits or computerized information; others move money in payment flows; still others move physical products. Each type of operation requires an infrastructure to support the transaction. Telecommunications infrastructures support moving bits. A payment infrastructure allows the movement of money. Moving physical goods requires physical infrastructure. The ease of taking e-commerce international depends mostly on the mix of infrastructures required.

Sawhney and Mandal argue that there is a hierarchy of difficulty in e-commerce depending on infrastructure requirements. Portals and infomediaries provide gateways to the Internet. Portals are primarily search engines to locate web sites while infomediaries go a step further by providing not only links but also information such as current news. They were also the first e-business forms to have a global presence.

At the next level are businesses such as Travelocity, digital music, and software vendors. Although they do not move physical objects, they still must rely on local infrastructure to take payments for their products. The technical and managerial challenge comes from dealing with issues such as credit card payments (fraud and lack of use in some areas), currency conversion, and a bewildering array of tax jurisdictions. Most difficult to globalize are e-commerce businesses that rely on a physical infrastructure. Like their brick-and-mortar counterparts, these businesses must ship goods that fulfill customer orders and manage their supply chains located throughout the world. In addition, they must deal with the challenges of receiving payments through a variety of payment infrastructures.

For e-businesses that also require a physical infrastructure in the countries where they operate, large multinational firms that enter e-commerce with an existing global presence often have an advantage. The have in place brick-and-mortar units or they have the resources to establish a physical base in each country of operation to maintain localized web sites. Smaller firms and firms new to the complexities of multinational commerce face more challenges in establishing an international presence.

Basic Opportunities and Threats of Multinational E-Commerce

In deciding whether to globalize their e-commerce operations—either as an existing brick-and-mortar company or as a pure e-commerce company—managers need to weigh the attractions and deterrents of international e-commerce.[32] Again, this is a traditional strategy formulation problem: they must consider the opportunities and threats before deciding on a strategy. However, the e-commerce environment has some unique characteristics. Consider the following attractions and deterrents.[33]

The major attractions of e-commerce globalization are:

- *Cost reduction.* It can be less expensive to reach international customers via the Web.
- *Technology.* The technology to reach anyone with an Internet-linked computer is readily available.
- *Efficiencies.* Electronic communication and processes can be more efficient.
- *Convenience.* The Web is in operation seven days a week and twenty-four hours a day regardless of location.
- *Speed of access.* Once a web site is running, a company's products or services can be accessed immediately from anywhere in the world.

Some deterrents include:

- *Return/receipt burden and cost of delivery.* If the pattern follows catalog sales, businesses should expect a 30 to 40 percent return rate for online purchases.[34]
- *Costs of site construction, maintenance, upgrades.* Web site construction and maintenance in multiple languages, currencies, and tax locations can cost companies millions of dollars per year.
- *Channel conflicts.* Distributors and retailers that sell a company's products may be undermined by competition from a company's web site that sells directly to end users. This conflict is a major fear of many automobile dealers if the

manufacturers were to sell directly from the factory. Consider what is happening to travel agents as more people buy tickets online directly from the airline companies.

- *Easily copied models.* Local competitors can easily see and copy a multinational's product, service, or business model if it is displayed on the Web.
- *Cultural differences.* It can be difficult to understand global customers and overcome cultural barriers and language differences on the Web. Web sites not only must be multilingual but also must present a format that is appropriate culturally.
- *Traditional cross-border transaction complexities.* These issues include pricing for exchange rates, different taxes, and government regulations.
- *Standard or local web sites.* Companies must decide whether to standardize or localize web sites to the local context.
- *Customer trust and satisfaction.* Companies must determine whether customers abroad will trust and are satisfied with e-commerce in general and their web sites in particular.

The following Case in Point gives an example of how one company overcame cultural differences, to succeed in Japan.

Picking a Market

One expert, Clay Shirky,[35] suggests that Web entrepreneurs should target countries based on two factors. First, attractive markets for e-commerce are those with market inefficiencies. Shirky claims that many formerly state-controlled markets have suboptimal economic performance. In these markets, e-commerce shopping allows buyers to obtain better quality and lower prices because they are free from state control. Second, target markets with attractive demographic characteristics. These target markets include locations with an Internet population of at least five percent, a high literacy rate (to predict future growth of the Internet population), a country that participates in at least one free trade agreement, and a government with a viable legal system.

In Shirky's opinion, e-commerce potential is great in South America because of the Mercosur trade group and in Southeast Asian countries with membership

---

C A S E   I N   P O I N T

Adapting E-commerce to Cultural Differences

Retailers agree that although Internet access is spreading and more consumers are becoming comfortable with e-commerce, significant cultural differences exist that pose serious challenges to e-commerce. Consider the case of Handango, which decided to expand to Japan after it noticed that Japanese customers were purchasing from its U.S. web sites. Although the company was encouraged to find that there are no shipping restrictions for its products, it quickly faced significant barriers. For instance, it found that Japanese consumers prefer to make online payments using a method called konbini. This method requires consumers to go to a local convenience store to make a cash payment. The clerk then transfers the money to the vendor's online account. Handango decided to form a partnership with a local consumer-electronics company to handle the marketing and sales aspect of its operations.

Source: Adapted from Bright, Becky. 2006. "E-commerce: How do you say "web"? Planning to take your online business international." Wall Street Journal, May 23, p. R11.

in the Asean trade group. He also suggests that the European Union is the next boom area for e-commerce because many countries such as France, Italy, and Germany retain market inefficiencies from pre-Union days. The open borders and common currency in the EU should be a fertile ground for e-commerce growth.

Not all countries are equally e-commerce ready. The population must have access to computers and infrastructure links to the Internet. Governments and financial institutions must be ready to protect and process e-commerce transactions. In Exhibit 10.9, you can see a ranking of the e-commerce readiness of selected countries. The e-commerce readiness scale is developed by the Economist Intelligence Unit[36] and is based on a number of factors that determine how suitable a market is to Internet-based opportunities. A score of 10 indicates perfect e-readiness.

It is important to note that the most recent e-readiness scale[37] shows that poorer countries are climbing the e-readiness scale much faster than wealthier countries. A comparison of 2006 to previous years also shows that most countries are experiencing significant improvements in the scale. This improvement suggests that Internet-based market opportunities will stay strong and that any multinational manager considering an e-commerce strategy must carefully consider this information.

The enormous growth in e-commerce shows that the benefits of global e-commerce clearly outweigh the risks. Firms increasingly use the Internet as a tool to globalize operations. In the rapidly growing Internet environment, however, the competition is heating up. Achieving sustainable competitive advantage is difficult when competitors can easily copy business models. The following Multinational Management Challenge shows some of the threats to the dominance of e-commerce by U.S. companies.

Multinational E-Commerce Strategy Implementation

Successful implementation of a multinational e-commerce strategy requires building an appropriate organization and developing the necessary technical capabilities to conduct electronic transactions. The following sections provide an overview of various options available to multinational managers.

EXHIBIT 10.9   E-Readiness Scale

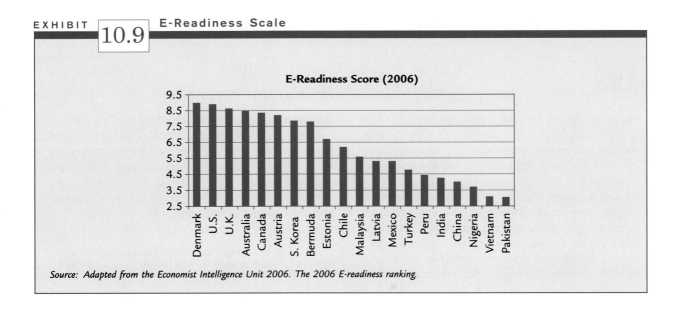

E-Readiness Score (2006)

Source: Adapted from the Economist Intelligence Unit 2006. The 2006 E-readiness ranking.

Multinational Management **Challenge**

Can U.S. Companies Stay on Top?

The United States hosts 90 percent of all commercial web sites, and 75 percent of all e-commerce takes place in the United States. The magazine, *The Economist*, asks: will the United States continue to dominate e-commerce? Maybe not. Although the existence of web sites that people can access from anywhere in the world makes crossing borders easier, *The Economist* cautions that going global may not be so easy.

Many barriers seem to exist. First, especially for retail trade, is the difficulty of delivery. As a result, some U.S. companies refuse orders from abroad. Second, at least for Europe, tax and regulatory barriers deter many U.S. e-commerce vendors. There is a perception among many Silicon Valley companies that Europe is prone to regulate everything, and e-commerce is not yet sufficiently developed to face such a challenge. Similarly, taxes in South America tend to be high on imported products. Third, many U.S. retailers left their domestic-only operations too late. Local companies in Europe and Asia are taking first-mover advantage to capture the estimated $9 billion of e-commerce retail sales in Europe and the estimated $6 billion in Asia. Finally, U.S. companies also are facing security and infrastructure issues in emerging markets such as Vietnam and the Ukraine.

Sources: Based on Bright, Becky. 2006. "E-commerce: How do you say "web"? Planning to take your online business international." Wall Street Journal, May 23, p. R11; Economist, The. 2000. "Survey e-commerce: first America, then the world," February 4, 2000.

The Multinational E-Commerce Organization

What is the organization of a multinational e-business? Amazon.com and Yahoo! provide the most likely models.[38] These organizations are three-tiered, mixing global and local functions. Corporate headquarters represents the global core that provides the vision, strategy, and leadership that drive the electronic marketing of worldwide products or services. Headquarters also provides shared services such as the network infrastructure. Managers at headquarters and in the shared functional areas have worldwide responsibility for their operations.

Local subsidiaries, which actually deliver the goods, take charge of functions better done locally, such as managing the supply chain and dealing with local regulations. These organizations try to solve the global–local dilemma with the global integration of similar technical functions such as web-server design while still making necessary local adaptations such as web-site translations.[39] Exhibit 10.10 illustrates the levels and functions of this type of organization.

Yahoo! provides the first Case in Point on page 496 of a successful mover of information within a multinational e-commerce model. Yahoo! shows an effective balance between the global and local requirements of an e-commerce site.

Technical Capabilities and Implementation Options For Multinational E-Commerce

Components of a successful multinational online presence require electronic capabilities and support throughout the value chain.[40] Such capabilities include:

- Software to process pricing in multiple currencies. The most sophisticated software not only supports payment-processing systems that show prices in

EXHIBIT **10.10**   **Organizational Structures of the Multinational E-Corporation**

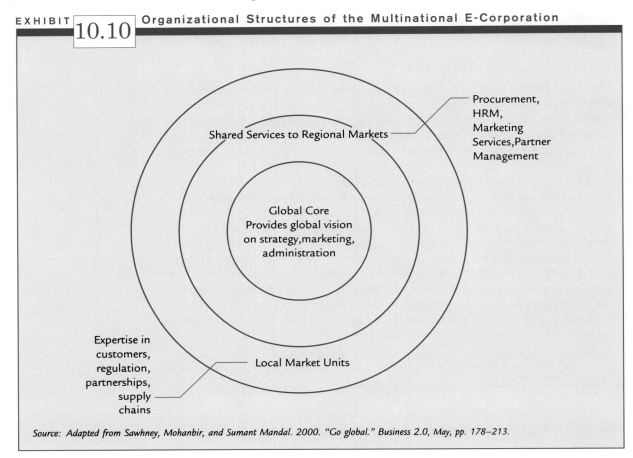

Source: Adapted from Sawhney, Mohanbir, and Sumant Mandal. 2000. "Go global." Business 2.0, May, pp. 178–213.

multiple currencies but also accepts payment in the customer's preferred currency.
- Systems that calculate and show purchase information on international shipping, duties, and local taxes such as the VAT (value-added tax common in Europe).
- Systems that check regulatory compliance with local and international laws.
- Ability to give support in multilingual service centers.
- Fraud protection.
- Electronic payment models in addition to credit cards (not used as commonly as in the United States).

Many areas of the world do not use credit and debit cards, which poses a significant problem for e-commerce. The second Case in Point on page 496 shows how 7-Eleven and other companies manage their electronic payment model without the use of credit cards.

Web sites: To Localize or Standardize

Standardized web site

Web sites that are similar in design and layout around the world.

As more multinationals use product-based web sites and corporate web sites to present, sell, and communicate with the public and their consumers, the issue of web site adaptation is becoming more critical.[41] Similar to the local–global dilemma discussed in Chapter, multinationals have to decide whether they want a **standardized web site** where the companies' web sites are fairly similar in layout

Yahoo!: Go Global; Act Local

Yahoo!, a leading Internet search engine, operates in 22 countries using 15 different languages. Evan Neufeld, director of international research for Jupiter Communications, calls Yahoo! the poster child for globalization. As of October 2005, traffic on the Yahoo! global network included more than 3.4 billion pages viewed per day on average. Yahoo! also had 411 million unique users visit the Yahoo! global web sites per month.

What is the Yahoo! formula? Yahoo! takes its basic model of site construction, making the look and feel similar everywhere, but modifies content and advertising as a country-level localization strategy. Yahoo! forms partnerships with local companies such as Spain's *Conzaón* and the BBC in England.

Conzaón provides Spanish audiences the society gossip they desire while the BBC provides U.K. users with news. In Europe, Yahoo! claims 20 million of the 38 million Internet users. In Europe alone, Yahoo! has 350 content partnerships. For e-commerce partners

overseas, Yahoo! favors local companies over U.S. companies.

Perhaps most surprising is the success of Yahoo! Japan. The highest ranking Japanese company in *BusinessWeek's* Info Tech 100, Yahoo! Japan made the bold move of launching a new product: Yahoo! Auction. With Japanese consumers' typical disdain for used good, most people predicted failure. However, CEO Inoue figured the Japanese were ready for a change. Yahoo! Auction now does $300 million in auction business each month.

Yahoo's success globally provides evidence of its superior global strategy. For example, in the first quarter of 2006, international revenues grew 32 percent to $470 million compared to the first quarter of 2005.

Source: Adapted from Businesswire. 2006. "Yahoo! reports first quarter 2006 financial results." April 18, p. 1; Kuni, Irene. 2003. "Online extra: Yahoo! Japan: King of the hill." BusinessWeek Online, June 23, 2003; Pickering, Carol. 2000. "The world's local yokel," Business 2.0, May, pp. 188, 193.

7-Eleven Shifts Thinking for Payments

E-commerce in many parts of the world is restricted because the use of credit cards is not common. How do you pay electronically without credit or debit cards? Even in an advanced industrial nation such as Japan, credit card use is much less common than in the United States. For example, in Japan, fewer than 10 percent of the transactions involve credit card payments.

In Japan, people often pay utility bills at convenience stores. Thinking creatively, 7-Eleven Japan took advantage of this existing payment structure for Web purchase payments. Japanese users of 7dream.com can select "Payment at 7-Eleven

Store" as an option, allowing them to pick up and pay for their online purchase at any of the 8,000 7-Elevens in Japan.

Similarly, Handango found that many of its German consumers would leave in the middle of their order. The company soon learned that Germans have a strong cultural bias against debt and using credit card. Handango eventually partnered with a local company to allow German customers to wire money directly from their bank accounts.

Source: Adapted from Bright, Becky. 2006. "E-commerce: How do you say "web"? Planning to take your online business international." Wall Street Journal, May 23, p. R11; Sawhney, Mohanbir, and Sumant Mandal. 2000. "Go global." Business 2.0, May, pp. 178–213.

and design around the world or a **localized web site** where the values, appeals, symbols, and even themes in the communication content is adapted to the local culture.[42]

For some companies, localization of web sites is minimal. Dell Computer has web sites in 50 countries using 21 different languages; however, it uses the same layout for the sites in all countries. In contrast, Chipshot.com, which sells golf

Localized web site

Web sites that are adapted to the local cultures.

equipment online, tailors its sites to local cultural needs. In Japan, to take advantage of the Japanese golfer's sensitivity to brand names, the Chipshot site shows brand names conspicuously and emphasizes the availability of custom-made clubs. By comparison, the U.S. site appeals to the more cost-conscious U.S. customers by emphasizing the 50-percent discount.[43]

Should companies standardize or localize? The practitioners and academic literature have been fairly silent on the subject. However, recent studies are starting to provide the guidance on the localization–standardization debate. Consider the following Case in Point examining McDonald's web sites around the world.

This study provides evidence of the influence of cultural factors on web site design and layout. Recent research also provides some guidance on appropriate web design. Exhibit 10.11 discusses high-context and low-context cultures and two of Hofstede's cultural dimensions and potential influence on web design and layout.

It also should be noted that some research suggests that cultural influences may not be as pervasive on web design.[44] Multinational companies need to determine the appropriate level of localization depending on the product, consumer preferences, and market features. However, if companies want a global web site, E. F. Sheridan,[45] president of the Web of Culture, suggests ten "mission-critical" factors that a corporate web site must use to communicate to a global audience. These factors include:

1. Link all international sites to the corporate web site.
2. If your site includes feedback or comment sections, include all nonelectronic local contact information. See http://www.novell.com for an example.

CASE IN POINT

McDonald's Web Sites Around the World

McDonald's multinational corporation currently operates in 119 nations. Given McDonald's effort to customize product offerings in the local context, it also is expected that the company will localize its web sites to satisfy local preferences. In an interesting study, Wurtz analyzed McDonald's web sites between high-context cultures (i.e., where communication is not direct but includes implicit messages contained in body language and silence) and low-context cultures (i.e., where communication occurs primarily through explicit statements through text and speech). Comparing high-context countries such as Japan, India, and South Korea with low-context countries such as Denmark, Germany, Finland, Norway, and the United States, Wurtz finds strong evidence of McDonald's web site adaptation to local cultures. For instance, the author finds more animation centered on people in high-context culture

web sites, showing preference for complexity in communication while low-context web sites are more static and use less animation. Navigation on low-context web sites tends to be more linear while high-context web sites have more new browser windows opening with less transparent guidance. The author also examines some aspects of Hofstede's cultural dimensions and how they influence web design. For instance, the highly individualistic Swiss and German web sites display images of individuals listening to music and relaxing (a very individual activity). In contrast, the Indian web site shows a man running with a child in a shopping cart, emphasizing the family ties and group approach typical of more collectivistic societies.

Source: Wurtz, Elizabeth. 2005. "A cross-cultural analysis of websites from high-context cultures and low-context cultures." Journal of Computer Mediated Communications, 11, pp. 25–43.

EXHIBIT **10.11** **Cultural Dimensions and Web Design**

Cultural Dimension	High	Low
High context vs. low context	• Provide subtle or obscure guidance for web page • Allow new browsers to open • Use animation and other cues to accommodate preference for complexity • Make fewer connections between product and individuals	• Use linear navigational guides • Restrict new browser windows • Design simple and easy to navigate web sites • Make connection between products and individual
Power distance	• Provide tall hierarchical web site structure • Provide less interaction with the company and its products and more interaction with other consumers • Use formal, ordered, and symmetric imagery to display authority (e.g., logos, crest)	• Implement flat hierarchical web site with few pages with coherent layout • Provide more access to company's products • Use fewer images to display authority
Individualism	• Use more imagery of the individual • Provide limited restricted access and more operational freedom	• Use images to display values congruent with the collective and the family • Display community work on pages

Source: Based on Mercado, Simon, K., Praveen Parboteeah, and Yushan Zhao. 2004. "Online course design and delivery: Cross-national considerations." Strategic Change, 13, 4, pp. 183–192; Wurtz, Elizabeth. 2005. "A cross-cultural analysis of websites from high-context cultures and low-context cultures." Journal of Computer Mediated Communications, 11, pp. 25–43.

3. Provide a prominent list of languages used by the company's web site. This list makes international use easier and shows a commitment to globalization. See http://www.lexmark.com for an example.
4. If your site includes downloads, use a page for global downloads for different languages.
5. Localize by language the parts of the parent company web site that receive the most access.
6. Provide a site map for the parent company's web site that includes links to all local content.
7. Provide the firm's privacy statement in all local languages.
8. Guard against local piracy by putting your policies in local languages. Many pirates of U.S. web material claim that they did not know it was illegal to copy since they did not understand English.
9. Localize your graphics as well as your written material.
10. Localize content management. Web sites need continual monitoring to update material. This is a particular challenge for the multinational company since it must be done in different languages.

Developing a global web site adds additional challenges to organizations beyond cultural sensitivity and language differences. Many organizations discovered that they needed to adapt their organizations to the information flow and customer demands created by web locations accessed from anywhere in the world. This often resulted in changes in organizational structure and changes in internal information systems to make the company more globally integrated.

The results of the Forrester Research survey reported in Exhibit 10.12 suggest that organizational challenges are among the most important issues affecting web-site globalization.

To Build or Outsource Technical Capabilities?

Similar to companies choosing an export strategy (direct or indirect exporting with the aid of export management companies), e-commerce companies that wish to globalize their operations have two basic options. They can run all e-commerce functions themselves or they can outsource these functions to e-fulfillment specialists called *e-commerce enablers*. The enablers provide services and software that translate web sites and calculate shipping, value-added taxes, duties, and other charges unique to each country. For example, NetSales (http://www.netsales.com/) offers a complete line of e-commerce services targeted at medium-sized businesses. Services range from supply procurement to setting up web-based stores.

The enablers of multinational e-commerce exist because many companies—even some that are very large—do not have the internal resources or capabilities to conduct all e-commerce functions. In addition, in such a rapidly changing, competitive environment, few companies have the time to develop such strategic capabilities. For example, Forrester Research estimates that 85 percent of U.S. e-retailers cannot fill international orders because they do not have the capability to deal with the complexities of shipping across borders. As such, even some very large companies such as Nike and Blockbuster outsource to enablers. Enablers take on functions such as receiving the customers' purchased goods, storaging, packing, and eventual shipping to the customer. As with good export management firms, successful order-fulfillment enablers

E-commerce enablers

Fulfillment specialists that provide other companies with services such as Web site translation.

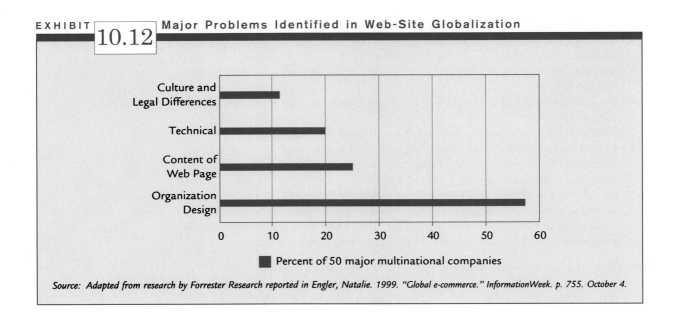

EXHIBIT **10.12**   Major Problems Identified in Web-Site Globalization

Percent of 50 major multinational companies

Source: Adapted from research by Forrester Research reported in Engler, Natalie. 1999. "Global e-commerce." InformationWeek. p. 755. October 4.

understand local business culture and know how to comply with taxation and regulatory issues.[46]

Many enablers now exist that specialize in helping companies globalize their e-commerce. Companies such as Global Site and Idion help create multilingual versions of web sites for their customers. These companies have automated the translation process so that updates to web sites can occur more rapidly. This type of service has become so popular that Forrester Research expects a 50 percent per year increase in this service.

The following Multinational Management Brief gives an overview of the services offered by NextLinx, one of the first global e-commerce enablers.[47]

In addition to e-commerce enablers that provide transaction services, numerous companies also offer web translations. Some of these companies have automated the translation process. One challenge of the translation process is to keep up with the frequent, often costly changes in global web sites. Culturally sensitive enablers also go beyond simple translations. Like any advertisement or promotion in different countries, the web site must be sensitive to cultural and religious differences. Colors, symbols, pictures, and variance in local use of the same language may cause different reactions in different countries.

Multinational Management **Brief**

Looking at a Global E-Commerce Enabler's Services

NextLinx identified long-term obstacles to international business that can be simplified by its services. These obstacles include:

- Export and import regulations and duties
- Complex border crossings
- Multi-region/country expertise needed
- Extensive documentation required
- Coordination of multiple transportation legs
- Total landed cost often unknown until after the shipment is delivered

The NextLinx software reduces the global e-commerce transaction to three phases on a web site. In the "pre-click" phase, the buyer reviews transportation options and costs and gets import duties, VAT, excise taxes and other governmental charges, and determines total landed cost. In the "click" phase, the buyer orders and determines door-to-door shipping. This phase also screens for customers with denied access to purchase and checks to determine if a license is required. In the "post-click" phase, documentation is printed and tracking of the shipment begins until it reaches the destination.

The NextLinx system covers 100 exporting and importing countries. It covers all 99 chapters of the Harmonized Tariff Schedule with all the HTS headings and sub-headings in the schedule. There are more than 19,000 HTS codes for both export and import. The software calculates customs duty rates including all trade preferential programs. It also calculates governmental charges such as VAT, excise taxes, merchandise-processing fees (MPF), and port charges. NextLinx can host the technology on its web site for a company, or it can provide software and technical support to clients who use their own servers.

Source: Adapted from http://www.nextlinx.com

Summary and Conclusions

This chapter introduced the basic concepts of e-commerce in general and multinational e-commerce in particular. It discussed the basic forms of e-commerce including B2C, B2B, C2C, and C2B. Presently, B2B dominates the Internet economy, but B2C is expected to eventually gain a major share of e-commerce transactions. Overall, e-commerce is expanding geometrically. Although the United States currently dominates e-commerce, statistics show that other areas of the world are quickly catching up.

The fundamentals of e-commerce strategy emphasize building on traditional business models and experimenting with cost reductions and areas of differentiation that Internet use might provide. There is no easy formula for building a successful e-commerce business. Innovative and creative managers will find ways to use e-commerce tools to enhance cost leadership or differentiation strategies. Because the World Wide Web makes e-commerce models transparent and easy to copy, only the most innovative and rapidly moving companies are likely to survive.

Companies conducting multinational operations via the Internet face most of the same challenges faced by brick-and-mortar multinational companies. The global-versus-local dilemma and the problems of conducting business in different cultural and institutional environments remain. The Web, however, provides instant access to the world for all companies willing to navigate the e-commerce world. It will probably become one of the most important drivers of globalization in the future.

Discussion Questions

1. Define e-commerce and discuss the types of e-commerce transactions.
2. Identify and discuss the levels of the Internet economy. How has the Internet created new types of businesses?
3. Compare and contrast the costs and benefits of a fully integrated-brick-and-mortar and e-commerce company.
4. What are the advantages of e-commerce businesses over traditional brick-and-mortar businesses when taking their operations global? What are the disadvantages?
5. Discuss the advantages and disadvantages of outsourcing global e-commerce activities to enablers.
6. Discuss the characteristics of a successful multinational web page.

Multinational Management **Skill Builder**

Build a Web Store

Step 1. Your instructor will divide the class into groups.

Step 2. Select an agricultural or industrial product produced in the region of the country where you are located. If possible, interview a small-business person concerning his or her perspectives on the international opportunities for the product. In the United States, one way of finding a potential business owner is through the small-business development centers attached to many U.S. universities. Your instructor may assign you a business or product.

Step 3. Using the steps shown in Exhibit 10.4, the chapter on small business management, and information from Web sources (such as those in Exhibit 10.6) and your library, identify a foreign market or markets for the product or products.

Step 4. Build a simulated or actual web site in your own language that shows the company's products or services. If you have the technical capabilities and are working with a real business, you can build a web store. Simple, no-cost or low-cost versions of web storefronts can be downloaded from sources such as http://www.authstores.com/. Periodically search the Web for additional free e-commerce sources as new sites frequently become available.

Step 5. Translate your web site into the language of the country or countries that represent your target market. Use the free translation software available on the Web (See the Internet locations for translations at the end of Chapter). Apply the ten steps noted in this chapter to make sure your site is culturally appropriate.

Step 6. Test your translation and site layout with native speakers. If it is a real site, wait for orders.

Step 7. Present your site and its performance to your class and to the small-business person, if possible.

Endnotes

[1] Andersen, Poul Houman. 2005. "Export intermediation and the Internet: An activity-unbundling approach." *International Marketing Review.* 22, 2: p. 147–164.

[2] ebusinessforum.com. 2000. "Ericsson: "The promise of purchasing cards.", http://www.ebusinessforum.com, December 18.

[3] Neff, Dale. 2001. *e-Procurement.* Upper Saddle River, N.J.: Prentice-Hall.

[4] Koh, Chang E., and Kyungdoo "Ted" Nam. 2005. "Business use of the Internet: A longitudinal study from a value chain perspective." *Industrial Management + Data Systems,* 105, 1/2: p. 82–95.

[5] Coppel, Jonathan. 2000. "E-commerce: Impacts and policy challenges." *OECD, Economics Department Working Papers,* No. 252, Paris, June 23.

[6] OECD. 2002. *Measuring the Internet Economy 2002.* Paris: Organization for Economic Cooperation and Development.

[7] OECD. 2006. *Measuring the Internet Economy 2002.* Paris: Organization for Economic Cooperation and Development.

[8] OECD. 2005. *Measuring the Internet Economy 2002.* Paris: Organization for Economic Cooperation and Development.

[9] Ibid.

[10] Barua, Anitesh, and Andrew B. Whinston. 2000. "Measuring the Internet economy" University of Texas, http://www.Internetindicators.com, June 6.

[11] Epstein, Marc J. 2005. "Implementing successful e-Commerce initiatives." *Strategic Finance,* March, 86, 9: p. 22–29; Venkatraman, N. 2000. "Five steps to a dot-com strategy: How to find your footing on the Web." *Sloan Management Review,* Spring, p. 15–28.

[12] Venkatraman, "Five steps to a dot-com strategy: How to find your footing on the Web."

[13] Gulati, Ranjay, and Jason Garino. 2000. "Get the right mix of bricks & clicks," *Harvard Business Review,* May–June, p. 107–114.

[14] Ibid.

[15] Beasty, Colin. 2006. "Retail's 2 worlds: Tips on integrating online and offline channels." *Customer Relationship Management, March,* 10, 3: p. 30–35.

[16] Ibid.

[17] Kim, Hyunwoo, Younggoo Han, Sehun Kim, and Myeonggil Choi. 2005. *Journal of Information Systems Education,* Spring, 16, 1: p. 55–64.

[18] Peslak, Alan R. 2006. "Internet privacy policies of the largest international companies." *Journal of Electronic Commerce in Organizations,* 4, 3: p. 46–62.

[19] Grimes, Roger. 2006. "E-commerce in crisis: When SSL isn't safe." *InfoWorld,* (May 1), 28, 18: p. 26.

[20] Claburn, Thomas. 2005. "New path of attack." *InformationWeek.* No. 1066. November 28.

[21] Gordon, Lawrence, and Martin P. Loeb. 2006. "Budgeting process for information security expenditures." *Communications of the ACM, January,* 49, 1: p. 121–125.

[22] Karat, Clare-Marie, Carolyn Brodie, and John Karat. 2006. "Usable privacy and security for personal information management." *Communication of the ACM, January,* 49, 1: p. 56–57.

[23] Fahmy, Dalia. 2005. "Making financial data more secure," *Institutional Investor,* December, p. 1; Grimes, "E-commerce in crisis: When SSL isn't safe."

[24] Chandra, Akhilesh, and Thomas Calderon. 2005. "Challenges and constraints to the diffusion of biometrics in information systems." *Communications of ACM,* December, 48, 12: p. 101–106.

[25] Mientka, Matt. 2006. "Behavioral biometric to improve e-commerce security." *AFP Exchange,* January/February, p. 32–33.

[26] Peslak, "Internet privacy policies of the largest international companies."

[27] Knight, Gary A. and Tamer Cavusgil. 2005. "A taxonomy of born-global firms." Management International Review, 45: p. 15–35.

[28] Ibid.

[29] Ibid.

[30] Rasmussan, Erik S., Tage K. Madsen, and Felicitas Evangelista. 2001. "The founding of the born global company in Denmark and Australia: Sensemaking and networking." *Asia Pacific Journal of Marketing and Logistics,* 13, 3: p. 75–107.

[31] Sawhney, Mohanbir, and Sumant Mandal. 2000. "Go global." *Business 2.0,* May, p. 178–213.

[32] Rosen, Kenneth T., and Amanda L. Howard. 2000. "E-retail: Gold rush or fool's gold?" *California Management Review,* Spring, 42, 3: p. 72–100.

[33] Cyr, Dianne, Carole Bonanni, John Bowes, and Joe Ilsever. 2005. "Beyond trust: Web site design preferences across cultures." *Journal of Global Information Management,* October–December, 13, 4: p. 25–54; Singh, Nitish, George Fassot, Hongxin Zhao, and Paul D. Boughton. 2006. "A cross-cultural analysis of German, Chinese and Indian consumers' perception of web site adaptation." *Journal of Consumer Behavior,* 5, p. 56–68; Singh, Nitish, Olivier Furrer, and Massimiliano Ostinelli. 2004. "To localize or standardize on the web: Empirical evidence from Italy, India, Netherlands, Spain and Switzerland." *Multinational Business Review,* 12, 1: p. 69–87.

[34] Rosen and Howard, "E-retail: Gold rush or fool's gold?"

[35] Shirky, Clay. 2000. "Go global or bust." *Business 2.0,* March 1, p. 145–146.

[36] The Economist Intelligence Unit. 2006. *The 2006 E-readiness Rankings.*

[37] Ibid.

[38] Sawhney and Mandal, "Go global."

[39] Ibid.

[40] Hudgins, Christy. 1999. "International e-commerce." *Network Computing,* (November 15), 10,23: p. 75–50.

[41] Singh, Fassot, Zhao, and Boughton, "A cross-cultural analysis of German, Chinese and Indian consumers' perception of web site adaptation."

[42] Singh, Furrer, and Ostinelli, "To localize or standardize on the web: Empirical evidence from Italy, India, Netherlands, Spain and Switzerland."

[43] Engler, Natalie. 1999. "Global e-commerce," *InformationWeek,* 755, October 4.

[44] Okazaki, Shintaro. 2004. "Do multinationals standardize or localize? The cross-cultural dimensionality of product-based web sites." *Internet Research,* 14,1: p. 81–94.

[45] Sheridan, E.F. 2000. http://www.Webofculture.com/corp/commandments.html

[46] Wilkerson, Phil. 2000. "Enabling global e-commerce." *Discount Store News,* (April 17), 39, 8: p. 15–16.

[47] Ghosh, Chandrani. 2000. "E-trade routes," *Forbes,* August 7, p. 108.

CHAPTER CASE

The Failure of Boo.com

Introduction

Boo.com was one of the most anticipated e-tailing sites around the world. The company was attempting to become a fashion merchandise seller in several different markets, with the dream of creating a global brand.

Surprisingly, after a glitzy launch during the end of 1999, Boo.com announced in mid-May 2000 that it had put the company's assets up for liquidation. During a period of one year, the company had spent $135 million with spectacularly poor results.[1] By April 1999, gross sales were only $500,000 a month, and Boo.com was spending $1 million more than it was earning every week. Only $500,000 of the initial investment remained.[2]

The demise of Boo.com stands as a spectacular landmark in the history of e-commerce. AOL vice president of e-commerce, Patrick Gates, said,[3] "Boo.com was one of the big reality checks for everyone. I don't think any of us were surprised specifically. I sensed that there would be some issues there based on the product mix and sort of high-flying technology. But that one made a lot of people look back and go, 'Wow.'"

The event contributed in large measure to dire predictions about B2C commerce and to widespread pessimism about the dot-com revolution. Soon after the closure of Boo.com, the Gartner Group, for example, announced that up to 95% of e-tailers could go out of business by mid-2001.[4] Similarly, Price Waterhouse Coopers announced that one in four British online firms would run out of cash by 2000.[5] Boo.com's failure also led to a widespread sentiment that selling apparel on the Web would not succeed, which forced even online retailers that had made steady progress, such as Dressmart.com, to fold.[6]

In addition to its historic significance, an analysis of Boo.com offers rich insights into everything that should be avoided when launching an e-tailing business. Analyzing the company reveals serious flaws on many fronts—from its Web site design to its promotion to its grandiose strategic ambition.

Background

Boo.com was founded by two Swedish entrepreneurs: Kajsa Leander, a fashion model, and Ernst Malmsten. Before Boo.com, they had created the Swedish Internet bookstore bokus.com in 1997 and sold it the following year. Boo.com was backed by Paris-based Europ@web, the private investment company of LVMH Chairman Bernard Arnault; 21 Investimenti of Italy, the private investment company of the Benetton family; Bain Capital Inc. of Boston; and the New York investment firm Goldman Sachs & Co.[7]

Boo.com first announced that it would launch by the end of May 1999; however, due to software problems, the Web site actually launched in November 1999. The company failed to meet its sales targets by January 2000. It fired 100 staff members and reduced its product prices by up to 40%. In May 2000, Rob Shepherd quit as chief technology officer, the third high-level personnel loss in a month. Finally, on May 17, 2000, after failed attempts at selling the site to other retailers and trying to get more funding from the shareholders, Boo.com announced that it was shutting down.

The rights to the name Boo.com were acquired by Fashionmall.com for 250,000 British pounds.[8] In February 2001, Boo.com recast itself as a fashion and style portal that provided fashion advice and reviews. It also provided links to small boutiques where customers could go to buy the products.[9] The new site was also less data-intensive making downloading easier.[10]

An Analysis of Firm Strategy

Ernst Malmsten, a cofounder, said, "We have been too visionary."[11] As implausible as it may sound, this statement may provide us a glimpse at the flaw in the firm's strategy.

Boo.com believed in the big-splash theory of firm strategy. The firm wanted to be a global fashion super retailer. The company hoped to have a major presence in multiple prominent fashion markets—at one point, it had offices in London, New York, Munich, Stockholm, Paris, and Amsterdam.[12] It aimed to leverage the power of the Internet by serving brands that were local powerhouses or global superstars to the consumers in these markets. And it intended to provide access to consumers in different multiple languages and transact business in multiple currencies.

The vision for the firm can be summarized in one word: grandiose. Although this strategy can be faulted on many counts, envisioning a global reach is not in itself a mistake. It is, however, problematic to hope to achieve that all at once. Because the company's Web site was launched simultaneously in several countries, the firm had to ensure that it had an effective presence in all of those countries. As a result, its resources were spread thin. The company may have been better served by starting small and spreading out over time.

The company also failed to consider those companies with strong brand names (e.g., Land's End, Nordstrom) that had already established strong presences in the markets that they wished to attack. Many of these companies had a long history in these markets due to catalog or bricks-and-mortar operations. Consequently, they had an advantage in resources, as well as in brand name.

Boo.com furthermore chose a product category, fashion goods, that is hard to sell on the Internet. Individuals like to touch and feel the fabric, try on a dress, and experience the product firsthand before buying it. In spite of these challenges, companies such as Land's End are successfully selling apparel online today by using systems such as virtual dressing rooms. Although Boo.com had a lot of functionality on its Web site, it did not adequately focus on the functionality that could best help its consumers.

The global vision for the company led to several execution problems. An ex-employee described a few.[13]

Multiple Currencies

If you want to trade globally, you can't only offer US dollars. As a result, you need to figure out a way to handle multiple currencies ranging from dollars to pounds to liras to francs, to deutschmarks, to kroners, etc. . . . If you are planning on doing this well, you have to peg your prices to a particular value. However, you have to realize that prices are not the same in every country and what may seem expensive in the US can be seen as cheap in other countries. This is where you have to make a decision as to whether you want to set a fixed price in the local currency or set a more dynamic price that is affected by currency exchanges and other fluctuations. It's a fascinating problem in and of itself but it's one that we discovered to be a big pain to deal with. In the end, Boo built a system that allowed us to set a different price for each country or set a single price for all countries and have that price be translated in the proper currency based on a set exchange rate. It was a bit of a kludge but it worked and, to this day, I haven't seen an e-commerce shop with a similar system.

A global e-tailer must worry about optimally setting prices in multiple markets. One price is not valid across all markets; the price must be set for each market in terms of the buying power of the market, its market size, and so forth. In addition, e-tailers must worry about the signals that the prices send. Price signals quality in the fashion business, and maintaining a consistent position across nations is certainly an important objective. All in all, developing a system that allowed them to set prices in multiple ways across countries was certainly one achievement of Boo.com.

Multiple Languages

First of all, forget translation software packages. They are still relatively immature and there is (at this point anyway) little hope that they will mature much beyond their current point in the near future. If you've taken any linguistics course, you know that grammatical rules can hardly be standardized for several languages. For example, something as simple as a verb can become a whole new set of problems. In English, there is a relatively small set of basic rules. The verb "to want" breaks down into "I want, you want, he wants, we want, you want, they want." Notice that there are only two basic variations here. In French, the same verb "vouloir" breaks down as follows: "Je veux, tu veux, il veut, nous voulons, vous voulez, ils veulent." In this case, there are 5 different variations. In Spanish, it's six . . . and so on. Take that problem and try to automate it and you are building a system that is bound to fail. The way we worked around it at Boo was to create a system where the copy was translated by hand by people who were fluent in the language. Unfortunately, another problem cropped up: British English and American English are EXTREMELY different. Considering that the assumption was that one version of each language was sufficient, problems cropped up and some of the perfectly normal British English stuff ended up being very offensive in the US. THAT was a major problem.

On the one hand, to be accepted by markets in different countries, the content has to be in different languages. Moreover, the language and product selection must be sensitive to the local cultures in order to truly appeal. Boo.com may have underestimated the cost of achieving this on the Web.

On-the-Fly Tax Calculation

This one almost killed me. In the US, it's relatively easy to deal with taxation. For the most part, the only taxes you have to pay are for states in which you have a physical presence. Where it gets tricky is when your servers are located in one area and your offices are in another. Technically, that is two locations. In the case of Boo, it got worse. For example, a sale to France was taxed three ways. Why? Quite simply because the company had offices in Paris, its servers were located in London, UK, and its distribution center was in Cologne, Germany. However, the interesting part of the problem was that we were making a sale but not delivering a good in the UK, delivering a good but not making a sale in Germany, and making a sale and delivering a good in France. This was just one example. Multiply that by the number of countries the company was doing business in and it soon got VERY complicated. Add to that the fact that certain goods were coming from China or Taiwan and the picture got so clouded that we had to bring in tax attorneys to help us on the details.

The Web has certainly complicated the matters of international taxation. To this day, there is no consistent set of global rules on taxation and the laws in this area are still emerging. Clearly, international coordination is necessary to solve some of these problems. Boo.com's vision was perhaps premature.

Integration with Multiple Fulfillment Partners

The main issue here was dealing with different file formats for DeutschePost (the European fulfillment company) and UPS (the company that did fulfillment for the US). What we ended up doing was create an EDI link to those guys (DeutschePost was not web-enabled yet) and create a set of filters for each of them. A simple answer to a simple problem but this little answer cost about 150 man hours of work as the content had to be migrated from the old (untagged) setup to the new one. Because the original database was originally set up wrong, we had to totally reorganize the schema and refit the content into it.

Working with multiple fulfillment partners can lead to new levels of complexity because the company has to work with different systems and cultures.

Perhaps the most telling sign of what went wrong can be found in a statement made by cofounder, Ms. Leander,[14] "We kind of forgot about the consumer." In other words, the company's grandiose vision was not put in place with the explicit intention of serving consumers and providing them value—that was a secondary purpose! Businesses often fail when they forget the consumer.

Problems with the Web Site

Boo.com had spectacular problems with its Web site when it first launched. The site was designed with excessive graphics, movies, audio, and video. Examples of such features included short movies that featured the brands for sale and a personal shopping assistant called Miss Boo who made remarks to assist shoppers. They tended to see Miss Boo as an annoyance because of the irrelevance of her comments. For example, when a user clicked on the Acupuncture Deep Greco Fashion Velcro shoe, Miss Boo popped up exclaiming: "Tie me up, tie me down in a shoe that looks like it's been attacked by Gulliver's Lilliputians."[15]

Every product on the Boo.com Web site had a 3-D image. Photographing the products to create these images cost up to half a million dollars a month.[16]

A company spokesperson explained, saying, "We realize we're selling clothing. But we're selling a lifestyle item, not a commodity, so we wanted to build a different type of experience. Some of it is around rich graphics, some of it is around rich elements of design. In some cases, this was not ideal for the customer experience. So we're taking this information and trying to make it better."[17] However, an analyst for Forrester Research rightly points out[18] that this was the wrong strategy for Web site design at the time because "99% of European and 98% of US homes lacked the high-bandwidth access needed to fully benefit from the site." The company rolled out a site for low-bandwidth users in February 2000, but the target market had already been alienated. Moreover, Boo.com was built using Macromedia's Flash program, which at the point of the launch, was loaded on the computers of only a small proportion of the population.

The initial response to the Web site was awful. An article in the *Wall Street Journal* reported:[19]

> *On Day 1, according to Boo, only 50% of consumers who typed in the address www.Boo.com actually made it onto the site. There were a variety of reasons: The site didn't run on some combinations of browser software and hardware, particularly Macintoshes. The abundance of graphics and animation made it extremely slow, even for customers with high-speed connections. Many of those with low-bandwidth connections found it impossible to access the site, or simply gave up, Boo says. And, worst of all, those who did manage to make it onto the site were unable to purchase anything because of a glitch in the checkout process that unexpectedly returned customers to the opening screen just before the transaction was completed.*

A Web site reviewer for the *Wall Street Journal* coined a new term, "Boo rage." She reported that she had spent three hours attempting to order a skirt.[20] Also, "the first 17 times I tried to submit my order, my browser crashed. I also endured pages that took forever to download, was randomly tossed off of the site, and was besieged by a ridiculous number of questions when registering."

The Web usability guru Jakob Nielsen wrote this scathing review in December 1999:[21]

> *Boo.com takes itself too seriously. Instead of making it easy to shop, the site insists on getting in your face with a clumsy interface. It's as if the site is more intent on making you notice the*

design than on selling products. Boo should be congratulated, though, on running a site that supports 18 countries equally well in terms of both language and shipping.

Screen Pollution
Boo insists on launching several of its own windows. My own browser window is left with the message "Nothing happens on this page, except that you may want to bookmark it." Fat chance, especially since the windows forced upon me are frozen and can't be adapted to my window or font preferences.

This site is simply slow and unpleasant. All product information is squeezed into a tiny window, with only about one square inch allocated to the product description. Since most products require more text than will fit in this hole, Boo requires the user to use a set of nonstandard scroll widgets to expose the rest of the text, 20 words at a time. Getting to a product requires precise manipulation of hierarchical menus followed by pointing to minuscule icons and horizontal scrolling. Not nice.

Miss Boo, the Shopping Assistant
She is prettier than Microsoft's Bob but just as annoying. Web sites do need personality, but in the form of real humans with real opinions and real advice. I prefer the interactive content experiments in the site's magazine section, such as a feature on the similarities between stone-age living and some current fashion products.

What's a Boobag?
It's a shopping cart, actually, and unlike other carts it contains miniature photos of your products. It is also possible to drape the items on a mannequin to see how they look as an outfit, though too much dragging and low-level interface manipulation is required.

In general, Boo.com became a victim of Internet time. Businesses move faster in Internet time; e-tailing systems take much longer to develop. In this case, the Web site was not fully designed when it was launched, which meant changes had to be made in public, reducing consumer confidence.

The Badly Designed Advertising Campaign

Another problem faced by Boo.com was that it overspent on advertising early on. It created a great deal of consumer interest, but then the Web site launch was delayed by about five months, during which time, consumers finally got fed up.

Anticipating a May 1999 launch, Boo.com announced a two-year $65 million advertising budget after hiring the London ad agency BMP DDB. The agency created a campaign showing geeky kids playing sports in cool clothes that would be available from Boo.com.[22]

According to Marina Galanti, the second marketing director, when the launch got delayed, the ad campaign was modified to make it "more about mood and attitude and less about sports." The launch was rescheduled for July and teaser ads began running in magazines. However, teaser ad campaigns work only when the firm knows exactly when the final product is going to be available. In this case, the tease campaign backfired because the site did not launch until November 1999. It also placed the spotlight on the company while it was still tinkering with the Web site.

The company believed in going on an all-out blitz rather than building the business gradually. As described in a *Wall Street Journal* article,[23] "the company launched press, television, cinema and outdoor campaigns in six countries and expanded to nine others, spending about $25 million—much of it still owed to the agencies that created and executed the ads."

After setting grandiose expectations, Boo.com seemed to have faltered in its marketing strategy. Panicked by low sales, the company abandoned its image as a high-end retailer and started offering huge discounts—but without modifying its advertising.[24]

It seemed to some that the company had simply not catered to its target market and had failed to make a connection. Simon Mathews, managing director of Optimedia International, a media planning firm, said, "Boo.com's advertising strategy was emblematic of what was wrong with its business." The focus was on showboating instead of selling a product with clear substance. They never gave people a real reason to buy their clothes."[25]

Poor Management Quality

Boo.com has also been criticized for poor management quality. The firm had few management controls and many of the personnel were consultants with little relevant business experience.[26] The company is also said to have been too enamored with the fashion industry: senior managers were rewarded with five-star hotels and first-class airline tickets to attend fashion shows in cities such as Paris and Milan. Early employees were also rewarded with Palm Pilots and other perks.[27]

But the poor management went further than simple extravagance, as an ex-employee recounts:[28]

> When I joined the company in August, the launch was behind schedule by three months and we had ten weeks to the Xmas season. The first thing I asked to see was the project plan. It didn't exist. People were working on bits and pieces of the project without communicating with other people they were affecting. Within a week, we put together a MS-project chart and things started to move properly.
>
> Lack of communications to and from the top was definitely a problem as well as a lack of understanding of Internet time. . . .
>
> Boo.com set out to do too many things and ended up doing none of them. The site was designed to create an immersive online retailing experience, but most users did not have broadband connectivity to benefit from it. The ad campaign built traffic to the site when it was not up. The management quality was poor and in the end, Boo's failure did not particularly surprise anyone who had worked for or with the company. Future attempts at building a global online apparel retailer will surely learn from the experiences of Boo.

The Future

Boo.com failed to create an immersive retailing experience online. The question for the future is will it ever be possible? Some studies now show that online users respond more to text than to pictures, which seems to support the approach taken by Amazon.com. But the jury is still out on this question.

CASE DISCUSSION QUESTIONS

1. Was Boo.com doomed more by its faulty strategy or by its poor implementation?
2. Can apparel ever be sold successfully on the Web? How about other fashion products such as jewelry and perfume?

3. What can the Web add to apparel sales that a catalog cannot?
4. What is the appropriate way to use graphics when designing a Web site?
5. Was Boo.com just ahead of its time? Will there ever be a global online retailer?

6. Will the impending broadband revolution help sites that want to create an immersive retail experience online?

CASE CREDIT

Sandeep Krishnamurthy, E-Commerce Management, 2003. South-Western, Mason: Ohio, p. 129–135. Used with permission.

CASE NOTES

[1] Keith Regan and Macaluso, "Boo.com Saga Ends with Asset Sale," *E-commerce Times,* May 30, 2000.

[2] Bryan Glick, "Boo.com's Fall Makes Realism the Fashion," May 24, 2000, http://www.vnunet.com/Analysis/1102339.

[3] John Weisman, "The Making of E-Commerce: 10 Key Moments, Part II," August 23, 2000, http://www.ecommercetimes.com/news/articles2000/000823-1.shtml.

[4] John Weisman, "The Making of E-Commerce: 10 Key Moments, Part II," August 23, 2000, http://www.ecommercetimes.com/news/articles2000/000823-1.shtml.

[5] Bryan Glick, "Boo.com's Fall Makes Realism the Fashion."

[6] Mick Brady, "The Web's Touchy-Feely Fashion Challenge," August 28, 2000, http://www.ecommercetimes.com/perl/story/4131.html.

[7] Cate T. Corcoran, "E-Commerce (A Special Report). Industry by Industry—More Than Style: Fashion sites need to be exciting and stylish; And, as this tale of two ventures shows, they also need to be practical," *Wall Street Journal,* April 17, 2000, p. R 68.

[8] Karen Holloway, "Boo.com Reborn as Lifestyle Portal," October 30, 2000, http://www.karenholloway.com/boo.htm.

[9] John Parker, "Boo.com Reborn," *Traffic World,* 265(9) (2001): p. 23.

[10] Scott Tillett, "It's Back from the Dead: Boo.com," *Internet Week,* 834 (2000): p. 11.

[11] John Weisman, "The Making of E-Commerce: 10 Key Moments, Part II," August 23, 2000, http://www.ecommercetimes.com/news/articles2000/000823-1.shtml.

[12] Erik Portanger and Stephanie Gruner, "Boo.com to Move Into Receivership As Funds Dry Up," *Wall Street Journal,* (2000): p. B16.

[13] Tristan Louis, "What I Learned at Boo.com," May 19, 2000, http://www.tnl.net/newsletter/2000/boobust.asp.

[14] Corcoran, "E-Commerce (A Special Report)."

[15] Corcoran, "E-Commerce (A Special Report)."

[16] Bryan Glick, "Boo.com's Fall Makes Realism the Fashion."

[17] Corcoran, "E-Commerce (A Special Report)."

[18] John Cassy and Mary O'Hara, "It All Ends in Tears at Boo.com," May 19, 2000, http://www.shoppingunlimited.co.uk/newsandviews/story/0,5804,222624,00.html.

[19] Corcoran, "E-Commerce (A Special Report)."

[20] Andrea Petersen, "Watching the Web: Buzzkill," *Wall Street Journal,* November 11, 1999, B, 19:p. 5.

[21] Jakob Nielsen, "Boo's Demise," May 2000, http://www.useit.com/alertbox/20000528_boo.html.

[22] Sarah Ellison, "Boo.com: Buried by Badly Managed Buzz," *Wall Street Journal,* May 23, 2000, p. B10.

[23] Ibid.

[24] Ibid.

[25] Ibid.

[26] John Cassy and Mary O'Hara, "It All Ends in Tears at Boo.com."

[27] Erik Portanger and Stephanie Gruner, "Boo.com to Move Into Receivership As Funds Dry Up."

[28] Tristan Louis, "What I Learned at Boo.com."

Enersis: Global Strategy in the Electric Power Sector

Introduction

Enersis, the Chilean multinational electricity company, has grown into a $US 3.7 billion (market capitalization) leader in the South American market by December of 1997. Beginning as the privatized version of the Santiago regional power distribution company, Enersis has become a true multinational, with major operating subsidiaries in Argentina, Peru, Brazil, and Colombia, along with those in Chile.

As the company prepares for the next century, conditions are either opportune for additional growth and profitability, or threatening with the possible arrival of major multinational electric companies from North America and Europe in the region. As the process of privatization of the sector proceeds throughout Latin America, Enersis is encountering increasing challenges from companies such as EDF (France), AES (US) and Iberdrola (Spain). Mr. Pablo Ihnen, CEO of Enersis, has a clear vision of the need for Enersis to expand through the region and to build a portfolio of businesses around the core electric generation and distribution activities.

At the same time that Enersis is exploring expansion opportunities abroad, the company is experiencing limitations on its ability to expand at home. As the largest electric power company in Chile, Enersis is always under public scrutiny for its pricing, service quality, and environmental protection issues. As one of the largest companies in the country, Enersis again is subject to constant public discussion. This reality makes it difficult for the company to pursue expansion activities in Chile, though recently Enersis did bail out a failing water utility (Lo Castillo), and other power generation projects have been started (such as a natural gas-powered plant in Atacama in northern Chile[1]).

Perhaps the greatest limitation on growth in the domestic market is its size; Chile's population of 14 million people is already fairly well supplied with hydro-electric power and some coal/gas thermo-electric power. The limit to domestic growth is very relative, however. In North American terms, the economic growth rate of Chile at more than 6% annually, with power needs at least matching that rate, is fairly attractive. Still, the need for increased electric power supply within Chile is expected to grow less rapidly than the demand elsewhere in Latin America.

Total capital investment in power generation in Latin America has been growing at a value of about $US 10 billion per year during the 1990s. Chile's investment in power generation has grown at about $US 600 million per year during that time, and appears likely to continue at this rate for the next five years. As Enersis expands in the rest of the region, capital investment needs are growing almost exponentially. Exhibit 1 depicts this environment.

If privatizations of state-owned power generation and distribution companies continue on the current path, the need for capital investment is expected to

EXHIBIT [1]   Installed Capacity (MW)

	1998	1999	2000	2001	2002	2003	% participation
Argentina	20,799	22,284	23,875	25,579	27,406	29,362	13
Bolivia	877	939	1,007	1,078	1,155	1,238	1
Brazil	61,591	65,988	70,700	75,748	81,156	86,950	37
Chile	6,712	7,191	7,705	8,255	8,845	9,476	4
Colombia	11,287	12,093	12,956	13,881	14,872	15,934	7
Ecuador	2,934	3,143	3,368	3,608	3,866	4,142	2
México	36,997	39,638	42,469	45,501	48,750	52,230	22
Perú	6,795	4,066	4,356	4,667	5,001	5,538	2
Venezuela	20,225	21,669	23,216	24,874	26,650	28,553	12
TOTAL	**165,216**	**177,012**	**189,651**	**203,192**	**217,700**	**233,244**	

reach $US 100 billion over the course of the next five years. To continue its role as the largest, highly profitable private power company in the region, Enersis needs a huge amount of additional financial resources.

The global (or regional) strategy being developed by Enersis was simply unthinkable only ten years ago. With the Latin American region in the late stages of an enormous external debt crisis and prolonged recession, the economic conditions were singularly unfavorable. The electric power industry at that time was almost entirely government-owned throughout Latin America. Chile was the first country in the region to privatize both the electric power generation industry and also the electricity distribution industry.

In December of 1997, as the leaders of Enersis considered the whirlwind process that had led the company to its current level of activities and internationalization, they realized that the process could not stop now. The competition in electric power generation was heating up in Brazil, in Colombia, and in other target markets for Enersis. The possible entry of foreign power providers was very real, and even in Chile competition was possible from providers in Argentina and Brazil. The distribution business was less subject to market entry, since all countries in the region had non-overlapping power grids, and thus new entrants would have to build an entire infrastructure to compete. Nevertheless, even in distribution Enersis wanted to compete with other firms to buy privatizing companies in South America, and the bidding was often cutthroat. Mr. Ihnen and other Enersis top managers began to wonder if the process that they had begun was really sustainable.

In addition to the competitive pressures, Enersis felt constrained by the government of Chile, which was very concerned about the monopoly power held by the company. With Enersis' 47% share in electric power generation and 45% share of electricity distribution in Chile, this was a very real concern. Thus far, Enersis had avoided any anti-trust violations, but the risk of becoming subject to a complicated investigation was significant.

Background on Enersis

Enersis is the Chilean energy company that was formed from the dismantling of the Compañia Chilena de Electricidad in 1981. In that year three new companies were formed, including: the Compañia Chilena de Generacion de Electricidad, Chilgener; the Compañia Chilena Metropolitana de Distribucion Electrica, Chilectra; and the Compañia de Electricidad de la Quinta Region, Chilquinta. These new companies were then privatized in 1987 in separate auctions.

The new owners of Chilectra included Chilean pension funds, company employees, institutional investors, and thousands of small shareholders. In 1988 the company changed its name to Enersis, which was structured to operate as a holding company. The principal operating subsidiary of Enersis was and is Chilectra, which is the main electricity distribution company in Santiago, the capital of Chile.

Soon after the privatization, Enersis began to move aggressively into a diversification program, mainly in other electricity-related activities. A major shareholding in Endesa, the largest electric power generating company in Chile was taken in 1990. Today Enersis owns 25% of Endesa, and is the largest single shareholder. A computer equipment and services subsidiary, Synapsis, was established to provide these services to the Enersis group. Manso de Velasco, a real estate and construction company, was acquired to be the main vehicle for buying land and building facilities for both Endesa and Chilectra throughout the country. The company's organization chart appears in Exhibit 2. The various operating companies are described in the next section.

Enersis in 1997 has become the largest privately-owned electric power generation and distribution company in Latin America. The company has operations that it manages in Chile, Argentina, Brazil, Colombia, and Peru. While focused principally on the electric power sector, Enersis is also active in real estate ventures through its subsidiary, Manso de Velasco.

To finance its growth, Enersis sold shares in the Chilean stock exchange, borrowed domestically and internationally, and sold ADRs in the US market, bringing its total financial structure in 1996 to 75% equity/25% debt, and a total asset value of $US 9.736 billion—December 1996. The distribution of shareholdings is shown in Exhibit 3 (p. 459).

Operating Companies and Affiliates

The initial business of Enersis, and still its single largest activity, is electricity distribution in the Santiago region of Chile through the operating company *Chilectra*. Chilectra Metropolitana was created in 1981 as part of the dismantling of the Compañia Chilena de Electricidad. In 1985, the company was placed into a privatization process, which resulted in Chilectra being 100% privately owned by 1987. The name of the overall company, as previously noted, was changed to Enersis in 1988, and Chilectra became its main distribution subsidiary.

Chilectra today is owned 75% by Enersis and the rest by individual and institutional shareholders through the Chilean stock exchange. Exhibit 4 (p. 459) shows the distribution of ownership of Chilectra, and demonstrates that this affiliate of Enersis has its own international capital structure, with ADRs issued in New York and a broad base of ownership among pension funds, foreign investment funds, and individual shareholders.

Chilectra purchases most of its electric power from domestic generating companies, led by Endesa (which also belongs to Enersis). Endesa provided 30.1% of Chilectra's electricity in 1997, followed by Chilgener with 24.1%, Pehuenche with 16.9%, Pangue with 14%, Colbun with 10.6%, and others with 4.3%. This portfolio of energy sources is expected to shift with the arrival of imported natural gas from Argentina. The natural gas will replace some of the Chilean system's use of coal for thermoelectric power generation.

EXHIBIT **2**   Enersis

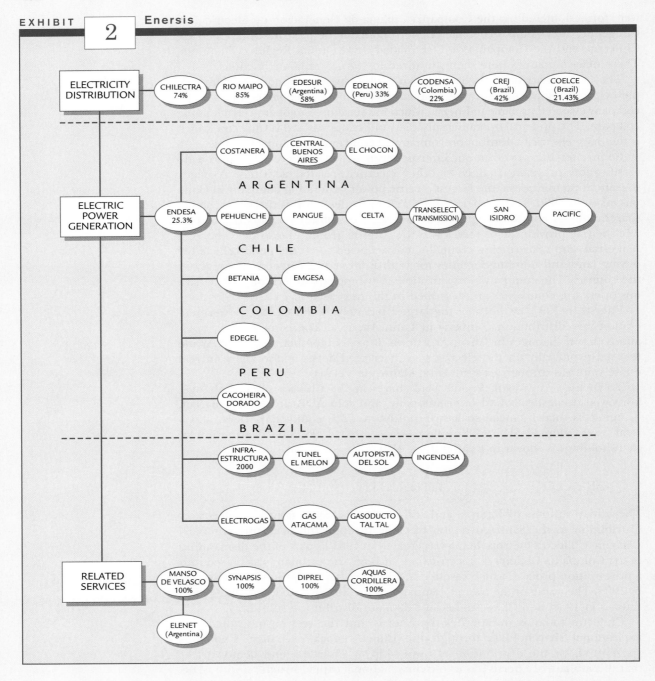

Rio Maipo

Rio Maipo is Enersis' second largest distribution system in Chile. This company was created from a division of Chilectra, with the goal of serving the Maipo Valley region. After sale of shares on the stock exchange, Enersis maintains 85% ownership of Rio Maipo.

Rio Maipo had approximately 255,000 customers at yearend 1997 and sold about 955 GWh of power during the year.

EXHIBIT 3   Ownership of Enersis, December 1997

Shareholder	Number of Shareholders	Number of Shares	%
Pension Funds	13	2,164,892,601	31.84
Employee Companies	5	1,981,587,840	29.16
ADRs	1	1,132,239,300	16.65
Foreign Equity Funds	19	150,909,038	2.20
Other Shareholders	13,153	1,370,371,221	20.15
TOTAL	**13,191**	**6,800,000,000**	**100.00%**

Source: Enersis Annual Report. 1997.

Edesur (Argentina)

Electricidad del Sur (Edesur) is the power distribution company for the southern half of the city of Buenos Aires, Argentina. Initially, in 1992, Enersis purchased 20% of the shares of Edesur in the privatization process. In 1995 Enersis purchased another 39% of Edesur, such that today Enersis holds 59% of the outstanding shares. As with the other distribution and generation companies, Enersis holds a majority of seats on the board of directors of Edesur, and thus is assured management control of the firm.

In 1997 Edesur had approximately 2,042,000 customers in the Buenos Aires region, producing revenues of about $US 66.9 million for the year. Edesur distributed 11,160 GWh of power during the year.

Edelnor (Peru)

In 1994 Enersis bought 33% of the Peruvian firm, Empresa de Distribucion Electrica del Norte, Edelnor, in a public auction. This investment gave Enersis control of the firm and the right to place a majority of directors on Edelnor's board.

Edelnor served about 805,000 customers in the northern district of Lima in 1997 and sold 3,256 GWh of electricity during the year.

EXHIBIT 4   Percent Ownership by Major Shareholder

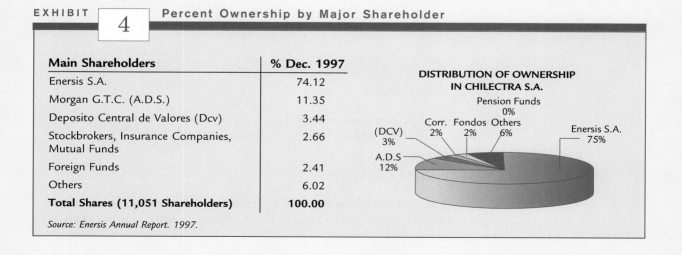

Main Shareholders	% Dec. 1997
Enersis S.A.	74.12
Morgan G.T.C. (A.D.S.)	11.35
Deposito Central de Valores (Dcv)	3.44
Stockbrokers, Insurance Companies, Mutual Funds	2.66
Foreign Funds	2.41
Others	6.02
Total Shares (11,051 Shareholders)	**100.00**

Source: Enersis Annual Report. 1997.

DISTRIBUTION OF OWNERSHIP IN CHILECTRA S.A.

Pension Funds 0%
Corr. Fondos 2%
Others 2%
Others 6%
(DCV) 3%
A.D.S 12%
Enersis S.A. 75%

Aguas Cordillera

This company is the main provider of drinking water and also of wastewater treatment in several districts of Santiago, Chile. Aguas Cordillera produces and distributes drinking water, and collects and disposes of wastewater, for a population of 310,000 people in the communities of Lo Barnechea, Vitacura, and part of Las Condes.

Compañia Electrica De Rio De Janeiro (Cerj-Brazil)

This company was acquired in 1996, and it distributes electricity through the state of Rio de Janeiro in Brazil. CERJ had 4.4 million customers at the end of 1997. During 1997, after one year under the management of Enersis, CERJ sold 6,424 GWh of electric power, 12% more than in the previous year. Energy losses were reduced by 4 percentage points, remaining at 25.3% at yearend 1997. CERJ had 1,340,573 clients at the end of the year, growth of 10.1% over the previous year.

Distribuidora De Productos Electricos Sa (Diprel)

The main business of Diprel is distribution and marketing of materials, products, and large-scale equipment to electric power companies. Since its creation in 1989, Diprel has followed a path of diversification of its products. In addition to equipment and materials for electric companies, Diprel now distributes similar products for construction, mining, and other industrial companies.

Diprel has been successful in penetrating the Chilean market through establishment of a major network of sales offices. The company is also developing a network of representatives throughout the rest of Latin America.

Codensa (Colombia)

Codensa distributes electricity to 1,536,035 clients in the city of Bogota; this constitutes about 24% of the entire country. The volume of power sold during 1997 was 7,929 GWh, with an energy loss of 23.8%.

Central Hidroelectica De Betania (Colombia)

This was Enersis' first investment in Colombia, in 1996. Betania has an installed capacity of 540 MW, and in 1997 generated 2,070 GWh.

Emgesa (Colombia)

Emgesa is the largest electric power generating company in Colombia. It has eight generating plants with a total of 2,458 MW of capacity. Emgesa produced 11,200 GWh of power during 1997.

Endesa (Chile)

The Empresa Nacional de Electricidad, S.A., *Endesa*, is the main electric power generating company in Chile. The government sold partial ownership to the private sector in 1989, when Enersis bought a 5% interest. Subsequently, additional share purchases have given Enersis a 25.3% holding in Endesa by 1995, and the right to place a majority of directors on Endesa's board. Endesa is now reported as a consolidated affiliate of Enersis on the holding company's books.

Endesa's main business is the generation of electric power, which it then transmits mainly through the Central Interconnected System (CIC). In addition, Endesa participates in the generating system in the northern part of the country as a part owner and operator of the Interconnected System of Norte Grande (SING). Exhibit 5 describes the production of electricity in Chile in 1996 and Endesa's role in it.

An interesting twist to Endesa's leadership in the Chilean power generation market is that it utilizes mainly hydroelectric power sources (i.e., rivers coming down from the Andes mountains). In the mid-1990s, Chile experienced a prolonged drought, which reduced the generating capacity of the hydroelectric plants and caused the country to become more dependent on thermoelectric power (from coal, oil, or natural gas). This drought caused Endesa to lose market share, since competitors were more able to deliver thermoelectric power during this time. Paradoxically, Endesa enjoys a major cost advantage when weather conditions are normal, since hydro power costs approximately one-tenth as much as thermo power to generate.

Endesa made its first foreign investment in Argentina in 1992, where it purchased the power plant, Central Costanera. With three plants operating in 1996, Endesa produced 9,513 GWh of electricity, constituting about 16% of total Argentine production.

In 1995 Endesa invested in Peru, buying 60% of the Empresa de Generacion Electrica de Lima, Edegel. Edegel has installed capacity of 689 MW of electricity, representing about 24% of total installed capacity in Peru. In 1995 Edegel produced about 2,650 GWh of electricity.

Ingenieria E Inmobiliaria Manso De Velasco

One of the key activities in generating and distributing electric power is the construction of power plants, transmission lines, and connections to users. While plant construction is contracted out to major construction firms, the

EXHIBIT 5   Installed Electric Power Capacity in Chile

	Capacity (MW)				Production (GWH)		
	Endesa	Total	% Endesa		Endesa	Total	%
SIC	2,641	4,594	57.5	SIC	12,868	22,421	57.4
SING	97	1,131	8.6	SING	30	5,545	0.5
TOTAL	**2,738**	**5,725**	**47.8**	**TOTAL**	**12,898**	**27,996**	**46.1**

Source: Endesa Annual Report. 1996.

engineering and construction of electric distribution lines and links was originally carried out within Chilectra. This last activity in 1988 was placed into the
wholly-owned subsidiary, Manso de Velasco.

Manso de Velasco continues to be the engineering and construction firm
used by Chilectra for constructing electricity distribution facilities. In addition,
Manso de Velasco has contracted to offer services to a wide range of outside
users, such as constructing lighting and power facilities for the Santiago metro
system and also installing lighting for public parks and gardens in the city.

Synopsis

Enersis has extensive activity in information technology to operate its power
generation and distribution businesses. This activity has been placed into the
subsidiary, Synapsis, which in addition sells information technology services to
outside clients.

Financial statements for Enersis and each of the major subsidiaries are
presented in the Appendices.

The Chilean Context

Chile is one of the most industrialized countries in Latin America. With a per
capita income of over $US 3000 per year, Chile ranks at the top of the Latin
American region. Its population is highly educated, with adult illiteracy at just 5
percent of the population. The country has embraced a free-market capitalist
economic model since the overthrow of the Marxist regime of Salvador Allende
in 1973. Initially under the military regime of Augusto Pinochet, Chile began to
liberalize its economy long before this policy framework became popular in the
region. The "Chicago Boys" trained by University of Chicago free-market
economists such as Arnold Harberger and Milton Friedman followed a highly
successful set of policies to reduce barriers to competition and to stimulate
investment. Tariffs were gradually lowered to a uniform 10% ad valorem by 1976,
the least restrictive in Latin America. The door was opened to foreign direct
investment in 1976, when Chile withdrew from the protectionist Andean Pact
integration group and implemented its own liberal foreign investment regime.

The results of this economic opening in the 1970s were clearly very positive.
To a certain extent they were assisted unintentionally by the rise in raw materials
prices that accompanied the oil crises. Chile's main export product has long been
copper, and copper prices rose dramatically in the late 1970s. This alone produced solid economic growth in the country during those years. When oil and
other raw materials prices dropped in the early 1980s, and when the foreign debt
crisis hit the region in 1982, Chile unfortunately was dragged down as well, and it
took several years until the economy rebounded. In comparison with other Latin
American countries, however, Chile did pull out of the crisis more rapidly. By
1986 GDP was growing by a positive 6 1/2% per year, and this continued through
the rest of the decade. In the early 1990s Chile's economy remained near the top
of the Latin American list, with an average growth rate of 7.4% per year.

Chile's government began in the 1970s a process of *privatization*, or sell-off of
state-owned companies, that has been followed in various degrees throughout
the rest of Latin America in the late 1980s and 1990s. At a time when the
economic model of import-substituting industrialization was widely followed in
the region, Chile turned its back to that view and aggressively began a process of
open markets and export-led growth. Since the government participated in the

economy as owner of well over half of industry, a major step to opening markets was the denationalization of companies. This was begun with the sale of Compañía de Cervecerías Unidas (beer), Cemento Melón (cement) and Celulosa Arauco (paper) in the late 1970s, and with subsequent sales of electric power, telephone, airline, and other government-owned businesses in the 1980s.

In the 1990s the Chilean model uses the government as regulator and overseer of the economy, much as in the industrial countries of Europe and North America—with a few key exceptions such as the national copper company, Codelco, which still remains in state hands.

Interestingly, there has been a very considerable consensus in Chile on the free-market economic policies that have been followed. This policy framework was closely associated with the Pinochet military regime, which, as any such government, was criticized for being authoritarian. Without debating that issue, it can be concluded that the Pinochet regime did indeed strongly support the open-market policy framework, and consistently maintained it through economic booms and recessions. When Pinochet stepped down as President in 1988, the elected government of Patricio Alwyn continued the economic policy framework, as have subsequent Chilean governments. The result was an economic performance (e.g., growth, inflation, balance of payments) superior to all other countries in Latin America from 1975 to 1995.

Recent History of Chile's Electricity Sector

The electric power sector in Chile is divided into three stages: generation, transmission, and distribution. The generation sector consists of companies that generate electricity from hydroelectric and thermal electric sources and sell their production to distribution companies, other regulated and unregulated customers, and to other generation companies. The transmission sector consists of companies that transmit high-voltage electricity from the generating companies. These companies are all subsidiaries of the main generation and distribution companies. Distribution companies purchase electricity from generating companies at the nodes of the countrywide system, typically at low voltage (23 kV or less), and then distribute it for sale to the public. Each of these segments is privately owned, with government regulation on pricing and oversight on service quality. Exhibit 6 describes the system.

The national electricity industry is divided into two large geographic grids, the Central Interconnected System (SIC) and the Interconnected System of Norte Grande (SING). In addition there are several other systems, including systems owned and operated by individual industrial companies (e.g., copper companies) for their own use, typically in remote areas.

As discussed above, Endesa dominates power generation in Chile, with approximately a 50% market share. Endesa owns and operates 16 power plants connected to the SIC and another three power plants connected to the SING.

At the level of distribution, there are eight major companies and several smaller ones. Their characteristics are described in Exhibit 7.

Chilectra and Rio Maipo are both part of the SIC network, which provides power to Santiago and to about 90% of Chile's total population.

Legal Framework

Chile's electricity law essentially allows private ownership of all stages of electric power production and distribution, with public-sector regulation and price

EXHIBIT 6   Stages in the Electric Power System

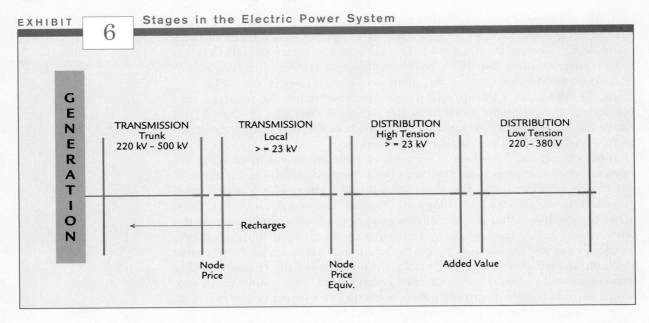

controls. The National Electricity Commission (CNE) sets prices and plans expansion of the system. The Superintendencia de Electricidad y Combustibles sets and enforces technical standards for the system. And finally, the Ministry of Economy has final authority over electricity prices, and it regulates the granting of concessions to electric generation, transmission, and distribution companies.

Probably one of the key continuing problems faced by Enersis was the complex system of price controls placed on the electricity sector. Negotiation of prices of power generation for sales to distributors and of power distribution for sale to final customers takes place on a four-year cycle, and in general prices fall behind costs by the end of each cycle. Endesa and Chilectra regularly seek to keep their output prices in a profitable range, but the negotiation process often is drawn out and leads to periods of very low profit.

EXHIBIT 7   Distribution of Electricity in Chile by Company

Company	Number of Customers	%	Sales GWH	%
Chilectra (ENERSIS)	1,099	36	6,676	50
CGE	498	16	1,918	15
Chilquinta	335	11	1,122	9
Rio Maipo (ENERSIS)	230	7	763	6
Saesa (COPEC)	319	10	939	7
Emec	151	5	426	3
Frontel (COPEC)	149	5	336	3
Emel	130	4	169	1
others	170	6	759	6
TOTAL	3,081	100	13,108	100

Source: Comision Nacional de Energia. 1995.

The electricity law seeks to provide objective criteria for electricity pricing and resource allocation. The regulatory system is designed to provide a competitive rate of return on investments in order to stimulate private investment, while ensuring electricity to all who request it. Under the law, companies engaged in electric power generation must coordinate their activities through the association of power suppliers, CDEC (Centro de Despacho Economico de Carga), for either the SIC or the SING, to minimize the operating costs of the electric system. Generation companies meet their contractual sales requirements with power that they either generate themselves or buy on the open market. Because Endesa's production in the SIC is primarily hydroelectric, its marginal cost of production is generally the lowest in the system, and therefore Endesa generates most of the power it sells there. Generation companies have to balance their contractual obligations with their delivery of power by buying any needed electricity at the spot market price, which is set hourly by the CDEC based on the marginal cost of production of the last generation facility utilized.

The main purpose of the two CDECs in operating the power assignment system is to ensure that only the most efficiently-produced electricity reaches customers. The CDECs also seek to ensure that every generation company has enough installed capacity to produce the electricity needed by its customers. Sales of electric power may be made through short-term or long-term contracts, or between generation companies, in the spot market. Generation companies may also contract to deliver power among themselves at negotiated prices. Generation companies are free to determine whether and with whom to contract, the duration of contracts, and the amount of electricity to be sold.

Sales of electricity to distribution companies for resale to regulated customers (customers with demand for capacity less than or equal to 2 megawatts) must be made at the node prices then in effect at the relevant locations or "nodes" on the interconnected system. Two node prices are paid by distribution companies: node prices for capacity and node prices for energy consumption. Node prices for capacity are calculated based on the annual cost of installing a new diesel fuel gas turbine generation facility. Node prices for energy are calculated based on the projected short-term marginal cost of satisfying the demand for energy at a given point in the interconnected system, quarterly during the succeeding 48 months in the SIC and monthly during the succeeding 24 months in the SING. To calculate the marginal costs, a formula is used that takes into account 10-year projections of the principal variables in the cost of energy such as water reservoir levels, fuel costs for thermoelectric power, maintenance, demand levels, etc.

A generation company may need to purchase or sell energy or capacity in the spot market at any time depending on its contractual requirements in relation to the amount of electricity that it is able to produce. These purchases and sales are transacted at the "spot marginal cost" of the interconnected system, which is the marginal cost of the last generation facility to be dispatched.

Energy supply prices are unregulated for final customers with a connected capacity greater than 2 MW (referred to as "large customers"), for temporary customers, and for customers that have special quality requirements. Customers not subject to regulated prices may negotiate prices freely with distribution and/or generation companies. All other customers are subject to the maximum prices established by the tariffs.

As far as electric power *distribution* is concerned, tariffs are established to allow distribution companies to recover their costs of operation, including allowed losses, and a return on investment. The operational costs include: selling, general and administrative costs of distribution; maintenance and operating costs of distribution assets; cost of energy and capacity losses; and expected return on investment of 10% per year in real terms including the cost of renewing all the facilities and physical assets used to provide the distribution services, including interest costs, intangible assets and working capital. The various costs are based on an average of those incurred by electricity distribution companies operating in Chile. Thus, more efficient companies may earn more than 10% returns, and less efficient ones less.

Key Competitors in Chile

The main competitor in Chile is most importantly Chilgener. Chilgener is a major competitor in power generation, with thermoelectric plants in Santiago, Valparaiso, and in Copaipo. In addition, Chilgener owns several electricity distribution companies operating in both the central and the northern power grids. Chilgener consistently bids for electric power projects in Chile and elsewhere in Latin America (especially Argentina) against Chilectra and Endesa. In a highly-publicized recent duel for construction of a natural gas pipeline between Argentina and Chile, a consortium led by Chilgener beat Enersis and gained a major new power source. Other smaller electric companies, such as Chilquinta, also compete domestically and abroad with Enersis.

Separate from the two major electric distribution grids, the electric companies serve "non-regulated clients," which are large-volume electricity users that are permitted to buy electricity directly from generating companies. The non-regulated clients are customers that use more than 2 MW hours of power—typically large industrial companies such as copper mines.

Global Strategy at Enersis

According to company documents, "The Company's business strategy is to use its accumulated utility experience and expertise to improve the profitability of its existing electric distribution and generation businesses in Chile, Argentina, Peru, Brazil, and Colombia, and to enhance the value of other businesses it may acquire in Latin America. The Company believes it has proven expertise in managing privatized utilities, including experience in reducing energy losses of distribution businesses, constructing and operating generation facilities, implementing proprietary billing and accounts receivable management systems, improving labor relations, increasing work force productivity, streamlining information systems, and operating under tariff and regulatory frameworks that reward efficient operations."

Following this broad statement in 1995, Enersis has continued to expand its activities in Latin America with the purchase of controlling interest in the Rio de Janeiro power distribution company, CERJ, and the Colombian power generation company, Betania. In addition, the company has diversified more widely in Chile, with the purchase of the water utility Lo Castillo in Santiago in 1996 and various real estate activities through the Endesa subsidiary, Infraestructura 2000.

Strategic Alliances of Enersis

Enersis has used strategic alliances frequently in its short history. When building the information systems part of its business, Enersis formed Synapsis as a joint venture with Unisys Corporation of the United States. After three years of operation, Enersis bought the partner's interest and now runs Synapsis as a wholly owned subsidiary.

In overseas ventures Enersis has worked exclusively with local partners in each country, as well as with other foreign investors on some occasions. For its initial foray into Argentina, a joint venture (Distrilec) was formed with Perez Companq (a large Argentine conglomerate) and PSI (from the U.S.) to own the power distribution company, Edesur. Likewise, when entering Peru to buy the power generation company, Edelnor, the company formed a joint venture with Endesa of Spain, Compañia Peruana de Electricidad, and Banco del Credito del Peru. Subsequently, when bidding for and winning the ownership of CERJ in Brazil, Enersis formed a joint venture with Endesa (Spain) and Electricidad de Portugal. No Brazilian partner participated in the consortium with Enersis on this occasion, but the consortium itself has Electrobras as a local partner in the total shareholding of CERJ. For capital and technology resources, Enersis has found the Spanish electric company, Endesa, to be a valuable partner in these and other projects.

As a policy, Enersis management asserts that strategic alliance partners will continue to be sought in each foreign venture undertaken, to assure knowledge of the local market and treatment as a local (at least partly local) company. The bias against foreign companies is particularly strong in Enersis' situation, for example, because Argentine companies and government agencies often view Chilean firms as smaller, less capable competitors, and because Peruvian companies and government agencies often view Chilean firms as antagonists, given the history of conflicts between the two countries. To defuse some of this opposition, in addition to gaining local market knowledge, Enersis will continue to work with local partners in future Latin American ventures.

Even as Enersis continues to actively use strategic alliances in its international ventures, the company maintains a clear policy of seeking to exert the highest possible degree of managerial influence in the businesses undertaken. It always follows an intention of long-term ownership, and generally obtains majority control of the board of directors (i.e., operational control) of affiliates.

Diversification Strategy

Enersis management has defined the strategy of the firm to be focused on the electric power industry and on related activities. These related activities began with the establishment of a subsidiary for information technology and one for real estate and construction activities. Since that time, additional activities have largely fallen into the categories of electric power generation and distribution outside of Chile and diversification into other sectors inside Chile. In 1996, the water company, Lo Castillo, was purchased. This move was justified as a step into additional infrastructure that accompanies electric power. In fact much of the distribution and physical facilities' construction are quite similar between the two businesses, so the diversification may be reasonably related to the core business after all.

Enersis, through Manso de Velasco, has spread its activities far from electric power, investing in construction of apartment buildings in Viña del Mar, a highway tunnel connecting Santiago with the coast (El Melon), and other ventures that have much to do with real estate and construction but virtually nothing to do with electricity other than relating to infrastructure development. While the real estate/infrastructure ventures do move the company away from power generation, these activities constitute substantially less than 10% of the total business, and the intention is to keep this type of diversification limited to a small percentage of total Enersis activity.

The Challenge of Operating Multinationally

Enersis has now been involved in business outside of Chile since 1992. This experience has not been without some missteps. For example, when expanding into Argentina, Enersis faced the inability to reduce staffing at the Edesur electricity distribution company, due to local labor rules. As well, there was a relatively low level of motivation of the labor force there, due to a history of state ownership of the electricity sector and the lack of performance-related incentives for the workers. It took Enersis managers more than two years to carry out the needed staffing reductions and to install modern performance measures and incentives.

As the Latin American region became more attractive for foreign investment during the 1990s, electric power utilities became important targets for foreign companies in the region. Once the threat of the external debt crisis had been extinguished by about 1991, interest began to pick up. At the beginning of the decade, Enersis had very few competitors when it bid for power companies that were being privatized in Argentina, Peru, and Brazil. By the middle of the decade, American companies such as Houston Energy, AES, Duke Power, and others had entered the bidding in Brazil, Mexico, and elsewhere. At the same time European power companies such as Iberdrola (Spain), Electricite de France, ENE (Italy) and Electricidad de Portugal also entered the fray.

Enersis found that the most useful strategy for dealing with the foreign competition, and being a foreign company itself outside of Chile, was to ally with a local power company in the target market and with one or more industrial-country companies. This package of Enersis management skills, local knowledge held by the local partner, and capital plus technology contributed by the U.S. or European partner, turned out to be a winning combination in bids for Edelnor in Peru, CERJ in Brazil, and Betania in Colombia.

A continuing problem for Enersis in overseas business is the fact that most electric power business remains in government hands throughout Latin America. This problem extends as well to the generation of electricity, where, for example, Argentine government-owned companies operate nuclear power plants that compete with Endesa to supply power to the distribution networks.

Appendix A Enersis S.A. and Subsidiaries Consolidated Statements of Income Years Ended December 31,1997 and 1996 (expressed in Thousands of Chilean Pesos—M$)

	1997	1996
Operating Results:		
Revenue from Operations	1,334,976,829	1,233,788,841
Cost of Operations	(857,443,897)	(763,248,909)
Gross Profit	477,532,932	470,539,932
Administrative and Selling Expenses	(115,128,805)	(124,625,967)
Net Operating Income	362,404,127	345,913,965
Other Income (Deductions):		
Interest Income	37,867,295	31,892,890
Equity in Income of Related Companies	31,999,177	17,610,537
Other Income	59,736,909	72,550,465
Equity in Loss of Related Companies	(987)	(9)
Amortization-Goodwill	(35,006,194)	(24,132,148)
Financial Expenses	(158,395,649)	(108,835,106)
Other Expenses	(43,947,488)	(29,052,406)
Monetary Correction	41,053,618	24,285,123
Non-Operating Income	(66,693,319)	(15,780,654)
Income Before Income Taxes and Minority Interest	295,710,808	330,133,311
Income Taxes	(57,002,970)	(40,701,164)
Income Before Minority Interest	238,707,838	289,432,147
Minority Interest	(157,945,493)	(179,094,920)
	80,762,345	110,337,227
Amortization-Negative Goodwill	22,753,925	2,307,295
Net Income	103,516,270	112,644,522
Liabilities and Stockholders' Equity Current Liabilities		
Due to Banks and Financial Institutions—Short-Term	56,328,049	79,321,790
Due to Banks and Financial Institutions—Current Installments	56,185,075	81,251,887
Bond Issues	39,622,264	52,059,672
Long-Term Obligation—Current Installment	6,097,099	9,682,682
Dividends Payable	18,714,200	48,621,825
Accounts Payable	80,828,450	62,828,616
Notes Payable	359,140	794,334
Miscellaneous Payables	43,054,841	44,174,656
Notes and Accounts Payable to Related Companies	7,519,838	5,337,297
Provisions	39,198,551	33,500,327
Withholdings	58,220,021	32,738,280
Deferred Income	6,253,329	19,733,523
Deferred Taxes	167,726	182,949
Other Current Liabilities	19,571,116	19,602,614
Total Current Liabilities	432,119,719	489,930,452

(*continued*)

Appendix A (*continued*)

	1997	1996
Operating Results:		
Long-Term Liabilities		
Due to Banks and Financial Institutions	1,707,736,423	969,611,840
Bond Issues	963,287,650	611,034,148
Notes Payable	28,725,949	24,893,286
Miscellaneous Payables	7,712,680	3,784,433
Provisions	19,301,360	8,558,077
Other Long-Term Liabilities	43,157,727	43,455,860
Total Long-Term Liabilities	2,769,921,789	1,661,327,644
Minority Interest	2,272,352,449	1,558,254,355
Stockholders' Equity		
Paid-In Capital	372,505,262	372,505,262
Premium on Sale of Own Shares	22,600,111	22,600,111
Other Reserves	21,594,889	22,163,444
Retained Earnings:		
Prior Years	232,469,742	196,759,783
Net Income for the Year	103,516,270	112,644,522
Interim Dividends	(46,665,681)	(43,883,980)
Total Retained Earnings	289,320,331	265,520,325
Total Stockholders' Equity	706,020,593	682,789,142
Total Liabilities and Stockholders' Equity	6,180,414,550	4,392,201,593

Source: Enersis Annual Report. 1997.

Appendix B Ownership of Eñersis as of 12/31/97

Shareholder	Number of Shareholders	Number of Shares	%
ENDESA Spain	5	1,981,587,840	29.16
Pension Funds	13	2,164,892,601	31.84
ADRs (Citibank as Depositary Bank)	1	1,132,239,300	16.65
Foreign Equity Funds	19	150,909,038	2.20
Stockbrokers, Mutual Funds, and Insurance Companies	97	364,098,443	5.35
Other Shareholders	12,665	1,006,272,778	14.80
TOTAL	**12,800**	**6,800,000,000**	**100.00**

As of December 31, 1997, Enersis S.A. was owned by 12,800 shareholders of record. The twelve largest shareholders of the company were:

Name of Shareholder	Number of Shares	%
Citibank N.A. (Depositary Bank)	1,132,239,300	16.65
A.F.P. Provida S.A.	424,999,771	6.25
Compania de Inversiones Luz y Fuerza S.A.	445,061,585	6.55

(*continued*)

Appendix B (*continued*)

Name of Shareholder	Number of Shares	%
Compania de Inversiones Chispa dos S.A.	445,061,585	6.55
A.F.P. Habitat S.A.	439,578,489	6.46
Compania de Inversiones Los Almendros S.A.	445,061,585	6.55
Compania de Inversiones Chispa Uno S.A.	445,061,585	6.55
A.F.P. Santa Maria S.A.	297,490,170	4.37
A.F.P. Proteccion S.A.	224,955,672	3.31
A.F.P. Cuprum S.A.	264,364,775	3.89
Endesa Desarollo S.A.	201,341,500	2.96
Compania de Inversiones Luz S.A.	194,412,126	2.86
Subtotal (12)	4,959,628,143	72.95
Other Shareholders (12,788)	1,840,371,857	27.05
TOTAL SHAREHOLDERS (12,800)	**6,800,000,000**	**100.00**

Source: Enersis Annual Report. 1997.

Appendix C Enersis's Subsidiaries

Compared Balance Sheets for the Years Ended 1996 & 1997 Consolidated Financial Statements (in th Ch$)

Company	Chilectra S. A.		Compania Electrica Del Rio Maipo S. A.		Ingenieria E Inmobiliaria Manso De Velasco S. A.	
	1996	1997	1996	1997	1996	1997
Assets						
Current Assets	95,932,965	113,655,826	6,905,251	5,103,062	80,165,281	57,556,408
Fixed Assets	164,847,753	178,162,696	23,685,481	26,250,384	59,234,937	61,332,698
Other Assets	379,964,688	437,704,746	744,612	633,057	68,835,658	71,321,779
Total Assets	640,745,406	729,523,268	31,335,344	3,198,650	208,235,876	190,220,885
Liabilities						
Short-Term Liabilities	58,650,663	82,328,872	7,339,729	6,480,372	100,203,749	83,691,072
Long-Term Liabilities	306,420,814	349,552,396	7,780,720	8,172,423	13,411,853	8,332,892
Minority Interest	123,453,124	12,323,641	0	0	16,522,817	18,695,577
Equity and Reserves	223,769,192	231,755,351	14,156,363	15,223,794	10,287,095	10,094,723
Subsidiary's Organization						
Cost	0	0	0	0	(104,700)	(155,125)
Accumulated Profits/Losses	11,628,679	23,463,597	906,555	908,673	57,375,144	60,480,194
Net Income	75,613,700	81,219,326	7,679,842	8,008,277	19,208,102	19,386
Less Interim Dividends	(47,682,766)	(51,119,915)	(6,527,865)	(6,807,036)	(8,671,184)	638
Total Liabilities and Equity	640,745,406	729,523,268	31,335,344	31,986,503	208,235,876	(10,304,986)

Compared Income Statements for the Years Ended 1996 & 1997

Company	Chilectra S. A.		Compania Electrica Del Rio Maipo S. A.		Ingenieria E Inmobiliaria Manso De Velasco S. A.	
	1996	1997	1996	1997	1996	1997
Operating Income						
Operating Revenues	292,409,961	278,601,779	36,909,063	35,611,809	55,715,923	61,322,185
Operating Costs	(204,231,674)	(189,633,558)	(26,344,032)	(25,452,716)	(33,144,910)	(38,505,737)
Operating Margin	88,178,287	88,968,221	10,565,031	10,159,093	22,751,013	22,816,448
Administrative and Selling Expenses	(27,950,367)	(22,535,093)	(3,635,883)	(2,653,949)	(5,834,837)	(4,168,383)
Operating Income	60,227,920	66,433,128	6,929,148	7,505,144	16,736,176	18,648,065

Compared Balance Sheets for the Years Ended 1996 & 1997 Consolidated Financial Statements (in th Ch$)

Company	Chilectra S. A.		Compania Electrica Del Rio Maipo S. A.		Ingenieria E Inmobiliaria Manso De Velasco S. A.	
	1996	1997	1996	1997	1996	1997
Non-Operating Income						
Non-Operating Revenues	64,013,747	74,206,722	3,781,890	3,456,969	9,132,738	7,365,254
Non-Operating Costs	(35,929,075)	(49,392,093)	(1,935,881)	(1,933,976)	(8,493,689)	(8,404,216)
Monetary Adjustment	458,642	3,231,872	146,227	642,586	2,744,554	3,394,882
Non-Operating Income	28,543,314	28,046,501	2,092,236	1,865,579	3,383,603	2,355,920
Income Tax	(11,296,447)	(11,569,453)	(1,341,542)	(1,362,446)	(1,499,578)	(2,192,476)
Minority Interest	(1,861,087)	(1,690,850)	0	0	(1,320)	(22,037)
Negative Goodwill Amortization	0	0	0	0	58,922	597,166
Net Income	75,613,700	81,219,326	7,679,842	8,008,277	19,208,102	129,386,638

Compared Balance Sheets for the Years Ended 1996 & 1997 Consolidated Financial Statements (in the Ch$)

Company	Chilectra S. A.		Compania Electrica Del Rio Maipo S. A.		Ingenieria E Inmobiliaria Manso De Velasco S. A.	
	1996	1997	1996	1997	1996	1997
Assets						
Current Assets	5,298,555	7,315,617	5,300,799	6,182,065	1,419	76,797
Fixed Assets	1,303,521	971,981	401,102	412,784	1,466	1,172
Other Assets	36,818	5,798	62,053	47,484	327	288
Total Assets	6,638,894	8,293,396	5,763,954	6,642,333	3,212	78,257
Liabilities						
Short-Term Liabilities	3,120,286	4,426,779	3,946,667	4,842,934	2,563	998
Long-Term Liabilities	97,082	60,452	129,139	106,039	0	0
Minority Interest	326	196	0	0	0	0
Equity and Reserves	3,519,754	3,519,754	1,374,800	1,374,800	65,987	69,561
Subsidiary's Organization Cost	0	0	0	0	0	0
Acumulated Profits/Losses	(1,236,720)	(98,554)	2,982	5,011	(62,432)	(65,338)
Net Income	1,138,166	2,060,079	2,043,231	2,088,050	(2,906)	5,082,808

(continued)

Appendix C (*continued*)

Compared Balance Sheets for the Years Ended 1996 & 1997 Consolidated Financial Statements (in th Ch$)

Company	Chilectra S. A.		Compania Electrica Del Rio Maipo S. A.		Ingenieria E Inmobiliaria Manso De Velasco S. A.	
	1996	1997	1996	1997	1996	1997
Less Interim Dividends	0	(1,675,310)	(1,732,865)	(1,774,501)	0	(5,009,772)
Total Liabilities and Equity	6,638,894	8,293,396	5,763,954	6,642,333	3,212	78,257

Compared Income Statements for Years Ended 1996 & 1997

Company	Chilectra S. A.		Compania Electrica Del Rio Maipo S. A.		Ingenieria E Inmobiliaria Manso De Velasco S. A.	
	1996	1997	1996	1997	1996	1997
Operating Income						
Operating Revenues	9,960,829	11,163,764	21,133,538	20,201,295	0	0
Operating Costs	(6,795,779)	(7,132,759)	(15,706,397)	(15,115,664)	0	0
Operating Margin	3,165,050	4,031,005	5,427,141	5,085,631	0	0
Administrative and Selling Expenses	(1,914,044)	(2,009,342)	(3,005,473)	(2,583,994)	(2,848)	(3,286)
Operating Income	1,251,006	2,021,663	2,421,668	2,501,637	(2,848)	(3,286)
Non-Operating Income						
Non-Operating Revenues	526,984	770,727	273,882	146,180	60	5,088,892
Non-Operating Costs	(316,216)	(169,111)	(192,207)	(226,786)	0	(4)
Monetary Adjustment	(95,182)	(199,020)	(48,717)	(14,779)	(118)	(2,794)
Non-Operating Income	105,586	402,596	32,958	(95,385)	(58)	5,086,094
Income Tax	(218,389)	(364,196)	(411,395)	(318,202)	0	0
Minority Interest	(37)	16	0	0	0	0
Negative Goodwill Amortization	0	0	0	0	0	0
Net Income	1,138,166	2,060,079	2,043,231	2,088,050	(2,906)	5,082,808

Source: Enersis Annual Report. 1997.

CASE DISCUSSION QUESTIONS

1. What are Enersis' main strengths? What is Enersis's main strategy?

2. What are some major problems/issues facing Enersis?

3. What has been Enersis's main strategic alliance focus? Why are they so reluctant to form strategic alliances with foreign companies? Do you see some problems with that strategy?

4. What should they do next? What are some issues with the way they decide to go?

CASE CREDIT

Copyright © 1999 Thunderbird, The American Graduate School of International Management. All rights reserved. This case was prepared by Professor Robert Grosse, Thunderbird, and Professor Carlos Fuentes, Universidad Gabriela Mistral, for the purpose of classroom discussion only, and not to indicate either effective or ineffective management.

Endnotes

[1] This project is actually fairly complex, including the construction of a natural gas pipeline across the Andes from Salta in Argentina to Mejillones in northern Chile, building a power plant in Mejillones, and connecting it to the national power grid (SING) at Atacama.

Enersis is co-owner of both the pipeline and the power plant, along with partner CMS. CMS operates the gas pipeline, and Enersis operates the power plant—which is connected to both the SIC and SING distribution networks.

Strategy Implementation for Multinational Companies: Human Resource Management

part four

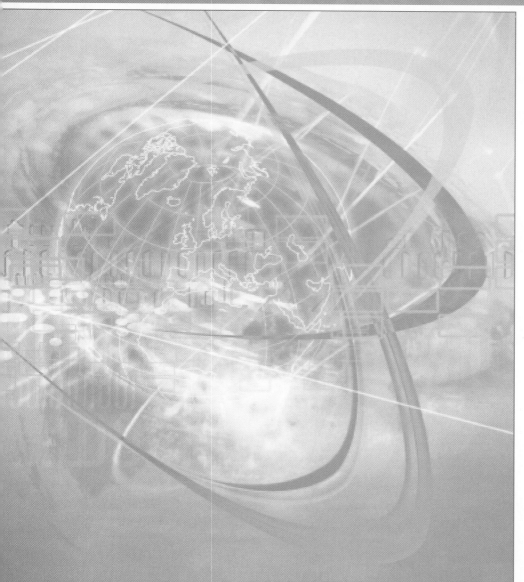

chapter 11

International Human
Resource Management

chapter 12

HRM in the Local Context:
Knowing When and How
to Adapt

Preview CASE IN POINT

Fast-Track Global Multinationals

U.S. companies and other multinationals around the world are increasingly relying on their expatriates to run their operations worldwide. As these companies search for new customers and markets abroad, they have a growing need for managers with the necessary skills for global assignments. One study showed that nearly half of the companies surveyed experienced an expansion of their expatriate workforce. That survey also showed that close to 21 percent of companies had expatriates leave the company in the middle of their assignment. It is clear that properly managing expatriates present both significant opportunities and challenges.

Companies that have serious ambitions to become key global competitors are devoting significant resources to manage international assignments. Consider DuPont's expatriate management program. DuPont routinely send its employees on international assignments. For example, engineers from Mexico and the United States may be sent to work on a chemical paint in China. Such international assignments pose challenges because DuPont has to deal with multiple nationalities within the same assignment. Instead of allowing each country or division to set its own policies, DuPont is finding that having standardized international assignment policy works well for its 300 to 400 international assignments each year. DuPont's Global Transfer Center of Expertise manages all aspects of the program from preparing the candidates for the international assignment to finding educational opportunities for the candidates' children.

As the global ambitions of U.S. companies grow, so do the global ambitions of managers. Now, many fast-track managers feel they must seek out global assignments as necessary steps in their careers. In many companies, such as Citicorp, Gillette, Texaco, 3M, General Motors, AT&T, General Electric, Procter & Gamble, Deloite Touche Tomatsu, and Ford, top managers are now being replaced by a new breed of executive. These new top managers have years of global experience and may not even be U.S. nationals. At 3M, for example, 75 percent of the top 100 executives have worked outside the United States. More than half of the top management group at Ford has worked outside the United States, perhaps not surprising for a company with 60 percent of its workforce in other countries. This new breed of top managers is changing U.S. corporate culture, espousing and insisting that managers have international experience. As one expert on international staffing noted, when an international opportunity arises, "Either you take up the offer or suffer the consequences later in your career."

Sources: Based on Business Wire 2006; Hube 2000 and Loeb 1995 and Oster et al. 1993 and Kiger 2002 Schoeff 2006 and SHRM 2003.

The Preview Case in Point shows that more multinationals are seeking internationally experienced managerial talent to run their operations in the global market. This emphasis on building internationally experienced management talent comes from the increasing popularity of global multinational strategies in response to a globalizing world economy.

A key ingredient of implementing any successful multinational strategy includes using compatible human resource management policies. This chapter discusses a number of crucial issues companies face when they apply human resource management practices in a global context. In combination with the next chapter on comparative views of human resource management, you will see how multinational managers select and implement appropriate human resource management policies to support their multinational strategies.

The chapter first presents a basic definition of international human resource management and shows how international human resource management differs from strictly domestic human resource management. The chapter then discusses how multinational companies must choose a mixture of employees and managers with different nationalities to set up operations in different countries. The chapter gives particular attention to the role, selection, training, and evaluation of multinational managers who are given international assignments. The chapter also explains issues regarding women with international postings and the particularly difficult conditions that face female expatriates. The chapter then outlines one of the most recent developments in human resource management—electronic human resource management—and its usefulness to international human resource management. The chapter concludes with a discussion of the four basic orientations to international human resource management and how each of these orientations best supports different multinational strategies.

International Human Resource Management Defined

Business organizations necessarily combine physical (e.g., buildings and machines) and financial assets as well as technological and managerial processes to do some type of work. However, without people, the organization would not exist.

Managing and developing human assets are the major goals of human resource management. **Human resource management (HRM)** deals with the entire relationship of the employee with the organization. The basic HRM functions consist of recruitment, selection, training and development, performance appraisal, compensation, and labor relations. They are defined as:[1]

- *Recruitment:* Identifying and attracting qualified people to apply for vacant positions in an organization.
- *Selection:* The process by which companies choose people to fill vacant positions in the organization.
- *Training and development:* The processes by which employees acquire the knowledge, skills, and abilities to perform successfully both in current jobs and in the future jobs they will have in their organizational careers.
- *Performance appraisal:* The system used by an organization to measure and assess employees' work performance.
- *Compensation:* The organization's entire reward package, including not only financial rewards and benefits, but also nontangible rewards such as job security.
- *Labor relations:* The continuing relationship between an employer and employees who are represented by labor organizations.

International Human Resource Management and International Employees

When applied to the international setting, the HRM functions become **international human resource management (IHRM)**. When a company enters the international arena, all the basic human resource management activities remain, but they take on added complexity. Two issues lead to this complexity for the multinational manager. First, the employees of multinational organizations include a mixture of workers of different nationalities. Second, multinational managers must decide how necessary it is to adapt the company's HRM policies to the national cultures, business cultures, and social institutions where the company is doing business.

Types of Employees in Multinational Organizations

IHRM must take into account several types of employees in the multinational organization. **Expatriate** employees come from a country that is different from the country in which they are working. Expatriate employees who come from the parent firm's home-country are called **home-country nationals.**

The expatriate workers who come from neither the host nor the home-country are called **third-country nationals.** Local workers come from the host-country, where the unit (plant, sales unit, etc.) is located. These workers are called **host-country nationals.** Usually, home-country and third-country expatriates belong to the managerial and professional staff rather than to the lower-level workforce. The globalization of the workforce also is breeding a special type of expatriate called the **inpatriate.** Inpatriates are employees from foreign countries who work in the country where the parent-company is located. Finally, recent trends, suggest a new breed of workers known as **flexpatriates.** Flexpatriates are employees who are sent on frequent but short-term international assignments.[2]

Given the high costs of expatriates, more and more companies are relying on flexpatriates on more short-term international assignments. Consider the following Focus on Emerging Markets.

Human resource management (HRM)
Functions are recruitment, selection, training and development, performance appraisal, compensation, and labor relations.

International human resource management (IHRM)
All HRM functions, adapted to the international setting.

Expatriate
Employee who comes from a country that is different from the country in which they working.

Home-country nationals
Expatriate employees who come from the parent firm's home-country.

Third-country nationals
Expatriate workers who come from neither the host nor home-country.

Host-country nationals
Local workers who come from the host-country where the unit (plant, sales unit, etc.) is located.

Inpatriate
Employees from foreign countries who work in the country where the parent-company is located.

Flexpatriates
Employees who are sent on frequent but short-term international assignments.

Focus on Emerging Markets

Rotational Assignments in Asia-Pacific

Recent surveys show that companies are increasingly relying on short-term intensive international assignments because of the excessive costs of full expatriate programs. For instance, because of the intense competition for skilled professionals in China and many emerging Asian countries, companies are using short-term rotational assignments to quickly develop and retain these skilled individuals. Such rotations involve moving flexpatriates from position to position in different countries.

Such rotation presents many advantages for companies. Short-term rotational assignments tend to be more cost efficient than full expatriate programs. Furthermore, by working for shorter durations in different countries, participants can accelerate learning by developing the necessary communication, team-building and decision-making skills to function in the global environment. Companies such as General Electric and Procter & Gamble use rotational assignments to develop their future leaders. They devise assignments tailored to their workers' abilities and potential.

Although many companies are sending expatriates on shorter assignments, their experiences suggest that many important issues need to be addressed to ensure that such programs work. For instance, because of the short-term nature of the assignment, it is better to send expatriates to countries that have cultures more similar to their own. Companies are finding that transfer of learning to China tends to work better if rotations are in other Asian countries. Companies also are still expected to be ready to address family, compensation and performance appraisal issues.

Source: Based on Fallon 2006 and Tahvanainen Welch and Worm 2005.

Adaptation of HRM Practices   An effective IHRM system has both company-wide HRM policies and procedures and HRM policies and procedures adapted to different country locations. Even for transnational companies, there often must be some adaptation of the firm's HRM practices to the traditions, national cultures, and social institutions of host countries. Adaptations of HRM practices are particularly necessary when dealing with non-managerial employees. These employees are usually host-country nationals who expect a multinational company's HRM practices to fit their local traditions. To avoid costly mistakes in HRM, effective management of host-country workers requires an in-depth knowledge of that country's HRM practices. Chapter 12 explores HRM practices in different countries in detail and provides background necessary to understand local HRM practices and to know when and how to adapt to local conditions.

This chapter next considers other issues that are pertinent to IHRM, including the choice between expatriate and local-country managers, the role of women as expatriates, and the usefulness of electronic human resource management to multinationals. Most of the issues discussed in the remainder of this chapter focus on IHRM practices for managers. The issues discussed in the next chapter are, in general, more relevant to IHRM practices for lower-level host-country national workers.

One of the most important IHRM issues relating to the implementation of multinational strategies is developing the correct HRM policies and procedures regarding the use of expatriate managers. These managers often will have ultimate responsibility for the firm's international operations and will implement much of a firm's multinational strategy. Consequently, the following section of this chapter focuses on IHRM issues with particular relevance to the use of expatriates.

Multinational Managers: The Expatriate or the Host-Country Manager

U.S. companies employ more than 7 million people outside the United States. Although most of these employees are lower-level workers, they require a significant number of managers. When are the management positions filled by expatriates? When are they filled by host-country nationals? Deciding how many expatriates or local managers to use depends mostly on a company's multinational strategy. Transnational strategists see their managerial recruits as employable anywhere in the world. Multidomestic strategists tend to favor local managers or use expatriates only for short-term assignments. Regardless of multinational strategy, management teams usually contain a mixture of expatriate and host-country nationals. For a particular position, a firm might approach its staffing decisions by answering questions such as:[3]

- *Given our strategy, what is our preference for this position (host-country, home-country, or third-country national)?* For example, a company with a regional strategy may favor the use of third-country nationals as country-level managers.

For expatriate managers (parent-country or third-country nationals):

- *Is there an available pool of managers with the appropriate skills for the position?* To use expatriate managers, a company must have qualified and available managers within its own ranks, or it must be able to recruit qualified parent-company or third-country managers to fill open positions.
- *Are these managers willing to take expatriate assignments?* Not all managers will take assignments abroad. Some managers believe that international assignments can hurt their advancement at home. Increasing numbers of managers have employed spouses, making it impossible to take an international assignment.
- *Do any laws affect our assignments of expatriate managers?* Some countries have strict restrictions on foreigners taking employment. Temporary work visas may be difficult or impossible for employees to obtain.

For host-country managers:

- *Do our host-country managers have the expertise for the position?* To use host-country managers, the local labor pool must have available managers with the training and expertise to fill open positions. Host-country managers often lack the expertise of managers from multinational companies.
- *Can we recruit managers with the desired skills from outside our firm?* Even if qualified managerial talent exists in a country, a foreign multinational might not have the reputation or the local connections to attract host-country managerial talent. For example, in Japan, many college graduates are reluctant to work for foreign multinationals because they do not provide the security of Japanese companies.

Is the Expatriate Worth It?

IHRM decisions regarding the use of expatriate managers must take into account the costs of such assignments. Total compensation of expatriate managers often is three to four times higher than home-based salaries and benefits. Extremely costly locations such as China can be even higher. In China, for example, a bilingual senior U.S. executive can expect a base salary approaching $400,000, hardship allowances as high as 35 percent of salary, two free houses (one in Hong Kong for the weekends and one in China), and chauffeur-driven cars.[4] An expatriate manager with a base salary of $100,000 and a family of four can cost as much as $360,000 in Tokyo, $275,000 in Hong Kong, $210,000 in Singapore and $250,000 in London. As the Case in Point below shows, expatriates assignments can sometimes carry unusual compensation packages.

The compensation packages of expatriates are dependent on the cost-of-living in the particular country to which the expatriate is sent. Mercer Human Resources Consulting develops a cost-of-living index that companies routinely use to determine how much they will pay their expatriates. The index uses New York as a base and compares prices in the country with New York by weighting price ratios in the expenditure patterns of the expatriate. The index then is a measure of the cost-of-living of American employees assigned to a foreign country. Exhibit 11.1 shows additional data on the cost-of-living index in 15 selected cities. As the exhibit shows, of the 50 cities surveyed by Mercer Human Resources Consulting, Tokyo is the most expensive city for multinational companies to send expatriates.

Even with such high costs, the success of an expatriate assignment is not guaranteed. U.S. companies in particular have poor records of expatriate success when compared with European and Japanese multinational companies. Surveys show that U.S. multinationals often have failure rates for managers in overseas assignments ranging from 10 to 40 percent[5] while other international surveys reveal that 83 percent of companies surveyed experienced expatriate failure.[6] A more recent study shows that 21 percent of companies surveyed had

C A S E   I N   P O I N T

Unusual Expatriate Expenses

As more multinationals extend their operations in remote locations around the world, they have to provide significant benefits to encourage expatriates to go to such locations. The following describes some of the more unusual benefits given to expatriates.

- In countries with extreme temperatures, expatriates are provided with clothing allowances. For instance, British expatriates in Russia often find that their wardrobe is not suitable for the freezing winters.
- Expatriates sent on assignment in South America rainforest areas are provided with suitable safari-style clothing.
- In parts of Sweden and Canada where it snows almost year round, expatriates are given allowances to have snow regularly cleared off their roof.
- Expatriates sent to non-English-speaking countries often are given allowances for Internet and other benefits, such as global news channels
- Expatriates sent to remote regions of China are given allowances to take shopping trips to bigger cities
- Expatriates sent to countries affected by war or other natural disasters, increasingly are being provided with extensive insurance coverage, with special emphasis on accidental death and disability, to deal with catastrophic situations.

Source: Based on Employee Benefits 2005 Mueller 2006.

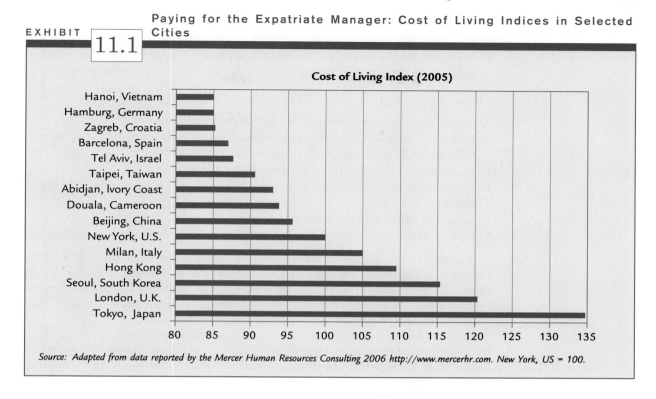

EXHIBIT 11.1 Paying for the Expatriate Manager: Cost of Living Indices in Selected Cities

Source: Adapted from data reported by the Mercer Human Resources Consulting 2006 http://www.mercerhr.com. New York, US = 100.

expatriates leave in the middle of their international assignments.[7] Clearly, ensuring expatriate success is a major challenge for companies.

Failure can often take many forms.[8] Some expatriates may be reassigned to the home-country for poor performance. Others may choose to return on their own because of their own or their family's difficulties adjusting to the local culture. Expatriates also may willingly choose to return because they find themselves ineffective in their jobs. Some companies also see expatriate failure when their expatriates end their assignments prematurely to take jobs with other companies.

Although it has been traditionally assumed that expatriates fail because they are not adequately prepared for their foreign assignments, there are other factors that account for failure. Often, such failures occur because companies don't have human resource management policies compatible with expatriate policies.[9] Many organizations tend to neglect appropriate human resource practices when they send their employees overseas.

Typical reasons for U.S. expatriate failure include individual, family, cultural, and organizational factors:[10] These include:

Individual

- Personality of the manager
- Lack of technical proficiency
- No motivation for international assignment

Family

- Spouse or family members fail to adapt to local culture or environment
- Family members or spouse does not want to be there

Cultural

- Manager fails to adapt to local culture or environment
- Manager fails to develop relationship with key people in the new country because of the complexities of cultivating networks with diverse people

Organizational

- Excess of difficult responsibilities of international assignment
- Failure to provide cultural training and other important pre-assignment training such as language and cultural acquisition training
- Company fails to pick the right people for the job
- Company promises but fails to provide the technical support domestic managers are used to
- Excess of difficult responsibilities of international assignment
- Failure of company to consider gender equity when considering candidates

Because of the problems associated with using expatriates, some U.S. multinational companies have questioned their use of expatriates. The high costs of locating expatriates in overseas assignments, the high costs associated with failed assignments, and the difficulties of finding U.S. managers with skills like language fluency combine to discourage some companies.

In contrast, however, many multinational companies, especially those with transnational or regional strategies, view international assignments in a broader, longer-term perspective. To compete successfully in the twenty-first century, such companies see international assignments as having a key strategic role. Consider the following benefits:

- *International assignments help managers acquire skills necessary to develop successful strategies in a global context.* **Strategic management in the next decades will require managers who understand global competition, customers, suppliers, and markets. Seldom can managers make effective strategic decisions without considering global implications. Without international-management experience, future top managers may not develop talents such as understanding foreign customers or foreign governments. Recognizing such challenges, companies such as Colgate-Palmolive provide a variety of international assignments both for high-potential managers and managers who recently have graduated from college.[11]**

- *Expatriate assignments help a company coordinate and control operations dispersed geographically and culturally.* **Expatriates with a shared vision and objectives for the corporation serve as links to communicate corporate needs and values to culturally and geographically diverse local subsidiaries. Expatriates also have firsthand knowledge of local situations and communicate local needs and strategic information to headquarters. In contrast, an overuse of host-country managers may create employees who identify primarily with the host-country subunit rather than with the global organization.[12]**

- *Global assignments provide important strategic information.* **Because of the length of typical expatriate assignments (two to five years) compared with short visits from headquarters, expatriate managers have sufficient time to gather complex information.[13] For example, in politically risky countries, an experienced expatriate manager can provide the top management of the parent-company with critical and timely information. This information might include key trends in the host-country's political, economic, and financial environments.[14]**

- *Global assignments provide crucial detailed information about local markets.* **Expatriates have incredible in-depth knowledge of local markets.**[15] This information need to be part of the strategic planning of companies as it can be extremely critical for companies that have wide geographic presence. For instance, Colgate-Palmolive's expatriates' detailed knowledge of local markets enabled them to determine that small sachets of detergent sell better in Africa than the typical 64-ounce bottle sold in the U.S. Similarly, interviews of 16 Austrian expatriates in Polish banks, revealed that the bankers acquired significant knowledge of local market conditions such as the legal system.[16]

- *Global assignments provide important network knowledge.* **Because expatriates meet many people such as clients, suppliers and people within the subsidiary,** they create an important network in the host-country. Because they are the main contact people between the host company and the parent-company, they also may develop a new network at the home company. Such networks can be very useful as they can create new business opportunities and help the subsidiary function smoothly.[17]

The tradeoff between the strategic benefits of international assignments and the high costs of using expatriates has led some companies to consider other options. The following section considers two other possibilities.

International Cadre and Flexpatriates: Other Choices

The high costs of expatriate managers and the need for managers who think and act globally create conflicting pressures for multinational companies. One reaction by multinational companies is to create a separate group of managers who specialize in international assignments. These international specialists are called the **international cadre** or *globals*. Another reaction by some multinational companies is to use flexpatriates on much shorter assignments, usually lasting less than one year.

Members of the international cadre have permanent international assignments. They are recruited from any country and are sent to worldwide locations to develop cross-cultural skills and to give the company a worldwide perspective.[18] Their main job is to promote sharing and learning by all organizational locations and by multinational employees of all nationalities.

Similar to the diplomatic corps of countries, members of the international cadre spends their career moving from one international assignment to another. They often develop their own international organizational culture, differing somewhat from their companies' main organizational culture.[19] For example, Colgate-Palmolive Co. calls its international cadre the "globalites." Rather than gaining ten years of experience before their first international assignment, as is common in most U.S. multinational companies, these Colgate-Palmolive managers are recent college graduates who expect to have long globe-hopping careers.[20] IBM uses a global database to search for talent for any project. Although preference is given to geographically closer managers or engineers, employees who indicate a willingness to move become eligible for global positions.[21]

The use of a permanent international cadre is more common for European firms than for U.S. multinationals. Perhaps because international issues are so pertinent in post-1992 Europe, many European companies believe it is necessary to develop an organizational culture that promotes international consciousness, tolerance, and cooperation at all levels of the organization.[22] Along

International cadre

Separate group of expatriate managers who specialize in a career of international assignments.

with using an international cadre, many European companies also attempt to give international experience to all managers at all levels and at a much earlier age. High-potential managers in particular are singled out for these international experiences.[23] For example, Unilever considers 75 percent of its managerial positions "international." If you take a job with Unilever, international assignments are part of the deal.[24]

More companies also are relying on flexpatriates to run their international operations. Flexpatriates are the frequent flyers who travel on short notice for shorter time durations while maintaining their family and personal lives at the home-country location.[25]

Flexpatriates serve key functions for the multinational companies. They often are sent to explore markets, consider problem areas in the foreign subsidiary, manage projects or even help with transfer of technology. Compared to expatriates, flexpatriates offer significant benefits for companies.[26] Flexpatriates offer more flexibility as employees are sent on a variety of much shorter assignments around the world. In contrast, expatriate assignments are of much longer duration. Flexpatriates also can still enjoy the many benefits of being an expatriate as they enjoy similar levels of challenge and autonomy. However, they do not experience many of the family and personal difficulties and stress associated with expatriate assignments. Most important, flexpatriate assignments are much less expensive than expatriate assignments since they involve no relocation or repatriation costs.

Despite the significant advantages, flexpatriates also can be problematic for companies. For instance, if the assignment exceeds six months, taxation issues can become complicated. Because they may have had little experience with flexpatriates, the local tax authorities may not have a system in place to accommodate such tax situations. In some cases, the companies may end up paying the flexpatriate's tax because of a reluctance to bear such burdens.[27] Additionally, because of the short nature of the assignment, the flexpatriate does not fully integrate into the local work environment and does not learn how to fully adapt locally. As flexpatriates rely on home work practices, they may be resented for neglecting the host-country culture.

Given the growing use of flexpatriates in companies, it is important to develop effective human resources policies to ensure a smooth flexpatriate experience. For instance, interviews of Finnish human resource managers described by Tahvanainen et al.,[28] reveal that many of the companies studied did not have adequate policies in place to manage their flexpatriates. Staff selection tends to be more informal while many companies tended to ignore pre-departure cross-cultural training. It is advisable for companies to apply many of the human resources policies discussed below for expatriates below (selection, compensation, training) to flexpatriates.

Next, the chapter considers how to use the expatriate manager to maximize strategic advantage.

The Expatriate Manager

Once a company makes the decision to use expatriate managers or to develop a full-time international cadre, successful multinational organizations develop IHRM policies that maximize the potential effectiveness of their expatriate managers. This section discusses the effective selection, training and development, performance appraisal, compensation, and repatriation of the expatriate multinational manager.

Selecting Expatriate Managers

Selecting the wrong person for any job can lead to failure and can be a major expense for the company. It is even more pronounced for expatriates because a failed expatriate assignment can cost the company from two to five times the assignee's annual salary.[29] In fact, it is estimated that each expatriate failure through early departure can cost a company more than $1 million.[30] Furthermore, it has even argued that improperly selected employees who cannot perform adequately but who remain on assignment can be even more damaging to the company than those assignees who leave prematurely.[31] Companies are, therefore, becoming more aware of the strategic need to select the right person for the job the first time. Consider the following examples in the Case in Point below.

Traditionally, multinational companies have assumed that domestic performance predicts expatriate performance. This assumption leads companies to search for job candidates with the best technical skills and professional competence. When these factors become the major, if not the only, selection criteria for international assignments, companies often overlook other important selection criteria.[32] What other criteria are important for selecting the best people for expatriate assignments?

Several experts on international IHRM have identified **key success factors for expatriate assignments.**[33] In addition to professional and technical competence,

> **Key success factors for expatriate assignments**
> Motivation, relational abilities, family situation, and language skills.

CASE IN POINT

Selecting the Right Person for the Assignment

More and more companies are realizing that it is critical for their success to send the right person abroad for the assignment. One key aspect of any successful selection program is advanced planning. To ensure successful selection, companies now are involving their human resource department in the process. Consider the following examples:

- Kellogg now has a system in place where managers are asked to select possible candidates for foreign assignments. HR and senior management then review the list and select individuals whom they consider to be ideal candidates. These candidates are then interviewed and surveyed based on their potential to do well on these assignments. The findings of the surveys, emphasizing potential risks and areas of concerns, are then presented to the candidates and their spouses. These candidates can then determine their chances of succeeding in the assignment.
- Apache Corporation, a natural gas and oil company with operations in Egypt, China and Poland, has implemented a formal system to identify potential candidates for expatriate assignments. Location managers are requested to report on their hiring

needs for the coming year. Employees are also surveyed to determine interested candidates. The company can then easily determine potential matches between employees and future open positions and whether they need to hire from outside.
- DuPont Corporation has developed a centralized expatriate program to take care of all human resource functions regarding expatriates. This program has allowed DuPont to better select and treat its 300 to 400 annual expatriates around the world.
- Key Equipment Finance, a leasing company based in Colorado used to select the best overall employees who often had long-term career goals incompatible with international assignments. However, Key Equipment Finance recently changed its selection procedures to find workers who had other skill sets but were willing to relocate. When these expatriates return, they still have growth room managing local markets.

Source: Based on Poe, Andrea C. 2002. "Welcome back." HRMagazine 45:3, pp. 94–101; Schoeff, Jr., Mark. 2006. "International assignments best served by unified policy." Workforce Management, Feb. 13, p. 36; Tyler, Kathryn. 2006. "Retaining repatriates." HRMagazine Mar 51:5, pp. 97–102.

the key success factors include relational abilities, family situation, motivation, and language skills. Consider the following:

- *Technical and managerial skills:* Often an expatriate assignment gives managers more tasks and greater responsibilities than similar-level assignments at home. Additionally, the geographical distance from headquarters can result in the manager having more decision-making autonomy. Only managers with excellent technical, administrative, and leadership skills have a strong likelihood of success in such positions.

- *Personality traits:* A foreign assignment inevitably comes with a host of unexpected problems and new situations. To be able to deal with such uncertainties and novelty, it helps if the expatriate is flexible, has a willingness and desire to learn new things, has the ability to deal with ambiguity, has an interest in other people and cultures, and has a good sense of humor. Extraversion also is critical to success.[34] Expatriates who are extraverts are more likely to be sociable and talkative. This trait can lead to higher motivation to communicate and develop relationships with locals. Such relationships with locals not only can help expatriates adjust better in the new country but also can provide access to important information regarding appropriate behavior in the new culture.

- *Relational abilities:* Relational abilities help employees avoid a major pitfall of international assignments, the failure to adapt to different cultures. People with good relational skills have the ability to adapt to strange or ambiguous situations. They are culturally flexible and sensitive to different cultural norms, values, and beliefs. They also have the ability to modify their own behaviors and attitudes to fit in with a new culture. They favor collaborative negotiation styles and avoid direct confrontation.

- *Family situation:* Selection for an international assignment also must consider the potential expatriate's family situation. An overseas assignment affects the spouse and children as much as the employee. A family situation favorable to the assignment is crucial for expatriate success. Key factors to consider include the spouse's willingness to live abroad, the impact of the potential posting on the spouse's career and the children's education, and the spouse's relational skills. Because of the increasing number of dual-career couples, multinational companies may need to provide two positions or compensation for the spouse's lost income to ensure a successful assignment.[35] The following Multinational Management Brief shows some of the programs companies now use to aid dual-career couples.

- *International motivation:* To overcome the challenges of more complex jobs, cultural differences, and strains on families, managers must be motivated to accept the expatriate position. Such motivation can come from a commitment to the company's international mission, an interest in the culture of the assignment country, and a good fit with the recruit's career stage. However, few good managers will accept an assignment that they perceive is detrimental to their career.

- *Stress tolerance:* The ability to tolerate stress is a crucial quality that can help an expatriate succeed on an international assignment.[36] Adapting to a new culture and work environment can be extremely stressful. Expatriates who can maintain their composure in the face of extreme stress are more likely to succeed in their new assignments.

- *Language ability:* The ability to speak, read, and write the host-country language enhances many of the other key success factors. Managers with good

Multinational Management **Brief**

Managing Dual Careers for the Expatriate

Ten years ago, the typical expatriate was a man with a spouse willing to forsake career to relocate to another country. Multinational companies now face many managers refusing international assignments for reasons related to their spouse's career. One survey found that sacrifice by their spouse is now the number one cause managers declining assignments. Furthermore, more expatriates are now paying attention to the work–family balance, and family matters often are important components of that balance. Companies like Motorola, HP, Royal Dutch Shell, and GE are responding. These firms give allowances for the spouse's career-building activities such as getting work permits or furthering education. Recent data show that 25 percent of the companies give spousal job search assistance, up from near zero in the early 1990s.

Consider some of the following examples:

- Royal Dutch Shell makes career counselors available for spouses and unmarried partners.
- Shell Oil Company created an information network with 44 centers for finding spouses jobs.
- Deloitte & Touche provides spouses a job-searching database on the company's intranet.
- 3M provides a one-time dislocation allowance for spouses and allows spouses who are employees to take personal leave.

The U.S government is also aware of the importance of helping family members of employees abroad. The Family Liaison Office of the U.S. State Department has set up the Strategic Networking Assistance Program (SNAP) in over 35 countries including Egypt, Singapore, Japan, and Mexico to help spouses find jobs. The program provides access to Local Employment Advisors (LEA) working closely with family members to help them find jobs. LEAs are responsible for developing a network of contacts that can be provided to family members for job searching purposes outside of the United States. The LEAs also provide one-on-one counseling, workshops and access to other published material.

Source: Based on Employee Benefits Magazine. 2006. "International: Cross-border perks: Small obstacle for monoliths." Feb. 10, p. S5; Latta, Geoffrey W. 1999. "Expatriate policy and practice: A ten-year comparison of trends." Compensation and Benefits Review, pp. 31, 35–39; Thaler-Carter, Ruth E. 1999. "Vowing to go abroad." HRMagazine, 44:12, pp. 90–96; U.S. Department of State. 2006. "Indexes of cost of living costs abroad." http://www.state.gov

language skills come better prepared to apply their technical and managerial skills. They have more success in dealing with local colleagues, subordinates, and customers. Knowledge of the local language also increases the understanding of the local culture and reduces the stress of adapting to a new cultural environment.

- *Emotional intelligence:* More recent research also suggests that emotional intelligence is a crucial success factor.[37] Emotional intelligence refers to the ability of being aware of oneself, understanding and relating to others and being empathetic and managing one's emotions. Expatriates inevitably need to relate to others and manage their own presence. Expatriates with higher emotional intelligence are more likely to be able to relate to locals and show the appropriate emotions to adjust locally.

Selecting an expatriate manager with the appropriate array of skills demands more effort than selecting domestic managers. There are more key success factors to consider in international assignments than in domestic assignments. Most successful multinationals use a combination of selection techniques to identify people with the appropriate talent for an expatriate posting. Some popular techniques include interviews, standardized tests of intelligence or technical knowledge, assessment centers (testing centers where candidates solve simulated managerial problems), biographical data, work samples, and references.

Exhibit 11.2 shows some of the characteristics of the key success factors and selection techniques used in the expatriate selection process.

The importance of the expatriate success factors is not equal for all expatriate job assignments. Each success factor has a different priority depending on four assignment conditions. These conditions are:[38] assignment length, cultural

EXHIBIT 11.2   Expatriate Success Factors and Selection Methods

Key Success Factors	Selection Methods					
	Interviews	Standardized Tests	Assessment Centers	Biographical Data	Work Samples	References
Professional/technical skills						
➤ Technical skills	✔	✔		✔	✔	✔
➤ Administrative skills	✔		✔	✔	✔	✔
➤ Leadership skills						
Relational abilities						
➤ Ability to communicate	✔		✔			✔
➤ Cultural tolerance and empathy	✔	✔	✔			
➤ Tolerance for ambiguity	✔		✔			
➤ Flexibility to adapt to new behaviors and attitudes	✔		✔			✔
➤ Stress adaptation skills	✔		✔			
International motivation						
➤ Willingness to accept expatriate position	✔			✔		
➤ Interest in culture of assignment location	✔					
➤ Commitment to international mission	✔					
➤ Fit with career development stage	✔			✔		✔
Family situation						
➤ Spouse's willingness to live abroad	✔					
➤ Spouse's relational abilities	✔	✔	✔			
➤ Spouse's career goals	✔					
➤ Children's educational requirements	✔					
Language skills						
➤ Ability to communicate in local language	✔	✔	✔	✔		✔

Source: Adapted from Black, J. Stewart, Hal B. Gregersen, and Mark E. Mendenhall. 1992. Global Assignments. San Francisco: Jossey-Bass; Ronen, Simcha. 1986. Comparative and Multinational Management. New York: Wiley.

similarity, required communication with host-country nationals, and job complexity and responsibility. Each of these conditions affects the selection criteria as follows:

- *Assignment length:* The amount of time an expatriate expects to remain in the host-country may range from short postings of a month or less to several years. Selection for short-term assignments usually focuses primarily on technical and professional qualifications.

- *Cultural similarity:* Cultures vary widely, but certain cultures are more similar to each other. The cultural similarity of Japan and Korea, for example, is higher than that of the United States and Taiwan or France and Saudi Arabia. Thus, finding the right French or U.S. expatriate for an assignment in the Middle East or Asia requires more emphasis on family factors, relational skills, and language skills. Managers from similar cultures usually find adaptation much easier.

- *Required interaction and communication:* Some jobs require more interaction and communication with host-country nationals such as subordinates, suppliers, customers, and joint-venture partners. Increased relational skills and knowledge of the host-country language and culture become more important in such situations.

- *Job complexity and responsibility:* People in jobs with more complex tasks and greater responsibilities often have significant effects on the success of projects. For this reason, professional and technical skills are always important. However, the more important the job to the organization, the more the candidate's skills and previous success in related work will count in the selection decision.

Exhibit 11.3 summarizes issues to consider in setting priorities during the expatriate selection process. Different success factors have more importance depending on the expatriate's job assignment conditions.

The efforts to ensure the best chance of the expatriate manager's success do not end with the selection process. Expatriates need training and development. Next, we consider training and development for the expatriate.

EXHIBIT 11.3   Selecting Expatriates: Priorities for Success Factors by Assignment Characteristics

Expatriate Success Factors	Assignment Characteristics			
	Longer Duration	**More Cultural Dissimilarity**	**Greater Interaction and Communication Requirements with Locals**	**More Complex or Responsible Job**
Professional/Technical Skills	High	Neutral	Moderate	High
Relational Abilities	Moderate	High	High	Moderate
International Motivation	High	High	High	High
Family Situation	High	High	Neutral	Moderate
Language Skills	Moderate	High	High	Neutral

Source: Adapted from Black, J. Stewart, Hall B. Gregersen, and Mark E. Mendenhall. 1992. Global Assignments. San Francisco: Jossey-Bass; and Tung, Rosalie L. 1981. "Selection and training of personnel for overseas assignments." Columbia Journal of World Business. 16 (1): pp. 68–78.

Training and Development

Cross-cultural training
Increases the relational abilities of future expatriates and, in some cases, their spouses and families.

Strong evidence shows that predeparture cross-cultural training reduces expatriate failure rates and increases expatriate job performance.[39] The main objective of cross-cultural training is to increase the relational abilities of the future expatriate and, when possible, the spouse and family of the future expatriate. The techniques used and the rigor of the training depend on the anticipated situations an expatriate might face in his or her assignment.

In spite of the evidence that training leads to successful expatriate assignments, many multinational companies still do not invest heavily in cross-cultural training.[40] This situation may be changing. U.S. multinational firms such as American Express, Colgate-Palmolive, and General Electric continually upgrade their international training concerns. A recent survey of 264 multinational companies by the consulting firm Windham International[41] with a total worldwide expatriate population of 74,709 found that approximately 63 percent now have cross-cultural training prior to expatriate assignments.

Training rigor
Extent of effort by both trainees and trainers required to prepare the trainees for expatriate positions.

Training rigor involves the extent of effort by both trainees and trainers required to prepare the trainees for expatriate positions.[42] Low rigor means that training lasts for a short period and includes techniques such as lectures and videos on the local culture and briefings concerning company operations. High-rigor training may last more than a month. It contains more experiential learning and extensive language training and often interactions with host-country nationals. Exhibit 11.4 shows various training techniques and their objectives as the rigor of the cross-cultural training grows.

EXHIBIT 11.4 Building Blocks of Cross-Cultural Training Rigor: Techniques and Objectives

Training Rigor (Low → High)

High

Techniques: Field trips to host country, meetings with managers experienced in host country, meetings with host country nationals, intensive language training.
Objectives: Develop comfort with host country national culture, business culture, and social institutions.

Techniques: Intercultural experiential learning exercises, role playing, simulations, case studies, survival language training.
Objectives: Build general and specific knowledge of host country culture, reduce ethnocentrism.

Techniques: Lectures, videotapes, reading background material.
Objectives: Provide background information on host country business and national cultures, basic information on company operations.

Low

Source: Adapted from Black, J. Stewart, Hal B. Gregersen, and Mark E. Mendenhall. 1992. Global Assignments. San Francisco: Jossey-Bass; Ronen, Simcha. 1986. Comparative and Multinational Management. New York: Wiley.

The same conditions that influence the priorities given to expatriate success factors in selection decisions also affect the requirements for an expatriate's training rigor. Increases in the length of the assignment, cultural dissimilarity between home and host-country, amount of required interaction and communication with local people, and job complexity/responsibility all suggest a need for increased training rigor as preparation for the overseas assignment.[43] Exhibit 11.5 shows how the rigor of training relates to the basic expatriate assignment conditions already discussed. Because a major reason for expatriate failure relates to family situations, training for a long assignment in a dissimilar culture may include training for all family members, not just the prospective expatriate.

As the Multinational Management Brief on page 530 shows, training cannot fully prepare expatriates to face life in the new country. Many companies are now relying on buddy programs to facilitate integration in the host-country.

Once expatriates are on assignment, IHRM does not stop. Multinational managers must have appropriate performance-appraisal techniques for employees in international assignments.

Performance Appraisal for the Expatriate

Conducting a reliable and valid performance appraisal of expatriate managers provides one of the greatest IHRM challenges for the international company. Seldom can a company transfer the same performance criteria and measures to a host-country operation.

Some of the issues that make expatriate performance appraisals difficult include:[44]

- *Fit of international operation in multinational strategy:* As discussed in Chapter 6, companies often enter international markets for strategic reasons other than the immediate profit of that particular international operation. Learning

EXHIBIT 11.5   **Training Needs and Expatriate Assignment Characteristics**

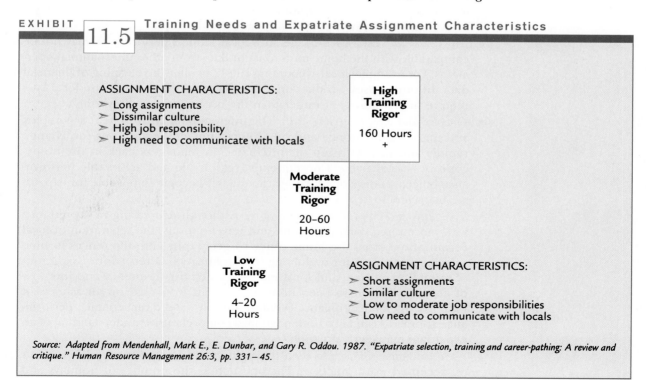

ASSIGNMENT CHARACTERISTICS:
➤ Long assignments
➤ Dissimilar culture
➤ High job responsibility
➤ High need to communicate with locals

High Training Rigor
160 Hours +

Moderate Training Rigor
20–60 Hours

Low Training Rigor
4–20 Hours

ASSIGNMENT CHARACTERISTICS:
➤ Short assignments
➤ Similar culture
➤ Low to moderate job responsibilities
➤ Low need to communicate with locals

Source: Adapted from Mendenhall, Mark E., E. Dunbar, and Gary R. Oddou. 1987. "Expatriate selection, training and career-pathing: A review and critique." Human Resource Management 26:3, pp. 331–45.

Multinational Management **Brief**

Expatriate Buddy Programs

According to surveys, some of the major challenges faced by expatriates when they start their assignments include such things as choosing schools for their children, finding housing, opening bank accounts, finding grocery stores, getting a driver's license and learning about the community. Unfortunately, many of these challenges cannot be easily addressed through pre-departure training. Expatriates usually must deal with such challenges when they start their foreign assignments.

Many global companies such as KPMG International and Balfour Beatty have implemented buddy programs to help expatriates better adjust to their new surroundings and deal with these challenges. In these programs, expatriates are assigned buddies in their host location. For instance, at Balfour Beatty, buddies receive cultural awareness training prior to the expatriates arriving. Once the expatriates arrive, they go through more cultural training with their buddies. Buddies also get time off work to help the newly arrived expatriates shop for houses and select schools. At KPMG, the buddies play an important networking role. They typically invite the expatriates to dinners and help them get adjusted socially. Other smaller companies motivate their expatriates through cash incentives to join local trade and social clubs. In general, global companies are finding that such buddy programs are useful to ensure that the expatriates adjust smoothly in their host locations.

Source: Krell, Eric. "Budding relationships." HRMagazine, 50, 6: pp. 114–118.

about a new market and challenging an international competitor may be strategic goals that put a subsidiary in the red but still serve a useful purpose for the organization. In these cases, local managers might look quite ineffective for a company that uses economic-performance measures such as return on investment, a standard profitability ratio (ROI).

- *Unreliable data:* Data used to measure local subunit performance may not be comparable with the home units' data or data from other international operations. For example, local accounting rules can alter the meaning of financial data. In other cases, production efficiency can look bad because local laws require full employment rather than the occasional use of overtime.
- *Complex and volatile environments:* The international environment is complex and unstable. Economic and other environmental conditions can change rapidly and in ways often unanticipated by managers back in the home-country headquarters. Consequently, reasonable and achievable performance objectives developed earlier can quickly become impossible for expatriate managers to achieve.
- *Time differences and distance separation:* Although decreasing in importance with more rapid communication and travel options, the separation of local organizations from the home office by geography and differences in time remains a problem for evaluating local managers. Often "out of sight, out of mind," expatriate and local managers lack the frequency and intensity of communication to keep home-office staff informed on all aspects of local management problems. Without intensive and direct contact, performance appraisals can fail to demonstrate a comprehensive understanding of an expatriate manager's situation.
- *Local cultural situations:* As seen throughout this text, countries differ widely on accepted work practices. Factors such as the number of holidays and

vacations, the expected hours of work, the training and types of local workers available, and the types of local managers available can directly affect the performances of expatriate managers. Although successful expatriate managers adapt quickly to the local cultural expectations, parent-country management and staff seldom have the same appreciation of the local situation. Good international performance appraisals must adjust for local cultural expectations regarding work.

To overcome the difficulty of conducting performance appraisals of international managers and other employees, experts suggest several steps to improve the process.[45]

- *Fit the evaluation criteria to strategy:* For example, if the objective is to enter a market for long-term position, it does not make sense to use short-term financial-performance measures.
- *Fine-tune the evaluation criteria:* Senior managers need to consider carefully all their objectives for the international operation. They need to visit local sites to understand more clearly the problems and situations faced by expatriate and local managers. Recently repatriated managers also can provide excellent knowledge about local circumstances.
- *Use multiple sources of evaluation with varying periods of evaluation:* The complexity of the international situation demands more information than similar appraisals done at home. As such, higher levels of management should rely on several sources of information. Exhibit 11.6 shows several common components of expatriate performance appraisals. These components include sources of evaluation information, evaluation criteria, and evaluation periods.

The next question considered is: How do multinational companies determine the fair and adequate compensation of expatriate managers?

Expatriate Compensation

Expatriate compensation presents significant challenges to companies. On the one hand, companies are being pressured to control the ever-growing costs associated with expatriate assignments with the knowledge that failure can

EXHIBIT 11.6 Evaluation Sources, Criteria, and Time Periods for Expatriate Performance Appraisals

Evaluation Sources	Criteria	Periods
Self-Evaluation	Meeting objectives Management skills Project successes	Six months and at the completion of a major project
Subordinates	Leadership skills Communication skills Subordinates' development	After completion of major project
Peer Expatriate and Host-country Managers	Team building Interpersonal skills Cross-cultural interaction skills	Six months
On-Site Supervisor	Management skills Leadership skills Meeting objectives	At the completion of significant projects
Customers and Clients	Service quality and timeliness Negotiation skills Cross-cultural interaction skills	Yearly

Source: Adapted from Black, J. Stewart, Hal B. Gregersen, and Mark E. Mendenhall. 1992. Global Assignments. San Francisco: Jossey-Bass.

reach exorbitantly high levels.[46] On the other hand, companies need to provide an appropriate compensation package not only to entice expatriates to relocate, but also to retain and motivate expatriate employees.

Compensation packages tend to include many common factors.[47] These factors include:

- *Local market cost of living:* One of the most important factors in determining the expatriate compensation is the cost of living in the country where the expatriate will be relocated. Often, companies will try to adjust the compensation levels so that the expatriate suffers no loss from relocation. As an example, expatriates sent to Japan may have close to 50 percent added to their home pay as services and goods allowances.

- *Housing:* Housing represents another key component in compensation packages. Many multinationals tend to provide some form of housing allowance with many companies providing free housing. Unlike providing cost-of-living allowances, providing comparable housing is much more difficult because there are major differences in acceptable sizes of houses. For instance, an American expatriate may easily move from a 3000-square-foot house in the United States to a smaller 1200-square-foot apartment in London. To provide an idea of housing costs, Exhibit 11.7 shows the average rent of two-bedroom unfurnished apartments in selected European cities.

- *Taxes:* How to deal with taxes is also an important aspect of compensation packages. Expatriates may face double taxation as they get taxed in the host-country as well as in the home-country. Although there are some exceptions, U.S. citizens and residents are taxed on their worldwide income.[48] As such, some multinationals often have to cover payment of taxes to ensure that their employees don't face double taxation.

- *Benefits:* Provision of similar home benefits such as pension and healthcare remains an important aspect of many compensation packages.[49] Many expatriates tend to be frustrated with their benefit packages when they are in the host-country. Often, the expatriate finds that the benefits are not similar to

EXHIBIT 11.7   Rent of a Luxury Two-Bedroom, Unfurnished Apartment

Source: Adapted from Mercer Human Resources Consulting 2006, http://www.mercerhr.com.

their home situation or are inadequate in the host-country. This situation suggests that more companies will need to find better ways to provide benefits to their expatriates. Recent events around the world also suggest the need for emergency benefits. Consider the following Multinational Management Brief.

As shown above, providing the appropriate compensation package can be a very daunting task. Some of the methods used to determine the level of benefits are discussed below.

The Balance-Sheet Approach

More than 85 percent of U.S. multinational companies commonly apply the **balance-sheet method** for determining expatriate compensation.[50] The balance-sheet method provides a compensation package that attempts to equate or balance an expatriate's purchasing power in the host-country with his or her purchasing power in the home-country.[51] The basic idea behind this approach is that the expatriate should not be in a better or worse position financially at the end of

Balance-sheet method
Attempts to equate purchasing power in the host country with the expatriate's purchasing power in his or her home country.

Multinational Management **Brief**

Providing Emergency Benefits

As more companies strive to take advantage of globalization opportunities while facing an increasingly competitive environment, they increasingly are finding it necessary to send expatriates to dangerous locations. Even the traditionally safer developed countries are not immune from dangers associated with emerging markets. Consider the recent bombings in both Madrid and London. As more countries face terrorism, war, natural disasters and other industrial accidents, companies are finding that they need to become better prepared to face such emergencies.

Although many multinationals choose to ignore foreign emergencies and develop policies only when they are hit by an emergency, more experts suggest a more proactive approach. These experts advise that multinationals to provide accidental death and disability (AD&D) benefits by working with insurers specializing in catastrophic coverage. Depending on where the expatriate is being sent, multinationals should provide policies and benefits that cover basics such as travel assistance (travel advisories, inoculations, and lost luggage). However, in some cases, more extensive programs such as catastrophe response may be necessary. Catastrophe response programs provide clearly defined procedures in the case of natural disasters or other human-made catastrophes. Some AD&D providers also provide event management programs where response plans are provided in case of emergency. Activities such as access to hospital or expatriate evacuations are planned ahead.

Providing AD&D benefits can be very advantageous to multinationals. Planning for emergencies ensures that injuries and loss of lives is minimized when such events do occur. With an AD&D plan, the responsibilities for providing support to an expatriate are in the hands of experts in case of emergencies. Often, multinationals find that responding to medical emergencies can be very complex. However, relying on AD&D programs ensures that expatriates are given the best possible care when emergencies do occur.

Source: Based on Employee Benefits Magazine. 2006. "Future strategy: Don't kid about cost of families joining workers." Jan 12, p. S39; Mueller, Stephen. 2006. "Shoring up protection for overseas employees." Risk Management, Mar 53:3, pp. 38–41; Houreld, Katharine. 2006. "Nigerian rebels fight for 'freedom'; Group tells foreign oil workers to leave delta or risk being killed" Washington Times Mar 9, p. A01.

the assignment. To balance the compensation received for the international assignment with compensation received in the home-country, multinational companies usually provide additional salary. This increased salary includes adjustments for differences in taxes, housing costs, and the costs of basic goods and services. Goods and services include items such as food, recreation, personal care, clothing, education, home furnishing, transportation, and medical care.[52] Exhibit 11.8 provides a simple view of how the balance sheet approach works.

Besides matching the expatriate's purchasing power, companies often provide other allowances and extra benefits called perquisites to the expatriate manager. These benefits cover the initial logistics of the international move (such as hotel costs while getting settled), compensation for lifestyle differences between the home and host-country, and incentives to take the assignment. Some of these additional allowances and perquisites include:[53]

- *Foreign-service premiums:* Multinational companies often provide 10 to 20 percent of base pay for accepting the individual and family difficulties associated

EXHIBIT 11.8   A Balance Sheet Approach to Expatriate Compensation

Domestic Assignment: Expenses and Spendable Income:		Expatriate Assignment: Expenses and Balanced Spendable Income + Allowances:
Base Salary	+	Base Salary
	=	
Taxes	=	Taxes
	+	
Goods and Services	=	Goods and Services
	+	
Housing	=	Housing
	+	
Spendable Income	=	Spendable Income

Allowances as an incentive to take position, foreign service premium, hardship pay, R&R

Allowances to balance extra tax payments

Allowances to cover cost of living differences, housing, children's education, medical costs, automobile, recreation, home leave travel

Allowances for moving expenses, settling in expenses, initial housing costs, and furnishing allowances with an overseas assignment. Approximately 78 percent of major U.S. multi-national companies pay this premium.

- *Hardship allowance:* This allowance provides extra money for a particularly difficult posting due to issues such as high risk or poor living conditions.
- *Relocation allowances:* Along with the basic costs of moving a family to an international assignment, many companies pay a flat amount equal to one month's salary at the beginning and end of the assignment to cover miscellaneous costs of relocating.
- *Home-leave allowances:* These allowances provide transportation costs for expatriates and their families to return to their home country once or twice a year.

Other Approaches

The high cost of expatriate compensation and the trend for multinational companies to have workers anywhere in the world doing similar work has resulted in companies developing modifications of the traditional balance sheet approach. Some companies simply pay home-country wages regardless of location. This approach, called the **headquarters-based compensation system,** works well when home-country wages are high compared with the local assignment's cost of living.[54] It can be a problem in high-cost locations such as Paris or Tokyo.

Many experts now recommend that companies wean expatriates gradually from dependence on perks and allowances that allow home-country managers to maintain the lifestyles they have at home, or sometimes to live better overseas.[55] These companies assume that there is nothing special about being an expatriate, especially for longer assignments.[56] After an initial period on assignment, allowances are reduced. Firms use local or regional markets to determine compensation. Such companies expect the expatriate to become an efficient consumer by adjusting to local lifestyles and costs of living. This approach is called the **host-based compensation system.**

The international cadre, those managers who work for global companies in a series of international assignments, presents different problems for compensation. To address the problem of compensation for multiple and continual global assignments, companies develop global pay systems. **Global pay systems** have worldwide job-evaluation and performance-appraisal methods designed to assess the worth of jobs to the company and equitably reward subordinates. To some extent, global pay systems resemble the balance-sheet system. Allowances still exist for differences in expenses such as cost of living, taxes, settling in, and housing. However, the system does not balance compensation to produce parity with lifestyles in the home-country. Rather, companies use a worldwide standard of compensation and make only necessary adjustments to that standard. The objective is to reduce waste from expatriate perquisites, eliminate the factor of steep differences in compensation from the decision to accept a given job, and promote compensation equity for all long-term international cadre managers.[57]

Although international cadre managers are not expected to "come home," most other types of expatriate managers return to their home company in their home-country. Returning home is not always as easy as many managers expect, and multinational companies often face the "repatriation problem."

The Repatriation Problem

Bringing expatriate employees home and back into full participation in the company remains a difficult problem for many organizations. For example, studies of North American companies found that 25 percent of managers completing

Headquarters-based compensation system

Paying home-country wages regardless of location.

Host-based compensation system

Adjusting wages to local lifestyles and costs of living.

Global pay system

Worldwide job evaluations, performance appraisal methods, and salary scales are used.

foreign assignments wanted to leave the firm.[58] Turnover may range from 33 percent to as high as 50 percent within two years after return.[59] A recent Cendant Mobility study also shows that approximately half of the companies surveyed had no repatriation program. This finding is especially troubling since U.S. employers often spend as much as $1 million to send an expatriate on an overseas assignment. It is therefore imperative for companies to try to retain returned expatriates.

The difficulties that managers face in coming back to their home countries and reconnecting with their old job form the **repatriation problem.** However, these difficulties can be solved with proper preparation and planning by the expatriate and the company.

Expatriates face at least three basic cultural problems when coming home.[60] Many of these problems relate to the phenomenon called "reverse culture shock" where people must relearn the subtleties of their own cultural norms, values, and beliefs. First, the expatriate must adapt to what is often a new work environment and organizational culture of the home office. This may lead to low work performance or turnover after the assignment. Second, expatriates and their families must relearn to communicate with friends and coworkers in the home and organizational cultures. Often, as part of adapting to their former host cultures, expatriates are unaware that they now use different communication patterns. Third, although surprising for people who have lived most of their life in their home country, many expatriates need time to adapt to the basic living environment, such as school, food, and weather.

There also are organizational problems for the expatriate and the company if repatriation is not. One survey reported that 61 percent of expatriates felt that they were not given the chance to use their international experience. After years in challenging international postings, three-quarters of expatriates reported that their present jobs were demotions. Often, there are no planned career paths for those expatriates returning home.[61] Three months after their return home, one-third of the former expatriates were still in temporary jobs.[62] Finally, expatriates also get used to the autonomy abroad and may no longer feel challenged when they return to the home office.

A variety of strategies exist that allow companies to have successful repatriations of their expatriates.[63] These include:

- *Provide a strategic purpose for the repatriation:* Use the expatriate's experiences to further organizational goals. Expatriates often provide excellent sources of information and experiences that companies should plan to use.
- *Establish a team to aid the expatriate:* The HRM department and the expatriate's supervisor can help plan for the expatriate's return. The returning expatriates can be provided with counseling so that they are aware of the challenges of repatriation as well as how business has changed at the local office. The team also can look for obvious reverse culture shock symptoms (boredom, fatigue, withdrawal, frustration, and isolation from co-workers) and can provide help as needed.
- *Provide parent company information sources:* Many companies assign mentors or sponsors who keep the expatriate informed of current changes in the company including job opportunities.
- *Provide training and preparation for the return:* This preparation can begin as early as six months before the return. Visits home and specific training for the next assignment help ease transition difficulties.
- *Provide a home-leave policy to encourage expatriates to make regular visits to the home office:* To make sure that expatriates stay connected to the home office,

Repatriation problem

Difficulties that managers face in coming back to their home countries and reconnecting with their home organizations.

companies can encourage and support regular visits to the local office. Companies also should include expatriates in corporate emails and newsletters to keep them in the loop.

- *Provide support for the expatriates and their families on reentry:* To ease the initial adjustments of coming home, companies can help find housing, provide time off for adjustments, and adjust compensation packages if necessary. Companies also may help the spouses of expatriates to find new jobs.

Even if companies have strong repatriation programs, they sometimes neglect an important aspect of an international assignment. Consider the following Multinational Management Brief.

Traditionally, in most multinational companies, international assignments have been male dominated. Why is this true? Is the practice continuing? Several issues arise when women take on international assignments.

International Assignments for Women

The most striking fact about women with international assignments is their paucity in numbers. Estimates are that only 12 percent of expatriate managers are women.[64] In North America, it is estimated that 14 percent of global assignees are women while women represent 45 percent of management in general.[65] In the U.K. it is estimated that only 9 percent of the expatriate population are women.[66] These data shows that while multinational companies are willing to promote women domestically, they are reluctant to post women overseas.[67] Personnel managers believe foreigners would be prejudiced against women managers.[68] In addition, of the women who do get international assignments,

---

Multinational Management **Brief**

Repatriation Programs and Promotions

Although repatriation programs can have significant long-term impact on companies, surveys show that they are the least developed areas of expatriate programs. The 2004 Cendant Mobility survey showed that only 49 percent of companies had repatriation programs. Even those companies that have repatriation programs often fail to consider one critical aspect: what to do when expatriates come back. The 2005 GEODESY survey revealed that almost one quarter of expatriates resigned within a year of returning to the home country. Such departures can represent significant losses for companies that have made substantial investments in their employees.

The most important factor dooming repatriation is that most companies fail to recognize that expatriates expect to be promoted when they return. However, the 2005 Geodesy survey showed that only 33 percent of expatriates are promoted while around 27 percent are not even guaranteed positions when they come.

To ensure that valuable expatriates are retained, some experts suggest that companies conduct post-assignment career planning even before the expatriates leave. This career planning will ensure that the expatriates know how they will be treated when they return. It also allows the expatriate to develop skills that may be needed upon repatriation.

Source: Based on PriceWaterhouseCoopers. 2005. "International assignments: Global policy and practice. Key trends 2005." PriceWaterhouseCoopers http://www.pwc.com; Tyler, "Retaining repatriates."

very few have top-management positions.[69] These findings are even more striking when one considers that North American companies use more women in international positions than do Asian or European companies.[70]

Why are the barriers so strong against women gaining international positions even in countries such as the United States where nearly half of the business-school graduates are women?

Culturally based gender-role expectations for women and men enter into many selection decisions. Some managers question whether family problems, a known predictor of expatriate failure, will be greater for women. They doubt whether women will be willing to take the time away from their families that is necessary to handle an expatriate position. They ask: How will the spouse fit in? What will happen if there are dual careers? Some even voice the concern that women are not tough enough to face the physical hazards, isolation, and loneliness of some international postings.[71]

However, the data tend to prove these prejudices wrong. Nancy Adler, a leading expert on women in international management, notes two important "myths" that lead HR executives and top-line managers to overlook qualified and motivated women for international postings. These are:[72]

- *Myth 1:* Women do not wish to take international assignments. In a survey of women graduating with MBAs, more than three-quarters said that they would choose an international position at some time during their career.
- *Myth 2:* Women will fail in international assignments because of the foreign culture's prejudices against local women. To address this myth, Adler surveyed more than one hundred women managers with international postings for North American companies. More than 95 percent of these women reported successful expatriate assignments, well above the average success rate for men.

Successful Women Expatriates: Foreign, Not Female

In a classic article, subtitled "A *Gaijin*, Not a Woman," Nancy Adler debunked one of the key myths regarding women as expatriates.[73] *Gaijin* is the Japanese word for foreigner. From her research, Adler concluded that it is a mistake to assume that people from foreign cultures, even traditionally patriarchal Asian cultures, apply the same gender-role expectations to foreign women that they apply to local women. It seems that people from even very traditional cultures can view foreign businesswomen so differently from the way they view local women that gender becomes irrelevant for business purposes. For example, one businesswoman working in the Sudan was surprised by the behavior of her Sudanese host. She asked him how it was possible that he could serve her food, give her a cushion to sit on, and wash her arms after the meal? Men never do these things for women according to traditional Sudanese gender-role expectations. The Sudanese host reasoned, "Oh, it's no problem. Women do not do business; therefore, you are not a woman."[74] After establishing a business relationship, according to Adler, the real issues that arise in cross-cultural interactions depend more on how people in the host-country culture react to people of the expatriate's nationality rather than to the expatriate's gender.

The following Case in Point describes a situation where a woman's business status determined how Japanese men responded to her.

The Woman's Advantage and Disadvantage

Some studies[75] suggest that women may have some advantages in expatriate positions, especially in Asia. Being unique has some benefits. Because so few

C A S E   I N   P O I N T

The Gender-Free *Meishi*

The Japanese and many other Asian cultures exchange business cards (*meishi* in Japanese) during introductions. *Meishi* serve to define status with one's company and determine how one should interact with business associates, even to the use of polite forms of language.

Two U.S. professors, a husband-and-wife team working on a research project in Japan, observed how the *meishi* determined the pattern of interaction with the woman. If the man was introduced first or the two were introduced as a married couple, Japanese businessmen and professors would focus attention on the man and treat the wife, politely but obviously, as *oksuma* (wife). However, if the woman also produced her *meishi* at the same time as the husband, the role of wife was ignored, and the Japanese responded to the woman in terms of her professional rank. She was *sensei* (a polite form of address for professors), and gender or marital status became irrelevant. It seemed particularly important, however, to initially establish professional rank. The Japanese seemed to have more difficulty moving a woman to professional status after they perceived her initially as a wife.

women have expatriate assignments, women who take expatriate positions report being more visible. Local businesspeople were more likely to remember them and often sought out these women more than the women's male colleagues. North American expatriate women also report that local businessmen from traditional cultures assume that the women are the "best," reasoning "Why else would you send a woman?"

Women also may be more likely to excel in relational skills, a major factor in expatriate success. Women report that local male managers can be more open in communication with a woman than with a man. Local men, even from traditional cultures, can talk at ease with a woman about an array of subjects that includes issues outside the domain of traditional "male only" conversations. Consequently, being both a businessperson and a woman gives expatriate women a wider range of interaction options than those available to expatriate men or to local women.[76]

Despite the many obvious advantages women expatriates enjoy, the situation is nevertheless bleak for many women expatriates. In-depth interviews with 50 European female expatriates revealed that they face much worse situations than their male counterparts.[77] Female expatriates are more likely to:

- *Face the glass ceiling:* Women expatriates have more difficulty being taken seriously at early stages of their career. They also are more likely to face isolation and loneliness.[78] They must work harder than their male counterparts, and constantly need to prove themselves. Studies have shown that, in some cases, women have to be at much higher positions than their male counterparts before they are assigned international positions.

- *Need to balance work and family responsibilities:* Because of socialization and childhood experiences, research suggests that women expatriates may have a higher burden than their male counterparts to balance family and home responsibilities. There is evidence that female expatriates may be more likely to have to choose between having an international career and a family, often because of very little support from the partner. It is, therefore, not surprising that women managers are less likely to be married or childless than their male counterparts.[79]

- *Need to worry about accompanying spouse:* **Many female expatriates felt that they could be successful only if the career of their spouse became secondary. However, because of societal norms, it is still difficult for male partners to accept that their spouse has the primary career. It also is not always easy for the company to accommodate the needs of the male partner because of visa regulations and other host-country work policies. It has also been found that female expatriates are more likely to have partners with professional careers and it is more difficult for the company to accommodate the needs of the partner.**[80]

Furthermore, even in societies where women may have advantages because they are viewed differently (e.g., *gaijin* in Japan), they still face significant barriers. For instance, although research found that western women had some advantages because they were seen as foreigners rather than women, it also found that these women faced significant barriers influencing their ability to adjust to the Japanese environment and to perform well at their jobs.[81] However, a more recent study argued that western women should have an easier time in Japan.[82] It reasoned that Japan has experienced many institutional changes such as a more flexible market, growth of foreign multinational presence, growth of women in the workforce and the 1986 Japan Equal Opportunity Act. These changes should result in some convergence between western and Japanese attitudes toward women and should provide for a better environment for women. However, results show that many of the barriers found in a similar study a decade ago are still strong. Foreign women managers still face cultural barriers, making it harder for them to adjust to their new jobs, perform well and become accepted in Japan.

As seen below, women will become an every-growing aspect of the expatriate population and companies can implement programs to ensure that women expatriates have an opportunity to flourish.

What Can Companies do to Ensure Female Expatriate Success?

Despite the disadvantages women face, the opportunities for women expatriate managers are expected to grow, particularly with global companies. Scholars see several factors leading to more women with international assignments.

Many global and multinational companies face an acute shortage of high-quality multinational managers.[83] At the same time, perhaps because of the rise in dual-career couples, fewer men are willing to take international assignments.[84] One way to solve this problem is to tap the available population of women managers. Freed from local cultural barriers that restrict the use of women managers, multinational companies can select the best people for the job regardless of gender. Because of potentially stronger relational skills, women managers often may be better qualified for international positions than their male colleagues.

Since women expatriates are likely to increase in proportion and they are as motivated and willing to take international assignments as men, companies must take the necessary steps to ensure that their female expatriates are successful. These steps are especially crucial given all of the barrier female expatriates face. Some potential steps include:

- *Provide mentors:* Because women expatriates face more barriers than their male counterparts, mentors can provide the necessary psychosocial support to face such obstacles.[85] Mentors can be informal and can provide guidance to the female expatriates. Mentors from the home office can provide the necessary support to facilitate re-entry back to the home office.

- *Provide opportunities for interpersonal networks as a form of organizational support:* Access to a network of colleagues in similar situation can be a source of social support and can provide contacts and other opportunities. Although it may be difficult for the female expatriates to gain access to the typical male-dominated networks,[86] the organization can take the necessary steps to develop formal professional networks of female managers.

- *Remove sources of barriers:* The organization should take the necessary steps to ensure that female expatriates are treated as fairly and equally as their male counterparts. The human resources department can be instrumental in ensuring that these female managers' unique needs also are considered. The organization also needs to take the necessary steps to educate their employees and change stereotypical attitudes toward women expatriates.

- *Provide support to cope with dual-career issues:* The organization should accept that women expatriates face peculiar and more difficult circumstances regarding their spouses than male counterparts do. It should provide the necessary counseling to ensure that the couple is aware of the difficulties an international assignment will represent to the family. The company also should help the spouse find an equivalent job or provide the necessary counseling.

Multinationals and Electronic Human Resource Management

As the previous sections demonstrated, the IHRM process is extremely complex relative to domestic HRM issues. Companies need to consider the various processes in the light of complications introduced by global operations. The crucial need to properly manage the expatriate experience also adds to the difficulty of IHRM. Below we consider electronic human resource management systems and how they can help the multinational company face IHRM challenges.

Because of rising pressures to contain costs, more and more companies are adopting **electronic human resources system (e.HR)**. e.HR involves the automation of various aspects of the human resources system of the company. As companies go global and rely on more international workers, e.HR can prove to be a very effective addition to IHRM. In this section, we discuss the strategic functions of e.HR and the steps to proper implementation.

Electronic human resources system (e.HR)

Automation of various aspects of the human resources system of a company.

Strategic Importance of e.HR

e.HR systems can be very cost effective for domestic organizations and even more beneficial for multinational companies. For multinationals and other companies involved in international operations, e.HR systems can provide the following strategic benefits:

- *Reduce HR and administrative system cost:* A properly designed e.HR program allows companies to considerably reduce costs. For instance, one of the functions of any HR department is to provide information related to benefits, pay inquiries and even training enrollment. e.HR can provide the necessary virtual location where expatriates can obtain valuable information at low cost to the organization.

- *Improve HR services to employees:* e.HR allows HR departments to improve HR services to employees and managers. By giving employees and managers quick access to valuable information, employee satisfaction with HR increases. Instead of waiting for days (and dealing with different time zones) to go through traditional HR routes, expatriates can readily access crucial information.

- *Employees take control of their own data:* e.HR also can allow employees to take control of their own personal data. Through e.HR, expatriates can update personal data (i.e., update family status changes), make payroll-related transactions (changes in withholding or deductions) and even view their pay stubs.[87] New hires also can use the self-service new-hire system to provide personal information and select benefits.

- *Repository of the wealth of knowledge and skills of expatriates:* Expatriates, through their foreign assignments, are likely to amass a wealth of knowledge about the culture and market conditions where they are serving.[88] Sophisticated e.HR systems can create an effective database of repatriate skills and knowledge. Such a database can be strategically valuable to companies as they scan new markets. Expatriates can rely on the database to scan the experiences of former expatriates as they face new challenges.

- *Employee tracking for career management and other HR purposes:* A successful e.HR system means that the company has at its disposal a database of all employees' vital information and skills. Organizations can use this database for expatriate career planning and for determining future hiring needs. Furthermore, an e.HR system can search for competencies and experiences that can help the organization identify potential candidates for foreign assignments.[89]

Proper Steps to e.HR Implementation

Although an e.HR program can be very valuable to a multinational company, it is costly and requires dedication for proper implementation. Companies can take several steps to enhance success. These include:

- *Develop business case to justify using e.HR or upgrading to e.HR:* HR departments need to provide evidence to justify investing in the technology needed to maintain an e.HR program. Important statistics may include the cost of a paper-based HR transaction relative to an e.HR based transaction. Consider the examples in the Case in Point on page 543.

- *Make the system customer-focused:* A sophisticated e.HR system should provide employees and managers with a painless way to produce the desired outcomes from the self-service system. For instance, if expatriates desire benefits information, they should be able to access the information easily.

- *Be proactive:* Companies need to anticipate changes and automate such changes. It also is important for companies to test changes before they are implemented.

- *Organize collected data in ways that are useful to the organization:* Pulling varied information together can be a challenging task, so organizations must

e.HR and Cost Savings

In the face of rising costs and the need to continuously monitor these costs, HR departments and companies must justify the need to maintain technologically-based e.HR systems. Companies are, therefore, finding more ways to track expenses to show cost savings. Consider the following examples:

- Texas Instruments initially tracked the expenses of its interactive phone centers and determined that an employee call to an HR person can cost from $4 to $30. By using a Web-based e.HR system, employees can now manage all of their HR and benefit programs for only a few cents per web transaction.
- Surveys in companies have shown that a paper-based travel and expense applications can cost

as much as $25 while automated Web-based systems cost only $5.
- Dow Chemical has been able to cut its recruiting costs by 25 percent and job advertising costs by 35 percent by implementing an automated resume-tracking and worker-profile system. Instead of reviewing hundreds of resumes, hiring managers can tap into the system's central repository to quickly identify qualified individuals. The new system has allowed Dow to cut hiring cycle time from an average of 95 days to only 30 to 35 days.

Source: Based on King, Julia. 2003. "Getting the right person at the right time." Computer World, February 3. http://www.computerworld.com; Jorgensen, Barbara. 2003. "e.HR is playing a larger role in corporate communications." Electronic Business, August, p. 36.

determine how the collected information can be used. For instance, if expatriate skills data are being collected, the company needs to have a system in place to fully benefit from that information.

e.HR systems can be beneficial to multinational companies in several ways. At a basic level, an e.HR system can act as a mere repository of information where expatriates can contribute their valuable international experiences to benefit future expatriates and the company. However, a sophisticated e.HR system can also result in major cost savings as expatriates are provided with 24-hour access to crucial information. If expatriates are concerned about how their retirement plan is doing, they no longer need to worry about contacting an actual HR person. They can consult the company site for such information. An e.HR system also can be designed so that expatriates can stay in touch with the home office. On such e.HR systems, expatriates can find updated newsletters, and communicate with local office colleagues through chat rooms and video/teleconferencing.

The final section, we look at the various types of IHRM orientations and how each of these orientations is appropriate for multinational strategies.

Multinational Strategy and IHRM

Multinational companies have several options to develop the appropriate IHRM policies for the implementation of multinational strategies. One way to ascertain a company's approach to IHRM is to examine its IHRM orientation or philosophy. Experts identify four IHRM orientations. These orientations are discussed next, followed by a consideration of how these orientations support the implementation of the four multinational strategies.

IHRM Orientations

IHRM orientation

Company's basic tactics and philosophy for co-ordinating IHRM activities for managerial and technical workers.

The four **IHRM orientations** are ethnocentric, polycentric, regiocentric, and global. These orientations reflect a company's basic tactics and philosophy for coordinating their IHRM activities for managerial and technical workers. Exhibit 11.9 shows how the IHRM orientations relate to some of the basic HRM functions.

EXHIBIT 11.9 IHRM Orientation and IHRM Practices for Managers and Technical Workers

IHRM Orientation

IHRM Practice	Ethnocentric	Polycentric	Regiocentric	Global
Recruitment and Selection	Home-country nationals for key positions selected by technical expertise or past home-country performance; host-country nationals for lowest levels of management only.	Home-country nationals for top management and technical-positions; host-country nationals for mid-level management positions; selection of home-country nationals similar to ethnocentric; selection of host-country nationals based on fit with home-country culture, e.g., home-country language ability.	Home-country nationals for top management and technical positions; regional country nationals for mid-level management and below.	Worldwide throughout the company; based on best qualified for position.
Training for Cross-Cultural Adaptation	Very limited or none; no language requirements.	Limited for home-country nationals. Some language training.	Limited to moderate training levels for home-country nationals; home and host-country nationals use language of business, often English.	Continuous for cultural adaptation and multilingualism.
Management Development: The Effects of International Assignments	May hurt career.	May hurt career of home-country nationals; host-country nationals' advancement often limited to own country.	Neutral to slightly positive career implications; international assignments of longer duration.	International assignments required for career advancement.
Evaluation	Home standards based on contribution to corporate bottom line.	Host standards based on contribution to unit bottom line.	Regional standards based on contribution to corporate bottom line.	Global standards based on contribution to corporate bottom line.
Compensation	Additional pay and benefits for expatriate assignments.	Additional pay and benefits for expatriate assignments; host-country compensation rates for host-country nationals	Due to longer assignments, less additional compensation for expatriate assignments.	Similar pay and benefit packages globally with some local adjustments.

Source: Adapted from Adler, Nancy J., and Fariborz Ghadar. 1990. "International strategy from the perspective of people and culture: The North American context." Research in Global Business Management 1, pp. 179–205; Heenan, D.A., and H.V. Perlmutter. 1979. Multinational Organization Development. Reading, MA: Addison Wesley.

Ethnocentric IHRM Orientation

An **ethnocentric IHRM** orientation means that all aspects of HRM for managers and technical workers tend to follow the parent organization's home-country HRM practices. In recruitment, key managerial and technical personnel come from the home-country. Local employees fill only lower-level and supporting jobs. Past performance at home and technical expertise govern selection criteria for overseas assignments in the ethnocentric IHRM company.[90]

Consistent with the use of home-country nationals for management and technical positions, evaluations and promotions use parent-country standards. The company assesses managers' performances using the same criteria and measures used for home-country units. Because of national context variations, companies may be forced to use different approaches for the evaluation and promotion of host-country managers. Such local adaptations, however, often have little effect on the ethnocentric company's procedures for promotions beyond the lowest levels of management. Limited by facilities and opportunities located in their country, host-country nationals usually face a ceiling or barrier limiting how far they may progress in the company.

When an ethnocentric IHRM company uses expatriates, training for the international assignment is often limited or nonexistent. Except for top country-level or region-level positions, most international assignments last only a short time, often only for marketing and sales contacts. The use of home-company evaluation and promotion standards, the lack of training, and the often short periods of expatriate assignments limit and discourage cultural adjustments for expatriates. Seldom, for example, do expatriate managers from the parent country know the host-country's language.

In the ethnocentric company, when international postings are available, they often have negative effects on the careers of managers or technical specialists. Since ethnocentric organizations usually concentrate key decision making at home, expatriate managers often feel that they have little success in communicating local needs to headquarters. Expatriates also tend to feel isolated and "out of the loop," with little opportunity to network with higher-level management.

An ethnocentric approach to IHRM is not necessarily good or bad. Some multinational strategies work perfectly well when a company uses ethnocentric IHRM policies. In choosing this or any other IHRM orientation, managers must consider the costs and benefits of the orientation in the context of their choice of a multinational strategy. Some benefits and costs of ethnocentric IHRM policies include[91]:

Benefits:

- *Little need to recruit qualified host-country nationals for higher management:* Local employees will hold only lower-level jobs or mid-level management jobs. Often a "glass ceiling" limits the advancement of host-country nationals.
- *Greater control and loyalty of home-country nationals:* These employees know that the home culture drives their careers. They seldom identify with the local country subsidiaries.
- *Little need to train home-country nationals:* Managers look to headquarters for staffing and evaluation and follow headquarters' policies and procedures.
- *Key decisions centralized:* Personnel decisions are made at headquarters.

Ethnocentric IHRM

All aspects of HRM for managers and technical workers tend to follow the parent organization's home-country HRM practices.

Costs:

- *May limit career development for host-country nationals:* High potential host-country nationals may never get beyond the glass ceiling, and talent is wasted.
- *Host-country nationals may never identify with the home company:* Host-country nationals are governed by local HRM practices, and they often realize that the glass ceiling exists. Therefore, they often have more allegiance to the local company than to the home company.
- *Expatriate managers are often poorly trained for international assignments and make mistakes:* Training is not valued and assignments are often short.
- *Expatriates may have limited career development:* International assignments are often viewed as hurting one's career, so they do not always attract the best people.

Regiocentric and Polycentric IHRM Orientations

Regiocentric IHRM
Regionwide HRM policies are adopted.

Polycentric IHRM
Firm treats each country-level organization separately for HRM purposes.

Firms with **regiocentric** or **polycentric IHRM** orientations have greater responsiveness to the host-country differences in HRM practices. These orientations are similar in that they emphasize adaptation to cultural and institutional differences among countries. They differ only in that the polycentric company adapts IHRM practices to countries while the regiocentric company adapts to regions. Given their similarity in IHRM philosophy, they are discussed together in this section.

Companies with polycentric IHRM orientations treat each country-level organization separately for HRM purposes. The home company headquarters ordinarily lets each country-level subsidiary follow local HRM practices. The regiocentric organization tends to adopt region-wide HRM policies. Consistent with these orientations, companies recruit and select their managers mostly from host countries or regions. Regiocentric companies may also look within the home company for key people who have mastered the cultures and languages of the countries in their regional locations. Qualifications for managers from the host-country follow local or regional practices. However, to communicate with the multinational's headquarters, host-country managers often need the ability to speak and write in the home company's national language.

Polycentric and regiocentric multinationals usually place home-country nationals in top-level management or technical positions. These home-country managers are used to control overseas operations or to transfer technology to host-country production sites.[92] As with the ethnocentric IHRM companies, HRM policies applied to home-country expatriates remain fixed at headquarters. In addition, unless headquarters values country- or region-specific international experiences, there remains a tendency for international assignments to have negative effects on the managerial careers of home-country nationals.[93]

Unlike the ethnocentric IHRM company, the polycentric IHRM company favors local procedures and standards for evaluations and promotions of most host-country managers. Decentralization from headquarters allows country or regional managers to assess their own human resource needs and develop local evaluation and promotion criteria. Local organizational cultures that differ from the home company's also influence the procedures used by organizations to evaluate and promote employees. Regiocentric IHRM companies act similarly to the polycentric companies but develop regional standards for evaluation and promotion.

Some benefits and costs of polycentric and regiocentric IHRM policies[94] include:
Benefits:

- *Using mostly host-country nationals or third-country nationals from the region reduces costs for training of expatriate managers from headquarters:* Successful expatriate assignments, especially in a widely different culture, require heavy investments in training.

- *The use of more host-country nationals and third-country nationals limits the number of home-country expatriate employees who face language barriers and adjustment problems:* Local managers speak their area's language. Third-country nationals from the region usually come from a similar culture and are more likely to have local language skills. Consequently, no investment in language training is necessary. The multinational company also faces fewer problems in managing expatriate adjustments to local cultures and in bringing home-company expatriates back into the headquarters organization.

- *Host-country employees and third-country nationals from the region are often less expensive than home-country expatriates:* The costs of expatriates are usually quite high.

Costs:

- *Coordination problems with headquarters based on cultural, language, and loyalty differences:* Even when host-country or regional managers speak the language of the multinational's headquarters, communication can still be difficult, and misunderstandings can result. Host-country managers may have more loyalty to their local organization than to the multinational parent.

- *Limited career-path opportunities for host-country and regional managers:* Similar to the case for companies with ethnocentric HRM practices, host-country and regional managers may face a glass ceiling for promotions. They may be limited to advancement within a country or region.

- *Limited international experience for home-country managers:* Because international experience often is not valued or rewarded, it does not always attract the best managers. Companies with limited managerial talent in international operations often face difficulties if their industry becomes more global with more international operations.

The frustrations and career barriers faced by host-country managers can hurt the development of local talent.

Global IHRM Orientations

Organizations with truly **global IHRM** orientations assign their best managers to international assignments.[95] Recruitment and selection take place worldwide, in any country where the best-quality employees can be found. The fit of the manager to the requirements of the job far outweighs any consideration of the individual's country of origin or country of job assignment. Capable managers adapt easily to different cultures and are usually bilingual or multilingual. In addition, the international assignment becomes a prerequisite for a successful managerial career in companies with global orientations.

Global IHRM

Recruiting and selecting worldwide, and assigning the best managers to international assignments regardless of nationality.

In companies with global orientations, managers are selected and trained to manage cultural diversity inside and outside the company. Employees inside their organization have culturally diverse backgrounds, and the company's multiple country locations provide culturally diverse customers, and suppliers.[96] Besides confronting issues of cultural diversity, global managers must meet the coordination and control needs of corporate headquarters.[97] To meet these challenges successfully, managers need continual training for cultural adaptation and development of the skills to balance local needs with overall company goals.[98]

As with other IHRM orientations, a global IHRM has its costs and benefits. Some benefits and costs of global IHRM policies[99] include:

Benefits:

- *Bigger talent pool:* The available talent pool of managers and technical specialists is not limited by nationality or geography.
- *Develops international expertise:* Multinational companies develop a large group of experienced international managers.
- *Helps build transnational organizational cultures:* Managers identify with the organizational culture more than with any national culture.

Costs:

- *Importing managerial and technical employees not always possible:* Host countries often have immigration laws that limit the use of foreign nationals or make their use very costly.
- *Added expense:* Training and relocation costs are expensive. Expatriate compensation is higher than for host-country employees.

Each IHRM orientation has strengths and weaknesses. A multinational's choice of an IHRM orientation depends for the most part on its multinational strategy. Next, we consider how the IHRM orientations support the four multinational strategies discussed in Chapter 6.

Finding a Fit: IHRM Orientation and Multinational Strategy

Exhibit 11.10 shows possible IHRM orientations that support the different multinational and participation strategies discussed earlier. Matching IHRM to the selected multinational strategy is a major component for successful strategy implementation. Like all strategic decisions for multinational companies, IHRM decisions are based on how the firm faces the global–local dilemma. Some IHRM decisions show a concern for local responsiveness when companies need people with a superior understanding of host-country issues. Other IHRM decisions reflect globalization pressures when companies need managers with world-class competence regardless of their passport nationality.[100]

Companies with multidomestic strategies concentrate on being responsive to local conditions. As a result, the country-by-country focus of polycentric IHRM provides the appropriate IHRM to maximize nation-level flexibility. In particular, the large use of host-country managers and employees provides a company with a built-in knowledge base of local conditions. That is, polycentric IHRM helps support the multidomestic strategy because local managers often better understand local customer tastes, distribution channels, government regulations, worker expectations, and other features unique to the local business environment.

EXHIBIT **11.10** **IHRM Orientations and Multinational Strategies**

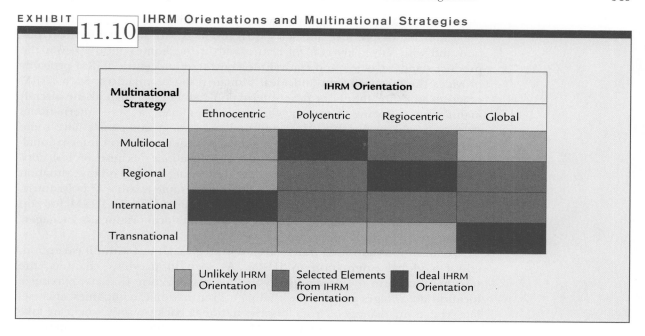

Multinational Strategy	IHRM Orientation			
	Ethnocentric	Polycentric	Regiocentric	Global
Multilocal				
Regional				
International				
Transnational				

☐ Unlikely IHRM Orientation   ☐ Selected Elements from IHRM Orientation   ■ Ideal IHRM Orientation

As shown in Exhibit 11.9, regiocentric IHRM practices also may work for multidomestic companies, but managers in such companies must assess their IHRM needs carefully by answering three key questions. Can they find third-country nationals who have the necessary knowledge of the business environment in the host-country? What kind of training and development are necessary to keep these managers performing at levels that equal or exceed host-country managers? What rewards keep these managers committed to their international assignments? Top management also must consider whether the investments in the selection, training, development, and retention of third-country expatriate managers provide sufficiently greater performance to offset the usually much lower costs of hiring local managerial talent.

The firm with a regional strategy has increased demands for coordinating activities of subunits located in different countries. Since these subunits are in one region of the world, the regiocentric IHRM strategy most closely supports the strategic intent of the company. Seldom would an ethnocentric IHRM orientation work for the firm with a regional strategy. However, some elements of a polycentric or global IHRM orientation may also support the regional strategy. For example, companies that emphasize regionally coordinated manufacturing may find the polycentric approach to IHRM satisfactory. Production facilities located in separate host countries can develop locally tailored HRM practices even though their products have regional sales or contribute components to regional products. In such cases, only the top managers in the region need a region-wide perspective and should be managed with regiocentric or global HRM policies. In contrast, companies that share R&D or product knowledge regionally may find that only regiocentric or more global IHRM practices can recruit, select, and develop the people with the right capabilities. In such cases, managers at all levels need knowledge of regional markets, governments, national cultures, languages, and social institutions to perform adequately.

The international strategy emphasizes globalization on the upstream end of the value chain—produce and sell global products with minimal local adaptation and with subsidiary control centralized in the home-country. Given the product standardization and centralized control, ethnocentric IHRM probably provides the most efficient and ideal human resource practices. Such IHRM practices work for the more pure international strategists, such as the aircraft manufacturer Boeing. However, for most companies, a pure international strategy is seldom possible. Most international-strategy companies have some products that require adaptation to regional or local needs. Most international-strategy companies have foreign production locations because of low cost, customer proximity, or politics. As such, depending on the unique situation faced by a company, there is usually a need to have some mixture of polycentric, regiocentric, or global IHRM practices. For example, while IHRM for top managers might follow an ethnocentric orientation, local production managers may be treated with a polycentric approach.

Organizations adopting transnational strategies, almost without exception, adopt a global orientation to IHRM. As seen in previous chapters, the transnational firm requires a highly flexible organization that can maximize location advantages in its value chain.[101] Transnational companies must select and train managers from diverse national backgrounds who can take assignments anywhere in the world. Multinational managers in transnational companies must be prepared to enter global corporate cultures that require managers to deal flexibly with diverse cultures and national social institutions.[102]

The success of any multinational strategy requires careful assessment of a firm's IHRM practices. Successful companies select IHRM orientations with a major focus on finding the orientation that best supports their multinational strategy. However, usually no one IHRM orientation exactly fits a company's multinational strategy, and few companies follow any IHRM orientation completely. Rather, each multinational company selects a general approach combined with specific IHRM practices and procedures from other orientations that fit its strategic needs. Since IHRM supports all levels of the value chain, a crucial mistake is to misalign an IHRM orientation with the company's multinational strategy.

Summary and Conclusions

This chapter introduced the basic HRM practices of recruitment, selection, training and development, performance appraisal, compensation, and labor relations. When these practices are applied to a company's international operations, they become IHRM or international human resource management. Besides basic HRM functions, two key issues in IHRM are the choice of the mixture of expatriate and host-country managers and knowing how to adapt home-company HRM practices to the host-country's situation. This chapter focused on HRM practices for expatriate employees. The next chapter reviews the differences in national

HRM practices. Knowledge of these national differences helps multinational managers adapt IHRM practices to local conditions.

Expatriate managers present challenges and opportunities to multinational companies. They are costly, often costing two to three times as much as host-country managers. They need special training to succeed although they are not always successful. However, expatriate managers are loyal to the home organization and they often have skills that are impossible to find with host-country managers. It is important for multinational companies to find ways to properly manage their expatriates in order to fully benefit from these expatriates' experience.

As companies face a global shortage of managers, they will start relying on their women managers to fulfill expatriate responsibilities. Multinationals, therefore, must become more aware of the significant barriers their women managers face in taking international assignments, and they must take the necessary measures in order to facilitate the female expatriates' experience.

Successful IHRM presents one of the most important challenges to multinational companies in the 21st century. Many globalization trends—the development of large-scale trading blocs, the opening of national boundaries for trade, and the increasing prevalence of international strategic alliances—offer multinational organizations the opportunity to use human resources unrestrained by political, linguistic, and cultural boundaries. Companies, large and small, that exploit international human resources most effectively will have strong competitive advantages in an increasingly global economy.

Discussion Questions

1. Identify the components of HRM and describe how they differ for IHRM.

2. Describe the types of nationals employed by multinational firms. Note likely situations when each type would be used.

3. Using the basic components of HRM as a guide, describe the likely practices used by a transnational firm.

4. Contrast the positive and negative issues for using short-term and international-cadre expatriate managers. Consider both the organization's perspective and the career implications for the individual manager.

5. Discuss the options available for expatriate compensation. Consider how these options might be used for a transnational and a multidomestic company.

6. Discuss how multinational companies can deal with the repatriation issue.

7. How can companies benefit from using women expatriates? Discuss some of the advantages women expatriates have over their male counterparts.

8. Discuss some of the major problems facing women expatriates. What can companies do to make the expatriate experience successful for their women expatriates?

9. What is electronic human resource management? Discuss how multinationals can benefit from using electronic human resource management systems.

Multinational Management **Skill Builder**

A Presentation

You are the vice-president of the human resource management department of a large multinational company. Your company has expatriates located around the world including countries such as Australia, Japan, Mexico, Malaysia, India, South Africa, and Chile. You just came back from an important meeting with other VPs and the CEO. The major emphasis during the meeting was on expatriates' dissatisfaction with their overseas assignment and overall cost reduction because of efficiency pressures. You have been instructed to report some solutions to these pressing problems. You have always believed that an e.HR system would be very beneficial to the company but your proposals have always been rejected because of your inability to prove potential cost savings from using the system. Your task is to present a more convincing case for the e.HR system. As you prepare your presentation, you know that you need to address the following issues:

Step 1. Using as many sources of information as possible, provide a list of possible types of information that you can use to show the cost savings potential of the new e.HR system.

Step 2. Demonstrate the types of information the new e.HR system will need to capture in order to be beneficial to the company.

Step 3. Demonstrate how capturing the new types of information can be beneficial to the company. In other words, you need to show how the collected data can be used.

Step 4. Show how the use of the e.HR system can also reduce expatriate dissatisfaction.

Step 5. Show how the use of an e.HR system makes sense in terms of the future plan of the company.

Step 6. Present your findings to the class.

Endnotes

1 Milkovich, George T., and Jerry Newman. 1993. Compensation. 4th ed. Homewood, Ill.: Irwin; Bohlander, George W., Scott Snell, and Arthur W. Sherman, Jr. 2001. *Managing Human Resources*, 12th ed. Cincinnati, OH: South-Western.

2 Mayerhofer, Helene, Linley C. Hartmann and Anne Herbert. 2004. "Career Management Issues for Flexpatriate International Staff." *Thunderbird International Business Review* Nov-Dec 46:6, pp. 647–666.

3 Black, J. Stewart, Hal B. Gregersen, and Mark E. Mendenhall. 1992. *Global Assignments*. San Francisco: Jossey-Bass; Quelch, John A. and Helen Bloom. 1999. "Ten steps to a global human resources strategy." *Strategy & Business*, First Quarter, pp. 2–13; Tung, Rosalie L. 1981. "Selection and training of personnel for overseas assignments." *Columbia Journal of World Business* 16:1, pp. 68–78.

4 Melvin, Sheila. 1997. "Shipping out." *The China Business Review*, 24, pp. 30–35.

5 Ashamalla, Maali H. 1998. "International human resource management practices: The challenge of expatriation." Competitiveness Review, 8, 2, pp. 54–65.

6 McFarland, Jean. 2006. "Culture Shock". Benefits Canada Jan 30:1, p. 31.

7 *Business Wire*, 2006. "International job assignment: Boon or bust for an employee's career?" March 13, p. 1.

8 Harzing, Anne-Wil and Claus Christensen. 2004. "Think Piece: Expatriate failure: time to abandon the concept?" *Career Development International* 9:6/7, pp. 616–626.

9 McCaughey, Deirdre and Nealia S. Bruning. 2005. "Enhancing Opportunities for Expatriate Job Satisfaction: HR Strategies for Foreign Assignment Success." *HR Human Resources Planning* 28:4, pp. 21–29.

10 Ashamalla, Maali H. 1998. "International human resource management practices: The challenge of expatriation." Competitiveness Review, 8, 2, pp. 54–65.; Harzing, Anne-Wil and Claus Christensen. 2004. "Think Piece: Expatriate failure: time to abandon the concept?" *Career Development International* 9:6/7, pp. 616–626.; McCall, Morgan W, and George P. Hollenbeck. 2002. "Global fatalities: When international executives derail." *Ivey Business Journal*, May/June, pp. 74–78.; McCaughey, Deirdre and Nealia S. Bruning. 2005. "Enhancing Opportunities for Expatriate Job Satisfaction: HR Strategies for Foreign Assignment Success."; Poe, Andrea C. 2002. "Welcome Back." *HRMagazine*, 45,3: pp. 94–101; Tung, Rosalie L. 1987. "Expatriate assignments: Enhancing success and minimizing failure." *Academy of Management Executive* 1:2, pp. 117–126.

11 Fink, Gerhard, Sylvia Meierewert, and Ulrike Rohr. 2005. "The Use of Repatriate Knowledge in Organizations." *HR Human Resources Planning* 28:4, pp. 30–36; Gregersen, Hal B. 1999. "The right way to manage expats." *Harvard Business Review* March/April, pp. 52–61; Lublin, Joann S. 1992. "Younger managers learn global skills." *Wall Street Journal*, March 3, p. B1; O'Connor, Robert. 2002. "Plug the expat knowledge drain." *HRMagazine*, October, pp. 101–107.

12 Korbin, Stephen J. 1988. "Expatriate reduction and strategic control in American multinational corporations." *Human Resource Management* 27:1, pp. 63–75.

13 Gregersen, Hal. B. 1999. "The right way to manage expats."

14 Boyacigiller, Nakiye A. 1991. "The international assignment reconsidered." In *Readings and Cases in International Human Resource Management*, edited by Mark Mendenhall and Gary Oddou pp. 148–155: PWS-KentBoston .

15 O'Connor, Robert. 2002. "Plug the expat knowledge drain."

16 Fink, Gerhard, Sylvia Meierewert, and Ulrike Rohr. 2005. "The Use of Repatriate Knowledge in organizations."

17 Ibid.

18 Quelch, John A. and Helen Bloom. "Ten steps to a global human resources strategy."

19 Torrington, Derek, and Nigel Holden. 1992. "Human resource management and the international challenge of change." *Personnel Review* 21:2, pp. 19–30.

20 Lublin, Joann S. "Younger managers learn global skills."

21 Quelch, John A. and Helen Bloom. "Ten steps to a global human resources strategy."

22 Torrington, Derek, and Nigel Holden. "Human resource management and the international challenge of change."

23 Scullion, Hugh. 1994. "Staffing policies and strategic control in British multinationals." International Studies of Management and Organization 24:3, pp. 86–104.

24 Quelch, John A. and Helen Bloom. "Ten steps to a global human resources strategy."

25 Mayerhofer, Hartmann and Herbert. "Career Management Issues for Flexpatriate International Staff."

26 Ibid

27 Tahvanainen, Marja, Denice Welch and Verner Worm. 2005. "Implications of Short-term International Assignments." *European Management Journal* Dec 23:6, pp. 663–673.

28 Ibid.

29 Poe, "Welcome Back."

30 Sims, Robert H. and Mike Schraeder. 2005. "Expatriate compensation: An exploratory review of salient contextual factors and common practices." *Career Development International* 10:2, pp. 98–108.

31 Selmer, Jan. 2002. "Practice makes perfect? International experience and expatriate adjustment." *Management International Review*, 42: 1, pp. 71–87.

32 Tung, "Selection and training of personnel for overseas assignments."

33 Gregersen, Hal. B. 1999. "The right way to manage expats."; Halcrow. Allan. 1999. "Expats: The squandered resource." *Workforce*, 3, July, pp. 28–30; Mendenhall, Mark, and Gary Oddou. 1985. "The dimensions of expatriate acculturation: A review." *Academy of Management Review* 10, pp. 39–47; Poe, "Welcome Back"; Tung, "Selection and training of personnel for overseas assignments."

34 Tye, Mary G and Peter Y Chen. 2005. "Selection of Expatriates: Decision-Making Models Used by HR Professionals." *HR Human Resource Planning* 28:4, p. 15.

35 Latta, Geoffrey W. 1999. "Expatriate policy and practice: A ten-year comparison of trends." *Compensation and Benefits Review*, pp. 31, 35–39.

36 Tye, and Chen. "Selection of Expatriates: Decision-Making Models Used by HR Professionals."

37 Gabel, Racheli Shmueli, Shimon L. Dolan and Jean Luc Cerdin. 2005. "Emotional intelligence as predictor of cultural adjustment for success in global assignments." *Career Development International* 10:5, pp. 375–395.

38 Tung, "Selection and training of personnel: Decision-making models used by HR professionals."

39 Black, J. Stewart, and Mark E. Mendenhall. 1990. "Cross-culture training effectiveness: A review and theoretical framework for future research." *Academy of Management Review* 15, pp. 113–36.; Forster, Nick. 2000. "Expatriates and the impact of cross-cultural training." *Human Resource Management Journal*, 10, pp. 63–78.

40 Forster, "Expatriates and the impact of cross-cultural training."

41 Winham International. 2000. "Survey highlights." http://www.windhamint.com.

42 Black, Gregersen, and Mendenhall. *Global Assignments.*

43 Mendenhall, Mark, and Gary Oddou. 1988. "Acculturation profiles of expatriate managers: Implications for cross-cultural training programs." *Columbia Journal of World Business* 21, pp. 73–79.; Tung, "Selection and training of personnel for overseas assignments."

44 Dowling, Peter J., Welch, Denice E. and Randall S. Schuler. 1999. *International Human Resource Management.* Cincinnati, OH: Southwestern.)

45 Black, Gregersen, and Mendenhall. *Global Assignments.*

46 Sims and Schraeder. "Expatriate compensation: An exploratory review of salient contextual factors and common practices."

47 *Employee Benefits.* 2006. "Sending perks overseas." Feb 10, p. S10.; Ibid.

48 Davis, Debra A. 2005. "Paying the Piper: Taxation of Global Employees." *Journal of Pension Benefits*, Autumn 13:1, p. 85.

49 Frazee, Valerie. 1998. "Is the balance sheet right for your expats?" *Workforce*, 3, pp. 19–23.

50 Overman, Stephenie. 2000. "In sync." *HRMagazine*, 45:3, pp. 86–92.

51 Sims and Schraeder. "Expatriate compensation: An exploratory review of salient contextual factors and common practices."

52 Dowling, Welch, Schuler, *International Human Resource Management*; Frazee, "Is the balance sheet right for your expats?".

53 Black, Gregersen, and Mendenhall, *Global Assignments.*

54 Ibid.

55 Frazee, "Is the balance sheet right for your expats?"; Overman, "In sync."

56 Sims and Schraeder, "Expatriate compensation: An exploratory review of salient contextual factors and common practices."

57 Overman, "In sync."

58 Gregersen, "The right way to manage expats."

59 Klaff, Leslie G. 2002. "The right way to bring expats home." *Workforce*, July, pp. 40–44; Poe, "Welcome back."

60 Black, Gregersen, and Mendenhall, *Global Assignments.*

61 Klaff, "The right way to bring expats home."

62 Gregersen, "The right way to manage expats."

63 Klaff, "The right way to bring expats home."; Gregersen, "The right way to manage expats."; Black, Gregersen, and Mendenhall, *Global Assignments*; Tyler, Kathryn. 2006. "Retaining Repatriates." *HRMagazine* Mar 51:5, pp. 97–102.

64 Lancaster, Hal. 1999. "To get shipped abroad, women must overcome prejudice at home." *Wall Street Journal*, June 29, p. B1.

65 Caligiuri, P.M. and Tung, R. 1999. "Comparing the success of male and female expatriates from a US based company." *International Journal of Human Resource Management*, 10: 5, pp. 163–179.

66 Harris, Hillary. 2002. "Think international manager, think male: Why are women not selected in international management assignments?" *Thunderbird International Business Review* 44: 2, pp. 175–203.

67 Linehan, Margaret. 2000. *Senior female international managers: Why so few.* Ashgate: Aldershot.

68 Jelinek, Mariann, and Nancy J. Adler. 1988. "Women: World-class managers for global competition." *Academy of Management Executive* 11:1, pp. 11–19.; Stroh, Linda K., Arup Varma, and Stacy J. Valy-Durbin. 2000. "Why are women left at home: Are they unwilling to go on international assignments?" *Journal of World Business*, 35, pp. 241–255.

69 Izraeli, Dafna, and Yoram Zeira. 1993. "Women managers in international business: A research review and appraisal." *Business and the Contemporary World*, Summer, pp. 35–46.

70 Linehan, *Senior female international managers: Why so few.*

71 Adler, Nancy J. 1993. "Women managers in a global economy." *HRMagazine*, September, pp. 52–55.

72 Ibid.

73 Adler, Nancy J. "Pacific basin managers: A *gaijin*, not a woman." *Human Resource Management* 26:2, pp. 169–191.

74 Solomon, Julie. 1989. "Women, minorities and foreign postings." *Wall Street Journal*, June 2, p. B1.

75 Adler, "Pacific basin managers: A *gaijin*, not a woman."

76 Adler, "Women managers in a global economy."

77 Linehan, Margaret and Hugh Scullion. 2001. "European female expatriate careers: critical success factors." *Journal of European Industrial Training*, 25: 8, pp. 392–418.

78 O'Leary, V.E., and J.L. Johnson. 1991. "Steep ladder, lonely climb." *Women in Management Review and Abstracts*, 6: 5, pp. 10–16.

79 Parasuraman, S.J. and J.H. Greenhaus. 1993. "Personal portraits: The lifestyle of the woman manager." In *Women in Management: Trends, Issues and Challenges in Management Diversity*, edited by E.A. Fagenson, London: Sage, pp. 186–211

80 Davidson, M.J. and C.L. Cooper. 1983. Stress and the Woman Manager. London: Martin Robertson.

81 Adler, "Pacific basin managers: A *gaijin,* not a woman."

82 Volkmar, John, and Kate L. Westbrook. 2005. "Does a decade make a difference? A second look at western women working in Japan." *Women in Management Review*, 20,(7): pp. 464–477

83 Thaler-Carter, Ruth E. 1999. "Vowing to go abroad." *HRMagazine*, 44:12, pp. 90–96.

84 Izraeli, Dafna, and Yoram Zeira. 1993. "Women managers in international business: A research review and appraisal."

85 Linehan and Scullion, "European female expatriate careers: critical success factors."

86 Davidson and Cooper, *Stress and the Woman Manager.*

87 Esposito, Michael and Jeff Novak. 2003. "Small steps, big savings." *Vendor Directory* http://workforce.com/hrdirectory.

88 O'Connor, "Plug the expat knowledge drain."

89 King, Julia. 2003. Getting the right person at the right time. *Computer World*, February 3 http://www.computerworld.com.

90 Mendenhall, Mark E., E. Dunbar, and Gary R. Oddou. 1987. "Expatriate selection, training and career-pathing: A review and critique." *Human Resource Management* 26:3, pp. 331–345.

91 Dowling, Peter J., and Denice E. Welch. 1988. "International human resource management: An Australian perspective." *Asia Pacific Journal of Management* 6:1, pp. 39–65; Reynolds, Calvin. 1997.

554   **Part 4**   Strategy Implementation for Multinational Companies

"Strategic employment of third-country nationals." *Human Resource Planning* 20,1: pp. 33–39.

[92] Adler, Nancy J., and Fariborz Ghadar. 1990. "International strategy from the perspective of people and culture: The North American context." *Research in Global Business Management* 1, pp. 179–205; Bohlander, Snell, and Sherman, Jr., *Managing Human Resources*.

[93] Adler and Ghadar, "International strategy from the perspective of people and culture: The North American context."

[94] Dowling and Welch, "International human resource management: An Australian perspective."; Reynolds, "Strategic employment of third-country nationals."

[95] Quelch and Bloom, "Ten steps to a global human resources strategy."

[96] Ibid.

[97] Bartlett, Christopher A., and Sumantra Ghoshal. 1998. *Managing Across Borders (2ed)*. Boston: Harvard Business School Press.

[98] Quelch and Bloom, "Ten steps to a global human resources strategy."

[99] Dowling and Welch, "International human resource management: An Australian perspective" Ibid.

[100] Adler, Nancy J., and Susan Bartholomew. 1992. "Globalization and human resource management." *Research in Global Strategic Management* 3, pp. 179–201.

[101] Bartlett and Ghoshal, *Managing Across Borders*.

[102] Black, Gregersen and Mark E. Mendenhall, *Global Assignments*.

The Road to Hell

John Baker, Chief Engineer of the Caribbean Bauxite Company of Barracania in the West Indies, was making his final preparations to leave the island. His promotion to production manager of Keso Mining Corporation near Winnipeg—one of Continental Ore's fast-expanding Canadian enterprises—had been announced a month before and now everything had been tidied up except the last vital interview with his successor, the able young Barracanian, Matthew Rennalls. It was vital that this interview be a success and that Baker should leave his office uplifted and encouraged to face the challenge of his new job. A touch on the bell would have brought Rennalls walking into the room but Baker delayed the moment and gazed thoughtfully through the window considering just exactly what he was going to say and, more particularly, how he was going to say it.

John Baker, an English expatriate, was forty-five years old and had served his twenty-three years with Continental Ore in many different places: in the Far East; several countries of Africa; Europe; and, for the last two years, in the West Indies. He hadn't cared much for his previous assignment in Hamburg and was delighted when the West Indian appointment came through. Climate was not the only attraction. Baker had always preferred working overseas (in what were termed the developing countries) because he felt he had an innate knack—better than most other expatriates working for Continental Ore—of knowing just how to get on with regional staff. Twenty-four hours in Barracania, however, soon made him realize that he would need all of this "innate knack" if he was to deal effectively with the problems in this field that now awaited him.

At his first interview with Hutchins, the production manager, the whole problem of Rennalls and his future was discussed. There and then it was made quite clear to Baker that one of his most important tasks would be the "grooming" of Rennalls as his successor. Hutchins had pointed out that, not only was Rennalls one of the brightest Barracanian prospects on the staff of

Caribbean Bauxite—at London University he had taken first-class honors in the B.Sc. Engineering Degree—but, being the son of the Minister of Finance and Economic Planning, he also had no small political pull.

The company had been particularly pleased when Rennalls decided to work for them rather than for the government in which his father had such a prominent post. They ascribed his action to the effect of their vigorous and liberal regionalization program, which, since the Second World War, had produced eighteen Barracanians at mid-management level and given Caribbean Bauxite a good lead in this respect over all other international concerns operating in Barracania. The success of this timely regionalization policy has led to excellent relations with the government—a relationship that had been given an added importance when Barracania, three years later, became independent, an occasion which encouraged a critical and challenging attitude toward the role foreign interests would have to play in the new Barracania. Hutchins had therefore little difficulty in convincing Baker that the successful career development of Rennalls was of the first importance.

The interview with Hutchins was now two years old and Baker, leaning back in his office chair, reviewed just how successful he had been in the "grooming" of Rennalls. What aspects of the latter's character had helped and what had hindered? What about his own personality? How had that helped or hindered? The first item to go on the credit side would, without question, be the ability of Rennalls to master the technical aspects of his job. From the start he had shown keenness and enthusiasm and had often impressed Baker with his ability in tackling new assignments and the constructive comments he invariably made in departmental discussions. He was popular with all ranks of Barracanian staff and had an ease of manner that stood him in good stead when dealing with his expatriate seniors. These were all assets, but what about the debit side?

First and foremost, there was his racial consciousness. His four years at London University had accentuated this feeling and made him sensitive to any sign of condescension on the part of expatriates. It may have been to give expression to this sentiment that, as soon as he returned home from London, he threw himself into politics on behalf of the United Action Party who were later to win the pre-independence elections and provide the country with its first Prime Minister.

The ambitions of Rennalls—and he certainly was ambitious—did not, however, lie in politics for, staunch nationalist as he was, he saw that he could serve himself and his country best (for was not bauxite responsible for nearly half the value of Barracania's export trade?) by putting his engineering talent to the best use possible. On this account, Hutchins found that he had an unexpectedly easy task in persuading Rennalls to give up his political work before entering the production department as an assistant engineer.

It was, Baker knew, Rennalls's well-repressed sense of race consciousness that had prevented their relationship from being as close as it should have been. On the surface, nothing could have seemed more agreeable. Formality between the two men was at a minimum: Baker was delighted to find that his assistant shared his own peculiar "shaggy dog" sense of humor so that jokes were continually being exchanged; they entertained each other at their houses and often played tennis together—and yet the barrier remained invisible, indefinable, but ever present. The existence of this "screen" between them was a constant source of frustration to Baker since it indicated a weakness that he was loath to accept. If successful with all other nationalities, why not with Rennalls?

But at least he had managed to "break through" to Rennalls more successfully than any other expatriate. In fact, it was the young Barracanian's attitude—sometimes overbearing, sometimes cynical—toward other company expatriates that had been one of the subjects Baker had raised last year when he discussed Rennalls's staff report with him. He knew, too, that he would have to raise the same subject again in the forthcoming interview because Jackson, the senior draftsman, had complained only yesterday about the rudeness of Rennalls. With this thought in mind, Baker leaned forward and spoke into the intercom. "Would you come in Matt, please? I'd like a word with you," and later, "Do sit down," proffering the box, "have a cigarette." He paused while he held out his lighter and then went on.

"As you know, Matt, I'll be off to Canada in a few days' time, and before I go, I thought it would be useful if we could have a final chat together. It is indeed with some deference that I suggest I can be of help. You will shortly be sitting in this chair doing the job I am now doing, but I, on the other hand, am ten years older, so perhaps you can accept the idea that I may be able to give you the benefit of my longer experience."

Baker saw Rennalls stiffen slightly in his chair as he made this point so added in explanation, "You and I have attended enough company courses to remember those repeated requests by the personnel manager to tell people how they are getting on as often as the convenient moment arises and not just the automatic 'once a year' when, by regulation, staff reports have to be discussed."

Rennalls nodded his agreement, so Baker went on. "I shall always remember the last job performance discussion I had with my previous boss back in Germany. He used what he called the 'plus and minus' technique. His firm belief was that when a senior, by discussion, seeks to improve the work performance of his staff, his prime objective should be to make sure that the latter leaves the interview encouraged and inspired to improve. Any criticism must, therefore, be constructive and helpful. He said that one very good way to encourage a person—and I fully agree with him—is to tell him about his good points—the plus factors—as well as his weak ones—the minus factors—so I thought, Matt, it would be a good idea to run our discussion along these lines."

Rennalls offered no comment, so Baker continued: "Let me say, therefore, right away, that, as far as your own work performance is concerned, the plus far outweighs the minus. I have, for instance, been most impressed with the way you have adapted your considerable theoretical knowledge to master the practical techniques of your job—that ingenious method you used to get air down to the fifth-shaft level is a sufficient case in point—and at departmental meetings I have invariably found your comments well taken and helpful. In fact, you will be interested to know that only last week I reported to Mr. Hutchins that, from the technical point of view, he could not wish for a more able man to succeed to the position of chief engineer."

"That's very good indeed of you, John," cut in Rennalls with a smile of thanks. "My only worry now is how to live up to such a high recommendation."

"Of that I am quite sure," returned Baker, "especially if you can overcome the minus factor which I would like now to discuss with you. It is one, which I have talked about before so I'll come straight to the point. I noticed that you are more friendly and get on better with your fellow Barracanians than you do with Europeans. In point of fact, I had a complaint only yesterday from Mr. Jackson, who said you had been rude to him—and not for the first time either.

"There is, Matt, I am sure, no need for me to tell you how necessary it will be for you to get on well with expatriates because until the company has trained up sufficient people of your caliber, Europeans are bound to occupy senior positions here in Barracania. All this is vital to your future interests, so can I help you in any way?"

While Baker was speaking on this theme, Rennalls had sat tensed in his chair and it was some seconds before he replied. "It is quite extraordinary, isn't it, how one can convey an impression to others so at variance with what one intends? I can only assure you once again that my disputes with Jackson—and you may remember also Godson—have had nothing at all to do with the color of their skins. I promise you that if a Barracanian had behaved in an equally peremptory manner I would have reacted in precisely the same way. And again, if I may say it within these four walls, I am sure I am not the only one who has found Jackson and Godson difficult. I could mention the names of several expatriates who have felt the same. However, I am really sorry to have created this impression of not being able to get on with Europeans—it is an entirely false one—and I quite realize that I must do all I can to correct it as quickly as possible. On your last point, regarding Europeans holding senior positions in the Company for some time to come, I quite accept the situation. I know that Caribbean Bauxite—as they have been doing for many years now—will promote Barracanians as soon as their experience warrants it. And, finally, I would like to assure you, John—and my father thinks the same too—that I am very happy in my work here and hope to stay with the company for many years to come."

Rennalls had spoken earnestly and, although not convinced by what he had heard, Baker did not think he could pursue the matter further except to say, "All right, Matt, my impression may be wrong, but I would like to remind you about the truth of that old saying, 'What is important is not what is true but what is believed.' Let it rest at that."

But suddenly Baker knew that he didn't want to "let it rest at that." He was disappointed once again at not being able to "break through" to Rennalls and having yet again to listen to his bland denial that there was any racial prejudice in his makeup. Baker, who had intended ending the interview at this point, decided to try another tack.

"To return for a moment to the 'plus and minus technique' I was telling you about just now, there is another plus factor I forgot to mention. I would like to congratulate you not only on the caliber of your work but also on the ability you have shown in overcoming a challenge which I, as a European, have never had to meet.

"Continental Ore is, as you know, a typical commercial enterprise—admittedly a big one—which is a product of the economic and social environment of the United States and Western Europe. My ancestors have all been brought up in this environment for the past two or three hundred years and I have, therefore, been able to live in a world in which commerce (as we know it today) has been part and parcel of my being. It has not been something revolutionary and new which has suddenly entered my life. In your case," went on Baker, "the situation is different because you and your forebears have only had some fifty or sixty years' experience of this commercial environment. You have had to face the challenge of bridging the gap between fifty and two or three hundred years. Again, Matt, let me congratulate you—and people like you—once again on having so successfully overcome this particular hurdle. It is for this very reason that I think the outlook for Barracania—and particularly Caribbean Bauxite—is so bright."

Rennalls had listened intently and when Baker finished, replied, "Well, once again, John, I have to thank you for what you have said, and, for my part, I can only say that it is gratifying to know that my own personal effort has been so much appreciated. I hope that more people will soon come to think as you do."

There was a pause and, for a moment, Baker thought hopefully that he was about to achieve his long-awaited "breakthrough," but Rennalls merely smiled back. The barrier remained unbreached. There remained some five minutes' cheerful conversation about the contrast between the Caribbean and Canadian climate and whether the West Indies had any hope of beating England in the Fifth Test before Baker drew the interview to a close. Although he was as far as ever from knowing the real Rennalls, he was nevertheless glad that the interview had run along in this friendly manner and, particularly, that it had ended on such a cheerful note.

This feeling, however, lasted only until the following morning. Baker had some farewells to make, so he arrived at the office considerably later than usual. He had no sooner sat down at his desk than his secretary walked into the room with a worried frown on her face. Her words came fast. "When I arrived this morning I found Mr. Rennalls already waiting at my door. He seemed very angry and told me in quite a peremptory manner that he had a vital letter to dictate which must be sent off without any delay. He was so worked up that he couldn't keep still and kept pacing about the room, which is most unlike him. He wouldn't even wait to read what he had dictated. Just signed the page where he thought the letter would end. It has been distributed and your copy is in your 'in tray.'"

Puzzled and feeling vaguely uneasy, Baker opened the "Confidential" envelope and read the following letter:

From: Assistant Engineer
To: The Chief Engineer, Caribbean Bauxite
    Limited
    14th August, 196_

ASSESSMENT OF INTERVIEW BETWEEN MESSRS. BAKER AND RENNALLS

It has always been my practice to respect the advice given me by seniors, so after our interview, I decided to give careful thought once again to its main points and so make sure that I had understood all that had been said. As I promised you at the time, I had every intention of putting your advice to the best effect.

It was not, therefore, until I had sat down quietly in my home yesterday evening to consider the interview objectively that its main purport became clear. Only then did the full enormity of what you said dawn on me. The more I thought about it, the more convinced I was that I had hit

upon the real truth—and the more furious I became. With a facility in the English language which I—a poor Barracanian—cannot hope to match, you had the audacity to insult me (and through me every Barracanian worth his salt) by claiming that our knowledge of modern living is only a paltry fifty years old whilst yours goes back 200–300 years. As if your materialistic commercial environment could possibly be compared with the spiritual values of our culture. I'll have you know that if much of what I saw in London is representative of your most boasted culture, I hope fervently that it will never come to Barracania. By what right do you have the effrontery to condescend to us? At heart, all you Europeans think us barbarians, or, as you say amongst yourselves, we are "just down from the trees."

Far into the night I discussed this matter with my father, and he is as disgusted as I. He agrees with me that any company whose senior staff think as you do is no place for any Barracanian proud of his culture and race—so much for all the company "clap-trap" and specious propaganda about regionalization and Barracania for the Barracanians.

I feel ashamed and betrayed. Please accept this letter as my resignation, which I wish to become effective immediately.
    c.c. Production Manager
    Managing Director

CASE DISCUSSION QUESTIONS

1. What are the strengths and weaknesses of the performance-review technique used by Baker?
2. Should Baker have anticipated Rennalls' reaction to his performance review? Why?
3. What issues of cultural sensitivity are germane for understanding the case? Was it the performance review or Baker's interaction style that prompted Rennalls resignation?
4. Why was Baker's extensive international experience not helpful in dealing with Rennalls?
5. If you were Baker, what would you do now?

CASE CREDIT

Prepared by Gareth Evans for Shell-BP Development Co. of Nigeria Ltd., Intercollegiate Case Clearing House, Soldiers Field, Boston, MA 02163.

HRM in the Local Context: Knowing When and How to Adapt

12

Preview CASE IN POINT

Following Local Traditions

The United States is the only industrialized country without government-mandatedvacation time. Employees in U.S. firms average just two weeks of vacation per year. In contrast, their European counterparts receive an average of five to six weeks of vacation annually. Countries such as Italy, France, Germany, Spain, Sweden, and others have regulations that guarantee workers at least a month of paid annual vacation. It is, therefore, not surprising that U.S workers are likely to work about 250 more hours than workers in Western Europe. While many U.S. managers see the European vacation as excessive, European managers counter that U.S. organizations have misplaced goals.

When Captura Software, an electronic finance service provider from Washington State, opened offices in London and Paris, HR manager Corkye Christensen knew that the company had to do more than follow the letter of the law. Average vacation time in most European countries is more than the 20 days mandated. Her first thought of trading extra vacation time for money wouldn't work—it is illegal in the EU. Captura's strategy is to blend with local traditions and nearly shut down in August. Even U.S. expatriates are allowed the extra vacation time of their local colleagues.

However, for ABC Electronic's flagship plant in Juarez, Mexico, the situation was different. ABC's decision to consolidate several religious holidays into a "Holy Week" and the decision to keep the factory running throughout July instead of shutting it down for the usual two-week break were major reasons why workers decided to go on strike. The imposition of U.S.-based policies was in conflict with local expectations and resulted in heavy losses for the company. ABC Electronic had to make several changes, including increasing wages and restoring the July break, to resolve the situation.

Sources: Based on Dowlatshahi, S. 2001. "Managing a labor strike at a maquiladora industry: A case study." International Journal of Operations and Production Management 21, 5/6:

pp. 728–748; Poe, Andrea C. 1999. "When in Rome . . . European law and tradition back generous vacation policies." HR Magazine, p. 44, HR Magazine Online Archive, http:// www.my.SHRM.org; Human Resource Management International Digest. 2002. "An ABC approach to handling a strike." 10, 1: pp. 26–27; Simmers, Tim. 2005. "Workers in U.S. labor longer with less vacation than others." Business Writer, December 10, p. 1.

T he Preview Case in Point shows several issues that can affect how multinational companies conduct business in a country. Other critical issues might include: How do you hire a worker in Mexico? What educational background can you expect from German workers? Can you lay off workers in Denmark? What would happen in Japan if you promoted a 30-year-old to supervise 40-year-old employees? What kind of relationships should you expect with unions in South Africa?

To avoid costly mistakes in HRM, multinational companies need to consider several key questions regarding local employees such as:[1]

- *How can we identify talented local employees?* Nations differ in terms of educational qualifications and formal certifications for job skills. Multinational companies must acquire the necessary knowledge to identify local talent.
- *How can we attract these prospective employees to apply for jobs?* In the United States, newspaper advertising is a popular technique for recruitment. However, in other nations, personal contacts are more important. A multinational company often must use local traditions to get the best candidates for jobs.
- *Can we use our home country's training methods with local employees?* Training methods are not always culturally transferable. To make training transcultural, both trainers and written material must be available in all languages.
- *What types of appraisal methods are customary?* Appraisal methods common in one country may not transfer to another country. For example, the Japanese use of age-graded promotions and raises may not be accepted by U.S. workers.
- *What types of rewards do local people value (e.g., security, pay, benefits)?* Cultural and institutional factors often lead people to value different combinations of rewards. In contrast to most European countries, for example, the United States is a society with high wages but low benefits.
- *How can we retain and develop employees with a high potential as future managers?* Countries differ in the training and development applied to lower-level managers with high potential. U.S. companies may identify these managers early in their careers and develop them through rapid promotion coupled with high rewards. In contrast, Japanese companies know that they have these managers for their whole career and may take a slower approach, emphasizing experience in many different functional jobs within the company.
- *Do any local laws affect staffing, compensation, and training decisions?* Multinational companies must learn about and work within the web of laws and government policies that govern work in their host countries.

All these questions deal with issues of human resource management (HRM) in different national settings. When multinational companies set up operations abroad or engage in strategic alliances with companies from other countries, managers often need to understand and adapt to local HRM customs and practices.

To show the impact of the national context (national and business cultures and social institutions) on human resource management, this chapter illustrates varied practices from the United States and other countries. The chapter builds on your understanding of international human resource management, discussed in Chapter 11. Reading both chapters will help you, the multinational manager, select and implement appropriate human resource management policies and, when necessary, adapt these policies to the local national environment.

Why Do Nations Differ in HRM?

Cross-national differences in HRM and the pressures to adapt to local conditions arise from the array of factors that make each nation unique. As we saw in Chapter 3, these factors are called the national context and include such things as the national culture, the country's available labor and other natural resources, the characteristics of political and legal institutions, and the types of managers available to firms. The national context also includes social institutions, national and business culture, factor conditions, and their combined effects on the business environment. Thus, the national context provides the unique setting for each nation in which managers make decisions regarding HRM practices. Exhibit 12.1 shows a model of how the national context leads to national differences in HRM policies and practices.

Chapters 2 and 3 showed that the values and norms associated with national and business cultures result in preferred ways of doing business. These preferences influence all aspects of the organization: strategies, organizational design, and human resource practices. Basic norms and values regarding gender, age, and family and friends influence HRM practices from recruitment to performance appraisal. For example, in more particularistic cultures, managers are more likely to hire people based on personal qualities (e.g., someone from a particular family or village) rather than on more universalistic criteria such as educational level.

Because countries differ widely regarding social institutions, multinational managers must select and implement HRM practices that meet the demands of a society's social institutions. Just as social institutions help structure the relationships among people, they help define the correct ways of doing business in any country. In the United States, for example, anti-discrimination laws, part of the legal social institution, prohibit many recruitment practices common in Japanese and Korean companies. In Japan, for example, the family system relies on women raising children so that men can work long hours at night or be away from home for long periods. As such, there are unwritten biases against women holding managerial positions after they have children.

The national context also includes the pool of resources available for firms. The resource pool represents all the human and physical resources available in a country. Examples include the quality of labor, the availability of scientific laboratories, and sources of fuel. If all countries had access to the same resources, there would be fewer differences across nations in management practices. Regardless of nationality, if firms could access the same resources, they would copy the strategies and organizations of the most successful competitors in the world. However, the national endowments of physical resources (e.g., supply of raw materials) and other resources (e.g., culturally based motivations to work, educational systems) are unique to each country.

Where does the resource pool come from? The resource pool represents the factor conditions associated with a country. Five key factors influence the

National context

National culture and social institutions that influence how managers make decisions regarding the strategies of their organizations.

Resource pool

All the human and physical resources available in a country.

EXHIBIT 12.1

How the National Context Leads to National Differences in Local HRM Practices

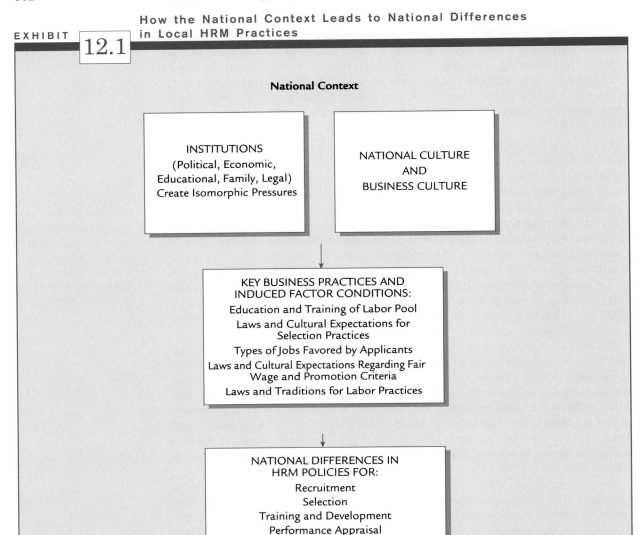

resource pool available to firms and, in turn, the management practices favored by firms in different nations:[2]

- *The quality, quantity, and accessibility of raw material:* For example, the extensive tracts of fertile land in the United States enable U.S. agricultural firms to compete with low price and high quality on the world market.

- *The quantity, quality, and cost of personnel available:* Germany, for example, has large pools of technically trained workers that support the development of industries and firms where high-quality differentiation strategies abound. In contrast, however, German workers are among the most highly paid in the world, thus making low-cost strategies difficult.

- *The scientific, technical, and market-related knowledge available to firms:* Both Japan and the United States, for example, have abundant stores of scientific and technical knowledge from universities and industry-based R&D. Additionally, in countries like China and Taiwan, the government is taking an active role to reshape the educational system in order to encourage people to get trained in more knowledge-oriented sectors.[3]

- *The cost and amount of capital available to firms for operations and expansion:* **This** factor addresses the question of how firms get financing to run their operations. For example, during the double-digit expansion of the Korean economy, Korean *chaebol* (conglomerates) relied mostly on heavy debt financing from government-controlled banks. More recently, in a post-1998 Korean economy reeling from the shock of failing *chaebol* and a weaker currency, Korean banks are less likely to loan money to debt-ridden companies.

- *The type, quality, and costs of supporting institutions such as the systems of communication, education, and transportation:* **Nations differ** widely in the supporting resources necessary to run a business. Trained workers are a critical resource. However, factors such as reliable phones and the ability to transport goods cheaply and predictably are also important.

Some resources occur naturally. These are called **natural-factor conditions.** For example, countries with extensive coal and gas reserves favor the development of industries and firms that require high energy consumption. For example, Canada has abundant sources of the water necessary for the efficient production of aluminum.

> **Natural-factor conditions**
> National resources that occur naturally, such as abundant water supply.

Other resources arise from cultural and institutional pressures. These are called **induced-factor conditions.** For example, the high cultural value placed on education in many Asian societies helps create a well-trained workforce for countries like Singapore and Korea. Social institutions such as the government also can affect induced-factor conditions. For example, the knowledge base available to the Japanese robotics industry is facilitated by the more than 180 Japanese universities that created robotics laboratories and the $20 million a year contributed to program development by the Japanese Ministry of International Trade and Industry.[4]

> **Induced-factor conditions**
> National resources created by a nation, such as a superior educational system.

In general, companies find competitive advantages by tapping into pools of national resources that are valuable and difficult to copy or rare.[5] "Valuable" means that the resource contributes quality or cost-competitive advantages to a company's product or service. "Difficult to copy or rare" resources are not easily imitated by competitors. When valuable, difficult to copy, or rare resources are unique to a nation, companies in that nation tend to take advantage of these resource pools and, in turn, develop similar strategies. Consequently, different resource pools also lead to basic national differences in strategies.

For example, Germany's technically trained workforce is a valuable resource for German industry.[6] As you will see in more detail later, it is a national system supported by a long cultural tradition of craftwork, existing educational institutions, and substantial government contribution to vocational training. As such, it is also difficult for firms in other countries to copy. Thus, many German companies often rely on this pool of technical workers to compete with differentiation strategies for products such as automobiles and cameras.

As the model shows, the national and business cultures combine with social institutions to affect the business environment and certain factor conditions. In turn, this national context determines the management practices and policies followed by most companies in a nation and the types of HRM adaptations necessary for multinational companies. As such, this chapter outlines the major characteristics of the national context that affect HRM. Throughout the chapter, you will see how the following issues affect national differences in HRM:

- *Education and training of the labor pool:* The type and quality of labor available to companies is a key issue in HRM. A country's educational system provides the raw human resource material for companies. How much training a person will need to be a qualified worker and the meaning of educational credentials for selection are examples of issues determined by a nation's educational system. A well-educated labor force is a factor condition induced by governmental and cultural support for education. Later, for example, you will see how the German system of specialized training dominates key aspects of German HRM. The following Case in Point discusses some of the recent efforts of the Taiwanese government to infuse creativity in its workforce.

- *Laws and cultural expectations for selection practices:* The laws of a country and the people's expectations that arise from the national and business cultures tell managers the "right" way to find new employees. In some nations, for example, you are expected to hire your relatives. In other nations, it might be against a company's policies to do so. In some nations, it is considered common and necessary to ask women job applicants if they plan to get married soon. However, asking a job applicant such a question in the United States would be illegal and discriminatory.

- *Types of jobs favored by applicants:* Japanese college graduates prefer to be hired by big companies. They are attracted to the security of working for a large company. Most Chinese businesses are family dominated, and family members expect to work for and with other family members. These examples illustrate cultural values and norms regarding the "best" and the "right" places to work.

- *Laws and cultural expectations regarding fair wages and promotion criteria:* Should older workers make more money than younger workers? Should men be promoted faster than women? Should people who enter the company together make the same salary and be promoted together? Should a worker's family

CASE IN POINT

Creativity Education in Taiwan

The Taiwanese Ministry of Education has played an important role in infusing creativity in the educational curriculum in Taiwan. Given the current global knowledge economy, Taiwan is predicting that creativity can be an important source of competitive advantage for the nation in the future. It is striving for the "Republic of Creativity" goal. As such, the Ministry of Education, in collaboration with most educational institutions such as universities, colleges, and high schools, has implemented various plans to encourage and cultivate creative talent in Taiwanese society. For instance, many universities have initiated creativity departments and created creativity degrees. As prominent examples, the National Taiwan University has created an innovation incubation center to promote innovation, value creation, and entrepreneurship. The National Taiwan Normal University is also offering a Masters degree in Creativity Development through its College of Education.

Will such efforts pay off? Will multinational companies relocate to Taiwan for R&D efforts in the future by taking advantage of such creativity efforts? It is still too early to determine how effective the programs are. However, such concerted efforts at all levels of Taiwanese society will likely benefit the nation in the long run.

Source: Based on Wu, Jing-Jyi, Stephanie Lo, and Pei-Chun Wang. 2005. (English Translation). Wu, Jing-Jyi, Ching-Mei Tseng, Han-Yi Wang, Chih-Jer Lin, and Wei-Wen Lin. 2004. Creative Education in Taiwan. Taipei: Ministry of Education (in Chinese).

situation influence his or her salary? Due to cultural expectations and institutional pressures, questions such as these are often answered differently in different national contexts. As such, values, norms, and institutional expectations influence compensation decisions and the relationship between performance appraisals and compensation. For example, U.S. multinational managers often find that the link between compensation and performance, considered legal and fair in U.S. companies, is considered less important in other nations.

- *Laws and traditions regarding labor practices:* The legal position and power of unions and the historical relationships between management and labor have profound influences on HRM practices regarding labor relations. For example, in some nations long-term historical precedents exist for labor–management conflict. Labor conflict, however, differs widely by national context. Additionally, the popularity of unions among workers differs by national context.

As these issues show, the regulatory environment has a significant impact on HRM practices and functions in different nations. Brewster, Wood, Brookes, and Ommeren[7] provide supporting evidence for this proposition. Using large-scale survey data from a large number of multinational companies based in Europe and Japan, they found that the regulatory environment determines the size of the HR departments. Basing their study on Whitley's[8] categorization of economies, they found that transitional economies of former communist countries of Central Europe tend to have smaller HR departments. In such countries, the transition to capitalism has been brutal, and there is an emphasis on cost cutting as well as staff reduction. As such, the HR function has taken a back seat to short-term organizational survival. In contrast, in countries like Japan that have strong institutional barriers against hiring or firing, companies find it difficult to increase or decrease staff members. Furthermore, Japan's government has an active role to regulate the labor market emphasizing job security and training. It is, therefore, not surprising to see that Japanese companies tend to have generally larger human resource management departments consistent with the many administrative and regulatory requirements of human resource practices.

The remainder of this chapter illustrates the impact of national context on HRM practices in several nations. These illustrations only hint at the extent of differences among national HRM practices. To understand any particular host country's HRM practices, multinational managers must pay careful attention to the values, norms, and laws that bear directly on HRM.

For comparison purposes, each basic task of HRM is treated by contrasting dominant practices in the United States with examples of practices from other nations. The HRM tasks considered, in order of presentation, are: recruitment, selection, training and development, performance appraisal, compensation, and labor relations.

Recruitment

Exhibit 12.2 summarizes the major steps in recruitment. First, managers determine that jobs are available. These vacancies may occur in anticipation of expansion or as replacements for workers leaving the organization. Second, employers determine the types of people and skills that are necessary for the job. Third, employers generate a pool of applicants for the job.

EXHIBIT **12.2**   **Steps in the Recruiting Process**

- ➤ Jobs Open
- ➤ Applicant Characteristics Identified
- ➤ Recruitment Strategies Applied
  - Walk-ins
  - Newspaper and other Advertising (e.g., Internet)
  - Job Positions Posted in Organization
  - State and Private Employment Services
  - Educational Institutions
  - Employee Referrals
- ➤ Applications Received

Source: Adapted from Bohlander, George W., Scott Snell, and Arthur W. Sherman, Jr. 2001. Managing Human Resources. Cincinnati: South-Western; Werther, William B., and Keith Davis. 1993. Human Resources and Personnel Management. New York: McGraw-Hill.

Recruitment strategies generate the applicant pool and include the following:

- Walk-ins or unsolicited applications.
- Advertisements placed in newspapers or on the Internet.
- Company web site job postings—listings of vacant positions on the firm's web site.
- Internal job postings—company listings of vacant jobs targeted at current employees.
- Public and private personnel agencies.
- Placement services of educational institutions.
- Current employee recommendations.

Managers hope that one or more of these recruitment strategies will generate a pool of applicants who are qualified for the vacant job.

Most national differences in recruitment occur in the preferences for using different recruitment strategies. National and business cultures have the dominant effects on the "right way" to find employees, but organizational and occupational cultures also have different norms regarding recruitment. For example, firms such as Procter & Gamble in the United States have strong norms favoring recruitment from within the firm. Social institutions such as educational systems also affect recruitment. In Japan, for example, personal contacts between university professors and managers are often a prerequisite for university students to get good jobs in big companies.

Recruitment in the United States

U.S. companies use all types of recruiting strategies. However, U.S. managers do not judge all recruitment strategies as being equally effective. Exhibit 12.3 shows recruitment strategies believed to be most effective for companies in the United States.

For all types of positions, U.S. managers see newspaper advertising as one of the most effective recruitment channels. College or university recruitment was judged among the most effective only for professional and technical jobs.

EXHIBIT **12.3**   **Most Effective Recruiting Sources for U.S. Companies (by job category)**

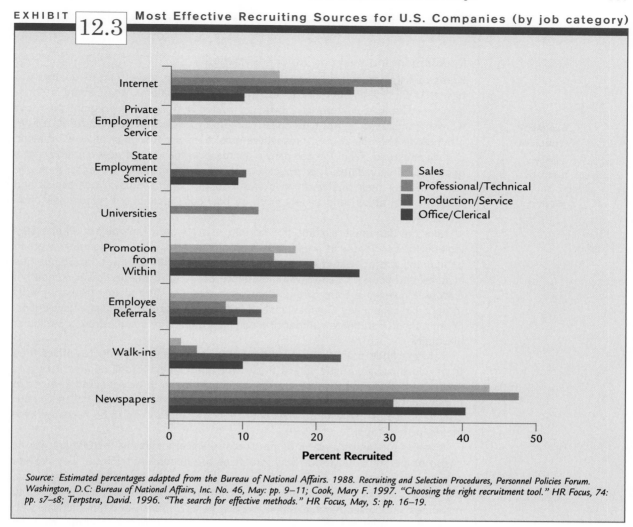

Source: Estimated percentages adapted from the Bureau of National Affairs. 1988. Recruiting and Selection Procedures, Personnel Policies Forum. Washington, D.C: Bureau of National Affairs, Inc. No. 46, May: pp. 9–11; Cook, Mary F. 1997. "Choosing the right recruitment tool." HR Focus, 74: pp. s7–s8; Terpstra, David. 1996. "The search for effective methods." HR Focus, May, 5: pp. 16–19.

Managers believed that employee referrals produced only marginal success. There is some concern in the United States that employee referrals result in the recruitment of only those employees with similar backgrounds to current employees. There is also a fear that recruitment by personal contacts (common in many other nations) may result in potential biases against certain groups, such as women and minorities.[9]

The belief in the United States that open and public advertisements are the most effective recruiting strategy reflects U.S. individualistic cultural values. Managers in the United States and other individualistic societies view potential workers as unique combinations of skills. These skills are purchased by the company on the labor market. Public advertisements of jobs maximize the pool of available talent and, from the workers' point of view, support egalitarian norms that all can compete for open jobs. In contrast, recruitment in collectivist societies tends to focus on the in-group such as the family and friends of those already in the organization.[10] Consider the following Multinational Management Brief regarding recruitment in Asian and African countries.

Multinational Management **Brief**

Recruitment in Asian and African Societies

Korea ranks moderately low on Hofstede's individualism scale (21st percentile) and has HRM practices more representative of collectivist cultures. Recruitment in Korea originated from a mixture of Confucian values and Western pragmatism. Most Korean companies recruit blue-collar workers by **backdoor recruitment,** a form of employee referral. That is, prospective employees are friends or relatives of those already employed. From the company's perspective, friends and relatives represent a good pool of candidates. If prospective employees are relatives or friends, then one can vouch for their trustworthiness and industriousness. Smaller companies and those in rural areas tend to rely more on backdoor recruitment rather than open recruitment.

Like the Japanese system, the Korean recruitment of managers emphasizes looking for candidates at prestigious universities. Also, like the Japanese, Korean companies prefer recent graduates to managers with experience. Companies assume that younger people will mold more easily to fit the particular company's culture. However, a form of backdoor recruitment occurs at this level, primarily through old school ties. Companies tend to favor graduates of particular universities. Often a disproportionate number of a company's managers come from a particular university.

Taiwan's HRM practices also are rooted in Confucianism. Confucian ethics tend to be more particularistic where those with the closest social connections (i.e., *guanxi*) are preferred over others. Confucianism tends to be reflected in a desire to maintain harmony at work and a more paternalistic management styles. Consequently, those people with *guanxi* connections are more likely to be recruited, promoted, or rewarded.

In many African nations hit by periods of political instability, recruitment also is based on personal networks. Such practices are necessary because they provide some order in an otherwise chaotic environment. Furthermore, some argue that the use of personal networks also allows marginal groups to have some access to resources and power. As an example, Algeria relies on family and other kinship networks for recruitment and selection processes. Recent research shows that the effect of the civil war and political instability has forced companies to develop an even narrower network for recruitment purposes. In an environment where use of physical force can be a threat, managers need to carefully develop trust to avoid such threats.

Source: Based on Chen, Shyh-jer, Lawler, John, & Bae, Johngseok. 2005 Convergence in Human Resource Systems: A Comparison of Locally Owned and MNC Subsidiaries in Taiwan. Human Resource Management, 44(3): pp. 237–256; Mellahi, Kamel, and Geoffrey T. Wood. 2003. "From kinship to trust: Changing recruitment practices in unstable political contexts." International Journal of Cross Cultural Management 3, 3: pp. 369–381; Steers, Richard M., Yoo Keun Shin, and Gerardo R. Ungson. 1989. The Chaebol: Korea's New Industrial Might. New York: HarperBusiness.

Backdoor recruitment
Prospective employees are friends or relatives of those already employed.

Recruitment around the World

Similar to companies' preference for recruitment strategies, individuals located around the world also have preferred ways to find jobs. These preferences evolve most likely from the norms associated with the national culture and social institutions. For instance, Korean workers looking for jobs know that many Korean firms prefer forms of backdoor recruitment. Consequently, they are more likely to resort to friends and family to find jobs.

To provide additional information on cross-cultural differences in preference for appropriate ways to find jobs, we analyzed data collected through the International Social Survey Program (ISSP) provided by the Inter-University Consortium for Political and Social Research.[11] The ISSP is a cross-national collaboration dedicated to the collection of important data related to work and work orientations.

The ISSP asked those respondents who were looking for jobs to indicate what they were using to look for the new job. The various types included in the survey were whether these respondents were registered with public and private agencies, whether they advertised on the newspaper, whether they responded to advertisements, whether they applied directly to employers, and whether they asked relatives or friends.

Comparisons of the various forms of recruitment confirm that both national culture and social institutions influence recruitment practices by encouraging people in different societies to have stronger preference for specific ways to look for jobs.

Exhibit 12.4 illustrates some of the country differences between whether individuals were registered with a public or private agency in their efforts to look for a job.

As the exhibit shows, individuals from, for instance, Sweden, Norway, Hungary, and France were more likely to be registered with a public agency as one of the ways to find a job. Such findings are not surprising considering that the governments of these countries are actively involved in the day-to-day operation of the country. Both former communist societies (e.g., Hungary, Slovenia) and

EXHIBIT 12.4   Preferred Ways To Look for a New Job: Public versus Private Agency

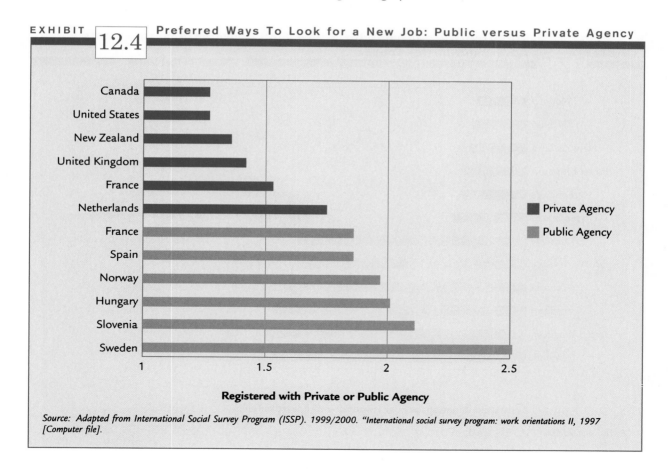

Source: Adapted from International Social Survey Program (ISSP). 1999/2000. "International social survey program: work orientations II, 1997 [Computer file].

socialist societies (e.g., Sweden, Spain) are heavily influenced by governmental regulations and policies. It is therefore natural that individuals from these societies rely on their governments as one of the ways to find a new job. In contrast, individuals in countries where governments play a lesser role (i.e., United States, United Kingdom, New Zealand) are more likely to rely on private agencies. Such results clearly demonstrate the influence of social institutions on preference for appropriate ways to find jobs.

Exhibit 12.5 shows which countries have the highest preference for advertising in newspapers and responding to newspaper advertisements.

Both advertising in newspapers and responding to advertisements reflect very open recruitment forms. In both cases, the potential employee is depending on open competition in the labor market and how his or her skills and qualifications compare to others. It is therefore not surprising to find that many individualistic countries (e.g., United Kingdom, United States, New Zealand) are found on that list. Individuals in such societies prefer such open means because these are the preferred recruitment methods. As mentioned earlier, societies high on individualism favor hiring the best person with the right skills for the job. One of the most likely ways to ensure that the best person is hired is through open advertisements where all potential pools of skills and qualifications can be considered.

When individuals rely on posting of advertisements or responding to newspaper advertisements, they are assuming that universalistic qualifications apply to all of them. The latter explains the presence of such feminine countries as Denmark, Norway, and the Netherlands where cultural norms favor egalitarian

EXHIBIT | 12.5   Preferred Ways to Look for a New Job: Answered Advertisements versus Advertised in Newspaper

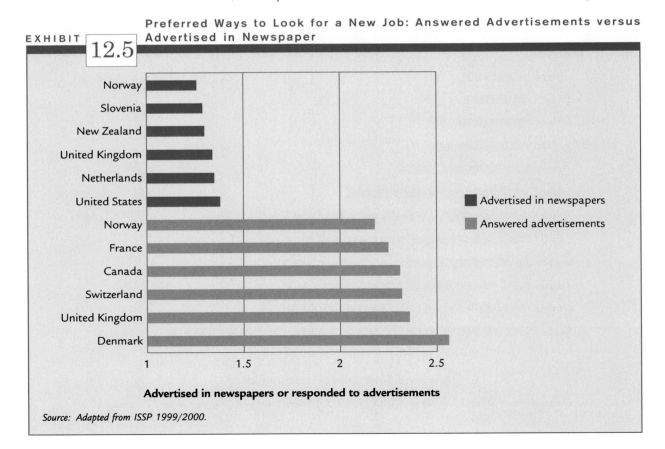

Advertised in newspapers or responded to advertisements

Source: Adapted from ISSP 1999/2000.

norms. Such results are also consistent with Trompenaar's[12] view of countries high on universalism (Canada, United States, Denmark) where the cultural expectation is based on equality.

Exhibit 12.6 shows individuals from the countries that have the highest preference for direct applications to companies compared with asking friends or relatives.

Exhibit 12.6 shows that individuals in countries that are high on individualism or femininity (e.g., Canada and Sweden) are more likely to apply directly for jobs. Direct applications are also reflective of open forms of recruitment and cultural norms of individual achievement and equality. In contrast, individuals in more socialist societies (e.g., Italy, Poland, and Hungary) prefer to ask friends or relatives as a means to get a job. The latter is not surprising because individuals in such societies rely more on friends, relatives, and other connections (i.e., relationships) for work advancement and other work opportunities. As such, they rely more on their personal connections as a means to find a job.

After attracting a pool of applicants, the next stage in the HRM process is selection.

Selection

Selection in the United States

U.S. experts on human resource management identify a series of steps in the selection process.[13] Exhibit 12.7 shows these steps, from the initial application to the final hiring.

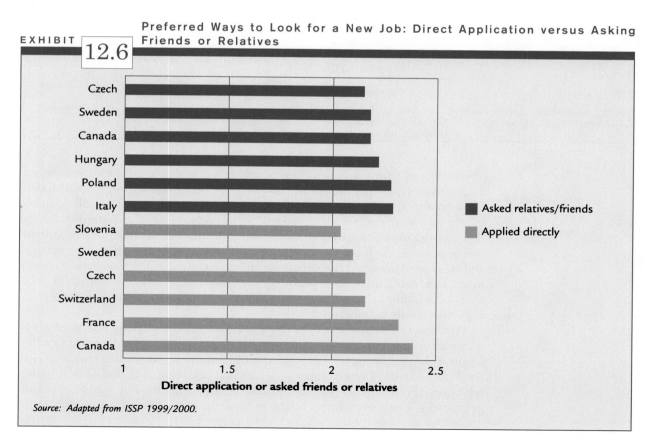

EXHIBIT 12.6

Preferred Ways to Look for a New Job: Direct Application versus Asking Friends or Relatives

Direct application or asked friends or relatives

■ Asked relatives/friends
■ Applied directly

Source: Adapted from ISSP 1999/2000.

EXHIBIT **12.7**   **Typical Steps in U.S. Personnel Selection**

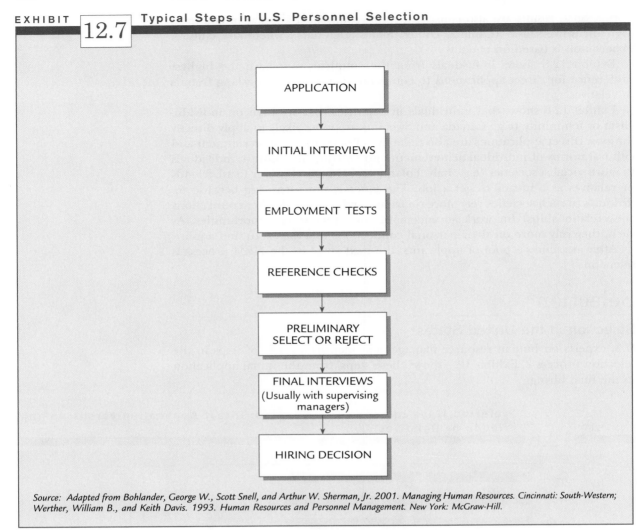

APPLICATION

↓

INITIAL INTERVIEWS

↓

EMPLOYMENT TESTS

↓

REFERENCE CHECKS

↓

PRELIMINARY
SELECT OR REJECT

↓

FINAL INTERVIEWS
(Usually with supervising
managers)

↓

HIRING DECISION

Source: Adapted from Bohlander, George W., Scott Snell, and Arthur W. Sherman, Jr. 2001. Managing Human Resources. Cincinnati: South-Western; Werther, William B., and Keith Davis. 1993. Human Resources and Personnel Management. New York: McGraw-Hill.

The aim of typical U.S. selection practices is to gather quality information on a candidate's job qualifications. The ideal selection then results in a match between the specific skills of the job applicant and the specific job requirements. As with the recruitment process, an individual is seen as a bundle of skills that the organization can purchase. The individualistic culture in the United States promotes a focus on individual achievements (e.g., education, natural ability, experience) and not on group affiliations such as the family. As a result, many U.S. companies have prohibitions against nepotism, the hiring of relatives. In addition, many U.S. companies have policies forbidding managers to supervise family members.

Previous work experience, performance on tests, and perceptions of qualifications from interviews help inform personnel or hiring managers about the applicant's qualifications. To avoid discrimination or favoritism, laws and cultural norms in the United States prescribe that information gathered during the selection process must be valid; that is, the information gathered from prospective employees must relate to performance on the vacant job. Job-qualification tests must predict job performance. For example, lifting

100 pounds would not be a valid selection test for most clerical jobs. Personal information gathered during the selection process, such as height and weight, must also be relevant to the job.

Next, we consider contrasting selection practices in collectivist national cultures.

Selection in Collectivist Cultures

Hofstede[14] captures the essence of hiring in collectivist cultures. He notes: "The hiring process in a collectivist society always takes the in-group into account. Usually preference is given to hiring relatives, first of the employer, but also of other persons already employed by the company. Hiring persons from a family one already knows reduces risks. Also relatives will be concerned about the reputation of the family and help correct misbehavior of a family member."

In many Asian and Latin American collectivist cultures, businesses are often small and family owned. The hiring of family members is a natural extension of family activities. However, modernization and urbanization challenge some of these traditions. In Mexico, for example, newspaper advertisements and executive-placement agencies are increasingly used in larger urban companies. In these larger companies, there are simply not enough relatives to fill all positions.[15]

In selecting employees, collectivist cultural norms value potential trustworthiness, reliability, and loyalty over performance-related background characteristics. Personal traits such as loyalty to the company, loyalty to the boss, and trustworthiness are the traits that family members can provide. However, larger and technically oriented companies may need professional managers and technicians with skills not available inside the family. In these cases, the selection process still prioritizes personal characteristics over technical characteristics. If one cannot have a family member, then the priority is to find employees who have the personality characteristics and background necessary to fit into the corporate culture. Younger male recruits are preferred because they have not been corrupted by another company's values, and cultural role expectations expect them to be more dedicated to work than women with children.

For example, in managerial selection in the collectivist Korean culture and the moderately collectivist Japanese culture, high school and university ties substitute for family membership. At Daewoo Corporation in Korea, the chairman and six of the eight top executives attended Kyunggi High School. Seoul National University graduates make up 62 percent of the highest executives in seven of Korea's most important *chaebol* (industrial conglomerates).[16] Graduates from two public (Tokyo and Kyoto) and two private (Keio and Waseda) universities dominate both business and public leadership in Japan. Executives who graduated from elite universities use their personal contacts with university professors to provide information on a recruit's worthiness to the company. Often, the recruit's area of study at the university is of much less concern than the more subjective assessments of fit with the company.

Next we consider selection in other countries.

Selection around the world

Because of the difficulty of collecting data, there are few studies that have compared selection practices around the world. However, the Best International Management Practices Project is to date the most comprehensive program designed to understand cross-cultural human resource management practices.[17] The project's main goals have been to survey around 40 countries to determine the best IHRM practices and how these practices relate to company success.

A comparison of current selection practices in 13 countries (Australia, Canada, China, Indonesia, Japan, South Korea, Mexico, Taiwan, the United States, and a number of Latin American countries) reveals that there may be some universal selection practices.[18] The study found that a common selection criterion in all 13 countries surveyed was a person's ability to perform technical aspects of the job. Results of the study also revealed that all managers rated personal interviews as the best screening tool to gauge a candidate's social skills. The latter suggests that in many societies, people are wary of offering jobs unless they have had a chance to personally see the candidate.

The study also revealed a number of important differences that reflect cross-cultural contexts. For instance, it was found that developed countries such as Australia, Canada, Germany, and the United States are more likely to view past work experience as the best way to infer evidence of technical skills. Another critical difference is that people in a number of Asian societies (China, South Korea, and Indonesia) tend to prefer that candidates take actual employment tests to demonstrate technical skills. This is perhaps a reflection of individualistic societies, which value individual skills as demonstrated by a person's qualifications (including past experience) while collectivist societies may not place as much emphasis on past skills.

Implications for the Multinational: Recruitment and Selection

The Best International Management Practices Project[19] findings suggest that for some recruitment and selection practices, there may be some more convergence around the world in the future. As part of the project, respondents were also asked which selection practices they felt should be used in the future. Findings suggest that managers of all 13 countries agreed that technical skills should be the most important criterion for selection purposes. The study also found that a person's potential to do a good job "even if the person is not that good when they first start" is also a criterion on which all countries agree.

However, despite some evidence of convergence, national context will likely continue to affect recruitment and selection practices. As such, recruitment and selection of host-country workers and managers requires that the managers of a multinational company understand and adapt to local practices. Thus, for example, foreign multinationals in the United States probably have the most success using the typical U.S. recruitment practices—advertising in newspapers and going to college campuses. In other countries, the multinational manager will also need to discover and use local recruitment and selection practices.

Adaptation to local recruitment and selection practices may not always be easy. In societies where backdoor or personal contacts are acceptable recruitment strategies, foreign multinational managers may not have access to the appropriate recruitment channels. In Japan, for example, most foreign multinational companies do not have the personal contacts with Japanese professors necessary to attract the best potential managerial talent. For U.S. companies, such recruitment methods may violate ethical codes that require competitive access to all open jobs.

What happens when a company does not follow local norms in recruitment and selection? First, it may not get the best potential employees. Second, it may

CASE IN POINT

Using e.HR for Recruitment

Global companies like Nike, KPN, and Siemens are all using e.HR systems to manage their HR functions around the world. Consider that Nike's European, Middle Eastern, and Asian headquarters gets almost 800 job applications a month for approximately 100 to 120 positions. Nike's policy is that each applicant is a potential employee and customer and has to be treated as such. However, before e.HR was implemented, there was tremendous stress on the HR department to quickly process the vitas to make hiring decisions. Unfortunately, reviews of the system showed that mistakes were made and that the cost of hires needed to be reduced while the level of talent needed to increase.

The new e.HR system at Nike has been helpful in addressing many of the problems. All applicants can now apply for specific jobs or for future job opportunities through the Nike web site. The web site is linked to other external recruiting web sites, which allows more potential applicants to be aware of job opportunities. Furthermore, for each new job position, the online system makes the first cut, and matches the candidates with the job requirements.

As such, Nike managers have access to a candidate short list rather than the large number of hard-copy vitas with the previous system. This system has enabled Nike to improve the quality of candidates it considers. Furthermore, applicants are encouraged to update their vita every six months to show their continued interest in the company. Nike has a constantly growing list of applicants for future positions. The database now contains around 8,500 vitas.

Nike has seen tremendous benefits with the implementation of the e.HR system. The company has saved close to 50 percent of recruitment costs. Furthermore, with the regular vita updates, Nike has relied less on external recruiters since it always has qualified applicants on hand. The system's ability to provide short lists based on the job requirements also has improved the quality of hires, and the time to fill vacancies has dropped from 62 to 42 days.

Source: Based on Pollitt, David. 2005. "Recruiting the right project managers at Siemens Business Services." Human Resources Management International Digest 13:7, pp. 28–30; 2005b. "E-recruitment gets the Nike tick of approval." Human Resources Management International Digest 13:2, pp. 33–5; 2006. "E-HR brings everything together at KPN." Human Resources Management International Digest 14: 1, pp. 34–5.

offend local cultural norms or break host-country laws. Thus, multinational managers must always assess the trade-off between following home practices that get what they believe are the "right" people for the job and the costs and benefits of following local traditions.

As we saw in Chapter 11, many companies are now making use of electronic human resources (e.HR) to manage their human resources. The use of e.HR has also proved to be very useful for the recruitment function. Consider the above Case in Point discussing e.HR for recruitment.

After identifying a pool of applicants and selecting those to be hired, the next step in the HRM process is training and development of the employees.

Training and Development

In any country, training and development needs vary widely. Different industries, technologies, strategies, organizational structures, and local labor market conditions affect an organization's training and development needs and programs. However, broad national differences in training and development do exist among countries.

The cross-national differences in training and development are most associated with institutional differences in national educational systems. Educational systems lead to large differences in recruits' qualifications in basic skills and in attitudes toward work. For example, more than 90 percent of the 25- to 34-year-olds in Norway, Japan, and Korea finished secondary school. Turkey and

Portugal had only 24 percent.[20] For another example, consider Germany. It has a strong technical-education program and an apprenticeship system that originated with the guild system of the Middle Ages.

Cross-cultural training and development differences are also associated with the degree of emphasis placed by the national governments.[21] For instance, the Australian government requires companies above a certain size to spend 1.5 percent of their payroll expenses on training. The Chinese government is also heavily involved in training; companies are encouraged to train their workers before they are offered full-time jobs. The Taiwanese have gone even further by establishing 13 public vocational-training institutes for those who do not have access to higher education.

Training needs are also determined by the particular business system in force in the country, which, in turn, impacts the emphasis on human resources functions. In that respect, Whitley[22] suggests that there are several forms of institutional frameworks that have implications for training. For instance, the industrial-districts model of regions (Northern Italy) or the large-firms model (e.g., Germany or Japan) all have important barriers that make it hard for companies to hire or fire. As a consequence, because of the difficulty of hiring or firing, companies in these countries focus on skills development. In such countries, there is a strong emphasis on training.[23] The compartmentalized model in both the United Kingdom and the United States is reflected in short-term contracting with stakeholders as well as emphasis on efficiency. As such, this focus on short-term contracting does not encourage emphasis on training. Another model is the transitional model typifying nations in Central and Eastern Europe. In such countries, more attention has been devoted to the need to cut costs. Furthermore, in many cases, these countries have had to get rid of the bloated staffs that were typical under communist rule. It is, therefore, not surprising to see that in these transitional countries, the emphasis on cost cutting and staff reduction also means that there is not much interest in training. Exhibit 12.8 summarizes the various models and emphasis on various human resources issues including training.

EXHIBIT 12.8   **Institutional Systems and Training around the World**

Models/HR Issues	Emphasis on Training	Ability to Hire or Fire	Strength of Unions	Extent to which the Government Regulates the Labor Market
Large Firms Model (Germany and Japan)	High	Low	High	High
Industrial Districts (Northern Italy)	Moderate	Low/Moderate	High	High
Corporatist (Sweden, Denmark and Netherlands)	High	Low	High	High
Transitional (Poland, Czech, and Hungary)	Low	Low	Low	Low
Compartmentalized (U.K. and U.S.)	Low	Low	Low	Low
Peripheral (Spain and Portugal)	Low/Moderate	Moderate/High	Moderate/High	Moderate/High

Source: Adapted from Chris Brewster, Geoff Wood, Michael Brookes, and Jos Van Ommeren. (2006). What determines the size of the HR function? A cross-national analysis. Human Resource Management, 45 (1), pp. 3–21.

In addition to social institutions' influence on training and development, cultural values regarding types of educational credentials and other personnel practices, such as lifetime employment, also influence training and development needs. For example, though threatened by economic practicalities and often maligned as inefficient, the Japanese retain the ideal of long-term employment. For companies like Ricoh, which continues to avoid layoffs at all costs, it allows management training and development to take place slowly, through extensive job rotations. Managers learn by doing. They have many different job assignments early in their careers.

Exhibit 12.9 gives an overview of work-related training systems in use throughout the world while Exhibit 12.10 gives some specific detail about training in a number of countries. Next, for a more detailed example, we will discuss training and development differences between the voluntary system of the United States and the cooperative system of Germany.

Training and Development in the United States

U.S. companies with more than 100 employees invest more than $60 billion in training costs.[24] Exhibit 12.11 shows the types of skills taught to employees by these U.S. organizations. The most popular training topics are management development and computer skills. However, other types of training, such as those needed for new methods and procedures, reach more people on all levels of the organization. In spite of the billions of dollars invested in training, training in the United States does not reach all workers. Estimates are that U.S. employers provide training only to one out of every fourteen workers.[25]

Because of perceived weaknesses in U.S. secondary education, the pressure on U.S. businesses to supplement basic educational training will also increase. Thirty percent of U.S. students do not finish high school. Many of those who do graduate do not have sufficient reading and mathematical skills for current and future jobs.[26] For example, 40 percent of the companies in Exhibit 12.11 already see the need to provide remedial and basic education.

EXHIBIT 12.9   Training Systems around the World

Type	Example Countries	Features and Sources of Institutional Pressures
Cooperative	Austria, Germany, Switzerland, and some Latin American countries	Legal and historical precedents for cooperation among companies, unions, and the government.
Company-Based Voluntarism/ High Labor Mobility	USA and the UK	Lack of institutional pressures to provide training. Companies provide training based on own cost-benefits.
Voluntarism/Low Labor Mobility	Japan	Low labor turnover encourages investment in training without institutional pressure.
State-Driven Incentive Provider	Hong Kong, Korea, Singapore, Taiwan, China, Australia	Government identifies needs for skills and uses incentives to encourage companies to train in chosen areas.
Supplier	Developing countries in Asia and Africa, transition economies	No institutional pressures for companies to train. Government provides formal training organizations.

Source: Adapted from International Labor Organization (ILO). 1999. World Employment Report 1998–99. Geneva: International Labor Office.

EXHIBIT 12.10   Key Specific Training and Development Characteristics of Selected Countries

Australia

➤ Government introduced 1990 Training Guarantee act—requires companiesto spend 1.5% of annual payroll expenses on training.

➤ More training provided at managerial level than blue-collar level.

➤ Not enough initiatives yet to assess effectiveness of training programs.

Canada

➤ Because of NAFTA, companies are facing increasing pressures to cut costs, and HR departments are being disproportionately affected.

➤ Use of outside consultants for training purposes is becoming increasingly prevalent.

➤ Only half of corporate HRM departments are involved in training.

China

➤ High degree of governmental intervention to encourage companies to train.

➤ Heavy emphasis on training and development of managers.

➤ Training programs are more likely to emphasize corporate values and interpersonal skills.

➤ Many multinationals (ABB, Ericcson, Procter & Gamble, Motorola) have established state-of-the-art campus training centers.

Japan

➤ Training and development is planned and executed in disciplined manner at all levels of the organization.

➤ Training for white-collar and blue-collar workers is fairly similar.

➤ Skills in coordination and communication are considered as important as technical skills in training programs.

Korea

➤ Emphasis is on molding current and future managers and workers to fit the corporate culture.

➤ Loyalty, dedication, and team spirit are emphasized rather than job skills.

➤ The Asian crisis has forced companies to cut down on training costs.

➤ Governmental policies require companies with more than 150 employees to establish training centers.

Mexico

➤ Increased levels of training being driven by standards established by international investors and other trade agreements (North American Free Trade Agreement, MERCOSUR).

➤ Major emphasis on on-the-job training and skill-development of lower-level employees.

➤ Training is seen as becoming increasingly important because often business and cultural practices collide on a variety of manufacturing and other techniques (i.e., JIT).

➤ Training methods such as on-the-job training are used to familiarize workers with job requirements.

Taiwan

➤ Government has built a vast educational system and established 13 vocational-training schools.

➤ New curricula stressing creativity and free thought is replacing traditional educational approaches based on memorization and job-specific skills.

➤ Taiwanese companies are seeing the importance of training as the country shifts to more knowledge-intensive sectors.

➤ Among different training practices, job rotation is perceived as most effective followed by in-house training and outside training.

➤ Emphasis on managerial rather than technical training.

Source: Adapted from Drost, Ellen A., Colette A. Frayne, Kevin B. Lowe, and J. Michael Geringer. 2002. "Benchmarking trainingand development practices: A multicountry analysis." Human Resource Management, 41, 1: pp. 67–86.

EXHIBIT **12.11**   **Skills Taught by U.S. Organizations**

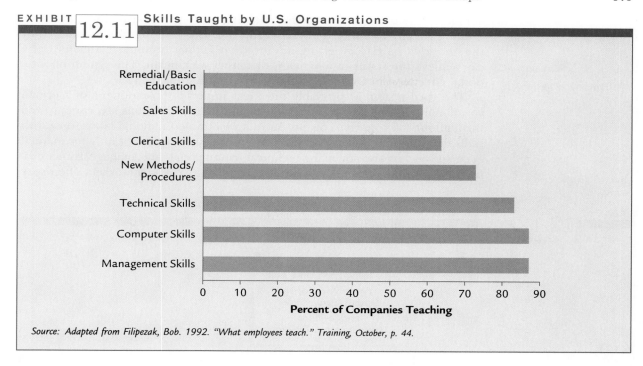

Source: Adapted from Filipezak, Bob. 1992. "What employees teach." Training, October, p. 44.

The shift in emphasis of the U.S. economy from manufacturing sectors to service areas is also predicted to be an important issue in the future. The service sector tends to be very capital and skill intensive and requires that employees have not only the appropriate technical skills but also critical thinking skills, team-building skills, and learning abilities on the job.[27] This suggests that there may be a widening gap between what companies emphasize in their training programs and the skills required for the future. A further issue compounding the problem is that recent pressures to cut costs have resulted in more U.S. companies outsourcing their training needs. Unfortunately, as more training is moving out of the organizations, their relevance and applicability to these companies' training needs is lessened.

Predictions of high needs for training have resulted in some calls from business and government for German-style apprentice programs. In such programs, the government requires industry to provide vocational training to workers in exchange for tax benefits. However, in the United States, training not specifically tailored for a company is often viewed as something that the employee may eventually take to a competitor. This makes some companies reluctant to invest in training without a more immediate and positive cost–benefit analysis regarding their own bottom line.[28]

Next we describe perhaps the most acclaimed model of vocational training.

Training and Vocational Education in Germany

German companies are renowned worldwide for their high-quality technical products. A sophisticated and standardized national system of vocational education and training provides a major human resource for German industry.

There are two major forms of vocational education in Germany. One form consists of general and specialized vocational schools and professional and technical colleges. The other form is called the **dual system.** The dual system

Dual system

Form of vocational education in Germany that combines in-house apprenticeship training with part-time vocational-school training and leads to a skilled-worker certificate.

combines in-house apprenticeship training with part-time vocational-school training leading to a skilled-worker certificate. This training can be followed by the *Fachschule,* a college giving advanced vocational training. Ultimately, one can achieve the status of a **Meister,** or master technician. The system of vocational education in Germany is summarized in Exhibit 12.12.

Meister
In Germany, a master technician.

The dual system is probably the most important component of German vocational training. The training and certificate qualifications are standardized throughout the country. This produces a well-trained national labor force with skills that are not company specific. Apprenticeships exist not only for manual occupations but also for many technical, commercial, and managerial occupations. Apprenticeships are not limited to the young. Older workers often seek

EXHIBIT 12.12   Skilled Worker Training in Germany

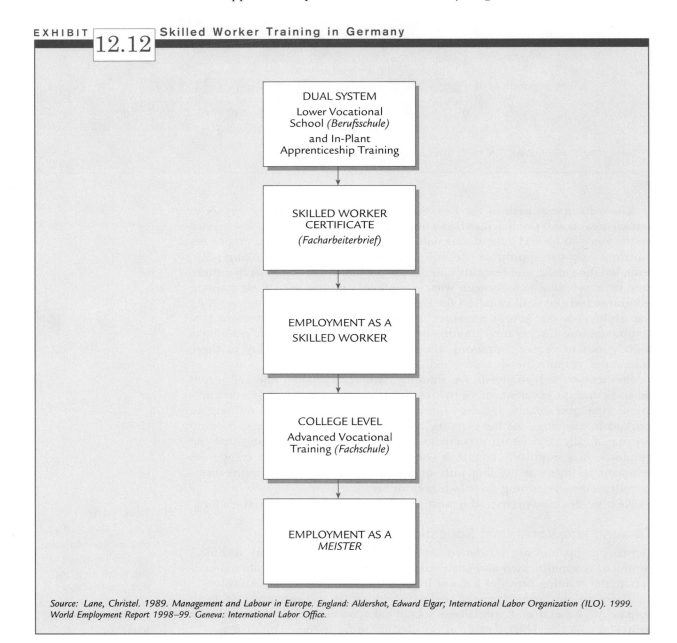

Source: Lane, Christel. 1989. *Management and Labour in Europe. England: Aldershot, Edward Elgar; International Labor Organization (ILO). 1999. World Employment Report 1998–99. Geneva: International Labor Office.*

apprenticeships and resulting certificates to enhance their development. There are nearly 400 nationally recognized vocational certificates.[29] Unions, organizations, and the government are now identifying new groups of certificates to represent qualifications for high-tech jobs in the new economy.

The dual system results from a collaboration of employers, unions, and the state. The costs are shared between companies and the state, with the companies paying approximately two-thirds of the costs. Employers have a legal obligation to release young people for vocational training. However, recently, cutbacks in German companies and high German unemployment have resulted in fewer apprenticeships being offered than there are workers applying. Many firms have cut the number of apprentices to cut costs or have called for more company-specific skills (see Exhibit 12.13). Emerging information-technology industries are also challenging the system as their job requirements are not served by the traditional German educational structure.[30]

Besides their national system of vocational education, German companies invest heavily in training, with four out of five workers receiving some in-house training. For example, at Mercedes Benz, the company's internal training center offers 180 vocational courses. Besides the 600 young people in vocational training and a modular management-development program, 4,000 employees per year take formal training at the company's training center.[31]

Training and development practices not only differ for entry-level workers, but the national context also affects the situation for managers. Next, we examine management development in the United States compared with that in Europe and Japan. Management development focuses on the programs that companies use to identify and groom managers for careers in an organization.

Management Development in the United States

Many U.S. companies have programs to identify and develop managerial talent. The objective is to develop quality managers who will spend their entire careers within the company. The prime steps include identifying managers with the talent for promotion and matching them with organizational needs for managerial talent.

Several techniques help identify and develop managerial talent.[32] Many U.S. companies charge senior-level managers with the responsibility of identifying

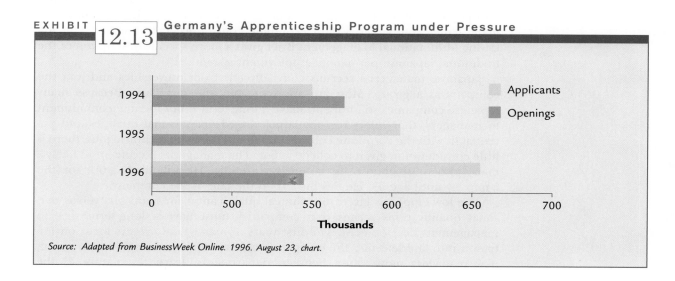

EXHIBIT 12.13   Germany's Apprenticeship Program under Pressure

Source: Adapted from BusinessWeek Online. 1996. August 23, chart.

managerial potential. Managerial performance appraisals often contain estimates of managerial readiness. Some companies use more direct approaches, such as assessment centers to identify managers. The assessment center is a testing procedure presenting individuals with a series of situations or problems. Observers judge how well potential managers respond to the situations or problems presented at each station in the assessment center. Managers may be promoted or identified as having high potential based on their performances in the assessment center. Mentoring occurs when a senior-level executive becomes the coach, guide, and advisor for a junior manager. This may be either a formal or an informal relationship. Some U.S. companies develop "fast-track" careers for junior managers destined for higher-level management. Usually, a company assigns fast-track managers to a variety of challenging positions early in their careers, and such managers, if successful, receive rapid promotions.

However, in an individualistic culture such as the United States, career management remains the responsibility of the individual. These individual goals may not correspond to filling the current organizational assignment or to participation in management development. Therefore, U.S. companies cannot assume the long-term loyalty of their better managers. Retrenchments, limited company growth, short career ladders, and even the relatively young age of superiors may prevent career advancement. Individual career opportunities may simply be better somewhere else, and good managers may resign.

Next, we examine management-development approaches used by the Japanese.

Management Development in Japan

An understanding of management development in Japan must be set in the context of a system undergoing increasing pressure to change, strong cultural traditions relating to age seniority, and the philosophy of **permanent employment**. The association of age with wisdom is a Confucian value that leads Japanese companies to believe that managers cannot be fully capable until they have reached a certain age. The philosophy of a permanent-employment system also arises from Confucian values of familial duties. The company, serving in the parent role, must protect and take care of the worker, and the worker in turn owes loyalty to the paternalistic company. The permanent-employment system also has institutional roots in law. Article 27 of the Japanese Constitution states, "All people shall have the right and obligation to work."[33] This is a point that many larger companies, within economic constraints, take literally. The following Multinational Management Brief gives a more specific description of the traditional Japanese permanent-employment system.

Japanese managerial recruits come directly from universities and join the company as a group. Most are approximately the same age. Because many Japanese companies still hope to make a long-term if not lifetime commitment to managers, they select recruits largely based on personal qualities and potential fit with the corporate culture. For all but the most technical jobs, there is little consideration given to college major. The managerial recruit (most likely a man) also must choose his company carefully. He will likely work for the company until age 55. He ties his fate to the fate of the company.

The low emphasis given to technical qualification for managers versus personal qualifications means that companies must have a long-term view to management development. The first years of managerial careers focus on initiation into and learning the company's culture. After an initial basic training, new managers move often between departments, learn the nature of the

Permanent employment

In Japan, continuous employment, often to the age of 55.

Multinational Management **Brief**

Permanent Employment in Japan: A System under Fire

Lifetime or permanent employment often received credit for producing the loyal and motivated workforce that supported the dramatic growth in the Japanese economy. It was touted as something to be imitated by companies from other nations. However, more recently, it has been criticized because Japanese organizations bloated with too many middle managers. Japanese companies are modifying the system but still feel committed to senior workers who came on board in a time of greater Japanese prosperity.

Basic characteristics of lifetime employment and current modifications include the following:

➤ Lifetime employment remains an ideal goal tempered by economic reality. Some estimate that only 15 to 18 percent of the workforce actually has lifetime security.

➤ It is mostly for men. Few Japanese women get the opportunity to enter career-track occupations.

➤ Lifetime employment is mostly a characteristic of large companies and, currently, only some of those large companies can afford it.

➤ Managers, more than workers, receive the protection of lifetime employment.

➤ The "lifetime" only lasts to approximately age 55 while most companies have a legal mandatory minimum retirement age of 60. Companies offer incentives for older employees (especially managers) to become part time or to take jobs with satellite companies.

Source: Based on Economist. 2006. "Greying Japan the downturn." January 9; Mroczkowski, Tomasz, and Masao Hanaoka. 1989. "Continuity and change in Japanese management." California Management Review, Winter, pp. 39–52; Takahashi, Shunsuke. 1993. "New trends on human resources management in Japan." In The Human Resource Yearbook 1993/1994 Ed., edited by Mary F. Cook, pp. 1.37–1.38. Englewood Cliffs, NJ: Prentice Hall; Thornton, Emily. 1999. "Corporate Japan: No room at the top." BusinessWeek Online, August 9; Yoshio, Higuchi. 2002. "The death of lifetime employment." Look Japan 48, 557: pp. 13–15.

company's business, and develop job skills. Managers may have more than ten different jobs before they have any real responsibility.[34] Learning the company's culture is also enhanced by extensive after-hours socializing and drinking with other managers. The typical Japanese manager may arrive at the office at 9 AM, leave work around 7 PM, and join his colleagues for drinks until 10 or 11 PM.

Traditionally, there has been little public or formal emphasis in Japanese companies on identifying high-potential managers early in their careers. For the most part, during the first 8 to 10 years, managers following a traditional Japanese system are promoted and paid the same as others in their age cohort. Most positions have a minimum age, and no one will be promoted before this age. However, some Japanese companies have kept secret files on their most promising juniors. They believe that identifying publicly a high-potential junior would be too disruptive to the social harmony of the group.

Although Japanese culture sanctions standing out from the group, economic reality is changing many organizations. Many companies are abandoning seniority and using merit as the basis for training and promotion purposes.[35] Consider that Asahi Breweries now ties evaluations to promotions for all managerial levels—a change accepted by younger managers but criticized by older managers—while Honda ties the bonus system to profitability and is gradually phasing out seniority as the criterion for pay and promotions. Similarly, Carlson

Goshn, CEO of Nissan, has implemented a performance-based incentive system at Nissan where highest achievers, rather than the most senior managers, get the highest rewards.[36]

Most management training and development focus on company-related skills. Unlike in the individualistic United States, the development of human resources is not considered an individual's personal investment; managers do not view their training and development as an accumulation of skills and competencies that can be marketed to other companies. With the mutual commitment of permanent employment, both the organization and employees accept that investment in management development is an investment for the well-being of the company.

In addition to technical issues such as marketing skills, Japanese managerial training contains what the anthropologist Thomas Rohlen calls a "spiritual" education.[37] Spiritual education emphasizes character development, such as the ability to persevere in difficult times, the acceptance of social responsibility, and the habit of cooperation. Toward this end, some Japanese companies have recently popularized military-style boot-camp training centers where managers undergo rigorous physical and psychological stress. As with military basic training, spiritual training sometimes includes hazing and self-deprecation, which are used to build stronger characters.

Having seen examples of training and development in different national contexts, we can now consider how these differences affect the multinational companies operating in different countries.

Implications for the Multinational: Training and Development

Before setting up operations in a host foreign country, multinational managers must consider the quality of the workers and sometimes the managers available in the host country. They must also examine the feasibility of exporting their company's training techniques to the host country. For example, a transnational company might need workers with basic skills in math and science to staff plants of the future. Rather than invest in basic education to train a low-cost workforce, the company can locate in countries with the best educational systems. Thus, for example, a multinational company with a requirement for technical workers might examine which educational systems produce the best students in mathematics and science.

No matter what the basic talent of host-country workers, training is an important component of the HR strategy. The following Case in Point describes efforts by multinational companies to increase diversity training among their employees.

Adaptation of management-development practices to different national contexts depends significantly on the intended use of host-country managers. If host-country nationals are limited to lower management levels, then multinational companies may follow local management-development practices. This would be a likely approach for a multilocal company with a polycentric IHRM orientation. Such companies develop local managerial talent for careers in one country. Host-country managers often never expect to work at the multinational organization's headquarters or in another country location.

In situations where multinational companies allow and expect host-country nationals to rise to higher levels of management, however, the parent

CASE IN POINT

Diversity Training

Most multinational companies are now finding that diversity training is essential if they want to compete globally. Consider the Chinese computing giant Lenovo's attempt to implement diversity training programs to unify its culturally and geographically diverse workforce. The company sees potential for competitive advantage in its diverse global workforce and is working hard to find ways to take advantage of such diversity. Lenovo employees go through intensive programs focused on training employees from different nationalities and backgrounds to work effectively together. Such training is also being positioned as crucial to long-term success rather than the usual approach that it is the right thing to do.

Many other companies are also implementing diversity training and see such training as crucial

not only to workforce integration but also to ensure fairness to all races, genders, and sexual orientations of employees around the world. For instance, IBM believes that the way to deliver superior products to the workplace is to have an environment where diverse employees can contribute without having to fear harassment or discrimination. As such, some of these companies are going as far as hiring diversity officers who report directly to the CEO. These companies are also taking deliberate steps to measure the effectiveness of such training and often are linking compensation to diversity goals.

Source: Based on Egodigwe, Laura. 2005. "Workplace-diversity training gets a new mandate; Touchy-feely approach gives way to fomenting cross-cultural strategies." Asian Wall Street Journal, November 14, p. 38; Childs, J.T. (Ted) Jr. 2005. "Managing workforce diversity at IBM: A global HR topic that has arrived." Human Resources Management 44, 1: pp. 73–77.

company's corporate culture dominates management-development policies, and such multinational companies expect managers of all nationalities to be, for example, Motorola or Ford managers—not British or Mexican or Malaysian.

Next, the chapter considers differences between performance appraisal in the United States and performance appraisal in collectivist cultures.

Performance Appraisal

Regardless of the national setting, all companies at some point must deal with the human resource problems of identifying people to reward, promote, demote, develop and improve, retain, or terminate. Not everyone can move up the ladder of the organizational pyramid. Not everyone can be a leader. Not everyone will perform at acceptable levels. Even in countries like Japan, with its high value for lifetime employment, the survival of the company now often requires layoffs.

The fundamental assumption in the West, and in particular, in the more individualistic cultures, is that performance-appraisal systems provide rational and fair solutions to these human resource problems. That is, ideally, appraisal systems provide management with objective, honest, and fair data on employee performance. Consequently, human resource decisions, such as pay or promotion, can be based on these performance-appraisal data. Although issues regarding seniority, experience, and security are not ignored, the cultural ideal is a meritocracy, where good performers get more rewards.

Performance Appraisal in the United States

The U.S. performance-appraisal system represents cultural values that espouse links among individual rights, duties, and rewards, as well as a legal system that promotes equal opportunity. Thus, the ideal U.S. performance-appraisal system is highly rational, logical, and legal.

The textbook view of the U.S. performance-appraisal system contains four elements: performance standards, performance measures, performance feedback, and human resource decisions related to remuneration, promotion, or termination.[38]

Performance standards reflect management's goals regarding acceptable quality and quantity of work output. These standards include work-related knowledge, quality, volume, and initiative. For example, a secretary may be expected to type a certain number of words per minute. Performance measures are techniques intended for objective and often comparative assessment of employees on the performance standards. The most popular measures use some form of rating scale.[39] The employee is rated on a variety of traits (e.g., work quality), usually by managers but occasionally by peers or subordinates. Teacher evaluations by class members and peer evaluations of contributions to a student-group project are examples of performance ratings.

Performance feedback usually occurs in a formal interview between superior and subordinate. Three methods are common in the United States.[40] First, in the tell-and-sell method, the supervisor gives feedback and explains the evaluation. Second, in the tell-and-listen method, the supervisor gives feedback and listens to the subordinate's reactions. Third, in the problem-solving method, the supervisor and subordinate work to identify problems and propose solutions for improvement.

What are the typical human resource consequences of the U.S. performance-appraisal system? Most U.S. organizations use performance appraisals for compensation decisions. Other major but less common uses include performance improvement, feedback, documentation, and promotion.[41]

Because of the concern in the United States that human resource decisions be fair and equitable to all individuals, performance-appraisal systems have institutionalized legal pressures to follow similar procedures. The following Multinational Management Brief summarizes the **U.S. legal requirements for appraisals.**

The U.S. performance-appraisal system is rooted in an individualistic culture and an institutional system that aspires to protect equal rights and equal opportunities. Cultural stories such as "the American dream of rags to riches" support the idea that all can achieve wealth and success through their own efforts. Next, we will see how the institutional systems and cultural values of other nations result in quite different aspects of work performance being valued and evaluated.

U.S. legal requirements for appraisals
Regulating performance-evaluation practices to ensure their fairness.

Performance Appraisals around the World

Although performance-appraisal practices vary widely among countries, they are undertaken with the common purpose of devising ways to control employees so that they give maximum performance.[42] However, while appraisals are based on similar notions in many countries, there are wide variations in terms of what they are used for. In that context, the Best International Human Resource Management Practices Project[43] provides extensive evidence on cross-national differences in performance-appraisal purposes in Australia, Canada, Indonesia, Japan, South Korea, Latin America, Mexico, China, Taiwan, and the United States.

Exhibit 12.14 shows the top five countries for each performance-appraisal purpose.

The project asked respondents to rate the importance of 12 purposes of performance appraisals. Results of the study revealed significant differences among countries in terms of these purposes. However, the most striking finding

Multinational Management **Brief**

The U.S. Legal Requirements for Performance Appraisals

Employee legal challenges to the fairness of HRM decisions resulting from perform-ance appraisals have resulted in a body of U.S. law that guides performance apprais-als. Here is a summary of the major factors:

➤ *Performance evaluations must relate clearly to the job and performance:* Evalua-tion systems must evaluate only performances on tasks or outcomes that the job is designed to achieve.

➤ *Performance standards must be provided in writing:* Access to specific written standards must be available to all concerned while working and before any appraisal.

➤ *Supervisors must be able to measure the behaviors they rate:* Systems that rate or evaluate a worker must be valid. This means that the company must be able to demonstrate that an evaluation system does measure what it is supposed to measure.

➤ *Supervisors must be trained to use evaluation measures:* Companies must be able to demonstrate that supervisors have the necessary skills and training to use evaluation tools such as interviews or observations.

➤ *Supervisors and subordinates must discuss appraisals openly:* Unlike in some Japanese firms, appraisals cannot be secret. There must be procedures in place to discuss appraisals.

➤ *Appeals procedures must be in place:* The employee must have some formal access to higher management or other appeal mechanism to challenge his or her superior's evaluation.

Source: Based on Bohlander, George W., Scott Snell, and Arthur W. Sherman, Jr. 2001. Managing Human Resources. South-Western;Cincinnati: Lindo, David K. 2003. "Can you answer their questions?" SuperVision 64, 1: pp. 20–22.

is that Australia, Canada and the United States are among the top five countries for all performance-appraisal purposes. These results are not surprising because these countries are very high on individualism where there is heavy emphasis on the individual development of the employee. As such, performance appraisals are seen as the most effective method to gauge how well an employee is doing and how that person's performance can be improved. However, it is also in-teresting to see countries and regions such as Taiwan and Latin America figure prominently on the list. This suggests possible explanations through the effects of social institutions such as the government and the trade agreements. As these countries are emulating Western-based systems through a desire to satisfy trade agreements and other competitiveness requirements, they are perhaps seeing performance-appraisal systems as critical.

It also is interesting to note that the more collectivist societies surveyed (e.g., China, Japan, Korea, Indonesia) were very unlikely to be among the top five countries for each performance-appraisal purpose. This suggests that perfor-mance appraisals may not be seen as important in such societies. In collectivist cultures, age and in-group memberships (usually family or social status) provide a large component of the psychological contract with the organization; that is, the employer and employee accept as correct and fair that human resource decisions should take into account personal background characteristics more

EXHIBIT **12.14**

Cross-National Differences in Purposes of Performance Appraisals: Top 5 Countries and Regions for Each Category

Performance Appraisal Purpose	Countries				
Determine pay	Taiwan	Canada	USA	China	Japan
Document performance	Australia	USA	Taiwan	Latin America	Canada
Plan development activities	Australia	Latin America	Canada	Taiwan	Mexico
Salary administration	Latin America	Taiwan	USA	Canada	Indonesia
Recognize subordinate	Australia	Taiwan	USA	Canada	China
Discuss improvement	Australia	Latin America	Canada	USA	Taiwan
Discuss subordinate views	Australia	Canada	Taiwan	USA	Mexico
Evaluate goal achievement	Australia	Latin America	Taiwan	Canada	Japan
Identify strengths and weaknesses	Latin America	Australia	USA	Canada	Taiwan
Let subordinate express feelings	Australia	Taiwan	Canada	China	USA
Determine promotion potential	Korea	Latin America	Taiwan	Australia	Japan

Source: Adapted from Geringer, J. Michael, Colette A. Frayne, and John F. Milliman. 2002. "In search of 'best practices' in international human resource management: Research design and methodology." Human Resource Management, 41, 1: pp. 5–30.

than achievement. Since who you are and how old you are may count more than how you perform, the usefulness of a Western-style performance-appraisal system is less clear. For example, if only family members are eligible for promotion, it makes little sense to evaluate all employees for management potential.

None of this implies, however, that information regarding performance is not communicated to people in collectivist cultures. Members of work groups often know the best and the worst performers. Because it is important to work for the benefit of the group, members may subtly praise or punish other workers based on work performance. Managers also may work indirectly to sanction poor performance. Behaviors such as withdrawing normal favors or working through intermediaries (who are often relatives) are common. For the Japanese, the supervisor can communicate negative feedback for poor work performance simply by ignoring his subordinate. Thus, even without formal appraisal systems, feedback occurs indirectly.

According to Hofstede,[44] managers in collectivist societies often avoid direct performance-appraisal feedback. An open discussion of performance may clash with the society's norm of harmony, which takes precedence over other values. For example, during the first 8 to 10 years of their careers, Japanese managers may never encounter the appraisal system. Even if one exists, it is often secret and lacks direct feedback to the employee. Instead, all beginning managers get the same salary and promotions, based on age and seniority. Reducing competition among managers and maintaining harmony among the group are higher-priority values than identifying or developing high-performers.

Steers, Shin, and Ungson[45] point out that the preference for seniority-based promotions, rather than appraisal-based promotions, is even greater among Koreans. They note that while job performance is important and most companies do have appraisal systems, seniority is most important for advancement. This follows "from the Confucian tradition that strives to preserve harmony (since it is unseemly for younger employees to supervise older ones). It is also easier to use seniority to make promotion decisions than to rely on imprecise personnel evaluation methods to discriminate between a group of high achievers."[46]

C A S E   I N   P O I N T

Performance Appraisals in Thailand

As more multinational companies enter Thailand, Thai workers are experiencing changes that reflect Western values. Thai workers no longer expect that managers possess all the power to run their companies. In fact, Thai workers expect to see more decentralization and a bigger role in decision-making. Consequently, experts advise that expatriates use the following basic tips when conducting performance appraisals for Thais:

➤ *Get to know your employee:* Experts suggest that the evaluator takes some time to get to know the employee. Specifically, given the nature of Thais, it may be worthwhile to ask about the family or hobbies or even sports.

➤ *Discuss the objectives of the performance appraisal:* Similar to Western performance appraisals, the evaluator should start with an overview of what the talk will be about. It is also advisable to

have an open meeting where subordinates can also share their views. Thais need to know that they can provide their view on contentious issues.

➤ *Balance strengths and weaknesses:* Managers should ensure that a balanced view of strengths and weaknesses are offered. Often, managers tend to spend too much time on weaknesses suggesting perhaps that appropriate feedback was not provided during the year.

➤ *Be patient and pay attention to facial and other cues:* Experts advise that managers be patient when conducting the performance appraisal. Special attention needs to be paid to facial cues, and evaluators need to make sure that they are properly understood, especially since Thai workers are likely to say "yes" and smile.

Source: Based on Financial Times. 2006. "Thailand expert discusses performance appraisal in cross cultural context." January 10, p. 213.

Perhaps because of the long-term orientation of Korean culture, Korean performance-appraisal systems focus on evaluating and developing the "whole man" for the long-term benefit of the company. They evaluate sincerity, loyalty, and attitude on an equal footing with job performance. Only for senior management, where the logic of an organizational pyramid dictates a smaller number of top positions, does the performance evaluation focus on actual performance and contribution to the company.[47]

However, there seems to be some evidence that more collectivistic societies may be using performance appraisals similar to the Western approaches. Consider the Case in Point discussing performance appraisals in Thailand.

At least from the more individualistic societies' perspective, performance appraisals provide the information necessary for promotion and compensation decisions. Next, we will see how compensation practices in other national contexts differ from the U.S. model.

Compensation

Compensation includes wages and salaries, incentives such as bonuses, and benefits such as retirement contributions. There are wide variations both among countries and among organizations within countries concerning how to compensate workers. A country's economic development, cultural traditions, legal institutions, and the role of labor unions all affect compensation. Consider these examples:

- Japanese workers earn more than three times the wages of workers in other East Asian countries such as Taiwan, Singapore, and Korea.[48]
- Although not required by law, South Korean and Japanese workers expect bonuses at least twice a year.

- In Denmark, more than 80 percent of employees belong to unions, and agreements between unions and employers' associations determine minimal and normal pay.[49]
- In the EU, there is a statutory minimum of four weeks of vacation. As an example, France has a law that guarantees workers five weeks of paid vacation on an annual basis.[50]

Compensation Practices in the United States

Conditions external and internal to the company affect the wages and salaries of workers and managers.[51] External factors include local and national wage rates, government legislation, and collective bargaining. Internal factors include the importance of the job to the organization, the affluence of the organization or its ability to pay, and the employee's relative worth to the business (merit).

Taking into account these external and internal factors, most U.S. companies develop formal and systematic policies to determine wages and salaries. The Personnel Policies Forum, a group of personnel managers representing companies of all sizes and from all industries, found that 75 percent of their member companies had formal written policies for wage and salary administration.[52] What are these policies? Consider the following additional results from the Personnel Policies Forum study.

To establish that their companies' wages and salaries are competitive in the labor market, the Personnel Policies Forum study showed that 94 percent of U.S. companies used data from comparative wage and salary surveys to determine compensation. Comparative wage and salary surveys tell companies how their compensation packages match up with those of competitors. Two-thirds of the companies check on comparative wage and salary data at least once a year. Nearly 40 percent assess their competitive wage and salary position more than seven times a year.

Perhaps more than any other society, the highly mobile U.S. labor market requires this hefty concern with external equity (i.e., Do we pay at or above market level?). The individualistic U.S. culture views careers as private and personal, and mobility, advancement, and higher wages often require leaving a company. Thus, unlike in countries such as Japan and Korea, where company loyalty often prevails over opportunities for higher remuneration, U.S. companies must rely on competitive wages to maintain a quality workforce.

Most U.S. companies also develop procedures to establish that people receive equitable pay for the types of jobs they perform. Seventy-five percent of the companies surveyed by the Personnel Policies Forum[53] have formal systems to evaluate how much particular jobs (independent of the people doing them) contribute to the company. A variety of methods helps establish a hierarchy of jobs based on their worth to the company. Issues such as responsibility, skill requirements, and the importance of the job's tasks to the organization contribute to the worth of a particular job. Those who occupy the higher-ranked jobs are paid higher.

Although the worth of a job to the company largely determines the base pay assigned to a certain position, raises in pay are determined mostly by merit.[54] As previously noted and discussed in more detail in the following section, this is particularly unlike the seniority-based systems of Korea and Japan.

As part of the total compensation package, benefits have grown substantially in the United States during the last few decades. Major employee benefits in the United States include pension plans, health-care benefits, insurance coverage, vacation pay, sick leave, and paid holidays. Social Security insurance, unemployment insurance, family leave, and workers' compensation insurance for work-related accidents are required by law. However, as the following Multinational Management Brief shows, U.S. benefits still lag behind those that a multinational company should expect to pay in Europe.

Next we will look at one of the most comprehensive studies on compensation practices and the perceived trend toward convergence.

Compensation around the world

Compensation packages vary widely among countries. The Best International Human Resource Management Practices Project[55] represents one of the most extensive cross-national studies of compensation practices to date. The researchers investigated cross-national variations in nine compensation practices in 10 countries (Australia, Canada, China, Indonesia, Japan, Korea, Latin America, Mexico, Taiwan, and the United States). Respondents were asked a number of questions pertaining to these compensation practices, both in terms of their assessment of the current state of practice and also the extent to which they felt that these practices should be used in the future.

Results of the study revealed some convergence in terms of compensation practices in these countries. For instance, managers of all countries and regions

Multinational Management **Brief**

A Comparison of Some Benefits in the United States and the European Community

➤ In the United States, paid holidays average around ten days a year. Most companies give a two-week vacation after one year of employment.

➤ The United States was one of the last developed countries to provide legal protection for maternity. The Family Leave Bill, passed in 1993, requires employers of more than 50 people to provide up to 12 weeks of unpaid leave for the care of newborns. However, in contrast to Europe, no paternity leave or subsidized child-care is provided.

➤ In Denmark, paid holidays accrue at 2.5 days a month. Maternity leave is four weeks before the birth and 24 weeks after the birth, with either parent taking the last 10 weeks.

➤ In Italy, there are 10 national public holidays a year along with paid vacations. Women are entitled to maternity leave of two months before and three months after the birth of a child.

➤ In the EU, law requires a minimum of 20 paid holidays, but most German workers have many more, averaging around 30. In the state of Bavaria, for example, German workers get the national average of six weeks' vacation along with Bavaria's 14 state holidays. Maternity leave is 14 weeks at normal salary.

Source: Based on Arkin, Anat. 1992. Personnel management in Germany: At work in the powerhouse of Europe." Personnel Management, February, pp. 32–35; Arkin, Anat. 1992. "Personnel management in Denmark: The land of social welfare." Personnel Management, March, pp. 32–35; Caplan, Janice. 1992. "Personnel management in Italy: It's the climate that counts." Personnel Management, April, pp. 32–35; Benjamin, Daniel. 1993. "Losing its edge: Germany is troubled by how little work its workers are doing." Wall Street Journal, May 6, pp. A1, A4; Foroohar, Rana. 2006. "Myth & reality." Newsweek International, February 27; Langer, Steven. 1993. "The Abbott, Langer & Associates compensation & benefits reports." In The Human Resource Yearbook 1993/1994 Ed., edited by Mary F. Cook, pp. 5.12–5.38. Englewood Cliffs, NJ: Prentice Hall; Poe, Andrea C. 1999. "When in Rome . . . European law and tradition back generous vacation policies." HR Magazine, 44, HR Magazine Online Archive, http://www.my.SHRM.org

felt that it was necessary that all but one of the nine compensation practices (pay incentives should be important, pay should be contingent on group/ organizational performance, incentives should be a significant amount of pay, job performances should be the basis of pay raises, benefits should be important, benefits should be more generous, pay should be based on long-term results) be used more in the future.[56] These managers also felt that less emphasis should be placed on using seniority as a determinant of pay decisions. Additionally, all managers felt that a properly designed compensation plan is key to harnessing employee performance conducive to organizational effectiveness.

These results are particularly striking given that the countries studied have wide variations in terms of both the national culture context and social institutions. However, they provide some practical guidelines for practicing managers. In general, it is suggested that managers make more effective use of the nine compensation practices listed above. For instance, given that the respondents felt that job performances should become more prevalent as the basis for pay raises, it is essential for HRM managers to implement systems that provide a stronger link between job performances and pay raises.

Despite the evidence of convergence in many areas, the study also revealed surprising results. For instance, the researchers expected that the more collectivist countries would have higher ratings for the compensation practice "pay is contingent on group or organizational performance." However, findings show that there were no major differences among collectivistic and individualistic countries in the study. Yet another perplexing result is that there were no significant variations among countries in terms of the compensation practice of using seniority as the basis for pay decisions.

This study suggests that there may be some convergence pressures regarding compensation practices. As further evidence of convergence, we will next see an example of the changing compensation system in Japan. In response to competitive pressures, 10 years of recession, and globalization of Japanese organizations, Japanese firms are moving toward a Western style of compensation management. However, it still differs from the U.S. approach in its emphasis on age and group harmony as factors to consider in pay packages.

Compensation in Japan

As with U.S. firms, Japanese companies determine base salaries to a large degree by the classification of positions. Positions have skill and educational requirements. Those who occupy the more demanding positions receive higher wages and bonuses depending on their classification.

There are two effects of seniority on the Japanese compensation system. First, besides educational qualifications, each position has minimum age requirements. As the Japanese worker gains in seniority he, and less often she, becomes eligible to move up to more valued and more highly paid positions. Second, seniority factors into pay decisions, but at a declining rate. That is, seniority counts more for pay raises earlier in one's career and diminishes after age 45. The logic of this system is that more money is required early, when family responsibilities such as buying a home or paying for children's education are highest. These responsibilities decrease after middle age. In fact, early in a career it is not uncommon for marital status and family size to affect wages or salary.

In more recent times, merit (as the Japanese interpret it) affects pay raises to a greater degree than under the traditional position/seniority system. As has been noted, the Japanese view of merit does not match exactly the Western view, stressing attitudes as much as job performance. However, experts on Japanese personnel policies predict that merit and achievement—at least Japanese style—will continue to have a greater impact on Japanese compensation and promotions.[57] Exhibit 12.15 shows the traditional compensation formula as it is being modified for pay raises in use in many Japanese companies today. The major shift that is occurring is the weight given to merit over seniority.

Economic pressures on the Japanese compensation system are growing.[58] This is partly due to the increasing costs of compensating a large management staff recruited from the baby-boom generation. As a result, some Japanese companies are taking the "radical" approach of basing management compensation only on merit. Honda was among the first to introduce this type of system, called the **nenpo system,** in 1992. At Honda, there are no cost-of-living raises, housing allowances, family allowances, or automatic pay raises. Instead, superiors determine a manager's pay by yearly performance evaluations that emphasize goals.[59] Although seniority remains important for holding certain positions, trends in Japanese human resource practices show a convergence with practices used in the United States and other Western nations. A recent survey shows that 90 percent of Japanese companies have or plan to introduce performance into their pay and promotion systems.[60]

Along with raises based on age, promotions, and merit, a significant component of Japanese compensation is the **bonus system.** Many Korean companies use similar systems. Bonuses come twice a year, usually during traditional gift-giving seasons. During the high of the Japanese boom economy, employees often received up to 30 percent of their base salary in the form of bonuses. Successful large companies paid up to 100 percent of base salaries in bonuses in particularly good years. However, with the current economic situation in Japan, such levels are now infrequent.

Nenpo system

New Japanese compensation system based on yearly performance evaluations that emphasize goals—although goals are not always the same as in Western companies.

Bonus system

In Japan, employees often receive as much as 30 percent of their base salary, usually given twice a year during traditional gift-giving seasons.

Implications for the Multinational: Performance Evaluation and Compensation

As with recruitment and selection, multinational companies must match their performance-evaluation system to their multinational strategies. For example, top managers for Japanese companies in the United States often report that they must adjust to the HRM practices of their Japanese parents. The U.S. managers are uncomfortable with ill-identified career paths and the lack of specialization. Moreover, many U.S. managers working for Japanese companies

---

EXHIBIT 12.15   **The Japanese Pay Raise Formula: Changing the Balance**

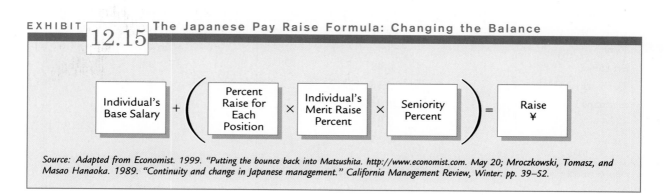

Source: Adapted from Economist. 1999. "Putting the bounce back into Matsushita. http://www.economist.com. May 20; Mroczkowski, Tomasz, and Masao Hanaoka. 1989. "Continuity and change in Japanese management." California Management Review, Winter: pp. 39–52.

believe that headquarters management posts are blocked by the glass ceiling. As Bill Bsand, executive vice president for Hitachi America, notes: "There are very few Americans who work for Hitachi in Japan and usually at a very low level."[61]

A multinational company with locations in several nations may need several different compensation systems, especially for host-country nationals. For each host country, worker compensation levels must match wage levels in the local labor market. Compensation also must meet local minimum-wage rates. Examining information, such as that reported in Exhibit 12.16 on pay rates for labor, can give multinational managers the general data necessary to estimate the costs of host-country workers and competitive wage and salary levels. Country-level comparative compensation data are available from many government, private, and international sources. Information on compensation laws is usually available from host-country governments. However, multinational managers must also consider regional differences within countries. Both labor costs and regional government laws may be different.

The relatively low cost of labor, managers, and engineers in Eastern European countries and India shows why many multinational companies seek location advantages in these countries. Children from these countries also score well in cross-national comparisons of math and science ability. This suggests that these locations will provide excellent future workers in technical occupations. However, multinational companies are also finding that it is harder to retain talented workers in India. Consider the following Focus on Emerging Markets.

However, some experts argue that competitive advantages based on wage rates are only short term. They look at the situation for many Japanese, South Korean, and Taiwanese companies that based their early competitive advantages on quality, low-cost labor. Most manufacturing companies in these countries have moved plants to cheaper locations in China or Southeast Asia. The implication for multinational companies is that, when local wage rates rise, the company will be forced either to keep pace or to seek another low-cost location.

Failure to meet local wage standards can result in poor workers and bad relationships with host governments. In addition, inadequate pay in other countries might bring negative reactions at home. For example, the Indonesian

EXHIBIT 12.16   Labor Costs and Hours Worked per Week in Selected Countries

Country	Average Cost of Labor per Hour in U.S. $	Average Hours Worked per Week
United States	20.32	38
Korea	8.09	47
Sri Lanka	0.48	43
Denmark	21.98	32
Germany	26.18	33
Greece	8.91	36
Japan	20.89	36

Source: Adapted from International Labor Organization (ILO). 2000. World Employment Report 1998–99. Geneva: International Labor Office; U.S. Department of Labor. 2003. Employment and Earnings, January 2001. Washington, D.C.: U.S. Government Printing Office.

Focus on Emerging Markets

Compensation Plans in Indian Multinational Companies

Although India boasts a plentiful supply of skilled labor, cultivating loyalty to retain such valuable workers has proved to be a difficult challenge. As local and multinational companies expand their presence in India, demand for talented employees is becoming fierce. As such, employees are becoming more readily willing to leave their companies to start new positions. As it is predicted that many sectors will face shortages in the future, many companies are starting to work harder to design compensation plans to retain their workers.

A survey by the Grow Talent Company shows that those companies that are successful at retaining their employees show respect for their employees through compensation and benefits. For instance, these companies use HR strategies such as "bring your spouse to the office" days or have big budgets to celebrate birthdays or weddings. Other companies are finding that engaging their workers' families also strikes a good work–family balance. Yet other multinational companies are finding that offering the possibility of attaining a Masters in Business Administration or some form of global experience cultivates loyalty.

Infosys, India's famous technology services firm, has also been able to retain employees through the Employee Relations Program. This program shows Infosys' commitment to work/life balance. The program includes counseling services, athletic competitive events, celebration of important cultural events, and even health fairs open to the employees' families. The company also celebrates the strong family ties inherent in Indian culture by inviting family members to visit its campus. This program has allowed Infosys not only to enjoy a very low attrition rate of 10 percent but also to prevent competitors such as IBM and Oracle from taking its trained employees.

Both domestic and multinational organizations are finding that good HR practices have important benefits. Often, the buzz about employers with good HR practices spreads rapidly through the labor-market grapevine. As such, these companies not only are able to better retain their workforce but also able to attract more applications for future positions.

Source: Based on Merchant, Khozem. 2006. "Companies in India offer a taste of the sweet life: Keeping skilled workers in a challenge in the buoyant Indian jobs market and businesses are offering an ever-growing range of perks to keep them happy." Financial Times, February 2; Workforce Management. 2006. "The 10 most forward-thinking leaders in workforce management." March 13.

suppliers of Nike manage to pay workers only $2.23 per day, less than the Indonesian minimum wage of $2.59 per day.[62] This and other potentially abusive labor practices have caused Nike and other U.S. offshore manufacturers to face criticism at home over labor abuses in low-wage countries.

In the next section, the chapter looks at labor relationships from a comparative perspective.

A Comparative View of Labor Relations

The patterns of labor relations in different nations arise not only from cultural differences but also from the unique histories of unionization in each country.[63] Historical factors, such as the state of technological development during early unionization and the time when governments recognized the legality of unions, influence current union structure and activities. Some unions were developed for ideological reasons such as overthrowing the capitalist system or representing religious values. Others developed simply to improve wages and working conditions. Management views of unions also differ from country to country. The astute multinational manager will be well versed in the history, structure, and ideology of unions in the countries in which her or his company operates. Consider some of the difficulties of labor relations in India as shown in the following Case in Point.

Before entering a country, one major HRM issue to consider is the popularity of unions. An indicator of union popularity is called union-membership density.

Union-Membership Density

Union-membership density

Proportion of workers in a country who belong to unions.

A strong indicator that multinational managers can use to tell how much unions influence companies in any country is the **union-membership density**. Union-membership density refers to the proportion of workers who belong to unions in a country. Estimates of union-membership density are always approximate because some reports do not consider white-collar workers or professional unions.

C A S E   I N   P O I N T

Dealing with Unions in India

India's free-market reforms have attracted multinational firms General Electric, Otis Elevator Co., and Unilever, to name only a few. However, these firms face a national context in which strong institutional pressures give power to unions and encourage union militancy.

India has more than 45 overlapping, sometimes conflicting, and most often confusing major labor laws. These laws allow unions to be formed by as few as seven people. Some companies must deal with as many as 50 different labor groups. The laws also make it difficult to fire employees or close money-losing operations. A company with more than 10 workers needs government permission to fire employees—something almost never given. In fact, Indian labor laws tend to be very highly protective of labor and have encouraged a very inflexible labor market.

How are multinational companies adapting? Siemens AG, Whirlpool Corp., and Philips Electronics NV are using golden handshakes to buy out workers. Rather than confronting unions directly, these companies offer workers voluntary retirement and payoffs. For example, with little fanfare, Siemens shed

1,300 of 7,500 employees from its bloated Indian operation for a maximum payout of $16,160—low by European standards but high for India. Many multinational managers sense that unions are ignoring such practices because of a growing realization by unions that Indian businesses must be more efficient to compete internationally.

Given the high prevalence of strikes and lockouts, some are arguing that Indian labor laws need to be revised to improve productivity and to make industries more profitable. They point to the experiences of China, which has transitioned from extreme job security to major reform in the labor laws. Currently, China has a relatively mobile labor market, and surveys show that Chinese workers have benefited from such changes. These experiences may be useful to India as it considers reforms.

Source: Based on Amjad, Ali. 2001. Labour Legislation and Trade Unions in Pakistan. Karachi: Oxford University Press; Economist. 2003. "Two systems, one grand rivalry." June 21, pp. 21–23; Hindu. 2006. "Needed: Labour reforms." February 28, p. 1; Rai, Saritha. 2006. "Airport workers across India strike to protest plan for privatizations." The New York Times, February 2, p. C5; Karp, Jonathan, and Michael Williams. 1997. "Firms in India use buyouts to skirt layoff rules." Wall Street Journal, October 13, p. A16.

Union membership in the United States has declined considerably over the last 30 years. However, European and other industrialized countries still have high proportions of workers who are union members. In major industrialized countries, union membership is declining but still averages greater than 50 percent. Some decline is due to the end of compulsory union membership in the transition economies of Eastern Europe. However, in countries such as South Africa, with the opening of unions to the formerly barred black population, unions have more than doubled in size.[64] Exhibit 12.17 gives a summary of unionization density in various parts of the world.

Some Historical and Institutional Differences

Historical conditions during the early days of unionization in a country and the unions' relationships with social institutions such as the government tend to influence the activities of contemporary unions. Consider the following differences among German, French, British, and U.S. unions observed by Professor Christel Lane.[65]

British unions began early in the 19th century, corresponding to the rise of major factory-based industries. Ignored early on by government, British unions developed without government interference. Not until the 1980s was there much legal control of management–labor conflict. If workers went on strike, neither the company nor the workers had any legal obligation to solve the conflict, such as honoring the workers' right to return to work. According to

EXHIBIT 12.17   **Union Density in Selected Countries**

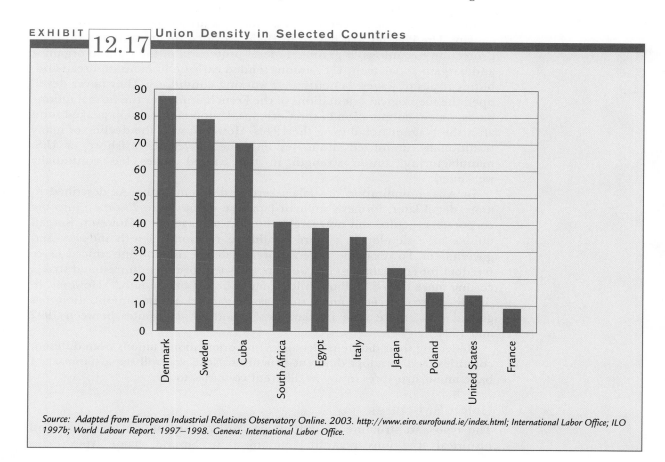

Source: Adapted from European Industrial Relations Observatory Online. 2003. http://www.eiro.eurofound.ie/index.html; International Labor Office; ILO 1997b; World Labour Report. 1997–1998. Geneva: International Labor Office.

Lane,[66] the lack of government intervention led management and workers to develop strong adversarial relationships that remain in existence in contemporary Britain. Lane characterizes the British situation as fragmented and highly conflictual.

Perhaps because German culture ranks high on uncertainty avoidance, labor relationships have a more orderly tradition. The government recognized the union movement in the mid-1880s. The strong role of the state served to develop more harmonious relationships between labor and management. The result in current-day Germany is a formalized, legalistic, low-conflict situation with centralized bargaining between large unions and large corporations. Lane argues that the government serves as an intermediary between unions and management.

French unions began much later and developed more slowly than did British or German unions. According to Lane,[67] there were many small companies, and this fragmentation of businesses retarded union growth. In some industries, legal recognition of the right to bargain collectively occurred as late as 1969.

The lack of legal protection of French workers and the difficulties of unionization led to highly militant unions. French unions often have strong ideological orientations. They adopt anti-capitalistic stances based on a belief in the unavoidability of class conflicts between owners and workers. The French ideological unions tend to compete for union members within the same organizations, the consequence of which sometimes has favored management. In many cases, management simply ignores the unions.

In the United States before 1926, there was little legal support for union activity. The Wagner Act, passed in 1935, provided the most important legal protection for unions. It granted federal protection of the right to organize and bargain collectively. U.S. unions tended early on to focus on bread-and-butter issues of wages, benefits, and working conditions. They never developed the ideological orientations of the French unions or the formal union–management cooperation of the Germans. Union membership peaked soon after the Wagner Act, during the 1940s. However, with the decline of many traditionally unionized industries and the movement offshore of U.S. manufacturing, union strength in the United States has continually weakened.

In Asia, unionization has taken several different paths. As described in more detail later, formerly militant Japanese unions were absorbed into the corporate structure and now largely support management. However, Korean unions have developed a more conflictive relationship with industry and government. For example, recent Korean labor legislation introduced more freedom for companies to fire workers. This led to student unrest and strikes costing more than $2 billion in lost output in just one month.[68] However, in tightly controlled economies such as Singapore, where unionization has gained little, there were no days lost to industrial disputes between 1992 and 1994.[69]

Reflecting their different ideologies and orientations, unions from different countries tend to adopt different structures. Next, you will see a summary of basic union structures in use in different countries today.

Union Structures

The type and structure of unions also reflect institutional pressures and historical traditions regarding unionization. Several major types exist.

Enterprise unions represent all people in one organization, regardless of occupation or location. **Craft unions** represent people from one occupational group, such as plumbers. **Industrial unions** represent all people in a particular industry regardless of occupational type. **Local unions** usually represent one occupational group in one company. However, they are often affiliated with larger craft or industrial unions. **Ideological unions** represent all workers based on some particular ideology (e.g., communism) or religious orientation. **White-collar or professional unions** also represent particular occupational groups. The nature of union structures also influences the collective-bargaining process and the general relationship between management and workers.

Exhibit 12.18 shows selected countries and the popular unions in these countries.

Enterprise unions are most often associated with Japanese labor relations, although they are not the only unions that exist now or have existed in Japan. However, most radical Japanese ideological and industrial unions were effectively crushed during the first half of the twentieth century and were replaced by enterprise unions. Sometimes critically called ''company'' unions, these unions have close associations with management. In fact, one-sixth of the executives in major Japanese companies were previously union executives.[70] Not surprisingly, there is often close cooperation between union and management, with unions viewing management goals as their own.

German unions favor the industrial form of organization. There are 17 major industrial unions, and collective bargaining generally takes place between the unions and employer associations (groups of employers). At the plant level, an elected **works council** negotiates directly with the employer over working conditions, although industry unions negotiate wages at the national or regional level. The following Multinational Management Brief shows how the works council is integrated into management decision making in Germany

Enterprise union
Represents all people in one organization, regardless of occupation or location.

Craft union
Represents people from one occupational group, such as plumbers.

Industrial union
Represents all people in a particular industry, regardless of occupational type.

Local union
Represents one occupational group in one company.

Ideological union
Represents all types of workers based on some particular ideology (e.g., communism) or religious orientation.

EXHIBIT 12.18   Popular Form of Unions in Selected Countries

Country	Craft	General	Industrial	White-collar	Professional	Enterprise
Australia	✓	✓	✓	✓		
Belgium			✓		✓	
Canada	✓		✓			
Denmark	✓	✓		✓		
England	✓	✓	✓	✓		✓
Finland			✓	✓	✓	
Germany			✓	✓		
Japan						✓
Netherlands		✓		✓		
Norway	✓		✓			
Sweden	✓		✓	✓		
Switzerland	✓		✓	✓		
United States			✓	✓		

Source: Adapted from Poole, M. 1986. Industrial Relations: Heritage and Adjustment. Oxford: Oxford University Press.

White-collar or professional union

Represents particular occupational group, similar to craft union.

Works council

In Germany, employee group that shares plant-level responsibility with managers regarding issues such as working conditions.

Co-determination

Surrender by management to workers of a share of control of the organization, traditionally reserved for management and owners.

Multinational Management **Brief**

Globalization of the Works Council

Co-determination, or, in German, Mitbestimmung, means that management surrenders to workers a share of the control of the organization reserved traditionally for management and owners. In Germany, co-determination exists at two levels. At the plant level, workers elect the works council. This group has certain prerogatives supported by law. Some decisions are shared with management, such as selection criteria. Some management decisions can be vetoed, such as reassignment. Finally, management must consult and inform the works council on other decisions, such as accident protection. These rights are detailed in the exhibit below.

At the level of the enterprise, industrial democracy in Germany gives many workers equal representation on the board of directors with those elected by the shareholders. In practice, however, most of these arrangements include policies that favor owners and managers in tight votes. For example, one of the worker-selected representatives must be a manager.

For the Volkswagen Group, the works council has followed its globalization with the formation of the World Works Council in 1999. Although the World Works Council does not have the participatory rights granted German groups by Germany's Industrial Constitution Law, it is funded out of corporate operations and has some powers to influence the Volkswagen Group's worldwide strategic decisions.

Examples of Decisions and Levels of Participation by German Works Councils

Co-Determined with Management	Veto Power over Management	Consulted; or Provided by Management Information
Compensation System	Selection Criteria	Major Business Plans
Piecework Rates	Training	Introducing New Technology
Job Design	Recruitment	Introducing New Equipment
Holiday Planning	Dismissal	Financial Information
Accident Prevention	Reassignment	

Source: Based on Lane, Christel. 1989. Management and Labour in Europe. Aldershot, England: Edward Elgar; International Labor Organization (ILO). 2000. "Globalization of works council activities." World of Work, 36. http://www.ilo.org/public/english/bureau/inf/magazine/36/

and is globalizing its influence following the globalization of German companies.

As noted previously, the most common objective of French unions is to organize all workers based on ideological positions. As such, union structure does not necessarily follow industry, occupation, or enterprise lines. Instead, one union will represent a variety of workers who adhere to the same ideological beliefs. Any one company may have several of these groups organizing workers.

The local union remains the major structural feature of U.S. unions. Most locals associate with some craft, industry, or mixed national union. There are approximately 170 national unions in the United States. Local craft unions tend to represent workers in a local region while local industrial unions tend to represent workers at the level of the plant. Although most collective bargaining takes place at the local level, in some instances, such as in the automobile industry, unions attempt to make company-wide or industry-wide agreements.

Implications for the Multinational: The Search for Harmony

When they use local workers, multinational companies have no choice but to deal with local labor practices and traditions. As a result, the impact of dealing with unions and related labor laws must be considered in any strategic decision regarding locating in another country. Consider these examples. In the United States, Japanese companies have avoided locations in the more union-friendly northern states, favoring instead southern locations with less union activism. The militant unions in Western Europe have led some multinational companies to look for locations in countries like the Czech Republic, where not only are wages lower but labor conflict also seems low.

The state of a country's labor relations is just one of many factors that must be considered in designing a multinational company's IHRM policies and procedures. However, like local wage rates and worker quality, a country's labor-relations patterns also influence location decisions. Where are the favorable locations? An international survey of managers rating their own countries' relationships between managers and employees gives some hints in Exhibit 12.19.

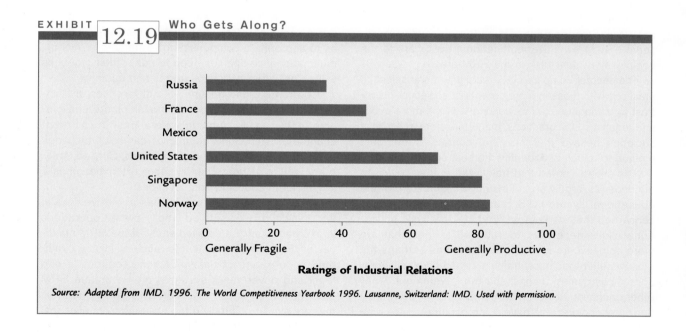

EXHIBIT 12.19   Who Gets Along?

Ratings of Industrial Relations

Source: Adapted from IMD. 1996. The World Competitiveness Yearbook 1996. Lausanne, Switzerland: IMD. Used with permission.

Summary and Conclusions

This chapter highlighted fundamental national differences in the HRM processes of recruitment, selection, training and development, performance appraisal, compensation, and labor relations. The chapter also showed how multinational operations are affected by the HRM practices prevalent in host countries.

To understand why HRM practices differ, the chapter presented a model of how the national context affects HRM practices. We saw that national culture, business culture, and key social institutions—education and the legal system—affect a nation's dominant HRM practices.

To show how the model works in different national contexts, the chapter provided numerous illustrations that contrasted U.S. HRM practices with those of other nations. Countries with collectivist cultures were often chosen for comparisons because of their cultural distances from the highly individualistic U.S. national culture. The contrasts purposefully showed large differences in HRM practices to give some sense of the variety of HRM practices in the world. However, no one chapter, or book for that matter, could explain adequately all the worldwide differences in human resource management. Thus, the examples given serve only to sensitize multinational managers to the complexity of their task in the HRM area.

The chapter compared U.S. recruitment and selection practices with those in more collectivist societies. In contrast to managers used to working with the more public and legalistic U.S. practices, managers from collectivist societies believe that personal contact is the best method to recruit and identify the best employees.

The chapter noted that training of entry-level workers depends largely on the institutional structure of the educational system. U.S. managers are increasingly concerned that workers do not have the basic educational skills necessary to succeed in jobs that are more complex. In contrast, Germany has perhaps the best system of technical training, based on a collaboration of companies, unions, and the government. Many other countries, however, including some of the transitioning economies and developing countries, have educational systems that produce potential workers with good mathematics and science skills.

Later in the chapter, we saw that management-development practices are embedded in cultural expectations regarding the relationship of managers with their organizations. U.S. companies face the dilemma of investing to develop top management talent and then risk that these managers will go to another company. In more collectivist national cultures, such as Japan and Korea, managers have more commitment to remain with the organization (they often have little choice). As such, companies can take a long-term view of investing in extensive management development and training.

To avoid legal ramifications of race, gender, and age biases, the discussion showed that U.S. performance-evaluation systems tend to be formal and public. In collectivist societies, in contrast, performance appraisal tends to be informal and more secret. In the United States, rewards—in particular, compensation—are linked to the results of performance appraisals. In collectivist societies, factors such as age, family situation, loyalty to the company, and relationship to the owners often influence rewards more than performance does.

Most multinational companies are attracted to production sites in countries where the wages are low but the talent pool is strong. As such, they tend to adopt host-country wage and salary levels. There are numerous sources of information that can provide guidance as to appropriate compensation strategies. In general, multinational companies need to adapt their practices to be consistent with local norms and customs.

Confronting and dealing with differences in traditions and volatility of labor relationships are unavoidable activities in running operations in different countries. Multinational companies can seldom change a country's traditions of labor relations. Consequently, the volatility of host-country labor often becomes a key factor in choosing host locations.

Whether a company establishes a joint venture in another country or sets up wholly-owned operations in another country, a detailed study of the HRM practices of the local environment is required. History, tradition, culture, and social institutions (education and legal and government systems) create unique HRM practices in each country. Moreover, even countries that are similar culturally often have different historical and traditional patterns of labor relations. Thus, a successful multinational manager comes prepared not only with knowledge of the local culture but also with an understanding of how HRM practices evolved to become part of a host country's business environment.

Discussion Questions

1. Describe and discuss the major factors in the national context that affect a nation's HRM practices.

2. Compare and contrast recruitment and selection strategies in the United States and in nations with more collectivist cultures. Discuss legal and cultural problems that multinational managers might face using a collectivist approach to recruitment and selection in the United States and using a U.S. approach in more collectivist cultures.

3. Some U.S. politicians have called for the development of a German-type apprenticeship-training system in the United States. If you were a manager of a U.S. Fortune 500 multinational company, how would you respond to this proposal and why?

4. Discuss the advantages and disadvantages of a permanent-employment system for managers.

Discuss how this system might work for non-Asian countries besides the United States.

5. You have been given the assignment of setting up a training program for first-level managers in a formerly government-owned Eastern European company. How would you go about developing a curriculum? Why?

6. Compare and contrast the appraisal and compensation systems in the United States and more collectivist-culture nations. Discuss legal and cultural problems that multinational managers might face using a collectivist approach to these systems in the United States and using a U.S. approach in more collectivist cultures.

7. Contrast the different types of unions and discuss the challenges each type might pose to a multinational manager.

Multinational Management **Skill Builder**

The HRM Component in a Multinational Company's Location Decision

Step 1. Read the following multinational problem.

You are now a vice president for human resources for the XYZ Company located in the United States. Your company manufactures components for industrial robots. Employees need U.S. high-school-level ability in reading and mathematics to maintain job skills.

You have just come from a meeting where the CEO has asked all functional-area vice presidents to prepare a report concerning the location advantages or disadvantages of country _____. Marketing and production VPs will look at issues such as potential market size, the availability of raw materials, and supply and sales distribution channels. Your job is to consider the nature of the labor force should your company decide to set up operations in _____. You will need to plan for a host-country national workforce of 200 production workers, 10 first-line managers, and 2 mid-level managers.

Step 2. Picking teams and countries.

Your instructor will divide you into teams of three to five people. Each team will choose a different country for a prospective location. Your team will act in the role of the vice

president for human resources and will prepare the report called for in Step 1. Your instructor may also require that you work within a specific industry.

This is a library research project. Your instructor may provide you with general data sources. You may also use information from the text.

Step 3. Prepare reports.

Reports may be written, oral, or both. A typical report analyzes the implications of economic, cultural, and institutional factors as they might affect all of the HRM functions discussed in this chapter. Below are some key topics that must be addressed. Your instructor may assign additional topics to consider.

A. Economic considerations:
   Comparative wage and salary levels of this country with other countries
   Employment levels, including workforce participation of women and youth
   Employer-provided benefits
   Characteristics of labor relations (e.g., likelihood of work stoppages)

B. Institutional conditions:
   Availability of educated workers
   Extent of government intervention in employment—wage levels, benefit

requirements, policies for layoffs,
mandated holidays, other labor legislation
Legal power of unions

   C. National and business cultures:
Effects of dominant religion and language
on labor relations
Cultural effects of the relationship of the
employee with the organization—long term,
family dominated, preference for larger or
smaller organizations, etc.
Traditions regarding union types and labor

   D. Analysis:
Costs and benefits of locating in this
country
Solutions for potential problems
Recommendation to the president

Step 4.   Present your findings.
Oral reports for this exercise will take
between ½ and 1½ hours, depending on
your instructor's requirements.

Sources: Adapted from Balfour, Alan. 1988–1989. "A beginning focus for teaching international human resources administration." Organizational Behavior Teaching Review, 13, 2: pp. 79–89.

Endnotes

[1] Black, J. Stewart, Hal B. Gregersen, and Mark E. Mendenhall. 1992. *Global Assignments.* Jossey-Bass;San Francisco: Reynolds, Calvin. 1997. "Strategic employment of third country nationals." *Human Resource Planning* 20,1, p. 33–39.

[2] Porter, Michael E. 1990. *The Competitive Advantage on Nations.* New York: Free Press.

[3] *Economist.* 2003. "Roll over, Confucius." January 25, p. 40.

[4] Porter, *The Competitive Advantage on Nations.*

[5] Barney, J.B. 1991. "Firm resources and sustained competitive advantage." *Journal of Management,* 17: pp. 99–120.

[6] Tregaskis, Olga, and Chris Brewster. 2006. "Converging or diverging? A comparative analysis of trends in contingent employment practice in Europe over a decade." *Journal of International Business Studies* 37, p. 111–126.

[7] Brewster, Chris, Geoff Wood, Michael Brookes, and Jos Van Ommeren. 2006. "What determines the size of the HR function? A cross-national analysis." *Human Resources Management* 45, 1: pp. 3–21.

[8] Richard Whitley. 1999. "Divergent capitalisms: the social structuring and change of business systems", Oxford University Press:Oxford .

[9] Bohlander, George W., Scott Snell, and Arthur W. Sherman, Jr. 2001. *Managing Human Resources.* Cincinnati: South-Western.

[10] Hofstede, Geert. 1991. *Cultures and Organizations.* London: McGraw-Hill.

[11] International Social Survey Program (ISSP). 1999/2000. "International social survey program: Work orientations II, 1997 [Computer file].

[12] Trompenaars, Fons. 1994. *Riding the Waves of Culture: Understanding Diversity in Global Business.* Chicago: Irwin.

[13] Bohlander, Snell, and Sherman, *Managing Human Resources;* Werther, William B., and Keith Davis. 1993. *Human Resources and Personnel Management.* New York: McGraw-Hill.

[14] Hofstede, *Cultures and Organizations.*

[15] Kras, Eva S. 1995. *Management in Two Cultures.* Yarmouth, Maine: Intercultural Press.

[16] Steers, Richard M., Yoo Keun Shin, and Gerardo R. Ungson. 1989. *The Chaebol: Korea's New Industrial Might.* New York: HarperBusiness.

[17] Geringer, J. Michael, Colette A. Frayne, and John F. Milliman. 2002. "In search of 'best practices' in international human resource management: Research design and methodology." *Human Resource Management* 41, 1: pp. 5–30.

[18] Huo, Y. Paul, Heh J. Huang, and Nancy K. Napier. 2002. "Divergence or convergence: A cross-national comparison of personnel selection practices." *Human Resource Management* 41, 1: pp. 31–44.

[19] Geringer, Frayne, and Milliman, "In search of 'best practices' in international human resource management: Research design and methodology."

[20] Organisation for Economic Co-operation and Development (OECD). 2000. *Education at a Glance: OECD Indicators.*

[21] Drost, Ellen A., Colette A. Frayne, Kevin B. Lowe, and J. Michael Geringer. 2002. "Benchmarking training and development practices: A multicountry analysis." *Human Resource Management* 41, 1: pp. 67–86.

[22] Richard Whitley. "Divergent capitalisms: the social structuring and change of business systems", Oxford University Press:Oxford.

[23] Brewster, Wood, Brookes, and Ommeren, "What determines the size of the HR function? A cross-national analysis."

[24] Van Buren, Mark E., and Stephen B. King. 2000. "ASTD's annual accounting of worldwide patterns in employer-provided training." *Training & Development.* Supplement, The 2000 ASTD International Comparisons Report, pp. 1–24.

[25] Cook, Mary F. 1993. *The Human Resources Yearbook 1993/ 1994 Edition.* Englewood Cliffs, N.J.: Prentice Hall.

[26] Ibid.

[27] Drost, Frayne, Lowe, and Geringer, "Benchmarking training and development practices: A multicountry analysis."

[28] Bondreau, John W. 1991. "Utility analysis in human resource management decision." In *Handbook of Industrial and Organizational Psychology,* edited by M. D. Dunnette and Latta M. Hough, pp. 1111–1143. 2d ed. Palo Alto: Consulting Psychology Press.

[29] Arkin, Anat. 1992. "Personnel management in Denmark: The land of social welfare." *Personnel Management*, March, pp. 32–35; International Labor Organization (ILO). 1999. *World Employment Report 1998–99.* Geneva: International Labor Office.

[30] *BusinessWeek Online. 1996.* August 23, chart; International Labor Organization (ILO), *World Employment Report 1998–99.*

[31] Arkin, "Personnel management in Denmark: The land of social welfare."

[32] Bohlander, Snell, and Sherman, *Managing Human Resources.*

[33] Schlender, Brenton R. 1994. "Japan's white collar blues." *Business Week,* March 21, pp. 97–104.

[34] Abegglen, James C., and George Stalk, Jr. 1985. *Kaisha: The Japanese Corporation.* New York: Basic.

[35] *Economist. 2006.* "Greying Japan the downturn." January 9.

[36] Millikin, John P., and Dean Fu. 2005. "The Global leadership of Carlos Ghosn at Nissan." *Thunderbird International Business Review* 47, 1: pp. 121–137.

[37] Terpstra, Vern, and Kenneth David. 1991. *The Cultural Environment of International Business.* Cincinnati: South-Western.

[38] Werther and Davis, *Human Resources and Personnel Management*.

[39] Locher, Alan H., and Kenneth S. Teel. 1988. "Appraisal trends." *Personnel Journal* 67, 9: pp. 139–145.

[40] Bohlander, Snell, and Sherman, *Managing Human Resources*.

[41] Ibid.

[42] Milliman, John, Stephen Nason, Cherrie Zhu, and Helen De Cieri. 2002. "An exploratory assessment of the purposes of performance in North and Central America and the Pacific Rim." *Human Resource Management* 41, 1: pp. 87–102.

[43] Geringer, Frayne, and Milliman, "In search of 'best practices' in international human resource management: Research design and methodology."

[44] Hofstede, *Cultures and Organizations*.

[45] Steers, Shin, and Ungson, *The Chaebol: Korea's New Industrial Might*.

[46] Ibid., p. 101.

[47] Ibid.

[48] U.S. Department of Labor. 1995. *Hourly Compensation Costs for Production Workers, June 1995*. Washington, D.C.: U.S. Government Printing Office.

[49] International Labor Organization (ILO). 1997. *World Employment Report 1996–97*. Geneva: International Labour Office.

[50] Simmers, Tim. 2005. "Workers in U.S. labor longer with less vacation than others." *Business Writer,* December 10, p. 1.

[51] Bohlander, Snell, and Sherman, *Managing Human Resources*.

[52] Bureau of National Affairs. 1988. *Recruiting and Selection Procedures, Personnel Policies Forum*. Washington, D.C: Bureau of National Affairs, Inc. No. 46, May: pp. 9–11.

[53] Ibid.

[54] Hansen, Fay. 1998. "Incentive plans are now commonplace in large firms."

[55] Geringer, Frayne, and Milliman, "In search of 'best practices' in international human resource management: Research design and methodology."

[56] Lowe, Kevin B., John Milliman, Helen De Cieri, and Peter J. Dowling. 2002. "International compensation practices: A ten-country comparative analysis." *Human Resource Management* 41, 1: pp. 45–66.

[57] Macharzina, Klaus. 2000. "Editorial: The Japanese model—out of date?" *Management International Review,* 40, pp. 103–106.

[58] *Economist,* "Greying Japan the downturn."

[59] Takahashi, Shunsuke. 1993. "New trends on human resource management in Japan." In *The Human Resource Yearbook 1993/ 1994 Ed.,* edited by Mary F. Cook, pp. 1.37–1.38. Englewood Cliffs, N.J.: Prentice Hall; Schmidt, Richard. 1997. "Japanese management, recession style." *Business Horizons,* 39, pp. 70–75.

[60] *Economist*. 1999. "Putting the bounce back into Matsushita." May 20, http://www.economist.com

[61] Lancaster, Hal. 1996. "How you can learn to feel at home in a foreign-based firm." *Wall Street Journal,* June 4, p. B1.

[62] *BusinessWeek Online*. 1996. "How Nike's pay stacks up." July 9, chart.

[63] International Labor Organization (ILO), *World Employment Report 1998–99;* Poole, M. 1986. *Industrial Relations: Heritage and Adjustment*. Oxford: Oxford University Press.

[64] International Labor Organization (ILO), *World Employment Report 1996–97;* International Labor Organization (ILO). 1997. *World Labour Report 1997–98*. Geneva: International Labour Office.

[65] Lane, Christel. 1989. *Management and Labour in Europe*. Aldershot, England: Edward Elgar.

[66] Ibid.

[67] Ibid.

[68] *Economist. 1997.* "The trouble with South Korea." January 18, pp. 59–60.

[69] IMD. 1996. *The World Competitiveness Yearbook 1996*. Lausanne, Switzerland: IMD.

[70] Abegglen and Stalk, Jr., *Kaisha: The Japanese Corporation*.

CHAPTER CASE
Management Appraisal at Attock Refinery Limited (A)

Mr. Adil Khattak, Assistant General Manager (Human Resources) and the senior management at Attock Refinery Limited (ARL) were re-evaluating the role of the HR systems in light of the internal and external changes that ARL was experiencing. Mr. Khattak, a handsome man with a striking presence, sat in his sparsely decorated office and reflected upon the state of the organization's Management Appraisal System. He had become increasingly concerned and his challenge was to examine the present system and make it responsive to the company's changing environment. While summarizing the views of the staff and management, Mr. Khattak noted that the appraisal system was perceived to be subjective, inadequate in differentiating between high and low performers, and only remotely linked to the reward system.

Organizational Background

The Attock refinery was set up under the name of Morgah in 1922 with initial capacity of 2,500 barrels per day (bpd). With the increase in indigenous crude oils, new plants with a capacity of 5,500 bpd were commissioned in 1940. Attock Refinery Limited (ARL) was incorporated as a Private Limited Company in November 1978 to take over the business of the Attock Oil Company (AOC) in relation to crude oil refining and supplying of refined petroleum products. It was subsequently converted to a Public Limited Company in June 1979 and was presently quoted on three stock exchanges of Pakistan.

Original paid up capital of the company was Rs 80 million, which was subscribed by the holding company, i.e., AOC, the Government of Pakistan, the investment companies and the general public. This was gradually increased to Rs 291.6 million by the issue of bonus shares over the last 5 years.

With additional discoveries of crude oil in the Potohar area in 1979, two new crude distillation units with refining capacity of 25,000 bpd were installed in 1980. Some of the old, unsafe and uneconomical units installed in the 1940's were closed to streamline the operations. Recently ARL had replaced an old 5,000-bpd Heavy Crude unit with one of 10,000 bpd. In addition, a Catalytic Reformer of 5,000 bpd had also been added for the production of Low Lead Premium Motor Gasoline. Prior to this, ARL was producing only Regular grade gasoline. Both units were equipped with the latest Distributed Control System for controlling of plant operations.

The company completed the upgrading project at an estimated cost of Rs. 2.696 billion. The installation of the new state-of-the-art plant was completed within the scheduled time. With this, the Refinery, besides processing 35,000 barrels of crude per day, would also produce low lead premium gasoline and 150,000 tons per annum of paving grade asphalt

The Refinery production depended on indigenous crude available in the northern and southern regions of the country. It was capable of refining all types of light and heavy crude produced in the Potohar area from different fields. Southern crude from Badin Block was also being processed at ARL.

The company produced a wide range of petroleum products including Liquefied Petroleum Gas, Low Lead Premium Motor Gasoline, Jet Fuels, Kerosene Oil, High Speed Diesel, Diesel Fuel Oil, various grades of road asphalt, Furnace Fuel Oil, Solvent Oil, Mineral Turpentine and Jute Batching Oil.

The organization had eight departments (see Exhibit 1). There were approximately 155 employees in the management staff and almost 550 in the non-management staff. Out of the 155 employees in the management staff approximately 60% had received engineering education, about 2% had management and accounting backgrounds respectively, and 36% had degrees in general education.

EXHIBIT **1**   **Attock Refinery Limited May 5, 1999**

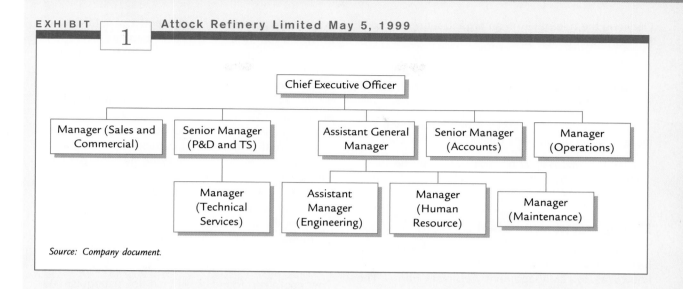

Source: Company document.

The Petroleum Industry and Arl's New Strategic Focus

Until recently, oil refining in Pakistan had been a government-regulated industry. The minimum return guaranteed by the government to the oil refineries was 10% net of taxes on issued capital. Returns over 40% were skimmed by the government. The Petroleum Policy announced in March 1994 removed the 40% limit on return if surplus percentage was to be used for development and expansion plans. There were indications that the government would further liberalize the oil and gas sector to attract foreign investment.

The petroleum industry in Pakistan was experiencing a major strategic shift due to internal and external environmental changes, specifically due to deregulation of the industry and entry of multi-national corporations. ARL had been forced to come out of its shell, where the sales were locked and returns guaranteed by the government. Shell (International) had already taken over the Pakistan Burma Shell (PBS) and there were moves by MOBIL and Askari Bank to take over Pakistan State Oil (PSO). It was now competing in a dynamic and competitive environment. In the words of Mr. Khattak:

In the coming years it will be survival of the fittest, PARCO is setting up a refinery in Multan with a capacity of 100,000 bpd. Once its open market competition, our monopoly in the north will not be there anymore. Some of our products would be surplus in the market. So one option is to focus on value added down stream products.*

While the Government of Pakistan remained a shareholder of ARL, the managerial control was with Attock Oil Company. Now the top management wanted the company to change its traditional work practices and become efficient enough to compete with any international player. The changing environment meant that the company would have to develop a fresh strategy and supporting systems to be able to compete effectively. The stated strategic objectives of ARL were expansion of refining capacity, up grading of technology, and optimization of facilities and processes leading to the introduction of value-added products. ARL aimed to gain market advantage in the North of the country through the development and implementation of supporting systems and human resources with a strong knowledge base.

After, Mr. Raziuddin, the present CEO took charge of ARL, he made efforts to change the entire culture of the company. He treated the workforce as a valuable asset and wanted to make sure that the employees were committed to their work and contributed significantly to organizational effectiveness.

---

*Downstream products include products such as petrol, high speed diesel, jet fuel, bitumen etc.

Outlining the role of HR in an organization's success Mr. Raziuddin observed:

> *The progress of any company depends on its Human Resources. In turn, development of Human Resources is integral and one of the most important functions of new corporate culture.*

While commenting upon the new challenges and increasing focus on HR's role, Mr. Khattak stated:

> *Now the emphasis is on cost-cutting, efficiency, gender equity, training and development and appraisal system.*

Management Appraisal System

The management appraisal system at ARL, was based on an appraisal instrument (see Exhibit 2) known as the "Management Appraisal Form." The appraisal was carried out annually and feedback was also provided to the employees towards the end of the year. Information and data on employee's performance was also gathered at the end of the year.

The appraisal process was carried out in five steps (see Exhibit 2). In the initial phase the instrument known as the "Management Appraisal Form" included the appraisee's personal details, summary of job description and the appraisal period. In the next section called Step 1, the appraiser evaluated the target employee according to five broad performance categories, namely, *what he accomplishes, how he works, what he is, what he knows,* and *what he feels.* A five point rating scale known as the appraisal code was used during this evaluation. Each of these categories was further divided into sub-categories. The subcategories collectively made up 32 performance dimensions.

Upon completion of Step 1, the appraiser was required to provide his comments on the employee's potential, his/her development needs and any preferences given by the employee about his/her career path.

The review committee set up for the appraisal purposes and comprising of the Assistant General Manager, Maintenance Engineering and Human Resources, Senior Manager Accounts, Manager Operations and Manager Human Resources, completed the remaining sections of the performance appraisal form. The review committee was required to analyze the elements of performance appraised in Step I and record significant findings. While doing this the committee had to comment on the employee's greatest strengths and also list the areas in which an employee's performance could and should be improved. Finally it had to identify an employee's training and development needs.

In Step III the over all performance of the employee was appraised and Step IV highlighted the employees capacity for advancement in his present organization unit. Here the review committee assessed what was the next suitable position for the employee, whether the employee had the potential for advancement, and if not, then what were the reasons. Finally the Chief Executive Officer gave his comments and signed the appraisal form.

Overall an employee was assessed against 32 performance dimensions using a 5 point rating scale. Appraising an employee on these dimensions was considered to be difficult by most appraisers. The appraiser found it difficult to distinguish between certain dimensions. There was considerable overlapping, as noted by Mr. Rana M. Akram, the Human Resource Manager:

> *We felt that 32 traits were overlapping and some of them were not even meaningful. Moreover if someone had to be rated as excellent, good or even below average we had to come up with long, de-scriptive sentences in English. So it was very difficult to come up with new phrases every year.*

The system was also perceived by the employees to be very qualitative and subjective. There were no quantifiable objectives against which the employees could be evaluated. Many employees believed that it was on the sole discretion of the appraiser to rate an employee as he wished. Sometimes the manager could not even justify the remarks that he made on an appraisee. One employee in the management staff was of the view:

> *The appraisal system uses a 1–5 scale. 1 being exceptional and 5 being below average. In addition to the scale, the appraiser also has to give his own remarks, i.e., he has to support his marking with his comments. Now if someone is given 2, the remarks that are given do not support that rating. Similarly sometimes the remarks are really good but the numbers are not according to the remarks.*

Performance appraisal was carried out annually. Since performance related data was not gathered regularly this sometimes led to problems. A manager recalled:

EXHIBIT **2**   Management Appraisal Form

ATTOCK REFINERY LIMITED   CONFIDENTIAL

Source: Company documents

APPRAISAL PERIOD
FROM
TO

MANAGEMENT APPRAISAL FORM

PERSONAL DETAILS

NAME		DATE OF BIRTH	QUALIFICATION	YEARS OF EXPERIENCE OUTSIDE THE COMPANY	DATE JOINED COMPANY
JOB TITLE	DEPARTMENT	LOCATION	Date Posted to Present Position	Positions Held During Review Period	
			Grade	Present Basic Salary:	
Generalist/ Specialist			Date coming to grade	Reports to	

Position Summary (Job Description) *

STEP 1 – APPRAISE THE ELEMENTS OF PERFORMANCE

Appraise those factors important to effective performance in the specific responsibilities of this position, using the appraisal code. Disregard factors not applicable. In the spaces provided, list and appraise other factors which are important to this position and / or comment on how effectively the employee performs his specific responsibilities

APPRAISAL CODE

1. Outstanding or exceptional performance (usually less than 10% of the total).
2. Performance which is definitely better than normally expected, producing results which exceed the requirements of the position (usually no more than 25% of the group).
3. Performance which consistently meets the requirements of the position (typical of a majority of personnel).
4. Performance which on the basis of comparative effectiveness requires certain improvement in one or more basic aspects of the work.
5. Inadequate performance

A. **WHAT HE ACCOMPLISHES – Consider the RESULTS of the employee's work and that of his subordinates and comment upon the extent the individual accomplished expected results during the review period along with the review of what has been achieved and reasons for success or failure in the space provided against comments.**

☐ **Quality of Work** – Caliber of work produced or accomplished compared with accepted standards of performance.

☐ **Quantity of Work** – Volume of acceptable work compared with what may reasonably be expected.

☐ **Cost Objective** – Effectiveness in meeting cost objectives and in operation at lowest cost, with minimum manpower, by most efficient methods.

☐ **Profit Objectives** – Effectiveness in meeting profit objectives and in generating and implementing money making ideas.

☐ **Developing People** – Effectiveness in selecting and appraising personnel setting high standards of performance; and motivating them to grow in their capacity to handle increasing difficult work.

☐ **Performance Objective** – Ability to meet performance objectives set by the Supervisors to carry out position responsibilities effectively.

Comments: *

B. **HOW HE WORKS – Consider the degree to which the employee applies sound METHODS in getting his job done.**

☐ **Planning** – Effectiveness in anticipating needs forecasting conditions setting goals and standards, planning and scheduling work, and measuring results.

☐ **Organizing** – Effectiveness in dividing the total work to be done into clear cut and manageable jobs and integrating all components into a harmonious, smoothly working whole.

☐ **Delegating** – Effectiveness in delegating work and assigning responsibility to subordinates and in establishing appropriate controls.

☐ **Working with Others** – Effectiveness of relationships with subordinates, associates, and superiors.

☐ **Communicating** – Effectiveness in keeping subordinates, associates, and supervisors adequately informed.

☐ **Analysis** – Effectiveness in thinking through a problem, in recognizing, securing, and evaluating relevant facts; and in reaching a conclusion.

☐ **Methods** – How does the individual go about getting the job done? How does he plan, delegate, follow through, communicate, work with people at various levels etc?

Comments: *

Source: Company document.

EXHIBIT 2   Management Appraisal Form (*continued*)

COMMENTS OF APPRAISER:

(i)   **POTENTIAL:** In your honest opinion in which category of potential does the individual fall?

High Potential?   Potential?   No Potential:

Comments: *

(ii) **DEVELOPMENT**: Has this individual, in your estimate, the ability to go beyond present responsibilities? Please estimate, to the best of your capability, the individual's development potential.

Comments: *

(iii) HAS THE EMPLOYEE EXPRESSED ANY PREFERENCE ABOUT HIS CAREER PATTERN? If so, please state; *

Date: Appraiser: Reviewed by:

STEP II: REVIEW & COMMENTS BY THE REVIEW COMMITTEE:

A.   **ANALYSE PERFORMANCE** (Analyse the elements of performance appraised in STEP I and record significant findings)

    a).   List the employees greatest strengths, as evidenced by specific examples of unusually good performance or of the kinds of work he does best. (The areas in which the employee excels are important indications of the direction in which his development should be planned). *

    b).   List the areas in which his performance can and should be improved. Be specific. (Definite knowledge of needs is necessary in making plans to assist the employee in improving his performance). *

B.   **IDENTIFY TRAINING AND DEVELOPMENT NEEDS**

    a).   In what areas and in which respects the employee feels he can improve his performance. *

    b).   Summarize the employee's training and development needs. Be as practical and specific as possible (Complete sections 1, 2, 3, below whichever is most appropriate).

        1.   Specify additional experience needs – jobs rotation, job enrichment, special assignments. *

        2.   Specify formal training needs – special attachments, in-house/in-country/foreign training Programme. *

        3.   Specify any other training and development plans. *

STEP III. APPRAISE OVER-ALL PERFORMANCE (CHECK (✓) appropriate box).

1. Outstanding or exceptional performance (usually less than 10% of the total)	2. Performance which is definitely better than normally expected, producing results which exceed the requirements of the position (usually no more than 25% of the group).	3. Performance which consistently meets the requirements of the position (typical of a majority of personnel).	4. Performance which on the basis of comparative effectiveness requires certain improvement in one or more basic aspects of the work.	5. Inadequate performance.
☐	☐	☐	☐	☐

EXHIBIT 2   **Management Appraisal Form (continued)**

C. WHAT HE IS– Consider the degree to which the employee's PERSONAL QUALITIES contribute to his effectiveness.

❑ **Leadership** – Effectiveness in developing in others the willingness and desire to work towards a common objective.

❑ **Judgement** – Soundness of conclusions, decisions, & actions.

❑ **Initiative** – Ability to take action without being told.

❑ **Drive** – Basic urge and energy to get things done?

❑ **Dependability** – Reliability in assuming and carrying out the commitments and obligations of his position.

❑ **Integrity & Honesty** – Degree of honesty and integrity demonstrated in performing the job.

Comments: *

D. WHAT HE KNOWS – Consider the employee's KNOWLEDGE in his functional and related fields and his understanding of environmental matters necessary to effective performance.

❑ **Assigned Work** – Knowledge of methods, techniques and skills in his functional field which are necessary to performance of his responsibilities.

❑ **Related Work** – Knowledge of related functions, the understanding of which has an influence on assigned work.

❑ **Knowledge of Industry practices**

❑ **Basic administrative skills**.

❑ **Company Philosophy and Objectives** – Knowledge of the Company and its objectives, organization structure, and management philosophy.

❑ **Development in Profession or Field** – Acquaintance with ideas, trends, techniques, and discoveries (both inside and outside the company) pertaining to his work.

❑ **Creative abilities** – Abilities to introduce/accept change

Comments: *

E. WHAT HE FEELS - Consider his general ATTITUDE towards the Company and his Colleagues as reflected in his work which contributes to effective performance.

❑ **Adaptability to Company's Culture** – Ability to adopt local culture and creating a sense of belonging.

❑ **Socializing** – Willingness and desire to mix up socially with Colleagues and other people concerning work.

❑ **Relationship with CBA** – Helpfulness in creating conducive and good working atmosphere with CBA.

❑ **Punctuality** – Regularity in attending work and other assignments.

❑ **Dedication** – Conscientious for accomplishment of job even some times beyond the call of duty.

❑ **Safety & Security** – Consciousness for fire prevention, safety and security of the Company's employees and property.

Other Factors: *

Comments: *

Dated: _____

_____
Signature of Appraiser

NAME:

POSITION:

Appraisee's own views about the appraisal.

EXHIBIT **2**   Management Appraisal Form (*continued*)

STEP IV – APPRAISE CAPACITY FOR ADVANCEMENT IN PRESENT ORGANIZATION UNIT (complete Section A, B, or C below, whichever is appropriate).

A. This employee is promotable. 1. The specific position(s) which appear to be the next step(s) ahead for him are:	(Indicate (✓) Readiness or Next Step Ahead		
	Ready Now	1-2 Years	3-5 Years

2. Does this employee appear to have the potential to advance beyond the next step(s) ahead?

☐ ☐ ☐   If practicable, name the position(s) which it is believed he has the potential to advance: *

Yes Can't No
     Judge
     Now

B. **This employee appears to have potential for advancement, but at this time the next step ahead has not been determined.**
Check (✓) appropriate reasons.

☐ New in present position, recently promoted, or similar reasons.

☐ Other reasons. (Specify) *

C. **It does not appear likely, at this time, that this employee will advance beyond his present position.**
Check ([ ]) appropriate reasons

☐ Own desire unwilling to change work locations, or similar reasons.   ☐ Specialized capabilities which are now fully utilized.

☐ Age, or limited time remaining for development and utilization of capabilities.   ☐ Other factors. (Specify) *

ANY OTHER COMMENTS OF REVIEW COMMITTEE. *

_____ _____ _____

Signature of Review Committee Members

STEP V – COMMENTS BY THE MANAGING DIRECTOR *

MANAGING DIRECTOR

*
_____

* The spaces have been eliminated as a result of page concerns.

One of my friends felt he had worked really hard throughout the year, but because he was unable to finish a task given to him by his supervisor towards the end of the year, he ended up getting a bad appraisal.

The system did not provide any formal feedback to the employees about their performance. While discussing this issue a manager offered the following comment:

This is how I believe it [appraisal] happens. The appraisal is written by the manager, it is given to the committee and then we are asked to sign it . . . but when everything is done then there is no need in asking us what we feel about it, whether it is good or bad.

Another manager observed:

The appraisal is bureaucratic, your appraisal is written and you don't know what it is. The last day your boss shares the appraisal with you and asks if you agree with it or not. You don't have a lot of choice other than to say that you do agree with it. You have to work for the same person in the coming year too. By disagreeing with his appraisal you actually start a dispute with him. You can't really argue with the appraiser, you can only agree or disagree.

The employees generally felt that there was no proper system of career progression in place at ARL. Promotion relied heavily on the sole discretion of the appraiser as opposed to being linked to the annual performance appraisal. There were employees who had performed well and yet had not been promoted for several years. "It is really the manager's will to promote or not to promote an individual," complained an executive. There was no separate assessment of promotional capabilities of an individual; it was in fact part of the same system. One member of the senior management staff felt that:

In the current system past performance is not really an indicator of future promotion; Elements of subjectivity are involved here.

For some managers the appraisal system was not adequately linked to the reward system. They were not sure as to how the increments were decided and on what grounds promotion recommendations were made. One manager shared his view:

We have two types of increments, normal and merit. The normal increment is 5%. The merit increment starts at 2.5% then 5% and so on. So if someone is given a 5% increment and someone else 2.5% then there is really no way of telling that on what grounds the increments were decided.

For some managers the problem was not with the appraisal form but with the individual's who completed the form. As one manager observed:

What I feel is that most of the people at higher level don't know how to fill an appraisal form. If you have a query and you want to question your appraisal then I believe there are very few people who can justify what they have written. For example once in my appraisal my boss gave me a low score on dependability, when I asked him why I got a low score then he told me that it was because I never called him for anything. So if I didn't call upon him too many times then I did a lot of work on my own at my own level, is this greater dependability or if I keep calling someone for guidance is that dependability? As far as I see things, there is nothing wrong with the appraisal system, what makes the difference is who is filling the appraisal. Whether you have a numeric or descriptive system that really isn't the problem. The main thing is that the people doing the appraisal should be fair enough and properly trained to write the right thing.

Conclusion

Mr. Khattak felt it important for the HR department to carefully consider the changing business environment and new organizational goals, in any new initiatives it would consider. He also wanted the department to address such issues as objectivity, differentiation and compensation. Pondering over the complexities that he and his HR team faced concerning the appraisal system in early 1999, Mr. Khattak was convinced that the matter deserved their immediate attention.

CASE CREDIT

This case was prepared by Assistant Professor Syed Aqeel Tirmizi and Faiza Imtiaz of the Lahore University of Management Sciences as a basis for class discussion rather than to illustrate either effective or ineffective handling of an administrative or business situation. © 2001 by World Scientific Publishing Co.

Management Appraisal at Attock Refinery Limited (B)

Amidst the changes in the company's managerial philosophy and strategy, concerns regarding the adequacy and utility of the current management appraisal system continued to surface in early 1999. The internal changes in ARL's management philosophy and the changes in its external environment were thought to have serious implications for the company's HR systems, including the current management appraisal system. The Administration and Personnel Department was renamed as the Human Resource Department. In addition as part of its new management philosophy the company adopted the Management by Objectives approach. Mr. Adil Khattak, Assistant General Manager Human Resources, felt that there was an urgent need to immediately address the issues regarding the appraisal system and to develop a new system that was in sync with ARL's new focus and vision. For this purpose, he advised Mr. Rana M. Akram, Manager HR and his team, to develop a new appraisal system and encouraged him to work closely with the senior management team.

The Proposed Appraisal System

Mr. Akram finalized the design and development of a new appraisal system in late 1999. After a series of presentations to the senior management, the new appraisal system was finalized and forwarded for approval to the Group CEO of Attock Oil Company (AOC).

The highlight of the new system was its MBO approach. A new appraisal instrument (see Exhibit 1) was developed. In addition to the system's focus on objectives, another new element that had been added was the quarterly feedback.

The Appraisal Form had five parts. Form A was the "Management Personnel Targets Appraisal Form" and was filled out by the immediate supervising officer. For each area of performance the employee together with his immediate supervisor established certain targets. These targets were assigned a weightage (W%) and assessed against predetermined verification criteria. Targets achieved were also assigned a rating (R). The net performance weightage was obtained by multiplying W% by R. After calculating the net result for all areas of performance the total rating points were calculated.

Form B was the "Management Personnel Performance Appraisal Form" and was also known as the Appraisal Record. In addition to basic demographics the form recorded an employee"s performance during the year on issues such as discipline, attendance, positive and negative activities, targets achieved and mid-term review.

The "Review of Personal Performance Form: C" was also filled out by the immediate supervising officer and was shown to the appraisee when completed. The form had 16 performance dimensions that were assigned different weights for different grades, which were represented in column "Weightage." An appraisee was rated on each dimension on a scale having five degrees each. The ratings given were put in column "Performance Rating (a)." To obtain the final rating point performance dimension "weightage" was multiplied with the given "performance rating." Final rating points were added up and divided by 100 to get the final aggregate rating. The number obtained was compared against the Scale for final aggregate rating in performance rating table (for more details see "Performance Rating Table") to get the final rating for performance dimension. This number was put in the requisite box and gave an individual's overall performance rating. Career advancement decisions were made for the individual. A four-member review committee completed the final part of the form.

EXHIBIT 1 Management Appraisal at ARL (B)

ATTOCK REFINERY LIMITED
MANAGEMENT PERSONNEL TARGETS APPRAISAL
FORM – A

(To be filled by the immediate controlling officer and shown to appraisee when completed)

APPRAISAL PERIOD: FROM _____ TO _____

NAME OF EMPLOYEE _____ DESIGNATION _____

SECTION / DEPARTMENT _____

SERVICE NUMBER _____

Sr. No	Area of Performance (1)	Yearly Targets (2)	Weightage (W%) (3)	Verification Criteria (4)	Targets Achieved (5)	Rating (R) (6)	Net Result (W%xR) (7)
1*							
2*							
3*							
4*							
5*							
6*							

Total Rating Points: _____

Weighted Average Rating = Total Rating Points ÷ 100

Signature (Appraisee)   Signature (Section Incharge / Head)   Signature (Department Manager)

WEIGHTED AVERAGE ON ACHIEVEMENT OF TARGETS

Weighted Average Rating $= (W_1\%xR_1+W_2\%xR_2+W_3\%xR_3+W_4\%xR_4+W_5\%xR_5+W_6\%xR_6) \div 100$

NOTE: In case the employee has not achieved the agreed targets or prescribed standards, due to some reason beyond his control, state the reason, which should not affect his overall performance evaluation. In that case the rating of last year shall be treated as the final rating. In-competence or non-cooperation of subordinates and colleagues, increased rate of absenteeism or mere rush of work should not be treated as reasons beyond control.

REMARKS, IF ANY:

_____   _____   _____
Appraisee   Section Incharge/ Head   Department Manager

Source: Company document

EXHIBIT | **1** | Management Appraisal at ARL (B) (*continued*)

NAME _____   SERVICE NUMBER _____

ATTOCK REFINERY LIMITED

ARL

MANAGEMENT PERSONNEL PERFORMANCE APPRAISAL RECORD

FORM-B

NAME OF THE EMPLOYEE   _____

SERVICE NUMBER   _____

DATE OF BIRTH   _____

ACADEMIC QUALIFICATIONS   _____

PREVIOUS EXPERIENCE   _____

DATE OF APPOINTMENT   _____

PRESENT DESIGNATION   _____

DESIGNATION ON APPOINTMENT   _____

DATE OF PROMOTION TO PRESENT POST _____

GRADE   _____

PRESENT BASIC PAY   _____

APPRAISAL RATING IN THE LAST TWO YEARS _____

1.   Performance as observed during the year

    a)   Attendance *   _____
    b)   Discipline *   _____
    c)   Counseling or warnings *   _____
    d)   Other activities (positive) * _____
    e)   Other activities (negative) * _____

2.   Any handicaps beyond control affecting the achievement of targets *_____

3.   Targets achieved *   _____

4.   Steps for the development of the employee taken during the year *_____

5.   Mid-term review *   _____

6.   Other remarks *   _____

DATE   **SIGNATURE**
                                                            (APPRAISER)

EXHIBIT 1 Management Appraisal at ARL (B) *(continued)*

NAME _____ SERVICE NUMBER _____

ATTOCK REFINERY LIMITED

MANAGEMENT PERSONNEL PERFORMANCE APPRAISAL

REVIEW OF PERSONAL PERFORMANCE

FORM - C

To be filled in by immediate controlling officer and shown to the appraisee when completed.

APPRAISAL PERIOD: FROM _____ TO _____

PERSONAL DETAILS

NAME & SERVICE NUMBER		DATE OF BIRTH	QUALIFICATION	YEARS OF EXPERIENCE OUTSIDE THE COMPANY	DATE JOINED COMPANY
JOB TITLE	DEPARTMENT	LOCATION	Date Posted to Present Position	Position Held During Review Period	
			Grade	Present Basic Salary	
Generalist/ Specialist			Date coming to Grade _____	Reports to	

POSITION SUMMARY (JOB DESCRIPTION)

HOW TO FILL THE FORM C:

- Performance dimensions have different weightage for different grades, which are represented in column, 'Weightage'.
- An appraisee will be rated on each dimensions on a scale, each having five degrees.
- Ratings given will be put in column 'Performance Ratings' (a).
- To get the final ratings points multiply performance dimension 'Weightage' with 'Performance Rating' given.
- Add all "Final Rating Points" to get the 'Final Aggregated Rating' and divide by 100.
- Check the 'Final Aggregated Rating Points' at the Scale in Table A to get the Final Rating for Performance dimensions.
- Put the Final Rating in the requisite box.

EXHIBIT **1**   **Management Appraisal at ARL (B)** *(continued)*

NAME _____   SERVICE NUMBER _____

Sr. No.	Performance Dimensions	Weightage (%) Management Grade Levels			Ratings	
		1&2	3&4	4A ≥	Performance (a)	Final Rating Points { (a) x Weightage }
1.	**JOB KNOWLEDGE** Possess knowledge of methods, techniques and skills and conversant with all phases of assigned job and related matters.	10	8	5		
2.	**EFFICIENCY ORIENTATION** Looks for the best use of resources: actively seeks ways to improve current methods, systems, processes and structures, demonstrates deep concern and is judicious with Company's funds, properties and interests, makes productive use of time to meet targeted standard levels.	7	6	5		
3.	**PLANNING & ORGANIZING** Anticipates needs, forecasts conditions, plans, organize and monitors results till completion of tasks assigned.	5	6	7		
4.	**DECISION MAKING** Takes rational, sound and timely decisions based on relevant information and facts.	4	6	7		
5.	**DEPENDABILITY** Carries out commitments and obligations of his position efficiently, expeditiously and honestly, takes quick and effective and reliable decisions after considering available options and their implications.	7	7	7		
6.	**DEVELOPING PEOPLE** Identifies and motivates others to improve their capabilities and standard of performance through training, counseling and job rotation process	5	6	7		
7.	**SAFETY CONSCIOUSNESS** Demonstrates concern for safety and complies with safety standards and requirements while performing duty	7	5	3		
8.	**COMMUNICATION SKILLS** Ability to listen carefully and to present facts and ideas verbally and in written form in clear, effective and convincing manner invoking positive responses.	5	7	10		
9.	**LEADERSHIP** Develops in subordinates the will and desire to work towards a common objective, assigns work to them and keeps track of progress and corrects deviations to achieve the desired goals.	3	7	10		
10.	**INITIATIVE** Does things before being asked to or forced by events and acts at the right time.	10	8	7		
11.	**PROBLEM SOLVING SKILLS** Logically breaking problems down into their essential elements, carrying out diagnosis and developing solutions	8	7	7		
12.	**TEAM SPIRIT** Exhibits team spirit in the performance of his duties to achieve overall common objectives	5	5	5		
13.	**INTERPERSONAL SKILLS** Building persuasive arguments based on logic / merits without hurting feelings of others.	5	5	5		
14.	**ADAPTABILITY** Ability to alter behaviour and opinions in the light of new information and responding constructively to changing situations.	5	5	5		
15.	**INNOVATION** Generates original and imaginative new ideas and suggests solution to problems to achieve improvement in work operations	7	6	5		
16.	**TENACITY** Remains stead fast and maintains stability of performance under pressure and stressful conditions and pursues tasks until completed	7	6	5		
	FINAL AGGREGATED RATING POINTS					

FINAL RATING	Name of the Appraiser _____
	Date _____
	Signature _____

APPRAISEE'S VIEWS

Name of Appraisee _____
Signature _____   Date: _____

EXHIBIT 1   Management Appraisal at ARL (B) (continued)

NAME _____   SERVICE NUMBER _____

PERFORMANCE REVIEW
(To be filled in by the Appraiser)

Given an overall assessment of performance highlighting noteworthy and key performance strengths after taking into consideration achievements against objectives, competency dimensions and any unexpected external / other factors during the year which not covered in the objectives. Indicate achievements as well as areas of improvement. *

DEVELOPMENT NEEDS / PLANS

1. List   the individual's greatest strengths as determined on the basis of overall performance assessment (This will provide an important indication of the direction in which development should be planned) *

2. List   the areas in which the appraisee needs improvement and development. Indicate briefly the step or plans for improvement such as training, job rotation, counseling, special assignments etc. *

3. Has the App   raisee expressed any preference about his career pattern? If so, please state. *

ASSESMENT / RATING POINTS:

- Outstanding   =   1
- Good   =   2
- Above Average   =   3
- Average   =   4
- Below Average   =   5

SUMMARY OF RATINGS

- Rating on performance standards / targets (Form – A)   =
- Rating on dimensions (Form – C)   =
- Final rating [30% (Form A) + 70% (Form C)   =

- Consensus of Average Rating Values)   =
  (Summation of total rating values divided by number
  of raters if more than one person has rated the employee)

PERFORMANCE RATING TABLE

Rating	Abbreviation	Increment Percent (%)	Rating Points	Description	Scale for Final Aggregated Rating
Outstanding	OS	12.5	1	The employee who excel in all aspects of their work	0.50 to 1.49 = 1
Good	G	10	2	The employees who excel in most aspects of their work	1.50 to 2.49 = 2
Above Average	AA	7.5	3	The employees who are qualified, competent and produce quality outputs	2.50 to 3.49 = 3
Average	A	5	4	The employees who meet average standards as to most job requirement but are deficient in the execution of a particular part of the job.	3.50 to 4.49 = 4
Below Average	BA	2.5	5	The employees whose work is unsatisfactory. They can be terminated if despite reasonable opportunity being given have not attained satisfactory work standards.	4.50 to 5.00 = 5

EXHIBIT 1   Management Appraisal at ARL (B) (continued)

NAME _____ SERVICE NUMBER _____

OVERALL PERFORMANCE RATING (To be Tick Marked)

OUTSTANDING - 1	GOOD - 2	ABOVE AVERAGE – 3	AVERAGE - 4	BELOW AVERAGE- 5

1. Is the individual promotable to the next grade or position ahead?

Yes

No

(To be Tick Marked)

Ready Now	1 to 3 Year	4 to 5 Year

POSITION / GRADE:

2. Is there any special impediment to his promotion to the next grade such as age, non-availability of position in the authorized strength, lack of basic qualifications, resistance to accept responsibilities, unwillingness to change work location etc?   _____ _____ _____ _____ _____

3. Does he appear to have the potentials to advance beyond the next position? (To be Tick Marked)

Yes	Can't Judge Now	No

If practicable name the position to which it is believed he has potential to advance.   _____

If the answer is no, state the reason.   _____ _____ _____ _____

REVIEWED BY DEPARTMENT MANAGER

Name of Appraiser: _____
Signature: _____
Date: _____

Name: _____
Designation: _____
Signature: _____
Date: _____

EXHIBIT 1   Management Appraisal at ARL (B) (*continued*)

NAME _____   SERVICE NUMBER _____

FINAL REVIEW AND ASSESSMENT OF APPRAISAL COMMITTEE

FINAL ASSESSMENT:
(To be Tick Marked)

OUTSTANDING- 1	GOOD -2	ABOVE AVERAGE – 3	AVERAGE - 4	BELOW AVERAGE- 5

COMMENTS: *

Signature   Signature   Signature   Signature
(Chairman – Appraisal Committee)   (Member)   (Member)   (Member)

REMARKS: *

Date: _____   **Chief Executive Officer**

The proposed system was implemented in the HR department on a trial basis in January 2000. One of the goals of the proposed system was to provide effective performance feedback to the employees. One of the executives who was on the team that designed the new system was of the view:

The main objective of the new system is to provide the employees proper feedback in terms of what the management wants. It is very important for the employee to know on what basis he has been appraised. Now that the subordinate and the immediate supervisor will jointly set the verification criteria there will not be any problems in terms of what the employee is expected to achieve.

Some managers felt that the new system would highlight employees' weaknesses and improvement needs.

Now we know the objectives an individual is required to achieve. So we have some benchmarks to evaluate him. The management can now pinpoint failures and highlight areas for improvement.

The system was also expected to resolve issues of increments and promotions. According to another manager:

We did not have the criteria against which we could promote someone or give him/her increment. Management had their own reasons for suggesting promotions and increments. Now the managers will have concrete factors for assessing performance and recommending promotions and increments.

One of the executives felt that the proposed system would put the employees in a better bargaining position.

From what I have heard and seen of the new system I feel that by indicating to the top management that these are my training needs, these are my targets, this is how I can contribute to the betterment of the organization I am in a better bargaining position. In the current system the appraisal is quite subjective. Your appraisal really depends on your appraiser's mood, your relationship with him etc. But now with predefined targets we can actually know what we were evaluated against.

It was hoped that by increasing the frequency of appraisals in the new system it would become more objective. Dr. Ilyas, Senior Manager–Technical Services, observed:

It is not fair to appraise someone at the end of the year. So in the new system we have suggested quarterly appraisals, or maybe semi-annual appraisals. This will make the appraisal more objective.

Dr Ilyas also observed that the past performance was a good predictor of future promotions and felt that the proposed appraisal system would permit adequate assessment for growth.

In the Final Analysis

By March 2000, no comprehensive data was available to gauge the extent to which the new performance management system addressed some of the concerns expressed earlier by various people since the new system was being implemented on a limited scale. Mr. Khattak and other senior managers hoped that the proposed system supported the new organizational strategy and would help the company align HR focus with its changing environment.

CASE DISCUSSION QUESTIONS

1. Discuss some of the challenges facing Attock Refinery Limited regarding its performance appraisal system.
2. What are some national culture and social institutional explanations for the performance appraisal challenges discussed in Part A of the case?
3. What are some of the major challenges facing the company as it tries to implement the changes discussed in Part B of the case? How does your discussion of national culture and social institutional factors influence these challenges?
4. What can be done to make the transition to the new system go smoothly?

Argentina Suites: A Case Study

Argentina Suites:
It's not just a facade, It's us!

— from an Argentina Suites brochure which pictures the hotel on the cover and the staff on the inside.

Section One: Background

Origins of Argentina Suites

In the mid-1980s an Argentine businessman went bankrupt before completing construction on a 160-unit apartment building in downtown Buenos Aires, the capital of Argentina. Abraham Sinclair, a wealthy Argentine doctor who had been a U.S. resident for over 30 years, was approached by his nephew, Marcelo, about purchasing the building. Abraham, who had made his fortune in the United States by combining a self-described "knowledge of money, interest in learning, and more than my share of good luck," already owned over 100 apartments in the city. Because of the depressed real estate market, the high inflation rate, and the strength of the U.S. dollar against the Argentine *austral*, Sinclair was able to purchase the 75,000-square-foot building for $900,000, which he believed to be an excellent price. He paid with U.S. currency that his daughter Natalie took from the United States to Argentina in her carry-on bag. She later said that though it would fit in the overhead compartment, she didn't let go of it throughout the entire flight.

What happened next was not clear, as Abraham, Marcelo, and Natalie each claimed to have had the original idea to convert the building into a hotel. It was clear, however, that with no market research, no hospitality experience, and rough financial projections calculated on the back of a coffee shop napkin that was thrown away at the end of the lunch, Abraham decided to enter the hotel business.

The next 18 months were spent making decisions concerning the hotel's development. Marcelo, an architect, was in Buenos Aires overseeing the construction. Natalie, who would be the general manager, split her time between Buenos Aires and a top-ranked business school in Chicago, where she was working on an MBA and staying in hotels whenever possible. Meanwhile, Abraham communicated decisions, solutions, and orders from his car phone in Detroit. He had no interest in acquiring an international franchise, as he felt it would limit his control and reduce profits.

Hotel Operations

The hotel opened in April 1987 with 65 units and a penthouse in the one finished tower. During the later stages of construction, Marcelo had been terminated and banished from the hotel by Abraham for accepting kickbacks and commissions. "But this is the way work is done in Argentina," he had protested upon being fired and not being invited to the grand opening. While Abraham was upset about this, he nevertheless decided that he would continue to employ other family members at the hotel. Natalie objected to this, citing the high rate of family-business failures as reason to go outside the family for department heads. Abraham told her, "Try to work with your relatives."

By 1990 the second tower was finished, and the property received a four-star rating. The hotel consisted of 160 units and average occupancy was 75 percent, most of which was business travelers. There were two 10-story towers and a third 3-story tower all connected by a long and narrow lobby. The hotel also had a restaurant that seated 120 patrons. The total cost of the project, including the purchase price, refurbishing, and furniture, fixtures, and equipment came to almost $3 million. Most offices were housed in a building to maximize revenue-producing space. The hotel had extremely low employee turnover due to the poor job market in Buenos Aires, high salaries, and a relaxed working environment. Natalie finished her MBA and was able to dedicate herself full time to the hotel.

In August 1991, Natalie resigned her position and was replaced by her then 70-year-old uncle, Geraldo. For the next several years, the hotel essentially operated without a general manager. Geraldo's role was more of a figurehead, which kept Monica, the head of marketing, and Maria, the head of administration, from battling for the official head position and office. Maria, Monica, and Coqui, head of personnel, ran the hotel, each overseeing different aspects of the operation and making the major decisions that were communicated to Geraldo for his authorization. It was a comfortable place for them since no one was watching what they did, no one was told what to do, and no one critiqued their work except for Abraham on his bimonthly visits, They were paid much more than they could have earned in any other company, worked the hours they wanted, made all the decisions, and had 100 employees working for them.

During the next several years, the city's hotel market changed considerably as the first new hotels in 20 years were built. (See Exhibit 1 for information regarding Argentina's hotel and tourism industries.)

Several five-star hotels had opened, including an Inter-Continental, a Park Hyatt, and a Caesar Park. Many international companies, including Marriott and Holiday Inn, had taken over management contracts at other well-established upscale hotels. In addition, Choice Hotels, Days Inn, and Radisson had recently announced plans to franchise hotels all over the country. Several four-star properties were also rumored to be under construction, including a Hampton Inn, an Embassy Suites, and a Hilton property. The 800-room Sheraton Hotel, built in 1973, was undergoing a major renovation and an expansion to include an additional 200-room luxury tower. All of these companies had sophisticated reservations and property management systems. This development was accompanied by an infusion of expatriate talent with expertise in management, marketing, and information technology. At the same time, there was an increase in international business travelers, and service quality was becoming a major competitive issue. Abraham's son, Max, returned to Argentina Suites as competition in the hotel market was intensifying. At 27, Max was several years younger than his sister Natalie.

The Return of Max

Max was very familiar with Argentina Suites. He had spent nearly four years, off and on, running its restaurant, and before that had worked in several other areas of the hotel. In 1994, he left Buenos Aires in order to pursue a master's

EXHIBIT   1   General Travel and Tourism Statistics: 1983–1993

Year	Tourism Receipts (US$ m)	Tourism Receipts as a Percentage of Total GDP	Visitor Arrivals from Contiguous Countries (000)	Visitor Arrivals from Other Countries (000)
1983	909	10.4	988	325
1984	1,127	12.2	1,286	323
1985	1,047	11.1	1,238	265
1986	1,129	14.1	1,419	356
1987	1,181	15.7	1,517	326
1988	1,384	13.2	1,612	507
1989	1,671	14.9	1,973	519
1990	1,976	13.8	2,117	612
1991	2,336	16.3	2,182	689
1992	3,090	20.2	2,204	827
1993	3,614	21.6	2,558	975
% Change 1983/93	297.6	—	159%	200%

Source: State Secretariat of Tourism.

Number of Hotels and Hotel Rooms by Main Location: 1995

	3-Star	4-Star	5-Star	Apart-Hotel
Number of Hotels				
Buenos Aries	292	53	10	27
Rest of Country	221	75	10	110
Number of Rooms				
Buenos Aires	7,474	5,215	2,657	1,645
Rest of Country	9,388	5,070	1,435	1,146

Source: State Secretariat of Tourism.

degree in hospitality management in the United States. Now, following graduation, he was returning to Buenos Aires to manage Argentina Suites even though he had in the past repeatedly rejected his father's request to do so. He realized that running Argentina Suites was the perfect opportunity to put his education into practice, especially because he understood its problems and would have the necessary ability and authority to fix them. He was willing to commit to one year, but he expected the work would occupy two years. At the most he would stay three.

Upon his arrival, Max realized he was very emotionally attached to the hotel and its employees. He began to feel a desire not only to understand, analyze, and manage the property but, for the first time, to make it a better place to stay, work, and own.

Max began to ask questions. He was able to obtain a consolidated income statement for the last several years from Monica, but was uncertain of its accuracy (see Exhibit 2, p. 562). When he asked her why energy costs, as a percentage of sales, had doubled since 1992, she said, "In the past, we secretly tapped into external power lines so that most of our energy was received without the accompanying cost." Max learned that when the nation's utility companies

EXHIBIT **2**   Edificio Argentina Consolidated Income Statements 1991–1995

	1991	1992	1993	1994	1995
Occupancy	73.0%	74.5%	83.0%	73.3%	73.2%
Average Daily Rate	$58.75	$86.47	$91.27	$105.00	$107.19
Revenue					
Rooms	$2,380,060	$3,560,354	$4,190,278	$4,236,737	$4,210,147
Food and Beverage	n/a	835,139	903,349	859,225	774,195
Telephone	249,510	375,367	483,961	534,820	500,784
Minor Operated Departments	111,822	174,253	180,024	147,542	136,996
Rental and Other Income	44,269	71,783	52,437	60,623	48,312
Total Revenue	$2,785,661	$5,016,896	$5,810,049	$5,838,947	$5,670,434
Departmental Expenses					
Rooms	$352,142	$507,855	$614,369	$738,708	$771,763
F&B	0	778,185	909,129	842,545	813,323
Telephone	0	0	0	0	0
Other Departmental Expenses	63,062	90,948	110,023	132,290	138,209
Total Departmental Expenses	$415,204	$1,376,988	$1,633,521	$1,713,543	$1,723,295
Total Departmental Profit	$2,370,457	$3,639,908	$4,176,528	$4,125,404	$3,947,139
Undistributed Operating Expenses					
Administration and General	$263,280	$379,700	$459,336	$552,297	$577,011
Marketing	58,544	84,432	102,140	122,811	128,307
Energy	0	0	0	0	0
Property Operations and Maintenance	129,527	186,803	225,981	271,716	283,875
Total Undistributed Operating Expenses	$451,351	$650,935	$787,457	$946,824	$989,193
Gross Operating Profit	$1,919,106	$2,988,973	$3,389,071	$3,178,580	$2,957,946
Income before Fixed Charges					
Value-Added Tax	$147,191	$253,779	$348,686	$300,969	$356,599
Brute Sales Tax (3% of Sales)	42,212	85,534	112,247	112,482	102,305
Property Taxes	46,235	56,001	55,821	55,229	53,884
Insurance	24,610	0	0	0	0
Reserve for Replacement	0	0	0	0	0
Avail. for Debt Service and Other Fixed Charges	0	0	0	0	0
Total Fixed Charges	$260,248	$395,314	$516,754	$468,680	$512,768
Net Operating Income	$1,658,858	$2,593,659	$2,872,317	$2,079,900	$2,445,158

were privatized in 1994, the new company detected that Argentina Suites was diverting electricity from its neighbors without charge, and the hotel received a fine equal to one year's energy usage. Since then, they had paid the appropriate amount each month.

Max was also informed of another scandal, this one involving the hotel and the country's Internal Revenue Service (DGI). Argentina Suites' accountant,

Osvaldo Olivera, had been altering bills for the past year or so. He did this by changing handwritten bills so that, for example, a $1,000 bill became a bill for $4,000. This allowed him to increase reported expenses and therefore decrease taxes. Monica assured Max that Olivera had undertaken this on his own, only letting Monica know about it several months after he had begun. Abraham had been notified when, a few months later, the DGI caught on when they detected an obviously changed bill and began an intense investigation/audit of the hotel.

This situation was partially rectified when the lawyer, Mario Boca, brought in several associates who arranged for the DGI to stop the investigation and clear the hotel of any wrongdoing. A fee of $300,000 was paid in exchange for consulting services. One year later, however, the DGI "pardon" had not been given. Mario said that they were asking for another $50,000.

Before taking any major action, Max wanted to spend some time observing the work processes and procedures currently in place. In the front office, he noted that reservations were taken by telephone and written in duplicate using carbon paper. No one seemed to understand why different companies and different individuals within companies received different rates. He also found that the guest history system consisted of individual registration cards that were stapled to the reservation sheet each time a guest returned to the hotel. These cards were often lost. In addition, the hotel had two computer systems—one for handling room inventory and one for handling guest information. There was no interface between the systems.

During his first week, Max caught a thief. Breakfast was included in the room rate for many guests, and the hotel compensated the restaurant for those guests who ate in the restaurant. When he reviewed past records, Max realized that the restaurant had billed the hotel for 100 percent of these clients although he knew that only 75 percent of them actually consumed breakfast. The assistant controller had been embezzling the other 25 percent for months and was immediately terminated; he refused to reveal the identity of his accomplices.

Curious about what roles the family management staff thought they played, Max asked them to write job descriptions. Maria told him that an American consultant hired by his father six months ago had had them write down their duties and responsibilities, but nothing had been done with this information. He did, however, create an organizational chart for the year 1995. (See Exhibit 3, p. 564). His father later told Max that he had met "the consultant," a controller for an eight-property midwestern hotel chain, on a ski lift in Aspen, and had asked him for an analysis of his hotel. Abraham had not been very pleased with the quality of the report. Max read each job description and decided to meet with each department head independently.

Section Two: Meetings with the Department Heads

Geraldo: General Manager

Geraldo Rabin, one of Abraham's brothers-in-law, was a former businessman. Because of his age, Abraham believed he would be a good authority figure. Geraldo said, "Our hotel needs a major renovation if we want to keep our clients from going to the new, more luxurious hotels." In fact, Geraldo, Maria, and Truco, the head of maintenance, had begun this process. They were replacing the 190 air conditioners, changing the wallpaper in 30 rooms, replacing

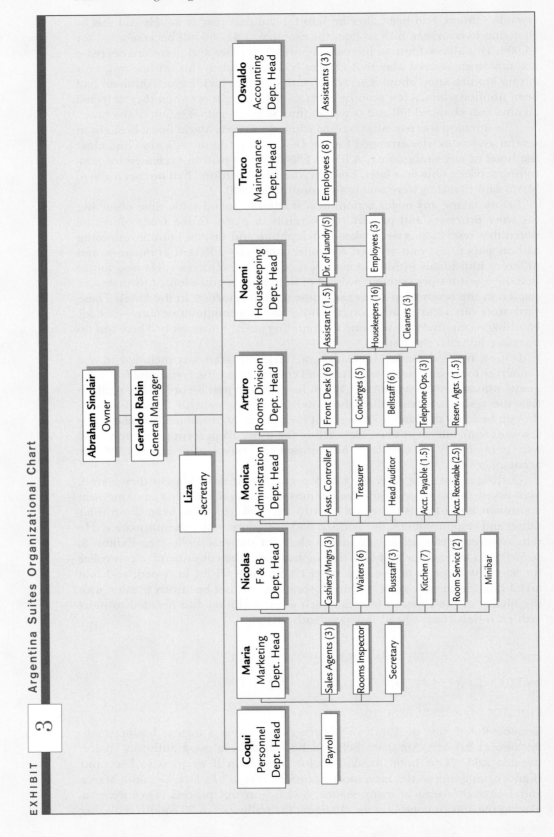

EXHIBIT 3   Argentina Suites Organizational Chart

Abraham Sinclair Owner

Geraldo Rabin General Manager

Liza Secretary

Coqui Personnel Dept. Head
- Payroll

Maria Marketing Dept. Head
- Sales Agents (3)
- Rooms Inspector
- Secretary

Nicolas F & B Dept. Head
- Cashiers/Mngrs (3)
- Waiters (6)
- Busstaff (3)
- Kitchen (7)
- Room Service (2)
- Minibar

Monica Administration Dept. Head
- Asst. Controller
- Treasurer
- Head Auditor
- Acct. Payable (1.5)
- Acct. Receivable (2.5)

Arturo Rooms Division Dept. Head
- Front Desk (6)
- Concierges (5)
- Bellstaff (6)
- Telephone Ops. (3)
- Reserv. Agts. (1.5)

Noemi Housekeeping Dept. Head
- Assistant (1.5)
- Dir. of Laundry (5)
- Employees (3)
- Housekeepers (16)
- Cleaners (3)

Truco Maintenance Dept. Head
- Employees (8)

Osvaldo Accounting Dept. Head
- Assistants (3)

the carpet in another 20 rooms, carpeting the hallways for the first time in order to improve the building's appearance and status, changing the light fixtures in the rooms where wallpaper was being replaced, and remodeling the lobby. Max listened, then asked for estimated prices for each change. The total was almost $500,000. This sum had neither been previously tallied nor were changes prioritized. They had prices for the air conditioners, but, according to Geraldo, they did not need to establish firm prices with the manufacturer of the wallpaper and carpet because, "The owner is a former business contact of mine, and we are always able to come to some agreement."

Liza: Executive secretary

Liza, Abraham's distant second cousin whom he hadn't seen in over 20 years, was Geraldo's secretary. She explained to Max that she had been trained to use the telex and facsimile machines. She also acted as hostess for the Thursday night happy hours. Her daughters, ages 15 and 17, worked in the concierge and bell stations.

Coqui: Head of Personnel

Coqui, son of a sister to whom Abraham had been estranged for 35 years, was named head of personnel. Abraham thought that this would largely be a paperwork role since Monica and Maria seemed to do the hiring, training, and managing of the staff. Geraldo had recommended Coqui for the job because he thought that Coqui's tough personality would help keep the employees in line. Because he had experience in sales, Abraham said he could help Maria in that department as well.

When Max asked about front office operations, Coqui responded, "Arturo is in charge of this area now. Your father ordered it last time he was here. I have no problem with that. I used to involve myself in the area because no one told me not to, and because Arturo doesn't have the character to be in charge. His personnel don't respect him or the rules. I've tried to force them to do what they're supposed to, but your sister spoiled them a lot and they won't change and it would be too expensive to fire all of them."

Max knew that a dismissed employee was entitled to one month's salary for every year employed, plus two months' salary as a bonus. Since the hotel had experienced very low turnover over the past eight years, this translated into an average of $10,000 for each employee.

Coqui also explained that while most employees were legally employed, there were still some employees that were in black (paid under the table), He said that while it was true that the government had begun to crack down on this behavior, "I have some friends in high places who usually keep these officials from inspecting our labor records."

"I've also started cutting costs," he said. "Like Noemi wants a 16th maid. She doesn't need that many; she knows that they're lazy and could clean more rooms. If it weren't for me we would spend a lot more money on unnecessary things and people. Since I've been overseeing maintenance and housekeeping, we've kept costs under control."

Maria: Head of Marketing

Marcelo's 40-year-old sister Maria, also an architect, was named head of marketing by Abraham. He believed that she was the right person for such a position because she was rather pretty, could be charming, had an outgoing, extroverted personality, and could carry on conversations with the American and Argentine businesspeople who were expected to be the hotel's primary clientele. Maria included the following activities among her 37 responsibilities:

1. caring about and loving the hotel
2. decorating and inspecting the hotel
3. establishing new business contacts
4. designing and purchasing employee uniforms
5. representing the hotel at international travel fairs
6. determining appropriate corporate and agency rates
7. public relations
8. personally linking the reservations and front desk departments

Max asked her about linking the reservations and front office departments. She said, "I do this, and I'm told that it's a good thing because I am able to modify rates and room designations on the spot because I know the companies and agencies using the hotel, our occupancy and rates, and because no one else understands the rate structure."

When Max asked her why there was not a clearer, more understandable rate structure, she said, "We never wanted too many people involved in this area." Maria was unable to produce an accurate profile of the hotel's primary customer base. She said that most were businesspeople from Argentina and the United States and stayed an average of 10 days. She also said that 50 percent of the guests in the hotel at any one time had stayed there previously. When Max asked if she could show him this using hotel statistics, she said that she could not because there was no computer program that kept track of such information.

"I'll try and find out how many new companies and travel agencies we've begun working with during the past five years if you want," she said. "I do know, however, that we still work with more than 90 percent of the ones we had before then. It's tough for me now that I fired 4 of my 5 girls. Remember, your father made me cut down on my staff."

She noted that one of her major concerns was the reservations agent, Patricia, who had had the position for over five years and had previously worked with Maria in the marketing department. Maria said that there was not any work done before 9 A.M. and that she thought Patricia should work from 9 to 5.

Patricia, however, thought that she could accomplish some tasks before 9 A.M., when the phones began ringing steadily. Patricia, and several front desk clerks, told Max that Maria wanted Patricia to come in at 9 A.M. because this way Maria, who usually arrived just before 9 A.M., could be the first to review the day's reservations and thus take a more important role in the area. They also said that Maria, who had personal troubles, was jealous of Patricia's happy marriage and home life.

Maria also asked Max to make sure his father didn't change the fact that the marketing department had two offices, one for her and one for her assistants, "Two offices command more respect and look more professional," she said.

Nicolas Fangio: Head of Food and Beverage

Nicolas Fangio, Monica's husband and a former bank employee, was now in charge of food and beverage. For the past two years, the hotel had leased out the restaurant, taking a percentage of profits in exchange for rent. Abraham had recently decided that the hotel was doing well enough to concentrate some effort in running the restaurant, and he had come up with a concept and name that he thought would work well. The family joked that owning a hotel was no longer enough, that Abraham wanted a good restaurant in which to entertain his family and friends.

The restaurant had originally been a mid-scale concept that offered decent food at slightly higher-than-average prices. Abraham's idea for the restaurant entailed many changes. He wanted to call the restaurant *Napoleon's* after the famous New York City steak house. This restaurant had a famous advertising campaign that said

> Only six restaurants in the world
> can prepare a perfect steak.
> Four are in Argentina.

Abraham believed that people would assume that his restaurant was one of the four. In order to resemble Napoleon's, $60,000 was invested in Italian marble and expensive wood, and fine china and glassware were purchased. The best meat available was used, and prices were high. An average meal, excluding wine, was $40; it had formerly cost about $10 to eat in the restaurant. When asked about the operations of the restaurant, Nicolas had little to say and deferred to Max on every issue.

Monica: Head of Administration

Another of Abraham's nieces, 40-year-old Monica, daughter of a deceased older brother whom Abraham had worshipped like a father, was named head of administration because of her accounting background. Monica had been working for Abraham for several years, managing his different real estate investments. Abraham believed it was a logical step for her to extend this role into controlling the finances of the hotel, especially since she was one of the few people that he fully trusted. He once said, in a somewhat joking manner, "Monica isn't smart enough to steel from me and get away with it."

"I know the administration department could use some changes," Monica admitted. "But I can't do this until the front office and marketing areas change. They make so many mistakes that we can't catch them all. Maria says that I have too many employees, but there's a lot more work here than she realizes. This isn't the United States, don't forget. We still have to call all our corporate and travel agent clients and pressure them to pay, and then when they do pay, we have to go over to their office and collect the cash. I am good, however, at making sure we don't pay our suppliers until the last possible minute and thereby control our cash better. And remember, in addition to running the hotel's administration department, I also manage your father's other real estate investments out of this office."

Arturo: Head of Rooms Division

Arturo was hired by Natalie when he was working as a front desk clerk at the nearby Sheraton Hotel. He was very good with guests but seemed to have little authority over his subordinates. As Max approached, he noticed Arturo smoking in the reservations area even though there was a large sign behind him that said:

> No Smoking. By order of the General Manager.

When questioned by Max, Arturo seemed unhappy. "I'd like to be given additional responsibilities, such as forecasting occupancy, room designation, and establishing a yield management policy," he said. "I'm supposed to be in charge of the front desk clerks, concierges, bellboys and, I think, reservations. But I'm not really in charge because Coqui, Maria, and Monica don't let me. They don't let me oversee the area or its employees. Please don't tell them I said that."

Noemi: Head of Housekeeping

Noemi, who had been at the hotel since shortly after its opening, said she was treated badly and felt unappreciated by the family. "I know I should spend more time on the floors checking the girls' cleaning, and I've started to do this more. But I need another housekeeper and they won't give me one. Coqui thinks that because he schedules my girls' shifts and days off, he knows what goes on here."

Truco: Head of Maintenance

Truco had been with Argentina Suites since construction began in 1985, He described several projects he would like to begin working on. Max asked for detailed plans including estimated prices, since he had been hearing rumors for years that Truco regularly received kickbacks and/or commissions on purchases and projects, though he had never seen any concrete proof. Truco said "I could arrange for this," and also mentioned that he had begun working part-time at a nearby retirement home since Coqui denied him a raise.

Osvaldo Olivera: Head of Accounting

Osvaldo, a former clothes salesman and Abraham's ex-wife's brother, was hired as head of accounting. His responsibilities were to control the amount of cash, credit card slips, and checks that entered or left the front office. He also checked the receptionist's cash box to ensure it equaled sales and/or expenses.

Olivera said he was looking forward to the installation of a computer system and agreed with Max that the hotel needed to include a statement of cash flow. "I need Monica to help me," he said. "She's the only one that knows where information is kept around here, and she slows me down. Do you think you could mention this to your father for me?"

Abraham had told Max recently that he would like to fire Olivera because he was very expensive. "His carelessness cost me three or four hundred thousand dollars."

Section Three: The Current Situation

Site Inspection

Max toured the hotel with Truco, Noemi, and Maria. They saw sinks with chipped enamel around the drain, loose light fixtures, the same painting hanging twice in the same room, mirrors hung too low, leaking faucets, flimsy mattresses, and creaking doors. Max noticed, for the first time, that every room had different carpet, wallpaper, bedspreads, chair fabrics, and other decorative pieces. Maria said this was a positive point. "When a guest comes to the hotel several times he likes to have a different looking room. If all the rooms were the same, he would get bored and perhaps go to another hotel."

"But don't you think a guest likes to know what to expect from his room?" Max asked,

"No, I don't think so. They like surprises, not knowing what to expect."

They showed him how they painted wallpaper when it began to deteriorate. This coat lasted two years after which it was painted again. They were very proud of how this system made the paper last from 5 to 6 years rather than 2 years. Geraldo's manufacturing friend no longer carried this wallpaper, but Maria had found some new wallpaper that she thought was very attractive. Max pointed out how it didn't match the new, blue carpet they had selected. She told him that it wasn't for those rooms but for the ones with gray carpet. He asked them if the paper could be painted when it began to look bad and they responded that it couldn't because of its glossy finish.

Truco also pointed out that there was no central fire/smoke detecting system. The sprinkler heads were simply glued onto the ceiling for appearance, and individual smoke detectors were present only in the hallways. Max knew that Argentine law did not require apartment buildings to have centralized fire/smoke systems, and that if it did, Argentina Suites would have found some way around this.

Next they turned their attention to the air conditioners which, for the most part, were the original ones installed eight years ago when the hotel opened. Max agreed with them that the air conditioners were too loud and did a poor job of cooling the rooms (and heating them in winter). Worse yet, they also informed him that the apartment building next door had a tenant who had filed a complaint with the city because of the noise, and that this had to be resolved somehow. To replace them would cost $1,000 each, and 190 would eventually be needed, Geraldo believed that 60 new ones were needed urgently, and the others could last 3 more months, Max asked if the 60 were to replace the ones in the rooms near the tenant who had complained. Only a few were; the rest were for the VIP rooms that were scattered around the hotel.

Maria suggested that more of the rooms be converted to VIP status. These were the larger rooms and had slightly nicer bathrooms. Max asked if there had been a study done on the actual prices that were paid for these rooms. There had not. Max knew that these VIP rooms were often used as "upgrades" for important companies or regular customers. He was not opposed to this, but he wondered if the investment was worth it given that they didn't know the effect on revenue.

Conversations with Employees

Max also spent time talking with some of the employees he had known before, as well as the few that had been hired in the last two years. They told him that the clientele had changed substantially in the last few years. American CEOs had begun to stay in the nearby more luxurious hotels, and lower level executives were the ones who now stayed at Argentina Suites. Max wondered if the restaurant, laundry, and telephone service were too expensive for these guests. They also showed Max how the employee dining room was falling apart and their bathrooms, which did not have doors between the stalls, were poorly lit, and had mold between the cracks in the tile.

However, as much as Max liked most of these employees, and believed they needed to be respected, he considered a lot of their actions to be unprofessional:

1. bellboys drinking soda in the lobby
2. employees with long hair and/or goatees
3. telephone operator smoking at her station

4. Coqui's assistant regularly wearing jeans
5. employees using the guest bathrooms on the lobby floor
6. assistant reservation agent, Geraldo's granddaughter, in street clothes in the hotel
7. employees ordering drinks, coffee, and snacks from the restaurant
8. employees regularly leaving their posts unattended
9. concierges sitting in chairs, almost hidden behind their desks
10. the entire front of the hotel, including the concierge desk and bellboy station, occasionally left unattended
11. guests opening the elevator and front door by themselves
12. evening front desk clerk and security guard playing cards

Conclusion

Max understood the larger context within which the hotel operated. The situation in Argentina was somewhat unique but in many ways similar to the business climate in Central and South America. The regional practices that had been acceptable and successful in the past, such as graft and nepotism, could not be continued successfully in the rapidly evolving and much more competitive multinational environment. Government policies were also changing to assure that businesses were run legitimately. In addition, technological change was posing a great threat to those companies that did not keep up.

Even with all its challenges, Max recognized that the hotel had some charm, and something about it worked well enough to attract a consistent set of clients. He could not dismiss the fact that the hotel's occupancy had not fallen even with the additional rooms in the city, and that its average daily rate (ADR) had even risen slightly, He believed that one reason for this was that the guests liked the customized, friendly service they received. Because the hotel had low employee turnover, many of the guests were on a first-name basis with them, and Max knew that they often brought gifts for the employees. Max also had seen some guest comment cards mentioning how they always looked forward to their stay at the Suites. Despite the positives, however, the hotel had many problems, and solving them would require many changes. The hotel was doing "fine" but Max felt that it could not maintain this performance long into the future if it continued to be operated in this archaic, inefficient, and unethical manner.

Max needed to convince both his father and his relatives that changes could benefit them all. Owning the hotel was largely an issue of ego with Abraham, yet he expected to profit from his investment. Max needed to prove that his modern management philosophy was in the best interest of everyone. He knew that running Argentina Suites would be a challenging test; the question was where to begin.

CASE DISCUSSION QUESTIONS

1. What are some of the major problems facing Argentina Suites? Identify cultural and social institutional factors explaining these challenges and the current business environment at Argentina Suites.

2. What recommendations would you make to Max to address the most critical problems? How can you make sure that the changes do not hurt the motivation of employees?

3. Should Max adopt any particular leadership style as he implements such changes? What problems should he expect?

4. What changes should Max implement to encourage an atmosphere of honesty, trust and ethical behavior?

CASE CREDIT

Strategy Implementation for Multinational Companies: Interaction Processes

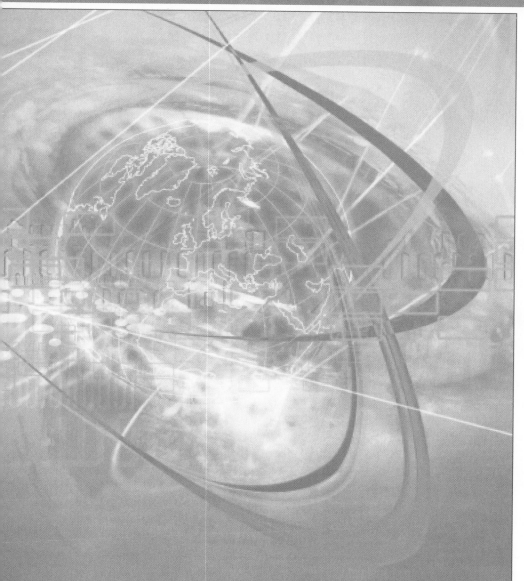

International Negotiation and Cross-Cultural Communication

13

Learning Objectives

After reading this chapter you should be able to:

- Understand the basics of verbal and nonverbal communication that may influence cross-cultural management and negotiation.

- Understand the basic international negotiation processes from preparation to closing the deal.

- Understand the basic tactics of international negotiation.

- Recognize and respond to "dirty tricks" in international negotiations.

- Know the differences between the problem-solving and competitive approaches to international negotiation.

- Identify the personal characteristics of the successful international negotiator.

Preview CASE IN POINT

Deals that Failed

When Kiel AG, a Swiss multinational conglomerate, discovered Georgia-based Edwards Engineering Inc. (EEI) for sale, Kiel's management felt that they had found the right company to acquire in the United States. There was a construction boom in the southeastern United States that Kiel viewed as a strategic opportunity. Moreover, EEI was a successful company, whose founder, Tom Edwards, was close to retirement and willing to sell.

Kiel made an initial offer close to the asking price, and the outlook for the purchase looked positive. Kiel president Herbert Kiel even came to the United States to conduct the negotiations personally. However, after four difficult days of negotiations, the Kiel team went home and talks ended.

What happened? In a typical U.S. American way, Edwards was open and friendly in the negotiations. He was eager to sell the business. He was direct and forthright about the strengths and weaknesses of his business. He made every effort to provide information requested and to adjust his proposals to Kiel's positions. But the U.S. style didn't work.

Edwards confused the Swiss. They approached the negotiations in a formal and measured way. They perceived Edwards' openness as dangerous and untrustworthy. They responded by asking to review documents and by hiring a major U.S. accounting firm to audit the EEI books. Edwards, on the other hand, found the audit insulting and time consuming. He was annoyed by Kiel's continuously polite but unresponsive answers to his proposals. Ultimately, neither side played the negotiation game the way the other expected. Distrust grew, and an otherwise good deal ended in failure.

Similarly, when Lee Iacocca was running Ford Motor Co., Ford made an attempt to buy Ferrari. The top executives at Ford went to personally meet Enzo Ferrari and came to an understanding that Ford would acquire the production side of the company so that it could use the name in the United States. The deal was then concluded with a handshake. Later, a team of Ford attorneys was sent to Italy with contracts to formalize the deal. However, Enzo Ferrari was disappointed with Ford as he expected that they had a "gentleman's" agreement—not an agreement with lawyers. Not surprisingly, the deal was voided.

Sources: Based on Bryan, Robert M., and Peter C. Buck. 1989. "When customs collide: The pitfalls of international acquisitions." Financial Executive 5: pp. 43–46; Goman, Carol Kinsey. 2002. "Cross-cultural business practices." Communication World, February–March, pp. 22–25; Copeland, L., and L. Griggs. 1985. Going International. New York: Random House; Whately, Arthur. 1994. "International negotiation case." In Management International, edited by Dorothy Marcic and Sheila Puffer, pp. 73–74. St. Paul: West.

International negotiation is the process of making business deals across national and cultural boundaries. International negotiation precedes any multinational business project. However, as we have just seen in the Preview Case in Point, without successful negotiation and the accompanying cross-cultural communication, there are seldom successful business transactions. The importance of proper negotiation is even more pronounced as many argue that nowhere do U.S. Americans pay more dearly for cross-cultural ignorance than in international negotiations.[1]

Consider some of the following examples where the successful outcome of the business opportunity depends on successful international negotiations. Companies that sell overseas must negotiate with foreign distributors and sales organizations. Companies that participate in international joint ventures must negotiate a contact to establish the alliance. Companies that receive raw materials from international sources must negotiate with local suppliers to provide raw materials at an acceptable cost. Companies that set up manufacturing operations in other countries often must negotiate with foreign governments to get necessary permissions. Finally, as in this chapter's Preview Case in Point, companies that wish to acquire businesses in other countries must negotiate successfully with the current owners.

As the world's market becomes increasingly global, U.S companies will need to become more adept at conducting international negotiations. Consider for example the possibility that the economic "center of gravity" of the world markets is going to shift to the emerging markets of China, Brazil, Turkey, India, and Mexico over the next 20 years.[2] These countries also are expected to show strong technology-driven growth and provide major opportunities for U.S. organizations. However, given the significant cultural differences between the United States and these countries, understanding how these differences affect international negotiations is increasingly crucial if the United States wants to take advantage of such opportunities.

This chapter provides a survey of the basic processes that guide international negotiation: successful preparation, building relationships with foreign partners, using persuasion tactics, gaining concessions, and reaching a final agreement. We will also consider how to identify and avoid the common "dirty tricks" of negotiators and what personal characteristics make a good international negotiator.

Successful communication across cultures is a prerequisite for international negotiation and for managing people from other cultures. Consequently, to identify some of the pitfalls of cross-cultural communication in negotiations and in cross-cultural management, the first section of this chapter provides a summary of important cross-cultural communication issues. After reading this first section, you will better understand the communication challenges involved in cross-cultural negotiation.

The Basics of Cross-Cultural Communication

Successful negotiation requires successful communication. Thus, successful international negotiation requires successful cross-cultural communication. Negotiators must understand (or have interpreted) not only the written and oral language of their counterparts but also other components of culturally different communication styles. Mistakes in cross-cultural communication often go unnoticed by the communicator, but these mistakes can do damage to international relationships and negotiations. Mistakes or misinterpretations of the subtle gestures of hand and face, the use of silence, what is said or not said, and the intricacies of dealing with age and status often prove pitfalls for the multinational businessperson.

To help you negotiate and communicate more successfully in your role as a multinational manager, we will review some of the major issues in cross-cultural communication. These include the relationship between language and culture, differences between high and low context cultures, cultural differences in communication styles, nonverbal communication through body movements and the use of personal space, when and how to use interpreters, how to speak to nonnative speakers of your language, and how to avoid cross-cultural communication errors based on faulty attributions.

Language and Culture

There are approximately 3,000 basic languages in the world, with many dialects.[3] Language is so essential to culture that many consider linguistic groups synonymous with cultural groups. Multinational managers should also note that many countries—Canada and Belgium, for example—have more than one national language. Even within political boundaries, these national languages often represent quite diverse cultural groups regarding communication and negotiation styles. In addition, the choice of the wrong language may touch on areas of extreme cultural sensitivity.

The interrelationship between language and culture is so strong that some experts suggest that a society's language determines the nature of its culture. This is known as the **Whorf hypothesis,** developed by the anthropologist and linguist Benjamin Lee Whorf.[4] Whorf argued that words provide the concepts for understanding the world. According to Whorf, all languages have limited sets of words. These restricted word sets, in turn, constrain the ability of the users to understand or conceptualize the world. Since language structures the way we think about what we see, it determines cultural patterns.

In his famous and, at the time, futuristic novel *1984*, George Orwell used Whorf's premise that those who controlled the available vocabulary would control the world. Not all experts agree with Whorf, and some argue the opposite. Culture comes first and requires the development of certain concepts and thus certain words. However, no one debates that there is a close interrelationship between language and culture. Most experts agree that the 21st century global leader must

Whorf hypothesis
Theory that language determines the nature of culture.

necessarily have language skills to be able to bridge cultural differences.[5] Consider the following Multinational Management Brief discussing the language pedagogical approach at the University of Pennsylvania's Lauder Institute.

High- and Low-Context Languages

The anthropologist Edward T. Hall[6] identified an important distinction among the world's languages based on whether communication is explicit or implicit. Hall focused on how different cultures use the context or the situation in which communication takes place to understand what people are saying. Languages in which people state things directly and explicitly are called **low context**. The words provide most of the meaning. You do not have to understand the situation in which the words are used. Languages in which people state things indirectly and implicitly are called **high context**. In the high-context language, communications have multiple meanings that one can interpret only by reading the situation in which the communication occurs. So important are the ideas of high and low context that many people refer to the entire culture as being high or low context.

Most Northern European languages, including German, English, and the Scandinavian languages, are low context. People use explicit words to communicate direct meaning. Thus, for example, if a German manager says "Yes," she means "Yes." In addition, most Western cultures attach a positive value to clear and direct communication. This is particularly apparent in negotiations, where low-context languages allow clear statements concerning what a negotiator wants out of the relationship.

In contrast, Asian and Arabic languages are among the most high-context languages in the world. In Asian languages, often what is left unsaid is just as important as what is said. Silent periods and the use of incomplete sentences require a person to interpret what the communicator does not say by reading the situation. Arabic introduces interpretation into the language with an opposite tack. Extensive imprecise verbal and nonverbal communication produces an

Low context language
One in which people state things directly and explicitly.

High context language
One in which people state things indirectly and implicitly.

Multinational Management **Brief**

Language Training

Most experts agree that language skills will become critical in the future to bridge cultural differences. Consider the Lauder Institute of Management's efforts at the University of Pennsylvania. The institute's mission is to provide language and cultural training to prepare future business leaders to bridge cultures. In that context, the Institute allows interested MBA students to earn a double degree: an MBA and an MA in international studies. Students pursue rigorous language training among one of the following eight crucial languages identified by the Institute: Arabic, Chinese, French, German, Japanese, Portuguese, Russian, and Spanish. Furthermore, most programs are experiential and follow the Five Cs (Communication, Culture, Connections, Comparisons, and Communities) in compliance with the National Standards for Foreign Language Learning. As an example, students from the Lauder Institute partnered with French students to study French companies. Feedback from the participants has been generally very positive indicating their improved language skills as well as a better ability to understand the cultures.

Source: Based on Babanoury, Claire. 2005. "Real world business language tasks in action." The Journal of Language for International Business, 16, 2: pp. 13–23; Babanoury, Claire. 2006. "Collaborative company research projects: A blueprint for language, C." The Journal of Language for International Business, 17, 1: pp. 15–28.

interaction where reading the situation is necessary for understanding. Exhibit 13.1 shows a ranking of languages by their degrees of high and low context.

Communication between high- and low-context people is a challenge for multinational operators. Translated words that have explicit meanings to a low-context speaker may have a multitude of meanings to a high-context speaker. For example, Japanese speech is full of words that encourage a speaker to continue and to repeat the message, often in a slightly different way. One of these words, *hai*, literally "yes" in English, means "yes" in the English sense only if other components of the situation also mean "yes." *Hai* can also mean: "Yes, I hear you," "Yes, say it again," "Yes, give me more information," "Yes, please continue with the conversation," or "Yes, I don't really want to say no, but it should be obvious to you that the answer is no." Such difficulties in translation suggest that, when negotiations take place between high- and low-context cultures, it is important that both sides realize that communication may have errors. Moreover, even good translations may require contextual interpretations for effective communication.

Differences in languages that have implications for international negotiations are not limited to high- and low-context languages. Consider the following Case in Point.

EXHIBIT 13.1   Country Differences in High-Context and Low-Context Communication

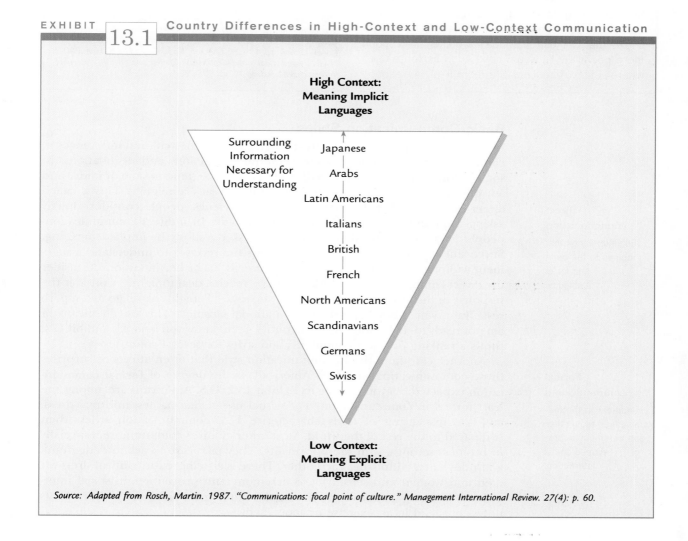

High Context:
Meaning Implicit
Languages

Surrounding Information Necessary for Understanding

Japanese
Arabs
Latin Americans
Italians
British
French
North Americans
Scandinavians
Germans
Swiss

Low Context:
Meaning Explicit
Languages

Source: Adapted from Rosch, Martin. 1987. "Communications: focal point of culture." Management International Review. 27(4): p. 60.

C A S E   I N   P O I N T

Differences between the Chinese and English Languages

As more companies try to take advantage of the tremendous opportunities presented by China, they will also have to deal with the challenges of language comprehension. Almost a quarter of the world's population including Chinese, Japanese, and Korean speakers read logographic characters that represent meanings rather than sound. In contrast, in many other languages such as those using Latin alphabets (English, Spanish), Arabic, and Hindi, the words represent sounds rather than meaning. This difference in reading process has been shown to have important implications for how people remember things or even how they process thoughts.

Such differences have important implications for how U.S. negotiators approach presentations to their Chinese counterparts. For instance, research shows that Chinese individuals are likely to respond more positively to visual cues such as fonts used whereas U.S. Americans are more likely to respond to the speaker's voice. As such, it is important for U.S. negotiators to use as many visual stimuli as they can to make their presentation more effective. Other research also shows that Chinese subjects were more likely to remember brands and to associate brand names with logos when information was presented visually. U.S. negotiators are thus also encouraged to rely on such visual information if they want their Chinese counterparts to remember aspects of their presentation. Instead of focusing on the presentation style of the negotiator, it may be more beneficial to improve the content of the presentation.

Source: Based Kambil, Amit, Victor Wei-the Long, and Clarence Kwan. 2006. "The seven disciplines for venturing in China." MIT Sloan Management Review, Winter, 47, 2: pp. 85–89; Lieberthal, Kenneth, and Geoffrey Lieberthal 2003. "The great transition." Harvard Business Review, October, pp. 13–27; Tavassoli, Nader T., and Jin K. Han. 2002. "Auditory and visual brand identifiers in Chinese and English." Journal of International Marketing, 10, pp. 13–28.

Basic Communication Styles

In addition to high- and low-context language use, other cultural differences in communication can influence cross-cultural interactions and negotiations. In some cultures, people speak very directly. That is, they tend to state opinions and ask questions that come right to the point and lack ambiguity. This is called **direct communication**. In contrast, in some societies, people consider directly asking a question or stating an opinion impolite. In indirect communication, people attempt to state their opinions or ask questions by implied meaning. Successful and polite communication allows the receiver to understand a statement without the communicator stating directly his or her intentions. Consider the direct communicator who asks: "Will we reach a deal tonight?" Consider the response of the indirect communicator who says: "Tonight we will go to a superb restaurant, which best represents our national cuisine." This usually means "I am not ready to do business with you until I get to know you better." Exhibit 13.2 shows a ranking of direct communication styles for several countries.

> **Direct communication**
> Communication that comes to the point and lacks ambiguity.

> **Formal communication**
> Communication that acknowledges rank, titles, and ceremony in prescribed social interaction.

Another cultural trait of communication style that often affects or surprises those communicating with U.S. Americans is the degree of **formal communication** expected. As you can see in Exhibit 13.2, U.S. Americans are among the least formal in communication. The casual use of first names, informal dress, and the dispensing of titles characterize U.S. communication styles when compared to the rest of the world. Most other cultures communicate, especially in business settings, with more formality. They take care to acknowledge rank and titles when addressing each other. There is also more formality of dress for men and women and sensitivity to ceremony and procedures in social interactions. In many countries, for example, adult men never wear short pants unless engaged in an exercise or sports activity.

EXHIBIT **13.2**   **Cultural Differences in Communication Styles**

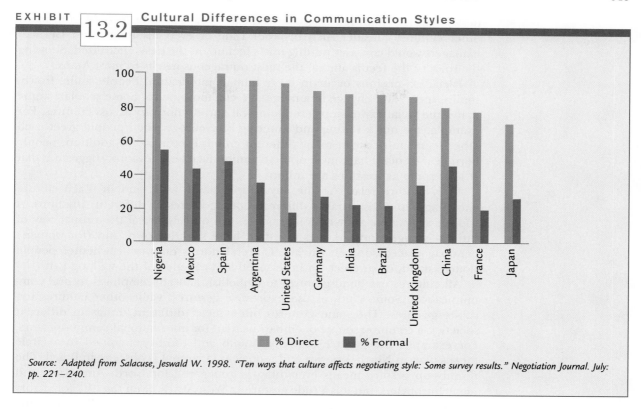

■ % Direct   ■ % Formal

Source: Adapted from Salacuse, Jeswald W. 1998. "Ten ways that culture affects negotiating style: Some survey results." Negotiation Journal. July: pp. 221–240.

At several points, we have noted that communication is more than verbal interaction. The next section provides background on the essential areas of nonverbal communication. Multinational managers and negotiators must be aware of cultural differences in both verbal and nonverbal communications.

Nonverbal Communication

Nonverbal communication means communicating without words. Often it is not necessary to say something orally to communicate with someone. People gesture, they smile, they gaze into another's eyes, they hug, they kiss—they engage in a whole array of behaviors that supplement or enhance spoken communication. The types of nonverbal communication considered here are body movements (called kinesics) and the use of personal space (called proxemics). We also consider forms of communication that rely on senses such as haptics or touching, oculesics (eye contact), and olfactics (smell).

Nonverbal communication
Face-to-face communication that is not oral.

Kinesics

Kinesics means communicating through body movements. Every culture uses body posture, facial expressions, hand gestures, and movement to communicate nonverbally. Most Asian cultures, for example, use bowing to indicate respect for older people or people of higher status. The person of lesser status must bow at a lower angle than the person of higher status.

It is easy to misinterpret the meanings of body movements in another culture. As with oral communication, there is no universal code for what body movements mean in all societies. For example, U.S. Americans communicate a relaxed atmosphere by "putting their feet up." The manager with his or her feet on the

Kinesics
Communication through body movements.

desk is saying, "I am relaxing, and you can, too." However, people from many other cultures consider such behavior rude or even insulting. Most German managers would consider putting one's feet up on the desk uncivilized. Showing the soles of the feet is among the most outrageous insults to most Arabs.[7]

Facial expressions occur in every human interaction. People smile, frown, squint, sneer, and engage in a range of facial movements. Some scholars argue that some facial expressions are biological and do not vary across cultures. For example, the quick raising and lowering of eyebrows when people greet each other seems to occur in many different cultural settings.[8] In addition, people born deaf or blind have most of the common facial expressions, suggesting that at least some expressions are inborn.[9]

Body posture relates to the way people stand, walk, and sit. Each culture encourages and discourages different body postures in different situations. A trip on a Japanese subway, for example, will quickly reveal the proper way of sitting—straight forward, legs together, head slightly down, and (for women) handbag placed squarely on lap. Cultural norms determine whether people slouch, stand, or sit erect, and the speed and cadence of the walking gait.

All cultures use hand gestures to embellish and add emphasis to oral communication. Some cultures use expressive gestures, while other cultures use subtle gestures. The same gestures often mean different things in different societies, a common source of embarrassment for international communicators. For example, the gesture with the thumb and forefinger joined in a circle means okay in North America and money in Japan but is obscene in Brazil. The thumbs-up gesture means everything is going well for North Americans and many Europeans, but it is a rude gesture in West Africa. Even the "V" for victory sign made with two fingers held upward, popularized by the British prime minister, Winston Churchill, during World War II, has a rude meaning for the British and the French if the palm is facing inward. Nodding the head means "Yes" in most of the world, but it means "No" in Bulgaria.[10]

The important point to remember for international negotiators and multinational managers is that it is easy to misinterpret gestures. A safe communication strategy minimizes the use of gestures. You should use only those gestures that you understand well. Eventually, as you get to know a culture better, acceptable and appropriate gestures will become second nature.

Proxemics

Proxemics focuses on how people use space to communicate. According to some experts on communication by space, all the basic senses allow people to perceive and sense differences in space.[11] Sight, smell, hearing, and touch all react to differences in space. Naturally, there are large cultural differences in how people react to the sounds, sights, smells, and personal contact associated with space. Each culture has appropriate distances for various levels of communication, and most people are uncomfortable if those distances are ignored. Violations of space may even be considered offensive.

The personal bubble of space around each individual may range from 9 inches to more than 20 inches. North Americans are most comfortable with 20 inches while groups from Latin and Arab cultures generally prefer a closer spacing. It is not uncommon to see a North American continuously backing up to maintain his or her "comfortable" 20 inches when interacting with someone from the Middle East or Latin America.

Personal space may also affect the design of offices. In the following Multinational Management Brief, the accompanying diagram shows a typical

Multinational Management **Brief**

The Typical Japanese Office

In the typical Japanese office, space is shared so that the workers and managers are all within hearing distance of each other. Unlike the typical U.S. office, the Japanese version has no separate rooms or partitions that divide the work area. Standard office desks are placed back to back and side by side. Workers often share the same phone and computer.

The closeness with colleagues provides a feeling of comfort for the Japanese that many Westerners find unnerving. Unlike most Westerners, the Japanese see no need for privacy during phone conversations or discussions with coworkers, or when concentrating on their work. In the reverse cultural situation, many Japanese salarymen who have expatriate assignments in the United States or Europe find the compartmentalization of buildings very uncomfortable.

The accompanying exhibit shows the layout of a typical Japanese office with the placement of a manager (Kachoo), first-line supervisors, and workers.

Seating in a Typical Japanese Office

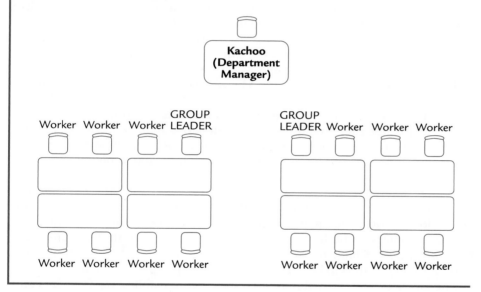

Japanese office, where the desks are in contact and managers work closely together. In contrast, Germans are even more protective of their personal office space than North Americans. They prefer heavy office furniture that people cannot move to get too close and invade their personal space. A German newspaper editor stationed in the United States was highly intolerant of the U.S. American habit of moving chairs closer in certain social situations. He finally reacted by having his visitor's chair bolted to the floor. This kept people at a comfortable and "proper" distance.[12]

Haptics or Touching, Oculesics, and Olfactics

Nonverbal communication also can occur through the various senses such as touching, smelling, and seeing. In that context, **haptics or touching** is communication through body contact. **Oculesics** refers to communication through

Haptics or Touching

Basic form of human interaction, including shaking hands, embracing, or kissing when greeting one another.

Oculesics

Communication through eye contact or gaze.

Olfactics

Use of smells as a means of nonverbal communication.

eye contact or gaze. Finally, olfactics is the use of smells as a means of nonverbal communication.

Haptics or touching is related to proxemics and is a basic form of human interaction. In greeting one another, people may shake hands, embrace, or kiss. In routine interaction, people may touch or pat each other in a variety of ways. The type of touching deemed appropriate is deeply rooted in cultural values. For example, Russian men often kiss other men outside their family as a form of greeting. Brazilian men hug in greeting. Japanese schoolgirls routinely walk holding hands with other girls although touching among strangers is less accepted. In some cultures, people expect a firm handshake, whereas in other cultures, the handshake is limp. Generally, Latin European and Latin American cultures accept more touching than do Germanic, Anglo, or Scandinavian cultures. Axtell[13] has classified the degree of touching among countries into categories such as no touching (e.g., Japan, United States, England, and many Northern European countries), moderate touching (e.g., Australia, China, Ireland, and India), and touching (e.g., Latin American countries, Italy, and Greece).

The degree of comfort with gaze and eye contact or oculesics also shows significant variations around the world. In some countries like the United States and Canada, people are very comfortable and expect eye contact to be maintained for a short moment during conversations. In contrast, in countries like China and Japan, eye contact is considered very rude and disrespectful. In fact, the way to show respect in such societies is by avoiding eye contact. Yet in other societies like France and the Middle East, maintaining eye contact for long periods of time is socially acceptable.

It is important for the negotiators to be aware of a society's degree of comfort with eye contact so that blunders do not occur during negotiations. For instance, it is necessary for U.S. negotiators to know that a prolonged stare from the French is not rude or hostile. Rather, it shows interest in the U.S. negotiators. Similarly, when negotiating with the Chinese, it is important to avoid direct gazing or eye contact so as not to place the Chinese negotiators in an uncomfortable position.

Finally, different countries have different views of smell or olfactics. Societies like the United States and United Kingdom tend to be very uncomfortable with body odors. In fact, U.S. Americans find such body odor offensive and will avoid talking to someone who has body odor. However, in contrast, Arabs are much more accepting of body odors and consider them natural.[14] As such, it is important for negotiators to be aware of such diverse perspectives on the smell and accept and adapt to such differences. Consider the following Case in Point comparing the French and Tunisians on various proxemics.

This section concludes our discussion of some basic forms of nonverbal communication. The following section builds on your knowledge of the cultural differences in communication. It deals with three practical issues in cross-cultural business communications: when to use interpreters, how to speak with someone whose language is not your own, and how to recognize and avoid incorrectly applying your own cultural assumptions to people's motivations.

Practical Issues in Cross-Cultural Business Communication

Cross-cultural negotiations and communications nearly always face a language barrier. One or both sides of the interaction must communicate in a foreign language. The international manager is always at an advantage if he or she speaks more than one language fluently. U.S. Americans are among the worst

C A S E   I N   P O I N T

Proxemics Differences between the French and Tunisians

Dion and Bonnin's study comparing the French and Tunisians provides interesting insights into how different cultures view their body and how they react to crowds. They argue that different cultures have different perceptions of their body. For instance, in more Western societies, people tend to view the body as a very obvious and clearly defined space, surrounded with some form of psychic distance. Body space is very valued and cannot be violated. In contrast, in Arab cultures, the body is considered as an extension of the community. As such, the Arab cultures have a different perception of their body as it does not have as clearly defined physical delineation.

To understand how people react to crowds, the researchers studied about 590 shoppers in two supermarkets located in France and Tunisia. Their findings are in sharp contrast to the common wisdom that different cultures have different preferences for crowds. In fact, they show that both the French and Tunisian shoppers have the same negative reaction to crowds. However, the way both groups react is fascinating. The French shoppers tend to react more aggressively if they perceive that other individuals are within their personal space. In contrast, the Tunisians accept that these intrusions are normal. However, they react psychologically by removing themselves both mentally and physically from the situation.

Source: Based Dion, Delphine, and Gaël Bonnin. 2004. "Une étude comparative des systèmes proxémiques français et tunisiens." Recherche et Applications en Marketing, September 19, 3: pp. 45–60.

when it comes to learning a second language. Europeans, in contrast, are much more likely to be bilingual or multilingual. U.S. businesspeople are fortunate that English is the most common language of business. However, even if English is the local business language and one speaks English, communication and understanding of the local culture always improve if one speaks the local language. As such, an important preparation for any international assignment is gaining at least rudimentary skills in the language of the country.

Using Interpreters

The increasing globalization of business means that the multilingual person is a valuable addition to any company. The following Multinational Management Brief describes the rising need for interpreters for business purposes in the multilingual European Union. With the gradual elimination of restrictions for doing business in Europe, nearly everyone who conducts business in Europe will need to communicate with people who speak another language.

To make sure that all parties understand agreements, international negotiation often requires the use of interpreters. The interpreter's role is to provide a simultaneous translation of a foreign language while a person speaks. This requires greater linguistic skills than speaking a language or translating written documents. Good interpreters not only are bilingual, but also have the technical knowledge and vocabulary to deal with technical details common in business transactions.

> **Interpreter's role**
> To ensure the accuracy and common understanding of written and oral agreements.

Even if some of the negotiators understand or speak both languages, it is often a good idea to use interpreters. It detracts from a team member's negotiation task if he or she must also serve as the negotiation team's interpreter. In addition, even if all members of the negotiating team are competent speakers of both languages, professional interpreters can be present to ensure the accuracy and common understanding of written and oral agreements.

However, the use of interpreters may not mean that the intended message is always conveyed efficiently. It is therefore important for any negotiator to meet

Multinational Management **Brief**

The EU's Boom Market for Linguists

The growth of the European Union and the increased desire for cohesion increases the demand for interpreters. With the recent addition of the 10 new states to the European Union, the demand for linguists has stayed strong at the headquarters in Brussels. However, the EU is finding it difficult to attract translators for the $48,000 annual salary. Additionally, the EU is also facing added challenges obtaining translators for the smallest countries. For instance, it has had major difficulties identifying a single candidate for Malta, a country of 400,000 people. To top everything, hired linguists face an overwhelming workload. They have to translate more than two million pages every year.

The European Union's need for interpreters has also increased in member offices. The European Union's offices throughout Europe have more than 3,000 full-time interpreters dealing with everything from trademarks to police work. To become an interpreter for the EU, one must pass an extremely difficult written and oral exam called a "concours." The pay is good, but interpreters spend half their time on the road and are often blamed for mistakes in negotiations. Along with their linguistic prowess, the best interpreters also have expertise in other fields; some are lawyers, engineers, and scientists.

Source: Based on Leonardi, Robert. 2006. "Cohesion in the European Union." Regional Studies, April, 40, 2: p. 155; Oster, Patrick. 1994. "The new Europe: A boom market for linguists." BusinessWeek, International Edition, May p. 9; Underhill, William. 2004. "EU parlez-vous Maltese?" Newsweek, March p. 22.

and work with the interpreter to ensure that negotiations proceed smoothly. For instance, it is advisable for U.S negotiators to have interpreters review their notes and other information they intend to share with the other party. Such proactive efforts may greatly help the U.S. negotiators anticipate problems. Axtell,[15] Chaney and Martin[16] suggest the following tips:

- Spend time with the interpreter so that he or she gets to know your accent and general approach to conversations.
- Go over technical and other issues with the interpreter to make sure that they are properly understood.
- Insist on frequent interruptions for translations rather than waiting at the end of statements.
- Learn about appropriate communication styles and etiquette from your interpreter.
- Look for feedback and comprehension by watching the eyes.
- Discuss the message beforehand with the interpreter if it is complex.
- Request that your interpreter apologizes for your inability to speak in the local language.
- Confirm through a concluding session with the interpreter that all key components of the message have been properly comprehended.

To simplify the increasing diversity of languages in business organizations, some multinational companies use one language as the corporate tongue. Increasingly, this language is English, since it is the most common second language. Examples of companies using English include Philips Electronics and DHL Worldwide Express. Using English allows these companies a more consistent corporate culture while dealing with the linguistic diversity of their employees and customers.

However, even these major multinational companies have permanent translators on staff to manage such issues as interaction with the international press, translation of local product information, and negotiations with other companies.

Although the use of company-wide languages simplifies some of the multinational's communication problems, it creates other linguistic challenges. One of the greatest challenges is communicating with nonnative speakers. The next section gives practical suggestions on how to communicate with nonnative speakers.

Communication with Nonnative Speakers

In the multinational organization, it is very likely that you will be speaking with and writing to employees, customers, and business associates in their second or even third language. In speaking with people using a nonnative language, communications scholars recommend several techniques. These techniques make communication easier and more accurate:[17]

➤ *Use the most common words with their most common meanings:* **A good source of these words is a book for a beginning language course.**

➤ *Select words with few alternative meanings:* **If this is impossible, use the word with its most common meaning.**

➤ *Strictly follow basic rules of grammar:* **Follow these rules more than you would with native speakers.**

➤ *Speak with clear breaks between words:* **It is often difficult for a nonnative speaker to hear distinct words, especially when there is background noise.**

➤ *Avoid "sports" words or words borrowed from literature:* **In U.S. English, for example, phrases such as "he struck out" should be avoided.**

➤ *Avoid words or expressions that are pictures:* **Some words or expressions, such as "knee deep in the big muddy" in U.S. English, require listeners to have a mental image of the picture to understand.**

➤ *Avoid slang:* **Slang is often based on age and region. The nonnative speaker may have learned the language from people from other regions. For example, British English slang is quite different from U.S. English slang.**

➤ *Mimic the cultural flavor of the nonnative speaker's language:* **For example, use more flowery communication with Spanish-speaking listeners than with Germans.**

➤ *Summarize:* **Paraphrase and repeat basic ideas.**

➤ *Test your communication success:* **Do not ask, "Did you understand?" Instead, ask your listener what he or she heard. Ask the listener to paraphrase what you have said.**

➤ *When your counterpart does not understand:* **Repeat the basic ideas using different words. Use more common nouns and verbs.**

➤ *Confirm important aspects in writing:* **Make sure all important information is written to avoid any misunderstanding or confusion.**

A multinational manager meets with all forms of verbal and nonverbal communication styles. Successful international communicators maintain flexibility and humor in adjusting to local communication patterns. Part of this adjustment comes from avoiding false or incorrect assumptions regarding the intentions of communicators. A considerable amount of communication is taken for granted, and therefore a simple gesture or word (even if translated) can be misinterpreted. The next section shows how you can avoid this common error.

Avoiding Attribution Errors

Attribution

Process by which people interpret the meaning and intent of spoken words or nonverbal exchanges.

Attribution is the process by which we interpret the meaning and intent of spoken words or nonverbal exchanges based on our own cultural expectations. In our own culture, without thinking, we know what a certain body movement or word tells us about a person's intentions and motivations. That is, we attribute a meaning to the communication based on our taken-for-granted cultural expectations. In our own culture, we need not think about these attributions. They are the basis of our everyday communication and understanding.

However, the main danger in cross-cultural communication comes from the ease of making mistakes of attribution. Applying our own cultural interpretations, we can easily misjudge the meaning of a touch, a gaze, a period of silence, or an ambiguous word. This is a common error because it is difficult, if not impossible, to process communications without being influenced by our own cultural framework. Even bilingual people may not understand perfectly how to view the world through the eyes of another culture. Consider the following Multinational Management Brief about attribution errors.

As we see in the Multinational Management Brief, attribution errors can happen anywhere and can have very embarrassing results for companies. The safest strategy in cross-cultural communication and negotiation begins with observation and guarded interpretations. Watch carefully what people from the other culture do in their interpersonal exchanges. Realize that one cannot always attach the same meanings to verbal and nonverbal interactions. Unless you are bilingual, it is often a good idea to avoid subtleties of a foreign language. For example, do not swear or use familiar (personal) words. Avoid complex nonverbal behaviors unless one understands their meanings explicitly.

Sensitivity to cross-cultural communication provides a solid foundation for a multinational negotiator. Next, building on the foundation of your understanding of the basic issues of cross-cultural communication, the chapter provides you with the essential background to develop your knowledge of international negotiations and prepare you to negotiate in the global business environment.

Multinational Management **Brief**

Attribution Errors

Many multinationals use international retreats as a way to promote camaraderie and inculcate the corporate culture across divisions around the world. However, when one multinational advertising firm tried to have a retreat in Orlando to promote cross-cultural teamwork, it made an attribution error that had very embarrassing results. The company managers decided that to encourage employees from around the world to get to know each other, they would require that employees share rooms with someone else around the world. The company managers made the room assignment, and when several Japanese female employees got to their rooms, they discovered that their roommates were German male employees. Unfortunately, the American planners had made the wrong attribution that individuals with name such as Jens and Tibor were female. The simple attribution error based on names was very embarrassing to the company and was cross-culturally unacceptable to the Japanese female employees.

Source: Based on McDonald, Duff. 2006. "Why we all hate offsites." Business 2.0, May, pp. 79–80.

International Negotiation

International negotiation is more complex than domestic negotiation. Differences in national cultures and differences in political, legal, and economic systems often separate potential business partners. Consequently, most international negotiators find it necessary to modify the negotiation styles of their home country. If they wish to succeed in the multinational arena, they must develop a style of international negotiation based on the flexible application of sound negotiating principles. The next section develops your understanding of basic negotiating principles by describing the steps in a successful international negotiation.

Steps in International Negotiations

Most experts recognize that the process of international negotiation includes several steps.[18] Although each international negotiation is unique and may combine two or more steps or repeat some, the negotiation process involves five steps leading to the final step, an agreement. The **negotiation steps** include preparation, building the relationship, exchanging information and the first offer, persuasion, concessions, and the agreement. Most important for international negotiation is preparation. The culturally naïve negotiator almost always fails to bring home an adequate agreement.

Exhibit 13.3 shows the negotiation steps. They are discussed in detail next.

Negotiation steps

Preparation, building the relationship, exchanging information, first offer, persuasion, concessions, agreement, and post agreement.

EXHIBIT 13.3   Steps in International Negotiations

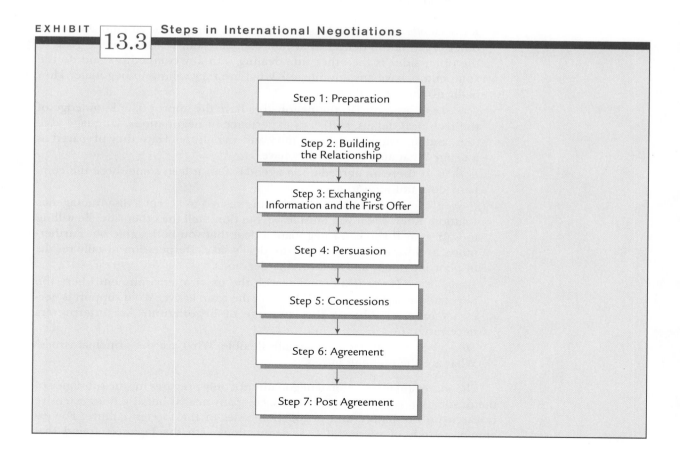

Step 1: Preparation

Step 2: Building the Relationship

Step 3: Exchanging Information and the First Offer

Step 4: Persuasion

Step 5: Concessions

Step 6: Agreement

Step 7: Post Agreement

Step 1: Preparation

A winning international-negotiating strategy requires significant preparation. Ahead of time, the well-prepared international negotiator gathers extensive information on the negotiation issues, on the setting in which the negotiation will take place, and on the firm and people involved. Prior to the negotiations, you must answer questions such as "Where do I stand?" in order to understand your company's position in the negotiation process. However, after you understand your own position, you also want to understand your counterparts' position in the negotiation process by answering questions such as "What do they want?" or "What is important to them?"

Experts on international negotiation identify numerous essential questions and issues to consider before the negotiation, including the following:[19]

> *Determine if the negotiation is possible:* To begin the negotiation process, you must believe that you have at least some areas of agreement with your negotiating counterparts.
> *Know exactly what your company wants from the negotiation:* What does the company hope to achieve in the negotiation? What are the minimally acceptable conditions of an agreement? Make a list of your specific needs or demands. Which specific demands have more negotiating power?
> *Be aware of what can be compromised:* It is very unlikely that you will get everything you want from the negotiation. It is therefore important that you think in advance of the compromise and concessions that you can make. By thinking ahead, you reduce the likelihood of giving up too much or making concessions on the wrong issues.
> *Know the other side:* What does the other side bring to the situation? Can the other organization deliver what your company wants? What are the goals of the other side? Is the other side dealing with any competitors and do the competitors have any advantages? What are they willing to negotiate? How badly do they want the deal?
> *Send the proper team:* Do the negotiators have the appropriate knowledge of the technical details, sufficient experience in negotiations, language abilities, and knowledge of the country and its culture? Have they prepared as a team? What authority do they have?
> *Agenda:* Is there an agreed-upon agenda? Can it lead somewhere the company does not want to go?
> *Prepare for a long negotiation:* Avoid being rushed to accept a disadvantageous solution. Know when you must leave, but don't tell the other side. Be willing to walk away if you can't negotiate a deal that you both agree on. Furthermore, avoid making a deal for the deal's sake. Desperation usually results in poor judgment and unfavorable decisions.
> *Environment:* Is the team familiar with the physical environment where the negotiations will take place? When will the team arrive? What support is necessary on site? What is the language of negotiation? Are interpreters necessary?
> *Strategy:* Plan a strategy but remain flexible. What are the principal issues? What are the opening moves?

The successful international negotiator not only prepares for the substance of the negotiation (e. g., technical details, company needs) but also does extensive research on the nature and negotiation styles of the foreign culture. For example, a study of successful U.S. negotiations with the Japanese found that careful preparations led to high-quality negotiations. Preparations that improved negotiations included reading books on Japanese business culture, hiring experts to train the negotiation teams, and practicing in simulated negotiations.[20]

A key aspect of negotiations that is often ignored is the location site of the negotiation. In many cases, location tends to favor one side over the other. However, negotiators can also take some steps to make sure that they benefit from being guests. Consider the following Case in Point.

While it is impossible to understand the negotiating styles of all the world's cultures, managers can anticipate certain differences among cultures in key negotiating processes. This section identifies some of the issues in negotiation most likely affected by cultural differences. These include cultural differences in the goals of the negotiation, the personal styles of the negotiators, the communication styles of the negotiators, the negotiators' sensitivity to timing and pacing of the negotiation, forms of agreement typical in the society, and the common types of organization of negotiating teams. The examples from different countries discussed next show the extreme differences in these areas.[21] Consider the following examples, realizing that many countries fall in between these cases.[22]

➤ *Negotiation goal—signing the contract or forming a relationship:* Most Chinese and Japanese businesspeople consider as the prime objective of negotiation the formation of relationships. A negotiation may produce signed agreements. However, the signed paper represents only the formal expression of the

CASE IN POINT

Negotiation Location: Is It Better to Be Host or Guest?

It is undeniable that location provides important advantages to the host that can heavily impact negotiation outcomes. Host negotiators control the location protocols and also have the advantage of feeling more comfortable in their familiar surroundings. Being at home also means that they have ready access to experts in order to get advice on aspects of the negotiation. Additionally, the host can lavishly treat the visitors that may create obligations on the part of the guest with respect to the negotiation outcomes. Hosts also control aspects of the physical environment, such as the room size, seating of people, and even timing of events including causing intentional delays. In contrast, guests may have jet lag and may be physically tired and unable to focus and react properly. Furthermore, the pressures of dealing with all of the stress, new food, and new climate may take a serious physical toll on the guests.

However, being a guest also has some advantages. A visit to the host company allows the visitor to get a good idea of the company's facilities and personnel. This can provide important information about the viability of any deal given the host company's degree of modernity and operations. Furthermore, a visit also allows the guest to really learn about the host's culture and lifestyle. Such knowledge may signal desire and commitment to make the negotiation a success. Finally, the effort of making the trip will likely save the host resources and also show seriousness regarding the negotiations.

Despite these advantages, being a guest is inherently harder than being a host. Some steps can nevertheless be taken to soften some of the hardships of being a guest. Visitors should arrive ahead of time to examine the negotiation site and have time to recover. Additionally, it is advisable to eat lightly and drink alcoholic beverages in moderation. Finally, it is also a good idea to be patient with the frustrations and hardships of being in a foreign country. These factors should not force the guest to short-circuit plans and make the deal as soon as possible to return home.

Source: Based on Mayfield, Jackie, Milton Mayfield, Drew Martin, and Paul Herbig. 1998. "How location impacts international business negotiations." Review of Business, Winter, pp. 21–24.

relationship between the companies, and sometimes of the personal relationships between the individual negotiators. The contract exists only as an initial step in the relationship, one that may lead to longer-term mutual benefits. In more legalistic societies, such as the United States, the detailed, signed contract is the most important goal of the negotiation. Commitment is less personally binding but relies instead on the force of law. The sanctity of the contract is a valued legal principle in U.S. courts.

➤ *Formal or informal personal communication style:* Business cultures differ widely on the acceptability of informal styles. Australians, like U.S. Americans, easily adapt to using first names and having informal conversations. As shown earlier in Exhibit 13.2, however, Nigerian, Spanish, and Chinese negotiators react negatively to the informality of using first names among short-term business acquaintances.

➤ *Direct or indirect communication style:* The extent to which communication is direct and verbal, rather than indirect and nonverbal, varies widely by culture, as we saw in the section on communication. The rules of politeness and styles of interaction in different cultures encourage or restrict the ability of negotiators to come directly to the point. For example, the Japanese will seldom say "No" directly. Instead, if something "is very difficult," it is probably impossible. Conversely, a speaker of a more explicit language might interpret such aversion to direct speech as an effort to hide something.

➤ *Sensitivity to time—low or high:* The pace of negotiation and the time given to each phase of negotiation intertwine with the objective of the negotiation. Cultures place different values on how much time is devoted to the negotiation in pursuit of negotiation goals. For U.S. Americans, signing the deal is a contract, and time is money. As a result, Americans tend to get down to business as soon as they can. In contrast, Asian cultures place value on creating a relationship rather than simply signing a contract. These cultures tend to want to take time to get to know the other parties better to determine whether a long-term relationship is worthwhile. Attempts to speed up negotiations tend to be viewed with suspicion that the other party may be trying to hide something.

➤ *Forms of agreement—specific or general:* A negotiated agreement may consist of general principles or very detailed documents that attempt to anticipate all possible outcomes of the relationship. In many countries, Japan for example, the preferred contract states only general principles and not detailed rules and obligations. The Japanese argue that, since it is impossible to foresee all possible contingencies, a detailed agreement is dangerous and unnerving. The contract may obligate someone to do something that eventually becomes impossible due to unforeseen circumstances. In contrast, broad agreements, preferably based on strong personal relationships, allow for fair adjustments if circumstances change. Pressing for legalistic, detailed coverage of all contingencies, as is typical of U.S. Americans, leads many people from other cultures to believe that their U.S. partners have little trust in the relationship. Exhibit 13.4 shows the differences among nations in cultural preferences for a broad or detailed contractual agreement.

➤ *Team organization—a team or one leader:* The senior U.S. negotiator often has, within specified boundaries, the final authority to make commitments for his or her company and to close the deal. This style of organization fits the U.S. mode of more rapid negotiations to reach a signed contract. In international negotiations, a small U.S. negotiation team with one leader

EXHIBIT 13.4　**Cultural Differences in Preference for Broad Agreements**

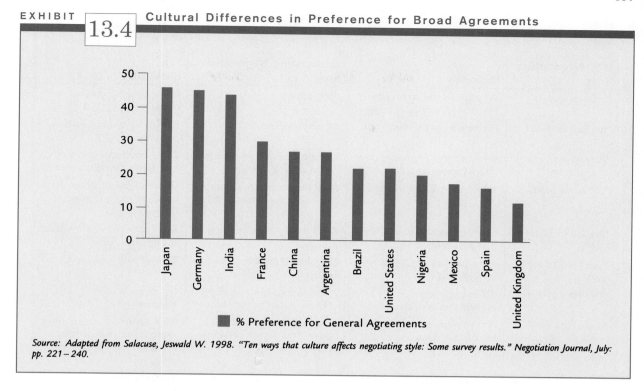

■ % Preference for General Agreements

Source: Adapted from Salacuse, Jeswald W. 1998. "Ten ways that culture affects negotiating style: Some survey results." Negotiation Journal, July: pp. 221–240.

faces a much larger team where the true decision maker might not be present or, if present, might say very little. Russians, Japanese, and Chinese prefer large teams and rely more on consensus decision making.

➤ *Attitude towards negotiation—win–lose or win–win:* Because of the role of culture, different nationalities tend to approach the negotiation with different mindsets. Some cultures view the process as one where both parties can benefit (win–win) while others see it as a necessity that one side wins while the other side loses (win–lose). For instance, Salacuse[23] reports that 100 percent of Japanese approached negotiations with a win–win mindset while only 33 percent of the Spanish executives surveyed had the same view. By understanding the approach, one can be aware of the situation one faces.

➤ *High or low emotions:* As we saw in Chapter 2, societies also differ in terms of acceptability and appropriateness of display of emotions. For instance, Latin Americans and the Spanish are said to usually show their emotions through negotiations while the Japanese and Germans tend to be more reserved. Knowing the appropriateness of emotional display is also necessary to ensure that the negotiations progress smoothly.

Lack of preparation for cultural differences in international negotiations can lead to many problems. For example, the negotiating style typical of the highly individualistic U.S. culture seldom works well in more collectivist cultures. Both U.S. managers and managers from other cultures negotiating with the United States should prepare to avoid some of the pitfalls of the U.S. negotiating style. Exhibit 13.5 contrasts some common U.S. negotiating characteristics with those from other national cultures. U.S. negotiators have what John Graham and Roy Herberger[24] call the "John Wayne" style of negotiation. As Exhibit 13.5 shows,

EXHIBIT **13.5**   **Preparation: Understanding Negotiators from Other Countries**

U.S. Negotiation Style	Rationale	Contrasting Negotiation Style	Rationale
"I can go it alone"	Why spend the money for more people than necessary?	*Bring a team*	More people provide social pressure
"Just call me John"	Formalities are unnecessary	*Be extremely formal*	Rank and status count in language
"Pardon my French"	Why bother? English is the international language	*Understand English but use interpreters anyway*	Gives extra time to listen and formulate responses
"Get to the point"	Why beat around the bush?	*Build the personal relationship and exchange information first*	Personal relationships and trust are more important than contracts
"Lay your cards on the table"	Give and expect honest information up front	*Don't reveal the real position at first*	A bit of trickery or avoiding saying No is okay
"Don't just sit there, speak up"	Long periods of silence are unacceptable	*Long periods of silence, especially in response to an impasse*	Time is necessary to react
"One thing at a time"	A final agreement is a sum of agreements on each issue	*A holistic approach with all points open for discussion until the end*	Issues are always interconnected
"A deal is a deal"	A commitment is final down to the last detail	*Today's commitment can be voided if tomorrow's circumstances are different*	Negotiations partners must understand that absolutes are impossible and things change
"I don't need to check with the home office"	Negotiators should have the authority to make the deal	*I must check with the home office first*	To complete the negotiation, you have to convince not only me but also my boss, on another continent

Source: Adapted from Graham, John L., and Roy A. Herberger, Jr. 1983. "Negotiators abroad—don't shoot from the hip." Harvard Business Review. 61: pp. 160–168.

U.S. negotiators are independent, aggressive, and direct. Although this style makes sense in the individualistic U.S. culture, it contrasts sharply with other negotiating styles from nations with other cultural values and norms. The following Multinational Management Brief shows what to expect in negotiations with Arabs.

After thorough preparation, a negotiator is ready to begin direct communication with his or her negotiating partners. In the next section, we will see how these interactions evolve in the negotiation process.

Step 2: Building the Relationship

Building a relationship

The first stage of the actual negotiation process, when negotiators concentrate on social and interpersonal matters.

After initial planning, the first stage of the actual negotiating process begins with **building a relationship** between the negotiating parties. At this stage, negotiators do not focus on the business issues. Rather, they concentrate on social and interpersonal matters. Negotiation partners get to know each other personally. They develop opinions regarding the personality characteristics of the negotiators: what they are really like, what their real goals are, and whether they can really be trusted.

This phase of the negotiation process often takes place at a location different from the formal negotiation place. The first step in a Japanese negotiation, for example, often occurs by drinking tea in a room outside the formal office. Only the exchange of business cards and small talk takes place during this encounter.

Multinational Management Brief

What to Expect when Negotiating with Arabs

There are five key characteristics of negotiations with people from Arab nations. These include:

1. *Arabs look at the world as subjective:* Reality is based on perception, not on facts. A common frustration for Westerners is that logical flaws in arguments have less impact than expected. If the facts do not fit someone's beliefs, then that person may reject the facts and consider only his or her own view of the situation. In particular, personal honor is more important than fact.

2. *The type of relationship expected:* A good personal relationship is the most important foundation of doing business with Arabs.

3. *Information on family and connections:* Social connections and networks are crucial in the highly personalized Arab societies. This should not be interpreted as useless information, but rather it may represent the key to finalizing a business deal.

4. *Persuasion:* For Arab negotiators, personalized arguments are more effective than logical arguments. Emphasis on friendship and personal appeals for consideration are common. Showing emotion by raising the voice, repeating points with enthusiasm, or even pounding the table is acceptable. Emotional argument shows the sincerity of the concern.

5. *The time required to complete the process:* From the perspective of Western business people, negotiations with Arab business partners take considerable time. Time is not fixed for Arabs. There are not fixed beginnings and endings of events. Everyone expects delays.

Source: Based on Nydell, Margaret K. 1997. Understanding Arabs: A Guide for Westerners. Yarmouth, Maine: Intercultural Press.

In most countries, including Japan, restaurants, bars, and cultural tours often provide the context for relationship-building activities.

The duration and importance of the relationship-building stage vary widely by national culture. U.S. negotiators are notorious in their attempts to "get down to business" after brief and perfunctory socializing.[25] German negotiators also get to the point quickly. When foreign negotiators bring up issues not related directly to the negotiation objective, U.S. negotiators often view this as a waste of time and an inefficient use of company resources. The pressure on U.S. managers is to get to the point, make the deal, and come home—particularly when they are overseas. International travel and hotels are costly, and many U.S. companies believe that a manager's time is better spent at home, getting on with implementing the negotiated deal.

The goal of U.S. negotiators is to get the details of the agreement on a written contract. This contract has specific requirements and specific due dates. As such, from this perspective, there is little need to develop personal relationships. In the U.S. legal view, "The partner must agree to a legally binding document." Other legal systems, however, do not see the contract as binding in its detail. For example, for many Chinese managers, a contract provides only the foundation on which to build the relationship, with details to be worked out later. As with most Asian societies, the Chinese believe that investing the time to build personal relationships must come first. Consider the following Multinational Management Brief.

Multinational Management **Brief**

Negotiating with the Chinese: The Role of Logic Paradigms

As more companies try to invest in China, they will face ever-increasing challenges. An important but often ignored component of negotiation is the role of logics. Logics, "the underlying assumptions, deeply held, often unexamined, which form a framework within which reasoning takes place," have important influences on predetermining how people interpret events and respond to situations. As such, an awareness of alternative logic paradigms (i.e., how different societies approach logic) is useful as it can help explain the biases and perspectives that help an individual understand the world. This knowledge is especially useful in understanding the Chinese approach to negotiations and the inherent importance for the Chinese to build relationships.

Most of Western thinking is based on formal logic whereby reasoning is an outcome of careful and rigorous deductive reasoning. The basic principles of formal logic are that entities cannot simultaneously co-exist in different forms (i.e., U.S. negotiators do not accept the idea that they can both win and lose at negotiations at the same time) and entities can be only one of two mutually exclusive things (i.e., U.S. negotiators cannot accept gray areas in negotiations). Formal logic thus makes the acceptance of contradictions nearly impossible as U.S. negotiators try to find satisfactory outcomes to negotiations (i.e., you can win or lose, get or lose the deal, etc.).

In contrast, the Chinese's thinking is based on dialectic logic, an approach that "embraces paradox and contradiction as the very vehicles through which positive change and growth occur." The basic principle of dialectic logic is that contradictions are an inescapable part of life. The resolution of such contradictions results in further contradictions, thus making permanence and stability unlikely. As such, the Chinese believe that life involves a ceaseless balance of contradictions.

These differences in logic paradigms have obvious implications for how U.S. and Chinese negotiators approach negotiations. For instance, the formal logic perspective implies that U.S. negotiators are more likely to approach the negotiation independently of the other team (i.e., an entity can only be one of two things) and take a competitive approach (i.e., we can only win or lose, and there is no middle ground). In contrast, the Chinese are more likely to accept the idea that they do not have a full knowledge of what needs to be done and that success is only possible through interdependence with the negotiating counterparts. Furthermore, formal logic focuses on reduction of ambiguity. Thus, the negotiation inherently centers on tasks and efficiency. In contrast, dialectic logic suggests that contradiction is not only necessary but also beneficial. This means that the Chinese are more likely to spend time on discovering and exploring new complexities. While the U.S. negotiators may be more focused on time and getting the job done within deadlines, Chinese negotiators are more likely to let the project unfold as is necessary.

The difference in logic paradigms also explains why Chinese negotiators prefer to take time to develop a relationship rather than merely focusing on the negotiation. The Chinese are more apt to work with the other party to explore contradictions and ambiguities. Additionally, the negotiation may be just the beginning of a long-term relationship. In contrast, for the U.S. negotiators, formal logic requires that they focus on achieving milestones as evidence of success. Such task-oriented focus minimizes the importance of relationships.

Source: Based on Graham, John L., and N. Mark Lam. 2003. "The Chinese negotiation." Harvard Business Review, October, pp. 28–39; Kambil, Amit, Victor Wei-the Long, and Clarence Kwan. 2006. "The seven disciplines for venturing in China." MIT Sloan Management Review, Winter, 47, 2: pp. 85–89; Horn, R. 1983. "An overview of trialectics within applications to psychology and public policy." In Trialectics: Toward a Practical Logic of Unity, edited by R. Horn, pp. 1–39. Basel, Switzerland: S. Karger; Palich, Leslie E., Gary R. Carinini, and Linda P. Livingstone. 2002. "Comparing American and Chinese negotiating styles: The influence of logic paradigms." Thunderbird International Review, 44, pp. 777–798.

Building a good relationship among the negotiating parties provides a foundation for working out an eventual deal. As we saw in the Multinational Management Brief, in many Asian societies, it is extremely important to build trust and relationships to be successful. Even in individualistic societies such as the United States, personal trust among negotiators is important. However, a business negotiation must eventually specify who is going to do what, when, and for what price. Thus, the next section shows how negotiators begin to address these issues.

Step 3: Exchanging Information and the First Offer

At this stage in the negotiation, both parties exchange information on their needs for the agreement. Parties exchange information that is **task-related information.** It pertains to the actual details of the proposed agreement. Typically, both sides make a formal presentation of what they desire out of the relationship. They present issues such as the quantity, characteristics, and price of a product. Both sides usually present their **first offer.** This is their first proposal of what they expect from the agreement.

At this stage, national and business cultures influence what information is given and requested, how the information is presented, and how close the initial offer is to the actually expected or hoped-for specifications in the agreement. Exhibit 13.6 shows a comparison among different nations regarding information exchange and first-offer strategies. Note, for example, the difference between the typical U.S. initial negotiation point (off the "real" goal by 5 to 10 percent) and the more extreme starting points used by Arab negotiators.

An important component of the information presentation stage is to ensure that the audience is properly understood and that the presentation is adapted to the audience's needs. There is some evidence that different cultures have different preferences for the type of information being presented,[26] and some countries in both Asia and Europe value depth. As such, it is critical for the negotiators to know the negotiation aspects in depth. If they display ignorance, the other party may be offended. However, in contrast, some cultures such as the Arab and Mexican cultures may focus more on relationships. In such cases, presenters may need to focus more on relational aspects of the presentation. If the information presented is too technical or difficult to understand, the other party may feel intimidated and more reluctant to make a deal,[27] and presenters must make sure that appropriate information is presented.

Task-related information
Actual details of the proposed agreement.

First offer
First proposal by parties of what they expect from the agreement.

EXHIBIT 13.6 Information Exchange and First-Offer Strategies

	Arabs	Japanese	Mexicans	Russians	U.S. Americans
Information Exchange	Focus is on information about the relationship and less on technological details	Extensive requests for technical information	Focus is on information about the relationships and less on technical details	Great attention to detail	Information is given directly and briefly, often with a multi-media presentation
First-Offer or Counteroffer	20 to 50% of goal	10 to 20% of goal	Fair for both parties and close to goal	Extreme and purposefully unfair	5 to 10% of goal

Source: Adapted from Chaney, Lillian H., and Jeanette S. Martin. 1995. Intercultural Business Communication. Englewood Cliffs, NJ: Prentice Hall; Yale, Richmond. 1992. From Nyet to Da: Understanding the Russians. Yarmouth, Maine: Intercultural Press.

After the first offer, the core of the negotiation begins. Negotiators move beyond first-offer strategies and attempt to reach accord on the actual nature of the agreement. The next section outlines some of the tactics used after both sides make initial offers.

Step 4: Persuasion

In the **persuasion** stage, each side in the negotiation attempts to get the other side to agree to its position. This is the heart of the negotiation process. Numerous tactics are available to international negotiators. While all negotiators use somewhat similar tactics to argue for their side, their emphasis and mix of tactics vary according to their cultural background. We will review two general types of tactics here, standard verbal and nonverbal negotiation tactics and some of the "dirty tricks" of international negotiation.

Verbal and Nonverbal Negotiation Tactics   John L. Graham, an expert on international negotiations, identifies several **verbal negotiation tactics** common in international negotiations.[28] These include:

> *Promise:* If you do something for me, I will do something for you.
> *Threat:* If you do something I don't like, I will do something you don't like.
> *Recommendation:* If you do something I desire, good things will happen to you (e.g., people will buy your product).
> *Warning:* If you do something I don't like, bad things will happen to you (e.g., other companies will know you cannot do business here).
> *Reward:* I am going to do something beneficial for you (without conditions).
> *Punishment:* I am going to do something you will dislike—without conditions (e.g., end the negotiations immediately).
> *Normative appeal:* This is the way we do or do not do business here (e.g., "You must learn the Japanese way").
> *Commitment:* I agree to do something specific (e.g., meet a delivery date).
> *Self-disclosure:* I will tell you something about myself or my company to show you why we need to close the deal.
> *Question:* I ask you something about your company or yourself.
> *Command:* This is an order that you must follow.
> *Refusal:* Just saying no.
> *Interruption:* I talk when you talk.

Exhibit 13.7 shows examples of cultural differences in these verbal negotiating tactics among Japanese, U.S., and Brazilian negotiators.

Cultural differences in nonverbal communication styles also influences negotiations. **Nonverbal communication** through such things as body posture, facial expression, hand gestures, and the use of personal space are a natural part of any international negotiation. For example, a hand gesture or a facial expression might be a subtle way to indicate agreement or disagreement with a proposal. In addition, foreign nonverbal communication might also create (purposely or not) situations that make a negotiator uncomfortable. For example, people from cultures with a comfortable speaking distance of one meter (about 3 feet) might have difficulty concentrating on negotiations when someone stands inside their comfort range.

Earlier in this chapter you learned that the interpretation of nonverbal communication is difficult for people of different cultural backgrounds. For example, in dealings with the Japanese, a proposal might be met with downcast

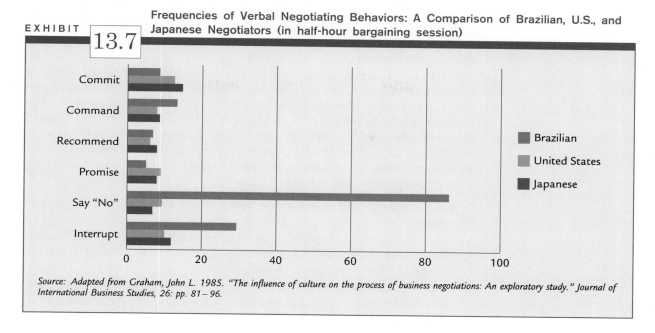

EXHIBIT **13.7**

Frequencies of Verbal Negotiating Behaviors: A Comparison of Brazilian, U.S., and Japanese Negotiators (in half-hour bargaining session)

Source: Adapted from Graham, John L. 1985. "The influence of culture on the process of business negotiations: An exploratory study." Journal of International Business Studies, 26: pp. 81–96.

eyes and no response. U.S. negotiators often interpret the Japanese silence as a rejection of the proposal. The Japanese, however, take whatever time they need to think and formulate a proper response. Unlike most U.S. negotiators, they feel no pressure to fill the gaps in conversation. Stressed by the silence, U.S. negotiators may continue to talk, causing the Japanese to hesitate even more. Feeling that their position is rejected, U.S. negotiators often offer unnecessary concessions.[29]

While many Asian societies use silence to communicate that they are still deliberating, other cultures allow hardly any time for introspection. Consider that one study found that, in thirty minutes of negotiation, the Japanese had more than five periods of complete silence of ten seconds or longer, nearly twice as many as U.S. negotiators. Brazilians, on the other hand, were never silent for more than ten seconds.[30]

The more direct tactics of negotiation are often supplemented by tactics that not all people consider fair. The next section shows you some of these tactics and possible responses.

"Dirty Tricks" in International Negotiations   There are many tactics in both international and domestic negotiations that people use to gain an upper hand. All negotiators want to get the best deal for their company, and they use a range of ploys or tactics to get what they want. However, people from different cultures consider some negotiating tactics **dirty tricks**. "Dirty tricks" are negotiation tactics that pressure opponents to accept unfair or undesirable agreements or concessions.[31]

The nature of cross-cultural negotiation makes the perception of dirty tricks almost unavoidable. Cultures differ on the norms and values that determine acceptable strategies for negotiation. As compared to U.S. Americans, Brazilians, for example, expect more deception and truth stretching during the initial stages of negotiation.[32] It is therefore also critical that special attention is paid to the presenters to detect whether information is being presented truthfully. Consider the following Multinational Management Brief.

Dirty tricks

Negotiation tactics that pressure opponents to accept unfair or undesirable agreements or concessions.

Multinational Management **Brief**

Spotting Deception

Research suggests that people are likely to lie 2.9 times in an average 10-minute business conversation. The potential for deception and deceit is even more pronounced in a negotiation in an international setting. It is therefore important that attention is paid to various cues and hints to determine whether information is being presented truthfully. Although experts have provided some advice for domestic negotiations, some of the verbal and nonverbal cues may also be relevant for international negotiations. Specifically, these experts suggest that negotiators may be lying if the following signs are observed:

➤ *Circumlocution:* Information is presented in a very ambiguous and long-winded manner.

➤ *Nose rubbing:* People experience the Pinocchio syndrome when they lie. Because blood rushes to the nose when a person is lying, it produces a sensation that can only be relieved by touching or rubbing the nose.

➤ *Omission, spin, and generalization:* It is also possible that information is presented selectively or broad generalizations are made through regular use of "always" and "never."

➤ *Smoke screens:* Questions and concerns are answered in ways that confuse or deceive.

Experts also suggest that only the most experienced negotiators tend to develop skills to be able to recognize the above cues to detect lies and intention to deceive.

Source: Based on Reynolds, Andrea. 2006. "How to spot a liar." Supply Management, January 11, 1: pp. 24–25.

In many countries, unlike the typical situation for U.S. negotiators, the negotiating team lacks the authority to complete a contract. Just when one party believes the deal is final, the other party responds by saying that "higher authority" must approve the contract before the deal is complete. The "agreement" often comes back with modifications, psychologically pressuring the other side to accept numerous "minor" modifications.

Some examples of common ploys in international negotiations (that some may consider dirty tricks) follow, with possible response tactics:[33]

➤ *Deliberate deception or bluffing:* Negotiators present flagrant untruths either in the facts they offer or in their intentions for the negotiation. For example, one foreign negotiating team spent a week in a hotel pursuing a deal, only to find out later that they were part of a dirty trick being played by the local company. The local company was already negotiating in earnest with another foreign company. It had brought in the second foreign company only to scare the negotiators from the first foreign company.
Possible response: Point out directly what you believe is happening.

➤ *Stalling:* Negotiators wait until the last minute before the international negotiating team plans to go home. They then push for quick concessions to close the deal.
Possible responses: Do not reveal when you plan to leave. When asked, say that you plan to stay "as long as it takes." Alternatively, state when you will leave, with or without the deal.

➤ *Escalating authority:* Negotiators make an agreement but then reveal that it must be approved by senior managers or the government. The objective is to put the other team under psychological pressure to make more concessions. *Possible response:* Clarify decision-making authority early in the negotiating process.

➤ *Good-guy, bad-guy routine:* One negotiator acts agreeable and friendly while his or her partner makes outrageous or unreasonable demands. The "good guy" suggests that only a small concession will appease the unreasonable "bad guy." *Possible response:* Do not make any concessions. Ignore the ploy and focus on mutual benefits of the potential agreement.

➤ *You are wealthy, and we are poor:* Often used by negotiators from developing countries, this tactic attempts to make concessions seem trivial. Smaller companies may also use this tactic when dealing with larger companies. *Possible response:* Ignore the ploy and focus on mutual benefits of potential agreement.

➤ *Old friends:* Negotiators act as if the companies and their negotiators have long-enduring friendships. They feign hurt feelings if their counterparts disagree or do not agree to their requests. *Possible response:* Keep a psychological distance that reflects the true nature of the relationship.

Successful international negotiators recognize and deal with dirty tricks and other ploys used in negotiations. Besides the possible strategies just noted, experts suggest other general responses to dirty tricks.[34] First, stick to your standards and avoid using the tricks yourself. This encourages negotiating counterparts to be more forthright. Second, point out the dirty tricks or ploys when they are used. This discourages the use of dirty tricks later in the negotiation. Third, try to avoid fighting back directly. Fourth, be ready to walk out of the negotiation if the other side fails to play fairly. This may involve some cost, but it is probably better than a bad deal for your company. Finally, realize that ethical systems differ by culture, and understand that your opponents may not feel that they are really doing something wrong or immoral.

Although negotiators use a variety of tactics to argue their points, the goal remains to make a business deal. In the next section, we will examine the final steps in negotiation that bring the process to a successful conclusion.

Steps 5 and 6: Concessions and Agreement

Successful negotiations result in the **final agreement**. The final agreement is the signed contract, agreeable to all sides. It must be consistent with the chosen legal system or systems. The safest contracts are legally binding in the legal systems of all the signers. Most important, people from different national and business cultures must understand the contract in principle. Partners must have a true commitment to the terms of the agreement, beyond whatever legal stipulations exist.

For most negotiations to reach a final agreement, each side must make some concessions. **Concession making** requires that each side relax certain demands to meet the other party's needs. It usually means giving in on the points of less importance to you to achieve your major objectives in negotiating the potential deal.

Final agreement
Signed contract, agreeable to all sides.

Concession making
Process requiring each side to relax some of its demands to meet the other party's needs.

Sequential approach

Each side reciprocates concessions made by the other side.

Holistic approach

Each side makes very few, if any, concessions until the end of the negotiation.

Styles of concession making differ among cultures. None are necessarily the most successful. Experts[35] point out that North American negotiators take a **sequential approach** to concession making. Each side reciprocates concessions made by the other side. North Americans have a norm of reciprocity, which means that one should meet a concession made by the other party by making one's own concession. In many cultures, however, people consider "giving in" a sign of weakness and an encouragement to extract more concessions. In addition, in the typical U.S. negotiating strategy, partners consider each issue as a *separate* point. Negotiators expect each side to give and take on the individual issues in sequence. They complete the agreement when the sequential concession making resolves all issues.

In contrast, a **holistic approach** is more common in Asia. The parties make very few, if any, concessions during discussions of each point in a potential agreement. Only after all participants discuss all issues can concession making begin. When dealing with holistic negotiators, North Americans are often perplexed to learn that a point that they believed was negotiated previously arises again in final discussion of the overall package.

To illustrate cross-national differences in concession making styles, Hendon, Roy and Ahmed[36] surveyed 10,424 executives from more than 21 countries over a 15-year period (1985-1999). They presented the executives with seven different patterns regarding a hypothetical situation where they are negotiating and have to distribute $100 within one hour. Their counterparts are not aware that they will give away $100. They also have to make distribution decisions at the end of each of the four 15-minute periods in an hour. Finally, they can give away exactly $100. The seven patterns presented to the executives are as follows:

- Pattern 1 – give away $25 at the end of each of the four 15-minute periods in an hour
- Pattern 2 – give away $50 at the end of each of the first two 15-minute periods, leaving no concession for the last two 15-minute periods in the hour
- Pattern 3 – give away $100 at the end of the negotiation, with no concessions during the first three 15-minute periods
- Pattern 4 – give away $100 at the end of the first 15-minute period, with no concessions for the remaining three 15-minutes periods
- Pattern 5 – give away increasing amounts in the order of $10, $20, $30, and $40 at the end of each of the 15-minute periods in that order
- Pattern 6 – give away decreasing amounts in the order of $40, $30, $20, and $10 for the end of each of the 15-minute periods in that order
- Pattern 7 – give away $50 at the end of the first 15-minute period, $30 at the end of the second 15-minute period, $25 at the end of the third 15-minute period, and take back $5 at the end of the negotiation

Results of the study shows that the various regions studied agreed on Patterns 4 and 7 as being their least favorite concession patterns. Executives from the 21 regions represented by the five regions of North America, British Commonwealth (e.g., the United Kingdom, Australia, South Africa), more developed Southeast Asian countries (i.e., Taiwan, Singapore, and Malaysia), less developed nations of South East Asia (i.e., Philippines, Papua, New Guinea), and Latin America overwhelmingly agreed that they disliked these patterns. Pattern 4 is known as the naïve negotiating style where the bottom line is revealed at the beginning of the negotiation. Practitioners do not recommend this style as it makes the negotiator vulnerable because the bottom line is revealed too fast. Pattern 7, known as the re-negotiation style, is also discouraged because it signals that the negotiator gave away too much at the beginning.

However, the results were more interesting in that the preferred concession patterns among these regions varied widely. For instance, the North Americans seemed to prefer Pattern 3 the most while none of the other regions liked this pattern. Pattern 3 is known as the tough hard-nosed concession style and is consistent with the macho culture of the individualist societies of North America. Concessions are made only at the end when everything else has failed. This strategy is, however, discouraged because concessions need to be made occasionally to break deadlocks and to get the negotiation progressing.

The less developed Southeast Asian region preferred Pattern 5 the most. Pattern 5 is known as the escalating pattern where higher levels of concession are made as the negotiation progresses. Although this seems to be a popular style, practitioners nevertheless discourage its use. The major problem with this style is that the negotiating counterpart may get greedy and expect more and more concessions. Furthermore, some may find it worthwhile to prolong negotiations in order to get more.

The British Commonwealth, advanced Asian, and Latin American nations all preferred Pattern 6. This is known as the de-escalation pattern where the negotiator is sending the message that fewer and fewer concessions can be made. However, if the negotiating counterpart is experienced, he or she may try to get as much as possible early in the negotiations.

These preference patterns suggest that negotiators can be better prepared by understanding the styles of their counterpart. Such knowledge can be invaluable as the appropriate strategies can be adopted to get the maximum advantage from the concession-making style.

Approaches to the negotiating steps discussed vary not only by culture but also by a general philosophy regarding negotiating strategy. The next section discusses two approaches to negotiation along with their implications for international negotiations.

Basic Negotiating Strategies

There are two basic negotiating strategies—competitive negotiating and problem-solving negotiating.[37] The competitive negotiator views the negotiation as a win–lose game. One side's gain must result in the other side's loss. Problem-solving negotiators, in contrast, search for possible win–win situations where the outcome of the negotiation is mutually satisfactory to both sides.

In **competitive negotiation,** each side tries to give as little as possible. They begin with high and often unreasonable demands. They make concessions only grudgingly. Competitive negotiators use dirty tricks and any plot that leads to their advantage. They spend more energy defending their positions while attempting to get the other side to make all the concessions.

Competitive negotiation seldom leads to long-term relationships built on mutual trust and commitment. Additionally, starting from inflexible positions often leads to outcomes that satisfy neither side. Thus, both sides develop negative attitudes toward each other, and often the "losers" seek revenge, reneging on the agreement when the opportunity arises.

The foremost tenet of **problem-solving negotiation** is separating positions from interests[38] Problem-solving negotiation means that negotiators should not think of defending their company's position as the major goal of the negotiation. Rather, they should seek out mutually satisfactory ground that is beneficial to

Competitive negotiation

Each side tries to give as little as possible and tries to "win" for its side.

Problem-solving negotiation

Negotiators seek out mutually satisfactory ground that is beneficial to both companies' interests.

both companies' interests. Problem-solving negotiators avoid dirty tricks and use objective information whenever possible. They often find that actively seeking to please both sides results in the discovery of new ways to achieve mutual gains.

Exhibit 13.8 summarizes and contrasts how the competitive negotiator and the problem-solving negotiator differ in their approaches, as discussed earlier in the chapter.

In international negotiations, there are three important points regarding the use of competitive or problem-solving strategies.

First, in cross-cultural bargaining, the ease of misreading the other side's negotiation strategy increases dramatically. For example, the formal politeness used by many Asian negotiators may look like problem solving to U.S. negotiators. The tendency of Brazilian negotiators to talk or to exaggerate may look like competitive bargaining to people from cultures with ritual politeness. However, in either of the examples, culturally based rules of social interaction can mask either a highly inflexible position or a true openness to problem solving.

Second, cultural norms and values may predispose some negotiators to one of the approaches. Exhibit 13.9 shows some recent evidence from a cross-national study on cultural differences in the preference for a problem-solving negotiation style.

Third, most experts on international bargaining recommend a problem-solving negotiating strategy. They believe that problem solving leads to better long-term contracts and relationships. Problem solving is more likely to achieve the multinational's goals of mutual benefits from international trade. In contrast, competitive negotiations exacerbate the inevitable conflicts and misunderstandings that occur in cross-cultural interaction.

EXHIBIT 13.8   Competitive and Problem-Solving Negotiation in the Negotiating Steps

Stages in Negotiation	Competitive Negotiating Strategy	Problem-Solving Negotiating Strategy
Preparation	Identify the economic or other benefits that the company needs from the deal. Know the position to defend.	Define the interests of the company. Prepare to overcome cross-cultural barriers to defining interests.
Relationship Building	Look for weaknesses in the other side. Find out as much as possible about your competition. Reveal as little as possible.	Separate the people in the negotiation from the problem. Change negotiators if necessary. Adapt to the other side's culture.
Information Exchange and First Offer	Give as little as possible. Give only task-related information. make your position explicit.	Give and demand objective information that clarifies interests. Accept cultural differences in speed and type of information needs.
Persuasion	Use dirty tricks and any ploys that you think will work. Use pressure tactics.	Search for and invent new options that benefit the interests of both sides.
Concession	Begin with high initial demands. Make concessions slowly and grudgingly.	Search for mutually acceptable criteria. Accept cultural differences in starting position and in how and when concessions are made.
Agreement	Sign only if you win and get an iron-clad contract.	Sign when the interests of your company are met. Adapt to cultural differences in contracts.

Source: Adapted from Adler, Nancy J. 1991. International Dimensions of Organizational Behavior, 2d ed. Boston: PWS–Kent; Kublin, Michael. 1995. International Negotiating. New York: International Business Press.

Cultural Differences in Preference for a Problem-Solving Negotiation Strategy

EXHIBIT **13.9**

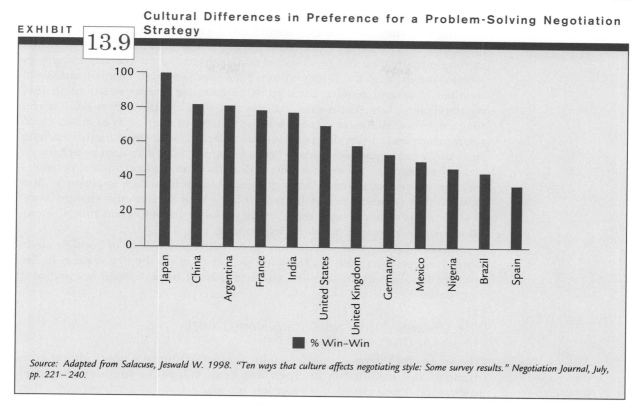

■ % Win–Win

Source: Adapted from Salacuse, Jeswald W. 1998. "Ten ways that culture affects negotiating style: Some survey results." Negotiation Journal, July, pp. 221–240.

Step 7: Post Agreement

A commonly ignored step by U.S. negotiators is the post-agreement phase. The **post agreement** phase consists of an evaluation of the success of a completed negotiation. Because of the inherent task orientation of U.S. negotiators, there is a tendency to ignore the benefits of post agreement as the U.S. negotiators get ready to move on to the next deal. Additionally, the short-term and impatient nature of U.S. negotiators also encourages them to ignore engaging in a post-agreement session.[39]

The post agreement stage can be very beneficial as it allows garnering of valuable insights into the strengths and weaknesses of the approach that was used during the negotiation. Such knowledge can be very important for organizational learning and success in future negotiations. By analyzing the various steps outlined earlier, the negotiators can determine where things went well and where improvements are needed. However, beyond information critical to learning, post agreement can also allow members of a negotiating team to further develop a closer relationship with their counterpart. As more U.S. companies increasingly negotiate with Asian countries, taking a long-term relationship approach is necessary. For instance, for the Chinese, agreement on a deal is not the end of the negotiation but rather the beginning of an opportunity to develop further trust and the relationship. As such, U.S. negotiators will need to become more adept at post agreement in order to further enhance their relationship-building skill.

How can learning be enhanced during the post-agreement stage? Lowenstein, Thompson and Gentner Lowenstein, Jeffrey, Leigh Thompson, and Dedre

Post agreement

Consists of an evaluation of the success of a completed negotiation.

Gentner.[40] suggest a formal training process. If companies are serious about learning from negotiations, they should invest in training those involved in negotiations. In addition to a case-based approach where complex information regarding one situation can be dissected and analyzed, they advise that companies look for use of "analogical" approaches. Such approaches are based on analysis of multiple cases and require participants to compare several situations to find commonalities. Lowenstein et al.[41] argue that such an approach is more useful than single case studies as they allow better transfer of learning (i.e., it is easier to apply principles to many different contexts rather than the more inertial learning from single cases) and also leads to better understanding of abstract principles. As such, after negotiators have concluded a deal, they can compare their experiences with previous negotiations to better grasp the lessons from their experiences. It is possible that common factors leading to failures or success may emerge. Such poshoc analyses may be very useful as they provide for important things to emphasize or deemphasize in future negotiations.

Superior products or services and good negotiations lead to good multinational business relationships. However, people must do the negotiating. In the next section, we will consider the characteristics of the successful international negotiator.

The Successful International Negotiator: Personal Characteristics

The successful international negotiator is comfortable in a multicultural environment and is skilled in interpersonal relationships. In addition, successful international negotiators have a variety of personal success characteristics that enhance their abilities to adjust to the stress of cross-cultural negotiations. These include:[42]

Personal success characteristics

Tolerance of ambiguous situations, flexibility, creativity, humor, stamina, empathy, curiosity, and knowledge of a foreign language.

➤ *Tolerance of ambiguity:* Even if they are familiar with the culture of their counterpart, an international negotiator is still a cultural bridge between people from different national and organizational cultures. Consequently, both the process of negotiation and the ultimate outcome are never entirely predictable. Individuals who take comfort in certainty of outcomes should probably avoid international negotiations. During the negotiation process, success requires that negotiators remain patient and nonjudgmental and "go with the flow."

➤ *Flexibility and creativity:* The international negotiator must expect the unexpected. Explicit goals for the outcome may not work. Unanticipated proposals may be offered. Counterproposals may not come. Even the site of the negotiation may be entirely different from the planned location.

➤ *Humor:* Situations arise in intercultural exchanges that are sometimes embarrassing or humorous. Humor often breaks tension and allows both sides to deal with cultural ambiguities. For example, a U.S. businesswoman in Japan was shocked to see a lobster, which she was eating at the time, demonstrate its freshness by attempting to walk off the plate. Her Japanese hosts were much amused at her shock. She joined in their laughter as they teased her about eating more "active" food.

➤ *Stamina:* Long travel, jet lag, different foods, different climates, hotel living, and culture shock stress the physical stamina of even experienced international negotiators. Negotiators must overcome these physical challenges and still listen, analyze, observe, and socialize during the negotiation exchange. Only those negotiators with a strong constitution succeed.

➤ *Empathy:* Empathy means putting yourself in the place of your foreign colleagues—understanding the world from their perspective. This does not mean that a negotiator must agree with his or her counterpart on all issues. Rather, the empathic person must have a sincere concern for the feelings and perspectives of the other party. Empathy facilitates the negotiation because it softens the impact of interpersonal errors and cultural misunderstandings.

➤ *Curiosity:* Curiosity opens the door to new information. Managers with a genuine curiosity and respect concerning other cultures often discover subtleties that a more task-oriented negotiator misses.

➤ *Bilingualism:* Knowing the counterpart's language is an asset. However, sometimes linguistic ability alone is not enough. Even people who speak a language fluently may not understand significant aspects of a country's business culture. In particular, a good negotiator needs to understand how the business culture affects styles of negotiation.

As this chapter shows, negotiation is a very important but complex activity for multinational companies. To illustrate the complexity of negotiations, this chapter concludes with a Focus on Emerging Markets discussing cultural contradictions of Indians and how one can approach negotiations with Indians.

Focus on Emerging Markets

Negotiating with Indians

As more companies enter the Indian market to take advantage of opportunities, there is an increased need to negotiate with Indians. However, as many companies have experienced, negotiating with Indians can be very complicated. In the 1990s, many independent power-producing companies abandoned negotiations to develop new power projects because the negotiations were so drawn-out. Even at country level negotiations, Indian officials are seen as tough, inflexible, and idealistic.

Why is negotiating so complex with the Indians? Experts suggest that Indian cultural values tend to include many contradictions. For example, Indians are known to be very individualistic and aggressive in some situations while very collectivistic and family-oriented in other situations. Furthermore, India is also a very old civilization with well-developed spiritual traditions. Such traditions have penetrated the Indian business mindset encouraging strong idealism. It is therefore not unusual for Indian negotiators to strive for very idealistic goals reflected often in unrealistic but best possible solutions. Additionally, companies have also found that personal relationships may not be as critical at the start of negotiations and may assume that the negotiations will proceed rapidly. However, these same companies soon found that relationships become more critical at the operational stage of negotiated projects. At later stages of the project, it is necessary to cultivate relationships to show sincerity.

Given the complexities of negotiating with Indians, practitioners provide the following suggestions to ensure that the negotiations proceed as smoothly as possible:

Focus on Emerging Markets

➤ *Patience:* Patience seems to be a critical necessity when negotiating with Indians. Indians will often prefer to look for the best possible situation. Fighting or hurrying this quest can only be angering and frustrating and won't necessarily result in quicker negotiations.

➤ *Work with the high idealism:* When negotiators are faced with the highly idealistic Indian, they may reject such views. However, Indians tend to react negatively to such rejection, becoming bitter. Negotiators are encouraged, instead, to find ways to show how their solution can be mutually beneficial.

➤ *Be flexible:* Contractual obligations are not seen the same way as in the United States. Because of decades of a chaotic business environment, Indians prefer more open-ended obligations. As such, the negotiators should be ready to accept changes within reason.

➤ *Understand that negotiated projects may not be implemented in a timely manner:* Negotiated projects may often take longer to be implemented because of deliberate actions or because of bureaucratic governmental obstacles. Negotiators should plan for such contingencies.

➤ *Encourage Indians to change their behavior:* Indian negotiators respond negatively to aggressive behavior. Experts suggest that negotiators should try to induce behavioral changes by making their Indian counterpart feel more secure. Often, the appropriate way to make Indians feel secure is by being humble and avoiding the use of pressure tactics.

Source: Based on Kumar, Rajesh. 2004. "Brahmanical idealism, anarchical individualism, and the dynamics of Indian negotiating behavior." International Journal of Cross Cultural Management 4, 1: pp. 39–58; Kumar, Rajesh. 2005. "Negotiating with the complex, imaginative Indian." Ivey Business Journal, March–April, pp. 1–6; Narlikar, Amrita. 2006. "Peculiar chauvinism or strategic calculation? Explaining the negotiating strategy of a rising India." International Affairs, 82, 1: pp. 59–76.

Summary and Conclusions

In this chapter, we examined the negotiating process and elements of cross-cultural communication in international business. The negotiating process involves preparation, building relationships with counterparts, persuading others to accept your reasonable goals through verbal and nonverbal negotiating tactics, making concessions, and finally, reaching an agreement. Successful negotiators prepare well and understand the steps of the negotiation processes. They also avoid the use of dirty tricks and competitive negotiating strategies.

The people who become successful negotiators are bilingual and have good cross-cultural communication skills. In addition, they are tolerant, flexible, empathic, and curious. They react to the stress of international negotiations with humor and stamina.

Oral cross-cultural communication demands that one learn the language or use interpreters, especially in complex negotiations. High-context languages also require that people learn to interpret situations that may not be apparent from analysis of the spoken component.

Nonverbal communications through body movements, proxemics, and touching vary widely for different cultural groups. International negotiators and managers must learn to interpret these behaviors in sensitive and empathic ways. This often requires looking at the world through the eyes of the other culture.

Avoiding attribution errors is a key to cross-cultural communication. International managers need sensitivity to their own behaviors and the behaviors of their foreign counterparts to avoid misinterpreting the meanings surrounding forms of communication. For example, a "dirty trick" in one culture may be a perfectly acceptable tactic in another culture.

Discussion Questions

1. Identify the steps in the negotiating process.
2. How does the U.S. "John Wayne" style of negotiation influence the steps in the negotiating process?
3. Pick two countries and discuss the cultural differences in the ways people might use verbal negotiating tactics.
4. What is an attribution? How do attributions influence cross-cultural communication?
5. How can attributions influence the perception of "dirty tricks"?
6. Identify some cultural differences in body movements. How might these influence a negotiating session?
7. How might a manager successfully influence his or her subordinates in a high-context culture?
8. Discuss each of the seven stages of negotiation. Which of these stages do you feel is the most important? Why?

Multinational Management **Skill Builder**

Negotiating an International Contract—a Simulation

Step 1. (1 minute) Read the following scenario.

This exercise simulates an international negotiation between Sportique Shoes, a North American manufacturer of athletic shoes, and Tong Ltd., a shoe manufacturer from the fictitious Southeast Asian country of Poreadon. Both countries are members of the WTO. Because of increasing price competition in the shoe industry, Sportique Shoes is seeking a low-cost manufacturing facility overseas. In preliminary correspondence, Tong Ltd. has offered the lowest price. It is also common knowledge that Poreadon has a high quality and motivated workforce.

A negotiating team from Sportique Shoes, charged with the task of beginning negotiations, arrives today to negotiate with the Tong Ltd. management team for a contract to manufacture Sportique's shoes for the next year.

Step 2. (10 minutes) Your instructor will divide the class into two teams. One team will represent the management of Sportique Shoes. The other team will represent the management team of Tong Ltd. Go to separate rooms or separate parts of one classroom.

Independent of the two teams, four people will be assigned the roles of World Bankers (2) and Administrators (2). These four people do not participate in the negotiation; rather, they observe, keep time, manage the finances, and take notes on the progress of the negotiation.

The objective of both the Sportique Shoes team and the Tong Ltd. team is to achieve the best contract for their company.

Step 3. (15 minutes) Each team will receive a packet of materials from the instructor. Read the Timeline, Negotiation Tasks, Cultural Background, and Negotiation Roles at this time. Decide who will play what roles.

Step 4. (10 minutes) Read the general rules for the following simulation:

A. The contract must cover four points:

1. Delivery dates for product shipments.
2. Quantity to be delivered at each shipment.

3. Price per 100 shoes manufactured.
4. Penalties for lateness.

B. Finances

1. Each team member must contribute $1.00 to each company's Capital Account. Your instructor may change or eliminate this requirement, depending on the particular circumstances of your course. The Capital Account is managed by each team's CFO.

2. The CFO delivers 40 percent of each company's Capital Account to the World Bank. The World Bank will finance future operations and requires this payment as an indication of good faith negotiations. The World Bank calls this money your Good Faith Account.

3. Forty percent of your Good Faith Account will be returned to each team after a successful contract is signed and delivered to your instructor. Should you fail to reach an accord in the time allocated, you will forfeit your entire Good Faith Account to the World Bank. It will be donated to a local charity. You may recover the additional 60 percent of your Good Faith Account by meeting certain objectives as stated in the Contract Negotiation Objectives.

C. General Contract Objectives and Financial Implications

1. Each team should try to negotiate a contract that is consistent with its cultural values and is economically favorable for its company.

2. Long-term financial gains and losses can result from what you negotiate. As in real life, these are not completely certain to you during the negotiation. However, the closer you are to reaching your objectives, the more likely it is that you will gain in the negotiations. For each point of negotiation, there are ranges of possible outcomes— some are neutral and both teams win, and some result in financial gain for one or the other side. After you negotiate your contract, your instructor will inform you of the economic results of your negotiations. For each point on which a team gained a favorable outcome, the other team will contribute 10 percent of its remaining Capital Account to the other team's Capital Account. For each point on which the contract results in balanced outcomes (you both win), the World Bank will contribute a flat fee of $1.00 to each company's Capital Account.

Step 5. (10 minutes) Read the Contract Negotiation Objectives provided by your instructor.
Step 6. (20 minutes) Plan a negotiation strategy with your team members.
Step 7. (10 minutes) Make a First Offer.
Step 8. (60 minutes) Negotiate!
Step 9. (30 minutes) World Bankers and Administrators balance accounts between teams. Entire group debriefs.

Endnotes

[1] Hise, Richard T., Roberto Solano-Mendez, and Larry G. Gresham. 2003. "Doing business in Mexico." *Thunderbird International Business Review* 45, pp. 211–224.

[2] De Mattos, Claudio, Stuart Sanderson, and Pervez Ghauri. 2002. "Negotiating alliances in emerging markets—Do partner's contributions matter?" *Thunderbird International Business Review* 44, pp. 710–728.

[3] Terpstra, Vern, and Kenneth David. 1991. *The Cultural Environment of International Business*. Cincinnati: South-Western.

[4] Whorf, Benjamin Lee. 1965. *Language, Thought, and Reality*. New York: Wiley.

[5] Babanoury, Claire. 2006. "Collaborative company research projects: A blueprint for language, c." *The Journal of Language for International Business* 17, 1: pp. 15–28.

[6] Hall, Edward T. 1976. *Beyond Culture*. Garden City, N.Y.: Anchor Press.

[7] Ferraro, Gary P. 1994. *The Cultural Dimension of International Business*. Englewood Cliffs, N.J.: Prentice Hall.

[8] Eibel-Eibesfeldt, I. 1971. "Similarities and differences between cultures in expressive movement." In *Behavior and Environment: The Use of Space by Animals and Men*, edited by Robert E. Hinde, pp. 297–312. London: Cambridge University Press.

[9] Ferraro, *The Cultural Dimension of International Business*.

[10] Axtell, R. E. 1991. *Gestures*. New York: Wiley; Chaney, Lillian H., and Jeanette S. Martin. 1995. *Intercultural Business Communication*. Englewood Cliffs, N.J.: Prentice Hall.

[11] Hall, Edward T., and Mildred Reed Hall. 1990. *Understanding Cultural Differences*. Yarmouth, Maine: Intercultural Press.

[12] Ferraro, *The Cultural Dimension of International Business*.

[13] Axtell, R. E. 1998. *Gestures*. New York: Wiley.

[14] Chaney, Lillian H., and Jeanette S. Martin. 2000. *Intercultural Business Communication (3rd edition)*. Englewood Cliffs, N.J.: Prentice Hall.

[15] Axtell, *Gestures*.

[16] Chaney, Lillian H., and Jeanette S. Martin. *Intercultural Business Communication (3rd edition)*. Englewood Cliffs, N.J.: Prentice Hall.

[17] Harris, Philip R., and Robert T. Moran. 1991. *Managing Cultural Differences*. Houston: Gulf.

[18] Adler, Nancy J. 1991. *International Dimensions of Organizational Behavior*, 2d ed. Boston: PWS-Kent; Graham, John L., and Roy A. Herberger, Jr. 1983. "Negotiators abroad—don't shoot from the hip." *Harvard Business Review* 61: pp. 160–168.

[19] Copeland, L., and L. Griggs. 1985. *Going International*. New York: Random House; Dolan, John Patrick. 2005. "Strategies to negotiate any sale." *Agency Sales* January, 35, 1: p. 24; Dolan, John Patrick. 2005. "How to prepare for any negotiation session." *Business Credit*, March, 107, 3: p. 18; Salacuse, Jeswald W. 1991. *Making Global Deals*. Boston: Houghton Mifflin.

[20] Tung, Rosalie L. 1984. "How to negotiate with the Japanese." *California Management Review* 26: pp. 62–77.

[21] Salacuse, *Making Global Deals*.

[22] Ibid; Salacuse, Jeswald W. 2005. "Negotiating: The top ten ways that culture can affect your negotiation." *Ivey Business Journal Online*, March–April, pp. 1–6.

[23] Salacuse, "Negotiating: The top ten ways that culture can affect your negotiation."

[24] Graham and Herberger, Jr., "Negotiators abroad—don't shoot from the hip."

[25] Salacuse, "Negotiating: The top ten ways that culture can affect your negotiation."

[26] Chaney and Martin, *Intercultural Business Communication*.

[27] Inman, William. 2006. "What are you talking about?" *Industrial Engineer* January, 38, 1: pp. 36–39.

[28] Graham, John L. 1985. "The influence of culture on the process of business negotiations: An exploratory study." *Journal of International Business Studies* 26: pp. 81–96.

[29] Adler, *International Dimensions of Organizational Behavior*.

[30] Graham, "The influence of culture on the process of business negotiations: An exploratory study."

[31] Adler, *International Dimensions of Organizational Behavior*.

[32] Graham, "The influence of culture on the process of business negotiations: An exploratory study."

[33] Adler, *International Dimensions of Organizational Behavior*; Elahee, Mohammad N., Susan L. Kirby, and Ercan Nasif. 2002. "National culture, trust, and perceptions about ethical behavior in intra- and cross-cultural negotiations: An analysis of NAFTA countries. *Thunderbird International Business Review* 44, pp. 799–818; Fisher, Roger, and William Ury. 1981. *Getting to Yes*. New York: Penguin; Kublin, Michael. 1995. *International Negotiating*. New York: International Business Press.

[34] Adler, *International Dimensions of Organizational Behavior*; Dolan, "How to prepare for any negotiation session."

[35] Adler, *International Dimensions of Organizational Behavior*; Kublin, *International Negotiating*.

[36] Hendon, Donald W., Matthew H. Roy, and Zafar U. Ahmed. 2003. "Negotiation concession patterns: A multi-country multiperiod study." *American Business Review*, January, pp. 75–83.

[37] Kublin, *International Negotiating*.

[38] Bazerman, Max H., and Margaret A. Neale. 1991. *Negotiating Rationally*. New York: Free Press.

[39] Palich, Leslie E., Gary R. Carinini, and Linda P. Livingstone. 2002. "Comparing American and Chinese negotiating styles: The influence of logic paradigms." *Thunderbird International Review* 44, pp. 777–798.

[40] 2003. "Analogical learning in negotiating teams: Comparing cases promotes learning and transfer." *Academy of Management Learning and Education* 2, pp. 119–127.

[41] Ibid.

[42] Kublin, *International Negotiating*.

Dell's Dilemma in Brazil: Negotiating at the State Level

In mid-March 1999, Keith Maxwell, Senior Vice President for Worldwide Operations, Dell Computer Corporation, looked out the window of his office at Dell's headquarters in Round Rock, Texas, and pondered the frustrating situation he faced in Brazil, where Dell had decided to locate its first manufacturing plant in Latin America.

In early 1998, Maxwell led the site selection team that visited five different states in Brazil in order to decide where Dell should locate its manufacturing plant.[1] In June 1998, after the team confirmed its initial findings and concluded its negotiations, Maxwell made the final recommendation to Michael Dell: the plant should be built in Brazil's southernmost state, Rio Grande do Sul. By mid-March 1999, Dell had already signed agreements with the local state government on the terms of the investment, the process of hiring local personnel to manage the plant had begun, and construction on the plant itself was scheduled to start soon.

Suddenly, however, the political climate in Rio Grande do Sul changed. A new governor, Olivio Dutra of the Partido dos Trabalhadores (Workers' Party),[2] took office in Rio Grande do Sul on January 1, 1999 and appeared likely to rescind the entire agreement. This was a setback, and Maxwell had to decide on a course of action to recommend: (1) leave Brazil entirely; (2) move the plant to another state; or (3) try to renegotiate with Governor Dutra.

Dell and the Brazilian Computer Market

As Maxwell considered the options, he reflected on the events that had led to this situation. Dell had

begun the process of selecting a site for its manufacturing plant in Brazil in 1998, after the company had experienced a long period of astonishing growth. Founded in 1984 by Michael Dell in his University of Texas dorm room, by 1999 Dell Computer Corporation had annual revenue of over $23 billion and a market capitalization of $98 billion. In just 15 years, the revenues Dell generated were the second largest in the world for personal computer manufacturers, just behind Compaq, and the company was still one of the fastest growing PC makers in the industry.

Most of Dell's success could be attributed to its revolutionary business approach, which had become known as the Direct Model. Following the Direct Model, Dell shipped its products to its customers directly from the factory, without any intermediary retailers. Dell also set up its supply chain of parts and components using the latest just-in-time (JIT) methods, which allowed the company to maintain minimal inventory. These highly efficient practices enabled Dell not only to get its products to customers faster than its competitors could, but also to reduce its costs substantially. The resulting ability to pass on these savings directly to customers created a tremendous competitive edge that enabled the company to control 25% of the U.S. market for personal computers, and 11% of the market worldwide.[3]

In order to maintain its rapid growth, Dell adopted a strategy of emphasizing international expansion. From its headquarters in Round Rock, Texas, the company expanded its operations to the point that by the late 1990s, it had offices in 34 countries around the world, sales in over 170 countries and territories, and manufacturing facilities in five countries, including Ireland and China. Although the company outsourced some of its manufacturing to contract manufacturers in Mexico, it did not have any manufacturing facilities of its own in Latin America when, in early 1998, it began evaluating possible sites for the construction of its own manufacturing plant in Brazil.

Brazil was a logical place for a manufacturing plant. In the late 1990s, sales of personal computers were growing faster in Latin America than anywhere else in the world and Brazil, the largest Latin American country with a population of over 170 million, was a very attractive market for the company. Despite the maxi-devaluation of the Brazilian currency, the *real*, in January 1999, Dell had decided to continue with its plans to invest in Brazil as part of its long-term strategy. Dell executives realized that having a plant in Brazil would be essential if the company were to enter the Brazilian market successfully. Although in 1992 the Brazilian government had abandoned its market reserve policy of allowing only domestic manufacturers to make computers in the country, Brazil's protectionist barriers for imports were still high. Moreover, Brazil was a member of Mercado Comun do Sul (Mercosul), the South American customs union that included Argentina, Uruguay, and Paraguay, with Chile and Bolivia as associate members. The benefit of Mercosul was that any company that produced at least 60% of a given product in any of the Mercosul countries would, with some exceptions, be able to export the product to any of the other Mercosul countries at zero tariffs. Clearly, Brazil's Mercosul membership was another plus for putting the plant in Brazil.

Once Dell had selected Brazil, however, the question remained as to exactly where the manufacturing plant would be located. Brazil had a federal system, with 26 separate states—each with its own governor and state legislature, as well as a federal district, and many of these states eagerly sought Dell's investment. Having chosen Brazil as the site for the new manufacturing plant in Latin America, Dell's executives would have still another decision to make.

Maxwell and the others on Dell's site selection team visited five different states in Brazil: São Paulo, Minas Gerais, Rio de Janeiro, Paraná, and Rio Grande do Sul. All of these states essentially met the requirements for levels of education and sufficient numbers of qualified personnel, adequate supply of electrical energy, and quality of telecommunications and transportation infrastructure. The main differences of interest to the Dell team were the special financial incentives each state offered, and the nature of the agency with which the

company interacted when making the investment decision.

Competition Between the States

The Guerra Fiscal In their exuberance during Brazil's transition to democracy, politicians elected to Brazil's Constituent Assembly approved a constitution in 1988 that gave states considerably more power than before. Among other things, states were authorized to collect state sales taxes, or Impostos sobre a Circulação de Mercadorias e Serviços (ICMS). Although the current average for these taxes was 12%, states had some leeway to reduce these taxes in order to attract investment.

In theory, individual states could not change their ICMS tax rates unless all states agreed to do so within the Conselho Nacional de Política Fazendária (CONFAZ), the representative body for the states on finance and taxation policy. Nevertheless, from the beginning, states made such changes without CONFAZ approval. Since the early 1990s, the competition between the states to lower their taxes and attract investment had become so fierce that journalists called it the "guerra fiscal," or taxation war.

Taxation rates mattered to large transnational corporations trying to decide where to invest. Competition among these companies was fierce, and a difference in sales tax meant that companies could offer their products at reduced costs without passing on the tax burden to consumers. Such incentives also compensated for extra costs associated with investing outside of the more industrialized and heavily populated locations of Brazil, especially the state of São Paulo, which traditionally received, by far, the greatest proportion of Brazil's foreign investment. Significantly, São Paulo itself did not offer this particular incentive—it did not need to do so.

But many in Brazil saw this policy as detrimental to the country's overall interests. Critics of the *guerra fiscal* argued that transnational corporations (TNCs) could use it to play one state against another for their own benefit, without concern for the welfare of the country as a whole. Poor Brazilian states, these critics maintained, were in no position to be giving tax concessions to large, wealthy transnational corporations.[4] Supporters of the policy, on the other hand, argued that without such incentives, the TNCs would not invest at all in states far from the more industrialized regions.[5] And as one supporter of the policy put it, "12% [the full taxation rate] of nothing is still nothing."[6]

The incentives Brazil's states could offer to attract foreign investment went beyond reductions in the ICMS. State governments could (and did, in many cases) also offer to provide free land on which to build infrastructure (usually roads or port facilities), and to provide government loans on highly concessional terms, including lengthy grace periods and low interest rates. As with the ICMS tax reductions, these incentives also came under harsh attack from critics. This was the environment that Maxwell and the Dell team had entered when they began their site selection process in Brazil.

Financial Incentives and Contrasting Approaches to Investment Promotion   During the site selection process, one of the team's chief concerns had been to investigate the prospects for obtaining financial incentives in each state. Upon actually visiting each state, however, the site selection team's initial and most important contacts were with the agency responsible for investment promotion. The nature of the working relationships Maxwell and the rest of the team established with these agencies also turned out to play a major role in the decision-making process.

Each state in Brazil that the Dell executives visited had a unique approach to promoting foreign investment; and in every state, the investment promotion organization responsible for meeting with the Dell team had a slightly different organizational structure and style. With the sole exception of Pólo-RS, Agência de Desenvolvimento (Pólo), the independent, private, nonprofit investment promotion agency that collaborated with the state government of Rio Grande do Sul, all of the state agencies the Dell executives encountered were government agencies. This made a difference in how these agencies interacted with Dell. While other states such as Minas Gerais offered Dell similar financial incentives, only in Rio Grande do Sul did the Dell executives, working with Pólo as an intermediary, encounter an investment promotion agency that they felt had made a concerted effort to understand Dell's specific needs. In other states, in contrast, Dell executives perceived that the government officials they were dealing with either did not sufficiently understand Dell's unique requirements, or were not sufficiently committed to attracting high-technology investment.

São Paulo, for example, was a state that initially attracted Dell. It had a large pool of skilled labor and, because of its large, relatively prosperous population, it was the principal market for computers in Brazil. São Paulo's sheer market size was the main reason that in the final selection process, two possible sites in the state, one in the city of São Jose dos Campos and the other in Campinas, were ranked high on the list, although still below Rio Grande do Sul.[7] But the Dell site selection team formed a negative impression of São Paulo when harried state government officials appeared to be somewhat indifferent to Dell's specific concerns.[8] Moreover, the state, which already had significant investment, had a policy of not offering special financial incentives.[9]

In Rio de Janeiro, the team encountered a different situation. The head of the Companhia de Desenvolvimento Industrial do Estado do Rio de Janeiro (CODIN), Rio de Janeiro's investment promotion agency, was accustomed to long drawn-out negotiations with automobile firms that sometimes lasted for a year or more. Consequently, he made a very low initial offer for financial incentives to Dell, expecting the company to come back with a counter offer. He was stunned when the Dell executives, accustomed to making decisions on a much speedier basis, never returned.[10]

In Paraná, the state government was not able to offer Dell the same financial incentives that Rio Grande do Sul offered.[11] In addition to that, Maxwell and others on the Dell team also perceived that the state was giving the same sort of presentation to them that it gave to all companies, regardless of the specific sector the company represented.[12]

Other than São Paulo, which was ranked high principally because of the size of its market rather than its investment promotion efforts, only Minas Gerais came close to winning the competition with Rio Grande do Sul for Dell's investment. In Minas, the Dell executives met with state government officials from various agencies, as well as with *técnicos* from the Instituto de Desenvolvimento Industrial, de Minas Gerais (INDI). Created in 1968, INDI had a unique structure. It was financed partly by the Companhia Energética de Minas Gerais (CEMIG), the state energy company—a mixed enterprise, 70% state-owned, 30% private—and partly by the Banco de Desenvolvimento de Minas Gerais (BDMG), the state-owned Minas Gerais Development Bank. While INDI was a government institution, then, the partially private ownership of one of INDI's supporting institutions, CEMIG, gave INDI more flexibility in hiring personnel than it would have had if it were purely a state-owned institution.[13] As a result, at least some of INDI's staff also received salaries that were considerably higher than those working in regular government agencies.[14] In this way, INDI was able to recruit highly qualified staff that specialized in at least six broadly diversified industrial sectors—mining and metallurgy; chemicals and nonchemical materials; industry and tourism; agroindustries; textiles, garments, leather, footwear, furniture, and publishing; and mechanics, electroelectronics and computers—who might otherwise have taken jobs in the private sector.[15]

It is a testament to INDI's effectiveness that members of Dell's site selection team made three separate visits to Minas Gerais to meet with state government officials. The final proposal that INDI prepared was only slightly less favorable than that of Rio Grande do Sul—the state that ultimately won Dell's investment. Minas Gerais was able to offer Dell a 70% reduction in the ICMS tax for 10 years; a loan for R$20 million (20 million *reais*), with a four-year grace period and a four-year repayment period; and free land for the plant site.[16] But in the end, Dell chose Rio Grande do Sul.

INDI was in some ways a victim of its own success. The agency's past achievements in attracting companies from the mining, steel, and automobile sectors had made such an impact on the state that when the Dell site selection team arrived, they had the impression that this was the primary focus of the government's activities. Historically, of course, Minas Gerais had always had a strong mining sector. (Minas Gerais itself means "General Mines" in Portuguese.) INDI's later success in attracting foreign investment from companies in the heavy capital equipment and automobile sectors further contributed to the state's industrial development. Observing the results of this prior industrialization, however, the Dell executives came away with the impression that Minas Gerais, especially in the vicinity of the Fiat plant and the greater metropolitan region of Belo Horizonte, was a heavy-industry, rust-belt region. This reinforced their sense that the government officials they were dealing with in Minas had grown accustomed to working with the large, capital-intensive, heavy-industry firms that were common in the mining and automobile industries, and would not fully be able to appreciate Dell's specific needs as a fast-paced, just-in-time-oriented, knowledge-intensive company.[17] Fair impression or not, the INDI staff were unable to change this view during the Dell executives' time in Minas Gerais, and it had a strong influence on the company's decision not to invest there.

Rio Grande do Sul, the Ultimate Choice

Rio Grande do Sul had not even been on Dell's short list when representatives from Pólo and the state government visited the company in early 1998 and convinced Dell's senior executives that the state deserved a closer look. But by June 1998—less than six months after that initial visit—Maxwell and the team had made the recommendation that Dell should establish a plant in Rio Grande do Sul.

Certainly, Rio Grande do Sul had a lot to offer. It had a well-developed, modern infrastructure; and as the first state to privatize its telecommunications company, its telecommunications infrastructure was among the more efficient in the country. In fact, a quick analysis indicated that, even before factoring in any incentives the state government might offer, lower costs in Rio Grande do Sul for the plant's overall facilities would already compensate for the additional expense associated with shipping computers to customers elsewhere in Brazil.[18] And although customers in São Paulo, for example, would have to wait a day longer to receive their computers from a plant in Rio Grande do Sul than they would if the plant were located in São Paulo itself, previous studies had indicated that this would not be a serious problem.[19]

Security was another factor. In terms of security from hijackings and robbery, the main road from Rio Grande do Sul to São Paulo, Dell's principal market, appeared to be considerably safer than many of the roads within the state of São Paulo itself. In addition, the Dell executives felt personally safe in and around the vicinity of Porto Alegre, Rio Grande do Sul's capital, where the plant would be located. Expatriate executives and suppliers from out of town might not know which areas to avoid in a large, unfamiliar city, but this was not really a serious problem in the greater metropolitan region of Porto Alegre, where the crime rate was relatively low.

Home to a number of well-regarded universities, Rio Grande do Sul had a well-educated population. It was one of the most prosperous of Brazil's states, with a standard of living that some rated as the highest in Brazil. In the end, too, the Rio Grande do Sul state government was able to offer very generous terms: a 75% reduction in the ICMS tax for 12 years, plus a R$20 million loan (over USD $16 million at the prevailing exchange rate), with a five-year grace period, to be paid back over a 10-year period.[20]

While offering generous incentives, the state government made sure that Dell would be providing benefits to Rio Grande do Sul as well. In the contract that the government signed with the company, Dell promised to develop joint research and development projects with local universities, such as the Universidade Federal de Rio Grande do Sul (UFRGS) and the Pontifícia Universidade Católica (PUC).[21] In addition to the company's R$128 million investment in its plant (USD $108.5 million), which alone would create beneficial linkage effects in the local economy in its construction and continued operation, Dell also promised to hire 260 direct employees in the first year and 700 employees within five years. If it did not, the contract would be nullified.[22]

These potential benefits help to explain why so many states in Brazil considered Dell's investment to be such a prize, and why Rio Grande do Sul was willing to offer such attractive incentives. Nevertheless, without Pólo's intervention Dell would not even have considered the state. Because Pólo played such an instrumental role in this outcome, further background on the agency itself is in order.

The Creation of Pólo Pólo originated in the early 1990s within the Federação das Associacoes do Rio Grande do Sul (FEDERASUL), which represented commercial enterprises in the state, and the Federação das Industrias do Rio Grande do Sul (FIERGS), which represented industries. Leaders within these two organizations proposed creating an independent, private agency to promote foreign investment that would be more flexible and nimble than a government entity. Funding for the agency would come from the private sector, but Pólo would work in conjunction with the state government to promote economic development in Rio Grande do Sul by attracting direct foreign investment in the state. Representatives from FEDERASUL

and FIERGS presented it to the two candidates for governor in the 1994 election: Olivio Dutra, a socialist from the Partido dos Trabalhadores (PT), and Antonio Britto, a pro-business moderate from the relatively centrist Partido do Movimento Democrático Brasileiro (PMDB). Although holding widely divergent political views, both candidates endorsed the idea, and thus Pólo was formally created in December 1995.

Pólo's founders sought to maintain a connection with the government by allowing the governor a key role in selecting the agency's president. This was done to ensure that the governor would maintain a close working relationship with the agency.[23] Ideally, both the government and the agency would work in concert to attract foreign investment that would contribute to the development of the state. However, this rule was changed in 1999, and the Board of Directors became solely responsible for selecting Pólo's president.[24]

The New High-Technology Emphasis Antonio Britto, the pro-business moderate, won the 1994 gubernatorial campaign and took office in January 1995. Having campaigned on a promise to promote foreign investment in areas that would bring jobs and economic development to Rio Grande do Sul, Britto was, for the most part, able to follow through with his plans. Using tax and other incentives aggressively, he was able to land large investments. "[25] In order to convince General Motors (GM) to establish a plant in the state, for example, Britto had offered substantial reductions in the ICMS state sales tax and generous loans at low interest rates, totalling hundreds of millions of dollars.[26]

José Cesar Martins, who became president of Pólo midway through Britto's administration in 1997, collaborated closely with the state government in an aggressive effort to attract more foreign investment like the GM plant. The agency maintained close contacts with several of what it called its "virtual" representatives: expatriate business people from Rio Grande do Sul working in New York City and San Francisco, who helped the agency by keeping tabs on investment trends and providing advice about how to deal with foreign investors. Martins also made sure that Pólo's staff participated in frequent investment forums and road shows around the world, in order to make contacts with potential investors and persuade them of the merits of investing in Rio Grande do Sul.

On one of these visits, Martins and other representatives from Pólo accompanied Governor Britto himself, as well as Nelson Proença, head of the Secretaria do Desenvolvimento e dos Assuntos Internacionais (SEDAI)—the state agency charged with attracting foreign investment to Rio Grande do Sul—to New York City for a series of meetings with potential investors. Marcelo Cabral, U.S. Managing Director for Banco Fator (a Brazilian investment bank) in New York City and one of Pólo's virtual agents in the U.S., had a substantial role in arranging this event.

A former equity analyst for Morgan Stanley, Cabral had extensive experience dealing with U.S. institutional investors who invested in Latin America, such as Scudder and Alliance Capital, and knew something about what made them tick. As an informal (virtual) advisor to Pólo, he explained to Martins that such investors would want to hear only briefly from the Governor and from Proença before speaking directly with managers of local companies looking for investment capital. To Cabral's surprise, Martins, a businessman himself, understood immediately and followed his suggestion.[27]

At the meeting, one of the investors that Cabral had invited argued that Rio Grande do Sul should seek to attract high-technology companies. Although Governor Britto was at first resistant to this idea, Nelson Proença, who had been an executive for IBM in Brazil for 10 years before working in the Britto government, was intrigued by this possibility. He reasoned that focusing on high-technology investment made a lot of sense given Rio Grande do Sul's unique characteristics: the large number of universities in the state already offering degrees in Computer Science and Electrical Engineering, and the overall high levels of education in the state's population as a whole.[28]

José Cesar Martins also thought the idea was worth pursuing. After discussing it further with Proença, Martins asked Cabral to help Pólo find a consultant in the area of high technology. From his extensive contacts in the financial community, Cabral knew the person to call was Duane Kirkpatrick, head of international operations for Robertson Stephens in San Francisco, one of the leading investment banks in the world in financing for high-technology businesses. Kirkpatrick agreed to serve as an outside consultant to Pólo to assess Rio Grande do Sul's prospects for attracting investment from high-technology companies.

After an extended visit to Rio Grande do Sul, Kirkpatrick came to the conclusion that high-technology investment would provide the state with high-wage jobs, in addition to linkages to the local economy. He also provided a number of suggestions about how Pólo and the state government of Rio Grande do Sul could attract such firms. Impressed, Pólo—in collaboration with Nelson Proença and Governor Britto—decided to focus future investment promotion efforts in this area.[29]

Rio Grande do Sul Makes the Short List: An Exchange of Visits As part of the new strategy, in February 1998, José Cesar Martins and a number of representatives from Pólo flew to San Francisco to attend a symposium for high-technology industries sponsored by Robertson Stephens bank. By this time, Pólo, with the help of Kirkpatrick and its virtual agents at Banco Fator (Marcelo Cabral and Dennis Rodriques), had already identified a list of high-technology companies that it would like to attract to Rio Grande do Sul. One of these was Dell Computer Corporation.

During the conference, Marcelo Cabral came upon an article in *América Económica* magazine about Dell's interest in building a manufacturing plant in Brazil, and he showed it to Martins. Demonstrating just how quick and flexible Pólo could be, Martins and his staff immediately left the conference, went back to their hotel and put in a call to Dell. When they got through to Tom Armstrong, Dell's Vice President of Tax and Administration, Armstrong told him that the company's preliminary site selection team, reporting to Keith Maxwell, had already been to Brazil three times and was closing its short list of potential sites in Brazil. "You are going to lose a big opportunity," Armstrong said. Martins protested, "But we are fast!" Martins told Armstrong that he, his staff, and Nelson Proença (who was in New York at the time) could be at Dell's headquarters the next day. They packed up, left the hotel, and were on a plane to Texas that night.

At Dell headquarters, the group was to be received by some of Dell's senior executives, including Daryl Robertson, Vice President of Dell Latin America, Tom Armstrong, and Keith Maxwell. But before the meeting at which Proença and Martins would make their pitch to Dell, they were given a tour of Dell's facilities and manufacturing plant in Round Rock. During this tour, something fortuitous happened. One of the workers in the plant, a skilled technician, happened to be Brazilian. The group stopped briefly to speak with him in Portuguese.

"I'll tell you how to win the hearts of Dell management," he told José Cesar Martins. "Tell them that Pólo is like the Irish Development Authority."[30] He explained that Dell's executives had had an excellent experience working with that organization. The Irish Development Authority (IDA) was Ireland's investment promotion agency. Dell executives had returned from a site selection trip to Ireland raving about how professional and helpful the IDA had been. Dell's experience with the IDA was an important factor in its decision to build a plant in Ireland.

Significantly, although Pólo had not consciously modelled itself after the IDA, it had many of the same characteristics. Pólo was entirely private, but worked in close collaboration with the government. It also had a targeted investment promotion strategy: it selected specific industries, and then focused on attracting investment from specific companies in those industries. Similarly, IDA's targeted investment promotion strategy allowed it to research an industry and specific companies thoroughly to anticipate any questions that site selection teams might have and address questions, concerns, or potential problems in advance, before the team even raised them. This is what made the organization so effective.

In its effort to focus on high-technology companies, Pólo clearly was pursuing a strategy similar to IDA's. In the meeting with Dell's senior management, then, José Cesar Martins did emphasize that Pólo was like the IDA. He noticed that this comment definitely caught their attention. The Dell executives listened attentively to presentations from Proença and Martins, and asked a number of penetrating questions about Rio Grande do Sul's level of education, rules regarding unions, and infrastructure. The Dell executives told the visitors that members of the site selection team had already visited São Paulo, Paraná, and Minas Gerais, but would like to return to Brazil to visit Rio Grande do Sul.

The site selection team came to Rio Grande do Sul sooner than expected, only about a week after that first meeting. Nevertheless, with only a short advance notice of the visit, Pólo called upon all its speed and agility. Notified over the weekend that the Dell executives were arriving Monday, Martins immediately called his staff and explained that they would have to make some urgent preparations for the meeting: charts would have to be prepared, statistics ready; in short, everything that would be relevant to Dell's concerns. Martins also called Proença, who convinced the governor to cancel meetings that Monday in order to give a presentation to the visiting Dell team. Thinking ahead, Martins made sure to hold the Monday meeting with Dell in a hotel, rather than in Pólo's offices, in order to avoid unwanted press attention at this delicate stage of the negotiations process.

It helped Pólo's case considerably that Martins was able to use his contacts in the business community to arrange private interviews for the Dell team with important business leaders in the state. These included high-level executives from three local companies: Gerdau, a steel conglomerate; Ipiranga, a gasoline distribution firm; and Rede Brasil Sul de Comunicações (RBS), a media company. Also present was one U.S. multinational, Coca-Cola, with which everyone on Dell's team would be familiar. A businessman himself, Martins was sensitive to the concerns of business executives. He knew that the Dell team would want to talk privately with local business executives in order to gain a perspective that was independent of Pólo and the state government officials.

The Pólo officials also made sure, on the first night the Dell executives were in town, to take them to visit a very popular local microbrewery called Dado Bier. They knew that the ambience of this popular local restaurant and bar would make a favorable impression on the Dell executives, and it did. To the visitors from Dell, the obviously well-educated, high-energy young clientele at Dado Bier seemed very similar to the kind of crowd that frequented such places in Austin, Texas.[31] This seemed to be just another indication that Dell would be able to find the kinds of employees it needed in Rio Grande do Sul. In addition to executives, engineers, and technicians, Dell's new plant in Brazil (which would also become its headquarters there) would need a large staff of personable, articulate, and technically proficient employees to take orders and handle technical questions over the telephone.

All of Pólo's quick, highly focused preparations worked. After listening to the presentations, speaking privately with business executives already in the state, and touring greater Porto Alegre for possible manufacturing sites, the Dell team said that they were interested.[32] They would send more teams later to examine potential sites more carefully, to ask additional questions, and to negotiate financial incentives. The Dell executives made clear that they would continue to negotiate with other states, but that they had decided that Rio Grande do Sul was definitely one of the leading candidates. To that extent, then, Pólo had been successful. Rio Grande do Sul would now just have to win against the other competing states.

In the end, of course, this was what happened. Tom Armstrong and Charlene Coor, as well as others at Dell whose job it was to confirm the site selection team's initial findings, made more visits and continued negotiations. Ultimately, determined to win high-technology investment for the state, the Britto government offered Dell the best terms for its investment. Less than six months after beginning negotiations with Pólo and the state government, Maxwell recommended to Michael Dell that the company should build its manufacturing plant in Rio Grande do Sul.

The Change in Government

Michael Dell agreed with this recommendation, and the company's plans to build its plant finally appeared to be set. But then the time came for another round of gubernatorial elections in 1998. Unfortunately, Britto's challenger—Olivio Dutra, once again—did not approve of the deal that Britto had negotiated with Dell. A member of Brazil's socialist Partido dos Trabalhadores, the Workers' Party, Dutra was against the government's granting of benefits to foreign transnational corporations. One of the main charges he had raised against Britto in his last campaign for governor was that "excessive" concessions granted to foreign transnational corporations would have to stop.

Dutra had served as mayor of Porto Alegre, where both he and the PT had a reputation for honest and effective government. Moreover, the Workers' Party was popular in 1998 as Brazil's financial crisis deepened and the federal government attempted to solve it with higher interest rates and other austerity measures. Perhaps not too surprisingly, then, Dutra won the 1998 election.

Since during his campaign Dutra had talked so much about the excessive benefits given to TNCs,

once he was in office he had to take action. During the first several weeks, he argued that the tax incentives granted to Dell, and also to Ford, which planned to build a multimillion dollar plant in the state and had been offered millions in incentives, would have to be renegotiated.[33]

Ford's attempts to negotiate with Dutra were futile. The new governor held fast to his position regarding the incentives by suspending the payment of loans the Britto government had promised the company.[34] Realizing that other states would offer the same incentives, and with minimal capital sunk into the project, Ford investigated its opportunities elsewhere. The state government of Bahia was quick to offer incentives identical to those the Britto administration had offered. Additionally, by locating its plant in Bahia, Ford would receive special incentives from the federal government for automobile manufacturers investing in the poorer northeastern states of Brazil.[35]

It helped Bahia's case considerably, of course, that the federal government was more than willing to intervene to make Bahia an attractive alternative to Rio Grande do Sul. Antonio Carlos Magalhães (ACM), President of the Brazilian Senate at the time, was an enormously influential politician from Bahia who was a key member of President Cardoso's governing coalition. It was ACM who pushed through the Congress a modification of the legislation on incentives for manufacturing automobiles in the northeast, so that Ford could still take advantage of it—even though the deadline for additional companies to do this had passed.[36] The federal government even approved additional incentives in order to make up for the extra costs Ford would face by putting its plant in Bahia rather than the more conveniently located Rio Grande do Sul. It was also significant that Brazil's national development bank, Banco Nacional de Desenvolvimento Econômico e Social (BNDES), provided a low interest loan of over US$300 million to Ford, more than it had planned to give for Ford's investment in Rio Grande do Sul. Again, the justification was that the additional amount was needed to make up for the extra costs associated with locating the plant in Bahia.[37] Realizing that Ford was now likely to withdraw from its plan to invest in Rio Grande do Sul, Dutra tried to negotiate with the company. But he was too late. Ford had already made its decision, and soon signed a contract with the Bahian state government.

The loss of Ford's investment was politically disastrous for Dutra. Residents of the town where the plant was to have been located protested.[38] The press lambasted the governor. And, of course, the political opposition had a field day lamenting the jobs that had been lost.

Nevertheless, Dutra had made his views very clear. It was at this point, by mid-March 1999, that Maxwell realized something had to be done.

Dell's Options

Maxwell considered his options again:

1. ***Dell could simply leave Brazil altogether.*** After all, the country had just experienced a massive devaluation in January 1999. Dell had continued with its plans in the immediate aftermath of the devaluation, demonstrating its faith in Brazil's long-terms prospects. But the country clearly had a significant degree of economic volatility, and even a fair amount of political volatility, or at least policy uncertainty, as Governor Dutra's recent actions indicated.

2. ***Dell could stay in Brazil but go to another state, such as Ford had done in Bahia.*** Certainly, the other states on the list that the site selection team had considered offered some interesting possibilities. Bahia would not be an option for Dell, but Minas Gerais might be. Minas met Dell's basic selection criteria and had offered an incentives package that was very similar to what Dell had received in Rio Grande do Sul.

   Minas Gerais had other benefits also. It did not have the same level of partisan differences, at least with regard to attracting foreign direct investment, that Rio Grande do Sul seemed currently to be experiencing. INDI, the state government's investment promotion agency, had seemed interested in working with Dell and knowledgeable about Dell's needs, if not quite to the same extent that Pólo had been. Perhaps the impression that members of the site selection team had—that Minas Gerais was too oriented toward the mining and automobile industries—had been misleading. After all, that did not mean

that the state could not also develop a niche in high-technology investment as well.

Dell had not yet begun construction on the plant in Rio Grande do Sul. As of yet, it really had no sunk costs that would make it difficult to leave the state and go elsewhere. Going to Minas was definitely still a possibility.

3. ***Dell could stay put and try to negotiate with the new governor.*** Fernando Loureiro was a talented Brazilian executive whom Dell had already hired to serve as its new Corporate Affairs Director in Brazil. He proposed that Dell could attempt to negotiate with the governor by showing how keeping Dell in the state could help him, or at least would not be inconsistent with his own goals and agenda.

   Loureiro's idea was that Dell executives could reason with the new governor by pointing out the harmony between the governor's objectives and Dell's. After all, Loureiro's argument went, Dell was a very different company from Ford. Unlike an automobile company, Dell did not manufacture something that damaged the environment; it manufactured computers. Computers provided people with access to the Internet. The Internet provided even people in poor slum areas access to information. This had a democratizing effect on society. Giving people everywhere access to information in this way could potentially create the conditions for a more just and egalitarian social order. Thus, Dell's goal to provide people with computers was in harmony with the governor's goal of working to create a more just and egalitarian society!

This last option seemed somewhat dubious to Maxwell. But, it was true that the governor had suffered a major political blow when Ford left. It would be very bad for him indeed if another major U.S. company decided to move to another state.

With such logic, perhaps the governor could be persuaded to let Dell keep all of its incentives. Loureiro had suggested this might be possible, provided that Dell offered to donate some computers to poor areas as a gesture of goodwill.

Should Dell take a chance on this last option or follow one of the others? Maxwell realized that there were risks either way. But he would be the one making the final recommendation to Michael Dell, and the decision would have to be made quickly.

CASE DISCUSSION QUESTIONS

1. Why does Dell want to invest in Brazil? Why is Dell considering a number of different states in Brazil?
2. How would you prepare to negotiate with the Brazilians?
3. What characteristics does Dell seek in a state where it will locate its investment?
4. Why does Dell select Rio Grande do Sul? What are some of the pros/cons of other states?
5. After Governor Dutra threatens to rescind the agreement with the previous governor, what are Dell's options? If you were Keith Maxwell, which option would you recommend and why?
6. What are some of the lessons of this case?

Appendix 1   Brazilian States

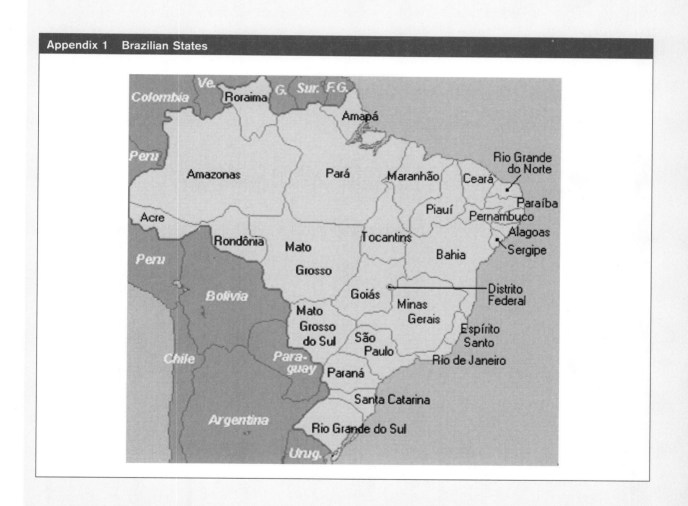

Appendix 2   Principal Site Options

	Rio Grande do Sul	Minas Gerais	São Paulo
General			
Population	10.2 Million	17.8 Million	37 Million
Area	281,749 Sq. KM	586,528 Sq. Km	1,522,000 Sq. Km
Demographic density	36.1 inhabitants / Sq. Km	30.5 inhabitants / Sq. Km	149.2 inhabitants / Sq. Km
Capital (population)	Porto Alegre (1.3 M)	Belo Horizonte (2.2M)	São Paulo (10.4M)
Economic Active population	53.5%	49.7%	47.6%
Life expectancy	71.7 years	70.4 years	70 years
Population Annual Growth	1.2%	1.4%	1.8%
Population distribution	Urban: 81.6%; Rural: 18.4%	Urban: 82%; Rural: 18%	Urban: 93.4%; Rural: 6.6%
Economic Indicators			
Total GDP	US$41.7 Billion	US$51.9 Billion	US$188.3 Billion
GDP per capita	US$ 4130	US$ 2928	US$ 5148
Commercial Balance	+ US$2.8 M	+ US$3.8 M	+ US$253 M
Principal Industries	Tobacco, Chemicals, Automobiles, Steel, Footwear, Foodstuffs	Metallurgy, General Engineering, Agribusiness, Minerals, Automobiles	Metallurgy, Automobiles, Foodstuffs, Engineering, Electronics
Infrastructure			
Homes with fixed telephone lines	67.9%	57.5%	77.9%
Paved roads	10,332 km	19,234 km	26,377 km
Incentives			
ICMS	75% reduction for 12 years	70% reduction for 10 years	N/A
Free land	no	Free land for plant site	N/A
Loan Agreements			
Amount	R$ 20 Million	R$ 20 Million	N/A
Grace period	5 year	4 year	N/A
Repayment period	10 year program	4 year program	N/A
Nature of Investment Agency	Pólo	INDI	Secretaria da Ciência e Tecnologia (SCT)
	Private, nonprofit agency	70% state-owned; 30% private	State institution

Source: Instituto Brasileiro de Geografia e Estatística (IBGE)

CASE NOTES

[1] The principal members of the initial team, in addition to Maxwell, included Daryl Robertson, Vice President, Dell Latin America; Tom Armstrong, Vice President, Tax and Administration; Kip Thompson, Vice President, Worldwide Facilities Management and Corporate Real Estate; and Charlene Coor, Director of International Tax.

[2] Brazil's Partido dos Trabalhadores (PT), the Workers' Party, is a leftist political party with a socialist ideology.

[3] "IDC Results Show Compaq Finished 1999 as Number One in Worldwide PC Market, but Dell Heads into Millennium Leading in the US," *PR Newswire*, January 24, 2000.

[4] Talita Moreira, "Business Leaders Praise Responses to Incentives Dispute," *Gazeta Mercantil Invest News*, <http://lexis-nexis.com/universe>, January 11, 2000; Denise Neumann et al., "Guerra Fiscal Abala Finanças dos Estados," *Estado do São Paulo*, July 13, 1997, p. 31; and Maria Quadros, "Governors Fail to Find Consensus on Fiscal War," *Gazeta Mercantil Invest News*, <http://lexis-nexis.com/universe>, January 28, 2000.

[5] Ricardo Caldeira, "Os Incentivos Fiscal Gera Desenvolvimento," *Gazeta Mercantil*, March 23, 1999, p. 2.

[6] Interview with Ricardo Hinkelman, Former Technical Adviser, SEDAI, Porto Alegre, November 10, 1999.

[7] Interview with Keith Maxwell, Senior Vice President, Dell Computer Corporation, Texas Round Rock, March 20, 2000.

[8] Ibid.

[9] Interview with Jorge Funaro, Chief of Staff, Secretariat of Science, Technology and Economic Development, São Paulo, November 15, 1999.

[10] Interview with Jorge Funaro, Chief of Staff, Secretariat of Science, Technology and Economic Development, São Paulo, November 15, 1999.

[11] Interviews with Fernando Sicuro, Technical Adviser of State Government of Paraná, and Clemente Simião, Coordinator, Secretariat of Industry, Commerce and Economic Development, State Government of Paraná, Curitiba, Parana, November 23, 1999.

[12] Maxwell, March 20, 2000.

[13] In fact, strictly speaking INDI did not have its own staff because all of INDI's personnel worked either for CEMIG, BDMG, or were outsourced from other agencies, and were technically on loan from these other institutions, Khoury Rolim Dias 2001, 2002.

[14] Interview with Romulo Ronan Fontes, Manager of Technical and Economic Studies Department, INDI, Belo Horizonte, November 26, 1999.

[15] INDI, <http://www.indi.mg.gov 2001>, January 23, 2002. Clearly, INDI, an older, larger, more established institution with a wider range of investment promotion activities, did not have what Pólo was able to develop in a very short time: a specific focus on attracting high-technology industries.

[16] Governo de Minas Gerais, Dell Proposal, Belo Horizonte, 1998.

[17] Maxwell, March 20, 2000.

[18] All computers were to be shipped by truck. This service was to be outsourced to local shipping companies.

[19] Telephone interview with Keith Maxwell, August 4, 2003.

[20] Guilherme Diefenthaeler, "O Dedo da Dell," *Amanha*, November, 1999, p. 39.

[21] Of course, in order to qualify for a tax incentive, the federal government gave to the computer industry known as the Proceso Produtivo Básico (PPB), which included a reduction of up to 50% of corporate income tax, companies such as Dell had to invest 5% of their total revenue in Brazil on research and development (R&D) within the country. At the time, at least 2% of this had to be invested in universities or other government-approved institutions; the rest could be invested inside the company. (Renato Bastos, "Computer Hardware and Peripherals," US Department of Commerce Industry Sector Analysis for Brazil, São Paulo, Brazil , 1998, p. 15.) As a result of these provisions, Dell would have to spend some money in Brazil on R&D in any case. The federal law, however, did not specify where in Brazil this expenditure on R&D would have to be made.

[22] "Alvorada Instala Pólo Tecnológico Com A Dell," *Jornal do Comércio*, August 21, 1998, p. 8; and Paulo Ricardo Fontoura, "Empresa Receberá Mais de 25 Anos de Incentivos Fiscais," *Gazeta Mercantil* August 26, 1998, p. 4.

[23] Interview with Telmo Magadan, former President of Pólo, Porto Alegre, December 17, 1999.

[24] Pólo-RS, Agência de Desenvolvimento, <http://www.polors.com.br>, January 11, 2000.

[25] Portas Abertas Para Novos Investimentos," *Zero Hora*, December 30, 1998, p. 11.

[26] Darcy Oliveira, "A Qualquer Custo," *Istoé*, April 14, 1997, pp. 34–6.

[27] Interviews with Marcelo Cabral, Former Managing Director of Banco Fator, Porto Alegre, December 17, 1999 and José Cesar Martins, former president of Polo, Porto Alegre, November 11, 1999 and December 15, 1999.

[28] Interview with Nelson Proença, Congressman, Chamber of Deputies, National Congress of Brazil, Brasília, December 5, 1999.

[29] Interviews with José Cesar Martins, November 11, 1999 and December 15, 1999; and Nelson Proença, December 5, 1999.

[30] Martins, November 11, 1999, and December 15, 1999.

[31] Telephone Interview with Keith Maxwell, August 4, 2003.

[32] Interviews with Miguelangelo Azário, Former Investment Analyst, Pólo, November 19, 1999, and November 1, 2001; Alex Martins, Former Director of Investments, Pólo, December 16, 1999, and Maxwell, March 20, 2000.

[33] Rosane de Oliveira, "A Opção e Seu Risco," *Zero Hora*, March 22, 1999, p. 10.

[34] Peter Fritsch, "Ford and GM Clash with Brazilian State—Dispute Over Incentives, Tax Breaks May Hurt Investment," *Wall Street Journal*, April 9, 1999, p. A11.

[35] Nelson Silveira, "Ford Promove Festa Política na Bahia," *Jornal do Brasil*, June 29, 1999, p. 16.

[36] Denise Madueño, "Governo Muda Lei Para Beneficiar Ford," *Folha de São Paulo*," June 30, 1999, p. 1.

[37] Denise Chrispim Marin, "Receita e Ford Já Negociam Incentivos à Fábrica da BA," *Folha de São Paulo*, July 14, 1999, p. 1.

[38] "Guiaba, De Luto, Grita 'Fica, Fica'; Prefeito Chora," *Folha de São Paulo*, April 30, 1999, p. 5.

14 Motivation in Multinational Companies

Preview CASE IN POINT

Motivating Workers in China

The move of multinational companies into China has created an intense competition for good workers. These multinational companies are finding that attracting the upwardly mobile Chinese professional with strong technical and international management skills is no easy task. As domestic companies reform their operations, they also are pursuing these same individuals. In a country where the average wage is $250 a year, money talks, especially in recruitment and retention. Skilled secretaries get monthly salaries that match or even double the yearly national average. When companies don't match the local market wages, job performance drops and turnover increases.

However, recent trends show that pay is no longer the best motivator for Chinese workers. As many of the safety nets (e.g., low-cost housing, healthcare, guaranteed jobs) that were part of the centrally controlled government have disappeared, budgeting for such items is slowly eating away at people's incomes. Additionally, corruption has become rampant. Chinese workers are becoming disenchanted with the uncertainties inherent in a capitalist society. As such, many job seekers are applying for civil-servant or other government jobs to benefit from job security.

Other surveys suggest that multinational companies have to become more creative to motivate their talented Chinese workers. As salary levels between cities and increases start to level off, multinational companies need to go beyond pay to motivate their workers. Some companies are finding that they need to provide adequate training programs while others are refining their performance management systems incorporating stronger pay for performance philosophies. A recent survey by Watson Wyatt also shows that Chinese workers are increasingly looking for safer and healthier work environments where the organization shows genuine concern for their professional development.

Sources: Based on Chen, Kathy. 2006. "Free Market Rattles Chinese; Economists' 'Ties' Questioned; Job Seekers Eye State Positions." Wall Street Journal, Jan 26, p. A9; Johnson, Mike.

1998. "Beyond pay: What rewards work best when doing business in China." Compensation and Benefits Review 30: pp. 51–56; Leininger, Jim. 2004. "The key to retention: Committed employees." China Business Review, January/February, 31: pp. 16–17, 38–39.

To implement multinational strategies successfully, earlier chapters showed how managers select the best organizational designs and the best international HRM policies. However, the best strategy, the best organizational design, and the best international HRM practices will not guarantee success. The multinational manager also must understand how to motivate and lead international employees with diverse cultural backgrounds and different expectations about work. This chapter focuses on motivation in the multinational enterprise. The next chapter will build on your understanding of motivation to identify leadership options in the multinational setting.

All managers must motivate their subordinates to accomplish organizational goals. However, as the Preview Case in Point shows, motivational techniques represent significant challenges for companies. Motivational methods based on pay used previously by multinational companies in China are no longer working. New trends suggest that these multinational firms need to constantly be aware of what workers seek in their work environment and adjust rapidly to satisfy these needs. As more multinational companies and domestic companies compete for the same talented workers, they are facing increased pressure to find new ways to motivate and retain these workers.

Multinational companies face an array of challenges to attract, retain, and motivate a workforce in a rapidly changing labor market. All multinational companies face the difficult task of motivating culturally diverse workers in an array of national settings. Furthermore, multinational companies also are facing new challenges as employees face an increasingly anxious and stressful workplace. These multinational companies need to constantly try new methods to motivate their workers. However, these new methods (e.g., humor, teams) may not always work, and multinational companies are only finding what works the hard way.

To provide the background necessary to understand how to motivate workers in multinational organizations, this chapter reviews international differences in work values and the meaning of work, discusses major theories of motivation and their multinational applications, and reviews U.S. and European views of designing jobs to produce high levels of motivation.

Work Values and the Meaning of Work

Before we can understand how to motivate or lead people from different national cultures, we must have some knowledge of what work means to people from different societies. There are two basic questions to answer: How important is work in people's lives? What do people value in work?

How Important Is Work in People's Lives?

To answer this question, several major international research projects studied thousands of workers from several countries. These studies included workers in all types of occupations: professional, managerial, clerical, service, and production workers.[1] The most recent study, the World Values Surveys and European Values Surveys (WVS/EVS),[2] contains information on people's attitudes toward work and life from 50 countries that include the majority of the world's population.

One question addressed in the Meaning of Work study is the degree to which people are attached to work or work centrality. **Work centrality** is "the degree of general importance that working has in the life of an individual at any given point in time."[3] Work centrality represents the importance of work in a person's life when compared with other activities, including leisure, family, community, and religion. Exhibit 14.1 shows the differences in work centrality for seven countries. Clearly, work has a dominant role in the lives of the Japanese.

Few studies have examined the country-level factors that lead to cross-national differences in work centrality. However, Parboteeah and Cullen[4] used a combination of national culture (Chapter 2) and social institutions (Chapter 3) to examine work centrality differences in 26 nations. They examined five social institutions, namely the extent of socialism, the degree of industrialization, the degree of union strength, the accessibility of education, and the extent of social inequality, and found that all five social institutions had negative effects on work centrality. In addition, the study also looked at three of Hofstede's[5] national culture dimensions. Results showed that uncertainty avoidance and masculinity had negative effects on work centrality. In contrast, the cultural dimension of individualism had positive effects on work centrality.

The study shows that the traditional attachment to work typical of most industrialized societies may be changing. Such changes are also consistent with Inglehart, Basanez, and Moreno's[6] observation of a postmodern shift in many

Work centrality

Overall value of work in a person's life.

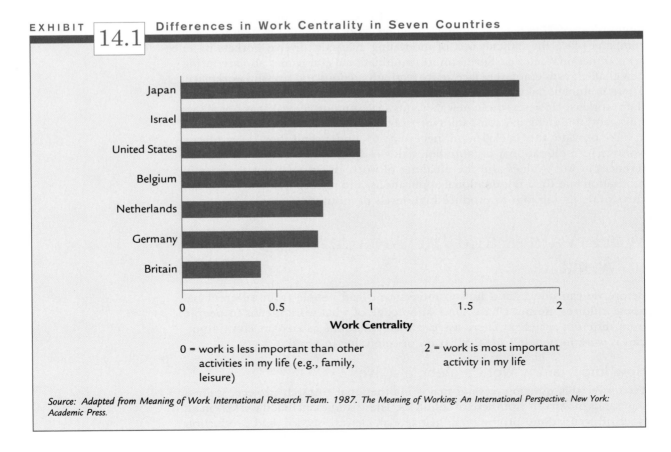

EXHIBIT 14.1   Differences in Work Centrality in Seven Countries

0 = work is less important than other activities in my life (e.g., family, leisure)

2 = work is most important activity in my life

Source: Adapted from Meaning of Work International Research Team. 1987. The Meaning of Working: An International Perspective. New York: Academic Press.

industrialized societies. They argue that industrialized societies have long strived on values that encouraged work centrality, economic achievement, individualism, and innovation but that these values have now reached their limits. In the post-industrialized societies, people are now more concerned with quality-of-life issues and individual self-expression.

Higher levels of work centrality are closely correlated with the average number of hours worked per week in the country (see Chapter 12 on national differences in human resource management for comparative data): People from countries with greater work centrality usually work more hours. The average Japanese worker, for example, puts in more hours than his or her counterpart in most other industrialized nations. Hence, managers may be able to apply management techniques that favor job-related incentives in order to motivate workers in societies with high work centrality.

In general, high levels of work centrality may lead to dedicated workers and effective organizations. However, as the following Multinational Management Brief shows, high levels of work centrality can also have adverse effects on workers. Evidence suggests that the number of hours worked by the Japanese is declining and many workers are complaining of burnout, perhaps indicating a change in work centrality for this country.[7]

Multinational Management Brief

Karoushi and Karojisatus—Sudden Death or Suicide from Overwork

The Japanese word "*karoushi*" translates in English as "sudden death from overwork." *Karojisatus* is suicide from overwork. As we saw in Chapter 12, the Japanese work more hours than people from most other countries do. They also have the highest work-centrality score.

This psychological and time commitment to working probably accounts for some of the Japanese economic growth. However, there is some indication that the benefits may have physical and psychological costs. As most of the managers who led Japan through its period of growth reach later middle age, the costs to them of long working hours and other Japanese business practices (long hours of drinking and smoking with colleagues after work) may be taking its toll. Early evidence suggests that death from work-related stress is on the rise. Police estimate the number of work-related suicides at 1,300 annually, but they have no official classification for this type of death. Some lawyers representing surviving family members put the estimate higher.

However, recent trends in the Japanese economy suggest that "*karoushi*" may slowly disappear from the Japanese work environment. Many young Japanese are rejecting the proud Japanese work ethic to join the Japanese NEETs (not in education, employment, or training). Additionally, other members of the younger generation are avoiding traditional corporate careers to become entrepreneurs and create their own wealth. Such trends suggest that, in the near future, Japanese corporations may have difficulties finding employees who are willing to dedicate the majority of their lives to work. Furthermore, as the Japanese population gets older (for the first time in Japanese history, the last census showed that deaths exceeded births), multinational companies in Japan will have a hard time finding the traditional and loyal workers that have always been part of the Japanese work environment.

Source: Based on Economist. 2006. "Greying Japan – The downturn." January 7; Caryl, Christian. 2006. "Turning un-Japanese." Newsweek, February 20; Kageyama, Yuri. 1998. "More overworked Japanese killing selves; Labor: As reflected in court cases, the deaths typically follow months of overtime with few or no days off and little sleep." The Los Angeles Times, July 20:7; Tubbs, W. 1993. "Karoushi: Stress-death and the meaning of work." Journal of Business Ethics 12, pp. 869–877.

Work obligation norms

Degree to which work is seen as an obligation or duty to society.

Besides understanding work centrality, it is also important to note the levels of **work obligation norms.** In general, societies that have high work obligation norms expect their citizens to view work as an obligation or a duty. These societies are more likely to have individuals adhering to this norm by working longer. Exhibit 14.2 shows the levels of work obligations in various societies surveyed by the World Values Survey.[8]

As Exhibit 14.2 shows, many of the emerging economies, such as India, Turkey, Poland, and Bulgaria, show very high levels of work obligation norms. Such findings are very encouraging for multinational companies that have substantial investments in these countries. Many of these emerging economies now have much stricter monetary and fiscal policies and more stable financial systems.[9] The high work obligation norms, coupled with a more structurally sound financial environment, suggest that multinational companies will face a workforce that has a very favorable view of work.

Exhibit 14.2 also shows that more developed economies such as the Netherlands, the United States, and Germany have much lower work obligation norms. Such results are consistent with Inglehart, Basanez, and Moreno's[10] post-industrialization shift. Decades of prosperity have reduced the importance of a strong work ethic, and individuals in these societies no longer view work as a duty.

EXHIBIT 14.2   **Work Obligations Norms for Selected Countries**

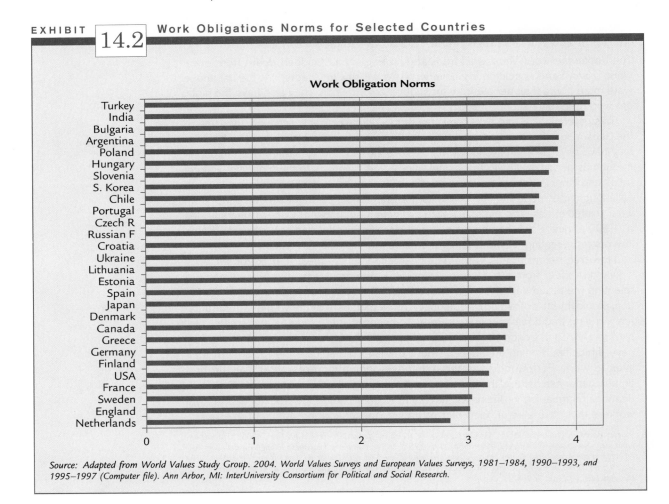

Source: Adapted from World Values Study Group. 2004. World Values Surveys and European Values Surveys, 1981–1984, 1990–1993, and 1995–1997 (Computer file). Ann Arbor, MI: InterUniversity Consortium for Political and Social Research.

What Do People Value in Work?

Besides examining the functions of work, the WVS/EVS study also looked at work values, namely what people expect from work. Two important work values are **extrinsic work values** and **intrinsic work values.** Through extrinsic work values, individuals express preference for security from their jobs with such aspects as income, job security, and less demanding work. In contrast, intrinsic work values express preferences for openness to change, the pursuit of autonomy, growth, creativity, and the use of initiative at work. Exhibits 14.3 and 14.4 show the extrinsic and intrinsic work values for selected countries of the World Values Survey.[11]

As Exhibit 14.3 shows, the most important finding is that people from different nations did not express the same preference for extrinsic and intrinsic

Extrinsic work values

Preference for security aspects of jobs such as income and job security.

Intrinsic work values

Preference for openness to change job aspects such as autonomy, being able to take initiative and be creative.

EXHIBIT 14.3   Preference for Extrinsic Work Values

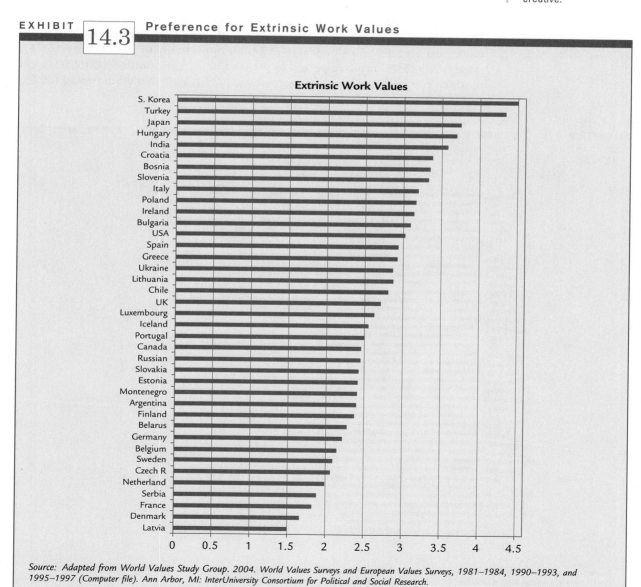

Source: Adapted from World Values Study Group. 2004. World Values Surveys and European Values Surveys, 1981–1984, 1990–1993, and 1995–1997 (Computer file). Ann Arbor, MI: InterUniversity Consortium for Political and Social Research.

work values. Most of the emerging economies (e.g., Turkey, Hungary, and India) rate extrinsic work values very highly. This probably reflects the situation in many of these countries where the security aspect of work is instrumental to survival. In contrast, many of the developed societies (e.g., the Netherlands, France, the United States) rate extrinsic work values much lower.

Similar to extrinsic work values, findings for intrinsic work values show that people from different societies have different preferences for such values (see Exhibit 14.4). A surprising finding, however, is that many of the countries that rated extrinsic work values highly also rated intrinsic work values highly. This may suggest that many of the emerging economies may view all work aspects positively while the more developed nations do not see work in a positive light. Consequently, when crafting their motivational strategies for a local workforce, multinational managers must not assume that people from different nations express the same preferences for work values.

The WVS/EVS research team asked workers to note what characteristics of a job they believe are important. The rankings of the work characteristics (for 50 countries) are: generous holidays (73%), an opportunity to use initiative (53%), good hours (53%), a job respected by people (50%), a responsible job (56%), a job in which you feel you can achieve something (42%), a job that is interesting (39%),

EXHIBIT 14.4   **Preference for Intrinsic Work Values**

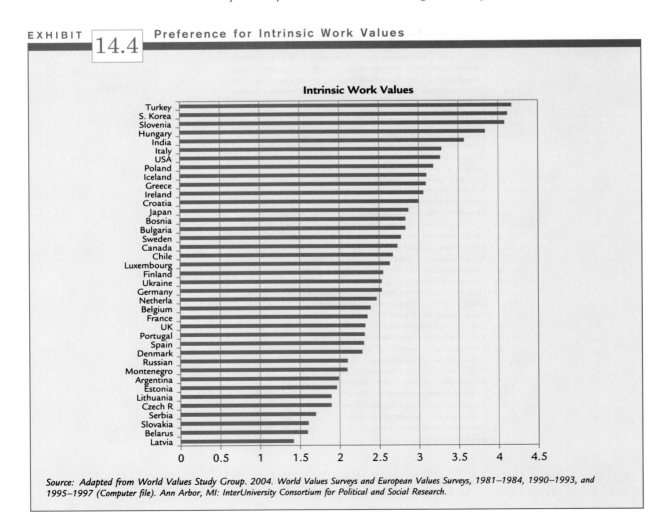

Source: Adapted from World Values Study Group. 2004. World Values Surveys and European Values Surveys, 1981–1984, 1990–1993, and 1995–1997 (Computer file). Ann Arbor, MI: InterUniversity Consortium for Political and Social Research.

a job that meets one's abilities (36%), good job security (30%), and good pay (19%).

Note that the reward of a generous holiday is almost a cultural universal: it is ranked first by nearly all countries. However, as one can see from Exhibit 14.5, the priorities given to different job characteristics do vary by country. Note, for example, that Japan and Russia differ from the world trend of giving a high priority to holidays. In spite of pay being a dominant function of work for many of the transitions and developing nations, no country rated pay as the most important work characteristic.

The earlier Meaning of Work study and the more current WVS/EVS study give us a good beginning picture of how work values differ in national contexts. They suggest the following conclusions:

- In some societies, work is very central and absorbs much of a person's life. People in such societies willingly work long hours and have a strong commitment to succeeding at work. However, in many industrialized countries that

EXHIBIT **14.5** Importance Rankings of Work Characteristics in Nine Countries

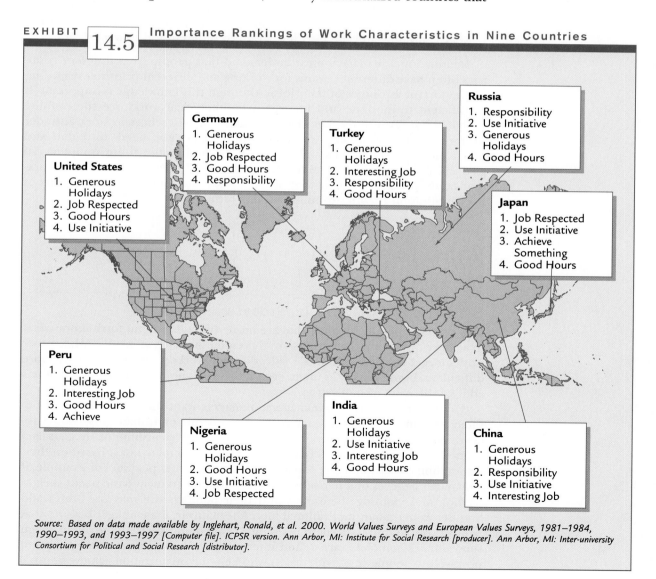

Russia
1. Responsibility
2. Use Initiative
3. Generous Holidays
4. Good Hours

Germany
1. Generous Holidays
2. Job Respected
3. Good Hours
4. Responsibility

Turkey
1. Generous Holidays
2. Interesting Job
3. Responsibility
4. Good Hours

United States
1. Generous Holidays
2. Job Respected
3. Good Hours
4. Use Initiative

Japan
1. Job Respected
2. Use Initiative
3. Achieve Something
4. Good Hours

Peru
1. Generous Holidays
2. Interesting Job
3. Good Hours
4. Achieve

India
1. Generous Holidays
2. Use Initiative
3. Interesting Job
4. Good Hours

Nigeria
1. Generous Holidays
2. Good Hours
3. Use Initiative
4. Job Respected

China
1. Generous Holidays
2. Responsibility
3. Use Initiative
4. Interesting Job

Source: Based on data made available by Inglehart, Ronald, et al. 2000. World Values Surveys and European Values Surveys, 1981–1984, 1990–1993, and 1993–1997 [Computer file]. ICPSR version. Ann Arbor, MI: Institute for Social Research [producer]. Ann Arbor, MI: Inter-university Consortium for Political and Social Research [distributor].

have traditionally been seen as valuing high work centrality (e.g., the United States, Japan), people may be changing their views of work. In contrast, less developed societies may have a workforce that places significant importance on the role of work in their lives.

- All people hope to receive certain benefits from work. Regardless of national context, money is a necessity, but it is not enough. Other emotional and practical benefits derived from work may have higher priorities. The benefits people hope to get from their jobs vary by national context.

- Societies differ in the degree to which they regard work as an obligation to society. Those societies that have high work obligation norms are more likely to have individuals working longer to conform to such duties.

- Many of the emerging economies that value extrinsic work values such as income and job security also place high value on intrinsic work values. Multinational companies need to provide jobs that not only provide adequate compensation but also provide job satisfaction.

- The first key to successful motivational strategies in multinational companies is understanding the differences among countries in the functions of work, work centrality, and the priorities given to different job characteristics.

Multinational managers must understand that people from different countries often have different reasons for working and different priorities regarding the important attributes of their jobs. Although this knowledge is important, is it sufficient to motivate and manage a multinational workforce successfully? Probably not. To use the knowledge of national differences in work attitudes for motivational purposes, a multinational manager also needs to understand how basic motivational principles work in the multinational environment. To give you this background, the next sections provide reviews of the basic work-motivation process, popular theories of work motivation, and applications of work-motivation theories to multinational settings.

Work Motivation and the National Context

The Basic Work-Motivation Process

Why do some people set goals that are more difficult and put forth more effort to achieve their goals than others? Why do some students seek "A's" while other students feel satisfied with "C's"? Why do some workers seek jobs that are more difficult and work harder at them, even if the pay is not higher? These questions address the issue of motivation.

Motivation concerns all managers. Managers want their subordinates motivated to achieve organizational goals. Toward this end, managers choose incentives (e.g., pay, promotion, recognition) and punishments (e.g., salary reduction), and design work (e.g., with simple or complex tasks) based on their assumptions and knowledge concerning what motivates people. For example, if a manager believes that her subordinates work only to meet basic needs such as feeding and clothing themselves and their families, she may use wages and bonuses as her major motivational tool. Alternatively, if a manager believes that people work to find fulfillment in doing a challenging job well, she might assign subordinates complex, varied, and interesting tasks. Managers usually respond positively to people (e.g., with raises) who help the organization achieve its goals and negatively (e.g., with bad evaluations) to employees who fail to help the organization achieve its goals.

The left side of Exhibit 14.6 gives a picture summarizing the psychological processes that most experts use to explain work motivation. A brief explanation of these underlying psychological processes follows.

Psychologists see **motivation** as a psychological process that results in goal-directed behaviors that satisfy human needs. Although **needs** differ for individuals and for cultural groups, all people seek to satisfy needs. A need is a feeling of a deficit or lacking that all people experience at some time. A need might be very basic, such as being hungry for the next meal. A need might be more complex, such as the need to be the best at whatever one attempts. To satisfy the hunger need, you may go to work to earn money to buy food. To satisfy an achievement need, you might practice ice skating daily with the ultimate goal of becoming an Olympic champion. In each case, a person uses

Motivation

A psychological process resulting in goal-directed behavior that satisfies human needs.

Need

Feeling of deficit or lacking that all people experience at some time.

EXHIBIT
14.6   The Basic Work Motivation Process and the National Context

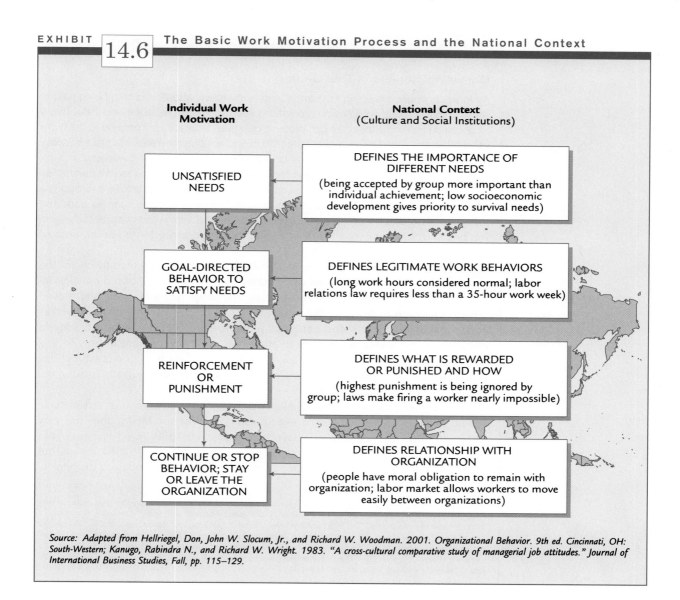

Individual Work Motivation

- UNSATISFIED NEEDS
- GOAL-DIRECTED BEHAVIOR TO SATISFY NEEDS
- REINFORCEMENT OR PUNISHMENT
- CONTINUE OR STOP BEHAVIOR; STAY OR LEAVE THE ORGANIZATION

National Context (Culture and Social Institutions)

DEFINES THE IMPORTANCE OF DIFFERENT NEEDS
(being accepted by group more important than individual achievement; low socioeconomic development gives priority to survival needs)

DEFINES LEGITIMATE WORK BEHAVIORS
(long work hours considered normal; labor relations law requires less than a 35-hour work week)

DEFINES WHAT IS REWARDED OR PUNISHED AND HOW
(highest punishment is being ignored by group; laws make firing a worker nearly impossible)

DEFINES RELATIONSHIP WITH ORGANIZATION
(people have moral obligation to remain with organization; labor market allows workers to move easily between organizations)

Source: Adapted from Hellriegel, Don, John W. Slocum, Jr., and Richard W. Woodman. 2001. Organizational Behavior. 9th ed. Cincinnati, OH: South-Western; Kanugo, Rabindra N., and Richard W. Wright. 1983. "A cross-cultural comparative study of managerial job attitudes." Journal of International Business Studies, Fall, pp. 115–129.

Goal-directed behavior

One that people use with the intention of satisfying a need.

goal-directed behaviors (i.e., work or practice) to satisfy unfulfilled or unsatisfied needs (i.e., hunger or the need for achievement). Goal-directed behaviors are behaviors that people use with the intention of satisfying a need.

Although satisfying needs is a general condition for human motivation, people use the work setting to satisfy many needs. For example, for most people, work is necessary to provide food and shelter. In addition, as you saw from the WVS/EVS study, working provides people with an opportunity to satisfy needs such as affording leisure, having interesting things to do, having responsibility, having a chance to use initiative, and developing relationships with other people. Many theories of work motivation have a basic assumption that people will work harder if they can satisfy more of their needs on the job.

The following Focus on Emerging Markets shows how the world-class Indian conglomerate Tata uses both satisfaction of needs and the work setting to motivate its workers.

Focus on Emerging Markets

Motivating Workers at Tata Group

As India continues attracting investment and world talent, attention is also being paid to some of India's most well-known corporations such as Infosys, Reliance, and Tata. These local companies show that they can produce goods and services to compete at the highest world-class level. This increased attention on Indian conglomerates has brought some interest in the Tata Group and its very unique approach to motivating workers.

The Tata Group has been around for more than 130 years and is still pursing its 19th century mission of making India an industrial power. Today, the Tata Group is a family conglomerate that is involved in various business sectors such as cars and steel, software and consulting, and even luxury hotels. However, despite thriving in the brutal global economy, the Tata Group has stayed true to its liberal roots of first taking care of its workers.

Consider, for example, the town of Jamshedpur, which was created by one of the founders of Tata. When the town was created in Calcutta, it was based on socialist principles. The company built schools, churches, parks, and a hospital, and it even provided housing to workers. In addition to satisfying many of the obvious worker needs, the company provided generous employee benefits. It cut the workday to eight hours and undertook efforts to make the work environment better. To this day, the steel mill and surrounding town is thriving as Tata tries to modernize. Furthermore, although India is generally prone to having regular strikes, Tata's steel arm has gone decades without a strike.

This concern for workers is similar across all of Tata's various businesses. Although many of the company's executives have Western MBAs, they are very aware of Tata's mission and view layoffs and downsizing as very "un-Tata." Tata works hard to ensure that their workers have access not only to basic needs but also to a good work environment. Such principles are still based today on the original founder's philosophical beliefs.

Source: Based Patel, Vibhuti. 2005. "India, Inc.: No longer just an outsourcing hub for low-level jobs, India is luring American talent and unprecedented new investments by tech giants Microsoft and Intel." Newsweek, Dec. 19, http://www.msnbc.msn.com/id/10455090/site/newsweek; Wehrfritz, George, and Ron Moreau. 2006. "A new kind of company: Tata coddles workers, not managers, keeps its distance from Wall Street—yet thrives in brutal global industries as a uniquely Indian kind of multinational." Newsweek, http://www.msnbc.msn.com/id/8359069/site/ newsweek; Worden, Skip. 2003. "The role of religious and nationalist ethics in strategic leadership: The case of J. N. Tata." Journal of Business Ethics, 47, pp. 147–164.

However, because most goal-directed behaviors take place in a social context, motivation includes more than satisfying needs; that is, when we do things that affect others, people react positively or negatively to what we do. In reinforcement theory, we call these reactions reinforcement and punishment. **Reinforcement** means that the consequences that follow a person's behavior encourage the person to continue the behavior. **Punishment** means that the consequences that follow a person's behavior encourage the person to stop the behavior. In the work setting, for example, managers use reinforcement, such as bonus pay, to encourage certain behaviors, such as higher daily output. Managers also use punishment, such as docking pay, to discourage behaviors, such as missing days of work. Based on whether they meet their needs at work and how managers react to their behaviors at work, employees may put more or less effort into work, feel satisfied or dissatisfied, or stay with or leave the organization.

National Context and Work Motivation: A Brief Introduction

Although certain basic needs are common to all humans (e.g., the need for food and shelter), the national context (culture and the social institutions) influences all steps of the motivational process. The right side of Exhibit 14.6 shows the effects of the national context on the work-motivation process. Each box contains two examples. One example shows an effect of national culture on the motivation process. The other example shows an effect of social institutions on the motivational process. More explanation and examples follow.

As we saw in both Chapter 2 and Chapter cultural values, norms, and supporting social institutions are important aspects of any society's business context. They influence the priority that people attach to work in general and the types of needs that people hope to satisfy at work. For example, early education and childhood games encourage people in collectivist societies to develop a need to belong to groups. The national context also helps define what behaviors at work provide legitimate ways to satisfy needs. For example, in countries such as Japan where work is central to a person's status and self-image, seeking a job in the largest and most prestigious company satisfies a need for achievement.

The national context influences reactions to goal-directed behaviors at work. For example, if a Japanese worker brags about her performance, she is likely to be sanctioned by her work group. The Japanese have a saying: "The nail that stands out gets hammered down." Finally, national culture and social institutions also influence the levels of satisfaction workers expect to receive in an organization and how committed workers are to their organization and its goals. For example, in countries where labor is well organized and militant, resistance to increases in work productivity is considered legitimate. Consider the Comparative Management Brief on page 700 where clearly the national cultural context influences the techniques that can be used to motivate Thai workers.

This brief overview of work motivation and the effects of the national context provide only an introduction to the complexities a multinational manager faces in the motivation of international workers. Next, to explore in more depth the challenges of motivating a culturally diverse workforce, the chapter expands on the basic model of work motivation. In the following sections you will see reviews of several motivation theories and a discussion of how the national context influences the application of each motivation theory and how the theory can be used by the multinational manager.

Reinforcement

Reactions to a person's behavior that encourage the person to continue the behavior.

Punishment

Consequences of a person's behavior that discourage the behavior.

Comparative Management **Brief**

Motivating Thais: Cultural Influences

As more multinational companies increase their investments in Thailand, being able to understand and motivate Thai workers is becoming more crucial. Consider that, for example, the Ford/Mazda AutoAlliance Thailand assembly plant, currently manufactures cars and pickup trucks for sale in more than 130 markets. Toyota is also seriously pursuing efforts to open a gearbox plant in Thailand. California-based Ducommun Technologies has also decided to establish its first non-U.S. facility in Thailand to manufacture microwave switches.

Hofstede's study revealed that Thailand has a high score on collectivism, moderately high scores on uncertainty avoidance, and a low score on masculinity. Motivational do's and don'ts garnered from practical experience in Thailand suggest that cultural influences may be very helpful in determining what works and what does not work.

The high score on collectivism suggests that Thais are very attentive to the needs of the in-groups. They generally function better in groups, and harmonious relationships are preferred. It is therefore not surprising to find that care must be taken not to openly criticize individual employees. Furthermore, senior Thais deserve *hai-kiat* (respect), and arguing with them in front of junior staff can be devastating. *Sia nah* (losing face) is the ultimate humiliation and has to be avoided.

The moderately high score on uncertainty avoidance implies that Thais prefer structure in their jobs and organizations to make things more certain and predictable. As such, unclear instructions or an organizational structure without clear lines of communications can be very demotivating. Managers are thus advised to provide clear structure to motivate their Thai employees.

Finally, the low score on masculinity or more feminine nature of the culture suggests a preference for family and quality of life as opposed to work. As such, it is imperative to understand Thais' appreciation of work and try to avoid training on weekends or expecting Thais to invest their personal time in the company. Motivational practices should focus around integration of the family.

Sources: Based on Hofstede, Geert. 2001. Culture's Consequences. London: Sage; M2 Presswire, 2006. "Research and markets: An analysis of the latest happenings in the automotive manufacturing industry from around the world." January 11; Niratpattanasai, Kriengsak. 2002. "How to make work miserable." The Bangkok Post, Nov. 22, p. 1; Sawyer, Christopher A. 2006. "Ford making Tracs for Thailand." Automotive Design & Production, Feb., p. 28; Thapanachai, Somporn. 2006. "Oldest Californian firm picks Saraburi." The Bangkok Post, Feb. 21, p. 1.

Need theory

Of motivation, assumes that people can satisfy basic human needs in the work setting.

Process theories

Of motivation, arising from needs and values combined with an individual's beliefs regarding the work environment.

Theories of Work Motivation in the Multinational Context

Why do we need work-motivation theories? Work-motivation theories attempt to show how the basic motivational processes apply to a work setting. Managers can use motivation theories to develop systematic approaches to motivating employees on the job. There are two basic types of motivational theories, **need theories** and **process theories.** The following section summarizes the major need theories of motivation. More than other motivational theories, need theories have the most international applications. A later section considers process theories.

Need Theories of Motivation

Need theories of motivation rest on the assumption that people can satisfy basic human needs in the work setting. That is, people are motivated to work because their jobs satisfy both basic needs, such as money for food and shelter, and higher-level needs, such as personal growth.

There are four popular need theories of motivation. These are Maslow's Hierarchy of Needs, ERG Theory, Motivator-Hygiene Theory, and Achievement Motivation Theory. Before considering the multinational applications of need theories of motivation, this section provides a brief review of each theory. You can find more detailed reviews of these and other theories of motivation in courses and texts in organizational behavior.

Exhibit 14.7 gives a summary and comparison of the four popular need theories. It also shows the characteristics of jobs that can satisfy the types of needs identified by these theories.

Maslow's Hierarchy of Needs

The psychologist Abraham Maslow[12] offered perhaps the most famous need theory of motivation. The **hierarchy of needs theory** states that people have five basic types of needs: physiological, security, affiliation, esteem, and self-actualization. Physiological needs include basic survival such as food, water, air, and shelter. Security needs include safety and the avoidance of pain and life-threatening

Hierarchy of needs theory

States that people have five basic types of needs: physiological, security, affiliation, esteem, and self-actualization.

EXHIBIT 14.7   Need Theories of Motivation

Source of Need Satisfaction on the Job	Maslow's Needs Hierarchy	ERG Theory	Motivator-Hygiene Theory	Achievement Motivation
➤ Advancement ➤ Use of Ability ➤ Meaningful Work ➤ Achievement ➤ Interesting Job	Self-Actualization	Growth	Motivators ➤ Advancement ➤ Growth ➤ Achievement	Need for Achievement
➤ Recognition ➤ Influence ➤ Esteem	Esteem			Need for Power
➤ Coworker Support ➤ Supervisor Support ➤ Social Interaction	Affiliation	Relatedness	Hygiene Factors ➤ Working conditions ➤ Job security ➤ Salary	Need for Affiliation
➤ Work Conditions ➤ Benefits ➤ Security	Security	Existence		
➤ Base Pay	Physiological			

Source: Adapted from Daft, Richard L. 1991. *Management*. 2d ed. Chicago: Dryden; Gordon, Judith R. 1987. *A Diagnostic Approach to Organizational Behavior*. Boston: Allyn and Bacon; Hellriegel, Don, John W. Slocum, Jr., and Richard W. Woodman. 2001. *Organizational Behavior*. 9th ed. Cincinnati, OH: South-Western.

situations. Affiliation needs include being loved, having friendship, and belonging to a human group. Esteem needs focus on respect, recognition by others, and feelings of self-worth. Self-actualization needs, the highest level in Maslow's theory, reflect needs of maximizing personal achievement.

Maslow believed that the five basic needs follow a hierarchy from lower-level or basic needs to higher-level needs. First people seek to satisfy lower-level needs, such as the physiological need for food and shelter. After they fulfill these lower-level needs, people seek to satisfy higher-level needs, such as the need for esteem. According to Maslow, once a need is satisfied, it no longer motivates. Thus, for example, if your base pay is adequate for survival, it has no motivational value. Then other characteristics of the work situation, such as working in teams to meet affiliation needs, become motivational. Current opinion on Maslow's approach suggests that, while there are two groups of needs representing higher- and lower-level needs, the need hierarchy does not work in sequence. Moreover, not all available jobs in a country provide the activities required to meet all levels of needs.[13]

Despite its simplicity, research shows support for parts of Maslow's predictions. In an innovative study, Hagerty[14] investigated Maslow's five needs in 88 countries spanning the periods of 1960 to 1994. The researcher categorized Maslow's five needs by considering crucial nation-level social institutions. Exhibit 14.8 shows that various measures used for each of Maslow's five needs.

Results of the study supported the basic proposition that individuals (and nations) will satisfy basic needs over time and progress to higher-level needs. Data analysis showed that over time most needs were increasingly being satisfied. Additionally, the study also showed that there may be some validity to the sequencing of needs as originally formulated by Maslow. However, the study failed to confirm the prediction that as nations expend effort on one level, growth slows down for other lower levels. In other words, Maslow predicted that individuals (and nations) can only expend effort to satisfy one level at a time, but the study did not support this prediction.

ERG theory

Simplified hierarchy of needs, including growth needs, relatedness needs, and existence needs.

Alderfer's ERG Theory

Clay Alderfer[15] developed **ERG theory** as a simplified hierarchy of needs having only three levels (see Exhibit 14.7 for a comparison with Maslow's theory). These needs include growth needs, relatedness needs, and existence needs. Growth needs are similar to Maslow's self-actualization and esteem needs. Work

EXHIBIT 14.8   Maslow's Hierarchy of Needs and Country Level Measures

Physiological needs	Safety needs	Belongingness and love needs	Esteem needs	Self-actualization needs
Daily calories available per person	Safety from war	Low divorce rate	Political rights	Tertiary education enrollment
GDP per capita	Safety from murder	Low child death rate	Women's participation in the workforce	Secondary education enrollment
	High life expectancy			Primary education enrollment

Source: Adapted from Hagerty, Michael R. 1999. "Testing Maslow's hierarchy of needs: National quality-of-life across time." Social Indicators Research, 46, pp. 249–271.

is motivating when it provides the opportunity for personal growth, such as by using one's creativity. Relational needs are similar to Maslow's affiliation needs. Getting support from one's work group satisfies relational needs. Existence needs are lower-level needs and represent basic survival needs.

In ERG theory, frustration of a need motivates behavior to satisfy the need. In addition, if a person cannot satisfy a higher-level need, she or he will seek to satisfy lower-level needs. For example, if the satisfaction of growth needs is impossible on the job, satisfaction of relational needs becomes the prime motivator.

Motivator-Hygiene Theory

Proposed by Frederick Herzberg,[16] **motivator-hygiene theory** assumes that a job has two basic characteristics, motivators and hygiene factors. Motivating factors include the characteristics of jobs that allow people to fulfill higher-level needs. For example, a challenging job might allow someone to meet his or her need for high levels of achievement. Hygiene factors include those characteristics of jobs that allow people to fulfill lower-level needs; for example, when good benefits and working conditions satisfy security needs.

Motivating factors arise from the content or the actual tasks that people perform on the job. Hygiene factors focus on the context or the setting in which the job takes place. Thus, for example, tasks that allow you to use your abilities are motivators. However, the size of your desk and color of your office are context or hygiene factors. Unlike other need theories, which assume that the desire to satisfy any type of need can motivate, Herzberg argued that satisfying lower-level needs at work (i.e., the hygiene factors) brings people only to a neutral state of motivation. To go beyond just a neutral reaction to the job, managers must build motivators into the context of a job (e.g., providing interesting tasks). Thus, only the opportunity to satisfy higher-level needs leads to increased motivation.

Huang and Van De Vliert's[17] study provides some insights into the application of Herzberg's theory to cross-cultural situations. They analyzed responses of more than 100,000 employees from 49 countries to investigate how intrinsic job characteristics (e.g., challenge, recognition, autonomy, and the job) and extrinsic job characteristics (e.g., pay, job security, and working conditions) impact job satisfaction. They found that, regardless of country, higher levels of extrinsic job characteristics made people more satisfied with their jobs. However, they also found that intrinsic job characteristics worked well only in certain countries. Hence, they found that intrinsic job characteristics are more motivating and satisfying in richer countries or countries with better governmental welfare programs. Such results are consistent with Herzberg's theory in that richer countries have less need for survival needs (i.e., hygiene factors) and are more motivated by intrinsic job factors (i.e., motivators) as such factors are more salient for them.

Achievement-Motivation Theory

The psychologist David McClelland[18] identified three key needs as the basis of motivation. These include needs for achievement, affiliation, and power (see Exhibit 14.7). However, most of McClelland's influential work focused on achievement motivation. **Achievement-motivation theory** suggests that some people (approximately 10 percent in the United States) have the need to win in competitive situations or to exceed a standard of excellence. High achievement-motivated people like to set their own goals. They seek challenging situations but avoid goals that they feel are too difficult. Because they like to achieve success in their goals, high achievers desire immediate feedback. They like to know how they are performing at every step leading to a goal.

> **Motivator-hygiene theory**
> Assumption that a job has two basic characteristics, motivators and hygiene factors.

> **Achievement-motivation theory**
> Suggestion that only some people have the need to win in competitive situations or to exceed a standard of excellence.

McClelland believed that achievement motivation is fixed in early childhood. He also believed that different cultures have different levels of achievement motivation. Some evidence supports McClelland's contention of different levels of achievement motivation in different cultures. However, there is no clear evidence regarding whether nations with more achievement-motivated people have better economic performance.[19]

Needs and the National Context

There are both similarities and divergence in the needs that people from different nations seek to satisfy from working. Similarities of needs across cultures occur because people tend to group needs into similar clusters or categories;[20] that is, regardless of national background, people see their work-related needs *grouped* in ways that match the broad groups proposed by need theories of motivation (see Exhibit 14.7).

However, national groups vary in two ways on how people see needs being satisfied at work. First, people from different nations do not give the same priorities to the needs that might be satisfied at work. For example, as shown in Exhibit 14.9, Hungarians give a high priority to satisfying physiological needs through higher base pay. This is not true for people from some other countries, such as China or Holland. Second, even if workers from different countries have

EXHIBIT 14.9

Rankings of the Importance of Job-Related Sources of Need Satisfaction for Seven Countries (H = upper third; M = middle third; L = bottom third; #1 = highest rank)

Job-Related Sources of Satisfaction for:	China	Germany	Holland	Hungary	Israel	Korea	United States
Self-Actualization Needs							
➤ Advancement	M	M	H	L	H	H	H
➤ Use of Ability	H	H	H	H	M	H	H
➤ Meaningful Work	M	H	M	M	M	M	M
➤ Achievement	#1	M	H	H	#1	#1	H
➤ Interesting Job	H	#1	#1	H	H	H	#1
Esteem Needs							
➤ Recognition	M	L	M	H	M	M	M
➤ Influence	M	L	M	L	L	L	L
➤ Esteem	H	M	M	M	H	L	H
Affiliation Needs							
➤ Co-Worker Support	M	H	H	M	M	H	L
➤ Supervisor Support	M	H	M	#1	H	H	M
➤ Interaction	L	L	M	M	L	L	L
Security Needs							
➤ Work Conditions	L	L	L	M	L	M	L
➤ Benefits	L	H	L	M	M	M	M
➤ Security	L	H	M	M	L	H	M
Physiological Needs							
➤ Base Pay	L	M	L	H	M	M	L

Source: Adapted from Elizur, Dov, Ingwer Borg, Raymond Hunt, and Istvan Magyari Beck. 1991. "The structure of work values: A cross cultural comparison." Journal of Organizational Behavior, 12, pp. 21–38.

similar needs, they may not give the same level of importance to satisfying these needs. For example, one cross-national comparison found that interesting work (something that satisfies growth needs) ranked as the most important work goal for Japanese, British, and Belgian workers. However, interesting work was still relatively more important for Belgian workers than it was for Japanese and British workers.[21]

Can multinational managers use need satisfaction as a motivational tool? Yes, it can serve as a motivational tool, if multinational managers take into account the particular needs that people in a nation seek to satisfy in the work setting. Consider the following Case in Point, which gives examples of companies that increased motivation by linking organizational goals to the local employees' needs.

What differences in need satisfaction might multinational managers expect to find in different countries? Exhibit 14.9 illustrates some of the differences in the priorities given to job-related sources of need satisfaction by people from several nations.[22] The exhibit divides the rankings of job-related sources of need satisfaction into three groups: High (H) for the top third, Middle (M) for the

CASE IN POINT

Finding the Right Needs in Central Eastern Europe

Central and Eastern European countries remain attractive destinations for foreign investment. Most major foreign investors coming from neighboring Germany and Austria, and U.S. investors see these growing markets as very lucrative. However, despite being in the region for a decade, foreign investors continue facing challenges.

For instance, taking over a formerly state-owned firm in Poland turned out to be a motivational challenge for the Finnish paper and power-equipment firm Ahlstrom Fakop. Morale and sales were low, and the new management searched for ways to improve the situation. The first try, offering incentive pay, produced no results. As workers recently jettisoned into a market economy, the East European employees of Ahlstrom Fakop had needs other than money. Decades of communism had produced an expectation of a guaranteed job. When told that their jobs were secure if sales and productivity targets were met, workers responded positively with increases in both. It seems that the anxiety produced by the transition to a market economy made keeping a job more important than bonuses for productivity.

When Dow Chemical took over a crumbling chemical plant in the former East Germany, it inherited a bloated workforce and the knowledge that it would need to lay off 400 workers. To ease the culture shock of the transition to a market-based company and to increase productivity, Dow built a motivational system based on trust and individual initiative. Many workers adapted well to the system, using the newfound independence to achieve higher levels of performance and promotions. However, some floundered, confused by managers who did not watch their every move and a distrust of those with power.

Recent trends suggest that many multinational companies are now facing a challenge of a new kind. After being there for a decade, many companies are finding that the pool of inexpensive talent is slowly drying up. Local companies have made substantial progress and are also competing with foreign companies for the same local talent. As a consequence, attracting and retaining talented employees is becoming one of the most important challenges. Such trends suggest that properly understanding Eastern European workers will become even more critical in the future.

Source: Based on Dougherty, Carter. 2006. "Eastern Europe at crossroads." International Herald Tribune, Jan. 19; Dougherty, Carter. 2006b. "Europe's young economies grow up but retain appeal: Even as costs rise, investors keep going east." International Herald Tribune, Jan. 18; Jacob, Rahul. 1995. "Secure jobs trump higher pay." Fortune, March 20, p. 24; Warren, Susan. 2000. "Five-year mission: For Dow, a dirty job in Germany presented a chance to clean up—to court eastern Europe, it wrestled a dinosaur from the Communist era—razing 'the glittering hall.'" Wall Street Journal, May 19, p. A1.

middle third, and Low (L) for the bottom third. Exhibit 14.9 also shows the job-related sources of need satisfaction in terms of Maslow's need hierarchy. For cross-referencing to other need theories, see Exhibit 14.7, which showed how Maslow's need hierarchy relates to other need theories.

As Exhibit 14.9 shows, people from different nations do not necessarily give the priorities suggested by need theories to the sources of need satisfaction at work. For example, although most need theories suggest that higher-level needs (e.g., self-actualization) should be most important, regardless of national background, many of the job-related sources of satisfying self-actualization needs had only moderate importance. Only the need for interesting work fell into the top third classification for all seven countries. High levels of potential need satisfiers on the job were found at all levels of the need hierarchy. In Germany, for example, perhaps because of the social institutional support for labor, job characteristics that could satisfy security and affiliation needs were as important as those related to self-actualization needs.

How can a multinational manager anticipate need differences in countries on which there is little information? Many multinational managers now work in emerging or formerly state-controlled economies where there is little available information on the often evolving employee attitudes toward work. In these cases, skillful multinational managers must anticipate worker needs based on cultural norms and values and institutional conditions. However, as Exhibit 14.8 shows, managers can also look at needs at the national level by considering important social institutions. Hagerty's[23] study suggests that managers may be able to motivate workers by providing for higher levels of social institutions not currently being satisfied. Hofstede's work[24] gives some additional hints on how a multinational manager might do this. Exhibit 14.10 shows some of the motivators at work identified by Hofstede for different types of national cultures

EXHIBIT 14.10   Hofstede's Dimensions of National Culture and Motivators at Work

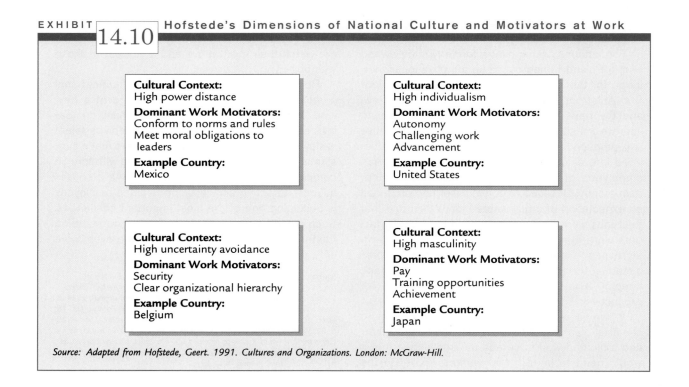

Cultural Context:
High power distance

Dominant Work Motivators:
Conform to norms and rules
Meet moral obligations to
 leaders

Example Country:
Mexico

Cultural Context:
High individualism

Dominant Work Motivators:
Autonomy
Challenging work
Advancement

Example Country:
United States

Cultural Context:
High uncertainty avoidance

Dominant Work Motivators:
Security
Clear organizational hierarchy

Example Country:
Belgium

Cultural Context:
High masculinity

Dominant Work Motivators:
Pay
Training opportunities
Achievement

Example Country:
Japan

Source: Adapted from Hofstede, Geert. 1991. Cultures and Organizations. London: McGraw-Hill.

(see Chapter 2). Hofstede's work suggests that emphasizing satisfying high-level needs at work may apply better to highly individualistic cultures. In addition, he cautions that need satisfaction may not be a motivator at all in some high power distance countries dominated by norms of service to the elite.

Applying Need Theories in Multinational Settings

Some points to consider in adapting need theories of motivation to the international context include the following:

- *Identify the basic functions of work in the national or local culture:* Where work is not central, people may satisfy their needs outside the work setting, limiting the use of need satisfaction as a motivational tool.

- *Identify the needs considered most important by workers in the national or local culture:* The evidence presented in this chapter shows that need priorities differ by national context. Managers should identify cultural differences in potential need satisfiers at work and focus on providing jobs that satisfy these needs.

- *Sources of need fulfillment may differ for the same needs:* Even if people from different cultures have the same needs, they may find different sources of fulfillment on the job. For example, people from different cultures may find interesting work most important, but they may have quite different ideas regarding what is interesting work. Hofstede's work suggests that individualism and power distance represent important dimensions of national culture that affect how people find need satisfaction at work.

- *Understand the limitations of available jobs to satisfy needs:* Although satisfying higher-level needs is possible in most industrialized countries, the same may not be true in many developing nations. Existing jobs may provide only the satisfaction of basic needs for survival.

To increase the motivation of host-country workers or to solve other motivational problems, multinational managers can also consider other approaches to motivation beyond need theories. Next, the chapter provides reviews of additional theories of motivation and their applications to multinational settings.

Process and Reinforcement Theories of Motivation

In this section, we briefly review the process theories of motivation known as *expectancy theory, equity theory,* and *goal-setting theory.* Process theories are more complex than need theories. They see motivation arising from needs and values *combined* with an individual's beliefs regarding the work environment. Besides the popular process theories, this section also reviews reinforcement theory and its application to multinational settings. These approaches to motivation receive fewer applications in the international setting than do need theories. However, we can draw some tentative conclusions regarding how these perspectives work in various national settings. For a complete review of these theories, students should consult any current organizational-behavior textbook.

Expectancy Theory

Victor Vroom[25] proposed a view of motivation that is more complex than simple need satisfaction. This theory and its later variants are known as **expectancy theory.** In this theory, Vroom proposed that work motivation is a function not only of an individual's needs or values but also of an individual's beliefs regarding what happens if you work hard. Expectancy theory assumes that part of

Expectancy theory

Assumption that motivation includes an individual's desire to satisfy his or her needs and their beliefs regarding how much their efforts at work will eventually satisfy their needs.

motivation is an individual's desire to satisfy his or her needs. However, the level of motivation also depends on people's beliefs regarding how much, or if, their efforts at work will eventually satisfy their needs.

The three factors that make up expectancy theory include expectancy, valence, and instrumentality. The theory often is presented in the form of the following equation:

$$Motivation = Expectancy \times Valence \times Instrumentality$$

Expectancy is an individual's belief that his or her effort will lead to some result. For example, if you believe that intensive study over a weekend will lead to a high grade, you have a high expectancy in that situation. *Valence* is the value you attach to the outcome of your efforts. For example, a student may value a high grade in a class compared to the pleasure of going skiing over a weekend. *Instrumentality* refers to the links between early and later results of the work effort. For example, continuing the grade analogy, instrumentality means the link between one outcome of studying, a grade on a test, and a later outcome, a final grade for a course. If the test was worth only 1 percent of the final grade, instrumentality would be low. That is, how one performs on a minor test has little effect on a final grade.

Thus, in the expectancy-theory perspective, motivation is much more than the value people attach to work outcomes. Beliefs regarding whether an effort will lead to success and whether the results of effort will lead eventually to valued outcomes also come into play.

Some suggest that expectancy theory serves best as a diagnostic tool to determine why workers are motivated or not motivated.[26] The manager must ask three questions. First, do workers believe that their efforts will lead to successful performance of a task? Second, do workers believe that present success at some task (e.g., no defects for a week) will lead to success at some future valued outcome (e.g., getting a raise)? Third, do employees value the outcomes that follow from their efforts at work?

Applying Expectancy Theory in Multinational Settings   There are two key issues in applying expectancy theory in the multinational company. The first is to identify which outcomes people value in a particular national or local cultural setting; that is, the multinational manager must find and use rewards that have positive valence for employees. The second is to find culturally appropriate ways of convincing employees that their efforts will lead to desirable ends.

In the Case in Point earlier in this chapter, we saw that the workers from one former Eastern Bloc country had a higher valence for secure jobs than they did for bonus pay. When managers from the Finnish parent company recognized this, they promised job security (the workers' ultimate goal) in return for the workers' putting more effort into productivity. As expectancy theory would predict, when workers became convinced that their efforts would lead to their valued goal of security, their motivation increased.

Equity theory

Proposal that people perceive the fairness of their rewards vis-a-vis their inputs based on how they compare themselves to others.

Equity Theory

Equity theory focuses on the fairness that people perceive in the rewards that they receive for their efforts at work. The rewards people receive from work can include, for example, pay, benefits, recognition, job perquisites, and prestige. Under this theory, the "efforts" people put into the job include not only the quality and quantity of their work but also such factors as their age, educational qualifications, seniority, and social status.[27]

Equity theory proposes that people have no absolute standards for fairness in the input/output (effort/reward) equation. Rather, people perceive the fairness of their rewards relative to their inputs, based on how they compare themselves to others. For example, if two people have the same experience, do the same job, but do not have the same pay, then one is in overpayment inequity and the other is in underpayment inequity. Equity theory predicts that workers who believe that they are under-rewarded reduce their contribution to the company (e.g., take longer breaks). Workers in an inequitable situation produced by over-rewards increase their work input, at least in the short run.

Chen, Choi, and Chi's[28] study of international joint ventures and compensation disparities provides some insight into applications and subtleties of equity theory in an international context. The study examined Chinese employees' perception of fairness compared with that of their expatriate counterparts in international joint ventures. As expected, it was found that local Chinese employees perceived less fairness when comparing their incomes with expatriates than when comparing with other locals. However, the study also showed that there are other factors that can neutralize part of the felt inequity. For instance, it was found that the local employees' perception of fairness increased if they were paid more than other local employees in other international joint ventures. Additionally, if the employees endorsed ideological explanations that expatriates are necessary and important to the Chinese economy and position in the global environment, their perception of fairness toward expatriates was higher. Finally, the study also showed that those employees who perceived that expatriates were interpersonally sensitive and nice to them perceived higher fairness with regard to these expatriates' compensation packages.

However, despite the significant validation that equity theory has received, research has expanded on the theory. Huseman, Hatfield, and Miles[29] suggest that people can be categorized into three groups: equity sensitives, benevolents, and entitleds. The equity-sensitive types tend to behave according to the original propositions of equity theory. Equity sensitives will tend to find ways to redress equity if they find that they are out of balance compared to others. Benevolents tend to be more tolerant of situations where they are under-rewarded. As such, although benevolents do not seek to be under-rewarded, benevolents are less likely to respond if they are placed in under-reward situations. In contrast, the third group, namely entitleds, tend to experience more dissatisfaction if they are under-rewarded. However, entitleds tend to be very comfortable with situations where they are over-rewarded. As such, it is argued that entitleds are more likely than the other two groups to seek over-rewards.

This expansion of equity theory has recently been tested in cross-cultural situations. In a cross-national comparison of Japanese and U.S. individuals, Allen, Takeda, and White[30] found that the Japanese were more likely to behave as entitleds than the U.S. Americans. For instance, they argue that because of high collectivism, the Japanese are more likely to strive to restore equity within the group to preserve harmony if they sense inequity. Chhokar, Zhuplev, Fok, and Hartman[31] also show that national culture has significant influences on whether specific countries perceived themselves as equity sensitives, benevolents, or entitleds. They found that the U.S American, Russian, and Indian subjects were more benevolence-oriented while the British and French were the most entitled-oriented. Although the high U.S. benevolence was surprising, the other results are consistent with the influences of culture.

Applying Equity Theory in Multinational Settings   The first issue to consider in multinational applications of equity theory concerns the importance of equity norms in a society. Developing reward systems based on equity norms may not be motivating when other norms for rewarding people have more importance than equity.

Psychologists identify three principles of allocating rewards that vary in their use in different cultural settings: the principle of equity (based on contributions), the principle of equality (based on equal division of rewards), and the principle of need (based on individual needs).[32] A recent review of cross-national reports on the three principles of reward allocation suggests the following:

- *Equity norms prevail in individualistic cultures:* In particular, managerial practices in the United States such as bonus pay, Management by Objectives, and most U.S. performance-appraisal systems use the equity norm. Rewards are based on performance. Good work deserves good pay.[33] In contrast, in societies where status comes from group membership rather than achievement, rewards based on performance may not make sense. High-status groups are expected to get higher rewards regardless of their performance levels.

- *Equality norms prevail over equity norms in collectivist cultures:* In societies with strong equality norms, at least for the members of one's group or team, group members prefer equal rewards for all. For example, one study of an Israeli company found that 40 percent of the workers perceived a bonus system as unfair even though it increased their income. They suggested that fair rewards should go to the team instead of to individuals.[34]

    However, as the Chen et al.[35] study shows, in some collectivistic societies like China, equity may be potentially becoming more important. As China has adopted a more open-door market-oriented economic approach, it is possible that employees are adopting more preference for equitable situations based on their performance. Managers must carefully assess local conditions to determine if equity is preferred.

- *The principle of need may prevail over equity in certain conditions:* One study found, for example, that Indian managers preferred rewards based on need over rewards based on either equality or equity.[36] Collectivist cultures in particular may place more value on other people's needs than on one's own contributions.

Exhibit 14.11 shows an example of how the "fairness" of equity or equality rewards can even affect students' responses to grades relative to contributions. The information comes from a study in which Korean, Japanese, and U.S. students assigned peer-evaluation grades for contributions to group projects. Although some equity norms seemingly worked for all students, U.S. students clearly linked rewards to performance much more than did the students from the two Asian societies.[37]

The second issue to consider in applying equity theory concerns cultural differences in beliefs regarding the sources of a person's contributions to work. In some cultures, age, social status, and family membership may be more important inputs to work than the actual effort and performance on the job. In many Asian countries, for example, most people would consider it very unfair if a younger worker received more pay than an older worker—particularly if she or he did the same job. Research suggests that, in addition to performance criteria, collectivist cultures judge pay fairness based on factors such as seniority, education, and family size.[38]

EXHIBIT 14.11 **Rewards from Peers for Contributions to a Student Group Project**

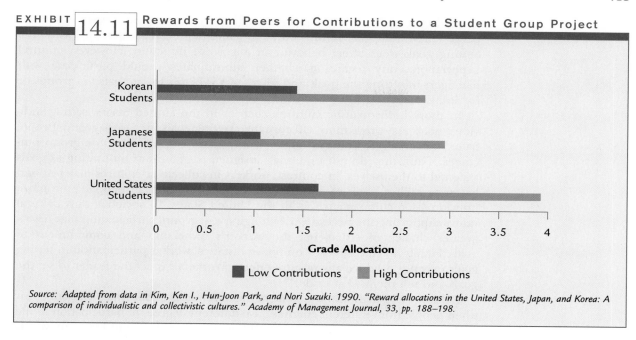

Grade Allocation

■ Low Contributions   ■ High Contributions

Source: Adapted from data in Kim, Ken I., Hun-Joon Park, and Nori Suzuki. 1990. "Reward allocations in the United States, Japan, and Korea: A comparison of individualistic and collectivistic cultures." Academy of Management Journal, 33, pp. 188–198.

A final issue to consider is whether the individuals in the country consider themselves as equity sensitives, benevolents, or entitleds. Although research on this issue is needed in more societies, multinational companies are well advised to be more sensitive to inequities and to take more immediate measures in countries with more entitleds. Limited cross-cultural research shows that the Japanese, French, and British displayed higher degrees of entitleds while the U.S. Americans, Russians, and Indians were more benevolents.

Goal-Setting Theory

Goal-setting theory assumes that people want to achieve goals. When they meet or exceed a goal, people feel competent and satisfied. When they fail to meet a goal, people feel dissatisfied. Thus, the mere existence of a goal is motivating.[39]

Goal-setting theory has several principles.[40] Goal-setting proponents argue that managers who follow these principles can motivate employees to meet organizational objectives. The principles of goal setting include:

- *Set clear and specific goals:* Employees need to know and understand what management expects them to accomplish.
- *Assign difficult but achievable goals:* If goals are too difficult, there is little incentive to try to achieve them. If goals are too easy, employees may not take them seriously.
- *Increase employee acceptance of goals:* At least in the United States, studies tell us that employees who participate in goal setting have a greater acceptance of managerial goals.[41]
- *Provide incentives to achieve goals:* Tying rewards (e.g., salary, bonuses) to goal achievement increases the acceptance of the goals.[42]
- *Give feedback on goal attainment:* To be motivated, people must understand how well they are doing to achieve their goals.

Goal-setting theory

Assumption that the mere existence of a goal is motivating.

Applying Goal-Setting Theory in Multinational Settings   Some experts believe that goal setting works to some degree regardless of location.[43] Setting goals does affect behavior in a positive direction. However, cultural expectations vary regarding whether subordinates should participate with managers in setting the goals and whether it is better to set goals for groups or for individuals.

In more individualistic cultures, such as in the United States, setting individual goals may prove more effective than setting goals for a work group. People from individualistic cultures do not easily share responsibility for group outcomes. Thus, they do not find goals assigned to groups as motivating as goals assigned to themselves. In contrast, workers in collectivist cultures may respond better to higher levels of participation in goal setting than people from more individualistic cultures such as in the United States. In societies with cultural values supporting the necessity of belonging to a group, participation may have a greater chance of enhancing the worker's ownership and commitment to goals. Finally, in cultures high on power distance, worker participation in setting goals may not produce any positive effects. Workers expect the leader to set the goals and tell them what to do.[44]

Exhibit 14.12 demonstrates some of the differences in outcomes that can occur when people from different cultures have different degrees of participation in the goal-setting process. This exhibit is based on a study of U.S. and Israeli university students.[45] Three groups of students performed simulated job tasks. For the first group, goals were assigned. For the second group, a representative from the group expressed the students' opinions on goals to the leader. For the third group, the whole group participated in setting goals. Because Israeli culture is more collectivist and lower on power distance than U.S. culture, the experimenters expected that goal assignment would not work very well for the Israeli students.

Participation in goal setting improved the performance of all groups. However, perhaps because U.S. students come from a highly individualistic and moderate power distance national culture, they performed almost as well with assigned goals as they did when given the opportunity to participate in goal

EXHIBIT 14.12   Cultural Effects on Performance by the Degree of Participation in Goal Setting

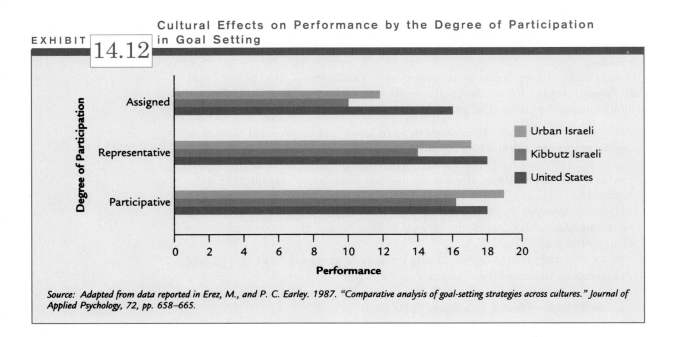

Source: Adapted from data reported in Erez, M., and P. C. Earley. 1987. "Comparative analysis of goal-setting strategies across cultures." Journal of Applied Psychology, 72, pp. 658–665.

setting. This was not true for the Israeli students, who come from a more collectivist and lower power culture. The Israeli students did much better with participation. The implication is that subordinate participation in goal setting is an effective motivational tool in more collectivist nations, but it is less important in individualistic or high power distance national cultures.

Reinforcement Theory

Most managerial applications of reinforcement theory focus on operant conditioning. **Operant conditioning** represents a basic way people learn. The famous psychologist B. F. Skinner identified most of the principles underlying operant conditioning.[46]

The operant-conditioning model proposes that behavior is a function of its consequences. That is, in its simplest application, if a pleasurable consequence follows a behavior, the behavior will continue. If an unpleasant consequence follows a behavior, the behavior will stop.[47] Unlike most other theories of motivation, operant conditioning focuses on observable behavior and not on the psychological processes (e.g., meeting needs) that affect people's motivation.

The operant-conditioning model has three steps. These steps are shown in Exhibit 14.13 with a managerial example. The antecedent comes first and

Operant conditioning
Model proposes that, if a pleasurable consequence follows a behavior, the behavior will continue, whereas if an unpleasant consequence follows a behavior, the behavior will stop.

EXHIBIT 14.13   Management Example of Operant-Conditioning Process and Types of Consequences

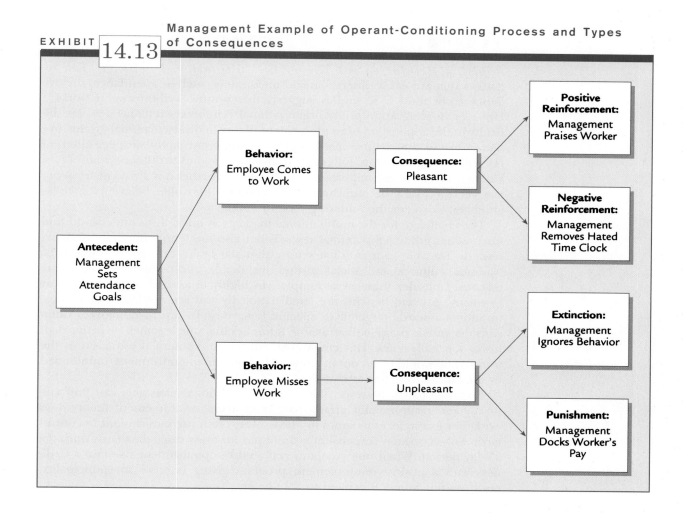

stimulates behavior. The behavior follows the antecedent, and the pleasant or unpleasant consequences follow the behavior. The exhibit shows a simple example based on work attendance. In the antecedent, management sets an attendance goal. The employee behaves by either coming to work or missing work. Management then provides pleasant or unpleasant consequences for the behavior.

Positive reinforcement occurs when management responds with a rewarding consequence. The consequence is deemed rewarding only if it increases the desired behavior. Not all people will respond to the same positively intended consequences in the same way. Although it often is confused with punishment, negative reinforcement increases desired behavior by eliminating some negative consequence. That is, people behave in a certain way to avoid something unpleasant. For example, you may put on a heavy coat to avoid the pain of extreme cold. Punishment occurs when something unpleasant occurs after a behavior. The exhibit shows that docking of pay is an unpleasant consequence that follows the behavior of not coming to work. Extinction occurs when a manager ignores a behavior. However, managers must be careful to avoid extinction when other rewards (e.g., a paid day off) may be operating.

Most management applications of reinforcement theory use positive reinforcement to encourage behaviors desired by management. To reinforce behavior, managers have an array of organizational rewards. These include material rewards (e.g., pay), benefit rewards (e.g., company car), status rewards (e.g., prestigious office), and social rewards (e.g., praise).[48]

Applying Reinforcement Theory in Multinational Settings   For behaviors that are easily observable and measurable, such as attendance, the evidence from most U.S. studies suggests that positive reinforcement works.[49] However, finding appropriate organizational reinforcers remains a major difficulty in the application of reinforcement theory to diverse national groups. We saw earlier in the chapter that people from different nations expect different rewards from work. Thus, different groups may respond to different reinforcers. Furthermore, it is also important to understand whether it is always necessary to use certain forms of punishment for certain observable behaviors such as absences. Consider the following Case in Point.

The challenge for the multinational manager is not only to understand how work values influence potential rewards but also to identify the organizational rewards available in a national setting that she or he can use as reinforcers. National cultures and social institutions define acceptable and legitimate rewards. Consider these two examples. In highly unionized countries such as Germany, pay and benefits are fixed nationally and are not available as organizational rewards targeted to specific behaviors. In Japan, employees often consider public praise embarrassing. It implies that one is somehow better than his or her colleagues. This embarrassment and the potential ostracism by the work group would result not in a reward but instead in punishment, unintended by the culturally ignorant manager.

Evidence exists, however, that when multinational managers can find culturally and institutionally appropriate reinforcers, reinforcement theory does work. For example, companies in Mexico City often use punishment to control tardiness—a one-day suspension without pay for every three days tardy during a 30-day period. When one company replaced the punishment system for tardiness with a positive-reinforcement program giving bonuses for punctuality, tardiness fell from 9.8 percent to 1.2 percent.[50]

CASE IN POINT

Should Absences Always Be Viewed Negatively?

Most Western-based academic research on absenteeism has tended to view absences as negative aspects of the work environment. It is typically assumed that absent workers are escaping stressful conditions at work and have necessarily low satisfaction with their jobs and low commitment to the employing organization. However, these assumptions may not be true of all cultures. Research now shows that different societies may have different views on the meaning of absence.

A study of Japanese airline employees found that absences can actually be of positive value to the organization. Because of the excessive workload that Japanese workers typically face, absences can be a proactive coping response to emotional exhaustion. As such, the study shows that absences provided workers with the means to buffer emotional exhaustion. Additionally, the study also showed that for those workers who were not absent, the more exhausted they felt, the lower their feelings of personal accomplishment. In contrast, for those workers who were absent more frequently, the study showed that the absences acted as a buffer and that higher levels of exhaustion were associated with higher levels of personal accomplishment.

Results of the study show that managers need to be aware of the role of absences in societies and not necessarily react negatively with punishment. The study also raises the provocative possibility that absences can be used to motivate workers.

Source: Based on Tourigny, Louise, Vishwanath V. Baba, and Terri R. Lituchy. 2005. "Job burnout among airline employees in Japan. A study of the buffering effects of absence and supervisory support." International Journal of Cross Cultural Management 5, pp. 67–85.

Exhibit 14.14 shows an example of how proper use of reinforcers can work in different national contexts. In this example, two groups of Russian workers at the Kalinin Cotton Mill responded positively to both extrinsic rewards and social rewards.[51] One group received extrinsic rewards. These rewards were U.S.-made products such as soap, jeans, T-shirts, and music tapes. The other group received the social rewards of recognition and praise. Both outcomes

EXHIBIT 14.14

Effects of Positive Reinforcement and Types of Rewards in a Russian Cotton Mill

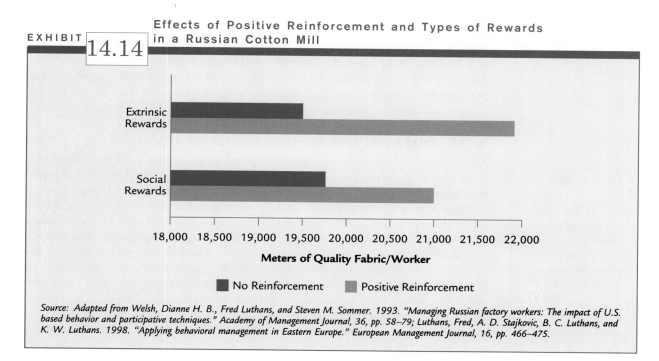

Source: Adapted from Welsh, Dianne H. B., Fred Luthans, and Steven M. Sommer. 1993. "Managing Russian factory workers: The impact of U.S. based behavior and participative techniques." Academy of Management Journal, 36, pp. 58–79; Luthans, Fred, A. D. Stajkovic, B. C. Luthans, and K. W. Luthans. 1998. "Applying behavioral management in Eastern Europe." European Management Journal, 16, pp. 466–475.

were similar to those found in U.S. studies. However, the Russian workers responded most positively to the U.S. products as rewards. This positive reinforcement increased the behaviors management desired.

Key Points in the Multinational Application of Process and Reinforcement Theories

The multinational manager should consider several key points when using process and reinforcement theories of motivation in different cultural settings. These include:

- *Expectancy theory:* The key is identifying the appropriate work rewards that have positive valence for employees in a national setting.
- *Equity theory:* The multinational manager must assess the importance and meaning of the principle of equity in a national context. A multinational manager may find equality norms or norms that base rewards on need to have equal or more importance than equity.
- *Goal-setting theory:* Depending on cultural norms, goal setting may be more effective when assigned to groups rather than individuals. Participation in goal setting may have more positive effects in collectivist cultures than in individualistic or high power distance cultures.
- *Reinforcement theory:* The rewards people value at work may influence the types of reinforcers useful to managers in different cultural contexts. In addition, the institutional environment, such as degree of economic development and the labor-relations system, affects the types of rewards available for managers in any society.

Motivation and Job Design: U.S. and European Perspectives

Job design attempts to make jobs more motivating by changing the nature of their functions and tasks. Early theories of job design focused primarily on making jobs more efficient through procedures such as time and motion studies. The objective was to make a job as fast and efficient as possible. There was little concern for the psychological state of the worker. Contemporary views of job design take into account the psychological effects on the worker produced by the types of tasks associated with a job. Theories that suggest ways to design jobs for high motivation focus on how job characteristics allow a worker to meet or satisfy motivating needs.

A U.S. Approach: The Job-Characteristics Model

Job-characteristics model

Suggests that work is more motivating when managers enrich core job characteristics, such as by increasing number of skills a job requires.

Although there are several approaches to redesigning work for increased motivational potential, one of the most popular in the United States is the **job-characteristics model.**[52] This model suggests that work is more motivating when managers enrich core job characteristics such as the different number of skills a job requires. In turn, these core job characteristics affect the psychological states of a worker that are critical to motivation. For example, one psychological state considered critical for motivation comes from whether the worker believes his or her job is meaningful. Proponents of the job-characteristics model argue that, if the core job characteristics lead to appropriate psychological reactions, then jobs have a high potential to motivate workers.

The job-characteristics model sees three critical psychological states as motivating. First, a person must believe that his or her job is meaningful. A meaningful job is perceived as important or valuable. Second, a person must believe that he or she is responsible or accountable for the outcome of his or her work. Third, a person must understand how well he or she has performed.

Core characteristics of a job that lead to the motivating psychological states include:

- *Skill variety:* A job with skill variety requires the use of different abilities and activities.
- *Task identity:* Task identity increases when a person can complete a whole piece of work from beginning to end.
- *Task significance:* Task significance increases when a job has important effects on other people.
- *Autonomy:* When people have autonomy, they control their own schedules and job procedures.
- *Feedback:* Feedback occurs when the job allows timely information on a person's performance.

Not all people respond positively to jobs with enriched job characteristics. Rather, the model suggests that jobs with high motivational potential work best for people who have a strong need for personal growth and have the appropriate knowledge and skills to perform the job well. Exhibit 14.15 gives a picture

EXHIBIT 14.15   A Motivating Job in the Job-Characteristics Model

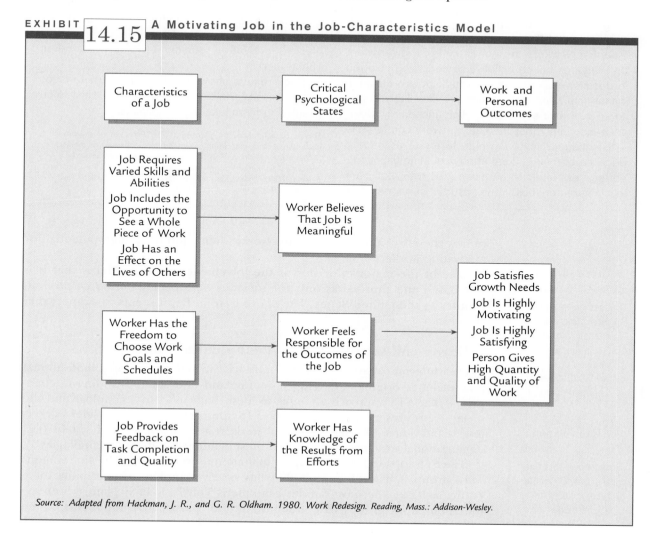

Source: Adapted from Hackman, J. R., and G. R. Oldham. 1980. Work Redesign. Reading, Mass.: Addison-Wesley.

CASE IN POINT

The Job-Characteristics Model: A Comparison of Mauritian and Australian Hotel Workers

Mauritius, a small island off the east coast of Madagascar, has a very vibrant tourism sector. Many of the world's leading hotel groups such as One & Only Resorts, Club Med, and Hilton Hotels have world-class resorts on the island. The tourism sector employs a significant part of the Mauritian employees, and these hotels work hard to motivate employees.

In an innovative study, Lee-Ross provides some insights into application of the job-characteristics model when comparing Mauritian and Australian hotel workers. The author argues that because Mauritian workers have high power distance, high uncertainty avoidance, and lower individualism than their Australian counterparts, they are less likely to be given jobs that display high levels of core job characteristics. For instance, the author argues that Mauritian workers are not likely to be given work that requires taking initiative or becoming involved in decision making because high power distance means that Mauritian workers are less likely to disagree with their supervisors. High uncertainty avoidance also imply that they are not very comfortable with situations involving high levels of autonomy. Because of their cultural attributes, Mauritian workers are less likely to be given jobs with high core job characteristics. The study supports this

argument, showing that Australian workers perceive higher levels of core job characteristics than their Mauritian counterparts.

However, although the job-characteristics model suggests that people who have higher levels of core job characteristics are more likely to be motivated (i.e., the Australians), the study showed that both Mauritian and Australian workers had similar levels of motivation. The authors suggest that the high power distance of Mauritians encourages them to agree with authority and even to be deferential to customers. This allows Mauritian workers to satisfy their predisposed cultural obligations of deference to those in positions of authority. By behaving consistent with their cultural predispositions, Mauritian hotel employees experience levels of motivation similar to their Australian counterparts.

Such results show that the job-characteristics model is clearly culture dependent and needs to be adapted to fit cultural predispositions.

Source: Based on Lee-Ross, Darren. 2005. "Perceived job characteristics and internal work motivation. An exploratory cross-cultural analysis of the motivational antecedents of hotel workers in Mauritius and Australia." Journal of Management Development, 24, pp. 253–266; Stott, Bridget. 2006. "Mauritius ready to open doors to paradise." The Observer, Feb. 19, p. 21.

of how the job-characteristics model works when a job has a high potential for motivating workers.

One of the major criticisms of the job-characteristics model is that it is U.S.-based and thus works only for societies that display similar cultural attributes to the United States. The above Case in Point seems to support that criticism.

A European Approach: Sociotechnical Systems

Sociotechnical systems (STS) approach
Focuses on designing motivating jobs by blending the social system (i.e., organizational structure, culture) with different technologies.

The **sociotechnical systems (STS) approach** to building a job's motivational potential was originally developed in England and some Scandinavia countries.[53] The STS approach attempts to mesh both modern technology and the social needs of workers. However, the STS approach does not consider workers just as individuals. Rather, individual workers are part of a social system (i.e., organizational structure, culture) that must blend with different technologies.[54]

Autonomous work group
Team or unit that has nearly complete responsibility for a particular task.

The STS approach focuses on the **autonomous work group.** The autonomous work group is a team or unit that has nearly complete responsibility for a particular task. The most famous example is Volvo's Kalmar plant, where autonomous work groups have responsibility for particular components of the automobile (e.g., doors). In autonomous work groups, worker teams control many aspects of their jobs traditionally governed by management; for example, the tasks assigned to individuals and the pace of work.[55]

The STS approach builds into a job many of the same motivational job characteristics proposed by the U.S. job-characteristic model just discussed. However, in a crucial difference with the U.S. approach, the team's tasks rather than the individual worker's tasks become the focus of job enrichment.[56] The team decides individual task assignments and thus increases skill variety. The team makes autonomous decisions on a variety of matters related to its job, such as which task to complete first. The team has task identity by producing a whole product. The team gets feedback from its work often by conducting its own quality inspections.

Choosing Job-Enrichment Techniques in Multinational Settings

How can a multinational manager choose the best techniques to design motivating work? Some experts suggest that the distinction between individualistic and collectivist cultures should determine the choice of job-enrichment techniques.[57] Approaches created in the United States tend to focus on how the *individual* reacts to core job characteristics. They have a cultural bias in favor of individualistic cultures. Approaches designed in more collectivist cultures, including the sociotechnical systems approach and the Quality Circles popular in Japan, focus on the job characteristics of the *team*. They have a cultural bias in favor of more collectivist cultures. Although proponents of both forms of enrichment can point to success stories in several nations, experts recommend a team focus for job enrichment in collectivist cultures and an individual focus in more individualistic cultures.

One explanation of why team-based job enrichment may not work well in individualistic cultures is that people from the more individualistic cultures just do not work as well in groups. Exhibit 14.16 gives an example of this phenomenon. It shows a comparison of three culturally diverse groups of managers working in groups or alone. As you can see, unlike the managers from the more collectivist cultures, U.S. managers performed much worse in groups than they did alone.

Why does performance drop off with the use of teamwork in more individualistic cultures? Some experts explain this by noting that people from individualistic cultures often engage in social loafing. **Social loafing** occurs when people put out less effort when they work in groups. They do this for three reasons. First, working in groups, people do not feel responsible for group outcomes and feel less pressure to perform. Second, workers in groups often believe that the group will make up any slack in their personal efforts. Third, especially in highly individualistic cultures such as the United States, people give their own work and interests priority over the group's. However, in individualistic cultures, some of the detrimental effects of social loafing on a group's performance decline when individuals rather than the groups are held accountable for performance. [58]

The following Multinational Management Challenge confirms the success of team-based job enrichment programs in some Japanese organizations. However, it also suggests that the success of these programs in individualistic cultures, such as in the United States, remains a challenge. Using team-based job designs in the United States and in other individualistic cultures may require that managers retain individual performance assessments even in the team-based company.

Social loafing

Term used when people put out less effort when they work in groups.

EXHIBIT **14.16**

Comparing the Performance of Chinese, U.S., and Israeli Managers Working Alone and in Groups

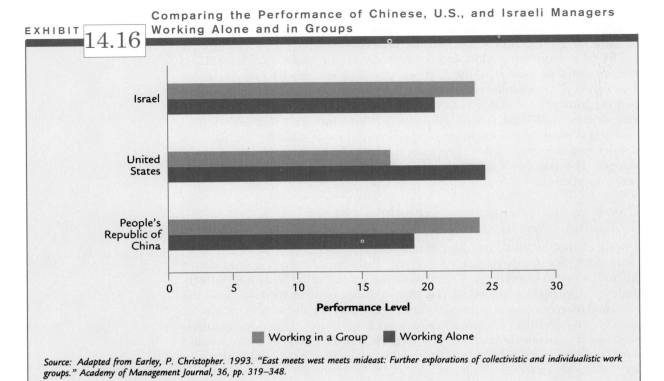

Performance Level

■ Working in a Group   ■ Working Alone

Source: Adapted from Earley, P. Christopher. 1993. "East meets west meets mideast: Further explorations of collectivistic and individualistic work groups." Academy of Management Journal, 36, pp. 319–348.

Comparative Management **Brief**

Team-Based Job-Enrichment Success Stories in Japan—Will They Work in the United States, Mexico, and the Czech Republic?

At Sony's plant in Kohda, Japan, teams of four workers do all the assembly and the final testing of camcorders. Output increased more than 10 percent from the former conveyer-belt assembly line. At an NEC telephone factory, eight-person teams work in a spider-like circle facing each other across a turntable. They pace their own work. Some group members build entire subcomponents and place them on a turntable in front of them. Other group members spin the turntable to get the components and produce the finished phones. Training costs increased because people had to learn new skills. However, 35 people now produce as many phones as 70 people did under the previous system.

Will this approach work in the United States? Companies like Dell Corp. believe so. They use assembly "cells" to assemble whole computer units and have been very successful. In spite of this successful incident, however, surveys of businesses show only moderate success by U.S. companies using these group-based approaches. One possibility is that, in the United States, the motivational benefits of group-based job enrichment work best for simple assembly jobs. In this type of work, when the assembly team is small, a manager can more easily identify, provide feedback to, and hold responsible the individual who is a slow performer. Other evidence suggests that, even in more collectivist cultures, groups will perform best when they receive both individual and group feedback.

Will this approach work in Mexico? Mexico is a more collectivist society than the United States, leading many multinational managers to expect that the self-managed teams would work well. However, a study of the experience of 243 Mexican executives found that nearly all had problems with the use of enriched jobs based on self-managed teams. Although the idea of working in groups appeals to the Mexican worker, other cultural values offset the effectiveness of the teams. A low tolerance of ambiguity (high uncertainty avoidance) and expectations regarding hierarchical authority make workers uncomfortable without direct supervision.

In the more collectivist Czech Republic, decades of communism have produced severe mistrust among people. However, ExxonMobil is finding ways to build successful teams among its Czech workers. ExxonMobil sponsors its workers by giving them time off and paying their fees to participate in several corporate training programs. By encouraging its staff to take team-building classes, ExxonMobil ensures that all employees build team management skills and have a common understanding of the process.

Sources: Based on Credit Management. 2006. "Building winning teams in Prague." p. 41; Earley, P. Christopher, Cristina B. Gibson, and Chao C. Chen. 1999. "'How did I do?' versus 'how did we do?' Cultural contrasts of performance feedback use and self-efficacy." Journal of Cross-Cultural Psychology, 30: pp. 594–619; Nicholls, Chantell E., Henry W. Lane, and Mauricio Brehm Brechu. 1999. "Taking self-managed teams to Mexico." Academy of Management Executive, 13: pp. 15–25; Williams, Michael. 1994. "Back to the past: Some plants tear out long assembly lines, switch to craft work." Wall Street Journal, October 24, pp. A1, A4.

Summary and Conclusions

Motivating workers in diverse cultural settings is a constant challenge for multinational managers. As companies both large and small become more global and transnational in their strategic and human resource orientations, the challenge of increasing worker motivation in multinational settings will become even greater. For a multinational company to remain competitive in the global environment, each company and its managers must find ways to motivate an increasingly diverse workforce.

As a guide to developing motivational techniques in multinational settings, this chapter addressed several key issues. First, the chapter showed some of the available information on international differences in work centrality, work obligation norms, and extrinsic and intrinsic work values in several different nations. Second, the chapter reviewed the basic processes of work motivation and how these processes are influenced by the national context. Third, the chapter reviewed classic theories of motivation (including need, process, and reinforcement theories) and the multinational applications of each approach. In these sections you also received specific and practical suggestions on how to apply these theories in different national contexts. Fourth, and finally, the

chapter considered both U.S. and European approaches to designing jobs with high motivational potential.

Most of the views of motivation discussed in this chapter were "made in the U.S.A." U.S. academics created the theories and performed much of the research supporting the theories. The approaches to motivation discussed here are also standard fare in U.S. university courses in organizational behavior. However, the dominance of U.S. perspectives as the "country of origin" for many motivational theories does not invalidate their multinational applications—if a manager makes appropriate adjustments for national contexts and various subcultures. Many of the psychological theories that underlie common U.S. approaches to motivation have "culture-free" assumptions and research support; that is, they attempt to explain human behavior independent of cultural setting.

However, even if psychological processes that underlie motivational theories are culture free, the applications of motivation theories are not. Even when people respond to work using the same underlying psychological processes, the national context continues to influence other factors, such as what people find rewarding at work and what people feel is fair and moral. For example, a U.S. American and a Brazilian may respond similarly to the psychological process of positive reinforcement. Their behaviors increase when consequences are pleasant. But this does not mean that they will view the same reinforcers offered by management as rewarding. As we saw throughout the chapter, nations vary widely in their predominant views regarding the functions and meaning of work and in the rewards that people hope to get from work.

A brief discussion of motivation can only sensitize the multinational manager to subtleties of applying any motivational technique in diverse national settings. Although a manager may begin his or her approach to motivating workers with an awareness of the broad stereotypes concerning national cultures, each job situation requires an understanding of the unique organizational, regional, and occupational cultures as well as the individual differences of each employee.

Discussion Questions

1. Compare the job-characteristics approach to job design and the sociotechnical systems approach. Pick a national culture with which you are familiar (besides your own) and discuss which approach would be most likely to succeed and why.

2. How might a country's educational and political systems affect the effectiveness of redesigning work as a motivational tool?

3. Discuss differences in the attributes of work considered most important in different nations. How might these differences influence the application to the work setting of expectancy theory and reinforcement theory?

4. Discuss the differences between need and process theories of motivation. Which type do you think is more applicable to multinational management and why?

5. Discuss the three principles of fairness of rewards. Do you think that equity theory could work in societies where other principles besides equity operate? If so, how would you apply equity theory as a manager in these countries?

6. Under what conditions would you recommend involving groups in setting goals? Discuss the cultural influences on goal setting using Hofstede's original four dimensions of national culture.

Multinational Management **Skill Builder**

Planning Motivational Strategies for Different Countries

Step 1. Read the following multinational problem.

You have just completed your first year as a management trainee for the XYZ company. Your company manufactures components for industrial robots. You have just come from a meeting with the vice president for personnel. She has told you that XYZ has decided to open a manufacturing plant in the country of _____. Because of your background in international business, top management has chosen you to be the new plant manager. The VP tells you that this is a significant opportunity and challenge since you would have to wait at least five more years to get this level of responsibility at home. Personnel experts are already in _____ (country) working on recruitment, selection, and training. Your major job will be to motivate the local workers

to reach the plant's full capacity as soon as possible. Given your knowledge of the local culture and social institutions, the VP asks you to prepare a report specifying the motivational strategies that you might use on your new assignment.

Step 2. Picking teams and countries.

Your instructor will divide you into teams of three to five people. Each team will choose or be assigned a different country for a plant location. Your team will act in the role of the new expatriate plant manager. If your instructor chooses, this may also be an individual assignment.

This project may be a library research project or an in-class assignment based on information from the text.

Step 3. Prepare reports.

Reports may be written, oral, or both. A report analyzes the likely effectiveness of motivational approaches given different economic, cultural, and institutional factors in the country in question.

Each report must discuss the strengths and weaknesses of applying the following motivational theories in the selected country:

- Need theory
- Expectancy theory
- Goal-setting theory

- Equity theory
- Reinforcement theory
- Job design

Step 4. Present your findings to the class.

Step 5. Class discussion.

Alternative approach: The whole class works with one country, and each team deals with one approach to motivation.

Endnotes

[1] Meaning of Work International Research Team. 1987. *The Meaning of Working: An International Perspective.* New York: Academic Press.

[2] World Values Study Group. 1994. *World Values Surveys and European Values Surveys, 1981–1984 and 1990–1993, and 1995–1997* (Computer file). Ann Arbor, MI: InterUniversity Consortium for Political and Social Research.

[3] Meaning of Work International Research Team, *The Meaning of Working: An International Perspective.*

[4] Parboteeah, K. Praveen, and John B. Cullen. 2003. "Social institutions and work centrality: Explorations beyond national culture." *Organization Science,* 14, pp. 137–148.

[5] Hofstede, Geert. 2001. *Culture's Consequences.* London: Sage.

[6] Inglehart, Ronald, Miguel Basanez, and Alejandro Moreno. 1998. *Human Values and Beliefs: A Cross-Cultural Sourcebook.* Ann Arbor: University of Michigan Press.

[7] Grant, Linda. 1997. "Unhappy in Japan." *Fortune,* January 13, p. 142.

[8] World Values Study Group. *World Values Surveys and European Values Surveys.*

[9] *Economist.* 2006. "Emerging economies – Climbing back." January 21.

[10] Inglehart, Basanez, and Moreno, *Human Values and Beliefs: A Cross-Cultural Sourcebook.*

[11] World Values Study Group. *World Values Surveys and European Values Surveys.*

[12] Maslow, A. 1970. *Motivation and Personality.* New York: Harper and Row.

[13] Pinder, C. C. 1984. *Work Motivation.* Glenview, Ill.: Scott, Foresman.

[14] Hagerty, Michael R. 1999. "Testing Maslow's hierarchy of needs: National quality-of-life across time." *Social Indicators Research,* 46, pp. 249–271.

[15] Alderfer, C. P. 1972. *Existence, Relatedness and Growth: Human Needs in Organizational Settings.* New York: Free Press.

[16] Herzberg, F., B. Mausner, and B. B. Snyderman. 1959. *The Motivation to Work.* New York: Wiley.

[17] Huang, Xu, and Evert Van de Vliert. 2003. "Where intrinsic job satisfaction fails to work: national moderations of intrinsic motivation." *Journal of Organizational Behavior,* 24, pp. 159–179.

[18] McClelland, David C. 1961. *The Achieving Society.* Princeton: Van Nostrand Reinhold.

[19] Ronen, Simcha. 1986. *Comparative and Multinational Management.* New York: Wiley.

[20] Ronen, Simcha. 1994. "An underlying structure of motivation need taxonomies: A cross-cultural confirmation." *Handbook of Industrial and Organizational Psychology,* 4, pp. 241–269.

[21] Harpaz, Itzhak. 1990. "The importance of work goals: An international perspective." *Journal of International Business Studies,* First Quarter, pp. 75–93.

[22] Elizur, Dov, Ingwer Borg, Raymond Hunt, and Istvan Magyari Beck. 1991. "The structure of work values: A cross cultural comparison." *Journal of Organizational Behavior,* 12, pp. 21–38.

[23] Hagerty, "Testing Maslow's hierarchy of needs: National quality-of-life across time."

[24] Hofstede, Geert. 1991. *Cultures and Organizations.* London: McGraw-Hill.

[25] Vroom, Victor H. 1964. *Work and Motivation.* New York: Wiley.

[26] Gordon, Judith R. 1996. *Organizational Behavior.* Upper Saddle River, N.J.: Prentice Hall.

[27] Adams, J. S. 1963. "Toward an understanding of inequity." *Journal of Abnormal and Social Psychology,* 67, pp. 422–436.

[28] Chen, Chao C., Jaepil Choi, and Shu-Cheng Chi. 2002. "Making justice sense of local expatriate compensation disparity: Mitigation by local referents, ideological explanations, and interpersonal sensitivity in China-foreign joint ventures." *Academy of Management Journal,* 45, pp. 807–817.

[29] Huseman, R. C., J. D. Hatfield, and E. W. Miles. 1987. "A new perspective on equity theory: The equity sensitivity construct." *Academy of Management Review,* 12, pp. 222–234.

[30] Allen, Richard, Margaret Takeda and Charles S. White. 2005. "Cross-cultural equity sensitivity: a test of differences between the United States and Japan." *Journal of Managerial Psychology,* 20, pp. 641–662.

[31] Chhokar, Jagdeep, Anatoly Zhuplev, Lillian, Y. Fok, and Sandra J. Hartman. 2001. "The impact of culture on equity sensitivity perceptions and organizational behavior citizenship behaviors: A five-country study." *International Journal of Value-Based Management,* 14, pp. 79–98.

[32] Erez, Miriam. 1994. "Toward a model of cross-cultural industrial and organizational psychology." *Handbook of Industrial and Organizational Psychology,* 4, pp. 559–607.

[33] Gluskinos, U. M. 1988. "Cultural and political consideration in the introduction of western technologies: The Mekorot Project." *Journal of Management Development,* 6, pp. 34–36.

[34] Ibid.

[35] Chen, Choi, and Chi, "Making justice sense of local expatriate compensation disparity: Mitigation by local referents, ideological explanations, and interpersonal sensitivity in China-foreign joint ventures."

[36] Berman, J. J., and P. Singh. 1985. "Cross-cultural similarities and differences in perceptions of fairness." *Journal of Cross-Cultural Psychology,* 16, pp. 55–67.

[37] Kim, Ken I., Hun-Joon Park, and Nori Suzuki. 1990. "Reward allocations in the United States, Japan, and Korea: A comparison of individualistic and collectivistic cultures." *Academy of Management Journal* 33, pp. 188–198.

[38] Hundley, Greg and Jooyup Kim. 1997. "National culture and the factors affecting perceptions of pay fairness in Korea and the United States." *International Journal of Organizational Analysis,* 5:4, pp. 325–341.

[39] Locke, E. A., and G. P. Latham. 1990. *A Theory of Goal Setting and Task Performance.* Englewood Cliffs, N.J.: Prentice Hall.

[40] Hellriegel, Don, John W. Slocum, Jr., and Richard W. Woodman. 2001. *Organizational Behavior.* 9th ed. Cincinnati, OH: South-Western.

[41] Erez, M., P. C. Early, and C. L. Hulin. 1987. "The impact of participation on goal acceptance and performance: A two-step model." *Academy of Management Journal,* 12, pp. 265–277.

[42] Locke, E. A., G. P. Latham, and M. Erez. 1988. "The determinants of goal commitment." *Academy of Management Review,* 13, pp. 23–39.

[43] Erez, M., and P. C. Earley. 1987. "Comparative analysis of goal-setting strategies across cultures." *Journal of Applied Psychology,* 72, pp. 658–665.

[44] Erez, "Toward a model of cross-cultural industrial and organizational psychology."

[45] Erez and Earley, "Comparative analysis of goal-setting strategies across cultures."

[46] Skinner, B. F. 1938. *The Behavior of Organisms: An Experimental Analysis.* New York: D. Appleton-Century Company.

[47] Luthans, Fred, and Robert Kreitner. 1985. *Organizational Behavior Modification.* Glenview, Ill.: Scott, Foresman.

[48] Hellriegel, Slocum, Jr., and Woodman, *Organizational Behavior.* 9th ed.

[49] Luthans and Kreitner, *Organizational Behavior Modification.*

[50] Herman, J. 1973. "Effects of bonuses for punctuality on the tardiness of industrial workers." *Journal of Applied Behavioral Analysis,* 6, pp. 563–570.

[51] Welsh, Dianne H. B., Fred Luthans, and Steven M. Sommer. 1993. "Managing Russian factory workers: The impact of U.S.-based behavior and participative techniques." *Academy of Management Journal.* 36, pp. 58–79.

[52] Hackman, J. R., and G. R. Oldham. 1980. *Work Redesign.* Reading, Mass.: Addison-Wesley.

[53] Trist, E., and H. Murry. 1993. *The Social Engagement of Social Science: An Anthology, Vol. II: The Socio-Technical Perspective.* Philadelphia: University of Pennsylvania Press; Thorsrud, E. 1984. "The Scandinavian model: Strategies of organizational democracy." In *International Perspectives on Organizational Democracy,* edited by B. Wilpert and A. Sorge, pp. 337–370. New York: Wiley.

[54] Cummings, T. G. 1978. "Self-regulating work groups: A socio-technical synthesis." *Academy of Management Review,* 3, pp. 625–634.

[55] Gordon, *Organizational Behavior.*

[56] Erez, M., and P. C. Earley. 1993. *Culture, Self-Identity, and Work.* New York: Oxford University Press.

[57] Ibid.

[58] Earley, P. Christopher. 1989. "Social loafing and collectivism: A comparison of the United States and the People's Republic of China." *Administrative Science Quarterly,* 34, pp. 565–581.

Chiba International, Inc.

Ken Morikawa, the general manager for administration of a Japanese manufacturing plant under construction in rural Georgia, was troubled. This morning his American personnel manager, John Sinclair, had walked eagerly across the temporary open-plan office and announced: "I've found a professor of Japanese at Georgia State University who is willing to help translate our corporate philosophy. I would like to hire him for the job."

Ken felt pressured. He thought that John Sinclair, like many Americans, was expecting too much of Japanese companies. The company philosophy that he, Ken, had learned to live by in Tokyo would continue to guide him, but he did not feel that Americans would welcome or even understand a Japanese company philosophy.

Ken had a very large task to do in supervising the building of a plant that might ultimately provide jobs for up to 2,000 employees in the area where very few workers had had any industrial experience. He wished to show that his was a company that cared about the welfare of its workers and their job security and could be trusted to treat them fairly and not to lay them off. He believed that such a philosophy, if it could be properly explained to workers and carefully implemented, would help to build a high morale among the employees and consequently improve productivity.

Ken also wanted to ensure that high morale would be maintained as the workforce expanded to full capacity. Indeed, aside from issues of ease of transportation and distribution, the characteristics of the local workforce, their "Japanese" work ethic, had been one of the primary reasons for establishing the plant here. He believed that the training costs involved in transforming very "green" workers were well worth it to avoid people who had picked up "bad habits" or had had their morale lowered in prior industrial jobs. In Japan, teaching company philosophy is an important part of the company's introductory training program. But will it work here?

Ken wondered if his new administrative duties were lowering his concern for personnel matters. Ever since he had had to read Alfred Sloan's My Years with General Motors during the company training program and had written a review that focused on human resource issues, he had held positions related to his field. Even though he had majored in mathematical economics in college, his first assignment had been in the personnel "design center," which controlled training and salary administration for white-collar employees. After two years he was sent to a district office as a salesman. He returned after 13 months to the employee welfare section of the personnel department at the head office, administering such programs as house loans and recreational activities. Eight years with the company had passed by the time he was sent to an American college to study personnel-related subjects and improve his English.

After receiving his MBA, he returned to the head office. His most recent assignment before coming to Georgia was in personnel development research, planning new wage systems. It was expected that in his new job in Georgia he would eventually hand the reins over to an American general manager and remain only in an advisory capacity. However, he felt that it was at this vital stage that the corporation depended on his human relations expertise to set the scene for future success. Was he neglecting an area in which he had been trained to be sensitive?

He brought the subject up at lunch with John Sinclair. "Let me tell you something, John. I have a hunch why the Japanese are more successful in achieving high quality and productivity than Americans have been recently. It has to do with application, rather than ideas. Many great ideas have come from the United States, but the Japanese concentrate on applying them very carefully. Americans emphasize creating something new and then moving on. The Japanese meticulously analyze a problem from all angles and see how a solution might be implemented.

"As they say, Rome wasn't built in a day. I'm not sure our American workers will understand what it really means to have a company philosophy. Let's take it slowly and see what kind of people we hire and then see what best meets their needs."

John, who had worked at a rather traditional U.S. company for 11 years and had become increasingly interested in how Japanese companies managed their U.S. employees, had been eager to join a Japanese company. He wanted to see in action such "Japanese" strategies as long-term employment, the expression of a company philosophy and careful attention to integrating the employees into the company. He answered comfortingly, "Ken, I know you hate conflict. But I also know that you think it is important to gather information. One of our purchasing agents, Billy, told me about a Japanese company that he recently visited, Chiba International. Apparently, they already have a fully developed company philosophy and I understand that they're doing very well with it. Why don't we go out to California and talk with their management and try and understand how and why they concentrated on communicating their philosophy."

"And soak up some sun, too," beamed Ken. "You're on!"

The Company

Chiba International, Inc., in San Jose, California, makes high-precision, sophisticated electronics parts used in the final assembly of customized and semi- customized integrated circuits-particularly the expensive memory chips used in computers and military hardware. In such products, reliability is everything, price a lesser consideration. The similar but cheaper parts that manufacturers use once a product reaches a high volume are left for others to make.

Chiba International is a subsidiary of Chiba Electronics Company. *Nihon Keizai Shimbun,* Japan's preeminent business paper, recently ranked Chiba Electronics as one of the foremost companies in Japan on the basis of its management earnings stability and performance, ahead of such better-known giants as Sony, Matshushita Electric and Toyota Motor. Chiba Electronics Co. has 70 percent of the $250-million-a-year world market for its products. Chiba International likewise has a 70 percent share of the $250-million-a-year U.S. market.

Chiba International started in the United States 12 years ago, with a small sales office. A manufacturing plant that had been losing $100,000 to $200,000 a month was acquired from an American competitor. The American management was terminated, and a team of Japanese, headed by a Canadian-born Japanese-reared executive, succeeded in turning it around within two years.

Today 14 of the 24 top executives and 65 of 70 salesmen at Chiba are Americans. All the employees in other categories are also American.

Chiba's Philosophy

"As the sun rises brilliantly in the sky,
Revealing the size of the mountain,
*   the market,*
Oh this is our goal.
With the highest degree of mission in
*   our heart we serve our industry,*
Meeting the strictest degree of customer
*   requirement.*
We are the leader in this industry and
*   our future path*
Is ever so bright and satisfying."

"That's a translation of our company song," said a high-ranking Japanese executive, one of the group of Japanese and American managers who had agreed to meet with Ken and John. "But we haven't introduced it to our employees yet. That's typical of the way we brought the company philosophy to our employees— slowly and carefully. Every line worker gets a leaflet explaining our company philosophy when he or she starts work. We don't have a specific training session on it, and we don't force them to swallow it. It's up to them to digest and understand it."

"What about when you acquire a company as you have done over the past few years?" asked John.

"The same thing. It's very gradual. If we force it, it causes nothing but indigestion. Here it has been easy; the work is very labor intensive, repetitive, tedious assembly. In other places the soil is different. At one, for example, almost all the employees are exempts. They understand the philosophy but won't necessarily go by it. Engineers and technical people also seem to be less receptive than people in sales, personnel, and administration. In other sites, though, where the technology is more similar to this, we have had no problem at all."

One of the other managers present in the group, this one American, interrupted to show Ken and John a copy of the leaflet. It was quite rhetorical in tone, and a few paragraphs struck them as particularly interesting.

Management Philosophy
Our goal is to strive toward both the material and spiritual fulfillment of all employees in the Company, and through this successful fulfillment, serve mankind in its progress and prosperity.

Management Policy
(...) Our purpose is to fully satisfy the needs of our customers and in return gain a just profit for ourselves. We are a family united in common bonds and singular goals. One of these bonds is the respect and support we feel for our fellow family coworkers.

Also, the following exhortation:

When there is a need, we all rally to meet it and consider no task too menial or demeaning; all that matters is that it should be done! We are all ready to sweep floors, sort parts, take inventory, clean machines, inspect parts, load trucks, carry boxes, wash windows, file papers, run furnaces, and do just about anything that has to be done.

Meetings

"Daily meetings at the beginning of each shift are held in the courtyard," explained the group. "All the workers stand in lines (indicated by metal dots in the asphalt). Each day, a different member of management speaks for about five minutes. On Mondays executives speak, on Tuesdays, personnel and administration are represented, Wednesdays are about safety concerns, and on Thursdays and Fridays, members of production and sales speak. They are all free to say whatever they like. The shift workers tend to develop favorites, especially among the more extroverted sales managers.

"Then a personnel coordinator delivers news about sports events and so on, and perhaps a motivational message, and goes on to lead the group in exercises for one minute. These calisthenics are voluntary, but most of the employees join in. After that, the large group breaks up for brief departmental meetings.

"Again, in the departmental meetings, a speaker is chosen for the day and speaks for about five minutes. Even people at the lowest exempt level find themselves speaking. Then the department manager discusses yesterday's performance, today's schedule and any other messages, such as that housekeeping is inadequate or that certain raw materials are in short supply.

"Once a month, there is an announcement of total company performance versus plans. This is important, as all company employees share at the same rate in the annual company bonus, which is based on profitability and usually equals about one month's salary or wages."

Another Japanese manager continued, "Years ago, there were complaints about having so many meetings, but I haven't heard any for a long time now. The employees like to hear important announcements and even less important ones, such as who is selling theater tickets, bowling league reports, and tennis match dates."

The American personnel manager chimed in: "I was the one who came up with the idea of exercises. I saw it on my visit to Japan. They are just a part of the rituals and symbols that you need in order to get better mutual understanding. The atmosphere was right and the timing was good. Even so, because they weren't mandatory, it took about one-and-a-half years until everyone joined in. Now most people understand the meaning behind it. If we were to stop it now, we'd get complaints.

"Besides the morning meeting, we have several other meetings. On Mondays, we have a very large liaison meeting for information sharing. All the executives attend: sales managers and staff managers, the plant manager and the assistant plant manager. On Tuesdays, we have a production meeting attended by the production managers and any staff involved with their problems. On Monday at four o'clock every second week we have a supervisors' meeting, mainly for one-way communication to them. On the alternating weeks we have a training meeting. The whole personnel department also meets every week.

"Less formally, we have many sales meetings about, for example, new products. We have combination sales and production meetings, which are called on an as-needed basis. Team meetings on the production line are also called whenever needed.

"All these formal meetings are supplemented by many company-sponsored activities. We have a company bowling league, tennis matches, softball, fishing, and skiing. We often organize discount tickets. We're planning the Christmas party. Each employee can bring a guest, so it costs us about $40,000. Our company picnic costs $29,000."

"It sounds very well worked out for the non-exempts," commented John. "How about for the exempts?"

Sales Force

They started with the largely American sales force.

"They're a very different species. They have tremendous professional pride. Most American sales engineers have a very arrogant take-it-or-leave-it attitude. Our attitude is almost the complete opposite. We try to serve our customers' needs, almost like a geisha girl, who makes her customer feel that he is the only one served by her.

"We try to communicate the following motto to them:

S *incerity*
A *bility*
L *ove*
E *nergy*
S *ervice*

Sincerity is the basic attitude you need to have, as well as the ability to convince the customer. You must love the products that you sell or you can't convince the customer. You must have energy because at the end of the day it's always the case that you could have done one more thing or made one more sales call. Finally, the mentality of serving the customer is the most important.

"We communicate that to our sales force and they like it, especially when they don't have to tell white lies to customers or put up with harassment from customers. We also want them to be honest with us, even about their mistakes. Quite often we depend on the salesmen's input for our understanding of customers, so an objective daily report by fax or phone is very important to us.

"No one in our company works on a commission basis, not even salesmen. We would lose market share for products that are difficult to promote. Also, the nature of different sales territories would make commissions unfair.

"Although we pay on straight salary only, we don't just have a unilateral sales quota. The salesman discusses his targets with his boss. They are purposely

set high, so good performance against goals is grounds for a merit increase the next year.

"We don't really have a marketing department. We feel that it is an expensive luxury and while we have a vice president in charge of marketing, his is almost a corporate sales staff function."

U.S. Management

John was curious about how American line managers reacted to working in a Japanese company.

A Japanese manager explained: "When Americans join us, they expect the usual great deal of internal politicking. They scan people in meetings, looking for those with real power, looking, to use our expression, for whose apple they should polish. It takes time for them to realize that it's unnecessary.

"When we interview American executives for a job, we do it collectively so five to ten interviewers are present. This usually puzzles the interviewee. He wonders whom he will report to. We reply that he will be hired by the company, although he may report to one individual. As in Japan, the company will take care of him, so it does not depend on his loyalty to one individual."

What about your company criteria for hiring managers?

"His way of thinking, not necessarily his ability. Although a Harvard MBA is welcomed, it is not essential. In fact, no one here has one. We don't provide an elegant fit to his social elite. There are no private offices. Salary and benefits are up to par for the location (and industry) but not especially high. We work long hours.

"We're looking for devotion and dedication as well as an aggressive attitude. We conduct two or three long interviews for an important position. We ask questions like 'What is your shortcoming?' We're interested not in the answer itself but in the kind of thinking behind it. We do make mistakes sometimes, but our batting average is good.

"Sometimes there's a very deep communication gap between Japanese management and U.S. management because we believe in dedication and devotion to the company. They do, too, but only to a certain point. We often tell them that the joy of working for the company can be identical to personal happiness with the family. I ask my wife for her understanding of that, and I work six days a week, from seven o'clock to ten o'clock. Their wives place demands on them to come home at six o'clock. U.S. executives put personal and family happiness first. I'm not telling you which is right. But it is second nature for me to think about the future of the company. So long as I have challenging assignments and job opportunities, I will put the company before my personal happiness."

What do American interviewees feel about all this?

"One problem is that they ask, 'What's my real future? Can I be considered for president?' There's no real answer because it probably will be a Japanese. However, we don't like to close those doors to a really capable American.

"The issue of communication between Japanese and Americans is still a problem. After the Americans go home, the Japanese get together at seven or eight o'clock and talk in Japanese about problems and make decisions without the Americans present. Naturally this makes the Americans feel very apprehensive. We're trying to rectify it by asking the Japanese managers not to make decisions alone and asking the Americans to stay as late as possible.

"More important, if we could really have our philosophy permeate the American managers, we Japanese could all go back to Japan and not worry about it. Our mission is to expedite that day by education and training.

"So far, however, there is a gap. Americans are more interested in individual accomplishment, remuneration and power. When they are given more responsibility, they don't feel its heavy weight, rather they feel that it extends their sovereign area so that they have more of a whip. That creates power conflicts among U.S. managers."

"Let me tell you, though," summarized the American personnel manager, "I like it. I was recruited by a headhunter. Now, I've been with the company five years and the difference from my former employer is astounding. I don't have to get out there and be two-faced, fudging to keep the union out, hedging for the buck. In general, it's hard to find an American employer that really sincerely cares for the welfare of the low-level employee. This company went almost too far in the opposite direction at first. They wanted to do too much for the employees too quickly, without their earning it. That way, you don't get their respect."

Financial People

"Our financial people throughout the company are proud because of our impressive company

performance. Only 20% of our financing is through debt, in contrast to many Japanese companies. We also have a rather unique way of treating some of our raw materials internally. We try to expense everything out. It's derived from our founder's very conservative management. We ask the question: 'If we closed down tomorrow, what would our liquid assets be?' In line with that, for example, internally we put our inventory at zero.

"We follow the 'noodle peddler theory.' The noodle peddler is an entrepreneur. He has to borrow his cart, his serving dishes and his pan to make ramen. He has to be a good marketer to know where to sell. He has to be a good purchasing director and not overbuy noodles, in case it rains. He could buy a fridge but he would need a lot of capital, the taste of noodles would deteriorate, and he would need additional manpower to keep an inventory of the contents of the fridge. The successful noodle peddler puts dollars aside at the end of the day for depreciation and raw materials for tomorrow. Only then does he count profits. That's also why we don't have a marketing department. The successful peddler doesn't have time to examine opportunities in the next town.

"This is the way a division manager has to operate. In order to maximize output with minimum expenditure, every effort is made to keep track on a daily basis of sales, returns, net shipment costs and expenses."

Open Communications

"I understand all that you've said so far," mused John, "but how exactly do you take all these abstract philosophical ideas and make them real?"

"Oh, open communications is the key. We have a fairly homogeneous workforce. Most are intelligent, some are even college graduates. Most are also very stable types with dependents or elderly parents they send money to.

"We're lucky, but of course it's not as homogeneous as in Japan, where everyone has experienced one culture. So here, the philosophy has to be backed up by a great deal of communication.

"We mentioned the meetings. We also have a suggestion box and we answer all the suggestions in print in the company newspaper. Also, one person from personnel tours the plant all day, for all three shifts, once a week, just chatting and getting in touch with any potential problems as they arise. It's kind of a secondary grievance system. We're not unionized and I guess we'd rather stay that way as it helps us so much with flexibility and job changes among our workforce.

"In the fall, when work is slow, we have many *kompas*. You may not know about this, John. A *kompa* is a small gathering off-premises after work. Eight to eighteen people participate, and the company pays for their time and refreshments. They're rarely social, they have an objective. For example, if two departments don't get along and yet they need to work together, they might hold a *kompa*. A *kompa* can take place at all levels of the company. Those groups that do it more frequently tend to move on from talking about production problems to more philosophical issues."

Appraisal and Reward Systems

"It all sounds great," sighed Ken, "just as good as Japan. But tell me, how does it tie in with wages and salaries, because people here are used to such different systems."

"Well, we don't have lifetime employment, but we do have an explicit no-layoff commitment. We are responsible for our employees. This means that employees also have to take responsibility and have broad job categories so we don't have to redo paperwork all the time. We have tried to reduce the number of job classifications to the raw minimum, so we have two pay grades covering 700 workers. At the higher levels, we have three pay grades for craftsmen and two for technicians."

John ventured, "I guess an example of your job flexibility in action is the mechanic you mentioned when we toured the plant."

"Yes, the person you spoke with was a dry press mechanic. He's doing menial labor this week, but his pay hasn't been cut, and he knows he wouldn't be taken off his job if it weren't important."

"We don't hire outside, if we can avoid it," added the personnel manager. "Only if the skill is not available in-house. The bulk of our training is on-the-job. We don't utilize job postings. We promote when a person's skills are ripe or when there is a need.

"The job of a 'lead' or team leader is the stepping-stone to supervisor. It's not a separate job status within our system, but the lead is given a few cents an hour extra and wears a pink, not a yellow, smock. The lead is carefully groomed for his or her position, and although a lead might be demoted because a specific need for them no longer existed, a lead would rarely be demoted for lack of skills or leadership ability.

"Rewards are for service and performance. Plant workers, unskilled and semi-skilled, are reviewed every six months. The lead completes the evaluation form (see Exhibit 1). This is checked or confirmed by the supervisor and the overall point score translates into cents per hour. There are two copies, one for the supervisor and one for the employee. Depending on the supervisor, some employees get a copy, some don't.

"The office clerical staff are all reviewed on April 1st and October 1st. A similar review form for managers is used to determine overall letter scores. All the scores are posted on a spread sheet and compared across departments, through numerous meetings of managers and personnel people, until the scores are consistent with one another. Then the scores are tied to dollars. Some managers feed back, some don't.

"Exempt staff are reviewed on April 1st, and as a separate process, the spreadsheet procedure just outlined is carried out. At least two managers review any exempt employee, but feedback is usually minimal. The reason is that we encourage feedback all year. If there are no surprises for your subordinate at review time, then you've managed well.

"Agreements on reviews for exempt personnel take place in many meetings at various levels. The process is very thorough and exceptionally fair, and contributes to the levels of performance we get."

Quality and Service

A question from John as to how Chiba International was doing as a result of all this elicited much pride.

"Turnover is 2 1/2 percent a month, which is very satisfactory for our kind of labor, given a transient society. We rarely have to advertise for new employees now. The community knows about us. But we do select carefully. The personnel department does the initial screening, and then the production managers and supervisors get together and interview people.

"The lack of available technically trained people used to be a big problem, but over the years we've developed the expertise internally. Our productivity is now almost as high as in Japan."

EXHIBIT 1

Employee's Name	Clock No.		Dept.		Shift		Over Last 6 Month Period				
							Days Absent	Number Tardies	Number Early Exit	Work Days Leave of Absences	
Employee's Job Title	Anniversary										

		Numerical Score			
Rate on Factors Below:		L	S	M	F
1. LOYALTY/EDUCATION	Faithful to the company cause, ideals, philosophy, & customers; a devoting or setting aside for company purposes.				
2. SPIRIT/ZEAL	Amount of interest & enthusiasm shown in work; full of energy, animation & courage; eagerness & ardent interest in the pursuit of company goals.				
3. COOPERATION	A willingness & ability to work with leaders & fellow employees toward company goals.				
4. QUANTITY OF WORK	Volume of work regularly produced; speed & consistency of output.				
5. QUALITY OF WORK	Extent to which work produced meets quality requirements of accuracy, thoroughness & effectiveness.				
6. JOB KNOWLEDGE	The fact or condition of knowing the job with familiarity gained through experience, association & training.				
7. SAFETY ATTITUDE	The willingness & ability to perform work safely.				
8. CREATIVENESS	The ability to produce through imaginative skill.				
9. ATTENDANCE	Includes all types of absence (excused or unexcused), tardies, early exits, L.O.A.'s from scheduled work.				
10. LEADERSHIP	The ability to provide direction, guidance & training to others.				

OVERALL EVALUATION OF EMPLOYEE PERFORMANCE:

Supervisor's Approval			Personnel Dept. Approval

Do Not Write Below This Line—For Human Resource Department Use Only

Present Base Rate	New Base Rate	Effective Date of Increase	Refer to instructions on the back side of this paper

Ken and John asked what other aspects of the company they had not yet discussed. They were told that quality, and, hence, customer service, was another central part of the philosophy.

"Our founder, Mr. Amano, firmly believes in zero defect theory. Doctor Deming taught us the concept of quality control. Unfortunately, many American companies did not emphasize this. During World War II, the concept of acceptable quality level was developed in the United States. The idea was that with mass production there will be some defects. Rather than paying for more inspectors on the production line, real problems, for example, with cars, could be identified by the consumer in the field and repaired in the field.

"We don't allow that. We have 100 percent visual inspection of all our tiny parts. They only cost $50 per 1,000 units. We inspect every finished package under a microscope, so we have 130 inspectors, which is about one-sixth of our production staff.

"The company's founder, Amano, has said to us, 'We try to develop every item our customers want. Being latecomers, we never say no, we never say we can't.' Older ceramic manufacturers would evaluate a proposal on a cost basis and say no. Yet we have been profitable from the start."

As the interview drew to a close, one Japanese manager reflected that Mr. Suzuki has a saying:

Ability x philosophy x zeal = performance.

If the philosophy is negative, performance is negative because it's a multiplicative relationship.

"But in our company, which now numbers 2,000, we must also start to have different kinds of thinking. The Japanese sword is strong because it is made of all different kinds of steel wrapped around one another. The Chinese sword is also very strong, but because it's all one material, it's vulnerable to a certain kind of shock. We must bear that in mind so that we have differences within a shared philosophy.

"We're thinking of writing a book on our philosophy, addressing such issues as what loyalty is, by piecing together events and stories from our company history. This would be a book that would assist us in training."

Ken and John walked out into the parking lot. "Whew!" sighed John. "It's more complicated than I had thought."

"Oh, yes! You need a great deal of patience," responded Ken paternally.

"So we'd better get started quickly," enthused John. "Where shall we begin? Perhaps I should call the translator."

CASE DISCUSSION QUESTIONS

1. Can Japanese motivation practices work in the U.S. without being adapted? Why or why not?
2. Which aspects of Japanese motivation practices do you see as most problematic for a U.S. workforce?
3. How should Ken and John adapt Chiba's California practices to their own situation in Georgia? What problems might they run into?
4. What aspects of the Japanese management approach used by Chiba are the most interesting or unusual?
5. Is it possible for U.S. employees to develop the same loyalty for the organization as their Japanese counterpart? What can Ken and John do to promote such loyalty?

CASE CREDIT

This case was written by Nina Hatvany and Vladimir Pucik for class discussion only. Used with permission of the authors. None of this material is to be quoted or reproduced without the permission of the authors.

Learning Objectives

After reading this chapter you should be able to:

- Know the characteristics of global business leadership.

- Understand traditional North American models of leadership, including trait theory, behavioral approaches, and contingency theory.

- Understand the Japanese performance-maintenance model, the Indian nurturant-task-oriented model, and Afro-centric model of leadership.

- Be able to apply the cultural-contingency model of leadership.

- Develop sensitivity to national cultural differences in preferred leadership traits and effective leadership behaviors.

- Understand how national culture affects the choice of leader influence tactics.

- Understand how national culture influences subordinates' expectations regarding appropriate behaviors and traits of leaders.

- Understand the role of transformational leadership in multinational settings.

- Understand how the national culture affects a leader's attributions regarding subordinates' behaviors.

- Understand the role of women global leaders for multinational organizations.

- Develop the ability to diagnose cultural situations and suggest appropriate leadership styles to fit the situation.

Preview **CASE IN POINT**

Same Problem—Different Styles

Consider the fictional example of the leadership styles of two CEOs, one from a U.S. pharmaceutical company and the other from a Japanese pharmaceutical company. They must lead their subordinates in dealing with a crisis regarding a potentially deadly batch of headache medicine produced by one of their overseas subsidiaries. Although the characters and companies are fictional, the styles are based on real leaders.

Ms. Moore, a U.S. American CEO

7:00 Ms. Moore, CEO of Thorndike Pharmaceuticals, leaves for work with her daughter.

7:30 Ms. Moore leaves her daughter at a private junior high school for girls.

7:45 Ms. Moore receives a cell-phone call from the Thorndike Pharmaceuticals European area manager to tell her of a death and the poisoning of several people in France as a result of taking tainted headache medication produced by their company. The European area manager asks what he should do. Moore says she will get back to him.

8:00 Ms. Moore calls her executive secretary and tells him to plan for an 8:30 videoconference with relevant U.S. and European managers and legal staff.

8:30 Ms. Moore has a videoconference with the management team and briefs its members on the crisis.

8:45 Corporate attorneys brief Ms. Moore and the top management team on legal options and liabilities.

Sakano-*san*, a Japanese CEO

Sakano-*san*, CEO of Kobe Pharmaceuticals, eats a breakfast of a raw egg and rice. Sakano-*san*'s wife wakes their two children in enough time for their 45-minute subway ride to school.

Sakano-*san* exchanges a polite bow with his driver and begins his limousine ride to Kobe Pharmaceuticals.

9:00 The director of public relations calls Moore, asking how she can deal with the press.

9:05 The plant manager of the French facility that produced the tainted drug calls and asks what he should do about the protesters outside the gate.

9:45 Fearing further deaths and injury, the VP of European operations temporarily shuts down all production of the tainted drug and recalls all drugs produced after a certain date.

10:00 Ms. Moore asks the finance and accounting department to figure out how much this is going to cost.

10:05 Top management and legal staff meet with Ms. Moore to give her an update.

10:30 Ms. Moore gives an interview to the press.

11:30 Ms. Moore has a hurried lunch at her desk. She takes calls from the legal department and from the VP for European operations during lunch.

For the remainder of the day, and to well after 8:00 P.M., Ms. Moore continues at this hectic pace of meetings and phone calls. She calls her husband at 4:00, reminding him to pick up their daughter at school.

Sakano-*san* meets with executives from Bayer to discuss an international joint venture.

Around this time, a trusted mid-level manager, a student of Sakano-*san*'s old Tokyo University professor, informs Sakano-*san* discreetly that a problem exists and that staff members are developing a solution. Sakano-*san* nods his understanding. Staff members engage in consensus building (*nemawashi*) to develop a plan of action to deal with the crisis.

Subordinates formally inform Sakano-*san* of the problem and their plan to deal with the crisis. He acknowledges the information and thanks them for their quick work.

With the knowledge that his staff is working on dealing with the crisis, Sakano-*san* continues his regular business day: a two-hour luncheon meeting with government officials to discuss long-term R&D goals for the industry. He ends his day talking with a chemical supply company CEO at 1:00 A.M. in a private bar in Tokyo's entertainment district, Ropongi.

Source: Based on the format in a fictional story in Doktor, Robert H. 1990. "Asian and American CEOs: A comparative study." Organizational Dynamics, Winter, pp. 46–56.

Leadership
Ability of an individual to influence, motivate, and enable others to contribute toward the effectiveness and success of the organizations of which they are members.

What is leadership? The Western-based view defines leadership as the influencing of group members to achieve organizational goals. However, if we want to examine leadership from a cross-cultural perspective, it is important to understand whether this definition is acceptable to most cultures. In that respect, the Global Leadership and Organizational Behavior Effectiveness project (GLOBE — described in more detail later) sheds some light on the issue. The project gathered about 200 researchers from 60 countries, and after hours of discussion, the GLOBE's universal definition of leadership emerged. The researchers agreed that leadership is "the ability of an individual to influence, motivate, and enable others to contribute toward the effectiveness and success of the organizations of which they are members."[1]

The European Foundation for Quality Management,[2] an important association dedicated to fostering quality in European companies, has also attempted to define leadership within the European context. It sees leadership as the process by which individuals "develop and facilitate the achievement of the mission and vision, develop values required for long-term success and implement these via appropriate actions and behaviors, and are personally involved in ensuring that the organization's management system is developed and implemented."[3]

As we see from the GLOBE and EFQM definitions, leadership is more than simply holding a management position. Excellent leaders motivate their employees to achieve more than minimal organizational requirements. Without good leaders, no company can achieve success. Consequently, most managers seek ways to improve their leadership skills, and the popular and academic press is filled with ideas on leadership. However, as we will see, there is no simple answer to the question, "What makes a great leader?" Many formal theories of leadership exist, and most people have their own beliefs concerning what makes a great leader.

Improving one's leadership skills in a domestic company is a difficult challenge. Becoming an excellent leader in a multinational company is an even greater challenge. This chapter shows that successful multinational leaders choose effective leadership styles based on an understanding of how national culture and a country's social institutions affect leadership. To achieve understanding, this chapter covers two important areas. First, it provides a summary of theories of leadership offered by experts from different countries. Second, the chapter offers key examples of how leaders of different national backgrounds behave in their home cultures. As the Preview Case in Point shows, and the chapter will point out, managers working in different cultures may achieve similar goals using widely different leadership styles.

Global Leadership: The New Breed

The rise of transnational companies and the dependence of even the smallest companies on international trade create a need for a new type of leader. Many of today's companies and more of tomorrow's companies will have units located all over the world and will draw workers and managers from all over the world. In such companies, people are expected to have the skills to be able to lead people from different nationalities. Such demands suggest that future leaders need to have the skills to deal with cross-cultural differences. Consider the following Case in Point and the substantial investment Intel is making to develop global leaders skilled in dealing with cross-cultural differences.

A **global leader** must have the skills and abilities to interact with and manage people from the diverse cultural backgrounds that populate his or her multinational company. Next, we consider some of the characteristics of this new breed of leader. Experts on managing cultural differences identify the critical characteristics of a global leader.[4] According to experts, the successful global leader:

> *Cosmopolitan:* **Is sufficiently flexible to operate comfortably in pluralistic cultural environments.**
> *Skilled at intercultural communication:* **Knows at least one foreign language and understands the complexities of interaction with people from other cultures.**
> *Culturally sensitive:* **Uses experience in different national, regional, and organizational cultures to build relationships with culturally different people while understanding his or her own culture and cultural biases.**

Global leader

One who has the skills and abilities to interact with and manage people from diverse cultural backgrounds.

Intel's Leadership Training Program

Intel, the Silicon Valley-based semiconductor giant, obtains 70 percent of its revenues from outside of the United States. It currently has more than 91,000 employees located in more than 48 nations. Given the global nature of its operations, Intel places crucial importance on the ability of its managers to deal with cross-cultural differences. In that context, it has a very innovative leadership program that requires all of its mid-level leaders to be exposed to different cultures.

The design of the leadership training program was the result of substantial cooperation among employees from places such as China, Russia, the United States, and Israel. Intel expects about 800 of its nearly 2,300 mid-level managers to attend the week-long seminar in a location different from their home base. To ensure that the managers get cross-cultural training, Intel also requires that 30 percent of the attendees come from other regions.

The program incorporates seminars emphasizing the development of leadership skills such as setting pace and implementing business plans. Although the seminars don't necessarily include cultural training, the program requires teams of six to nine mid-level leaders from various regions to create new product proposals at the end of the training. In doing so, Intel forces the participants to consider cultural differences by working with individuals from many different societies. Such experiences ensure that attendees have a chance to deal with cultural differences as they work on the project.

Source: Based on Fraueheim, Ed. 2005. "Crossing cultures." Workforce Management, November, p. 1; Thomke, Stefan H. 2006. "Capturing the real value of innovation tools." MIT Sloan Management Reviews, Winter, 47: pp. 24–32.

> *Capable of rapid acculturation:* **Rapidly acculturates or adjusts to strange or different cultural settings.**
> *Knowledgeable about cultural and institutional influences on management:* **Understands how national culture and a country's social institutions affect the entire management process.**
> *A facilitator of subordinates' intercultural performance:* **Uses a deep understanding of cultural differences in work and living to prepare subordinates for successful overseas experiences.**
> *A user of cultural synergy:* **Takes advantage of cultural differences by finding a synergy that combines the strengths of each cultural group and by using performance standards understandable across cultural groups. This results in higher levels of organizational performance than that produced by culturally homogeneous companies.**
> *A promoter and user of the growing world culture:* **Understands, uses, and takes advantage of the international advances in media, transportation, and travel that support the globalization of international business.**
> *A commitment to continuous improvement in self–awareness and renewal:* **Understanding and questioning one's self.**

Emotional intelligence

The ability of the global leader to accurately perceive his or her emotions and to use those emotions to solve problems and to relate to others.

A growing body of literature suggests that **emotional intelligence** is also an important trait of a global leader should have.[5] Emotional intelligence refers to the ability of the global leader to accurately perceive his or her emotions and to use those emotions to solve problems and to relate to others. Those leaders who are higher on emotional intelligence tend to have a better ability to use their emotions to devise strategies to achieve goals. Given that a large part of being a global leader is being able to relate to others, multinational companies should seek out emotional intelligence when hiring leaders.

The remainder of this chapter provides a background on leadership that multinational managers can use to improve their global leadership skills. Few managers will reach the levels and experience of truly global managers. But all managers can benefit by gaining a better understanding of leadership and by using this knowledge to develop more of the strengths of a global leader.

Three Classic Models: A Vocabulary of Leadership

The following sections survey three basic models of leadership. These models include leadership traits, leader behavior, and contingency leadership models. Knowledge of these basic views of leadership will help you understand the basic terms used to describe leadership options in a multinational setting.

Similar to the motivation theories discussed in the previous chapter, most, but not all, of these leadership models originate from North America. However, this chapter focuses on the multinational applicability of leadership models, not just on their North American applications.

Leadership Traits

Trait models of leadership evolved from the debate regarding whether leaders are born or made. Early leadership theorists looked at successful leaders in business, politics, religion, and the military, such as Alexander the Great and Muhammad. They concluded that such leaders were born with unique characteristics that made them quite different from ordinary people. This view of leadership is known as the **great-person theory**.

Although leadership theorists never identified an exact list of leadership traits, decades of research did discover some differences between leaders and their subordinates.[6] At least in the United States, successful leaders exhibit the following traits: higher intelligence and self-confidence, more initiative, more assertiveness and persistence, greater desire for responsibility and the opportunity to influence others, and a greater awareness of the needs of others. However, unlike the great-person theory of leadership, contemporary views of leadership traits do not assume that leaders are born. Although leaders are different, aspiring leaders can achieve this difference through training and experience.

> **Great-person theory**
> Idea that leaders are born with unique characteristics that make them quite different from ordinary people.

Leadership Behaviors

U.S. Perspectives on Leadership Behaviors

Although leaders have different traits than their subordinates, North American studies of leadership traits have concluded that traits alone do not make a leader. The *behaviors* leaders use to manage their employees may be more important. Classic studies of leadership behaviors in the United States came from two U.S. universities, The Ohio State University and the University of Michigan. Based on hundreds of studies of North American managers, these teams of researchers identified two major types of leadership behaviors.[7] One type of leadership includes behaviors that focus on completing tasks by initiating structure. Leaders who have a principal concern for initiating structure are called task-centered leaders. A **task-centered leader** gives specific directions to subordinates so that the subordinates can complete tasks. These leaders

> **Task-centered leader**
> One who gives subordinates specific standards, schedules, and tasks.

Person-centered leader

One who focuses on meeting employees' social and emotional needs.

Autocratic leadership

Leaders make all major decisions themselves.

Democratic leadership

Leader includes subordinates in decision making.

Consultative or participative leadership

Leader's style falls midway between autocratic and democratic styles.

establish standards, schedule work, and assign employees tasks. A second type of leadership behavior focuses on meeting the social and emotional needs of employees. These consideration behaviors represent the style of a **person-centered leader**. Consideration behaviors include actions such as showing a concern for subordinates' feelings and taking subordinates' ideas into account.

The distinction between person-centered and task-centered leader behaviors also applies to how leaders make decisions. Leaders who adopt an **autocratic leadership** style make all major decisions themselves. Those who employ a **democratic leadership** style include subordinates in the decision making. Most experts accept that a range of leader behaviors exists between the authoritarian leader, who makes all decisions, and the purely democratic leader, who abdicates all decision making to the group.[8] A **consultative or participative leadership** style often falls midway between the autocratic and democratic leadership styles.

Taking a somewhat broader perspective than just leadership behavior, Rensis Likert, a famous management and leadership theorist, identified four styles of management that also reflect a similar distinction between the task and the person.[9] These patterns are exploitative/authoritative, benevolent/authoritative, consultative, and participative. Exhibit 15.1 shows how each management style relates to a manager's general leadership orientation, preferred motivational techniques, communication style, decision-making style, and controlling style.

Based on the early studies of U.S. workers, we can conclude that leaders choose behaviors that focus on initiating structure for task completion or on meeting the social and emotional needs of workers. Which style of leader behavior is best? Perhaps it all depends on the situation. In later sections, you will see that contemporary U.S. leadership theories challenge the assumption that

EXHIBIT 15.1   Likert's Four Styles of Management

Management Behaviors	Exploitative Authoritative (System 1)	Benevolent Authoritative (System 2)	Consultative (System 3)	Participative (System 4)
General Leadership Style	Autocratic, top-down	Paternalistic but still autocratic	Less autocratic, more attention to employees	Employee-centered
Motivation Techniques	Punishments, some rewards	More rewards, but still punishment dominated	Reward dominated	Employees set own goals and appraise results
Communication Style	Downward, little use of teamwork	Downward, with some limited teamwork	Employees give opinions	Extensive multiway communication both laterally and vertically
Decision-Making Style	Decisions made at top of organization	Management sets boundaries	Management consults but makes final decision	Group or team makes most decisions
Control Mechanisms	Process and output managed from the top	Management sets boundaries	More output control than process	Team appraises results

Source: Adapted from Likert, R., and Jane Likert. 1976. New Ways of Managing Conflict. New York: McGraw-Hill.

one style of leadership behavior fits all situations. Before considering that issue, however, we will look at leadership through the eyes of the Japanese.

Japanese, Indian, and Afro-Centric Perspectives on Leader Behaviors

The **performance–maintenance (PM) theory** of leadership represents a Japanese perspective on leader behavior. Created in Japan, but similar to many U.S. leadership theories, PM theory has two dimensions.[10] The performance function (P) is similar to task-centered leadership. It represents a style of leadership where the manager guides and pressures subordinates to achieve higher levels of group performance. The performance (P) side of PM leadership has two components. First, the leader works for or with subordinates to develop work procedures, called the planning component. Second, the leader then pressures employees to put forth more effort and to do good work, called the pressure component. The maintenance function (M) is similar to person-centered leadership. It represents behaviors that promote group stability and social interaction.

One key difference exists between the Japanese PM approach to leader behavior and the U.S. perspective on task- and person-centered leadership. The Japanese PM leader focuses on influencing groups. The U.S. approach to task- or person-centered leadership focuses on how the leader influences individuals.

PM theory suggests that groups perform best when both P and M are present. That is, a leader can pressure a group to achieve higher levels of performance as long as the leader also supports the social interaction needs of the group, the M function. The theory suggests that the positive effects of combining the P and M leadership components should work in all cultural settings. However, in adapting to national differences, many Japanese companies use modified versions of PM theory to manage their overseas operations.[11]

Researchers have also attempted to understand preferred leadership behaviors in India.[12] Although early theories based on Western models failed, Sinha's[13] **nurturant-task-oriented leadership (NT) theory** has provided a better understanding of Indian leadership. Unlike Western-based models, the NT theory combines elements of task behaviors, arguing that the preferred leader in India is both person-centered and task-centered. Ideal Indian leaders are expected to nurture their subordinates by showing affection and care and by making efforts to develop their subordinates. However, the Indian leader is also expected to be concerned about task accomplishment. As such, the preferred Indian leader is seen as both paternalistic and authoritative[14] whereby he or she guides and cares for subordinates in return for complete obedience, respect and loyalty.

As both examples above show, the Japanese and Indian styles of leadership tend to emphasize person-centered leadership styles compared to the U.S.-based perspective. The **Afro-centric model of leadership** also emphasizes person-centered leadership, and is based on the concept of *Ubuntu,* which is an African philosophy based on collectivism and group-centeredness in contrast to individualism.[15] In a study comparing whites and blacks in South Africa, Booysen[16] found that subjects in the black sample were more people-focused, consistent with their belief in *Ubuntu.* The researchers found that blacks scored higher on collectiveness, humane orientation, and gender egalitarianism compared to whites. As such, white managers had responses that were more congruent with Western task-oriented styles while blacks tend to be more people focused.

Performance–maintenance (PM) theory
Japanese perspective on balancing task- and person-centered leader behaviors.

Nurturant-task-oriented leadership (NT) theory
Indian leadership theory combining both task- and person-centered leader behaviors.

Afro-centric model of leadership
African leadership model emphasizing person-centered styles based on collectivism and group-centeredness.

The next section presents an overview of a more complex view of leadership, called contingency theory. It shows the historical progression of leadership theory beyond the simple trait and behavior models.

Contingency Theories

The early models of leadership tended to look for leadership universals: Managers and researchers wanted to know which leadership traits or behaviors defined excellent leadership in all situations. After years of study, experts concluded, "it all depends"; no one leadership style works best for all situations. This conclusion led to an approach to leadership known as **contingency theory.** Contingency theories assume that different styles and different leaders are more appropriate for different situations. To lead successfully, managers must choose different leadership styles in different situations.

How does contingency theory work? To illustrate the logic of the contingency approach to leadership, this section reviews two important North American contingency theories of leadership, Fiedler's theory of leadership and path-goal theory. For additional reviews of other similar contingency theories of leadership, students should consult standard organizational-behavior textbooks. The contingency theories discussed next identify several factors that influence the effectiveness of different leadership styles in different situations. They also provide the basic framework that multinational managers can use to adapt their leadership styles to work in different national contexts.

Fiedler on Leadership Effectiveness

Fred Fiedler, an expert on leadership, developed one of the most popular early contingency views of leadership.[17] **Fiedler's theory of leadership** proposed that managers tend to be either task- or person-centered leaders. The success of these leadership styles depends on three contingencies or characteristics of the work situation: the relationships between the leader and his or her subordinates (e.g., the degree to which the subordinates trust the leader); the degree to which subordinates' tasks are easily and clearly defined (e.g., tasks for assembly-line work usually are clearly defined); and the officially granted organizational power of the leader (e.g., the formal power of a position such as a ship's captain).

As with all contingency theories, effective leadership occurs when the leadership style matches the situation. What situations suggest a task- or person-centered leadership? Exhibit 15.2 shows predicted effectiveness of task- and person-centered leadership in different conditions. Task-centered leadership works best when the work situation includes a positive relationship between the leader and subordinates, highly structured tasks, and higher levels of organizational power. It also works best in just the opposite conditions, such as when the job requirements are unclear. Person-centered leadership is required in mixed conditions, such as when a leader has low formal power but has good relationships with subordinates.

The theory's logic suggests that task-centered leadership works best in situations that are favorable or unfavorable for a leader. In favorable situations, the leader does not need to worry about the psychological needs of subordinates. They already feel positive about their work, the tasks are clear, and the leader is powerful. The leader tells people what to do, and they do it willingly. In unfavorable situations, such as when job requirements are unclear or subordinates are uncooperative, the leader must focus on getting subordinates to complete the job. In mixed situations, however, employee commitment and satisfaction become more important, and a successful leader must focus more time on people rather than on just getting tasks done.

Contingency theory

Assumption that different styles and different leaders are more appropriate for different situations.

Fiedler's theory of leadership

Proposal that success of task- or person-centered leader depends on relationships between the leader and his or her subordinates; the degree that subordinates' tasks are easily and clearly defined; and the officially granted organizational power of the leader.

EXHIBIT 15.2   Predictions of Leader Effectiveness under Different Conditions

Leadership Style	Leader Effectiveness		
Person-Centered	Ineffective	Effective	Ineffective
Task-Centered	Effective	Ineffective	Effective
Contingency Conditions	➤ good relations between leader and group ➤ structured tasks ➤ low power in leader's position ➤ (generally favorable for the leader)	Mixed	➤ poor relations between leader and group ➤ unclear job requirements ➤ low power in leader's position ➤ (generally unfavorable for the leader)

Source: Adapted from Fiedler, F. E. 1978. "Contingency model and the leadership process." In L. Berkowitz (ed.), Advances in Experimental Social Psychology. 11. New York: Academic Press, pp. 60–112.

Path–Goal Theory

Another popular contingency theory, **path–goal theory**, identifies four types of leadership styles that a manager might choose depending on the situation. These styles include:

> *Directive style:* Give subordinates specific goals, schedules, and procedures.
> *Supportive style:* Show a concern for satisfying subordinates' needs and establishing good relationships.
> *Participative style:* Consult with subordinates; ask for suggestions; encourage participation in decision making.
> *Achievement-oriented style:* Set goals; reward goal accomplishment.

In path-goal theory, the key contingency or situational factors that determine the choice of the best leadership styles are the nature of the subordinates and the characteristics of the subordinates' tasks. Exhibit 15.3 presents a simplified overview of path–goal theory.

What can we learn from path–goal theory? The theory proposes many outcomes regarding the complex interactions between leadership and the contingency factors. As such, a complete review of path–goal theory is beyond the scope of this chapter. However, some key leadership suggestions based on path–goal theory include the following:[18]

> When subordinates have high achievement needs, successful leaders adopt the achievement-oriented style.
> Subordinates with high social needs respond best to the supportive leadership style.
> When the subordinates' job is unstructured, the theory suggests using a directive style (the leader details very specific job tasks and requirements) or an achievement-oriented style (the leader gives subordinates responsibility to discover solutions).

Path–goal theory

Four types of leadership styles that a manager might choose depending on the situation.

Traits, Behaviors, and Contingencies

So far, this chapter has reviewed basic North American, Japanese Indian and Afro-centric views of leadership based on leadership traits, leadership behaviors, and contingency theory. We know that leaders have different characteristics than

15.3 A Simplified Model of Path–Goal Theory

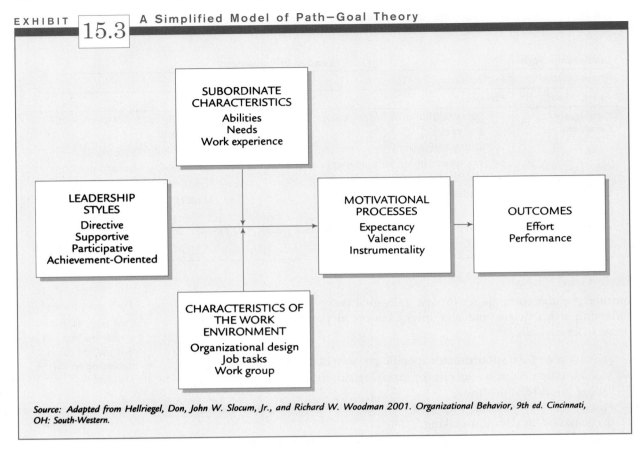

Source: Adapted from Hellriegel, Don, John W. Slocum, Jr., and Richard W. Woodman 2001. Organizational Behavior, 9th ed. Cincinnati, OH: South-Western.

their subordinates. However, it seems that leaders can develop these characteristics if they do not come naturally. Leaders have a variety of behaviors that they can use to get the job done. These range from a task- to a person-centered style and include decision-making styles from autocratic to democratic.

Most experts now believe that there is no consistent leadership trait or behavior that works in all situations. The contingency theory of leadership suggests that a successful leader must diagnose the situation and pick the behaviors or develop the leadership traits that fit best. The next sections will build on your knowledge of leadership concepts and contingency theory to help you understand how national culture and social institutions such as the educational system affect the choice of an appropriate leadership style for a multinational manager.

National Context as a Contingency for Leadership Behaviors

Most experts on leadership in multinational companies argue that a contingency perspective is required[19]—that is, successful leadership in multinational companies requires that managers adjust their leadership styles to fit different situations. This adjustment must occur not only in response to traditional contingency factors, such as subordinates' characteristics, but also in response to the cultural and institutional contexts of the multinational manager's country locations.

The following Focus on Emerging Markets illustrates the effects of culturally contingent management behavior by showing some of the preferred leadership

Focus on Emerging Markets

Leadership Styles in Latin America and Mexico

Recent trends suggest that many of the Latin America countries are slowly emerging from crisis and enjoying robust growth. Most of these countries have mature economies with sound financial and economic policies. Such changes are encouraging more investments. As more multinational companies begin operating in Latin America, they will need to adapt their leadership styles to the cultural demands of employees.

Many Latin American countries share a common cultural heritage because of their similar Spanish colonial history. As such, many Spanish institutional traditions, such as authoritarianism and paternalism, are still strong today. Hofstede (1980) also found that many Latin American countries share high power distance, high uncertainty avoidance, and high masculinity. Such historical and cultural facts have implications for leaders.

The traditional Latin American leader, *el patron*, is expected to be autocratic and directive, seldom delegating work or using teams. Such leaders will use the formal top-down organizational hierarchy to communicate, will be more relationship oriented, and will be expected to be aggressive and assertive. An exploratory study in Argentina, Chile, the Dominican Republic, Mexico, Peru, Puerto Rico, and Venezuela confirms that the leaders in these countries were more likely to adhere to the *el patron* behaviors.

These studies suggest that appropriate leadership behaviors and styles are dependent on the culture. In a study using two plants of a U.S. manufacturer, one in the United States and the other in Mexico, two researchers from the University of San Diego found that different leadership styles produced the same level of success.

The exhibit below shows their results based on the classification of management styles developed by Likert and discussed earlier. Neither plant used a participative management style. The U.S. plant achieved success with a consultative management style. The Mexican plant succeeded by using a management style falling into the authoritative range on all of Likert's management behaviors. Since both plants performed equally well, it suggests that national culture may be an important contingency factor in choosing a leadership or management style. Furthermore, the results also confirm the more authoritative nature of leadership styles and behaviors in Latin American countries.

Likert's Management Styles in Mexican and U.S. Plants

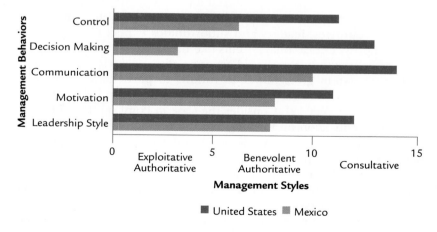

Source: Based on Economist. 2006. *"Climbing back." January p. 21; Morris, Tom, and Cynthia M. Pavett. 1992. "Management style and productivity in two cultures." Journal of International Business Studies, First Quarter, pp. 169–179; Romero, Eric J. 2004. "Latin American leadership: El patrón & el lider moderno." Cross Cultural Management 11, 3: p. 25.*

behaviors in selected Latin American countries. It also shows one U.S. company that had equally successful plants in Mexico and the United States, using two different management styles.

The first step in understanding how to adjust one's leadership to a multinational situation comes from understanding what local managers do to lead successfully in their own countries. The second step is using this knowledge to modify one's leadership style appropriately to fit a particular national context. That is, although it is unlikely that an expatriate manager can ever lead in exactly the same way as local managers, knowledge of how successful local leaders behave can be highly useful to suggest necessary modifications in a multinational leader's behavior.

As a guide both for understanding leadership behaviors in different national contexts and for modifying one's own leadership behaviors in different cultural contexts, the next section presents a **national-context contingency model of leadership**. This model shows how culture and related social institutions affect leadership practices. Exhibit 15.4 presents a summary of this model.

National-context contingency model of leadership

Shows how culture and related social institutions affect leadership practices.

The National-Context Contingency Model of Leadership: An Overview

Similar to the classic contingency theories of leadership discussed earlier, the model shown in Exhibit 15.4 begins with the basic contingency assumption that to be successful, leaders must modify their behaviors or develop particular leadership traits, depending on two key contingencies. The first contingency is the characteristics of their subordinates. The second contingency is the nature of their work setting.

In the multinational setting, however, the basic components of the contingency leadership model (leader behavior and traits, subordinates' characteristics, and the work setting) are affected by the national context. As you remember, the national context includes the national culture, business culture, and social institutions.

The following points briefly outline how leadership behaviors, traits, and contingencies are affected by the national context:

> *Leader behaviors and traits:* National culture, business culture, and social institutions define the array of preferred and acceptable leader behaviors and traits for managers. Consider the following examples. In high-power-distance countries, leaders and subordinates expect the manager to act with authority. Educational systems like the French *grandes écoles* train managers to believe that they should act as an elite social class. If the host country's legal system gives power to unions to participate in management decisions, then managers must adjust their leadership behaviors to this situation (see Chapter 12). Consider the Case in Point on page 746 regarding the role of education on forming executive leadership in China and India.

> *Subordinates' characteristics:* As discussed in detail in Chapter 14, national and business cultures influence workers' needs and levels of achievement motivation. Additionally, a country's socioeconomic development and institutional support for education affect the quality and availability of training and education for workers (see Chapter 12). Consequently, a leader must modify his or her style to fit the types of workers available in a particular nation.

> *Work setting:* Culture and social institutions affect the choices managers make in designing organizations and subunits. These organizational characteristics in turn affect the leader's options in the work setting: that is, task

EXHIBIT 15.4   A National-Context Contingency Model of Leadership

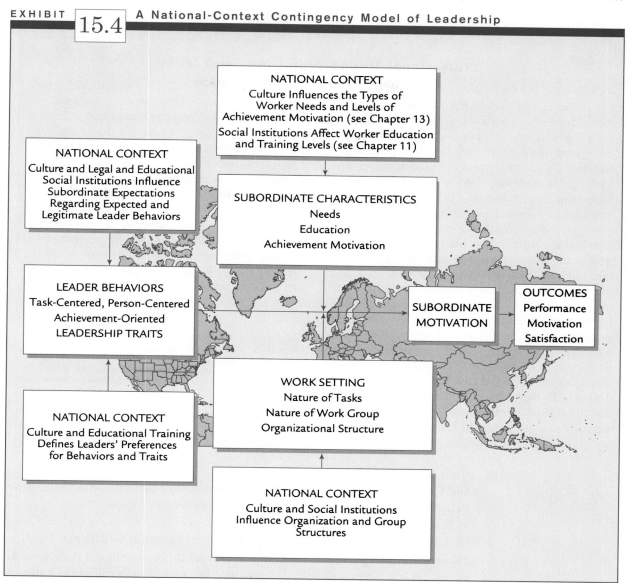

characteristics, such as routine work, and organizational characteristics, such as formalized jobs, constrain leadership options. In fact, the organizational context can be so powerful that, in some situations, certain leader behaviors may not even be necessary.[20] For example, a highly formalized organization may not require much direct leader supervision.

The next sections expand on the cultural-contingency model of leadership. They provide more examples and detail on how national culture, business culture, and social institutions affect the choice of leader behaviors or traits in different countries. In addition to this discussion, your previous readings provide you with the knowledge of how the national context affects the two leadership-contingency factors of subordinate characteristics and the work situation. Chapter 12 on national differences in human resource management practices

C A S E   I N   P O I N T

Professional Managers in China and India

As both India and China dominate trade, more attention is now being paid to the people leading their major domestic companies. Observers agree that India is producing far more professional managers with global name recognition. Consider, for example, Nandan Nilekani, CEO of Infosys, credited with transforming his company into a global information technology powerhouse, or CEO Ratan Tata's transformation of Tata into a global competitor.

Why is India producing far more globally recognizable leaders than China? Many credit India's high quality and extremely competitive educational system. In fact, India's first business school, the Indian Institute of Management, was started in 1961 in collaboration with Harvard and MIT. The country now has a large number of Indian Institute of Technology, providing top-notch business education. Some even argue that the IITs have one of the hardest entrance examinations in the world. The result is that Indian managers are getting access to excellent MBA programs, with more than 600 programs graduating about 5,000 students annually. China has only 95 programs and is graduating fewer students.

India also has had far more experience dealing with Western-style global business markets. The Indian economy was never as closed as the Chinese, and while the Chinese government was expelling multinational companies, India was hosting a large number of well-known multinational firms. Such experiences have made Indian managers more comfortable with Western business practices. Furthermore, more than half of the Indian gross domestic product (GDP) comes from the entrepreneurial-minded private sector while only 33 percent of the Chinese GDP comes from the private sector. As such, the Indians have had much longer experiences with a vibrant private sector and Western-style leadership practices.

Source: Based on Mazumdar, Sudip. 2006. "Grades and politics." Newsweek, Jan. p. 23. http://www.msnbc.msn.com; Patel Vibhuti. 2005. "India, Inc.: No longer just an outsourcing hub for low-level jobs, India is luring American talent and unprecedented new investments by tech giant Microsoft and Intel." Newsweek, Dec. p. 19. http://www.msnbc.msn.com; Punoose, Rukhmini. 2005. "India's edge." Newsweek, Oct. p. 31. http://www.msnbc.msn.com; Wehfritz, George, and Ron Moreau. 2005. "A new kind of company." Newsweek, July p. 4. http://www.msnbc.msn.com.

and Chapter 14 on motivation in the multinational organization discuss how the national context influences the nature of subordinates' characteristics.

Leadership Traits and Behaviors in the National Context

There is considerable evidence that people from different cultural backgrounds prefer certain traits and behaviors in their leaders. That is, different cultures have different images of what distinguishes successful leaders. However, there is also evidence that some leader behaviors and traits are cultural universals. That is, they are endorsed or accepted by almost all people. The following section provides more detail on cross-national differences in leadership. Following that presentation, you will see some of the traits and behaviors that seem successful in numerous national contexts.

Dorfman[21] suggests that leadership has different evaluation connotations in different societies. The United States places a very important premium on leadership, which is seen as a desirable quality having a positive connotation. In contrast, other societies seem to place less emphasis on leadership. In Japan, for example, CEOs typically attribute organizational success to their subordinates rather than their own leadership. In Holland, where people are mostly preoccupied with consensus and equality, the concept of leadership is also thought to be over-emphasized.

In addition to differences in evaluations of leadership, Geert Hofstede[22] points out that attributes and characteristics of leaders do not necessarily translate well into other national contexts. In Germany, for example, it is the engineer and not the manager who is the cultural hero. Doctorate degrees are more important than business degrees. In France, the distinction between management and worker reflects social class distinctions between *cadres* and *non-cadres*. Becoming a member of the *cadre* requires graduating from one of the *grandes écoles* and, most often, coming from the correct social-class background. In Holland, a desired leadership trait is modesty, in contrast to the trait of assertiveness usually valued in the United States. In the Chinese family business, the leader is the patriarch, the oldest male head of the family. Consider the evolution of the traditional Nigerian view of leadership discussed in the following Case in Point.

The very latest research on cross-national differences in leadership is a project called GLOBE (Global Leadership and Organizational Behavior Effectiveness). The GLOBE study (see Chapter 2) contains insights regarding leadership that can help the multinational manager develop a leadership style to navigate successfully through a maze of cultural settings. Led by Robert House, nearly 200 researchers from 60 countries are looking at what makes a leader successful and to what extent leader behaviors and traits are contingent on the national context.[23] Prior to this comprehensive study, we had studies that only considered leadership in a few countries at one time.

The GLOBE research team assembled a list of more than 100 leader behaviors and traits. They asked people from countries representing the majority of the world's population and from every continent whether these traits or behaviors inhibit a person's leadership or contribute to leadership success. The first task of the team was to see which leadership traits and behaviors are "culturally endorsed." By culturally endorsed, they mean which traits and behaviors are considered best for a leader in a particular national context.

The GLOBE team found that numerous leader behaviors and traits are culturally endorsed in some societies but not others. These are the culturally contingent aspects of leadership that vary by the national context. Exhibit 15.5 shows a listing of these leader characteristics separated into three groups. The groups divide the traits and behaviors by the range of variance across cultures.

C A S E   I N   P O I N T

Oga: A Traditional Nigerian View of Leadership in the Modern Organization

In Nigerian society, the concept of *oga* means master. It is broadly used in superior–subordinate relationships in all phases of life. Bosses are called *oga*. Teachers are called *oga*. Domestic employees call their employers *oga*. Traditionally, *oga* connoted a status with divine or ascribed authority. Royalty, kings, heads of the family, and religious leaders had *oga*. *Oga* also included a concept of reciprocity. The *oga* was obligated to provide for the well-being of subordinates.

The concept of *oga* evolved during the British colonial period. European expatriates took on the title of *oga*. With this adaptation, the concept lost its more spiritual connotations. In modern organizations, managers are still called *oga*. It shows deference and respect. Thus, it remains a concept of authority. However, the use of *oga* as a title communicates to superior and subordinate to activate the traditional view that they have reciprocal relationship obligations. The deference of the subordinate has the cultural expectation of a paternalistic caring from the superior.

Source: Based on Ogbor, John O. 2000. "Organizational leadership and authority relations across cultures: Beyond divergence and convergence." International Journal of Commerce & Management, 10, pp. 48–73.

EXHIBIT **15.5**   **Culture Contingent Leadership Traits and Behaviors**

Large Range of Cultural Differences	Moderate Range of Cultural Differences	Small Range of Cultural Differences
Cunning	Class conscious	Self-sacrificing
	Autonomous	
Subdued	Ruler	Compassionate
	Domineering	
Provocateur	Group competitor	Intuitive
Sensitive	Habitual	Enthusiastic
	Individualistic	
Evasive	Willful	Worldly
	Micro-manager	
Ambitious	Elitist	Logical
Group conflict avoider	Self-effacing	Able to anticipate
	Formal	
Status-conscious	Procedural	Unique
	Self-sacrificing	
Risk taker	Compassionate	Sincere
	Intuitive	
Independent	Enthusiastic	Orderly
	Worldly	
Cautious	Logical	Indirect
	Able to anticipate	
	Unique	
	Sincere	
	Orderly	

Source: Adapted from House, R. J., Paul J. Hanges, S. Antonio Ruiz-Quintanilla, Peter W. Dorfman, Mansour Javidan, Marcus Dickson, Vipin Gupta, and 170 GLOBE Country Co-Investigators. 1999. "Cultural influences on leadership and organizations: Project GLOBE." Advances in Global Leadership. 1: pp. 171–233.

The greater the differences among cultures the more the culturally accepted leadership is contingent on the national context. In turn, larger variations among countries mean that successful multinational managers most likely must moderate their leadership styles to succeed in different national contexts.

The GLOBE team also found that most people, regardless of cultural background, believe that some traits and behaviors lead to outstanding leadership while other traits and behaviors prevent managers from leading successfully. We consider these traits and behaviors cultural universals because they seem to work for everyone regardless of cultural or national background. Exhibit 15.6 shows a list of the universally acceptable or disliked behaviors and traits identified by the GLOBE study. The implication for the multinational manager is that one can adopt these traits or behaviors and behave within cultural expectations almost anywhere in the world.

Another way of looking at the leadership traits and behaviors is to consider groups of traits and behaviors that represent different leadership styles. Earlier

EXHIBIT 15.6

Culture Free Positively and Negatively Regarded Leadership Traits and Behaviors from 60 Countries

Positively Regarded Traits and Behaviors		Negatively Regarded Traits Behaviors
Trustworthy	Dependable	Loner
Just	Intelligent	Asocial
Honest	Decisive	Not cooperative
Plans ahead	Effective bargainer	Non-explicit
Encouraging	Win–win problem solver	Egocentric
Positive	Skilled administrator	Ruthless
Dynamic	Communicator	Dictatorial
Motivator	Informed	
Confidence builder	Team Builder	

Source: Adapted from Den Hartog, Deanne N., Robert J. House, Paul J. Hanges, Peter W. Dorfman, S. Antonio Ruiz-Quintanna, and 170 associates. 1999. "Culture specific and cross-culturally generalizable implicit leadership theories: Are attributes of charismatic/ transformational leadership universally endorsed?" Leadership Quarterly, 10, pp. 219–256.

in the chapter you saw the classic distinctions among leadership styles focusing on the person versus the task leader and the degree of participation. The GLOBE research team identified leadership styles that are particularly relevant for looking at leadership in different cultural settings. Some are similar to the classic leadership style distinctions. We consider five here: team-oriented, self-protective, participative, humane, and autonomous.

The team-oriented style characterizes a leader who is an integrator, is diplomatic and benevolent, and has a collaborative attitude about the team. The self-protective leader is self-centered, status conscious, procedural, and a face-saver. The participative leader is a delegator and encourages subordinate participation in decisions. The humane style characterizes leaders who have modesty and a compassionate orientation. Finally, the autonomous leader is individualistic, independent and unique, and is expected to act in self-interested fashion.

To compare the various leadership behaviors, we use the GLOBE's study grouping of countries by clusters.[24] Clusters are convenient to summarize information regarding how countries are similar as well as how they differ.[25] We consider ten clusters, namely the Anglo cluster, the Confucian Asia cluster, the Eastern Europe cluster, the Germanic Europe cluster, the Latin America cluster, the Latin Europe cluster, the Middle East cluster, the Nordic Europe cluster, the Southern Asia cluster, and the Sub-Saharan cluster. Exhibit 15.7 shows the countries included in each cluster.

Exhibit 15.8 shows how each of these styles varies across clusters representing a large sample of nations representing Asia, Africa, Europe, the Middle East, and North America. As can be seen in the exhibits, there are differences in the various leadership styles based on cultural differences. For instance, it is not surprising to find that team-oriented leaders are preferred in Latin European, Eastern European, and Southern Asian societies. Latin European societies have had a history of socialist governments corresponding with collectivism rather than individualism.[26] Similarly, Southern Asian societies are high on collectivism, and those leaders who are willing to be collaborative and diplomatic are more likely to succeed.[27] Thus, the high collectivism in these societies suggests

EXHIBIT 15.7   GLOBE's Study Clusters and Countries Included in Each Cluster

Anglo	Latin Europe	Eastern Europe	Latin America	Confucian Asia
Australia	Israel	Albania	Argentina	China
Canada	Italy	Georgia	Bolivia	Hong Kong
Ireland	Portugal	Greece	Brazil	Japan
New Zealand	Spain	Hungary	Colombia	Singapore
South Africa (White)	France	Kazakhstan	Costa Rica	South Korea
United Kingdom	Switzerland (French)	Poland	El Salvador	Taiwan
U.S.A.		Russia	Guatemala	
		Slovenia	Mexico	
			Venezuela	

Nordic Europe	Germanic Europe	Sub-Saharan Africa	Middle East	Southern Asia
Denmark	Austria	Namibia	Qatar	India
Finland	Switzerland	Nigeria	Morocco	Indonesia
Sweden	Netherlands	South Africa (Black)	Turkey	Philippines
	Germany (former East)	Zambia	Egypt	Malaysia
	Germany (former West)	Zimbabwe	Kuwait	Thailand
				Iran

Source: Adapted from Gupta, Vipin, Paul J. Hanges, and Peter Dorfman. 2002. "Cultural clusters: Methodology and findings." Journal of World Business, 37, pp. 11–15.

EXHIBIT 15.8   Culturally-Contingent Beliefs Regarding Effective Leadership Styles

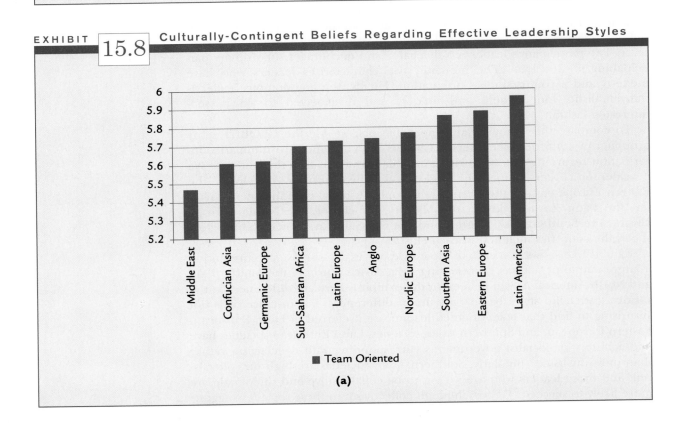

(a)

EXHIBIT
15.8

Culturally-Contingent Beliefs Regarding Effective Leadership Styles (*continued*)

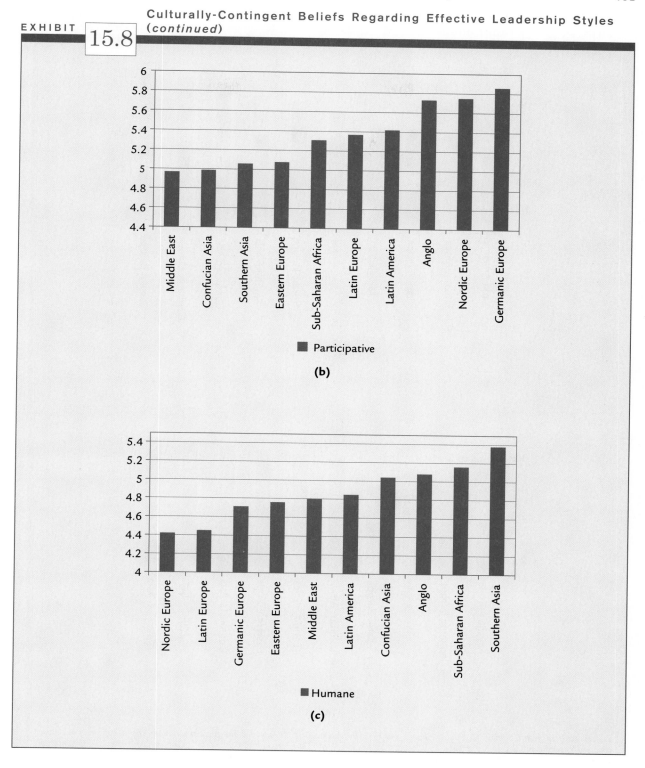

Participative

(b)

Humane

(c)

EXHIBIT 15.8

Culturally-Contingent Beliefs Regarding Effective Leadership Styles (*continued*)

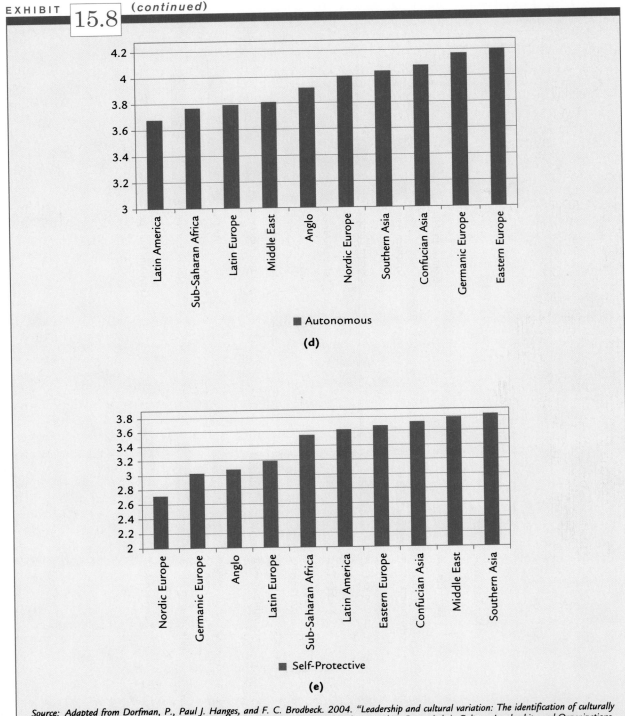

(d) Autonomous

(e) Self-Protective

Source: Adapted from Dorfman, P., Paul J. Hanges, and F. C. Brodbeck. 2004. "Leadership and cultural variation: The identification of culturally endorsed leadership profiles. In R. J. House, P. J. Hanges, M. Javidan, P. W. Dorfman, and V. Gupta (eds.), Culture, Leadership, and Organizations. Thousand Oaks, CA: Sage Publications, pp. 669–720.

that leaders who respect the group and the collective are more likely to succeed. It is nevertheless surprising that the Eastern European societies have preference for high team-oriented leaders. However, these societies have had long periods of communism where people have had to rely on each other to satisfy basic needs. It is also possible that the presence of many multinational companies in these countries and the use of teams are gradually encouraging Eastern Europeans to view team-oriented leaders in a better light.

The participative leader is one who delegates and encourages subordinates to participate in decisions. With regards to this dimension of leadership, Exhibit 15.8 shows that the Anglo, Nordic European, and Germanic European clusters have the highest score on the dimension. Germanic and Nordic European countries all have systems that emphasize economic developments through cooperation between workers and employers rather than more confrontational means.[28] This desire for cooperation and harmony between labor and capital translates into more effective leaders being seen as those who are willing to listen to their subordinates and accept their input. Anglo cultures tend to be very individualistic. Individualism is synonymous with people valuing their freedom and having a say in decisions that affect them. As such, those leaders who allow subordinates to have their say through participative leadership are more likely to be viewed as effective.[29] Furthermore, all of the above cultures have low power distance where subordinates are encouraged to have a say in decision-making.

The humane-oriented leader is a fair, altruistic, friendly, generous, and caring leader to others.[30] All country clusters rate the humane leader highly, suggesting that this leadership orientation is almost universally seen as a very desirable trait in successful leaders. Exhibit 15.8 shows that the Southern Asian cluster scored the highest on this leadership dimension. The latter can be attributed to the generally benevolent and humane orientation that most of the Southern Asian societies such as India, Thailand, and Malaysia value.

As far as the autonomous leader is concerned, it is interesting to note that most country clusters see autonomy as generally impeding effective leadership. Results were also similar for the self-protective leader. The clusters with the highest score on autonomy are the Germanic and Eastern European clusters. Their scores, however, were slightly higher than 4, indicating that these clusters were generally indifferent as to the propensity of autonomous leadership to either contribute to or impede effective leadership. The scores for the self-protective leadership were all fairly similar and were all lower than 4, indicating that all country clusters felt that self-protective leadership that involved being self-centered impeded effective leadership. Taken together, results for autonomous and self-protective leadership are consistent with Den Hartog et al.'s[31] findings that certain leadership characteristics such as being a loner or egocentric are negatively regarded universally.

Why do leaders from different countries have different characteristics and use different behaviors to achieve the same organizational ends? These differences occur because the national context produces differences in the repertoire of behaviors and traits available to managers to express their leadership styles. Both superiors and subordinates see the leader's task or person orientation based on culturally and institutionally defined sets of leader behaviors; that is, each national context has its own acceptable ways to communicate a leader's concerns for tasks or people. As such, to lead successfully in multicultural companies, managers must be particularly sensitive in using locally appropriate leadership behaviors to communicate their intended leadership styles.

The next section shows that even the basic tactics leaders use to manage subordinates vary by the national context.

National Context and Preferred Leader-Influence Tactics

Beyond broad approaches to leadership behaviors, one can look more specifically at the tactical behaviors leaders use to influence subordinates. U.S. managers favor seven major **influence tactics**.[32] These include the following:

Influence tactics

Tactical behaviors leaders use to influence subordinates.

> *Assertiveness:* Example behaviors include being forceful, directive, and demanding.
> *Friendliness:* Example behaviors include being friendly, humble, and receptive.
> *Reasoning:* Example behaviors include using logical arguments, providing reasons, and using plans.
> *Bargaining:* Example behaviors include offering favors and exchanges.
> *Sanctioning:* Example behaviors include using threats, rewards, and punishments.
> *Appeals to a higher authority:* Example behaviors include appeals for help to higher authorities and sending problems to higher authorities.
> *Coalitions:* Example behaviors include building support for ideas by networking and using friendships.

What influence tactics are used in other national contexts? One research study found that most managers, regardless of cultural background, use the same general types of influence tactics. However, different nationalities favor specific influence tactics.[33] For example, the British prefer bargaining while the Japanese favor reasoning. Exhibit 15.9 shows the favored types of tactics for Taiwanese, Japanese, Australian, and British managers.

Although influence tactics are clearly used by leaders around the world, more recent studies indicate that in some countries decreased use of influence tactics may also be effective. Consider Kozusznik's[34] study of Polish managers. The author argues that the Polish leadership style tends to be characterized by overuse of forceful leadership influence tactics. Polish managers tend to cling to both hard (e.g., forceful influence tactics to create barriers to undesirable behaviors) and soft (e.g., persuasion communication, consultation, personal appeals) influence tactics to manage their workers. It is argued that using either approach to influence can be damaging as managers need to adapt to the new environment characterizing the globalization. For instance, given the increased presence of multinational companies and the consequent use of teamwork, it may be necessary for leaders to use less influence. The authors examined the effectiveness of both **deinfluentization** and self-monitoring techniques on perception of effectiveness. Not surprisingly, managers who exhibited both high deinfluentization behaviors (e.g., suppressing the need to influence others by listening to others, waiting for others to talk, using less persuasion, and offering more space to others) and high self-monitoring behaviors (e.g., being sensitive to others by using cues to manage their own presence) were seen as more effective. Such results suggest that multinational companies may need to start assessing the effectiveness of influence tactics in countries where autocratic leadership styles are more prevalent. The new global work demands may require less aggressive influence tactics and the retraining of managers.

Deinfluentization

Reduced use of influence tactics.

EXHIBIT **15.9**   Preferred Leader Influence Tactics in Four Countries

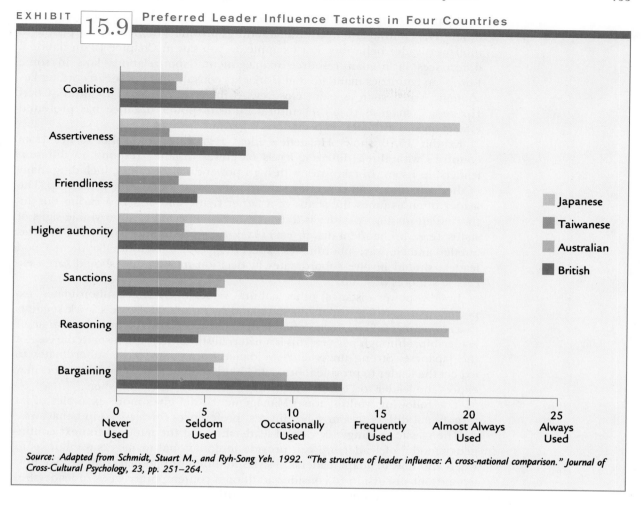

Source: Adapted from Schmidt, Stuart M., and Ryh-Song Yeh. 1992. "The structure of leader influence: A cross-national comparison." Journal of Cross-Cultural Psychology, 23, pp. 251–264.

National Context and Subordinates' Expectations

Leaders cannot lead without the cooperation of subordinates. In addition to influencing the expected leader traits and the range of legitimate leader behaviors, the national context also affects subordinates' expectations regarding who can be a leader, what a leader "should" do, and what a leader may or may not do. All levels of culture—national, business, occupational, and organizational—influence the types of leader behaviors considered appropriate or fair by subordinates. For example, at the level of organizational culture, even universities differ in the range of leader behaviors students perceive as acceptable for professors. At some universities, two 25-page papers for a semester class represent a "fair" expectation. At other universities, students would resent this assignment and perceive it as "unfair."

We saw earlier that subordinates of different nationalities classify certain behaviors differently, as different leader behaviors communicate the leader's person or task orientation. Subordinates also accept or reject certain behaviors as legitimate prerogatives of leadership. For example, North American workers consider leadership behaviors associated with applying pressure to work, considered normal in Japan, as harsh or punitive.[35]

Subordinates' expectations

Expectations regarding what leaders "should" do and what they may or may not do.

What makes different behaviors acceptable in one country but not in another? The cultural and institutional settings provide a framework for people to interpret leader behaviors. For example, as you saw in Chapter 12 on national differences in human resource management, labor-relations laws in some European countries mandate that managers consult with workers regarding key strategic issues, such as plant closures. At the level of national culture, Geert Hofstede[36] suggests that the cultural value of power distance has profound effects on subordinates' expectations regarding leaders.

Exhibit 15.10 shows Hofstede's ideas regarding how subordinates from countries with three different levels of power distance respond to different leadership issues. In countries with high power-distance values, including many of the Latin and Asian countries, subordinates expect autocratic leadership. The leader often assumes the status of a father figure and acts as a caring but authoritarian master. A leader is different and is expected to show visible signs of status (e.g., a chauffeur-driven car). In low power-distance countries, such as Sweden and Norway, subordinates expect the leader to be more like them. Good leaders should involve subordinates in decision making and should forgo excessive symbols of status.

Besides power distance, other cultural values likely affect subordinates' expectations regarding leadership styles and behaviors. Hofstede's work suggests that strong masculinity norms often lead to the acceptance of more authoritarian leadership, although perhaps this is a paternalistic authoritarianism in the case of the Japanese. Strong uncertainty-avoidance norms may cause subordinates to expect the leader to provide more detail in directions. For example, workers may expect the leader to "tell us exactly what you want, how, and when."[37]

The following Multinational Management Brief gives more examples of international differences in subordinates' preferences for leadership behaviors.

The classic contingency view of leadership and the national-context contingency model of leadership can provide multinational managers a guide as to when and how to adapt leadership styles to different national contexts. We now extend our discussion to consider additional contemporary views of leadership and their applications to multinational settings.

EXHIBIT 15.10   Subordinates' Expectations under Three Levels of Power Distance

Low Power Leadership Issue	Medium Power Distance (Great Britain)	High Power Distance (United States)	Distance (Mexico)
Subordinates' Dependence Needs	Weak dependence on superiors	Moderate dependence on superiors	Heavy dependence on superiors
Consultation	Strongly expected as part of superior's role	Expect consultation but will accept autocratic leadership	Expect autocratic leadership
Ideal Superior	A democrat	A moderate democrat	A benevolent autocratic or a paternalistic father figure
Laws and Rules	Apply to superiors and subordinates	Apply to all, but superiors have some privileges	Superiors are above the law and take advantage of privileges
Status Symbols	Viewed as not appropriate	Accepted as symbolic of authority	Very important contributions to the authority of superiors

Source: Adapted from Hofstede, Geert. 1980. "Motivation, leadership, and organization: Do American theories apply abroad?" *Organizational Dynamics*, Summer, pp. 42–63; Hofstede, Geert. 1984. *Culture's Consequences.* Newbury Park, Calif.: Sage.

Multinational Management Brief

National Differences in Leadership Preferences

Workers from 13 countries were given two descriptions of the ideal manager. These descriptions represented cultural norms and values that contrast styles of analysis. In some cultures, the "best" way to analyze a complex phenomenon is to dissect it into specifics. This means that the phenomenon should be broken down into parts, units, facts, etc. In other cultures, the "best" way to analyze a complex phenomenon is to see patterns and relationships in the whole—not the parts that make up the whole.

The two descriptions of the ideal leaders were:

The specifics leader:

➤ Gets the job done

➤ Gets the information, people, and equipment to accomplish tasks

➤ Gives subordinates autonomy to accomplish tasks

➤ Intervenes only as necessary

The integrated-whole leader:

➤ Gets subordinates working well together

➤ Knows the answers to most questions at work

➤ Guides subordinates continually

➤ Helps subordinates solve work and nonwork problems

➤ Acts as a father figure

Which type of leader is preferred where? The accompanying exhibit shows the percentage of people from 13 countries that preferred the specifics-oriented leader.

Preferences for the "Specifics" Leader in Thirteen Countries

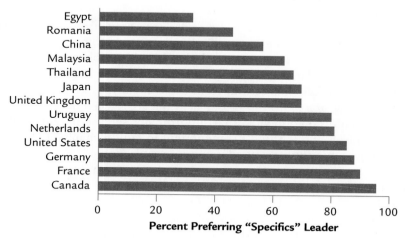

The information in the exhibit suggests that employees in most Western nations prefer leaders with the behaviors described as the specifics leader. This leader deals with specific job-related tasks rather than a broad approach to the worker and the work situation.

Source: Based on Hampden-Turner, Charles M., and Fons Trompenaars. 1996. "A world turned upside down: Doing business in Asia." In Pat Joynt, and Malcolm Warner (eds.) Managing across Cultures. London: International Thomson Business Press, pp. 275–305; and Trompenaars, Fons, and Charles Hampden-Turner. 1998. Riding the Waves of Culture. New York: McGraw-Hill.

Contemporary Leadership Perspectives: Multinational Implications

The next section of the chapter reviews two contemporary approaches to leadership: transformational leadership and the attribution approach to leadership. It considers how these views of leadership apply in multinational settings.

Transformational Leadership

In asking what makes some leaders truly great and different, some leadership experts have concluded that there are two basic forms of leadership. Most ordinary leaders use **transactional leadership**. Transactional leadership means that managers use rewards or punishments to influence their subordinates—that is, if you do what the manager wants, he or she rewards you. If you fail do to what she or he wishes, the manager punishes you. According to the leadership experts, transactional leadership does work. However, it does not lead to truly great organizations.[38]

Some experts argue that to achieve a really great organization managers must adopt a higher form of leadership known as **transformational leadership**. Of importance to the multinational manager is the finding by the GLOBE researchers that transformational leadership is considered superior in almost all societies. What makes a transformational leader? What do transformational leaders do that separates them from ordinary leaders?

Studies identify several behaviors and characteristics of transformational leaders.[39] The transformational leader:

> *Articulates a vision:* **Presents in vivid and emotional terms an idealized vision of the future for the organization—what it can and should become—and makes this vision clear to followers.**

> *Breaks from the status quo:* **Has a strong desire to break from tradition and do things differently; is an expert in finding ways to do things differently; challenges subordinates to find new solutions to old problems.**

> *Provides goals and a plan:* **Has a vision that is future oriented and provides clear steps for followers to transform the company.**

> *Gives meaning or a purpose to goals:* **Places the goals in emotionally laden stories or a cultural context so that subordinates see the need to follow the leader's ideals and to share a commitment to radical change; helps subordinates envision a future state of a better organization.**

> *Takes risks:* **Is willing to take more risks with the organization than the average leader.**

> *Is motivated to lead:* **Seeks leadership positions and displays strong enthusiasm for the leadership role; acts as a role model.**

> *Builds a power base:* **Uses personal power based on expertise, respect, and the admiration of followers.**

> *Demonstrates high ethical and moral standards:* **Behaves consistently and fairly with a known ethical standard.**

Although the detailed study of transformational leadership is new, the German sociologist Max Weber recognized the existence of transformational leadership throughout history.[40] This type of transformational leadership he called "charisma," and he noted that it existed in all cultures. According to Weber, Jesus

---

Transactional leadership

One where managers use rewards or punishments to influence their subordinates.

Transformational leadership

One where managers go beyond transactional leadership by articulating a vision, breaking from the status quo, providing goals and a plan, giving meaning or a purpose to goals, taking risks, being motivated to lead, building a power base, and demonstrating high ethical and moral standards.

Christ and Muhammad were among the first transformational leaders. Most people also consider leaders such as Martin Luther King, Jr., Adolf Hitler, Mao Zedong, and Lee Iacocca as representative of transformational leaders—regardless of whether people accept the goals and behaviors of these leaders as ethical.

Transformational leaders succeed because subordinates respond to them with high levels of performance, personal devotion, reverence, excitement regarding the leader's ideas, and a willingness to sacrifice for the good of the company.[41] However, true transformational leaders are rare. They seem to arise when organizations need change or face a crisis. In the following Case in Point, you can see how Carlos Ghosn of Nissan is a transformational leader and is moving his company into new levels of competition.

Although transformational leaders exist in all countries, the same leadership traits and behaviors may not lead to successful transformational leadership in all countries. The charisma of transformational leadership requires tapping into basic cultural values and evoking national cultural myths and heroic deeds.[42] For example, Hitler built part of his charisma by tapping into the heroic myths and symbols of German culture while Gandhi capitalized on Indian culture in his struggles with the British.[43] In addition, traits associated with charisma—such as risk-taking—and behaviors necessary to communicate a transformational vision may have different consequences in different national settings.

Den Hartog et al.[44] provide perhaps the most definitive test of the proposition that transformational or charismatic leadership is universally endorsed as the key to effective leadership. As part of the GLOBE project, they examined data from 62 different cultures and found that charismatic leadership attributes such as motive arouser, encouraging, trustworthy, positive, confidence builder, and motivational were all perceived as universal attributes. Although no attempts were made to link these differences to cultural factors, the study nevertheless shows that there may be some aspects of transformational leadership that are viewed similarly in many cultures.

As part of the GLOBE project mentioned earlier,[45] researchers also looked at whether possessing traits of a charismatic leader contributed to effective

---

CASE IN POINT

Transformational Leadership at Nissan

As we will see in the chapter's closing case, Carlos Ghosn took over a severely failing Nissan and turned around the company, producing profits just two years after he started in the position. Such a turnaround surprised both critics and supporters alike.

How did he do it? Ghosn's transformational style was instrumental in helping him turn around Nissan. He is among the few non-Japanese individuals leading a Japanese company. When he took over Nissan, he knew that he could only transform the company by working through the Japanese culture. He spent the time getting to know each and every worker in the company. He also articulated a clear vision that resulted from long discussions with hundreds of managers. He knew that a complete transformation would be possible only if he got the approval of the Japanese workforce.

Clearly, Ghosn is a transformational leader. He possesses many of the transformational qualities discussed earlier. Furthermore, in a short period of two years, he was able to implement dramatic changes while at the same time building respect for his leadership style. His commitment to make changes by listening to Nissan's employees and by respecting the Japanese culture and Nissan's organizational culture shows his transformational qualities.

Source: Based on Barabba, Vincent. 2005. "Using experience to teach yourself." Strategy & Leadership, 33, pp. 55–64; Millikin, John P. and Dean Fu. 2005. "The Global Leadership of Carlos Ghosn at Nissan." Thunderbird International Business Review 47: pp. 1, 121–137.

leadership. The charismatic leader is decisive, performance-oriented, a visionary, an inspiration to subordinates, and is willing to sacrifice for the organization. Exhibit 15.11 shows the ranking of the various country clusters as described in Exhibit 15.7.

Exhibit 15.11 clearly shows that charismatic leadership is a universally desirable leadership trait. The GLOBE's study scores can potentially range from 1 (substantially impedes leadership) to 7 (substantially facilitates leadership) with a middle point of 4 (neither impedes nor facilitates leadership). The actual scores for the various country clusters range from a high of 6.04 for the Anglo culture to a low of only 5.35 for the Arabic cluster. Clearly, these results are consistent with Den Hartog et al.'s[46] findings that those leaders who are perceived as charismatic are more likely to be seen as successful.

Next, we will examine one final perspective on leadership and its application to multinational operations.

Attributions and Leadership

Attributional approach to leadership

Emphasis on what leaders believe causes subordinates' behaviors.

The **attributional approach to leadership** emphasizes the leader's attributions regarding the causes of subordinates' behaviors. We all make attributions when we observe someone's behavior and attach a reason or motivation to that behavior. For example, when a student walks quickly across campus, we may assume (correctly or incorrectly) that she is late for class, or we might believe that the student is hungry and going to lunch.

The most important attribution for leaders concerns the attribution of responsibility for work performance. In determining how to respond to subordinates' behaviors, leaders make two key distinctions in attributions: the external attribution and the internal attribution. The external attribution explains a person's behavior based on factors outside the person and beyond the

EXHIBIT 15.11   **GLOBE Study and Charismatic Leadership**

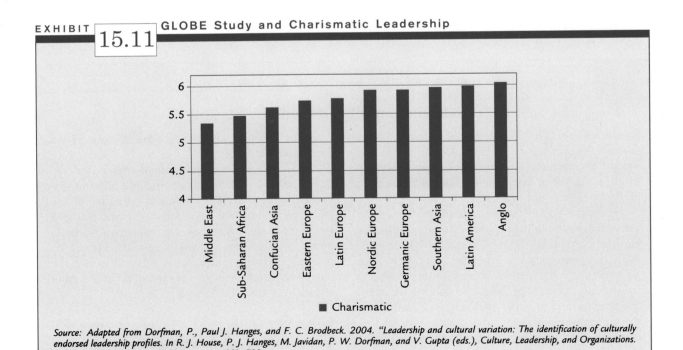

Source: Adapted from Dorfman, P., Paul J. Hanges, and F. C. Brodbeck. 2004. "Leadership and cultural variation: The identification of culturally endorsed leadership profiles. In R. J. House, P. J. Hanges, M. Javidan, P. W. Dorfman, and V. Gupta (eds.), Culture, Leadership, and Organizations. Thousand Oaks, CA: Sage Publications, pp. 669–720.

person's control (e.g., natural disasters, illness, faulty equipment). For example, a leader uses an external attribution when she assumes an employee was late because of a severe storm. The internal attribution explains a person's behavior based on the characteristics of the person (e.g., personality, motivation, low ability). For example, a leader makes an internal attribution when he assumes an employee was late because he is lazy.

Once a leader makes an attributional decision regarding a subordinate, the leader responds to the subordinate based on that assumption. If the leader perceives the cause of a subordinate's behavior to be based on an internal attribution, he or she tends to correct or reward the worker. If, on the other hand, the leader perceives the cause of a subordinate's behavior to be based on an external attribution, the leader modifies the work environment. Consequently, according to this view, successful leadership requires making the correct attributions regarding subordinates' behavior.[47]

In most Western nations, people have a greater tendency to assume an internal attribution. That is, managers more often believe that people behave in certain ways because of internal motivations, such as laziness or ambition, and not because of outside factors, such as poor working conditions. This assumption is so strong in Western culture that it is called the **fundamental attribution error.**[48]

Similar to the problem faced in international negotiation, where mistakes in attribution represent a major source of misunderstanding, the challenge for the multinational leader is to understand the cultures of subordinates sufficiently well to avoid serious attribution errors. The Multinational Management Challenge on p. 762 shows how a U.S. manager working in Mexico and his Mexican subordinate imposed their own culturally biased attributions regarding the use of time, authority, and interpersonal relations. This illustration shows what can happen when superiors and subordinates attach the wrong motivations to each other's behaviors. How would you advise these managers?

Fundamental attribution error

Assumption by managers that people behave in certain ways because of internal motivations rather than outside factors.

Global Women Leaders: The Future?

As more and more women are assuming positions of leadership in organizations,[49] it is becoming increasingly important for companies to ensure that they have systems in place to adequately manage and benefit from their women leaders. It is widely argued that most leadership research has been based primarily on males, often reflecting U.S. individualistic norms.[50] However, as companies face new economic, ethical, social, and political pressures, women global leaders are seen as having particular characteristics and traits that are becoming increasingly important for companies to successfully navigate these new realities.

Why are women global leaders seen as being more desirable to deal with today's economic and competitive realities? **Women global leadership** is seen as a spread of traits or qualities that are associated with women to the process of leading worldwide organizations.[51] As the business environment shifts from mass production to mass customization, women global leaders are seen as having the skills and qualities necessary to develop deep relationships to understand markets and customers. Given that the traditional male leadership model typifies abilities based on efficiency, hierarchy, tough-mindedness, and assertiveness, women leaders are seen as having the necessary "orientation toward more participative, interactional, and relational styles of leading"[52] that companies need to effectively function today.

Women global leadership

Application of traits or qualities that are associated with women to the process of leading organizations worldwide.

Multinational Management **Challenge**

Getting Attributions Right

Paul Jones makes some observations regarding his leadership challenges during his first year as a manager in Mexico. Jones's observations are countered by the perceptions and attributions of Sr. González, a subordinate manager at Jones's plant.

Paul Jones:	Sr. González:
First day: "It is well past 9:00 A.M. and the office staff just arrived. I must emphasize punctuality at the next staff meeting."	"Mr. Jones wants us to behave as if we were robots. He seems crazy about the clock. Doesn't he realize that there are legitimate reasons to be late?"
"I just toured the plant, and González pointed out various problems. He really pressed me to meet all the supervisory staff, but there are many more pressing problems."	"Mr. Jones did not take the time or make the effort to meet the supervisors. Doesn't he realize that this neglect really hurt their feelings?"
Second month: "My managers keep asking me for advice, or, worse, asking me to solve their problems. Don't they realize that this lack of taking responsibility reflects poorly on their performance?"	"Mr. Jones does not seem to realize that many managers feel he is the boss and he must make the decisions."
"I had to correct a first-line supervisor today when he was incorrect in teaching a worker how to operate a machine. The whole plant seemed to stop and listen. These people need to get over their fear of criticism."	"Mr. Jones's actions today created an extreme embarrassment for one of my supervisors. Jones criticized him in public! Now all the supervisors are afraid to do anything, for fear of a public reprimand."
"I thought things were looking up. My managers recently produced a beautiful document on how to improve procedures. Three weeks later, much to my astonishment, only one manager had made any attempt at implementation."	"Doesn't Mr. Jones realize that the managers were waiting for him to tell them when to begin?"
"I figured maybe I should try a 'U.S.-style' meeting—shirt sleeves, feet up on the desk, and open communication. However, the managers just stood around looking embarrassed. I don't understand."	"Mr. Jones did not act like a plant manager at all. Can you imagine a plant manager putting his feet up on the desk? How uncivilized!"

Source: Kras, Eva S. 1995. Management in Two Cultures. Yarmouth, Maine: Intercultural Press.

Women global leaders provide other key advantages for companies. They are more likely to provide unity that accommodates the needs of most key stakeholders in organizations. Compared to their male counterparts, women leaders are likely to develop broadly based support for their actions rather than the traditional hierarchical support.[53] As such, as more global companies are facing stronger pressures to become more ethical and socially responsible, women leaders are seen to have better qualities and skills to help them achieve these goals. Additionally, as these companies also face diversity at a global level (both in terms of employees and customers), women leaders are seen to be better able to understand these new perspectives. Finally, scholars of leadership have also argued that women are more likely to possess transformational characteristics to lead.[54] As we discussed earlier, because transformational leadership emphasizes closer relationships with followers, women leaders are seen to possess a greater propensity to be transformational leaders because of their higher caring and nurturing qualities.

The effectiveness of women as leaders is supported by surveys. Professor Beverley Alimo-Metcalfe surveyed a large number of employees in both the private and public sector in England on women leadership. Her research found that both males and females rated women as more effective in 11 different dimensions of leadership, including such dimensions as being decisive, acting with integrity, encouraging others' potential, and networking.[55] The survey also found that women were rated as more effective in terms of transformational leadership, the ability of leaders to inspire and motivate workers to bring their best. Given that such qualities are highly conducive to more successful organizations, the survey suggests that organizations that do not promote their women managers to senior positions are at a disadvantage.

C A S E   I N   P O I N T

Global Women Leaders

Recent events point to the rise of women leading major democracies. Consider Angela Merkel, Germany's first woman chancellor; Michelle Bachelet, the first woman president in the very conservative country of Chile; Simpson Miller, Jamaica's first female prime minister; and Tarja Halonen, Finland's first female president.

Many global companies are also taking drastic strategic steps to ensure that women are given the appropriate environment in order to flourish as leaders. For instance, Xerox has been recognized numerous times as one of the "Top 30" companies for executive women. Currently, about 27 percent of the vice presidents at Xerox are minority or majority women. Xerox offers a work environment promoting female leadership in the organization. The company emphasizes training and professional development programs geared toward women. Furthermore, it also partners with independent organizations such as the Women's Alliance. It is, therefore, not surprising to see that nearly one-third of Xerox's corporate officers, including the current chairperson and CEO, are women.

General Electric (GE) is also cultivating female leadership at a global level. It launched the GE Women's Network in India and regularly provides opportunities for Indian women to interact with GE leaders

and learn from their experience. Participants are given the chance to interact with valuable role models and learn about job opportunities. Additionally, GE only recruits from universities that have more than 20 percent women candidates. Such efforts show GE's desire to develop its female leaders. Other large multinationals such as Motorola, Coca-Cola, and Pepsi also are implementing programs to ensure that their Indian subsidiaries have work environments where Indian women can develop as global leaders.

Accenture, a leading global management consulting company, also recognizes women leaders. It presents annual awards, the Government Women's Leadership Awards, celebrating excellence in women leadership. These awards are given to women who are selected for "outstanding achievements, leadership, and ingenuity." Such awards also bring prominence to women leaders.

Source: Based on Agrawal, Shaleen. 2006. "Women rising: India Inc. is still largely a men's club. But an increasingly large number of companies are taking steps to make it more gender-diverse." Business Today, March 12, p. 88; Business Wire. 2006. "Accenture celebrates excellence in the public sector at third-annual government women's leadership awards tea; Three outstanding women in government and small business honored." Jan. p. 17; Business Wire. 2006. "Xerox workplace ranks among 'top 30' for executive women." March p. 7; Pittsburg Post Gazette. 2006. "Chiefs who happen to be women: Liberia, Chile, Germany, Finland—Are female leaders a global trend?" Jan. p. 18.

As the Case in Point shows, as more women are leading some of the world's major democracies, women global leaders are poised to become increasingly important to multinational companies in the future. Successful companies are going to be those companies that can harness the creative potential of their women leaders to successfully cope with the environmental realities and difficulties of today's business world. Similar to some of the guidelines to develop women expatriates (as discussed in Chapter 12), companies should develop systems to provide an environment where women leaders can develop their full potential.

Getting Results: Should You do What Works at Home?

Most of what we have discussed so far in this chapter suggests that leadership works differently in different national contexts. This contingency view of leadership suggests that managers cannot assume that the leadership styles or traits that worked successfully in their home countries will result in equally successful leadership in a foreign country.

What happens if leaders do not adapt to local conditions? The results of at least one study suggest that home-based leadership styles do not work very well in other cultural settings.[56] Based on this study, Exhibit 15.12 shows the correlation between managerial performance and leadership behaviors for two groups of U.S. managers, one working in the United States and one working as expatriates in Hong Kong. A +1.0 indicates a perfect correspondence between the leadership behavior and the performance of the leader's unit; a 0 indicates no relationship; and a negative number indicates that leader's behavior reduced performance levels. As you can see from the example, typical U.S. leadership behaviors did not work as well in Hong Kong as in the United States. In particular, the highly involved "hands-on" leadership style that worked very well in the United States had little impact on the performance of Hong Kong workers.

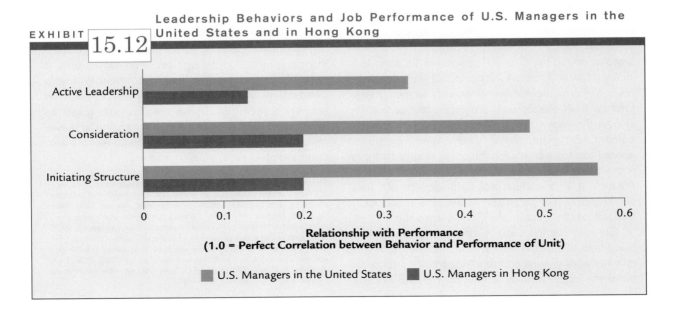

EXHIBIT 15.12   Leadership Behaviors and Job Performance of U.S. Managers in the United States and in Hong Kong

Relationship with Performance
(1.0 = Perfect Correlation between Behavior and Performance of Unit)

■ U.S. Managers in the United States   ■ U.S. Managers in Hong Kong

One potential reason that many managers (especially from the United States) fail in international assignments may be their inability to modify their behavior and adopt leadership styles congruent with the cultural setting. This difficulty in adaptation is not surprising. As noted in Chapter 12 on international human resource management, selection for an expatriate assignment usually requires prior success as a manager in the home country. Thus, before getting an international assignment, most expatriate managers likely demonstrated successful leadership in their home countries. As a result, without adequate cross-cultural training and awareness, many previously successful managers will continue to use in their international assignments the same leadership behaviors that worked well at home.

The Cultural Context and Suggested Leadership Styles

Probably because of the extreme variability among cultures and nations, there are few prescriptive theories of multicultural leadership; that is, there is no simple formula identifying how to lead in every national context. However, some writings by Geert Hofstede and Carl Rodrigues suggest some general recommendations.[57] Using the dimensions of national culture considered most important by Hofstede for organizations—power distance and uncertainty avoidance—Exhibit 15.13 shows these experts' recommended leadership styles for different cultural settings.

Power distance is important for leadership because it affects both subordinates' and superiors' expectations regarding the leader's degree of

EXHIBIT 15.13   National Culture and Recommended Leadership Styles

Cultural Context: Low Power Distance and Low Uncertainty Avoidance
Leader Type: "The Democrat"
Recommended Leadership Styles: Supportive, Participative, and Achievement
Example Country: Great Britain

Cultural Context: High Power Distance and Low Uncertainty Avoidance
Leader Type: "The Master"
Recommended Leadership Styles: Directive and Supportive
Example Country: China

Cultural Context: Low Power Distance and High Uncertainty Avoidance
Leader Type: "The Professional"
Recommended Leadership Styles: Directive, Supportive, and Participative
Example Country: Germany

Cultural Context: High Power Distance and High Uncertainty Avoidance
Leader Type: "The Boss"
Recommended Leadership Style: Directive
Example Country: France

Source: Adapted from Hofstede, Geert. 1991. Cultures and Organizations. London: McGraw-Hill; Rodrigues, Carl A. 1990. "The situation and national culture as contingencies for leadership behavior: Two conceptual models." Advances in International Comparative Management, 5, pp. 51–68.

directiveness or task orientation. In high-power-distance countries, leaders generally behave more autocratically. Subordinates also feel, "You are the boss, so tell us what to do." Hofstede[58] suggests that managers from low-power-distance countries can usually adjust to a high-power-distance country without much difficulty. They must develop a more authoritarian leadership style. However, he suggests that it is more difficult for managers from high-power-distance countries to become less authoritarian and more participative or person-centered.

The uncertainty-avoidance norm also affects the range of acceptable leadership styles.[59] In high-uncertainty-avoidance national cultures, both leaders and subordinates often feel more comfortable when the leader removes ambiguity from the work setting. In countries such as France, this may take the form of *le directeur* telling subordinates exactly what to do. In countries such as Germany, substitutes for leadership such as professional training may make the work setting predictable and allow leaders more discretion for participation.

Ultimately, each multinational manager must diagnose the institutional, organizational, and cultural situations that may affect the success of his or her leadership style. Too many contingencies exist to predict what may work in all situations faced by multinational managers. However, successful global leaders remain flexible and highly sensitive to the national context.

Summary and Conclusions

All managers who work for multinational companies should strive to become global leaders, unconstrained by national or cultural limitations and able to adjust to any national context. Toward this goal, this chapter has provided background information on the nature of leadership, information crucial to understanding leadership options in a multinational setting.

First the chapter defined leadership and introduced the concept of the global leader. The chapter then reviewed three classic North American views of leadership based on leadership traits, leadership behaviors, and contingency theory. Trait theories identify the personal qualities of leaders. Leadership-behavior theories identify the behaviors that signify certain leadership styles; these styles are usually considered person-centered or task-centered. Contingency theories identify characteristics of the supervisor, organization, and subordinates that determine the appropriate leadership style in a given situation. The chapter also showed that the Japanese and Indians have similar views of leadership.

The national-context contingency model of leadership extended traditional contingency theories to show how culture and social institutions affect the leadership process. Culture affects the preferences that leaders have for certain leadership styles. Culture

and the nation's social institutions affect subordinates' expectations regarding the leadership behaviors considered fair or appropriate. Using the most recent findings from the GLOBE study, you saw numerous examples of national differences in preferred leadership traits and behaviors.

The national context also affects leadership contingencies indirectly. Culture and social institutions, such as a nation's educational system or economic system, influence the characteristics of the workforce available in a country and the nature of typical companies there. In turn, the types of workers available in a country and the typical designs of organizations and jobs limit the successful leadership options for the multinational manager. In addition to developing a national-context contingency view of leadership, the chapter reviewed the international implications of contemporary views of leadership, focusing on the transformational leader and leadership attributions. The chapter also discussed women global leaders and strategic necessity of organizations to develop systems to ensure that their environment is conducive to women leaders flourishing.

Finally, the chapter applied elements of the national-context contingency model of leadership to suggest leadership styles for expatriate managers in selected countries. Specifically, we showed that the power-distance norm and the uncertainty-avoidance norm suggest different choices in leadership styles. Although it is impossible to identify all cultural and situational factors that affect the choice of leadership style, a careful reading of this chapter should sensitize the multinational manager to the array of complex cultural issues facing the global leader of today.

Discussion Questions

1. Define leadership. How might people from different national cultures define leadership? What are the implications of these definitions for multinational leaders working in these countries?
2. Discuss how the cultural norms of power distance and uncertainty avoidance affect the preferred leadership styles in different nations.
3. Pick a national culture with which you are familiar and identify leadership traits and behaviors that would be detrimental to organizational effectiveness.
4. From the perspective of the subordinates, discuss why culturally inappropriate leadership behaviors might be de-motivating.

5. Discuss whether transformational leadership qualities are culture-free. That is, are transformational leaders similar regardless of cultural background, or are there different types of transformational leaders for each cultural group?
6. How can women's leadership styles better prepare multinational companies to face today's competitive challenges? What can multinational companies do to fully develop the potential of their female leaders?
7. Compare and contrast the U.S. leadership-style model with the Japanese performance-maintenance model and the Afro-centric model. Use national culture dimensions to explain your findings.

Multinational Management Skill Builder

Leadership Challenges in Mexico

You have been approached by a U.S. multinational company that is considering opening a manufacturing facility in Mexico. The company will most likely employ Mexican employees although management will come from the United States. Your consulting services are required to ensure that the U.S. management and leadership is effective in the Mexican environment. After gathering the necessary information, you need to prepare a presentation to answer the following questions:

Step 1. What sources of cultural and social institutional differences between the United States

and Mexico are likely to pose significant challenges to U.S. managers as they lead Mexican workers?
Step 2. What specific forms may these challenges take?
Step 3. What do you propose to help your client and its managers face these problems? Are there specific forms of training or immersion programs you would recommend?

Endnotes

[1] Dorfman, P. 2003. "International and cross-cultural leadership research." In J. Punnett, and O. Shenkar (eds.) *Handbook for International Management research*, 2d ed. Ann Arbor, MI: University of Michigan.

[2] European Foundation for Quality Management. 2006. http://www.efqm.org

[3] McCarthy, Grace. 2005. "Leadership practices in German and UK organizations." *Journal of European Industrial Training* 29, 2/3: pp. 217–261.

[4] Harris, Philip R., and Robert T. Moran. 2000. *Managing Cultural Differences*. Woburn, MA: Gulf Professional Publishing; Rosen, Robert, Patricia Digh, Marshall Singer, and Carl Phillips. 2000.

Global Literacies: Lessons on Business Leadership and National Cultures. New York: Simon & Schuster.

[5] Alon, Ilan, and James M. Higgins. 2005. "Global leadership success through emotional and cultural intelligences." *Business Horizons*, 48, pp. 501–512.

[6] Yukl, Gary. 1998. *Leadership in Organizations.* Englewood Cliffs, N.J.: Prentice Hall.

[7] Likert, R. 1961. *New Patterns of Management.* New York: McGraw-Hill; Stogdill, Ralf M., and Alvin E. Coons. 1957. *Leader Behavior: Its Description and Measurement.* Columbus: Bureau of Business Research, Ohio State University.

[8] Tannenbaum, R., and W. H. Schmidt. 1958. "How to choose a leadership pattern." *Harvard Business Review*, March-April, pp. 95–102.

[9] Likert, R. 1967. *Human Organization: Its Management and Value.* New York: McGraw-Hill.

[10] Peterson, M., Mary Yoko Brannen, and Peter B. Smith. 1994. "Japanese and U.S. leadership: Issues in current research." *Advances in International and Comparative Management*, 9, pp. 57–82.

[11] Misumi, J., and M. F. Peterson. 1985. "The performance-maintenance theory of leadership: Review of a Japanese research program." *Administrative Science Quarterly* 30, pp. 198–223.

[12] Dorfman, P. and Robert J. House. 2004. "Cultural influences on organizational leadership: Literature review, theoretical rationale, and GLOBE project goals." In R. J. House, P. J. Hanges, M. Javidan, P. W. Dorfman, and V. Gupta (eds.) *Culture, Leadership, and Organizations.* Thousand Oaks, CA: Sage Publications, pp. 51–73.

[13] Sinha, J.B.P. 1984. "A model of effective leadership styles in India." International Studies of Management and Organization, 14, 3, pp. 86–98.

[14] Dorfman and House, "Cultural influences on organizational leadership: Literature review, theoretical rationale, and GLOBE project goals." In R. J. House, P. J. Hanges, M. Javidan, P. W. Dorfman, and V. Gupta (eds.) *Culture, Leadership, and Organizations.*

[15] Littrell, Romie F., and Stella M. Nkomo. 2005. "Gender and race differences in leader behaviour preferences in South Africa." *Women in Management Review*, 20, 8: pp. 562–580.

[16] Booysen, L. 2001. "The duality of South African leadership: Afro-centric or Eurocentric." *African Journal of Labor Relations*, Spring/Summer, pp. 36–63.

[17] Fiedler, F. E., and J. E. Garcia. 1987. *New Approaches to Effective Leadership.* New York: Wiley.

[18] House, R. J., and M. L. Baetz. 1979. "Leadership: Some empirical generalizations and new research directions." *Research in Organizational Behavior* 1, pp. 341–424.

[19] House, R. J., N. S. Wright, and R. N. Aditya. 1997. "Cross-cultural research on organizational leadership: A critical analysis and a proposed theory." In P.C. Earley and M. Erez (eds.), *New Perspectives in International Industrial Organizational Psychology.* San Francisco: New Lexington, pp. 536–625; Rodrigues, Carl A. 1990. "The situation and national culture as contingencies for leadership behavior: Two conceptual models." *Advances in International Comparative Management*, 5, pp. 51–68.

[20] Kerr, S., and J. M. Jermier. 1978. "Substitutes for leadership: Their meaning and measurement." *Organizational Behavior and Human Performance*, 22, pp. 375–404.

[21] Dorfman, "International and cross-cultural leadership research." In J. Punnett, and O. Shenkar (eds.) *Handbook for International Management research*, 2d ed.

[22] Hofstede, Geert. 1993. "Cultural constraints in management theories." *Academy of Management Executive*, 7, pp. 81–93.

[23] House, R. J., Paul J Hanges, Mansour Javidan, Peter W Dorfman, and Vipin Gupta. 2004. *Culture, Leadership, and Organizations.* Thousand Oaks, CA: Sage Publications; Brodbeck, Felix, and 44 associates. 2000. "Cultural variation of leadership prototypes across 22 European countries." *Journal of Occupational and Organizational Psychology*, 23, pp. 1–29; Dorfman, "International and cross-cultural leadership research." In J. Punnett, and O. Shenkar (eds.) *Handbook for International Management research*, 2d ed.

[24] Dorfman, P., Paul J. Hanges, and F. C. Brodbeck. 2004. "Leadership and cultural variation: The identification of culturally endorsed leadership profiles. In R. J. House, P. J. Hanges, M. Javidan, P. W. Dorfman, and V. Gupta (eds.) *Culture, Leadership, and Organizations.* Thousand Oaks, CA: Sage Publications, pp. 669–720.

[25] Gupta, Vipin, Paul J. Hanges, and Peter Dorfman. 2002. "Cultural clusters: Methodology and findings." *Journal of World Business* 37, pp. 11–15.

[26] Jesuino, Jorge Correia. 2002. "Latin Europe cluster: From south to north." *Journal of World Business* 37, pp. 81–89.

[27] Gupta, Vipin, Gita Surie, Mansour Javidan, and Jagpdeep Chhokar. 2002. "Southern Asia cluster: Where the old meets the new?" *Journal of World Business* 37, pp. 16–27.

[28] Szabo, Erna, Felix C. Brodbeck, Deanne N. Den Hartog, Gerard Reber, Jurgen Weibler, and Rolf Wunderer. 2002. "The Germanic Europe cluster: Where employees have a voice." *Journal of World Business* 37, pp. 55–68.

[29] Ashkanasy, Neal M., Edwin Trevor-Roberts, and Louise Earnshaw. 2002. "The Anglo cluster: Legacy of the British empire." *Journal of World Business* 37, pp. 28–39.

[30] House, Hanges, Javidan, Dorfman, and Gupta, *Culture, Leadership, and Organizations.*

[31] Den Hartog, Deanne N., Robert J. House, Paul J. Hanges, Peter W. Dorfman, S. Antonio Ruiz-Quintanna, and 170 associates. 1999. "Culture specific and cross-culturally generalizable implicit leadership theories: Are attributes of charismatic/transformational leadership universally endorsed?" *Leadership Quarterly*, 10, pp. 219–256.

[32] Kipnis, D. S., M. Schmidt, and I. Wilkinson. 1980. "Intraorganizational influence tactics: Explorations in getting one's way." *Journal of Applied Psychology* 65, pp. 440–452.

[33] Schmidt, Stuart M., and Ryh-Song Yeh. 1992. "The structure of leader influence: A cross-national comparison." *Journal of Cross-Cultural Psychology* 23, pp. 251–264.

[34] Kozusznik, Barbara. 2005. "Deinfluentization and self-monitoring as influence regulation tactics of Polish women and men managers." *Women in Management Review*, 21, 2: pp. 131–142.

[35] Peterson, Brannen, and Smith, "Japanese and U.S. leadership: Issues in current research."

[36] Hofstede, Geert. 1984. *Culture's Consequences.* Newbury Park, Calif.: Sage.

[37] Ibid.

[38] Bass, Bernard M., and Bruce J. Avolio. 1994. *Improving Organizational Effectiveness through Transformational Leadership.* Thousand Oaks, Calif.: Sage.

[39] Ibid.; Conger, J. A., and James G. Hunt. 1999. "Overview—Charismatic and transformational leadership: Taking stock of the present and future (Part I)." *Leadership Quarterly* 10, pp. 112–117; Conger, J. A. 1991. "Inspiring others: The language of leadership." *Academy of Management Executive* 5, pp. 31–45.

[40] Weber, M. 1947. *The Theory of Social and Economic Organization.* New York: Oxford University Press.

[41] Greenberg, Jerald, and Robert A. Baron. 1995. *Behavior in Organizations.* Englewood Cliffs, N.J.: Prentice-Hall.

[42] Kets de Vries, M. F. R. 1988. "Origins of charisma: Ties that bind the leader to the led." In J. A. Conger, and R. N. Kanungo (eds.) *Charismatic Leadership.* San Francisco: Jossey-Bass, pp. 237–252.

[43] Erez, Miriam P., and Christopher Earley. 1993. *Culture, Self Identity and Work.* Oxford: Oxford University Press.

[44] Den Hartog, House, Hanges, Dorfman, Ruiz-Quintanna, and 170 associates, "Culture specific and cross-culturally generalizable implicit leadership theories: Are attributes of charismatic/transformational leadership universally endorsed?"

[45] House, Hanges, Javidan, Dorfman, and Gupta, *Culture, Leadership, and Organizations.*

[46] Den Hartog, House, Hanges, Dorfman, Ruiz-Quintanna, and 170 associates, "Culture specific and cross-culturally generalizable implicit leadership theories: Are attributes of charismatic/transformational leadership universally endorsed?"

[47] Heneman, R. L., D. B. Greenberger, and C. Anonyuo. 1989. "Attributions and exchanges: The effects of interpersonal factors on the diagnosis of employee performance." *Academy of Management Journal* 32, pp. 466–476.

[48] Mullen, B., and C. A. Riordan. 1988. "Self-serving attributions for performance in naturalistic settings: A meta-analytic review." *Journal of Applied Social Psychology*, 18, pp. 3–22.

[49] Adler, Nancy. 2001. "Global leadership: Women leaders." In M. E. Mendenhall, T. M. Kuhlmann, and G. K. Stahl (eds.) *Developing Global Business Leaders*. Westport, CT: Quorum Books, pp. 73–98.

[50] Ibid.

[51] Fondas, N. 1997. "The origins of feminization." *Academy of Management Review* 22, pp. 257–282.

[52] Ibid.

[53] Adler, Nancy. 2001. "Global leadership: Women leaders." In M. E. Mendenhall, T. M. Kuhlmann, and G. K. Stahl (eds.) *Developing Global Business Leaders.*

[54] Schyns, Birgit, and Katrin Sanders. 2005. "Exploring gender differences in leaders' occupational self-efficacy." *Women in Management Review*, 20, 7: pp. 513–523.

[55] Hope, J. 2003. "The leading ladies: Why most men would prefer a female boss." *Daily Mail*, January 9, p. 45.

[56] Black, J. Stewart, and Lyman W. Porter. 1991. "Managerial behaviors and job performance: A successful manager in Los Angeles may not succeed in Hong Kong." *Journal of International Business Studies*, First Quarter, pp. 99–113.

[57] Hofstede, Geert. 1991. *Cultures and Organizations*. London: McGraw-Hill; Rodrigues, "The situation and national culture as contingencies for leadership behavior: Two conceptual models."

[58] Hofstede, *Cultures and Organizations.*

[59] Ibid.

CHAPTER CASE

The Global Leadership of Carlos Ghosn at Nissan

> *"I did not try to learn too much about Japan before coming, because I didn't want to have too many preconceived ideas. I wanted to discover Japan by being in Japan with Japanese people."[1] "Well, I think I am a practical person. I know I may fail at any moment. In my opinion, it was extremely helpful to be practical [at Nissan], not to be arrogant, and to realize that I could fail at any moment."*
>
> Carlos Ghosn, 2002[2]

Introduction

Nissan had been incurring losses for seven of the prior eight years when, in March 1999, Carlos Ghosn (pronounced GOHN) took over as the first non-Japanese Chief Operating Officer of Nissan. Many industry analysts anticipated a culture clash between the French leadership style and his new Japanese employees. For these analysts, the decision to bring Ghosn in came at the worst possible time because the financial situation at Nissan had become critical. The continuing losses were resulting in debts (approximately $22 billion) that were shaking the confidence of suppliers and financiers alike. Furthermore, the Nissan brand was weakening in the minds of consumers due to a product portfolio that consisted of models far older than competitors. In fact, only four of the company's 43 models turned a profit. With little liquid capital available for new product development, there was no indication that Nissan would see increases in either margin or volume of sales to overcome the losses. The next leader of Nissan was either going to turn Nissan around within two to three years, or the company faced the prospect of going out of business.

Realizing the immediacy of the task at hand, Ghosn boldly pledged to step down if Nissan did not

show a profit by March 2001, just two years after he assumed duties. But it only took eighteen months (October 2000) for him to shock critics and supporters alike when Nissan began to operate profitably under his leadership.

Background of Carlos Ghosn

Born in Brazil in 1954 to French and Brazilian parents, both of Lebanese heritage, Carlos Ghosn received his university education in Paris. Following graduation at age 24, Ghosn joined the French firm, Compagnie Générale des Etablissements Michelin. After a few years of rapid advancement to become COO of Michelin's Brazilian subsidiary, he learned to manage large operations under adverse conditions such as the runaway inflation rates in Brazil at that time. Similarly, as the head of Michelin North America, Ghosn faced the pressures of a recession while putting together a merger with Uniroyal Goodrich. Despite his successes in his 18 years with Michelin, Ghosn realized that he would never be promoted to company president because Michelin was a family-run company. Therefore, in 1996 he decided to resign and join Renault S.A., accepting a position as the Executive Vice President of Advanced Research & Development, Manufacturing, and Purchasing.

Ghosn led the turnaround initiative at Renault in the aftermath of its failed merger with Volvo. Because he was so focused on increasing margins by improving cost efficiencies, he earned the nickname "Le Cost-Killer" among Renault 's top brass and middle management personnel. Three years later, when Renault formed a strategic alliance with Nissan, Ghosn was asked to take over the role of Nissan COO in order to turn the company around in a hurry, just as he had done earlier in his career with Michelin South America. For Ghosn this would be the fourth continent he would work on, which combined with the five languages he spoke, illustrates his capacity for global leadership.

Background of Nissan

In 1933, a company called Jidosha-Seizo Kabushiki-Kaisha (which means "Automobile Manufacturing Co., Ltd." in English) was established in Japan. It was a combination of several earlier automotive ventures and the Datsun brand which it acquired from Tobata Casting Co., Ltd. Shortly thereafter in 1934, the company name was changed to Nissan Motor Co., Ltd. After the Second World War, Nissan grew steadily, expanding its operations globally. It became especially successful in North America with a lineup of smaller gasoline efficient cars and small pickup trucks as well as a sports coupe, the Datsun 280Z. Along with other Japanese manufacturers, Nissan was successfully competing on quality, reliability and fuel efficiency. By 1991, Nissan was operating very profitably, producing four of the top ten cars in the world.

Nissan management throughout the 1990s, however, had displayed a tendency to emphasize short-term market share growth, rather than profitability or long-term strategic success. Nissan was very well known for its advanced engineering and technology, plant productivity, and quality management. During the previous decade, Nissan's designs had not reflected customer opinion because they assumed that most customers preferred to buy good quality cars rather than stylish, innovative cars. Instead of reinvesting in new product designs as other competitors did, Nissan managers seemed content to continue to harvest the success of proven designs. They tended to put retained earnings into equity of other companies, often suppliers, and into real-estate investments, as part of the Japanese business custom of *keiretsu* investing. Through these equity stakes in other companies, Ghosn's predecessors (and Japanese business leaders in general) believed that loyalty and cooperation were fostered between members of the value chain within their *keiretsu*. By 1999, Nissan had tied up over $4 billion in the stock shares of hundreds of different companies as part of this *keiretsu* philosophy. These investments, however, were not reflected in Nissan's purchasing costs, which remained between 20–25% higher than Renault's. These *keiretsu* investments would not have been so catastrophic if the Asian financial crisis had not resulted in a devaluation of the yen from 100 to 90 yen = 1 US dollar. As a result, both Moody's and Standard & Poor's announced in February 1999, that if Nissan could not get any financial support from

another automobile company, then each of them would lower Nissan's credit rating to "junk" status from "investment grade".

Clearly, Nissan was in need of a strategic partner that could lend both financing and new management ideas to foster a turnaround. In addition, Nissan sought to expand into other regions where it had less presence. In March 1999, Nissan President and Chief Executive Officer Yoshikazu Hanawa found such an alliance opportunity with Renault, which assumed a 36.8% stake in Nissan, allowing Nissan to invest $5.4 billion and retain its investment grade status. Hanawa was also able to get Renault's top management to agree to three important principles during negotiations:

1. Nissan would maintain its company name
2. The Nissan CEO would continue to be selected by the Nissan Board of Directors
3. Nissan would take the principal responsibility of implementing a revival plan.

It was actually Hanawa who first made the request to Louis Schweitzer, CEO of Renault, to send Carlos Ghosn to Nissan to be in charge of all internal administration and operations activities.

Why would Renault agree to all of these conditions in this bailout of Nissan? Renault was also looking for a partner, one that would reduce its dependence on the European market and enhance its global position. In 1997 85% of Renault's revenue was earned in Europe, 32.8% of which came from its domestic (French) market. Renault also had high market share in Latin America, especially Brazil. On the other hand, Nissan has the second largest market share in Japan and a strong market share in North America (see Appendix 2, Nissan' market share). Nissan lacked, however, market share and distribution facilities in Latin America. By creating the new alliance, Nissan and Renault expected to balance their market portfolios and become more competitive. Renault wanted a partner that was savvy and established in the North American and Asian markets. Furthermore, the merger of Daimler and Chrysler in May 1998 gave Renault a sense of urgency about finding a partner to compete more effectively on a global scale. As a result, Renault and Nissan agreed to a Global Alliance Agreement on March 27, 1999, with Carlos Ghosn designated to join Nissan as COO.

Addressing National Culture Issues

When Ghosn went to Japan, he knew that industry analysts were reasonable in doubting whether a non- Japanese COO could overcome Japanese cultural obstacles, as well as effectively transform a bureaucratic corporate culture. Ghosn was going to have to address several Japanese cultural norms in order to transform the company back into a successful one.

The following are some of the issues he faced.

Consensus Decision-Making and its Relationship to Career Advancement Since the war, the Japanese business culture for decades had been producing leaders who were very good at reaching consensus and working cooperatively within a department (a derivative of the *mura-shakai* consensus based society system). Thus, the conventional wisdom in Japan was that conscientiousness and cooperation were the key elements to maintaining operational efficiency and group harmony. This paradigm often resulted in delays to the decision making process in an effort to achieve consensus.

As an unintended consequence of the emphasis on conscientiousness, Japanese professionals tended to avoid making mistakes at all costs in order to protect their career growth. This can result in frequent informal informational meetings and coalitions (called *nemawashi*) that occur between professional departments prior to a decision-making meeting. Through these informal contacts, participants try to poll the opinions of other participants beforehand in order to test which positions have the strongest support so that their position is aligned with the position most likely to be influential. Then, at the time for a meeting with their superiors, participants tender their aligned positions one by one to the ultimate decision maker with the feeling that if the decision maker agrees to the consensus, then no one individual can be identified later for originating a faulty position if that decision results in failure. Rules and conformity replace process.

In Japan, age, education level, and number of years of service to an organization are key factors determining how an employee moves up the career ladder. Due to a cultural tenet called *Nennkou-Jyoretu*, placing power in the hands of the most knowledgeable and experienced, promotions are normally based on seniority and education. In practice, the only things that usually thwart these time- and education-based promotions are performance errors that reflect poorly on the team and any behavior that causes disharmony among team members. When something goes wrong, the most senior person accepts responsibility while accountability at lower levels is diffused.

This part of Japanese culture had been useful to reinforce control over operations and enhance quality and productivity. During the postwar period of the company's growth, it contributed to great working relationships among everyday team members at Nissan, but these norms, by the mid 1990s, were actually impeding the company's decision making. Specifically, these cultural norms severely hampered risk-taking and slowed decision making at all levels. Existing teams of employees routinely spent much time on concepts and details, without much sense of urgency for taking new action, due in part to the risks involved with actions that could result in failure. This mindset contributed to a certain degree of complacency with market position and internal systems at Nissan, undermining the company's competitiveness.

In a related cultural issue, as employees became increasingly aware that Nissan was not performing well, the Japanese culture of protecting career advancement led to finger pointing rather than acceptance of responsibility. Sales managers blamed product planning. Product planning blamed engineering. Engineering blamed manufacturing and so on.

When Ghosn first arrived in Japan, he was surprised to learn that, while most of the employees sensed that there was indeed a problem within the company, they nearly always believed that their respective departments were operating optimally. The consensus was that other departments and other employees were creating the company's problems. Ghosn also learned that many of the employees of the company did not have a sense of crisis about the possibility of bankruptcy at Nissan because of the Japanese business tradition, which implied that large troubled employers would always be bailed out by the government of Japan. This view was based on the long standing partnership between the government and the major businesses to ensure employment and expand exports to world markets. The businesses for their part were committed to providing lifetime employment to their workers.

Addressing Corporate Culture Issues

Not only were there Japanese cultural norms for Ghosn to contend with, but there were procedural norms at Nissan, both formal and informal, which were holding the company back. First, once decisions were made at Nissan, the follow-up during implementation was often not effective. This was not usually the case in other Japanese companies. Second, top management had developed tunnel vision regarding its strategic focus on regaining market share, as opposed to restoring margin per unit sold. This was in part due to a focus on what was best for maintaining the company's size and its employees, i.e. more units to produce, rather than what was best for customers (newer, better products to meet market demands) or for investors (higher earnings and higher stock value). Additionally, in an unusual break from Japanese business culture, there were communication problems between the layers of the organization. Staffs seemed relatively uninformed of key corporate business decisions, while top management seemed out of touch with what policy execution issues were present at the middle and lower management levels.

Ghosn realized that Nissan's fundamental problem was the lack of vision from management and the persistent problem of ignoring the voice of Nissan's customers.[3] Furthermore, he identified the following problems at Nissan:

1. Lack of a clear profit orientation
2. Insufficient focus on customers and too much focus on competitors
3. Lack of a sense of urgency
4. No shared vision or common long term plan
5. Lack of cross-functional, cross-border, cross-cultural lines of work.[4]

Carlos Ghosn's Philosophies of Management

Despite all of his doubters, Ghosn embraced the cultural differences between the Japanese and himself, believing fervently that cultural conflict, if paced and channeled correctly, could provide opportunity for rapid innovation. He felt that by accepting and building on strengths of the different cultures, all employees, including Ghosn himself, would be given a chance to grow personally through the consideration of different perspectives. The key, he reiterated many times, was

that no one leader should try to impose his/her culture on another person who was not ready to try the culture with an open mind and heart. In this vein, Carlos Ghosn came to Japan knowing that if he were to start imposing reforms by using the authority of his company position, rather than work through the Japanese culture, then the turnaround he sought would likely backfire.

What he did bring with him was three overriding principles of management that transcended all cultures. And he used these as a backdrop to give employees structure as to their efforts of determining the proper reforms. These three principles are as follows:

1. Transparency—an organization can only be effective if followers believe that what the leaders think, say, and do are all the same thing
2. Execution is 95% of the job. Strategy is only 5%—organizational prosperity is tied directly to measurably improving quality, costs, and customer satisfaction.
3. Communication of company direction and priorities—this is the only way to get truly unified effort and buy-in. It works even when the company is facing layoffs.

The First Months in Japan and the Cross-Functional Teams

When you get a clear strategy and communicate your priorities, it's a pleasure working in Japan. The Japanese are so organized and know how to make the best of things. They respect leadership.

Ghosn Middleton[5]

Even though Ghosn expected that his attitude toward cultural respect and opportunism would lead to success, Ghosn was pleasantly surprised by how quickly Nissan employees accepted and participated in the change of their management processes. In fact, he has credited all of the success in his programs and policies (described below) to the willingness of the Nissan employees at all levels to change their mindsets and embrace new ideas.

Perhaps it was the way he started that set the foundation among the employees. He was the first manager to actually walk around the entire company and meet every employee in person, shaking hands and introducing himself. In addition, Ghosn initiated long discussions with several hundred managers in order to discuss their ideas for turning Nissan around. This began to address the problems within the vertical layers of management by bringing the highest leader of the company in touch with some of the execution issues facing middle and lower management. It also sent a signal to other executives that they needed to be doing the same thing.

But he did not stop there. After these interviews, he decided that the employees were quite energetic, as shown by their recommendations and opinions. With this in mind, Ghosn opted to develop a program for transformation which relied on the Nissan people to make recommendations, instead of hiring outside consultants. He began to organize Cross-Functional Teams to make decisions for radical change. Part of his interest in doing this in-house was to address the motivation and horizontal communication issues that he encountered throughout the organization. He felt that if the employees could accomplish the revival by their own hands, then confidence in the company as a whole and motivation would again flourish. In a sense he was making it clear that he was also putting his own future in their hands because he had publicly stated several times that the Nissan company had the right employees to achieve profitability again in less than two years.

Before the strategic alliance occurred between Renault and Nissan, Renault had made an agreement with Hanawa to remain sensitive to Nissan's culture at all times, and Ghosn was intent on following through on that commitment. First and foremost, when he chose expatriates to accompany him from Renault to Nissan, he screened carefully to ensure that those expatriates would have his same cultural attitudes toward respecting Nissan and the Japanese culture. And, after completing his rounds of talking with plant employees, he chose not to use his newfound understanding of the problems to impose a revival plan. Instead, Ghosn mobilized existing Nissan managers by setting up nine Cross-Functional Teams (CFTs) of approximately 10 members each in the first month. Through these CFTs, he was allowing the company to develop a new corporate culture from the best elements of Japan's national culture.

He knew that the CFTs would be a powerful tool for getting line managers to see beyond the functional or regional boundaries that defined their direct responsibilities. In Japan, the trouble was that employees working in functional or regional departments tend not to ask themselves as many hard questions as they should. Working together in CFTs helped managers to think in new ways and challenge existing practices.

Thus, Ghosn established the nine CFTs within one month of his arrival at Nissan. The CFT teams had responsibility for the following areas: Business Development, Purchasing, Manufacturing and Logistics, Research and Development, Sales and Marketing, General and Administrative, Finance and Cost, Phase-out of Products and Parts, Complexity Management, and Organizational Structure.

Ghosn had the teams review the company's operations for three months and come up with recommendations for returning Nissan to profitability and for uncovering opportunities for future growth. Even though the teams had no decision making power, they reported to Nissan's nine-member executive committee and had access to all company information. The teams consisted of around ten members who were drawn from the company's middle management.

Ten people could not cover broad issues in depth. To overcome this each CFT formed a set of subteams. These sub-teams also consisted of ten members and focused on particular issues faced by the broad teams. CFTs used a system reporting to two supervisors. These leaders were drawn from the executive committee and ensured that the teams were given access to all the information that they needed. To prevent a single function's perspective from dominating, team had two senior voices that would balance each other.

One of the regular members acted as a pilot who took responsibility for driving the agenda and discussion. The pilot and leaders selected the other members. The pilots usually had frontline experience as managers.

The CFTs also prescribed some harsh medicine in the form of plant closures and employee reductions. The CFTs would remain an integral part of Nissan's management structure. They continue to brief the CEO; however the team's missions have changed somewhat. They are to carefully watch the on-going revival plan and try to find further areas for improvement.

Since the members of the teams were often mid-level managers who rarely saw beyond their own functional responsibilities, this new coordination had high impact on participants. Specifically, it allowed them to understand how the standard measures of success for their own departments were meaningless to Nissan unless they were framed in a way that connected to other departments to result in customer attraction and retention. In many cases, these mid-level managers enjoyed learning about the business from a bird's eye perspective and felt fully engaged in the change process, giving them a sense of responsibility and ownership about turning Nissan around.

As Ghosn explained in a speech in May 2002, "The trouble is that people working in functional or regional teams tend not to ask themselves as many hard questions as they should. By contrast, working together in cross-functional teams helps managers to think in new ways and challenge existing practices. The teams also provide a mechanism for explaining the necessity for change and for projecting difficult messages across the entire company."[6]

Ghosn did have one great stroke of luck that helped him reinforce the need for change. At approximately the same time as he was arriving in Japan, Yamaichi, the major financial house in Japan, went bankrupt and was not bailed out by the Japanese government. Before that, Japanese employees, including Nissan's, did not worry about corporate problems because the government was always saving the day. This recent turn of events helped to develop a sense of urgency among Nissan employees. Ghosn, to his credit, used the Yamaichi example whenever he could to continue to motivate his employees, repeating that their fate would be no different if they did not put all of their effort into figuring out, and then executing, the best way to turn Nissan around.

Reforms in Full Swing

Within the first six months, the fruit of the CFTs and the increased sense of urgency were apparent. Management (especially Ghosn) was increasingly perceived as transparent among all levels of employees, which Ghosn attributed to his respect for protecting Nissan's identity. In addition, decisions were being made faster; and there was increased communication and understanding about what was important to management. There was, however, very little implementation yet, only planning. Having received from the CFTs the recommendations, which included plant closures and reduced headcount, Ghosn created

and communicated what he called the Nissan Revival Plan (or NRP) in October of 1999. From that point forward he stressed implementation and follow-up, rather than planning and reexamining decisions. Other CFTs were formed, but the bulk of his efforts lay in ensuring high-quality execution of the decisions that were laid out in the plan.

Ghosn's main focus areas included: (1) development of new automobiles and markets, (2) improvement of Nissan's brand image, (3) reinvestment in research and development, and (4) cost reduction.

Reducing Redundancies To achieve these results, the closing of five factories and the reduction of 21,000 jobs (14% of Nissan's workforce) were planned. Job cuts would occur in manufacturing, management, and the dealer network.[7] Since Japanese business culture had tended to have lifelong employment as a principle, Ghosn endured strong criticism from the media, including being labeled as a *gaijin*, a foreigner. In addition, Ghosn fired several managers who did not meet targets, regardless of the circumstances. Many industry analysts cited his demotion of Vice President of Sales and Marketing in Japan, Mr. Hiroshi Moriyama, as unacceptable and reckless. They contended that falling revenues and dissipated market share were due to Nissan's aging product line rather than to Moriyama's performance. In addition to the media and industry analysts, the government, also expressed concern about the layoffs, but Prime Minister Keizo Obuchi responded by offering subsidies and programs to help the affected workers.[8]

Keiretsu Partnerships As one of the biggest changes of the NRP, Nissan broke away from the Japanese cultural norm of *keiretsu* investments. However Nissan maintained customer-supplier relationships with those former *keiretsu* partners. As it turned out, Nissan regained billions in tied up capital to use for debt servicing and new product development without losing any significant pricing advantages. In fact, because Ghosn put such an emphasis on reducing purchasing costs, Nissan actually began to substantially lower its costs after the *keiretsu* investments were sold.

Reorganization Another major component of the NRP was the restructuring of the organization toward permanent cross-functional departments, which each serviced one product line. As a result, the staffs gained better visibility of the entire business process and began to focus on total business success and customer satisfaction, as opposed to misleading performance goals that could be taken out of context. In addition, Ghosn also eliminated all advisor and coordinator positions that carried no responsibilities and put those personnel in positions with direct operational responsibility. Employees were disciplined much more strongly for inaccurate or poor data than misjudgment, thereby stimulating risk-taking behavior and personal accountability. Ghosn also made it clear, however, that engineers were not to reduce product cycle times or do anything that would negatively impact product quality or reliability. He repeated this often to drive home the point that the way to restore the power of the Nissan brand was through each individual customer's experience.

For higher-level staff, Ghosn created a matrix organization to improve transparency and communication. Within this matrix, he assigned each staff member two responsibilities: functional (e.g., marketing, engineering) and regional (e.g., domestic, North America). The result was that each staff member would have two bosses, thereby building awareness of both functional and regional issues. Ghosn also put an emphasis on cross-functional department members having very clear lines of responsibility and high standards of accountability. Every report, both oral and written, was to be 100% accurate. Ghosn is quoted as saying, "Right from the beginning, I made it clear that every number had to be thoroughly checked. I did not accept any report that was less than totally clear and verifiable, and I expected people to personally commit to every observation or claim they made."[9]

Performance Evaluations and Employee Advancement Ghosn also put focus on performance by introducing a performance based incentive system. These incentives included cash incentives and stock options for achievements that could be linked directly to successful operating profits and revenue. This was a large departure from the traditional Japanese compensation system, in which managers usually received no stock options or bonuses. Under Ghosn's compensation system, the highest achievers got the highest rewards. And promotions were no longer limited to age, length of service, or educational level. For example, a female factory worker who had only a high school diploma was promoted to be a manufacturing manager based on her strong abilities to perform the work, relating promotion and salary increase to the ability to perform challenging or demanding tasks. The promotion of some younger leaders over older, longer-serving employees caused some problems regarding lack of cooperation. But just as Ghosn saw cultural differences as growth opportunities, he thought these tests of authority were growth experiences for young managers.

The First Three Years

The NRP was achieved in March 2002, one year ahead of schedule.[10] One success was a 20% reduction in purchasing costs. This was a result of achieving a purchase price from *kereitsu* suppliers that matched the prices offered by Renault's suppliers. In addition, the supplier base shrunk by 40% and the service suppliers decreased by 60%.[11]

Prior to NRP, seven plants produced automobiles based on 24 platforms. After NRP, four plants produced automobiles based on 15 platforms.[12]

The Near Future—Implementation of Nissan 180

On May 9, 2002, Ghosn stated in a speech for an annual business review, "The Nissan Revival Plan is over. Two years after the start of its implementation, all the official commitments we took have been overachieved one full year ahead of schedule . . . Nissan is now ready to grow." He went on in the speech to set out the goals for a new plan, one he called "Nissan 180" which would focus on profitable growth. All new goals were to be accomplished by April 1, 2005. The one in "Nissan 180" represents an additional 1,000,000 car sales for Nissan worldwide; the eight, an 8% operating profitability with no changes in accounting standards; and the zero represented zero automotive debt. In addition, the plan called for an increase of global market share from 4.7% presently to 6.1%, a further reduction of purchasing costs by 15%, and a significant increase in customer satisfaction and sales satisfaction ratings. In 2002, mid-career hires (400) outnumbered college recruits (280). Because hiring outside managers might create animosity among managers within Nissan, this practice reflects a sharp change in hiring decisions. "We're moving to a system where it doesn't matter if you've been in the company ten years or 40 years . . . . If you contribute, there will be opportunity and reward," said Kuniyuki Watanabe, Nissan's Senior Vice President for Human Resources.[13]

Not only was Ghosn aggressively launching the Nissan 180 program to transition out of the Nissan Revival Plan program, but he was also pushing a new, customer-focused initiative called "Quality 3-3-3". He said that this program focuses on three categories of quality: product attractiveness, product initial quality and reliability, and sales & service quality.

Challenges for Ghosn and Nissan

As Ghosn contemplates the future, he knows that the transformation has really just begun. How could the momentum and the energy that his employees exhibited be maintained now that they had all reached the goals that were seemingly Herculean just over two years ago. Would there be a letdown of effort and results by Nissan employees, or would Ghosn be able to mobilize them to get to the next level of profitable growth and reestablishment of brand power and market share?

He was aware that current succession plans called for him to return to Renault as its new CEO, replacing Louis Schweitzer in 2005. Before this could happen, Ghosn would be challenged to find an adequate replacement who could take Nissan to new heights of accomplishment as planned. Could the new approaches that had been so successful become part of the Nissan culture without his continued guidance? Would the success of the NRP spoil the sense of urgency that helped reinforce the need for change allowing Nissan to slip back into old habits? How could he find someone to carry forward the need to create a sustainable pattern of customer focus and profitable growth?

CASE DISCUSSION QUESTIONS

1. Why was Nissan struggling in the 1990s? What are some unique characteristics of the Japanese economy that contributed to these problems?

2. What are some elements of traditional Japanese culture that impeded Nissan's success? Which of these cultural elements are specific to Nissan?

3. How did various part of Nissan feel about Ghosn? How did he go about enlisting the support of Nissan's employees? How did his own management philosophy and style contribute to making the changes happen?

4. What was the role of cross-functional teams and how were they designed? Do cross-functional teams contradict some elements of traditional Japanese culture?

5. Discuss some important lessons garnered from Goshn's cross cultural leadership style.

CASE NOTES

[1] "Decision-Making and Coordination Structures of the Alliance," 20 October 1999, http://www.nissanglobal.com.

[2] "Nissan President Carlos Ghosn Talks about His Company's Recovery," *Nikkei Business*, 20 May 2002, http://nb.nikkeibp.co.jp/Article/1142.

[3] p. 155, Carlos Ghosn (2001) (August 10, 2002).

[4] p. 26, (2000) (August 8, 2002).

[5] , John. *ExpressExec.com*, http://www.expressexec.wiley.com/ee/ee07.01.07/sect0.html, Acquired on Internet, 7 August 2002.

[6] Ghosn, Carlos, "Saving the Business without Losing the Company," *Harvard Business Review*, Vol. 80, No. 1, January 2002.

[7] "Nissan's Napoleon," *Worldlink*, 11 July 2002, http://www.worldlink.co.uk.

[8] Barr, C.W. "Get Used to It: Japanese Steel Themselves for Downsizing. Mitsubishi and Nippon Telephone Have Added 30,000 Layoffs to Nissan's 21,000 Announced Oct. 19," *Christian Science Monitor*, Nov. 12, 1999.

[9] Ghosn, Carlos. "Saving the Business without Losing the Company," *Harvard Business Review*, Vol. 80, No. 1, January 2002.

[10] 2002 News, "Nissan Announced NRP Will Conclude One Year Earlier than Planned," http://www.nissan-global.com.

[11] Nissan 180, "Fiscal Year 01 Business Review," http://www.nissan-global.com.

[12] Nissan 180, "Fiscal Year 01 Business Review," http://www.nissan-global.com.

[13] Raskin, Andy. "*Voulez-Vous* Completely Overhaul This Big, Slow Company and Start Making Some Cars People Actually Want *Avec Moi?*" *Business 2.0*, January 2002.

[14] http://www.google.co.jp/search?q=cache:NNR0tavWLwAC:www.ai-online.com/articles/-0302coverstory.asp+carlos+Ghosn,+background&hl=ja&ie=UTF-8

Appendix 1 Summary of Results of NRP

The turnaround at Nissan was phenomenal, with the following statistics:

- From seven out of eight years of operating losses to profitability within the first 12 months. Since 1999, Nissan has shown four consecutive semi-annual operating profits, and the year 2001 was marked by the best-ever, full-year earnings at Nissan. The current operating margin is 7.9%, over 3% greater than committed to in the NRP.
- Net automotive debt is the lowest it has been in 24 years (down from $10.5 billion to $4.35 billion).
- The company developed eight new car models to be launched by late 2002/early 2003, including the award winning, revamped Altima, and the new 350Z.
- Supplier costs were reduced by 20%, as per the NRP, mainly through sourcing and other strategies to minimize exchange rate issues, as well as the reduction of the number of parts suppliers by 40% and the number of service providers by 60%.
- Five plants have been closed, according to the NRP.
- Headcount was reduced by 21,000, according to the NRP, mainly through natural turnover, retirements, pre-retirement programs, and by selling off non-core businesses to other companies.

Appendix 2 Nissan and Renault Profile

The Renault Group - 2000

Revenues:
EUR 40.2 billion

Global Production : 2,427,178 units
Passenger cars + Light Commercial Vehicles

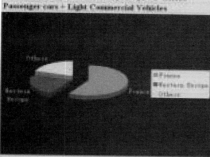

Shareholders' equity at December 31, 2000:
EUR 913,632,540.27

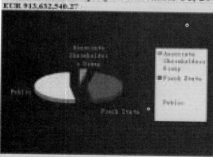

Global Sales : 2,356,778 units
Passenger cars + Light Commercial Vehicles

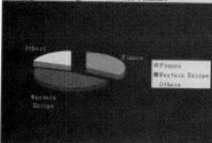

The Nissan Group - 2000
(April 2000 - March 2001)

Revenues:
JPY 6,090 billion / US$ 49.1 billion /EUR 55.9 billion
(Exchange rate at 2001/03/30 :
$1 = JPY 124 ; 1 EUR = JPY 109)

Global Production : 2,613,948 units
Passenger cars + Light Commercial Vehicles

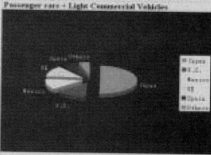

Shareholders' equity at March 30, 2001:
JPY 957,939 million

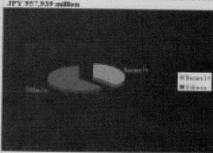

Global Sales : 2,632,010 units
Passenger cars + Light Commercial Vehicles

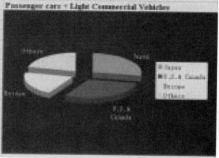

Appendix 3 Carlos Ghosn's Background[14]

1954	Born in Brazil, March 9
1974	Receives chemical Engineering degree from École Polytechnique, Paris
1978	Graduates from École des Mines de Paris. Joins Michelin
1981	Becomes plant manager at Le Puy plant, France
1984	Becomes head of R&D
1985	Becomes COO of South American operations. Turns company around
1989	President and COO of North American operations
1990	Named CEO of North American operations
1996	Joins Renault as Executive VP of advanced R&D, car engineering and development, power train operations, manufacturing, and purchasing. Gains nickname, "Le Cost-Killer"
1999	Named Nissan president and COO

Grupo UNIKO

In March of 1995, Rubén Galván, director of Grupo UNIKO (UNIKO), faced a threatening competitive and economic environment. The Mexican auto parts industry faced increasing competition due to a shrinking economy and the passage of the North American Free Trade Agreement (NAFTA). The massive devaluation of the Mexican peso spurred a financial crisis that negatively impacted most of Mexican industry. Most importantly, the economic crisis resulted in the contraction of the market for vehicles and consequently in the demand for auto parts. UNIKO had to implement a strategy that would assure the group's survival and continued performance in Mexican and international markets. Galván had to decide how to position UNIKO for global competitiveness.

Grupo UNIKO has chosen to focus on achieving long-term fundamental competitiveness through a focused corporate vision: "becoming a group of companies deploying a service spirit in an environment of continuous development and creativity." (Exhibit 1).

Galván broadly defines fundamental competitiveness as the ability to satisfy and exceed customer expectations while maintaining high levels of quality and technological competence. UNIKO's customer focus, however, encompasses more than simply catering to its clients. In fact, UNIKO defines its customers as its clients, shareholders, personnel, and community (Exhibit 2).

UNIKO's management believes that the group as a whole will attain fundamental competitiveness by meeting the needs of all its customers. Therefore, UNIKO's goal is to optimize critical processes across functional areas, identified according to all of its customers' demands and needs, while maintaining high quality products and levels of technology. UNIKO must foster an environment that is conducive to change and to the implementation of its "customer focus."

Company Background

Grupo UNIKO is a collection of companies in the manufacture of auto-parts for both Mexican and international original equipment manufacturers (OEMs)

EXHIBIT 1   **UNIKO's Vision**

> ➤ To become a group of companies deploying a customer service spirit in an environment of continuous development and creativity.
>
> ➤ Our customers' perception of the quality and competitiveness of the company will be forged with the honesty, congruency, and enthusiasm of the leaders.
>
> ➤ The processes of any kind, applied to satisfy our customers' expectations will be reliably structured and systemized to guarantee success.

EXHIBIT **2**   UNIKO's Customers

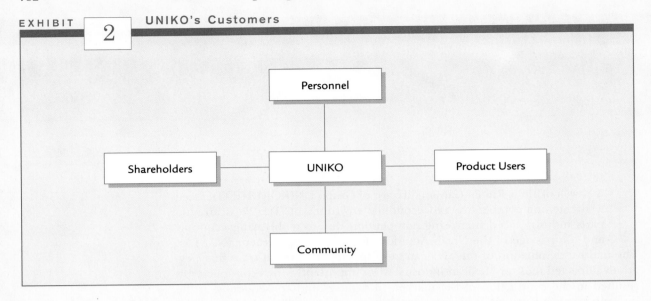

and distributors (aftermarket). As of 1994, exports accounted for only 20 percent of sales while the OEMs and aftermarket accounted for 50 percent and 30 percent, respectively. UNIKO's principal products include Constant Velocity (CV) crankshafts, pistons and related parts, pick-up boxes, valves, and valve lifters. UNIKO is composed of a number of manufacturing subsidiaries (Pistones Moresa, Vel-con, Fomasa, Morestana, Alfisa, Copresa, and Morinsa) and Tecnysia, a systems automation firm. These companies are owned by UNIK, a holding group and subsidiary of DESC, one of the largest Mexican business conglomerates (Exhibit 3).

Grupo UNIKO resulted from the restructuring of SPICER S.A. in January 1994. Before the 1994 restructuring, SPICER was a collection of auto parts companies

EXHIBIT **3**   Mexican Business Conglomerate DESC

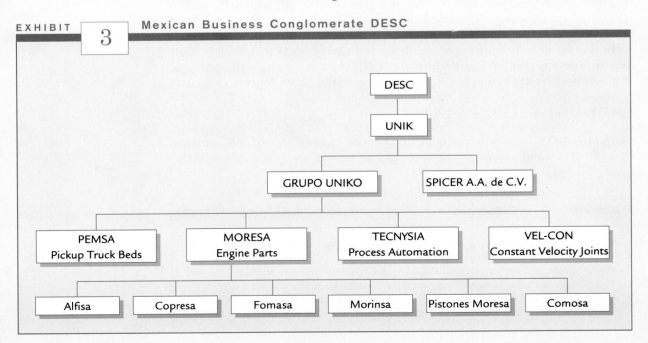

similar to Grupo UNIKO but with a much larger product base. SPICER was a partnership between DESC and the U.S.-based DANA Corporation. The partnership's history traces back to the 1960s, when DANA Corporation joined the Senderos Trouyet Group (now DESC) in a joint venture. In January 1994, DANA Corporation decided to dilute and re-focus its investment to concentrate on its primary fields of interest. This resulted in the formation of UNIK, Grupo UNIKO's parent company, and SPICER S.A. SPICER S.A. manufactures universal joints, axles, drive-shafts, transmissions, and clutches. DANA retained 49 percent ownership of SPICER, and gave up its interest in all but one (Vel-con) of the companies under UNIK.

A critical feature of Grupo UNIKO is its strategic alliance and partnership with several foreign firms. UNIKO is supported by technical agreements with world leaders in the automotive industry. Its foreign technology partners include:

➤ TRW, U.S.A.: Shareholders of MORESA and provider of technical assistance for Valves,
➤ GKN, Europe: Shareholder of Vel-con and provider of technical assistance for CV joints,
➤ UNISIA-JECS, Japan: Provider of technical assistance for Pistons,
➤ FANUC, THK, and PHD, U.S.A.: Provider of technical assistance on Automation, and
➤ AERCOLOGY, U.S.A.: Provider of technical assistance on Environmental Control Systems.

Aside from this technical support, each of Grupo UNIKO's companies has fully developed its own technological capacity in order to provide the best combination of local resources to achieve competitive potential.

UNIKO's Total Quality Philosophy

UNIKO's total quality philosophy (Exhibit 4), shared with the parent company UNIK, dictates that the group must be committed to exceeding the expectations of its four customers (clients, shareholders, personnel, and community), and must emphasize the projection of a consistent company "image" and strategy. Total quality is related to UNIKO's vision (Exhibit 1). In addition, UNIKO's vision involves using customer perception as a platform for the improvement of plans and products and implementing processes in a reliable, structured, and systematized manner. Galván believes that enforcing UNIKO's total quality philosophy will guarantee customer satisfaction and future competitiveness.

EXHIBIT 4   UNIKO's Quality Policy

➤ To serve our customers is the only reason for existence of the company.
➤ Our customers' perception must be the platform to design improved plans.
➤ The expectation of our customers must be exceeded.
➤ It is the leader's task to establish the conditions, plans, structure, and system to assure customer satisfaction.
➤ It is everyone's task to apply our best effort as individuals and through teamwork to achieve the goals.
➤ The key processes shall be robust and continuously updated to optimize response time and value to our customers.

The total quality philosophy is ingrained in the company's strategic objectives that include:

➤ Participation
➤ Productivity
➤ Zero downtime or unscheduled stops
➤ Zero unrecycled scrap and rework
➤ Zero inventory
➤ Zero changeover time

Specifically, the total quality philosophy dictates the following strategies for meeting the needs of each of its customers:

Clients

Total quality demands that UNIKO provide clients with competent service, competitive price, quality, and technological creativity in manufacturing processes, product design and development.

Shareholders

UNIKO aims to meet shareholders' demands for profitability, sales growth, and image. UNIKO's management hopes to achieve a return on investment greater than 15 percent through long-term planning and careful preparation of investment strategies. Similarly, UNIKO hopes to increase sales by creating and implementing an integrated marketing strategy. The projection of a consistent corporate image is a critical aspect of UNIKO's competitive strategy. Rubén Galván has emphasized the importance of maintaining an image of high quality and technological competence. He has admitted that some investments in technology were made mainly to meet customers' wants and expectations, not to satisfy any overriding technical requirement. However, UNIKO also views its investments in technology and automation as a way to achieve discipline and consistency in its processes and quality.

Personnel

Because personnel are also customers, UNIKO has both a short-term and long-term vision on people development. Special emphasis is placed on building a satisfied, productive, and skilled workforce because UNIKO considers it to be the source of current and future competitive advantage. Consequently, UNIKO strives to meet the current and future needs of its workforce, emphasizing long-term people development. Long-term people development involves the use of continuous in-house training. Moreover, UNIKO makes an effort to improve the working environment in its plants, as well as to provide competitive income commensurate with skill levels. Management prefers to increase skills and consequently wages in order to improve the quality of its workforce and reduce turnover. Similarly, UNIKO provides subsidized services such as cafeterias, medical care, and safety.

Community

Rubén Galván states that UNIKO seeks to "establish roots" in the communities in which it operates. Community activities are aimed at creating a "family" environment with the families of its workers as well as other people in the community. Their "community focus" emphasizes active participation, family programs, respect for the environment, and good citizenship. Active participation entails attention to visitors, support to charities, and promotion of symposiums. Family programs include ceremonies, weekend workshops where employees' families obtain handicraft-making skills, as well as the distribution of a company newsletter, "Communiko." UNIKO places strong emphasis on preserving and protecting the environment. Its main concerns involve noise emissions, waste in the plants, and hazardous waste. The firm follows all Mexican, and most U.S., environmental standards and regulations.

Leadership

Effective leadership is a "key issue, a pivot" on which the success of these policies depends, argues Galván. UNIKO stresses leadership in its managers. A "genuine leader" (Exhibit 5) is defined as honest, forward looking (able to conceptualize the vision as shown in Exhibit 1), inspiring (able to explain and energize others with that vision), and competent, both as an individual, and within teams. UNIKO's corporate culture stresses an atmosphere of trust and teamwork, and managers are urged to advance it through respect for employees and with a hands-on egalitarian supervisory style.

The Mexican Auto Parts Industry

The performance of the Mexican auto parts industry has long been tied to that of the Mexican auto industry as a whole. From 1962 to 1983, the industry was

EXHIBIT **5**   UNIKO's Leadership

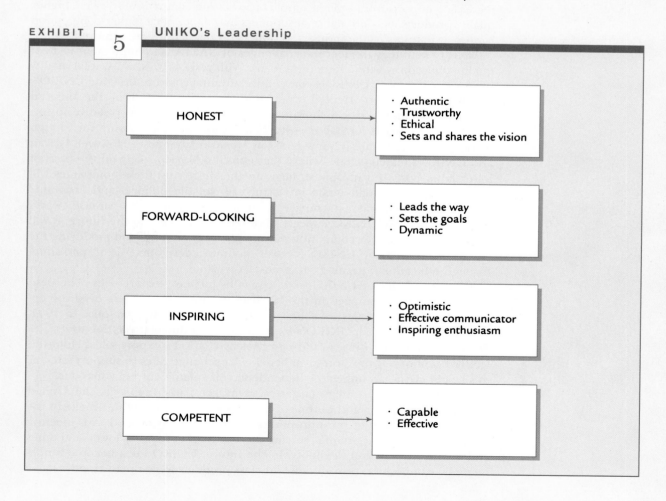

heavily restricted to promote domestic production (import-substitution strategy). For example, required local content level for domestic market vehicles was 60 percent. These local content restrictions, coupled with domestic ownership restrictions (majority Mexican capital), created an industry that was quite small and (by world standards) parochial and inefficient.

The industry is currently in a transitional phase characterized by a trend towards deregulation and liberalization. Beginning in 1989, automotive imports were finally allowed and many domestic content and ownership restrictions were lifted. Local content requirements in terms of value-added in Mexico were reduced to 36 percent. Auto imports were allowed to rise to 15 percent of the market in 1991, with an increase to 20 percent in 1993. With the passage of NAFTA, the 49 percent foreign ownership restriction was lifted in 1999 and all tariffs on imports will be gradually eliminated by 2005.

NAFTA and the Mexican Peso Devaluation

NAFTA and the December 1994 Mexican peso devaluation caused UNIKO to speed up the integration and implementation of its competitive strategy. NAFTA will put added pressure on auto parts suppliers who lack adequate investment in plant, equipment, and technology and who are unable to serve all the needs of assemblers in Mexico. First, NAFTA will further liberalize the auto parts industry by reducing local content requirements, making Mexican firms vulnerable to increasing imports from foreign suppliers possessing competitively priced, higher quality products. Second, national suppliers may experience higher competition from new entrants to the industry as ownership restrictions are removed.

UNIKO's strategy to meet the challenges of NAFTA is to implement its total quality philosophy with a long-term focus. With respect to NAFTA, total quality involves maintaining UNIKO's competitive advantage and redirecting UNIKO's efforts towards export-oriented production. According to Galván, the Mexican auto part suppliers' critical short-term competitive advantage (relative to foreign competition) is low labor costs. NAFTA will open the doors for foreign investors seeking to take advantage of low Mexican labor costs. However, Galván and UNIKO's management believe that entering Mexico solely on the basis of lower labor costs is a myopic strategy. In the short run, these companies will have to cope with inadequate infrastructure, volatile political and economic conditions, and inadequate service from suppliers not up to par with world standards. Because UNIKO expects labor costs to increase in the future, it will attempt to maintain its competitive advantage by developing and modifying the talent of its people. UNIKO stresses in-house development of personnel through educational training programs.

The second tier of UNIKO's strategy is to increase export sales. The peso devaluation and its impact on the Mexican economy has underscored the importance of export sales as a hedge against currency fluctuations. In 1994, Galván recognized that UNIKO's exposure to peso fluctuations, due to its U.S. dollar denominated debt, would be offset by UNIKO's export sales. However, UNIKO cannot rely on short-term beneficial exchange rates to support sales, as this would create an unhealthy dependence on volatile currency markets.

UNIKO's export strategy targets aftermarket parts supply in the United States, Latin America, and Europe. UNIKO is seeking to establish a niche in the aftermarket because of the transportation difficulties associated with meeting OEM needs. Most importantly, serving the aftermarket requires lower lead times and greater production flexibility. In the future, UNIKO must become fundamentally competitive, providing world class products at competitive prices.

UNIKO's Manufacturing Facilities and Corporate Philosophy

UNIKO's plants follow the focused factory design concept. Each plant is relatively small and produces an individual product line. The average workforce is around 400, and no plant has more than 1,000 employees. The relatively small size of these plants is designed to promote close, cooperative working environments and to take advantage of efficiencies of scale. A smaller workforce is more easily monitored by management. Because the company's workers are located in different facilities, instead of housed in one large plant, the strength of the workers' union is minimized. The focused factory concept is carried even further in the manufacture of pistons. Aftermarket production is located at the Morinsa factory, which is separate from OEM production at Pistones Moresa.

Rubén Galván admits that not all of UNIKO's plants have equal quality standards or similar levels of modern technology investment, that is, the same level of competitiveness. He estimates that 80 percent of UNIKO's plants are not up to world standards for competitiveness and that 60 percent are not as modern as Pistones Moresa and Vel-con (UNIKO's two most modern plants). Galván recognizes that in order for UNIKO's plants to become fundamentally competitive, they must be willing to restructure in a way that permits the implementation of the UNIKO vision. Galván believes that it is not the lag in technology that puts the less competitive plants in danger, but the inability or unwillingness of the people in the plants to accept change and adopt the total quality philosophy.

Technology and People: Finding the Appropriate Mix

Grupo UNIKO has implemented in its organization a mix of technological and human assets that it feels are appropriate for Mexico.

Technology

In the field of high-precision parts manufacturing, technology means automated machining and Computerized Numerical Control (CNC) equipment. UNIKO has an in-house division, Tecnysia, that custom develops such systems for the firm. Tecnysia upgrades and adapts second-hand U.S. and European robotics with custom electronic control systems. This approach is more cost effective than buying new systems and paying outside vendors to adapt them to UNIKO's purposes. It also allows for the development of special-use tools and machinery proprietary to the firm, an advantage not easily duplicated by its competition.

The use of an inside vendor to design systems is as much a part of UNIKO's technology development strategy as any other cost factor. UNIKO is trying to build a capability for technology. "We're trying to grow roots, not just be a low-cost opportunity," says Rubén Galván.

UNIKO needs to use automated manufacturing systems. Automated systems create quality and, when properly designed and configured, can perform complex machining operations at high speed without error. However, the "atmosphere of discipline" that automation creates for the customer is equally important. Many customers demand a high level of automation, because automation is perceived as a hallmark of quality. Customer perceptions and needs must drive improvements. This is part of UNIKO's quality policy. The use of in-house technology also develops workforce skills.

People

UNIKO believes in investing in its workforce. Training is a primary component of this policy. At the firm's Cedei training centers, workers receive basic theory training in pneumatics, hydraulics, electronics, and electrical and mechanical systems. This training starts before they ever step on to the factory floor. They also receive instruction on how to operate machinery and controls. Most employees also receive extensive diagnostic and preventative maintenance training. Such training in both theory and systems avoids the information obsolescence, which is common in machine-specific instruction programs.

Tecnysia works with line employees to design and install new equipment and systems. This process requires knowledgeable employees with broad-based skills. Workers are encouraged to redesign their own jobs, in order to increase both efficiency and quality. This demands high skill levels. Furthermore, implementing the firm's quality philosophy requires that key processes be continuously updated. Continuous upgrading of manufacturing, design, and development processes are required to satisfy the needs of UNIKO's clients.

Outside observers still might wonder why UNIKO has invested so much in its workers, given the low Mexican wage rates and huge labor pool. Labor costs are a big advantage for UNIKO (vis-à-vis U.S. and European competitors). But the firm's leadership has realized that this advantage is not a long-term one. As the Mexican economy develops, Mexican labor rates will eventually rise to parity with those in the industrialized world. In line with the firm's ambition to become a long-term leader, it must develop labor as a resource and not as a commodity. "Training is the key to our development," says Galván.

In order to retain skilled workers, UNIKO realizes that compensation is an important factor. Employees are rewarded through initial hourly pay of over three times the national minimum wage, with a regular series of increases, a program of subsidized meals through the company cafeteria, free comprehensive health care, family education, and limited profit sharing.

Highly trained workers are valuable. Good benefits help keep them. UNIKO has largely succeeded in its goal to retain its human investments. Company-wide, UNIKO's employees stay an average of 8–10 years.

Plant working environment is also an important factor in employee retention and motivation. The firm does not use any type of time-based supervision. Management has discovered that the timecard system, formerly used throughout the firm, cost more to implement than the absenteeism it was designed to curtail. Current absenteeism levels are below industry standards.

UNIKO has discovered that its employees are concerned about the safety and environment of their working area. The company uses sensor technology and extensive training to avoid on-the-job accidents. Working areas are kept clean, are well lit by natural and artificial light, and are decorated with plants and artwork created by employees and their families at the company-run continuing education facilities. Managers make themselves approachable to line employees by involving themselves in day-to-day plant floor operations. Galván espouses management by "walking around." He believes that his managers must maintain regular contact with operations to detect problems as soon as they occur. A good manager must, in Galván's words, develop "a sense of smell" for trouble.

A Closer Look: Pistones Moresa and Vel-con

Pistones Moresa and Vel-con are two of UNIKO's most modern, technologically advanced plants.

Pistones Moresa

The Pistones Moresa plant is located in Celaya, about 260 kilometers from Mexico City. It is a modern facility that produces aluminum pistons for original equipment manufacturers. Most of the automotive companies in Mexico, including Chrysler, Nissan, GM, Ford, and Volkswagen are customers of Pistones Moresa.

The plant is maintained as a clean, open, well-lit facility. Artwork from employees is displayed in offices and on various walls throughout the factory. Clean, lively fish tanks can be seen from many of the offices. The plant atmosphere helps to maintain positive employee morale and provides an impression of quality and professionalism to both employees and visitors.

Piston Manufacturing Press

The piston manufacturing process consists of (1) production of piston castings and (2) machining of the castings.

1. *Production of piston castings*

Pistons are cast from aluminum alloy of specified composition. Currently, castings used are produced at the plant or are shipped from UNIKO's Alfisa plant in Huehuetoca. Management plans to eventually produce all of the required castings on site.

The castings made at the plant are produced in one of two automated cellular stations. Each station contains three large vats of liquid aluminum alloy mounted on a rotating platform. A pair of robotic arms alternately removes liquid from one of the vats while the others are refilled and tested for proper aluminum alloy composition. Testing is performed in a nearby room with state of the art chemical and optical analysis. Each robotic arm pours liquid alloy into a casting mold. Two molds, each with four cavities, are alternately filled by a single robotic arm. This alternate filling speeds up the manufacturing process since one mold can be filled while the other cools to the proper temperature. Once a mold has cooled to the proper temperature, the castings are automatically removed.

2. *Machining of the castings*

The majority of the plant's operations are concentrated on machining the rough castings to specified dimensions. The plant contains a total of 12 machining lines: six manual, four semi-automatic, and two recently installed fully-automatic lines. The semi-automatic lines are set up in a U-shaped structure that allows individual workers to perform more than one operation.

Two technicians are required to maintain the operation of the automatic lines. Each of the machine stations has its own control panel and lights to indicate if the machine is running properly (green) or if there is some sort of problem (red). If a problem develops in one of the machines, the entire line is shut down until it can be resolved by one of the technicians.

To maintain tight tolerances in the final product, and to avoid any expansion or contraction of the metal, the pistons must be kept at a constant temperature of 20°C throughout the milling process. The pistons are bathed in a solvent solution prior to each stage in the machining process, and held in the solution until they reach the exact temperature for machining. The solution is also used to cool the cutting heads.

Once the machining is completed, workers check each of the pistons to ensure they are within the required weight tolerances. If the weight is too great, small amounts of material are machined from the piston in order to reduce its weight to a specified level.

Workers at the end of the lines insert offset pins (produced at UNIKO's Copresa plant near Mexico City) into the pistons and then package them for shipping.

Additional Characteristics of the Plant

The automated machining lines are not dedicated to individual customers. In fact, minimal changeover time on these lines allows several models to be produced during a given shift. Changeover time for the manual lines is much greater, which results in more dedication of these lines to specific products. Pistones Moresa is continuing to work towards a goal of 100 percent flexibility in all of its lines.

To maintain levels of product quality on the manual lines comparable to that of the automated lines, the manual lines are operated at a slower production rate. The manual lines run at about half of the speed of the fully automated line. By operating at a level lower than the maximum possible rate, workers are able to maintain required levels of product quality.

Pistones practices predictive (not preventive) maintenance to keep machines up and running. Engineers chart equipment performance to head off the kind of irregular or atypical failures that preventive maintenance is able to forestall.

Vel-con

The Vel-con plant is located near Pistones Moresa and produces Constant Velocity (CV) joints for front-wheel-drive and four-wheel-drive vehicles. Unlike pistons, CV joints are composed of a number of different components assembled at the plant. The facility produces in excess of 120 different product assemblies. Vel-con has an information center inside the main factory floor entrance where employees can peruse sales, quality, and product charts, along with other displays and reviews. The facility has a similar environment to that of Pistones, with extensive natural lighting and a large amount of greenery.

Market Information

Vel-con produces 55 percent of its products for the original equipment manufacturer market and 45 percent for the aftermarket. They have a 97 percent OEM market share and control 87 percent of the aftermarket. Aftermarket parts are manufactured to the same exacting quality standards demanded by OEM consumers. Price is the primary selling point in the aftermarket.

In general, domestic (Mexican) steel quality is lower than that of other countries, so most steel bar stock is imported. The plant has almost 60 suppliers and over 153 distributors for its finished products. Average inventory for finished goods is 30 days.

Production Techniques

Production is not labor intensive, but instead relies heavily on automation. Emphasis is placed on having one interrelated and flexible production line rather than separate stations. Each line can handle components for up to four different types of joints at a time. Components are tracked through a system of magnetically coded assembly platforms, each of which carries four units. Vel-con is currently working on the development and installation of parallel assembly lines to increase the flexibility of this process.

Vel-con conducts most of its development work separate from Tecnysia. The in-house engineering staff allows the division to move from idea to finished process in about two months. Vel-con also charts each employee's skill level and encourages them to learn as many skills as possible. This allows management to move workers from one task to another in response to changes in production volume or special setup needs.

Environmental Issues

All of the plant's waste products are thoroughly treated. The machine tools are constantly bathed in a solution of water and a chemical solvent that carries away heat and metal shavings. At a plant facility, the shavings are collected for recycling and the solvent is extracted for reuse. Oil, which is washed from the tools, is removed in a bacterial holding tank. The remaining wastewater is settled out and chemically purified. The facility's power plant meets EPA emissions standards.

A Competitive Balance

UNIKO has adopted a mixture of high technology and human skill in its production processes. Advanced technology is essential to survival in the newly globalized auto parts market. Skilled personnel give the firm flexibility and allow it to constantly update and improve its processes. Through a combination of strategic alliances, export-derived capital, and forward focused leadership, UNIKO is reinventing itself. It is in transition from being a fairly typical producer of highly technical products in a parochial market to becoming a world-class fabricator of competitive parts for global assemblers. UNIKO is adapting to the changing needs and faces of its customers, becoming, in the process, a customer-driven company. UNIKO's leadership realizes the promise and perils posed by NAFTA and it's making the investments necessary to weather these and other uncertainties of the Mexican economy. The ultimate challenge, however, is for all of UNIKO's plants to complete the transition and become globally competitive.

Source: Stephen M. Hills, G. Keong Leong, and P. Roberto Garcia, *Cases in International Business: A Focus on Emerging Markets.* West Publishing Co., St. Paul, MN:1996. Copyright © 1996 by West Publishing Co. Used with permission of the authors.

CASE DISCUSSION QUESTIONS

1. The director of Grupo UNIKO, Rubén Galván, does not believe that new technology and its financing are the main problems confronting the Mexican auto-parts industry. In contrast, he believes that the most important problem is human resources. Show how the case reflects Galván's belief.

2. Previous policies of import substitution in Mexico allowed auto-parts firms to develop in an environment in which they did not have to be terribly sensitive to their customers. Firms were relatively paternalistic, and the workforce was not presumed to have much interest in managerial decisions. Show how UNIKO has departed from these old assumptions in some instances but in others reflects past practices.

3. Show how the current approach can be problematic given Mexico's cultural values. What can be done to make the transition to the current approach easier?

4. Based on Mexico's culture and suggested leadership styles discussed in the text, assess Galván's approach to leadership.

Old Corporate Ways Fade as New Korean Generation Asserts Itself

Until a few years ago, there was an unwritten rule about working hours at South Korea's leading food and beverage company. "Everyone sat at their desks, fidgeting and waiting for their superiors to leave. Assistant managers waited for managers to leave. The managers waited for the bosses upstairs to leave," said Kim Jang-ok, 40, a customer service manager at Cheil Jedang Corp.

So for Kim, Lee Wook-jae presents a cultural shock. Lee, a 27-year-old assistant marketing manager, doesn't wait for the bosses. He leaves when he pleases. He also comes to work in khaki pants and an open-necked shirt, a cell telephone dangling from a cord around his neck. His black hair is dyed chestnut brown with yellow strains. "I want to be judged by what I do for the company, not by my hairstyle," Lee said.

Thanks to young office workers such as Lee, a growing number of companies are abandoning South Korea's rigid corporate culture for a global one. Staid old "Korea, Inc." isn't dead. Most companies still prefer top-down management. Sons inherit businesses from fathers. Most employees address each other by their titles. Suits with ties are standard attire in most offices. The rise of Internet startups with their casual, egalitarian ways, the new generation of assertive youths entering the job market, and the disintegration of some of the country's top conglomerates has also undermined old hierarchies.

Lee, who majored in business management at the Ohio State University, is among thousands of Koreans returning home every year armed with U.S. college diplomas and Western ways. "When I first dyed my hair some months ago, everyone in the office looked at me as if I did something wrong," said Lee. "After a while, they accepted it. Now they even comment on how well my latest color came out."

Women are making halting progress, too, in male-oriented corporate Korea. They still earn less and are promoted less, but "We no longer deliver coffee for male workers. That ended three or four years ago. We get more chances to demonstrate our abilities," said Kim Yoon-hee, 28, a colleague of Lee's at Cheil Jedang. "Still, many men look uncomfortable to talk business with women," she said. "When I sit down for contract negotiations, for example, some of the men across the table first give me a look that says, 'What is this woman doing here?'"

The old system was shaken to its roots during the Asian economic crisis of the late 1990s. People began questioning whether staffers trained to think alike were flexible enough to react to sharp global market changes. "It was not uncommon for the one-man boss to shout at a lower-ranking official briefing him, 'Who's this fool? Get out!'" said Choi Hae-pyong, describing his management experience at an electronic components arm of South Korea's largest conglomerate, Samsung. At 39, Choi is beyond dying his hair, but is still adventurous enough to have quit Samsung last year with two colleagues to start their own business, making components for flat-panel computer screens. At Samsung, he said, "They put brutal pressure on employees to force good results. But under such a system, you try to keep the status quo and not make any mistakes. You don't try to be creative.

"Now I no longer have the safety of working in big business. But at least now I work for myself. I feel good," Choi said.

These days, more companies are urging their employees to get lean and creative. Big corporations such as Cheil Jedang, LG Electronics and SK encourage workers to shed sober suits and stiff ties. They also have abolished many executive posts, to speed up decision making. At Cheil Jedang, gone are big desks and long titles for managers. Individual merit determines wage increases and promotion. Workers who used to say "Mr. Manager Kim" now say "Mr. Kim." Employees in casual attire sit with legs crossed and talk business—in a stark contrast to other big business offices where employees still work in suits and ties, and young staffers bow to the boss or stand at attention. "In the past, everybody dressed and looked more or less the same. Everybody got promoted at the same time and had the same salary increases," said Kim, the customer service manager. "In the old days, you got to the senior managers only when you were summoned," he said. "Now, we see young employees going directly to senior managers with opinions. For example, they come to me to ask for more responsible jobs, rather than the dull work of typing data into the computer."

Until recently, working for the nation's top conglomerates conferred status. Now, more college graduates prefer Internet startups and foreign businesses. "Loyalty to the company used to be a big motto and your life centered on what you did at the company," said Ha Il-won, a mid-level manager at a construction arm of the SK conglomerate. "But the Asian financial crisis shattered our illusion about lifetime employment at one company. We became more individualistic." Previously, companies hired students with good school grades and required them to pass a written test. Today, many recruiters are just as likely to choose independent people who have traveled or worked abroad.

"Interviewers were more interested in listening to what I had to say than asking standard questions. They asked me what I thought of anti-globalization activists," said Park Ji-sook, 24, a French major who was hired by LG Electronics while protests were going on against the World Trade Organization meeting in Seattle in late 1999. Park said she spoke well of the activists' success in attracting media attention to their demands through the well-publicized protests.

The company made her an editor of its Internet Web site.

CASE DISCUSSION QUESTIONS

1. What institutional factors are driving changes in Korean business culture?

2. How can organizations in a culture that values respect for age differences manage the changes that occur when organizational necessities require that younger mangers supervise older managers?

3. How will Korean companies manage more individualistic employees without loosing the competitive advantage of a loyal workforce?

Source: Choe, Sang-Hun. 2001. Associated Press. http://www.asianweek.com/2001_02_02/biz4_koreanbizculture.html

Achievement versus ascription How a society grants or gives status.

Achievement-motivation theory Suggestion that only some people have the need to win in competitive situations or to exceed a standard of excellence.

Afro-centric model of leadership African leadership model emphasizing person-centered styles based on collectivism and group-centeredness.

Anchor partner A partner that holds back the development of a successful strategic alliance because it cannot or will not provide its share of the funding.

Asia-Pacific Economic Cooperation (APEC) A confederation of 19 nations with less specific agreements on trade facilitation in the Pacific region.

Attitudinal commitment The willingness to dedicate resources and efforts and face risks to make the alliance work.

Attribution Process by which people interpret the meaning and intent of spoken words or nonverbal exchanges.

Attributional approach to leadership Emphasis on what leaders believe causes subordinates' behaviors.

Autocratic leadership Leaders make all major decisions themselves.

Autonomous work group Team or unit that has nearly complete responsibility for a particular task.

B2B Business-to-business transactions.

B2C Business-to-consumer transactions.

Back stage of culture Aspects of culture that are understood only by insiders or members of the culture.

Backdoor recruitment Prospective employees are friends or relatives of those already employed.

Back-front hybrid structure Splits the value chain into worldwide product divisions for upstream activities and geographical units for downstream activities.

Balance-sheet method Attempts to equate purchasing power in the host country with the expatriate's purchasing power in his or her home country.

Benevolent trust The confidence that the partner will behave with good will and with fair exchange.

Bonus system In Japan, employees often receive up to 30 percent of their base salary, usually given twice a year during traditional gift-giving seasons.

Born-global firms Firms that generate a significant portion of their revenues from international sales the day they are founded.

Brick-and-mortar Traditional or non-virtual business operation.

Buddhism Religious tradition that focuses primarily on the reality of world suffering and the ways one can be freed from suffering.

Building a relationship The first stage of the actual negotiation process, when negotiators concentrate on social and interpersonal matters.

Bureaucratic control system Focuses on managing organizational processes through budgets, statistical reports, standard operations procedures, and centralization of decision making.

Business culture Norms, values, and beliefs that pertain to all aspects of doing business in a culture.

Business-level strategies Those for a single business operation.

C2B Consumer-to-business transactions.

C2C Consumer-to-consumer transactions.

Calculative commitment Alliance partner evaluations, expectations, and concerns regarding potential rewards from the relationship.

Capabilities The ability to assemble and coordinate resources effectively.

Capitalist or market economy System where production is decentralized to private owners who carry out these activities to make profits.

Christianity Religion based on the life and teachings of Jesus.

Co-determination Surrender by management to workers of a share of control of the organization, traditionally reserved for management and owners.

Coercive isomorphism Social institutions coerce or force organizations to adopt certain practices.

Cognitive social institution Refers to the widely shared knowledge regarding how things are done in a society.

Collectivism A set of cultural values that views people largely in terms of the groups to which they belong.

Commitment In a strategic alliance, occurs when partners take care of each other and put forth extra effort to make the venture work.

Comparative advantage That arising from cost, quality, or resource advantages associated with a particular nation.

Compensation Organization's entire reward package, including not only financial rewards and benefits but nontangible rewards, such as job security.

Competitive advantage When a company can outmatch its rivals in attracting and maintaining its targeted customers.

Competitive negotiation Each side tries to give as little as possible and tries to "win" for its side.

Competitive scope How broadly a firm targets its products or services.

Competitive strategies Moves multinationals use to defeat competitors.

Competitor analysis Profiles of your competitor's strategies and objectives.

Complementary skill One that enhances but does not necessarily duplicate an alliance partner's skills.

Concession making Process requiring each side to relax some of its demands to meet the other party's needs.

Consultative or participative leadership Leader's style falls midway between autocratic and democratic styles.

Contingency theory Assumption that different styles and different leaders are more appropriate for different situations.

Contract manufacturers Produce products for foreign companies following the foreign companies' specifications.

Control system Vertical organizational links, up and down the organizational hierarchy.

Convenient relativism What occurs when companies use the logic of ethical relativism to behave any way they please, using the excuse of differences in cultures.

Convergence Increasing similarity of management practices in different nations.

Coordination system Horizontal organizational links.

Copycat businesses Those following the "Me too" strategy, whereby they adopt existing strategies for providing products or services.

Corporate-level strategies How companies choose their mixture of different businesses.

Counter-parry Fending off a competitor's attack in one country by attacking in another country, usually the competitor's home country.

Country clusters Groups of countries with similar cultural patterns.

Craft union Represents people from one occupational group, such as plumbers.

Credibility trust The confidence that the partner has the intent and ability to meet promised obligations and commitments.

Cross-cultural training Increases the relational abilities of future expatriates and, in some cases, their spouses and families.

Cultural beliefs Our understandings about what is true.

Cultural control system Uses organizational culture to control behaviors and attitudes of employees.

Cultural norms Prescribed and proscribed behaviors, telling us what we can do and what we cannot do.

Cultural Paradoxes Situations contradicting cultural prescriptions.

Cultural relativism A philosophical position arguing that all cultures, no matter how different, are correct and moral for the people of those cultures.

Cultural rituals Ceremonies such as baptism, graduation, or the tricks played on a new worker, or the pledge to a sorority or fraternity.

Cultural stories These include such things as nursery rhymes and traditional legends.

Cultural symbols These may be physical, such as national flags or holy artifacts. In the workplace, office size and location can serve as cultural symbols.

Cultural values Values that tell us such things as what is good, what is beautiful, what is holy, and what are legitimate goals for life.

Culture The pervasive and shared beliefs, norms, and values that guide the everyday life of a group.

Customer contact techniques Trade shows, catalog expositions, international advertising agencies and consulting firms, government-sponsored trade missions, and direct contact.

Decision-making control Level in the organizational hierarchy where managers have the authority to make decisions.

Defensive competitive strategies Attempts to reduce the risks of being attacked, convince an attacking firm to seek other targets, or blunt the impacts of any attack.

Deinfluentization Reduced use of influence tactics.

Democratic leadership Leader includes subordinates in decision making.

Deontological ethical theory Focus on actions that, by themselves, have a good or bad morality regardless of the outcomes they produce.

Differentiation strategy Strategy based on finding ways to provide superior value to customers.

Direct communication Communication that comes to the point and lacks ambiguity.

Direct contact Face-to-face interaction of employees.

Direct exporting More aggressive exporting strategy, where exporters take on the duties of intermediaries and make direct contact with customers in the foreign market.

Dirty tricks Negotiation tactics that pressure opponents to accept unfair or undesirable agreements or concessions.

Dispersed subunits Subsidiaries located anywhere in the world where they can most benefit the company.

Distinctive competencies Strengths that allow companies to outperform rivals.

Dominant partner The partner that controls or dominates strategic and operational decision making.

Dual system Form of vocational education in Germany that combines in-house apprenticeship training with part-time vocational-school training, and leads to a skilled certificate.

e.HR system Automation of various aspects of the Human Resources system of a company.

E-commerce enablers Fulfillment specialists that provide other companies with services such as Web site translation.

E-commerce security Degree to which customers feel that their private and personal information are safeguarded by companies collecting such information.

E-commerce The selling of goods or services over the Internet.

Economic analysis Of an ethical problem, focuses on what is the best decision for a company's profits.

Economic system System of beliefs (concerning work, property, and wealth), activities (extraction, production, and distribution), organizations (business firms, labor unions) and relationships (ownership, management) that provide the goods and services consumed by the members of a society.

Education Organized networks of socialization experiences which prepare individuals to act in society.

Elephant-and-ant complex Occurs in strategic alliances when two companies are greatly unequal in size.

Emerging Markets Rapidly growing countries between developing and developed economies.

Enterprise union Represents all people in one organization, regardless of occupation or location.

Entrepreneur Person who creates new ventures that seek profit and growth.

Entry wedge Company's competitive advantage for breaking into the established pattern of commercial activity.

Equity theory Proposal that people perceive the fairness of their rewards vis-a-vis their inputs based on how they compare themselves to others.

ERG theory Simplified hierarchy of needs, including growth needs, relatedness needs, and existence needs.

Escalation of commitment Companies continue in an alliance relationship longer than necessary because of past financial and emotional investments.

Ethical analysis One that goes beyond focusing on profit goals and legal regulations.

Ethical convergence Refers to the growing pressures for multi-national companies to follow the same rules in managing ethical behavior and social responsibility.

Ethical relativism Theory that each society's view of ethics must be considered legitimate and ethical.

Ethical universalism Theory that there are basic moral principles that transcend cultural and national boundaries.

Ethics gap Idea that U.S. political and legal social institutions create greater coercive and normative pressures for U.S. businesses to follow ethical standards.

Ethnocentric IHRM All aspects of HRM for managers and technical workers tend to follow the parent organization's home-country HRM practices.

Ethnocentrism When people from one culture believe that theirs are the only correct norms, values, and beliefs.

European Union (EU) Austria, Belgium, Britain, Denmark, Finland, France, Germany, Greece, Ireland, Italy, Luxembourg, the Netherlands, Portugal, Spain, and Sweden, plus Norway and Switzerland in the related European Free Trade Area.

Expatriate Employee who comes from a different country from where he or she is working.

Expectancy theory Assumption that motivation includes an individual's desire to satisfy his or her needs and their beliefs regarding how much their efforts at work will eventually satisfy their needs.

Explicit Knowledge Knowledge that can be found in records or databases and that can be easily transferred.

Export department Coordinates and controls a company's export operations.

Export Management Company (EMC) Intermediary specializing in particular types of products or particular countries or regions.

Export Trading Company (ETC) Intermediary similar to emc, but it usually takes title to the product before exporting.

Extrinsic Work Values Preference for security aspects of jobs such as income and job security.

Fair exchange In a strategic alliance, occurs when partners believe that they receive benefits from the relationship equal to their contributions.

Fiedler's theory of leadership Proposal that success of task- or person-centered leader depends on relationships between the leader and his or her subordinates; the degree that subordinates' tasks are easily and clearly defined; and the officially granted organizational power of the leader.

Final agreement Signed contract, agreeable to all sides.

First offer First proposal by parties of what they expect from the agreement.

First-mover advantage That of the entrepreneur who moves quickly into a new venture and establishes the business before other companies can react to the opportunity.

Foreign Corrupt Practices Act (FCPA) Forbids U.S. companies to make or offer illegal payments or gifts to officials of foreign governments for the sake of getting or retaining business.

Foreign direct investment (FDI) Multinational firm's ownership, in part or in whole, of an operation in another country.

Foreign direct investment (FDI) Multinational firm's ownership, in part or in whole, of an operation in another country.

Foreign subsidiary Subunit of the multinational company that is located in another country.

Formal communication Communication that acknowledges rank, titles, and ceremony in prescribed social interaction.

Formal international cooperative alliance A nonequity alliance with formal contracts specifying what each company must contribute to the relationship.

Front stage of culture The easily observable aspect of culture.

Full-time integrator Cross-unit coordination is the main job responsibility.

Functional structure Has departments or subunits based on separate business functions, such as marketing or manufacturing.

Fundamental attribution error Assumption by managers that people behave in certain ways because of internal motivations, rather than outside factors.

General Agreement on Tariffs and Trade (GATT) Tariff negotiations between several nations that reduced the average worldwide tariff on manufactured goods.

Generic strategies Basic ways that both domestic and multinational companies keep and achieve competitive advantage.

Geographic structure Has departments or subunits based on geographical regions.

Global culture Managerial and worker values that view strategic opportunities as global and not just domestic.

Global IHRM Recruiting and selecting worldwide, and assigning the best managers to international assignments regardless of nationality.

Global integration solution Conducting business similarly throughout the world, and locating company units wherever there is high quality and low cost.

Global leader One who has the skills and abilities to interact with and manage people from diverse cultural backgrounds.

Global mindset One that requires managers to "think globally, but act locally."

Global pay system Worldwide job evaluations, performance appraisal methods, and salary scales are used.

Global platform Country location where a firm can best perform some, but not necessarily all, of its value-chain activities.

Global start-up or born-global firm Company that begins as a multinational company.

Globalization drivers Conditions in an industry that favor transnational or international strategies over multilocal or regional strategies.

Globalization The worldwide trend of economic integration across boarder allowing businesses to expand beyond their domestic boundaries.

Global–local dilemma Choice between a local-responsiveness or global approach to a multinational's strategies.

Goal-directed behavior One that people use with the intention of satisfying a need.

Goal-setting theory Assumption that the mere existence of a goal is motivating.

Great-person theory Idea that leaders are born with unique characteristics that make them quite different from ordinary people.

Greenfield investments Starting foreign operations from scratch.

Haptics or Touching Basic form of human interaction, including shaking hands, embracing, or kissing when greeting one another.

Headquarters-based compensation system Paying home country wages regardless of location.

Hierarchy of needs theory States that people have five basic types of needs: physiological, security, affiliation, esteem, and self-actualization.

High-context language One in which people state things indirectly and implicitly.

Hinduism Acceptance of the ancient traditions of India that are based on the Vedic scriptures.

Hofstede model of national culture A cultural model mainly based on differences in values and beliefs regarding work goals.

Holistic approach Each side makes very few, if any, concessions until the end of the negotiation.

Home country nationals Expatriate employees who come from the parent firm's home country.

Host country nationals Local workers who come from the host country where the unit (plant, sales unit, etc.) is located.

Host-based compensation system Adjusting wages to local lifestyles and costs of living.

Human resource management (HRM) Functions are recruitment, selection, training and development, performance appraisal, compensation, and labor relations.

Hybrid structure Mixes functional, geographic, and product units.

ICA International cooperative alliance.

Ideological union Represents all types of workers based on some particular ideology (e.g., communism) or religious orientation.

IHRM orientation Company's basic tactics and philosophy for coordinating IHRM activities for managerial and technical workers.

IJV and ICA performance criteria Often must include criteria other than financial, such as organizational learning.

IJV negotiation issues Include points such as equity contributions, management structure, and "prenuptial" agreements regarding dissolution of the relationship.

IJV International joint venture.

Implicit Knowledge Knowledge that resides within employees and dependent on the organization's context.

Independent management structure Alliance managers act more like managers from a separate company.

Index of economic freedom Determines the extent of governmental intervention in a country.

Indirect exporter Uses intermediaries or go-between firms to provide the knowledge and contacts necessary to sell overseas.

Individualism The relationship between the individual and the group in society.

Induced-factor conditions National resources created by a nation, such as a superior educational system.

Industrial society Characterized by the dominance of the secondary or manufacturing sectors.

Industrial union Represents all people in a particular industry, regardless of occupational type.

Industrialization Cultural and economic changes that occur because of how production is organized and distributed in society.

Influence tactics Tactical behaviors leaders use to influence subordinates.

Informal international cooperative alliance An agreement not legally binding between companies to cooperate on any value-chain activity.

Inpatriate Employees from foreign countries who work in the country where the parent company is located.

Interdependent relationships Continuous sharing of information and resources by dispersed and specialized subunits.

Internal versus external control Beliefs regarding whether one controls one's own fate.

International business ethics Those unique ethical problems faced by managers conducting business operations across national boundaries.

International cadre Separate group of expatriate managers who specialize in a career of international assignments.

International cooperative alliance (ICA) An agreement for cooperation between two or more companies from different nations that does not set up a legally separate company.

International division Responsible for managing exports, international sales, and foreign subsidiaries.

International Entrepreneurship Discovery, evaluation and exploitation of new market opportunities at the international level.

International franchising Comprehensive licensing agreement where the franchisor grants to the franchisee the use of a whole business operation.

International human resource management (IHRM) All HRM functions, adapted to the international setting.

International joint venture (IJV) A separate legal entity in which two or more companies from different nations have ownership positions.

International sales intensity Amount of international sales divided by total sales of the company.

International strategic alliance Agreement between two or more firms from different countries to cooperate in any value-chain activity from r&d to sales.

International strategies Selling global products and using similar marketing techniques worldwide.

Internet hosts Computers connected to the Internet with its own IP address.

Interpreter's role To ensure the accuracy and common understanding of written and oral agreements.

Intrinsic work values Preference for openness to change job aspects such as autonomy, being able to take initiative and be creative.

Islam Religion based on the submission of the will to Allah (God).

ISO 9001:2000 The current name for the technical and quality standards of the International Organization for Standardization.

Job-characteristics model Suggests that work is more motivating when managers enrich core job characteristics, such as by increasing number of skills a job requires.

Key success factors (KSFs) Important characteristics of a company or its product that lead to success in an industry.

Key success factors for expatriate assignments Motivation, relational abilities, family situation, and language skills.

Kinesics Communication through body movements.

Knowledge Management Systems and mechanisms to ensure that the right form of knowledge is available to the right individual at the right time.

Labor relations Ongoing relationship between an employer and those employees represented by labor organizations.

Leadership Process of influencing group members to achieve organizational goals.

Legal analysis Of an ethical problem, focuses on only meeting legal requirements of host and parent countries.

Less developed countries (LDCs) The poorest nations, often plagued with unstable political regimes, high unemployment, and low worker skills.

Levels of culture These include national, business, and occupational and organizational culture.

Liability of foreignness Challenges facing small companies due to lack of knowledge of local market.

Liability of newness A large percentage of new businesses fail within a year.

Liability of smallness The challenges facing small businesses in getting access to necessary resources to internationalize.

Liaison role Part of a person's job in one department to communicate with people in another department.

Licensing Contractual agreement between a domestic licenser and a foreign licensee (licenser usually has a valuable patent, technological know-how, trademark, or company name that it provides to the foreign licensee).

Local union Represents one occupational group in one company.

Localized website Websites that are adapted to the local cultures.

Local-responsiveness solution Responding to differences in the markets in all the countries in which a company operates.

Location advantages Dispersing value-chain activities anywhere in the world where the company can do them best or cheapest.

Long-term orientation A basic orientation toward time that values patience.

Low-context language One in which people state things directly and explicitly.

Low-cost strategy Producing products or services equal to those of competitors at a lower cost than competitors.

Market transition Changes societies go through as they move from socialism to a market based economy.

Masculinity Tendency of a society to emphasize traditional gender roles.

Meister In Germany, a master technician.

Metanational structure An evolution of the transnational network structure that develops extensive systems to encourage organizational learning and entrepreneurial activities.

Micro-multinational Company that uses web technology and the Internet to go global from the day it is founded.

Mimetic isomorphism Organizations purposefully copy the strategies of the most successful organizations.

Minireplica subsidiary Smaller version of the parent company, using the same technology and producing the same products as the parent company.

Mixed economy Combines aspects of capitalist and socialist economies.

Moral languages Description of the basic ways that people use to think about ethical decisions and to explain their ethical choices.

Motivation A psychological process resulting in goal-directed behavior that satisfies human needs.

Motivator-hygiene theory Assumption that a job has two basic characteristics, motivators and hygiene factors.

Multidomestic strategy Emphasizing local-responsiveness issues.

Multinational company Any company that engages in business functions beyond its domestic borders.

Multinational management The formulation of strategies and the design of management systems that successfully take advantage of international opportunities and respond to international threats.

National context National culture and social institutions that influence how managers make decisions regarding the strategies of their organizations.

National culture The dominant culture within the political boundaries of the nation-state.

National-context contingency model of leadership Shows how culture and related social institutions affect leadership practices.

Natural-factor conditions National resources that occur naturally, such as abundant water supply.

Need theory Of motivation, assumes that people can satisfy basic human needs in the work setting.

Need Feeling of deficit or lacking that all people experience at some time.

Negotiation steps Preparation, building the relationship, exchanging information, first offer, persuasion, concessions, and agreement.

Nenpo System New Japanese compensation system based on yearly performance evaluations that emphasize goals—although goals are not always the same as in Western companies.

Neutral versus affective The acceptability of expressing emotions.

New ventures Entering a new market; offering a new product or service; or introducing a new method, technology, or innovative use of raw materials.

Nonverbal communication Face-to-face communication that is not oral.

Nonverbal communication Face-to-face communication that is not oral.

Normative isomorphism Organizations indirectly copy the designs, cultures, and strategies of other organizations by conforming to professional and technical norms.

Normative social institution Refers to the values and norms promulgated by the social institutions.

North American Free Trade Agreement (NAFTA) A multilateral treaty that links the United States, Canada, and Mexico in an economic bloc that allows freer exchange of goods and services.

Nurturant-task-oriented leadership (NT) theory Indian leadership theory combining both task and person-centered leader behaviors.

Occupational cultures Distinct cultures of occupational groups such as physicians, lawyers, accountants, and craftspeople.

Oculesics Communication through eye contact or gaze.

Offensive competitive strategies Direct attacks, end-run offensives, pre-emptive strategies, and acquisitions.

Olfactics Use of smells as a means of nonverbal communication.

Operant conditioning Model proposes that, if a pleasurable consequence follows a behavior, the behavior will continue, whereas if an unpleasant consequence follows a behavior, the behavior will stop.

Organizational culture The norms, values, and beliefs concerning the organization shared by members of the organization.

Organizational design How organizations structure subunits and use coordination and control mechanisms to achieve their strategic goals.

Organizational isomorphism Pressure from social institutions to follow similar paths in management practices.

Output control system Assesses the performance of a unit based on results, not on the processes used to achieve those results.

Participation strategies Options multinational companies have to enter foreign markets and countries.

Particularism Dealing with other people based on personal relationships.

Passive exporter Company that treats and fills overseas orders like domestic orders.

Path-goal theory Four types of leadership styles that a manager might choose depending on the situation.

Performance appraisal System to measure and assess employees' work performance.

Performance–maintenance (PM) theory Japanese perspective on balancing task- and person-centered leader behaviors.

Permanent employment In Japan, continuous employment, often to the age of 55.

Personal success characteristics Ability to tolerate ambiguous situations, flexibility, creativity, humor, stamina, empathy, and knowledge of a foreign language.

Person-centered leader One who focuses on meeting employees' social and emotional needs.

Persuasion Stage when each side in the negotiation attempts to get the other side to agree to its position.

Pervasive The idea that culture affects almost everything we do, everything we see, and everything we feel and believe.

Political Risk Impact of political decisions on a multinational's profitability.

Polycentric IHRM Firm treats each country-level organization separately for HRM purposes.

Porter's Five Forces Model Technique to assess forces at work in an industry.

Postindustrial society Emphasis on the service sectors.

Power distance Expectations regarding equality among people.

Pre-industrial society Agriculture dominates and shapes the economic environment.

Prescriptive ethics for multinationals Suggested guidelines for the ethical behavior of multinational companies.

Primary Stakeholders Those stakeholders directly linked to a company's survival, e.g., customers, suppliers, employees and shareholders.

Privatization Transfer of state ownership to private individuals.

Privatization The sale of government-owned businesses to private investors.

Problem-solving negotiation Negotiators seek out mutually satisfactory ground that is beneficial to both companies' interests.

Process theories Of motivation, arising from needs and values combined with an individual's beliefs regarding the work environment.

Product structure Has departments or subunits based on different product groups.

Profit center Unit controlled by its profit or loss performance.

Proxemics The use of space to communicate.

Punishment Consequences of a person's behavior that discourage the behavior.

Recruitment Process of identifying and attracting qualified people to apply for vacant positions in an organization.

Regiocentric IHRM Regionwide HRM policies are adopted.

Regional strategy Managing raw-material sourcing, production, marketing, and support activities within a particular region.

Regional trade agreements Agreements among nations in a particular region to reduce tariffs and develop similar technical and economic standards.

Regulative social institution Constrains and regularizes behaviors through its capacity to establish rules, to inspect and review conformity, and to manipulate consequences to reinforce behaviors

Reinforcement Reactions to a person's behavior that encourage the person to continue the behavior.

Religion Shared set of beliefs, activities, and institutions that have basis upon faith in supernatural forces.

Religiosity Indication of the importance of acceptance of the core philosophies of religion in one's life.

Repatriation problem Difficulties that managers face in coming back to their home countries and reconnecting with their home organizations.

Resource pool All the human and physical resources available in a country.

Resources Inputs into the production or service processes.

Secondary Stakeholders Those stakeholders that are indirectly linked to a company's survival, e.g., media, trade associations and other special-interest groups.

Secure server An Internet host that allows users to send and receive encrypted data.

Selection Process by which companies fill vacant positions in the organization.

Sequential approach Each side reciprocates concessions made by the other side.

7d culture model A seven dimension cultural model based on beliefs regarding how people relate to each other, how people manage time, and how people deal with nature.

Shared cultural values, norms, and beliefs The idea that people in different cultural groups have similar views of the world.

Shared management structure Occurs when both parent companies contribute approximately the same number of managers to the alliance organization.

Small-business advantage Fast- moving entrepreneurs can use their competitive advantage of speed. Being first to market, they can capture significant sales before larger competitors react.

Small-business stage model Process of internationalization followed by many small businesses.

"Small" business UN definition: less than 500 employees. Popular press definition: less than 100 employees. U.S. Small Business Administration's definition: varies by industry and uses both sales revenue and the number of employees.

Social Inequality Degree to which people have privileged access to resources and positions within societies.

Social institution A complex of positions, roles, norms, and values organizing relatively stable patterns of human resources with respect to sustaining viable societal structures within a given environment.

Social loafing Term used when people put out less effort when they work in groups.

Social responsibility Idea that businesses have a responsibility to society beyond making profits.

Socialist or command economy Production resources are owned by the state and production decisions are centrally coordinated.

Sociotechnical systems approach Focuses on designing motivating jobs by blending the social system (i.e., organizational structure, culture) with different technologies.

Specialized operations Subunits specializing in particular product lines, different research areas, or different marketing areas.

Specific versus diffuse The extent to which all aspects of an individual's life are involved in their work relationships.

Split-control management structure Partners usually share strategic decision making but split functional-level decision making.

Standardized website Websites that are similar in design and layout around the world

Stereotyping When one assumes that all people within a culture behave, believe, feel, and act the same.

Strategic complementarity One that complements the alliance partners.

Strategy formulation Process by which managers select the strategies to be used by their company.

Subordinates' expectations Expectations regarding what leaders "should" do and what they may or may not do.

Sustainable Strategies not easily defeated by competitors.

Switching costs Expenses involved when a customer switches to a competitor's products.

SWOT The analysis of an organization's internal strengths and weaknesses, and the opportunities or threats from the environment.

Task force Temporary team created to solve a particular organizational problem.

Task-centered leader One who gives subordinates specific standards, schedules, and tasks.

Task-related information Actual details of the proposed agreement.

Team Permanent unit of the organization designed to focus the efforts of different subunits on particular problems.

Technological leadership Being first to use or introduce a new technology.

Teleological ethical theory One that suggests that the morality of an act or practice comes from its consequences.

Third country nationals Expatriate workers who come from neither the host nor home country.

Time horizon The way cultures deal with the past, present, and future.

Training and development Giving employees the knowledge, skills, and abilities to perform successfully both in current jobs and in future jobs.

Training rigor Extent of effort by both trainees and trainers required to prepare the trainees for expatriate positions.

Transactional leadership One where managers use rewards or punishments to influence their subordinates.

Transformational leadership One where managers go beyond transactional leadership by articulating a vision, breaking from the status quo, providing goals and a plan, giving meaning or a purpose to goals, taking risks, being motivated to lead, building a power base, and demonstrating high ethical and moral standards.

Transition economies Countries in the process of changing from government-controlled economic systems to capitalistic systems.

Transnational strategy Two goals get top priority: seeking location advantages and gaining economic efficiencies from operating worldwide.

Transnational subsidiary Has no companywide form or function—each subsidiary does what it does best or most efficiently anywhere in the world.

Transnational-network structure Network of functional, product, and geographic subsidiaries dispersed throughout the world, based on the subsidiaries' location advantages.

TRIAD The world's dominant trading partners: European Union, United States, and Japan.

Turnkey operation Multinational company makes a project fully operational and trains local managers and workers before the foreign owner takes control.

U.S. legal requirements for appraisals Regulating performance-evaluation practices to ensure their fairness.

Uncertainty avoidance How people react to what is different and dangerous.

Union membership density Proportion of workers in a country who belong to unions.

Universalism Dealing with other people based on rules.

Utilitarianism Argument that what is good and moral comes from acts that produce the greatest good for the greatest number of people.

Value chain All the activities that a firm uses to design, produce, market, deliver, and support its product.

Verbal negotiation tactics Promises, threats, recommendations, warnings, rewards, punishments, normative appeals, commitments, self-disclosures, questions, commands, "No" (refusals), interruptions.

White-collar or professional union Represents particular occupational group, similar to craft union.

Whorf hypothesis Theory that language determines the nature of culture.

Women global leadership Spread of traits or qualities that are associated with women to the process of leading organizations worldwide.

Work centrality Overall value of work in a person's life.

Work obligation norms Degree to which work is seen as an obligation or duty to society.

Works council In Germany, employee group that shares plant-level responsibility with managers over issues such as working conditions.

World Trade Organization (WTO) A formal structure for continued negotiations to reduce trade barriers and a mechanism for settling trade disputes.

Worldwide geographic structure Has geographical units representing regions of the world.

Worldwide matrix structure Symmetrical organization, usually with equal emphasis on worldwide product groups and regional geographical divisions.

Worldwide product structure Gives product divisions responsibility to produce and sell their products or services throughout the world.